D0164131

MICROECONOMICS

A MODERN APPROACH

FIRST EDITION

ANDREW SCHOTTER

NEW YORK UNIVERSITY

SOUTH-WESTERN
CENGAGE Learning™

Australia · Brazil · Canada · Mexico · Singapore · Spain · United Kingdom · United States

SOUTH-WESTERN
CENGAGE Learning™

Microeconomics: A Modern Approach

Andrew Schotter

VP/Editorial Director: Jack W. Calhoun

Editor-in-Chief: Alex von Rosenberg

Sr. Acquisitions Editor: Steve Scoble

Developmental Editor: Katie Yanos

Executive Marketing Manager: Brian Joyner

Sr. Content Project Manager: Colleen A. Farmer

Technology Project Manager: Deepak Kumar

Manufacturing Coordinator: Sandee Milewski

Production Technology Analyst: Emily Gross

Production Service: Newgen

Sr. Art Director: Michelle Kunkler

Cover and Internal Designer: Jennifer Lambert/
Jen2Design

Cover Image: © Getty Images

Printer: Edwards Brothers

© 2009 South-Western, a part of Cengage Learning

ALL RIGHTS RESERVED. No part of this work covered by the copyright herein may be reproduced, transmitted, stored or used in any form or by any means graphic, electronic, or mechanical, including but not limited to photocopying, recording, scanning, digitizing, taping, Web distribution, information networks, or information storage and retrieval systems, except as permitted under Section 107 or 108 of the 1976 United States Copyright Act, without the prior written permission of the publisher.

For product information and technology assistance, contact us at
Cengage Learning Academic Resource Center, 1-800-423-0563

For permission to use material from this text or product, submit all requests online at **www.cengage.com/permissions**
Further permissions questions can be emailed to
permissionrequest@cengage.com

Library of Congress Control Number: 2007938680

Student Edition ISBN 13: 978-0-324-58444-8
Student Edition ISBN 10: 0-324-58444-X
Student Edition Package ISBN 13: 978-0-324-31584-4
Student Edition Package ISBN 10: 0-324-31584-8

South-Western Cengage Learning
5191 Natorp Boulevard
Mason, OH 45040
USA

Cengage Learning products are represented in Canada by Nelson Education, Ltd.

For your course and learning solutions, visit **academic.cengage.com**
Purchase any of our products at your local college store or at our preferred online store **www.ichapters.com**

Printed in the United States of America
1 2 3 4 5 6 7 11 10 09 08

To Anne

Brief Contents

Contents

Preface

As a professional economist, I often suffer through the following scenario: I go to a cocktail party and meet a stranger who eventually asks me what I do for a living. After I say I teach economics, the response I get is almost always the same, "Oh, I took an economics course in college and it was the worst thing I ever took. I did not understand a thing."

While I might be smug about how difficult economics is and therefore how smart I must be to understand some of it, such smugness must be tempered by the fact that the people at these cocktail parties are usually quite bright and accomplished. What is worse is that I do not notice the same response when my biology or neuroscience friends are asked the same question. So the remaining hypothesis is that we economists somehow fail to teach economics correctly.

One reason why we fail is obvious. Traditional undergraduate courses and texts present economics as a dead science, one with no unsolved puzzles and no unanswered questions. This is odd, because graduate education in microeconomics is filled with such puzzles and questions, and we teach graduate students to evaluate and criticize theories rather than merely to accept them. The same is true in other sciences, yet somehow we permit our undergraduates to gain the impression that previous generations of economists have solved all the puzzles and answered all the questions and that their task as students is simply to learn a set of established principles. As a result, most undergraduates look on their microeconomics text as something akin to the Bible—as a source of divine wisdom. The truth, however, is that economics is an amazingly dynamic science that periodically undergoes waves of change that sweep out old ideas and bring in new ones. For example, one could argue that economics is now undergoing a "behavioral revolution" in which ideas and concepts from psychology and neuroscience are making inroads into how we economists think about our science. Unfortunately, although there are some fine microeconomics books that do a good job of explaining economic principles, few discuss the exciting things that are happening on the frontiers of our science.

Another reason economists fail to teach economics correctly may be that economics, as opposed to biology and neuroscience, has historically been assumed not to be an experimental science. As a result, standard microeconomic theory textbooks are written without any mention of whether the theories presented fare well when tested under controlled circumstances. In other words, students are required to take what they learn as an article of faith. Given this expectation, it is no wonder that economics looks dead: If it cannot be subjected to controlled testing, it becomes an "as if" science with very little that can be refuted.

The past twenty-five years has seen the emergence of a new methodology for economics that involves a concerted effort to test theory under controlled laboratory circumstances. This has injected a huge amount of excitement into economics because not only can we learn a set of elegant theories, but we can also devise how these theories can be tested in the lab and in the field and how such experimental evidence might lead us to change our theories. This process breeds certain energy into the field, energy that is lacking in all extant economics textbooks and which I would like to add here.

A Fresh Approach

This book attempts to deal with the concerns just outlined by taking a distinctively modern approach to undergraduate education in microeconomics. I see no reason why undergraduates should not be swept up in the excitement over such issues as finding a solution to the free-rider problem, dealing with economic problems from the perspective of game theory, using controlled laboratory experiments to test economic postulates, or dealing in a rigorous way with problems of moral hazard, adverse selection, and asymmetric information. Of course, I am not proposing that a microeconomics text should skimp on the presentation of the fundamentals, such as supply-and-demand analysis and perfectly competitive markets. What I am saying is that a microeconomics text should be like a good meal; it should consist not only of staples such as meat and potatoes but also of some interesting side dishes. Otherwise, the meal will be rather dull and the diners may quickly lose their appetites.

However, giving students a sense of the excitement of new approaches to solving economic problems is only part of the reason why we should make some basic changes in the intermediate microeconomics course. There is also a need to nurture a spirit of critical analysis in students. *The development of critical thinking skills should start in our undergraduate economics courses, not wait for graduate studies. Theories taught should be understood but their deficiencies should be made obvious.* I will never forget the comment of one early reviewer of this text who wanted to rid the book of all critical remarks about the theories presented, stating that "being critical can only confuse students." Again, the difference between science and faith is critical thinking.

Another problem that I have encountered in intermediate microeconomics textbooks is that there seems to be no overriding principle that ties together the various chapters of the text. One finds a wide array of theories mixed together with many real-world examples, mathematical applications, and explanatory diagrams but with no underlying theme or themes to unify this massive amount of material. I think that there is a better way to present intermediate microeconomics to students. This book offers a consistent unifying model that runs through every chapter. I have been able to use such an approach because I define microeconomics somewhat differently here than other authors do in their books. For me, microeconomics is a tool that helps us understand why societies have the various economic institutions that they have. For example, I believe that microeconomics helps us to understand why the United States has insurance companies, regulated monopolies, and paper money. It is the role of microeconomics to explain how these institutions, among others, were created by the individual utility-maximizing actions of a myriad of social agents.

The Structure of the Book

This book is divided into eight sections. Section 1 sets the stage for the text by introducing the unifying theme of the book: how economic institutions develop to solve problems that arise in a society. In this section we encounter a primitive society that lacks any institutions except the state and property rights. All that exist are people living in a basically agrarian society and consuming the goods that grow on their property. These agents, their preferences, their level of rationality, and the way they deal with uncertainty (through insurance) is described in Section 2. As the book progresses, this society becomes more and more institutionally complex. Its agents create institutions to handle the problems that inevitably accompany advances in the nature and level of its economic activities. For example, in Section 3 our economic agents discover how to produce goods; hence we need to discuss technology and cost. In Section 4, after firms have been established, we discuss the theory of games and decision making in general, because our emerging firms will be forced to interact with one another in the marketplace once they are established. Section 5 discusses markets (perfectly competitive, oligopolistic, and monopolistic). With markets established, Section 6 looks at the theory of exchange, and Section 7 investigates what happens when such markets either fail to exist or perform poorly. Finally, our last section looks at the tensions in market economies among the factors of production: land, labor, and capital.

The net result of presenting the content of the course within the framework of a unified model is that the students can relate the theory they are learning to a society and its people. In effect, all the chapters of the book form one large-scale application of microeconomic theory. In my teaching experience, this approach has been very successful with students because it allows them to view microeconomics in more human terms than is usually the case.

One note of caution: For this approach to work properly, it is essential that students read Section 1. Otherwise, they will not understand the model as it develops in the remainder of the book.

How This Book Differs from Others

This book breaks with tradition in a number of different ways.

Cohesive Narrative. As I have already noted, this book tells one continuing story that ties all the chapters together. Rather than treating intermediate microeconomics as a series of unrelated topics, it presents the content of the course within the context of a society that starts out in a primitive state of nature and gradually develops the characteristics and institutions of a modern economy. While I have found that this approach has great pedagogical advantages, I am sure that some instructors will not be inclined to teach the subject in such a manner. To these people, I would say that they should feel free to play down (or ignore) the narrative in class. You will find that you can continue to teach supply-and-demand analysis and all the usual topics without becoming involved in the model presented in the text. It will be there as a frame of reference for your students when they do their reading assignments and will help put class lectures in a context.

Experimental Teasers. Most chapters in the book begin with what I call an "experimental teaser," which is a published experiment whose results are either intriguing or puzzling, and the reader is asked to think about the teaser before reading the chapter. In the course of the chapter, the groundwork for resolving the teaser is laid so that its resolution can be presented formally. I find these teasers make the topics discussed come alive and present students with something to get excited about. In addition, experimental evidence is many times offered as either confirmation for the theories presented or as evidence that they need to be modified.

An Emphasis on Game Theory and Strategic Analysis. The analytical tools used in this book also require some discussion. The book is written in a simple, straightforward manner that should be comprehensible to a wide variety of students, but it does require that students be willing to think. One of the major analytical tools used here is game theory. Chapter 11 introduces students to the fundamentals of game theory and shows them how it can serve as a tool for strategic business analysis.

Game theory is then used throughout the remaining chapters as a means of understanding the different strategies of the various parties to a situation. My experience has been that presenting economic and social problems to students in the form of games is a very effective way to help them grasp such problems in their entirety.

Of course, until recently, intermediate microeconomics books have given very limited coverage to game theory. Often they simply mentioned it in passing or relegated it to an appendix of the chapter on oligopoly. Today, with the increasing interest in game theory, a few books are giving it more coverage, but none make extensive use of it as a tool for strategic analysis as this book does.

Encouragement of Critical Thinking. To help students see economics as a dynamic science, I devote a considerable amount of space to criticisms of the theories presented. In some chapters this is done through a device that I call "consulting reports." These reports suggest possible solutions to problems that our model society faces, such as how to regulate natural monopolies. Usually, the solution provided by a consulting report reflects the views of a well-known economist. After each report, I examine the theory it propounds, raising criticisms that have probably occurred to the students and citing the arguments of other economists who support the theory or disagree with it.

In most cases, I intentionally leave some doubt as to which side of the controversy has won. I hope that this approach to presenting microeconomic theory will stimulate debate in the classroom and encourage students to develop a spirit of critical analysis. Rather than simply accepting the theories they encounter because these theories were devised by famous economists, it is important that students look at every economic plan with a critical attitude, analyze its strengths and weaknesses, come to their own conclusions, and then have the confidence to defend their conclusions even though they may differ from the opinions of "experts."

Broad Coverage of Experimental Economics. As stated above, this book is unique in the amount of coverage it gives to experimental economics. It is my belief that the future of microeconomics will be heavily connected with the use of experimental tools, as will its teaching. These tools have already proven themselves quite valuable in shedding light on some difficult theoretical issues. Therefore, at many junctures in the book, I present the results of experiments that relate to issues that are being discussed. Sometimes these experimental results form the basis for a consulting report, and sometimes they are cited as part of the critical analysis of a theory that was first proposed in a consulting report. For example, I use the preference-reversal experiments of Kahneman and Tversky to warn students that although the theory of expected utility seems logical and consistent, it may not prove to be a good predictor of real human behavior. The question of whether people (or experimental subjects) actually take a free ride when the opportunity is available to them is discussed in the chapter on public goods (Chapter 25).

Of course, I also subject experimental results to criticism. Students should view conclusions drawn from empirical data with a critical eye, just as they view theoretical ideas.

Some Nontraditional Chapters That Can Enrich the Course. There are several chapters in this book that are not normally found in texts for the intermediate microeconomics course. I think that these chapters enrich the course, but it is not necessary to teach them. For example, I devote an entire chapter to the internal organization of the firm (Chapter 13). In this chapter I investigate the issues of how best to organize work within a firm and how best to compensate workers. Because these issues are currently of great concern in business, some instructors may want to cover them. Similarly, I devote a chapter to the topic of entry prevention (Chapter 20), in which students learn how monopolists and oligopolists defend their markets against potential entrants and how potential entrants try to overcome these defenses. For instructors and students who are especially interested in strategic business analysis, this can be a valuable chapter. Other chapters in this book that might seem unconventional are the ones on natural monopoly and the economics of regulation (Chapter 18) and on time inconsistency and dynamic decisions (Chapter 12).

I strongly believe in the principle of free disposability. If the nontraditional chapters do not fit the objectives of your course or if there is little time available, eliminate them or cover them very briefly. I have written these chapters in such a way that they can be omitted without damaging the logic of the book. The same is not true for the chapter on game theory (Chapter 11). Because this chapter provides a foundation for the applications of game theory that appear in later chapters, I would urge you to give it at least limited coverage in your course.

I have relegated topics that involve fairly difficult quantitative material to the appendixes of some chapters. Instructors with students who are more advanced, have a better math background, or are willing to work harder may want to use these appendixes.

Fresh Examples and Problems. Throughout this text, I have tried to use examples that differ from those appearing in other books. For instance, instead of the example of cars that are "lemons," which is so often used to present the topic of asymmetric information and market failure, I have substituted the example of car mechanics who offer expert opinions to partially informed car owners. Similarly, to present the topic of adverse selection, I have used the example of tipping in restaurants. I have also attempted to make the end-of-chapter exercises and problems fresh and interesting.

One additional note about the exercises and problems: Although the use of calculus is not required in any of this material, some exercises and problems have been written so that students who are familiar with calculus can easily use it if it helps them.

Media Notes. Finally, scattered throughout the text are a set of "media notes" that report real world examples of the material discussed in the text. These are included to demonstrate the relevance of what we are discussing to events in the real world, some important and some frivolous. They are meant to enlighten and also to entertain.

Supplements

Instructor's Manual. The Instructor's Manual consists of two parts: Lecture Notes and Solutions. The Lecture Notes section outlines and summarizes the material for each chapter to assist with class preparation. The Solutions section contains the answers to all of the in-text exercises and problems.

Test Bank. The Test Bank contains comprehensive true/false, multiple choice, and short answer questions for the key terms and concepts presented in each chapter of the text.

PowerPoint Presentation. The PowerPoint presentation contains slides of key talking points and important tables and figures for each chapter of the text.

Website. The text website, accessible at academic.cengage.com/econ/schotter, contains key term quizzing for students, as well as access to the Instructor's Manual, Test Bank, and PowerPoint presentation for instructors.

Acknowledgments

I owe a debt of gratitude to the following list of reviewers, whose keen insights and thoughtful comments helped to shape this text:

Richard Beil, Auburn University

Calvin Blackwell, College of Charleston

John R. Bowblis, Rutgers University–New Brunswick

Ariaster B. Chimeli, Ohio University

Shin-Yi Chou, Lehigh University

Rachel T. A. Croson, University of Pennsylvania

Amlan Datta, Texas Tech University

Martin Dufwenberg, University of Arizona

Jeffrey C. Ely, Northwestern University

Thomas S. Friedland, University of California

Craig Gallet, California State University–Sacramento

Rajeev Goel, Illinois State University

Jim Holcomb, University of Texas–El Paso

Billy Jack, Georgetown University

Mark R. Johnson, Tulane University

Paul Johnson, University of Alaska–Anchorage

Kate Krause, University of New Mexico

Debashis Pal, University of Cincinnati

Salim Rashid, University of Illinois

Lee Redding, University of Michigan–Dearborn

Brian Roberson, Miami University

Jeffrey O. Sundberg, Lake Forest College

Jennifer VanGilder, California State University–Bakersfield

Jonathan Willner, Oklahoma City University

Gilbert N. Wolpe, Newbury College

Ben Young, University of Missouri–Kansas City

In addition, there were many people who helped create and edit this text, and others who found errors in earlier texts that I corrected here. To start, I would like to thank Marina Agranov, Wolly Ehrblatt, Erkut Ozbay, and especially Ashok Mathew, whose hard work made writing this text a much easier task. A number of others helped greatly in making this book as error free as possible. Most importantly, I would like to thank Dirk Engelmann who, along with his students, found a too-large number of mistakes and typos in an earlier version of the text. In addition, a number of students have e-mailed me some corrections that I gladly took into account in the text. These include William Doyle, Felipe Valencia, Akio Yasuhara, Alan Mehlenbacher, Ying Jin, A. Radin Ahmed, E. R. de Regt, and Karmentha Naidoo. Anna Ingster was also very helpful in discovering some ambiguities in the text. I would like to thank Laura Pilossoph for her work on the glossary.

Finally, let me thank all of the people at South-Western who have made the process of publishing this book go as smoothly as it has and who have guided me along the way. These include Steven Scoble and Steve Momper, who were instrumental in acquiring the book for South-Western; Katie Yanos, my Developmental Editor, who guided the project through its many stages; Starratt Alexander and Colleen Farmer, Content Project Managers, and Jamie Armstrong, Production Coordinator, who brought the book physically to life; Michelle Kunkler, Senior Art Director, who made it look attractive; Laura Cothran, Editorial Assistant, who assisted with all the logistics; and Brian Joyner, Executive Marketing Manager, who made you, the reader, aware of it.

Andrew Schotter

About the Author

Andrew Schotter is Professor of Economics, Faculty of Arts and Sciences, New York University, and Director of the Center for Experimental Social Science. From 1983 to 1988 he was codirector of the C. V. Starr Center for Applied Economics at New York University and has served as chair from 1988 to 1993 and from 1996 to 1999. Professor Schotter received his B.S. degree from Cornell University and his M.A. and Ph.D. degrees from New York University. His areas of special interest in teaching are microeconomic theory, game theory, and experimental economics. His areas of special interest in research are applications of game theory to economics; microeconomics; experimental economics; and theories of economic and social institutions.

These interests are reflected in the many articles that Professor Schotter has contributed to economics journals and in the books he has written and edited. In addition to *Microeconomics: A Modern Approach*, he is the author of *Free Market Economics: A Critical Appraisal* and *The Economic Theory of Social Institutions.* He has edited *Selected Economic Writings of Oskar Morgenstern* and (with Steven Brams and Gerhard Schwödiauer) *Applied Game Theory*, and is the editor, along with Andrew Caplin, of the *Handbook of Economic Methodology*, a book series to be published by Oxford University Press.

Professor Schotter's wide-ranging professional activities have also included serving as a member of the editorial board of the *American Economic Review* and *Experimental Economics* and as an Associate Editor for *Games and Economic Behavior;* doing consulting work for businesses and financial institutions; giving testimony before the Joint Economic Committee of the United States Congress on the cost of the tort system; and serving as a visiting scholar at the University of Paris, the University of Venice, the Institution for Advanced Studies in Vienna, the Russell Sage Foundation, and Tel Aviv University. In 1993 he was given the Kenan Enterprise Award for his contributions to the economic theory of free markets.

Professor Schotter is married to Anne Howland Schotter, a Professor of English Literature at Wagner College in New York. They have two children, Geoffrey and Elizabeth, who lent their names to the two archetypes of economic agents in the model society their father has created to illustrate microeconomic theory in this book.

Introduction

Section 1 of this textbook is entirely taken up by the introductory chapter. Unlike most introductory chapters, however, it is my feeling that this one should be read. This is so because this text is slightly different from your average microeconomics textbook and, as a result, the approach taken needs some explanation. This is what I attempt to do in this section. I outline what types of problems microeconomics tries to solve, give the reader a quick guide through the chapters, and explain the emphasis that the book places on experimental evidence in support of the theories explained. I urge you to read the introduction because it properly motivates the material in the rest of the book, and I also urge you to read the material under each section heading because it helps tie the various sections of the book together and reminds you of what has been discussed previously in the book.

CHAPTER 1
**Economics and Institutions:
A Shift of Emphasis**

Economics and Institutions: A Shift of Emphasis

Microeconomics and Institutions

Imagine that you are an executive with a large firm. You wake up one morning and, stumbling out of bed, realize that the day is going to be an unpleasant one. You rush to get a head start on the commuter traffic, but by 7 A.M. you are caught in a massive traffic jam on the expressway. As your car sits idling on the right side of the road, you watch the barely moving vehicles ahead of you and contemplate the rest of your day.

At 9 A.M. you have an appointment with a representative of your firm's insurance company to find out whether that company will renew your firm's product liability insurance with the same deductible as before. At 10 A.M. you are scheduled to meet with a representative of the local utility company to discuss some proposals for cutting energy usage that might decrease your firm's high utility costs. Because the utility company is a publicly sanctioned monopoly, your firm cannot simply purchase its electricity from another company with lower rates. At 2 P.M. a committee that you head will be meeting to vote on some difficult issues. The committee members are deeply divided, and you hope that a majority will emerge on each issue. At 4 P.M. your firm will inform its executives about their yearly bonuses. This event always creates tension because the bonuses are based on top management's assessment of the performance of each executive during the past year.

After work, you will go to your health club. You need the exercise, but the main reason for your visit is that you paid a large annual membership fee and feel guilty about not using the club enough. This story, as simple as it is, illustrates the wide variety of institutions that shape our economic, social, and political lives. Let us now investigate the subject of institutions more closely.

Institutional Arrangements: Preordained or Arbitrary?

With all the pressure and anxiety that most of us face in our daily activities, we rarely stop to think about why things are arranged as they are. For example, why do we drive on the right side of the road instead of the left side? Why are companies willing to sell us liability insurance? Why do these companies demand a deductible for the liability insurance? Why does the government allow only one utility company to sell electricity in an area? Why do most committees make their decisions by a simple majority vote rather than by a two-thirds majority vote or a unanimous vote? Why do some employers pay bonuses in addition to salaries? Why are many bonus plans based on individual performance rather than company performance or departmental performance? Why do most health clubs charge a big annual membership fee in advance? Why can't consumers in the state of Washington buy locally grown apples?

Most of us take the institutional arrangements in our society for granted and never question them. But these arrangements need not be as they are, and sometimes other societies have very different institutional arrangements. We could drive on the left side of the road as people do in England and Japan, be unable to buy liability insurance, have several utility companies competing to sell electricity in each area, require that committees use a two-thirds majority vote or a unanimous vote to reach decisions, earn salaries but no bonuses, and pay small fees each time we use the facilities of a health club.

Why are things arranged the way they are? Are the institutional arrangements that define our lives preordained or could they have evolved differently? There is no one simple answer to these questions. Clearly, some of the institutional arrangements that we see around us are arbitrary because other societies faced with the same problems have found different solutions. Yet there are probably more similarities than differences in institutional arrangements. Often, institutional arrangements that appear quite different because of variations in surface details actually fulfill the same function for an economy. For example, in Japan, employees receive a large part of their compensation in the form of bonuses, which are based on the performance of their firms. The better a firm does, the more its employees earn. In the United States, we typically award bonuses on the basis of each employee's performance and not the performance of the firm or a department or division of the firm.[1] Hence, the details of the U.S. and Japanese compensation systems are different, but both serve the same function—to motivate employees at work.

Microeconomics: A Tool for Understanding Institutions

One major purpose of microeconomics is to help us explain the institutional structures in an economy. This book will do just that by giving the reader the technical apparatus with which to make sense out of what, on the surface at least, appears to be a chaotic world composed of a myriad of institutions, customs, and conventions to which we adhere but do not fully understand. The question that microeconomics asks is, How do individuals, in an attempt to maximize their own self-interest, create a set of economic institutions that structure their daily lives?[2] Note, however, that this question views institutions as being created endogenously, or in an unplanned manner, by the agents in society. An equally interesting question, known to economists as the mechanism design question, is how a planner can design a set of institutions that leads to results he or she considers best for society. We will deal mostly with the first question but will touch on the second later in the text.

The other major purpose of microeconomics, the one on which microeconomics textbooks have traditionally focused, is to answer the question of how scarce resources are allocated by one type of institution—markets (be they perfectly or imperfectly competitive). Before addressing the broader institutional question, let us more closely investigate the conventional textbook analysis of resource allocation.

---

[1] It is interesting to note that increasing numbers of U.S. firms are now adopting compensation systems that give more emphasis to group achievement and less emphasis to individual achievement.

[2] This question is dealt with using a game theory approach in Andrew Schotter, *The Economic Theory of Social Institutions* (Cambridge, England: Cambridge University Press, 1981).

Conventional Microeconomics

The following classic definition of economics was written by the noted British economist Lionel Robbins.[3] It is the definition that appears most often in the introductory chapters of microeconomics textbooks.

> The economist studies the disposal of scarce means. He is interested in the way different degrees of scarcity of different goods give rise to different ratios of valuation between them, and he is interested in the way in which changes in ends or changes in means—from the demand side or the supply side—affect these ratios. Economics is the science which studies human behavior as a relationship between ends and scarce means which have alternative uses.[4]

The Problem of Allocating Resources

To gain a better understanding of the problem of allocating scarce resources, consider the following two situations. First think of a typical country auction where a set of goods have to be allocated to the people showing up to bid. Clearly, if the auction is to be efficient, it should allocate the goods to those who value them the most. So the person who likes the baby grand piano and is willing to pay the most for it should receive it at the end of the auction, while the person who likes the power tools and is willing to pay the most for them should receive them. Of course, the auctioneer does not care about allocating goods to those people who value them most; he or she cares about maximizing the revenue received from the auction. So the question here is whether the auction rule used by the auctioneer to sell the goods leads to an efficient or optimal allocation. (Think of eBay and ask yourself the same question: Do eBay auctions determine optimal allocations?)

Another more complicated situation is that faced by a typical family in managing its personal finances. Every month the parents earn a certain amount of income. This is the amount the family has available to spend on goods and services. The problem of allocation arises because each member of the family has a different idea about how the money should be spent. One parent wants to make some home improvements, and the other parent wants to buy a new car. The older child wants to spend all the money on electronic games, and the younger child wants to use it for ice cream and candy. A decision must be made about how this limited income is to be spent.

Economics helps us understand both how the family's income *ought* to be spent (in order to maximize a given objective) and how it *will* be spent (given a good description of the decision-making process that determines spending). When we rely on economists to tell us how allocation decisions ought to be made, we are asking them to lead us along the road of normative or welfare economics. When we want economists to inform us on how the allocation process will actually work, we are asking them to take us down the path of positive economics. (Normative or welfare economics deals with what ought to be rather than what is and involves prescriptive statements that may be based on value judgments. Positive economics deals with what is rather than what ought to be and involves descriptive statements that are objective and verifiable.)

normative (welfare) economics
The type of economics that deals with prescriptive rather than descriptive statements.

positive economics
The type of economics that deals with descriptive rather than prescriptive statements.

---

[3] Lionel Robbins, Baron Robbins of Clare Market (1898–1984), was a professor of economics at the London School of Economics from 1929 until 1961. During the Second World War, he was the director of the economics section of the British Cabinet Office. In 1961, he became the chairman of the *Financial Times*, a British financial newspaper.

[4] Lionel Robbins, *An Essay on the Nature and Significance of Economic Science* (London: Macmillan, 1932).

Allocation Strategies

Let us continue with the family analogy to explore the problem of resource allocation. How ought a family spend its money? One response is, "Any way the family pleases." In a country like the United States, which is founded on the sanctity of the individual and the family, such an answer might be the end of this normative inquiry. However, even though no external authority (state or community) has the right to intervene in the decision-making process within a family, we could still ask the leaders of the family (usually the parents) what their goals are and advise them as to the most efficient way to achieve those goals. For example, say that one child is a happy-go-lucky child who extracts the most joy out of every situation, while the other child is a morose naysayer. Further, say that the parents devote their entire lives to making their children happy. Their overriding objective is to maximize the sum of the happiness of their children. If so, should more money be spent on the negative child or the positive child? What rule would tell us if the parents have allocated their limited budget correctly between the two children? Is equal spending always optimal?

Economics tells us that the optimal way for these parents to allocate their funds between their children depends on the *incremental happiness*—or, as we will call it later, *incremental utility and marginal utility*—that each dollar allocated to a child brings. If the happy child is a very efficient happiness-producing machine in the sense that each dollar allocated to him or her creates exquisite happiness and more happiness than the last dollar, while the morose child gets little enjoyment from toys or anything else the parents buy for him or her, the parents might as well spend all their money on the happy child. Why throw good money after a non-responsive child? On the other hand, the happy child may start out in such a perfect state of happiness that there is no need to spend additional dollars, while the unhappy child may be made substantially happier by the purchase of toys or other items. Clearly, the allocation would be different in this situation. The rule of economists is this: Distribute the dollars until the last dollar spent on each child increases their utility equally. Under normal circumstances, this rule will lead the parents to divide the money they spend between the two children. This is how a family ought to spend its money if you ask an economist for advice *once the objective for spending the money is specified*. Economists, however, have no intrinsic expertise in specifying the objective.

The Effect of Institutions on the Allocation Process

How the family will spend its money is another question. To answer this question, we must know the institutional details of the process the family uses to make allocation decisions. If this process is dictatorial, one person will make all the decisions. For example, if the family functions in the manner of a patriarchal Victorian family, the money will be spent according to the patriarch's tastes. If the process is democratic, all members of the family will play a role in allocation decisions by voting. The economist would have to study the voting rules used and the tastes of the voters (family members) in order to understand this type of allocation process. If the resources were allocated through some kind of internal family market (whatever that might look like), then the economist would look for an equilibrium allocation in this market. Because economists are most familiar with studying markets, they would probably have the most to say if markets were the allocating institution used.

Although the institutional question involves an investigation of the allocative role of markets, it is really more concerned with how these markets came into being in the first place and how they can be designed to increase economic welfare. Hence, the positive question of modern institutional economics is why we have the current set of institutions we have, while the welfare question is how we can design (or redesign) economic institutions to increase economic welfare.

Economic Institutions Defined

The term institution has several different meanings. An institution can be a convention of behavior that is created by society to help it solve a recurrent problem. For example, when a waiter or waitress serves us a meal in a restaurant, we leave a tip because it is the conventional thing to do. Tipping does have an economic purpose, and it is the job of microeconomists to explain what this purpose might be, but we leave a tip without really knowing its purpose. We are simply following a convention of our society. Under this definition, institutional behavior is conventional behavior, and institutions are conventions.[5]

Institutions can also be defined as sets of rules that constrain the behavior of social agents in particular situations.[6] For example, the U.S. Congress is called an institution. When we apply this term to Congress, we usually think of something very concrete—the national legislative body of the United States, consisting of the Senate and the House of Representatives. However, Congress is really a collection of abstract rules specifying how governmental decisions will be made. The passage of bills requires a simple majority, an override of a presidential veto requires a two-thirds majority, and seniority is important in committee appointments. These are just a few of the many rules that determine how Congress functions in making decisions. When we view institutions as sets of rules, we are led to look at the normative question of how best to choose these rules so that the outcomes that result from our institutions are optimal.

Finally, people often use the term *institution* in a loose, nontechnical sense to mean an organization—usually a large, well-established organization. For example, banks are called financial institutions and universities are called institutions of higher learning. This use of the term *institution* is vague; and in most cases, one of our two other meanings would also apply.

In this book, we will normally use the term **economic institutions** to mean conventions developed by a society to help it solve recurrent economic problems or sets of rules created to govern economic behavior. However, occasionally we will be guilty of using the term to mean simply organizations that serve an economic purpose.

economic institutions
Conventions developed by a society to help it resolve recurrent economic problems; sets of rules created to govern economic behavior.

The Emphasis of This Book

The objective of this book is to demonstrate how all the tools assembled in the toolbox of modern microeconomic theory can be used to help explain the world. We will, of course, explore the function and purpose of competitive markets and study how these markets allocate scarce resources. However, this book has a broader emphasis. It presents the competitive market as just one among a variety of

---

[5] For a fuller exposition of this view of institutions, see Schotter, *The Economic Theory of Social Institutions;* David Lewis, *Convention: A Philosophical Study* (Cambridge, MA: Harvard University Press, 1969); and Edna Ullman-Margalit, *The Emergence of Norms* (New York: Oxford University Press, 1978).

[6] For a summary of this view, see Leonid Hurwicz, "Mechanisms and Institutions," in *Economic Institutions in a Dynamic Society: Search for a New Frontier*, ed. Takashi Shiraishi and Shigeto Tsuru (London: The Macmillan Press Ltd., 1989).

mechanisms that can be used to solve the problems of allocation that societies face. This book attempts to explain how the institutions we observe around us came into being, how they function once they are in place, and how they might be designed to achieve predetermined goals, like maximizing welfare. The natural starting point for our analysis is a society in an institutional state of nature with no productive capabilities. This book presents a unified model of how such an economy develops and grows over time.

Economic Models

economic models
Abstract representations of reality that economists use to study the economic and social phenomena in which they are interested.

Economic models are abstract representations of reality that economists use to study the economic and social phenomena in which they are interested. Economists are famous for the models they build and infamous when those models fail to yield reliable predictions. Of course, economists are not the only scientists who build models. When new space vehicles are developed, rocket scientists build scaled-down versions and test them in wind tunnels to see how they will fly. These scaled-down space vehicles are created on the basis of models and are built to see how the real ones will behave. Note that a model is not reality but a representation of reality—in this case, a physical representation of reality.

Mathematical Models

In economics, we do not have the luxury of being able to construct a scaled-down version of the U.S. economy or the New York Stock Exchange to study their physical properties (although experimental studies of small-scale stock markets have been done). Hence, we try to represent these phenomena abstractly. One way to do this is to build a mathematical model—to develop an equation to represent each segment of an economy and then see how the various segments of the economy behave in response to one another. The interaction of the equations in the model simulates interrelationships in the economy.

Analogies as Models

Another way to understand an economic reality is to make an analogy between that reality and something else—something we know how to analyze. For example, consider the U.S. automobile market. Every year, Ford, General Motors, Chrysler, and foreign companies build cars and compete for a share of this market. Price is one of their major competitive tools. Consumers look at the features of the various cars and the prices and decide which cars they want to buy. These decisions determine the profits of the automobile manufacturers. In a sense, these automobile manufacturers are playing a *price game* among themselves in which, given their car designs, they compete for market share by choosing a price strategy. In this game, the players are the automobile manufacturers, their strategies are their prices, and their rewards are their profits. If seeing the automobile market as a game helps us to understand how this market functions, then the game analogy is a helpful economic model. Game theory—the study of games of strategy and the strategic interactions that such games reveal—was developed specifically to help us explore the analogy between economic and social reality and the games people play.

game theory
The study of games of strategy and the strategic interactions that such games reveal.

Natural and social scientists are not the only people who engage in model building. Poets and novelists use models to help their readers understand the realities they are trying to convey in their writings. For example, when the Scottish poet Robert Burns said, "My love is like a red, red rose," he was building a model of his love by means of an analogy (or a simile). Burns used the model of his love as a red, red rose to make that love more vivid and real to the reader.

This book uses an analogy to provide an understanding of the microeconomic reality in which we live. Our model is in the form of a narrative, but it is just as much a model as a scaled-down space shuttle, a set of equations representing the U.S. economy, a market game, and the red, red rose about which Robert Burns wrote.

Testing Theories—Economics as an Experimental Science

In science, the proof of the pudding is in the eating. In other words, how good a theory is can be measured by how well it explains the real world. Theories that are elegant on an esthetic basis can easily fail empirically to explain what they purport to explain. This raises the question of how we as economists attempt to prove the theories that we create.

Historically it has been the case that economics has shared a very rich and sophisticated empirical tradition in which real world data—that is, data collected by censuses, government agencies, and others—has been used to get estimates of the key parameters that define our models. This data is not generated by the scientists but rather by political agencies whose aim is political and not theoretical. To this day, employing statistical and econometric techniques on such data serves as the central empirical tool used by economists.

Over the past 25 years, however, economics has proven itself to be amenable to experimental investigation. In an economic experiment, volunteer recruits arrive at an experimental lab, usually consisting of a set of networked computers, and engage in a multi-person decision-making experiment played for real money. The experiment is supposed to replicate an economic environment specified in theory so that any prediction of the theory should be observable in the lab. The experiment is designed to directly test the theory, and hence the data generated are relevant to doing so. While the stakes are lower in a laboratory experiment than in the real world and while the subject pool is limited—undergraduate students rather than, say, business professionals—economic theory is silent on whether this should make a difference in the predictions of the theory. In other words, there is no $100 economic theory that says that rational behavior only kicks in if the stakes being played for are above $100, just as there is no $1,000,000 economic theory that says behavior shifts when the stakes get very large. Economic theory assumes perfectly rational behavior with perfectly calculating agents for any stakes and any population of people. That is its beauty. While this may obviously be false, this is one of the things we can learn in the lab and must be considered a limitation of the theory and not of experimental methods.

If economics is to be considered a behavioral science, then it should be able to predict the behavior of laboratory subjects interacting in the same replica economic environments that are specified in our theories. Put differently, if you create a theory and then cannot observe the behavior postulated by the theory in the lab no matter what you do, you might want to rethink the validity of your theory.

In this book we focus heavily on experimental economics. As you will see, almost every chapter is started with an experimental puzzle, called a teaser, which is supposed to get you thinking about the topic of that chapter. These experiments many times raise puzzles for the reader to think about as the material in the chapter unfolds. They are eventually explained and resolved.

I have used this experimental material for two reasons. One is that it has proven to be a good tool to get students interested in the material. While economic theories can be rather abstract, the concreteness of a well-designed experiment quickly makes the issues under investigation easy to grasp. Second, seeing a theory tested also serves to make it more real. Questioning an experimental design can often help a student understand the theory well because if you do not understand a theory, it would be hard to devise an experiment to test it.

None of this emphasis on experiments should detract from the usefulness or centrality of standard economic tools that are typically used to test theories. They remain the central methodology for the profession. However, it is my feeling that experiments can more often serve as a better rhetorical and motivating device for students.

The Model Used in This Book and an Outline of the Chapters

The model used in this book begins with a society that is in a primitive state of nature and follows this society as it gradually evolves into a modern economy. Throughout the process of evolution, this society develops institutions to deal with recurrent economic problems and to govern economic behavior.

The book is divided into eight sections, and in the material heading of each section I describe how the material there fits into our overall model. The first section contains only one chapter—this introduction. We will now describe the rest of the book going section by section.

Section 2: Preferences, Utilities, Demands, and Uncertainty

The Starting Point: A Primitive State of Nature. The narrative of our book opens in Chapter 2 with a society containing a set of primitive social agents. They live in a world where there are no productive capabilities because no one has yet discovered how to turn one type of good (inputs) into another type of good (outputs). Their world resembles the Garden of Eden in the sense that the food they eat grows on trees and the only decision they must make is how much time to spend picking fruit and how much time to spend relaxing. Chapter 2 describes their world and their tastes and behavior. In short, Chapter 2 presents the physical and behavioral characteristics of the society that we will follow throughout the remainder of this book.

Chapter 3 introduces the concept of an indifference curve, one of the central tools we will use throughout the text, and demonstrates how it can be used to describe the behavior of economic agents.

To lay the groundwork for the analysis of markets and other institutions, Chapter 4 investigates the theory of individual demand curves as they are derived from the tastes and preferences of the social agents in our model. This chapter supplies the theoretical foundation upon which much of our later analysis of institutions is built. Chapter 5 applies the concepts studied in the previous chapters to the problem of economic welfare, a central concern for all of economics.

In each of the first five chapters of the book, we make the assumption that there is no uncertainty in the world. We know, however, that uncertainty surrounds us. Farmers plant crops not knowing what the weather will be that year, people invest in the stock market not knowing if another crash will occur, and people buy houses not knowing whether lightning will strike and burn their houses down. To guard against such uncertainties, people create institutions that provide risk-sharing arrangements, and some agents offer to sell insurance. Chapters 6 and 7 introduce the concept of uncertainty (Chapter 6) and demonstrate (Chapter 7) how this problem leads to the creation of insurance companies and other risk-sharing institutions.

Section 3: Production and Costs

In Chapters 2 through 7, no one in our model produces anything, but in Chapter 8 one of the inhabitants finally discovers how to combine various inputs (capital and labor) to produce a product that all the agents in the society want to consume. Chapter 8 describes the technology of production this inhabitant has discovered. Because profit-maximizing production is a balancing act between costs and revenues, Chapter 9 investigates the type of cost functions that are generated by the technology introduced in Chapter 8. Finally, because some decisions are made in the long run while others are made in the short run, in Chapter 10 we discuss the difference this fact has for long- and short-run cost curves.

Section 4: Decision Theory—Static and Dynamic Decisions

After our entrepreneur understands her cost situation, she must plan her market strategy. Chapter 11, therefore, presents some of the tools of modern game theory and discusses the concepts that our entrepreneur must know in order to make rational decisions about her entry into the world of business and the strategic situation she will face in dealing with her employees.

Economic decisions come in many flavors, however. While in Chapter 11 we look at static decisions—that is, decisions that are typically made at one point in time and affect a decisions maker's payoffs at one point in time as well—in Chapter 12 we investigate dynamic decisions, which are those made over time and that provide a stream of benefits for the decision maker instead of just a one-shot payoff. This leads us into a discussion of how to discount future payoffs in order to compare them to present ones and some problems of what is called time inconsistency.

Before business begins, however, our entrepreneurial pioneer must decide what form of enterprise to create. For example, should a conventional firm be established, and if so, how should it be organized—as a partnership or in a hierarchical fashion? Chapter 13 applies some of the tools we have derived in this section and addresses this problem, investigating not only the best internal structure for the firm but also different incentive schemes that might be used to motivate work by the firm's employees. Our entrepreneur finally decides to start a firm with a conventional hierarchical structure, and in Chapter 13 we see the emergence of this firm and the reasons for its creation.

Section 5: Markets and Market Structures

After our entrepreneur completes all the preliminary activities needed to establish her firm, production and sales begin. Because she is the first person ever to do such a thing, it is natural that, at least for a while, our entrepreneur will be a monopolist. Therefore, you might think that we should start our analysis of markets by discussing the theory of monopoly, monopoly pricing, and the welfare aspects of having an industry organized monopolistically. While this may be natural, we are going to make an institutional leap and assume, in Chapter 14, that when our entrepreneur starts to produce, there is a full set of competitive market institutions already existing. (In Chapter 21, we actually describe the process through which such markets emerge.)

We do this for two reasons. First, competitive markets lead to results that are optimal from a welfare point of view and hence provide a benchmark by which to compare other forms of market institutions, such as a monopoly, an oligopoly, etc. Second, it is conventional for textbooks to start with perfect competition and then treat the theory of monopoly and oligopoly as special cases. While my own preference is not to do this, as I did not in previous editions, I am yielding to convention here. Consequently, in Chapter 14 we study the theory of perfectly competitive markets in the short run, while in Chapter 15 we study the properties of these markets in the long run. Finally, because a common analogy is made between a market and an auction, we study some particular auction institutions in Chapter 16.

natural monopoly
A situation that occurs in industries where the cheapest way to obtain a given quantity of output is to have only one firm produce it.

Chapter 17 treats the theory of monopoly, while in Chapter 18 we encounter another type of monopolistic situation—a natural monopoly. This situation occurs in industries where the cheapest way to obtain a given quantity of output is to have only one firm produce it. To illustrate such a situation, Chapter 18 presents the example of a firm that supplies water to a group of consumers. This firm is the only source of water for the consumers.

In Chapter 18, we investigate the question of whether a monopoly is sustainable against entry into its market by competing firms. As we explore the example of the water company, we find that a societal problem arises because consumers realize that if the company continues as a monopoly, they will have to pay very high prices for the water they need. This displeases the consumers so much that they create a commission to regulate the monopoly, and we have the first public utility regulatory commission. The rest of Chapter 18 provides an analysis of the various ways that society can regulate the water company as a public utility. By the end of this chapter, we have another new institution—a regulated natural monopoly.

In Chapter 19, another producer appears. This firm makes a type of generic good called gadgets. The technology for this good is not such that it will lead the producer to be a natural monopolist. Hence, there is no need for society to regulate this firm. What this firm must worry about is the problem of entry into its market by other firms because such entry can be expected to lower the profits of an incumbent monopolist. Clearly, to understand the circumstances under which entry into a market can be prevented, we must first understand the consequences of successful entry for the incumbent firm and the entrant. Chapter 19 describes the characteristics of oligopolistic industries—industries in which a small number of firms dominate a market.

In Chapter 20, we investigate strategies the gadget producer can use to keep competing firms out of its industry, and we also explore the role that credible threats have in entry prevention. Unfortunately for the gadget producer, it does not succeed in preventing the entry of other firms into its market. In fact, not only do we see in Chapter 20 what happens to an industry as entry occurs, but we also investigate what happens when the number of entrants gets larger and larger so that we can eventually have an infinite number of firms. This is the condition that defines the perfectly competitive market, which we studied in Chapter 14. Here we see the contrasting welfare implications of having an industry organized as a monopoly, an oligopoly, or a perfectly competitive market.

Section 6: Welfare, Exchange, and General Equilibrium

As you remember, in Chapter 14 we made the assumption that perfectly competitive markets existed through which to exchange goods. Chapter 21 explains how such markets might emerge. Markets arise because our social agents realize one day that they might be better off spending some of their time trading the different kinds of goods with one another. They have different tastes, and the kinds of goods each one is endowed with might not provide the bundle that will make each of them most happy. In a two-person world, this trading will take place through a process of bilateral negotiations whose equilibrium outcomes are described in the early part of Chapter 21. As the chapter progresses, however, the population of our model grows so that instead of just one agent of each type, there are eventually two agents of each type, then four, and so on. Eventually, we assume that an infinite number of agents exist. As the economy grows, the process of bilateral bargaining is replaced by a process of multilateral bargaining, and when the number of agents in the economy gets very large, impersonal competitive markets emerge. Hence, in Chapter 21 we see the creation of a new economic institution—competitive markets. Chapter 22 takes the analysis of Chapter 21, in which there is trade but no production, and introduces production into it. In a general equilibrium context, Chapter 22 reviews the economic foundations of the free-market argument and its welfare implications. It also briefly outlines the circumstances under which freely created institutions (like competitive markets) might fail to determine optimal outcomes for a society. Chapters 23, 24, and 25 examine these circumstances in greater depth.

Section 7: Breakdowns and Market Failure

After discussing the benefits of perfectly competitive markets in Section 5, Chapters 23, 24, and 25 consider some sobering counterexamples to the optimality of such markets. In the remaining chapters of this book, the society in our model encounters a number of situations where free, perfectly competitive markets fail. As a result, this society engages in a policy debate about the best course of action available to remedy the failed markets. This debate involves ideological issues and divides the society between those who think that intervention by the government is the most effective way to handle the problems caused by market failure and those who still believe that the government should do nothing because market forces can be relied on to eventually provide solutions. Chapter 23 introduces the concept of **incomplete information** as one of the causes of uncertainty and market failure. According to this concept, producers and consumers are not fully informed about the characteristics of all goods consumed and produced in the economy. Therefore, some markets fail because there is no mechanism to transmit information fully. To help solve this problem, various agents in our model society develop institutions such as reputation, guarantees, and investment in market signals. Chapter 23 investigates the efficacy of these institutional solutions.

In Chapter 24, our society begins to understand that industrialization has its disadvantages as well as its benefits. The air and water are becoming polluted, and people demand that something be done about this problem. Various schemes are proposed—taxes, quotas, environmental standards, and effluent charges. In addition, our social agents begin to question who should be held liable for the damage inflicted on others and whether a law should be passed to impose liability on one party. In this context, the famous Coase theorem is introduced and analyzed.

In Chapter 25, our social agents face a new problem. For the first time, they feel the need to build a social project that will provide its benefits free of charge to everybody and exclude no one. Initially, it is suggested that people voluntarily contribute by placing what they feel is an appropriate amount in collection boxes located in the main square of the town. Much to their disappointment, our social agents discover that people are taking a **free ride**—enjoying a public good paid for by others—rather than contributing. The failure of this voluntary system creates the need for a coordinating body that will have the power to levy taxes to pay for

incomplete information
A situation in which producers and consumers are not fully informed about the characteristics of all goods consumed and produced in the economy and that can cause uncertainty and market failure.

free ride
The process of enjoying the benefits of a public good without contributing to its construction.

social projects and will therefore help solve the free-rider problem. This coordinating body is the state.

Chapter 25 also explores issues that arise in connection with the role of the state in selecting and funding social projects. If the aim of the state is to maximize the welfare of society, then it must face the problem of how it will decide on the optimal level of this "public good" to purchase and how the purchases will be financed. Such a problem leads the government in our model to investigate a wide variety of tax and subsidy schemes or mechanisms that can be used to overcome the free-rider situation.

At the end of Chapter 25, we see that as our model develops, conflicts will arise among the various interest groups in society. These interest groups must reach a compromise between their own preferences and the broader needs of society. We therefore investigate the role of government as an arbiter of conflicts among interest groups, and we examine the search for a reliable method to help these groups make appropriate social decisions.

Section 8: Input Markets and the Origins of Class Struggle

In Chapter 26, we extend our analysis of interest group politics by looking at the tensions that arise in free-market economies from the sometimes conflicting interests of the various factors of production—land, labor, and capital. Because there are many questions in such economies about the fairness of the returns received by land, labor, and capital, we investigate the manner in which these returns are determined and analyze the economic arguments that are used to justify these returns.

Three Fundamental Institutions

Before we begin the analysis of our model, we will assume that there are some primitive institutions that exist in all societies and that these institutions are already present in our model when we first encounter it in Chapter 2. In other words, we will assume that this society existed for a time before our story starts and that during that time, three fundamental institutions developed: the state, property rights, and economic consulting firms. At first glance, the last of these institutions—economic consulting firms—seems far less fundamental than the other two and probably appears to be an odd choice. However, its importance will soon become clear. Let us look at each of these institutions in turn.

The State

While life in the society described in Chapter 2 is quite primitive, life was even more primitive in the time before our narrative starts. In fact, picture this society at its earliest stage as existing in a raw state of nature. The English philosopher Thomas Hobbes called life in such a society "nasty, brutish and short," which we will take to mean that people have no respect for one another's lives or property. People obtain whatever food they can by gathering fruit and plants and by stealing from one another. The concept of property rights has not as yet arisen.

How did the institution of the state develop in such a society? Assume that people have staked out land for themselves and protect this land by fighting because others do not respect their claims to ownership unless force is used. At this stage, land theft is not a problem because the concept of "might makes right" has imposed at least some equilibrium in the division of land. However, the food-gathering system does not work as well. People spend part of each day picking fruit and harvesting plants and the other part of the day robbing others and protecting themselves against robbery. This process is wasteful because the time could be more efficiently spent if it were all devoted to gathering food. (Robbery is merely a redistribution of already existing food, and protection is entirely wasteful because it creates no new fruit and plants to consume.) Therefore, it would be best for society if all people simply agreed to consume what grows on their land and not to rob one another. In this way, they would not have to waste time and effort on protection. Unfortunately, in a primitive state of nature, such an agreement would not be stable. If society as a whole refrains from robbery and protection, it is in the interest of individuals to take advantage of the situation and rob others. In a primitive state of nature, robbery is a natural result of any restraint on the part of the peaceful majority in using force to protect its property.

What will such a society do to deal with the problem of robbery? We might expect that the agents in this society would form protective associations—groups of people who join together and agree not to rob one another but, instead, to rob people outside their group.[7] There are two benefits to joining a protective association. First, there are fewer people by whom one has to fear being robbed; and, second, there is a savings of time and effort when several neighbors band together for protection rather than each doing it alone. If the savings are large enough, it will be most beneficial if everyone in the society forms one grand protective association and agrees not to rob anyone else in the association. This grand protective association and the promises made by it function like a system of property rights. Such an arrangement is stable because if people break their promises and rob someone else, they will be punished by the protective association either through ostracism or through confiscation of their property. This grand protective association actually fills a role in its society that is equivalent to what we call the *state*, which is merely a voluntary, all-inclusive group whose aims, among other things, are to protect private property and enforce the "promises" that civilized people make to one another when they agree to be members.

In the rest of our narrative, we will assume that this grand protective association (or the state) was formed sometime in prehistory or at least before the economic history of the society we will be studying in this book. All members of this society will be members of the grand association and are assumed to adhere to its rules, which, of course, include respect for the property rights of others. The people also grant the state the right to make laws, levy taxes, and raise an army—all the common functions of government. We have now described the creation of our first economic institutions—the state and property rights.

Property Rights

While political theory usually describes the creation of the state and property rights as emerging from the type of primitive state of nature envisioned by the English philosophers John Locke and Thomas Hobbes, economists have explained the benefits of property rights with an additional justification more related to economic efficiency than to the fear of robbery. To understand this reasoning, assume that in our state of nature there exists a lake that is shared by two neighbors. Neither

---

[7] See Robert Nozick, *Anarchy, State, and Utopia* (New York: Basic Books, 1975), and Schotter, *The Economic Theory of Social Institutions* for a full description of the emergence of the state.

neighbor owns the lake. It is simply a common resource for the two of them.[8] To emphasize the efficiency rationale for property rights, let us say that when these two neighbors catch fish from the lake, neither attempts to rob the other. Thus, they do not need property rights to be able to keep what they catch.

Assume that the neighbors can fish with two different intensities—high or low. Fishing with high intensity involves fishing many hours a day or using nets or even dynamite to catch fish, whereas fishing with low intensity involves fishing fewer hours a day or using only a pole. As we might expect, fishing with high intensity produces larger catches. However, there is a trade-off in this situation. Larger catches provide more fish to exchange for other goods like food, clothing, and tools, but larger catches also deplete the supply of fish at a rate that prevents the remaining fish from reproducing fast enough to maintain a plentiful stock of fish in the lake. If the size of the fish population ever becomes so small that it goes below a certain critical level, all fish life will disappear from the lake. For the purposes of our analysis, we will assume that this critical level is reached when at least one neighbor fishes with high intensity. Thus, fishing with high intensity produces short-run gains and long-run hazards.

The two neighbors must decide how intensively to fish. Assume that if both neighbors fish with low intensity, each will catch enough fish to exchange for a wide variety of goods. We will summarize the value of these goods to the two neighbors by assigning it the number 20, which means that the payoff to each neighbor when both fish with low intensity is 20. If they both fish with high intensity, the lake will be ruined because the fish population will fall below the critical number necessary for viable life. We will assume that the payoff in this case is 4 for each neighbor.

If one neighbor fishes with high intensity and the other with low intensity, the lake will be ruined in the future, but the one who fishes with high intensity will bene-fit greatly because he will be able to catch many fish today and reap a short-run gain. The one who shows restraint will be doubly hurt because the lake will be ruined by his greedy neighbor and he will not even have received a good short-term payoff. In this situation, we will assume that the payoff is worth 30 for the neighbor who fishes with high intensity and 2 for the neighbor who fishes with low intensity. (These pay-offs demonstrate that the neighbors are somewhat short-sighted because the one who fishes with high intensity seems to totally discount the fact that his fishing will even-tually ruin the lake.) Table 1.1 describes the situation faced by the two neighbors.

In this table, the first number in each cell represents the payoff to neighbor 1 and the second the payoff to neighbor 2. Note that if neighbor 1 decides to fish with low intensity and neighbor 2 with low intensity, then the payoff to each is 20, as shown in the cell at the upper left corner of the matrix. If both neighbors decide to fish with high intensity, each has a payoff of 4, as shown in the cell at the lower right corner.

Table 1.1	**The Payoffs from Fishing at High and Low Intensities.**	
	NEIGHBOR 2	
	Fish with low intensity	**Fish with high intensity**
Neighbor 1 **Fish with low intensity**	20, 20	2, 30
Fish with high intensity	30, 2	4, 4

---

[8] This explanation for the existence of property rights is the same as that offered by Garrett Hardin, "The Tragedy of the Commons," *Science*, 162 (December 1968): 249–54.

The cells at the lower left and upper right corners indicate the payoffs when one neighbor chooses high-intensity fishing and the other neighbor chooses low-intensity fishing. Note that the two neighbors would be better off if each fished with low intensity because only in that case would they both receive a payoff of 20 (and society would get a payoff of 40). However, if one neighbor shows restraint, the other neighbor can get a payoff of 30 by fishing with high intensity.

The question now arises as to how each neighbor will behave when the lake is a common resource (no one owns it) and the payoffs are as previously described. The answer is simple. Each will fish with high intensity. The reason is that the decision to fish with high intensity is best for each neighbor, no matter what the other neighbor does. To see why this is true, consider the situation of neighbor 1. If he thinks that neighbor 2 will fish with low intensity, then his best response is to fish with high intensity and receive a payoff of 30 rather than a payoff of 20. Similarly, if neighbor 1 thinks neighbor 2 will fish with high intensity, his best alternative is also to fish with high intensity because then at least he obtains many fish in the short run, knowing that the lake will be ruined in the long run. His payoff will only be 4, but that is greater than the payoff of 2 he would get if he fished with low intensity and neighbor 2 fished with high intensity. Hence, fishing with high intensity is the best one neighbor can do no matter what the other does, and because this is true for both neighbors, both will fish with high intensity. As a result, the lake will be ruined and the sum of the payoffs to both neighbors will be only 8.

The reason we have such a poor solution to this problem is that no one owns the lake. Because of the lack of ownership, neither neighbor can afford to show restraint, knowing that the other will not refrain from high-intensity fishing. Let us now say that the lake is not a common resource but rather the private property of one person—neighbor 1. If this is the case, neighbor 1 will clearly fish with an intensity equal to twice his low-intensity fishing and thereby receive a payoff of 40 (twice the payoff of 20 for low-intensity fishing). Note also that if one neighbor owns the lake, he will not ruin it with high-intensity fishing because he need not fear the actions of another user. Hence, the existence of property rights increases the payoff to society. When the lake was a common resource, the payoff to the two users was only 8; but now that the lake is owned by one person, the payoff is 40. Societal benefits have increased although the distribution of these benefits has become more inequitable.

Property rights do not necessarily lead to unequal income distribution. For example, assume that both neighbors owned fishing rights to the lake. In this case, one neighbor could turn to the other and say, "Look, if we do not coordinate our actions, we will ruin this lake and our livelihoods. Why don't you sell me your rights? I will pay you 5 not to fish in the lake. You will benefit from this arrangement because your payoff will be only 4 if you don't sell and we both fish with high intensity, which you know we will." The second neighbor says, "I think it's a great idea for me to sell you my rights. However, I'd like you to pay me 35 and keep 5 for yourself because you will receive a payoff of 40 if you own the lake. In that way, you will benefit and so will I." Note that in this bargaining, any agreement that gives each party a payoff of at least 4 and adds up to 40 will make both parties better off than they would be without the sale. Hence, a split of 20-20 is possible here, which means that property rights can generate payoffs just like the ones that would be received if both neighbors acted in the socially optimal way in using the lake to fish.

Whatever the final split in benefits, it is clear that the existence of property rights enhances the efficiency of economic activities by giving people the appropriate incentives to manage what were previously common resources. This increased efficiency is one of the major benefits achieved by the creation of a state that will enforce the rights of people to own private property.

Economic Consulting Firms

Throughout this book, the society in our model will have at its disposal a number of economic consulting firms. Whenever this society reaches a point where a major decision must be made, its agents will call on some consultants for advice, which will come in the form of consulting reports. The opinions given in these reports will rarely be accepted without argument. Instead, they will lead to dialogues between the consultants and the social agents about the economic theories on which the consultants have based their advice. Sometimes, the consulting reports will also rely on the results of laboratory experiments that were conducted to test the economic theories being discussed. The consultants will use the results of such experiments to support their opinions.

Obviously, while the state and property rights are real institutions that we might find in a primitive society, economic consulting firms are not. They are a pedagogical device that we will use in this book to make a critical examination of a wide variety of economic theories and some of the laboratory experiments designed to test these theories.

The consulting reports and the dialogues they engender demonstrate the fragile nature of particular economic models and the sensitivity of the results they produce to their underlying assumptions. The critical nature of the dialogues between the consultants and the social agents is meant to inject a healthy note of skepticism into our analysis of economic theories. Economics is not a dead science in which all known problems have solutions and all existing solutions are effective. Quite the contrary is true. We will therefore subject every theory we discuss in this book to criticism.

Conclusion

In the next section, we encounter the model that we will be using throughout this book to study microeconomics. Our model starts with a society in a primitive state of nature. This society has no economic or social institutions except the three fundamental institutions that we have just discussed—the state, property rights, and economic consulting firms. We will become familiar with the conditions that exist in this society and the psychological makeup of its inhabitants. Our understanding of the characteristics of this society will provide a foundation for analyzing its gradual development into a modern economy with the types of economic and social institutions that we see in our own society.

SECTION 2

Preferences, Utilities, Demands, and Uncertainty

Economies consist of people. This point is so simple and obvious that one can easily overlook its importance. Human behavior plays a key role in every economy. The decisions that shape an economy—decisions about consumption, production, savings, and investment—are made by people.

No two individuals are alike, but there are certain regularities of behavior that are similar across people. In this section, we will turn our attention to such behavioral regularities and see what they can tell us about consumer preferences and decision making.

The setting for our analysis of consumer behavior is a primitive society, one devoid of social institutions or other cultural artifacts. We will begin this section in Chapter 2 by discussing the characteristics of the goods existing in our primitive society and the characteristics of its inhabitants. Underlying this discussion are seven assumptions about our primitive society. Some of these assumptions concern the psychological makeup of the inhabitants, specifically their feelings about one another and about the consumption goods available to them. Other assumptions concern the rationality of the inhabitants, specifically how they go about making choices. Still other assumptions concern the types of consumer goods available in this society. These serve as a description of our agents' *preferences*.

From the assumptions that we make about the psychology and rationality of the inhabitants of our primitive society, we will derive an analytical construct called an *indifference curve*, which graphically represents the consumer preferences of the inhabitants. These indifference curves, studied in Chapter 3, represent the *utility functions* that are associated with our inhabitants' preferences. Throughout the remainder of this book, we will use indifference curves as a convenient tool for analyzing consumer behavior. Keep in mind that the type of indifference curves we produce to describe a person's preferences will always depend on the assumptions that we make about the psychology and rationality of that person.

It should also be noted that the person we are discussing in this and later chapters is *homo economicus*—economic man (person). This fictional individual contains many qualities that we all share but is characterized primarily by a dedication to the principles of rationality.

At the end of Chapter 3, we will discuss how the consumers in our primitive society go about choosing bundles of goods from those available to them. We will examine the characteristics of an *optimal bundle of goods*—the bundle that most satisfies a consumer's preferences (maximizes the consumer's utility) after taking into account any constraints such as available income or time. These constraints make it necessary for the consumer to choose bundles from an *economically feasible consumption set*—the set of bundles the consumer can afford.

Through Chapter 3, our primitive society lacked any institutions except the state and property rights. In Chapter 4, we will assume that our primitive society has developed competitive markets so that we can continue our examination of consumer behavior in a setting that is more institutionally advanced and therefore closer to a modern economy. We will not discuss how these markets arose in our primitive society until later in the book, when we study the process of market entry and perfectly competitive markets.

From an operational standpoint, perfectly competitive markets exist when any economic agent can exchange as much of a given commodity as he wishes for another commodity at a fixed, predetermined (equilibrium) price. One key characteristic of such markets is that they are anonymous. The identity of the actual traders is not important. A Smith or a Jones can trade on the same terms as a Rockefeller. Another key characteristic is uniform pricing for a commodity no matter what the size of the trade. The unit price of the commodity is the same whether a trade involves 100 units or 100,000 units. There are no quantity discounts in a perfectly competitive market. Big and small traders are treated alike.

When competitive markets exist, it is easier to predict consumer behavior, as we will see in Chapter 4. Such behavior is characterized by a consumer's *demand function*, which we will now be able to derive, given our study of consumer preferences and decision making in Chapters 2 and 3. A demand function shows the relationship between the quantity of any particular good purchased and the price of that good if other factors such as consumer income and the prices of substitute and complementary goods remain constant. Demand functions will be presented as *demand curves*, which depict in graphic terms the quantities of a good that consumers would be willing to purchase at various prices. We will observe how demand curves result from the utility-maximizing behavior of our agents.

The demand functions that we derive for our agents will allow us to analyze how their behavior will change in response to changing income and changing prices. In Chapter 4, we will examine various properties of demand curves and investigate a method of measuring *consumer surplus*—the gain that a consumer receives from purchasing a good at a certain price. We will then use this measure to study how the benefits obtained from purchasing a good change as its price changes. In Chapter 5, we present a variety of applications of consumer demand theory.

In Chapter 6, we introduce uncertainty into the analysis. This is essential because in the real world we are not fully informed about all of the relevant parameters we face. For example, part of our environment is random. Hence, when a farmer plants his crops, she does so without knowing what the weather is going to be during the growing season. While she may have some long-range forecasts that allow her to assign probabilities to various possibilities, she nevertheless must make her choices *ex ante* before knowing what the weather will be. People make investments without knowing how the economy will fare in the future. Clearly, if we are going to present a comprehensive theory of decision making in economics, we must at some point introduce uncertainty into our analysis. This is done in Chapter 6.

Finally, Chapter 7 applies the tools of uncertainty analysis to studying the very important institution of insurance. This chapter offers a number of applications.

2 Consumers and Their Preferences

EXPERIMENTAL TEASER 1

SOCIAL PREFERENCES

Homo economicus (economic man) is assumed to satisfy a set of behavioral and psychological assumptions upon which economists build a model of his behavior. This is the model we will study in this chapter and this book. Experimental evidence has raised some questions about whether this model actually predicts behavior well.

Consider the following experiment performed by Elizabeth Hoffman, Kevin McCabe, Keith Shachak, and Vernon Smith.* Experimental subjects are brought into a laboratory and randomly assigned to one of two groups. One group is called the dividers and the other the receivers. Each divider is given $10 and randomly matched with one receiver whose identity he or she does not know. The divider is asked to split these ten dollars between himself and the randomly drawn receiver in any way he wants. He can keep it all for himself or he can give some to this other person.

Do you think that college undergraduates would give any of this money away? If so, does such behavior violate the assumptions associated with *Homo economicus*? If instead of randomly being assigned to be a divider or a receiver subjects engaged in a contest—say, solving puzzles—with the winner being made the divider and the loser the receiver, would the mean amount offered go up? Would the amount offered vary with the divider and receiver knowing each other's names? Would the mean amount offered change if the experiment were double blind—that is, neither the subjects nor the experimenter knew what any subject decided to give? Stick around and we will give you the answers to these questions at the end of the chapter.

---

* See Elizabeth Hoffman, Kevin McCabe, Keith Shachak, and Vernon Smith, "Preferences, Property Rights and Anonymity in Bargaining Games," in *Games and Economic Behavior,* Volume 7, 1994, pp. 346–80.

The Consumption Possibility Set

A Primitive State of Nature: People and Goods

When our analysis starts, people are living in a primitive state of nature with few institutions and no economic activity except the gathering of food. In fact, economic life is bleak and monotonous. It totally lacks the rich diversity of institutions and activities that we see in our own economic world. There are no banks, insurance companies, corporations, or antitrust laws; and most important, there are no markets of any type. The only institutions that exist are the three fundamental ones that we discussed in Chapter 1: the state, property rights, and economic consulting firms. As this society evolves and its economy grows, we will see how additional institutions emerge in response to attempts by the society's agents to solve a variety of problems that arise.

At the beginning, the inhabitants of our primitive society are all simple economic agents who do not know how to produce any goods and who divide their time between relaxing and picking apples and raspberries, the only two goods available for their consumption. As we might expect, these economic agents have few choices to make. They must decide how much of their time to spend at leisure and how much to spend picking fruit, and they must decide what mix of fruit (bundle of goods) they want to consume at any given point in time. Put differently, they must decide which bundle of goods, taken from the set of bundles that is feasible for them to consume, is best in the sense that it would make them most happy.

As a first step in analyzing how decisions about consumption are made, we will examine the consumption possibility set for the economic agents in our primitive society. This is the set of bundles feasible for the agents to consume. To keep our discussion simple, we will assume that there are just two economic agents in our primitive society. Figure 2.1 provides a graphic representation of their consumption possibilities. For convenience, let us refer to the two available types of goods—the apples and the raspberries—as good 1 and good 2. We will assume that these goods are available in positive quantities ranging from 0 to $+\infty$. The quantities of good 1 (x_1) appear along the horizontal axis of Figure 2.1, and the quantities of good 2 (x_2) appear along the vertical axis of this figure.

Point *a* in Figure 2.1 represents a possible bundle of goods to be consumed by either one of our two agents. It contains 20 units of good 1 and 12 units of good 2. Point *b* represents a bundle that contains 50 units of good 1 and 50 units of good 2. Notice that the set of consumption possibilities depicted in Figure 2.1 is bounded from below by the horizontal and vertical axes because only positive amounts of each good are available for consumption. (It is impossible to consume negative quantities of any good.) Conversely, Figure 2.1 depicts consumption possibilities as unbounded from above, which would mean that our agents could consume infinite positive amounts of all goods. However, consumption of infinite quantities is not really possible because our agents simply do not have enough time to consume huge amounts of goods. Furthermore, after markets are created and goods are assigned prices, the consumption of our agents will be limited by their incomes. We will deal with the problem of the lack of realism in boundless consumption possibilities when we reach Section 2.3 of this chapter.

consumption possibility set
The set of bundles feasible for the agents to consume in a society.

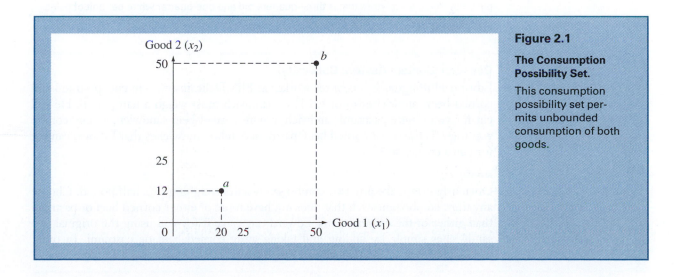

Figure 2.1

The Consumption Possibility Set.

This consumption possibility set permits unbounded consumption of both goods.

What we are looking for here is the set of consumption bundles of goods 1 and 2 from which our agents can feasibly choose their consumption bundles.

The Convexity Property of Consumption Possibility Sets

The consumption possibility set will contain all the feasible bundles available for our agents to consume. Clearly, physical reality will place restrictions on what this set might look like. To be complete in our treatment of consumption possibility sets but not dwell on excessive detail, let us quickly discuss three assumptions that we will impose on the consumption possibility sets of our agents. First, we assume that goods are infinitely divisible, so in our world it will be possible to consume $\frac{1}{10}$ of an apple or $\frac{1}{1,000}$ of a raspberry. (This is called our divisibility assumption.) Second, we assume that it is possible to add consumption bundles so that if you can consume bundle a containing 20 apples and 16 raspberries and also consume bundle b containing 2 apples and 100 raspberries, then you can consume bundle $a + b = 22$ apples, 116 raspberries. (This is called our additivity assumption.)

Using additivity and divisibility, we can derive another property of consumption sets, which is called convexity. By convexity we mean that it is possible to combine two bundles to produce a third by consuming fractions of them. For example, say it is possible to consume bundle a containing 20 shirts and 16 oranges and also to consume bundle b containing 2 shirts and 100 oranges. Then convexity says it is possible to consume a bundle like c that contains, for example, $\frac{1}{2}$ of a and $\frac{1}{2}$ of b (that is, $c = 11$ shirts and 58 oranges). In fact, convexity says that if bundles a and b are available for you to consume, then so is any bundle c formed by taking a fraction λ of a and $1 - \lambda$ of b where $0 \leq \lambda \leq 1$; that is, $c = \lambda a + (1 - \lambda)b$. Bundle c is called a convex combination of bundles a and b.

divisibility assumption
The assumption on consumption sets that states that goods are infinitely divisible.
additivity assumption
The assumption on consumption sets that states that it is possible to add consumption bundles.
convexity
The property of consumption sets that implies that it is possible to combine two bundles to produce a third by consuming fractions of them.

Example 2.1

A CONVEX SET OF COLORS: SHADES OF PINK

Schoolchildren have worked with convex sets all their lives. For example, say a child has a bottle of white paint and a bottle of red paint. The set of colors he or she can mix using these two basic components is convex and represents all shades of pink between pure white and pure red. As the fraction (λ) of white paint mixed into the red paint gets smaller (approaches 0), the color of the mixture approaches pure red. As the fraction of white paint mixed into the red paint gets larger (approaches 1), the color of the mixture approaches pure white. Shocking pink may involve a mixture that is three-quarters red and one-quarter white per unit of paint.

SOLVED PROBLEM 2.1

Question (Content Review: Convexity)
Edward Huffington is a counter worker at Eli's Delicatessen. He cuts pastrami and corned-beef sandwiches to order. Each sandwich must weigh a half pound. He will cut for you a pure pastrami sandwich, a pure corned-beef sandwich, or any combo you want. Is the set of corned beef–pastrami combo sandwiches that Edward can cut for you a convex set?

Answer
Obviously it is. Take any two combo sandwiches weighing one half pound. Choose any third combo sandwich that does not have more of either corned beef or pastrami than either of the originals, and Edward can make it for you using the original two sandwiches simply by adding and taking away corned beef or pastrami. In other words, you choose any mixture and Edward will create the sandwich for you.

Question (Application and Extension: Convexity)

Maria is the best auditor at the IRS. She has 3 cases on her desk and 1 hour to look at them. If she spends the hour looking only at the folder from the Sleaze Corporation, she will discover 8 instances of fraud and 6 instances of bribery. If she spends the full hour looking at Slime-Ball Inc., she will catch 2 instances of fraud and 4 instances of bribery. Finally, she can look at the folder of Murder Inc., where she will find 14 instances of fraud and 2 of bribery (not to mention many murders, but that is not her concern).

If she spends a fraction λ of her time on any folder, she will find exactly λ of the fraud and bribery cases she would have found had she spent the entire hour. For example, if she spent a half hour on the Sleaze Corporation's folder, she would find 4 instances of fraud and 3 instances of bribery.

a) On a graph with cases of fraud on the horizontal axis and cases of bribery on the vertical axis, locate the 3 points associated with spending a full hour on each folder.

SOLVED PROBLEM 2.2

Figure 2.2

A Convex Set.

The triangle represents the set of all bribery and fraud cases that can be detected.

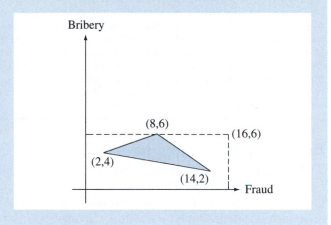

b) If Maria splits her 1 hour evenly to look at the 3 cases, what is the set of fraud and bribery cases she can find? Is this set convex?

Answer

The set of feasible fraud-bribery cases found is depicted as the shaded region in Figure 2.2. As you can see, this is a convex set because any point in the set can be achieved by taking a convex combination of two other points in the set.

Rationality

Now that we know some key facts about the physical world in which our economic agents live, we must investigate their psychological makeup. What type of people are they? We will begin by assuming that our agents have *preferences* among the available consumption bundles and that these preferences constitute a complete binary ordering of the elements of their consumption possibility set. When we say that a complete binary ordering of preferences exists, we mean that if any two bundles in the consumption possibility set (hence the term *binary*) are chosen, say bundles *a* and *b*, then our agents will be able to rank them—to tell

complete binary ordering
An assumption on consumer preferences that implies that if any two bundles in the consumption possibility set (hence the term binary) are chosen, say bundles *a* and *b*, then our agents will be able to rank them—tell whether they prefer *a* to *b* or *b* to *a* or whether they consider *a* to be exactly as good as *b*.

whether they prefer *a* to *b* or *b* to *a* or whether they consider *a* to be exactly as good as *b*. This will be true for *all possible bundles* (hence the term *complete*). As a result, it will never be the case that our agents will tell us that they cannot decide which bundle is at least as good as any other bundle because they will always have well-defined opinions. Moreover, we will assume that this ordering satisfies two properties called *reflexivity* and *transitivity*, which we will discuss soon. These restrictions on preferences constitute a minimal rationality assumption that can be summarized as follows.

> **Rationality Assumption 1: A Complete Binary Ordering.** For any bundles *a* and *b* in a consumption possibility set, *a* is at least as good as *b*, *b* is at least as good as *a*, or *a* is exactly as good as *b*. When *a* is exactly as good as *b*, we say that our agent is *indifferent* between *a* and *b*.

Counter Example 2.1

TIM DUNCAN, ALLEN IVERSON, AND FAVORITE CHILDREN

The assumption of a complete ordering does not always hold true. In certain situations, people are unable or unwilling to make a comparison and express a preference. For example, if we were to ask basketball fans whether Tim Duncan or Allen Iverson is the better basketball player, they might answer that they cannot rank the two players because it would be like *comparing apples and oranges*. What they would mean is that each player is so different from the other that it is impossible to make a meaningful comparison. Likewise, most parents would be unwilling to express a preference between their two children because they believe that they should love each of their children equally.

While we will use the assumption of a complete ordering in this text as it is used throughout economic theory, we must recognize its shortcomings.

Binary Relationships among Goods

To be as precise as possible in defining our next assumption, let us say that the binary preference relationship our agents have over the set of bundles feasible for them to consume is called the *R* relationship. *R* will mean the "at-least-as-good-as relationship." Hence, when we see the statement *aRb*, we will read it as "Bundle *a* is at least as good as bundle *b*." For example, if bundle *a* consists of 2 pounds of apples and 1 pound of raspberries and bundle *b* consists of 1 pound of apples and 3 pounds of raspberries, the statement *aRb* will mean that our agent feels that a bundle containing 2 pounds of apples and 1 pound of raspberries is at least as good as a bundle containing 1 pound of apples and 3 pounds of raspberries.

Our next assumption about preference relationships is simply that any bundle is at least as good as itself. This assumption is known as reflexivity.

> **Rationality Assumption 2: Reflexivity.** For any bundle *a*, *aRa*.

Because this assumption is obviously satisfied for our work here (that is, any bundle is at least as good as itself), we will not discuss this assumption further.

An even more useful assumption is transitivity—the assumption that consumer preferences are consistent. This assumption means that if our agents think that bundle *a* is at least as good as bundle *b* and that bundle *b* is at least as good as bundle *c*, then they also think that bundle *a* is at least as good as bundle *c*. We can summarize this assumption as follows.

> **Rationality Assumption 3: Transitivity.** If *aRb* and *bRc*, then *aRc*.

If this assumption holds true, then we say the *R* relationship is transitive. The transitivity assumption is actually the essence of what is meant by rationality in economic theory.

reflexivity
An assumption on consumer preferences that states that any bundle is at least as good as itself.

transitivity
An assumption on consumer preferences, and the property of preference relationships that states that if agents think that bundle *a* is at least as good as bundle *b* and that bundle *b* is at least as good as bundle *c*, then they also think that bundle *a* is at least as good as bundle *c*.

Example 2.2

FINDING AN INTRANSITIVE SUCKER

While the transitivity assumption may sound reasonable on logical grounds, there is a better justification for it based on the theory of markets and what we observe in the real world. To demonstrate that transitivity might be a good description of what people are actually like, let us see what could happen if people did not have transitive preferences—preferences that are consistent.

Say a person exists whose preferences are intransitive. For instance, assume the person prefers good *a* to good *b*, good *b* to good *c*, but good *c* to good *a*, and this person is willing to pay at least $1 to switch from one good to a preferred good. Further assume that this person currently has good *b* but that you have goods *a* and *c*. Let us consider how these preferences can yield bad outcomes. You offer the person a trade of good *a* for his good *b*. You say, "I will give you good *a* if you give me good *b* plus $1." Because the person prefers good *a* to good *b* even though it will cost him $1, he accepts the deal and receives good *a*. You then have $1 and goods *b* and *c*. However, you find out that the person prefers good *c* to good *a*, so you offer the following deal: "I will give you good *c* if you give me good *a* plus $1." Again, the person accepts the deal. You have then collected $2 and hold goods *b* and *a*, while the person with the intransitive preferences has paid out $2 and holds good *c*. Finally, you learn that the person prefers good *b* to good *c*, and you therefore offer the following deal: "I will give you good *b* if you give me good *c* plus $1." Once again, the person accepts the deal. You now have $3 and goods *a* and *c*.

As a result of these deals, we see that the person has paid out $3 and has returned to his starting position—again holding only good *b*. You can now start the trading process over again and become infinitely rich (or at least take all the other person's wealth by repeated trading). Clearly, intransitive preferences have led to a ridiculous situation. Because we rarely observe such strange behavior, we might conclude that people's preferences are transitive in the real world.

Note that our economic definition of rationality is narrower than its everyday meaning. When we describe economic agents as rational, we essentially mean that they know what they like and behave accordingly. Excluded from this notion of rationality is any evaluation of the preferences themselves. That is, economics takes people's preferences as given and assumes that rational agents maximize their satisfaction in the most efficient way.

rationality
The assumption that economic agents know what they like and behave accordingly, that is, that an agent's preferences exhibit completeness, reflexivity, and transitivity.

The Economically Feasible Set

Time Constraints

At this point, we have described our consumption set as one that is bounded from below by the horizontal and vertical axes and allows for the possibility of zero consumption of any good (that is, it includes the origin). However, our consumption set is unbounded from above, which leads to the assumption that our agents can consume infinite positive amounts of the two goods available to them—an assumption that is clearly unreasonable. To make our analysis more realistic, we need only recognize that agents cannot consume infinite amounts of goods for a variety of reasons. For example, consumption usually takes time, and in any given day, there is not enough time to consume more than a finite amount of each good. To see how time constraints can limit consumption, let us assume that consumption of certain goods—goods 1 and 2—can only take place during daylight hours and that it stays light for exactly 12 hours a day. Let us also assume that it takes 2 hours to consume 1 unit of good 2 and 4 hours to consume 1 unit of good 1, as we see in Figure 2.3. If one of our agents spends all her time consuming good 2, she can consume only 6 units a day, while if she spends all her time consuming good 1, she can consume only 3 units a day.

Because it takes a fixed amount of time to consume each of these two goods and the amounts differ, one good is more "expensive" than the other. If our agent decides to consume 1 unit less of good 2, she releases 2 hours that become available to consume good 1. With those 2 hours, she can consume $\frac{1}{2}$ unit of good 1. Hence, in terms of time, good 1 is twice as expensive as good 2 because it takes twice as long to consume that good. Put differently, when our agent consumes 1 unit of good 1, she is sacrificing the consumption of 2 units of good 2.

Look again at Figure 2.3. Note that by dividing time in various proportions between the two goods, the agent can consume any bundle on or below the straight line between points a and b. The agent is on the straight line if all 12 of the available hours are used for consumption, and she is below the straight line if fewer than 12 hours are used. In fact, that straight line represents all the bundles that take exactly 12 hours to consume. Also note that all the goods on the line between a and b are available for consumption because of our assumption of convexity, which is one of the reasons we made it. Finally, note that because of the time constraint, our agent is unable to consume bundles such as c that lie outside the newly bounded consumption set. Hence, we can now say that the set of consumption bundles available to our agent is a set bounded from below by the fact that negative consumption is impossible (which is why the horizontal and vertical axes represent the lowest possible level of consumption) and bounded from above by a time constraint. The available consumption set is depicted by the shaded area marked F in Figure 2.3.

Figure 2.3

The Economically Feasible Consumption Set: Time Constraints.

The time available to the agent permits her to consume only bundles represented by points in the shaded triangle F.

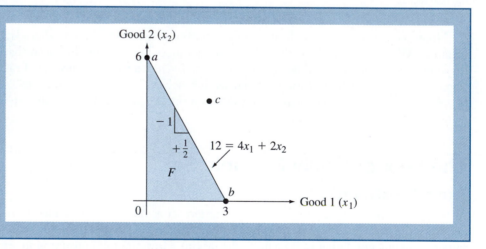

SOLVED PROBLEM 2.3

Question (Content Review: Time Constraints on Consumption Sets)
In Figure 2.3, if the consumer were at point b and decided to spend 4 fewer hours consuming good 1, how many more units of good 2 could he consume?

Answer
The answer here is quite simple. It takes 4 hours to consume 1 unit of good 1 and 2 hours to consume 1 unit of good 2. By switching 4 hours away from the consumption of good 1, the consumer will lose 1 unit of good 1; but because it takes only 2 hours to consume a unit of good 2, he gets to consume 2 more units in exchange.

Income or Budget Constraints

Later in this book we will see how income or budget constraints place an upper bound on the set of goods available for consumption by our agents. At that point, our model will contain a market for each good and our agents will work and earn an income. By a market, we mean a place where agents can go and exchange one good for another at a fixed price. Of course, in the primitive society that we are now studying, there are no markets and our agents have no incomes. However, in order to take a brief look at the effect of income constraints, let us assume that markets and incomes do exist in our primitive society. Let us also assume that the price of good 2 is 1 and the price of good 1 is 2 and that each agent earns an income of 6. In Figure 2.4 we see the same economically feasible set that we determined in Figure 2.3, but the set now has a different interpretation. If the agent spends all his income on good 2, he will consume 6 units; that is, he will be at point a in Figure 2.4. If he spends all his income on good 1, he will consume 3 units and be at point b. If he divides his income between the two goods, he will be at some point on the straight line between points a and b. Because the straight line represents all bundles whose cost exactly equals the agent's income, its equation is $2x_1 + 1x_2 = 6$ and its slope is -2, the negative of the ratio of the price of good 1 to the price of good 2 (x_1 is the amount of good 1 consumed and x_2 is the amount of good 2 consumed). For example, take bundle d in Figure 2.4, where d consists of 2 units of good 1 and 2 units of good 2. If the agent consumes this bundle, its cost will be

$$\text{Cost of } d = 2 \cdot (2 \text{ units of good 1}) + 1 \cdot (2 \text{ units of good 2}) = 6$$

Bundles such as c will not be feasible in this case because they will cost more money than our agent has. However, bundles such as e will be within the agent's budget.

No matter how we decide to place an upper bound on the consumption possibility set, the result leaves us with a reduced set of consumption bundles that are feasible to consume. We call this reduced set the **economically feasible consumption set**.

market
A place where agents can go and exchange one good for another at a fixed price.

economically feasible consumption set
The reduced set of consumption bundles economically feasible to consume; that is, each bundle satisfies the budget constraint.

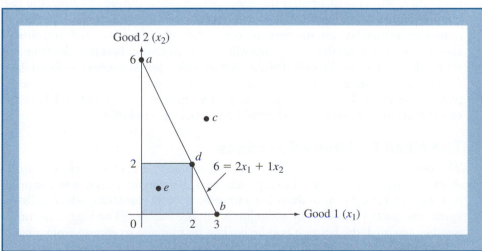

Figure 2.4

The Economically Feasible Consumption Set: Income Constraints.

If the agent is constrained by income rather than time, then the upper boundary of this area now represents the limitations of the agent's income rather than his time.

SOLVED PROBLEM 2.4

Question (Content Review: Income Constraints on Consumption Sets)

In Figure 2.4:

a) If the consumer has an income of 20 rather than 6, how many units of good 1 can be purchased if the consumer spends all of her money on that good?

Answer

If the consumer has an income of 20 and spends all of her money on a good like good 1 with a price of 2, she can buy 10 units.

b) If the price of good 1 is reduced to 1 and the consumer's income is reduced to 4 instead of 6 as depicted in the figure, can the consumer still purchase bundle d?

Answer

The answer is yes. Lowering the price of good 1 to 1 means that the budget line can be written as Income $= 1x_1 + 1x_2$. If the income of the consumer is now 4, the budget line would be $4 = 1x_1 + 1x_2$. Bundle d involves 2 units of good 1 ($x_1 = 2$) and 2 units of good 2 ($x_2 = 2$), the total cost of which is 4. Hence, the consumer can still consume bundle d if the price of good 1 and the consumer's income are reduced as described.

Rationality and Choice

Our three rationality assumptions—completeness, reflexivity, and transitivity—along with the properties of the economically feasible consumption set, are basically all that is needed to allow our agents to make the choices they must make as our analysis develops. What we mean is simply this: Given the definition of the economically feasible consumption set and the complete, reflexive, and transitive preference relationship R, it can be shown that there exists a set of bundles that are *best* in the sense that they are at least as good as any other available bundles.

If preferences were not complete, such a best set of consumption bundles might not exist because there might be bundles that could not be ranked. Similarly, if preferences were not transitive, such a best set of consumption bundles might not exist because our agents might find themselves in a situation in which their preferences would cycle around the consumption set. If transitivity held, the best bundle would exist. This example shows that our preference relationship, with its minimum rationality assumptions of completeness, reflexivity, and transitivity, allows us to be certain that our agents will be able to choose best bundles from any set similar to the economically feasible consumption set. We can therefore take it for granted that in any situation of constrained choice of the type depicted so far (where consumers have to choose a best alternative from a closed and bounded set), our agents will have a well-defined best choice or set of choices.

The Need for Utility Functions

utility function
A representation of an agent's preferences that tells the agent how good a bundle is by assigning it a (possibly ordinal) utility number.

The preference relationship is useful to us right now; however, to make our analysis easier later on, we will want to represent an agent's preferences not by the primitive idea of binary relationships but rather by a utility function, which tells the agent how good a bundle is by assigning it a utility number. The bigger the utility number assigned, the better a bundle is. The best bundle to choose from a set of available bundles would then be the one that was assigned the biggest utility number by the agent's utility function or, more precisely, the one that maximized the utility function over the feasible set of consumption bundles.

The intuitive meaning of *utility* is simply the level of satisfaction the agent receives from the consumption of a particular bundle of goods. It is important to note, however, that the use of utility functions does not require any additional assumptions beyond those involved in the description of the consumer's preferences. In particular, it is not necessary that utility levels be observable or measurable. The point is simply that if an agent's behavior is governed by preferences satisfying certain properties, then that agent behaves *as if* seeking to maximize some single-valued index of satisfaction, which is a function of consumption levels of *all* the goods over which the agent has preferences. Knowing an agent's preferences, however, does not enable us to identify this function uniquely. As we will see, a particular set of preferences can be represented by an infinite number of utility functions.

The Continuity Assumption

We will want our utility functions to be what mathematicians call *continuous*. To do this, we will make one more assumption, known as continuity, which basically states that if two bundles are close to each other in the feasible set, then they will be assigned utility numbers that are close to each other as well.

Another way to state this assumption is to say that for every feasible bundle, there exists another feasible bundle that is exactly as good as it is. Say, for example, that you have a bundle consisting of twelve oranges and six apples and that someone else, the only other person in the world, has two raspberries and three apples. If the other person wants to buy one of your oranges, then continuity would say that there would exist some quantity of apples that, if received in exchange for your orange, would make you indifferent between trading and not trading. Note the emphasis on indifference here. While there certainly may be an amount of apples that would make you more than willing to make the trade, we are looking for an amount that will make you exactly indifferent. That is what continuity requires.

continuity
The assumption on utility functions that states that if two bundles are close to each other in the feasible set, then they will be assigned utility numbers that are close to each other as well.

Question (Application and Extension: Continuity)

Consider a political activist who cares about two things and two things only in the world—liberty and chocolate. She judges all countries first and foremost by how much liberty they afford their people and secondly by how much chocolate they have available to buy. If such an activist were to compare life in two countries, then if one country offered its citizens more liberty than the other, the activist would prefer it no matter what the difference in chocolate consumption was. You cannot trade off liberty for chocolate. Only if two countries are equally free would the activist actually consider their chocolate consumption. (Such preferences are called *lexicographic preferences* and take their name from the dictionary, where words are listed alphabetically.) Are the activist's preferences continuous?

Answer

To answer this question, let us draw a simple diagram (see Figure 2.5).

In this diagram, we see the amount of liberty in a country on the horizontal axis (imagine we could actually measure it) and the amount of chocolate on the vertical axis. Consider point A containing a certain amount of liberty α and a certain amount of chocolate β. If preferences are continuous, there must be another point in this space that contains an amount of liberty and chocolate that this activist likes exactly as much as point A. No such point exists, however. To see this,

SOLVED PROBLEM 2.5

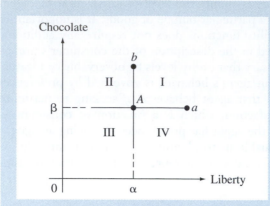

Figure 2.5

Lexicographic Preferences.

No point in the diagram presents a bundle of liberty and chocolate indifferent to A.

start at α and verify that if you move in any direction, you will make the person either strictly worse off or strictly better off, but there is no direction to move in which indifference might lie. For example, say we move in the direction of point a along the line Aa. Then, because any move to the right of A will involve more liberty, it will be strictly preferred to A no matter how small the change. Any move toward point b along the line Ab will also be strictly preferred to a because it has the same amount of liberty but more chocolate. Any move in Area I will also be strictly preferred to A because it involves more of both. Likewise, movements in Area III are all strictly worse than A. Movements in Area IV, however, where indifference is likely to lie, are all strictly better than A because they involve more liberty even though they contain less chocolate (remember that we do not compare chocolate until we first compare liberty and then only if they are tied in amount). By a similar argument, all points in Area II are strictly worse than A. Hence, you cannot find a point that is indifferent to A, and so the preferences described are not continuous.

The Existence of Continuous Utility Functions

Our rationality and continuity assumptions allow us to derive the existence of a continuous utility function for each of our agents. In short, it can be proved that if economic agents have preferences that are complete, transitive, reflexive, and continuous, then there exists a continuous utility function that *agrees* with the underlying preferences of the agent in the following sense: If a consumer prefers bundle a to bundle b, then her utility function will assign a utility number to a that is greater than the utility number assigned to b. The reason utility functions are so convenient is that when a consumer is given a choice among a set of alternative bundles, we no longer have to ask her in a binary fashion which of the bundles she prefers in order to find the bundle that is best for her. This can be quite cumbersome when the set of bundles is large. For example, say that there were only four bundles to choose from; a, b, c, and d. If you were to use only preferences to decide which bundle was best, the consumer would have to make all binary comparisons: a vs. b, b vs. c, c vs. d, etc. There are six such comparisons. By using a utility function, all the consumer has to do is to evaluate each bundle separately and tell us how much utility is associated with each bundle. We can then simply select the bundle that yields the greatest utility number.

Additive and Multiplicative Utility Functions

The following examples highlight the difference between *additive* and *multiplicative* utility functions.

Example 2.3

ADDITIVE UTILITY FUNCTIONS: APPLES AND RASPBERRIES

Say that there are two goods in the world, goods x and y, and some economic agent has the following simple utility function:

$$U = x + y$$

This utility function is an example of an **additive utility function** because it simply adds the number of units of goods x and y that are consumed and uses the total of the units to define the total utility of a bundle. For instance, if good x is apples and good y is raspberries, then consuming 100 apples and 4 raspberries yields 104 units of utility, consuming 200 raspberries and 200 apples yields 400 units of utility, and so on. A raspberry lover might have the following type of additive utility function:

$$U = x + 100y$$

In this case, consuming 100 apples and 4 raspberries yields 500 units of utility, which reflects the relative importance of raspberries in this person's life.

additive utility function
A utility function that has the property that the marginal utility of one extra unit of any good consumed is independent of the amount of other goods consumed.

Note that with additive utility functions, the enjoyment that a person receives from one type of good (say good x) is independent of the enjoyment or utility he receives from another type of good (say good y). The goods enter such utility functions in an *additive* and *separable* manner. With these functions, a person need not consume both goods to get positive levels of utility. The same is not true of multiplicative utility functions.

Example 2.4

MULTIPLICATIVE UTILITY FUNCTIONS: APPLES AND RASPBERRIES

Let us again say that there are two goods in the world, good x (apples) and good y (raspberries). However, we now have an economic agent with a different utility function:

$$U = xy$$

This utility function is an example of a **multiplicative utility function** because the amount of enjoyment the agent receives from good y (raspberries) directly depends on how many units of good x (apples) he consumes. For example, consuming 4 raspberries and 100 apples yields 400 units of utility, while consuming 5 raspberries and 100 apples yields 500 units of utility. Note that such a person will receive no utility unless *both* goods are simultaneously purchased. In this case, the goods do not enter the utility function in a separate fashion.

multiplicative utility function
A utility function in which utility is a function of the products of the various units of goods consumed. In such utility functions, the marginal utility of consumption for any good depends on the amount of other goods consumed.

Which utility function—the additive function or the multiplicative function—is most descriptive of reality? This is not for us to say. Basically, economists do not argue about people's tastes, but clearly these different utility functions will have very different consequences for the way our agents behave in the economy and consume goods. Note, finally, that for a given set of preferences, R, we may have many utility functions that are consistent with it. Still, given any set of bundles, each of these utility functions would yield identical choices. In terms of choice they are equivalent.

Cardinal and Ordinal Utility

The concepts of utility function and utility number are more subtle than we have implied. For example, when we say that a person's utility function assigns a utility number to each available bundle, what properties do we think this utility number has? In economics, this question has been answered by differentiating between two types of utility measurements: *cardinal* and *ordinal*.

cardinal utility
Utility is said to be measurable in the cardinal sense if not only the utility numbers assigned to bundles but also their differences are meaningful.

Utility is said to be measurable in the cardinal utility sense if not only the utility numbers assigned to bundles but also their differences are meaningful. For example, say that you presently have a chocolate bar to which your utility function assigns the number 10 and someone offers you a compact disc to which your utility function assigns the number 30. These numbers imply that a compact disc is three times as good as a chocolate bar to you because the disc has been given a utility number that is three times as large as the number given the chocolate. Hence, your utility is said to be cardinal in a strong sense. A slightly weaker cardinal measurement will be very useful for us in this book, especially when we look at the topic of uncertainty in the world and the economic effects of uncertainty.

ordinal utility
Utility is measurable in the ordinal sense if the utility numbers we assign to objects have no meaning other than to represent the ranking of these goods in terms of a person's preferences.

Utility is measurable in the ordinal utility sense if the utility numbers we assign to objects have no meaning other than to represent the *ranking* of these goods in terms of a person's preferences. For example, say that you like a BMW more than a Saab. If you had an ordinal utility function representing your preference between these two objects, it would have to assign the BMW a larger number. With ordinal utility functions, however, the nature of the number is not important as long as it is larger. Hence, a perfectly legitimate ordinal utility function might assign the BMW a number of 90 and the Saab a number of 89, or it might assign the BMW a number of 1,000,000 and the Saab a number of 1. In both cases, the ordinal utility functions would represent the fact that you value the BMW more highly than the Saab. The actual utility numbers assigned are unimportant as long as they preserve the ranking of the objects.

In much of what we do in the first part of this book, we need not assume that utility is measurable in the cardinal sense but only in the weaker ordinal sense. From a scientific point of view, this is beneficial because one looks for the weakest set of assumptions under which a theory will perform and make accurate predictions. If we can temporarily dispense with the stronger assumption that utility is cardinal, we might as well do so. However, we will return to this assumption later when it becomes necessary to predict behavior.

SOLVED PROBLEM 2.6

Question (Application and Extension: Continuous Utility Functions)

A student entertainment council committee must decide which of three sets of concerts it wants to bring to campus. Plan 1 provides 6 reggae bands and 3 rap groups. Plan 2 provides for 5 reggae and 5 rap, while plan 3 calls for 7 reggae and 2 rap.

There are three student commissioners on the council, Commissioners Allen, Baxter, and Cooper. Commissioner Allen has utility function $u_A = xy$, where x is the number of reggae bands and y is the number of rap groups. Commissioner Baxter has utility function $u_B = x^{1/2}y^{1/2}$, and Commissioner Cooper has utility function $u_C = 2x + y$. If each commissioner votes for his or her favorite plan (the one that gives him or her the highest utility), which plan will be selected by the council if they use a majority voting rule to decide on all issues?

Answer

The answer to this question is quite simple. Each commissioner will choose the plan that is best for him or her. Assuming that each will vote honestly, we see that each commissioner will evaluate the plans as follows:

Commissioner Allen: $u_A = xy$

$$u_A(\text{Plan1}) = (6)(3) = 18$$
$$u_A(\text{Plan2}) = (5)(5) = 25$$
$$u_A(\text{Plan3}) = (7)(2) = 14$$

Thus, Commissioner Allen will vote for plan 2.

Commissioner Baxter: $u_B = x^{1/2}y^{1/2}$

$$u_B(\text{Plan1}) = (6)^{1/2}(3)^{1/2} = 4.24$$
$$u_B(\text{Plan2}) = (5)^{1/2}(5)^{1/2} = 5$$
$$u_B(\text{Plan3}) = (7)^{1/2}(2)^{1/2} = 3.74$$

Commissioner Baxter will vote for plan 2.

Commissioner Cooper: $u_C = 2x + y$

$$u_A(\text{Plan1}) = (2)(6) + 3 = 15$$
$$u_A(\text{Plan2}) = (2)(5) + 5 = 15$$
$$u_A(\text{Plan3}) = (2)(7) + 2 = 16$$

Commissioner Cooper will vote for plan 3.

Therefore, when put to a vote, plan 2 will be selected by a vote of two to one over plans 3 and 1. Note that Commissioners Allen and Baxter preferred the plans in the same order. This is because $u_A = xy$ and $u_B = x^{1/2}y^{1/2}$ represent the same preferences. In ordinal terms they are identical.

Psychological Assumptions

We can derive the existence of utility functions for our economic agents strictly from the rationality assumptions stated earlier in this chapter. However, to gain a better understanding of the choices that our agents will make, we should discuss what type of people they are—what kind of psychological makeup they have. We will make three psychological assumptions about our agents.

Psychological Assumption 1: Selfishness

Our first psychological assumption is selfishness—that people are interested only in their own utility or satisfaction and make their choices with just that in mind. Hence, when people judge any allocation of goods for the economy, they look at it only in terms of how much they will receive from the allocation. While this assumption does not rule out sympathy for other human beings, it tells us that sympathy does not influence the decisions that people make.

> **selfishness**
> A psychological assumption about agents that states that they are interested only in their own utility or satisfaction and make their choices with just that in mind.

Example 2.5

AMBIGUOUS UNSELFISHNESS

Some economic activity that looks unselfish on the surface still satisfies the selfishness assumption if one takes a long-term view of the situation. For example, consider the actions of office workers who set up a voluntary coffee club. They agree to pay 50 cents for each cup they drink and to make coffee when the pot is empty. Clearly, when no one is looking, it is possible to drink the last cup, not make any more coffee, and not contribute the 50 cents owed for the cup that was consumed. Despite their ability to cheat and make a "clean get-away," people usually do not take advantage of the opportunity. Compliance with the voluntary rules of the coffee club is not motivated by unselfishness but by a fear that failing "to do one's part" will break the socially beneficial norm of contribution and cause the coffee club to cease operations. Of course, this would deprive everyone in the office of the advantage of convenient and cheap cups of coffee.

Selfish people are capable of acting in what appears to be a socially considerate manner while pursuing their own self-interests. Are the members of the coffee club unselfish or not? You decide.

Psychological Assumption 2: Nonsatiation

nonsatiation
A psychological assumption about consumer preferences that states that more of anything is always better.

Our second psychological assumption is nonsatiation, which means that more of anything is always better. For example, say that there are two bundles of goods—bundles a and b. If bundle a contains at least as much of all goods as bundle b and more of at least one good, then bundle a must be strictly preferred to bundle b. Geometrically, this can be explained as shown in Figure 2.6.

Consider bundle b in Figure 2.6 and the set of bundles in the shaded area labeled U_b. U_b contains all the bundles that have at least as much of *both* goods as bundle b. Using our assumption of nonsatiation, it follows that our agents would rank all bundles in U_b as being better than b. Because a is a bundle in this set, it is also ranked as being better than b. The assumption of nonsatiation means that as we give people more and more goods, each additional good increases their utility (happiness). Hence, our analysis refers only to *goods* and not to economic "bads" that diminish utility. This restriction implies no loss of generality, however, because we can indirectly incorporate bads into our analysis by defining as goods any services involving the removal of things that diminish utility (for example, a service such as disposal of hazardous wastes).

Psychological Assumption 3: Convexity of Preferences

convexity of preferences
A psychological assumption about preferences that states that if a consumer is indifferent between a goods bundle x and a goods bundle y, then he would prefer (or be indifferent to) a weighted combination of these bundles to either of the original bundles x or y.

Our third assumption, convexity of preferences, is an assumption about the benefits of diversifying one's bundle of goods and not having an overload of a single type of good. Most simply, it can be explained as follows. Say that an agent has an initial choice of two bundles, a and b. Bundle a is exactly as good as bundle b in the eyes of the agent. Someone offers the agent a new bundle created by mixing goods from the original two bundles—say by taking half of a and half of b.

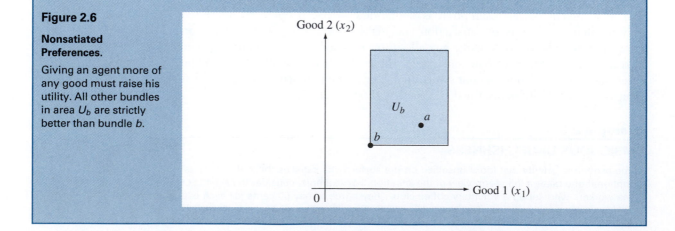

Figure 2.6

Nonsatiated Preferences.

Giving an agent more of any good must raise his utility. All other bundles in area U_b are strictly better than bundle b.

Then according to the convexity assumption, the resulting bundle *c* would be at least as good as either of the original bundles (*a* and *b*) from which it is made. For convexity to hold, this assumption must be true for any original bundles that are equally good and for any mixtures derived from those original bundles. In short, convexity states that mixtures of bundles are at least as good as the indifferent components from which those mixtures were made. This assumption will prove to be very important to us in our later work. Note that the convexity of preferences is not related to the convexity property of the consumption possibility set discussed earlier.

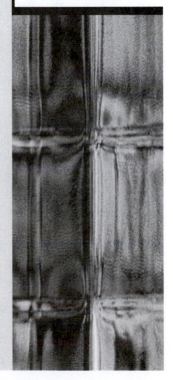

SOLVED PROBLEM 2.7

Question (Content Review: Preferences)

What assumption(s) rule out the following phenomena?

Elizabeth is indifferent between a bundle consisting of 6 raspberries and 7 apples and a bundle consisting of 3 raspberries and 10 apples. She is also indifferent between a bundle consisting of 3 raspberries and 10 apples and a bundle consisting of 5 raspberries and 6 apples.

Answer

Nonsatiation. If transitivity holds, then Elizabeth appears to be indifferent between a bundle consisting of 6 raspberries and 7 apples and a bundle consisting of 5 raspberries and 6 apples. However, if nonsatiation holds, then Elizabeth must prefer 6 raspberries and 7 apples to 5 raspberries and 6 apples because the former bundle has more of each good. Thus, nonsatiation has been violated.

RESOLVING
TEASER 1

In Teaser 1 you were asked to imagine what you would do if you were the divider in the experiment where your task was to split $10 between you and an anonymous receiver. You can imagine this game being played in several ways, as was done by researchers Hoffman, McCabe, Shachak, and Smith.

In one scenario, you simply come into the lab and are randomly allocated a position of receiver or divider and then play the game. In another, you and another student first compete for the right to be the divider by answering quiz questions, with the winner of the contest earning a "property right" to the favored divider position. In another set of treatments, the game is played in a double-blind manner rather than the typical single-blind way. In single-blind experiments, the divider's identity would be hidden from the receiver but the experimenter (professor) would know what the divider gave his counterpart. In double-blind treatment, not only does the receiver not know who his divider was but neither does the experimenter, and that fact is known to the divider when he makes his or her division.

This game, called the Dictator game, has been played often with the surprising result that undergraduate student subjects tend to give significant portions of the $10 to their anonymous partners. I say surprising because this is not what economic theory, as we have postulated it, would predict. If people are selfish, they evaluate all allocations only in terms of what they are getting. They do not care what others get. In addition, if they are nonsatiated, then the more they get, the better. If you put these two together, you get the prediction that no economic agent of the type we have described would give anything away. Yet they do. So what's wrong?

(Continued)

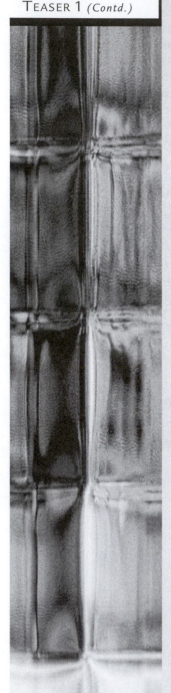

The answer may be that real people in the real world are not actually selfish. They may have what are called other-regarding preferences—that is, they may care what others, in addition to themselves, get. This possibility was explored by Ernst Fehr and Klaus Schmidt in "A Theory of Fairness, Competition and Cooperation," (The Quarterly Journal of Economics, August 1999, pp. 817–68) and by Gary Bolton and Axel Ockenfels in "ERC: A Theory of Equity, Reciprocity and Competition" (American Economic Review 2000, 90, pp. 166–93). These authors posit a very simple idea, which they incorporate into a simple utility function. For example, in the Fehr-Schmidt paper, the idea is that people are averse to inequality of any form. If they get less than others, they feel envious, and if they get more, they feel guilty. If there are only two people in the world, person I and person J, then an inequality-averse person would have a utility function of the following type: $U_i(x) = x_i - a(x_j - x_i)$ if $x_j > x_i$ and $U_i(x) = x_i - b(x_i - x_j)$ if $x_i > x_j$, where $b \leq a$ and $0 \leq b \leq 1$. Note what this says. If there were no other person in the world and person I received x dollars, he would value it at x. However, if there were another person, J, then person I would look to see what J was getting. If person I was getting less than person J, person I's utility would be decreased by the envy term, a, multiplied by the amount by which he was jealous. But if person I was getting more than person J, his utility would be decreased by the guilt term, b, multiplied by the amount of excess.

Obviously, this type of utility function would explain why some students give some money away, and how much they give away depends on the relationship between their a's and b's. For any fixed level of income for themselves, they would prefer a world of equality, but if that is not possible, then they will tolerate inequality but only up to some point. Such people violate the selfishness axiom introduced earlier, but clearly such people exist. You probably are one of them.

Now back to the experimental teaser. The amount that the divider gives, in general, is significantly more than $0, but it depends on the treatment. For example, when the right to be the divider is allocated randomly, only 20% of subjects offer $0 to their anonymous receiver, with a similar proportion offering $5. When subjects have to compete for the right to be the divider, however, 40% offer $0, with another 40% offering $1 or $2. More amazing, when the experiment is done using a double-blind protocol, about 66% offer $0 or $1, while only 0.5% offer $5. This would seem to imply that we are actually more selfish deep down and are willing to show it when we think no one is looking or when we can find an excuse to justify it (like winning a contest).

In summary, the selfishness hypothesis has received some very strong challenges in recent years. In general, experimental studies have documented that people do incorporate feelings for others into their behavior and hence presumably into their utility functions. The exact way this is done may be complicated, however. In the Hoffman et. al experiments described above, it appears that people are looking for excuses to be selfish, which, in this experiment, come in the form of either winning a contest and "earning" the right to keep more or being able to hide their selfishness from others.

Conclusion

Our ultimate goal in studying consumer behavior is to derive the demand function for a consumer, and our discussion so far takes us part of the way. We have done this by studying preferences and now must go on to look at how these preferences manifest themselves in our major analytic tool, the indifference curve.

Summary

This chapter has started our discussion of the consumer. Put simply, the job of the consumer is to consume, to choose bundles of goods to consume from the set of feasible bundles available to him or her. After describing those bundles from which the consumer must choose, we then went on to look at the types of consumers we will be studying. These turn out to be people who satisfy certain basic assumptions of rationality (i.e., they have complete, continuous, and transitive preferences defined over the set of available bundles) and their preferences. They are also selfish and nonsatiated. People with such preferences could be assumed to have their preferences represented by a utility function. This means that they behave as if they were choosing the bundle that awards them the highest utility if consumed, which is equivalent to thinking that we walk around the world with a utility function in our heads that assigns a utility number to each possible bundle we could consume and then choose that bundle with the higher utility. Remember, however, that there may be many utility functions that represent the same preferences.

Exercises and Problems

1. Which assumption or assumptions about consumer preferences or behavior explain the following phenomena?
   a) A person has a wardrobe with shirts of many colors.
   b) In maximizing his utility, given prevailing prices and his income, a consumer exhausts his entire budget.

2. What assumption or assumptions rule out the following phenomenon: Geoffrey has a bundle consisting of 6 apples and 8 raspberries. He states that if he is given 1 more apple, he will ask for 3 more raspberries to keep himself indifferent between his old bundle and the new bundle that he will have after he receives the 1 additional apple.

3. Which, if any, of the properties that we discussed in the section titled "The Consumption Possibility Set" are not satisfied by the consumption sets depicted in Figure 2.7? Does the convexity property hold for any of these sets? Explain your answer.

Figure 2.7

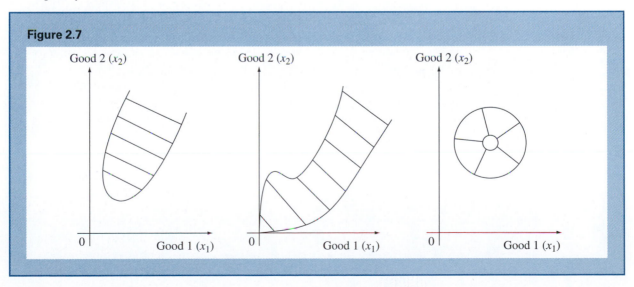

4. We sometimes say that an individual with strong internal conflicts is divided into "several different people." Assume that Geoffrey and Elizabeth fall into such a category.

a) Geoffrey's internal conflicts divide him into three different people—the greedy Geoffrey, the health-conscious Geoffrey, and the diet-conscious Geoffrey. To make up his mind between any pair of goods, Geoffrey takes a majority vote of his three internal selves. Let us say that Geoffrey has three goods to consume—apples, chocolate, and meat—and that his three internal selves have the following binary preferences:

Greedy Geoffrey:	chocolate *R* apple *R* meat
Health-conscious Geoffrey:	apple *R* meat *R* chocolate
Diet-conscious Geoffrey:	meat *R* chocolate *R* apple

If we consider Geoffrey's preferences after he takes the majority vote of his internal selves, which, if any, of the assumptions that we discussed in the "Rationality" section of this chapter are violated by the ordering that results from the vote?

b) Say that Elizabeth is also divided into three internal selves, and her internal selves have the following preferences:

Greedy Elizabeth:	apple *R* chocolate *R* meat
Health-conscious Elizabeth:	apple *R* meat *R* chocolate
Diet-conscious Elizabeth:	apple *R* meat *R* chocolate

Say that Elizabeth decides between each pair of goods differently than Geoffrey. She uses a unanimity criterion—one good is better than another only if *all* internal selves believe it to be. Which, if any, of the assumptions that we discussed in the "Rationality" section of this chapter are violated by the ordering that results?

Utilities—Indifference Curves

CONSISTENT CHOICES

Consider the following experimental task given to subjects in an experiment run by James Andreoni and John Miller.*

A student is brought into the room, given a certain amount of money, and asked to choose which bundle of goods he or she most prefers from those he or she can afford. Each good has a fixed price. So, for example, the student may be given $100 and told that good 1 costs $1 and good 2 costs $4. He obviously can afford to buy, say, 100 units of good 1, 25 units of good 2, or any combination of goods 1 and 2 whose cost is not more than $100. One such bundle, for example, is 40 units of good 1 and 15 units of good 2 because that would cost exactly $100 = $1 × (40 units) + $4 × (15 units). After the student completes this task, he or she is given another one with a different amount of income and different prices and told to choose again. This is repeated eight times.

To help the student in the experiment, he or she is presented with a series of what we will call budget lines and asked to choose which combination of goods along the budget line they want most. For example, take the case illustrated in Figure 3.1.

In this case, the subject has $100 and faces prices that are $1 for good 1 and $1 for good 2. (We know this because if he spends all his money on good 1, he can buy 100 units; and the same is true for good 2, so each good must cost $1. We will explain this more clearly in the chapters in this section.) The subject will be given these budget

Figure 3.1

Budget Line.

Points on the budget line indicate all the bundles of goods that the consumer can afford.

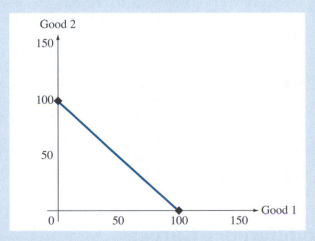

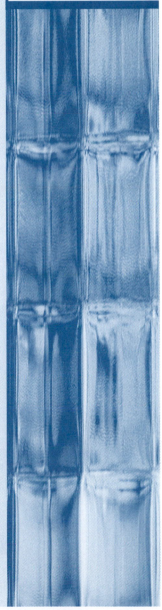

* See James Andreoni and John Miller, "Giving According to GARP: An Experimental Test of the Consistency of Preferences for Altruism," in *Econometrica*, vol. 70, no. 2 (March 2002, pp. 737–53)

EXPERIMENTAL
TEASER 2 *(Contd.)*

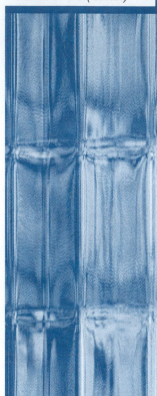

lines one at a time and asked to choose a bundle for each one. Look at Figure 3.2 and the dots presented there.

In this figure, we see one subject (Subject 40) and three of the budget lines he or she faced. The dots on each budget line are the choices made by this subject in each budget price situation. As we can see, this subject chose A when he faced the thick budget line, C when he faced the dashed budget line, and B when he faced the thin budget line.

Do these choices look strange to you? If so, what is strange about them? Do you think that people who choose in this manner are likely to have well-behaved demand functions? Actually, the choices made by this student subject violate some basic assumptions that economists like to impose on people when they make choices. What do you think those assumptions are?

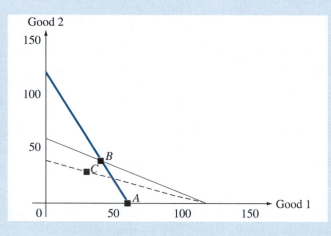

Figure 3.2

Alternative Budget Lines.

The subject faces different budget lines, indicating different incomes and relative prices, and is asked to choose a bundle from each one.

EXPERIMENTAL
TEASER 3

AGE AND CONSISTENT CHOICE

The experiments described above were run on college-age subjects. By and large, they demonstrate that people who reach that age make consistent choices. But how do we get to the point where our choices are consistent? Are we born with that ability, or do we learn it as we grow? This question has been investigated by William Harbaugh, Kate Krause, and Timothy Berry.* They compared 7-year-olds with 11- and 21-year-olds. What do you think they found? Also, does market experience improve one's ability to make consistent choices? If so, then we might expect in the real world that choices would be consistent because people tend to have a lot of experience with markets as they interact in the economy. See what John List and Daniel Millimet have to say about this.†

---

* William Harbaugh, Kate Krause, and Timothy Berry, "GARP for Kids: On the Development of Rational Choice Behavior," *American Economic Review,* 2001, 91(5): 1539–45.

† John List and Daniel Millimet, "Bounding the Impact of Market Experience and Rationality: Evidence from a Field Experiment with Imperfect Compliance," *Mimeo,* 2005.

Indifference Curves

Given our discussion in Chapter 2, we are now in a position to discuss the main analytical tool that we will use throughout a major portion of this book—the indifference curve. The existence of indifference curves and the shape that they take follow from the assumptions about rationality and psychology that we made in the previous chapter. To understand what an indifference curve is, consider Figure 3.3.

Indifference Curves Derived and Defined

Take point a in Figure 3.3, which is a feasible bundle of goods 1 and 2. More precisely, bundle a contains 10 units of good 1 and 20 units of good 2. Now let us find another bundle in this space, say bundle b, that is *exactly as good as* bundle a for the consumer. Suppose that the consumer is indifferent between bundles a and b. We know that a bundle such as b exists because we have assumed that preferences are continuous (see the discussion of the continuity assumption in the "Rationality and Choice" section of Chapter 2). Now let us look again at Figure 3.3 and find *all* the bundles in the space that are exactly as good as bundle a. The line drawn through all these bundles is called an indifference curve because it represents a locus of bundles that are all exactly as good as one another in the eyes of the consumer. She is indifferent between these bundles. A diagram, such as Figure 3.3, on which indifference curves are depicted is called an indifference map.

Because we are using only ordinal utility here, we are free to take any numbers we want to label the utility levels associated with the indifference curves in Figure 3.3. Let us use 100 for the utility level of the first indifference curve. We know from the existence of a utility function that all the bundles on an indifference curve must be assigned the same utility number. Why? Because a utility function assigns a number to each bundle, and the number assigned should be an accurate reflection of the consumer's preferences. If the consumer is indifferent between bundles, her utility function must assign the same utility number to all bundles. In the case of the first indifference curve in Figure 3.3, all bundles have a utility level of 100.

Now let us look at bundle w in Figure 3.3. This bundle contains more of goods 1 and 2 than does bundle a. Therefore, bundle w and all bundles that are exactly as good as it to the consumer form a second indifference curve, which is associated with another level of utility. We will use 140 for the utility level of the second indifference curve because we know that all bundles along this indifference curve must be preferred to the ones along the first indifference curve where bundle a lies. (Remember, bundle w has more of all goods than does bundle a and the consumer is nonsatiated.)

indifference curve
A curve or locus of bundles in the consumption set for a consumer among which the consumer is indifferent.

indifference map
A set of indifference curves for a consumer.

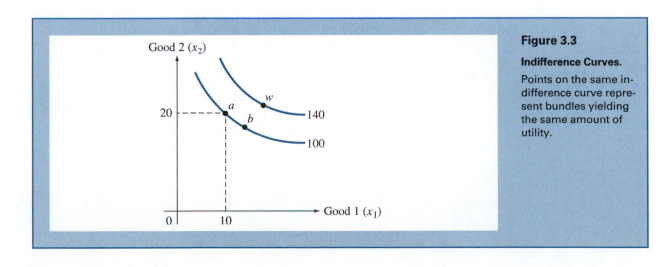

Figure 3.3

Indifference Curves.

Points on the same indifference curve represent bundles yielding the same amount of utility.

Note the following general points about indifference maps. Every bundle of goods is on some indifference curve, and the indifference curves that are farther from the origin contain higher levels of utility.

The Shape of Indifference Curves

When we look at Figure 3.3, we see that both of the indifference curves have a particular shape. They slope down and to the right, are bowed in toward the origin, and do not cross each other. These shapes follow from the nonsatiation and convexity assumptions we discussed in Chapter 2, as we can now observe.

> **Indifference curves cannot slope upward. (This rule follows from the nonsatiation assumption.)**

To see why indifference curves cannot slope upward, let us consider Figure 3.4.

Look at point a in Figure 3.4. The space in this figure has been divided into four regions by drawing lines parallel to the horizontal and vertical axes through a. The four regions are identified by the letters B, C, D, and E. What we are interested in knowing is where in this space the indifference curve must be. To obtain this information, let us look for the location of some other bundle that is exactly as good as bundle a for our consumer. Clearly, such a point cannot lie in region B because all bundles in that region contain either more of goods 1 and 2 than does bundle a (consider bundle x, for instance) or more of one good and the same amount of the other good (consider bundle y). From our assumption of nonsatiation, however, all these bundles must be considered strictly better than bundle a for our consumer. Hence, no bundle in region B can yield exactly as much utility as bundle a. What about region D? Here, just the opposite is true. All bundles in region D contain either less of both goods than bundle a or the same amount of one good and less of the other good. Hence, all the bundles in region D must be considered strictly worse than bundle a. That leaves only regions E and C as possible regions in which we can find bundles that yield exactly the same amount of utility as bundle a. Hence, the indifference curves must run through these regions and slope down and to the right.

> **Indifference curves cannot cross each other. (This rule follows from the transitivity and nonsatiation assumptions.)**

To see why indifference curves cannot cross each other, we will look at what would happen if they did. Consider Figure 3.5.

Figure 3.4

Indifference Curves Cannot Slope Upward.

If an indifference curve ran from a to x, then bundle x would be no better than bundle a despite containing more of both goods. This upward slope of the indifference curve would be a violation of the nonsatiation assumption.

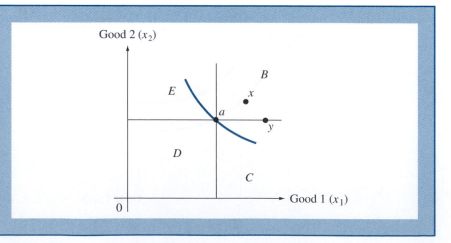

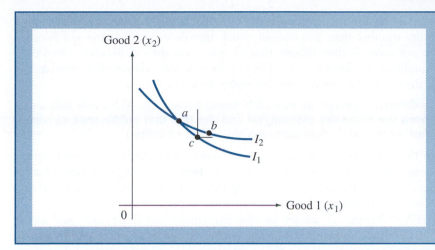

Figure 3.5

Indifference Curves Cannot Cross Each Other.

If indifference curves I_1 and I_2 crossed at a, then by transitivity of preferences bundle b would be no better than bundle c despite containing more of both goods. This crossing of indifference curves would be a violation of the nonsatiation assumption.

In Figure 3.5, we see bundle a and two indifference curves, labeled I_1 and I_2, which cross each other at a. We also see two other bundles labeled b and c, with b on indifference curve I_2 and c on indifference curve I_1. According to the definition of an indifference curve, if bundles a and b are on the same indifference curve, they must be equally good in the eyes of our consumer. The same must be true for bundles a and c. According to the assumption of transitivity, however, if bundle c is rated exactly as good as bundle a and bundle a is rated exactly as good as bundle b, then bundle c must be exactly as good as bundle b. But bundle b contains more of all goods than does bundle c, which means that bundle b must be strictly better than bundle c according to the assumption of nonsatiation. Hence, if we are going to satisfy the assumptions of transitivity and nonsatiation, the indifference curves in Figure 3.5 cannot cross each other.

> **Indifference curves farther from the origin contain higher levels of utility. (This rule follows from the nonsatiation assumption and the fact that indifference curves do not cross.)**

To see why indifference curves that are farther from the origin contain higher levels of utility and, hence, should be labeled with larger utility numbers, let us consider Figure 3.6.

In Figure 3.6 we see two bundles labeled a and w. Because bundle w contains more of goods 1 and 2 than does bundle a, it must be strictly preferred by our

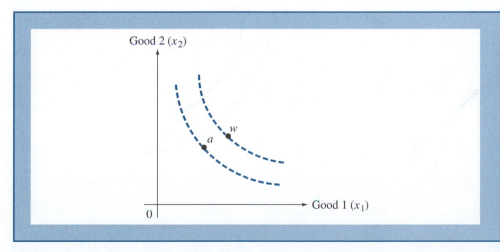

Figure 3.6

Indifference Curves Farther from the Origin Represent Higher Utility Levels.

Bundle w must be preferred to bundle a because it contains more of both goods.

consumer. Hence, the indifference curve on which bundle w lies must be given a larger utility number than the one on which bundle a lies. Because indifference curves do not cross, it then follows that all points on the indifference curve containing bundle w receive a larger utility number. It also follows that indifference curves farther from the origin represent higher levels of utility.

> **Indifference curves are bowed in toward the origin. (This rule follows from the convexity assumption and the fact that indifference curves farther from the origin contain higher levels of utility.)**

We know that indifference curves must slope down and to the right if our assumption of nonsatiation is to be satisfied. There are two ways that indifference curves can do this, as shown in parts A and B of Figure 3.7. However, the curve illustrated in part A violates the assumption of the convexity of preferences.

In part A of Figure 3.7, we see indifference curves that slope down and to the right but do so in such a manner that they are bowed out from the origin. In part B, we see just the opposite situation—the indifference curves bow in toward the origin. Because of the assumption of the convexity of preferences and the fact that indifference curves farther from the origin contain higher utility levels, it is necessary that indifference curves have a bowed-in shape. To understand why this is true, consider points a and b in both diagrams. From the convexity assumption, we know that if bundles a and b are exactly as good as each other, then bundle c, which is a mixture of a and b, must be at least as good as either of them. However, in part A of Figure 3.7, we see that if the indifference curves had a bowed-out shape, bundle c would not be at least as good as bundles a and b because bundle c is on a lower indifference curve than bundles a and b, which implies that bundle c contains a lower level of utility. Note that the opposite situation occurs in part B, where bundle c is on a higher indifference curve, as it must be if the convexity assumption is to hold.

Figure 3.7

(a) Bowed-out indifference curves violate the convexity of preferences. Bundle c is a weighted average of bundles a and b, but it yields a lower utility level because it is on an indifference curve that is closer to the origin. (b) Bowed-in indifference curves satisfy the convexity of preferences. Bundle c, a weighted average of bundles a and b, yields a higher utility level.

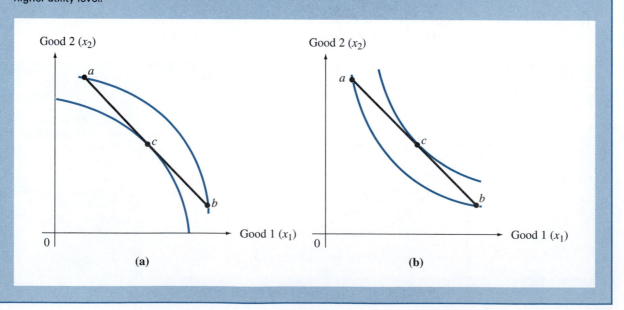

The Marginal Rate of Substitution

There is another interpretation of the bowed-in shape of indifference curves that is more intuitive and will be useful to us later in this book. What exactly does it mean for an indifference curve to have a bowed-in shape? To answer this question, look at Figure 3.8.

Consider bundle d on indifference curve I_1 in Figure 3.8. If we take ten units of good 1 away from our consumer, how much of good 2 would we have to give her in order to keep her on the same indifference curve? In the diagram, this increase in good 2 and decrease in good 1 moves the consumer from bundle d to bundle c. If we let $-\Delta x_1$ be the amount of good 1 taken away from the consumer and Δx_2 be the amount of good 2 required to compensate her for that loss, then $-\Delta x_2/\Delta x_1$ is a measure of what economists call the marginal rate of substitution of good 2 for good 1 ($\text{MRS}_{\text{good 2 for good 1}}$). (Actually, this term should be used only as Δx_2 and Δx_1 get very small.) The marginal rate of substitution is the ratio in which the consumer, at a particular point on the indifference map, would be willing to exchange one good for another—the rate of exchange that would just maintain the consumer's original utility level. The steepness of the indifference curve at any point is a measure of this marginal rate of substitution when Δx_2 and Δx_1 are both small, that is, when the change we are looking at in x_1, Δx_1, approaches zero. Convexity implies that as we move along the indifference curve and, hence, keep the consumer at the same level of utility, the marginal rate of substitution decreases. This property of diminishing marginal rates of substitution simply means that as we continually take a constant amount of good 1 away from the consumer, we must compensate her with greater and greater amounts of good 2.

We can observe diminishing rates of substitution in Figure 3.8. At point d, the consumer has a lot of good 1 and relatively little of good 2 (to be precise, the consumer has 110 units of good 1 and only 9 units of good 2). Note that at point c, when we take 10 units of good 1 away, we need to give the consumer only 1 unit of good 2 to compensate her. Now look at point b, where the consumer has 20 units of good 1 and 60 units of good 2. In this case, when we take 10 units of good 1 away from the consumer, we must give her 40 units of good 2 to compensate for the loss. In short, as the consumer acquires more and more of good 2, it has less and less value as a substitute for the loss of the same 10 units of good 1. That is what convexity of preferences implies, and that is why convex indifference curves bow in toward the origin.

marginal rate of substitution
The ratio at which a consumer, at a particular point on the indifference map, would be willing to exchange one good for another; the rate of exchange that would just maintain the consumer's original utility.

diminishing marginal rates of substitution
The property of indifference curves stemming from their convexity that implies that if we move along the indifference curve, hence keeping the consumer at the same utility level, the marginal rate of substitution decreases.

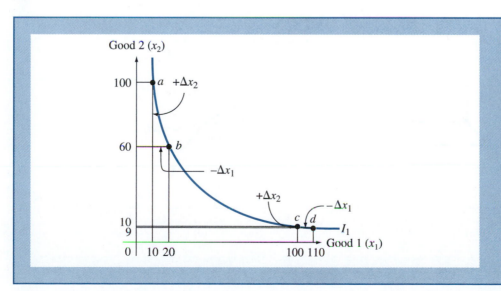

Figure 3.8

Convex Preferences and the Marginal Rate of Substitution.

As the consumer is given bundles containing more and more of good 2, she values an individual unit of good 2 less and less.

Indifference Curves and Tastes

By looking at a person's indifference map, we can learn something about that person's taste for goods. To more fully understand how indifference curves depict tastes, consider the indifference curves shown in parts A and B of Figure 3.9. Each of these indifference curves represents a different person's taste for two goods.

Flat Indifference Curves: Goods that Yield No Utility. In part A of Figure 3.9, we see an indifference curve that is flat. This flatness implies that if we take one unit of good 1 away from the consumer at point a, then we need not compensate

Figure 3.9

(a) Flat indifference curves. The good measured on the horizontal axis is yielding no utility for the consumer. (b) Straight-line indifference curves: perfect substitutes. The same amount of good 2 is always needed to compensate the consumer for the loss of one unit of good 1. (c) Right-angle indifference curves: perfect complements. Adding any amount of only one good to bundle a yields no additional utility. (d) Bowed-out indifference curves: nonconvex preferences and the marginal rate of substitution. As the consumer is given bundles containing more and more of good 2, he values an individual unit of good 2 more and more.

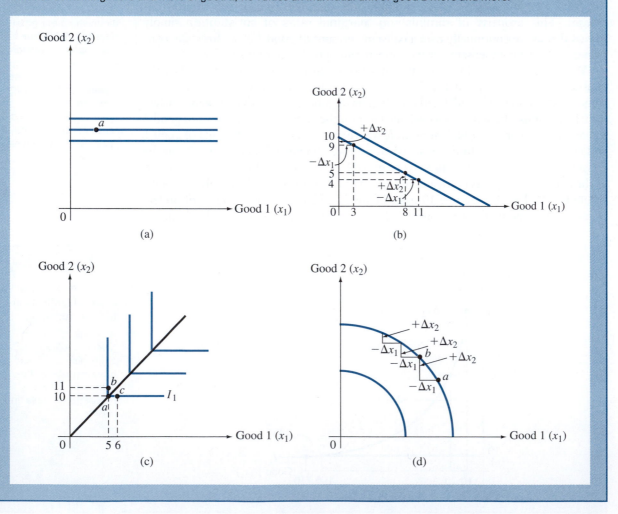

him for this loss with any amount of good 2 to keep him on the same indifference curve or generate a level of utility equal to his original level at point *a*. This situation can be true only if good 1 yields zero utility for the consumer because only then will it be unnecessary to compensate him for the loss of good 1. Such a situation should occur only if we weaken our nonsatiation assumption to allow for zero marginal utilities.

Straight-Line Indifference Curves: Goods that Are Perfect Substitutes.

Part B of Figure 3.9 provides a contrast to part A. In part B, we see preferences in which goods 1 and 2 are perfect substitutes for each other. By perfect substitutes, we mean that no matter how much of goods 1 and 2 the consumer is consuming (that is, no matter at what point we are on the indifference curve), whenever we take away a certain amount of good 1 from the consumer, we can always compensate him with the same constant amount of good 2 to keep him on the same indifference curve. In part B, this means that any time we take 3 units of good 1 away from the consumer, we must give him 1 unit of good 2.

perfect substitutes
Two goods are perfect substitutes if the marginal rate of substitution between them is constant along an indifference curve. In a two-good world, the indifferent curve for perfect substitutes is a straight line.

Right-Angle Indifference Curves: Goods that Are Perfect Complements.

Part C of Figure 3.9 shows preferences in which the consumer can continuously increase the amount of utility he derives from goods 1 and 2 only by increasing his consumption of them in constant proportions. For example, note that the consumer achieves utility level I_1 if he consumes goods 1 and 2 in the ratio of 2:1 (or, in this figure, by consuming 10 units of good 2 and 5 units of good 1). If the consumer consumes 11 units of good 2 while continuing to consume 5 units of good 1 (and is therefore at point *b*), he has not increased his utility level. Likewise, consuming 6 units of good 1 and 10 units of good 2 also does not increase his utility level. His tastes demand that the goods be consumed in strict proportion. Such goods are called perfect complements.

perfect complements
Two goods are perfect complements if they must be consumed in a fixed ratio in order to produce utility. In a two-good world, perfect complements have right angle indifference curves.

Bowed-Out Indifference Curves: Nonconvex Preferences.

Part D of Figure 3.9 presents indifference curves that bow out and violate the convexity assumption. Remember that Figure 3.8 showed a diminishing marginal rate of substitution. Here we have the opposite situation—an increasing marginal rate of substitution between goods 2 and 1. As we successively take away constant amounts of good 1 from the consumer, starting at point *a* (that is, as we move along the indifference curve from point *a* to point *b*), the amount of good 2 that we must give the consumer to compensate him for a loss of 1 unit of good 1 decreases. Thus, good 2 becomes a better and better substitute for good 1 as the consumer receives more and more of it. In a sense, as the consumer acquires more of good 2, each additional unit of that good is more desirable to him. Heroin addicts would have indifference curves such as this—the more they consume of the drug, the more they want each additional "fix."

Question (Content Review: Indifference Maps)
Draw indifference curves for the following person:

Mary says, "I don't care whether it's Coors or Budweiser, as long as it's beer."

SOLVED PROBLEM 3.1

Answer

By her statement, it appears as if Coors and Budweiser are perfect substitutes for Mary. Hence, she would have an indifference map that looks like that depicted in Figure 3.10.

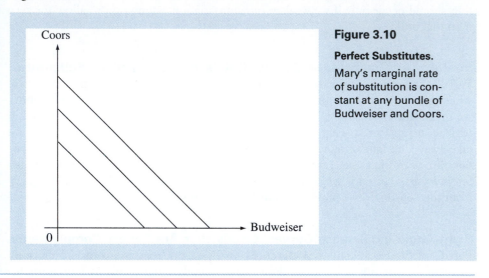

Figure 3.10

Perfect Substitutes.

Mary's marginal rate of substitution is constant at any bundle of Budweiser and Coors.

Optimal Consumption Bundles

As we discussed in Chapter 2, the set of consumption bundles available for our consumers to consume is bounded from below by the physical reality that it is not possible to consume negative quantities of any goods (as represented by the horizontal and vertical axes). The set is bounded from above by the economic reality that it may be impossible to consume certain bundles because they may require either more time or (when markets exist and people can earn incomes) more money than our consumers have. Which bundle will our consumers choose as the one that maximizes their utility if they have a choice of any point in the economically feasible set? In other words, what is each consumer's optimal consumption bundle? To help us answer this question, we will consider Figure 3.11.

Figure 3.11 shows the economically feasible consumption set (which is labeled F) and the set of indifference curves of a consumer. If the consumer wants to choose the bundle in F that makes her most happy (maximizes her utility), then the consumer would select the bundle that places her on the highest indifference curve possible. Bundle e is such a bundle. Let us examine some of the other bundles to see why they would not be optimal. A bundle such as k, while containing a higher level of utility, is not economically feasible. A bundle such as m clearly cannot be the best because there are other bundles like n that contain more of both goods and, hence, are better (according to the nonsatiation assumption). With the exception of e, bundles on line BB', such as x, are simply on lower indifference curves and, therefore, contain lower levels of utility.

optimal consumption bundle
The bundle the consumer chooses in order to maximize his utility within the economically feasible set; the bundle that is best according to his or her preferences.

Characteristics of Optimal Bundles

Note that point e in Figure 3.11 is characterized by the fact that it is the only point in set F at which an indifference curve is tangent to budget line BB'. But

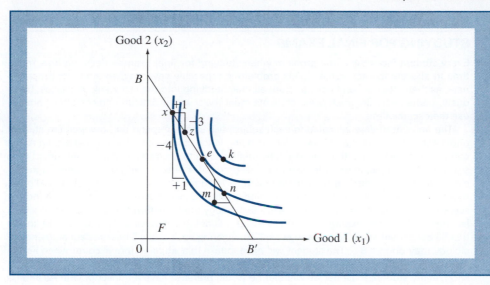

Figure 3.11

The Optimal Consumption Bundle.

At the optimal point e, the indifference curve is tangent to the boundary BB' of the economically feasible consumption set.

what does this mean? For one thing, it means that the slopes of the indifference curves and budget lines at that point are equal. However, the slope of the indifference curve measures how much of good 2 the consumer must be given in order to compensate her for the loss of 1 unit of good 1. It is the marginal rate of substitution of good 2 for good 1, while the slope of line BB' tells us how much of good 2 she will be *forced* to give up (either by the market or by the time required to consume goods 1 and 2) in order to get another unit of good 1. This ratio is, in essence, the *price* of good 1 in terms of good 2. Hence, if we denote $-\Delta x_2/\Delta x_1$ as the ratio of the amounts of good 2 that our consumer must be given to compensate for the loss of Δx_1 units of good 1, then the marginal rate of substitution equals $-\Delta x_2/\Delta x_1$. Because the slope of budget line BB' represents the ratio of the prices of goods 1 and 2, the price ratio equals p_1/p_2. At the optimal bundle e, the marginal rate of substitution equals the price ratio p_1/p_2.

Now it should be clear that the equality of the marginal rate of substitution and the price ratio is a condition that must be satisfied when identifying an optimal bundle if our consumer's indifference curves have the bowed-in shape we have assumed and if the consumer finds it optimal to consume positive quantities of both goods. The following example in Figure 3.11 illustrates why this condition must be satisfied. Assume that we are at a bundle such as x that has a marginal rate of substitution unequal to the price ratio. Bundle x is located at a point where we see a rather steep slope for the indifference curve and a rather high marginal rate of substitution as compared to a rather flat price ratio. Assume that the marginal rate of substitution for bundle x is 4/1, which means that our consumer is willing to give up 4 units of good 2 in exchange for 1 unit of good 1, while the price ratio of the two goods is 3/1, which means that our consumer must give up only 3 units of good 2 in order to receive 1 unit of good 1. In such a situation, our consumer is clearly better off exchanging 1 unit of good 1 for 3 units of good 2 because that exchange yields a higher level of utility. (She is better off because she gave up less than the maximum she was willing to give up.) As a result of this situation, our consumer would be placed on a higher indifference curve (at point z). Hence, x cannot be an optimal bundle.

Example 3.1

STUDYING FOR FINAL EXAMS

Every student faces the same problem when studying for final exams—deciding how much time to allocate to each subject. This problem is especially severe when students procrastinate, as they often do, and have to cram all their studying into the last week of classes. Obviously, under such circumstances, students must make some difficult choices about how to use their scarce time.

The amount of time allocated to each subject will clearly depend on how well the student understands the subject and how well he is doing in the course. If he has earned a solid A in a course up to the point of the final exam, he might decide to spend a substantial amount of time studying that subject in order to ensure a final grade of A. Alternatively, the student might decide that he can "coast" in the course where he is earning an A and that he should allocate more time to a course in which he is earning a C but hopes to bring it up to a B. Behind the scenes in this decision-making process is a technology that transforms time allocated to a subject into a grade. For example, say that a student is doing very well in economics and knows that 5 hours spent studying that subject will surely bring an A, while 5 hours spent studying sociology may bring a B−. The student will have to take this situation into account when he decides how much time to allocate to preparing for the final exam in each of the subjects. In short, every student must decide whether he would prefer to have a transcript with As and Cs that shows uneven performance, sometimes excellent and sometimes poor, or a transcript with Bs that shows performance that is consistently good but never outstanding.

To help us structure our analysis of the problem of choosing an optimal allocation of time, assume that a student has taken only two courses this semester and has a total of 10 hours available to study for final exams. Given her performance in the courses up to finals week and her abilities in the two subjects, she has preferences about the amount of time she will spend studying each subject. These preferences are depicted in part A of Figure 3.12, where we see a set of indifference curves for this student.

Along each indifference curve, the student is indifferent between the number of hours allocated to each subject. Note, however, that this does not mean that along the indifference curves the grades received will be the same. For example, at point a on indifference curve I, the student allocates only 1 hour to studying subject 1 but nine hours to studying subject 2,

Figure 3.12

Optimal Allocations of Time.

(a) Studying for finals: an optimal allocation of time. For this student, the optimal allocation of time is at point b, where the indifference curve is tangent to the time (hours–budget) constraint. (b) Studying for finals: a different optimal allocation of time. For another student, the optimal allocation is different. In this case, the student cares more for subject 1 than for subject 2, so she allocates more time to studying subject 1 than to studying subject 2.

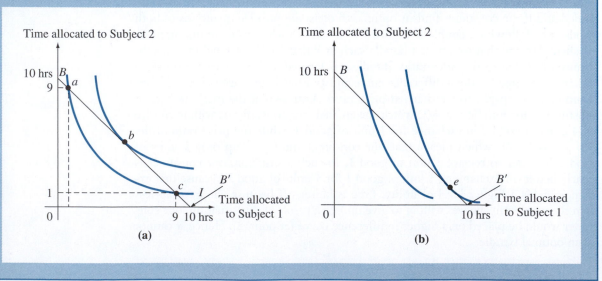

which might result in the student receiving a grade of C− in subject 1 and a grade of A in subject 2. At point *c*, the student allocates 9 hours to subject 1 and 1 hour to subject 2 and might receive a grade of B+ in subject 1 and a grade of B− in subject 2. All that indifference curve *I* tells us is that the student is indifferent between these two sets of grades.

What is the optimal allocation of time for this particular student? That question can be answered only by looking at the relationship of the slope of the indifference curve to the time (hours–budget) constraint. Line *BB'* is the time constraint in this situation because it indicates that there are 10 hours available for studying and that every hour taken away from studying subject 1 makes an hour available for studying subject 2. Therefore, the slope of the budget line is −1.

Obviously, the optimal allocation of time occurs at point *b* in part A of Figure 3.12, where the indifference curve is tangent to the budget line. At that point, the rate at which the student wants to substitute time to study subject 2 for time to study subject 1 equals the rate at which such time must be transferred according to the time constraint: −1. For the sake of argument, let us say that at point *b*, our student receives a grade of B in each subject. Clearly, given the student's preferences, she would like to be known as a solid B student and, therefore, finds this allocation most satisfactory.

Now let us consider another student who is facing the same problem but has preferences as indicated in part B of Figure 3.12. Clearly, this is a student who cares very much about subject 1 but relatively little about subject 2. The steep slope of her indifference curve at almost any point means that the student is willing to give up many hours studying subject 2 in order to obtain even a little more time to study subject 1. One possible explanation for this strong preference might be that the student is majoring in subject 1 and is just taking subject 2 as an elective for a pass/fail grade. Obviously, such a student will want to spend almost all her time studying subject 1, as indicated by point *e* in part B of Figure 3.12.

In summary, we can say that there is no universally optimal method of allocating time when studying for final exams. The optimal allocation depends on the amount of time a student has available, the type of grades the student wants to earn, and other factors. However, given a student's indifference map, we will always find that the optimal allocation of time is situated at a tangency point between an indifference curve and the budget (time constraint) line.

SOLVED PROBLEM 3.2

Question (Application and Extension: Optimal Allocations of Time)

Freddy, just like the two students in Figure 3.12, is also studying for his finals. He has a total of only eight hours, which he must divide between two subjects. Assume Freddy is a philosophy major and wants to go to graduate school to study philosophy. Hence, he cares tremendously about how well he does in his undergraduate philosophy course. He faces two finals: one in his favorite course—Philosophy 301, Philosophy of Final Exams, taught by the professor from whom he wants to get a letter of recommendation—and the other in Calculus II, a distribution requirement. Both tests are in the morning (only eight hours away), and Freddy, as usual, has not started studying yet. He knows, however, that he has been paying attention in both courses and that if he spends 0 hours on a subject, he will receive an F, 2 hours will get him a D, 4 hours a C, 6 hours a B, and 8 hours an A. So, for example, spending 2 hours on philosophy and 6 hours on calculus will yield grades of D in philosophy and B in calculus. Given his interests, we can represent his utility function as $u(x, y) = 3x + y$, where x is the number of hours spent on philosophy and y is the number of hours spent on calculus. How much time will Freddy spend on each subject?

Answer

With this linear utility function as depicted in Figure 3.13, Freddy cares about doing well in philosophy so much more so than in calculus that his optimal choice is to choose point *f* and spend all his time on philosophy and none on calculus.

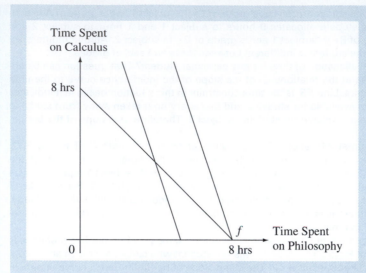

Figure 3.13

Study for Final Exams.

Freddy spends all his time studying philosophy so he can get an A. He fails calculus.

This will result in an A in philosophy but an F in calculus. Thus, for this student, it is optimal to fail calculus. The solution can also be depicted by the following table.

Hours Allocated to Philosophy (x)	Hours Allocated to Calculus (y)	Utility = $3x + 1y$
0	8	8
1	7	10
2	6	12
3	5	14
4	4	16
5	3	18
6	2	20
7	1	22
8	0	24

Obviously, allocating all 8 hours to philosophy is optimal.

Example 3.2

THE ECONOMICS OF TIPPING

You check into a hotel and a porter carries your bags to your room. How much should you tip? A hair stylist cuts your hair. What is the appropriate tip? A waitress serves you a meal in a restaurant. What tip should you leave? In the analysis below, we will use indifference curves—our basic tool for analyzing consumer behavior—to find an answer to questions of this type. The answer that we come up with may seem bizarre. In fact, no universally agreed-to theory of tipping exists, and the phenomenon is a true economic anomaly. It certainly will not fit our picture of the psychological makeup of consumers because our analysis will violate the selfishness assumption that we made earlier. More precisely, we will consider leaving a tip an altruistic act—one that reflects the tipper's concern about the utility (happiness)

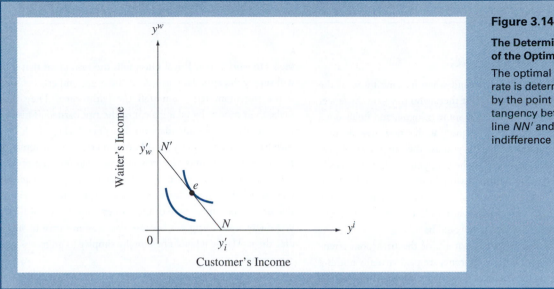

Figure 3.14

The Determination of the Optimal Tip.

The optimal tipping rate is determined by the point of tangency between line NN' and an indifference curve.

of the tippee. Some people believe that tipping is motivated by fear of embarrassment. "Stiffing" (failing to tip) a server can lead to an embarrassing confrontation. However, it will be our assumption that people leave tips because they care about their servers.

Assume that customer i in a restaurant cares about the utility of her waiter in the sense that her utility function depends not only on her own income but also on the waiter's income.[1]

Consider Figure 3.14. In this diagram we have placed the income of the customer on the horizontal axis and the income of the server on the vertical axis and have depicted the customer's indifference curve. To determine the tip that a person will leave given his or her tastes, we devise the following "categorical imperative tipping rule": Give the tip that, *if left by all other customers*, would provide the server with the income that you feel is best, considering your preferences and your income.

In the mind of our customer, this tipping rule transforms the tip she will give into an estimate of the server's income. First, the customer estimates the number of meals she expects the waiter to serve given the restaurant's reputation and price. We will call this D. If the average price of meals served is p, the income of the waiter will be $y^w = (tip\ percentage) \cdot D \cdot p$. Note that given the demand for the meal and the price of the meal, the categorical imperative tipping rule transforms each tip percentage into income for the customer and income for the waiter as depicted by line NN' in Figure 3.14.

Here, we see the customer starting out with income y'_i. Line NN' shows how the incomes of the customer and the waiter are determined by the tipping rate of the customer. Clearly, if no tip is left, the waiter will receive no income and the customer will stay at income y'_i, point N in Figure 3.14. If the tipping rate is set at such a high rate that the customer transfers all her income to the waiter, we will be at point N', where the customer has no income and the waiter is doing extremely well.

To choose an optimal tipping rate, then, our customer must select the point on line NN' that is best — that places her on the highest indifference curve consistent with line NN'. That occurs at point e. The tipping rate consistent with point e is, therefore, the optimal one for the customer to set.

---

[1] Our analysis here borrows heavily from the work of Robert Scott in "Avarice, Altruism, and Second Party Preference," *Quarterly Journal of Economics* 86, no. 1 (February 1972).

MEDIA NOTE

(BATHROOM) TIPPING

You go to a fancy restaurant and when its time to go to the bathroom you find an attendant there who turns on the faucet for you, offers you a towel and some cologne, and holds open the door when you leave. The question that now arises is, how much do you tip him or her? If you use the categorical imperative tipping rule described in the text, you would have to estimate how much this attendant would earn if all people tipped as you did. However, there is a piece of information missing. What salary does this person earn without a tip? You might guess minimum wage, but you would be wrong.

It turns out that most, if not all, of the bathroom attendants in fancy New York restaurants are paid virtually nothing and rely on tips for their entire income. What is worse, the company that supplies them, Royal Flush Bathroom Attendants of Manhattan, takes 25%–30% of their tips. The way it

seems to work is that Royal Flush tells the restaurant that they will supply the attendant, as well as the soaps and creams, etc., if the restaurant lets them staff the bathrooms. They then make their money by taking a cut of the tips earned. This can be devastating to the attendant on slow days during which they earn $15 for an entire day's work. It also creates a dilemma for the tipper because once this gets incorporated into the tipping rule described above, the customer would have to dramatically increase what he or she leaves in order to leave the optimal tip. Further, if you knew some of the money went to Royal Flush, you might want to tip less because you may not care to subsidize them. Maybe it would be morally simpler to go to less chic restaurants.

Source: Adapted from "Restroom Attendants Gain Ally in Bid for Back Pay and Tips" as appeared in the *New York Times,* October 8, 2004

MEDIA NOTE

IS TIPPING AN ECONOMIC PHENOMENON?

Tipping is a significant economic activity. Twenty-six billion dollars are paid as tips per year in the United States, and there are more than 30 jobs that are considered tip worthy. However, is tipping best explained by economic theory or is it mostly a psychological phenomenon best explained by psychologists?

Two factors suggest that economic theory alone may not be the best tool to use to explain tipping. First, tipping is viewed as an anomalous activity by economists because tipping after the service has been provided has no impact in the quality of the service provided. In addition, if the reason for tipping is to induce better service, one would think that better service would call forth better tips. But research shows a very weak connection between the size of tips and the quality of service. This finding is even true for customers who repeatedly patronize a restaurant because even they don't vary the tips in accordance to service and, by their own admission, the

decision to tip is not affected by the future probability of visiting the restaurant.

There is a large body of evidence that suggests that the psychological view of tipping is correct. For example, tipping is less prevalent in countries where inequality between people is less culturally acceptable, suggesting that tipping is an activity diners engage in to reduce their own discomfort.

Other evidence suggests that waiters who stand out of the crowd by wearing something unique increase their tips by 17%. Also, giving a positive weather forecast when presenting the bill will increase a waiter's tip by 19%. Putting a smiling face on a bill will increase a waitress's tip by 18% but will decrease a male waiter's tip by 9%. There is not much in economic theory to explain these outcomes.

So is tipping an economic phenomenon used to monitor waiters or a psychological one used to make you feel good about yourself? Perhaps both.

Source: Adapted from "Your Pound of Flesh, Sir," as appeared in *Financial Times,* April 9, 2005.

Revealed Preference

Notice the logic of what we have done up until now. We have started with the preferences of the consumer, insisted that these preferences satisfy certain assumptions, and asked what choices the consumer would make given his assumed preferences. But a person's preferences are not observable. What we can observe are his choices. So it makes some sense to ask the opposite question, which is, given a consumer's choices, can we infer that those choices were made by a consumer of the type we have assumed up until now, that is, a consumer with complete, transitive, and continuous preferences?

The answer is yes, but only if his or her choices satisfy some consistency criteria. So, instead of insisting that preferences be constrained to satisfy certain axioms or assumptions and then demonstrating that rational choices result, in this section of our analysis we insist on choice being constrained to be consistent in some manner and then go back and ask what the underlying preferences look like that are consistent with these choices. This is called the reveal preference theory because the object of analysis is to ask what the choices of the consumer reveal about his or her preferences. Our discussion here will help us answer the questions raised in the experimental teaser to this chapter.

Let us start with a simple concept. Say we observe a consumer in two situations described by how much income he has and what prices he faces. For example, say that in situation 1, he has $100 and can buy apples and pears each at $1 a piece. In that situation, say he buys 50 apples and 50 pears, which constitute bundle x (50 apples, 50 pears). (Note that the consumer can exactly afford this bundle because it exactly exhausts his income.) Now say that the consumer faces another situation in which he has $200 to spend but the price of apples has risen to $4 while the price of pears has stayed at $1 each. Say the consumer now buys 35 apples and 60 pears, bundle y (35 apples, 60 pears), the cost of which is exactly $200. Such a consumer, we will claim, acted in a strange manner because notice that after the prices changed, he chose bundle $y = (35\ apples,\ 60\ pears)$, which he could have afforded in the first situation but chose not to take. If he did not like that bundle in the first situation (and chose $x = (50\ apples,\ 50\ pears)$), then why the sudden reversal? The problem is that by choosing $x = (50\ apples,\ 50\ pears)$ over $y = (35\ apples,\ 60\ pears)$ in the first situation when both were affordable (at prices of $1 each), he revealed a direct preference for x over y; but in the new situation when his income and the prices changed, he revealed a preference for the opposite bundle. We would like to rule such reversals out. This is done by the Weak Axiom of Revealed Preference.

> **Weak Axiom of Revealed Preference (WARP):** If bundle x is ever directly revealed to be preferred to bundle y when the two bundles are not identical, then y can never be directly revealed to be preferred to x.

Note that in the definition of the Weak Axiom of Revealed Preference, we used the concept of x being revealed to be directly preferred to y. This occurs when we have a direct comparison of two situations. However, we may require something stronger. Say that bundle x is revealed to be directly preferred to bundle y and that bundle y is revealed to be directly preferred to another bundle z (in a similar binary comparison); then, by transitivity, we will claim that x is revealed to be preferred to z. However, because the relationship between x and z is indirect—it occurred through y—we will say that x has been indirectly revealed to be preferred to z. If this is true for all bundles in our consumption space, then such behavior satisfies the Strong Axiom of Revealed Preference

> **Strong Axiom of Revealed Preference (SARP):** If bundle x is revealed to be preferred to bundle y (either directly or indirectly) and bundle y is different from x, then bundle y cannot be directly or indirectly revealed to be preferred to x.

Note that the strong axiom is stronger than the weak because it requires that the preference for x over y not be reversed even by a sequence of binary comparisons, that is, not even indirectly. So the SARP imposes transitivity on revealed choices.

Weak Axiom of Revealed Preference (WARP)
The axiom that states that if bundle x is ever directly revealed to be preferred to bundle y when the two bundles are not identical, then y can never be directly revealed to be preferred to x.

Strong Axiom of Revealed Preference (SARP)
The axiom that states that if bundle x is revealed to be preferred to bundle y (either directly or indirectly) and bundle y is different from x, then bundle y cannot be directly or indirectly revealed to be preferred to x.

Finally, the SARP has been modified to allow for the possibility that the person making choices may have convex indifference curves but not strictly convex ones. This has yielded the Generalized Axiom of Revealed Preference (GARP).

It has been shown in various forms that if a consumer satisfies a version of the SARP—that is, if his actions are consistent in that manner—then those choices must come from a consumer who has the type of utility function we have described above. In other words, we have successfully reversed the process and instead of constraining preferences and describing choices, we have constrained choices and derived an underlying utility function. These are the types of choices that would be made by a decision maker with convex preferences and a continuous, nonsatiated utility function.

RESOLVING
TEASER 2

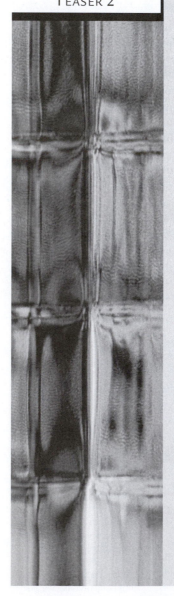

Now that we have learned about revealed preferences and the concepts of transitivity of preferences, etc., it should be clear why the subject we discussed in our teaser, Subject 40, was not making choices according to the assumptions of economic theory. In fact, he or she violated WARP, SARP, and GARP.

To see this, note that when Subject 40 chose allocation A, he or she was choosing from the thick budget line; C was chosen when the budget line was dashed; and B was chosen when the budget line was thin. This means that A was chosen when C was affordable, but then C was chosen when A was affordable, violating WARP. In addition, notice that C is indirectly revealed to be preferred to B (because C is directly revealed to be preferred to A, but A is directly preferred to B), but B is directly revealed to be preferred to C, which violates SARP and GARP. With these violations, we cannot expect this person to make the kind of transitive choices we need for our analysis here. In fact, we will rule such choices out in what we do in this text, yet we realize that they may exist out there in the real world for some (irrational?) people. But let us be more precise about the actual experiment Andreoni and Miller performed.

This experiment was actually run to test people's preferences for altruism. While altruism is not a good you can buy in a store, it is something that has a price and therefore one can purchase it. Let us call an altruistic act one that helps someone else but at a cost to you. (Obviously, if I could make you a billionaire by also making myself a millionaire, doing so is not really an altruistic act. If I intentionally make you a billionaire and suffer a loss in the process, then my actions can be called altruistic.)

To make this more concrete, say that you are given $100 and asked to split it between yourself and some stranger drawn at random. Say that every dollar you give up can be transferred one for one to the other person. So if you transfer $10 to him or her, he or she gains $10 and you lose $10. The cost of being altruistic here is 1. Now say that you have to give up $40 to transfer $10 to the other person. In this case, the cost of altruism has obviously gone up from 1 to 4.

In the Andreoni-Miller experiment, the researchers give subjects a number of different amounts of money and vary the cost of altruism. They are interested in how many people exhibit rationality in the sense that they do not violate the axioms of WARP, SARP, and GARP. They find that over 10% of subjects do violate the axioms. If we now take the ones who do not violate them, we can use the data generated by their choices to estimate their actual utility functions. Remember that a utility function tells a story about a person's preferences. In this case, if you showed me your utility function, I could tell you what your attitude is toward altruism and toward the person you were allocating money to.

(Continued)

For example, say that you considered the person who receives money from you to be a perfect substitute for yourself—your clone, in fact, whom you care for just as much as you care for yourself. In other words, for any given dollar, you do not care if you keep it or give it away to that person (your indifference curves are straight lines with slope −1). In such a case, given the price of altruism, you would give all the money to the person and would get the biggest utility from it. For example, say that the price of altruism is ¼, meaning that for every dollar you give up, your counterpart gets $4. In such a case, if you gave your cohort all the money, he or she would receive $400, while if you kept it, you would have $100. Because you think your cohort is just as worthy as yourself, obviously it would be best to give away all the money. In fact, 6.2% of subjects did this. Now assume that you are perfectly selfish and don't care at all about your cohort. Then, obviously, for any price of altruism, you would keep all the money, and 22.7% of the subjects did that. Finally, let us say that you get utility from a dollar only if your cohort gets exactly the same amount of money. You are an egalitarian and get utility only to the extent that you consume dollars in the ratio of 1:1 with your cohort. In that case, you would split the $100 in such a way as to equalize the amounts going to you and your cohort, and 14.2% of subjects had these preferences.

GARP FOR KIDS

Experimental Teaser 3 asks a question that is answered in another interesting experimental paper written by William Harbaugh, Kate Krause, and Timothy Berry* titled "GARP for Kids: On the Development of Rational Choice Behavior." The questions are, do we get more rational as we get older and is there a time before which we tend to violate GARP but after which we do not?

In this paper, they describe an experiment similar to that done by Andreoni and Miller with two differences. One is that they used 31 second graders, 42 sixth graders, and 55 college undergraduates, with average ages of 7, 11, and 21 years, respectively, instead of only college undergrads. Second, they offered them boxes of juice and bags of chips as goods instead of money.

They found that the average violation of GARP is different for the three age groups, but it is more pronounced when we move from second graders to sixth graders than when we move from sixth graders to college undergraduates. For example, the average number of violations per subject, out of 11 choices per subject, was 4.3 for second graders, 2.1 for sixth graders, and 2.0 for college undergraduates. While these seem high, if the subjects had simply chosen randomly, we would have observed around 8.5 violations. So while these subjects violated GARP, they did not choose randomly.

Does Experience in Markets Lead Kids to Be More Rational?

One standard criticism of experimental findings where subjects violate GARP is that in the real world, such irrational people would be weeded out by markets or markets would teach them to change their behavior because it would be costly for them to behave in such a way. John List and Daniel Millimet tested this on 11-year-olds. They performed the same experiment as Harbaugh, except they did it with some kids who had experience with trading cards in a market and others who did not. They found that those with market experience had fewer violations.

* William Harbaugh, Kate Krause, and Timothy Berry, "GARP for Kids: on the Development of Rational Choice Behavior," *American Economic Review* 91 (December 2001): 1539–1545.

Conclusion

The purpose of our discussion of preferences and utilities is to eventually analyze how consumers behave in markets. In other words, the process is to go from preferences to utilities to demands. Having now laid the foundation for this, we will proceed in our next chapter to look at consumer behavior in markets—individual and market demand.

Summary

This chapter has introduced the concept of an indifference curve, which is a major analytical tool of economists. We have derived the basic properties of indifference curves from the assumptions we made in Chapter 2 about the preferences of consumers. Given such consumers and a set of consumption bundles from which to choose (called the economically feasible consumption set), we then derived the conditions necessary to define an optimal consumption bundle. We concluded that an optimal bundle is a bundle for which the marginal rate of substitution equals the ratio of the prices of the goods in the bundle. Finally, at the end of the chapter, we turned our analysis on its head. Instead of talking about consumer preferences and then proceeding to their choices, we looked at the choices they made and, using the revealed preference theory, tried to induce what their preferences must be.

Exercises and Problems

1. Draw indifference curves for the following people.
    a) John says, "I get no satisfaction from 1 ounce of vermouth *or* 3 ounces of gin, but 1 ounce of vermouth *and* 3 ounces of gin (a martini) really turn me on."
    b) Steve says, "I will not cut my hair to please my boss unless she pays me. My price is $300 plus $1 for every $\frac{1}{8}$ inch of hair that is cut. In other words, for every $1 above $300 that the boss pays me, I will cut $\frac{1}{8}$ inch off my hair."
    c) In part b of this problem, what is the marginal rate of substitution between dollars and hair in the region below and above $300?
    d) Ann says, "I enjoy beer and pretzels, but after 12 beers, any additional beer makes me sick."

2. Assume that there are two goods in the world: apples and raspberries. Say that Geoffrey has a utility function for these goods of the following type, where r denotes the quantity of raspberries and a the quantity of apples.

$$U = 4r + 3a$$

    a) Draw the indifference curves that are defined by this utility function.
    b) What is the marginal rate of substitution between the raspberries and the apples when Geoffrey consumes 50 raspberries and 50 apples? What is the marginal rate of substitution between these two goods when Geoffrey consumes 100 raspberries and 50 apples? What do the answers to these questions imply about the type of goods the apples and raspberries are for Geoffrey?

c) If the price of raspberries is $1 per unit, the price of apples is $1 per unit, and Geoffrey has $100 to spend, what bundle of raspberries and apples would he buy? Would the marginal rate of substitution be equal to the ratio of the prices of these goods in the optimal bundle? If not, why not?

d) If the unit prices of the raspberries and the apples are $4 and $3, respectively, what bundle of raspberries and apples would Geoffrey buy with his income of $100?

3. Assume that there are two goods in the world: apples and raspberries. Say that Geoffrey has a utility function for these goods of the following type, where r denotes the quantity of raspberries and a the quantity of apples.

$$U = r \cdot a$$

a) Draw an indifference curve that is defined by this utility function and has a utility level of 2,500.

b) What is the marginal rate of substitution between the raspberries and the apples when Geoffrey consumes 50 raspberries and 50 apples? What is the marginal rate of substitution between these two goods when Geoffrey consumes 100 raspberries and 50 apples?

c) If the price of raspberries is $1 per unit, the price of apples is $1 per unit, and Geoffrey has $100 to spend, what bundle of raspberries and apples will he buy? Is the marginal rate of substitution equal to the ratio of the prices of these goods in the optimal bundle? If not, why not?

d) If the unit prices of the raspberries and the apples are $4 and $3, respectively, what bundle of raspberries and apples will Geoffrey buy with his income of $100?

If the price ratio of apples to raspberries is ¾, the optimal conditions are

$$\frac{r}{a} = \frac{3}{4} \tag{3.3}$$

$$4r + 3a = 100 \tag{3.4}$$

By substituting (3.3) in (3.4), we obtain the following:

$$4r + 4r = 100 \Rightarrow r = 12.50$$
$$3a + 3a = 100 \Rightarrow a = 16.67$$

Therefore, Geoffrey will consume 12.5 raspberries and 16.67 apples at the optimum.

4. A savings bank is an institution that permits people to deposit a certain amount of money today and have it earn interest so that they can withdraw a greater amount in the future. For example, say that our society creates a savings bank that allows people to deposit $100 today and get back $110 next year if the money is continuously kept in the bank. (We will assume that our savings bank pays a flat 10% interest rate with no compounding.) A study of consumer attitudes in our society shows that people have preferences between spending money today and saving money today in order to have more money tomorrow. Say that there are three different Elizabeths (Elizabeths 1, 2, and 3) who each have $100 and must decide how much of this $100 to consume today and how much to place in the savings bank and let grow at 10%.

a) Assuming that all their preferences can be represented by indifference curves that are bowed in toward the origin, draw three diagrams indicating the optimal consumption bundle for each of the Elizabeths. Assume that Elizabeth 1 consumes the entire $100 today, Elizabeth 2 consumes $40 today and deposits $60 in the bank, and Elizabeth 3 deposits the entire $100 in the bank. (The two goods on the axis of each diagram should be "consumption today" and "consumption tomorrow.")

b) What is a common name for the slope of the budget line in these three diagrams?

5. Consider the indifference map for a consumer that is shown in Figure 3.15.

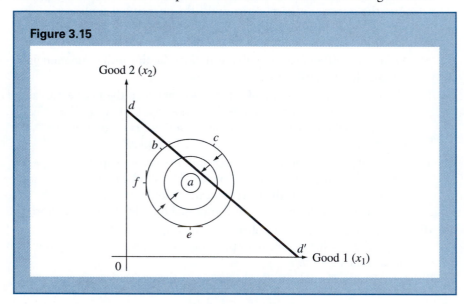

Figure 3.15

a) In terms of utility, what does point *a* represent?

b) What is true of the marginal utility of good x_2 at point *f*?

c) What is true of the marginal utility of good x_1 at point *e*?

d) What is the marginal rate of substitution at points *e* and *f*?

e) What assumption have we made to rule out such indifference curves?

f) Given the budget line *dd'*, is point *a* an optimal consumption bundle if the consumer can freely dispose of goods that are not wanted? If so, are the optimal marginal conditions satisfied?

g) If the consumer can freely dispose of goods (that is, if our assumption of free disposal holds true), is the consumer still indifferent between bundles *c* and *b*? If not, why not?

6. Suppose that Geoffrey is facing the following budget constraint:

$$M = p_1 x + Y \quad \text{if } x \le x^*$$
$$M' = p_2 x + Y \quad \text{if } x > x^*$$

The price of good Y is equal to 1; the price of good x is p_1 up to quantity x^* but switches to p_2 thereafter; M is Geoffrey's income; and $M' = M + (p_2 - p_1)x^*$ can be called Geoffrey's "virtual" income after the price change.

a) Draw Geoffrey's economically feasible consumption set when $M = 10$, $p_1 = 2$, $p_2 = 5$, and $x^* = 3$.

    b)   Draw Geoffrey's economically feasible consumption set when $M = 20$, $p_1 = 4, p_2 = 2$, and $x^* = 2$.

    c)   If the indifference curves for Geoffrey are bowed in and convex, would the optimal consumption bundle in part A of this problem always be unique? Would the optimal consumption bundle in part B of this problem always be unique?

7. Geoffrey and Elizabeth walk into a record store. Geoffrey (whose nickname is Mister Convex) has indifference curves that exhibit diminishing marginal rates of substitution for classical and rap music records. Elizabeth, who is known as Miss Concave, has indifference curves that exhibit increasing marginal rates of substitution for these types of records. The classical and rap music records sell at the same price, and both Geoffrey and Elizabeth have the same budget. When they leave the store, one person has bought only rap music records and the other person has bought some of both types of records. Who bought what? Draw two diagrams that illustrate these choices and indicate the equilibrium bundles.

Demand and Behavior in Markets

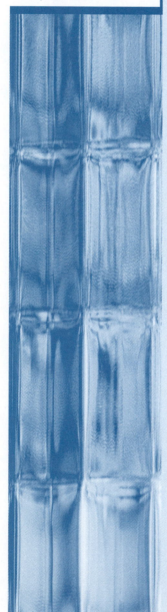

COMPENSATED DEMAND CURVES—WHAT IS THE DEMAND CURVE OF RATS FOR ROOT BEER?

The theory of the consumer, as we have described it, may look so complicated that it could not be a good description of the way people behave. For example, it implies that people can maximize their utility even when the situations they face are very complex. If we as humans are not capable of such complicated behavior, then the theory should certainly fail. But what if we could show that even lower animals like rats and pigeons are capable of behaving as if they were following the prescriptions of demand theory? If this were true, then certainly one could not argue that the theory is too complicated for humans.

Consider the following experiment. John Kagel, Howard Rachlin, Leonard Green, Ray Battalio, Robert Baseman, and W. R. Klemm* took a rat and placed it in an experimental chamber with two identical levers symmetrically placed on one side of the cage. When either of the levers was pushed, a nozzle above the lever would dispense a certain amount of a liquid. For exposition, let's say that the left lever dispensed root beer and the right dispensed Tom Collins mix. (Rats like both of these more than water in the sense that if you give them two bowls, one with water and the other with either one of these drinks, they will drink the root beer or the Tom Collins mix first.) Within a given time period, the rat was allocated a total number of pushes (for example, 300) on both levers. As long as the rat had more lever pushes available, a white light was lit on the top of each lever telling the rat that more pushes were available. When the number of pushes had been exhausted, the light would go out. (It turns out that 300 pushes were not enough to satiate the rats; in the experiments they always exhausted the 300 pushes before the time period ended.) When a lever was pushed, an amount of liquid was dispensed into a cup below the lever and remained there for five seconds, more than enough time to consume it. The amount of root beer or Tom Collins mix dispensed with one push of the lever was controlled by the experimenter.

Now how does this experiment relate to the theory of consumption? If the rat was a consumer, what would his income be and what prices would he face? Do you think that the rat will violate WARP (the Weak Axiom of Revealed Preference discussed in Chapter 3)? Will the rat have a downward sloping demand curve? You will be surprised, but you will have to wait until the end of the chapter to find out.

* John Kagel, Howard Rachlin, Leonard Green, Ray Battalio, Robert Baseman, and W. R. Klemm, "Experimental Studies of Consumer Demand Behavior Using Laboratory Animals," *Economic Inquiry* 13 (March 1975): 1, pp. 22–38.

The typical object of attention in economics is the demand function, and this is the final stop on our attempt in this section of the book to study the path from preferences to utilities to demands. What we are interested in demonstrating is that demand curves do not fall from heaven but rather are determined by a process of utility maximization, which itself is based on the primitive notions of preferences.

We study demand function in this chapter in a world where competitive markets exist. What this means is that we will study a consumer who faces fixed prices—one price for each good—and has a given income to spend on these goods. The fixed price assumption is a defining characteristic of perfectly competitive markets, which imply that no bargaining exists in such markets because no economic agent is big enough or has the power to affect the price determined by the market. They are parameters outside of our control.

When competitive markets exist, it is easier to predict consumer behavior, as we will see in this chapter. Such behavior is characterized by a consumer's *demand function*, which we will now be able to derive, given our study of consumer preferences and decision making in Chapters 2 and 3. A demand function shows the relationship between the quantity of any particular good purchased and the price of that good if other factors such as consumer income and the prices of substitute and complementary goods remain constant. Demand functions will be presented as *demand curves*, which depict in graphic terms the quantities of a good that consumers would be willing to purchase at various prices. We will observe how demand curves result from the utility-maximizing behavior of our agents.

The demand functions that we derive for our agents will allow us to analyze how their behavior will change in response to changing income and changing prices. We will examine various properties of demand curves and investigate a method of measuring *consumer surplus*—the gain that a consumer receives from purchasing a good at a certain price. We will then use this measure to study how the benefits obtained from purchasing a good change as its price changes.

Individual Maximization and Impersonal Markets

Institutions arise to solve problems that societies face, and perhaps one of the most important problems they face is the problem of exchange. When societies grow large, the process of exchange is performed through the intermediation of competitive markets. As we have noted already, one of the salient features of these markets is that they are anonymous. Personalities do not matter. Everyone trades at the same *fixed* and *predetermined* prices. In short, competitive markets are impersonal markets. The problem that all agents must solve in an economy with impersonal markets is deciding how much of a particular good they wish to consume or produce given the prices of all goods existing in the economy.

impersonal markets
Markets in which the identity of the traders and their size in the market do not affect the price at which they trade.

The agents in our primitive society will play two roles in the economy as it develops over time. They will be consumers and producers. However, at this point in our narrative, no one in our primitive society has yet discovered how to produce anything. Because we will not encounter production until Chapter 5, we will use this chapter to investigate how our agents will behave *when they function as consumers in impersonal markets*. Note that their behavior will be quite different from the behavior we would expect to see in markets with small numbers of agents where price formation is a more personal activity (where there is face-to-face bargaining between two agents). In such situations, threatening, bluffing, cajoling, and strategizing are common, and impersonal prices are nonexistent. When markets are large and competitive, however, consumer behavior takes the form of simple maximization of utility. Given income and tastes, the consumer merely chooses the bundle of goods that provides the most happiness *given the prices prevailing in the market*. Let us consider this maximization process in more detail.

The Problem of Consumer Choice

In an economy, consumers are described by two characteristics: tastes and income. A consumer's tastes can be summarized by her utility function or the shape of her indifference curves, and a consumer's income can be represented by the size of her economically feasible consumption set. For the purposes of this discussion, we will assume that each of our agents has available a certain number of dollars that she receives during each pay period.[1] The problem for the agent is to decide, given her tastes, income, and the prevailing prices in the market, how much of each good she wants to consume. As we know from our study of consumer preferences and decision making in Chapter 2, this problem can be summarized as shown in Figure 4.1.

In Figure 4.1, we see an agent with indifference curves marked I_1, I_2, and I_3 who faces the relative prices depicted by the slope of budget line BB' and who has an income with a value of 20. As we can observe, the current relative prices of goods 1 and 2 are in the ratio of 1:1. By the term relative prices, we mean that the market requires an agent to forgo one unit of good 2 in order to receive one unit of good 1. A relative price of 3:1 means that the agent would have to give up three units of good 2 to get one unit of good 1. When prices are stated in terms of dollars, we can find the relative prices of goods by comparing how many dollars an agent must give up to get various goods. For example, if the price of good 2 is $3 and the price of good 1 is $1, then in order to obtain good 2, an agent must give up three times the number of dollars required to obtain good 1. The relative price of goods 2 and 1 is therefore 3:1.

With $20 of income at our agent's disposal and a relative price ratio of 1:1, we can think of the price of good 1 as being $1 and the price of good 2 as also being $1. If our agent spends all her income on good 1, she can buy 20 units. If she spends all her income on good 2, she can also buy 20 units. Bundles of goods 1 and 2 that add up to 20 are depicted by budget line BB' in Figure 4.1. Our agent can consume any bundle of goods lying on or below budget line BB'. With tastes depicted by the indifference curves in the figure, our agent will maximize her utility at point *e* because only at that point on her budget line is the marginal rate of substitution equal to the price ratio.

We will refer to the quantity of a good that people seek to purchase at a given price as the quantity demanded of that good. The issue that concerns us in this chapter is how in large impersonal markets the quantity demanded of any single good will vary as the relative prices of goods vary. To examine this issue, we

relative prices
The ratio that tells how much a consumer in a market would have to forgo of one good in order to receive units of another good.

quantity demanded
The quantity of a good that people seek to purchase at a given price.

---

[1] This income could come from some work that one agent does for another agent. However, because we are assuming that no production yet exists in the economy of our primitive society, we will have to leave the source of the income undefined.

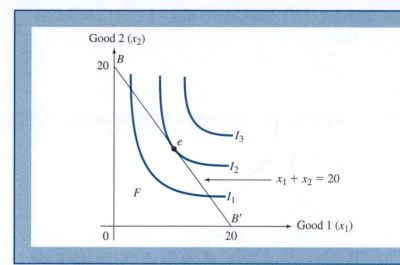

Figure 4.1

Optimal Consumption Bundle.

Feasible consumption bundles are represented by all points on and below the budget line—BB'. The utility-maximizing feasible bundle, point e, is on the highest attainable indifference curve, I_2, which is tangent to BB' at e.

will perform a simple thought experiment in which we will try to answer the following types of questions: If we change the price of good 1, say by decreasing it, but we hold the price of good 2 and the agent's dollar income constant, how will the amount of good 1 consumed by the agent change? Will the agent consume more of good 1 as its price decreases? If so, why? What will happen to the quantity demanded of good 1 as we change the price of good 2? What will happen to the quantity demanded of goods 1 and 2 if we keep the prices of both goods constant but change the agent's dollar income? Under what circumstances will the agent consume more of a good as its price decreases? What determines the sensitivity of the quantity demanded to a price change? Finally, we will look at the question of how we can measure the loss or gain to an agent when the price of a good changes.

Income Expansion Paths

To begin our analysis of demand and consumer behavior in large impersonal markets, consider Figure 4.2.

In this figure, we again see a diagram of the budget set of an agent with his indifference curve tangent to budget line BB' at the optimal point, which is labeled e. Now, however, we also see other budget lines—CC' and DD'—that have the same one-to-one slope as BB'. This shift of the budget line represents a situation in which, for some reason, our agent receives more dollar income but faces the same set of relative prices for goods 1 and 2 as he did before.

Suppose that instead of receiving an income of $20 during each pay period, our agent receives $40. With the price ratio remaining 1:1, the new budget line, CC', retains the same slope as BB'. If the agent decides to spend all his income on good 1, he can now buy 40 units of this good. Similarly, allocating all income to good 2 allows the agent to buy 40 units of that good. If the agent splits his income between the two goods, he can buy any bundle on budget line CC', where all bundles have a value of $40. When facing budget line CC', the agent will again choose that bundle at which the marginal rate of substitution of good 2 for good 1 is equal

Figure 4.2

Income Expansion Path.

As the agent's income rises, his budget line shifts outward, from *BB′* to *CC′* to *DD′*. Successively higher budget lines are tangent to successively higher indifference curves. The income expansion path is the locus of these tangencies (optimal consumption bundles) as income varies.

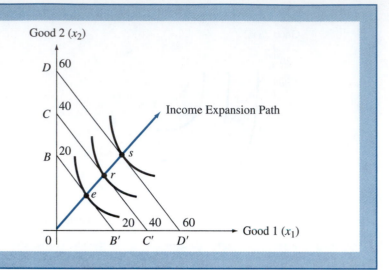

to the slope of the budget line. This point is labeled *r*. Now, assume that the income of the agent increases to $60. As a result, the budget line shifts to *DD′*, which has the same slope as *BB′* and *CC′* but is located farther out in the Good 1–Good 2 space. On budget line *DD′*, the optimal bundle is *s*.

If we connect all the optimal points in Figure 4.2 (*e*, *r*, and *s*), we can determine the income expansion path for the agent. This path shows how a consumer changes his quantity demand of specified goods (in this case, goods 1 and 2) as his income changes. Notice that along the income expansion path, the marginal rate of substitution of good 2 for good 1 is equal to the slope of the budget line (a slope of –1) and the path traces the locus of tangencies between the sequence of budget lines and the indifference curves.

income expansion path
The path connecting optimal consumption bundles that shows how a consumer changes his quantity demanded of specified goods as his income changes and prices remain constant.

SOLVED PROBLEM 4.1

Question (Content Review: Budget Constraints)

A student entertainment committee for a college is given $12,000 to bring in rock bands and speakers for the entire year. Rock bands typically cost $4,000, and speakers typically cost $1,000.

a) Write the equation for the budget constraint of the committee.

Answer

The equation for the budget constraint of the committee is $12,000 = $4,000 (number of rock bands) + $1,000 (number of speakers).

b) Assume that rock bands become more expensive and now cost $6,000. Write the new budget constraint.

Answer

After the increase in the price of rock bands, the budget constraint is $12,000 = $6,000 (number of rock bands) + $1,000 (number of speakers).

c) Draw a diagram representing the budget constraint before and after the change in the price of rock bands.

Answer

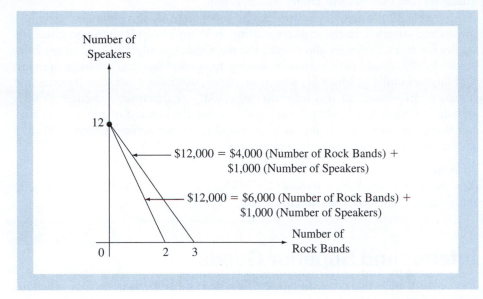

d) In terms of speakers, what is the cost of inviting a rock band to campus both before and after the increase in the price of rock bands?

Answer

The cost (opportunity cost) of inviting a rock band to campus is either the 4 or 6 speakers you cannot have as a result of the invitation.

e) Draw a diagram representing the change in the budget constraint of the committee if the college only gives it $8,000 and if the prices are $4,000 for rock bands and $1,000 for speakers.

Answer

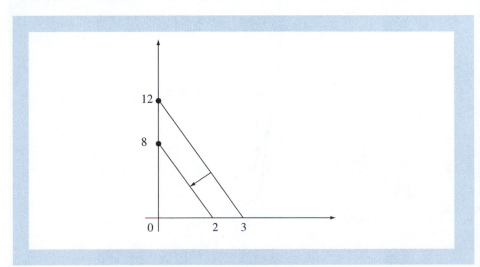

SOLVED PROBLEM 4.2

Question (Content Review: Utility Maximization)

Assume that Wally exists in a world where there are only three goods: apples, oranges, and bananas. In the markets existing in Wally's world, you must give up 3 apples for every 2 oranges you receive but must give up only 1 banana to get 2 oranges. Wally spends all of his money buying apples and bananas (he hates oranges) and buys a bundle at which his marginal rate of substitution between bananas and apples is 3:1. Based on this information, could you determine whether Wally's bundle is a utility-maximizing bundle and whether the amount of apples he is buying is representable as a point on his demand curve for apples? (Assume Wally's preferences satisfy our convexity assumption.)

Answer

Yes. Note that at Wally's bundle, his $MRS_{of\ bananas\ for\ apples} = 3:1$, which exactly equals the price ratio of bananas to apples.

Inferior and Superior Goods

Figure 4.3 depicts two different types of income expansion paths, each of which involves a different type of good.

In this figure, we are interested in the demand for good 1 only. We want to see how that demand will vary as the income of the consumer increases but the relative prices remain constant. Note that the income expansion path in Figure 4.3(a) slopes upward and curves to the right, which shows that whenever the income of

Figure 4.3

Superior and Inferior Goods.

(a) Income expansion path: superior good. As his income increases, the agent demands more and more of good 1.
(b) Income expansion path: inferior good. As his income increases, the agent demands less and less of good 1.

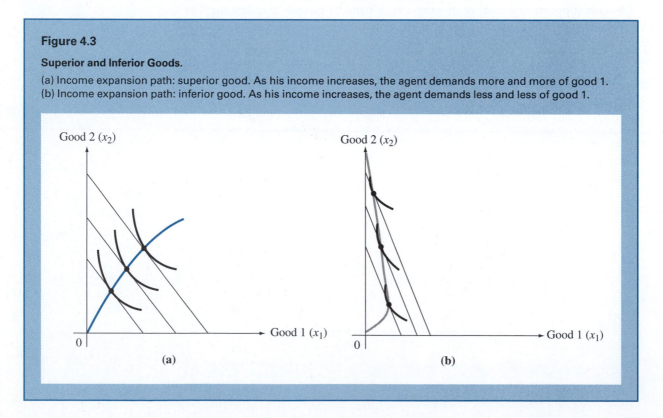

(a)   (b)

Figure 4.4

Income and Tastes.

(a) Income and tastes. Good 1 is a superior good, while good 2 is an inferior good. (b) Income and tastes. Good 1 is an inferior good, while good 2 is a superior good.

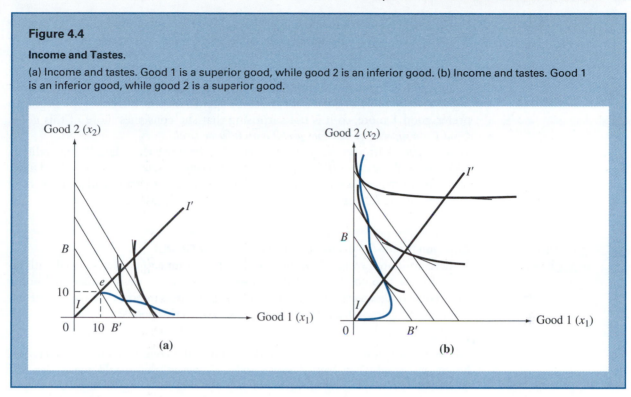

our agent increases, he consumes more and more of good 1. Economists use the term **superior good** to describe this type of good—a good for which demand increases as the income of the consumer increases and the relative prices remain constant.[2]

In Figure 4.3(b), we see just the opposite situation. Here, as the income of our agent increases, he eventually consumes less and less of good 1. Economists call this type of good an **inferior good**—a good for which demand decreases as the income of the consumer increases and the relative prices remain constant.

What determines whether a good is inferior or superior for a consumer? Keep in mind that goods that are superior for some people may be inferior for other people. Whether a good is inferior or superior for a specific consumer depends on the properties of the good and, more important, on the preferences of the consumer. Figure 4.4 illustrates the relationship between income and tastes.

In Figure 4.4(a), we see the original budget line from Figure 4.2 along with bundle *e*, which was optimal at that income and at the price ratio of 1:1. Note that at those relative prices, the agent bought equal amounts of the two goods (10 units of good 1 and 10 units of good 2) and spent half of her income on each good ($10 on good 1 and $10 on good 2). If we assume that the agent continues to divide her income equally between goods 1 and 2 as that income grows, her income expansion path will be a straight line as depicted by line *II′*. However, such a line cannot be an income expansion path for our agent because along that line the indifference

superior good
A good for which demand increases as the income of the consumer increases and the relative prices remain constant.

inferior good
A good for which demand decreases as the income of the consumer increases and the relative prices remain constant.

---

[2] What we have defined here as a *superior good* is sometimes also referred to as a *normal good.* However, we will use the term *normal good* to mean a good for which the quantity demanded decreases as the price of the good increases. See the discussion in the "Normal Goods and Downward-Sloping Demand Curves" section.

curves are not tangent to the budget lines. What is happening here? The answer is simply that as the consumer is becoming more wealthy in terms of income, her tastes are changing (that is, her indifference curves are "rotating"). Note that along line *II′*, the indifference curves for our agent are cutting the line more and more steeply, indicating that good 1 is becoming more valuable because the agent is willing to give up more of good 2 for it. As the agent's income increases, she begins to prefer good 1 more, so it is not surprising that she consumes more of this good. *Good 1 is a superior good, while good 2 is an inferior good.*

In Figure 4.4(b), just the opposite is true. As we move along line *II′*, the indifference curves along curve *II′* become flatter, reflecting a preference for good 2. Under these circumstances, it is not surprising that our agent buys more and more of good 2 as her income increases. *Good 2 is a superior good, while good 1 is an inferior good.*

SOLVED PROBLEM 4.3	**Question (Content Review: Inferior and Superior Goods)** If there are only two goods in the world and a consumer is never satiated with either of these two goods (i.e., if the consumer always gets positive marginal utility from consuming an extra unit of these goods regardless of how much he or she has consumed previously), can both of the goods be inferior goods? **Answer** Obviously not. If both goods are inferior, then as the consumer's income increases, he or she would buy less of *both* goods. However, this would mean that the consumer is not spending all of his or her growing income, which would not be rational because (given nonsatiation) the consumer could increase his or her utility by buying more. Thus, in a two-good world, it is *not* possible for both goods to be inferior.

Homothetic Preferences and the Characteristics of Goods

homothetic preferences
Preferences for which the resulting indifference curves have the property that, along any ray from the origin, the marginal rate of substitution between two goods remains constant. This implies that consumers will increase the purchases of goods proportionately as their incomes increase and prices stay constant.

Our analysis of income and tastes leads us to ask what kinds of preferences would cause consumers to increase their purchases of goods 1 and 2 proportionately as their incomes increase. These preferences must produce indifference curves that do not "rotate" as the consumer gets wealthier but, instead, have the same slope along any line from the origin (such as line *II′*). Preferences of this type are called homothetic preferences.

When a consumer has homothetic preferences, all goods are superior and purchased in the same proportion no matter what the consumer's income. In a world where all consumers have homothetic preferences, we might think of rich people as simply expanded versions of poor people. The tastes of such rich people do not change as their incomes change. They allocate their incomes exactly the way they did when they were poor. They just buy proportionately more of each good as their incomes grow.

Price-Consumption Paths

price-consumption path
The curve representing how consumption will vary when one price changes but all other prices and the consumer's income remain constant.

Now that we have investigated how consumption varies when income changes but relative prices remain constant, we should examine how consumption will vary when one price changes but all other prices and the consumer's income remain constant. Such a relationship is represented by the price-consumption path.

Changing Relative Prices

In Figure 4.5, we again see our agent facing budget line BB' and choosing bundle e, where his indifference curve is tangent to the budget line. The slope of BB' is -1 because the price ratio of good 1 to good 2 is 1:1. Now let us say that good 1 becomes relatively *less expensive*. By this, we mean that any agent can go to the market and, instead of exchanging 1 unit of good 1 for 1 unit of good 2, he can obtain several units of good 1 for 1 unit of good 2. For example, assume that the agent receives 2 units of good 1 whenever he gives up 1 unit of good 2. This situation is depicted in Figure 4.5 as a rotation of budget line BB' around point B so that the budget line becomes flatter at each amount of good 1. We will call this new budget line BB^*. Note that the income of our agent remains at \$20. If he wants to spend all of this income on good 2, he will be able to buy the same 20 units as before because the price of good 2 has not changed. However, our agent will now be able to buy 40 units of good 1 because it is half as expensive as it used to be. This is why budget line BB^* rotates or pivots around point B.

Now let us consider what happens if good 1 becomes relatively *more expensive*. Assume that instead of obtaining 1 or 2 units of good 1 in exchange for 1 unit of good 2, our agent receives only a half unit of good 1 for 1 unit of good 2. In that case, budget line BB' will rotate or pivot inward around point B toward budget line BB''. At an income of \$20, the agent can again buy 20 units of good 2, but now he can buy only 10 units of good 1. These examples and the previous examples demonstrate that changes in the price ratio of goods lead to rotations of the budget line around a point on the old budget line, while increases in income that leave relative prices constant *shift* the budget line outward or inward parallel to itself, keeping the slope intact.

Deriving the Price-Consumption Path

Figure 4.6 depicts the reaction of our agent to varying prices by showing how her consumption bundle changes as the price of one good changes.

When the price of good 1 decreases so that BB^* is the relevant budget line, the optimal bundle for our agent moves from point e to point g, where the indifference curve is tangent to the new budget line. When the price of good 1 increases so that BB'' is the relevant budget line, the optimal bundle for our agent moves

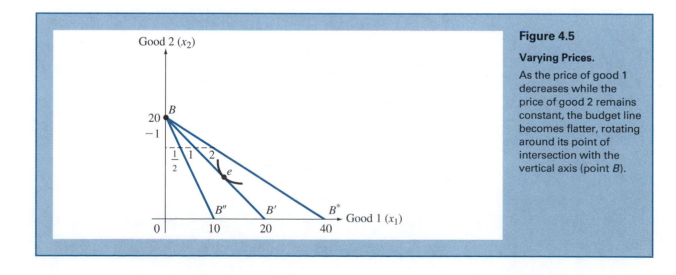

Figure 4.5

Varying Prices.

As the price of good 1 decreases while the price of good 2 remains constant, the budget line becomes flatter, rotating around its point of intersection with the vertical axis (point B).

Figure 4.6

Price-Consumption Path.

As the price of good 1 varies, the price-consumption path traces the locus of tangencies between budget lines and indifference curves.

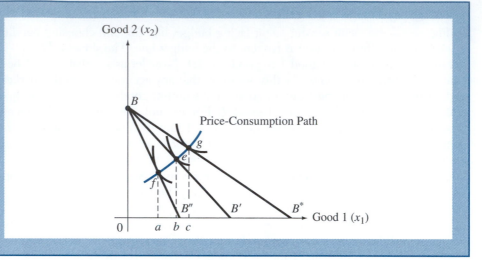

from point e to point f, where again the tangency condition holds. If we connect these tangency points, they trace the price-consumption path for the agent—the locus of optimal bundles that results when the price of one good changes but the prices of other goods and the agent's income remain constant.

Demand Curves

Demand curve
A curve that represents graphically the relationship between the quantity of a good demanded by a consumer and the price of that good as the price varies.

The price-consumption path gives us all the information we need to construct the demand curve for a good. This demand curve represents graphically the relationship between the quantity of a good demanded by a consumer and the price of that good as the price varies. Figure 4.7 shows the demand curve for good 1. Let us look at the changes in the quantity of good 1 consumed as its price changes from $p_1 = 2$ to $p_1 = 1$ to $p_1 = \frac{1}{2}$.

The price of good 1 appears along the vertical axis of Figure 4.7, and the quantity of good 1 demanded by our agent appears along the horizontal axis. The curve plotted in the figure shows how the demand for good 1 changes as its price changes, assuming that the income of the agent and the price of good 2 remain

Figure 4.7

Demand Curve for Good 1.

The demand curve for good 1 associates the optimal quantity of good 1 with its price, while holding income and other prices constant.

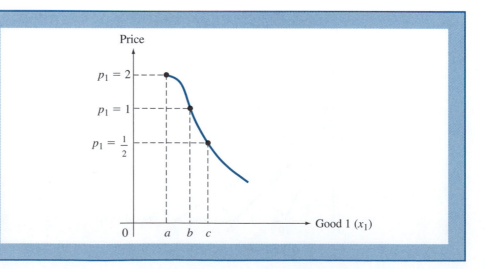

constant. As we can see, the demand curve for a good is the image of the agent's price-consumption path when we focus our attention on good 1 alone and plot the relationship between the demand for good 1 and *its* price. Note that every point on the demand curve, by being a point on the price-consumption path, is also a tangency point of the agent. Demand curves are generated by the utility-maximizing behavior of agents. They follow from the attempts of the agents to make themselves as satisfied with their consumption as they can possibly be, given their limited budgets.

SOLVED PROBLEM 4.4

Question (Content Review: Demand Functions)

Bernie has preferences regarding egg rolls and sushi. His utility function can be expressed as $u(e, s) = es$, where e is egg rolls and s is pieces of sushi. The price of sushi is $3 per piece, and egg rolls are $2 each. Bernie has a total income of $80. Of the following bundles, determine which is on Bernie's demand curves for egg rolls and sushi: a) 25 egg rolls and 10 pieces of sushi, b) 15 egg rolls and 10 pieces of sushi, c) 20 egg rolls and $13\frac{1}{3}$ pieces of sushi.

Answer

Given $u(e, s) = es$ for Bernie, the $MRS_{Sushi\ for\ egg\ roll}$ equals the ratio of the marginal utility of sushi to the marginal utility egg rolls. Therefore, to complete this problem, we must know what the marginal utilities are. For this utility function, $MU_{sushi} = e$ and $MU_{egg\ roll} = s$. This is easy to see because the additional amount of utility Bernie gets from one more piece of sushi is $e(s + 1) - es = es + e - es = e$. Likewise, the additional amount of utility he gains from one more egg roll is the amount of sushi he already has (s).

For a bundle to be on Bernie's demand curve, it must satisfy two conditions. The marginal rate of substitution must be equal to the price ratio, and the bundle must also be on the budget constraint. The first condition in this problem can be expressed by

$$\frac{e}{s} = \frac{p_s}{p_e}$$

while the budget constraint is

$$p_s s + p_e e = I$$
$$3s + 2e = 80$$

The first bundle is on the budget constraint but does not satisfy the marginal rate of substitution condition. $(3)(10) + (2)(25) = 80$, but $\frac{25}{10} \neq \frac{3}{2}$. So this bundle is not demanded by Bernie at these prices and income.

The second bundle satisfies the marginal rate of substitution condition but not the budget constraint. $(3)(15) + (2)(10) \neq 80$, but $\frac{15}{10} = \frac{3}{2}$. Thus, this bundle is also not demanded by Bernie at the given prices and income.

The third bundle satisfies both conditions. $(3)(\frac{40}{3}) + (2)(20) = 80$, and $\frac{20}{1} / \frac{40}{3} = \frac{60}{40} = \frac{3}{2}$. This is the bundle that Bernie will demand.

Demand and Utility Functions

Because the demand curve is generated by utility-maximizing behavior, let us look behind such behavior and try to envision what type of utility functions might give rise to it. This examination of demand and utility functions will give us a better understanding of the reason we made the assumption about the convexity of preferences in Chapter 2.

Nonconvex Preferences and Demand

In Figure 4.8(a), we see an agent's indifference map with a shape that violates the convexity assumption. When faced with a budget line such as BB', this agent could not maximize his utility by picking point e, where the indifference curve is tangent to the budget line, because a point like f would place the agent on a higher indifference curve and yet not violate the agent's budget constraint. Point f, therefore, must involve more utility. For an agent with nonconvex preferences, the optimal consumption bundle would occur at the *corner* of the feasible set—at either point h or point k.

Note that agents with nonconvex preferences would maximize their utility by spending all their incomes on only one good. This is not surprising, however, because we know that the assumption of convex preferences involves the idea that mixtures of equivalent things are better than the components. In this particular case, we see that when prices are depicted by budget line BB', the agent will spend his entire budget on good 2. When the price of good 1 increases, the agent remains at point B. (If the agent preferred to buy only good 2 when the price of good 1 was lower, he would certainly do so after the price of good 1 rose.) When the price of good 1 decreases enough, however, say to the prices shown by budget line BB^*, the agent will *jump* from consuming all of good 2 to consuming only good 1. For any price ratio less than this one, the agent will continue to consume only good 1. His price-consumption path is depicted by the dark lines in Figure 4.8(a). Note

Figure 4.8

Nonconvex Preferences and Demand.

(a) Nonconvex preferences and demand: indifference map. Nonconvex preferences imply optimal consumption bundles at the corners of the feasible set—either point h or point k. (b) Nonconvex preferences and demand: demand curve. Nonconvex preferences imply jumps in the demand curve.

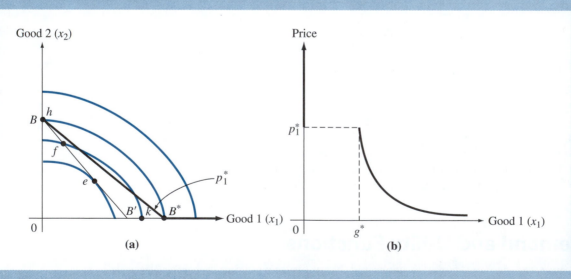

that part of this path is a point along the vertical axis and part is a segment of the horizontal axis, showing that at any given price ratio, the agent is spending all of his income on only one good, which may be either good 1 or good 2.

Figure 4.8(b) depicts the demand curve of this agent, which is the image of the price-consumption path just described. Note that there is a zero demand for good 1 as long as its price is above p_1^*. At p_1^*, however, the demand jumps from zero to g^*, which is what we saw happening in the agent's price-consumption path as well. Such jumps in the demand function can create problems for our analysis. In Chapter 6, when we derive the existence of competitive markets, we will see that such markets would fail to exist if we assumed that people had nonconvex preferences. For this reason, nonconvex preferences will be ruled out in most of our analysis in the remainder of this book.

Nonstrictly Convex Preferences and Demand

Nonconvex preferences are not the only type of preferences that can be responsible for odd-looking demand curves. Consider the indifference curves depicted in Figure 4.9(a).

In Figure 4.9(a), we again see an indifference map for an agent along with a set of budget lines. These preferences are convex (they are bowed into the origin), but they differ from typical indifference curves because they consist of a set of flat portions along which the marginal rate of substitution is constant. Note that at the price ratio that determines budget line BB', the agent chooses the consumption bundle e. However, because this bundle occurs at a kink point of the indifference

Figure 4.9

Nonstrictly Convex Indifference Curves and Demand.

(a) Nonstrictly convex indifference curves and demand: price-consumption path. When preferences are nonstrictly convex, the price-consumption path may include points of nontangency between the budget line and the indifference curve (point e) as well as segments in which all points are tangent to the same curve (segment hj). (b) Nonstrictly convex indifference curves and demand: demand curve. Nonstrictly convex preferences may imply a demand curve with flat segments.

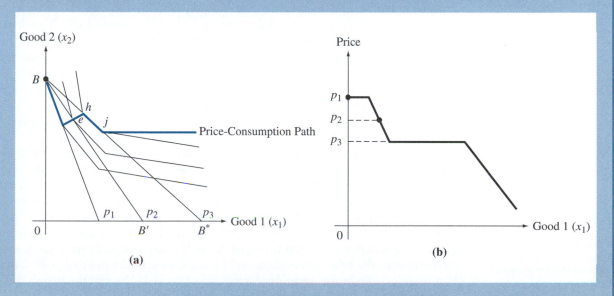

(a)

(b)

curve, the condition that the marginal rate of substitution must equal the slope of the budget line is not satisfied. To the left of point *e*, the marginal rate of substitution is steeper than the budget line, while to the right of point *e*, it is flatter. Still, at those prices, there is only one bundle that is the best to consume. This is not true, however, when the agent faces a steeper price ratio as depicted by budget line *BB**. Here the budget line is tangent to an entire segment of the indifference curve, which means that at those prices the agent is indifferent to any bundle on segment *hj* of the budget line.

The price-consumption path is shown in Figure 4.9(a), and the corresponding demand curve appears in Figure 4.9(b). Note that the demand curve now has flat segments, indicating that at various prices there are numerous quantities that could be demanded.

In summary, if our demand analysis deviates from the rather restrictive assumptions we made in Chapter 2 (assumptions such as the convexity of preferences, nonsatiation, and selfishness), we may generate some odd-looking demand curves. By accepting those assumptions, we can guarantee that our demand curves will not jump and that they will have a unique quantity demanded at every price.

Income and Substitution Effects

The Income Effect

Now that we have derived demand curves for agents with nonconvex preferences and have investigated what the utility functions of these agents might look like, we should examine the properties of *well-behaved* demand functions. By *well-behaved*, we mean demand functions derived for agents who have the types of preferences we assumed in Chapter 2 (strictly convex, nonsatiable, and selfish) and who have utility functions that are consistent with those preferences. One simple question that we can ask at the start of this discussion is whether demand curves must slope down and to the right or whether it is possible for them to slope upward so that as the price of the good under consideration increases, more of that good is actually demanded. To answer this question, let us consider Figure 4.10.

In Figure 4.10(a), we see our agent at point *e*, where our analysis begins. At this point, our agent is maximizing her utility by finding that bundle at which the indifference curve I_1 is tangent to the existing budget line marked *BB'*. Now let us assume that the price of good 2 and the agent's income remain constant but the price of good 1 *decreases*. As we know, this will cause budget line *BB'* to rotate outward, determining budget line *BB''*. At the prices depicted by budget line *BB''*, the agent chooses bundle *f* on indifference curve I_2. If we look only at the amount of good 1 the agent buys in the shift from *BB'* to *BB''*, we see that the decrease in the price of good 1 causes the agent to increase her demand for good 1. Such behavior generates a downward-sloping demand curve, as we see in Figure 4.10(b).

But why does an agent consume more of a good, like good 1, when its price decreases? Basically, there are two reasons. One reason is that a decrease in the price of a good an agent is consuming has the *same effect as an increase in the agent's real income*. The agent can now buy the same quantity of good 1 as she did before the decrease in its price and still have some income left over to buy additional goods. The agent may buy more of good 1 simply because her income has increased and good 1 is a superior good. On the other hand, if good 1 is an inferior good, then an increase in the agent's income caused by a decrease in the price of good 1 may lead to a decrease in the agent's consumption of good 1. We call the impact of an income-induced change in demand the income effect.

income effect
The impact of an income-induced change in demand caused by a change in price.

Figure 4.10

Income Effects, Substitution Effects, and Demand.

(a) Income and substitution effects. The income effect of the price change is measured by the parallel shift of the budget line from *DD′* to *BB′*. The substitution effect is measured by movement around the indifference curve from point *e* to point *g*. (b) Downward-sloping demand curve.

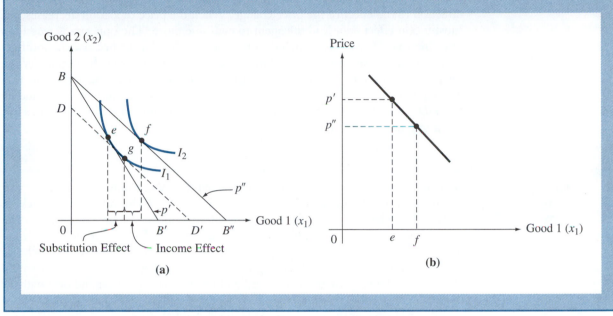

(a)   **(b)**

The Substitution Effect

Even if we try to nullify the income effect by taking enough income away from the agent to make her exactly as well off as she was before the decrease in price (that is, place the agent back on the indifference curve where she started), we must still consider the possibility that the agent will change her consumption of goods 1 and 2. Because good 1 has become cheaper relative to good 2, whose price has remained constant, we might expect the agent to *substitute* good 1 for good 2 and consume more of it. Such an attempt to substitute a good whose price has decreased (like good 1) for another good whose price has remained constant (like good 2) because of the price change, after having nullified the implicit income effect, is referred to as a substitution effect.

The Income and Substitution Effects Combined

Let us look at Figure 4.10(a) again and see how the substitution effect works. As we discussed previously, our agent starts at point *e* and moves to point *f* after the price change. Now notice that at point *f*, our agent is on a higher indifference curve than she was at point *e*. She is on I_2 instead of I_1. This shift occurs because the decrease in the price of good 1 has increased the agent's real income, making it possible for her to achieve a higher level of utility. To nullify this income effect, we must take away enough income from our agent *at the new prices* to place her back on her original indifference curve, where point *e* was chosen. We therefore shift budget line *BB″* down in a parallel fashion (keeping the new prices fixed) until we reach a tangency between indifference curve I_1 and the new budget line *DD′* at point *g*.

substitution effect
The change in demand that results from an attempt to substitute a good whose price has decreased for another good whose price has remained constant after having nullified the implicit income effect.

By letting prices change from those depicted by BB' to those depicted by BB'' (or DD') but taking away enough income from our agent so that she cannot achieve a higher level of utility (be on a higher indifference curve), we nullify the income effect. We can then be sure that any change in the consumption of good 1 is due to the substitution effect. Therefore, the move from point e to point g is caused by the substitution effect. Note that this effect must always be opposite in direction to the effect of the price change. When the price of a good decreases, the substitution effect *must* lead the agent to consume more. The opposite is true for a price increase. The substitution effect produces such behavior because the indifference curve is convex and exhibits diminishing marginal rates of substitution. When the price line becomes flatter (as when the price of good 1 decreases), the new tangency point in the situation where the income effect has been nullified (see budget line DD') must be to the right of point e. The substitution effect simply causes our agent to move around the original indifference curve.

SOLVED PROBLEM 4.5	**Question (Application and Extension: Compensating Variations in Income)** Sammy is currently consuming a bundle consisting of 5 CDs and 2 baseball tickets. CDs and baseball tickets both cost $10 per CD or ticket. After Sammy's favorite team wins the World Series, the owner of the team decides to raise ticket prices to $15 per ticket. Mark, a philanthropist and friend of Sammy, offers Sammy a choice of two options. Mark will either a) give Sammy the amount of money that would allow him to buy exactly the same bundle of tickets and CDs as he did originally or b) give Sammy enough money so that he will be able to have exactly the same level of utility as he did at the old prices. Which will Sammy choose? **Answer** Sammy will choose option a. To see why, look at Figure 4.11. Originally, Sammy is at a point like point a on indifference curve I. If Mark gives him enough money

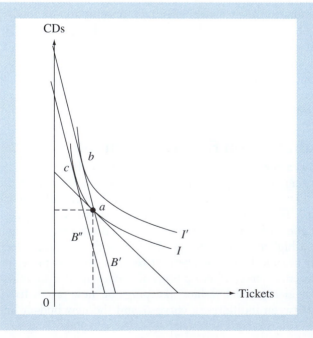

Figure 4.11

Compensating for Price Changes.

Sammy moves from indifference curve I to I' when he is given enough money to purchase his original bundle a after the prices change.

to afford his original bundle, Sammy's new budget constraint will be like B'. With that constraint, he will prefer bundle b over any other he can afford, including the original bundle a. Thus, with this plan Sammy will be better off in the end than he was originally, moving from indifference curve I to higher indifference curve I'. If Sammy accepted plan b, he would opt for a bundle like bundle c but would be no better off than he was originally, as he would still be on indifference curve I. (Remember, plan b only promises to restore Sammy to his original utility level.)

Normal Goods and Downward-Sloping Demand Curves

We now know that the shift from point g to point f in Figure 4.10(a) is due to the income effect and that this shift shows how much our agent changes her consumption of good 1 because the decrease in its price has made her better off. In this case, both the income and substitution effects cause our agent to want to consume more of good 1 as a result of its fall in price. That need not be the case, however, as Figure 4.12 indicates.

In Figure 4.12, we again start with a situation in which the agent's indifference curve is tangent to his budget line at point e. Again, we decrease the price of good 1 by rotating the budget line from BB' to BB'' and our agent moves to point f. Let us now separate the income and substitution effects by taking away enough income from our agent after the price change to place him back on indifference curve I_1. The shift in our agent's purchases of good 1 from point e to point g when the price of good 1 decreases is again caused by the substitution effect. Note, however, that point g in Figure 4.12 is to the right of point f. When we include the income effect, our agent actually consumes less of good 1. Good 1 must therefore be an inferior good because the increase in income resulting from the new price led to a *decrease* in consumption of the good. In this case, then, the income and substitution effects have worked in opposite directions. While the substitution effect has caused our agent to purchase more of good 1, the income effect has led him to

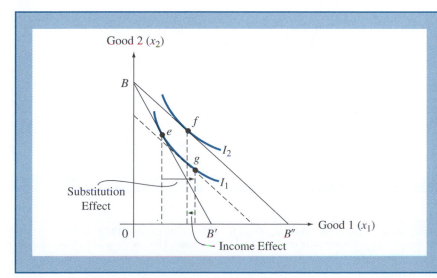

Figure 4.12

Income and Substitution Effects Work in Opposite Directions.

The substitution effect of a decline in the price of good 1 causes an increase in demand for the good, the move from e to g. Because good 1 is an inferior good, this is partly offset by the income effect, a decrease in demand for the good from g to f.

consume less. Note, however, that the net result is an increase in the demand for good 1 (point f is still to the right of point e). Hence, the demand curve for good 1 is still downward sloping. We will call a good whose demand curve is downward sloping a normal good. Keep in mind that such a good can be either an inferior or a superior good, as Figures 4.10 and 4.12 indicate.

normal good
A good whose demand curve is downward sloping.

Giffen Goods and Upward-Sloping Demand Curves

Demand curves need not slope downward. Clearly, if the income effect in Figure 4.12 had overpowered the substitution effect, the net result would have been a decrease in the consumption of good 1 when its price fell. This situation would lead to an upward-sloping demand curve. Any good with an upward-sloping demand curve is called a Giffen good.[3] To see how such a demand curve occurs, consider Figure 4.13.

Giffen good
A good whose demand curve is upward sloping.

We again start with our agent facing the prices depicted by budget line BB' and choosing bundle e. After the price of good 1 decreases, however, our agent moves to bundle f, which contains less of good 1 than bundle e. The lowering of the price of good 1 has caused demand for the good to fall rather than rise. To discover the substitution effect, let us move budget line BB'' back until it is tangent to indifference curve I_1 at bundle g. As usual, the move from e to g is the substitution effect and causes our agent to consume more of good 1. The income effect is shown by the shift from g to f. Note that not only does the income effect cause our agent to consume less of good 1, indicating that good 1 is an inferior good, but this effect is so powerful that it is actually of a greater absolute magnitude than the substitution effect. As a result, the reaction of our agent to a decrease in the price of good 1 is a move from e to f. When looked at in terms of good 1 alone, this

Figure 4.13

Giffen Good.

The decline in the price of good 1 causes a decline in the demand for that good because the substitution effect (the move from e to g) is more than offset by the income effect (the move from g to f).

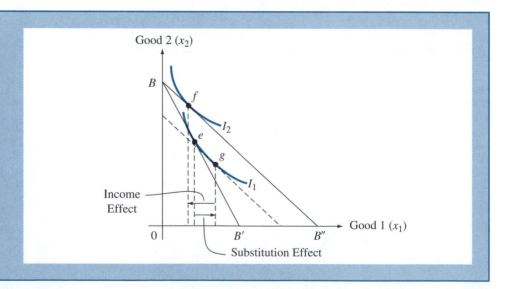

---

[3]   Giffen goods are named after the British economist Sir Robert Giffen (1837–1910), who first observed that an increase in the price of a good could cause demand for the good to increase. Giffen made this observation when he was studying the effect of rising prices for bread on the budgets of the poor.

reaction means a lowering of the demand for good 1 as its price falls. Such a reaction would produce an upward-sloping demand curve, and any good with such a demand curve is a Giffen good.

Example 4.1

GIFFEN GOODS: MARGARINE VERSUS BUTTER AND RICE VERSUS MEAT

Until recently, margarine was often used as an example of a Giffen good. It was argued that people would consume margarine when they were poor but would substitute butter when their incomes rose. It was also argued that if the price of margarine were to fall dramatically, this change might release enough income to allow additional consumers to substitute butter. Therefore, a decrease in the price of margarine could lead to a decrease in its consumption. Because butter is high in cholesterol and many consumers are anxious to avoid such foods, margarine is probably no longer a Giffen good. Health-conscious consumers now prefer margarine to butter regardless of their income and regardless of any changes in the price of margarine.

Rice is another food that can help us understand the nature of Giffen goods. In Asian countries, rice forms the bulk of the diet. If people are poor and consequently spend most of their income on rice, a decrease in its price can cause a decrease in its consumption. When people spend such a large part of their income on a single food, a fall in its price has a relatively large income effect. As the incomes of these people rise, they may decide to eat less rice and substitute other foods like chicken and fish in order to vary their diet. This substitution may cause the consumption of rice to fall, and, if so, rice will be a Giffen good.

Note that in order for a good to be a Giffen good, it must be an inferior good. However, not all inferior goods are Giffen goods.

Table 4.1 indicates the relationship between the concepts of inferior and superior goods and the types of goods classified as normal and Giffen goods.

Table 4.1	**Identifying Normal and Giffen Goods.**	
Type of Good	**Substitution Effect**	**Income Effect**
Normal	Opposite to price change	The good is either superior or inferior but with an income effect that is less powerful than the substitution effect.
Giffen	Opposite to price change	The good is inferior. The income effect is more powerful than the substitution effect.

MEDIA NOTE

GIFFEN GOODS?

Consider the amazing increase in incomes that occurred in the United States during the later 1980s and 1990s. Increases in stock prices created billionaires by the dozens who went about spending lavishly. They bought mansions, jets, and all sorts of other luxury goods. According to the author of this article, these goods were bought precisely because their cost went up. So in the article, they were labeled Giffen goods. One leading example is the purchase of Johnnie Walker Black, an expensive scotch that is only slightly better than the cheaper Johnnie Walker Red. Another is the Nokia Vertu cell phone, which costs $19,450.

The question for us is, does the fact that people spent more for luxury goods indicate that those goods were Giffen goods? Actually, the answer is no because a Giffen good is defined as one for which the consumer increases his purchases as the prices increase, *"holding the income of the consumer constant and merely changing prices."* In the example here, people were buying more expensive goods, at least partially because their incomes rose, so this is not a good test.

Source: Adapted from "Supersize American Dream: Expensive? I'll Take It," as appeared in the *New York Times,* December 16, 2002.

Compensated and Uncompensated Demand Curves

compensated demand function
A hypothetical demand curve in which the consumer's income is adjusted as the price changes so that the consumer's utility remains at the same level.

uncompensated demand function
A demand function that represents the relationship between the price of a good and the quantity demanded, which includes both the substitution and income effects of price changes.

Now that we have analyzed the substitution and income effects, we are able to make a distinction between two different but related types of demand functions—compensated and uncompensated demand functions. Both of these types of demand functions represent a relationship between the price of a good and the quantity demanded, but a compensated demand function is a hypothetical construct in which the consumer's income is adjusted as the price changes so that the consumer's utility remains at the same level. In short, the income effect of price changes is removed from a compensated demand function, and real income is held constant. An uncompensated demand function (which is what we have studied above) includes both the substitution and income effects of price changes. The concepts of compensated and uncompensated demand functions will be useful to us when we study the topic of consumer surplus later in this chapter.

Obviously, the primary difference between compensated and uncompensated demand functions is the presence or absence of the income effect that results from price changes. As we know, when the price of a good changes, the consumer is affected in two ways. First, he is affected because the good purchased in the past now has a new price (the substitution effect). Second, he is affected because as the price changes and his dollar income stays the same, his real income changes (the income effect). The compensated demand function nullifies the income effect and shows us how the quantity of a good that is purchased varies strictly as a result of the substitution effect.

Deriving Compensated Demand Functions

To see how compensated and uncompensated demand functions are derived, consider Figure 4.14.

In Figure 4.14, the agent starts on budget line BB' where, given indifference curve U_0, she chooses bundle e as the optimal bundle. If we now decrease the price of good 1 so that the relevant budget line is BC', then our agent will move from

Figure 4.14

Deriving Compensated Demand Curves.

The compensated demand function for good x_1 is determined by varying the slope of the budget line—for example, going from budget line BB' to GG' and recording the optimal quantities of x_1 determined by the tangencies between the new budget lines and the original indifference curve U_0.

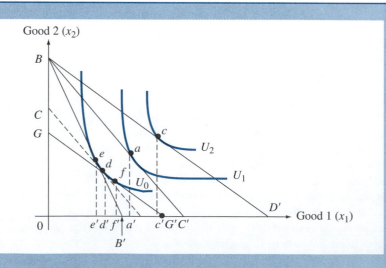

bundle e to bundle a. Note that this shift from e to a is caused by both the income and substitution effects. Final consumption of good x_1 has increased from e' to a', and our agent's utility has increased from U_0 to U_1.

We can eliminate the income effect after the price has changed by taking enough money away from our agent to place her back on the original indifference curve U_0 and then looking at the demand for x_1 at that point. We move budget line BC' back in a parallel fashion toward the origin until a tangency is reached at point d, where d' units of good x_1 are demanded. Therefore, demand has increased from e' to d'. This shift from e' to d' is solely the result of the substitution effect because we have removed the income effect.

If we now lower the price of good x_1 further, we see that a tangency is reached at point c on indifference curve U_2, where c' units of x_1 are demanded. When we again nullify the income effect associated with the price change, GG' becomes the relevant budget line. We then see that a tangency is reached between U_0 and GG' at f, and that f' units of x_1 are demanded.

To derive the compensated demand function for our agent, we need only to plot the relationship between the price of good x_1 and the quantity demanded after the income effect is removed. Figure 4.15 shows this relationship.

In Figure 4.15, the various prices of good x_1 that were presented in Figure 4.14 appear on the vertical axis, and the quantities demanded appear on the horizontal axis. Note that at the price associated with budget line $BB'(P_{BB'})$, e' units of good x_1 are demanded, but as the price decreases to $P_{BC'}$ and $P_{BD'}$, the compensated demand for good x_1 increases to d' and f', respectively.

Figure 4.15 also shows the uncompensated demand function, which relates the various prices for good x_1 ($P_{BB'}$, $P_{BC'}$, and $P_{BD'}$) to the demands for that good (e', a', and c', respectively).

The Relationship of Compensated and Uncompensated Demand Functions

It should be obvious that compensated and uncompensated demand functions are not equivalent. They differ because of the presence or absence of the income effect. Note, however, that the compensated and uncompensated demand curves in

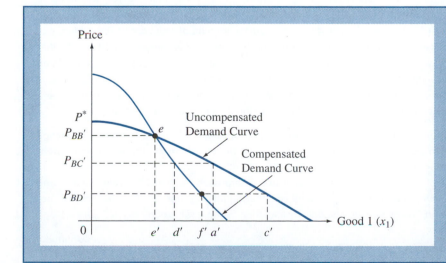

Figure 4.15

Plotting Compensated and Uncompensated Demand Curves.

The compensated demand curve indicates the demand for good x_1 at each price, say $P_{BC'}$, after the consumer has been compensated for the income effect of the change in price from $P_{BB'}$ to $P_{BC'}$. The uncompensated demand curve indicates the demand without compensation for the income effect of the price change.

Figure 4.15 cross at point e, where they both define bundles that yield a utility level of U_0. As prices change, the utility level for our agent changes along the uncompensated demand curve but not along the compensated demand curve. Hence, in both cases, when prices are $P_{BB'}$, the optimal choice for our agent is bundle e at utility level U_0. Therefore, both demand curves cross at point e.

Note that, to the left of point e, the uncompensated demand curve lies below the compensated demand curve because the income effect of an increase in the price of a superior good leads to a decrease in demand. On the other hand, when the price of a superior good decreases, the income effect of that decrease leads to an increase in demand and the uncompensated demand curve therefore lies above the compensated demand curve.

Inferior and Superior Goods and Compensated and Uncompensated Demand Curves

Is it possible to tell whether a good is superior or inferior simply by observing the relationship between its compensated and uncompensated demand curves? The answer to this question is yes. Consider Figure 4.15 again. Good x_1 in this figure must be a superior good because, starting at point e, as its price decreases, the uncompensated demand for the good is greater than the compensated demand. This situation implies superiority because the agent's income rises while the price falls. Note that the agent purchases more of good x_1 when his income rises, and the amount purchased is beyond the increase in the compensated demand with the income effect removed. Therefore, the good must be superior. The opposite is true of a price increase above $P_{BB'}$.

See the resolution to Experimental Teaser 4 below for some empirical support of compensated demand theory.

RESOLVING
TEASER 4

COMPENSATED DEMAND CURVES

Now how does the experiment listed in the teaser relate to the theory of consumption we have just studied? In our theory, the consumer allocates his fixed income to the purchase of two goods whose prices are fixed in the market. So in this experiment, what constitutes an income and what constitutes prices? After some thought, you should come to the realization that in this rat world, a rat's income is the number of pushes it has on the lever (in this case, 300), and the prices are the amount of root beer or Tom Collins mix dispensed per push. For example, if one push on either lever dispenses 0.1 ml of either liquid, we can say that the prices of root beer and Tom Collins mix are the same. When the amount of Tom Collins mix per push increases to 0.5 ml, then the Tom Collins mix decreases in price. In other words, the scarce commodity here is pushes on levers, and the price of a liquid is the inverse of the amount of that liquid you get for a given push.

Question: Another way to define the price of root beer or Tom Collins mix is to change the number of lever pushes necessary to dispense an equal amount of liquid from either nozzle. Is this equivalent? Explain.

The first experiment performed was one where each rat had 300 lever pushes, and each lever push dispensed 0.05 ml of either liquid. In other words, the prices of root beer and Collins mix were equal. The situation facing a rat is depicted in Figure 4.16.

(Continued)

Figure 4.16

Compensated Demands of Rats.

As the price of Tom Collins mix falls, rats consume more.

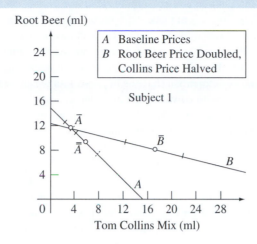

Root Beer (ml)

| A | Baseline Prices |
| B | Root Beer Price Doubled, Collins Price Halved |

Subject 1

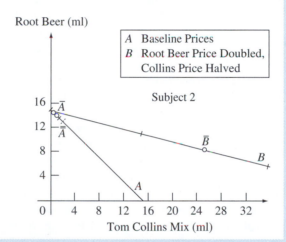

Root Beer (ml)

| A | Baseline Prices |
| B | Root Beer Price Doubled, Collins Price Halved |

Subject 2

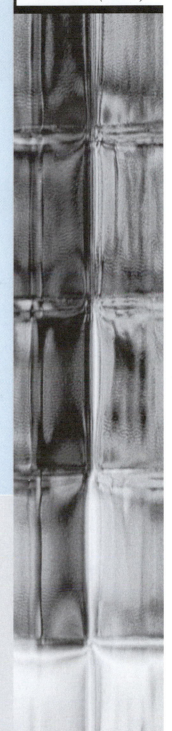

As we see in this figure, at the beginning of the experiment, the rat could choose any bundle of root beer or Tom Collins mix on or below line *A*. If we look at the actual purchases of a real experimental rat subject (call him Willard), we see that when facing these prices, Willard chose bundle $\bar{A}$. What Kagel and his associates did next was to change the prices faced by Willard by increasing the mount of Tom Collins mix dispensed per lever push from 0.05 ml to 0.1 ml and by reducing the amount of root beer to 0.025 ml. In this way, they dramatically changed the prices facing the rat, making Tom Collins mix cheaper and root beer more expensive. However, after making these changes, they increased the number of lever pushes available to Willard by an amount that, after the price change, allowed Willard exactly enough lever pushes to buy bundle $\bar{A}$, if he still desired.

Hence, in this experiment, when we observe the demand for root beer by rats, we observe the "compensated demand curve" of the rat; this is due to the fact that after each price change, we compensate the rat for the change in prices. (Note that this compensation is not quite the same as the one we looked at before in the sense that

(Continued)

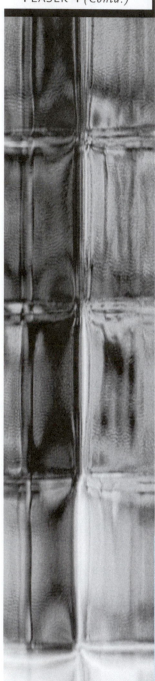

RESOLVING
TEASER 4 *(Contd.)*

in the past, when we compensated consumers for a price change, we gave them enough money to place them on the same indifference curve. Here we compensate them by giving them enough or taking away enough lever pushes to allow them to buy the same bundle they bought before. While this way of compensating is more practical because we cannot observe a person's utility level, the two are generally equivalent for small changes in prices.) As we know from our discussion of compensated demand curves, when the price of a good goes up, the consumer must always consume less of it. Why? You'll recall that this is because there can be no income effects when we compensate consumers for changes in prices. After the price and income changes are implemented, therefore, the budget line faced by Willard is depicted in Figure 4.16 as line *B*.

The results of the experiment for Willard are presented in Figure 4.16. When Willard faced budget line *A*, he chose bundle $\bar{A}$. When the prices were changed and he was compensated for the change, he chose bundle $\bar{B}$, which contains more Tom Collins mix. After Willard got used to the new budget and price situation, the experimenter changed the prices once again back to their original relationship, and Willard chose point $\bar{\bar{A}}$, meaning that when the prices and incomes returned to the original relationship, Willard practically returned to his original consumption (give or take a few milliliters either way). This is a check for the consistency of Willard's behavior. (Note that Willard does not satisfy the Weak Axiom of Revealed Preference because he revealed himself to directly prefer $\bar{A}$ to $\bar{\bar{A}}$ in the first situation when they were both available but then reversing himself in the second situation and choosing $\bar{\bar{A}}$ again when they were both affordable. Still, the violation was rather small because both bundles are close to each other.

After they demonstrated that Willard behaved in a manner basically consistent with compensated demand theory, the researchers lowered the prices several more times and estimated his demand function, which appears in Figure 4.17.

This experiment should teach you that the theory of demand has some very testable hypotheses embedded in it, all of which can be tested on humans or even rats if one is clever. The experiment is interesting because it shows how little high-powered intelligence is required for the theory to work. While economic theory is clothed in terms of maximization and so on, the intuitive appeal of the theory is not lost on animals of lower intelligence.

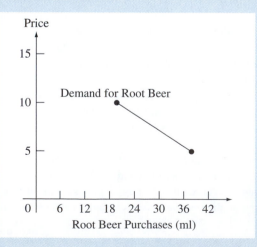

Figure 4.17

Compensated Demand Function of Rats.

Compensated demand function slopes downward.

Conclusion

We have now made the progression from preferences to utilities to demand. That is, we have shown how we can start with the primitive concepts of consumer preferences and show how these preferences can be represented by utilities and then use the resulting utility functions to derive demand functions for our economic agents. The point, of course, is to show that demand functions are not arbitrary but rather come from a process of utility maximization where the underlying utility functions are preference based. This is what we have accomplished so far, so in our next chapter we will apply these concepts to a set of real-world problems.

Summary

This chapter has studied the theory of demand using the underlying institutional assumption that competitive markets exist so that each person, given his or her income, faces prices that are fixed and beyond his or her control. We have seen how the process of utility maximization determines a well-defined demand curve for our consumers. We derived what are called compensated as well as uncompensated demand functions and also showed how the process of utility maximization is influenced by both a substitution and an income effect. This leads to the notions of normal and Giffen goods. We are now in a position to use these demand functions in all of the discussions that follow.

APPENDIX A

THE DEMAND CURVE

As we explained in the text, demand curves are not dropped from heaven upon individuals but rather are the result of their attempts to maximize their utility given their incomes. The demand curve for any individual can therefore be obtained directly from the problem of maximizing the utility function of the individual subject to a budget constraint.

To be more specific, let $u(x_1, x_2)$ be a utility function defined over the consumption of an amount x_1 of good 1 and an amount x_2 of good 2. Let W be the income of the individual and p_1 and p_2 be the prices of goods 1 and 2.

The budget constraint for the problem is

$$W = p_1 x_1 + p_2 x_2$$

That is, the amount $p_1 x_1$ is spent on good 1, the amount $p_2 x_2$ is spent on good 2, and the sum of these two amounts is the income W.

The individual's problem is to choose the quantities x_1 and x_2, given income W and prices p_1 and p_2, to maximize utility $u(x_1, x_2)$ subject to the budget constraint.

Formally, the problem is

$$\underset{\{x_1, x_2\}}{\text{Max}} \ u(x_1, x_2)$$
$$\text{s.t.} \ W = p_1 x_1 + p_2 x_2$$

Define a new problem called the Lagrangian Problem, which combines the utility function and the constraint of the problem as follows:

$$L(x_1, x_2, \lambda) = u(x_1, x_2) + \lambda(W - p_1 x_1 - p_2 x_2)$$

Then we can maximize the Lagrangian with respect to x_1, x_2, and λ; the first order of necessary conditions yields a system of equations:

$$\frac{\partial L(x_1, x_2, \lambda)}{\partial x_1} = \frac{\partial u(x_1, x_2)}{\partial x_1} - \lambda p_1 = 0$$

$$\frac{\partial L(x_1, x_2, \lambda)}{\partial x_2} = \frac{\partial u(x_1, x_2)}{\partial x_2} - \lambda p_2 = 0$$

$$\frac{\partial L(x_1, x_2, \lambda)}{\partial \lambda} = W - p_1 x_1 - p_2 x_2 = 0$$

This system of equations can be solved for the equilibrium demand functions, x_1 and x_2, and the equilibrium value of λ, the marginal utility of income:

$$x_1^* = x_1(W, p_1, p_2)$$
$$x_2^* = x_2(W, p_1, p_2)$$
$$\lambda^* = \lambda(W, p_1, p_2)$$

x_1^* and x_2^*, which are both functions of W, p_1, and p_2, are the equilibrium demand functions.

Consider now an explicit example. Let $u(x_1, x_2)$ be multiplicative; that is, $u(x_1, x_2) = x_1 x_2$. Then the Lagrangian is

$$L(x_1, x_2, \lambda) = x_1 x_2 + \lambda(W - p_1 x_1 - p_2 x_2)$$

The maximization problem reduces to

$$\operatorname*{Max}_{\{x_1, x_2\}} x_1 x_2 + \lambda(W - p_1 x_1 - p_2 x_2)$$

The first order conditions are

$$\frac{\partial L}{\partial x_1} = x_2 - \lambda p_1 = 0 \Rightarrow x_2 = \lambda p_1$$

$$\frac{\partial L}{\partial x_2} = x_1 - \lambda p_2 = 0 \Rightarrow x_1 = \lambda p_2$$

$$\frac{\partial L}{\partial \lambda} = W - p_1 x_1 - p_2 x_2 = 0 \Rightarrow W = p_1 x_1 + p_2 x_2$$

Substitute for x_1 and x_2 in the budget constraint:

$$p_1 \cdot \lambda p_2 + p_2 \cdot \lambda p_1 = 2\lambda p_1 p_2 = W$$

$$\Rightarrow \lambda = \frac{W}{2p_1 p_2}$$

$$\Rightarrow x_1^* = \frac{W}{2p_1} \text{ and } x_2^* = \frac{W}{2p_2}$$

Note that both the demand curves are downward-sloping; in fact,

$$\frac{\partial x_1}{\partial p_1} = -\frac{W}{2} \cdot \frac{1}{p_1^2} < 0 \text{ and } \frac{\partial x_2}{\partial p_2} = -\frac{W}{2} \cdot \frac{1}{p_2^2} < 0$$

The price elasticity of demand is constant and equal to 1:

$$\xi_1 = \frac{\partial x_1}{\partial p_1} \bigg/ \frac{x_1}{p_1} = -\frac{\dfrac{W}{2} \cdot \dfrac{1}{p_1^2}}{\dfrac{W}{2p_1^2}} = -1$$

Symmetrically, for x_2, we have $\xi_2 = -1$.

Finally, the equilibrium level of utility is obtained by substituting the equilibrium demands of x_1 and x_2 in the utility function and is given by:

$$u^* = \frac{1}{4} \cdot \frac{W^2}{p_1 p_2}$$

Exercises and Problems

1. John has a utility function in which he consumes only gin and vermouth. He must have one ounce of gin and two ounces of vermouth to make a perfect martini. This perfect martini is the only thing that gives him utility, and if he has excess gin or vermouth, they are thrown away. Each martini yields him one unit of utility. Say that the price of gin is $1 an ounce and the price of vermouth is 50 cents an ounce.

   a)   How much would it cost John to attain a utility level of 45? of 50? of 70?

   b)   Assume that John has an income of $10. What is the maximum utility that he can achieve with this income?

   c)   Assume that Saddam Hussein, instead of invading Kuwait in 1990, had invaded the vermouth-producing region of Italy and the price of vermouth went up to $2 an ounce. How much utility can John achieve at this new price?

   d)   Compare the situation before and after the increase in the price of vermouth. What price-compensating variation in income is needed to compensate John for the price increase?

2. Assume that Elizabeth has a utility function of $U = x \cdot y$, so that her utility equals the product of the quantities of x and y she consumes. Her marginal utilities of the goods x and y are $MU_x = y$ and $MU_y = x$, respectively. She tells her friend Miriam that no matter what her income, she always spends an equal amount of it on each good. If the price of good x is $p_x = 2$, the price of good y is $p_y = 4$, and her income is $100, she will buy 25 units of good x and 12.5 units of good y.

   a)   Is Elizabeth a utility maximizer if she follows her simple rule of thumb? Prove your answer.

   b)   Assuming that Elizabeth is a rational maximizer, derive the demand for good x when her income is $1,000 and the price of good y is held constant at $p_y = 1$. (Determine how many units of good x she will buy as the price of good x varies but the price of good y and her income remain constant.)

3. Russell has a utility function of $U = x + y$ and a budget of $600. Assume that the price of good y is $p_y = 1$. Derive Russell's demand for good x as its price varies from $p_x = 0.25$, to 0.5, to 0.75, to 1, to 1.25, to 1.5, to 1.75, and to 2.

4. There is an island called Homothetica in which all people have the same homothetic utility function of $U = X^{1/2} Y^{1/2}$ over goods X and Y. There are three income groups on the island, and these groups have incomes of $500, $1,000, and $2,000, respectively. Say there are 500 people in each income group. At prices p_x and p_y, say that the poorest people consume 20 units of good X and 40 units of good Y each.

    a)   What are the prices of good X and good Y?

    b)   If the supply of goods X and Y on Homothetica totals 50,000 units and 200,000 units, respectively, will there be any excess demand or excess supply of either of these goods at the prices you calculated in part A?

5. Jeffrey is five years old. He likes candy and hates spinach. He is allowed 2 candy bars a day, but his mother offers him 1 additional candy bar for every 2 ounces of spinach he eats.

    a)   On these terms, Jeffrey eats 3 ounces of spinach and 3.5 candy bars each day. Using indifference curves, illustrate his optimal choice.

    b)   Suppose that Jeffrey's mother does not give him 2 "free" candy bars each day but still gives him 1 candy bar for every 2 ounces of spinach he eats. Would his spinach consumption be greater or smaller than in part A? Explain your answer.

Some Applications of Consumer Demand, and Welfare Analysis

5

WORK-LEISURE TRADEOFFS

Cab drivers have good and bad days. Let's say you are a taxi driver and have rented your cab from a fleet owner for 8 hours (9 A.M. to 5 P.M.). You are having a great day, so by 1 P.M. you have already made as much as you typically make for the whole day. Do you quit and say, "Great! Now I can relax for the rest of the day," or do you stay on and really make a killing? What does economic theory say you might do? What do cab drivers actually do when they are surveyed? These questions will be answered later when we report the results of the survey done by Colin Camerer, Linda Babcock, George Loewenstein, and Richard Thaler.*

_____

* Colin Camerer, Linda Babcock, George Loewenstein, and Richard Thaler, "Labor Supply of New York City Cab Drivers: One Day at a Time," *Quarterly Journal of Economics* 112 (May 1997): No. 2, pp. 408–41.

WILLINGNESS TO PAY AND WILLINGNESS TO ACCEPT

One day you go into your attic and find an unopened Bob Dylan album in perfect condition. You take it to a collector you trust and find out the record is worth $120. The next day a friend of yours offers you $120 for the record and you reject it, despite the fact that while you like Dylan you would never pay $120 for one of his records.

Such situations are common, and I am sure you have come upon them in your own life. The reason economists find them so irrational is that in the theory of the consumer, a consumer is supposed to be able to reach a point of indifference between possessing and not possessing a good. In other words, if I ask you, the consumer, how much you would be willing to pay for a good, your answer (if truthful) should be an amount of money that, if I offer the good to you for that price or less, you would be willing to spend. But if I ask for more than that amount, you would not be willing to buy the good. Such an amount of money is called the consumer's willingness to pay. Now, let's say that you accidentally come upon the good, as in our example above. If after finding the good I were to ask you how much you would be willing to accept in order to give up the good (i.e., ask you for the willingness to accept), then your answer should be the same. In other words, your willingness to accept payment in order to give up a good should be the same as your willingness to pay to get the good. If not, something seems wacky. Is there a difference between people's willingness to accept and willingness to pay? If so, what explains it? We will review the experimental results of Daniel Kahneman, Jack Knetsch, and Richard Thaler† to help us explain this phenomenon.

_____

† Daniel Kahneman, Jack L. Knetsch, and Richard H. Thaler, "Experimental Effects of the Endowment Effect and the Coase Theorem," *Journal of Political Economy* 98 (December 1990): No. 61, pp. 1325–47.

The consumer analysis described in the preceding chapters can be applied to countless situations. It is the central tool for much of what economists do. In this chapter, we will concern ourselves with applying what we have learned above to a variety of situations using concepts we have already learned as well as some we develop here.

Application 1: Work and Leisure

Let us assume that the society in our model contains labor markets as well as markets for goods. In the labor markets, the goods exchanged are hours of work and dollars. The participants in these markets are the workers who supply the hours and the firms that have a demand for such hours. In this application, we are concerned about the supply decisions of the workers. To investigate these decisions, consider Figure 5.1.

In Figure 5.1, we see the amount of leisure taken by an agent along the horizontal axis and the amount of income the agent receives along the vertical axis. Because leisure is the opposite of work, as our agent purchases more and more leisure, he devotes less and less time to work. To make our analysis easier, let us concentrate on the agent's work-leisure choice and assume that every hour worked yields $1\frac{2}{3}$ dollars. Consequently, every hour not spent working and therefore spent at leisure would cost $1\frac{2}{3}$ dollars. In this sense, the cost of each hour of leisure is what our agent will have to give up by not working for that hour. The amount forgone is the opportunity cost of time. By working, our agent can transform 1 hour of his time into $1\frac{2}{3}$ dollars. This is why the budget line in Figure 5.1 has a slope of $-1\frac{2}{3}$. The budget line indicates that if our agent decides not to work but rather to devote all of his time to leisure, he will be at point *m* and will have 24 hours of leisure and zero dollars of income. If our agent decides to work full time, he will be at point *w* and will have zero hours of leisure and $40 of income. Given the opportunity cost of his time, our agent has to choose how much of his time to spend working and how much to spend relaxing. This choice will be determined by both the opportunity cost of time and our agent's taste for leisure or distaste for work. Such preferences are depicted by the indifference curves presented in Figure 5.1. Note that at the current opportunity cost, or at the current implicit wage, our agent chooses to work for exactly 12 hours.

opportunity cost
The cost of engaging in any activity or the opportunity forgone by choosing that particular activity.

Figure 5.1

Work and Leisure.

A higher wage (cost of leisure) has both a substitution effect (the movement from *e* to *g*) and an income effect (the movement from *g* to *f*).

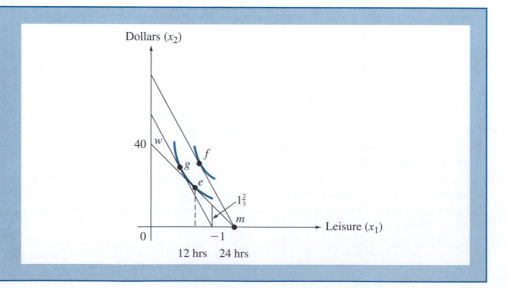

Let us now assume that the implicit wage available to our agent increases, as depicted by the rotation of the budget line around point m in the figure. This new budget line reflects the fact that our agent now faces a higher implicit wage in the market. At this new wage, our agent moves from point e to point f and actually works less. So, an increase in the implicit wage has led to fewer hours of work and more hours of leisure. We can explain this result by using our familiar analysis of income and substitution effects.

When the available wage increases, it means that the cost of leisure also increases. It is more costly for our agent to do nothing. Such a change leads our agent to work harder because of a substitution effect. (We know that a substitution effect always functions in a way opposite to the price change. Therefore, an increase in the cost of leisure means that our agent will devote more hours to work.) As a result of the substitution effect, our agent moves from e to g in Figure 5.1 and consumes less leisure. However, there is also an income effect in this situation. Because the available wage has now increased, our agent will have more income even if he maintains his old work pattern. With this increased income, our agent will be in a position to work fewer hours. The income effect is shown in the figure by our agent's move from g to f. In this case, because leisure is a superior good and work is an inferior good, the income effect is more powerful than the substitution effect and our agent works less hard as his wage increases.

See the Experimental Evidence feature at the end of this section for an additional application of consumer analysis to work-leisure choice.

Application 2: Crime and Punishment

As our primitive society grows, it will eventually have to contend with the problem of crime and crime prevention. An economist looks at crime as a rational act of an economic agent who faces the problem of allocating time between legal and illegal activities. For example, assume that we are studying a person who must decide whether to be a criminal or not. In either case, this agent will work eight hours a day and must allocate these eight hours between legal and illegal activities. If he works at a job that involves legal activities, he will earn an hourly wage of w_h. We will call this amount the *honest wage*. If he works as a drug dealer or a numbers runner or engages in some other illegal activities, his wage will be w_d. We will call this amount the *dishonest wage*. Our agent is a moral person and therefore has preferences about how he earns his income. However, money is still money to him once he earns it, so dishonest dollars are just as good as honest ones. Finally, if he engages in illegal activities, there is a chance that he will be caught and sent to jail. Obviously, this risk makes illegal activities less attractive to him. Let us represent the cost of our agent's risk of being put in jail by an amount π, which is subtracted from his dishonest wage. Clearly, π will depend on such factors as the number of police officers, the efficiency of the police, and our agent's distaste for spending time in jail.

One of the most interesting aspects of economics is that it sometimes allows us to uncover counterintuitive results or paradoxes that, on the surface, seem impossible. In this application, we will see such a paradox, which we will call the *paradox of crime prevention*.

Income and Crime

To understand how our agent makes a choice between legal and illegal activities, let us look at Figure 5.2.

Figure 5.2

Income and Crime.

Each line such as *BB'* represents the income the agent can earn for each allocation of his time between legal and illegal activities, given a different level of the honest wage w_h and the dishonest wage w_d.

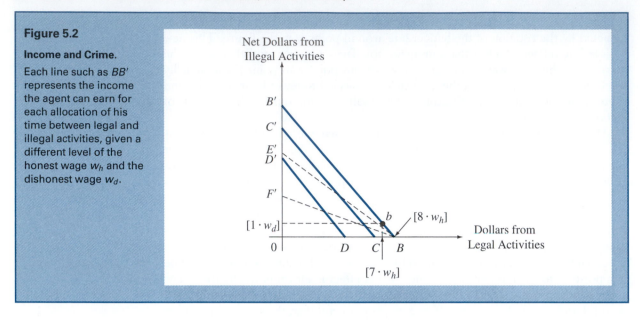

On the horizontal axis of Figure 5.2, we see the amount of money our agent will receive from legal activities, while on the vertical axis we see the amount he will receive from illegal activities. The parallel budget lines marked *BB'*, *CC'*, and *DD'* represent lines along which all eight hours of our agent's workday are allocated. Each pair of wages, w_h and w_d, determines a different line. Consequently, as the wages increase proportionately, these lines shift out in a parallel fashion. For example, our agent will be at point *B* along budget line *BB'* if he spends all his time working at legal activities when both the honest and dishonest wages are high. If he again allocates all his time to legal activities but the honest and dishonest wages are lower, he might be at point *C*. Budget lines *CC'* and *DD'*, therefore, have lower absolute wages than budget line *BB'* but identical relative wages.

If our agent devotes seven hours to legal activities and one hour to illegal activities, he will receive a mixture of honest and dishonest wages and will move to point *b* in Figure 5.2. At point *b*, our agent's income will consist of an honest wage for seven hours of work and a dishonest wage for one hour of work.

Changes in the Dishonest Wage

Let us hold the honest wage constant and vary the values of the dishonest wage. Assume that society increases the cost of committing crime either by increasing the probability that the criminal will be caught or by increasing the jail sentence the criminal will receive if caught. This new policy will increase π and lower $w_d - \pi$, the net dishonest wage. Such a policy will also change the ratio of honest and dishonest wages, which can be represented in Figure 5.2 by rotating budget line *BB'*. Note that now, if our agent spends all eight hours working legally, his income will remain at *B*, but as the rate of the dishonest wage decreases to *BE'* or *BF'*, our agent will earn less and less when he shifts his time to illegal activities.

paradox of crime prevention
Illustrates the fact that policies aimed at reducing crime may actually increase it if crime is an inferior enough good and the income effect of the crime prevention policies is big enough.

The Paradox of Crime Prevention

We are now in a position to understand the **paradox of crime prevention**. As one might imagine, the amount of crime in a society will depend on the relative wages earned from legal and illegal activities, and these relative wages can be influenced by social policy. Ultimately, the impact of any crime prevention policy will depend on how each agent who is contemplating crime balances the income and substitution effects. The paradox of crime prevention illustrates the fact that policies aimed at reducing crime may actually increase it if crime is an inferior enough good and the income effect of the crime prevention policies is big enough. Figure 5.3 illustrates this paradox.

In Figure 5.3, our agent starts on budget line BB', where he chooses point a as an optimal bundle of honest and dishonest wages. Note that at point a, a fairly large amount of the agent's income is being received from illegal activities. (Actually, the fraction of time spent on crime at point a is measured by the ratio of $aB : BB'$, so as a moves closer to B', the fraction of time spent on crime approaches 1. It will equal 1 at B'.)

When society increases the cost of committing crimes, π increases and the net dishonest wage $(w_d - \pi)$ falls. This change can be shown by rotating BB' to BC'. At this new wage, the agent chooses the bundle of honest and dishonest wages depicted by point c. Note, however, that $cB/C'B > aB/BB'$, meaning that our agent allocates more time to illegal activities after the crime prevention policy is initiated than before. Obviously, this policy has not had the intended result. In fact, it has had the opposite effect.

The paradox of crime prevention is easily explained in terms of the income and substitution effects. Note that at the original equilibrium, point a, our agent derives a considerable portion of his income from crime. In fact, most of his income comes from crime. Therefore, when the social policy reduces the benefits of crime, the agent's income is severely reduced. If crime is an inferior good, our agent will purchase more of it when his income falls; that is, he will commit more crime. To see an illustration of this situation, look at Figure 5.3 again. As a result of the crime prevention policy, our agent moves from point a to point c. This move is made in two stages. The substitution effect shifts the agent from a to b, leading to a reduction in crime. This change occurs because crime has become less remunerative—the net dishonest wage has fallen. However, our agent moves from b to c as a result of the income effect. Because so much of his income was derived from crime before the crime prevention policy was implemented, the reduction of the dishonest wage impoverishes our agent and forces him to work harder (commit more crime) to compensate.

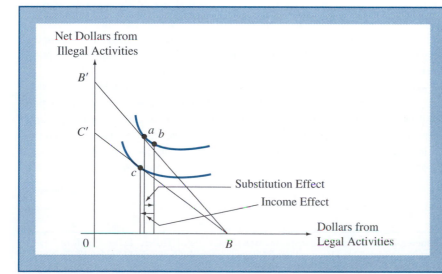

Figure 5.3

The Paradox of Crime Prevention.

Increasing the cost of committing crime (π) lowers the dishonest wage ($w_d - \pi$) and rotates the budget line from BB' to BC'. The substitution effect (from a to b) is more than offset by the income effect (from b to c), resulting in a net increase in the time allocated to illegal activities.

RESOLVING
TEASER 5

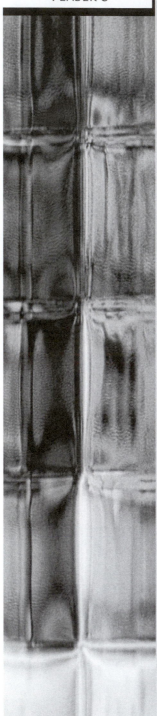

WORK-LEISURE CHOICE

In Application 1 of this section, we talked about the trade-off that workers face when they decide to supply their labor to the market. In that application, the trade-off existed between labor and leisure at one point in time. In real life, however, workers face a different trade-off—how to trade off income earned and leisure today versus income earned and leisure tomorrow or next week or even next year. This is an intertemporal trade-off, and depending on how people view it, it can lead to drastically different results in their behavior.

To illustrate this point, let's look at an intriguing real-world experiment on the labor supply decision of New York City cab drivers performed by Colin Camerer, Linda Babcock, George Lowenstein, and Richard Thaler.[1] In this experiment, Camerer and his colleagues looked at how much labor New York City cab drivers supplied on the different days that they drove by looking at the time sheets they filled out as their days progressed. These time sheets allow an investigator to derive how much revenue drivers received during the day and how long they worked. Let us assume that all cab drivers try to maximize their utility, which depends on how much income and leisure they have. We then must determine over what time horizon they maximize their utility. For example, say that when cab drivers are working, there are some good days and some bad days. That is, there are some days when many people want a taxi and fares are good (perhaps when it rains or a convention is in town), and there are days when there are few fares. Let us further assume that good days and bad days are not correlated, so if Tuesday is a good day, it implies nothing about whether Wednesday will be good as well. According to economic theory, if cab drivers even have as short a planning horizon as two days (that is, if they care about their consumption and leisure over two days instead of just one), then if the first day is a good day, they will work longer on that day and take their leisure on the second day. The reason is simple. If the implicit wage of driving a cab is high (if the cab drivers are having a good day), then they will work harder that day because the cost of leisure is very high on a good day. The cab drivers will then plan to take more leisure on the second day, which is expected to be a "normal" day with the average implicit wage. The cost of leisure is high on day 1 and low on day 2; hence, it makes sense to work when the wage is high and shirk when the wage is low.

Camerer and his colleagues found just the opposite! Upon checking the time sheets of drivers, they noticed that when the implicit wage was high and cab drivers were having a good day, they tended to leave work early and enjoy leisure. In fact, the labor supply elasticities (i.e., the percentage change in the hours worked for a given percentage change in the wage) response was negative and ranged from −0.503% to −0.269% for the three data sets they reviewed. This means that increasing the implicit wage on a given day by 1 percent led to a decrease in the amount of labor supplied of between 0.503% and 0.269%.

The explanation offered by Camerer is quite straightforward and intuitive. It appears that cab drivers have a day-by-day time horizon. When they come to work on a given day, they seem to have a target income for which they are aiming. If they reach that target early in the day because they have done well, instead of continuing to work (which is what they should do if they were looking ahead), they quit and take their leisure on that day. This simple income target is justifiable on several grounds. Most

(Continued)

---

[1] Colin Camerer, Linda Babcock, George Lowenstein, and Richard Thaler, "Labor Supply of New York City Cab Drivers: One Day at a Time," *Quarterly Journal of Economics* 112 (May 1997): No. 2, pp. 409–41.

immediately, however, it is a simple rule to administer—much more simple than the complicated intertemporal maximization rule implied by economic theory. Its major defect is that its myopia may lead to regret in the future when a day is slow but drivers have to keep driving to make their target incomes.

Measuring the Price Sensitivity of Demand

Although we study demand theory so that we can systematically analyze the behavior of consumers and increase our understanding of utility maximization, we also study this theory because it will play a central role in our investigation of the theory of markets in later chapters. One particular feature of demand functions—their elasticity—will be of great importance. Therefore, it is worth our while to stop and examine elasticity of demand.

Elasticity of demand measures the sensitivity of consumer demand for a product to changes in its price. This analysis of the price sensitivity of demand is done in percentage terms to allow us to make easy comparisons between different goods. More precisely, the elasticity of demand measures the percentage change in the demand for a good that results from a given percentage change in its price. Clearly, we need to express price sensitivity in percentage terms because the prices of goods differ. For example, a $1 change in the price of a BMW car will not lead to any change in its demand, while a $1 change in the price of an ice cream cone will probably have a dramatic effect on its demand. This does not mean, however, that demand for BMWs is not price sensitive. A 10% change in the price of a BMW means a difference of about $3,000, while a 10% change in the price of a $1.50 ice cream cone results in a difference of only 15 cents. When price changes are expressed in percentage terms, we see that BMWs may actually have more price sensitivity than we originally thought. Let us investigate this elasticity measure more closely.

Price-Elasticity Demand Curves

As we discussed at the beginning of this section, the price elasticity of demand measures the relative sensitivity of demand to changes in the price of a good. We can analyze the price sensitivity of a particular good by looking at the percentage change in the quantity demanded that results from a given percentage change in the price of the good. When a 1% change in the price of a good leads to a more than 1% change in the quantity demanded, the demand for the good is called elastic. When a 1% change in the price leads to a less than 1% change in the quantity demanded, the demand is called inelastic. When a 1% change in the price leads to exactly a 1% change in the quantity demanded, we say that the demand has a unitary elasticity. To understand elasticity, inelasticity, and unitary elasticity more precisely, let $\Delta q/q$ be the percentage change in the quantity demanded of a good, and let $\Delta p/p$ be the percentage change in the price. Then, letting ξ denote the elasticity of demand, we see that

$$\xi = \frac{\left(\dfrac{\Delta q}{q}\right)}{\left(\dfrac{\Delta p}{p}\right)} = \frac{\left(\dfrac{\Delta q}{\Delta p}\right)}{\left(\dfrac{q}{p}\right)}$$

Note that because the demand curve is usually downward-sloping, $\Delta q/\Delta p$ (the slope) is negative, as is ξ. When the demand is elastic, $|\xi| > 1$; when it is inelastic,

elasticity of demand
Measures the percentage change in the demand for a good that results from a given percentage change in its price.

elastic demand
A characteristic of demand for a good where, at a given price, a 1% change in the price of a good leads to a more than 1% change in the quantity demanded of that good.

inelastic demand
A characteristic of demand for a good where, at a given price, a 1% change in the price leads to a less than 1% change in the quantity demanded.

unitary elastic demand
A characteristic of demand for a good where, at a given price, a 1% change in the price leads to exactly a 1% change in the quantity demanded.

$|\xi| < 1$; and when it has unitary elasticity, $|\xi| = 1$. Further, when demand is linear ($q = a - bp$), we know that $\Delta q/\Delta p = -b$ because $-b$ measures the slope of the demand curve. Hence, for a straight-line or linear demand curve, we have the following formula:

$$\xi = -(b)\left(\frac{p}{q}\right)$$

Using this formula, we can see that the elasticity of demand for a straight-line demand curve varies along its length despite the fact that the slope of the curve is unvarying. For an illustration of this, look at Figure 5.4. Let us take a point near ($P^{\max}$, 0) on the demand curve in this figure—say (P', ϵ).

At that price, we know that p is quite high, while q is almost zero. Hence, p/q is very large and so the elasticity of demand ($|\xi| > 1$) must therefore also be large. At a point close to (0, A), say (ϵ, A'), just the opposite is true. Here, q is very large, while p is almost zero. Hence, p/q is small and so is $|\xi|$ ($|\xi| < 1$). Thus, we see that while the elasticity of demand starts out large and is greater than 1 near $P^{\max}$, it falls throughout the length of the demand curve until, at last, near its intersection with the horizontal axis, it is small and less than 1. Because ξ varies continuously, as p/q does, there must be some point along the demand curve, call it point μ, where $|\xi| = 1$. Therefore, the existence of a straight-line demand function does not imply the constancy of the elasticity of demand along the length of the curve. In fact, for most demand functions, the elasticity varies with the price and the quantity demanded. This fact complicates the task of forecasting the future values of economic variables because the magnitude of the response to price changes does not remain constant.

Elasticities can vary from 0 to $-\infty$. There are some special elasticities for demand functions that will be of importance to our work later on. First, let us take a look at perfect inelasticity. When the demand curve has zero elasticity, quantity does not adjust to changes in price. No matter what price is charged, the same quantity will be demanded. This situation is illustrated in Figure 5.5(a), where we see a demand curve that is perfectly vertical and is known as a perfectly inelastic demand curve. Now, let us look at perfect elasticity. Figure 5.5(b) presents a demand curve that is perfectly horizontal. Here, an infinite amount is demanded at price p so that the price does not change as different quantities of the good are offered for sale. This is a perfectly elastic demand curve.

perfectly inelastic demand curve
A demand curve that is perfectly vertical, representing zero quantity response to a price change.

perfectly elastic demand curve
A demand curve that is horizontal and in which a zero quantity will be sold at any price above a given price p while, at price p, any quantity can be sold.

Figure 5.4

Elasticity along a Linear Demand Curve.

The elasticity $\xi = -b(p/q)$ along a linear demand curve $q = a - bp$ increases in absolute value with p/q.

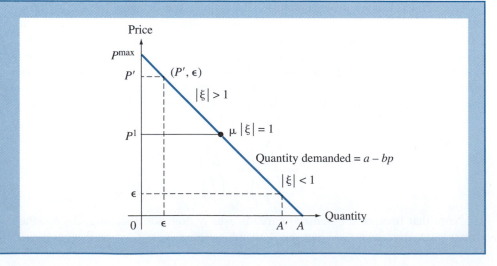

Figure 5.5

Perfectly Elastic and Perfectly Inelastic Demand Curves.

(a) Perfectly inelastic demand curve. With zero elasticity, the quantity demanded is constant as prices change.
(b) Perfectly elastic demand curve. With infinite elasticity, the quantity demanded would be infinite for any price below p and zero for any price above p.

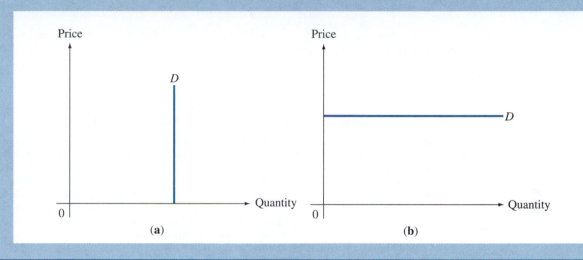

(a) (b)

Question (Extension and Application: Elasticity of Demand)

Barney has a demand for hamburgers represented by the linear demand curve $q = 50 - 2p$, where q is the quantity of hamburgers demanded and p is the price. The current price of hamburgers is $10, so Barney's current quantity demanded is $q = 50 - (2)(10) = 30$. At this point on his demand curve, what is Barney's elasticity of demand?

SOLVED
PROBLEM
5.1

Answer

We can proceed with this problem in two ways, which will result in identical answers. First, we can determine elasticity of demand by seeing by what percentage Barney's demand for hamburgers will change with a 1% increase in price. Because the original price is $10, a 1% increase would make the price $10.10. Plugging this price into the demand curve, we get a new quantity demanded: $q' = 50 - (2)(10.1) = 29.8$. Then $\Delta q = q' - q = -0.2$, so the percentage change in quantity is

$$\frac{\Delta q}{q} = \frac{-0.2}{30} = -0.67\%$$

Calculating the elasticity, we get

$$\xi = \frac{\dfrac{\Delta q}{q}}{\dfrac{\Delta p}{p}} = \frac{-0.67\%}{1\%} = -\frac{2}{3}$$

A second way we can approach the problem is to use the equivalent expression for elasticity

$$\xi = \frac{\dfrac{\Delta q}{\Delta p}}{\dfrac{q}{p}}$$

recognizing that $\Delta q/\Delta p$ is the slope of the demand curve. Looking at the demand curve, we see that the slope is -2. Thus, we can also calculate elasticity as

$$\xi = \frac{\dfrac{\Delta q}{\Delta p}}{\dfrac{q}{p}} = \frac{-2}{\dfrac{30}{10}} = -\frac{2}{3}$$

Note that because $|\xi| = \frac{2}{3} < 1$, Barney is on the inelastic portion of his demand curve for hamburgers.

Example 5.1

THE FREE MARKETEER'S CHILD AND THE NINTENDO HABIT

Let us assume that Joan, a strong free-market advocate, and Bob, her husband, are raising their child according to strict market principles. They have set a price for each activity that the child might want to engage in at home. The child uses money from his monthly allowance to pay for these activities. For example, the child might have to pay $2 to watch television for an hour and $100 to play a Nintendo game for an hour. The prices that the parents have set for the various activities are designed to control the child's behavior—to encourage certain activities and discourage others. Some activities, like reading, that the child may not like but the parents consider especially valuable have a negative price (income supplement) attached to them. For instance, an hour spent reading a book might earn the child a supplement of $50 to his allowance.

Say that the parents want to cut down on the child's Nintendo playing and have estimated that his demand for Nintendo hours has an elasticity of -1.5. At the current price of $100 an hour, the child plays 200 hours of Nintendo a month. The parents would like to decrease this amount of time by 40 hours. How much would the price of Nintendo playing have to be increased in order to decrease the child's playing time by the desired 40 hours? We can obtain an approximate answer to this question by using the elasticity formula. In this case, we know that the elasticity of demand is -1.5 and therefore that $(\Delta q/\Delta p)(p/q) = -1.5$. We also know that $p = \$100$, $q = 200$ hours, and the desired change in q, $\Delta q = -40$. Placing this information in the elasticity formula allows us to find the approximate answer that we are looking for because we know that $(-40/\Delta p)(100/200) = -1.5$. Solving for Δp leads to the answer $\Delta p = 40/3 = 13.33$. Therefore, if these free-market parents want to reduce their child's Nintendo playing by 40 hours a month, they will have to increase the price of Nintendo time by $13.33 to $113.33 an hour.

SOLVED PROBLEM 5.2

Question (Content Review: Elasticity of Demand)

1. This question refers to the free-market parents discussed previously. Assume that the parents did not know the price elasticity of demand of their child for Nintendo but wanted to estimate it so that they could control him better. They perform the following experiment over a series of months. They keep his allowance and the price of all other goods he buys constant but systematically change the price of Nintendo playing to see what happens. They generate the following data:

Price of Nintendo Playing	Number of Hours Played
$50 per hour	300 hours
$75	250
$100	200
$125	150
$150	100

a)   Plot these points on graph paper.

Answer

As we see in Figure 5.6, these data generate a perfectly straight line. Every time the price is raised by $25, the amount of Nintendo playing decreases by 50 hours. Note that there is nothing random about the child's demand curve. The boy is very precise in his Nintendo playing.

Figure 5.6

The Demand for Nintendo Time.

The demand curve for Nintendo time is downward sloping.

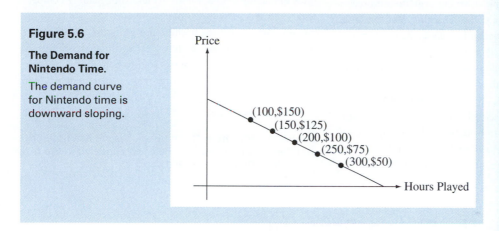

Price

(100,$150)
(150,$125)
(200,$100)
(250,$75)
(300,$50)

Hours Played

b)   Write an equation for the demand curve.

Answer

We can see that the slope of the demand curve is −2. Hence, the demand curve must have the following form:

$$q = A - 2p$$

To know the demand curve fully, we need to know the intercept, A. That is easily done. First, find the price that makes demand zero. Because every time we increase the price by $25 the quantity consumed decreases by 50 hours and because at price $150 the demand is 100, we would conclude that at price $200, demand would be zero. But then the following would be true:

$$0 = A - 2(200)$$

Solving for A, we find that $A = 400$, so the demand curve has the following formula:

$$Q = 400 - 2p$$

c)   What is the elasticity of demand at the point where the price is $100?

Answer

Because demand is a straight line, $\Delta q / \Delta p$ is a constant and is equal to the slope of the demand curve. Therefore, elasticity of demand at the point where price equals $100 is

$$\xi = \frac{\Delta q / q}{\Delta p / p} = \frac{\Delta q}{\Delta p} \cdot \frac{p}{q} = (-2)\left(\frac{100}{200}\right) = -1$$

MEDIA NOTE

PRICE ELASTICITY

Just before Christmas, during the holiday shopping season, Leonard Riggio, chairman of Barnes & Noble, interrupted a meeting with several major publishers to urge them to reconsider prices. He basically said that charging less for books would yield more profit. Book prices above $25, he argued, could be lowered to below $20 with no loss of profit.

Obviously this debate could be solved very easily if publishers did a good job of estimating the price elasticity of demand for the books they are selling. Some publishers think that the elasticity is rather low. For example, consider the statement of Stephen Rubin, publisher of the Doubleday Broadway group at the Random House division of Bertelsmann, who said, "I am just convinced that there is no difference between $22 and $23.

Let's face it: price is not a factor if it is a book that you really want."

That statement would be true if there were not substitutes to reading a book for enjoyment. But reading competes with a variety of other entertainments like going to the movies, eating out with friends, and going to concerts. So if the cost of reading rises with respect to these substitutes, we can expect the number of books sold to fall. The existence of substitutes for books, therefore, makes their demand more elastic.

What do you think?

Source: Adapted from "Some Book Buyers Read the Price and Decide Not to Read the Rest," as appeared in the *New York Times,* December 16, 2001.

The Slutsky Equation

Slutsky equation
An equation that decomposes a change in demand as a result of a price change in one good, holding all other prices and incomes constant, into income and substitution effects.

We can use an equation called the Slutsky equation[2] to summarize the impact that a change in price will have on demand. This equation portrays the income and substitution effects we have been discussing. It will be useful in some of our later work. If we let Δx_1 denote a change in the quantity demanded of good 1, let Δp_1 denote a change in the price of that good, and let ΔW denote a change in income, then the Slutsky equation can be written as follows:

$$\frac{\Delta x_1}{\Delta p_1} = \left(\frac{\Delta x_1}{\Delta p_1}\right)_{[\text{utility constant}]} - x_1 \left(\frac{\Delta x_1}{\Delta W}\right)_{[\text{price constant}]}$$

Note that $\Delta x_1/\Delta W$ is the change in demand that results when there is an increase in an agent's income. The first term in this equation represents the substitution effect because it shows what happens to demand when the price of good 1 changes and we nullify the effect of that change on the agent's income, thereby putting him back on the indifference curve where he started, as we saw in Figures 4.10(a) and 4.12 in the previous chapter. The second term in the equation represents the income effect. It shows how an agent would change her consumption of good 1 because of an income change if prices remained constant. We also saw this effect in Figures 4.10(a) and 4.12. Note that the term expressing the income effect is multiplied by the amount of good 1 purchased so that, as we might expect, the more of a good an agent consumes, the greater will be the income effect on that good when its price changes.

The Slutsky equation is useful for representing the elasticity of demand. Because the percentage change in the quantity demanded of good 1 given its current level of demand is $\Delta x_1/x_1$, while the percentage change in the price of the good is $\Delta p_1/p_1$, if we multiply the top of the Slutsky equation on both sides by p_1/x_1,

---

[2] This equation is named after Eugene Slutsky (1880–1948), a Russian economist who is known for his work on demand theory. Slutsky also made significant contributions to econometric theory.

multiply the term expressing the income effect by W/W, and then rearrange terms, we find the following:

$$\text{Elasticity} = \overbrace{\left(\frac{\Delta x_1}{\Delta p_1} \cdot \frac{p_1}{x_1}\right)}^{\eta_{11}}{}_{\text{[utility constant]}}$$

$$- \overbrace{\frac{\Delta x_1 p_1}{W}}^{k_1} \overbrace{\left(\frac{\Delta x_1}{\Delta W}\right)_{\text{[price constant]}} \cdot \left(\frac{W}{x_1}\right)}^{\xi_{1w}}$$

In this formula, the term η_{11} is the response in the demand for good 1 when we change its price but remove the income effect caused by this change so as to keep our agent on the same level of utility. (The first 1 in the subscript of η_{11} is the good, and the second 1 in the subscript is the good whose price has changed.) The term η_{11} actually represents the elasticity of the compensated demand curve or the demand curve that would result if, after every price change, we changed the agent's income appropriately to keep her on the original indifference curve. The term $k_1 \epsilon_1 W$ in the equation is the income elasticity of demand of good 1 weighted by k_1, the fraction of the agent's income spent on good 1. By the income elasticity of demand, we mean the percentage change in the demand for a good that results from a 1% change in the agent's income.

income elasticity of demand
The percentage change in the demand for a good that results from a 1% change in the agent's income.

Question (Application and Extension: Elasticity of Compensated Demand)
As we know, compensated demand curves are not observable, but that doesn't mean that we can't infer something about them. Say that a professor has an elasticity of demand for books equal to −2, and she spends 15% of her income on books (some professors would rather read than eat). If the income elasticity of books is 1.5, what is the elasticity of the professor's compensated demand?

SOLVED PROBLEM 5.3

Answer
We know that the formula for the elasticity of demand derived from the Slutsky equation is

elasticity of demand
= elasticity of the compensated demand curve
−(fraction of the consumer's income spent on the good)
×(the consumer's income elasticity of demand)

If the fraction spent on books is 0.15, the income elasticity is 1.5, and the full elasticity is 2, then

$$-2 = (\text{compensated elasticity}) - (0.15)(1.5)$$

So the elasticity of the compensated demand curve is

$$\text{compensated elasticity} = -2 + 0.15(1.5) = -2 + 0.225 = -1.775$$

Properties of Demand Functions

Now that we have derived demand functions from the utility-maximization process, we might want to ask the following question: What should a demand curve look like if it is for an agent who has the types of preferences we assumed in Chapter 2 (preferences that are strictly convex, nonsatiable, and selfish)? In this section, we will examine some very simple properties of a demand function for such an agent.

Demand Property 1: Price and Income Multiplication

The demand for a good by an agent who maximizes his utility, taking prices p_1 and p_2 as given, and who has an income of W is identical to the demand for the good when both the prices and the income of the agent are multiplied by a constant λ. According to this price and income multiplication property, if we multiply all the prices in an economy and the income of its agents by the same factor λ, then the demand for the good will not change. To see that this is true, consider Figure 5.7.

In Figure 5.7, our agent is facing fixed prices with a budget line depicted by BB'. In this situation, our agent chooses bundle e, where his indifference curve is tangent to the budget line. If we were to multiply all prices by a factor of, say, $\lambda = 2$, the budget line would move back parallel from BB' to $B'''B''$. At such prices, the agent would choose bundle f. Therefore, doubling all prices would certainly have an effect on demand, as we know from the income expansion path. However, if we were to double the agent's income, we would move the budget line back to BB' and the optimal consumption bundle back to bundle e. Multiplying all prices *and* income by the same factor leaves demand unaffected.

The price and income multiplication property can also be called the no-money illusion property because it implies that people are not tricked by the *level* of prices as long as their incomes increase appropriately and relative prices remain unchanged. If everyone's income rises as fast as the price level during a period of inflation, then demands will be unchanged.

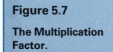

Figure 5.7

The Multiplication Factor.

Multiplying all prices by the same factor shifts the budget line from BB' to $B'''B''$. Multiplying prices and the agent's income by the same factor has no effect on the budget line.

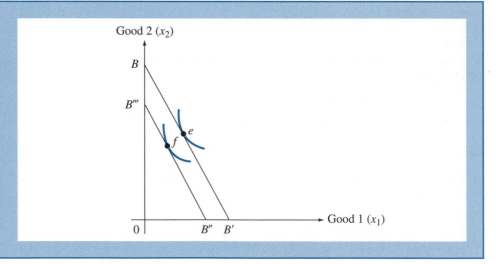

SOLVED PROBLEM 5.4

Question (Application and Extension: Price and Income Multiplication)
Sam has been asked to move from Bucharest, Romania, to New York City. Sam consumes only two things—hot dogs and soda. In Bucharest, hot dogs cost $2 each and sodas are $1; Sam has a total of $20 to spend. Sam has utility function $u(s, h) = sh$, where h is his demand for hot dogs and s is his demand for sodas. In

New York, the price of a hot dog and a soda is twice what it is in Bucharest, but his company gives him twice as much income to make the move. Will Sam be just as well off in New York as he is in Bucharest?

Answer

Note that after Sam moves from Bucharest to New York, if he spends all of his money on hot dogs, he will be able to buy 10 of them (i.e., $4 each and Sam has $40). Likewise, if he spends all of his money on soda, he can buy 20 cans ($2 each and he has $40). Also note that the price ratio of hot dogs to soda is 2:1. So in real terms, Sam is in exactly the same situation as he was in Bucharest. Given that his tastes have not changed, Sam will buy the same bundle of goods in New York as he did in Bucharest and, hence, he will be exactly as well off. This demonstrates Demand Property 1.[3]

Demand Property 2: Ordinal Utility

If we represent an agent's preferences by an ordinal utility function, then the way we number the agent's indifference curves does not affect the demands made by the agent. To observe this property, consider Figure 5.8.

In Figure 5.8, we see budget line BB' and an indifference map for the agent. Next to each indifference curve are two numbers, each of which represents a different way of numbering the agent's ordinal utility function curve. Under one calibration, our agent chooses bundle e and reaches a maximum utility level of 100. Under the other calibration, he chooses the same bundle and remains at the same utility level, but this level is labeled 5. Note that the labeling has no effect on the bundle chosen.

Demand Property 3: Budget Exhaustion

From our nonsatiation assumption in Chapter 2, we know that a consumer will always spend his entire income on the consumption of goods. In other words, the budget of a consumer will be exhausted because he is never satiated and, therefore,

---

[3] A more sophisticated approach would be to solve for Sam's demand functions for hot dogs and soda (see Appendix A in Chapter 4 for details). As derived in Appendix A, the demand for soda and hot dogs can be written as $s = I/2p_s$ and $h = I/2p_h$, where p_h is the price of hot dogs, p_s is the price of sodas, and I is Sam's income. If we plug in the appropriate values for prices and income, we see that Sam's quantity demanded in Bucharest for hot dogs is

$$h = \frac{I}{2p_h} = \frac{20}{(2)(2)} = 5$$

and his quantity demanded for sodas is

$$s = \frac{I}{2p_s} = \frac{20}{(2)(1)} = 10$$

If Sam moves to New York, he gets double the income but must pay double the price for hot dogs and sodas; thus, now $p_h = \$4$, $p_s = \$2$, and $I = \$40$. We can see that Sam's quantities demanded are unchanged:

$$h = \frac{I}{2p_h} = \frac{40}{(2)(4)} = 5$$
$$s = \frac{I}{2p_s} = \frac{40}{(2)(2)} = 10$$

Figure 5.8

Ordinal Utility Property.

Regardless of the utility numbers assigned to the three indifference curves, as long as utility increases with movement away from the origin, the agent maximizes his utility by moving to point *e*.

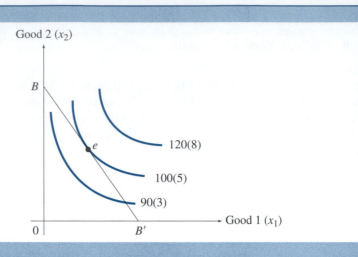

will always be able to increase his utility by consuming more. This means that if we were to give a consumer a small percentage increase in income, all the additional income would be spent on the goods available. If we let ϵ_{1Y} and ϵ_{2Y} be the income elasticities of demand for goods 1 and 2, respectively, then the budget exhaustion property can be formulated as follows:

$$k_1\epsilon_{1Y} + k_2\epsilon_{2Y} = 1$$

Note that k_1 and k_2 are the fractions of the consumer's budget spent on goods 1 and 2, respectively.

Consider the following example of the budget exhaustion property of demand functions: If we assume that a consumer spends 60% of his income on good 1 and 40% on good 2 and that the income elasticity of demand for good 1 is 0.3, then the income elasticity of demand for good 2 must be 2.05 because $0.60(0.3) + 0.4(2.05) = 1$, as our formula indicates.

The budget exhaustion property and the price and income multiplication property together can furnish us with some very useful information about the characteristics of demand for a consumer. For example, assume that there are three goods in our model economy instead of the two we have discussed up to now. Also assume that an agent spends his income on the three products in the following way: 60% on good x, 20% on good y, and 20% on good z. Say that the income elasticity of demand for good y is 1.5, while the income elasticity of demand for good z is 3. Then, if the government wants to increase the consumption of good x by 3%, it must subsidize the agent's income by 18%. This fact is easily determined by using the budget exhaustion property of demand functions. In the case of the three goods, the budget exhaustion property is formulated as follows:

$$k_x\epsilon_{xY} + k_y\epsilon_{yY} + k_z\epsilon_{zY} = 1$$

Note that k_x, k_y, and k_z indicate the fraction of income spent on goods x, y, and z, and ϵ_{xY}, ϵ_{yY}, and ϵ_{zY} indicate the income elasticity of demand for goods x, y, and z. Because we know that $k_x = 0.6$, $k_y = 0.2$, $k_z = 0.2$, $\epsilon_{yY} = 1.5$, and $\epsilon_{zY} = 3$, we see that, using the budget exhaustion property, $0.6(\epsilon_{xY}) + 0.2(1.5) + 0.2(3) = 1$, or $0.6(\epsilon_{xY}) + 0.3 + 0.6 = 1$. This implies that $\epsilon_{xY} = 0.10/0.60 = 0.166$. With such income elasticity, it is clear that if we want to increase the consumption of good x by 3%, we must increase income by 18%.

From Individual Demand to Market Demand

Markets are made up of many individual buyers and sellers. Up to this point, we have discussed how to derive demand curves for the individual agents in an economy. Now the question that arises is how we aggregate individual demand curves into a market demand curve. This type of demand curve or demand function relates the price of a good on the market to the total demand for that good by all individuals who contemplate buying it. We will examine the subject of market demand in this section.

market demand curve
The aggregate of individual demand curves.

To illustrate how we derive a market demand curve for a product from the utility-maximizing behavior of the individual consumers in a society, we will group all goods available in the society except one (say, jam) into a single composite good. We will assume that the relative prices of all the goods that make up the composite good remain constant and fixed. By forming this composite good, it will be possible for us to present the demand for the remaining good, jam, on a two-dimensional graph. What we want to know is how the demand for jam will change as we change its price but keep the price of the composite good and the income of the consumers constant.

The market demand for jam is easily derived by "adding up" the individual demand of all consumers in society. To see how this is done, consider Figure 5.9. Note that this figure is divided into four segments, (a), (b), (c), and (d).

In Figure 5.9, there are three individual demand curves: one for person i, one for person j, and one for person k. Note that each of these curves was derived from a process of utility maximization, as depicted in Figure 5.6 in the previous chapter. For the purposes of our discussion, we will assume that persons i, j, and k are the only people in society, and we will determine the market demand curve for jam by adding their individual demand curves *horizontally*. Let us choose price P_1 arbitrarily and look at how much of the good each person is willing to buy at that price.

Figure 5.9

Deriving Market Demand from Individual Demand.

The market demand curve D is the horizontal summation of the individual demand curves D_i, D_j, and D_k.

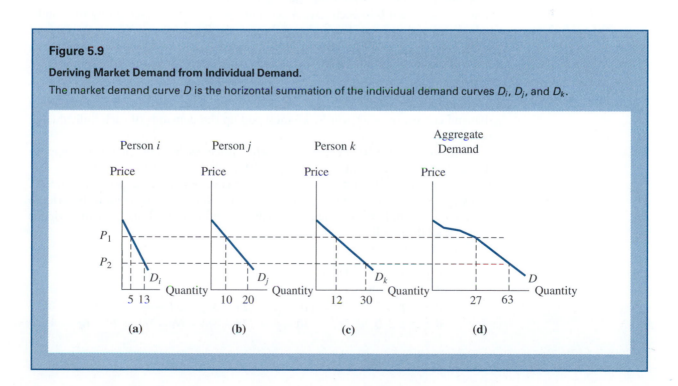

As we see, at price P_1, person i is willing to buy 5 units (Figure 5.9[a]), person j is willing to buy 10 units (Figure 5.9[b]), and person k is willing to buy 12 units (Figure 5.9[c]). Hence, at price P_1, we know that society is willing to buy 27 units $(5 + 10 + 12 = 27)$. As a result, Figure 5.9(d) shows that we have an aggregate market demand of 27 units of jam at price P_1. Let us now decrease the price to P_2 and repeat the calculation. At price P_2, person i wants to buy 13 units, person j wants to buy 20 units, and person k wants to buy 30 units. Hence, at price P_2, the aggregate market demand for jam is 63 units $(13 + 20 + 30 = 63)$. We now have another point on our market demand curve for jam in Figure 5.9(d). Repeating this process for many prices traces a market demand curve, as Figure 5.9(d) indicates.

Of course, the process of deriving the market demand curve that we have described here is purely hypothetical. Because one does not know the utility functions of all people in a society, it is impossible to know what the actual market demand curve for jam might look like. To alleviate this problem, we could attempt to estimate the market demand for jam. For example, we could look at the demand curve for jam and see how demand varied over time as the price of jam varied. This estimated relationship would serve as an approximation of the demand curve. If the good in question is totally new, we would have to perform some market research—for example, circulate questionnaires asking people about their individual demand for the good. We would want to know how much of the good people think they would buy at various prices. It is not necessary to survey everyone in society because we can make inferences from the answers we receive from a representative sample of the population. The concept of elasticity of individual demand curves carries over to market demand curves. However, we must recognize that we are talking about the properties of an aggregate market demand and not the demand of any single individual.

SOLVED PROBLEM 5.5

Question (Content Review: Aggregating Individual Demand Curves)

Tim, George, and Bob each have a demand for oysters represented by their individual demand curves. Tim's demand curve is $D_T = 10 - p$, George's demand curve is $D_G = 6 - 2p$, and Bob's demand curve is $D_B = 24 - 3p$, where p is the price of oysters. Find the aggregate demand for oysters for these three people.

Answer

To find the aggregate demand for oysters, we must "horizontally" add these demand curves. In other words, we must add up the demands of each individual at each price.

The first step is to determine at what price each individual will begin to demand a positive amount. For Tim, $p = 10$, while for George and Bob, $p = 3$ and $p = 8$, respectively. Therefore, no one will demand oysters if the price is above 10. If the price is between 8 and 10, then only Tim will demand oysters. If the price is between 3 and 8, both Tim and Bob will demand oysters. Finally, if the price is below 3, all three will demand oysters.

Thus, the aggregate demand, D_A, is

$$\begin{aligned}
&\text{if } p > 10 & &D_A = 0 \\
&\text{if } 10 \geq p > 8 & &D_A = 10 - p \\
&\text{if } 8 \geq p > 3 & &D_A = (10 - p) + (24 - 3p) = 34 - 4p \\
&\text{if } 3 \geq p > 0 & &D_A = (10 - p) + (24 - 3p) + (6 - 2p) = 40 - 6p
\end{aligned}$$

Expenditure Functions

From our analysis in the preceding sections, we see that when consumers have the type of preferences assumed in Chapter 2, their behavior can be summarized by a set of demand curves with the properties of price and income multiplication, ordinal utility, and budget exhaustion. If consumers have the right preferences, we can say even more about their behavior because we can use expenditure functions to describe that behavior. Expenditure functions have certain interesting and useful properties.

An expenditure function identifies the minimum amount of income that we must give a consumer in order to allow him to achieve a predetermined level of utility at given prices. We can call the predetermined level of utility u^*, when the prices the consumer faces are p_1 and p_2. Just as we derived a demand function from the process of utility maximization, given the consumer's income and the prices, we can derive an expenditure function by a process of income minimization, given the predetermined level of utility for the consumer and the prices. To illustrate how we can derive such a function, consider Figure 5.10.

In Figure 5.10, we see an agent described by two indifference curves and facing a set of two different price lines. To start our analysis, let us focus on indifference curve I_1, which involves a level of utility equal to u^*. Look at price line p, whose slope represents the relative prices of p_1 and p_2 for our two goods. If these are the prices that our agent faces, we can ask the following question: At prices p_1 and p_2, what is the minimum amount of income we would have to give this agent to allow him to reach a level of utility equal to u^*? To answer this question, we want to find the budget line that is the lowest possible at the given prices and that will allow our agent to purchase one of the bundles of goods on indifference curve I_1 (because any such bundle entails a utility level of u^*). Clearly, budget line B_1B_1 is such a line, and at prices p_1 and p_2, bundle e is the optimal (or cost-minimizing) bundle. Note that bundle e involves the purchase of 10 units of good 1 and 15 units of good 2. The cost of bundle e is therefore as follows:

$$\text{Cost(bundle } e) = (p_1 \cdot 10) + (p_2 \cdot 15)$$

Now that we know the minimal cost of achieving a utility level of u^* when the prices are p_1 and p_2, what is the minimal cost of achieving u^* when the prices are different? For example, say that the prices are p_1' and p_2'.

expenditure function
The function that identifies the minimum amount of income that we must give a consumer in order to allow him to achieve a predetermined level of utility at given prices.

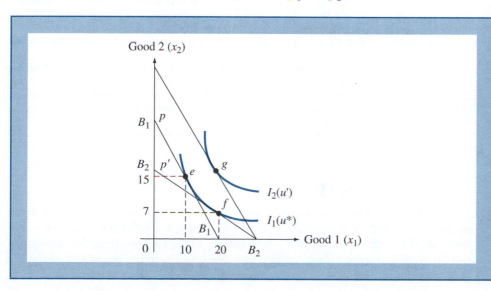

Figure 5.10

Derivation of an Expenditure Function.

At prices measured by price line p, bundle e is the lowest-cost bundle that yields utility equal to u^*.

In this case, the cost-minimizing way to achieve u^* is to choose point f on budget line B_2B_2. Note that the cost of bundle f is as follows:

$$\text{Cost(bundle } f) = (p_1' \cdot 20) + (p_2' \cdot 7)$$

We now know the minimal cost of achieving a utility level of u^* when the prices are p_1' and p_2' instead of p_1 and p_2. By a similar method, we can discover the minimal cost of achieving u^* at any given prices. We can also see how the minimal cost of achieving a given utility level changes as we keep prices constant but change the amount of utility we expect our agent to attain. For example, at prices p_1 and p_2, we know that the minimal cost of achieving u^* is Cost(bundle e). Keeping prices constant, we can see from Figure 5.10 that if we want to allow our agent to achieve a utility level of u' on indifference curve I_2, we must give him enough income to allow the purchase of bundle g. Therefore, the minimal cost of achieving utility level u' at prices p_1 and p_2 is Cost(bundle g).

In a similar manner, we can define the minimum amount of income that must be given to a consumer to attain any given level of utility at any given set of prices. More precisely, we can write an expenditure function as follows:

$$E = E(p_1, p_2, u)$$

This formula indicates the minimum amount of expenditure (E) necessary to achieve a utility level of u at prices p_1 and p_2. To make this process more concrete, consider the problem described in Example 5.2.

Example 5.2

RASPBERRY-APPLE COBBLERS AND EXPENDITURE FUNCTIONS

Let us say that a person loves to eat raspberry-apple cobblers but will only do so if the raspberries and apples are used in the ratio of 3 ounces of apples to 1 ounce of raspberries. Any units of apples and raspberries beyond these proportions yield no additional utility and are thrown away. (Apples and raspberries are strict complements in yielding utility from cobblers.) Assume that each cobbler uses exactly 3 ounces of apples and 1 ounce of raspberries. Further assume that each cobbler eaten yields 1 unit of utility and that the utility of cobblers is linear in the number eaten, so if the person eats 1,000 cobblers, he will receive 1,000 units of utility. Say the price of raspberries is $6 per ounce and the price of apples is $1 per ounce. This is all the information we need to derive an expenditure function for the consumer. We know that the cost of achieving a utility level of 1 is the cost of buying 3 ounces of apples ($3) and 1 ounce of raspberries ($6), which totals $9. Therefore, because utility is linear in cobblers eaten, we know that the cost of achieving 10 units of utility is $90. If the price of raspberries decreases from $6 to $3, the cost of each cobbler and each unit of utility will be reduced from $9 to $6.

In this example, we see that if we specify the utility level we want and the prices of apples and raspberries, we can find out how much income our consumer will need to achieve the desired utility level, which is precisely what an expenditure function is supposed to tell us. This fact will be useful to us later when we use expenditure functions to define the concept of a price-compensating variation in income.

Consumer Surplus

As we will see later in this book, it is sometimes useful to have a monetary measure of the benefit that an agent receives from consuming a good at a certain price. For instance, if we can measure the benefit that an agent receives from her consumption of good 1 at price p_1, we can also measure how much the agent will lose if the government imposes a tax of t per unit on good 1, thereby increasing its price from

p_1 to $p_1 + t$. We can determine this loss by measuring the benefits of consumption at prices p_1 and $p_1 + t$ and then calculating the difference between the two amounts. To understand how we go about making such a measurement, let us explore the concept of **consumer surplus**—the net gain that a consumer achieves from purchasing a good at a certain price per unit. We will begin our discussion by considering Figure 5.11(a).

In Figure 5.11(a), we see an agent who consumes two goods, labeled Y and 1. Good Y is not a typical good because it is called *income* and represents a composite of all the goods on which consumers could spend their money if they did not spend it on good 1. Look at point A, where at price ratio p', our agent is not buying any of good 1 but rather is spending all her money on the composite good, Y (income). At point A, the slope of the indifference curve measures the marginal rate of substitution between income and good 1. We see that at point A, our agent is willing to give up v units of income in order to obtain her first unit of good 1. If our agent actually makes this purchase, she will end up on the same indifference curve where she started out. Therefore, v measures the maximum amount that our agent is willing to pay to receive the first unit of good 1.

To make our analysis easier, let us assume that our agent is only interested in consuming good 1 in integer quantities—in whole units, such as 1, 2, or 3. In Figure 5.11(b), the quantity of good 1 purchased appears on the horizontal axis and its price appears on the vertical axis. Figure 5.11(a) showed that our agent was willing to pay *at most* a price of v for the first unit of good 1, so we know that she will demand at least 1 unit of the good if the price is v or less but will not purchase

consumer surplus
The net gain that a consumer achieves from purchasing a good at a certain price per unit.

Figure 5.11

Willingness to Pay and Consumer Surplus.

(a) Maximum willingness to pay. The marginal rate of substitution (minus 1 times the slope of the indifference curve) measures the agent's willingness to pay for one more unit of the good measured on the horizontal axis in terms of units of the good measured on the vertical axis. (b) Consumer surplus. The area under the demand curve and above the price measures the agent's total willingness to pay for the quantity of the good she is consuming minus the amount she must pay.

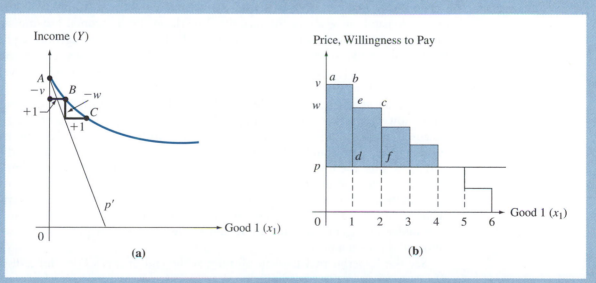

(a)   (b)

any units if the price is higher. This fact yields segment *ab*, the first segment on the demand curve in Figure 5.11(b).

Now, let us go back to point *B* in Figure 5.11(a) and see how much income our agent is willing to give up to purchase the second unit of good 1, *having already bought the first unit*. By looking at the slope of the indifference curve at point *B*, we find that our agent is willing to give up *w* units of income to obtain one more unit of good 1. Therefore, it must be that *w*, the amount our agent is willing to pay for the second unit of good 1, is less than *v*, the amount she was willing to pay for the first unit of good 1, because convex preferences mean a diminishing marginal rate of substitution of good 1 for income. Note again that if our agent actually gives up *v* amount of income for the first unit of good 1, then she will be back on her original indifference curve at point *B*. (Point *B* in Figure 5.11(a) is represented by point *b* in Figure 5.11(b), which shows the maximum amount of income that our agent is willing to give up to buy the second unit of good 1.) If our agent actually pays *w* amount of income to purchase the second unit of good 1, she will also end up on her original indifference curve.

Let us complete our analysis of consumer surplus by repeatedly moving along our agent's indifference curve and looking for her maximum willingness to pay. The curve generated by this process appears in Figure 5.11(b). In fact, this figure merely shows the demand curve for our agent because the height of a demand curve at a particular quantity represents the maximum an agent is willing to pay for that unit. Now let us assume that our agent is in a market where the price of good 1 is fixed at *p*. From our discussion of consumer surplus up to this point, we know that for the first unit of good 1, our agent is willing to pay at most *v*. However, if the market allows her to pay less for that good, then our agent will be better off. Figure 5.11(b) indicates how much better off our agent will be in this case. The rectangle *0ab*1 represents the maximum amount that our agent is willing to pay for the first unit of good 1, while the smaller rectangle *0pd*1 represents how much the agent is required to pay for the first unit by the market. Because the market price is less than the price our agent is willing to pay, she achieves a net gain (consumer surplus), and that gain is measured by the rectangle *pabd*.

Our agent also achieves a gain when she purchases the second unit of good 1. We know from Figure 5.11(a) that she is willing to give up *w* units of income to obtain the second unit of good 1 after having purchased the first unit. The height of the demand curve above the quantity 2 mark on the horizontal axis measures her maximum willingness to pay for that second unit. Because our agent is required to pay only the fixed price *p* for every unit purchased, we know that the rectangle *def* in Figure 5.11(b) measures the net gain (consumer surplus) she achieves when she purchases the second unit of good 1 at price *p*.

A similar analysis can be made for the third, fourth, and fifth units of good 1. Note, however, that at price *p*, our agent will purchase only five units of this good because her maximum willingness to pay for the sixth unit is less than the fixed price *p*. Our agent would rather not buy the sixth unit of good 1 and will end her purchases after the fifth unit. The sum of the rectangles above the price line is a measure of the consumer surplus of our agent because it shows the net gain she achieves from purchasing the good at price *p* per unit. The consumer surplus achieved by an agent when she buys quantity q' of a good at price *p* is equal to the area under the agent's demand curve and above the constant price line between zero and the q'-th unit.

See the Experimental Evidence feature at the end of this section for a discussion of some anomalies about willingness to pay.

SOLVED
PROBLEM
5.6

Question (Application and Extension: Consumer Surplus)

Bob is a drug addict. His demand for cocaine is given by

$$Q = 100 - 3p$$

where Q is the quantity demanded and p is the price paid. The market price for cocaine is \$10 a bag. At that price, what is Bob's consumer surplus of consuming cocaine?

Answer

Let's answer this question using some algebra and a little high school geometry. Look at Figure 5.12, where we have drawn the demand curve as having a slope of $-\frac{1}{3}$. The intercept on the y axis can be found by solving the price that will make the quantity demanded equal to 0—in other words, by solving $0 = 100 - 3p \Rightarrow p = 33.3$. At $p = 10$, Bob buys 70 bags $(Q = 100 - 3(10) \Rightarrow Q = 70)$. Now the consumer surplus is the area of the triangle marked CS in the diagram.

Figure 5.12

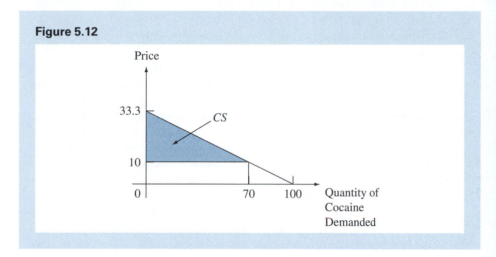

Note that this triangle has a base of 70 and height of 23.33 (33.3−10). Thus, the area of the triangle CS, which is a measure of the consumer surplus, is

$$\text{Area } CS = \frac{1}{2}(23.3)(70) = \$815.5$$

This is a dollar measure of the value that Bob is getting from consuming those 70 bags of cocaine at \$10 each.

RESOLVING
TEASER 6

THE DISPARITY BETWEEN WILLINGNESS TO PAY AND WILLINGNESS TO ACCEPT

As we have just seen earlier in this section, the concept of a consumer's maximum willingness to pay plays an important role in much of the theory of the consumer and is crucial to developing the concept of consumer surplus. Therefore, it would be nice to know that such a concept is based on a firm foundation and is not subject to either

(Continued)

RESOLVING
TEASER 6 *(Contd.)*

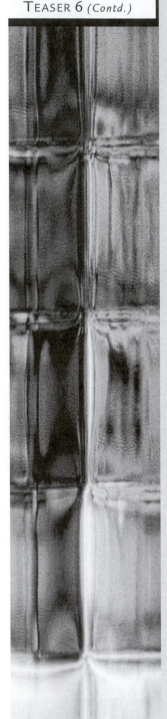

small or large irrationalities on the part of consumers. Unfortunately, this is not necessarily the case. The situation described in Experimental Teaser 6 shows that there may be a discrepancy between a person's willingness to pay and his or her willingness to accept. This phenomenon has been called the endowment effect by Richard Thaler. I will summarize an experiment by Daniel Kahneman, Jack Knetsch, and Thaler[4] to illustrate the endowment effect in a market context.

Forty-four undergraduates at Cornell University were used as subjects in their market experiment. In the experiment, 22 of the subjects were randomly given Cornell coffee mugs, which sell for $6.00 at the bookstore. Those subjects given the mugs were clearly sellers, and the others were buyers. After the mugs were distributed, the subjects received worksheets upon which they were to state their willingness to buy or sell at various prices. For example, if you were a seller, you would be asked your willingness to sell (accept payment) for the good at various prices, from $0.25 to $8.75 in 50-cent increments. For example, two lines on a seller's form would appear as follows:

At a price of $8.75, I will sell _____ I will not sell _____.
At a price of $8.25, I will sell _____ I will not sell _____.

The subject was supposed to check his or her willingness to sell at these various prices. A similar sheet was given to the buyers.

After these sheets were collected, the information on them was aggregated to form demand and supply curves and the price consistent with the intersection of these derived curves. This was, then, the market-clearing price for the experiment, and all buyers willing to pay that price or more bought the good, while all those willing to sell at that price or less sold the good. The payoff for the sellers was the amount of money they received from the sale (minus how much they valued the mug), while the payoff to the buyers was the value of the mug they received minus the utility of the money given up to get it. Those who made no sales received nothing.

What should the theory predict? (Think about that before reading on.) Well, if economic theory is correct and mugs were randomly given out, there should be no difference between the tastes of the 22 people who received mugs and the 22 who did not. Hence, we would think that the supply and demand curves would be rather symmetrical and that the median willingness to pay of the buyers should be approximately equal to the median willingness to accept of the sellers. As Figure 5.13 will show, this was far from the case.

As we see in the figure, the recorded willingness to accept numbers was much higher than the recorded willingness to pay numbers. There seems to have been an endowment effect occurring because once people were given a mug, they seemed to demand more money to give it up than those who did not. Also note that the theory expects that approximately 11 mugs should be sold (because it is equally likely that a random buyer should value a mug more than a random seller) while, in fact, only 3 were sold. This again indicates how unwilling sellers were to give up their mugs.

What explains this phenomenon? While one can think of many explanations, I will offer only the one that comes from what Daniel Kahneman and Amos Tversky[5] called *Prospect Theory.* In this theory, people are averse to losses in the sense that they view a loss more importantly than a gain. For example, if you have a certain wealth, you

(Continued)

---

[4] Daniel Kahneman, Jack L. Knetsch, and Richard H. Thaler, "Experimental Effects of the Endowment Effect and the Coase Theorem," *Journal of Political Economy* 98 (December 1990): No. 61, pp. 1325–47.

[5] Daniel Kahneman and Amos Tversky, "Prospect Theory: An Analysis of Decision Making Under Risk," *Econometrica* 47 (March 1979): No. 2, pp. 263–92.

Figure 5.13

Supply and Demand Curves for the Experimental Markets

Rather than being symmetrical, these supply and demand curves exhibit an endowment effect.

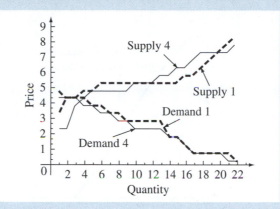

would look upon that wealth as a status quo from which you would judge gains and losses. Marginal increases in your wealth above that status quo would not be judged as important as marginal losses from it. If this is the case, then a subject, after being given the mug, would incorporate the mug into his or her status quo wealth and then would judge the loss of the mug more seriously than the money to be received from its sale. Does this completely explain the anomaly? I will leave that for you to consider.

Approximate Versus Exact Measures of Consumer Surplus: Compensated Versus Uncompensated Demand

When we say that consumer surplus can be measured by the area under the demand curve, we must be careful to specify which demand curve we are talking about—the compensated or uncompensated demand curve. The **exact measure of consumer surplus** is determined by the area under the *compensated demand curve*, while the **approximate measure of consumer surplus** is determined by the area under the *uncompensated demand curve*.

Accepting the area under the uncompensated demand curve as a measure of consumer surplus raises a problem. In attempting to measure consumer surplus, we are searching for a dollar index of how much a consumer benefits from being able to purchase a good at a given price. Dollars are being used to measure utility. Now consider the uncompensated demand curve in Figure 5.14.

Figure 5.14 depicts both an uncompensated demand curve and a compensated demand curve. (Remember that the compensated demand curve for a superior good is necessarily the steeper of the two curves because it excludes the income effect, which decreases demand for the good when its price rises and increases demand for the good when its price falls.) Using the uncompensated demand curve in Figure 5.14, we measure the consumer surplus at price p' as the area $p*Bp'$. We have seen in Figure 5.11(b) that this surplus can be approximated by adding the surpluses received on the units purchased from 1 to b as we decrease the price. However, with the uncompensated demand functions, there is an income effect because the consumer becomes wealthier as the price falls. The marginal utility of the dollars used to measure the surplus is, therefore, getting smaller and smaller. As a result, we are adding surpluses for units with dollars of varying worth. Representing utilities with dollars does not work if the value of the dollar changes during the analysis.

exact measure of consumer surplus
A measure of consumer surplus determined by the area under the compensated demand curve.

approximate measure of consumer surplus
A measure of consumer surplus determined by the area under the uncompensated demand curve.

Figure 5.14

Exact and Approximate Measures of Consumer Surplus.

The exact measure of consumer surplus at price p' is the area $\tilde{p}B'p'$ under the compensated demand curve above price p'. The approximate measure is the area $p*Bp'$ under the uncompensated demand curve.

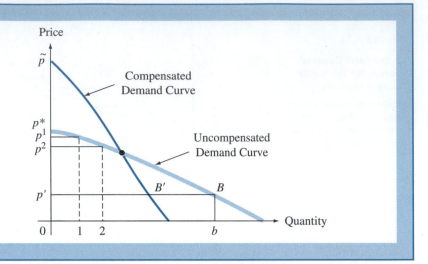

For compensated demand functions, measuring utility with dollars of changing value is not a problem because, throughout the analysis, the consumer's wealth (at least in terms of utility) is held constant. As we see in Figure 5.14, the two measures of consumer surplus differ because the triangle $\tilde{p}B'p'$ is not equal in size to the triangle $p*Bp'$.

In the real world and in this text, we will be forced to work with uncompensated demand functions because these are the only ones we can observe by looking at data on prices and quantities. (Compensated demand functions exist only in the minds of consumers.) Fortunately, however, economists have demonstrated that the error in measuring consumer surplus with uncompensated demand functions instead of compensated demand functions is small.[6] Consequently, in the remainder of this book, we will measure consumer surplus as an area under the uncompensated demand curve, even though we recognize that the result will be just an approximation.

Measures of Consumer Gain

Changes in Consumer Surplus

In the previous section, we viewed consumer surplus as a measure of the net gain a consumer achieves from purchasing a good at a given price (p). However, we could also ask what the gain (or loss) is to the consumer when the price of the good is changed from p to $p + \Delta p$. Clearly, our measure of consumer surplus will allow us to answer this question. All we need to do is take the consumer surplus of the agent at price p and compare it to the consumer surplus at $p + \Delta p$. For example, consider Figure 5.15, where we have an agent who initially faces a price of p for good 1, but then the price of p is increased by Δp.

When the price is p, the consumer surplus of our agent is represented by the area $acpa$ in Figure 5.15. When the price increases to $p + \Delta p$, we see a smaller consumer surplus of $ad(p + \Delta p)a$. The difference between these two areas (the shaded portion of Figure 5.15) measures the loss to our agent that results from a rise in the price of good 1.

---

[6] See Robert Willig, "Consumers' Surplus Without Apology," *American Economic Review* 66 (Sep. 1976): No. 4, pp. 589–97.

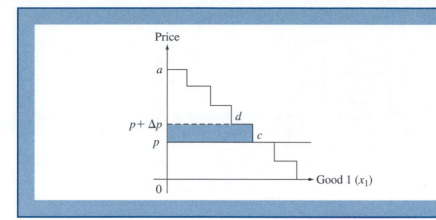

Figure 5.15

Change in Consumer Surplus.

When the price increases, the change in the area under the demand curve and above the price measures the welfare loss caused by the price change.

Question (Application and Extension: Change in Consumer Surplus)
Consider Ellen's demand schedule for telephone calling cards:

Quantity	Price
1	10
2	9
3	8
4	7
5	6
6	5

SOLVED PROBLEM 5.7

If a firm is selling these cards at \$6 and then a tax is placed on them that raises their price to the consumer to \$8, what is the loss in consumer surplus to Ellen?

Answer
At p = \$6, Ellen bought 5 calling cards. Her consumer surplus on those 5 units was

$$\text{Consumer surplus} = (\$10 - 6) + (\$9 - \$6) + (\$8 - \$6) + (\$7 - \$6)$$
$$+ (\$6 - \$6)$$
$$= \$10$$

This \$10 summarizes the fact that Ellen received a \$4 benefit from consuming the first calling card at \$6 because she valued it at \$10 (her willingness to pay) but only had to pay \$6 for it, benefited \$3 from consuming the second unit, and so on. When the price is raised to \$8, her consumer surplus falls to

$$\text{Consumer surplus} = (10 - 8) + (9 - 8) + (8 - 8) = 3$$

Thus, she loses \$7 as a result of the increase.

Price-Compensating Variation

Another way to think of the loss or gain to a consumer that results from a price change is to ask how much income we must give or take away from the consumer *after the price change* (that is, at the new prices) to compensate him for the change. In other words, how much income would we have to give or take away to make the

Figure 5.16

Price-Compensating Variation in Income.

ZB is the amount of income that must be given to the agent after the price increases from *p* to *p'* in order to restore him to I_1, the indifference curve he was on before the price change.

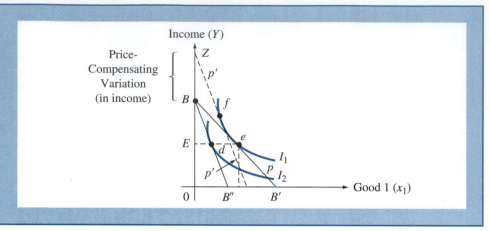

price-compensating variation in income
A measure of how much income must be given to a consumer after a price change to leave him or her at the same level of utility he or she had attained before the price change occurred.

consumer just as well off after the price change as he was before it? Because this amount of income would restore the consumer to his previous level of utility, it is a measure of the loss or gain to the consumer from the price change. Such a measure is called a price-compensating variation in income. Figure 5.16 provides an illustration of this measure.

In Figure 5.16, we will again assume that our agent lives in a society that has only two goods, which are labeled good 1 and income. Income is a composite good made up of all the goods other than good 1 on which our agent can spend his money if he does not spend it on good 1. Our agent starts out on budget line BB' and is at point *e* on indifference curve I_1. At a price of *p* for good 1, our agent chooses to give up *BE* units of income to obtain *Ee* units of good 1. Now let us increase the price of good 1 from *p* to *p'* so that the new budget line facing our agent is BB''. Our agent chooses a new bundle at point *d*. However, point *d* lies on indifference curve I_2, which is a lower indifference curve than the one on which point *e* lies, so we know that our agent is worse off as a result of the price increase in good 1. How much worse off is he? To answer this question, we must determine how much income our agent would need after the price change (at the new relative prices) to restore him to his previous level of utility.

Let us look again at Figure 5.16. If we take the new budget line BB'' and shift it out until it becomes tangent to the old indifference curve I_1, our agent is at point *f*. At this point, where the tangency occurs, our agent is indifferent between having income $0B$ and facing prices *p* and having income $0Z$ and facing prices *p'*. Therefore, the difference between $0Z$ and $0B$ (which is *ZB*) is the amount of income we must give our agent *after the price of good 1 has changed* to compensate him for the loss. This amount measures his loss as a result of the price change. If our agent does not receive this amount of income, he will suffer, but *ZB*, the price-compensating income variation, will eliminate his suffering.

Price-Compensating Variations and Expenditure Functions

The expenditure functions that we derived earlier in this chapter can be of great use to us in calculating the magnitude of price-compensating variations. For example, let us assume that the prices of the two goods in our economy are p_1 and p_2 and that at those prices our agent achieves a utility level of u^* with an expenditure of E. Now assume that the price of good 1 increases to $p_1 + \epsilon$. We would like to know by how much we must compensate our agent in order to make him as well off after the price change as he was before it occurred. In other words, what price-compensating variation would be necessary to restore our agent to his original level of utility? We can easily calculate this variation in income by using the idea of an expenditure function. We know that originally $E = E(p_1, p_2, u^*)$. Now we can calculate the expenditure needed to achieve u^* when the prices are $p_1 + \epsilon$ and p_2 as $E' = E(p_1 + \epsilon, p_2, u^*)$. The price-compensating variation in income needed as a result of the change in the price of good 1 is therefore as follows:

$$\text{Price} - \text{compensating variation} = E' - E$$
$$= E(p_1 + \epsilon, p_2, u^*) - E(p_1, p_2, u^*)$$

The difference between E' and E indicates by how much we must increase our agent's income to allow him to remain at the same level of utility after the price of good 1 changes.

Example 5.3

PRICE-COMPENSATING VARIATIONS AND EXPENDITURE FUNCTIONS: RASPBERRY-APPLE COBBLERS

To see how to work with expenditure functions, let us return to our previous example of the person who eats raspberry-apple cobblers and derive her expenditure function. Remember that this person gets satisfaction only from cobblers that contain apples and raspberries in the proportion of 3:1. Hence, when the prices are $6 per ounce for raspberries and $1 per ounce for apples, it costs $90 for this person to achieve a utility level of 10. (She must eat 10 cobblers, each costing $9.) If a tax is now placed on apples so that their price increases from $1 to $4 per ounce, then each cobbler will cost $18 and it will now cost $180 for the person to achieve a utility level of 10. (She will have to consume 10 cobblers, each costing $18.) The difference of $90 between these amounts ($180 − $90) indicates the price-compensating variation that must be paid after the price change to make the person just as well off after that change as she was before it (measured at the new price level). Hence, the derivation of an expenditure function can be a handy tool in calculating price-compensating variations.

Conclusion

In this chapter, we concluded our discussion of how consumers behave in markets. We did not explain how the institution of markets arose, but we will turn our attention to this topic in future chapters. We will then see that markets emerge to help the people in our primitive society solve a problem—how to exchange goods efficiently. Once the institution of markets has emerged, we will observe how, as the number of people in the economy becomes large, this institution takes on the characteristics of perfectly competitive markets identical to the ones studied here.

Summary

After deriving demand functions in Chapter 4, this chapter investigated their properties by discussing the concept of the elasticity of demand. Finally, toward the end of the chapter, we applied our demand analysis to the study of welfare economics by presenting a number of concepts aimed at measuring the benefits consumers receive from purchasing a good at a particular price. We learned that these concepts—exact and approximate consumer surplus and price compensation variation—can also be used to measure the impact of a price change on the welfare of a consumer.

APPENDIX A

THE EXPENDITURE FUNCTION

The expenditure function indicates the minimum amount of income required to allow an individual to reach a certain level of utility. Using the same notation as in Appendix A in Chapter 4, let $\bar{u}$ represent a fixed level of utility; as before, the choice variables are x_1 and x_2, but the objective here is for the consumer to find the cheapest way to obtain utility level u given prices p_1 and p_2. In other words, the consumer must minimize $W = p_1 x_1 + p_2 x_2$ subject to the constraint $u(x_1, x_2) = u$.

Formally, the problem is

$$\underset{\{x_1, x_2\}}{\text{Min}} \; p_1 x_1 + p_2 x_2$$
$$\text{s.t. } u(x_1, x_2) = \bar{u}$$

Note that the roles of the objective and the constraint are reversed from what they were in Appendix A of Chapter 4. There the consumer tries to maximize utility given a budget constraint, while here the consumer tries to minimize the expenditure needed to reach a predetermined utility level. The Lagrangian of this problem is

$$L(x_1, x_2, \bar{u}) = p_1 x_1 + p_2 x_2 + \lambda(\bar{u} - u(x_1, x_2))$$

The first order necessary condition for a minimum is

$$p_1 = \lambda \frac{\partial u}{\partial x_1}$$
$$p_2 = \lambda \frac{\partial u}{\partial x_2}$$
$$\bar{u} = u(x_1, x_2)$$

Solving for the optimal values of x_1 and x_2, x_1^* and x_2^*, we get

$$x_1^* = x_1(p_1, p_2, \bar{u})$$
$$x_2^* = x_2(p_1, p_2, \bar{u})$$

Finally, the expenditure function is the minimized value of the objective function:

$$e(p_1, p_2, u) = p_1 x_1^* + p_2 x_2^*$$

Consider a specific example where $u(x_1, x_2) = x_1 x_2$. Here, the problem to be solved is

$$\underset{\{x_1, x_2\}}{\text{Min}} \; p_1 x_1 + p_2 x_2$$
$$\text{s.t. } x_1 \cdot x_2 = \bar{u}$$

The minimization problem is

$$\underset{\{x_1, x_2\}}{\text{Min}} \; L(x_1, x_2, \bar{u}) = p_1 x_1 + p_2 x_2 + \lambda(\bar{u} - x_1 x_2)$$

The first order conditions are

$$p_1 = \lambda x_2 \quad p_2 = \lambda x_1$$
$$\text{and } \bar{u} = x_1 x_2$$

which simplify to yield

$$x_1 = \sqrt{\left(\frac{p_2\,\bar{u}}{p_1}\right)} \quad x_2 = \sqrt{\left(\frac{p_1\,\bar{u}}{p_2}\right)}$$

Substituting in the objective, we have

$$e(p_1, p_2,\,\bar{u}) = 2\sqrt{p_1 p_2\,\bar{u}}$$

which is the expenditure function. So fixing $\bar{u} = 200$, $p_2 = 8$, $p_1 = 1$, we find that a minimum income of 80 is needed to achieve this prescribed utility level, that is, $80 = 2\sqrt{8 \cdot 1 \cdot 200}$.

APPENDIX B

PRICE-COMPENSATING VARIATIONS

In the previous section, we obtained the general expression for the expenditure function and calculated this function for a specific example of multiplicative utility. The method of analysis for price-compensating variations can be presented easily in the context of the example.

Suppose that at prices p_1 and p_2, the utility level that is attained after maximization is $\bar{u}$. Using $u = x_1 x_2$, we know that it requires an expenditure of $e(p_1, p_2, \bar{u}) = 2\sqrt{p_1 p_2\,\bar{u}}$ to achieve a utility level of $\bar{u}$. Suppose now that p_1 changes to $p_1 + \epsilon_p = p_1'$.

Then, the expenditure required to attain the same utility level u is

$$e' = e(p_1', p_2,\,\bar{u}) = 2\sqrt{p_1' p_2\,\bar{u}} = 2\sqrt{(p_1 + \epsilon_p)p_2\,\bar{u}}$$

The price-compensating variation in income—that is, the change in income that will make the individual as well off as before the price change—is equal to

$$e' - e = 2\sqrt{(p_1 + \epsilon_p)p_2\,\bar{u}} - 2\sqrt{p_1 p_2\,\bar{u}}$$
$$= 2(\sqrt{p_1 + \epsilon_p} - \sqrt{p_1})\sqrt{p_2\,\bar{u}}$$

Because this is the additional amount we must give the consumer to compensate for the change in prices while keeping the utility level at u, it is identical to the price-compensating variation we defined in the text.

Exercises and Problems

1. David has to work in order to earn a living. He is paid an hourly wage. (He receives a fixed amount for each hour he works.) He uses his income to purchase various necessities of life. For the sake of simplicity, suppose that David's consumption needs are fulfilled by one "composite" good called C. He has to divide his time between work and leisure, but he enjoys leisure and dislikes work. He can devote at most 24 hours a day to leisure. Therefore, if he wants to enjoy leisure for L hours, he can work for only $(24 - L)$ hours. Suppose that David's preferences for consumption and leisure are given by the utility function $U(C, L)$ such that he derives positive marginal utility from both "commodities." Also

suppose that the price of C is $1 per unit and the wage rate is w per hour; that is, w is the real wage. Further suppose that David's wage rate of w per hour is for the first eight hours a day and that he receives an overtime wage of w' per hour for any extra time he works, such that $w' > w$. The relevant budget constraints are shown in Figure 5.17.

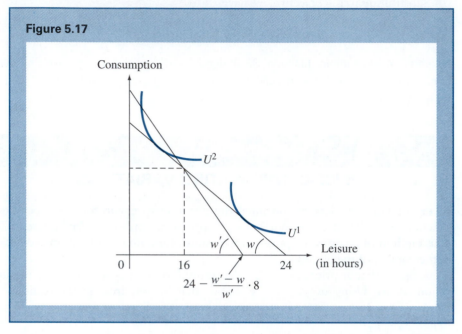

Figure 5.17

a) If David's preferences are represented by an indifference curve like U^1, would he choose to work for more than 8 hours? Explain your answer.

b) If, instead, David's preferences are represented by an indifference curve like U^2, would he choose to work overtime? Explain your answer.

Uncertainty and the Emergence of Insurance

MEASURING YOUR RISK AVERSION

How you make decisions in a world with uncertainty will depend on how averse you are to risk. Economists define risk aversion in one particular way that we will discuss later. In order to measure a person's level of risk aversion, Charles Holt and Susan Laury* devised the following test. In it you will be shown a set of 10 decisions where you are asked to choose between lottery pairs with one lottery labeled A and one lottery labeled B. For example, one pair of lotteries might contain lottery A, which offers you a 40% chance of gaining $200 and a 60% chance of gaining $160, and lottery B, which offers a 40% chance of gaining $385 and a 60% chance of gaining only $10. For each pair from 1 to 10, you will be asked to state which you prefer. More precisely, look at the ten pairs of lotteries below, which are run by throwing a ten-sided die and choosing lottery A or B depending on what number is shown face up.

	Option A	Option B	Your Choice A or B
Decision 1	200 if throw of die is 1 160 if throw of die is 2–10	385 if throw of die is 1 10 if throw of die is 2–10	
Decision 2	200 if throw of die is 1–2 160 if throw of die is 3–10	385 if throw of die is 1–2 10 if throw of die is 3–10	
Decision 3	200 if throw of die is 1–3 160 if throw of die is 4–10	385 if throw of die is 1–3 10 if throw of die is 4–10	
Decision 4	200 if throw of die is 1–4 160 if throw of die is 5–10	385 if throw of die is 1–4 10 if throw of die is 5–10	
Decision 5	200 if throw of die is 1–5 160 if throw of die is 6–10	385 if throw of die is 1–5 10 if throw of die is 6–10	
Decision 6	200 if throw of die is 1–6 160 if throw of die is 7–10	385 if throw of die is 1–6 10 if throw of die is 7–10	
Decision 7	200 if throw of die is 1–7 160 if throw of die is 8–10	385 if throw of die is 1–7 10 if throw of die is 8–10	
Decision 8	200 if throw of die is 1–8 160 if throw of die is 9–10	385 if throw of die is 1–8 10 if throw of die is 9–10	
Decision 9	200 if throw of die is 1–9 160 if throw of die is 10	385 if throw of die is 1–9 10 if throw of die is 10	
Decision 10	200 if throw of die is 1–10	385 if throw of die is 1–10	

(Continued)

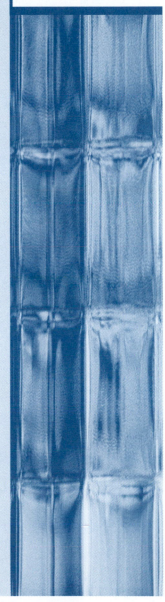

* Charles Holt and Susan Laury, "Risk Aversion and Incentive Effects in Lottery Choices," *American Economic Review* 92 (December 2002): No.5, pp. 1644–55.

EXPERIMENTAL
TEASER 7 *(Contd.)*

Most people prefer lottery A for the first several decisions and then switch to lottery B from then on. If you switch from liking lottery A to liking lottery B after the fourth decision, that is, at decision 5, then you are behaving as if you are "risk neutral." If you switch from lottery A to lottery B before the fifth, you are "risk preferring," and if you switch later, you are called "risk averse." Why do you think this is so?

Uncertainty and the Need for Insurance

As the economy of our primitive society develops and becomes more advanced, a number of institutions will emerge. Each institution will arise to solve a different type of problem that the society faces. For example, money will emerge to facilitate trade, regulatory commissions will emerge to control the excesses of monopolies, competitive markets will emerge to provide an efficient means of exchanging goods, and collusive oligopolies will emerge in an attempt to maintain high profits in certain industries. Another very important institution that will arise in this economy is insurance. The reason for its absence until now is simple. Up to now, there has never been any uncertainty in the society that our economic agents inhabit.

The introduction of insurance makes sense only in a society where something is uncertain or unknown. If all events and contingencies are completely predictable, there are no risks to insure; and as a result, no one will want to buy or sell insurance. However, when uncertainty exists, insurance solves a problem for society. Say that you own a house and are aware that lightning may strike the house someday and damage it. The lightning may even start a fire that will burn down the house. You may therefore be willing to pay some money to insure your house so that if lightning does strike, you will receive funds to repair or rebuild the house. Another agent may be willing to make a bet with you that your house will not be hit by lightning. She will ask you to pay her a certain amount, say $1,000, today in return for a promise that if your house burns down tomorrow, she will pay you $200,000 so that you can rebuild the house. Hence, uncertainty may cause one agent to want to buy insurance and another agent to want to sell insurance.

In this chapter, we will investigate the prerequisite for insurance by examining how economic agents make decisions in the face of uncertainty. We will investigate how its economic agents behave when we introduce uncertainty into this society. In Chapter 7, we observe how they behave when insurance develops to help them deal with the problems that arise from uncertainty. However, before we can examine such issues, we must discuss how to use the concepts of probability and probability distributions to represent the uncertainty that our agents will face.

Representing Uncertainty by Probability Distributions

Some events that will occur are not known with certainty but rather probabilistically. For example, if we sit in a room and measure the height of each person who enters that room, then the height of any entrant will be a random event. It may be 5 feet, 6 feet, or 5 feet 11 inches. However, we know that the heights of people are distributed in some manner and if we have sufficient information about this distribution, we can place a probability on the event that the next person coming through the door will be any particular height. A probability distribution tells us the likelihood

Probability distribution
The distribution that tells us the likelihood that a given random variable will take on any given value.

that a given random variable will take on any given value. For instance, let us say that there are only three possible heights that people can be—4 feet, 5 feet, and 6 feet. If each of these heights is spread equally throughout the population, one-third will be 4 feet, one-third will be 5 feet, and one-third will be 6 feet. Then, with an infinite number of people, the likelihood that the next person who walks through the door will have any one of these heights is as shown in Table 6.1.

Table 6.1 defines the probability distribution for three possible events that can occur—the person who enters the room is 4 feet tall, 5 feet tall, or 6 feet tall. This probability distribution is presented in graphic terms in Figure 6.1.

We see the three possible events on the horizontal axis in Figure 6.1 and the associated probabilities on the vertical axis. Because there are a finite number of events, we will use the term discrete probability distribution to describe such a probability distribution.

discrete probability distribution
A probability distribution with a finite number of events.

At this point, we might want to ask the following question: What is the *expected* height of the next person who walks into the room? In other words, if we draw a person at random from the population and have to predict what his or her height will be, what is the best prediction we can make? To come up with this prediction, we simply multiply the probability of a height by its value. For example, because there are three possible heights, each of which is equally likely to occur (that is, each has a one-in-three probability of occurring), the expected height of the next person to arrive is calculated as follows.

$$
\begin{aligned}
\text{Expected height} = {} & (\text{Probability of person being 4 feet tall}) \cdot (4 \text{ feet}) \\
& + (\text{Probability of person being 5 feet tall}) \cdot (5 \text{ feet}) \\
& + (\text{Probability of person being 6 feet tall}) \cdot (6 \text{ feet}) \\
= {} & (1/3)(4) + (1/3)(5) + (1/3)(6) = 5 \text{ feet}
\end{aligned}
$$

Table 6.1	The Probability Distribution for Three Different Heights that Are Spread Equally throughout a Hypothetical Population.	
	Height	**Probability**
	4 feet	1/3
	5 feet	1/3
	6 feet	1/3

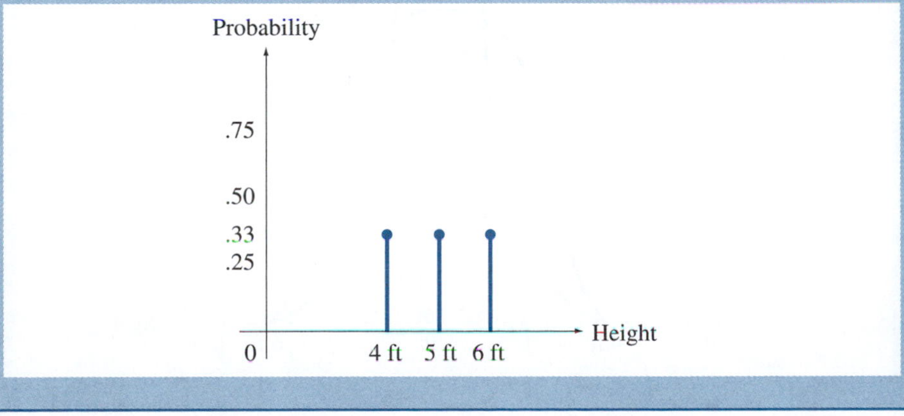

Figure 6.1

Discrete Probability Distribution.

The length of the vertical line segment over a point on the horizontal axis represents the probability of the associated event.

In general, the *expected value, mean,* or *weighted average* of a discrete random variable is the sum of the various values that the random variable can take on multiplied by the associated probability, or $EV = \Sigma \pi_i \upsilon_i$, where π_i = the probability of event i occurring and υ_i = the value of event i when it occurs. Two requirements that we will place on a probability distribution are (1) $1 \geq \pi_i \geq 0$, and (2) $\Sigma \pi_i = 1$, so that all events have a nonnegative probability of occurring (requirement 1) and the sum of the probabilities equals 1 (requirement 2), meaning that some event must happen (in this case, the person who walks into the room is 4 or 5 or 6 feet tall).

In the example that we are discussing here, the number of events (heights) is finite and the probability distribution is simply the three vertical bars that we see in Figure 6.1. If, however, the number of events (heights) were infinite, then the probability distribution would look like one of the curves in Figure 6.2. Such a probability distribution is called a **continuous probability distribution**.

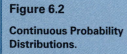

continuous probability distribution
A probability distribution with an infinite number of events.

Properties of Distribution

The two curves in Figure 6.2 describe how likely it is that a random variable will take on any specific value. Note that distribution A is "skinnier" than distribution B, which means that in B there is more of a chance that the random event can take on an extremely high or low value. In A, the value acquired by the random event is more likely to be within some prescribed bounds. Hence, we can say that there is more variability in the B distribution than in the A distribution. It will be useful for us to obtain a measure of this variability. One such measure, called the **variance** of the distribution, determines variability by looking at the expected squared deviation of the random variable from its mean. More precisely, if we let $\bar{x}$ be the mean of a discrete random variable, then the variance is defined as $\sigma^2 = \Sigma \, \pi_i (\upsilon_i - \bar{x})^2$. To calculate a variance in an infinite distribution of heights, we must take all the

variance
A measure that tries to capture the variability of a random variable by looking at the expected squared deviation of the random variable from its mean.

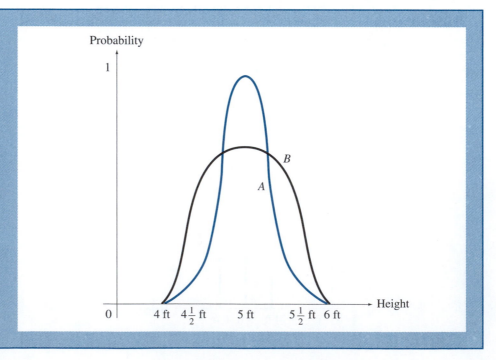

Figure 6.2

Continuous Probability Distributions.

There is an infinite number of possible events, represented by the points on the horizontal axis. The area under the curve between any two points represents the probability of an event in that set.

actual heights in the population, find the difference between these heights and the mean height of the population, square each such deviation, multiply each by π_i, and then add the results. As we will see later, the variance of a random variable will help us define what we mean by the concepts of risk and a risky situation.

The Mean and Variance of a Random Variable

There are certain facts about the mean and variance of a random variable that will be helpful for us later in our analysis of uncertainty. More precisely, let us define the following properties of random variables. We will assume that we have n random variables that are identical in the sense that they have the same probability distribution describing their behavior but are independent of one another. We will let $x_1, x_2, \ldots, \ldots x_i, \ldots x_n$ denote these variables, and we will let the mean of each of these random variables be $\bar{x}$ and the variance be σ^2. Next, we will define a new random variable, y, as the mean of the n individual random variables, or $y = (x_1 + x_2 + \ldots + x_n)/n$. We can demonstrate that the mean of y ($\bar{y}$) equals $\bar{x}$ and the variance of y equals σ^2/n.

This property of random variables will be used later in our discussion of risk pooling. To illustrate what it means, let us say that five people each face a gamble that will pay them either $100 or $0 with a 50% chance of obtaining one result or the other. To put it another way, each of these people faces a gamble whose mean or expected value is $50 [$50 = 0.50($0) + 0.50($100)] and whose variance is 2,500 [$2,500 = 0.50(0 - 50)^2 + 0.50(100 - 50)^2 = 0.50(2,500) + 0.50(2,500)]$. Now let us say that these people agree to a scheme in which each of them will play his or her gamble and will put its proceeds into a pot, the sum of which will be shared equally by everyone. If we let x_i be the outcome of the gamble for person i, then each person's share will be $y = (x_1 + x_2 + x_3 + x_4 + x_5)/5$. As a result of this scheme, to earn a share of the payoff from a gamble, each participant can be expected to receive $50 on *average*, and the variance of the shared earnings will be $500 = 2,500/5$.

SOLVED PROBLEM 6.1

Question (Content Review: Calculating Variances)

Saint Francis Church is holding a lottery to help raise funds for the construction of a new bingo hall. Suppose the chances of winning the various cash prizes are as follows:

Prize	Probability
$ 0	0.74
$ 10	0.15
$ 50	0.10
$100	0.01

Henry is not a churchgoer and does not like bingo, but he likes to play lotteries whenever he thinks it's worth his while. If the church is selling tickets for $25 each and Henry's preferences are risk neutral—that is, Henry will buy a ticket only if the expected value of the payoff is greater than or equal to its price—will Henry buy a ticket? What is the variance of payoffs in this lottery?

Answer

Henry will not buy a ticket. The expected payoff of this lottery is

$$E\pi = (0.74)(\$0) + (0.15)(\$10) + (0.10)(\$50) + (0.01)(\$100) = \$7.50 < \$25$$

The variance of the lottery is

$$\sum_i \pi_i(x_i - \bar{x})^2 = 0.74(0 - 7.5)^2 + 0.15(10 - 7.5)^2 + 0.10(50 - 7.5)^2$$
$$+ (100 - 7.5)^2$$
$$= \$308.73$$

Decision Making under Conditions of Uncertainty: Maximizing Expected Utility

In the previous chapters, our agents were always faced with a choice between known bundles of goods. When the world becomes uncertain, however, the object of choice for our agents is no longer known bundles. Instead, it is risky prospects or gambles that offer these bundles as prizes. For example, let us say that we are given a choice between two risky investments, A and B, as described in Table 6.2.

Note that in this situation, the decision maker does not know what will happen after she makes a choice between investments A and B because the outcome depends on random elements that are out of her control. One investment (A) involves planting wheat in the northern part of her country, and the other investment (B) involves planting wheat in the southern part of her country. Let us assume that the most important random variable in this situation is the weather for the coming year in the two regions. The values for this random variable are dry (event 1), wet (event 2), cold (event 3), very cold (event 4), and very wet (event 5). Table 6.2 shows the probability of each event occurring in each region and the associated payoff if the event does occur. By looking at the two investments in this manner, we see that they represent two different probability distributions over the payoffs of $10, $20, $30, $40, and $50. Figure 6.3 presents these probability distributions in graphic form.

As we can see, with investment B, our agent has no chance of obtaining the highest payoff of $50, but she also has no chance of receiving the lowest payoff of $10. On the other hand, with investment A, she has a possibility of "striking it rich" by earning $50 or "striking out" by earning $10. Given this analysis of the risk and reward involved in each investment, which one should our agent choose?

As we might expect, our agent's first inclination is to choose the investment that provides the largest expected monetary value. This approach seems to make sense. Most people would want to have the investment from which they can *expect* the greatest return, and they therefore would compare possible investments on this basis. To find out whether investment A or investment B offers the better expected

expected monetary value
The expected monetary return of a lottery, gamble, or investment, determined by taking a weighted average of the monetary prizes offered using the associated probabilities as weights.

Table 6.2	Two Risky Investments Involving Wheat Production in Different Geographic Areas.		
INVESTMENT A PLANT WHEAT IN THE NORTH		**INVESTMENT B** PLANT WHEAT IN THE SOUTH	
Payoff	**Probability of Event**	**Payoff**	**Probability of Event**
$10	0.10 (event 1)	$10	0 (event 1)
$20	0.30 (event 2)	$20	0.30 (event 2)
$30	0.20 (event 3)	$30	0.40 (event 3)
$40	0.20 (event 4)	$40	0.30 (event 4)
$50	0.20 (event 5)	$50	0 (event 5)

Figure 6.3

Two Investments in Wheat Production.

Investment A and investment B offer two different probability distributions over the payoffs $10, $20, $30, $40, and $50.

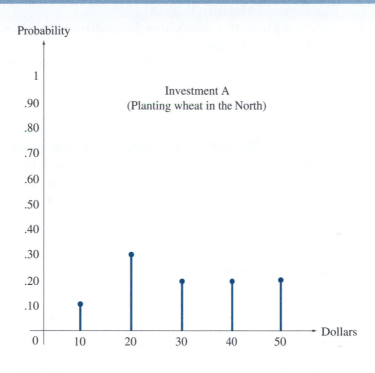

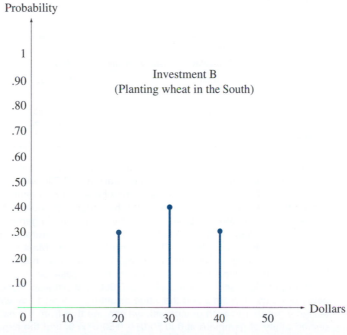

return, we simply multiply the payoffs from each investment by their associated probabilities and then add the results. Of course, the expected monetary value that we derive for each investment merely defines the mean of the random variable described by the investment. In this case, the expected monetary value is $31 for investment A and $30 for investment B.

Expected Monetary Value(A)
$$= \$10(0.10) + \$20(0.30) + \$30(0.20) + \$40(0.20) + \$50(0.20) = \$31$$
Expected Monetary Value(B)
$$= \$10(0) + \$20(0.30) + \$30(0.40) + \$40(0.30) + \$50(0) = \$30$$

On the basis of this calculation, our agent will choose investment A because its expected monetary value is greater than the expected monetary value of investment B.

Why Not Maximize Expected Monetary Returns?

Although it seems logical to use expected monetary value as the criterion for making investment decisions under conditions of uncertainty, this approach is actually filled with contradictions. To help us understand the problems, we will consider two examples.

Example 6.1

THE SADISTIC PHILANTHROPIST

Let us say that a patient leaves a doctor's office with the sad news that he has exactly two days to live unless he is able to raise $20,000 for a heart operation. The patient spends the next two days calling relatives and friends but is not able to raise a penny. With one hour left to live, the patient walks dejectedly down the street and runs into a sadistic philanthropist. Instead of offering the patient $20,000 outright, this philanthropist offers him a choice between two gambles. In gamble A, he will receive $10,000 with a probability of 0.50 and $15,000 with a probability of 0.50. In gamble B, the patient will receive nothing ($0) with a probability of 0.99 and $20,000 with a probability of 0.01. These gambles are summarized in the following table.

	Gamble A				Gamble B		
Prize	Probability	Utility Dollars		Prize	Probability	Utility Dollars
$10,000	0.50	0		$ 0	0.99	0
$15,000	0.50	0		$20,000	0.01	1
Expected monetary value: $12,500	Expected utility: 0			Expected monetary value: $200	Expected utility: 0.01	

Obviously, if our patient is a maximizer of expected monetary value, he will want to choose gamble A because its expected return is $12,500, whereas gamble B's expected return is only $200. However, there is a catch here. If our patient chooses gamble A, then it is certain that he will die in one hour, but if he chooses gamble B, he has at least a 1% chance to live. Hence, the money to be received by our patient in gamble A is worthless because he will die, while gamble B promises a chance to live. Therefore, most people would say that gamble B is the better choice. The reason is obvious. Most people are interested in more than just obtaining an amount of money. They are also interested in what that money will bring in terms of happiness or satisfaction. In this case, because $20,000 is needed for a life-saving operation, any amount below $20,000 is worthless. Hence, if we *arbitrarily* call the value or utility of death 0 and the value or utility of living 1 (we will explain later how we can assign a number to such outcomes), we can see that from the patient's point of view the expected utility of gamble A is 0 $[0.50(0) + 0.50(0) = 0]$ and the expected utility of gamble B is 0.01 $[0.99(0) + 0.01(0) = 0.01]$. If people act so as to maximize their expected utility, then gamble B is better than gamble A and it is the one that will be chosen by our patient.

The point of this example, then, is that when making decisions in situations involving uncertainty, agents do not simply choose the option that maximizes their expected monetary payoff; they also evaluate the utility of each payoff. We might say that they behave as if they are assigning utility numbers to the payoffs and maximizing the expected utility that these payoffs will bring. Let us now examine another illustration of this point by considering the famous St. Petersburg Paradox and the solution to it first proposed by Daniel Bernoulli.[1]

expected utility
The expected utility of a lottery, gamble, or investment, determined by taking a weighted average of the utility of the monetary prizes offered using the associated probabilities as weights.

SOLVED PROBLEM 6.2

Question (Application and Extension: Maximizing Expected Utility)

The partnership of Barney, Baxter, and Benjamin, attorneys-at-law, takes on civil cases for individuals wishing to sue. Marcy, a potential client, comes to their offices and asks them to represent her in a suit against a chemical plant that has been dumping toxins into a river near Marcy's house. After listening to Marcy's situation, the three partners meet to decide if they should take the case. They all agree that if they take the case, there is a 30% chance they will win big and make $4,000,000 for the firm, a 30% chance they will win small and make $1,000,000, and a 40% chance they will lose and win nothing. If they do take the case, they must forgo another case in which they believe that they will win $1,210,000 with certainty.

The partners always decide whether or not to take a case by majority vote. Assume that Barney has utility function $u(x) = x^2$, Benjamin has utility function $u(x) = x$, and Baxter has utility function $u(x) = x^{1/2}$, where x is the total amount of money taken by the partnership. Will the partners take the case? How will each partner vote?

Answer

Barney's expected utility for Marcy's case is $(0.3)(4,000,000)^2 + (0.3)(1,000,000)^2 = 5,100,000,000,000$, while his utility for the sure case is $(1,210,000)^2 = 1,464,100,000,000$. Thus, Barney will vote to take Marcy's case.

Benjamin's expected utility from Marcy's case is $(0.3)(4,000,000) + (0.3)(1,000,000) = 1,500,000$. His utility from the sure case is $1,210,000$, so he will also vote to take Marcy's case.

Baxter's expected utility from Marcy's case is $(0.3)(4,000,000)^{1/2} + (0.3)(1,000,000)^{1/2} = 900$, while his utility from the sure case is $(1,210,000)^{1/2} = 1,100$, so Baxter will vote not to take Marcy's case.

Therefore, the partners will take Marcy's case by a two-to-one vote.

Example 6.2

THE ST. PETERSBURG PARADOX

If a person cared only about maximizing the expected monetary value of a gamble, then she would be indifferent between two gambles having identical expected monetary values. Let us say that such a person is given a choice between the following two gambles: Gamble 1 offers a 100% chance of receiving a payoff of $100 and no chance of receiving a zero payoff; that is, it will produce a payoff of $100 for sure. Gamble 2 offers a 50% chance of receiving a payoff of $200 and a 50% chance of receiving a zero payoff. This type of person would just be

---

[1] Daniel Bernoulli (1700–1782) was a Swiss mathematician. His proposition that the willingness of a person to accept a risk depends on the expected utility of the payoff as well as its expected monetary value is known as Bernoulli's Hypothesis.

willing to pay $100 to take part in gamble 2 because she would be paying $100 to buy something worth exactly $100 to her on average. We use the term *fair gamble* to describe a gamble in which a person must pay exactly its expected monetary value in order to participate in it. If people actually behaved as maximizers of expected monetary value under conditions of uncertainty, then they would be willing to accept any fair gamble.

Daniel Bernoulli proposed the following game to demonstrate that people are *not* maximizers of expected monetary value. Let us say that we will flip a fair coin until it lands heads up. The coin has a 50:50 chance of landing heads up on any given flip (and hence a 50:50 chance of landing tails up). The *first* time the coin lands heads up, we will stop flipping it and determine the payoffs as follows: If the coin lands heads up on the first flip, we will pay $2; if it lands heads up on the second flip, we will pay ($2)^2; if it lands heads up on the third flip, we will pay ($2)^3; and so on. Because there is a 50% chance of the coin landing heads up on any given attempt and because all attempts are independent of each other, the probability that the coin will land heads up on the first flip is $\frac{1}{2}$. The probability that it will land heads up on the second flip is $\left(\frac{1}{2}\right)^2$ (that is, the probability of the coin landing tails up and then heads up is $\frac{1}{2} \cdot \frac{1}{2}$). The probability that the coin will first land heads up on the third flip is $\left(\frac{1}{2}\right)^3$, and so on. If we now look at the expected monetary value of this gamble, we see that it is the sum of terms like $\$2 \cdot \left(\frac{1}{2}\right) + \$2^2 \cdot \left(\frac{1}{2}\right)^2 + \$2^3 \cdot \left(\frac{1}{2}\right)^3 + \dots + \$2^n \cdot \left(\frac{1}{2}\right)^n + \dots$, which is equal to $1 + 1 + 1 + 1 + \dots$ (the dots imply that this is an infinite series). In short, because we will flip the coin an infinite number of times if we must and because each flip has an expected return of 1, the expected monetary value of such a gamble is infinite.

This result implies that if a person is a maximizer of expected monetary value, she should be willing to pay an infinite amount of money to take part in the gamble. However, in reality, people are not willing to pay an infinite amount of money to participate in a gamble that gives them a very small chance of winning a large amount of money. Hence, this example makes it seem unlikely that people are maximizers of expected monetary value.

Maximizing Expected Utility: Cardinal Utility

From the examples that we have just looked at, it would appear that when people are faced with risk, they assess the possible payoffs in terms of utility and then choose the gamble that yields the payoff with the highest expected utility. Such a hypothesis is called the expected utility hypothesis. It is the main behavioral assumption that economists use in analyzing the choices that people make under conditions of uncertainty. Previously, we noted that when people attempt to evaluate a risk, they act as if they are assigning utility numbers to the expected payoffs. To be more precise, we can say that people act as if they have *cardinal* utility functions. How can we be sure that people really behave this way? And if they do, how can we operationally estimate such utility functions? We will now investigate cardinal utility in order to be able to answer these questions.

expected utility hypothesis
The hypothesis that states that when people are faced with risk, they assess the possible payoffs in terms of utility and then choose the gamble that yields the payoff with the highest expected utility.

Ordinal and Cardinal Utility

In Chapter 2, we defined ordinal and cardinal utility functions. Up to this point, we have not made use of the concept of cardinal utility because ordinal utility was strong enough to meet our needs. Remember that with ordinal utility, the actual utility numbers assigned to objects or choices are of no importance. All that matters is that when we prefer one object or choice to another, we give it a higher ordinal utility number.

For example, let us say that we are shown three objects—a candy bar, an orange, and an apple—and we are asked to indicate the order of our preference. Our ordinal utility function assigns the candy bar a utility number of 100, the orange a utility number of 50, and the apple a utility number of 70. Hence, if we are then given a choice between the candy bar and the orange, we will select the candy bar because it provides us with more utility—it is the object with the highest utility number. If our ordinal utility function assigns utility numbers of 5 to the candy bar, 2 to the orange, and 4 to the apple, the results are the same. If we are again given a choice between the candy bar and the orange, we will choose the candy bar. In this sense, the utility numbers assigned to objects or choices by an ordinal utility function are irrelevant as long as the order of the numbers accurately indicates a person's preferences, with the most desired object given the highest utility number, the next most desired object given the next highest utility number, and so on.

The Need for Cardinal Utility. When there is uncertainty in the world, we need a stronger utility concept than ordinal utility. We need what economists have called a cardinal utility because, as we will soon see, it will be necessary to place more restrictions on the types of utility numbers we use. To illustrate this point, let us again take the two ordinal utility functions for the candy bar, the orange, and the apple. However, we will now assume that we are being given a choice between the certainty of having the apple and a 50:50 chance of obtaining either the candy bar or the orange. In other words, we are being asked to decide between having "a sure thing" (the apple) or taking a gamble, which will give us an object that we want more (the candy bar) with a specified probability or an object that we want less (the orange) with another specified probability.

Let us say that we are maximizers of expected utility but have only an ordinal utility function. If we use the scale of numbers from our first ordinal utility function, we see that the utility of the sure thing is 70 and the *expected utility* of the gamble is $\frac{1}{2}(100) + \frac{1}{2}(50) = 75$. Hence, this ordinal utility function would lead us to choose the gamble because the gamble provides a greater expected utility than the sure thing. However, if we use the scale of numbers from our second ordinal utility function, we find that the utility of the sure thing is 4 and the expected utility of the gamble is $\frac{1}{2}(5) + \frac{1}{2}(2) = 3\frac{1}{2}$. Hence, this ordinal utility function indicates that we should make the opposite decision and choose the sure thing (the apple) rather than the gamble (the candy bar or the orange). The reason for such conflicting results is that ordinal utility is not a strong enough concept to use in decision making under conditions of uncertainty. It gives different answers depending on which scale of utility numbers one happens to choose, and that is obviously unsatisfactory. This is precisely why economists developed the concept of cardinal utility. They needed a stronger utility function that would allow them to make consistent decisions when there is uncertainty.

In Chapter 2, we listed a number of assumptions that, if satisfied, would guarantee the existence of ordinal utility functions with particular convenient properties for the people we find in this book. In a similar manner, we can provide a list of conditions that will ensure that these people also have cardinal utility functions. However, for our purposes here, we will simply assume that the people we are dealing with have appropriately defined cardinal utility functions for which the hypothesis of expected utility holds; and as a result, these people will prefer gambles with a higher expected utility over gambles with a lower expected utility.

Constructing Cardinal Utility Functions. With *cardinal* utility functions, it is possible to prove that people make choices between risky alternatives or gambles by first assigning a cardinal utility number to each of the prizes and then choosing the gamble that maximizes their expected utility.[2]

---

[2] For a proof of the existence of the expected utility property and cardinal utility functions, see John von Neumann and Oskar Morgenstern, *The Theory of Games and Economic Behavior* (Princeton: Princeton University Press, 1947).

Let us assume that an agent is considering gambles that yield prizes A_1, A_2, A_3, ... , A_n, and this agent prefers A_1 to A_2 to A_3... to A_n. Hence, A_1 is the best prize and A_n is the worst prize. What we want to do is find the agent's cardinal utility for each of these prizes; that is, we want to know the utility number he assigns to each of the prizes. To obtain this information, let us take the best prize, A_1; the worst prize, A_n; and some intermediate prize, A_k. Our first step is to find the utility number this agent attaches to A_k. We will arbitrarily assign a utility number of 0 to the worst prize, A_n, and a utility number of 1 to the best prize, A_1. These two numbers will be the only arbitrary element we add to the process. Now let us form a gamble $G = G(p, A_1; (1-p), A_n)$, in which there is a probability of p of obtaining the best prize and a probability of $(1-p)$ of obtaining the worst prize. Next, we will take A_k and ask the agent what probability he will need to make him indifferent between the certainty of having A_k and the gamble G. According to a continuity assumption similar to the one we used to define ordinal utility in Chapter 2, such a probability must exist. For argument's sake, let us call this probability p_1 and call the cardinal utility attached to A_k $U(A_k)$ and $U(A_k) = p_1(1) + (1 - p_1)0 = p_1$. If $p_1 = 0.60$, then $U(A_k) = 0.60$.

At this point, we have three utility numbers—0, 1, and 0.6—which are attached to prizes A_n, A_1, and A_k, respectively. To find any other utility number, we proceed in the same manner as we did to determine the utility number for A_k. For example, if we want to know what utility number is attached to prize A_2, which is between A_1 and A_k, we form the gamble $G' = G(p, A_1; (1-p), A_k)$ and find the probability that will make the agent indifferent between A_2 and G'. If such a probability is 0.40, then $U(A_2) = 0.40[U(A_1)] + 0.60[U(A_k)] = 0.40(1) + 0.60(0.60) = 0.76$.

If we continue this process, we can assign a utility number to each prize. Notice that the utility numbers reflect the intensity with which our agent prefers one prize to another. We elicited this information by asking the agent for probability numbers that measure such intensities. But what about the arbitrary way in which we started this process by assigning a utility number of 0 to the worst prize, A_n, and a utility number of 1 to the best prize, A_1? This arbitrary assignment established the scale of our cardinal utility function and defined its *zero point*. The 0 assigned to the worst alternative and the 1 assigned to the best alternative set the extremes between which all other utility numbers fall. The actual numbers used are not important. We could just as well have assigned 100 as the utility number for the worst alternative and 1,000 as the utility number for the best alternative. All other utility numbers would then fall between these two extremes. Note especially that the zero point—the number of the worst alternative—need not be 0. In our example of a cardinal utility function, we chose to use zero for this point because it seemed most natural, but it was not necessary for us to do so.

The utility numbers we derived in our example were unique to the agent except for the fact that they contained an arbitrary zero point and scale. A different arbitrary zero point and scale would not have changed the nature of the cardinal utility function that we constructed for this agent. The proper analogy to make is between the Fahrenheit and Celsius scales used to measure the heat of an object. Both measurements differ only with respect to the zero temperature and the scale they use. For example, in the Celsius scale, we know that zero is the point at which water freezes; but in the Fahrenheit scale, this temperature is called 32°. Similarly, the boiling point for water is reached at 100° in the Celsius scale and 212° in the Fahrenheit scale. We can always convert a measurement from Fahrenheit to Celsius by dividing the Fahrenheit measurement by one constant and adding another constant to it. Still, any calculations or decisions that we would make using measurements from the Fahrenheit scale would be the same as we would make using measurements from the Celsius scale. They are just two different representations of the same phenomenon—the heat of an object. The same is true of any two different representations of cardinal utility derived from the process explained in this section.

SOLVED
PROBLEM
6.3

Question (Application and Extension: Utility Functions)

Professor Judgewell has four students whom he likes to various degrees. The students are Mr. A, Mr. B, Ms. C, and Ms. D. All of them are applying to medical school, and he writes a letter of recommendation for each student. After reading the letters, the medical school is confused as to how much he likes each of them. They call him and ask the following set of questions. First, they ask him simply to rank the students, and he ranks them in the order of A, B, C, and D, with A being his favorite. Next they ask him the following question: If he could have B in his class for sure or a lottery giving him A (his favorite) with probability x, and D (his least favorite) with probability $(1 - x)$, what value of x would make him indifferent between B for sure and the lottery? (He answers 0.4.) Then he is asked the following question: If he could have C in his class for sure or a lottery giving him B (with probability y) and D with probability $(1 - y)$, what value of y would make him indifferent? (He replies that $y = 0.3$.) Setting the value of D in the professor's utility function equal to 0 and the value of A equal to 1, construct the professor's (cardinal Von Neumann-Morgenstern) utility function.

Answer

Let $U(A) = 1$ and $U(D) = 0$. Then we know that $U(B) = x[U(A)] + (1 - x) U(D)$. Because Professor Judgewell stated that $x = 0.4$, we know that $U(B) = x(1) + (1 - x)(0) = 0.4$. Knowing that, we now know that $U(A) = 1$, $U(B) = 0.4$, and $U(D) = 0$. We also know that the professor is indifferent between C and a 0.3 chance of B and a 0.7 chance of D. Thus, we know that $U(B) = y[U(B)] + (1 - y) U(D) = 0.3(0.4) + 0.7(0) = 0.12$. The professor's utility function can be summarized as follows:

Student	Utility
A	1.00
B	0.40
C	0.12
D	0.00

Utility Functions and Attitudes toward Risk

Just as we learned something about the preferences of an economic agent under conditions of perfect certainty by looking at an indifference curve, we can gain information about an agent's attitude toward risk by observing what economists call his or her Von Neumann-Morgenstern utility for money.

Risk Neutrality

We can classify some agents as having a neutral attitude toward risk. For example, let us consider Figure 6.4.

In Figure 6.4, dollars appear on the horizontal axis and the utility generated by those dollars is shown on the vertical axis. The straight line in this figure is the

Figure 6.4

Risk Neutrality.

Because the utility function is a straight line, the agent exhibits constant marginal utility of income. The expected utility of a gamble is equal to the utility of a certain payoff that is equal to the expected monetary value of the gamble.

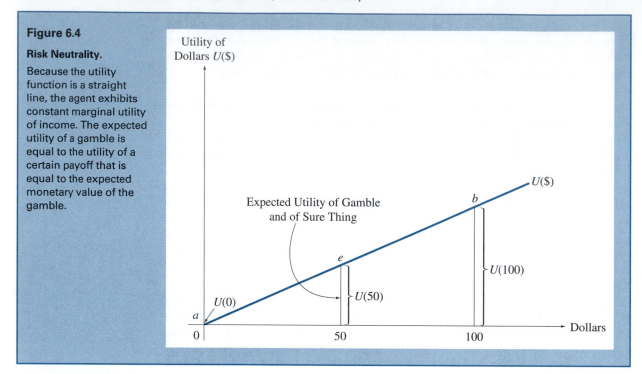

agent's utility function. It tells us how much utility he will receive from any given level of dollars. Note, however, that because the utility function is a straight line, every time the agent obtains one more dollar, his utility increases by the same amount. To put it another way, the marginal utility of an additional dollar is constant, no matter how many dollars the agent already has.

risk neutral
A characteristic of an agent who has a linear utility function, which implies that he will choose between gambles strictly on the basis of their expected monetary value. A risk-neutral agent will be indifferent to a "fair gamble" (a gamble that asks a decision maker to put up an amount equal to the gamble's expected monetary return in order to play).

As we will soon see, an agent who has a linear utility function like this agent is **risk neutral**. By risk neutral, we mean that the agent will choose between gambles strictly on the basis of their expected *monetary* value. In other words, we tend to think of some gambles as being riskier than others if the variances of their returns are greater. For example, gamble G^1, which offers a prize of $50 for sure, is less risky than gamble G^2, which offers a prize of $100 with a probability of 0.50 and no prize with a probability of 0.50. A sure thing is obviously less risky than a gamble. However, a risk-neutral agent will be oblivious to such uncertainties and will look only at the expected return on the two gambles. Hence, if offered a choice between gambles G^1 and G^2, this agent will be indifferent.

In Figure 6.4, the expected utility of gamble G^2 is presented as point e. To understand how the expected utility of this gamble is derived, notice that the height at point b represents the utility of a prize of $100—U($100)—to our agent and the height at point a represents the utility of no prize—U($0)—to our agent. Therefore, the expected utility of gamble $G^2 = (0.50)U($0) + (0.50)U($100)$. In fact, point e in Figure 6.4 is halfway between points a and b on the utility function.

Now let us look at the expected utility of gamble G^1. Its prize of $50 for sure—U($50)—is measured by the height of the utility function at point e. Consequently, we see that an agent with this utility function will be indifferent between having $50 for sure (gamble G^1) and a gamble whose expected value is $50 (gamble G^2). The fact that gamble G^2 has more variance in its returns does not influence the agent's decision. He is neutral to risk and therefore willing to accept a "fair gamble."

Risk Aversion

Let us now consider an agent with a different attitude toward risk—an agent who has an aversion to risk. The utility function for such an agent appears in Figure 6.5.

The utility function for the agent portrayed in Figure 6.5 is not a straight line but rather a curved one. The fact that the line is curved in such a way that its slope is decreasing means that this agent exhibits diminishing marginal utility for income, which, as we will see, indicates that she is risk averse. Unlike her risk-neutral counterpart, such an agent will not be indifferent between a sure thing and a gamble, each of which has the same expected monetary value.

To understand why this agent reacts aversely to risk, let us assume that she has the same choice as our risk-neutral agent had. She can choose between having a prize of $50 for sure and taking a gamble with a 50% chance of obtaining a prize of $100 and a 50% chance of obtaining no prize. In Figure 6.5, the height at point *b* again represents the utility of a prize of $100 and the height at point *a* again represents the utility of no prize ($0). The expected utility of the gamble is a weighted average of these two utilities and again occurs at point *e*, which is halfway between points *a* and *b* on the straight line. Now, however, point *d* represents the utility of having a prize of $50 for sure, and point *d* is greater than point *e*. Hence, our agent will want to take the sure thing—the prize of $50—and will want to reject the fair gamble offering an expected return of $50. This agent is averse to the risk involved in the gamble, as indicated by her diminishing marginal utility of income, which the curved utility function in Figure 6.5 depicts. Because the marginal utility of income is falling, additional dollars received toward the $100 range of income are of less importance or marginal worth than the dollars received at the lower end of the income range. As a result, our agent is not willing to sacrifice a sure $50 for the mere chance of gaining more dollars but dollars with less value (a lower marginal utility). She discounts those dollars and does not want to subject herself to risk to obtain them. In other words, risk-averse agents reject fair gambles.

risk averse
A characteristic of an agent who has a concave utility function (diminishing marginal utility). A risk-averse agent will reject a "fair gamble" (a gamble that asks a decision maker to put up an amount equal to the gamble's expected monetary return in order to play).

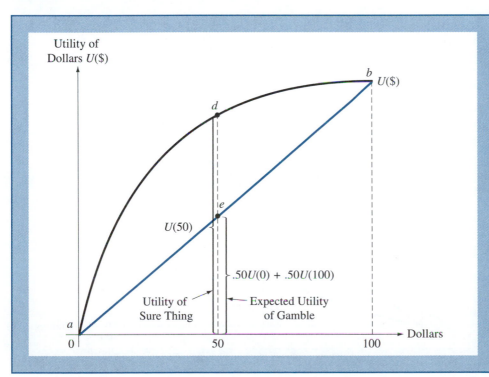

Figure 6.5

Risk Aversion.

Because the slope of the utility function is decreasing in the payoff, the agent exhibits diminishing marginal utility of income. The expected utility of a gamble is less than the utility of a certain payoff that is equal to the expected monetary value of the gamble.

MEDIA NOTE

RISK AVERSION

There is probably no place in the world where risk plays a more important place than in currency markets. The price of a currency is set by many factors, but how risky it is to hold a country's currency is certainly an important factor. This can be seen in the price of the Australian dollar whose price fell in an increase in international risk aversion in May 2004.

This occurred because one can think of holding a currency as holding a lottery ticket. If the variance associated with this lottery increases, then a risk-averse economic agent will value his currency holdings less and wish to switch them for something more secure like gold or a less variable currency like the Swiss franc. The flight from the Australian dollar led to its fall because the value of a currency is set by the forces of supply and demand on world markets, but the cause was risk aversion.

Source: Adapted from "Dollar Slips on Risk Aversion" as appeared in *The Australian,* May 19, 2004.

risk preferrers
A characteristic of an agent who has a convex utility function (increasing marginal utility). A risk-preferring agent will pay a premium to accept a "fair gamble" (a gamble that asks a decision maker to put up an amount equal to the gamble's expected monetary return in order to play).

Risk Preference

Finally, there are some agents who actually prefer fair gambles to sure things. These agents are called risk preferrers. A utility function for such an agent is shown in Figure 6.6.

Note that the utility function in Figure 6.6 becomes steeper as the agent's income increases. Hence, a risk-preferring agent has increasing marginal utility for income. To understand risk preference better, let us again say that the agent is given a choice between the certainty of having a prize of $50 and a gamble that involves receiving a prize of $100 with a probability of 0.50 or receiving no prize with a probability of 0.50. In Figure 6.6, point *b* again represents the utility of having a prize of $100 and point *a* again represents the utility of having no prize ($0).

Figure 6.6

Risk Preference.

Because the slope of the utility function is increasing in the payoff, the agent exhibits increasing marginal utility of income. The expected utility of a gamble is greater than the utility of a certain payoff that is equal to the expected monetary value of the gamble.

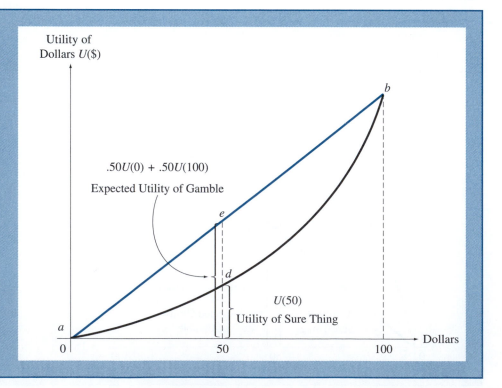

Therefore, we find that the expected utility of the gamble appears at point e midway between points a and b. Point d again represents the utility of having a prize of $50 for sure. However, in this case, point e is greater than point d. Hence, an agent with this type of utility function will want to take a gamble whose expected monetary value is $50 rather than accepting a sure $50. The agent prefers the risk of a fair gamble.

Question (Content Review: Choice Under Uncertainty)

Jim has to invest in two Internet stocks—Zombie.com and Oyvey.com. His broker tells him that the potential profit for each stock over the next year is as follows:

Zombie		Oyvey	
Payment	Probability	Payment	Probability
10	0.2	10	0.10
20	0.2	20	0.10
30	0.2	30	0.60
40	0.2	40	0.10
50	0.2	50	0.10

Jim's utility function appears as follows:

$	U($)
10	20
20	30
30	35
40	37
50	38

a) Which investment will Jim take?

Answer

Given our assumptions about expected utility, Jim will choose the investment that maximizes his expected utility. With his first utility function, his expected returns are

$$\text{Expected Utility}(\text{Zombie}) = 20(0.2) + 30(0.2) + 35(0.2) + 37(0.2) + 38(0.2)$$
$$= 4 + 6 + 7 + 7.4 + 7.6 = 32$$
$$\text{Expected Utility}(\text{Oyvey}) = 20(0.1) + 30(0.1) + 35(0.6) + 37(0.1) + 38(0.1)$$
$$= 2 + 3 + 21 + 3.7 + 3.8 = 33.5$$

Consequently, Jim will invest in Oyvey.

b) If Jim had a utility function of the following type, which investment would he take?

$	U($)
10	20
20	30
30	50
40	80
50	120

Answer

Given the second utility function for Jim and carrying out the same calculations, we find

$$\text{Expected Utility(Zombie)} = 20(0.2) + 30(0.2) + 50(0.2)$$
$$+ 80(0.2) + 120(0.2)$$
$$= 4 + 6 + 10 + 16 + 24 = 60$$
$$\text{Expected Utility(Oyvey)} = 20(0.1) + 30(0.1) + 50(0.6)$$
$$+ 80(0.1) + 120(0.1)$$
$$= 2 + 3 + 30 + 8 + 12 = 55$$

In this case, Jim will choose Zombie.

c) What is it about Jim's second utility function that leads him to reverse his investment decision?

Answer

The reason that Jim changes his preference for investments with the change in his utility function is that his first utility function is concave like the one in Figure 6.3, while the second one is convex like the one in Figure 6.6. What this means is that while in the first utility function additional dollars have decreasing marginal utility, in the second they have increasing marginal utility. Hence, with the second utility function, Zombie looks good because it gives Jim a larger chance of getting big payoffs, which have an exaggerated value for Jim (a payment of 50 has a utility of 120 attached to it as opposed to a utility of 38 attached to it by the first utility function). Hence, Jim likes Zombie under his second utility function because only it offers him a bigger chance of getting those payments he really values.

RESOLVING
TEASER 7

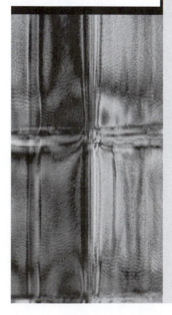

MEASURING RISK AVERSION

Now that you know what we mean when we categorize a person's attitude toward risk, you can see how the Holt-Laury test can be used to do so. Note that in the 10 decision problems offered in the test, the expected monetary value is greater for lottery A than lottery B in the first 4. This reverses itself on decision 5, where lottery B has a higher expected monetary value. Because a risk-neutral person chooses only on the basis of expected monetary returns, such a person would choose lottery A in decisions 1–4 but switch to lottery B from decision 5 onward. Note also that lottery A always contains less extreme payoffs than lottery B in that it pays either 200 or 160 with various probabilities. It is the safer option. Past decision 4, however, it is also the decision with the smaller expected payoff, so a risk-averse decision maker would be one that would be willing to trade off some expected payoff for a more secure reward. Hence, if you are risk averse, you would keep choosing A past decision 4 for some time. A risk preferrer would do the opposite. He or she would be so eager to get the big prize, 385, that he or she would switch much earlier to B. So by noting when a subject decides to switch from A to B, Holt and Laury can infer something about the subject's attitude toward risk.

If you want to give yourself this test, go to Charles Holt's Vecon Web page at http://veconlab.econ.virginia.edu/admin.htm.

The Desire to Buy Insurance: Risk Aversion

In addition to characterizing an agent's attitude toward risk, cardinal utility functions can be of use to us in analyzing more applied questions about insurance and about risk taking in general. To understand the value of cardinal utility functions in such areas, let us consider Figure 6.7.

Figure 6.7 is identical to Figure 6.5. It depicts the utility function of an agent who is averse to risk. Let us assume that this agent owns a house that has a current value of $100 and that she is aware of the possibility that the house may burn down, in which case the land it is on will be worth $20. Let us also assume that from previous history, we know that there is a 20% chance that the agent's house will burn down. Therefore, we can say that during the next period, the agent is actually facing a gamble in which she will have a house worth $100 if it does not burn down or she will have land worth $20 if the house does burn down. Obviously, if the probability that the house will burn down is 0.20, then the probability that it will not burn down is 0.80. Hence, we can represent the agent's gamble as $G(\$20, 0.20; \$100, 0.80)$. The utility of this gamble is indicated by point e in Figure 6.7. If the agent does nothing, her current state (ownership of the house) is worth the height $e'e$ to her in terms of utility. However, note that $e'e$ and $g'g$ are the same height, which means that $e'e$ contains exactly the same amount of utility for our agent as having $80 for sure.

Our agent can obtain $80 for sure if someone is willing to sell her insurance on the house for a yearly premium (price) of $20. If our agent's house does not burn down by the end of the year, then the insurer simply keeps the $20 premium and that is the end of the deal. If the house does burn down, then the insurer must pay our agent $80 so that her worth will again be $80: $20 (value of the land) + $80 (proceeds of the insurance policy) − $20 (insurance premium). Hence, no

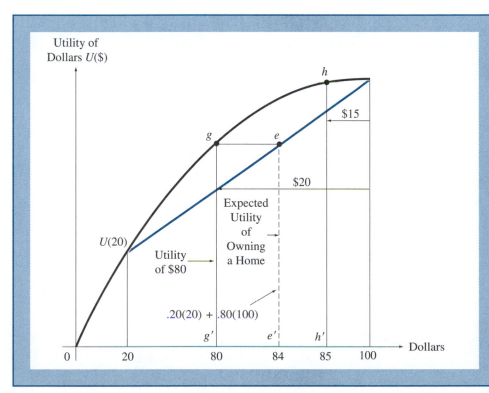

Figure 6.7

Risk Aversion and Insurance.

The homeowner is indifferent between buying insurance, which yields the utility represented by height $g'g$, and not buying insurance, which yields the expected utility represented by height $e'e$.

matter what happens, our agent is worth $80 at the end of the year. If no fire occurs, she still has her $100 house less the $20 insurance premium; or if a fire does occur, the insurance company pays her $80 plus she has the land worth $20 (from which we subtract the $20 premium for the insurance). Either way, our agent ends up with $80.

Note that a risk-averse agent, such as the one portrayed in Figure 6.7, is willing to buy insurance because she is indifferent between owning the house with no insurance and paying to have the house fully insured. Both situations yield the same utility. Of course, if our agent can obtain insurance for less than $20, say for $15, then she will be better off with insurance than without it. Let us look again at Figure 6.7. If our agent pays only $15 to be fully insured, her utility will be equivalent to having $85 for sure. This amount of utility, which is depicted by the height $h'h$, is greater than the utility of the gamble faced by our agent if she does not buy insurance, which is depicted by the height $e'e$.

But what about someone who prefers risk? Would such a person be willing to purchase insurance? Clearly not. To understand why, let us consider Figure 6.8.

In Figure 6.8, we see an agent whose utility function for income demonstrates a risk-preferring attitude. Let us say that this agent also owns a house that is worth $100 and faces a 20% chance that the house will burn down, leaving only a $20 value for the land, just as was the case previously. Again, the height $e'e$ represents the utility of the gamble the agent takes when she owns a house with no insurance. As a result of this gamble, she again faces an expected loss of $16 because there is a 20% chance that the house will burn down and she will lose $80. In the previous case, the agent was risk-averse and was therefore willing to pay up to $20 to insure her house. However, in this case, our risk-preferring agent will pay only $10 for such insurance. Thus, our risk-preferring agent is indifferent between a situation in which she is fully insured at a cost of $10 and a situation in which she has no

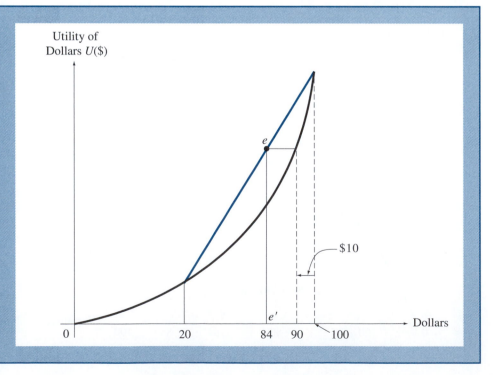

Figure 6.8

Risk Preference and Insurance.

The homeowner prefers not buying insurance, which yields a utility equal to height $e'e$, rather than buying insurance, which yields an expected utility equal to the value of the utility function at an income of $84, given a fair premium of $16.

insurance and simply accepts the gamble described before. In fact, such a person will not pay a *fair premium* of $16 to obtain insurance and avoid the gamble. This type of behavior is not unexpected from someone who enjoys risk.

Conclusion

The world we live in is uncertain. Knowing this calls forth a need to be able to make decisions with less than full information about the state of the world. When our agents know how to do this, they will have learned the basic tools of decision making under uncertainty, and in our next chapter, we will use these tools to see how they influence the rise of institutions like insurance companies, etc.

The theory of expected utility is not without its detractors. Many scholars have attacked the theory as not descriptive of how real people go about making decisions. In the next chapter, we will look at these criticisms more closely.

Summary

In this chapter, we took a look at how our analysis changes when we introduce uncertainty into the world. We found that the first thing needed was a strengthening of our concept of utility. To solve this problem, we introduced the concept of cardinal utility. We found that risk aversion is a property of a person's utility for money and is associated with a concave utility function. In contrast, people with convex utility functions will be risk preferrers, while people with linear functions will be risk neutral. In our next chapter, we will apply these concepts to problems in buying and selling insurance and also take up various criticisms of the theory of expected utility.

Exercises and Problems

1. Consider the following payoffs for two investments, A and B, and the associated probabilities of earning these payoffs.

Investment A		Investment B	
Probability	Payoff	Probability	Payoff
0.10	$0	0.20	$49
0.20	50	0.20	49
0.40	60	0.20	49
0.10	40	0.20	49
0.20	100	0.20	49

   a)   What are the mean and variance of returns from these two investments?

   b)   Which investment has the highest expected monetary return?

   c)   Albert has the following utility function for money: total utility = $5\sqrt{\$}$. Which of the two investments would he prefer?

2. Marge likes money and has a utility function of $U = (\$)^2$. She goes to Atlantic City to play roulette and bets her money on number 16. (There are 36 numbers on the roulette wheel, and the wheel is fair. Thus, each number has one chance in 36 of winning.) If Marge's number comes up, she wins $50. If the number does not come up, she loses her money and her wealth is decreased by the size

of her bet. Let us say that her wealth is $10, so a win at roulette will increase her wealth to $60 minus the amount of the bet, and a loss will reduce it to $10 minus the amount of the bet.

a)   Graph Marge's utility function.

b)   What is the maximum amount of money Marge will want to bet?

c)   What bet would make this a fair gamble for a risk-neutral casino? Is the bet greater or less than Marge's bet? What explains the difference?

3. In a country called Acirema, there are three types of citizens: (1) people in jail who were caught committing crimes; (2) people who are "honest," that is, who did not commit a crime and are therefore not in jail; and (3) people who committed crimes but who were not caught and are therefore not in jail (these are mostly politicians). Assume that the citizens of Acirema derive utility only from income (status and other factors mean nothing) and that they all have Von Neumann-Morgenstern utility functions. Also assume that this country pays a guaranteed income of $10,000 to each honest person and $1,000 to each criminal in jail and that the value of committing a crime and not being caught is $13,000. Finally, assume that with the country's present police force, the probability of being caught when committing a crime is 75%.

a)   Can we deduce, without ambiguity, the shape of a criminal's utility function? If so, what shape does it have?

b)   Can we deduce the shape of an honest person's utility function? If so, what shape does it have?

c)   If we sell insurance to criminals to pay them an income if they get put in jail, will we have any business? Why or why not?

4. Assume that a scientist runs an experiment in which people are faced with two choices. Choice A offers a 25% chance to win $240 and a 75% chance to lose $760. Choice B offers a 25% chance to win $250 and a 75% chance to lose $750. The scientist finds that everyone who participates in the experiment chooses B. In a more complicated experiment, the same subjects are asked to choose A or B *and* C or D. Choice A offers a sure gain of $240. Choice B offers a 25% chance to win $1,000 and a 75% chance to win zero. Choice C offers a sure loss of $750. Choice D offers a 75% chance to lose $1,000 and a 25% chance to lose zero. The scientist finds that 73% of the subjects choose A and D and 3% choose B and C. The remainder choose either A and C or B and D. The scientist claims that the results of her experiments violate the axioms of choice under conditions of uncertainty. Is she right? Discuss.

Uncertainty—Applications and Criticisms

INSURANCE PRICING

Congratulations. You have finished college and found a job. Unfortunately, while it is a great job, it does not offer you health insurance. Hence, the burden of paying for health insurance is on your shoulders. But before you begin shopping around for the best offer, you will find the following questions helpful in making your decision:*

1. How much will you be willing to pay for health insurance that will cover any medical expenses caused by any disease? How much extra will you be willing to pay for such insurance if it includes coverage for any accidents as well?

2. How much will you be willing to pay for insurance that will cover any medical expenses that have resulted from either a disease or an accident?

3. How much will you be willing to pay for insurance that will cover any medical expenses that have resulted for any reason whatsoever?

   As you can see, options 1 and 2 are the same. Both give you the same coverage (after adding the extra accident insurance for option 1); hence, the price you are willing to pay for each will be the same. The third option gives you a broader coverage than the two first choices, so you ought to be willing to pay a much larger sum for such insurance. What do you think that people are willing to pay when these options are explained to them?

---

* See Eric J. Johnson, John Hershey, Jacqueline Meszaros, and Howard Kunreuther, "Framing, Probability Distortions and Insurance Decisions," *Journal of Risk and Uncertainty* 7 (August 1993): no. 1, pp. 35–51.

EXPECTED UTILITY

Consider the following problem offered subjects by Daniel Kahneman and Amos Tversky.* Choose between A, which involves receiving $1 million with certainty, and B, which involves receiving $5 million with a probability of 0.10, $1 million with a probability of 0.89, and nothing ($0) with a probability of 0.01. Now choose between the following: C, which involves receiving $1 million with a probability of 0.11 and nothing with a probability of 0.89, and D, which involves receiving $5 million with a probability of 0.10 and nothing with a probability of 0.90.

(Continued)

---

* Daniel Kahneman and Amos Tversky, "Prospect Theory: An Analysis of Decision under Risk," *Econometrica* 47 (March 1979): no. 2, pp. 263–91.

EXPERIMENTAL
TEASER 9 *(Contd.)*

What choices should you make if you are an expected utility maximizer? What choices do you think most people make when faced with these choices? Are they the same? If not, why not?

If you chose A from the first pair of lotteries and D from the second, then your behavior violates the predominant economic theory of choice under uncertainty, the expected utility theory. Don't feel bad, however, because a majority of people, when asked this question, choose the same way. What do you think is so wrong with these choices?

The Creation of Insurance and Insurance Markets

Given the fact that risk-averse people might be willing to buy insurance, how might the institution of insurance have developed? What we will now do is provide a plausible example of how this institution might have come into existence. To do so, let us consider a primitive agrarian society in which production has not yet developed and the inhabitants gather fruit (apples and raspberries) each morning. There are two types of people in this society, whom we will call Geoffreys and Elizabeths. Each day they sell the fruit they pick on the market at a price of $1 a pound for apples and $6 a pound for raspberries. Now let us assume that because of the existence of some fruit-eating insects, there is a 10% chance that the stock of apples and raspberries picked each morning will be destroyed. Let us further assume that these insects affect only the part of the country where the Geoffreys store their goods. If each Geoffrey picks 8 pounds of apples and 2 pounds of raspberries a day, we know that his daily income is $20 (8 pounds of apples · $1 per pound + 2 pounds of raspberries · $6 per pound). However, because of the possibility that insects will ruin his stock of fruit, each Geoffrey faces a gamble in which there is a 90% chance that his income will be $20 and a 10% chance that it will be zero. In short, each Geoffrey faces a gamble with an expected value of $18 and an expected loss of $2. If all Geoffreys are risk-averse, then Figure 7.1(a) will describe their current situation.

In Figure 7.1(a), we see our now familiar diagram of the utility function of a risk-averse agent. This time, the expected value of the agent's gamble is $18 and the associated utility is indicated by the height $e'e$. As we can see, any Geoffrey would be willing to pay up to $4 to insure himself against the risk of having insects destroy his daily stock of fruit if such insurance were offered. But who will offer it? To answer this question, let us assume that every Elizabeth is a risk preferrer and has a utility function similar to the one described in Figure 7.1(b). If this is the case, then every Elizabeth starts with a daily income of $38 because she has a no-trade bundle of 6 pounds of raspberries and 2 pounds of apples valued at the equilibrium prices of $P_{raspberries} = 6$, $P_{apples} = 1$. The utility of such an income is represented by the height $b'b$ in Figure 7.1(b).

Let us now assume that every Elizabeth is contemplating the sale of insurance to some Geoffrey at a price of π. This means that the Elizabeth would offer the following deal to some Geoffrey: "Look, if you pay me π, I will pay you $20 if you lose your daily stock of fruit because of insects. However, if you suffer no loss, then I will pay you nothing." If the Geoffrey accepts this offer, the Elizabeth will no longer have $38 for sure. Instead, she will face a gamble in which she will

Figure 7.1

Risk-Averse Geoffreys and Risk-Preferring Elizabeths.

(a) *Risk-averse Geoffreys.* Geoffrey is indifferent between not buying insurance and having an expected utility equal to height $e'e$, and buying insurance for a premium of $4 and having a certain utility equal to the value of the utility function at an income of $16.

(b) *Risk-preferring Elizabeths.* Elizabeth will not sell insurance to Geoffrey at a zero price because she prefers a certain utility equal to height $b'b$ rather than an expected utility equal to height $d'd$.

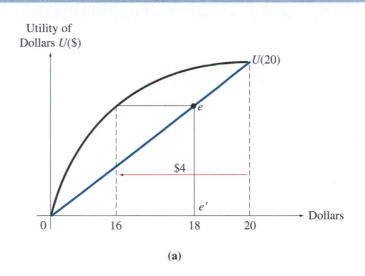

(a)

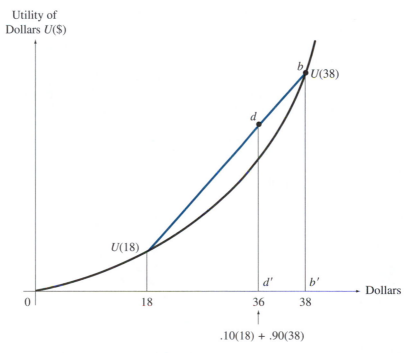

(b)

have $38 + \pi$ with a probability of 0.90 if no insects attack the fruit picked by her Geoffrey, or $18 + \pi$ with a probability of 0.10 if insects destroy her Geoffrey's stock of fruit and she has to pay him $20.

At what price (for what insurance premium π) would an Elizabeth be willing to sell insurance to a Geoffrey? To find the answer to this question, let us say that the price of insurance is zero. As we have already seen, if the Elizabeth sells insurance to a Geoffrey, she will transform her present sure income into a risky one because there will be a 90% chance that she can keep her $38 and a 10% chance that she will have to pay $20 to the Geoffrey. The expected utility of such a gamble is represented by the height $d'd$ in Figure 7.1(b). However, the height $d'd$ is clearly less than the height $b'b$, which represents the utility of the current situation in which the Elizabeth does not sell insurance and therefore has the certainty of keeping her income of $38. Hence, at a zero price, the Elizabeth will clearly not want to sell insurance to a Geoffrey.

However, there is a price at which the Elizabeth would be willing to sell insurance. To find the lowest such price, let us consider Figure 7.2.

In Figure 7.2, we see the Elizabeth at her no-sale point, the utility of which is represented by the height $b'b$. However, let us now assume that the price of insurance is $1.50. In this case, there is a 90% chance that insects will not attack the fruit picked by the Geoffrey and that there will be no need to pay any money to the Geoffrey. As a result, the Elizabeth's income will grow to $39.50. There is a 10% chance that insects will destroy the Geoffrey's stock of fruit, which means that the Elizabeth will have to pay him $20 and her income will shrink to $19.50: $38 (original income) − $20 (insurance payment to the Geoffrey) + $1.50 (insurance premium received from the Geoffrey). The expected utility of this gamble is represented by the height $k'k$ in Figure 7.1(b). However, because the height $k'k$ is equal to the height $b'b$, we can conclude that the Elizabeth will be indifferent between not insuring a Geoffrey and insuring him at a price of $1.50. Therefore, $1.50 is the lowest price at which any Elizabeth would be willing to sell insurance to any given Geoffrey. Of course, the Elizabeths would be willing to sell insurance at a higher price.

We know that any Geoffrey would be willing to pay as much as $4 in order to buy insurance. Hence, there are clearly trading gains to be made in the sale of insurance policies by the Elizabeths to the Geoffreys. The price of these insurance

Figure 7.2

Willingness to Sell Insurance.

Elizabeth is indifferent between not selling insurance and having a certain utility equal to height $b'b$, and selling insurance at a premium of $1.50 and having an expected utility equal to height $k'k$.

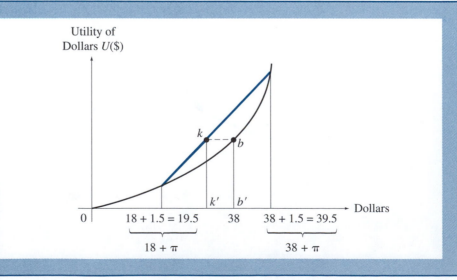

policies will be set somewhere between $1.50 and $4, depending on the deal negotiated between each pair of traders.

Risk Pooling: The Growth of Insurance Companies

The example that we just looked at indicates that the need for insurance arose because there are many uncertainties in the world. It also indicates that the profitability of insurance exists because people have different attitudes toward risk. Some people, like the Geoffreys, are risk averse; and other people, like the Elizabeths, are risk preferrers. However, this explanation only tells us why one individual would sell insurance to another. It does not tell us why there are large insurance companies that sell insurance to many people. Let us now investigate this question.

Although each Geoffrey can find an Elizabeth to insure him, there may be other methods of avoiding risk that the Geoffreys can collectively develop. One such method is **risk pooling** or **self-insurance**. To understand how such an institution might develop, let us again look at the behavior of a risk-averse agent. Figure 7.3 depicts the utility function of such an agent.

In Figure 7.3, we see that our risk-averse agent faces two gambles, both of which yield the same expected *monetary* return. One gamble, which is illustrated in

risk pooling (self-insurance)
A method of avoiding risk whereby groups come together to form a pool so as to share a risk if anyone in the group experiences a negative event.

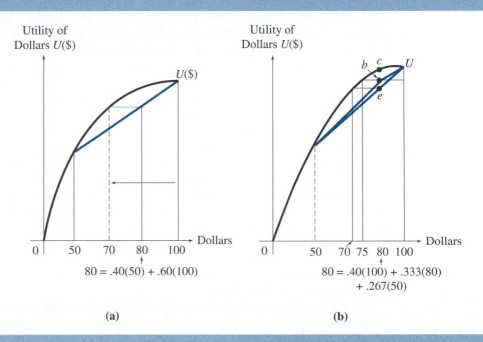

Figure 7.3

Risk and Variance.

(a) The gamble yields $100 with a probability of 0.60 and $50 with a probability of 0.40 for an expected monetary value of $80 and a variance of $\sigma^2 = 0.40 \cdot (50 - 80)^2 + 0.60 \cdot (100 - 80)^2 = 600$. (b) The gamble yields $100 with a probability of 0.40, $80 with a probability of 0.333, and $50 with a probability of 0.267 for an expected monetary value of $80 and a variance of $\sigma^2 = 0.40 \cdot (100 - 80)^2 + 0.333 \cdot (80 - 80)^2 + 0.267 \cdot (50 - 80)^2 = 400.3$.

$80 = .40(50) + .60(100)$

$80 = .40(100) + .333(80)$
$\qquad + .267(50)$

(a)

(b)

(a), will produce a gain of $100 with a probability of 0.60 and a gain of $50 with a probability of 0.40. Such a gamble has an expected monetary value of $80 and a variance of returns of $\sigma^2 = 0.40(50 - 80)^2 + 0.60(100 - 80)^2 = 360 + 240 = 600$. Note that we can reinterpret this gamble by saying that the agent has an asset with a value of $100 and there is a 60% chance that the asset will retain its value and a 40% chance that the value will decrease to $50. Under these circumstances, our agent would be willing to pay a premium of up to $30 in order to obtain insurance that will give him $50 if the asset decreases in value.

In Figure 7.3(b) we see the other gamble that our agent faces. In this gamble, using our latest interpretation, the agent has an asset worth $100 and there is a 40% chance that the asset will retain its full value, a 33.3% chance that the value will be reduced to $80, and a 26.7% chance that the value will be reduced to $50. Note that the expected monetary value of this gamble is exactly the same as the expected monetary value of the previous gamble:

$$\text{Expected monetary value} = (0.40)(\$100) + (0.333)(\$80) + (0.267)(\$50) = \$80$$

However, the variance of this gamble has decreased because

$$\sigma^2 = (0.40)(\$100 - \$80)^2 + (0.333)(\$80 - \$80)^2 + (0.267)(\$50 - \$80)^2 = 400.3$$

As we can see in Figure 7.3(b), this decrease in variance makes the second gamble more attractive to our agent than the first one. In the second gamble, the risk the agent faces is a combination of three possible events: the value of the asset remains at $100 (with a probability of 0.40), the value of the asset decreases to $80 (with a probability of 0.333), or the value of the asset decreases to $50 (with a probability of 0.267). The first gamble involves only two possible events: the value of the asset remains at $100 or the value of the asset decreases to $50. Point *b* in part (b) indicates the expected utility of the second gamble. Note that this point is higher than point *e*, which represents the expected value of the first gamble. The reason for this difference is that the first gamble offers no chance that the asset's value will be $80. The only alternatives it provides are a 60% chance that the asset will be $100 and a 40% chance that the asset will be $50. In fact, if we were to take the 0.333 probability weight associated with the $80 return and distribute it to the $100 and $50 returns so that their probabilities are again 0.60 and 0.40, we would come back to point *e*. Hence, as we shift probability to the $80 prize *and keep the expected monetary return to the gamble constant*, we move point *e* upward and toward point *c*. At point *c*, there is no variance in the gamble. The agent receives $80 for sure or, to put it another way, the agent knows for sure that the asset will be reduced in value by $20.

The fact that our agent prefers point *b* to point *e* tells us that risk-averse agents will always prefer a gamble whose variance is smaller if it yields the same expected monetary return. We should also note that with the second gamble, our agent is willing to pay less for insurance than the $30 maximum he was willing to pay before. He is now willing to pay only a maximum of $25. This result can be summarized by a proposition that we will call the **mean-preserving spread proposition**: If a risk-averse agent is faced with two gambles, both of which have the same expected monetary return but different variances, the agent will always choose the gamble whose variance is smaller. In other words, the gamble with the smaller variance will have a greater expected utility and the agent will therefore want to pay less to insure against that gamble.

To see how the mean-preserving spread proposition helps us explain the existence of risk pooling or self-insurance, let us say that two of the Geoffreys in our previous example decide not to buy insurance but rather to pool (combine) their

mean-preserving spread proposition
The proposition that states that if a risk-averse agent is faced with two gambles, both of which have the same expected monetary return but different variances, the agent will always choose the gamble whose variance is smaller.

risks. They say to each other, "Let us agree that we will pick our fruits as usual and store them as usual. No matter what happens, we will share the resulting income or loss equally. Hence, if the fruits the two of us pick are destroyed by insects, we will both bear the loss. If each of our stocks of fruit remains undamaged, then, of course, neither of us will suffer a loss. However, if one of us has the bad luck to lose his stock of fruit because of insect damage and the other retains an undamaged stock, we will share the resulting income equally."

If we investigate this arrangement more closely, we will see that the expected monetary value it produces for the two Geoffreys is the same as the expected monetary value they would obtain if no pooling existed. More precisely, if we assume that the probability of one person's stock of fruit being destroyed is independent of whether the other's stock of fruit has been destroyed, then the probability that both will be destroyed is $(0.10)(0.10) = 0.01$. The probability that neither will be destroyed is $(0.90)(0.90) = 0.81$. The probability that only one will be destroyed is $(0.10)(0.90) + (0.10)(0.90) = 0.18$ because there are two ways that this can happen depending on whose stock of fruit is or is not destroyed. If both are destroyed, the Geoffreys will have a joint loss of $40 and no joint income. If neither stock of fruit is destroyed, the Geoffreys will have a joint income of $40 and no joint loss. If only one stock of fruit is destroyed, the joint income will be $20 and the joint loss will be $20. Because each Geoffrey has an equal share of the joint income or loss resulting from the risk-pooling arrangement, the expected monetary loss from the arrangement is as follows:

$$
\begin{aligned}
\text{Expected monetary loss (risk pooling)} \\
= (0.81)(0/2) + (0.18)(20/2) + (0.01)(40/2) \\
= 0/2 + 3.6/2 + 0.4/2 \\
= 1.8 + 0.2 \\
= 2
\end{aligned}
$$

When no risk pooling exists, the expected monetary loss is as follows:

$$
\text{Expected monetary loss(no risk pooling)} = (0.10)(20) + (0.90)(0) = 2
$$

Although both of these arrangements produce the same expected monetary loss, their variances differ. With the risk-pooling arrangement, the variance in losses to any individual is as follows:

$$
\sigma^2_{\text{risk pooling}} = (0.81)((0/2) - 2)^2 + (0.18)((20/2) - 2)^2 + (0.01)((40/2) - 2)^2 = 18
$$

With no risk pooling, the variance in losses to any individual is as follows:

$$
\sigma^2_{\text{no risk pooling}} = (0.90)(0 - 2)^2 + (0.10)(20 - 2)^2 = 36
$$

In short, we see that risk pooling has cut the variance in losses dramatically while keeping the mean intact. Hence, according to the mean-preserving spread proposition, our agents must be better off with risk pooling than without it.

The beneficial effect of risk pooling is not surprising because we know that if we have n people, each of whom faces a risk with a mean of x and a variance of σ^2, then the mean loss per person is again x and the variance is σ^2/n. Hence, when we move from one individual who bears risk by herself to two individuals who pool their risks, the mean loss for the population of individuals remains the same but the variance is cut in half. Note that as the population in the pool grows larger, the variance in the mean loss approaches zero. For large numbers of people, we become increasingly sure that we will have a mean loss of exactly two per person.

We can now see that even in the simple economy with which we are dealing here, there is room for the emergence of insurance companies. An economic agent who is willing to sell insurance to a large enough number of other agents can reduce his risk almost to zero because he knows that he will have to pay only $n \cdot 2$ to cover damage each year. No individual agent can reduce her own risk in this manner. She would therefore be willing to pay up to $4 to obtain insurance. Any agent who is willing to sell insurance in this economy and charge $4 for it can make $n(4 - 2) - $ (the cost of issuing insurance) in profits each year. Under these circumstances, there should be many agents who are willing to start an insurance company. In fact, as long as there are profits to be made in selling insurance, we can expect that firms will continue to enter the insurance industry. However, as more competition develops, the price of insurance should decrease from $4 to $2, at which point insurance companies will no longer earn profits. As we will see in Chapter 15, in the long-run competitive equilibrium of the insurance industry, profits will fall to zero.

In summation, insurance and an insurance industry emerge in a society as its agents face the uncertainties in their lives and try to come to terms with these uncertainties.

RESOLVING
TEASER 8

Look back at the questions posed in the teaser, and let us think of them as actual insurance options you are faced with. As we said before, options 1 and 2 are the same. Both give you the same coverage (after adding the extra accidents insurance for option 1), hence the price you are willing to pay for each will be the same. The third option gives you a broader coverage than the first two choices, so you ought to be willing to pay a much larger sum for such insurance.

However, the findings from a survey run by Johnson et al. are quite surprising. The questions were divided among three groups of university hospital employees. The average sum group 1 was willing to pay was $89.10, the second group's average was $47.12, and the third's was $41.53. All the differences are significant. The authors attribute these differences to the effect of isolating vivid causes. When the insurance causes are broken down to individual cases, people tend to overestimate the probability of each happening and thus, when aggregating the causes, they price the insurance much higher.

The authors also point out that status quo bias affects insurance choice. *Status quo bias* is the term given to the fact that people have resistance to changing their current situations even if the new one offered to them is better. In order to show that insurance choice is affected by status quo bias, the authors presented the following natural experiment.

Legislative changes in the states of Pennsylvania and New Jersey have introduced, at the same time, the option for a reduced right to sue in cases of car accidents in exchange for lower insurance rates. Both states have mandatory car insurance laws, but in New Jersey the default option was the reduced right to sue while in Pennsylvania the default was the full right to sue. If drivers in New Jersey wanted to have the full right, they were able to purchase it with an additional cost. If drivers in Pennsylvania wanted to reduce the right to sue, they could have done so as well. The changes in each state were virtually costless. Moreover, the states do not differ much in the rate of accidents, that is, the probability of being in an accident. Nevertheless, in New Jersey 20% chose the full right to sue (meaning 80% chose the reduced right), while in Pennsylvania the number was 75%.

(Continued)

RESOLVING
TEASER 8 *(Contd.)*

Given the fact that there is no significant difference between the policies or the probabilities of accidents, the result above is puzzling. If the reduced right to sue is the better policy (given costs and probability of accidents), then the New Jersey drivers and Pennsylvania drivers should choose it, and if not, the full-right policy should be the favorable option. However, we see that drivers in each state chose to remain with their default options. This is clearly a case in which status quo bias affected choices simply due to the fact that there are no alternative explanations. According to the authors, if Pennsylvania had chosen to make the reduced-right policy the default option, the state would have saved the drivers over $200 million in auto insurance costs.

How Could Expected Utility Be wrong?

Expected utility theory is the foundation upon which the theory of decision making under uncertainty is built. My aim in the previous chapter was to convince you of its logical foundation. But science does not progress by setting out a set of logical assumptions or axioms, deducing conclusions from those assumptions, and then walking away. The proof of the pudding for any theory is in the testing. So how has expected utility theory done when tested?

Basically, it has done well. I say this not because there do not exist many important studies indicating that it is flawed, but rather because individual behavior is such a hard thing to predict, especially in the lab, it is not surprising that expected utility theory should fail and fail often. Despite its many failures, the theory does organize a wide variety of behavior both in the lab and in the real world and furnishes a good starting point for investigation. In that sense, it is very useful.

Having said all this, it seems very clear that expected utility theory is a fragile concept. It requires that people assess probabilities in an unbiased manner and obey all of the axioms stated before assigning utilities to prizes. If any of this is wrong, then we can expect behavior to violate the theory. We will call these violations of probability rules and violations of utility value formation and discuss them in turn here.

Violation of Probability Rules

People are not machines. When they are told that they have a 99% chance of dying, they process that probability with some emotional baggage that is not part of the laws of probability. Likewise, they may have problems distinguishing between small probabilities. However, expected utility theory relies heavily on the proper manipulation of probabilities (and ultimately values as well). Let us look at some situations that clearly highlight the fact that people may not be able to process probabilities in a totally rational manner.

Violations of the Conjunction Law: The Linda Problem.[1] Consider the following scenario given to subjects by Daniel Kahneman and Amos Tversky:

Linda is 31 years old, single, outspoken, and very bright. She majored in philosophy. As a student, she was deeply concerned with issues of discrimination and social justice and also participated in anti-nuclear demonstrations.

---

[1] Amos Tversky and Daniel Kahneman, "Extensional versus Intuitive Reasoning: The Conjunction Fallacy in Probability Judgment," *Psychological Review* 90 (October 1983): no. 4, pp. 293–315.

Kahneman and Tversky gave this scenario to subjects and then asked them to rank several statements about Linda by their probability of being true. The statements were as follows:

1. Linda is a teacher in elementary school.

2. Linda worked in a bookstore and takes yoga classes

3. Linda is active in the feminist movement (F).

4. Linda is a psychiatric social worker.

5. Linda is a member of the League of Women Voters

6. Linda is a bank teller (T).

7. Linda is an insurance salesperson.

8. Linda is a bank teller and is active in the feminist movement (F&T).

Look at statements 3, 6, and 8. According to the laws of probability, it can never be more likely that Linda is both a bank teller and a feminist than either of these alone (i.e., either a bank teller or a feminist), yet 90% of subjects asked said that 8 was more likely than either 3 or 6 alone. The reason is that the description of what Linda is like made it seem that, whatever she did, she would be a feminist, so being a bank teller and a feminist struck them as more likely certainly than being a bank teller alone. It was more representative of her being a bank teller and a feminist than simply a bank teller.

Ambiguity Aversion: The Ellsberg Paradox[2].

In an experiment, people were asked to imagine that there were two urns, A and B, each containing a large number of red and black balls. Urn A is known to have 50% red balls and 50% black balls, but no one knows the proportion of red balls and black balls in urn B. People were further told to imagine that they could earn $100 by first choosing a color and then choosing a ball that matched it from one of the urns. They were then asked which urn they would rather take the ball from. Most people said that they would choose from urn A, the urn with the known probabilities, rather than from urn B, the "ambiguous urn." However, they admitted that they were indifferent between attempting to select a red ball or a black ball from urn B if that were the only urn available, thereby indicating that they treated urn B as being made up of 50% red balls and 50% black balls.

The result of this experiment violates the expected utility theory, which tells us that the origin of one's uncertainty should not affect one's choice. Yet we see that the people who participated in this experiment treated the composition of urns A and B as identical despite their preference for the known urn A rather than the ambiguous urn B.

Violation of Base Rates.

In many cases, the probability of an event is subjective. That means that the event may not have occurred enough in the past to form an objective probability assessment based on frequencies of occurrence. Kahneman and Tversky offered a famous example of one type of bias called the base-rate bias. To illustrate this bias, consider the following example.

---

[2] This problem is taken from the famous Ellsberg Paradox, which can be found in Daniel Ellsberg. "Risk, Ambiguity, and the Savage Axioms," *Quarterly Journal of Economics* 75 (November 1961): no. 4, pp. 643–68.

A cab was involved in a hit-and-run accident at night. Two cab companies, Green and Blue, operate in the city. You are given the following data:

a. 85 percent of the cabs in the city are green, and 15 percent are blue.

b. A witness identified the cab as blue.

The court tested the reliability of the witness under the same circumstances that existed that night and concluded that the witness correctly identified each one of the colors 80% of the time and failed 20% of the time. What is the probability that the cab involved in the accident was blue rather than green?

The median and modal response to this question from subjects was 0.80. But this response does not seem to take into account the fact that the overall fraction of blue cabs in the city (the base rate) is only 15%. A consistent use of the laws of probability would answer the question of "What is the probability of the cab being blue given that the witness with 80% accuracy says it's blue" by saying it was 0.41 because that analysis would start at 0.15 (the overall or unconditional probability of any cab being blue) and then increase that probability using the witness's report and his or her accuracy. Such failure to appropriately use base rates can lead to unexpected choices.

Nonlinear Probability Weights. If people obey the expected utility theory, then the psychological weight they attach to the probability of getting any prize in a lottery should simply be the probability itself. But this need not be the case. People may have a hard time evaluating and differentiating between low and high probabilities and may attach importance to these probabilities that are not equal to the probabilities themselves. For example, people tend to think that low probability events are more likely than they are and make a distinction in their minds between events that are certain and those that are close to but are not certain. They downplay or underweigh the latter. Put these two facts together and you have a relationship between probability and the weights people attach to them that is not linear but rather assigns too much weight to very low probabilities and too little to high probabilities.

Framing. One implication of the expected utility theory is that how a problem is presented to people should not matter as long as the prizes and the probabilities with which they occur are the same. This unfortunately is not quite true as, again, Kahneman and Tversky demonstrate. Consider the following set of three connected problems.

Problem 3.1. In problem 3.1, people were asked whether they preferred A, a sure win of $30, or B, an 80% chance to win $45. A was the choice of 78% of the people involved in the experiment, and B was the choice of 22%. Thus, these people overwhelmingly chose the sure thing even though the alternative offered a high probability (80%) of winning a greater amount of money.

Problem 3.2. Problem 3.2 involved a two-stage game. In the first stage, there was a 75% chance to end the game without winning anything and a 25% chance to move to the second stage. For the people who reached the second stage, there was a choice between C, a sure win of $30, and D, an 80% chance to win $45. People had to make this choice before the outcome of the first stage was known. Again, the result was strongly in favor of the safer alternative: 74% of the people selected C and 26% selected D.

Problem 3.3. In problem 3.3, people were asked to choose between E, a 25% chance to win $30, and F, a 20% chance to win $45. Here the preferences were more evenly divided: 42% of the people selected E and 58% selected F.

Note that problems 3.2 and 3.3 are identical in the sense that they offer people the same probability of winning the same prizes. Both offer a 25% chance of winning $30 and a 20% chance of winning $45, despite the fact that these probabilities and prizes are achieved in two stages in problem 3.2 and in one stage in problem 3.3. Problem 3.1 differs in both its probabilities and prizes. Despite this difference, people tended to treat problems 3.1 and 3.2 as if they were the same. They chose A and C in almost the same proportions. However, people treated problems 3.2 and 3.3 as if they were different.

According to the theory of expected utility, if two situations offer a decision maker the same prizes with the same probabilities (no matter how those probabilities are arrived at—whether in one or two stages), then the decision maker's choices should be identical in both situations. Clearly, the Kahneman-Tversky experiments that are labeled "Problem 3" indicate that people care about more than just final prizes and final probabilities when they make choices. They care about the ways that these probabilities are generated, which violates the theory of expected utility.

All of the situations above make it clear that a theory that relies on people processing probabilities in an unbiased and unemotional manner may lend itself to disconfirmation in both laboratory experiments and in the real world. Let us now take a look at the other component of expected utility theory, the construction of values, to see if there may also be problems there.

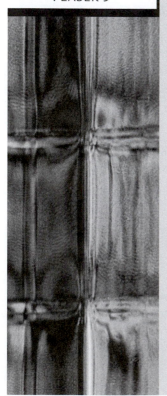

RESOLVING
TEASER 9

EXPECTED UTILITY - The Kahneman-Tversky Experiments

Remember that Experimental Teaser 9 described the following experiment. People were first asked to choose between A, which involved receiving $1 million with certainty, and B, which involved receiving $5 million with a probability of 0.10, $1 million with a probability of 0.89, and nothing ($0) with a probability of 0.01. When given this choice, most people selected A. By subtracting the 0.89 probability of receiving $1 million from A and B, Kahneman and Tversky determined the following pair of gambles and again asked people which one they would prefer: C, which involved receiving $1 million with a probability of 0.11 and nothing with a probability of 0.89, and D, which involved receiving $5 million with a probability of 0.10 and nothing with a probability of 0.90. Because the 0.89 probability of receiving $1 million was subtracted from both gambles A and B, we would not expect to see any change in people's preferences when they are asked to choose between C and D. However, most people reversed their original decision by choosing D (the equivalent of B) instead of C (the equivalent of A). Kahneman and Tversky say that these people reversed their decision because in gamble A they exaggerated the importance of the certainty of obtaining $1 million relative to probabilities less than 1. In short, it seems that these people attached weights to probabilities that are not proportional to the probability number. Hence, Kahneman and Tversky concluded that people do not maximize their expected utility by multiplying it by probabilities but rather use probability weights in place of raw probabilities. This can lead people to make conflicting choices when faced with gambles of the same type.[3]

---

[3] This problem is the famous Allais Paradox, which is named after the Nobel Prize–winning French economist Maurice Allais, who first raised doubts about the predictive content of the expected utility theory.

Constructing Values. Expected utility theory asks us to evaluate and assign utilities to outcomes or prizes in absolute terms. In other words, the theory asks decision makers to decide on what the utility to them is of, say, $100 or $20 or $1,000. Psychologically, this may not make total sense. We may view our current wealth as a status quo and view increments to it as gains and decrements to it as losses, and we may actually evaluate these gains and losses differently. To illustrate how this may happen, consider the following set of problems used by Kahneman and Tversky.

They told people to assume that there was disease affecting 600 people, and they had two choices:

- Program A, where 200 of the 600 people will be saved.

- Program B, where there is a 33% chance that all 600 people will be saved and a 66% chance that nobody will be saved.

The majority of people selected A, showing a preference for certainty. The researchers then offered them another choice:

- Program C, where 400 of the 600 people will die.

- Program D, where there is a 33% chance that nobody will die and a 66% chance that all 600 people will die.

Most people now selected D, seeking to avoid the loss of 400 people.

Notice how the framing makes the difference. A and C are the same and B and D are the same in terms of final outcomes, but they are viewed differently because they start at a different status quo. In program A, 200 people are said to be saved so that looks like a gain, while in Program C, 400 are said to die so it looks like a loss, yet the cases are identical.

Prospect theory predicts that changing the sign on a set of choices will result in people's changing their preferences even if the final outcomes and the probabilities attached to them are the same. Evidence has been found for this effect, which is called the reflection effect.

For another example, consider a choice between lotteries A and B where, in each lottery, we have the probability of a certain amount and the amount itself, so lottery A gives a 25% chance of winning $6,000 and a 75% chance of winning $0:

$$A : (0.25, \$6,000; 0.75, \$0) \text{ or}$$
$$B : (0.25, \$4,000; 0.25, \$2,000; 0.50, \$0)$$

Now consider a choice between A′ & B′:

$$A' : (0.25, -\$6,000; 0.75, \$0) \text{ or}$$
$$B' : (0.25, -\$4,000; 0.25, -\$2000; 0.50, \$0)$$

At first, B was chosen by 82% of subjects who participated in this experiment. But when the sign of the values involved was reversed, A′ was the more popular choice (chosen by 70% of subjects).

Thus, based on the reflection effect, it appears that to change people's preferences one simply has to change the sign of the events in question. The resolution of this puzzle was offered by Kahneman and Tversky, who suggest that the way people go about assigning values to utilities of prizes is by first defining for themselves a status quo outcome and judging all other outcomes as either gains or losses from this status quo. More importantly, while the marginal utility of increments from the status quo is considered to be decreasing, the marginal utility of decrements below the status quo is increasing, meaning that people tend to view gains as

the reflection effect
The prediction that changing the sign on a set of choices will result in people's changing their preferences, even if the final outcomes and the probabilities attached to them are the same.

if they had diminishing marginal utility but losses as if they had increasing marginal utility. This may lead people to exhibit a great deal of loss aversion, which is behavior not explicitly predicted by the expected utility theory.

MEDIA NOTE

SIMIAN ECONOMICS

Economists talk about *Homo economicus*—the rational economic agent. Indeed, when subjects are faced with a simple problem of buying goods in exchange for money, changes in prices affect their behavior as predicted by the expected utility theory. However, when faced with a choice whose outcomes are uncertain—that is, there is risk involved in the decision—people tend to be more risk averse then the theory would predict.

Keith Chen, from Yale School of Business, and colleagues have decided to look into the question of whether this discrepancy is a result of cultural conditioning or has a deeper biological origin. They have decided that the best way to do this is to use monkeys, especially the capuchin monkey.

First, the monkeys were taught the meaning of money. They were given metal discs that were used in exchange for food. Then, the monkeys were given 12 discs and were allowed to trade one at a time for either a piece of apple, a grape, or a cube of jelly at the price of one item per disc. After the price was established, it was changed by doubling the apple portions, thus halving the price of apples. Furthermore, the disc endowment went from 12 to 9. The monkeys reacted exactly as the theory predicted, within 1% error margin.

The next step was to test the monkeys' risk attitudes. This was done using three trading regimens, in each of which the monkeys had to choose between two different options, or "salesmen." Two salesmen stood at two different locations around the cage and always traded apples for discs. In the first

regimen, the first salesman always offered one piece of apple per disc. The second offered two pieces half of the time and only one piece the other half. Nevertheless, the monkeys quickly learned that the second salesman offered a better deal overall and preferred to trade with him.

In the second regimen, the first salesman offered one piece of fruit but, half of the time, would add a bonus piece once the disc was handed over. The second salesman behaved exactly as in the first regimen. The monkeys learned this behavior of the salesmen and quickly reversed their preferences, opting to trade with the first salesman rather than the second, even though the average outcomes were identical.

In the third trading scheme, the first salesman again offered only one piece of apple per disc with no bonuses, while the second salesman showed two pieces of apple but always took the second piece of apple away before handing over the goods, thereby creating the illusion of a loss. In this regimen, the monkeys preferred the first salesman over the second more strongly than before. The link between the last two treatments was the monkeys' loss aversion, even though in theory there was no loss.

The fact that monkeys respond to incentives as predicted by economic theory, while certainly not invalidating the role of culture on behavior, does imply that the biological foundation for economic theory among humans is on solid ground (unless we are too smart for our own good).

Source: Adapted from "Monkey Business-Sense: Simian Economics," as appeared in *The Economist*, June 25, 2005

Brain Evidence. If people make decisions on the basis of expected utility, could the brain be organized to calculate it? In other words, might there be a part of the brain that calculates utilities, a second that calculates probabilities, and a third that multiplies them together?[4] While economic theory does not need this to be true—it is an "as if" theory that requires only that people act as if they were maximizing expected utility—neuroscientists or, more precisely, neuroeconomists like Paul Glimcher and Michael Platt actually believe that the brain is organized in exactly that way. They have done a series of intriguing experiments in which monkeys make choices by moving their eyes and staring at certain portions

---

[4] For a full examination of the newly emerging field of neuroeconomics see Paul Glimcher, *Decisions, Uncertainty, and the Brain: The Science of Neuroeconomics*, MIT Press/Bradford Press, 2003.

of a visual field. By measuring the firing rates of the neurons that influence the eye movements of these monkeys and seeing how they vary as either the reward or probability of reward for correct eye movements varies, Platt and Glimcher present evidence that makes it appear that these neurons fire in proportion to the expected returns associated with right and left eye movements. While neuroeconomics, the application of neuroscience to economics, is in its infancy as a field, it has created a great deal of excitement and anticipation about what is likely to come.

Why Use the Expected Utility Theory?

After even a brief sampling of the results of the Kahneman-Tversky experiments, the following question naturally arises: If the expected utility theory seems to be so deeply flawed, why do people still use it? One response might be that the role of theory in the social sciences is to help us organize the data generated by human decision makers. Therefore, despite the anomalies pointed out by Kahneman and Tversky, the expected utility theory is still a very useful tool because it helps us organize our thinking about economic decision making under conditions of uncertainty. No theory about human behavior can make accurate predictions all the time, but the expected utility theory still serves a useful purpose as an analytical tool. This answer may not be satisfactory to everyone. Some people will probably object that we do not need an "incorrect" theory to help us organize our thoughts. However, even flawed theories can offer benefits as long as we are aware of their limitations.

Conclusion

In this chapter, we have surveyed some problems that exist with the expected utility theory and viewed the development of insurance as a spontaneous event that occurs in a society because people need a means of coping with the uncertainties in their lives. However, insurance could not arise if people did not have different attitudes toward risk and if there were not advantages to pooling risks.

Once insurance companies exist, the forces of supply and demand should cause a competitive equilibrium to emerge, just as it usually emerges with tangible products. However, these results cannot be guaranteed. There are situations that arise where individual initiative cannot be relied on to create optimal institutions. In later chapters, where we study the problems or moral hazard and self-selection, we will take a look at such situations and will find that some of them involve problems with insurance.

Summary

This chapter has presented an example of how people, if left alone to create the institutions they desire, can produce results that benefit everyone in society. The creation of insurance and other risk-sharing arrangements improves the expected utility of all agents in society. According to the assumption that we used in this chapter, insurance arose because there are uncertainties in the world and people who are averse to the risk that results from such uncertainties gain by purchasing insurance.

In much of our analysis, we used the theory of expected utility. According to this theory, people will attempt to maximize their expected utility when making economic decisions under conditions of uncertainty. However, at the end of the chapter, we surveyed some experiments in which Kahneman and Tversky tested the expected utility theory and proved that it was less than completely convincing.

Exercises and Problems

1. Joey Gamble makes his living buying risky lotteries. Let us say that he buys some of these lotteries from Dewey, Cheatum, and Howe, who are partners in a law firm. The three partners have the following utility functions for the prizes available in the lotteries.

	Utility Functions		
Money	Dewey	Cheatum	Howe
$ 0	0	0	0
$ 5	5	12.5	7
$10	10	18	12.6
$15	15	22.5	14
$20	20	24	14
$30	30	25	14

In this table, the column on the left lists the dollar amount of the lottery prizes and each column on the right shows the utility of those dollars to the three law partners.

a) If the first lottery offers a 50% chance of winning a prize of $30 and a 50% chance of winning no prize ($0), what is the minimum amount of money that each of the three law partners would have to be paid in order to sell in this lottery?

b) What is the risk premium that each of the three law partners would sacrifice in order to sell the lottery?

c) Let us say that Joey Gamble wants to sell the three law partners insurance on their houses. Each of the houses currently has a value of $30, but if they burn, their value will fall to zero. There is a 90% chance that the houses will not burn and a 10% chance that they will burn. How much would each lawyer be willing to pay to insure his house?

2. Jane owns a house worth $100,000. She cares only about her wealth, which consists entirely of the house. In any given year, there is a 20% chance that the house will burn down. If it does, its scrap value will be $30,000. Jane's utility function is $U = \sqrt{\text{wealth}}$.

a) Draw Jane's utility function.

b) Is Jane risk averse or risk preferring?

c) What is the expected *monetary* value of Jane's gamble?

d) How much would Jane be willing to pay to insure her house against being destroyed by fire?

e) Say that Homer is the president of an insurance company. He is risk neutral and has a utility function of the following type: $U = \$$. Between what two prices could a beneficial insurance contract be made by Jane and Homer?

Production and Cost

As economies develop, they become more institutionally rich. For example, the economy we have discussed so far is institutionally barren (except for the creation of competitive markets and insurance companies). Its inhabitants produce nothing and merely consume goods that appear to have been dropped from heaven. However, as we progress through this book, our economic agents will learn to trade with each other. Initially, they may do this through a set of face-to-face barter deals, but, as the population grows, competitive markets will emerge to help them exchange their goods through impersonal trades in which prices are set anonymously. Money will come into existence to facilitate the trading process by providing a medium of exchange accepted by all agents. Before we can discuss the creation of these institutions, however, we must introduce production into our analysis because that will serve as the foundation upon which many of these institutions are created.

In Chapter 8, we will investigate the development of production and its technology in our primitive society. We will see how one of the inhabitants finds a way to use goods and resources at her disposal to produce new goods that she can sell to others. This marks the beginning of a new economic activity—production. We will also examine the technology that is available in this society to transform existing goods or inputs into new goods called outputs.

To introduce production and the technology responsible for it, we create a fiction in which one person in society accidentally stumbles upon a process that produces a product—jam. Thinking that other people would want to buy this product, she decides to produce it on a weekly basis and sell it to consumers in order to earn profits for herself. Thus, she becomes the first entrepreneur in our primitive society.

As an initial step in getting her business underway, our jam maker experiments with the various possible ways of producing her product and analyzes the results. These efforts lead to another important event—the discovery of technology.

We examine the activities of our jam maker to see how different combinations of inputs—capital and labor—can be used to produce various quantities of output. The objective of this analysis is to find input combinations that could produce the desired output in ways that are technologically feasible and technologically efficient.

In Chapter 9, we will see our jam maker pursue the entrepreneurial process one step further and investigate the costs of producing her product. We will base much of our discussion of production costs on two assumptions. The first of these assumptions is that every technology is associated with a particular type of cost function, just as every set of consumer preferences has a particular utility function associated with it. Our second assumption is that every producer is motivated by a desire to produce in the cheapest possible way in order to maximize profits when the goods are sold. We will derive the optimal conditions of production from this assumption.

Finally, in Chapter 10, we will examine the effect that time has on production decisions. We will derive both *short-run* and *long-run cost functions*. When we study concepts such as *fixed costs*, *variable costs*, *total costs*, *average costs*, and *marginal costs*, we will discuss them in terms of both their short-run and long-run meanings.

Another area that we will discuss in this chapter is the interrelationship of various types of costs: *total costs*, *average costs*, and *marginal costs*. We will also investigate the cost functions of special types of technologies—the Leontief and Cobb-Douglas technologies. We will analyze important properties of these technologies such as their returns to scale and elasticity of substitution.

At the end of this chapter, our jam maker will have at her disposal all the information about technology and costs that she will need to start production.

The Discovery of Production and Its Technology

Up until this point in the book, no one has ever produced anything. All that we have discussed is how, if goods existed in a market, people would choose the bundles of those goods they liked most and how they would change those bundles as prices and incomes varied. But the way people get income is through producing goods that people want and selling those goods at a profit. This is what we will discuss in this and the next chapters.

Discovering Production

The Discovery of Production and the Rise of an Entrepreneur

To set the stage for the discovery of production, let us go back to the primitive society we investigated in earlier chapters. Because no one produced any goods in those chapters, let us assume that the goods available in this type of Garden of Eden society were fruits that grew on trees on the land that people owned. If my land has only apple trees and yours has only cherry trees, then, if we have tastes for both fruits, it is likely that we will trade and that markets will be established where we can do so.

Finally, assume that one day a member of this society accidentally leaves the fruit she has traded for in a stone bowl lying over an open fire and goes away for a few hours. When she returns, she discovers that her fruit has boiled down into jam, a food no one else has yet made in this society. She tastes the jam and finds that it is delicious. She allows several friends to taste the jam, and they like it so much that they ask how they can obtain some for themselves.

The accidental discovery of how to produce jam leads this member of our primitive society to become an entrepreneur. She reasons that other people would probably be willing to buy jam, so it might be profitable for her to spend time making jam. She also reasons that by having some of her fellow pickers supply her with fruit rather than gathering it herself, she can produce a greater amount of jam. She then concludes that she and her helpers might gain more from the production and sale of jam than from merely harvesting and trading raw fruit.

Seeing an opportunity to profit from her discovery, our entrepreneur makes contracts with six of her fellow pickers to gather fruit for her. She decides to spend each Monday morning making a 45-cubic-inch bowl to use in making jam, which she estimates will last for one week.

Measuring Opportunity Cost, Investment, and Profits

Obviously, the time that our entrepreneur plans to spend making a bowl each week could be spent picking fruit, just like everyone else does in our primitive

opportunity cost
The cost of engaging in any activity or the opportunity forgone by choosing that particular activity.

society. Hence, spending her time making jam has a cost for our entrepreneur—the amount of fruit she could have gathered during that time. The cost of engaging in any activity is the opportunity forgone by choosing that particular activity. This important concept is called the opportunity cost of a decision. To make this concept more precise, assume that our entrepreneur could earn $7.60 an hour harvesting fruit. Therefore, every hour she spends making a bowl means that she sacrifices $7.60. If it takes her an entire five-hour morning every Monday to make the weekly bowl, the opportunity cost to our entrepreneur is $38.[1]

Because our entrepreneur will spend only one morning (Monday morning) in the week making a bowl, she will have the remaining days of the week available to pick fruit. Thus, by sacrificing the opportunity to pick fruit one morning a week in order to produce a bowl, she will end up with both fruit and jam each week. This is the essence of investment: a sacrifice of consumption today (not picking fruit on Monday) for the sake of greater consumption tomorrow (the ability to eat fruit *and* jam later in the week).

Banks and credit markets do not yet exist in our model. But if they did, our entrepreneur could take out a one-week loan for $38 every Monday to cover the cost of making a bowl. She could then *buy* fruit on the market to produce the jam. By the end of the week, she would be able to pay the bank back *with interest*.

If our jam maker is actually going to start a business, she must believe that she will be able to recover her opportunity cost. As we have seen, she can earn an income of $38 a day by picking fruit. Thus, her income for a week (five days) of work would be $190. If our entrepreneur cannot earn at least $190 a week, she will have no incentive to start the business. Her jam-producing enterprise must therefore yield a return of at least that amount after paying for bowls, the fruit supplied by the pickers, and so on. We will call a return that is just sufficient to recover an entrepreneur's opportunity cost—just sufficient to induce her to enter the business—the normal profit for that business. Our entrepreneur's normal profit is $190 a week. Any profit above $190 will be considered an extra-normal profit because it is a profit beyond the amount needed to keep our entrepreneur in the business of producing jam.

normal profit
A return that is just sufficient to recover an entrepreneur's opportunity cost.

extra-normal profit
Any return above the normal profit to an entrepreneur.

SOLVED PROBLEM 8.1

Question (Content Review: Opportunity Cost)
You have a baby-sitting job on Saturday night earning $6.50 an hour; you will baby-sit for 4 hours. Your friend (who has nothing better to do) asks you to come over to watch the NBA Finals game. You say okay and cancel your baby-sitting job.

a) How much did it cost you to watch the NBA Finals?

Answer
Obviously, it cost you $26.

b) Now assume that the situation is reversed. You are scheduled to watch the NBA Finals at your friend's house and you are offered the baby-sitting job. You agree to baby-sit. The people for whom you are baby-sitting have no TV. What is the cost to you of agreeing to baby-sit?

---

[1] This $38 is actually the daily amount that each Elizabeth earns in our model in Chapter 7. Every morning the Elizabeths pick six pounds of raspberries and two pounds of apples with equilibrium prices of $6 and $1, respectively. Thus, the daily bundle is worth $38 [6($6) + 2($1) = $38]. We will assume that our entrepreneur in this chapter is one of the Elizabeths from Chapter 7.

Answer

Because the opportunity cost of any activity is what you are forced to give up to do it, the cost of baby-sitting to you is the lost enjoyment you would get from watching the NBA Finals.

The Production Function and Technology

When she sets up her firm, our jam producer will soon discover that she cannot simply produce jam or any other product out of thin air. In order to produce outputs, you need inputs, and these inputs can be combined only in certain ways in order to produce outputs. The set of constraints defining how one can combine or convert inputs into outputs is called a technology. Hence, the right way to view a technology is as a constraint on the process of production.

There is a direct analogy between the concept of a technology in the theory of the producer and that of preferences in the theory of the consumer because preferences are also a constraint on how happy a person can be. They define how one can combine consumption goods into the production of utility. Similarly, just as we used the underlying concept of preferences along with some rationality and taste assumptions to derive a utility function for a consumer in the theory of the consumer from Chapter 2, we will use in this chapter the concept of a technology along with some underlying assumptions about technology to derive the concept of a production function. This production function will completely summarize all there is to know about the technology facing our producer.

Rather than being overly formal, let us simply state the assumptions we will place on technology intuitively in an effort to jump quickly to our main concept of the production function, which is the construct we will use in the remainder of the book. Just as we listed seven assumptions that lead to the construction of a utility function in the theory of the consumer, we will examine assumptions here about technology, which will lead to the construction of a production function.

The first assumption, called the no free lunch assumption, is rather famous. This assumption simply means that you cannot get something in this world for nothing; more specifically, you cannot get any output from a production process without inputs. The second assumption, called the nonreversibility assumption, basically states that you cannot run a production process in reverse. For example, if you have a process that makes sausages out of pigs, you cannot reverse the machine, put in some sausage, and get a pig back. We will also assume that our production technology has free disposability, which means that if we can produce a certain output with a given combination of inputs, then with those inputs we can always produce strictly less. (For example, we can produce the original amount as we had before and then throw away the excess at no additional cost or without using any more inputs.)

Our final three assumptions, additivity, divisibility, and convexity, are assumptions we have seen before in a slightly different context. Additivity says that if we can produce an output of x using one combination of inputs (capital and labor) and another level of output of y using another combination of these inputs, then we can feasibly produce the output $x + y$. Likewise, divisibility says that if we can produce an output level of z using b units of capital and c units of labor, then we could produce, for example, $\frac{1}{2}z$ using *some* combination of the amounts of capital and labor. Our last assumption is convexity. This assumption says that if there is a production activity y that produces a certain amount of output z using capital and

---

technology
The set of technological constraints on production defining how one can combine or convert inputs into outputs.

no free lunch assumption
The assumption that you cannot get any output from a production process without inputs.

nonreversibility assumption
The assumption that states that you cannot run a production process in reverse.

free disposability assumption
The assumption that states that if we can produce a certain output with a given combination of inputs, then with those inputs we can always produce strictly less.

additivity assumption
The assumption that states that if we can produce an output of x using one combination of inputs (capital and labor) and another level of output of y using another combination of these inputs, then we can feasibly produce the output $x + y$.

divisibility assumption
The assumption that states that if an input combination y is a feasible input combination, then so is λy where $0 \leq \lambda \leq 1$. In other words, if it is feasible to produce a product using 4 units of labor and 8 units of capital, then it is feasible to produce using a constant fraction of those inputs, for example, 2 units of labor and 4 units of capital, if $\lambda = 1/2$.

convexity assumption
The assumption that states that if there is a production activity y that produces a certain amount *(Continued)*

of output z using capital and labor in particular amounts and another activity w that produces the same quantity using different amounts of these inputs, then we can always produce at least z by mixing these activities and using y a fraction of the time and w a fraction of the time.

production function
A function that describes the maximum amount of output a producer can produce given a certain level of inputs.

isoquant
The set of bundles that most efficiently produce the same output given a production function.

labor in particular amounts and another activity w that produces the same quantity using different amounts of these inputs, then we can always produce z by mixing these activities and using y a fraction λ of the time and w a fraction $(1 - \lambda)$ of the time.

These assumptions allow us to derive the concept of a production function, which is a function that describes the maximum amount of any output a producer in our economy can get most efficiently, given a certain level of inputs. In other words, a production function summarizes the technology a producer faces in the economy by describing the technology as a constraint on the producer's ability to produce. In the case of two inputs, this constraint is presented in the form of a function as follows:

$$\text{Output} = f(\text{input}_1, \ \text{input}_2)$$

Recall that we described the utility function of a consumer as a set of indifference curves representing the utility levels associated with different bundles of goods. Similarly, as shown in Figure 8.1, we can depict the production function by a set of isoquants or an isoquant map with each isoquant defining the combination of inputs that are required to produce a given level of output.

Figure 8.1 shows a series of curves called isoquants because any combination of inputs (capital and labor) along a given isoquant produces the same amount of output. We have drawn our isoquants to look identical to indifference curves (that is, they are bowed in toward the origin and smooth) because the same assumptions that produced the shape of the indifference curves when we were dealing with preferences can be used to derive isoquants with the same smooth shape. Isoquants can be more precise, however, because the numbers associated with them have cardinal meanings; that is, they are units of real output. For example, all of the combinations of inputs yielding 100 units of output can be found along the curve labeled I_{100}. All of the combinations of inputs along curve II_{200} yield an output of 200 units, and this output is physically twice as much as the 100 units on curve I. Remember that when we dealt with ordinal utility functions, the absolute values of the numbers associated with each curve were not meaningful; only their relationships to one another were. Here, numbers have a strict meaning and represent physical units.

Figure 8.1

Isoquants.

All combinations of inputs along the same isoquant yield the same output.

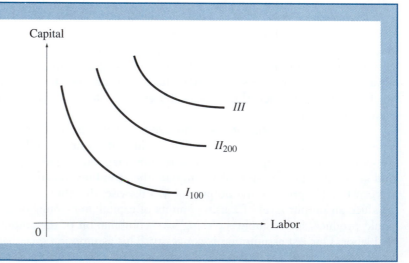

The Marginal Rate of Technical Substitution

For reasons similar to those described in Chapter 3, we can assume that isoquants never cross each other and that the isoquants farther from the origin define outputs that are greater than those of the isoquants closer to the origin. Similarly, just as the slope of an indifference curve measures what we have called the *marginal rate of substitution* between consumption goods, the slope of an isoquant measures what is called the *marginal rate of technical substitution* between production inputs. We will provide a formal definition of this concept later on. However, one difference between an indifference map and an isoquant map, as mentioned previously, is that the numbers indexing indifference curves are just ordinal numbers representing rankings of preference; but, with isoquants, the numbers indicate real levels of output. Let us start our discussion by considering Figure 8.2.

Assume that our producer is at point α in Figure 8.2. She is using 3 units of capital (input x_2) and 9 units of labor (input x_1) to produce 7 units of output. She might ask herself the following question: If I were to subtract 1 unit of capital from this activity, how many units of labor would I have to add in order to keep my output constant? What she is ultimately asking is this: At what rate can I substitute units of labor for units of capital when I am already using 9 units of labor and 3 units of capital? As we can see in Figure 8.2, the subtraction of 1 unit of capital moves our producer from point α to point β, which contains 2 units of capital and 9 units of labor. As a result, output decreases from 7 units to 4 units. This change in output defines the marginal product of capital.

The marginal product of any factor of production (input) measures the amount by which output changes when we change the use of that input by 1 unit but hold all other inputs constant. In this sense, marginal product measures output in physical units and is therefore sometimes called marginal *physical* product to distinguish it from marginal *value* product, which measures output in monetary units. In the example we are using here, the subtraction of 1 unit of capital decreases the amount of output produced by 3 units (output falls from 7 units to 4 units). Thus, because this third unit of capital is responsible for 3 units of output, we say that the marginal product of capital is 3. Clearly, the marginal product of capital at point α

marginal product of capital
The amount by which output would increase if we added one more unit of capital to production, holding all other inputs fixed.

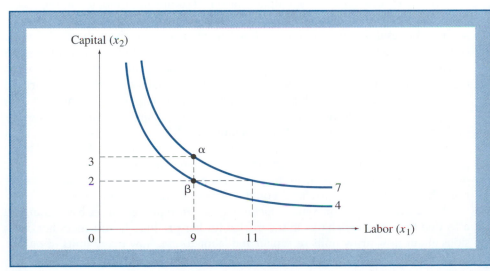

Figure 8.2

Marginal Rate of Technical Substitution.

The absolute value of the isoquant's slope measures the rate at which one input can be substituted for the other while keeping the output level constant.

is positive, because the marginal product of an input measures the amount by which the output produced increases if we add 1 unit of that input and *hold the use of all other inputs constant*. This is exactly what we do when we move from point α to point β. We denote the marginal product of input x_2 at point α as shown in the following equation. In this case, Δ stands for change.

$$\text{Marginal product of input } x_2 \text{ at point } \alpha = \frac{\text{(change in output)}}{\text{(change in the use of input } x_2 \text{ given } x_1)} = \frac{\Delta y}{\Delta x_2}$$

Let us say that $\Delta y / \Delta x_2 = 3$. Hence, the subtraction of 1 unit of capital led to a decrease of 3 units of output, meaning that the marginal product of the third bowl (unit of capital) at point α was 3 units of output. As we saw already, the subtraction of this input places our producer at point β. Once she is at point β, we can ask how many units of labor she must add in order to restore her output to 7 units. Let us assume that the answer is 2 units of labor. Thus, if our producer adds 2 units of labor at point β, her output will increase by 3 units, or $\Delta y / \Delta x_1 = \frac{3}{2}$. This merely measures the marginal product of labor. The ratio of the marginal product of labor to the marginal product of capital measures the absolute value of the slope of the isoquant at point α *if* we assume that the subtraction of capital and the addition of labor we make at this point become very small. Such a ratio provides the formal definition of what we have called the **marginal rate of technical substitution** (MRTS) as −1 times the slope of the isoquant at a given point, or the rate at which one input can be substituted for another while keeping the output produced constant. More precisely, we can express this rate as follows:

marginal rate of technical substitution
The rate at which one input can be substituted for another while keeping the output produced constant.

$$\text{Marginal rate of technical substitution of } x_2 \text{ for } x_1 \text{ at point } \alpha = \frac{\text{Marginal product of } x_1}{\text{Marginal product of } x_2} = \frac{\dfrac{\Delta y}{\Delta x_1}}{\dfrac{\Delta y}{\Delta x_2}}$$

Because a production function really describes a relationship between inputs and outputs, it would be helpful to represent all of these variables—outputs as well as inputs—together in one graph. Figure 8.3 does just that for a case in which there are two inputs and one output. The output appears on the vertical axis.

In Figure 8.3, we see that the two inputs (capital and labor) are placed on the floor or the input surface, while output is placed vertically or pointing out into space. Note that when 1 unit of capital and 6 units of labor are used at point y_1 on the input surface, the result is 4 units of output. If we move to point y_2 where there are 2 units of capital and 3 units of labor, we can produce the same output and reach the same height in output space. Suppose we plot the set of input combinations that each yield exactly 4 units of output (the isoquant with 4 units of output) on the input surface. Then, because each such combination traces an identical output and reaches into output space at a common height, we would trace a line of equal height on the surface of the production function. This line is identified as WW' in Figure 8.3. Inputs yielding larger outputs trace higher lines on the surface of the production function. Dropping these lines on the surface of the production function (projecting them onto the input surface) traces the isoquant map. Hence, isoquants are sets of input combinations that each yield an equal height on the surface of the production function.

As we will see later, the type of technology an entrepreneur faces has a dramatic effect on the way she behaves in the market for her product. It influences her decisions about how many units of capital and labor to use, how many units of output to attempt to produce, and even whether to stay in business or get out.

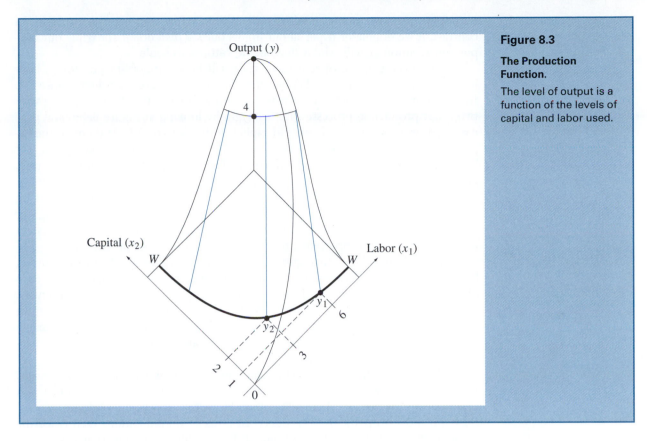

Figure 8.3

The Production Function.

The level of output is a function of the levels of capital and labor used.

Describing Technologies

A producer typically will have many possible output levels from which to choose. Moreover, each output level can be achieved using various combinations of inputs. Although the production function determines the efficient output-input combinations, by itself it cannot tell us which efficient combination is best from the viewpoint of our entrepreneur to help her maximize her profits. In order to discuss the choice of an optimal output-input combination, we must first examine some ways of describing the technology available to a producer. In general, technologies are characterized by two attributes: their returns to scale and their elasticity of substitution. Let us consider each of these concepts.

Returns to Scale

When we talk about the returns to scale of a technology, we are really asking this question: *What will happen to our output if we multiply all our inputs by the same factor?* A technology's returns to scale measures the ratio between the resulting change in the output level and the proportionate change in the levels of *all* the inputs. For example, by reference to the returns to scale of the technology, we can see what will happen to output if we double the use of capital *and* labor simultaneously. If, when we double the use of capital and labor, we also double the amount of output produced, we say our technology has constant returns to scale. If we double or triple all our inputs but *more than* double or triple the amount of

returns to scale
Measures the ratio between the resulting change in the output level and the proportionate change in the levels of all the inputs.

constant returns to scale
A feature of a technology that is such that when all inputs are increased by a fixed multiple λ, output increases by the same multiple; that is, if all inputs are doubled, then so is the resulting output.

increasing returns to scale
A feature of a technology that is such that when all inputs are increased by a fixed multiple λ, output increases by more than that multiple; that is, if all inputs are doubled, then the resulting output increases by more than a factor of two.

decreasing returns to scale
A feature of a technology that is such that when all inputs are increased by a fixed multiple λ, output increases by less than that multiple; that is, if all inputs are doubled, then the resulting output increases but by less than a factor of two.

output we produce, our technology will exhibit increasing returns to scale. In contrast, if we double or triple all our inputs but *less than* double or triple our output, our technology will exhibit decreasing returns to scale.

Because the concept of returns to scale will be an important one for us later in this book, let us spend a little more time discussing it here. Consider Figure 8.4. In this figure we see a set of isoquants describing a production function along with two other production processes. Let us begin by looking at Figure 8.4(a) and process p_1, a process that uses labor and capital in the ratio of 6:1. At point A, the inputs are 6 units of labor and 1 unit of capital. At the isoquant on which point A is located, we can expect this combination of inputs to produce 4 units of output. Now if we double the inputs, we move out along process p_1 until we reach point B, where the inputs are 12 units of labor and 2 units of capital. At the isoquant on which point B is located, we see that the output should be 8 units. By doubling our inputs, we have doubled our output. However, if a technology is to exhibit constant returns to scale, this proportionality effect must be true for *all* processes.

Now look at point C in Figure 8.4(a), where we again see 4 units of output, but this time it was produced with 2 units of capital and 3 units of labor. The ratio of labor to capital is now 3:2. If we double the inputs here, we move to point D, where we produce 8 units of output. Once again, we have doubled the amount we produced before the proportionate increase. Hence, the technology depicted in Figure 8.4(a) exhibits constant returns to scale because all of its processes are characterized by the same proportionality.

In Figure 8.4(b), we see a technology that exhibits *increasing* returns to scale. If we start at point A, we again find that our inputs are 6 units of labor and 1 unit of capital and we produce 4 units of output. However, now when we double our inputs and move to point B, we produce 10 units of output—more than twice the amount of output that we had at point A. Because doubling our inputs *more than* doubles our output, this technology has increasing returns to scale.

Figure 8.4(c) provides an example of a technology with *decreasing* returns to scale. Note that when we double our inputs and move from point A to point B, we

---

Figure 8.4

Returns to Scale.

(a) Constant returns to scale. Doubling the levels of labor (from 3 units to 6 units) and capital (from 2 units to 4 units) also doubles the level of output (from 4 units to 8 units). (b) Increasing returns to scale. Doubling the levels of both inputs more than doubles the output level. (c) Decreasing returns to scale. Doubling the levels of both inputs less than doubles the output level.

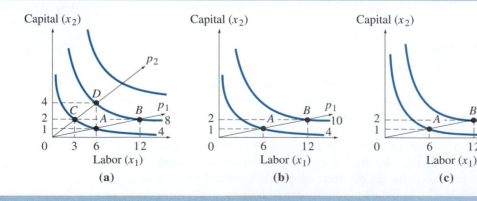

less than double our output. At point A, we produced 4 units of output, but after the doubling of the inputs, our output at point B is only 6 units.

Increasing returns to scale can arise for a number of reasons. One reason is that as the size of a firm and its output increase, workers are able to specialize in certain tasks, which increases their productivity. Another reason is that certain capital inputs do not make sense when used in small-scale production but will create great savings if they are used in large-scale production. For example, certain types of machinery are very efficient when used to produce large quantities, but they are too costly when production is limited to small quantities. The use of computerized procedures and other mass production techniques may be efficient only when the output level is large. Changes in physical conditions can also account for increasing returns to scale. For example, let us say that an oil pipeline company doubles the diameter of the pipe it uses to supply oil to customers, and the firm thereby more than doubles the flow of oil through the pipeline. If the pipeline is the only input to production, a doubling of the diameter of that input will lead to more than a doubling of output, which means increasing returns to scale.

SOLVED PROBLEM 8.2

Question (Extension and Application: Returns to Scale)

Consider the following three production functions:

$$q = f(K, L) = K^{1/2}L^{1/2}$$
$$q = f(K, L) = K^{1/4}L^{1/4}$$
$$q = f(K, L) = K^{2}L^{2}$$

Demonstrate that the first function has constant, the second has decreasing, and the third has increasing returns to scale.

Answer

If we double inputs and get double the output, we would say that there are constant returns to scale. Let's look at the first function. If we double inputs

$$f(2K, 2L) = (2K)^{1/2}(2L)^{1/2}$$
$$= 2K^{1/2}L^{1/2}$$
$$= 2q$$

we get twice the initial output. Hence, this particular function does have constant returns to scale.

If we double inputs and less than double our output, then we have decreasing returns to scale. For function 2, we see that

$$f(2K, 2L) = (2K)^{1/4}(2L)^{1/4}$$
$$= 2^{1/2}K^{1/4}L^{1/4}$$
$$< 2q$$

Therefore, this function has decreasing returns to scale.

If doubling the inputs more than doubles the output, we would say that we have increasing returns to scale. For function 3, if we double both inputs, then

$$f(2K, 2L) = (2K)^{2}(2L)^{2}$$
$$= 16K^{2}L^{2}$$
$$> 2q$$

Therefore, this function has increasing returns to scale.

All of the production functions are examples of what we will call Cobb-Douglas production functions. A simple rule to use to see if a Cobb-Douglas production function has increasing, constant, or decreasing returns to scale is to look at the sum of the exponents. If $\alpha + \beta > 1$, then returns are increasing; if $\alpha + \beta = 1$, then returns are constant; and if $\alpha + \beta < 1$, then returns are decreasing (where α is the exponent of K and β is the exponent of L).

SOLVED PROBLEM 8.3

Question (Extension and Application: Production and Returns to Scale)

Alpha Corporation employs a technology using inputs capital, K, and labor, L, to produce shirts. The technology is $q = K^2L^2$, where q is the number of shirts produced. Alpha Corporation needs to produce 10,000 shirts. It owns 10 factories currently, any one of which has enough capacity to produce the entire amount. Is Alpha Corporation better off producing the entire amount at one factory or splitting up production across several factories?

Answer

To answer this question, we do not have to know anything about the costs of the inputs; we need only look at the production function. Alpha's production function has increasing returns to scale. To see this, double the inputs and see by how much the output increases.

$$(2K)^2(2L)^2 = 2^2K^22^2L^2 = 16K^2L^2 = 16K^2L^2 = 16q$$

So, doubling the inputs multiplies the output by 16. Because the production function has increasing returns to scale, each additional unit of production is cheaper and cheaper to produce. Therefore, Alpha Corporation is better off producing all the shirts at one factory.

Elasticity of Substitution

elasticity of substitution
A measure of how easy it is to substitute one input for another in producing a given level of output.

Return to scale is one of two major attributes that economists use to characterize technologies. The other major attribute is elasticity of substitution, which measures how easy it is to substitute one input for another in producing a given level of output. Clearly, for a profit-maximizing enterprise, such a fact of technological life is important. As we will see in the next chapter, firms will want to produce given levels of outputs at the least possible cost and will want to adjust their use of inputs as the prices of the inputs change.

The elasticity of substitution measures the percentage change in the ratio of inputs used that will occur for a given percentage change in the ratio of input prices. For example, say there is only one process that will produce outputs, and this process involves the use of labor and capital in the ratio of 6:1. In such a case, we cannot substitute any units of labor for units of capital or vice versa. We must use the two inputs in exactly the specified proportion. As the prices of the inputs change, there will be no response in terms of the ratio of inputs used. The elasticity of substitution here is zero. On the other hand, if a 1% change in the ratio of input prices leads to a 1% change in the ratio in which these inputs are used, we would say that the elasticity of substitution is one. In the next chapter, we will investigate the concept of the elasticity of substitution more extensively.

Time Constraints

The Immediate Run, the Short Run, and the Long Run

Our ultimate goal in this chapter and the next is to determine the optimal combination of inputs to be used by our entrepreneur in her jam-making business and to determine how much output she should attempt to produce given the market price of jam. To find the most appropriate level of input and output, we must be more precise about the conditions she will face. We must know how much time she will have to adjust her inputs to their optimal level. For example, assume that at present she has one bowl available and that she has made contracts with six pickers to supply her with fruit. With this capital and labor, she can produce four pounds of jam a week. Also assume that there was a jam craze in our society during recent years, but this craze has ended and the demand for jam has greatly decreased. If we ask our entrepreneur how she will respond to this decreased demand *by tomorrow*, she will say that in such a short period of time she cannot change anything because she has a one-week contract with her pickers and she has recently made a new bowl. Hence, she will not be able to adjust her inputs at all. Producers may be faced with a period of time so short that they are unable to vary any of their inputs to meet changes in demand or other changes. We will call such a period of time the immediate run.

If given a longer period of time (say one week) in which to adjust input levels, our entrepreneur will be able to dispose of some units of labor (not renew the contracts of some of the pickers). However, she will not be able to do anything about the bowl—her capital—until the bowl wears out. During this week, capital is a fixed factor of production because its level cannot be adjusted, but labor is a variable factor of production because its level can be adjusted. The time period during which at least one factor of production is fixed is called the short run. In this case, the short run is a week. The period of time long enough to vary all factors of production (in this case, labor and capital) is called the long run.

The exact time periods covered by the immediate run, the short run, and the long run vary according to the circumstances of each producer. These periods also change as the circumstances of a producer change. For example, suppose that the pickers who work for our jam maker obtain one-month contracts rather than one-week contracts. This change will alter the period of time that constitutes the short run for our jam maker.

The Relationship Between Time Constraints and the Production Function

The reason we are discussing the concept of time constraints is that they have a dramatic effect on the manner in which our entrepreneur will decide on her optimal level of production. In fact, defining the period of time we are considering for such decisions helps define what we will call the short-run and long-run production functions. We will not discuss the immediate run any longer because this time period is too short to allow a producer to make decisions about inputs and outputs.

Remember that the production function we defined earlier, before introducing time constraints, permitted the producer to vary the levels of both inputs (labor and capital). We will now call this production function the long-run production function, reflecting the fact that the producer has a long enough period in which to adjust the inputs so that she can approach their optimal levels. However, with a short-run production function, the producer can change only one input—labor. Capital is a fixed factor. Our producer cannot add or subtract any units of capital. In contrast, labor is a variable factor in both a short-run and a long-run

immediate run
A period of time so short that producers are unable to vary any of their inputs to meet changes in demand or other changes.

fixed factor of production
A factor of production whose level cannot be adjusted in the time period under investigation.

variable factor of production
A factor of production whose level can be adjusted.

short run
The time period during which at least one factor of production is fixed.

long run
The period of time long enough to vary all factors of production.

long-run production function
The production function that allows the producer to vary the levels of all inputs in an effort to produce a given quantity.

short-run production function
The production function that allows the producer to vary the levels of some but not all inputs in an effort to produce a given quantity.

production function. Hence, during the short run, a producer has only partial control over input and therefore over the way she can achieve optimal output. With a fixed amount of capital, say $\bar{x}_2$, output can be decreased only by decreasing the number of units of labor. Figure 8.5 describes a short-run production function.

We know that not all input combinations in Figure 8.5 are available to us because production will occur during a time period so short that we cannot vary the amount of capital we use. In fact, our production possibilities are depicted solely by the set of input combinations that involve $\bar{x}_2$ units of capital. Such a set is shown by line $\bar{x}_2 B$ plotted on the floor of the input surface. The corresponding output is traced by curve $\bar{x}_2 C$. This curve is therefore the short-run production function for the units of output. Because the amount of capital is fixed, output is determined by the amount of labor used. Given that fact, we can plot the relationship between labor used and output (holding $\bar{x}_2$ or capital constant at $\bar{x}_2$). The resulting graph, which is called the total product curve, is shown in Figure 8.6.

In Figure 8.6, we see the relationship between labor used and output when *the amount of capital is constant.* As we would expect, when we increase the use of labor, the output produced increases. Initially, this growth in output occurs at an increasing rate—each additional worker adds more output than the previous one. However, when we reach point E, the growth in output takes place at a decreasing rate—each additional worker adds less output than did his or her predecessor. This change from an increasing to a decreasing rate of growth in output occurs because we are holding capital constant and are not allowing it to increase along with the labor used. Eventually, when we reach a certain number of units of labor, each

total product curve
The total product curve represents the amount of output that results as we add more and more units of a variable factor to the production of a good, holding one input constant—for example, how much output we get at different levels of labor inputs holding capital fixed at a given level.

Figure 8.5

Short-Run Production Function.

With the level of capital fixed at $\bar{x}_2$, the output level is a function solely of the level of labor.

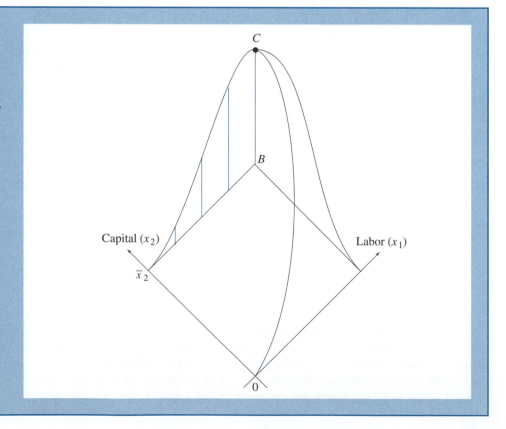

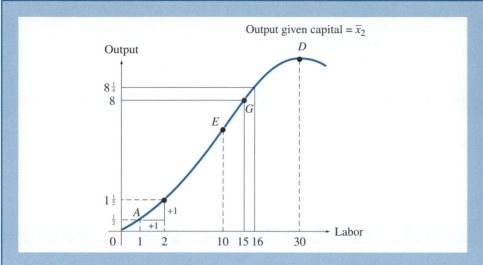

Figure 8.6

Short-Run Production Function in Labor-Output Space.

The level of the fixed input, capital, is suppressed.

additional unit becomes less crucial to the process of producing output *given that we have only a fixed amount of capital.*

The decrease in the rate that output grows when we increase the usage of labor but hold capital constant illustrates the principle of **decreasing returns to factor**. Note that this principle should not be confused with the principle of decreasing returns to scale of the technology because the latter is a long-run concept that describes what can happen to output as we increase *all* factors of production (labor and capital) in proportion. The concept of decreasing returns to a factor of production is a short-run concept that describes what happens to output when one factor of production is fixed and the other factor grows. (There are technologies that produce diminishing returns to each factor but increasing returns to scale.) Eventually, we may have so many units of labor that they actually begin to interfere with one another. When that point is reached, any more units of labor that we add will result in negative incremental output. Such a point is reached in Figure 8.6 at point D, where we see that after 30 units of labor have been used with $\bar{x}_2$ units of capital, the 31st unit actually reduces the output.

The increase in the amount of output produced that results when we add one more unit of labor but hold all other inputs constant is the definition we used earlier for the marginal product of labor. Note that this marginal product can be measured at any point by looking at the slope of the curve depicting the short-run production function. For example, in Figure 8.6 at point A, we see that when we increase the number of units of labor from 1 to 2, the amount of output we can expect to produce increases from $\frac{1}{2}$ unit to $1\frac{1}{2}$ units. Hence, the marginal product of the second unit of labor is 1, which means that the marginal product of the first unit must have been $\frac{1}{2}$. At point G, where we are already using 15 units of labor, the addition of a sixteenth unit only increases our output by $\frac{1}{4}$ of a unit. Clearly, Figure 8.6 depicts a technology in which the marginal product of 1 input (labor) at first increases and then decreases when we hold the other input (capital) constant.

Because the marginal product of labor is simply the slope of the short-run production function at any point, we can graph this **marginal product curve** just as we did the total product curve in Figure 8.6. Figure 8.7 depicts the marginal product curve. Comparing Figures 8.6 and 8.7 demonstrates the relationship between the total and marginal products. Figure 8.7 portrays what we will call the marginal

decreasing returns to factor
The decrease in the rate that output grows when we increase the usage of one factor but hold the usage of all others constant.

marginal product curve
The graph of the marginal product of a factor of production.

Figure 8.7

Marginal Product.

The slope of the short-run production function measures the change in the output level resulting from the introduction of 1 additional unit of the variable input—labor.

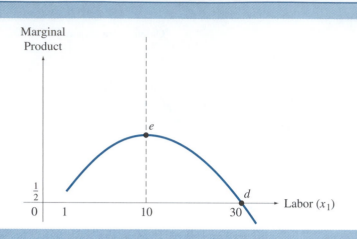

product curve associated with the short-run production function for the total product curve presented in Figure 8.6. Note that in Figure 8.6 as we add the first unit of labor, output increases by $\frac{1}{2}$ from 0 to $\frac{1}{2}$. When we add a second unit, output increases by 1 unit, which is a greater increase than the first. Hence, the rate of increase in the slope of the *total* product curve is increasing for the first unit of labor. In Figure 8.7, this fact is depicted by a positive value for the marginal product of the first unit of labor. The next unit of labor is even more productive, presumably because the two workers represented by these units of labor can use teamwork to make each of them more productive.

EXPERIMENTAL EVIDENCE

AN EXPERIMENT TO DO WITH YOUR FRIENDS

Here is an experiment you can do with your friends. The purpose is to explain what it means to have decreasing returns to a factor.

Place a stack of white paper and one pair of scissors on a table. Instruct your friends on how to make paper airplanes from the paper—a task that requires first cutting the paper down to the proper size with scissors, then folding it, and so on. (You must use the scissors; you cannot rip it with your hands.)

Now, when the experiment starts, just let the paper and the scissors sit there for 3 minutes. Count how many airplanes will be built. (Obviously, none.) Thus, you get zero output when you use no people. Now let one of your friends come up to the table and count how many of the airplanes he or she can make in 3 minutes. Next allow two people to come up and make airplanes and count their 3-minute output. Clearly, with two people you might be able to make more than twice the amount that only one person makes because one can

be cutting and the other folding. After 3 minutes, let three people come up, and so on. Remember that there will be only one pair of scissors. To record the data from the experiment, make a table that appears as follows:

EXPERIMENTAL TABLE	
People	Output/Three Minutes
0	
1	
2	
3	
4	
5	
6	
7	
8	

The question is, what do you think will happen to the rate at which output increases as you add more and more people but keep the number of scissors fixed at 1? What is the fixed factor?

Notice that the slope of the total product curve is steeper after we have added the first unit of labor. Hence, the point on the marginal product curve associated with this point is positive and higher than the point where the first unit of labor appears. As we continue to add more units of labor, each additional one is more productive than its predecessor until we reach point E in Figure 8.6 (point e in Figure 8.7) or until we have 10 units of labor. At that point, the last unit of labor is the most productive yet, but each successive unit of labor is less productive. Hence, after 10 units of labor, the marginal product curve falls continuously but is still positive until it reaches point D in Figure 8.6 (point d in Figure 8.7). At that point, the marginal product of the last unit of labor added (the 30th unit) is zero. If we add a 31st unit, it will actually reduce the amount of output produced, possibly because, as mentioned previously, the worker represented by this unit of labor might simply interfere with the other workers.

Question (Content Review: Production)

Consider the following table, which gives a snapshot of the production function of a firm:

SOLVED PROBLEM 8.4

Number of Machines, K	Number of Workers, L					
	1	2	3	4	5	6
1	110	195	235	270	300	310
2	160	235	280	302.5	317.5	330
3	200	265	300	317.5	327.5	332.5
4	230	275	315	335	345	350
5	245	300	327.5	342.5	352.5	355
6	255	315	332.5	345	355	356

The table has rows and columns, with the rows indicating how much capital is used and the columns indicating how much labor is used. The numbers in each cell tell you what output you would get if you used that amount of capital and labor. For example, with 3 machines and 1 unit of labor, you would get 200 units of output.

a) Is there increasing, decreasing, or constant returns to labor when capital is fixed at 3 machines? Where do you look to check?

Answer

When there are 3 machines, there are decreasing returns to labor. We see this by looking across row three and noticing that every time we add another worker (but keep the number of machines fixed at 3), we increase output but at a lesser and lesser rate. For example, holding capital fixed at 3, adding the second worker increases output by 65, but adding the third increases it only by 35. Thus, we have decreasing returns to the factor.

b) What is the average product of labor when there are 6 machines and 3 workers?

Answer

When there are 6 machines and 3 workers, their output is 332.5. So the average output per worker is $110.83 = \frac{332.5}{3}$.

c) Draw the short-run production function for this firm when capital is fixed at $K = 5$.

Answer

The short-run production function for the firm when capital is fixed at $K = 5$ is the total product of labor curve. This can be drawn by looking across the row associated with $K = 5$ and graphing the output for each unit of labor. The diagram appears as follows:

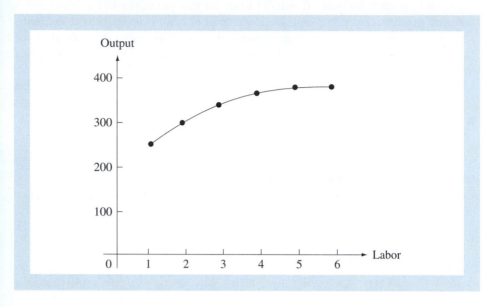

Conclusion

This chapter has laid the groundwork for an examination of questions about the optimal use of inputs and the profitability of an enterprise. We will use the analytical techniques presented in this chapter to answer the following questions about our entrepreneur's jam-making business in the next chapter: What is the optimal combination of inputs for her to use? How much output should she attempt to produce each week? Given the demand for her product, will she be able to operate profitably enough to stay in business, pay her pickers, and reimburse herself for the time she spends making jam each week (pay back her opportunity cost)?

Summary

This chapter has investigated the technology with which our entrepreneur can pursue her interests in producing a product. We have seen how the basic processes available to her to produce output combine to form a technology that can be described most succinctly as a production function. We examined this production function by using the concept of an isoquant, and we defined both the long-run and short-run forms of production functions. We also saw how the concepts of a total product curve and a marginal product curve are derived. Finally, we examined two important properties of a production function: returns to scale and elasticity of substitution.

APPENDIX A

THE PRODUCTION FUNCTION

As we noted in Chapter 5, a production function specifies the maximum output we get from given levels of input. It describes our technology. In this appendix, we illustrate some properties of production functions using the Cobb-Douglas production function, which is a commonly used specification for the production function in theoretical as well as in empirical work. We will look at returns to scale, elasticity of substitution, and interpretations of various properties of the production function.

The general form of the Cobb-Douglas production function is

$$Q = AK^\alpha L^\beta$$

where A is a positive constant, $0 < \alpha < 1$, $0 < \beta < 1$, and K is the amount of capital and L the amount of labor used to produce output Q.

Returns to Scale

The returns to scale of a production function indicate what happens to output when all units are increased proportionately. For the Cobb-Douglas production function, the returns to scale are simply equal to $\alpha + \beta$. More precisely, the Cobb-Douglas production function is homogeneous of degree $(\alpha + \beta)$. Suppose we change K to λK and L to λL; then, the new output $= A(\lambda K)^\alpha(\lambda L)^\beta = \lambda^{\alpha+\beta} \cdot AK^\alpha L^\beta = \lambda^{\alpha+\beta}Q$.

Further, if $\alpha + \beta = 1$, then the function is said to be linearly homogeneous and it has constant returns to scale. When $\alpha + \beta > 1$, then the production function has increasing returns to scale, and when $\alpha + \beta < 1$, it has decreasing returns to scale.

When the production function has constant returns to scale (CRS), we can write

$$Q = AK^\alpha L^{1-\alpha}$$

Marginal Rate of Technical Substitution

The marginal rate of technical substitution is the rate at which one input must be replaced by the other to maintain the same level of output. It describes the slope of the isoquant. To determine the marginal rate of technical substitution, we set the total derivative $dQ = 0$.

$$dQ = \frac{\partial Q}{\partial K}dK + \frac{\partial Q}{\partial L}dL = 0$$
$$\Rightarrow A\alpha K^{\alpha-1}L^{1-\alpha}dK + A(1-\alpha)K^\alpha L^{-\alpha}dL = 0$$

Hence, the absolute value of the marginal rate of technical substitution between capital and labor is (the absolute value of)

$$\frac{dK}{dL} = \left(\frac{1-\alpha}{\alpha}\right) \cdot \frac{K}{L}$$

Elasticity of Substitution

The elasticity of substitution also describes the substitution possibilities of a technology but does so in percentage terms rather than in absolute terms. It describes the curvature of the isoquant. The elasticity is measured by the following expression:

$$\varepsilon_{KL} = \frac{d\ln(K/L)}{d\ln(MRTS)}$$

The numerator of this term is

$$d\ln\left(\frac{K}{L}\right) = d\left(\frac{K}{L}\right) \bigg/ \frac{K}{L} = \frac{dK}{K} - \frac{dL}{L}$$

and the denominator of this term is

$$d\ln MRTS = \frac{dMRTS}{MRTS} = \frac{1-\alpha}{\alpha}\left(\frac{LdK - KdL}{L^2}\right) \bigg/ \frac{1-\alpha}{\alpha}\left(\frac{K}{L}\right)$$

$$\Rightarrow d\ln MRTS = \frac{dK}{K} - \frac{dL}{L}$$

Hence, the elasticity of substitution is unity for the Cobb-Douglas production function.

Properties of Cobb-Douglas Production Functions with Constant Returns to Scale

Consider once more the constant returns to scale Cobb-Douglas production function with $\alpha + \beta = 1$. In this case, we can write the production function in per capita terms as follows:

$$\text{Define } q = \frac{Q}{L} \quad \text{and} \quad k = \frac{K}{L}$$

Then

$$Q = A\left(\frac{K}{L}\right)^{\alpha} L^{\alpha}L^{1-\alpha} = ALk^{\alpha}$$

$$\Rightarrow q = \frac{Q}{L} = Ak^{\alpha}$$

The average products of the inputs are

$$APL = \frac{Q}{L} = Ak^{\alpha}$$

$$APK = \frac{Q}{K} = \frac{Q}{L}\frac{L}{K} = Ak^{\alpha}\frac{1}{k} = Ak^{\alpha-1}$$

The marginal products are

$$MPL = \frac{\partial Q}{\partial L} = AK^{\alpha}(1-\alpha)L^{-\alpha} = (1-\alpha)A\left(\frac{K}{L}\right)^{\alpha} = (1-\alpha)Ak^{\alpha}$$

$$MPK = \frac{\partial Q}{\partial K} = A\alpha K^{\alpha-1}L^{1-\alpha} = \alpha A\left(\frac{K}{L}\right)^{\alpha-1} = \alpha Ak^{\alpha-1}$$

Assume that each input is paid its marginal product. Then the share of capital in output is

$$\frac{K \cdot MPK}{Q} = \frac{\alpha KAk^{\alpha-1}}{LAk^{\alpha}} = \alpha$$

and the share of labor in output is

$$\frac{L \cdot MPL}{Q} = 1 - \alpha$$

Hence, the exponent of each input variable reflects that input's relative share in the total product.

The elasticity of output with respect to capital is

$$\varepsilon_{QK} = \frac{\partial Q}{\partial K} \bigg/ \frac{Q}{K} = \alpha$$

and the elasticity of output with respect to labor is

$$\varepsilon_{QL} = \frac{\partial Q}{\partial L} \bigg/ \frac{Q}{L} = 1 - \alpha$$

Hence, the exponents of each input variable also reflect the elasticity of output with respect to that input.

Finally, A is an efficiency parameter—it reflects the level of technology in the economy. Higher values of A imply that larger amounts are produced with the same input combination but have no impact on substitution possibilities or returns to scale.

Exercises and Problems

1. Consider a production function with the isoquant shown in Figure 8.8.

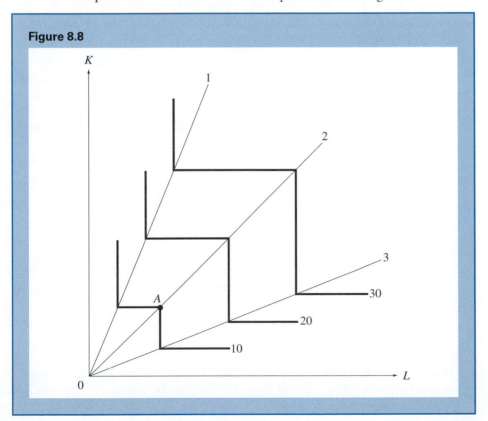

Figure 8.8

    a) What assumption or assumptions about technology does this production function violate?

    b) Is point A the efficient combination of inputs to choose for producing 10 units of output?

    c) Prove that the output expansion path will be either 1 or 3 for any set of prices.

    d) Prove that path 2 will never be used.

2. A good recipe for a French dish called ceviche requires 16 ounces of fillet of red snapper, 3 ounces of lime juice, 1 ounce of coriander, and 8 ounces of Bermuda onion. This combination of inputs is expressed in the following production function:

$$y = \text{Min} \left\{ \frac{z_1}{16}, \frac{z_2}{3}, z_3, \frac{z_4}{8} \right\}$$

In this production function, z_1 is fillet of red snapper, z_2 is lime juice, z_3 is coriander, and z_4 is Bermuda onion. The unit of measure for each input is the ounce, and the unit of measure for ceviche (the output) is the quantity produced by the recipe. If a restaurant has on hand 32 ounces of snapper, 9 ounces of lime juice, 5 ounces of coriander, and 48 ounces of onion, how many "units" of ceviche can it produce?

3. We can produce fasteners (Y) by combining nuts (Z_1) and bolts (Z_2). If the quantity of bolts is fixed at 10 units, the total production function is $Y = \text{Min} \{Z_1, 10\}$.

    a) In one diagram, graph the total product curve for the fasteners.

    b) In another diagram directly below the first one, graph the associated marginal product curve for the fasteners.

4. Construct a total product curve for a function that exhibits diminishing marginal product throughout. Then construct another total product curve for a function that exhibits initially constant and subsequently diminishing marginal product. Below the graphs of these two total product curves, derive the corresponding average and marginal functions. Check to see that the curves you have drawn are consistent with what you know about the relationship between the average and marginal product curves.

5. Assume that you have exactly 100 hours of labor to allocate between producing good X and good Y. Your output of goods X and Y depends solely on the hours of labor you spend in the following way:

$$X = \sqrt{L_X} \quad \text{and} \quad Y = \sqrt{L_Y}$$

    a) If you can sell your output of goods X and Y at the fixed prices $P_X = 10$ and $P_Y = 5$, how much of goods X and Y would you produce to maximize your profits?

    b) Now assume further that you have the following utility function:

$$U = 10\sqrt{X}\sqrt{Y}$$

If you can trade a bundle of goods X and Y that you produce in the market at fixed prices of $P_X = 10$ and $P_Y = 5$, what bundle would you produce and what bundle would you consume to maximize your utility? Are you a net demander and a net supplier of the two goods? Draw a diagram to depict what is happening.

6. Consider the isoquant map shown in Figure 8.9.

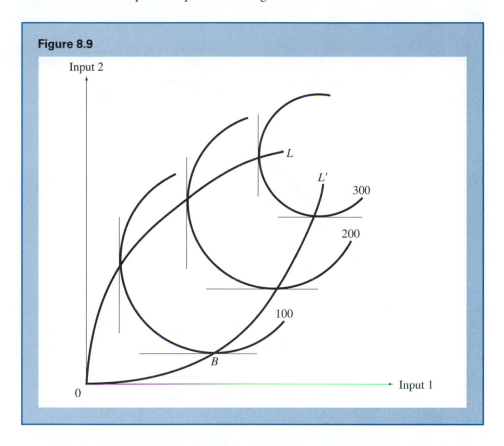

Figure 8.9

a) What is the marginal product of input 1 along line $0L'$? What is the marginal product of input 2 along line $0L$?

b) Why would it never be efficient to produce goods outside the lens-shaped area?

c) Would it ever be efficient to produce 100 units of output at point B? How would your answer change if you had already bought the amount of inputs 1 and 2 consistent with point B and there was no free disposability of inputs?

7. Are the returns to scale of the following production functions increasing, decreasing, or constant?

a) $Q = KL/4$

b) $Q = K + L$

c) $Q = Min(K/6, L/3)$

8. Consider Figure 8.10, which shows a short-run production function.

a) At what point is output per worker maximized in the short-run production function? Explain.

b) How much would the firm be willing to pay worker 101 to leave the job?

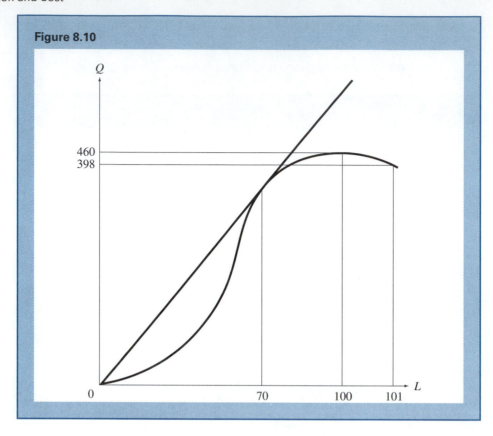

Figure 8.10

9. Which set of isoquants (*a*, *b*, or *c*) in Figure 8.11 shows the following: constant returns to scale? increasing returns to scale? decreasing returns to scale?

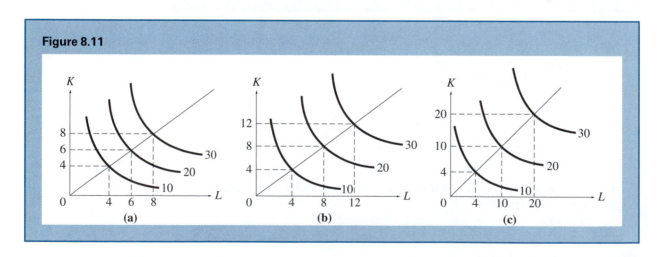

Figure 8.11

Cost and Choice

Just as we studied the theory of preferences in order to be able to derive a consumer's utility function, we also studied technology in order to study a firm's cost function. In this chapter, we use the theory of production developed in Chapter 8 to derive various types of cost functions for our budding entrepreneur. These cost functions serve as a shortcut for the technology used by the firm and allow it to decide how much output it will want to produce in an effort to maximize its profits. Because all of the firm's decisions will involve a balancing act between revenues on one hand and costs on the other, it is essential that we pause here and study the cost functions of a firm.

How Costs Are Related to Output

One fundamental question that any producer must answer is this: How are my costs related to my output? Obviously, determining the optimal output will require an understanding of the relationship between the cost of the output and the revenue (benefits) that will result when the output is sold. The demand curve for a product will tell us how much revenue the producer will receive by selling various quantities. (Remember that a demand curve indicates the quantity that consumers will buy at each price. We can determine the revenue the producer will receive by simply multiplying the price by the quantity.) Now we must derive a relationship between cost and quantity that will tell us how much it will cost to produce each quantity of a product. This relationship, which we will call a cost function, describes the *cheapest* or *most efficient* way to produce any given output.

cost function
The function that demonstrates the relationship between cost and quantity that will tell how much it will cost to produce each quantity of a product.

The Relationship Between Cost Functions and Production Functions: Production Functions with Fixed Proportions

The shape of a cost function is closely related to the type of production function available. For example, let us assume that the technology faced by our jam maker is such that she needs one picker and one bowl to produce each pound of jam. Let us also assume that there can be no substitution of bowls for pickers. Figure 9.1 depicts this technology. Note that because our jam maker needs pickers and bowls in a fixed, one-to-one proportion, her production function is represented by a series of isoquants, each of which is a right angle.

Let us now be more precise about the details of this jam-making technology. Each bowl takes a morning (five hours) to construct and will last only long enough to produce 1 pound of jam before falling apart. Gathering the fruit needed for 1 pound of jam requires the work of one picker for a morning. Thus, our producer will have to pay for one bowl and one picker in order to make each pound of jam. What is the cheapest way for her to obtain these inputs? Assume that our producer's

Figure 9.1

A Simplified Jam-Making Technology.

Production of 1 pound of jam requires 1 picker and 1 bowl, with no possibility of substitution.

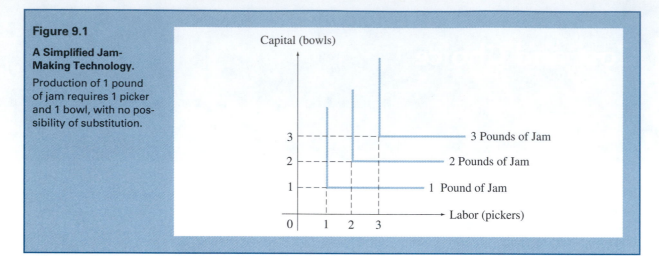

opportunity cost for constructing a bowl is $38 and assume that she can hire a laborer for $20 each morning ($4 an hour). The way for her to produce jam *most cheaply* is to hire one laborer to make the bowl and another laborer to pick the fruit, paying each of them $20 for a morning of work. It will therefore cost $40 to produce 1 pound of jam. Figure 9.2 depicts the cost function associated with this example.

Because the cost of producing 1 pound of jam (one unit of output) is $40, we can write the cost function for this example as shown below if we let X stand for the number of pounds of jam we want.

$$\text{Cost of Producing } X \text{ Pounds of Jam} = 40X$$

Obviously, if it costs $40 to produce 1 pound of jam, it will cost $120 to produce 3 pounds of jam and $400 to produce 10 pounds of jam. This example is very limited. It involves the cost function for only one specific production function, but its derivation raises some points that will be important when we study the derivation of cost functions in more general circumstances. One lesson that we can draw from this example concerns efficiency and the choices that producers make. Remember that cost functions define a relationship between cost and output that

Figure 9.2

The Cost Function for Our Simplified Jam-Making Technology.

With constant returns to scale and no substitution among inputs, the cost function is a straight line.

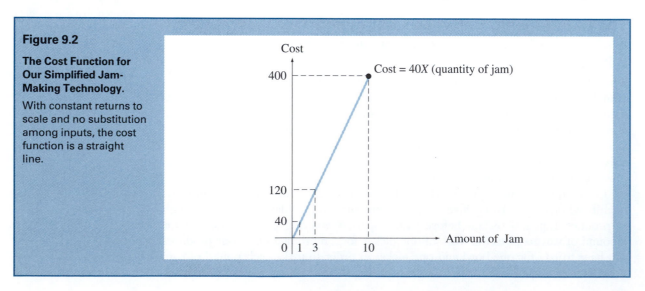

describes the *cheapest* or *most efficient* way to produce any given output. Thus, when we refer to a cost function, we are assuming that the producer wants to maximize profits and will therefore try to produce any given quantity at its lowest cost. This use of the lowest cost option is called "efficiency," and the cost curves for products are the loci of efficient points.

Another lesson that emerges from this example is that the effort to produce most cheaply involves finding the least-cost way to combine inputs in order to attain any given level of output. In our simple jam-making example, the producer had no choice as to how to combine inputs because the technology required the use of one bowl and one picker for each pound of jam. To put it another way, the elasticity of substitution in the technology was zero. If substitution possibilities had existed, then our producer would have had to know the right combination of inputs in order to produce each amount of jam in the most efficient manner.

Question (Content Review: Cost and Output)

SOLVED PROBLEM 9.1

Great Northern Steel must choose between two technologies to produce steel I-beams. Technology 1 is a Leontief technology, $q = \text{Min}\{2K, 3L\}$. This means that to find out how much output you'd get if you had, say, 5 units of capital and 3 units of labor, you find the minimum of 2(5) and 3(3), which is 9. So with 5 units of capital and 3 units of labor, you'd get $\text{Min}\{2 \cdot (5), 3 \cdot (3)\} = \text{Min}\{10, 9\} = 9$ units of output. Technology 2 is also Leontief, $q = \text{Min}\{K, 4L\}$. Great Northern must choose one of these technologies to produce 100 I-beams. Capital, K, and labor, L, both are priced at $10 per unit input. Which technology should Great Northern choose?

Answer

Both technologies are Leontief and are thus constant-returns-to-scale production functions. Looking at technology 1, we see that the cheapest way to produce one I-beam is to use $\frac{1}{2}$ unit of capital and $\frac{1}{3}$ unit of labor:

$$q = \text{Min}\left\{2\left(\frac{1}{2}\right), 3\left(\frac{1}{3}\right)\right\} = \text{Min}\{1, 1\} = 1$$

So to produce one I-beam, the cost is $10 \times \frac{1}{2} + \$10 \times \frac{1}{3} = \$8.33$. Because the technology is a constant-returns-to-scale production function, each I-beam costs the same amount to make. Thus, the total cost of producing 100 I-beams is $100 \times \$8.33 = \$833$.

The cheapest way to produce one unit with technology 2 is to use 1 unit of capital and $\frac{1}{4}$ unit of labor:

$$q = \text{Min}\left\{1, 4\left(\frac{1}{4}\right)\right\} = \text{Min}\{1, 1\} = 1$$

So to produce one I-beam with this technology, the cost is $10 \times 1 + \$10 \times \frac{1}{4} = \$12.50$. This means that 100 I-beams would cost $100 \times \$12.50 = \$1,250$ to produce. Therefore, given the prices of the inputs, technology 1 is the cheapest way to produce I-beams.

Let us now turn our attention to the derivation of cost functions for a general technology in which it is possible to substitute inputs for each other. We will see how our jam maker will find the optimal combination of inputs to produce her desired output. In discussing the derivation of cost functions for this producer, we will again use the more general terms *capital*, *labor*, and *output* rather than *bowls*, *pickers*, and *jam*.

The Optimal Combination of Inputs with Substitution Possibilities

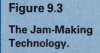

optimal combination of inputs
The mixture of inputs that produces a particular level of output at the lowest cost.

The optimal combination of inputs is the mixture of inputs that produces a particular level of output at the lowest cost. The optimal way to combine inputs to produce units of output will obviously depend on the time a producer has available to adjust her inputs. For example, assume that our jam maker is producing 12 units of output a week and suddenly decides to produce 35 units. If she cannot acquire additional capital fast enough, she will have to use her existing capital and merely hire more labor to produce more output. This may not be the most efficient—cheapest—way to produce output. However, if our producer has enough time, she will be able to acquire more capital *and* hire more labor, which will probably allow her to achieve her desired level of output at less cost.

Because the available time affects the choices that producers make, we will derive two types of cost functions: one for the long run and one for the short run. With the long-run cost function, we will be able to vary all inputs and will therefore seek the optimal combination of inputs in this context. With the short-run cost function, we will look for the least-cost way to produce any desired quantity of output *given that we cannot vary at least one input*. (In this case, the fixed input will be capital.)

The Optimal Combination of Inputs in the Long Run: Isocost Curves and Isoquants

Let us assume that a general production function describes the technological possibilities facing our jam maker as she attempts to produce units of output. Figure 9.3 portrays this production function as a set of isoquants. In our analysis of jam production, we will also assume that there are only two inputs: capital and labor.

As Figure 9.3 indicates, our jam maker can produce the same output using many different combinations of her two inputs. For example, we see that if she uses 3 units of capital and 9 units of labor, she can produce 7 units of output. She can

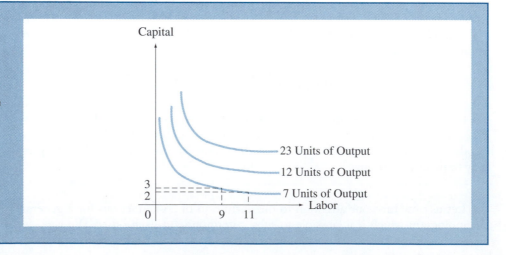

Figure 9.3

The Jam-Making Technology.

Each isoquant is the locus of capital-labor combinations yielding a particular output level.

also, however, produce 7 units of output with 2 units of capital and 11 units of labor. In fact, the isoquant labeled 7 depicts an infinite number of input combinations that she can use to produce 7 units of output. The question that our jam maker will inevitably ask herself is, If I want to produce 7 units of output, what is the least-cost combination of inputs that I can use? Clearly, the answer to this question will depend on the cost of the inputs. For example, if units of capital are free but units of labor are expensive (say capital magically appears), then certainly our jam producer will want to use many units of capital and few units of labor in order to produce output. In other words, she will want to *economize on the use of labor*.

We know the cost of inputs in the economy of our primitive society. For every unit of output (pound of jam), acquiring capital (to construct a bowl) and labor (to pick fruit) will cost $20 each ($4 an hour for five hours). Hence, units of capital are just as expensive as units of labor in this economy. The relative price of these inputs is depicted in Figure 9.4 as a series of lines stretching from the vertical axis to the horizontal axis.

Consider the line marked 400 (line *AB*) in Figure 9.4. All combinations of inputs along that line are equally expensive—they cost $400. The equation for line *AB* is therefore $w_c c + w_l l = 400$, where c and l denote the number of units of capital and labor used by the producer and w_c and w_l denote the prices or unit costs of capital and labor. The slope of line *AB* is $-w_l/w_c$, or -1 times the ratio of the unit costs of capital and labor. We call lines such as line *AB* isocost curves. (Remember that *iso* means "equal.")

Isocost curves show the various combinations of two inputs that can be purchased with a certain sum of money. For example, with $400, our jam maker can buy 20 units of capital and no units of labor (and be at point *A* on line *AB*), or she can buy 20 units of labor and no units of capital (and be at point *B*). She can also use $400 to buy 10 units of capital and 10 units of labor and be at point *C* on line *AB*. All combinations of two inputs along this line have the same cost, and hence line *AB* is an isocost curve. Note that isocost curves farther away from the origin have greater costs because they contain more inputs.

The slope of an isocost curve depicts the relative costs of the inputs (actually, the negative of the relative costs). On line *AB*, however, both inputs are equally costly. The ratio of the cost of labor to the cost of capital is therefore 1:1, which can be demonstrated by looking at point *A* on line *AB*, the isocost curve labeled 400. If our producer buys one less unit of capital (19 bowls instead of 20 bowls),

isocost curves
Curves in which all combinations of inputs on the curve are equally expensive. If input prices are fixed, such a curve is a straight line.

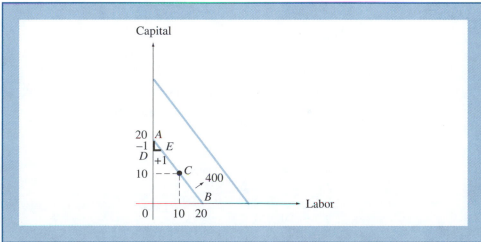

Figure 9.4

Isocost Curves and the Optimal Combination of Inputs.

Line *AB* is the locus of capital-labor combinations costing $400.

she will save $20 and move from point *A* to point *D*. If she then buys one unit of labor (so that she has one picker instead of zero pickers), it will cost her $20 and will move her from point *D* to point *E*. Hence, our producer will end up back on the 400 isocost curve. The slope of the curve is therefore −1, which represents the fact that whenever our producer gives up 1 unit of one type of input, she releases enough dollars to purchase 1 unit of the other type of input. Therefore, as we noted previously, we can say that the slope of the isocost curve equals −1 times the ratio of the costs of the inputs, or $-w_l/w_c$.

Figures 9.3 and 9.4 contain all the information we need to describe the optimal manner in which our jam maker can combine inputs in order to produce a given output. These figures also allow us to describe the cost associated with any given level of output. We can now state the following simple rule about optimal input combinations: In order to produce any given amount of output in the least-cost way, choose the combination of inputs that is located on the lowest isocost curve tangent to the isoquant associated with the desired level of output. Let us now examine this rule more closely. Consider Figure 9.5.

Figure 9.5 depicts several isoquants superimposed on a set of isocost curves. One isoquant depicts all the input combinations that will produce 25 units of output. We will assume that this is our jam maker's desired level of output.

Finding the Least-Cost Combination. To find the least-cost way to produce 25 units of output, let us start by looking at the isocost curve labeled 100. None of the input combinations along this curve contains enough inputs to produce 25 units of output. Now look at the isocost curve labeled 700. Clearly, there are two input combinations on this curve that will produce 25 units of output (points α and β). However, neither of these input combinations is the least-cost way to obtain the desired output because there are two input combinations on the isocost curve labeled 600 that will produce 25 units of output at a lower cost (points φ and λ). A look at point φ on the isocost curve labeled 500 reveals another input combination that will produce 25 units of output at an even lower cost. This must be the optimal input combination because no other input combination in the triangle *BAO* below the 500 isocost curve can produce 25 units of output, but any input combination above line *AB* must be on a higher isocost curve and hence must be more costly. We can see from Figure 9.5 that the least-cost input combination at point φ on the 500 isocost curve consists of 20 units of labor and 5 units of capital.

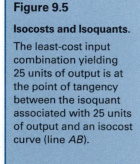

Figure 9.5

Isocosts and Isoquants.

The least-cost input combination yielding 25 units of output is at the point of tangency between the isoquant associated with 25 units of output and an isocost curve (line *AB*).

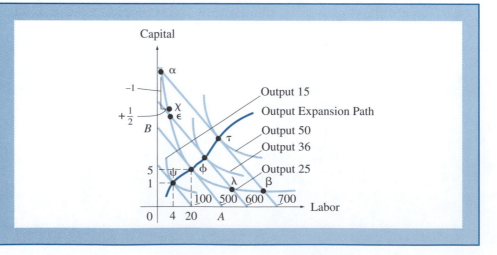

The Marginal Conditions for a Least-Cost Input Combination. Let us examine point φ a little more closely. As our rule about optimal input combinations states, φ is a point of tangency between the 500 isocost curve (the lowest isocost curve containing enough inputs to produce the desired output) and the isoquant for that level of output. What facts characterize this point? We know that the slope of the isocost curve at this point is equal to the negative of the relative input costs, or w_l/w_c. The slope of the isoquant at point φ is, as we saw in Chapter 8, −1 times the marginal rate of technical substitution of units of capital for units of labor, or the negative of the ratio of the marginal products of labor and capital at this point (marginal product of labor/marginal product of capital = [Δ output/Δ labor] ÷ [Δ output/Δ capital]). Hence, at the point of the optimal input combination, we know that the marginal rate of technical substitution equals the ratio of the prices of the inputs. We can express this relationship as follows:

$$MRTS_{capital/labor} = \frac{w_{labor}}{w_{capital}}$$

To understand why this condition must hold at the point of the optimal input combination, consider point α in Figure 9.5. As we discussed previously, the set of inputs at this point can produce 25 units of output. However, notice that our tangency condition is not satisfied. In fact, at point α, the ratio of the marginal products of labor and capital is greater than the ratio of the prices of these inputs. For the sake of argument, let us assume that at point α the marginal product of capital is 1, while the marginal product of an additional unit of labor is 2. Hence, $MP_{labor}/MP_{capital} = 2$. We know that the ratio of the input prices is 1:1. Hence, at point α, $2 = MP_{labor}/MP_{capital} > w_{labor}/w_{capital} = \frac{1}{1}$.

To show that point α cannot be a least-cost way to produce 25 units of output, let us say that we decide to use one less unit of capital. We will then save $20 and produce one less unit of output. However, because at point α the marginal product of an additional unit of labor is 2, we need buy only $\frac{1}{2}$ unit of labor in order to produce the output lost when we decide to use one less unit of capital. (We move from point α to point χ, in Figure 9.5.) Because $\frac{1}{2}$ unit of labor costs only $10, we see that if we were to move from α to χ, we would be able to produce the same 25 units of output and save $10. Hence, point α cannot contain the least-cost input combination because it is not a tangency point.

Question (Content Review: The Optimal Combination of Inputs)

Consider the following table showing the output associated with various combinations of inputs for a firm.

Number of Machines, K	NUMBER OF WORKERS, L					
	1	2	3	4	5	6
1	110	195	235	270	300	310
2	160	235	280	302.5	317.5	330
3	200	265	300	317.5	337.5	342.5
4	230	275	315	335	345	350
5	245	300	327.5	342.5	352.5	355
6	225	315	332.5	345	355	356

Look at the combination of 2 units of capital and 2 units of labor. We see that, given the technology, the firm can produce 235 units of output. If we define the marginal product of labor or capital at a given point as the additional amount of output that would be forthcoming if we added one more unit of either capital or labor, holding the other fixed, then

a) What is the marginal product of labor at the (2, 2) point?

Answer

The marginal product of labor at that point is 45 because when we add one more unit of labor (holding capital fixed at 2), we increase output from 235 to 280.

b) What is the marginal product of capital?

Answer

The marginal product of capital is 30 for analogous reasons. Output increases from 235 to 265 when the third machine is added, holding labor fixed at 2.

c) Note that there are two ways to produce exactly 235 units of output. Which way is more efficient if the price of capital, P_C, = 1 and the price of labor, P_L, = 2?

Answer

Obviously, the most efficient way to produce 235 units of output is to employ 2 units of capital and 2 units of labor because the alternative option—3 units of labor and 1 unit of capital—is more costly. Hence, the first method costs $6 and the second costs $7.

Deriving the Long-Run Cost Function. We now know that it will cost $500 for our jam maker to produce 25 units of output in the optimal or least-cost manner, using 20 units of labor and 5 units of capital. This fact appears in Figure 9.6, which shows the quantity of output on the horizontal axis and the cost of producing that output on the vertical axis.

The curve in Figure 9.6 depicts the long-run cost function faced by our jam maker. We have derived the first point on this cost curve by placing a ϕ at the coordinates (25, 500) to indicate that she needs 20 units of labor and 5 units of capital

Figure 9.6

A Long-Run Cost Function.

The long-run cost function associates the cost of the least-cost input combination, when all input levels are variable, with each possible level of output.

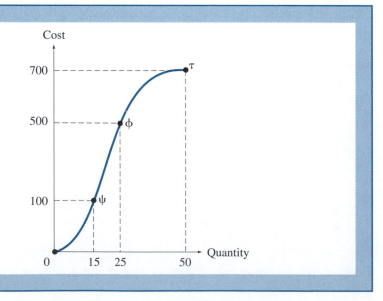

at a cost of $500 to produce 25 units of output. Now look back at Figure 9.5. Say that instead of 25 units, our jam maker wants to produce 15 units of output. As we can see from Figure 9.5, the optimal input combination for 15 units of output occurs at tangency point ψ. This input combination consists of 4 units of labor and 1 unit of capital and costs $100. In Figure 9.6, we can place another point, ψ, on the long-run cost curve to represent the least-cost way to produce 15 units of output. Now let us say that our jam maker wants to produce 50 units of output. Figure 9.5 tells us that the optimal input combination for this level of output is at tangency point τ and the associated cost is $700. We can therefore record point τ on the long-run cost curve in Figure 9.6. In a similar fashion, we can determine the least-cost way of producing any level of output.

Earlier, we defined the relationship between cost and quantity as the cost function. Note that, *given the input prices*, the curve containing the tangency points between the isocost curves and the isoquants (the dark line in Figure 9.5) represents the set of input combinations that produces any given output level at the least cost. This curve is called the output expansion path. A cost function is generated by placing a cost on each input combination and its associated output level. This function is the image of the expansion path in the cost-output space. Figure 9.6 presents the cost function associated with the technology described in Figure 9.5.

output expansion path
The curve containing the tangency points between the isocost curves and the isoquants, presenting the set of input combinations that produces any given output level at the least cost.

SOLVED PROBLEM 9.3

Question (Application and Extension: The Optimal Combination of Inputs)

Greenstreet Ltd. produces teapots. It has a production function $q = K^{1/2}L^{1/2}$, where K is the amount of capital used, L is the amount of labor, and q is the quantity of teapots produced. Labor costs $5 per unit, and capital costs $2 per unit. The marginal product of capital, given this production function, is $MPK = \frac{1}{2}K^{-1/2}L^{1/2}$. Greenstreet is currently employing 50 units of labor and 375 units of capital in production. Is Greenstreet producing efficiently?

Answer

Greenstreet is not producing efficiently. The marginal rate of technical substitution for this firm is

$$MRTS = \frac{MPL}{MPK} = \frac{\frac{1}{2}K^{1/2}L^{-1/2}}{\frac{1}{2}K^{-1/2}L^{1/2}} = \frac{K}{L} = \frac{375}{50} = 7.5$$

while the price ratio is

$$\frac{w_L}{w_K} = \frac{5}{2} = 2.5$$

Greenstreet could reallocate its inputs and produce more output but still incur the same cost as it currently is experiencing. Greenstreet is currently producing $50^{1/2} \times 375^{1/2} = 136.93$ teapots at a cost of $5 \times 50 + 2 \times 375 = $1,000$. If Greenstreet were to switch to using 250 units of capital and 100 units of labor, it would also be incurring a cost of $1,000 but would satisfy the efficiency condition because

$$MRTS = \frac{K}{L} = 2.5 = \frac{w_L}{w_K}$$

With this efficient combination of inputs, Greenstreet would be producing $100^{1/2} \times 250^{1/2} = 158.11$ teapots.

Figure 9.7

The Optimal Combination of Inputs in the Short Run.

Let relative input prices be given by the slope of isocost lines AA, $A'A'$, and so on, and let capital be fixed at $\bar{x}_2$ units. Then the least-cost way to produce a particular level of output, say 100 units, is with the number of units of labor given by the x_1 coordinate of point a on the lowest isocost line intersecting the isoquant corresponding to 100 units of output.

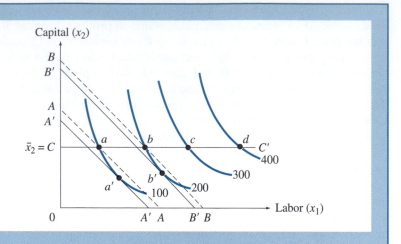

The Optimal Combination of Inputs in the Short Run

When a producer is operating in the short run, she does not have the flexibility to combine inputs in an optimal way as she would in the long run because at least one of her factors of production or inputs is fixed. In such a case, the producer finds the optimal input combination by using the smallest amounts of the variable factors of production—those that are not fixed and are therefore under her control—that yield the desired output level. We will explore the issue of short-run behavior more fully in Chapter 10, but for now let us look briefly at this issue by referring to Figure 9.7.

Figure 9.7 shows an isoquant map in which each of the isoquants is indexed to a different level of output. Along the vertical axis we see the amounts of capital (x_2) used in production, and along the horizontal axis we see the amounts of labor (x_1). Note that the capital is fixed at $\bar{x}_2$, and this fact is represented by the horizontal line CC'. To find the optimal combination of inputs to use in this short-run situation, we move along line CC'. For example, if the desired level of output is 100 units, then point a is the optimal input combination. This is true because the producer is constrained to choose points along line CC', and a is the first point along that line where 100 units can be produced.

Note that at point a the isoquant is not tangent to isocost curve AA, which goes through this point, so we know that point a cannot satisfy the marginal conditions for long-run optimum production outlined previously. In fact, in the long run, if both labor and capital can be varied, the producer will choose point a' as the point at which to produce 100 units of output. Point a' involves less cost because it is on isocost curve $A'A'$. This example demonstrates that producing in the short run is always at least as costly as producing in the long run and, in general, more costly.

The short-run cost function for this producer can be found by associating the cost of points a, b, c, d, and so on with the related outputs of 100 units, 200 units, 300 units, 400 units, and so on.

Special Technologies and Their Cost Functions

As we have just seen, the cost function of our jam maker's enterprise is closely related to the type of production function by which the firm is constrained. The reason is simple: Given fixed relative input prices, different production technologies will generate different output expansion paths and different cost functions. Let us now investigate some special types of production technologies and see how they result in different cost functions.

The Leontief Technology

Think of a technology as a simple process that uses 1 unit of capital and 6 units of labor in order to produce 1 unit of output. In other words, capital and labor must be used in the proportion of 1:6 in order to produce output. This type of production function is known as the Leontief production function.[1]

We can express this technology as follows if we let y denote the units of output and we let min( ) denote the minimum of the terms in parentheses.

$$y = \min\left(\frac{1}{6} \text{ labor}, \ 1 \text{ capital}\right)$$

What this technology tells us is that for any combination of inputs, we can find the amount of output that will be produced if we first take the number of units of capital we have and multiply it by 1 and then take the number of units of labor we have and multiply it by $\frac{1}{6}$. The resulting output is the smaller of these two numbers. To examine this technology more closely, let us consider Figure 9.8.

In Figure 9.8, we see the isoquants associated with the Leontief production function. Note that because the isoquants are right angles, there is only one efficient way to produce any given output—by using the capital and labor inputs in the ratio of 1:6. Look at point A, where we have 1 unit of capital and 6 units of labor and we produce 1 unit of output. $[y = \min((\frac{1}{6})6, 1(1)) = \min(1, 1) = 1]$.

At point B, we again have 1 unit of capital, but the amount of labor has increased to 8 units. This input combination produces 1 unit of output. Notice that even though we now have more labor, the output remains the same as it was at point A. Without more capital, the additional units of labor do not produce any more output. To put it another way, moving from point A to point B by adding more units of labor does not increase output. This behavior must mean that the marginal product of labor along the portion of the isoquant from A to B is constant and equal to zero. Similarly, when we move from point A to point D, the marginal product of capital is zero. We can therefore say that no substitution is available in this technology unless we use inputs in the proper proportions. Otherwise, the marginal product of additional inputs is zero.

Look again at Figure 9.8. To produce more output than the 1 unit we have at point A, we must add *both capital and labor* and we must maintain the ratio of 1:6 between these inputs. Thus, at point C we have 2 units of capital and 12 units of labor and produce 2 units of output.

As we discussed in Chapter 8, to describe a technology, we must calculate its returns to scale and its elasticity of substitution. Clearly, with the Leontief technology, we have constant returns to scale because doubling *all* inputs doubles the output (moving from point A to point C in Figure 9.8), while tripling all inputs triples the output (moving from point A to point E), and so on. It is also clear that the

Leontief production function
A production function in which inputs (capital and labor) must be used in a certain fixed proportion to produce output.

---

[1] The Leontief technology is named for the economist Wassily Leontief, a professor of economics at New York University, who was born in Russia in 1906. Leontief joined the faculty of Harvard University in 1931 and became a professor of economics there in 1946. He won the Nobel Prize in Economics in 1973. He is well known for his work on the interdependencies of the various sectors of an economy. He devised the technique of input-output analysis in which the interrelationships in an economy are represented by a set of linear production functions.

Figure 9.8

The Leontief Production Function.

With no possibility of input substitution, the isoquants are L-shaped.

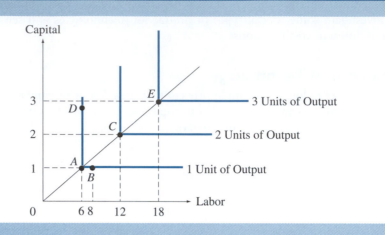

Leontief technology has a zero elasticity of substitution because it does not allow us to use inputs in any ratio except the ratio of 1:6.

The fact that the Leontief technology does not permit the substitution of capital for labor is disturbing. In the real world, not one but many processes are available to produce output, and each uses capital and labor in different proportions. We should therefore be able to substitute one input for another. However, the Leontief technology at least gives us a rough approximation of the constraints involved in producing output.

The Cost Function of the Leontief Technology. What kind of cost function would be related to a Leontief production function? To find the answer to this question, let us construct a cost function for the Leontief technology as we learned to do previously. Figure 9.9 depicts the isoquants for this type of production function along with a set of isocost curves. Given our cost assumptions, we know that the ratio of the cost of capital to the cost of labor is 1:1. Let us now determine the optimal combination of inputs to use in producing one unit of output—the input combination that will produce the output in the least-cost way.

Figure 9.9

Optimal Input Combinations in the Leontief Technology.

With L-shaped isoquants, there are no points of tangency between isoquants and isocost curves. The optimal input combination is at the corner of an isoquant (point A).

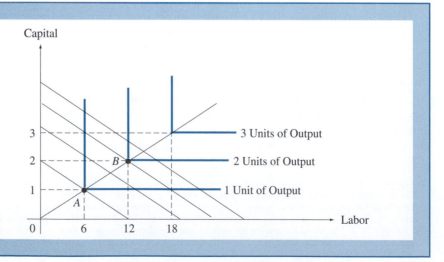

Previously, we said that the optimal input combination for a given amount of output is the one located on the lowest isocost curve tangent to the isoquant associated with the desired level of output. This input combination will be at a point where the marginal rate of technical substitution equals the ratio of the input prices. We can describe such a relationship as follows:

$$MRTS_{capital/labor} = \frac{\text{Marginal Product}_L}{\text{Marginal Product}_C} = \frac{w_L}{w_C}$$

Note that point A in Figure 9.9 cannot satisfy this condition of being the least-cost way to produce one unit of output. The curvature of the isoquant at point A is not tangent to the isocost line there and can never be tangent to it because the isoquant is at a right angle. In this case, we can generalize the condition of the optimal input combination by looking at the marginal rate of technical substitution to the left and to the right of point A. To the left, the isoquant is vertical, meaning that the marginal rate of substitution is infinite. To the right, the marginal rate of substitution is zero. At point A, we therefore have the following:

$$MRTS_{right\ of\ A} < \frac{w_{labor}}{w_{capital}} < MRTS_{left\ of\ A}$$

Point A satisfies this generalized condition. Because each of the inputs (capital and labor) costs \$20, the cost of producing 1 unit of output is $6(20) + 1(20) = 140$. Thus, we can now say that it costs \$140 to produce 1 unit of output in the least-cost way, using the Leontief technology. If our entrepreneur wants to produce 2 units of output, she can do this most cheaply at point B in Figure 9.9, where 12 units of labor and 2 units of capital are used. The output at this point will cost \$280 $(12(20) + 2(20) = 280)$. Note that with the Leontief technology, the output-expansion path is a straight line and the returns to scale are constant. Doubling each input doubles the output, tripling each input triples the output, and so on. The associated cost function must therefore be a straight line, as we see in Figure 9.10.

The Cobb-Douglas Technology

Clearly, the Leontief technology is very special. It assumes there is only one process for producing output and requires the use of capital and labor in a fixed ratio.

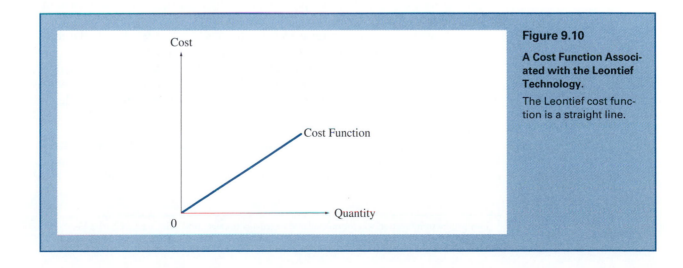

Figure 9.10

A Cost Function Associated with the Leontief Technology.

The Leontief cost function is a straight line.

Cobb-Douglas production function
A production function of the form (with two inputs, capital and labor)
$y = Kx_{capital}^{\alpha}x_{labor}^{\beta}$.

The Cobb-Douglas production function does not suffer from these drawbacks, so let us now turn our attention to this technology.[2]

Consider the following algebraic description of the output-producing technology:

$$y = Kx_{capital}^{\alpha}x_{labor}^{\beta}$$

In this expression, K is merely a constant that shows how productive the technology is because it multiplies the output produced using the inputs $x_{capital}$ and x_{labor}. The α and β are coefficients that will help us to represent certain facts about the technology, such as the elasticity of substitution and the returns to scale.

To illustrate what this Cobb-Douglas production function means, let us say that we have 9 units of labor and 1 unit of capital and that $\alpha = \frac{1}{2}, \beta = \frac{1}{2}$, and $K = 2$. Then we would produce the following amount of output:

$$y = 2(1)^{1/2}(9)^{1/2} = 6$$

In other words, if we use 9 units of labor and 1 unit of capital in this technology, we will obtain 6 units of output. Note that we can also produce 6 units of output by using 9 units of capital and 1 unit of labor, which indicates that substitution of inputs is possible with the Cobb-Douglas technology. Figure 9.11 illustrates what the isoquants for this technology look like.

If we examine the isoquants for the Cobb-Douglas production function in Figure 9.11, we see that point A contains the input combination of 9 units of labor and 1 unit of capital and is on the isoquant representing an output level of 6. We also see that point B uses 9 units of capital and only 1 unit of labor and produces the same 6 units of output. Note that point C is another location where we can produce 6 units of output, but in this case, we are using 81 units of labor and $\frac{1}{9}$ unit of capital because $y = 2(\frac{1}{9})^{1/2}(81)^{1/2} = 6$.

There are other interesting features of the Cobb-Douglas technology. For instance, given $\alpha = \frac{1}{2}$ and $\beta = \frac{1}{2}$, if we multiply each input by 2, our output will double because

$$y = K(2x_{capital})^{1/2}(2x_{labor})^{1/2} = (2)^{(1/2)+(1/2)}K(x_{capital})^{1/2}(x_{labor})^{1/2}$$
$$= 2K(x_{capital})^{1/2}(x_{labor})^{1/2}$$

Thus, if we use 9 units of labor and 1 unit of capital, we will obtain 6 units of output; and if we use 18 units of labor and 2 units of capital, we will obtain 12 units of output. In fact, any time we multiply our inputs by a factor λ, our output will increase by the same multiple. Hence, with a Cobb-Douglas technology, when $\alpha + \beta = 1$, we have constant returns to scale. Similarly, when $\alpha + \beta > 1$, the technology exhibits increasing returns to scale because the output increases by more than the factor used to multiply the inputs. For example, when $\alpha + \beta > 1$, we double our inputs, and the output more than doubles. The opposite is true when $\alpha + \beta < 1$. In that case, the technology exhibits decreasing returns to scale. In short, $\alpha + \beta$ is a measure of the returns to scale.

homothetic production function
A production function that has the property that whenever we multiply inputs by a factor λ, the marginal rate of technical substitution remains the same between all inputs.

The Cobb-Douglas Production Function as an Example of a Homothetic Production Function. The Cobb-Douglas production function is an example of a homothetic production function. Mathematically, a production function is

---

[2] This production function was formulated and tested against statistical evidence by Charles W. Cobb and Paul H. Douglas in 1928. Cobb was a mathematician at Amherst College, and Douglas was an economist at the University of Chicago. Douglas later became a U.S. Senator.

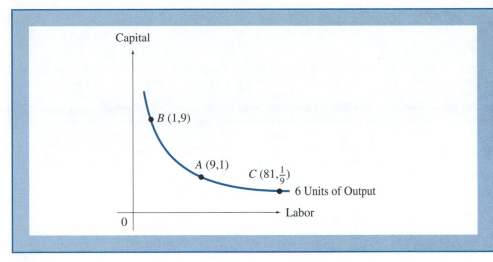

Figure 9.11

Isoquants Associated with the Cobb-Douglas Technology.

The possibility of input substitution at any input combination implies isoquants that are smooth curves bowed in toward the origin.

homothetic if, whenever we multiply its inputs by a factor λ, we simply obtain the same output we started with multiplied by some function of λ. To illustrate, let us say that we use 1 unit of labor and 9 units of capital as our inputs. The resulting output will then be $y = Kx_{capital}^{\alpha} x_{labor}^{\beta} = K9^{\alpha}1^{\beta}$. If we now multiply all inputs by λ, our units of output will be $Y = [\lambda^{\alpha+\beta}] K9^{\alpha}1^{\beta}$.

In short, when we multiply all our inputs by λ, we receive as output the same initial units, $K9^{\alpha}1^{\beta}$, multiplied by $[\lambda^{\alpha+\beta}]$. *When* $\alpha + \beta = 1$, multiplying our inputs by λ simply multiplies our output by λ as well. This particular type of homothetic production function is called a homogeneous production function, where the degree of homogeneity is $\alpha + \beta$. Hence, when $\alpha + \beta = 1$, the Cobb-Douglas production function exhibits constant returns to scale. It is a production function that is homogeneous to a degree of 1 because $\alpha + \beta = 1$.

The Relationship of Different Cobb-Douglas Production Functions to Their Associated Cost Functions.

Figure 9.12 shows three different representative Cobb-Douglas production functions. These production functions are labeled (a), (b), and (c). The associated cost functions for these production functions are labeled (d), (e), and (f).

In Figure 9.12(a) we see the isoquants of a Cobb-Douglas production function in which there are constant returns to scale ($\alpha + \beta = 1$). In fact, assume that $\alpha = \frac{1}{2}, \beta = \frac{1}{2}$, and $K = 2$. Figure 9.12(a) also depicts a set of isocost curves along each of which the cost is constant and the slope is -1. In this figure, we see that the least-cost way to produce 18 units of output occurs at point A, where the input combination is 9 units of labor and 9 units of capital. We know that point A is the least-cost way to obtain this output because the isoquant of the production function is tangent to the isocost curve (that is, the slopes of both equal -1).

If we double the inputs that appear at point A of Figure 9.12(a), we move to point B, where the inputs are 18 units of labor and 18 units of capital. This input combination produces 36 units of output, double the output we had at point A, which indicates constant returns to scale.

Also notice that because Cobb-Douglas production functions are homothetic, as we move out along a ray from the origin, such as the ray from 0 to point B, the marginal rate of technical substitution at any isoquant along the ray does not change. While point A, the least-cost way to produce 18 units of output, uses

homogeneous production function
A particular type of production function that has the property that whenever we multiply its inputs by a factor λ, we simply obtain the same output we started with multiplied by λ^K where K is the degree of homogeneity.

Figure 9.12

Cobb-Douglas Production Function.

(a) A Cobb-Douglas production function: constant returns to scale. Moving from point A to point B doubles both input levels and doubles the output level. (b) A Cobb-Douglas production function: increasing returns to scale. Moving from point A to point B doubles both input levels and more than doubles the output level. (c) A Cobb-Douglas production function: decreasing returns to scale. Moving from point A to point B doubles both input levels and less than doubles the output level. (d) A cost function associated with the Cobb-Douglas technology: constant returns to scale. Constant returns to scale imply a straight-line cost function. (e) A cost function associated with the Cobb-Douglas technology: increasing returns to scale. Increasing returns to scale imply a concave cost function. (f) A cost function associated with the Cobb-Douglas technology: decreasing returns to scale. Decreasing returns to scale imply a convex cost function.

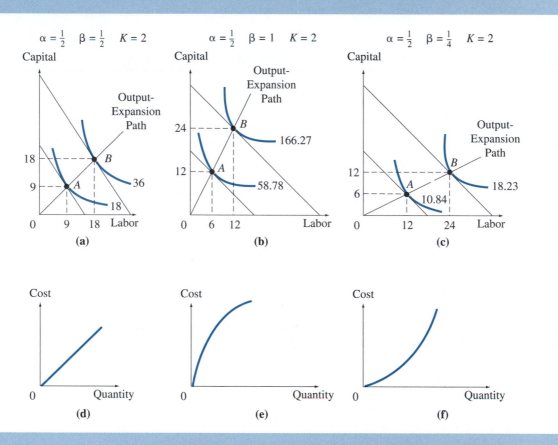

9 units of capital and 9 units of labor as inputs, point B, the least-cost way to produce 36 units of output, uses 18 units of capital and 18 units of labor as inputs. Thus, point B involves twice the inputs and twice the output of point A and is in fact tangent to the isocost curve. In short, the expansion path of any homothetic production function is a straight line from the origin, as we see in Figure 9.12(a).

Figure 9.12(d) depicts the cost function associated with the production function in (a). What we see in Figure 9.12(d) is a straight-line cost curve, which illustrates the fact that a constant-returns-to-scale production function will determine a linear total cost function. The reason that we have this type of cost function is simple.

If we double or triple all inputs in production in order to double or triple our output and if the relative prices of the inputs remain constant, then the multiplication of the output implies a comparable multiplication of costs.

Let us now look at the relationship between the production function depicted in Figure 9.12(b) and the cost function in (e). In (b) we have a Cobb-Douglas production function that displays increasing returns to scale ($\alpha + \beta > 1$). To be more precise, let us assume that $K = 2$ and $\alpha = \frac{1}{2}$, but $\beta = 1$. At point A of this figure, we use 12 units of capital and 6 units of labor to obtain 58.78 units of output. In addition, because the production function exhibits increasing returns to scale, when we double our inputs, we more than double our output. We can see this in Figure 9.12(b) by comparing points A and B. At point A we use 6 units of labor and 12 units of capital to produce 58.78 units of output. At point B we use twice as much of each input (12 units of labor and 24 units of capital) to produce more than twice as much output (166.27 units of output).

Figure 9.12(e) illustrates the effect of increasing returns to scale on the shape of the cost function associated with the Cobb-Douglas production function shown in (b). Note that while the cost function in (e) is increasing, it is doing so at a decreasing rate and is no longer linear, as it was when we had a production function with constant returns to scale (see Figure 9.12[d]). The reason the cost function has its present shape is obvious. Because the technology can double or triple output without doubling or tripling the inputs, at fixed input prices, costs will rise less than proportionately with the output. In short, when output doubles or triples but the inputs used less than double or triple, there is a saving on costs.

Figure 9.12(c) depicts a Cobb-Douglas production function with decreasing returns to scale ($\alpha + \beta > 1$), and Figure 9.12(f) illustrates the associated cost function. As we would expect, this production function and its cost function have features that are opposite to the ones we saw in (b) and (e), where the technology had increasing returns to scale and costs rose less than proportionately with output. In Figure 9.12(c), a comparison of points A and B shows that a doubling of inputs produces less than double the amount of output. As a result, when we look at the cost function in Figure 9.12(f), we see that cost rises at an increasing rate as we produce more output.

Question (Application and Extension: A Cobb-Douglas Production Function and Its Associated Costs)

The Ozzie Corporation produces plastic toy guitars using a Cobb-Douglas production function of the following type:

$$q = K^{1/2}L^{1/2}$$

Say the cost of capital is 4 and the price of labor is 2: $w_K = 4$, $w_L = 2$. Ozzie is offered an opportunity in the future to fill three contracts for 1,000, 2,000, and 5,000 guitars but does not know its cost of producing them. Derive its long-term costs for these quantities.

Answer

From Solved Problem 9.3, we know that with this Cobb-Douglas production function the marginal rate of technical substitution is $MRTS = K/L$. To produce efficiently, Ozzie must use inputs such that $MRTS = w_L/w_K = \frac{2}{4}$. In other words, because capital is twice as expensive as labor, for this production function Ozzie

SOLVED PROBLEM 9.4

will use twice as much labor as capital in its production. So to produce 1,000 units of output in the least-cost manner, it must satisfy two conditions:

$$q = K^{1/2}L^{1/2} = 1,000, \text{ and } L = 2K$$

Hence, substituting $2K$ for L, we find $q = K^{1/2}(2K)^{1/2} = K\sqrt{2} = 1000$, or $K = 1,000/\sqrt{2} \approx 707.21$. Therefore, in order to produce 1,000 guitars, Ozzie needs 707.21 units of capital. Because Ozzie will use twice as many units of labor, it will need approximately 1,414.42 units of labor. At a price of $4 per unit of capital and $2 per unit of labor, we see that the cost of 1,000 guitars is $2,828.84 + $2,828.84 = $5,657.68. To find the cost of producing 2,000 or 5,000 guitars, note that this production function has constant returns to scale. Hence, it will cost twice as much to produce 2,000 guitars and five times as much to produce 5,000, or $11,315.36 and $28,288.40, respectively.

The Elasticity of Substitution of the Cobb-Douglas Technology.
Because the Cobb-Douglas technology has substitution possibilities, it appears more realistic than the Leontief technology. However, we do not yet know exactly what these substitution possibilities are and why they are important. Therefore, let us now take a closer look at the elasticity of substitution of the Cobb-Douglas technology.

The Reasons for Input Substitution.
Why would a producer ever want to substitute capital for labor or labor for capital? Why not use the same ratio of capital to labor to produce any level of output, as in the Leontief technology? Because the relative prices of capital and labor may vary, producers sometimes want to change the combination of inputs they use to produce output so that they can continue to operate in the least-cost way. For example, if capital becomes very expensive and labor is cheap, a producer will want to use more units of labor and fewer units of capital *if the technology permits* this substitution. The elasticity of substitution, which we defined in Chapter 8, measures how freely we can vary our inputs as their relative prices change but the amount of output produced remains constant. Basically, the elasticity of substitution measures the percentage change in the ratio of the inputs used as the producer experiences a given percentage change in the ratio of the prices of the inputs. More precisely, if we let $k = x_{capital}/x_{labor}$ be the ratio of units of capital to units of labor used and if we let $w = w_{capital}/w_{labor}$ be the ratio of the prices of capital and labor, the elasticity of substitution, σ, can be written as shown below. Figure 9.13 illustrates the concept of elasticity of substitution.

$$\sigma = \frac{\left(\frac{\Delta k}{k}\right)}{\left(\frac{\Delta w}{w}\right)}$$

In Figure 9.13, we see one isoquant for a production function. If the prices of capital and labor are described by the slope of the isocost line marked $(w_c/w_l)^1$, then we know that point A is the least-cost way to produce the given level of output because, at the given prices, point A is the point of tangency between the isocost line and the isoquant lines. Note that at point A, capital and labor are used in the ratio indicated by $(x_c/x_l)^1$. This ratio is equal to the slope of line $0A$ because that slope equals $(CA/0C)$, where $CA = x_c^1$ and $0C = x_l^1$. At point B, we see a

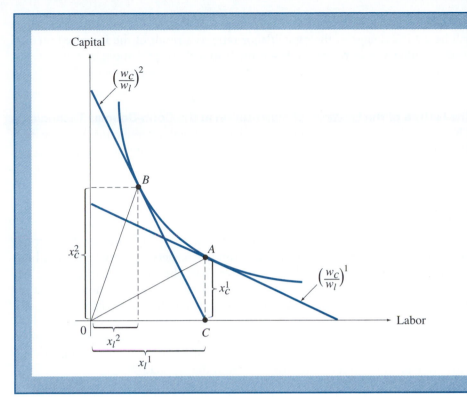

Figure 9.13

The Elasticity of Substitution.

For the Cobb-Douglas technology, the input ratio changes 1% in response to a 1% change in the input price ratio.

situation where prices have changed, as indicated by the isocost line marked $(w_c/w_l)^2$. So the input combination used now has a capital-to-labor ratio of $(x_c/x_l)^2$ as shown by the slope of line $0B$. The elasticity of substitution measures the percentage change in the ratio of inputs used in moving from $(x_c/x_l)^1$ to $(x_c/x_l)^2$ as prices changed from $(w_c/w_l)^1$ to $(w_c/w_l)^2$.

Question (Content Review: Elasticity of Substitution)

Let us assume that a corporation's output can be represented by a production function $q = f(K,L)$, where q is the output of the company and K and L are the amounts of capital and labor used. Let us say that at the present time, the capital/labor ratio used to produce the firm's current output level is $K/L = \frac{1}{3}$, while the ratio of the cost of capital to the cost of labor is 4:2. Say that the government decides to force firms to provide medical benefits for all of their workers—a legal requirement that will raise the cost of labor to the employer relative to capital by 10% (i.e., $\frac{\Delta w}{w}$ changes by 10%). If the elasticity of substitution of the production function is 1.5, how much will that change in the future the capital/labor ratio that the firm now uses to produce output?

Answer

The formula for the elasticity of substitution is

$$\sigma = \frac{\Delta k/k}{\Delta w/w}$$

where k is the capital/labor ratio and w is the ratio of capital costs to labor costs. From the problem, we know that $\sigma = 1.5$, while $\frac{\Delta w}{w} = 0.10$. Hence, we need only

SOLVED PROBLEM 9.5

solve for $\frac{\Delta k}{k}$ in the equation $1.5 = \frac{\Delta k/k}{.10} \Rightarrow \frac{\Delta k}{k} = 1.5 \cdot 0.10 = 0.15$. Therefore, there will be a 15% change in the capital/labor ratio as a result of the increased medical costs. In other words, relative to labor, the firm will use 15% more capital.

The Nature of the Elasticity of Substitution in the Cobb-Douglas Technology. The exact elasticity of substitution in a Cobb-Douglas production function is 1. More precisely, this means that a 1% change in the relative cost of the inputs will lead to a 1% change in the ratio of the inputs used.

Conclusion

All the pieces are beginning to fall into place for our jam maker as she attempts to become the first entrepreneur in our primitive society by starting its first business venture. In the previous chapter, we saw how she discovered the technology that she will use to produce her product. In this chapter, we saw how she learned to analyze costs so that she can produce efficiently and thereby maximize her profits. She is now able to derive the cost function associated with production, and she is able to find the least-cost way to produce at any given level of output. An understanding of technology and production costs will be of major importance to our entrepreneur as she prepares for her entry into the market.

Summary

In this chapter, we have discussed the cost and production concepts necessary to understand how to maximize profits by producing efficiently—in the least-cost way. We have examined the conditions that determine the optimal combination of inputs in both the short run and the long run. We have also discussed two special production technologies: the Leontief and Cobb-Douglas technologies. We have looked at the important properties of these technologies, such as their returns to scale and their elasticities of substitution, and we have examined the cost functions of these technologies.

APPENDIX A

THE COST FUNCTION

A cost function tells us the minimum cost necessary to produce a given level of output. (Note how similar cost functions are to the expenditure functions we studied in Chapter 5. Mathematically they are identical. Cost functions are calculated by solving a cost-minimization problem subject to the condition that the output is fixed at some level.)

Assume that the production technology is generalized Cobb-Douglas; that is, output $Y = AK^\alpha L^\beta$. Further, let W_1 be the cost of capital and W_2 be the wage rate, so that these are the factor prices. The total costs are therefore $W_1 K + W_2 L$. We assume that there are no fixed costs.

Then the cost-minimization problem is to choose the amounts of inputs K and L to minimize the total production costs of producing an output level $\overline{Y}$

subject to the constraints imposed by the production technology, namely, $\overline{Y} = AK^\alpha L^\beta$.

Formally, the problem is

$$\text{Min}_{(K,L)} \ W_1 K + W_2 L$$
$$\text{s.t. } \overline{Y} = AK^\alpha L^\beta$$

The Lagrangian for this problem is

$$\Im = W_1 K + W_2 L + \lambda(\overline{Y} - AK^\alpha L^\beta)$$

The first-order conditions are

$$\frac{\partial \Im}{\partial K} = 0 \Rightarrow W_1 = \lambda \alpha A K^{\alpha-1} L^\beta$$
$$\frac{\partial \Im}{\partial L} = 0 \Rightarrow W_2 = \lambda \beta A K^\alpha L^{\beta-1}$$
$$\frac{\partial \Im}{\partial \lambda} = 0 \Rightarrow \overline{Y} - AK^\alpha L^\beta = 0$$

which imply

$$\frac{W_1}{W_2} = \frac{\alpha}{\beta} \cdot \frac{L}{K}$$
$$\text{and } \overline{Y} = AK^\alpha L^\beta$$

Solving for K and L, we get

$$K = \left(\frac{\overline{Y}}{A}\right)^{1/(\alpha+\beta)} \left(\frac{\alpha}{\beta} \cdot \frac{W_2}{W_1}\right)^{\beta/(\alpha+\beta)}$$
$$L = \left(\frac{\overline{Y}}{A}\right)^{1/(\alpha+\beta)} \left(\frac{\beta}{\alpha} \cdot \frac{W_1}{W_2}\right)^{\alpha/(\alpha+\beta)}$$

Then the cost function is given by

$$C(\overline{Y}) = W_1 \left(\frac{\overline{Y}}{A}\right)^{1/(\alpha+\beta)} \left(\frac{\alpha}{\beta} \cdot \frac{W_2}{W_1}\right)^{\beta/(\alpha+\beta)} + W_2 \left(\frac{\overline{Y}}{A}\right)^{1/(\alpha+\beta)} \left(\frac{\beta}{\alpha} \cdot \frac{W_1}{W_2}\right)^{\alpha/(\alpha+\beta)}$$

While this may look complicated, it is simply a function telling us that if we specify the factor costs W_1 and W_2 and the output level $\overline{Y}$ we desire, then, given the technology as described by α and β, $C(\overline{Y})$ tells us the minimum cost needed to produce that output.

In the linearly homogeneous case, when $\alpha + \beta = 1$, $\beta = 1 - \alpha$, and $Y = AK^\alpha L^{1-\alpha}$, then

$$C(Y) = W_1 \frac{Y}{A} \left(\frac{\alpha}{1-\alpha} \cdot \frac{W_2}{W_1}\right)^{1-\alpha} + W_2 \frac{Y}{A} \left(\frac{1-\alpha}{\alpha} \cdot \frac{W_1}{W_2}\right)^{\alpha}$$
$$C(Y) = W_1^\alpha W_2^{1-\alpha} \frac{Y}{A} \left(\left(\frac{\alpha}{1-\alpha}\right)^{1-\alpha} + \left(\frac{1-\alpha}{\alpha}\right)^{\alpha}\right)$$

The cost function calculated above is the long-run cost function—in other words, it is the expression for the cost of producing output Y when both capital and labor are variable.

In the short run, one or the other (typically capital) is not variable; that is, $K = \overline{K}$. Hence, the cost-minimization problem becomes one of choosing the amounts of labor needed to

$$\text{Min}_{(L)}\ W_1 \overline{K} + W_2 L$$
$$\text{s.t.}\ Y = A\overline{K}^\alpha L^\beta$$

In this case, for any fixed Y and $\overline{K}$, we see that

$$L = \left(\frac{Y}{A\overline{K}^\alpha}\right)^{1/\beta}$$

Hence, the short-run cost function $C_{SR}(Y)$ is

$$C_{SR}(Y) = W_1 \overline{K} + W_2 \left(\frac{Y}{A\overline{K}^\alpha}\right)^{1/\beta}$$
$$= W_1 \overline{K} + W_2 \left(\frac{1}{A\overline{K}^\alpha}\right)^{1/\beta} Y^{1/\beta}$$
$$= \text{a fixed cost} + \text{a variable cost}$$

The short-run average cost is

$$SRAC(Y) = \frac{C_{SR}(Y)}{Y}$$
$$= \frac{W_1 \overline{K}}{Y} + \frac{W_2}{(A\overline{K}^\alpha)^{1/\beta}} Y^{1-\beta/\beta}$$

where the first term is the short-run average fixed cost and the second term is the short-run average variable cost. The short-run marginal cost is

$$SRMC(Y) = \frac{\partial}{\partial Y} C_{SR}(Y)$$
$$= \frac{W_2}{(A\overline{K}^\alpha)^{1/\beta}} Y^{(1-\beta)/\beta} \frac{1}{\beta}$$

Exercises and Problems

1. Assume that a firm produces 90 units of output using 9 units of input X and 9 units of input Y. The firm's technological possibilities can be represented by the production function $Q = 10X^{1/2}Y^{1/2}$, whose marginal products are $MP_x = \frac{Q}{2X}$ and $MP_y = \frac{Q}{2Y}$.

   a) If the price of X is \$8 and the price of Y is \$16, is the input combination of 9 units of X and 9 units of Y the most efficient way to produce 90 units of output?

   b) What must the *ratio* of input prices be for this input combination to be efficient?

   c) Assume that the price of X is \$1 and the price of Y is \$2. Derive the least-cost way to produce 400 units of output. (*Hint*: Remember that at an efficient input combination, the ratio of the marginal products—the marginal rate of technical substitution—equals the ratio of the input prices.)

2. A medical center produces health services using two inputs: hospital beds and labor. There is a government regulation restricting the number of beds to B. Assume that the medical center is currently using B beds and L units of labor to

produce Q_1 units of health services. Also assume that the medical center plans to expand its output to Q_2 units of health services. Prepare a diagram to show how this government regulation restricting the number of hospital beds would affect the efficiency of delivering health services. (*Hint*: Show the expansion paths with and without this government regulation.)

3. A college student is considering whether to operate a lawn-mowing business for the summer or work in a business owned by her family. Her time is worth $\$w_1$ per hour, and she can work as many hours as she chooses in the family business at this rate. If she starts her own business, she will have to buy gasoline for her lawn mower at a price of $\$w_2$ per gallon. She can rent a small mower for $\$w_3$ per hour. The mower cuts a 12-inch swath of lawn and uses $\frac{1}{3}$ gallon of gasoline per hour. With this mower, she can cut 10,000 square feet of lawn in an hour. (Use 10,000 square feet as the unit of measurement for output.) Our college student can rent a large mower for $\$w_4$ per hour. This mower uses 1 gallon of gasoline per hour and cuts 3 units of lawn per hour.

   a) Verify that the production functions for the two mowers are as follows:

   $$y = \text{Min}\{z, 3z_2, z_3\}$$
   $$y = 3 \cdot \text{Min}\{z_1, z_2, z_4\}$$

   Assume that z_1 is hours of labor, z_2 is gallons of gasoline, and z_3 and z_4 are the hours of the small mower and the large mower, respectively.

   b) Derive the cost functions.

   c) Show that using the small mower is a cheaper way to cut grass if $2w_1 < w_4 - 3w_3$. Why is this result *independent* of the price of gasoline?

   d) How high a price must our college student receive for cutting a unit of lawn in order to induce her to set up her own lawn-mowing firm rather than work in the family business?

4. Assume that a firm uses two types of input in the production of a certain commodity. What is the maximum output if the marginal product of input 1 is $MP_1 = 100X_2 - X_1$ and the marginal product of input 2 is $MP_2 = 100X_1 - X_2$, the total amount that can be spent on inputs is $\$1,000$, the price of input 1 is $\$2$, and the price of input 2 is $\$5$?

5. Suppose that a firm has long-run total costs of $\$1,000$ for producing 100 units of output. The two inputs for production are labor and capital. Labor costs $\$10$ per unit, and capital costs $\$10$ per unit. The firm is currently producing 100 units of output and is using the cost-minimizing combination of $50L$ and $50K$ for labor and capital.

   a) On an isoquant diagram, show that an increase in output from 100 units to 150 units will result in higher short-run than long-run total costs, average costs, and marginal costs.

   b) Show that a decrease in output from 100 units to 50 units will result in higher short-run than long-run total costs and average costs but higher long-run than short-run marginal costs.

   c) Give an intuitive explanation for these relationships between the short-run and long-run cost curves.

6. Suppose that a firm produces a product with two inputs: labor and capital. Labor costs $\$3$ per unit of input, and capital costs $\$5$ per unit. The firm maximizes output subject to the constraint that it does not spend more than $\$1,000$.

a) Draw a graph depicting the firm's cost constraint. Give the firm a set of convex isoquants, and show an optimum for the firm on the graph. Label the optimal quantities of capital and labor and the isoquant associated with the optimum so that the firm is producing 100 units of output.

b) Using the same isoquants that you used in part A, show an optimum for the firm that minimizes costs subject to the constraint that $y = 100$. What is the level of costs at the new optimum? How do the optimal quantities of capital and labor here compare to those you found in part A?

c) Suppose that the firm must pay higher wages, and its labor cost therefore rises to $5 per unit. Show the effect of this increase on the quantity of labor demanded under the following conditions:

   i. The firm maximizes output subject to the constraint that costs are $1,000.

   ii. The firm minimizes costs subject to the constraint that $y = 100$.

Cost Curves

Any economic decision is a balancing act between costs and benefits. If an appropriate decision is going to be made, we must have the right costs calculated. But as we have seen, decisions are made with different time horizons. Some decisions must be made in environments where certain factors of production are fixed, the short run, while others have the luxury of longer time horizons, the long run. Because different constraints are binding on the decision maker during these two different time frames, it is not surprising that short-run cost curves differ from their long-run counterparts. In this chapter, we study each type of curve. As you will see, these curves play a major role in our analysis of markets.

Short-Run and Long-Run Cost Functions

Fixed and Variable Costs

Let us return to the operations of our jam maker and assume that she must decide exactly how many units of capital to purchase for her next week's production. Remember that our jam maker's capital consists of bowls. Each bowl takes a morning to construct and can be used for just one week, no matter how intensively, before it becomes useless. Up until that time, it works perfectly (like the old One Horse Shay buggy that worked perfectly until the horse suddenly died). Therefore, once our jam maker commits herself to purchasing a certain amount of capital, the only way she will be able to increase her output during the next week will be to increase the amount of labor she uses. Hence, within any week, the cost of capital will be a fixed cost for our jam maker because it will not vary with the amount of output she attempts to produce. The cost of the labor, however, will be a variable cost because it will change according to how many units of output she attempts to produce.

Clearly, in the short run, jam production will involve both fixed costs and variable costs. Fixed costs are the costs of the fixed factors of production—the costs that do not change with the level of output. Our jam maker's fixed costs are the costs of the units of capital she must use during any week because she purchased them previously. Variable costs are the costs of the variable factors of production—the costs that change with the level of output. Our jam maker's variable costs are the costs of the units of labor she decides to use during any week. Of course, after each week's production is over, she will be able to change both the amount of capital and the amount of labor she uses, so in the long run, all costs will be variable.

In this case, the short run is one week and the long run is any period beyond a week. Our jam maker will have to investigate both her long-run and short-run cost functions so that she can behave rationally in both time periods.

In Figure 10.1, we see a representative production function. Say that at the beginning of a particular week, our jam maker has $\bar{x}$ units of capital that she purchased the previous week and has committed herself to using that amount in the production

fixed costs
The costs of the fixed factors of production; the costs that do not change with the level of output.
variable costs
The costs of the variable factors of production; the costs that change with the level of output.

Figure 10.1

Long- and Short-Run Production Functions.

(a) A long-run production function. In the long run, both inputs are variable and output is a function of capital as well as labor. (b) A short-run production function. In the short run, capital is fixed and output is a function only of labor.

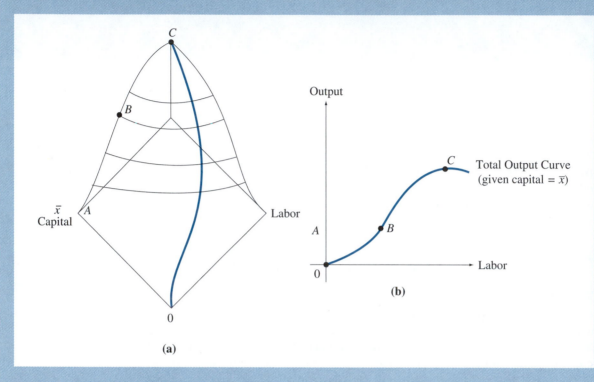

(a)

(b)

of jam this week. The curves labeled *ABC* in Figure 10.1(a) and 10.1(b) describe her short-run production function for the week. Labor and output have been plotted in Figure 10.1(b). Note that, with the amount of capital constant, our jam maker's short-run production function exhibits increasing returns to the use of labor until point *B* and decreasing returns to the use of labor thereafter.

Short-Run Cost Concepts

We can now describe a number of cost concepts that are relevant to our jam maker when she contemplates her behavior in the short run. First, let us construct a short-run total cost function that we can deduce from the short-run production function illustrated in Figure 10.1(b). Then we will construct a short-run marginal cost (SRMC) function (i.e., a function that indicates the incremental cost of producing the $q + 1$st unit of output given that we have already produced q units) and a short-run average cost (SRAC) function (i.e., a function that indicates the average cost of producing any q units of output). These three functions are presented in Figure 10.2.

short-run total cost function
A function that describes the total cost of producing any given level of output with a given fixed amount of capital.

The Short-Run Total Cost Function. The curve in Figure 10.2(a) represents a short-run total cost function—a function that describes the *total* cost of producing any given level of output with a given fixed amount of capital. Note that if our jam

Figure 10.2

Short-Run Cost Function.

(a) A short-run total cost function. Total cost is the sum of the fixed and variable costs. (b) Short-run marginal and average cost functions. Marginal cost is the slope of the total cost function. Average cost is the slope of the ray from the origin to a point on the total cost function.

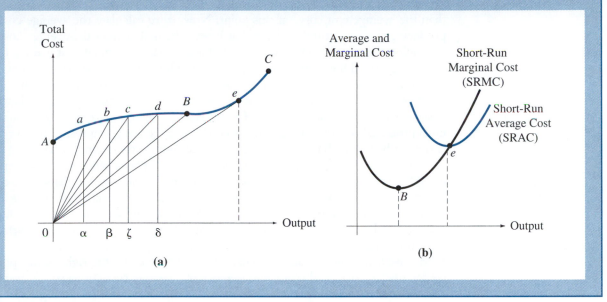

(a)

(b)

maker does not attempt to produce any output and therefore does not hire any labor, she still must pay for the capital she bought—her fixed costs. The magnitude of these fixed costs is represented by the height of the short-run total cost function at the point of zero units of output in Figure 10.2(a). If we want to find the average cost of producing α units of output, we will first look at the total cost of producing α, which is indicated by the distance α*a* in the diagram, and then we will divide that amount by the units of output produced, which is indicated by the distance 0α. The average cost is therefore total cost/total quantity or α*a*/0α. But α*a*/0α is nothing more than the slope of line 0*a* emanating from the origin and going through point *a*.

Note that in Figure 10.2(b), given the assumed technology, the short-run average cost curve is U-shaped just like the short-run marginal cost curve. This cost behavior can also be seen in Figure 10.2(a), where at low output levels, like β, the slope of line 0*b* is rather steep, meaning that the average cost is high. The reason for this type of cost behavior is that when we produce only a few units, much of the cost of each unit must be used to pay the fixed costs that we incurred. These fixed costs must be covered no matter how many units of output we produce. The average cost continues to fall as we move to output levels ζ and Δ (lines 0*c* and 0*d*) because the short-run marginal costs are falling here, and more important, we are now spreading the fixed costs over more and more units of output. The average cost of producing output is also equal to the marginal short-run cost at point *e* because, at this point, the slope of ray 0*e* is, in fact, the slope of the total cost curve.

Because average cost reaches its minimal level at point *e*, we can now state the following rule about the relationship between marginal and average costs: Given the assumed technology, the short-run average total cost of production is equal to the short-run marginal cost of production at that level of output where the average cost is minimized.

This relationship between marginal and average costs is easy to prove. Consider any output level y and calculate the average cost of production up to that point. If the next unit produced, $y + 1$, has a greater cost than the average of all other units produced up to that point, it means that the marginal cost of $y + 1$ is greater than the average of the first y. Hence, the marginal cost curve is higher than the average cost curve at this point. Now, if we calculate the average cost of producing the $y + 1$st unit, we see that it must be higher than the average cost of producing the yth unit whenever the $y + 1$st unit has a marginal cost greater than the average of all the units produced before it. Thus, when the short-run marginal cost of a unit is greater than the average cost (when the short-run marginal cost curve is above the average cost curve), the average cost must be rising. Likewise, when the short-run marginal cost of a unit is lower than the average cost of all the units produced before it, it must decrease the average cost. As a result, the average cost must be falling (but must still be above the short-run marginal cost).

To illustrate this point, let us consider a baseball player whose batting average is .300 over 50 games. If in the 51st game (the marginal game) he bats .500, then this marginal addition to his average will increase it. If our baseball player bats .200 in the 51st game, then his average will fall. Now consider a point where the short-run marginal and average cost curves are equal (see point e in Figure 10.2[b]). To the left of this point, we see that the marginal cost curve is below the average cost curve, and hence the average cost curve must be falling. To the right of this point, we see that the marginal cost curve is above the average cost curve, so the average cost curve must be rising. Because the average cost curve falls in the region to the left of the point where the two cost curves are equal and rises in the region to its right, the average cost curve must reach its minimum at this point.[1]

Types of Short-Run Average Cost Functions.

Types of Short-Run Average Cost Functions. Because the short run is the period of time during which fixed costs exist, we can define cost functions that relate to the fixed and variable costs incurred during this period. For example, in Figure 10.3, we have plotted the *short-run average fixed cost function* and *short-run average variable cost function* as well as the short-run average total cost function.

The short-run average fixed cost function is easily explained. Because the fixed costs of production do not change in the short run, the average fixed cost associated with any level of output is simply the total fixed cost divided by that number of units. As output increases, the average fixed cost associated with any given quantity decreases because we are simply dividing an unchanging total amount (the total fixed cost) by a larger and larger denominator. Eventually, as we produce more and more units, the component of the average cost of production that is attributable to the fixed cost falls to zero.

short-run average fixed cost function
The function that gives the average fixed cost associated with any level of output. Because the fixed costs of production do not change in the short run, the function is given by the total fixed cost divided by the number of units.

---

[1] A simple proof can be offered with the use of calculus. Let $C(q)$ be the total cost of producing quantity q. The average cost of producing any quantity q is therefore $AC = C(q)/q$. If we find that q is where the average cost is minimized, we then know that the following condition holds by simply differentiating AC with respect to q.

$$\frac{d(AC)}{dq} = \frac{dC}{dq} q - C(q) = 0, \;\; or \;\; \frac{dC}{dq} = \frac{C(q)}{q}$$

This condition simply means that at the quantity that minimizes the average cost of production, the marginal cost equals the average cost.

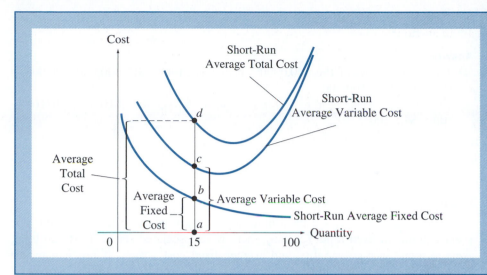

Figure 10.3

Some Short-Run Average Cost Curves.

Average fixed cost is always decreasing in output. Average variable and total costs may be U-shaped.

For instance, let us say that our jam maker purchases 1 unit of capital at a cost of $20 and intends to use this capital for her next week's production. Thus, her total fixed cost for the week will be $20. If she produces 1 unit of output during that week, then her average fixed cost will be $\frac{20}{1} = 20$. If she produces 2 units of output, her average fixed cost will be $\frac{20}{2} = 10$. If she produces 100 units of output, however, her average fixed cost will be only $\frac{20}{100} = 0.20$. This is a good example of why the average fixed cost curve asymptotically moves toward zero.

The remaining costs in the short run are the variable costs, which in our jam maker's case are the costs associated with labor. Because units of capital are fixed in number in the short run, the application of more and more units of labor means diminishing returns to the labor factor. It also means that the curve representing this short-run average variable cost function will have the U-shape that we observed previously. However, because the average total costs in the short run are simply the average fixed costs plus the average variable costs, any point on the curve representing the short-run average total cost function must be the vertical sum of the short-run average fixed and variable curves.

For example, let us look at our jam maker's average cost of producing 15 units of output in the short run. As we see in Figure 10.3, the distance *ab* represents the average fixed cost (average cost of capital) associated with that level of output, while the distance *ac* represents the average variable cost (average cost of labor). The distance *ad*, which is the average total cost, is equal to *ab* + *ac*. Note that when our jam maker produces 100 units of output, only a very small portion of her average total cost is attributable to fixed costs (or units of capital) because the costs incurred for the original units of capital are now spread over many units of output. This is why the average variable cost curve and the average total cost curve become closer and closer as the quantity of output increases—the average fixed cost is moving toward zero.

short-run average variable cost function A function describing the average cost of producing units of output counting only the cost of those factors of production that can vary in the short run.

Question (Content Review: Average Costs)

Suppose that it cost eBay, the online auction house, $10 million to get established. Also suppose that it currently has 100,000 auctions simultaneously occurring. Assume further that the marginal cost of adding another auction, once the basic programming is done, is $40. What is the average cost of the 100,000th auction?

SOLVED PROBLEM 10.1

What is the average cost of the 100th auction? What is the marginal cost of the 100th auction?

Answer

a) The average cost of the 100,000th auction is $140 = \$10,000,000/100,000 + 100,000 \times \$40/100,000$.

b) The average cost of the 100th auction is $100,040 = \$10,000,000/100 + 100 \times \$40/100$.

c) The marginal cost is $40.

Long-Run Cost Concepts

As we have seen, capital is a fixed input for our jam maker in the short run. For every amount of fixed input (capital), there is an associated set of short-run total, average total, average variable, and average fixed cost curves. If our jam maker knew exactly how many units of output she would produce before she purchased any capital, she would choose the amount of capital that would minimize the average cost of producing the output. For example, if she knew that she would be producing only a few units of output, she would purchase just a small amount of capital. Obviously, there is no point in bearing a very large fixed cost to produce only a few units of output. Similarly, if our jam maker knew that she would be producing many units of output, she would want to obtain many units of capital. With a substantial quantity of output, even a large fixed cost becomes insignificant. Let us use this logic and the technique of cost curve analysis to determine optimal amounts of capital for different levels of output. Consider Figures 10.4 and 10.5.

In Figure 10.4, we see a series of short-run cost functions, each of which is defined by a certain amount of capital. For example, curve 1 is the short-run total cost function that results from the use of 5 units of capital, curve 2 results from the use of 10 units of capital, and curve 3 results from the use of 15 units of capital. Note that for quantities of output below *a* units, it is cheaper to use 5 units of capital than 10 units or 15 units. Curves 2 and 3 involve too much fixed cost for a low level of output. It is not worthwhile to use capital so intensively with very small amounts of output. Between quantities *a* and *b*, we see that the optimal amount of capital is 10 units. When producing these increased quantities of output, it is cheaper to substitute capital for labor—to use more units of capital and fewer units

Figure 10.4

Short-Run Total Cost Functions and a Long-Run Total Cost Function.

Long-run cost is the minimum short-run cost of producing that quantity of output.

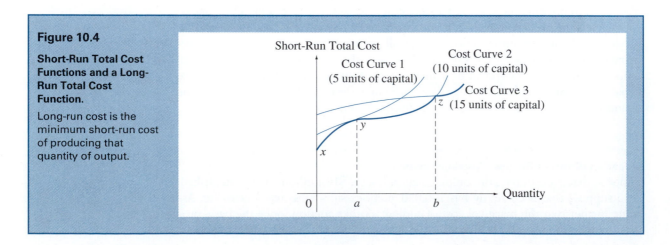

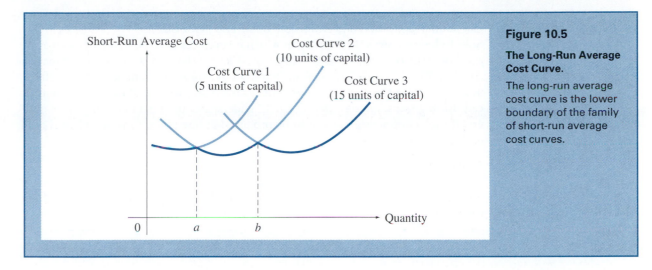

Figure 10.5

The Long-Run Average Cost Curve.

The long-run average cost curve is the lower boundary of the family of short-run average cost curves.

of labor. For quantities above *b*, it is cheaper to use 15 units of capital. When we say that it is "cheaper" to use one amount of capital rather than another, we mean that the average total cost of production is lower.

Now, look at Figure 10.5. Here we see the three average cost curves associated with the total cost curves for the three different amounts of capital. Note that for quantities of output below *a* units, the short-run average total cost curve associated with 5 units of capital is below the other two short-run average total cost curves. At point *a*, these two are equal so that for larger quantities we see that our jam maker will switch first to 10 units of capital and then at point *b* will switch to 15 units of capital. For every quantity of output desired, there is an optimal capital stock or number of units of capital that minimizes the average cost of producing the desired output. In other words, for every quantity of output, there is an optimal short-run total cost curve and average cost curve.

The Long-Run Total Cost Function. In the long run, we can vary the capital we use in order to choose the short-run average cost curve that we want to be on. What then do the long-run total, average, and marginal cost curves look like? In the long run, our total cost of producing any given quantity can never be greater than the cost of producing that amount in the short run because any combination of capital and labor that we use in the short run can also be used in the long run. Thus, the long-run curve lies below the short-run curve.

To better understand the meaning of this relationship between short-run and long-run costs, let us consider Figure 10.4 again. For quantities of output below *a*, the optimal amount of capital is 5 units. Thus, in the long run, if our jam maker knows that she wants to produce *a* units of output, she will purchase 5 units of capital. After *a*, she will switch to 10 units of capital and move along that curve until point *b*, where she will switch to 15 units of capital. The long-run total cost of producing any quantity of output is simply the smallest possible short-run total cost of producing that quantity. The long-run total cost function is therefore represented by curve *xyz*, which is made up of the minimal points of all the short-run total cost curves. Curve *xyz* has a scalloped shape only because we have assumed that there are just three quantities of capital available. Actually, if units of capital were infinitely divisible so that we could use any given amount, this curve, by a similar logic, would be smooth and upward sloping.

long-run total cost function
A function describing the total cost of producing units of output when no factor of production is fixed so that each can vary accordingly.

SOLVED PROBLEM 10.2

Question (Application and Extension: Costs and Plant Size)

Solo Industries owns three plants at which it produces gliders. Plant 1 has an average cost function $AC_1 = 200 - 24q + q^2$. Plant 2 has an average cost function $AC_2 = 200 - 32q + 2q^2$, and plant 3 has an average cost function $AC_3 = 200 - 40q + 3q^2$. Solo receives three different contracts to produce gliders. One contract calls for 8 gliders, the second calls for 12 gliders, and the final one calls for 18 gliders. If each contract's gliders must be produced at one plant, to which plant should each contract be assigned?

Answer

To assign each plant a contract, we want to see where it is cheapest to produce each contract. The following table represents the cost of filling each contract in each plant.

	THE AVERAGE COST OF FILLING CONTRACTS		
	Plant 1	Plant 2	Plant 3
Contract 1	72	72	72
Contract 2	56	104	152
Contract 3	92	272	452

Looking at the table, we see that Solo is indifferent as to which plant will produce contract 1 because the cost of producing gliders is the same (72) at all three plants. However, this is not the case for the other contracts. For them it is clear that producing contract 2 in plant 2 and contract 3 in plant 1 is best. So the cheapest way to fill the three contracts is to fill contract 1 in plant 3, contract 2 in plant 2, and contract 3 in plant 1 for a total cost of 268. Any other allocation is more costly.

---

long-run average cost function
A function describing the average cost of producing units of output when no factor of production is fixed so that each can vary accordingly.

long-run marginal cost function
A function describing the marginal cost of producing units of output when no factor of production is fixed so that each can vary accordingly.

short-run marginal cost function
A function that indicates the incremental cost of producing the $q + 1$st unit of output given that we have already produced q units.

The Long-Run Average Cost Function. The long-run average cost function (LRAC) is constructed in a way that is similar to the short-run average cost function. In Figure 10.5, we see a series of short-run average cost curves, each of which is associated with a different level of capital.

Again, if we want to produce a quantity of output equal to or less than a, we will choose 5 units of capital and be on the corresponding average cost curve. For quantities between a and b, we will choose 10 units of capital and be on the short-run average cost curve corresponding to that level of capital. We will follow the same procedure for larger quantities. In the long run, we can choose the short-run cost curve that we want to be on. Clearly, our jam maker will select the cost curve that will give her the lowest average cost in the long run. *The long-run cost curve is the lower boundary of a series of short-run cost curves* (see the dark curve in Figure 10.5).

The Long-Run Marginal Cost Function. Now that we have defined the long-run average cost function, we can define the long-run marginal cost function (LRMC) by logic similar to that used in deriving the short-run marginal cost function. We would expect the long-run marginal cost curve to intersect the long-run average cost curve at its lowest point. Such a curve is shown in Figure 10.6 along with a series of short-run average and marginal curves.

The question that remains is this: What is the relationship between the long-run and short-run marginal cost curves? This relationship can be defined as

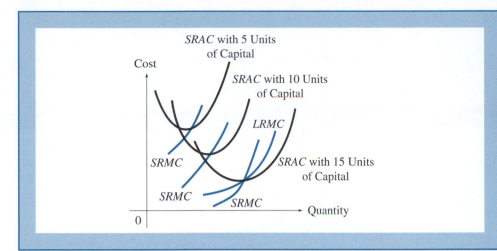

Figure 10.6

Long-Run and Short-Run Cost Functions.

The long-run marginal cost curve intersects the long-run average cost curve at its lowest point.

follows: At that quantity where the short-run average cost of production is equal to the long-run average cost of production, the long-run marginal cost of production equals the short-run marginal cost of production. For smaller quantities, the long-run marginal cost is greater than the short-run marginal cost; for larger quantities, the long-run marginal cost is less than the short-run marginal cost. We will use Figure 10.7 to explain this relationship.

In Figure 10.7, we again see a series of short-run average cost curves and an associated long-run average cost curve. Consider quantity a. At this quantity of output, we notice that the long-run average cost curve is tangent to the short-run average cost curve labeled $SRAC_1$. Thus, the long-run and short-run average costs for quantity a are equal, which is indicated by point A'. Directly below this point, the long-run and short-run marginal cost curves cross at point A. This intersection shows that the long-run and short-run marginal costs for quantity a are equal at point A. However, note that for smaller quantities of output (quantities below quantity a), the long-run marginal cost is above the short-run marginal cost; for larger quantities of output, we have the opposite situation. This is what our characterization of the relationship between long-run and short-run marginal cost curves means graphically. But why is it true? We can use Figure 10.8 to examine the reason.

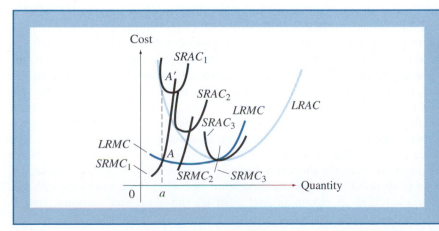

Figure 10.7

The Relationship between Long-Run and Short-Run Marginal Cost Functions.

At a quantity a, where $SRAC = LRAC$, it is also the case that $SRMC = LRMC$. At quantities below a, $SRMC < LRMC$, while at quantities above a, $SRMC > LRMC$.

Figure 10.8

Long-Run and Short-Run Marginal Costs.

The optimal long-run input combination is $\bar{z}$ units of labor and $\bar{x}$ units of capital yielding q' units of output. The short-run cost of increasing the quantity from q'' to q' is less than the long-run cost. In the short run, $\bar{x}$ units of capital are already available and the producer must only add more units of labor. In the long run, she must add more capital as well. The short-run cost of increasing the quantity from q' to q^* is greater than the long-run cost. In the long run, the producer will increase output by adjusting the capital optimally, but in the short run, she can adjust only labor.

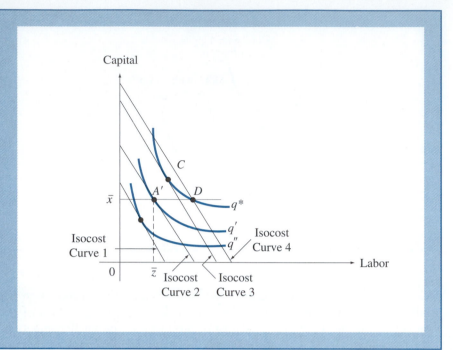

short-run expansion path
A curve that depicts the locus of labor-capital combinations that would be used to produce varying amounts of output in the short run when one factor is held constant.

In Figure 10.8, we see an enterprise with $\bar{x}$ units of capital. This means that in the short run, no matter how many units of output our entrepreneur wants to produce, she must use $\bar{x}$ units of capital. She can vary only the number of units of labor. Hence, the short-run expansion path for this situation is the straight dark line labeled $\bar{x}A'D$ because, given that $\bar{x}$ is fixed, $\bar{x}A'D$ depicts the locus of labor-capital combinations that would be used to produce varying amounts of output. The short-run expansion path is horizontal because we are not allowed to vary capital in the short run as we want to expand or contract our output. Now consider point A'. At that point, q' units of output are produced and the optimal long-run combination of inputs is $\bar{z}$ units of labor and $\bar{x}$ units of capital. Therefore, at this quantity, the optimal way to produce q' units of output is the same in the short run as in the long run, so the total and average costs must be equal here. Point A' in Figure 10.8 corresponds to point A' in Figure 10.7.

Now look at the isoquant associated with quantity q'' in Figure 10.8. This is the set of bundles that most efficiently can produce the output q'' given a production function. Any bundle along the isoquant produces that quantity. If we want to increase the quantity of output from q'' to q' in the long run, we will have to increase our inputs by adding more units of labor *and* more units of capital. In the short run, however, we already have the necessary amount of capital. Therefore, in the short run, to increase the quantity from q'' to q', we only need to add more units of labor. This is why for quantities of output below q', the short-run marginal cost is lower than the long-run marginal cost. In moving from q' to q^*, we see that in the long run we will go from point A' to point C and, hence, from isocost curve 2 to isocost curve 3. In the short run, because we have too few units of capital, we will move from point A' to point D and from isocost curve 2 to isocost curve 4. Thus, for quantities of output greater than q', the short-run marginal cost is greater than the long-run marginal cost.

Conclusion

Before our entrepreneur can actually start production, she must, in addition to knowing her cost situation, acquire knowledge of market strategy and planning. If she is going to succeed in the business world, producing efficiently will not be enough. She will have to learn how to think strategically in order to stay one step ahead of her competition. In the next chapter, we will examine a number of concepts from the theory of games that will be of great help to our entrepreneur when other firms are created and she must interact with these firms in the market.

Summary

As we have seen in this chapter, due to the different time horizons used in short- and long-run analyses, short- and long-run cost curves can differ. We have derived each of them and discussed their properties. As we have said before, because economic decisions are made by balancing costs and benefits (usually marginal costs and marginal benefits), it is important to make sure that for the problem at hand we are using the right cost concepts. The distinction between short- and long-run costs concepts is essential in this endeavor.

Exercises and Problems

1. A trucking firm's output is measured by the number m of truck-miles moved per day. The firm's operating costs are as follows:
    i. Wages of truckers, $\$w$ per hour
    ii. Cost of gasoline, $\$p$ per gallon
    iii. Fuel consumption, $g = A + Bs$, where g is gallons of gasoline per truck-mile, s is the speed at which a truck is driven, and A and B are constants
    a) Derive the total variable cost function of the firm if it has an unlimited number of trucks.
    b) What does the cost function look like if the firm has only one truck and that truck can be driven for a maximum of 10 hours per day?

2. Assume there is a fixed cost of $\$1,000$ for renting a computer chip plant. The first 300 chips are produced for $\$5$ each, and each additional unit after the first 300 chips costs $\$8$.
    a) What is the cost of producing 120 units?
    b) What is the average cost of producing the 150th computer chip?
    c) What is the average cost of producing the 400th computer chip?

3. Find the expression for the average fixed cost, average variable cost, and average cost functions where the total cost function is
    a) $TC = 3 + 4q$
    b) $TC = 10 + q^2$
    c) $TC = 100 - 3q + 10q^2$

4. Mutual Industries owns three plants at which it produces exactly the same cars. Plant 1 has cost function $TC_1 = 300 - 10q + 50q^2$. Plant 2 has cost function

$TC_2 = 50 + 10q^2$, and plant 3 has cost function $TC_3 = 1000 + 20q$. Mutual decides to produce 5 cars in the least costly way.

a) If only one plant is available for production, which plant will be chosen? Find its cost.

b) If production can take place in different plants, how many cars will be produced in each plant? Find the costs.

Decision Theory – Static and Dynamic Decisions

Hiring employees for a new or existing firm and dealing with them, trying to enter an industry currently dominated by another firm, exploiting the monopoly power of a new product, and trying to preserve market share by preventing other firms from entering one's industry are all situations that many entrepreneurs and corporate managers face in today's business world. As we will see, the first entrepreneur in our primitive society will soon have to cope with such situations. One way to handle these situations is to treat them as games of strategy played between a firm's management and its employees or between the managements of rival firms. In such games, each agent (player) takes one of several possible actions and then receives a payoff, which depends on the actions taken by all the agents involved in the game. In this section, we investigate the process of making decisions in strategic environments and environments in which one has to make decisions over time.

In Chapter 11, we will examine the theory of games and see how it is applied to many different types of situations. We will then use game theory as a major analytical tool throughout most of the remaining chapters of this book. In Chapter 12, we turn our attention to the problem of making decisions over time and discuss what new issues are introduced by the introduction of time. In Chapter 13, we give you a taste of what it is like to apply game theory to a problem by applying it to a problem that our entrepreneur of the last section will have to face—that of how to properly set up a firm and give the right incentives to workers.

Game Theory and the Tools of Strategic Business Analysis

BACKWARD INDUCTION

Consider the following game used in an experiment by Tom Palfrey and Richard McKelvey.*

In this game, two players alternate moves. At each stage a player can either move down (take) and stop the game or move to the right (pass) and allow the game to continue and let the other player make a move. On the first move player 1 can either move down and stop the game, which would determine payoffs of 0.40 for him- or herself, and 0.10 for player 2, or move right and let the game go to player 2, who also has the choice of moving down or to the right. If player 2 moves down, he or she gets 0.80 and player 1 gets 0.20. If player 2 moves to the right, player 1 will move again, etc. Note that the payoffs increase over time for both players, so if the game continues to the end, player 1 will earn 6.40 while player 2 will earn 1.60, which is better for both of them than stopping at move 1.

An experiment using this game was performed by Tom Palfrey and Richard McKelvey, and we will discuss their results later. For now, think of answering the following questions.

1. How would this game be played by two fully rational players who know the other is rational and know the other knows that he or she is rational? Would play continue to the end where both players will benefit, or will it stop sooner? Game theory predicts it will stop at the first stage. Why? Does trust have anything to do with how people play this game?

2. In the McKelvey-Palfrey experiment, what do you think happened? Does the particular one-shot game in which the players care only about their individual monetary returns accurately model behavior in this situation?

---

* Richard D. McKelvey and Thomas R. Palfrey, "An Experimental Study of the Centipede Game," *Econometrica* 60 (July 1992): no. 4, pp. 803–36.

In case you have not noticed by now, economics is about decision making. However, decision problems come in many stripes and colors. There are those problems, like ones we studied earlier in this book, where decision makers are asked to make choices in a world of perfect and complete information and certainty. The consumer choice problems we studied in Chapters 2–5 were like this. Then there are those choices that are made in a world of uncertainty (Chapters 6 and 7), where the decision makers are uncertain about some aspect of the world they are in but know the probabilities with which various events can occur. This is like a "game against nature" where you are playing an opponent who is indifferent to your welfare but who simply acts randomly in a prescribed manner. (You may think of playing roulette as a game against nature because whether you win is uncertain but you cannot say that the wheel being spun cares about whether you win or not.) Your task here is to choose optimally given the random nature of your opponent.

Finally, there are games of strategy. In games of strategy, you are in a decision making problem under uncertainty, but the uncertainty involves the actions of a real, live opponent who is out to maximize his or her payoff and who may or may not care about your welfare. So in these situations, you cannot act optimally until you make a conjecture about what your opponents are likely to do, and they must make a conjecture about not only what you are likely to do but what they think you think they are likely to do, etc. The central question of games of strategy is where this "I think that he thinks that I think" process will end.

Game theory allows us to describe and analyze social and economic situations as if they were games of strategy. We will therefore begin this chapter by defining what a game of strategy is and discussing how we would expect any such game to be played by rational economic agents. We will find that game theory makes it possible to predict the *equilibria* for games—those states in which no player will want to change his or her behavior given the behavior of the other players in the game.

There are several different types of equilibria for games. However, in this chapter, we will concentrate on equilibria that are sustained by credible threats made by the players. Economists use the term *subgame perfect equilibria* to describe such equilibria for reasons that will become clear as we proceed. We will also distinguish between different types of games depending on the information available to the players. We will identify games of *complete* and *incomplete information* (see Appendix) and games of *perfect* and *imperfect information*.

At various points in the chapter, we will also discuss the results of laboratory experiments conducted by economists to test game theory.

MEDIA NOTE

PRACTICAL GAME THEORY

Take a classic economic textbook example of a market. In these cases firms are usually passive entities that make decisions solely on cost/benefits analyses. Apply this way of thinking to the real world and you are bound to fail. Firms are not passive. They are constantly changing strategies either to take advantage of a situation or as an answer to some other competitor action. Take, for example, the company Square D, a player in the commercial buildings components market. This company had an innovative procedure that would enable it to be ahead of the competition. But the procedure needed time to be implemented, and secrets like that are hard to keep in the business world. What should a company that needs some time do? It had chosen to plant false rumors and information in the newspapers in order to throw the competitors off course. This move was a success. Using cost/benefit analyses wouldn't have suggested such a strategy.

This is where game theory comes into play. When using game theory, managers have to take into account the effects of their actions on the other players in the markets. How will the other player react? Also, managers can use game theory analysis to gain an insight into what is the best answer to threats made by other firms.

Adam Brandenburger, an economist at NYU's Stern School of Business, argues that game theory can also do something far more powerful. Using scenarios, it can help managers imagine how their industry would evolve if they were not part of it. This makes them aware of what it is that they in particular have to offer, while reminding them of other firms' strengths.

An insight like this can bring cooperative rivalry between firms. Take, for example, the companies Oracle, Netscape, and Sun, which are pushing the standardization of the Java programming language. The success of it will enable these three firms to open a bigger market for their products (network computing) while slowing their rivals (Microsoft). While this doesn't mean that firms that think this way always come out on top, game theory does allow a fresher look on the market, thus discovering new business opportunities.

Source: Adapted from "Movers and Shakers," as appeared in *The Economist,* January 22, 1998

Games of Strategy Defined

What do we mean by a game of strategy?[1] A person is engaged in a game of strategy with someone else (or with several other people) when his utility or payoff is affected not only by the actions that he takes but also by the actions that his opponents take. For example, chess is obviously a game of strategy because whether a player wins, loses, or draws depends not only on his choices but also on those of his opponent. Many economic situations can also be viewed as games of strategy. For example, the profits of an automobile company like Ford depend not only on its own pricing decisions but also on the pricing decisions of its competitors such as General Motors, Chrysler, Honda, and Toyota. Similarly, political conflicts often have the characteristics of games of strategy. For example, before and during the Persian Gulf War of 1991, Saddam Hussein's prestige depended not only on his military actions but also on those of President George Bush and the other leaders of the United Nations coalition.

More precisely, a game of strategy is an abstract set of rules that constrains the behavior of players and defines outcomes on the basis of the actions taken by the players. Under this interpretation, the game *is* the rules, and in order to have a well-defined game of strategy, we must have a well-defined set of rules constraining people's actions. What must these rules specify? First, they must tell us who the players are and whether chance will have a role in the game (such as in the shuffling of a deck of cards before a poker game). When chance does have a role and will therefore affect the outcome of a game, it is common to view this role as the moves of an imaginary "chance player." (For example, we might consider poker as a game in which the chance player makes moves by determining the cards held by the real players, who make their moves by placing bets, and so on.)

The rules of a game of strategy must also tell us the order in which the players will make their moves and the choices that will be available to the players. We must know who will move first, who will move second, and so on; and we must know what choices each player will have when his turn to move comes up. We must also know what information the players will have when they make their moves. Finally, the rules of a game of strategy must tell us how much utility each player will receive depending on the choices of all the players in the game. When we buy a board game like Monopoly, the accompanying instructions give us this type of information.

game of strategy
A multiperson decision problem in which an abstract set of rules constrains the behavior of players and defines outcomes on the basis of the actions taken by the players.

Using Game Trees to Describe Games

The rules and payoff contingencies of a game can be presented by using what game theorists call a game tree. This diagram provides a detailed description of the rules of the game and is therefore known as the game's extensive form. To understand how a game tree or extensive form represents the rules of a game, consider the following simple example.

game tree
A visual depiction of an extensive form game that presents the rules and payoff contingencies of the game.
extensive form
A description of a game of strategy that provides a detailed description of the rules of the game.

---

[1] The theory of games was first applied to economics by John von Neumann and Oskar Morgenstern in *The Theory of Games and Economic Behavior* (Princeton, NJ: Princeton University Press, 1944). Von Neumann (1903–1957) was a mathematician at the Institute of Advanced Study in Princeton, and Morgenstern (1902–1977) was an economist at Princeton University. Von Neumann invented game theory in 1928 when he proved his famous mini-max theorem.

Example 11.1

IBM VERSUS TOSHIBA: THE RULES OF THE "OPERATING SYSTEM GAME"

Let us assume that there are only two computer companies in the world, IBM and Toshiba. In producing their computers, these companies must decide whether to make their machines compatible with each other by using the same operating system, such as DOS or UNIX. Clearly, compatibility would be beneficial to both companies because it would allow them to sell their peripherals, such as disk drives, to accompany the other firm's computers. However, because of the way the two companies have developed their products in the past, each would like the other to adjust to its computer environment in order to achieve compatibility. For example, say that IBM would prefer to use DOS and Toshiba would prefer to use UNIX.

To describe the game played between these two companies, let us say that IBM has a head start on Toshiba in developing its new computer and can announce this product in advance of Toshiba. Therefore, say that on January 3 of a given year, IBM holds a news conference and commits itself to use either a DOS or UNIX operating system. After hearing IBM's commitment, Toshiba decides to hold a news conference in March and announce its own plans. Once both companies have made their commitments, production plans will be set. The payoff for each of the corporate players in this game will be as follows. If both use DOS, the outcome will be a victory for IBM because its operating system will become the industry standard. If both companies select UNIX, Toshiba will do relatively better. However, no matter which operating system the two companies choose, it is important that they make the same selection because compatibility of their computers is better for both of them than noncompatibility.

To make the consequences of these decisions clear, let us assume that if both IBM and Toshiba choose the DOS system, IBM will earn $600 million and Toshiba will earn $200 million. If they both use Toshiba's version of the UNIX system, Toshiba will earn $600 million and IBM will earn only $200 million. If they do not choose the same operating system and, as a result, their equipment is not compatible, we will assume that each will earn only $100 million. Figure 11.1(a) contains a game tree that portrays this strategic situation or *game*.

The game tree in Figure 11.1(a) describes all the rules of the game involving the choice of the new operating system. Note that the game tree informs us who the players are. In this case, there are two players—IBM and Toshiba. Both are real players. There are no chance players in this situation. However, as a convention, when there is a chance player (for example, a chance or random device like the shuffle of a deck of cards), we will designate that player as player 0. Also note that the game tree tells us which player moves at each decision point in the game (at each *node* of the game tree). We see that the game starts with IBM making a choice, and then Toshiba makes a choice. The fact that the game tree ends after Toshiba's choice means that there are only two moves in the game. At each node of the game tree, we see the choices (*branches* of the tree) available to the player in that move. For example, at the first node of the game tree in Figure 11.1(a), we see that IBM has two choices. It can select either DOS or UNIX. Depending on IBM's decision, Toshiba will be at a node either on the left side or the right side of the game tree. At each of these nodes, Toshiba, like IBM, has two choices. The figures in parentheses at the end of each path through the game tree indicate the financial results of the choices available to the players. The figure at the top is the payoff to IBM, and the figure at the bottom is the payoff to Toshiba.

We can divide games into two categories: games of perfect information and games of imperfect information. These terms describe how much each player knows about the previous choices of the other players when reaching a decision point in a game.

Games of Perfect and Imperfect Information: What Players Know When They Make Their Choices

In some games, the players know *everything* that happened in the game up to the point when their turn to move occurs and they must make a decision. This condition is shown in the game tree by the fact that each node of the tree is distinguishable to the player moving there. In the game described by Figure 11.1(a), when

Figure 11.1

Game Tree Diagram for (a) Game of Perfect Information and (b) Game of Imperfect Information.

(a) Player 2 (Toshiba) knows whether player 1 (IBM) moved to the left or to the right. Therefore, player 2 knows at which of two nodes it is located. (b) Player 2 (Toshiba) does not know whether player 1 (IBM) moved to the left or to the right. Therefore, player 2 does not know whether it is located at node 2 or node 3.

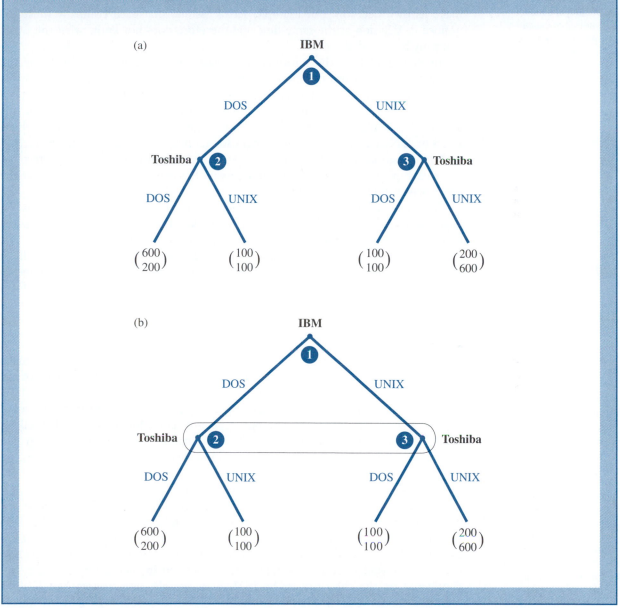

Toshiba makes its choice of an operating system, it knows whether IBM chose DOS or UNIX in the previous move. A game of this type is called a **game of perfect information** because when any player makes a move, she knows all the prior choices made by the other players.

In some games, however, we must assume that when any player reaches a decision point, she does not know all the choices of the other players who preceded

game of perfect information
A game in which, when any player makes a move, he knows all the prior choices made by all the other players.

game of imperfect information
A game in which, when a player reaches a decision point, she does not know all the choices of the other players who preceded her.

information sets
The sets that indicate what a player knows when it is her turn to make a move in a game tree.

her. Such games are called games of imperfect information. To represent the information available to a player in this case, we must add information sets to the game tree. These sets indicate what a player knows when it is her turn to make a move. Figure 11.1(b) presents the same game tree that we saw in Figure 11.1(a), except that this game now has a different information structure because Toshiba *does not know* what operating system IBM has selected when it, Toshiba, must make its own decision. For example, let us assume that each company must announce its decision at the same time and therefore does not know what the other company has decided.

In Figure 11.1(b), the information structure of the game is depicted by the oval placed around the two nodes of the tree that represents Toshiba's possible moves. This oval is the information set indicating that Toshiba has imperfect information when its turn to move comes up because it does not know whether it is at node 2 or node 3. In other words, Toshiba does not know whether IBM chose DOS or UNIX as the operating system for its new computer. In Figure 11.1(a), each information set contains only one node. Information is therefore perfect because each player knows exactly where it is on the game tree and exactly what the other player did previously in the game.

In games of both perfect and imperfect information, the game tree tells us the payoff to the players conditional on any path taken through the game tree, that is, conditional on any combination of choices made by the players in the game. For example, if IBM chooses DOS and Toshiba chooses DOS, the payoffs will be 600 ($600 million) to IBM and 200 ($200 million) to Toshiba. If IBM chooses DOS and Toshiba chooses UNIX, then each player will receive a payoff of 100 ($100 million).

Describing Games in Their Normal Form

Obviously, when a game involves either many players or a few players who make many moves, the game tree can become complicated. To keep the analysis of the game from getting too difficult in these circumstances, it is common to simplify the presentation of the game by defining a strategy, or pure strategy, for each player. By a strategy, we mean a complete plan of action for the player that tells us what choice he should make at any node of the game tree or in any situation that might arise during the play of the game. In our discussion of player strategies, we will now shift our method of analyzing games from the extensive form that we used previously to what is called the normal form.

pure strategy
A complete plan of action for the player that tells us what choice he should make at any node of the game tree or in any situation that might arise during the play of the game.

normal form game
A representation of a game of strategy defined by the number of players in the game, the set of strategies each player has, and the payoffs to each player contingent on one strategy choice for each player. This game is often presented as a matrix game when the players have a small and finite number of strategies.

To understand the difference between the two forms, let us look again at the extensive form of the game between IBM and Toshiba, which is portrayed in Figure 11.1(a). Because IBM moves first in this game and does not move again, it has two possible strategies here: use DOS or UNIX as the operating system for its new computer. Toshiba's strategies, however, are defined in such a way that they are contingent on the choice made by IBM. For example, one strategy for Toshiba might be, "Choose DOS if IBM chooses DOS, but choose UNIX if IBM chooses UNIX." Let us denote this strategy as (DOS | DOS, UNIX | UNIX). The action indicated after each vertical bar is the action of IBM, while the action indicated before each vertical bar is the proposed action of Toshiba, conditional on IBM's action. We can then define four strategies for Toshiba as (DOS | DOS, UNIX | UNIX), (DOS | DOS, DOS | UNIX), (UNIX | DOS, DOS | UNIX), and (UNIX | DOS, UNIX | UNIX).

Note that by combining the strategies of the players, we define a complete path through the game tree. For example, let us assume that IBM chooses DOS

Table 11.1	Normal-Form Game between IBM and Toshiba (payoffs in millions of dollars).			
		TOSHIBA		
		(DOS | DOS, DOS | UNIX)	(DOS | DOS, UNIX | UNIX)	(UNIX | DOS, UNIX | UNIX)	(UNIX | DOS, DOS | UNIX)
IBM	**DOS**	600, 200	600, 200	100, 100	100, 100
	UNIX	100, 100	200, 600	200, 600	100, 100

and Toshiba chooses (DOS | DOS, DOS | UNIX). The two players then proceed through the game tree on the path in which IBM chooses DOS and so does Toshiba. This path yields a payoff of 600 ($600 million) for IBM and 200 ($200 million) for Toshiba. Thus, for any combination of strategies, there is a pair of payoffs: one for IBM and one for Toshiba. Obviously, working with strategies simplifies our analysis because we can now reduce the game between IBM and Toshiba to the matrix shown in Table 11.1.

This matrix represents the strategic situation of our two players and tells us what payoff each of them will receive depending on the strategies chosen. The first amount in any cell of the matrix is the payoff to IBM, and the second amount is the payoff to Toshiba. For example, say that IBM decides to use the strategy of choosing DOS, while Toshiba uses the strategy (UNIX | DOS, DOS | UNIX). This strategy can be stated from Toshiba's point of view as follows: "If IBM chooses DOS, we will choose UNIX. If IBM chooses UNIX, we will choose DOS."

Looking at Figure 11.1(a), we see that the strategy we just described will result in a payoff of $100 million for IBM and $100 million for Toshiba. Note that we are not saying that it would be wise for IBM or Toshiba to choose DOS or UNIX. Certainly, each of these players would rather receive a payoff of $600 million or $200 million than a payoff of $100 million. All that we are doing in the normal form of a game is specifying the results of each pair of strategies that the players may choose.

Example 11.2

MATCHING PENNIES: A ZERO-SUM GAME

To increase our knowledge of the extensive and normal forms of games, let us consider the common children's game called "matching pennies." In this simple game involving two children, each child places a penny in her hand without allowing the other child to see which side of the coin is face up—"heads" or "tails." Then, simultaneously, each child opens her hand to reveal whether her coin shows heads or tails. If both coins are facing the same way—either heads or tails—child 1 pays child 2 a penny. If not, child 2 pays child 1 a penny.

This is clearly a game of imperfect information because each child moves (opens her hand) without knowing what the other child has done (how the other child has placed the coin in her hand). The extensive form of this game appears in Figure 11.2.

The game tree in Figure 11.2 shows that child 1 moves first by choosing either heads or tails. Then child 2, who does not know what child 1 did (note the information set at this decision point), must make her move. The payoffs depend on the path the players take through the game tree. When both children choose heads or both choose tails, child 2 receives a payoff of +1 and child 1 receives a payoff of −1 (terminal nodes 1 and 4). When the coins do not match (terminal nodes 2 and 3), the payoffs are the opposite. Note that because the payoffs always add up to zero, this type of game is called a zero-sum game. The gain of one player equals the loss of the other player.

The normal form for this game is quite simple. Because both children have only two possible strategies, choosing heads or tails, their payoffs can be described as shown by the matrix in Table 11.2.

zero-sum game
A game in which the gain of one player equals the loss of the other player.

Figure 11.2

Extensive Form of the Game of Matching Pennies.

Child 2 does not know whether child 1 chose heads or tails. Therefore, child 2's information set contains two nodes.

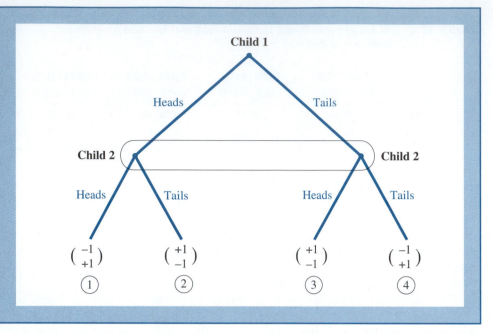

Table 11.2	A Game of Matching Pennies.		
		PLAYER 2	
		Heads	**Tails**
Player 1	**Heads**	−1, +1	+1, −1
	Tails	+1, −1	−1, +1

Question (Content Review: Extensive and Normal Form Games)

Consider the following situation based on the O. Henry story "The Gift of the Magi."

Bob and Alice are in love, but they are very poor. Their anniversary is approaching, and each wants to get the other something nice to celebrate it. Because they are so poor, they can't afford much, but they both possess something of which they are very fond; each would like to complement the other's special possession with a gift. Alice has long, lovely hair, and Bob would like to get her a comb for it. Bob has a beautiful pocket watch, and Alice would like to get him a chain for it.

They leave their home on the morning of their anniversary, each facing two choices. Alice can cut her hair and sell it to a wig factory and use the funds to buy Bob a watch chain, while Bob can sell his watch and use the proceeds to get Alice a comb. Alternatively, they can do nothing and simply exchange cards with each other, which at least will express how much they care about each other. Neither knows what the other will do.

Their payoffs are as follows: If they both sell their possessions, they will each get a payoff of −100 because not only will they each lose their prized object, but they also will not get the satisfaction of helping the other. If one sells and one does not, the one who sells at least gets the satisfaction of doing something nice for the other and, hence, gets a payoff of +50. The other, who does not sell and only buys a card, receives a payoff of +25—while that person gets something nice and gives a card, he or she feels a little guilty about not sacrificing for the other. If they both exchange cards, then they get a payoff of +10 each.

a) Draw the extensive form of the game associated with this story.

Answer

The extensive form of the game appears as in Figure 11.3.

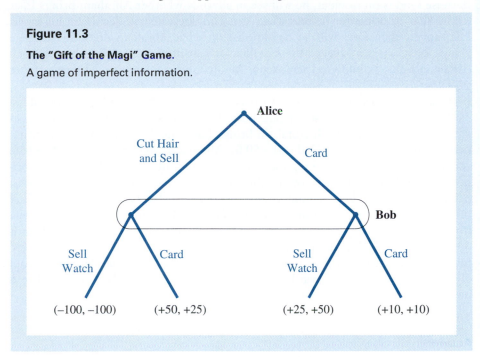

Figure 11.3

The "Gift of the Magi" Game.

A game of imperfect information.

b) Is this a game of perfect or imperfect information?

Answer

Note that because neither player knows what the other has done before moving, the game is one of imperfect information.

c) Write the normal form of the game.

Answer

The normal form of the game appears as in Table 11.3.

Table 11.3	The "Gift of the Magi" Game.		
		BOB	
		Sell Watch	**Buy Card**
Alice	**Sell Hair**	−100, −100	+50, +25
	Buy Card	+25, +50	+10, +10

d) Do you know what happened in the actual story? If you do, was it rational?

Answer

In the story, we get the worst of all outcomes. Alice sells her hair, and Bob sells his watch. As we will see later in this chapter, this outcome is not an equilibrium for the game.

SOLVED PROBLEM 11.2

Question (Application and Extension: Extensive Form Games)

Consider the following situation based on an old biblical story. Abraham is told to bring his son Isaac for sacrifice. Abraham, a devout believer, cannot understand why God has told him to do this, and he contemplates disobeying his command. Hence, Abraham has two choices: to bring Isaac, or to refuse to bring him. Because God is omniscient, he will see in advance whether Abraham brings Isaac to the altar or not; after he sees what Abraham does, he will decide on his move. His moves, therefore, will be conditional on what Abraham does. If Abraham brings Isaac, he can accept the sacrifice or substitute a sheep in his place. If Abraham refuses, then God can excuse Abraham or punish him. The payoffs are as follows.

If Abraham brings Isaac and God excuses him, then both will get a payoff of $+100$ because this is the best outcome possible. God has seen that Abraham is obedient and Isaac is spared. If Abraham brings Isaac and God accepts the sacrifice, then the payoff is $+90$ for God and -50 for Abraham. God has seen that Abraham is obedient and, therefore, does not wish to hurt him by accepting Isaac as a sacrifice. Hence, God's payoff is lower. Abraham is hurt by losing his son but at least has shown he is obedient to God. (Let's not consider what Isaac thinks about all of this.) If Abraham does not bring Isaac and God punishes him, this is the worst possible scenario—both get a payoff of -100 because God has seen that Abraham is not obedient and Abraham is punished. If Abraham does not bring Isaac and God forgives him, then each gets a payoff of -10; God has seen that Abraham is not obedient, Abraham has shown his infidelity, and the fact that Isaac is still alive is not a complete victory for him.

a) Draw the extensive form of this game.

Answer

The extensive form of this game appears as in Figure 11.4.

Figure 11.4

The God-Abraham Game.

God can see if Abraham is willing to sacrifice before he moves.

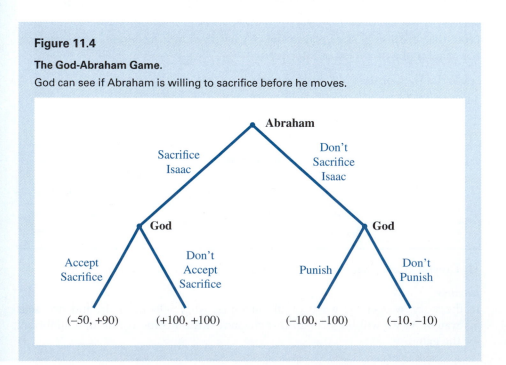

b) Is this a game of perfect or imperfect information?

Answer

Because any player making a move knows exactly what the other has done before him, this is a game of perfect information.

c) Write down all of Abraham's strategies. Write down all of God's strategies.

Answer

Abraham's strategies are simple—either to sacrifice Isaac or not to sacrifice him. For God, the strategy space is slightly larger because he must make his strategy conditional on what Abraham has done. God has four strategies:

- Accept the sacrifice of Isaac if Abraham brings him, and punish Abraham if he does not (Accept and Punish)

- Accept the sacrifice of Isaac if Abraham brings him, but do not punish Abraham if he does not (Accept and Don't Punish)

- Don't accept the sacrifice of Isaac if Abraham brings him, but punish Abraham if he does not (Don't Accept and Punish)

- Don't accept the sacrifice of Isaac if Abraham brings him, and do not punish Abraham if he does not (Don't Accept and Don't Punish)

d) Write the normal form of the game.

Answer

Given the payoffs listed, the normal form of the game associated with this story is as shown in Table 11.4.

Table 11.4	The God-Abraham Game.				
				GOD	
		Accept and Punish	**Accept and Don't Punish**	**Don't Accept and Punish**	**Don't Accept and Don't Punish**
Abraham	Sacrifice	−50, +90	−50, +90	+100, +100	+100, +100
	Don't Sacrifice	−100, −100	−10, −10	−100, −100	−10, −10

e) What outcome occurred in the Bible?

Answer

In the Bible, the outcome is the strategy pair Sacrifice and Don't Accept/Don't Punish with an associated payoff of +100, +100.

Equilibria for Games

The reason that we analyze any game is to discover what its equilibrium will be if it is played by rational people. When we apply the term **equilibrium** to a game, we mean a state in which no player will wish to change his or her behavior given the behavior of the other players. More specifically, we mean that the players will have a choice of strategies and that the strategy selected by each of them will be such

equilibrium
A state in which no player will wish to change his or her behavior given the behavior of the other players.

that no player will have any incentive to change his or her choice. In short, once an equilibrium is achieved in a game, no matter how it is achieved, it will continue without change.

In order to use the concept of equilibria for games in our analysis, we must be more precise about what this concept involves. We know that an equilibrium is made up of an array of strategy choices for a game (one strategy choice for each player), and we know that after the choices are made, they will not change. By "will not change," we might mean that no individual players or groups of players will have any incentive to change their actions *if they assume that their opponents also will not change their actions*. However, most of the games that we will study will involve situations where each player must make his or her strategy choice in isolation and must not consult with any of the other players. Such games are called **noncooperative games** because there is no possibility of formal or binding cooperation and coordination among the players.[2] Obviously, when we want to discover the equilibrium for a game in which all players will make their choices by themselves, we will not consider the incentives of *groups* of players to alter their behavior given the choices of others. Instead, we will consider only the incentives of the *individual* players.

To understand what an equilibrium for a game might be like, consider again the matrix for the game between IBM and Toshiba (Table 11.1). Look at the cell entry showing the payoffs of (200, 600), which are in boldface type. We will examine the idea that the pair of strategies associated with this pair of payoffs [UNIX and (UNIX | DOS, UNIX | UNIX)] is, when taken together, an equilibrium pair of strategies for the game. To see if this claim is correct, let us first consider the position of IBM. If Toshiba chooses (UNIX | DOS, UNIX | UNIX) as a strategy, then Toshiba is saying that it will select UNIX as the operating system for its new computer no matter what IBM does. Faced with this strategy, IBM will have a choice between a payoff of 100 ($100 million) if it selects DOS and a payoff of 200 ($200 million) if it selects UNIX. Clearly, the *best response* that IBM can make if Toshiba selects (UNIX | DOS, UNIX | UNIX) as a strategy is to choose UNIX. Hence, if IBM thinks that Toshiba will select (UNIX | DOS, UNIX | UNIX), it will choose UNIX.

Similarly, if Toshiba thinks that IBM will choose UNIX, it will receive a payoff of 100 ($100 million) if it selects (DOS | DOS, DOS | UNIX) as its strategy and a payoff of 600 ($600 million) if it selects (UNIX | DOS, UNIX | UNIX). If Toshiba thinks that IBM will choose UNIX, selecting (UNIX | DOS, UNIX | UNIX) is its best response (or at least as good a response as any other). Put differently, if IBM expects Toshiba to select (UNIX | DOS, UNIX | UNIX) and Toshiba expects IBM to select UNIX, then these are exactly the choices they will make because each of these choices is the best response to the other player's strategy (or at least the best response to each player's expectation of the other player's actions).

Nash Equilibria

The Nash equilibrium is a fundamental concept in game theory.[3] It describes an outcome in which no player wishes to change his behavior (strategy choice) given the behavior (strategy choice) of his opponents. More formally, we can define a Nash equilibrium in the following manner.

noncooperative games
Games in which there is no possibility of communication or binding commitments.

Nash equilibrium
A set of strategies, one for each player, in which no player wishes to change his behavior (strategy choice) given the behavior (strategy choice) of his opponents.

---

[2] We will not discuss cooperative games here. However, we should note that cooperative games are games in which it is assumed that the players can talk to each other and make binding contracts. For games of this type, we use a different concept of equilibrium.

[3] The Nash equilibrium is named for the U.S. mathematician and economist John F. Nash, who first proposed it in 1951.

Let us say that $s^* = (s_1^*, \ldots, s_n^*)$ is an array of strategy choices, one for each of our n players, where s_1^* is the strategy choice of player 1, s_2^* is the strategy choice of player 2, and so on. In addition, let us say that $\pi_i(s_1^*, \ldots, s_n^*)$ is the payoff to player i when s^* is chosen, where i can be any player $i = 1, 2, \ldots, n$. We can now give the following formal definition of the Nash equilibrium: An array of strategy choices $s^* = (s_1^*, \ldots, s_n^*)$ is a Nash equilibrium if $\pi_i(s_1^*, \ldots, s_i^*, \ldots, s_n^*) \geq \pi_i(s_1^*, \ldots, \hat{s}_i, \ldots, s_n^*)$ for all strategy choices $\hat{s}_i$ in S_i (that is, the set of all possible strategies from which player i can choose) and all players i.

This definition has a simple explanation. Consider the expression $\pi_i(s_1^*, \ldots, s_i^*, \ldots, s_n^*)$ on the left side of the inequality in the definition. This is the payoff to player i when he chooses s_i^* and all other players make their expected choices in s^*. On the right side of the inequality, $\pi_i(s_1^*, \ldots, \hat{s}_i, \ldots, s_n^*)$ indicates the payoff to player i when he chooses to deviate from s^* and select another strategy, namely $\hat{s}_i$, while all the other $n - 1$ players continue to make their choices in s^*. What the equilibrium condition tells us is that no player i can benefit from such a deviation, regardless of what strategy, like $\hat{s}_i$, he thinks of choosing from the strategy set S_i. In other words, if no one can benefit from deviating from s^* once it is established, then no one will and s^* will be an equilibrium.

MEDIA NOTE

A MOVIE REVIEW BY THE AUTHOR

A Beautiful Mind but Poor Game Theory

A year or so ago I went to see the film *A Beautiful Mind*. In a crucial scene in the film, Russell Crowe, playing John Nash, is out with three of his friends at a bar when they spot a beautiful blonde woman with four brunette friends who are not as beautiful. This scene supposedly represents the moment that Nash realized his concept of the Nash equilibrium.

Because the blonde was surrounded in the dating arena by four less beautiful women, Nash realized that if they all tried to approach the blonde, three would fail for sure, and then those that did would so offend the brunettes that they would meet no one. So Nash proposed that the optimal thing to do (the Nash equilibrium?) was for each guy to ignore the woman who most attracted them, the blonde, and coordinate in approaching the brunettes. This way they would each have a greater chance of success.

There is something terribly wrong here, however, and that is that the equilibrium proposed by Crowe in the film is not a Nash equilibrium. If I am one of the four guys and we all agree that we will ignore the blonde and approach the brunettes, then I have an incentive (as do all the other guys) to double cross my friends and approach the blonde because I would be the only one speaking to her. In other words, ignoring the blonde is not a best response to all the others' ignoring the blonde. It is not a Nash equilibrium.

Maybe director Ron Howard should have hired a game theorist to check the scene out.

Dominant Strategy Equilibria

The concept of a Nash equilibrium is simply the definition of an equilibrium situation. To understand this concept, we must initially suppose that the players in a game have somehow arrived at a certain (Nash equilibrium) configuration of strategy choices. We then consider only the possible one-person, or unilateral, deviations from this configuration in which each player contemplating such a deviation assumes that all the other players are *not* contemplating a change in strategy. Under these circumstances, the Nash equilibrium concept tells us that no player will have an incentive to actually make the deviation being contemplated, so the configuration of strategy choices will remain unchanged. What the Nash equilibrium concept does not tell us is how or why a certain configuration of strategy choices would ever be selected in the first place.

prisoner's dilemma game
A 2 × 2 matrix game in which each player has a dominant strategy determining an equilibrium that is Pareto dominated.

For certain games, however, we can say something about why a particular equilibrium emerges. Consider the matrix shown in Table 11.5, which applies the famous prisoner's dilemma game to the problem of price-setting by oligopolistic firms (see Chapter 19 for a fuller discussion of this problem). In the example that we are using here, the firms involved are Ford and General Motors.

For the purposes of this game, assume that Ford and General Motors build cars that are almost identical, so price is the variable that consumers look at when deciding which type of car to buy. The first entry in each cell of the matrix is the payoff to Ford, and the second is the payoff to General Motors. Each firm has two possible strategies for pricing its cars: set a high price or set a low price. The matrix shows the consequences of these pricing strategies for each firm.

Note that if both Ford and General Motors set a high price, they are colluding against the consumer and each therefore reaps a good profit of $500 million. However, if one firm sets a high price, then the other firm can achieve an advantage by *cheating* and setting a low price. The firm with the low price will steal virtually the entire market and earn a profit of $700 million for itself, while leaving its competitor with a profit of only $100 million. If both firms set a low price, then they share equally in an expanded market, but because of the low price, each earns a profit of only $300 million.

In Table 11.5, the only combination of strategies that produces a Nash equilibrium is the one in which both Ford and General Motors set a low price and receive a profit of $300 million each. If either firm expects the other to set a low price, its best response is also to set a low price. This is the only combination of strategies that yields an equilibrium despite the fact that the two firms would be better off if both set high prices, in which case each would earn a profit of $500 million. The problem with the combination of high-price strategies is that each firm has an incentive to cheat when the other sets a high price.

The low-price equilibrium can also be justified on other grounds in this example. Note that setting a low price is best for each firm *no matter what it expects the other firm to do*. To see why this is true, let us examine Ford's decision. (General Motors is in a symmetrical situation, so its calculations will be the same.) If Ford expects General Motors to set a high price, then its best response is to cheat and set a low price because it will then earn $700 million instead of $500 million. On the other hand, if Ford expects General Motors to set a low price, its best response is again to set a low price but for a different reason—to avoid setting a high price and losing a large portion of the market. In this case, Ford's payoff will be $300 million instead of $100 million. Clearly, no matter what Ford expects General Motors to do, it is better off setting a low price. When one strategy is best for a player *no matter what strategy the other player uses*, that strategy is said to dominate all other strategies and is called a dominant strategy. In the game that we just examined, both firms have a dominant strategy, which is to set a low price. The equilibrium in such a game is therefore called a dominant-strategy equilibrium.

dominate
Strategy A dominates strategy B if it gives a higher payoff than B no matter what the opposing players do.

dominant strategy
A strategy that is best for a player no matter what the opposing players do.

dominant-strategy equilibrium
The equilibrium in a game in which all players use their dominant strategies.

Table 11.5	A Prisoner's Dilemma Price-Setting Oligopoly Game (payoffs in millions of dollars).		
		GENERAL MOTORS	
		High Price	**Low Price**
Ford	**High Price**	500, 500	100, 700
	Low Price	700, 100	300, 300

Example 11.3

THE SECOND-PRICE AUCTION

The second-price auction is an example of a real-world game with a dominant-strategy equilibrium. The rules for this auction are as follows. Each participant must write her bid for the good she wants on a piece of paper and seal the paper inside an envelope. She submits the envelope to the auctioneer. The winner is the person who submitted the highest bid that is opened by the auctioneer. The unusual feature of this type of auction is that the price of the good to the winner is not the price she submitted but the price submitted by the *second highest* bidder. For instance, assume that a Monet painting is up for sale at an auction, and there are two bidders. If bidder 1 submits a bid of $1 million and bidder 2 submits a bid of $600,000, then bidder 1 will win the good at a price of $600,000. Notice that the payoff to a bidder is zero if the bidder does not win the good at the auction and is equal to the value the bidder placed on the good minus the winning price (the net value) if the bidder wins.

One might think that because each bidder wants to buy the painting at the lowest possible price, each will submit a bid below her true maximum valuation for the painting. This conjecture is wrong, however. In a second-price auction, each participant has a *dominant strategy* of bidding her true maximum valuation for the good. For example, say that you value the Monet at $1.2 million and someone else values it at $900,000, but you do not know the other person's valuation and she does not know yours. Then, in a second-price auction, your dominant strategy is to submit a bid of $1.2 million and her dominant strategy is to submit a bid of $900,000. Strategically, submitting a lower bid can never help and may actually hurt a participant in this type of auction.

To see why *honesty is the best policy* in such an auction, let us look at your role as a bidder for the Monet painting. We will assume that your true maximum valuation for the painting is $1.2 million and that this is the amount of your bid. If your opponent bids less than $1.2 million, you will win. If your opponent bids more than $1.2 million, you will lose. Suppose that your opponent's bid is higher than $1.2 million. Clearly, if you lower your bid, there will be no change in your payoff. It will still be zero. On the other hand, if you raise your bid above your true valuation of $1.2 million, you will either continue to lose because your bid remains the second highest or win but receive a negative payoff because the price that you will have to pay to win will be more than the maximum value of the painting to you. Consequently, if your opponent bids more than $1.2 million, then your bid of $1.2 million is at least as good as any other bid and strictly better than some bids.

If your opponent bids less than $1.2 million, the same domination holds. If you increase your bid above your true valuation of $1.2 million, you will still win and, because of the second-price rule, you will pay the amount that your opponent bid, which is less than $1.2 million. So nothing is gained by raising your bid if your opponent is bidding below your true valuation. If you decrease your bid so that it is below $1.2 million, then either you will still win with this lower bid and pay the same price or you will lose with the lower bid, in which case you will receive a zero payoff instead of the positive net earnings from winning. Consequently, bidding your true valuation is at least as good as any other strategy if your opponent's strategy is to bid below that amount. A similar argument holds if your opponent's bid is $1.2 million, exactly the same as your bid. Thus, bidding your true maximum valuation is a dominant strategy in a second-price auction because no matter what your opponent does—whether her bid is above or below your bid—you are always at least as well off bidding your true valuation as you are bidding any other amount.

Question (Content Review: Dominant Strategies)

Consider the game shown in Table 11.6.

SOLVED
PROBLEM
11.3

Table 11.6	A Dominant-Strategy Equilibrium.			
		PLAYER 2		
	1	**2**	**3**	**4**
1	40, 20	90, 300	200, 100	55, 22
2	30, 25	85, 55	100, 50	10, 10
3	38, 55	75, 65	44, 60	40, 60
4	22, 98	85, 200	155, 195	33, 155

(Player 1 labels rows 1–4)

a) Does player 1 have a dominant strategy?

Answer

Strategy 1 is dominant for player 1. No matter what player 2 does, player 1 would have been better off choosing strategy 1.

b) Does player 2 have a dominant strategy?

Answer

Strategy 2 is dominant for player 2.

c) What is the equilibrium of the game?

Answer

Given that each has a dominant strategy, the equilibrium is one where player 1 chooses strategy 1 and player 2 chooses strategy 2. We have an equilibrium in dominant strategies.

Solving Games by Elimination of Dominated Strategies

dominated strategy
A strategy that is dominated by another strategy.

Rational players should never use a dominated strategy, a strategy that is dominated by another strategy. Therefore, when we encounter a rational player in a game, we might assume that this player will never use such a strategy and might eliminate it from his set of possible strategies. One way to try to discover the equilibria of games is to first eliminate all dominated strategies, thereby *reducing* the game, and then search the reduced game for equilibria. To see how this procedure might work, consider Table 11.7, which shows the payoffs in a game where there are two players, each of whom has two possible strategies. Note that the first number in each cell is the payoff to player 1 and the second number is the payoff to player 2.

In this game, strategy 2 for player 2 *weakly dominates* strategy 1 because strategy 2 is *just as good as* strategy 1 when player 1 chooses strategy 1 and *strictly better than* strategy 1 when player 1 chooses strategy 2. If player 1 thinks that player 2 is rational, he will expect that player 2 will never use strategy 1. Player 1 will then eliminate strategy 1 from the set of possible strategies that player 2 could use. This leaves player 1 with a choice between strategy 1, which gives each player a payoff of 4, and strategy 2, which gives him a payoff of 6 and gives player 2 a payoff of 3. If player 1 is rational, he will choose strategy 2 because, *after the elimination of the dominated strategy 1 for player 2*, strategy 2 dominates strategy 1 for player 1. By eliminating the dominated strategies (in this case, weakly dominated strategies), we have arrived at an equilibrium with a payoff of (6, 3).[4]

At the end of this section, we present some experimental evidence that may cause you to think a little harder about the domination relationship.

Table 11.7	**A Game with Two Players Who Each Have Two Possible Strategies.**		
		PLAYER 2	
		Strategy 1	**Strategy 2**
Player 1	**Strategy 1**	4, 4	4, 4
	Strategy 2	0, 1	6, 3

---

[4] As we will see later, the strategy pair (1, 1) is also an equilibrium in this game.

EXPERIMENTAL EVIDENCE

SOLVING GAMES BY ELIMINATION OF DOMINATED STRATEGIES

It seems obvious that a rational player should never use a dominated strategy. However, in reality, when we play a game, we do not know if our opponent is rational enough or smart enough to figure out that some of his strategies are dominated. When such doubts arise, it is no longer clear that the equilibrium we derived through the elimination of dominated strategies is the one that we will observe in the real world. To investigate this conjecture, Schotter, Weigelt, and Wilson conducted an experiment in which they had 20 pairs of undergraduate subjects repeatedly play the game described in Table 11.7 with different opponents.[5] The experiment showed that the students who took the role of player 1 chose strategy 1 57% of the time, while their opponents who took the role of player 2 actually chose their dominated strategy 20% of the time. In other words, many of the subjects who assumed the role of player 1 clearly suspected that their opponents might not be smart enough or rational enough to figure out that they should never use strategy 1. Therefore, in order to avoid the possibility of the zero payoff shown in the lower left corner of Table 11.7, they decided to *play it safe* and choose strategy 1, which guaranteed them a payoff of 4.

An unexpected finding of the Schotter, Weigelt, and Wilson experiment was that when they had a *different* 20 pairs of subjects play the extensive form of the same game, the results were totally different. To these 20 pairs of subjects, the game was described in extensive, or game tree, form as shown in Figure 11.5.

Note that the strategic situation presented in extensive form in Figure 11.5 is exactly the same as the one described in normal form to the first group of subjects. However, among the second group, only 9% of the sub-

---
[5] For a more detailed discussion of this experiment, see Andrew Schotter, Keith Weigelt, and Charles Wilson, "A Laboratory Investigation of Multi-Person Rationality and Presentation Effects," *Games and Economic Behavior* 6 (May 1994): no. 3, pp. 445–68.

Figure 11.5

Extensive Form of the Game Played in the Schotter, Weigelt, and Wilson Experiment.

When the same game was presented to one group of subjects in normal form and to another group of subjects in extensive form, the results were different. The method of presentation apparently affected the way that each group viewed the strategic situation and, therefore, caused them to play the game differently.

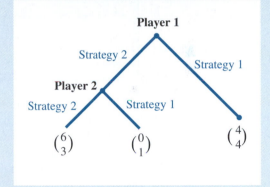

jects who took the role of player 1 chose to *play it safe* and opt for strategy 1 with its (4, 4) payoff. The other 91% who assumed this role acted as if they thought their player 2 opponent could figure out the fact that one of his strategies was a dominated strategy.

This difference in how the two groups perceived the ability of player 2 to recognize a dominated strategy may have occurred because strategy 1 for player 2 is more visibly dominated by strategy 2 in the extensive form of the game than in the normal form. If this is the reason for the difference, it leads to the conclusion that the way we present a game to people (in its normal or extensive form) will influence the way they play the game. However, this idea runs counter to conventional thinking in game theory because the strategic situation is identical in both cases.

Solving Games by the Iterated Elimination of Dominated Strategies

When games get larger, we can use the process of eliminating dominated strategies in an iterated manner. For example, consider the game matrix shown in Table 11.8a.

Table 11.8

(a) Eliminating Dominated Strategies.

		PLAYER 2		
		1	**2**	**3**
Player 1	**1**	2, 0	2, 4	0, 2
	2	0, 6	0, 2	4, 0

(b) One Step of Elimination.

		PLAYER 2	
		1	**2**
Player 1	**1**	2, 0	2, 4
	2	0, 6	0, 2

(c) Two Steps of Elimination.

		PLAYER 2	
		1	**2**
Player 1	**1**	2, 0	2, 4

Let us assume that each player in this game is rational, knows that the other is rational, and knows that the other knows she is rational, etc. In other words, it is commonly known that each player is rational. Thus, if you were player 1 in this game, you would know that player 2 will never use strategy 3 because strategy 2 dominates it, and a rational player will never use a dominated strategy. Hence, we can eliminate strategy 3 from the game entirely, and the game will look like Table 11.8(b) after the first elimination of dominated strategies.

However, by the same logic, player 2 will realize that player 1 will never use strategy 2 because it is dominated by strategy 1 in the reduced game. Hence, we can eliminate strategy 2 for player 1, reducing that game as shown in Table 11.8(c).

Now, however, it is clear that strategy 2 dominates strategy 1 for player 2, and the process stops with player 1 choosing strategy 1 and player 2 choosing strategy 2.

This process of the iterated elimination of dominated strategies solves the game uniquely when domination occurs at each iteration and it is strict. By strict we mean that when a strategy dominates another, it does so in the sense that the strategy that is dominated is strictly worse than the other, no matter what the opponent does. If for some strategies of an opponent one strategy is exactly as good as another but for others it is strictly better, that strategy is said to weakly dominate the others. When a game has weak domination and we use this iterative process to solve it, we may get multiple solutions, depending upon the order of elimination. Whenever a game arrives at a unique outcome using the strong or weak version of the iterative elimination of dominated strategies, we call the game *dominance-solvable*.

SOLVED PROBLEM 11.4

Question (Application and Extension: Iterated Elimination of Dominated Strategies)

Solve the following game using the iterated elimination of dominated strategies. In this game, each of 10 people chooses a number between 0 and 100. The average of these numbers is computed, and this average is multiplied by $p = \frac{2}{3}$. We will call the resulting number x. The person whose number is closest to x wins a big prize, while all others receive nothing.

Answer

In the equilibrium of this game, all players choose zero. We can demonstrate this by using the iterated elimination of dominated strategies. To do this, consider the fact that it is dominated to ever choose between 66.66 and 100. This is so because the highest x can be is 66.66, and that occurs only when everyone chooses 100. Thus, x can never be in the interval between 66.66 and 100. Choosing a number within this interval is dominated by choosing 66.66. So if all players are rational (and know that the others are), we can eliminate that interval. Thus, the highest anyone would choose now is 66.66. By a similar logic, however, if no one will choose above 66.66, the largest that x can be is $(\frac{2}{3}) \cdot 66.66 = 43.99$. Hence, choosing in the interval between 43.99 and 66.66 is now dominated as well. This logic continues until we reach zero. Clearly, if all choose zero, no one will have any incentive to raise his or her chosen number, and because zero is the lowest number available, it must be an equilibrium. (Assume the prize is split under these circumstances.)

Question (Application and Extension: Iterated Elimination of Dominated Strategies)

Solve the following game, in Table 11.9(a), using the iterated elimination of dominated strategies. Does it make a difference in what order you eliminate strategies?

SOLVED PROBLEM 11.5

Table 11.9

(a) Eliminated Weakly Dominated Strategies.

		PLAYER 2		
		1	2	3
Player 1	1	20, 0	10, 1	4, −4
	2	20, 2	10, 0	2, −2

(b) Reduced Game Eliminating Column 3 First.

		PLAYER 2	
		1	2
Player 1	1	20, 0	10, 1
	2	20, 2	10, 0

Answer

There is no unique solution to this game using iterative elimination of dominated strategies because the domination in this matrix is weak. For example, look at player 1's choices. Strategy 1 weakly dominates strategy 2 because the payoffs associated with strategy 1 are identical to those associated with strategy 2 as long as player 2 chooses strategies 1 and 2. Only if player 2 chooses strategy 3 is strategy 1 strictly better for player 1. Hence, strategy 1 weakly dominates strategy 2 for player 1. So if we start the elimination process with player 1, we would eliminate strategy 2 first. In that case, in the reduced game, player 2 would choose strategy 2 and the process would be over. The solution would be strategy 1 for player 1 and strategy 2 for player 2. However, what if we started with player 2? In that case, player 2 would eliminate strategy 3, which is strictly worse than strategies 1 and 2. This elimination would leave the reduced matrix shown in Table 11.9(b).

Note, however, that because this game has no dominated strategies for either player, the process of elimination would end here and we would not arrive at the same solution as we did before. Hence, when domination is weak, the outcome is not guaranteed to be unique.

See the Experimental Evidence feature at the end of this section for an application of eliminating dominated strategies.

EXPERIMENTAL EVIDENCE

AN APPLICATION OF ELIMINATING DOMINATED STRATEGIES

People choose numbers between 0 and 1,000 (consider the following game identical to that of Solved Problem 11.4) and then the mean of these numbers, $\bar{x}$, is calculated. After the mean is calculated, it is multiplied by $\frac{2}{3}$, and that player whose chosen number is closest to $(\frac{2}{3}) \cdot$ (the mean) wins a big prize. (Call this game the Guessing Game.)

Now let's use our knowledge of the game in Solved Problem 11.4. First notice that choosing a number larger than 666.66 can never be a smart thing to do, as it is dominated. It is dominated because the largest that $(\frac{2}{3}) \cdot$ (the mean) can ever be is 666.66, which will occur only when everyone chooses 1,000. Hence, to solve the game, the first thing you should do is eliminate the range 666.66 to 1,000 as dominated. This requires one level of reasoning. Next, however, if everyone realizes that all others will not choose in the range 666.66 to 1,000, then we should eliminate the range 444.44 to 666.66 using the same reasoning: If no one will choose above 666.66, then the highest that $(\frac{2}{3}) \cdot$ (the mean) could be is 444.44, which would occur when everyone chooses 666.66. So we should eliminate all choices from 444.44 to 666.66. These choices are dominated after we have eliminated the first range of 666.66 to 1,000. If we continue in this manner, we see that the only equilibrium is for everyone to choose zero. The game has been solved by iteratively eliminating dominated strategies.

Therefore, this game has a very precise prediction: All people should choose 0. Rosemarie Nagel[6] has run a number of experiments on this game and has found that while the very sharp prediction of the theory cannot be supported by the data generated by her subjects, over time they seemed to have learned to move in the right direction—toward zero. For example, Nagel

ran a number of guessing games in which subjects chose numbers between 0 and 100 and p was set at either $\frac{1}{2}$ or $\frac{2}{3}$. The game was repeated four times to allow subjects to learn. The results were simple. Figures 11.6 (a) and 11.6(b) present histograms of the choices made in the first period of each experiment. If the theory had

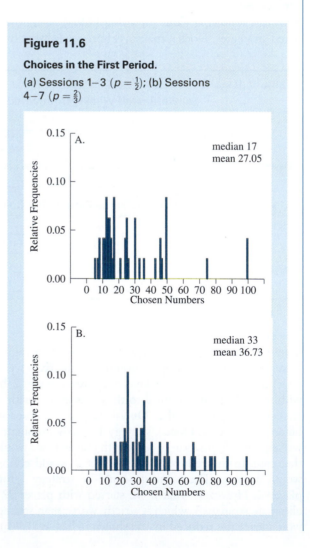

Figure 11.6

Choices in the First Period.

(a) Sessions 1–3 ($p = \frac{1}{2}$); (b) Sessions 4–7 ($p = \frac{2}{3}$)

A.
median 17
mean 27.05

B.
median 33
mean 36.73

[6] See Rosemarie Nagel, "Unraveling in Guessing Games: An Experimental Study," *American Economic Review* 85 (December 1995): no. 5, pp. 1,313–26.

predicted well, then all of the choices should have been zero. Clearly, however, this was not the case in either the $p = \frac{1}{2}$ or $p = \frac{2}{3}$ experiments. What is true, however, is that the larger p is, the greater the choices of the subjects are, even though this does not make sense from the point of view of theory. For any $p < 1$, the only equilibrium is 0. For example, the median choice of the subjects in the $p = \frac{1}{2}$ experiment is 17, while it is 33 in the $p = \frac{2}{3}$ experiment. (Try to think of why people choose higher when p is greater. There is no right answer; just put yourself in the place of the subject and ask what you would have done and why.)

As the experiment was repeated, however, the choices of the subjects moved down toward zero but never actually got there. For example, in the $p = \frac{1}{2}$ experiment, nearly half of the subject choices were less than 1 by the fourth period. For the $p = \frac{2}{3}$ experiment, however, only 3 out of 48 subjects made such low choices by the fourth and final period. On average, choices in every round moved down and toward zero.

So what can we conclude? This experiment demonstrates that, although people do have an ability to think strategically and eliminate dominated strategies from their play, it is not at all clear that they can go through the long string of logical deletions of dominated strategies called for by this theory. While they seem to learn over time, the theory still leaves many observations unexplained.

Games with Many Equilibria

Not all games have equilibria that can be determined by the elimination of dominated strategies, and many games have multiple equilibria or several arrays of strategy choices that satisfy the definition of a Nash equilibrium. For example, let us consider a coordination game. Table 11.10 presents one interpretation of such a game, which we will call "the telephone game."

Let us say that there is a small town with a local telephone company that has only one telephone line. Because of its limited capacity, the telephone company rations access by restricting telephone calls to a maximum length of five minutes. If a call is not completed at the end of five minutes, the telephone company cuts it off. To continue the conversation, one of the parties involved must redial the other party. This leads to a problem: Which party should call back? Should it be the original caller (the person who made the first call), or should it be the original callee (the person who received the first call)?

If telephone calls are expensive, we can assume that each person will prefer to wait and have the other person call him back. This creates two strategies for each player: call back or wait. If both wait, no call is placed and the payoff to each player is zero, as shown in the cell at the lower right corner of the game matrix. If both try to make the call, then each receives a busy signal. The result is that no call goes through, and each player again has a zero payoff, as shown in the cell at the upper left corner of the game matrix. However, if one player makes the call and the other waits, then the payoff to the caller is 3 and the payoff to the callee is 6. The callee receives the higher payoff because he saves the expense of the telephone call. What is the equilibrium for such a game? In other words,

coordination game
A game in which the players have a common interest in reaching an equilibrium yet, if there are multiple equilibria, their preferences may differ as to which is the best. At the equilibrium of a coordination game, no player wishes any other player to change their actions.

Table 11.10	**The Telephone Game: A Coordination Game with Two Nash Equilibria.**		
		PLAYER 2 (ORIGINAL CALLEE)	
		Strategy 1 (call back)	Strategy 2 (wait)
Player 1 (original caller)	Strategy 1 (call back)	0, 0	3, 6
	Strategy 2 (wait)	6, 3	0, 0

who should call and who should wait? To answer this question, let us look at Table 11.10 again.

Clearly, it is in the interest of these two players to coordinate their strategies so that one chooses strategy 1 and the other chooses strategy 2. Only through coordination can they both obtain a positive payoff. However, let us say that they cannot agree about how to coordinate their strategies. Both prefer strategy 2, which yields a payoff of 6. (Remember that the payoff from strategy 1 is only 3.)

In this game, there are two Nash equilibria. One occurs if player 1 chooses strategy 1 and player 2 chooses strategy 2; and the other occurs if player 1 chooses strategy 2 and player 2 chooses strategy 1.[7] To verify that these two sets of strategies are, in fact, Nash equilibria, let us consider what happens when player 1 chooses strategy 1 and player 2 chooses strategy 2. In this case, if player 1 thinks player 2 will choose strategy 2, he obviously will want to choose strategy 1 because that choice will give him a payoff of 3 instead of the zero payoff that would result if he also selected strategy 2. Similarly, if player 2 thinks player 1 will choose strategy 1, he will want to choose strategy 2 because the payoff of 6 from that choice is better than the payoff of zero that would result if he also selected strategy 1. The same is true of the equilibrium that occurs when player 1 chooses strategy 2 and player 2 chooses strategy 1.

What this example proves is that games may have many equilibrium outcomes. In its original form, game theory did not deal with the issue of which one of the many outcomes players will actually choose. More recently, game theory has been broadened to include refinement concepts that make it possible to narrow down the choice of equilibria when many exist. We will not investigate these modern refinement concepts except where they are of immediate relevance to our analysis.

refinement concept
A refinement concept places a set of extra constraints on a Nash equilibrium in order to select among multiple equilibria if they exist or to simply make the equilibrium more plausible.

Example 11.4

MATCHING NUMBERS: A COORDINATION GAME WITH MANY EQUILIBRIA

Assume that someone offers two players the following coordination game. Each player must choose a number between 1 and 10. If the numbers selected by the two players match (are the same), then each player is paid that amount in dollars. If the numbers do not match, each player receives nothing. This game has the normal form shown in Table 11.11.

The matrix in Table 11.11 lists the payoffs from all the possible strategies that can be used in the game described above. Notice that the only positive numbers appear along the diagonal of the matrix. These positive numbers indicate the payoffs to the players when both follow a strategy of choosing the same number. For example, when both players choose 3, their payoff is $3 each, and when both choose 7, their payoff is $7 each. Away from the diagonal, the payoffs are zero, which indicates that the players must coordinate their strategies in order to benefit from the game.

The game outlined here has ten Nash equilibria. These equilibria occur when both players choose the same number from one to ten, no matter what the number is. The payoffs along the diagonal are the equilibrium outcomes. Each of these pairs of strategies results in a Nash equilibrium because neither player would want to deviate from her matching selection and receive a payoff of zero.

---

[7] Actually, there is another possible equilibrium in such a game. This equilibrium occurs in what are called *mixed strategies*, where a player uses his two strategies with certain probabilities. Mixed strategies will be illustrated by another game that we will discuss later in this section (in Example 11.5).

Table 11.11	**The Normal Form of Matching Numbers: A Coordination Game with Ten Nash Equilibria.**									
					PLAYER 2					
		1	**2**	**3**	**4**	**5**	**6**	**7**	**8**	**9**	**10**
	1	1, 1	0, 0	0, 0	0, 0	0, 0	0, 0	0, 0	0, 0	0, 0	0, 0
	2	0, 0	2, 2	0, 0	0, 0	0, 0	0, 0	0, 0	0, 0	0, 0	0, 0
	3	0, 0	0, 0	3, 3	0, 0	0, 0	0, 0	0, 0	0, 0	0, 0	0, 0
	4	0, 0	0, 0	0, 0	4, 4	0, 0	0, 0	0, 0	0, 0	0, 0	0, 0
	5	0, 0	0, 0	0, 0	0, 0	5, 5	0, 0	0, 0	0, 0	0, 0	0, 0
Player 1	**6**	0, 0	0, 0	0, 0	0, 0	0, 0	6, 6	0, 0	0, 0	0, 0	0, 0
	7	0, 0	0, 0	0, 0	0, 0	0, 0	0, 0	7, 7	0, 0	0, 0	0, 0
	8	0, 0	0, 0	0, 0	0, 0	0, 0	0, 0	0, 0	8, 8	0, 0	0, 0
	9	0, 0	0, 0	0, 0	0, 0	0, 0	0, 0	0, 0	0, 0	9, 9	0, 0
	10	0, 0	0, 0	0, 0	0, 0	0, 0	0, 0	0, 0	0, 0	0, 0	10, 10

EXPERIMENTAL EVIDENCE

COORDINATION GAMES

Experiments with coordination games like the one in Example 11.4 have produced some interesting results. It would be natural to assume that the players in such a game would always choose the best equilibrium (the one with the [10, 10] payoff), but experimental evidence has indicated that this is not necessarily the case. In a number of experimental studies conducted by Van Huyck, Battalio, Beil, and others, student subjects played coordination games that were similar in structure to the one described in Example 11.4.[8] Like this game, the games in the experiments all had Nash equilibria that could be unanimously ranked from worst to best. What these studies found, contrary to expectations, was that the subjects did not converge on the best equilibrium as the game was repeated. Rather, these studies showed that the outcome of the first round tended to perpetuate itself. For instance, if in the first round of their game, a pair of subjects played to a (4, 4) equilibrium, this would be the equilibrium that emerged at the end of the experiment. The choice of equilibrium was more dependent on the history of play than on the payoff properties of the various equilibria. This result runs counter to the traditional view in game theory that the outcome of a game should depend on its strategic properties and payoffs and not on any historical accidents that might occur while it is being played.

---

[8] For more information about some of these experiments, see John van Huyck, Raymond Battalio, and Richard Beil, "Tacit van Huyck, Raymond Battalio, and Coordination Failure," *American Economic Review* 80 (March 1990): 234–48.

Not every game produces Nash equilibria in such a simple, clear-cut manner as the game described in Example 11.4. Let us now consider Example 11.5, which illustrates a game with what are called *mixed strategy equilibria*.

Example 11.5

WAR: A GAME WITH NO EQUILIBRIA IN PURE STRATEGIES

Assume that two generals face each other in battle. Each general has two strategies available: to retreat or to attack. The payoffs shown in Table 11.12 represent the benefits that the armies of these generals will receive from the four possible combinations of strategic choices. For instance, if general 1 retreats and general 2 attacks, there will be no battle and the two armies will receive payoffs of 6 each. (We will assume that there are strategic reasons for each set of

Table 11.12	A Game with No Equilibria in Pure Strategies.		
		GENERAL 2	
		Retreat	**Attack**
General 1	**Retreat**	5, 8	6, 6
	Attack	8, 0	2, 3

payoffs, but we will not delve into the explanations because they are not relevant to our discussion.)

At first glance, the pair of strategy choices that provides the (6, 6) payoff might seem to be a Nash equilibrium. However, this game has no Nash equilibrium in pure strategies. By a pure strategy, we mean a rule specifying the action to take—in this case, either to retreat or to attack. When we say that the game described here has no Nash equilibrium in pure strategies, we mean that there is no pair of strategies, one for general 1 and one for general 2, that constitutes an equilibrium for the game. For instance, take the pair of strategies with the (6, 6) payoff, where general 1 chooses to retreat and general 2 chooses to attack. This is not a Nash equilibrium because one player has an incentive to deviate from his strategy choice. If general 1 chooses to retreat, the best response for general 2 is also to retreat, which will give him a payoff of 8. This payoff is greater than the payoff of 6 he will receive if he attacks when general 1 retreats. However, the pair of strategies in which each general chooses to retreat is also not a Nash equilibrium. The payoff from this pair of strategies is (5, 8), but general 1 will want to deviate from the strategy of retreat. If he attacks when general 2 retreats, he will receive a payoff of 8, which is greater than the payoff of 5 he obtains when both he and general 2 choose to retreat. The other two pairs of strategies—(attack, retreat) and (attack, attack)—with payoffs of (8, 0) and (2, 3), respectively, will also not produce Nash equilibria. (To verify this claim, think through the consequences of the strategy choices that are involved.)

There is a way to produce Nash equilibria in games like the one described in Example 11.5. To do so, we must expand the definition of a strategy to include not only the choice of an action (such as to attack or retreat) but also the probability of the action being chosen. For instance, let us assume that instead of simply attacking or retreating, general 1 decides that he will choose between these two pure strategies by spinning the type of spinner that comes with a board game. As a result, he has a probability of p of retreating and a probability of $1 - p$ of attacking. Similarly, let us assume that there is a probability of q that general 2 will retreat and a probability of $1 - q$ that he will attack. By expanding the choices of the generals to include probability mixtures for strategies, we are allowing them to use mixed strategies—strategies that define probability mixtures for all the possible pure strategies in the game (in this case, to retreat or attack).

The set of mixed strategies available to choose from in our current example is the set of all p's such that $0 \leq p \leq 1$ or all q's such that $0 \leq q \leq 1$. In general, if players have n pure strategies, a mixed strategy is any probability distribution over these strategies or any set of p's (or q's) $(p_1, ..., p_n)$ such that $p_1 \geq 0, p_2 \geq 0, ..., p_n \geq 0$ and $p_1 + p_2 + ... + p_n = 1$.

Let us return to Example 11.5 and assume that general 2 chooses probabilities q and $1 - q$ for the pure strategies of retreat and attack, respectively. If general 1 then chooses retreat as his strategy, his expected payoff from that strategy, according to Table 11.12, will be $q(5) + (1 - q)6 = 6 - q$.[9]

mixed strategies
Strategies that define probability mixtures over all or some of the pure strategies in the game.

---

[9] These payoffs are actually what economists call Von Neumann-Morgenstern utilities, as discussed in Chapter 6.

The expected value of a strategy is the probability-weighted payoff the player can expect to receive. Note that if $q = 1$, general 2 will always retreat. Thus, if general 1 also retreats, he will have a sure payoff of 5. If $q = 0$, general 2 will always attack, and hence a retreat by general 1 will yield a sure payoff of 6 for him. When $0 \leq q \leq 1$, general 1 will sometimes (with a probability of q) receive his (retreat, retreat) payoff of 5 and sometimes (with a probability of $1 - q$) receive his (retreat, attack) payoff of 6. Similarly, the expected payoff from the choice of the attack strategy by general 1 is $q(8) + (1 - q)2 = 2 + 6q$.

Now, if general 2 chooses q, such a choice makes the expected payoff of one strategy for general 1 greater than the expected payoff of the other strategy; and the strategy with the greater payoff will be chosen with a probability of 1. For example, let us say that general 2 chooses a mixed strategy of $q = \frac{1}{2}, 1 - q = \frac{1}{2}$. If general 1 chooses to retreat, his expected payoff will be $\frac{1}{2}(5) + \frac{1}{2}(6) = 5\frac{1}{2}$. However, if general 1 chooses to attack, his expected payoff will be $\frac{1}{2}(8) + \frac{1}{2}(2) = 5$. Clearly, if general 2 chooses the mixed strategy of $q = \frac{1}{2}, 1 - q = \frac{1}{2}$, then the best response by general 1 is to choose to retreat. Knowing this, general 2 will surely abandon his mixed strategy and retreat. Hence, a situation in which general 2 uses a strategy of $q = \frac{1}{2}, 1 - q = \frac{1}{2}$ cannot be part of a mixed strategy equilibrium.

Finding Mixed Strategy Equilibria. The principle that underlies the example we just investigated is that if one player in a game uses a mixed strategy that leaves the other player with a unique pure strategy best response, a mixed strategy equilibrium does not exist. The only situation in which a mixed strategy equilibrium arises is one where the mixed strategies chosen leave both players indifferent between the payoffs they expect to receive from their pure strategies. For instance, in the game described in Example 11.5, let us say that general 2 uses the mixed strategy of $q = \frac{4}{7}, 1 - q = \frac{3}{7}$. Then the expected payoff for general 1 from using either of his pure strategies is the same. The expected payoff from retreating is $\frac{4}{7}(5) + \frac{3}{7}(6) = \frac{38}{7} = 5\frac{3}{7}$, and the expected payoff from attacking is $\frac{4}{7}(8) + \frac{3}{7}(2) = \frac{38}{7} = 5\frac{3}{7}$.

In this case, general 1 does not care which strategy he uses. Consequently, he might as well choose his strategy randomly. However, if he decides to retreat with a probability of $p = \frac{3}{5}$ and attack with a probability of $1 - p = \frac{2}{5}$, this would make general 2 indifferent between his two strategies because each would yield him a payoff of $4\frac{4}{5}$. A situation in which all players choose their mixed strategies in order to make their opponents indifferent between the expected payoffs from any of their pure strategies is called a **mixed strategy equilibrium**.[10]

To illustrate the principle of solving games for mixed strategy equilibria, consider the following problem.

mixed strategy equilibrium
An equilibrium where players use mixed strategies.

Question (Application and Extension: Mixed Strategy Equilibria)

Michael Jordan and his biggest fan, Dave, live next door to each other. Dave idolizes Michael, but Michael can't stand Dave. Dave likes Michael so much that he

SOLVED PROBLEM 11.6

---

[10] To actually calculate a mixed strategy equilibrium for general 2, note that using general 1's payoff, the expected payoff to general 1 from retreating is $q(5) + (1 - q)6 = 6 - q$ and the expected payoff to general 1 from attacking is $q(8) + (1 - q)2 = 6q + 2$. Setting these two expected payoffs so that they are equal to each other and will therefore make general 1 indifferent between them yields $6 - q = 6q + 2$. Solving for q, we find that $7q = 4$ or $q = 4/7$. A similar calculation can be made for general 1's mixed strategy equilibrium.

wants to dress like him every day (he wants to be like Mike). This annoys Michael so much that he wants to dress as differently as possible from Dave.

Both Michael and Dave work for the AirGod Shoe Company. Dave always has to get to work before Michael, so he must leave his house each morning before Michael leaves his. Therefore, each morning Michael is able to see what Dave is wearing.

Assume that Michael's preferences can be represented as follows:

U (Wear red|Dave wears blue) = 2

U (Wear blue|Dave wears red) = 1

U (Wear red|Dave wears red) = -1

U (Wear blue|Dave wears blue) = -2

Assume that Dave's preferences can be represented as follows:

U (Wear red|Michael wears red) = 2

U (Wear blue|Michael wears blue) = 1

U (Wear red|Michael wears blue) = -1

U (Wear blue|Michael wears red) = -2

a) If Michael sees that Dave is wearing red when he goes to work, what will he do?

Answer

Clearly, Michael doesn't like to match Dave; so if he sees Dave wearing red, he will wear blue.

b) If neither is able to see what the other wears to work, what will the equilibrium outcome be?

Answer

If Michael is unable to see what Dave wears, the two men are essentially playing a simultaneous move game that has no pure strategy, so the only equilibrium is in mixed strategies. A mixed strategy equilibrium requires that the expected payoffs of wearing each color are equal for each man. Let's take a look at the game in the normal form, as shown in Table 11.13.

Table 11.13	The "I Want to Be Like Mike" Game.		
		DAVE	
		Wear Red	**Wear Blue**
Michael	**Wear Red**	(−1, 2)	(2, −2)
	Wear Blue	(1, −1)	(−2, 1)

Let d_r be the probability that Dave wears red. Therefore, the probability that Dave wears blue is $1 - d_r$. The expected payoff to Mike of wearing red is

$$E\pi_m(\text{wear red}) = d_r(-1) + (1 - d_r)(2)$$
$$= 2 - 3d_r$$

Likewise, Mike's expected payoff for wearing blue is

$$E\pi_m(\text{wear blue}) = d_r(1) + (1 - d_r)(-2)$$
$$= -2 + 3d_r$$

Equating these two expected payoffs, we get

$$2 - 3d_r = -2 + 3d_r$$
$$4 = 6d_r$$
$$d_r = \frac{2}{3}$$

Thus, if Dave chooses red and blue with probability $\frac{2}{3}$ and $\frac{1}{3}$ respectively, then Michael will be indifferent between wearing red and blue himself and will be willing to mix his strategies. Likewise, let m_r be the probability that Michael wears red and use the same procedure to solve for Dave's equilibrium strategies.

$$E\pi_d(\text{wear red}) = m_r(2) + (1 - m_r)(-1)$$
$$= -1 + 3m_r$$

$$E\pi_d(\text{wear blue}) = m_r(-2) + (1 - m_r)(1)$$
$$= 1 - 3m_r$$

Setting the two equal to each other, we get

$$-1 + 3m_r = 1 - 3m_r$$
$$2 = 6m_r$$
$$m_r = \frac{1}{3}$$

So if Michael wears red with probability $\frac{1}{3}$, Dave will be indifferent between wearing red and blue and will be willing to mix strategies. The equilibrium mixed strategies for the players are Dave $= (\frac{2}{3}, \frac{1}{3})$ and Michael $= (\frac{1}{3}, \frac{2}{3})$.

MEDIA NOTE

GAME THEORY

An art collector from Japan had to decide which auction house, Christie's or Sotheby's, would handle the sale of his $20 million collection. He was reluctant to split the collection between the two houses or to sell through a private dealer. Instead he opted for the tried-and-true method of resolving differences and had the two auction houses play the game rock, paper, scissors.

The auction houses were informed that they had a week to come up with a strategy. As opposed to the payoff of such a game in the playground, a right decision in this game would be worth millions of dollars in commission to the house that won.

Sotheby's attitude to this situation was that the game is a game of chance and thus didn't pay too much attention to strategy. Christie's took a different approach to the problem. The president of Christie's in Japan engaged in extensive research

during the week, but the most useful advice came from 11-year-old twins who play the game constantly in school.

The twin's advice was to start with scissors because "rock is too obvious and scissors beats paper." They also gave advice for a second round in case a tie was involved in the first—stick to scissors because everyone expects you to switch to rock (The girls also took into account that the sides involved were novices.)

At the end of the week, both sides met and gave their decision. Christie's won in the first round (Sotheby's chose paper).

Did the advice offered constitute an equilibrium strategy for the game? The answer is no, and you should know why. Think it over.

Source: Adapted from "Rock, Paper, Payoff: Child's Play Wins Auction House an Art Sale," as appeared in the *New York Times,* April 29, 2005

Credible Threats

When game theory was first developed, there was a belief that the extensive and normal forms of games were equivalent tools for strategic analysis and produced equivalent results. In recent years, however, this belief has changed, especially under the influence of Reinhard Selten.[11] We have come to understand that the two ways of viewing a game are not quite the same. To illustrate this point, let us consider the game tree depicted in Figure 11.7.

In Figure 11.7, we see the extensive form of a game that we will call "the rotten kid game." The scenario for this game is simple. It is a Saturday afternoon, and player 1 (a difficult child) wants to go see the latest action movie. However, player 2 (one of his parents) has decided that the family will visit Aunt Sophie. Player 1 starts the game. He can either go to Aunt Sophie's house (move to the left) or refuse to go (move to the right). If player 1 moves left (L), the game is over and each player receives a payoff of 1. If player 1 moves right (R), then player 2 continues the game. She either punishes player 1 by keeping him at home and not allowing him to do anything (she moves to the left), or she relents and the family goes to the movie (she moves to the right). If player 2 moves L, both players receive a payoff of −1. If player 2 moves R, then player 1 receives a payoff of 2 and player 2 receives a payoff of zero.

This game involves a threat by player 2 (one of the parents) to punish player 1 (the child) if he refuses to go to Aunt Sophie's house. However, as we will see later, this is not a credible threat. Because player 1 is a "rotten kid," he will cry and scream constantly if he is kept at home and not allowed to watch television or play with his toys. Therefore, to obtain some peace after player 1 refuses to go to Aunt Sophie's house, player 2 will not carry out her threat. Instead, she will relent and take the family to the movie. Knowing this, the child will refuse to go.

Table 11.14 presents the normal form of this game. Notice that if we look at the normal form, we see that both players have two strategies available—move to the left (L) or move to the right (R).

In the normal form of this game, there are two equilibria. One occurs if both players move L, and the other occurs if both players move R. There is only a weak incentive for player 2 to adhere to the first of these equilibria and not deviate from it because if player 1 chooses L, it does not matter what choice player 2 makes. Despite this fact, each of the equilibria that emerges from the normal form of the game satisfies the definition of a Nash equilibrium: No player can do strictly better by deviating from his or her choice.

In the extensive form of the game, as depicted in Figure 11.7, we see that while both of the equilibria are Nash equilibria, one of them (the one that results when both players choose L) is less satisfactory than the other. The reason that this equilibrium is less satisfactory is that it relies on a noncredible threat for support—the threat made by player 2 against player 1.

To gain a better understanding of noncredible threats, let us think of the (L, L) equilibrium in Figure 11.7 in terms of the following statement that player 2 makes to player 1: "I want you to choose strategy L when the game starts because that move will give me a payoff of 1. If you choose strategy L, you will also receive a payoff of 1. However, if you deviate and choose strategy R, I will then choose L, in which case you will receive a payoff of −1. Therefore, you better choose L or else." The equilibrium produced by this threat is a Nash equilibrium for the

noncredible threat
A threat in a strategic game that is not believable or would not be carried out if called upon.

---

[12] Reinhard Selten is a German economist, game theorist, and Nobel Prize winner who teaches at the University of Bonn.

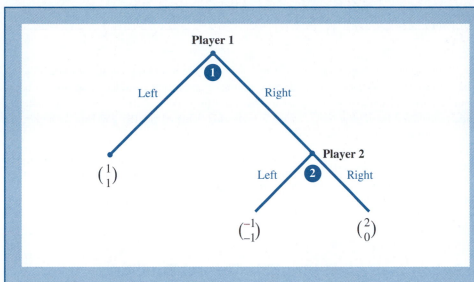

Figure 11.7

Credible (and Noncredible) Threats in the Extensive Form of a Game.

The (L, L) equilibrium relies on a noncredible threat by player 2 to move to the left if player 1 moves to the right.

Table 11.14	The Rotten Kid Game: The Normal Form of the Game in Figure 11.7.		
		PLAYER 2 (A PARENT)	
		Left (punish child)	**Right (relent)**
Player 1 (a difficult child)	Left (go to Aunt Sophie's house)	1, 1	1, 1
	Right (refuse to go to Aunt Sophie's house)	−1, −1	2, 0

following reason. Given the threat from player 2, the best response of player 1 is to choose L; and when player 1 chooses L, it does not matter what player 2 does because she will never have the opportunity to make a move.

The problem with this equilibrium is that *player 2's threat is not credible*. For example, say that player 2 makes the statement quoted previously, but despite her threat, player 1 moves R instead of being frightened into moving L. If player 1 does defy the threat, then player 2 will be at node 2 in the game tree (Figure 11.7) and will be faced with a choice of either carrying out her threat and receiving a payoff of −1 or moving R and receiving a payoff of zero. If player 2 is rational, she will prefer a payoff of zero to a payoff of −1. Only spite would cause her to carry out her threat under these circumstances. Therefore, if player 2 is rational, she will never act on her threat. Clearly, the (L, L) equilibrium is not satisfactory because it involves a noncredible threat.

MEDIA NOTE

GAME THEORY, INSURANCE, AND TERROR

Since the attack on the World Trade Center on 9/11/2001, businesses have had to worry about insuring themselves against terror attacks. One might think that the premiums for high-profile buildings in high-risk areas like New York City might be extremely high, far higher than comparable buildings in less famous areas. In fact, insurance companies have

MEDIA NOTE *(Contd.)*

set the price of insurance for landmark buildings in New York City so high that many owners have decided to go without such insurance. When one thinks about it, however, from a strategic point of view, the price differentials should not be so great because, while high-profile buildings are likely to be more attractive to terrorists, they are also more likely to have more security around them, while more mundane targets will not. In a perfect game–theoretic world, the protection should adjust so as to make the terrorist indifferent as to which building he attacks, thereby making the insurance premiums identical.

The situation in the insurance industry is quite different. Because insurance companies consider these risks to be incalculable, many firms do not offer terrorist insurance and there is a growing demand that the government step in and issue it.

Source: Adapted from "Can the Risk of Terrorism Be Calculated by Insurers? 'Game Theory' Might Do It Today, Bush Will Prod Congress to Act Soon on Terror Insurance," as appeared in the *Wall Street Journal,* April 8, 2002

Subgame Perfect (Credible Threat) Equilibria

The statement made by player 2 that was quoted previously specifies a plan of action that applies to the entire game tree. It tells us what she will do no matter what choices player 1 makes. If player 1 moves R instead of L, the game will proceed to node 2; and we can consider the remaining portion of the game tree at that point to be a subgame of the larger game. Nash equilibria are often supported by one player's expectation that if the game proceeds to a particular subgame, his or her opponent will take a certain action—carry out a threat. However, we want to narrow the set of equilibria down to those that rely only on credible threats.

Considering a threat to be credible is the same as saying that if the game ever progresses to the point where the threat is supposed to be carried out (in this case, in the subgame starting at node 2), the threat will, in fact, be acted on. In our example, player 2 will not carry out her threat in the subgame starting at node 2 because she has no incentive to actually take this action, even though it is specified in her strategy. The strategies of players 1 and 2 therefore do not produce an equilibrium in the subgame starting at node 2. These considerations lead us to define a subgame perfect equilibrium as follows: A set of strategies, one for each player, is a subgame perfect equilibrium if the actions prescribed by these strategies for the players once they reach any subgame constitute a Nash equilibrium for that subgame.

We will not consider an exact definition of a subgame here. For our purposes, it will be sufficient to define a subgame as any node on the game tree along with all the branches emanating from that node.

subgame
The remaining portion of the game tree at a given node of the larger game.

credible threats
Threats that, if the game ever progresses to the point where the threat is supposed to be carried out, will, in fact, be acted on.

subgame perfect equilibrium
A set of strategies, which constitute a Nash equilibrium, where the actions prescribed by these strategies for the players once they reach any subgame constitute a Nash equilibrium for that subgame.

backward induction
The process of solving a game by going to its end and working backward.

Backward Induction and Subgame Perfection

In games of perfect information, there is a simple way to locate subgame perfect equilibria. We can use backward induction, the process of solving a game by going to its end and working backward, to figure out what each player will do along the way. To understand this process, consider the game tree depicted in Figure 11.8.

In this game, player 1 moves first and can move either to the left (L) or to the right (R). If he moves L, player 2 has a choice of moving L or R, but no matter what she does, the game will end and each player will receive a payoff of 4. If player 1 moves R, player 2 again has a choice of moving L or R. However, both of

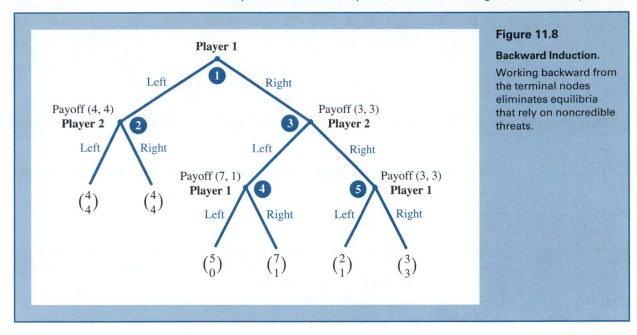

Figure 11.8

Backward Induction.

Working backward from the terminal nodes eliminates equilibria that rely on noncredible threats.

these choices lead to another move by player 1, who will then end the game by moving either L or R. The payoffs at the end of the game tree tell us what happens to the players depending on the path they take through the tree when they make their choices.

To find the subgame perfect equilibria in this game, let us work backward from the last move. For example, let us say that the game progresses to node 5, at which point player 1 will make the last move. If he decides to move R, he and player 2 will each receive a payoff of 3. If he moves L, he will receive a payoff of only 2 and player 2 will receive a payoff of only 1. If player 1 is rational, he will move R at node 5 and obtain a payoff of 3. Therefore, we can replace the subgame starting at node 5 with the payoff (3, 3). Similarly, if the game progresses to node 4 rather than node 5, this will be the last move for player 1. If he chooses R, he will receive a payoff of 7 and player 2 will receive a payoff of 1. If player 1 chooses L, he will receive a payoff of 5 and player 2 will receive a payoff of zero. Clearly, if player 1 is rational, he will move R.

Let us now look at node 3 of the game tree, where player 2 makes the move. When she contemplates this move, she knows that if she chooses R at node 3, player 1 will then move R at node 5 and her payoff will be 3, but if she chooses L at node 3, player 1 will move R at node 4 and her payoff will be 1. The value of node 3 to player 2 is therefore 3, and we can replace that node with the payoff of (3, 3) because we now know that if the game ever progresses to that node, it will then proceed to the terminal node, which has the payoff of (3, 3). Finally, let us look at node 1, where player 1 starts the game. He now knows that if he chooses R, the game will progress to node 3 and will eventually end at node 5, where he will receive a payoff of 3. If player 1 chooses L at node 1, it is obvious that the game will end at node 2, where he will receive a payoff of 4. Therefore, if player 1 is rational, he will move L at node 1.

The strategy in which player 1 moves L at node 1, player 2 moves R at node 3 (if she ever reaches that point, which she will not if player 1 chooses L at node

1), and then player 1 moves R at node 5 (if he ever reaches that point) is a subgame perfect equilibrium and is arrived at through a process of backward induction. This process picks out the credible threat equilibria because it goes to the end of the game first, determines what the players will do in all subgames, and brings these contingencies back to the first move of the game. After the first move is made, it is assumed that later moves will be rational if the players ever reach those points.

RESOLVING
TEASER 10

THE CENTIPEDE GAME

From our discussion of backward induction, it should be clear that game theory predicts that play of the centipede game should stop on the first move. The reason is simple. Think of player 2 at the last move. He or she has a choice between moving down (taking) and getting a payoff for him- or herself of 3.20 or moving to the right and getting a payoff of 1.60. Clearly, he or she will move down at that point, so we know the game will end there. At that termination, player 1 will get a payoff of 0.80. Now look at the next-to-last move where Player 1 moves and has a choice between moving down and getting a payoff of 1.60 and passing the game on to player 2, whom we know will move down and give player 1 a payoff of 0.80. Given this fact, player 1 will stop the game at the next-to-last move and get 1.60 for himself. If we continue this logic backward, we see that the game will end on the first move, where player 1 will get 0.40 and player 2 will get 0.10.

In the Palfrey-McKelvey experiment, the researchers played this game with many pairs of subjects repeatedly. The surprising result was that while game theory predicted that every play of the game would end at the first move, in fact only 6% of the games did. This is a dramatic rejection of the predictions of the theory. Why did it occur? Well, one reason is that game theory is a theory of how perfectly rational people will play games with other perfectly rational people where it is commonly known that all people are perfectly rational. If some people think that others are not that rational, they may behave differently. Second, notice that there is an opportunity for all players to do better in this game than having it end on the first move. If player 1 passes on the first move, then as long as player 2 does not take at that point, he or she will never regret that decision because from that point on his payoff will be higher than taking at move 1. Hence, if player 1 trusts that player 2 will not take on his or her first turn, it may be worthwhile to not take.

Rationality and Equity

The Traditional View

As we discussed in Chapter 2, economists use certain assumptions about human behavior in their work—that people are rational and selfish. Game theorists also make these assumptions. Hence, when they view a game, they base their strategic analysis strictly on the payoffs the players will receive. Game theorists further assume that each player is interested in his own payoff and cares about the payoffs of his opponents only to the extent that those payoffs will influence his opponents' actions.

EXPERIMENTAL EVIDENCE

THE ULTIMATUM GAME AND BACKWARD INDUCTION

This traditional view of human behavior in games has recently been challenged by experimental evidence. A number of economists have conducted experiments indicating that when people play games, they do, in fact, care about the equity of the outcomes of these games. Obviously, the results of such studies violate the traditional assumptions of selfishness and rationality. The most famous of these experiments was performed in Germany by Guth, Schmittberger, and Schwarze.[12] In their experiments, subjects were asked to play a simple game called an ultimatum game. In this two-person game, player 1 divides an amount of money, c, between himself and his opponent. He does this by specifying the amount of c that he wants to keep for himself. The remainder goes to his opponent, player 2. Let us call a_1 the amount that player 1 wants for himself and $c - a_1$ the amount that he leaves for player 2. Player 2 can either accept or reject the division of the money proposed by player 1. If player 2 accepts the proposed division, player 1 receives a_1 and player 2 receives $c - a_1$. If player 2 rejects the proposed division, both players receive a zero payoff.

---

[12] See Werner Guth, Rolf Schmittberger, and Bernd Schwarze, "An Experimental Analysis of Ultimatum Bargaining," *Journal of Economic Behavior and Organization* 3 (December 1982): no. 4, pp. 367–88.

If we use backward induction to analyze this game, it becomes clear that a *rational* player 1 will offer player 2 as small an amount of c as possible. In the last stage of the game, player 2 is given a choice between something positive and zero. If she is rational, she will accept whatever money player 1 offers her because *something is better than nothing*. Using the traditional assumptions of game theory about human behavior, we would therefore predict that the money in this game would be split in such a way that player 1 would receive almost all of it and player 2 would have to be content with a trifling sum.

Interestingly, this is not the result observed in the experiments conducted by Guth, Schmittberger, and Schwarze. These experiments found that the subjects who took the role of player 1 asked for only about 50% or 60% of the total money available despite the strategic advantage they had. They did not exploit this advantage to the fullest, which runs counter to the behavior we would expect based on our backward induction solution of the game. Furthermore, subjects who took the role of player 2 often rejected proposed divisions of the money when they felt that their share was *too low*. In other words, they were willing to receive no payment at all if they felt the amount offered them was *unfair*. Obviously, these subjects did not have the expected rational reaction that something is better than nothing.

Conclusion

This brief introduction to game theory presented some of its basic concepts and techniques. We will now begin to use game theory as a tool for strategic analysis. We will see how it can be applied to strategic situations that business enterprises face in their attempts to enter and control markets. In Chapter 13, we will put some of the concepts of game theory to work as we analyze the efforts of the jam maker in our primitive society to deal with one of the biggest problems faced by business enterprises—how to motivate people to work.

ultimatum game
A two-person game in which player 1 divides an amount of money, c, between himself and his opponent and the opponent either accepts or rejects the proposal.

Summary

In this chapter, we began our study of game theory by defining games of strategy as abstract sets of rules that constrain the behavior of players and specify their payoffs on the basis of the actions they and their opponents take. We found that games can be classified in various ways. For example, they can be classified according to their payoff structure, such as zero-sum games, in which the payoffs always add up to zero. Games can also be classified on the basis of the information players have about them, as in games of complete and incomplete information (see Appendix) and games of perfect and imperfect information. Still another way to classify games is according to whether the rules allow the players to communicate with each other, as in cooperative games, or forbid such communication, as in noncooperative games.

Using the idea of a best response, we defined an equilibrium for games as a Nash equilibrium—a state in which no player has any incentive to change his or her behavior given the behavior of the other players. We learned that a game offers an array of strategy choices, one for each player, and when the choices made are such that no player has any reason to change his choice, a Nash equilibrium has been achieved. We investigated a number of examples of equilibria for games, including one example in which there was no Nash equilibrium in pure strategies. To arrive at a Nash equilibrium in this case, we had to use mixed strategies—pure strategies with probabilities. We also examined the difference between credible and noncredible threats in games, and we looked at subgame perfect equilibria—equilibria that are supported by credible threats made by the players.

At several points during the chapter, we discussed various experiments that economists have conducted to test key assumptions of game theory. We found that the studies of Schotter, Weigelt, and Wilson indicate that the way a game is presented (in the extensive or normal form) will influence the way it is played, and the studies of Guth, Schmittberger, and Schwarze indicate that in the real world players may be less selfish than game theory has traditionally assumed.

APPENDIX A

GAMES OF INCOMPLETE INFORMATION

In this chapter, we dealt only with games of complete information. We assumed that the players were fully informed about the games in which they were involved. We also assumed that each player knew that the other players had this information. In short, we took it for granted that all information about a game was *common knowledge* among the players.

The assumption of complete information implies in particular that any given player in a game knows the rules and the entire game tree or matrix of the game, including the payoffs for the other players. This is a bold assumption because in real life there are many game-like situations in which the people involved do not know all there is to know about the situation. For example, the players in such "games" often do not know the payoff functions of their opponents. In other words, each player does not understand the motivation of the other players in the game. He does not know what makes his opponents "tick." Obviously, in such a game—a game of incomplete information—it would be much more difficult to find an equilibrium, especially for the players themselves because they cannot assess the incentives of their opponents to deviate from a particular array of strategies.

Determining a Bayes-Nash Equilibrium

Before we investigate what an equilibrium might be for a game of incomplete information, let us first restate the problem slightly so that we can think of it in a different way. Let us represent the fact that any player in such a game does not know what his opponents are like by assuming that he is facing a set of players of different types and that he knows the probabilities attached to each type. As a player in a game of incomplete information, he knows what type of player he is, but he can only know what types of players his opponents are probabilistically. For example, he might know that an opponent could be one of two types—either type a or type b. He might also know that the probability of her being type a is p and the probability of her being type b is $1 - p$. His opponent has the same limited amount of information. She knows what type of player she is but only knows her opponent's type probabilistically. She knows that there is a probability of q that her opponent is type a and a probability of $1 - q$ that he is type b.

We might think of a game of incomplete information as being played in stages. In stage 1, each player is assigned a type, possibly by chance—for example, by drawing a piece of paper with a type written on it from a hat. The composition of the pieces of paper in the hat reflects the probability of picking a piece of paper with a certain type recorded on it—in this case, with either an "a" or a "b" recorded on it. (For example, there may be 10 pieces of paper—5 with the letter "a" and 5 with the letter "b." When a player picks a piece of paper at random, there is a 0.5 chance that it will contain an "a" and a 0.5 chance that it will contain a "b.")

In stage 2 of the game, each player reads the type recorded on the piece of paper picked at random but does not reveal this information to the other player. After learning what type he or she is, each player then chooses a strategy for the game. Note that a strategy in this game is slightly different from a strategy in the games we discussed before. In this game, a strategy is a rule that specifies what action a player will take depending on the type recorded on the piece of paper drawn. For example, let us assume that there are two possible types a player can be—type a or type b—and there are two possible actions that a player can take in the game—action 1 or action 2. A strategy for this particular game of incomplete information might be a rule that states, "Take action 1 if you are type a, and take action 2 if you are type b."

Now that we have an idea of the kind of strategy that is needed for a game of incomplete information, we can describe what a Nash equilibrium might be like in such a game. The equilibrium that we are looking for is a special type of Nash equilibrium known as a **Bayes-Nash equilibrium**.[13] We can define a Bayes-Nash equilibrium as follows: Given an array of strategies (or action rules) $s^* = (s_1^*, \ldots, s_n^*)$ for an n-person game of incomplete information, a Bayes-Nash equilibrium occurs when each player, given the specified strategies for all types of players and given the probabilities about what types the other players in the game might be, cannot increase his or her expected payoff by deviating from s^*.

Bayes-Nash equilibrium
An equilibrium defined for a game of incomplete information that takes into account the fact that a player may be facing opponents of different, random types.

An Example of a Bayes-Nash Equilibrium

To gain a better understanding of the Bayes-Nash equilibrium, let us consider the following game. This game involves two players whom we will designate players 1 and 2. Let us assume that the players are of two possible types, a and b, and that each player has two possible strategies, which we will call strategies 1 and 2. The payoffs in this game differ according to the type of player involved and the type of opponent the player faces. Table 11.15 contains four matrices showing the payoffs from all the possible combinations of player types. For example, matrix 1

---

[13] The Bayes-Nash equilibrium is named after Thomas Bayes, an eighteenth-century English clergyman who was instrumental in the development of probability theory and proposed a formula for changing probabilities as new information about an event accrues.

Table 11.15   The Possible Payoffs of a Game of Incomplete Information.

MATRIX 1				MATRIX 2		
	Player 2a				Player 2b	
	Action 1	Action 2			Action 1	Action 2
Player 1a Action 1	4, 7	3, 0	**Player 1a** Action 1		4, 0	3, 6
Action 2	3, 6	5, 1	Action 2		3, 1	5, 7

MATRIX 3				MATRIX 4		
	Player 2a				Player 2b	
	Action 1	Action 2			Action 1	Action 2
Player 1b Action 1	5, 7	5, 0	**Player 1b** Action 1		5, 0	5, 6
Action 2	2, 6	1, 1	Action 2		2, 1	1, 7

indicates the payoffs that will occur if both players are type a. Matrix 2 indicates the payoffs that will occur if player 1 is type a and player 2 is type b.

Assume that players 1a and 2a are selected for the game. Matrix 1 depicts the payoff for this combination of players. However, because we are dealing with a game of incomplete information, the players are unsure about the payoffs of their opponents. Player 1 knows his own payoffs, but he does not know whether his opponent—player 2—is type a or type b, so he does not know if the payoffs for the game appear in matrix 1 or matrix 2. Similarly, player 2 knows what her payoffs are, but she does not know whether her opponent—player 1—is type a or type b. As a result, she does not know whether matrix 1 or matrix 3 contains the payoffs for the game.

To derive the equilibrium for this game, let us look at each player individually, starting with player 1. We have already said that he has drawn type a and will therefore receive the payoffs indicated by matrix 1 or matrix 2. If his opponent is also type a, matrix 1 will be the relevant matrix. Note that in this matrix, player 2a has a dominant strategy, which is to take action 1. Thus, player 1a knows that if he is facing player 2a, his opponent will choose action 1. If, however, player 1a is facing player 2b, matrix 2 is the relevant matrix, and player 1a knows that there is another dominant strategy, which will cause player 2b to choose action 2.

As we discussed previously, the probability of player 2 being either type a or type b is 0.5. Given this probability, let us now calculate the expected payoff to player 1a from taking either action 1 or action 2. If player 1a chooses action 1 and his opponent is type a, matrix 1 indicates that player 2a will choose action 1, and as a result, player 1a will receive a payoff of 4. On the other hand, if player 1a chooses action 1 but his opponent is type b, then according to matrix 2, player 2b will choose action 2, which will lead to a payoff of 3 for player 1a. Hence, if player 1a selects action 1, we can summarize his expected payoff as follows.

Expected payoff for player 1a from choosing action 1 = 0.5(4) + 0.5(3) = 3.5

If player 1a chooses action 2 and his opponent is type a, matrix 1 indicates that player 2a will select action 1, which means that player 1a will receive a payoff of 3. If player 1a chooses action 2 but his opponent is type b, matrix 2 shows that player 2b will select action 2, in which case the payoff to player 1a will be 5. When player 1a chooses action 2, we can summarize his expected payoff as follows.

Expected payoff for player 1a from choosing action 2 = 0.5(3) + 0.5(5) = 4

Now let us assume that player 1 draws type b. He will therefore receive the payoffs that appear in matrix 3 or matrix 4. If his opponent is type a, matrix 3 is the relevant matrix for the game. Note that in this matrix, player 2a has a dominant strategy, which will cause her to choose action 1. If, however, player 1b has an opponent who is type b, matrix 4 is the relevant matrix and the dominant strategy for player 2b is to choose action 2. Again, the probability of player 2 being either type a or type b is 0.5. Using this probability, let us calculate the expected payoff to player 1b from selecting either action 1 or action 2.

If player 1b chooses action 1, matrix 3 indicates that player 2a will choose action 1 and the resulting payoff to player 1b will be 5. On the other hand, if player 1b chooses action 1 but his opponent is type b, matrix 4 shows that player 2b will choose action 2. In this case, the payoff to player 1b will be 5. We can summarize the expected payoff to player 1b from selecting action 1 as follows.

Expected payoff for player 1b from choosing action $1 = 0.5(5) + 0.5(5) = 5$

If player 1b chooses action 2 and his opponent is type a, matrix 3 tells us that player 2a will choose action 1, which will mean a payoff of 2 for player 1b. If player 1b chooses action 2 but his opponent is type b, matrix 4 indicates that player 2b will choose action 2. As a result, player 1b will receive a payoff of 1. We can summarize the expected payoff to player 1b from selecting action 2 as follows.

Expected payoff for player 1b from choosing action $2 = 0.5(2) + 0.5(1) = 1.5$

The foregoing analysis of player 1's position in this game of incomplete information shows us that if he is type a, he is better off choosing action 2, but if he is type b, he is better off choosing action 1. Such an analysis allows us to describe player 1's strategy for the game because it tells us exactly what he will do in stage 2 of the game regardless of which type he draws.

If we apply this kind of analysis to player 2's position, we will also discover her strategy for the game. For example, we will find that if she is type a, her best choice is action 1, which will give her a payoff of 7, whereas if she is a type b, her best choice is action 2, which will give her a payoff of 6.

We now have two strategies for this game of incomplete information—one strategy for each of the players. Player 1's strategy is to choose action 2 if he is type a and to choose action 1 if he is type b, while player 2's strategy is to choose action 1 if she is type a and to choose action 2 if she is type b. These two strategies are equilibrium strategies for the game because each was derived by using the assumption that there is a probability of 0.5 that the opposing player is type a or type b. We know that these strategies are a best response to such a probability because that is exactly how these strategies were derived. Hence, if player 1 is using his strategy and is type a or type b with a probability of 0.5 and the same is true of player 2, then neither player will have any incentive to deviate. Thus, given the distribution of types, these two strategies form a Bayes-Nash equilibrium for the game.

APPENDIX B

REPEATED GAMES

Until now, we have assumed that a game is played once and only once by a group of players, regardless of whether it is a game of complete or incomplete information. We know, however, that in real life people play the same games over and over again as time passes. For example, each year, General Motors and Ford, the two leading U.S. automobile manufacturers, repeat a game in which they both choose prices and styles for their cars and then compete for market share. While this game changes somewhat over time, we can think of it as essentially a repetition of the same game. Another example of a repeated game is the annual budget battle that we see within many organizations. Year after year, the various departments of these organizations compete for their share of the budget, often using exactly the same set of strategies they used previously. Clearly, repeated games are an important class of games in the real world.

What precisely do we mean by a repeated game? We can define such a game as one in which a fixed set of players repeatedly play the same game against each other. In this appendix, we will analyze games played repeatedly over time that do not change and are not affected by the previous outcomes.

repeated game
A game in which a fixed set of players repeatedly play the same game against each other.

The Prisoner's Dilemma Game

Let us consider an example of a repeated game that involves two players—the famous prisoner's dilemma game. The matrix in Table 11.16 depicts the payoffs from this game.

This game has a payoff structure that is identical to the payoff structure of the pricing game described in the "Equilibria for Games" section. The typical scenario used to explain the prisoner's dilemma game is as follows: Two people commit a crime and are apprehended by the police. These prisoners know they are guilty, but they also know that the police do not have the evidence to convict them of a serious crime unless one of them talks. If they both keep quiet and do not confess, the police can convict them of only a lesser offense (loitering at the scene of a crime) and put them in jail for a minimal amount of time. Assume that this outcome yields a payoff of 6 to each player, as shown in the upper left cell of the matrix. If player 1 confesses and player 2 does not, then player 1 is released in exchange for his testimony, while player 2 is convicted of the serious crime of robbery and receives a long jail sentence. This outcome yields a payoff of 12 for player 1 and a payoff of 2 for player 2, as indicated in the lower left cell of the matrix. If player 2 confesses and player 1 does not, then the payoffs are reversed. Player 1 receives a payoff of 2 and player 2 receives a payoff of 12, as shown in the upper right cell of the matrix. If both prisoners confess, they are allowed to plea bargain and receive an intermediate sentence, which yields a payoff of 4 to each of them, as shown in the lower right cell of the matrix.

When the two prisoners arrive at the police station, they are separated and kept apart. Because they are not allowed to communicate and make binding agreements, these prisoners are involved in a noncooperative game. What set of strategies will form an equilibrium for this game? An examination of the matrix of payoffs in Table 11.16 makes it clear what each prisoner should do.

If player 1 thinks his partner in crime will not confess, he can also refuse to confess and receive a minimal jail term, which will yield him a payoff of 6. However, his best choice is to confess so that he can be released, in which case he will

Table 11.16	The Payoffs from the Prisoner's Dilemma Game.		
		PLAYER 2	
		Do Not Confess	**Confess**
Player 1	Do Not Confess	6, 6	2, 12
	Confess	12, 2	4, 4

receive a payoff of 12. If player 1 thinks player 2 will confess, then confessing is again his best response because he will be able to plea bargain and obtain an intermediate sentence, which gives him a payoff of 4 instead of the 2 he would receive by not confessing. In short, confessing is the best choice he can make *no matter what the other player does*. This means that confessing is a dominant strategy for player 1. Because the game is symmetric, confessing is also a dominant strategy for player 2. Thus, if the two players follow their dominant strategies in the game, both of them will confess. However, this situation raises a problem. If both players confess, the payoff to each is only 4, while if both players do not confess, the payoff to each will be 6. In other words, the dominant strategy of each player leads to an outcome that is not Pareto optimal. Both players would do better if they did not confess, but neither trusts the other not to double-cross him by confessing; thus, confessing is a dominant strategy for both players.

Repeated Games with Finite Horizons

Based on what we know about the dominant strategy of each player in the prisoner's dilemma game, if this game is played only once, we would predict that each player would confess. Should we expect to see different behavior if the game is repeated 100 times or 100,000 times by the same set of players? Our first reaction might be to answer yes to this question. We might reason that if the players have more time to observe the results of their strategic interaction, they may demonstrate good faith and build up mutual trust. In a game that will be played only once, there is no future, and hence the players can expect no payoff from restraint in the short run. This logic seems compelling, but it is not correct.

If we use a backward induction argument like the one described in the "Credible Threats" section, we can see that adding a longer horizon to the problem so that we can repeat the game many times does nothing to change the equilibrium outcome. Whenever the game is played, each player will confess. Repeating the prisoner's dilemma game over a long horizon does not turn it into a cooperative game and thereby alter its equilibrium outcome. However, this does not mean that if we were to observe such a game actually being played over and over again in real life or in a laboratory, we would find that people always confess. In fact, laboratory experiments by Rapoport and Chammah tested just this question and found that in the initial stages of a game, people did cooperate by not confessing. This cooperation broke down in the later stages of the game, but it did at least exist during some portion of the game's history.[14] From the standpoint of both logic and game theory, this should not happen.

To understand why we would expect the players to confess at each stage, let us look at the last period of a game with a long horizon. In this period, there is no future for the players to consider, so the situation is identical to the situation we find when a game will be played only once. Both players will confess because they will not trust each other and will therefore use their dominant strategy for the game. But this means that when the players are in the next-to-last period of the game, they will again feel that there is no future because what will happen in the final round is already determined. Hence, the players will have no reason to build trust at that stage of the game. The next-to-last period therefore becomes like the last period, and both players will confess. By continuing to use this backward

---

[14] Anatol Rapoport and Albert Chammah, *Prisoner's Dilemma* (Ann Arbor, MI: University of Michigan Press, 1965).

induction method of analysis until we reach the first round of the game, we can demonstrate that the players will choose to confess in all periods. The same argument would hold if the game were repeated a million times. Whenever we have a game with a finite horizon—a finite number of stages—backward induction determines the outcome.

finite horizon game
A repeated game with a finite number of repetitions.

infinite horizon game
A game repeated over an infinite horizon.

discount factor
Measures how much a player values future payoffs relative to current payoffs.

Repeated Games with Infinite Horizons

What happens when a game has an infinite horizon—is infinitely repeated? Such a game is called a supergame. As we will see, when a game lasts forever, there are equilibria in which the players cooperate at every stage of the game as long as their discount factors are not too low. A discount factor measures how much a player values future payoffs relative to current payoffs.

To gain a better understanding of games with infinite horizons, let us assume that players 1 and 2 are involved in such a game. (Obviously, their lives will be limited in length, so they will not be able to play the game for an infinite period. We will simply assume that they represent groups that will continue the game indefinitely. For example, the president of the United States might feel that he is making decisions for an entity that will always exist even though it will be governed by others in the future.) At every stage of the game, the two players will make choices, and based on those choices, each of them will receive a payoff. However, because some of the payoffs will be received in future periods, we need a way to compare the payoffs that are received today to the payoffs that will be received tomorrow. Presumably, any payoff received today is better than the same payoff received tomorrow. The players always have the option of waiting until tomorrow to enjoy a payoff received today, but in the meantime, they can use that payoff to their advantage. For example, say that the payoffs in a game are in dollars. Clearly, if a player receives a dollar today, he can either enjoy it immediately by using it to buy something he wants or deposit that dollar in the bank and earn interest on it, thereby having more than a dollar to enjoy five years from now.

To carry this analogy further, assume that a player has A dollars and puts this amount in the bank for one year at an interest rate of r percent a year. At the end of one year, he will have $A(1 + r)$ dollars. Therefore, A dollars today are worth $A(1 + r)$ dollars one year from now. If the player puts A dollars in the bank for two years, letting the amount grow at r percent a year, he will have $A(1 + r)$ $(1 + r)$ or $A(1 + r)^2$ dollars after two years. In general, we can say that A dollars today are worth $A(1 + r)^t$ dollars t years from now.

Now let us evaluate a stream of payoffs into the future. Turning this analysis around, we can ask the following question: What is the present value of B dollars paid to a player t years in the future? To obtain B dollars t years from now, he would have to put only $B/(1 + r)^t$ dollars in the bank today. Therefore $B/(1 + r)^t$ is the present value of B dollars t years from now. To apply these concepts to games of strategy, let us say that players 1 and 2 are involved in a game that will be played over an infinite horizon and are using a strategy array that, if adhered to, will yield them a payoff stream of $a = (a_0, a_1, \ldots, a_t, \ldots)$, where a_0 is the payoff in the current period (0), a_1 is the payoff in period 1, and a_t is the payoff in period t. The dots indicate that because this is an infinite game, the payoff stream stretches into the infinite future. If we denote the current period of time as period 0, the value to the players of this payoff stream today is $a_0/(1 + r)^0 + a_1/(1 + r)^1 + a_2/(1 + r)^2 + \ldots$ or $\pi_i = \sum_{t=0}^{\infty} a_t/(1 + r)^t$, where $\sum_{t=0}^{\infty}$ means "add" the terms to the right from period 0 to infinity.

This expression represents the payoff to a player in such an infinitely repeated game, where the payoff stream is the one indicated above. Note that the payoff today, in period 0, is simply $a_0/(1+r)^0$ or a_0 because $(1+r)^0 = 1$. Tomorrow's payoff is worth $a_1/(1+r)^1$ today, and the payoff in period t is worth $a_t/(1+r)^t$. Note that as t becomes large, because $r \geq 0$, $a_t/(1+r)^t$ goes to zero. This means that payoffs in the distant future are not considered important by decision makers today. If we let $\delta = 1/(1+r)$ be called the discount factor of a player, it is clear that as δ becomes smaller, the player cares less and less about future payoffs (because any future payoff, a_t, will be multiplied by δ^t, and as δ^t becomes small, the value of a_t today becomes small).

Finally, let us note that if a player were to receive the same payoff $\bar{a}$ period after period forever, then that player would receive the payoff $\pi_i = \sum_{t=0}^{\infty} \delta^t \bar{a}$. Although this is a sum over an infinite horizon, its value is not infinite because as time passes, the value of the payoff $\bar{a}$ in the far distant future becomes negligible. In fact, it can be shown that this sum is equal to $\bar{a}/(1-\delta)$, which is the present value of an infinite stream of payoffs, each one of exactly $\bar{a}$.

With this background information, let us now return to the prisoner's dilemma game. We want to demonstrate that in a game with an infinite horizon, it is possible to have cooperation between the players at all stages of the game. (Of course, as we have already seen, cooperation at all stages is not possible in a finite game.) Let C be the action of confessing and DC be the action of not confessing. Let the following be the strategy of each player.

1. Do not confess in period 0.

2. Continue not to confess as long as your opponent does not confess.

3. If your opponent ever cheats and confesses, then confess at every stage of the game from that point until the end of time.

If this strategy is used by both sides in the supergame, it represents an implicit agreement to cooperate at every stage and to punish a player forever if he does not cooperate. The term **trigger strategy** is used to describe this type of strategy because one deviation triggers an infinite punishment. It is also called a **grim strategy** because the punishment for deviation is so drastic.

If each player uses such a strategy, then the pair of strategies constitutes a Nash equilibrium for the supergame if the discount factor of the players, Δ, is large enough. To test the validity of this claim, let us say that in the supergame both players use the strategy outlined above. Therefore, at every stage of the game, these players will receive the payoff associated with not confessing, which we will denote as (DC, DC). The present value of obtaining this constant payoff forever is $(DC, DC)/(1-\delta)$ or, using the numbers in Table 11.16, $6/(1-\delta)$. If the strategy described above has produced a Nash equilibrium, then there must be no incentive for either player to deviate from this strategy. Let us now check to see if there is an incentive to deviate. For example, let us say that player 1 contemplates cheating in period t by confessing to the police. His strategy will then be as follows: "I will choose DC for all periods until period t. In period t, I will deviate and choose C. From that point on, however, I know that my opponent will try to punish me forever by choosing C. Therefore, my best response to such a punishment is to choose C also, and that is what I will do from period $t+1$ on." Such a deviation strategy will yield player 1 a payoff stream of $a_1^1(DC, DC), \ldots, a_{t-1}^1(DC, DC), \ldots, a_1^t(C, DC), a_1^{t+1}(C, C), a^{t+2}(C, C), \ldots$. What this tells us is that if player 1 plans to deviate in period t but player 2 adheres to the original strategy, then player 1 will receive the payoff from cooperation for all periods

trigger strategy (grim strategy)
A type of strategy in an infinite horizon repeated game where one deviation triggers an infinite punishment.

until period t. In period t, when he deviates and double-crosses player 2, he will receive a payoff of $a_1(C, DC)$ for that period. From then on, his payoff will be the much less desirable one that results when both players choose to confess: $a_1(C, C)$. The following question now arises: Is such a deviation profitable given that the other player will not change her planned strategy? Put differently, is the payoff that player 1 will receive during the period when he double-crosses player 2 sufficiently enticing to make him want to risk a poor payoff in the infinite number of periods that will follow?

To define the conditions under which no deviation is profitable, let P_1 be the payoff to player 1 in the supergame. If player 2 adheres to her strategy, then player 1's payoff from deviating when discounted to the beginning of the game is $P_1 = \sum_{\rho=0}^{t-1} \delta^\rho a_1(DC, DC) + \delta^t a_1(C, DC) + \sum_{\rho=t+1}^{\infty} \delta^\rho a_1(C, C)$. The payoff from adhering to the proposed strategy is $P_1 = \sum_{\rho=0}^{\infty} \delta^\rho a_1(DC, DC)$.

Note that until period t, these two strategies yield the same payoff because they both dictate the same actions. In period t, however, the payoffs differ. If we look at this situation from the perspective of period 0, would it be profitable to plan to deviate in period t? Such a deviation is profitable if $\delta^t a_1 (C, DC) + \sum_{\rho=t+1}^{\infty} \delta^\rho a_1(C, C) \geq \sum_{\rho=t}^{\infty} \delta^\rho a_1(DC, DC)$. The term on the left side of the inequality shows the payoff stream from deviating in period t, and the term on the right side of the inequality shows the payoff stream from not deviating. This inequality can be rewritten as $\delta^t(a_1(DC, DC)/(1-\delta) \leq \delta^t a_1(C, DC) + \delta^{t+1} a_1(C, C)/(1-\delta)$.

After algebraic manipulation, we find that a deviation is profitable if and only if

$$\delta < \frac{a_1(C, DC) - a_1(DC, DC)}{a_1(C, DC) - a_1(C, C)}$$

Using the payoffs from the prisoner's dilemma game that are depicted in Table 11.16, we see that deviation is profitable if

$$\delta < \frac{12 - 6}{12 - 4} = \frac{6}{8}$$

The more that players discount the future (the smaller δ is), the more likely it is that infinite cooperation will not be an equilibrium strategy. Such players tend to care more about the big payoff they will receive when they deviate than the infinite stream of poor payoffs that will result from deviation.

Exercises and Problems

1. Consider the following (not so unrealistic) scenario for a conflict between Iraq and the United States in the Persian Gulf area.

   - Iraq moves first and decides whether or not to invade Kuwait.

   - If Iraq does not invade Kuwait, the game is over and Iraq receives a payoff of 0, while the United States receives a payoff of 1,000.

   - If Iraq invades Kuwait, the United States must decide whether or not to send troops to Saudi Arabia.

   - If the United States does not send troops to Saudi Arabia, then the game is over and the payoff is 1,000 for Iraq and 100 for the United States.

   - If the United States sends troops to Saudi Arabia, Iraq must decide whether or not to leave Kuwait.

- If Iraq leaves Kuwait, the game is over and the payoff is −1,000 for Iraq (which is humiliated) and 500 for the United States.

- If Iraq decides to stay in Kuwait, the United States must decide whether or not to attack Iraq.

- If the United States does not attack Iraq, the game is over. The presence of U.S. troops in Saudi Arabia is viewed as a farce and the United States suffers a great loss of prestige, while Iraq claims to have conquered "the evil intruder." Iraq therefore receives a payoff of 1,000, and the United States receives a payoff of −700.

- If the United States attacks Iraq and wins the resulting war, the game is over. However, because the United States wins with great casualties, the payoffs are $U^* = -500$ for the United States and $I^* = -900$ for Iraq.

    a. Present this story as a two-person in extensive form; that is, draw the game tree. What is the subgame perfect equilibrium?

    b. If $I^* = -500$ and $U^* = -900$, what is the subgame perfect equilibrium for the game?

    c. If $I^* = -900$ and $U^* = 150$, what is the subgame perfect equilibrium for the game?

2. Assume that there is a game called "picking the last stone from a pile of four stones." This game has three players, A, B, and C, who have four stones set in front of them. The rules of the game are as follows: A moves first and takes one or two stones, B moves next and takes one or two stones, then C moves and takes one or two stones, and finally A picks up the last stone if there is one left. Whoever picks up the last (fourth) stone wins.

   a) Draw the extensive form of the game.

   b) What are the subgame perfect equilibria for this game?

   c) Is it ever possible for player A to win this game? Explain your answer.

3. Consider a town consisting solely of one straight main street along which all the stores are located. Let us depict this situation as follows: The town starts at A and ends at B. People are distributed equally along the main street so that there are as many people between 0 and $\frac{1}{4}$ as there are between $\frac{3}{4}$ and 1, or, for that matter, on any two segments of the same length. Two gas stations that are identical in all respects (including price and level of service) want to locate along the main street. Assume that the inhabitants of the town will patronize the gas station that is closest to them. Where, along the main street, will the gas stations position themselves? That is, what are their positions at the Nash equilibrium for this game?

4. Suppose that there is a game called "the dollar auction game." This game involves auctioning a dollar bill to two individuals. The rules of the game are as follows: Bidding starts at $0.05 and increases in five-cent increments. A bidder can drop out of the auction at any time by raising a white card that says "Surrender." When this happens, the dollar bill goes to the bidder who did not drop out and the price is the amount of his last bid. The loser, however, must also pay the auctioneer the amount of his last bid. For example, assume that player 2 bids $0.80 and player 1 bids $0.85. Then player 2 drops out, player 1 wins the dollar for $0.85 cents, and player 2 must pay $0.80 to the auctioneer. Is there a Nash equilibrium for this game? If not, why not?

5. Let us say that there is a game called "the sealed bid mechanism game." In this game, a buyer and a seller will exchange a good produced by the seller. Before making the exchange, the seller finds his cost (C) for the good, which can be any amount between 0 and 100 with equal probability. This cost is known to the seller but not to the buyer. The buyer, on the other hand, finds the value (V) of the good to her, which can also be any amount between 0 and 100 with equal probability. The seller knows nothing about the value of the good to the buyer. Keeping her information about the value of the good *private*, the buyer submits bid B. The seller submits asking price C. If $B > C$, a transaction takes place at price P, which is the average of the bid and the asking price; that is, $P = (B + C)/2$. If $B \leq C$, no transaction occurs. When a transaction takes place, the payoffs to the buyer and the seller are $\Pi_B = V - P$ and $\Pi_s = P - C$, respectively. The payoffs to the buyer and the seller are zero if no transaction occurs.

   a) Define a strategy for the buyer and the seller in this game.

   b) Show that the following strategy pairs form a Nash equilibrium for this game.

$$\text{If } V \geq 50, \text{ bid } 50.$$

   Buyer's Strategy :

$$\text{If } V < 50, \text{ bid } 0.$$
$$\text{If } C \leq 50, \text{ ask } 50.$$

   Seller's Strategy :

$$\text{If } C > 50, \text{ ask } 100.$$

   c) Using exactly the same argument as above, show that, in fact, the following strategy pairs form a Nash equilibrium for this game. Consider X as any number between 0 and 100 (including these two numbers).

$$\text{If } V \geq X, \text{ bid } X.$$

   Buyer's Strategy :

$$\text{If } V < X, \text{ bid } 0.$$
$$\text{If } C \leq X, \text{ ask } X.$$

   Seller's Strategy :

$$\text{If } C < X, \text{ ask } 100.$$

   (*Hint*: See if there is any incentive to deviate.)

6. Consider the following three-person game in which player 1 chooses the row, player 2 chooses the column, and player 3 chooses the matrix that will be played.

	L	R			L	R
l	6, 3, 2	4, 8, 6		l	8, 1, 1	0, 0, 5
r	2, 3, 9	4, 2, 0		r	9, 4, 9	0, 0, 0

The first number in each cell is the payoff to player 1, the second number is the payoff to player 2, and the third number is the payoff to player 3. Find the Nash equilibrium for this game.

7. Consider the following game in which player 1 chooses a row and player 2 chooses a column.

	L	C	R
T	3, 1	0, 5	1, 2
M	4, 2	8, 7	6, 4
B	5, 7	5, 8	2, 5

a) Does player 1 have a dominant strategy?

b) Does player 2 have a dominant strategy?

c) What is the Nash equilibrium for this game? Is it *ever* possible for either player to use a strategy other than his dominant strategy? Explain.

8. Consider a game called "the chain store game." In it, a company operates a chain of stores in 20 towns. In each of these towns, there is a potential competitor—an entrepreneur from the area who might raise money at the local bank in order to establish a second store of the same kind. Thus, the game has 21 players: the chain store company, which we will call player 0, and its potential competitor in each town k (which we will call player k), where k is numbered from 1 to 20. At the moment, none of the 20 potential competitors has enough capital to take on the chain store company. But with the passage of time, these entrepreneurs will be able to raise the money they need from their local banks. Assume that player 1 (in town 1) will be the first to acquire the necessary capital, then player 2 (in town 2), and so on. Thus, the game will be played over 20 periods. In period 1, player 1 must decide between two options: going in or staying out (opening or not opening a second store to compete with the chain store in his town). If he chooses to stay out, he does not open the store and player 0's decision becomes irrelevant. As a result, player 0 receives a payoff of 5 and player 1 receives a payoff of 1. If, however, player 1 chooses to go in, player 0 must choose between being cooperative or aggressive (being accommodating or fighting the entry of the second store). If the decision is to fight, both players receive a payoff of zero, while if the decision is to be accommodating, both players receive a payoff of 2. Similarly, in period 2, player 2 must choose between going in or staying out, and if she chooses to go in, player 0 must choose between being cooperative or aggressive. This game will continue for 20 periods. Thus, in each period k, the payoffs to player 0 and the potential competitor, player k (in town k), are the ones given in the following matrix.

	In	Out
Cooperative	2, 2	5, 1
Aggressive	0, 0	5, 1

The first number in each cell of the matrix is player 0's payoff, and the second number is player k's payoff. The total payoff that player 0, the chain store company, receives in the game is the sum of its payoffs in the 20 periods. Each potential competitor receives a payoff only in the period when he or she is involved in the game.

a) What is the subgame perfect equilibrium for this game?

b) Does it seem likely that this equilibrium will occur if the game is actually played for money in a laboratory or in real life?

9. Assume that there is a two-person game with the payoffs depicted in the following matrix.

		Player 2	
		Left	Right
Player 1	Top	+1, −1	−1, +1
	Bottom	−1, +1	+1, −1

Also assume that player 2 uses the strategies of moving to the left and moving to the right with a probability of 0.5 for each.

a) Calculate the expected payoff to player 1 when he uses the strategy of moving to the top and when he uses the strategy of moving to the bottom.

b) Now suppose that player 1 uses the strategies of moving to the top and moving to the bottom with a probability of 0.5 for each. Calculate the expected payoff to player 2 when she moves to the left and when she moves to the right.

c) When each player uses each of the two strategies with a probability of 0.5, does the pair of mixed strategies constitute a Nash equilibrium? Explain your reasoning.

Decision Making Over Time

EXPERIMENTAL
TEASER 11

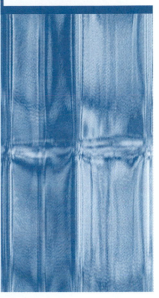

WAGE PROFILES

Everyone likes a raise in salary. Raises are supposed to show us that we are doing a good job and that we are appreciated. This implies that people should like an increasing wage profile over ones that decrease, that is, a stream of wages on the job that increase over time as opposed to ones that decrease. For example, say that you are 35 years old and thinking of taking one of two jobs. Both jobs offer you the same total amount of money over the next 30 years (say that you are not expecting to leave the job once you take it and will retire there at age 65). One job starts out with a low salary and increases that salary each year, albeit at a decreasing rate, so that you earn big raises in your middle years at the job but smaller raises as you near retirement. The other profile offers you a high salary now but decreases your wage each year until you retire. If both profiles pay you the same total amount over the 35 years, which would you prefer?

When asked this question in a survey by George Loewenstein and Nachum Sicherman,* most people preferred the increasing wage profile. This is counter to economic theory's belief that people choose so as to maximize their discounted present value. Why?

* George Loewenstein and Nachum Sicherman, "Do Workers Prefer Increasing Wage Profiles?" *Journal of Labor Economics* 9 (January 1991): no. 1, pp. 67–84.

EXPERIMENTAL
TEASER 12

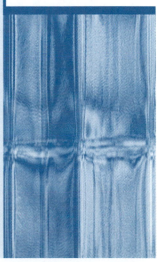

TIME INCONSISTENCY

Say that you were offered a choice today between getting $100 in four weeks or $110 in five weeks. To make this choice, you would have to assess how you felt about these amounts and the delays in getting them. Then say you were asked to choose between $100 today and $110 in one week. Note that here the delay between the $100 and $110 is the same as before; it just happens now rather than in one month. According to orthodox economic theory, these choices must be consistent. If you choose the delayed $110 in five weeks, you should also choose to wait for the $110 when offered the choice today. Such choices are "time consistent."

An experiment done by Kris Kirby and R. J. Herrnstein* indicates that people are often "time inconsistent" in their choices. They choose the $100 today but claim to want the $110 in five weeks. What type of people would be vulnerable to such a reversal? Do you think that there is any part of your life where you exhibit similar behavior? I suspect there is.

* Kris Kirby and R.J. Herrnstein, "Preference Reversals due to Myopic Discounting of Delayed Reward," *Psychological Science* 6 (March 1995): no. 2, pp. 83–89.

One limitation of our analysis so far is that we have not included time in the decision making problems we have discussed. We know, however, that this is a shortcoming because, in life, we make choices today that will have consequences for us tomorrow or the day after. In fact, many times we need to sacrifice money or utility today in order to increase our satisfaction in the future. If this is the case, however, then we must have a way of comparing money received today to that received in the future because we will often need to know whether a sacrifice made today will be worth it when we receive benefits, say, one year from now. For example, if I invest $1 today and receive $2.25 three years from now, is that a good deal?

Whether it is a good deal or not depends on how we view (or discount) the future. Clearly, if given a choice between $1 today and $1 in one year, people would choose to take the dollar today. (We could always put the dollar in our mattress and wait one year and be no worse off.) So it appears as if we have a preference for the present over the future. The questions to ask are the following: How do we incorporate that preference into decision making, and are such preferences consistent? This is what we will discuss in this chapter.

Discounting the Future

As we have said above, people tend to have a preference for the present. To see why this may be, assume that a decision maker has A dollars and puts this amount in the bank for one year at an interest rate of r percent a year. At the end of one year, he will have $A(1 + r)$ dollars. Therefore, A dollars today are worth $A(1 + r)$ dollars one year from now. If you offered to give the decision maker A now or less than $A(1 + r)$ in one year, he or she would reject it and choose to have A now instead because he or she could put that A in the bank and receive $A(1 + r)$ in one year. If the player puts A dollars in the bank for two years, letting the amount grow at r percent a year, he will have $A(1 + r)(1 + r)$ or $A(1 + r)^2$ dollars after two years. In general, we can say that A dollars today are worth $A(1 + r)^t$ dollars t years from now, given a yearly fixed interest rate r.

Now let us evaluate a stream of payoffs into the future. Turning this analysis around, we can ask the following question: What is the "present value" of B dollars paid to an individual t years in the future? To obtain B dollars t years from now, he would have to put only $B/(1 + r)^t$ dollars in the bank today. Therefore $B/(1 + r)^t$ is the present value of B dollars t years from now. Now say that you are contemplating an investment that will yield you an income stream of $a = (a_0, a_1, \ldots, a_t, \ldots)$, that is, a stream that yields you a_0 in period 0, a_1 in period 1, and a_t in period t. The dots indicate that because this is an infinite sequence, the payoff stream stretches into the infinite future. If we denote the current period of time as period 0, the value to the decision maker of this payoff stream today (π_i) is $a_0/(1 + r)^0 + a_1/(1 + r)^1 + a_2/(1 + r)^2 + \ldots$ or $\pi_i = \sum_{t=0}^{\infty} a_t/(1 + r)^t$, where $\sum_{t=0}^{\infty}$ means "add" the terms to the right from period 0 to infinity.

This expression represents the value today to a decision maker of receiving a certain stream of income in the infinite future, where the payoff stream is the one indicated above. Note that the value of the payment today, in period 0, is simply $a_0/(1 + r)^0$ or a_0 because $(1 + r)^0 = 1$. Tomorrow's payoff is worth $a_1/(1 + r)^1$ today, and the payoff in period t is worth $a_t/(1 + r)^t$. Note that as t becomes larger, because $r \geq 0$, $a_t/(1 + r)^t$ goes to zero. This means that payoffs in the distant future are not considered important by decision makers today. If we let $\delta = 1/(1 + r)$ be called the discount factor of a player, it is clear that as δ becomes smaller, the player cares less and less about future payoffs (because any future payoff, a_t, will be multiplied by δ^t, and as δ^t becomes small, the value of a_t today becomes small).

Finally, let us note that if a player were to receive the same payoff $\bar{a}$ period after period forever, then that player would receive the payoff $\pi_i = \sum_{t=0}^{\infty} \delta^t \bar{a}$. Although this is a sum over an infinite horizon, its value is not infinite because as time passes, the value of the payoff $\bar{a}$ in the far distant future becomes negligible. In fact, it can be shown that this sum is equal to $\bar{a}/(1 - \delta)$, which is the present value of an infinite stream of payoffs, each one of exactly $\bar{a}$.

The important point of discounting is that it matters when you get your money and not just how much you will be getting. For example, say you are offered two income streams A and B. In one, A, you get $100 in year 1 and $330 in year 2, while in the other, B, you get $300 in year 1 and $121 in year 2. Assume that the market rate of interest is 10%. Note that stream A gives you more money overall in that it gives you $430 over the two years while the second, stream B, gives you only $421. These are in undiscounted dollars, however, and do not take into account when you will get the money.

Now let's take discounting into account and see if we change our minds. With a discount rate of 10%, the discounted present value of stream A is $W_A = \$100/(1.10) + \$330/(1.10)^2 = \$90.90 + \$272.72 = \$363.62$, while that of stream B is $W_B = \$300/(1.10) + \$121/(1.10)^2 = \$272.72 + \$100 = \$372.72$. So, if we include discounting in our analysis, we would and should prefer the smaller income stream because it is the one that gives us the most money early on, when we are discounting by a factor of only $1/(1.10)$, rather than later when we discount by $1/(1.10)^2$. The point is that while we get more money in stream A, we get it late. And judging these streams from the vantage point of today, those dollars are discounted relatively heavily.

SOLVED PROBLEM 12.1

Erkut is offered two wage streams from two different jobs, both for 8 years.

The first job is as a consultant in a consulting firm and offers $150 in the first year and then an increase of $50 in each following year—that is, $200 in the second year, $250 in the third year, and so forth. The second position, as a professor in the local college, comes with a fixed income of $300 in each year. Which job should Erkut choose if he discounts his future income using a 15% discount rate? What would he choose if his discount rate were 5%?

Answer

While the consulting firm offers more money overall ($2,600 compared to $2,400), it is not necessarily true that Erkut should prefer it over the college position because we need to consider the discounted value of these offers. Let us assume that Erkut's discounting rate is 15% and calculate the discounted value of each offer.

The consulting firm proposal's discounted value is

$$\frac{150}{1.15} + \frac{200}{(1.15)^2} + \frac{250}{(1.15)^3} \cdots + \frac{450}{(1.15)^7} + \frac{500}{(1.15)^8} = \$1,297.13$$

The local college proposal's discounted value is

$$\frac{300}{1.15} + \frac{300}{(1.15)^2} + \frac{300}{(1.15)^3} \cdots + \frac{300}{(1.15)^7} + \frac{300}{(1.15)^8} = \$1,346.20$$

We can see that under a discount rate of 15%, Erkut would prefer to be a professor rather than a consultant.

What would be Erkut's choice if his discount rate were 5% rather than 15%?

To answer this we need to calculate the discounted values again, using a 5% discount rate.

The consulting firm proposal's discounted value is

$$\frac{150}{1.05} + \frac{200}{(1.05)^2} + \frac{250}{(1.05)^3} \cdots + \frac{450}{(1.05)^7} + \frac{500}{(1.05)^8} = \$2,017.98$$

while the local college proposal's discounted value is

$$\frac{300}{1.05} + \frac{300}{(1.05)^2} + \frac{300}{(1.05)^3} \cdots + \frac{300}{(1.05)^7} + \frac{300}{(1.05)^8} = \$1,938.96$$

In this case Erkut would take the consulting firm offer and renounce academic life for the next 8 years (at least).

RESOLVING
TEASER 11

It should be obvious now why the results of the Loewenstein and Sicherman survey indicate a problem for present value maximization. To be more precise, let us explain exactly what they did.

In their experiment, 40 adults were presented with a questionnaire specifying seven different wage streams. The wages were for five years, and the participants were asked to consider these sequences as their only source of income in those years. While the income streams' total monetary sums were identical ($125,000 in total), they varied in their allocations across the years. One sequence was declining (more in the beginning, less toward the end), one was constant ($25,000 each year), and the rest were increasing in various degrees. The subjects were asked to rank the sequences with 1 (best sequence) to 7 (the worse sequence).

Given a positive discounting rate, $0 < \delta < 1$, the best sequence to a present value maximizing subject is the declining sequence and the second best is the flat stream. However, the subjects in this experiment chose the opposite to the dictates of economic theory. Only 7.3% of the subjects exhibited present value maximization behavior. When comparing the declining sequence with its mirror image increasing sequence, the majority of the subjects preferred the increasing sequences over the declining (that is, they ranked the increasing sequences higher).

The second part of the experiment included only two income sequences, one increasing and one decreasing. After choosing between the two, the subjects were presented with an argument that favored one sequence over the other and that gave an explanation why the chosen sequence was better. The argument for the declining sequence used a present value maximization argument, while the argument for the increasing sequence was more psychological (it is more satisfying to get a bigger income from year to year; it is hard to save money; there is no need to put money away in the beginning in order to spend more in the future).

The responders' overall reaction to the arguments was again opposite to present value maximization. A total of 68% of the subjects found the argument favoring increasing wages more persuasive, as opposed to 30% who found the declining

(Continued)

sequence argument more persuasive. Nevertheless, the percentage of subjects who chose the declining stream rose from 7% to 22%.

In their conclusion, the authors suggest that this preference for an increasing wages profile is what makes the wages observed in the market different from what the theory predicts. They also suspect that such preferences are not limited to wage profiles. They present various cases that seem to contradict conventional economic theory but can be explained in view of their experimental findings. Still, it needs to be examined how we can adjust the current theory in order to accommodate Lowenstein and Sicherman's findings.

Time Consistency

One aspect of the analysis of intertemporal choice as outlined above is that if a decision maker uses the discounting functions we described above to make his or her choices, then his or her decisions will be "time consistent." The following is an explanation. Say that today you are given an investment opportunity. The opportunity asks you to pay $c in 10 years and receive b dollars in year 11. You are asked today if you want to make that decision. (You will actually pay the money, $c, in 10 years and receive the benefit $b in 11 years, so before those times you pay and receive nothing.) According to what we have said so far, you would think about the problem as follows. From today's vantage point, the cost of c that you will incur 10 years from now is worth $\$c[1/(1+r)^{10}]$, while the benefit you will get in 11 years is worth $\$b[1/(1+r)^{11}]$. For the sake of argument, say that $b[1/(1+r)^{11}] > c[1/(1+r)^{10}]$ so that if asked now, the decision maker thinks that the deal is a good one because $b[1/(1+r)^{11}] - c[1/(1+r)^{10}] > 0$. Note that if the decision maker was asked to invest $c today and receive $b in a year from now, he or she would accept this offer as well. This is because $b[1/(1+r)^{11}] > c[1/(1+r)^{10}]$ implies that $b[1/(1+r)] > c$ by dividing both sides by $[1/(1+r)^{10}]$.

So for this decision maker, the passage of time does not reverse his or her decisions. He or she would choose to invest if the decisions were made today and also if the decisions were made today but happened 10 years in the future. Such a person has time-consistent preferences.

The reason the person is time consistent stems from the stationarity axiom of standard economic theory. It states that given two goods separated by a fixed time but both in the future, relative preference between those goods is unaffected by how far in the future they may be (Fishbum & Rubinstein, 1982[1]; Koopmans, 1960[2]; Loewenstein & Prelec, 1991[3]; Strotz, 1955[4]). In plainer language, the stationarity axiom says that if you would like a chocolate bar next Tuesday twice as much as an apple next Wednesday, you would like them in the same ratio for successive Tuesdays and Wednesdays a month, a year, or 10 years from now. This

[1] Peter C. Fishbum and Ariel Rubinstien, "Time Preference," *International Economic Review* 23 (October 1982): no. 3, pp. 677–94.

[2] Tjalling C. Koopmans, "Stationary Ordinal Utility and Impatience," *Econometrica* 23 (April 1960): no. 2, pp. 287–309.

[3] George Loewenstein and Drazen Prelec, "Negative Time Preference," *American Economic Review* 107 (May 1991): no. 2, pp. 573–97.

[4] Robert H. Strotz, "Myopia and Inconsistency in Dynamic Utility Maximization," *The Review of Economic Studies* 23 (1955): no. 3, pp. 165–80.

axiom implies that a deferred good is discounted in value by a constant fraction per unit time. This is what the discounting functions we explained above, called exponential discounting functions, do.

Not all people have such time-consistent preferences, however. For example, think of the investment problem we just studied in the following way. Say that there are two people inside my head called Me-today and Me-in-10-years. Let's say that Me-today is very impatient and wants to consume as much as possible today, but this same person, when viewing the future, thinks that that choice will be ruled by his alter-ego, Me-in-10-years, who he thinks is more patient. Then it is entirely possible that such a person, when asked today if he or she would want to invest in 10 years, would today say yes because that choice is made by Me-in-10-years and not Me-today. Now say that 10 years passes and the time has come to pay $-c$ dollars for the investment. When that time comes, however, it is no longer Me-in-10-years who exists but rather Me-today (moved 10 years into the future) who is too impatient and refuses to invest. Such behavior is called time-inconsistent behavior because the passage of time has reversed the decisions made previously.

The exponential discounting model we present in this book, as shown above, is free of such time inconsistency problems, but it is one of the few models that is. Other discounting functions, most notably the "hyperbolic model," exhibit inconsistencies, and there is a large body of experimental and real world data that support them.

If you think you are immune to such time inconsistency problems, consider the following. Have you ever tried to lose weight? Say that today you are offered a choice between an apple, which is good for you, and a candy bar, and you know that tomorrow you will face the same choice. Because the choice is offered to you now, you may give in to temptation and eat the candy bar instead of the apple, swearing to yourself that tomorrow you will choose the apple and not the candy. When tomorrow comes, you are again offered the same choice and again you give in and choose the candy bar. Why? Because when you are asked to make a choice tomorrow, the past is irrelevant and the person who is making the decision again has a choice between a candy bar and an apple that will be consumed on the spot. So even though this is tomorrow from the perspective of the you who made a decision yesterday, it is today for the you who has to choose now. You are back in the same position, and it is very likely you will make the same choice.

To explain time inconsistency one last way, consider the following hyperbolic discount function, $\Phi(t) = (1 + \alpha t)^{-\tau \backslash \alpha}$, and its graph in Figure 12.1 for values of $\alpha = 3$ and $\tau = 1$. This function tells us how much we discount payoffs (utility) received in the future. Note that the slope of this function, measured as a rate of decline, changes as we move through time. For example, if we call time 0 today, then we see, looking at the curve on the left, that the rate of decline of the hyperbolic function (what is called the discount rate) is steep. This means that a decision maker with such a discount function would view utility received today as very different from (far superior to) that same utility received tomorrow. Such a decision maker is very impatient. At time period 25, however, the slope of the discount function is rather flat, indicating that when viewed from the perspective of today, there is not much difference between money and utility received in period 25 versus period 26.

Now say you are sitting at time period 0, looking at your leftmost curve, and you are asked a question about whether you would like $1 in time period 25 or $1.05 in period 26. Because your discount curve is flat at that point, you might

time inconsistency
A decision maker exhibits time inconsistency if, when faced with identical intertemporal choices that are simply separated by time (i.e., $10 today versus $25 in three weeks or $10 in one year versus $25 in one year and three weeks), the choices made differ.

hyperbolic preferences
A particular way to discount future payoffs that leads to time-inconsistent behavior.

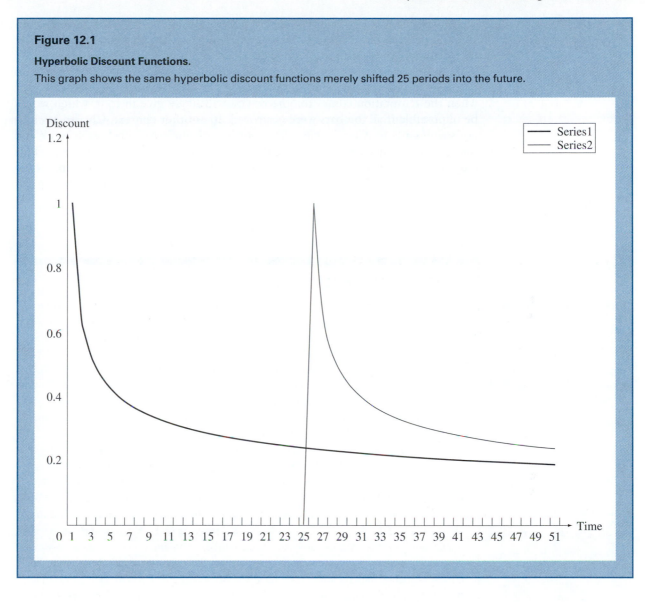

Figure 12.1

Hyperbolic Discount Functions.

This graph shows the same hyperbolic discount functions merely shifted 25 periods into the future.

very well be willing to wait because, when viewed from time period 0, money in those two periods looks pretty much the same. So let's say that you temporarily respond that you would rather wait until period 26, but you reserve the right to change your mind when you get there. Now say 25 periods have passed and in the 25th you are reminded of your past decision. At this point, the future is the present and your time preferences are measured not by the leftmost curve anymore but rather by the curve on the right. This curve is simply the original one shifted over 25 periods so that the slope of the curve today is again steep. If you were now asked to choose, it is very likely you would choose not to wait because your discount function indicates great impatience (because the slope is so steep). Hence, it is very likely that when period 25 comes around, you will reverse your previous tentative decision and take the money in period 25. This preference reversal is called time inconsistency.

So how can you control yourself? One way is to choose a commitment device. If you understood your inconsistency, you could make a contract with your friend that states that if you ate a candy bar tomorrow, you would have to pay $100 to him or her or do something that is distasteful to you. Another way is to eat the candy bar today but throw out all the others you have, knowing that when the temptation comes tomorrow you will likely give in to it, which would be impossible if all the bars were destroyed. In another context, Christmas clubs are savings plans at work that take a portion of one's paycheck each week and put it in a savings account so that the family can buy gifts at Christmas. This club serves as a commitment device for savings for people who know that, on a weekly basis, the temptation to buy now and not save may be too strong for them to overcome.

RESOLVING
TEASER 12

TIME INCONSISTENCY

A great body of experimental evidence has been built up over the years supporting the hyperbolic model. When asked questions about the future and the present, people have consistently demonstrated exactly the types of time inconsistencies discussed above.

One of the first experiments that documented this reversal with humans is Kirby and Herrnstein's. Their experiment consisted of three different treatments. In the first two, the rewards given to the subjects were monetary rewards (4 pairs were considered), while in the third experiment the rewards were actual goods (sports radio, Swiss army knife, etc.) ranked by the subjects for desirability.

The experiment has two parts; in each part, the subjects need to choose a preferable option from two choices. In the first part, the choice is between an immediate small reward (SER) and a large delayed reward (LLR). Here, the experimenters want to find out how far in the future the large reward needs to be in order for the subjects to prefer the small reward (the different treatments use different methods in order to find the shortest delay). After finding this time frame, the subjects go to the second stage of the experiment. In this part, the time difference between the small and the large reward is kept fixed and equal to the delay found in the first part. The difference is that the choice is pushed into the future so that instead of having the option of having the small prize today, that choice is pushed into the future with the larger prize pushed to the same fixed distance after that. This is done until the subjects prefer the large reward over the small reward, reversing their initial choices.

An example is in order. Suppose that you are a subject in this experiment, and the small reward is $100 and the large reward is $110. In the first part, the choice you face will be either $100 today (small immediate reward) or $110 sometime in the future. This means that in the first part, a question you will face will be, "Would you like to have $100 today or $110 in a week?" As long as you choose the large reward, the experimenters will increase the time lag between the small and the large reward until you have chosen to receive $100 today. Denote the time lag and let us assume that, for this example, you prefer $100 today over $110 in a month, that is D = 1 month. In the second stage of the experiment, you no longer receive the $100 today but rather are offered it at some point in the future. You now must decide between $100 X days from

(Continued)

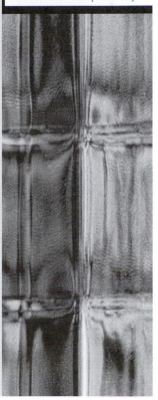

now or $110 $X + D$ days from now. The experimenters increase X as long as you prefer the small reward while keeping D fixed, until you indicate that you prefer the $110 over the $100. For example, the questions that would be asked are, "Would you prefer $100 in one month or $110 in 2 months?" or "Would you prefer $100 a year from now or $110 a year and a month from now?" As you can see, the time difference between the two offers remains constant and equal to what was found in the first part of the experiment.

According to exponential discounting, if you have preferred receiving the smaller reward today over a larger reward at time D from today, you will always prefer the smaller reward over the larger reward regardless of when the smaller reward is offered as long as the difference between the rewards remains D. This means that if you prefer $100 today over $110 in a month, you will prefer $100 a decade from now over $110 a month and a decade from now, etc. If you have switched—that is, you prefer $100 today over $110 in a month but prefer $110 in 7 months over $100 in 6 months—it is as if you have reversed your preferences.

Out of 36 subjects, 34 showed such reversals. All 34 subjects confirmed that they preferred that larger, late reward when the delays for both rewards were long. Furthermore, all the subjects were satisfied with the decision they made when the payoff trial was revealed and payment was made.

These results show that the assumption of exponential discounting in economics is problematic because, under such an assumption, the reversals documented cannot occur. Instead, the experiment's results indicate that people are impulsive in their choices and that immediate gratification needs to be included in the theory. Hyperbolic discounting models are a step in modeling such phenomena into traditional economics.

Searching for the Lowest Price: Why Wealthy People Refuse to Shop for Bargains

This chapter has discussed decision problems that involve making choices over time. At first we discussed how people view the future by looking at how they discounted it using either exponential or hyperbolic discounting functions. This led us to a discussion of the circumstances under which people make consistent choices over time.

In the remainder of this chapter, we continue our discussion of dynamic intertemporal choice. We deal with a number of problems that all of us face in our lives at one time or another. For example, many of us, at one time, will have to face the problem of searching for a job. All of us have already faced the problem of shopping for the best price on a durable good we are planning to buy, like a computer or CD player. When doing such shopping, we are constantly worried about stopping our search too soon and, as a result, accepting a price that is too high or a wage that is too low. On the other hand, we also fear searching too long and wasting time and money in the process, especially if our prolonged search does not turn up a lower price or higher wage. To search optimally means steering a path between these two evils in an efficient manner.

To understand the problem and see how our principle of backward induction introduced in Chapter 11 can help us in this endeavor, let us say that you are looking to buy a new computer and there are three stores in your town—store A, store B, and store C. Assume that there are only two prices for the computer, $$P_1$ and

P_2, with $P_2 > P_1$, and that there is a 50-50 chance that any given store will sell the computer you want at the lower price. Using these probabilities, we can define the average price in the market as $E(P) = 0.5P_2 + 0.5P_1$.

Assume further that it costs you K to search in any given store (this could represent the cost of your time, which could be considerable if you were a billionaire, or the actual cost for transportation to get to the store) and that the stores will be searched in the order A, B, C. Depending on the cost of the good being bought and the opportunity cost of your time, two cases can be defined: If you have a high opportunity cost of time (for example, assume you are a busy billionaire), then it might make sense to assume that $K > P_2 - E(P)$, while if you are a normal person, we might expect $K < P_2 - E(P)$. Let us investigate these two cases one at a time.

Case 1: The Billionaire—$K > P_2 - E(P)$.

To derive the optimal search rule for a billionaire in this context, let us use backward induction and find out what the billionaire would do if he or she had rejected all prices and arrived in store C still looking for a computer to buy. Put differently, let us go to the end of the problem and work our way back. Arriving in store C, clearly the billionaire shopper would accept any price because all previously rejected stores must have high prices and there are no more stores to shop in. Hence, if the shopper arrived at store C, he or she could expect to pay the average price, or $E(P)$. So it is easy to know what the shopper will do in the last period, and that is one of the reasons we want to start our analysis there.

Now, *knowing what will be done in the last period or in store C*, let us move back one store and see what will happen when the shopper arrives in store B. Given that the low price will always be accepted, the only question is whether to reject the high price if it is offered and continue to store C. This decision is made easier by the fact that we know the shopper will accept any price offered at C. The average price, as we know, is $E(P)$, but if the shopper continues to store C, that will cost K. So the cost to the consumer of rejecting the high price at store B and continuing is $K + E(P)$. The cost of accepting the high price at store B, however, is P_2. So the shopper will stop at store B only if $P_2 < K + E(P)$ (or equivalently, $K > P_2 - E(P)$). By assumption this is true, so we know that at store B the consumer will accept the high price.

Now we know that if the shopper arrives at store C, he or she will accept any price, as is also true at store B. So let us move back to store A and see what the shopper will do there. The expected price at B is $E(P)$, and it will cost K more to get to B. Consequently, the expected cost of rejecting a price at A and continuing the search to B is $K + E(P)$. The cost of accepting the high price at store A, however, is P_2. So the shopper will stop at store A only if $P_2 < K + E(P)$ (or equivalently, $K > P_2 - E(P)$). Again, by assumption this is true, so we know that at store A the consumer will accept the high price.

These considerations lead to the conclusion that a shopper with high opportunity costs for his or her time will accept any price offered at store A and not shop around at all. So the optimal shopping rule for a billionaire shopper in this situation is, "Do not shop around but accept the first price offered."

Case 2: A Normal Shopper—$K < P_2 - E(P)$.

We will analyze the search strategy for a shopper with low opportunity costs of time (a normal shopper) in the same manner as we did the billionaire. We start at the end and analyze what would happen if the shopper arrived at store C without having bought any computer at stores A and B. Obviously, if this were the case, the shopper would accept any price offered at store C and could expect to pay $E(P)$. Moving back to store B, we know that the shopper would accept the low price, so let's see what happens if the high price is offered. Taking the high price would cost P_2. Rejecting it would mean shopping at store C, where we know the shopper can expect to pay $E(P)$ and pay K to get there. So if $P_2 > K + E(P)$, it would be better to reject the high price and search at C. By assumption, $P_2 > K + E(P)$ is true in this case, so at store B the high price would be rejected.

Now, let us move the analysis back one more step to store A. Here we know that the low price will be accepted. So the only question is what will happen if the high price is offered. To figure this out, the shopper will have to compare the cost of stopping at accepting the high price, P_2, with the cost of searching and moving to B, which is $K +$ cost. At B the shopper will accept the low price if it is offered. Hence, there is a 0.5 chance that this price will be offered and accepted. The expected cost of this happening is $0.5P_1$. However, we have derived the fact that if the high price is offered, it will be rejected and the search will continue to store C. That will cost $K + E(P)$, and because there is a 0.5 chance that will occur, the expected cost of that event is $0.5[K + E(P)]$. Hence, the shopper at store A will stop and accept the high price if $P_2 < K + 0.5P_1 + 0.5[K + E(P)]$.

In case 2, the optimal rule is more complicated and can be summarized as follows: "At any store, always accept the low price. If you receive the high price at store A, reject it if the cost is low enough. At store B, always reject the high price, and at store C, accept any price."

Note how optimal search proceeds. At any point in the process, the searcher is always weighing whether to stop and accept the price at that stage or proceed optimally. Because the decision maker has used backward induction to figure out the cost of not stopping but proceeding in an optimal manner, at any point in time the decision maker can choose an optimal action. This principle is called **Bellman's Principle of Optimality,** named for the mathematician David Bellman.

The result of our analysis then is to derive the fact that wealthy people do not shop around for bargains while normal people might very well do so. Observing wealthy people buying at the first shop they visit is not an indication that they reject sound economic advice; they may simply have a high opportunity cost for their time. It is proof that they act rationally but simply have a different opportunity cost for their time.

Bellman's Principle of Optimality
The idea that, in a dynamic economic problem, at any point in time the decision maker can choose an optimal action by comparing the value of stopping versus continuing in an optimal fashion.

Intergenerational Giving: A Strange Inheritance Problem

One of the problems most of us face sooner or later is deciding how much we want to leave our children in inheritance. The problem is even more complex because some of what we leave our children will be left to their children, so we must simultaneously decide how much we want to leave our children, our grandchildren, and perhaps even later generations.

We can capture the inheritance problem in a stylized fashion by the following example, to which our backward induction method is again perfectly suited. Say that you are a parent living in period 1 with a child who continues to live in period 2 after you die and a grandchild who lives in period 3 and continues to live after your child dies. In the economy in which you live there are two goods, x and y, whose prices are $p_x = p_y = 1$. You have a utility function, $U_1(x, y, U_2)$, defined over the two goods x and y and the utility of your child U_2 as follows: $U_1 = 3x + 2y + U_2$. Your child cares about consuming goods x and y but also cares about the utility of his child, as portrayed by the following utility function: $U_2 = 4x + 3y + U_3$. Finally, your grandchild will have a utility function of $U_3 = 1x + 5y$.

Say that you have wealth of $1,200. You must decide how much of this wealth to use purchasing goods x and y, which will make you happy, and how much to leave for your child, whose utility you also care about.

The solution can be achieved by using backward induction, going to period 3 where your grandchild will live and working your way backward in the problem. In period 3 your grandchild will take any money bequeathed to her and use it strictly to buy good y because each unit of good y purchased yields 5 units of utility while good x yields only 1 unit of utility. Knowing this fact, let us move one period back to period 2 and see how your child will behave. The child's utility has the grandchild's utility as an additive term, and we therefore know that any dollar left the grandchild will generate 5 units of utility for the grandchild and 5 units of utility for the child. Because the child can get only 3 units of utility for every dollar spent on y and 4 for any dollar spent on x, the child will bequeath all his funds to the grandchild. Now, knowing the behavior of the child, let us go back to the first period and see how you will behave.

The parent gets no direct satisfaction from the utility of the grandchild. However, the parent does care about her child, who gets 5 units of utility for every dollar spent on the grandchild. Because the parent can get only 3 units of utility for every dollar spent on good x and 2 units of utility for every dollar spent on good y, the parent will bequeath all her funds to the child, who will then bequeath them to the grandchild, who will spend the $1,200 on good y. The result is that the parent and the child consume nothing but give all they have to the grandchild.

Note that this is particularly interesting because the parent does not care directly at all about the grandchild yet is leaving the grandchild all of her wealth. Obviously this occurs because the parent does care about the child, who in turn cares about the grandchild.

Searching for Wages

The labor market is constantly in a state of flux, with workers continually losing their jobs, searching for new ones, and regaining employment. Obviously, if the rate at which workers are losing their jobs is greater than the rate at which they obtain new employment, then the stock of unemployed workers will rise. Conversely, if the rate at which workers are finding new jobs is faster than the rate at which people are being laid off, the stock of unemployed workers will fall. Clearly then, the more we know about how workers search for jobs and accept them, the more we will be able to understand about the workings of the labor market and explain its unemployment statistics.

To make our analysis more precise, let us assume that Elizabeth has just lost a job and must search for a new one. She can search as many times as she wants, but each time she searches costs her $5. Any firm in the market can offer only one of ten different wages—$5, $10, $15, $20, $25, $30, $35, $40, $45, or $50—so each new firm she searches will offer one of these wages drawn randomly. Elizabeth, however, does not know which one of these wages is going to be offered to her by any firm. What she does know is that each firm is likely to offer her any one of these wages with equal probability, so any firm at which she searches is as likely to offer a wage of $5 as it is a wage of $25 or $50. Finally, any wage offered to her during her search will always remain available to her to take later on, so if she rejects a wage today, she will be able to return to that company and accept it later. (This assumption is not so restrictive because despite Elizabeth's ability to "recall" wage offers, it is never optimal to do so.)

Given these facts, what is the optimal way to search in this market? We know that for most economic decisions, an economic agent should continue doing any activity as long as the marginal benefits from persisting in that activity are greater than or equal to the marginal cost. In this context, it is clear what the marginal cost of search is—it is $5. What is not so clear is the marginal benefit of one more search. To understand this, let us say that Elizabeth has already received a wage offer of $20. In fact, let us say that on her very first search she receives a $20 offer. Should she continue to search any more? The answer is yes, but let us see how we arrive at that answer.

To begin, we know that having received an offer of $20, Elizabeth will never accept anything less than $20 if it is offered to her in the future. The gain from one more search is the expected increase above $20. With our assumptions about the probability of different wage offers, we know that each of the wages has a $\frac{1}{10}$ chance of being offered. Hence, if Elizabeth searches one more time, there is a $\frac{1}{10}$ chance of her getting a $25 offer and hence a gain of $5, a $\frac{1}{10}$ chance of getting an offer of $30 and hence a gain of $10, and so on. The expected gain from one more search is as follows: [Expected gain from one more search | a wage of $20] = [($25 − $20)/10 + ($30 − $20)/10 + ($35 − $20)/10 + ($40 − $20)/10 + ($45 − $20)/10 + ($50 − $20)/10] = 10.5.

So if Elizabeth's current wage offer is $20, her expected gain from one more search is $10.50. Because that gain is greater than the cost search of $5, one more search is advisable. Thus with a wage of $20, her search will continue. Finding the optimal way to search, then, is equivalent to finding that wage, called the **optimal reservation wage**, such that if that or more is offered, it will be accepted, while if a wage of less than the optimal reservation wage is offered, it will be rejected. The optimal reservation wage is therefore that wage at which the expected marginal benefits from searching one more time exactly equal the cost of one more search. All wages below the optimal reservation wage are rejected, while all above it are accepted. As we just saw, $20 is not an optimal reservation wage because at $20 the expected marginal gain from one more search is greater than the marginal cost of undertaking that search.

In this problem, we can see that $30 is the optimal reservation wage because at $30 the marginal benefits from one more search are as follows: [Expected gain from one more search | a wage of $30] = [($35 − $30)/10 + ($40 − $30)/10 + ($45 − $30)/10 + ($50 − $30)/10] = 5, which is exactly what the marginal search cost is.[5]

From our discussion, it should be obvious that if search costs were to rise, the optimal reservation wage must fall. For example, verify for yourself that if the cost of searching were $18, the optimal reservation wage would be $10.

optimal reservation wage
The wage set by a worker searching for a job such that if that wage or more is offered, it will be accepted, and the worker will stop searching.

---

[5] More formally, if $f(w)$ is the probability density function from which wages are drawn and c is the marginal cost of search, then the optimal reservation wage is set by finding that R^* such that

$$\int_{R^*}^{\infty} (w - R^*)f(w)dw = c.$$

MEDIA NOTE

UNEMPLOYMENT INSURANCE AND JOB SEARCH

As we have said many times, because economic agents make decisions by equating marginal costs and benefits, whenever you change one of those you alter decisions. Paul Kersey and Tim Kane, Ph.D., at the Heritage Foundation suggest that when this principle is applied to unemployment insurance, it implies that the May 2004 proposal to extend the length of time people can collect unemployment insurance should be rejected. Their argument is simple. First they say that at the time of the repeal, May 2004, the economy was not in a sufficiently bad state to warrant the extension. This is not their main point, however. Rather it is that by extending the length of unemployment insurance, we are decreasing the marginal cost of not getting a job to an unemployed worker. Hence, if the marginal benefits for continuing to search stay the same and the marginal costs decrease, we can expect longer spells of unemployment because it is less costly not to take a job.

The authors contend that the extension would not only increase spending by roughly $1 billion per month but was unnecessary given the fact that the market seemed to be strengthening. They also contend that extending benefits sets up the wrong incentives since it subsidizes the unemployed and will lead to longer unemployment spells as a result.

Source: Adapted from "The Wrong Time to Extend Unemployment Insurance," as appeared in *Heritage Foundation Reports,* May 4, 2004

EXPERIMENTAL EVIDENCE

OPTIMAL SEARCH

There have been a number of experimental tests of the theory of optimal search. One of the earliest was by Schotter and Braunstein.[6] In these experiments, subjects performed a number of search tasks, one after the other, using a computer. While these experiments were very complex and had subjects perform a number of different search tasks, we will concentrate on one in which subjects searched for a wage from a distribution of wages that was uniform over the interval [0, 200] with a constant search cost of 5. A distribution is uniform over an interval if the probability of getting any wage in that interval is positive and equally likely, while the probability of getting any wage outside that interval is 0. Figure 12.2 illustrates what we mean.

In this figure, we see that the probability of getting any wage in a subinterval (say [100, 120]) is equal to the area of the rectangle above that interval (*abcd*) divided by the area of the entire rectangle above the interval [0, 200] (rectangle 0200*ef*). Note that the area of the entire rectangle is equal to 1 because that area represents the probability that the wage received is some wage between 0 and 200, which we know must happen for sure.

To figure out the expected gain from one additional search, it helps to recognize that if the searcher is currently setting a reservation wage of w^* and rejecting all wage offers below that wage, the expected gain from searching again is simply the probability of getting a higher wage on that additional search multiplied by the expected value of that wage minus the reservation wage. But for a uniform distribution, if w^* is the reservation wage and a wage higher than w^* is offered, its expected value is $(w^* + 200)/2$. This is seen in Figure 12.3.

Note that, in this diagram, if the searcher sets a reservation wage of w^*, then the expected value of a higher wage offer is $E(w \mid w > w^*)$ and is one-half the distance between the reservation wage w^* and the end of the interval [0, 200], or $(w^* + 200)/2$. Now, the probability that a wage greater than w^* will actually be offered is $(200 - w^*)/(200 - 0)$, so the expected gain from one more search is $[(200 - w^*)/200] \cdot [E(w \mid w < w^*) - w^*]$. Hence, to find the optimal reservation wage in this example when the marginal search cost is 5, we solve $[(200 - w^*)/200] \cdot [E(w \mid w > w^*) - w^*] = 5$ for w^*. Because $E(w \mid w > w^*) = (200 + w^*)/2$, we can rewrite our condition above as $[(200 - w^*)/200] \cdot [(200 + w^*)/2 - w^*] = 5$. Solving for w^* indicates that $w^* \approx 155$. Hence, if people

[6] Andrew Schotter and Yale Braunstein, "Economic Search: An Experimental Study," *Economic Inquiry* 19 (January 1981): no. 1, pp. 1–25.

Figure 12.2

Uniform Probability Distribution Defined over the Interval [0, 200].

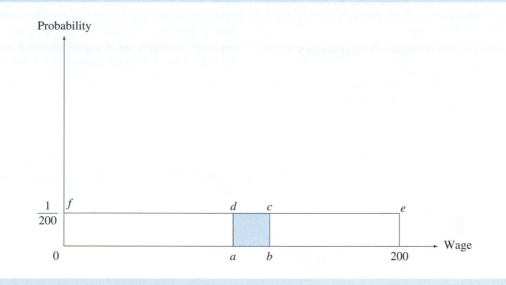

Figure 12.3

Expected Value of a Wage Greater Than Reservation Wage (w^*) over Interval [0, 200] Is Equal to $(w^* + 200)/2$.

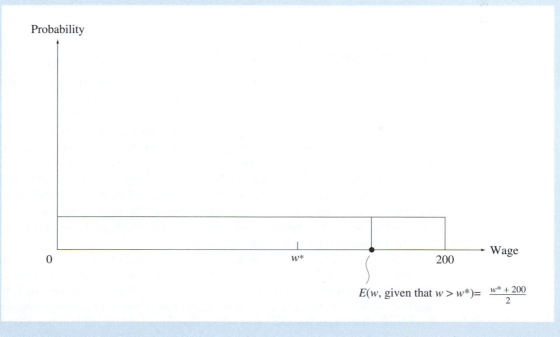

$$E(w, \text{ given that } w > w^*) = \frac{w^* + 200}{2}$$

(Continued)

searched optimally in this experiment, we should expect to observe the following behavior:

1. Searchers should never accept wages below $155 and should stop, no matter how long they have been searching, as soon as a wage of $155 or more has been offered them.

2. Searchers should never reject wages above $155.

3. Searchers should be willing to accept a payment of $155 and not search at all; w^* should be the minimum payment we need to give searchers not to search.

The Schotter and Braunstein[7] experiment offered strong support for the theory of optimal search. For example, when subjects were questioned about the amount of money they would hypothetically accept rather than search (their reservation wage), they responded with an average amount of $156.75, which was amazingly close to the $155 optimal reservation wage. Now it is one thing to respond to a hypothetical question and yet another to behave in a manner that is consistent with a theory. If searchers were going to reject all wages below $156.75 and accept wages above that level, we would expect them, on average, to be accepting wages equal to approximately $170. In fact, the Schotter and Braunstein subjects accepted wages that were, on average, $170.38. Finally, subjects in this particular experimental trial had an average "highest rejected" wage of $125.57, which is consistent with the idea that no wages above $155 would be rejected but all below $155 would be.

_____
[7] Ibid.

Conclusion

Time and space have not permitted us to pursue the problem of dynamic choice as much as we might have liked in this text. Just as introducing uncertainty was a major step toward realism in the types of problems decision makers face, introducing time also brings us closer to reality. The important message about dynamic choice problems is that they need to be simplified. While at first blush they seem far too complex to be analyzed intelligently, we have tried to show that there are tricks available to the analyst that allow a dramatic simplification of these problems, which permits us to employ simple yet optimal decision rules for dynamic problems.

Summary

This chapter investigated how to incorporate time into our analysis. We first discovered that, because some rewards we receive from the decisions we make occur at different times in the future, we need some way to discount these future payments and costs in order to compare them to benefits and costs incurred or received today. In doing this we need a discount function, and in this chapter we investigated two types of function, called the exponential and the hyperbolic discount functions. These functions can be used to compare future benefits and costs to those received today, but they differ in what we call their time consistency. The exponential functions exhibit time consistency but the hyperbolic does not, which means that hyperbolic-based decisions made today about the future are likely to be reversed when the future actually rolls around.

Armed with these notions about discounting, we then looked at how decisions are made when, instead of being made once and for all, they are made over time as new information is revealed. We looked at various types of search problems and learned how to break these complex problems down into manageable decision problems that compare the value of choices made today with those that would emerge tomorrow if we proceeded in an optimal way. This led us to investigate an optimal reservation wage policy for economic search problems and a simplified version of what is called dynamic programming.

Exercises and Problems

1. Kyle and Dorothee are friends. Even though they share a vast range of interests, Kyle is a hyperbolic discounting economic agent and Dorothee is an exponential one. The following table has the discounting factors of both.

Time	Hyperbolic Discounting Factor	Exponential Discounting Factor
0	1	1
1	0.9	0.56
2	0.81	0.54

a) Kyle and Dorothee decide to strike a deal. A year from now Dorothee will loan $1,000 to Kyle, and in return Kyle will give $1,100 back to Dorothee 2 years from now. Is this deal acceptable on both sides at time 0, given the discounting factors specified above?

b) Would the deal go through if Kyle would pay $1,000 in 2 years? How about $1,200? What is the minimal sum Kyle is willing to give Dorothee so that the deal will be acceptable on both sides?

c) Suppose that the deal from (a) went through. Now a year has passed and Dorothee comes up to Kyle with the following suggestion. Instead of going through with the original contract, Kyle will pay Dorothee $400 and Dorothee will tear the contract up. Will Kyle agree to this kind of trade? What will happen if Dorothee asks for $500? And how about $200?

2. Let's go back to Erkut from Solved Problem 12.1. Erkut had two job offers in front of him, a position as a consultant in a consulting firm and a position of a professor in a local college. Each job is a contract for 8 years. However, instead of starting to work in either job immediately, Erkut decided to go to graduate school for 4 years and then go out to the job market. The job offers will wait for him after he finishes with school. The consulting company offer is $150 in the first year and an increase of salary by $50 every year after that, that is, $200 in his second year, $250 in his third year, and so forth. The professor appointment will pay $300 in the first year and $325 every year after that. Again, both jobs are guaranteed for 8 years. Erkut is an exponential discounting kind of a guy.

a) With a discount rate of 15%, which job will Erkut choose now (remember that he will only start to get paid at the end of the fifth year)?

b) After 4 years, Erkut has finished his schooling and needs to rethink his steps. Again he can only choose from the above-mentioned jobs, and their conditions haven't changed. What will Erkut choose now? Did his choice change after 4 years? Can you explain why?

c) Now assume that Erkut is a hyperbolic discounting guy (rather than an exponential) with the following discounting factors:

Time	Discounting Factor	Time	Discounting Factor
1	0.5623	7	0.5102
2	0.5432	8	0.5068
3	0.5323	9	0.5038
4	0.5247	10	0.5012
5	0.5189	11	0.4988
6	0.5142	12	0.4966

(How to use this table: If Erkut receives $100 at the seventh year, then today this $100 is worth $100 · 0.5102 = $51.02).

<u>Discount factor seventh year</u>

What job will he choose when he starts graduate school? What job will he want after he finishes graduate school? Explain your results.

3. Geoffrey wants to buy a new CD. There are four music stores (called 1, 2, 3, and 4) in his town that carry the CD he wants. Geoffrey does not know the particular price that any individual store will charge, but he does know that the price will be $9.50, $14.00, or $18.50 at any store with equal probability. Because Geoffrey can't drive himself, he must take public transportation to get to each store, which will cost him $1.25 per trip. He has decided to search the stores in order: first 1, then 2, 3, and finally 4. Assume initially that Geoffrey will not be able to return to any store that he has already visited.

   a) What is Geoffrey's optimal search strategy?

   b) If now Geoffrey could go back to a store he had already visited, would it ever be to his advantage to go back to a store at which he had previously rejected a price of $14.00 and buy the CD at that price?

   c) Suppose now that public transportation won't take Geoffrey to stores 3 and 4, so to get to each of them he will have to take a taxi, and suppose that store 1 is close enough to his home that Geoffrey can walk to it. Therefore, it will cost him nothing to go to store 1, $1.25 to go to store 2, $5.00 to go to store 3, and $5.00 to go to store 4. What will Geoffrey's optimal search strategy be now? Assume again that Geoffrey will be unable to return to any store he has already visited.

   d) Before Geoffrey ever even leaves his house, how much money should he expect to spend if he follows his optimal search strategy in part a? What about in part c? Which scenario has a higher expected cost to Geoffrey? Explain.

4. Robert is unemployed and looking for a job. He doesn't care what kind of job he gets, only that it pays well. He knows that the wages of all jobs for which he qualifies are distributed uniformly on the interval [$0, $100].

   a) Assuming it costs Robert $2 per job interview and that he won't learn the wage he'll be offered until the interview is complete, what should Robert's optimal search strategy be?

   b) If Robert's cost of search goes up to $5 per interview, what should his optimal search strategy be?

   c) Now let's assume that Robert has only $20 with which to search for a job and that interviews will cost him $5 each. Therefore, Robert will only be able to search a finite number of times. What procedure should we employ to determine Robert's optimal search strategy? What is his optimal strategy assuming that once Robert rejects an offer, it will no longer be available to him? What happens to Robert's reservation wage as he approaches his final period for searching? Explain.

5. Joe is stranded on a desert island. He has only 1,000 cans of beans to eat, and there is no other food source on the island. Joe knows he'll live for only three more periods, and he wants to make himself as well off as possible for his remaining life. Assume that Joe's utility each period depends on how much he consumes in that period and how much he will consume in the next period according to the relation $U_t = c_t^{1/2} + c_{t+1}^{1/2}$. (Because Joe will live only three periods, this means that $U_3 = c_3^{1/2}$.)

   a) What is Joe's optimal savings and consumption plan? (*Hint*: In solving this problem, let y_t be the amount of beans Joe has at the beginning of period t, and let s_t be the amount he chooses to save in period t. Convert the utility function of period t into terms of y_t and s_t and solve for optimal savings.)

   b) Now assume that the salty sea air causes part of Joe's food stock to go bad each period. If we call this rate of deterioration δ, then this means that if Joe saves s_t cans of beans in period t, then he will have only $y_{t+1} = (1 - \delta)s_t$ cans of beans for period $t + 1$. What now is Joe's optimal consumption and savings plan if $\delta = 0.1$? What if $\delta = 0.5$?

   c) Now assume that Joe can protect his food from the elements, so he doesn't have to worry about the deterioration of his food stock. However, there is a giant iguana on the island that loves to eat canned beans. The iguana is a clever beast and can manage to avoid any attempt by Joe to capture or kill him, so Joe must hide his beans to protect them from the iguana. Assume that Joe knows that even if he does hide his beans, the iguana is so clever that it still has a probability P of finding them and eating the entire stock. This means that if Joe tries to save s_t cans of beans in period t, his expected supply at the beginning of period $t + 1$ is $E(y_{t+1}) = P(0) + (1 - P)(s_t) = (1 - P)(s_t)$. This implies that Joe's utility will actually be of the form $U_t = c_t^{1/2} + E(c_{t+1}^{1/2})$. What is Joe's optimal savings and consumption plan? If $P = 0.1$ what should s_1 be? What if $P = 0.5$?

6. Edward I has decided that he should leave some of his money to his son, Edward II. He knows that Edward II is a lazy but good-hearted person who, while he won't work to earn more money, will still pass on some of his inheritance to his son, Edward III. It is obvious to Edward I that Edward III is not only lazy but is greedy as well and will not pass any money on to any children he may have. Assume that Edward I's utility is of the form $U_I = x_I U_{II}$, where x_I is Edward I's consumption of goods and U_{II} is the utility of Edward II. Edward II's utility is of the form $U_{II} = x_{II}^{1/2} U_{III}^{1/2}$, and Edward III's utility is $U_{III} = x_{III}$.

   a) If the price of x_I, x_{II}, and x_{III} are all equal to 1 for all Edwards and Edward I has an initial wealth of $5,000, what is the optimal schedule of bequests and consumption for the Edwards?

   b) What will the optimal schedule be if the price of x is 2?

13

The Internal Organization of the Firm

CHAPTER

EXPERIMENTAL TEASER 13

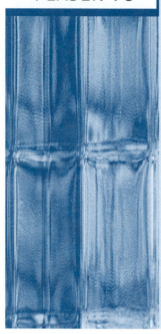

GROUP INCENTIVES

Bosses are always thinking of how they can get more work out of their employees. One of the problems that gets in the way is the fact that it is hard to monitor how hard a worker works. As a result, it may be optimal to offer group incentives, that is, give a bonus to all workers in a group if the group performs well. This happens often in the corporate world.

One common way to do this is to set a goal for the group and, if they meet or exceed it, give them a bonus or allow them to share in the profits above the stated threshold. The question is whether this is the best possible way to increase output.

An experiment run by Andrew Schotter and Haig Nalbantian* tested this scheme. In their experiment, groups of 6 experimental subjects were formed into a laboratory firm and asked to contribute costly "effort." The more effort the group contributed, the higher the revenues would be. If the group produced revenues that met or exceeded a fixed revenue target, they would all share equally in the revenue created. If they failed to meet the target, they would get nothing. How do you think this scheme would work? What problem might it run into, and why might it be a poor performer? Can you think of a better scheme? We will discuss ways to approach these questions later.

---

* Haig R. Nalbantian and Andrew Schotter, "Productivity Under Group Incentives: An Experimental Study," *American Economic Review* 87 (June 1997): no.3, pp. 314–40.

Business enterprises take many forms. Some are simple organizations that operate with few formal rules and little structure, while others are complex organizations with many procedures and an elaborate hierarchical structure consisting of a chief executive and other officers at the top, several levels of managers in the middle, and workers at the bottom. Some business enterprises hire productive services and supervise them internally under the supervision of their own managers, while other business enterprises obtain most of these services from outside the organization on a contractual basis. When services for production are hired and supervised within a business enterprise by its managers, that organization is said to be a *firm*. When a business enterprise uses the market to provide it with most of the services it needs in order to produce and uses contracts to ensure that it receives these services, the organization is not a firm in the conventional sense.

In this chapter, we will investigate the internal organization of the firm. We will begin by examining how entrepreneurs decide whether to create a firm. We will then discuss various methods that firms can use to reward employees for their efforts. Because these efforts have a strong effect on profitability, it is important that firms motivate their employees to do well on the job. Motivational strategies also help firms to deal with a *moral hazard* problem—the problem of employees who do not provide the expected level of effort for the pay they are receiving unless their activities are closely monitored.

The Decision to Start a Firm

Let us return to our primitive society and examine the next stage in the development of its economic institutions. In earlier chapters, we saw how the first entrepreneur—the potential jam maker—emerged in this society. Now she has learned about the technology and costs of production, and she wants to set up a business enterprise. The question that she must consider is what type of organizational structure this enterprise should have. One possible approach is to hire employees, pay them by the week to produce for her, and supervise them to make sure they do the required work. Another possible approach is to enter into contracts with the individual workers and pay them on the basis of their output. Under this arrangement, the workers will not be employees but rather will be independent contractors providing their services to the enterprise. (We will discuss the problems with this arrangement later.)

To obtain capital goods such as the bowls that will be used to make the jam, our entrepreneur also has two options. Her first option is to hire employees, provide them with all the tools needed to produce the capital goods, and then supervise the employees to make sure they do a satisfactory job. Her second option is to contract with individual workers to produce the capital goods outside the organization and supply them to her in finished form. If our entrepreneur relies on the market to provide her with both labor and capital, then, in a sense, she will not create the type of organization we know as a firm. According to the classical definition, a **firm** is an entity that transforms inputs into outputs. It acquires and manages inputs (labor and capital) in order to produce outputs (goods or services that it sells).

firm
A business entity that hires labor and capital to produce a product.

CONSULTING REPORT   13.1

ORGANIZING WORK IN BUSINESS ENTERPRISES

The consultants tell our entrepreneur that she must understand that there are costs and benefits involved in both methods of organizing work in business enterprises (the firm and the market), and she must weigh these costs and benefits before coming to a decision. For example, by contracting for finished capital goods, she does not have to worry about supervising their production. All that she has to do is inspect the finished goods and see if they are satisfactory. However, entering into and maintaining contracts with many independent contractors at the same time may be quite costly. As the size of the enterprise grows, these costs may become prohibitive. On the other hand, in some cases, it is more expensive to hire and supervise large numbers of employees to produce capital goods within the firm than it is to contract out the work. The consultants advise our entrepreneur that a firm should be established only if organizational costs such as supervision will be less than the transaction costs that will result from having goods produced outside the business by contractors.

The consultants then explain to our entrepreneur that it is not necessary for her to make an either/or decision about all the activities of her business. They tell her that she can decide to have some activities performed within the firm and others performed outside of it by contractors. The decision about whether to rely on the firm or the market to carry out a particular activity depends on the nature of the activity. Again, costs and benefits must be weighed in order to make a decision. ●

To help evaluate the different organizational structures, our entrepreneur hires a consulting firm. This firm bases its opinions on the work of two famous economists—Ronald Coase and Oliver Williamson.[1]

When the consultants speak of the *nature of an activity*, they are referring to the distinction between general inputs and specific inputs. For example, the fruit pickers we discussed in Chapter 8 could be used to gather the fruit needed to make jam, and they could also be used to gather fruit for their own consumption. We can therefore classify the labor of the pickers as a general input because it has a number of alternative uses. In contrast, bowls are an example of a capital good that has only one use in our primitive society—jam making. We can therefore classify this capital good as a specific input.

The distinction between the two types of inputs is important because bargaining with the suppliers of specific and general inputs involves different problems. In the case of a specific input, once time is spent producing the good, that time is completely wasted if the good cannot be sold. For example, suppose that someone agrees to produce a bowl for our jam maker at a price of $20. However, after the bowl is finished, the jam maker states that she is willing to pay only $10 for it. Because the bowl is worthless elsewhere, its producer will probably take the $10. The bargaining situation between the jam maker and the bowl producer can be described as a game in extensive form. The game tree in Figure 13.1 depicts the strategic situation faced by the two players in such a game.

To motivate the game, assume that it cost $20 for the bowl producer to make a bowl and that the bowl producer can get either a high price or a low price. The high price is $40 and the low is $30. Further, assume that the profit of the jam maker is $30 if she pays the high price and $40 if she pays the low price (this is the same as assuming that the revenues from selling jam are $70). In Figure 13.1, the jam maker moves first and offers either a high or a low price. If it is a low price and that is rejected by the bowl producer, the game ends and the payoffs are $0 for the jam maker as well as $0 for the bowl maker because there is no deal and the opportunity to profit is missed by not producing the bowl. If the low price is accepted and the bowl is made, then the payoffs are $40 for the jam maker and $10 for the bowl producer, which are their profits.

Now look at what happens if the high price is offered. Here, if it is rejected, the game ends with payoffs of $0 for both the jam maker and for the bowl producer, which again are their lost opportunity profits. If the bowl is built, then the jam maker can insist on changing the price or keep the price at the same level. If it is lowered and the bowl is sold, the profit to the jam maker is $40 and the profit to the bowl producer is $10. If the bowl producer decides to reject the sale, then they lose those profits, so the payoffs are $0 and −$20. If the high price is kept, then the corresponding payoffs are $30 and $20 if the bowl is sold and $0 and −$20 if not.

Consider the following strategy for the bowl producer: *I will build the bowl only if I am offered the high price. However, if I am offered the high price and I build the bowl but am then asked to accept a reduced price, I will not sell the bowl.* This strategy is

general inputs
A capital good that has many uses.

specific inputs
A capital good that has only one specific use.

---

[1] Ronald Coase and Oliver Williamson are both noted for their many contributions to the theory of the internal organization of the firm. An article by Coase, "The Nature of the Firm" (*Economica* 4 [November 1937]: no. 16, pp. 386–408), was a seminal work in this area. The voluminous writings of Williamson, which are summarized in his two books *Markets and Hierarchies: Analysis and Antitrust Implications* (New York: The Free Press, 1975) and *The Economic Institutions of Capitalism* (New York: The Free Press, 1985), have carried on the work started by Coase and expanded it in significant ways. The British-born Coase, who taught at the University of Chicago Law School, won the Nobel Prize in Economics in 1991.

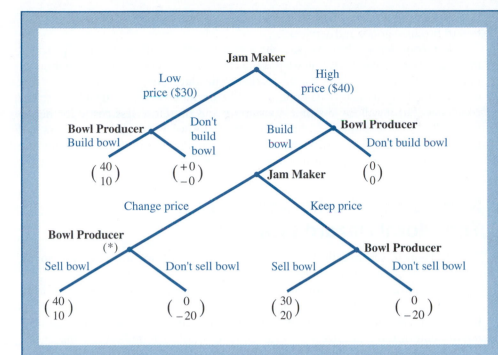

Figure 13.1

The Bowl-Contracting Game.

The jam maker moves first by choosing to pay either a low price or a high price for the bowl. The bowl producer moves next by deciding whether to build the bowl at the price offered. If the bowl producer decides to build the bowl, the jam maker must then choose between keeping the price at its original level and changing the price. Finally, the bowl producer must decide whether to sell the bowl, given the price set by the jam maker.

designed to frighten the jam maker into a strategy of offering the high price and not reducing that price later. On the surface, the bowl producer's threat seems to be a strong one. Failure to obtain a bowl at a high price would be costly to the jam maker. Having forfeited her profit, she gets a payoff of $0. However, this pair of strategies does not constitute a subgame perfect equilibrium for the game. The threat of the bowl producer not to sell if he is asked to take a reduced price is not credible. For example, say that the jam maker offers the high price and the bowl producer therefore goes ahead and builds the bowl. Then the jam maker refuses to pay the promised price and asks for a reduction. This action puts the players at the node of the game tree marked with an asterisk (*) in Figure 13.1. At this point, the bowl producer is faced with a take-it-or-leave-it situation. If he refuses to sell, he receives a payoff of −$20; and if he sells, he receives a payoff of $10. Clearly, if the bowl producer is rational, he will decide not to carry out his threat because this threat will result in a negative payoff. Therefore, his threat is not credible, and his strategy cannot be part of a subgame perfect equilibrium.[2]

Knowing that his bargaining position is weak, any bowl producer would ask for some type of guarantee before entering into a contract. For instance, he might ask for a retainer that will at least cover the cost of constructing the bowl. Even in our primitive society, such a contract will be costly to prepare and will involve the bowl producer and the jam maker in long hours of negotiation. Monitoring compliance with the contract will also take time. Later, as society develops, lawyers will

---

[2] Actually, the bowl producer has more leverage in this situation than indicated here. Once the bowl is built and the jam maker is ready to start production, the bowl producer can ask for an increased price because it would be very difficult for the jam maker to obtain another bowl on short notice. Revenues will be lost if the jam maker cannot find a bowl quickly. This situation can be depicted by expanding the game tree to allow for another move on the part of the bowl producer, but for the purposes of our discussion here, it is not worth complicating the situation to include the additional move.

be employed to prepare such contracts, which will add to the cost of using contractors to produce goods and services.

After considering this analysis, our entrepreneur follows the advice provided in Consulting Report 13.1. She weighs the costs and benefits of her two options—establishing a firm or relying on the market to produce the goods and services that she will need for her jam-making business. She decides to set up a firm because she concludes that it will be less time-consuming and therefore less costly for her to hire and supervise employees than to contract the work to outside suppliers and then monitor compliance with the contracts. She also concludes that having the work performed within the firm will give her more control over quality.

Motivating Workers to Work: The Moral Hazard Problem

The decision to set up a firm, while solving some problems for an entrepreneur, creates a number of other problems. For example, in many enterprises it is not possible to monitor the production process. What is measurable is the output or profit of the enterprise but not the individual effort of each employee. Very large firms like AT&T are able to calculate their profits at the end of the year but may find it too difficult or too expensive to monitor the actions of each mid-level manager.

moral hazard
Occurs whenever there are incentives for economic agents who cannot be monitored to behave in a manner contrary to what is expected of them.

If the efforts of employees cannot be measured, how can a firm be sure that they put forth the expected amount of effort? In fact, if they are paid a fixed monthly or weekly salary, why would they work at all if their efforts cannot be monitored? A very real hazard exists here—a moral hazard—because employees may be tempted to act unethically and take money without carrying out the duties they are being paid to perform. A moral hazard occurs whenever there are incentives for economic agents who cannot be monitored to behave in a manner contrary to what is expected of them. (We will discuss moral hazard problems in Chapter 23 as well as in this chapter.)

MEDIA NOTE

PAYING FOR PERFORMANCE

One interesting fact about corporate tax law is that if a CEO's pay exceeds $1 million per year, then the corporation can receive a tax deduction only if the received salary was related to the performance of the corporation. This is one of the reasons that when firms do poorly in a given year, companies must scramble to justify CEO raises and bonuses in performance terms. One way is to simply redefine the performance standards. For example, a CEO's bonuses may kick in at a lower rate of return for the firm than had previously been set.

Such changes are often made in midyear as data arrives indicating that the original targets will not be met. Amazing. This helps to explain why you often hear that corporate CEOs received huge bonuses despite failing performance.

Source: Adapted from, "Executive Compensation," as appeared in the *New York Times,* May 25, 2003

Solutions to the Moral Hazard Problem of Workers Not Working

Can a firm prevent the moral hazard problem of workers not working from becoming a reality? To help her deal with this problem, our entrepreneur again decides to seek professional advice. She has a number of questions about how to organize and manage the firm and how to compensate employees, which will have an effect on the moral hazard problem. For example, should her firm have a hierarchical structure and attempt to monitor the activities of its employees closely? Should the employees be paid a fixed weekly or monthly wage, or should they receive a share of the firm's revenue? To answer these questions, she contacts several consulting firms that specialize in planning employee compensation.

A Plan Combining the Efficiency Wage and Monitoring

The first consulting firm that our entrepreneur talks with bases its advice on the work of Guillermo Calvo, Carl Shapiro, and Joseph Stiglitz.[3]

To understand the logic behind the plan proposed by the consultants, assume that each worker's utility function can be represented as $u(w, e) = w - \psi \cdot (e)$, and let $\bar{w}$ be the wage offered to all workers, which is assumed to be above their opportunity wage $w(\bar{w} > w)$, or the wage he or she could earn at the next-best work opportunity. The firm should hire enough inspectors so that each worker will have a probability p of being caught shirking if, in fact, he does shirk his duties.

Assume that workers will shirk if and only if they perceive they will be *better off* doing so. To understand what "better off" might mean, let us say that their effort as workers can be measured in e units (effort units) and that the firm expects them to work with an effort level of e^*. If they use an effort level below e^* ($e < e^*$) and are caught, they will be fired and earn w instead of $\bar{w}$. Workers do not like to work because it is tiring. To represent this fact, let us assume that for every effort unit they expend working, their final dollar payoff is decreased by ψ units. Thus, their cost of working is $c = \psi \cdot (e)$. Given the specified conditions, workers have only two choices: either to work with an effort level of e^* or to work with an effort level of 0. If the workers are going to shirk, they might as well have some fun doing it because the firm will treat all shirkers the same way—it will fire them.

Let us now look at the factors that will determine how the workers behave. The expected payoff to a worker is simply a weighted average of the worker's payoff when he is caught and when he is not caught. The weights are the probabilities of being caught and of not being caught if shirking occurs. We can define the probabilities and payoffs as follows:

$$E\pi(\text{shirking}) = p \cdot (w) + (1 - p)\bar{w} - \psi \cdot (0) = p \cdot (w) + (1 - p)\bar{w}$$

What this expression tells us is that if a worker shirks and uses an effort level of 0, his expected payoff ($E\pi$) will be the sum of *three* amounts. The first amount, which is $p \cdot (w)$, represents the fact that there is a probability of p the worker will be caught if he is shirking and he will then be awarded a payoff of w. The expected payoff to him in this situation is therefore $p \cdot (w)$. The probability of not being caught shirking is $(1 - p)$, in which case the worker will receive $\bar{w}$. Therefore, the second amount, $(1 - p)\bar{w}$, represents the expected payoff from shirking and not being caught. Whether the worker is caught shirking or not, his cost of effort is $\psi \cdot (0)$ or 0 because he is not putting out any effort. Thus, $\psi \cdot (0)$ is the third amount.

[3] See Guillermo Calvo, "The Economics of Supervision," in Haig Nalbantian, ed., *Incentives, Coopera-tion, and Risk Sharing* (Totowa, NJ: Rowan and Littlefield, 1987); and Carl Shapiro and Joseph Stiglitz, "Equilibrium Unemployment as a Worker Discipline Device," *American Economic Review* 74 (June 1984): no. 3, pp. 433–44.

opportunity wage
The wage an agent could earn at the next-best work opportunity.

CONSULTING REPORT   13.2

MOTIVATING WORKERS WITH THE EFFICIENCY WAGE AND MONITORING

The consultants suggest that our entrepreneur institute the following plan for compensating her workers and monitoring their activities: Pay your workers *more* than their opportunity wage and have inspectors check (monitor) their job performance at random intervals. If the inspectors find workers shirking their duties, fire them on the spot. The fired workers will probably receive only their opportunity wage elsewhere and will thereby have to take a cut in pay. If the wage paid to the workers is set correctly, this plan will induce them to work at the expected level of effort despite the fact that they are not continuously monitored. ●

The expected payoff if the worker exerts effort at a level of e^* is

$$E\pi(e = e^*) = \bar{w} - \psi \cdot (e^*)$$

(Note that the worker will never exert more effort than e^* because the firm pays no premium for such hard work.)

The expression shown here has a simple explanation. If the worker exerts effort at a level of e^*, he will be paid $\bar{w}$ whether he is monitored or not. He is assured of receiving a payoff of $\bar{w}$, but from this amount we must subtract the cost of his effort, which is $\psi \cdot (e^*)$. The worker will therefore shirk or not depending on whether

$$E\pi(\text{shirking}) \gtrless E\pi(e = e^*),$$

or will not shirk as long as

$$p \cdot (w) + (1 - p)\bar{w} < \bar{w} - \psi \cdot (e^*)$$

If the wage offered the workers is far above their opportunity cost (that is, if $\bar{w}$ is sufficiently greater than w), then it is better for the workers to perform their duties with full intensity ($e = e^*$) rather than shirk and take a chance of being caught. The workers have to be made to feel that their job is so good that it is not worthwhile for them to run the risk of being fired. Solving the above condition as an inequality, we find that $(\bar{w} - w) \geq \psi \cdot (e^*)/p$ is the *nonshirking condition*. If the difference in the wage paid and the opportunity wage (the opportunity cost of labor) is less than $\psi \cdot (e^*)/p$, workers will shirk. If it is greater, they will not shirk. Therefore, $w + (\bar{w} - w)$ is called the **efficiency wage**.

efficiency wage
Wages paid by a firm to its workers that are above the market-clearing level in order to increase their productivity or efficiency.

The problem with this type of plan for motivating workers is that the costs of monitoring job performance and paying the efficiency wage may be excessively large. For example, if our entrepreneur hires enough inspectors so that the probability of detecting shirking by any worker is $\frac{1}{10}$ and if the marginal cost of effort is 1 and e^* is 2, then $\bar{w} - w$ would have to be 20. In other words, if $w = \$20$, each worker would have to be paid \$40 in order to induce him not to shirk his duties. A 100% premium must be paid to bribe the workers to put forth the expected level of effort. In addition, there is the cost of the inspectors who must monitor the workers. Obviously, this is an expensive way for a firm to solve the moral hazard problem of workers not working.

SOLVED PROBLEM 13.1

Question (Content Review: Work or Shirk?)
Rosie works in an aircraft-manufacturing plant. Rosie's contract calls for her to install 20,000 rivets to earn \$1,000. It is difficult to monitor workers' performance at the plant, so there is only a 30% chance that a worker will be caught shirking his

or her riveting duties. When a worker shirks, she exerts no effort. If caught shirking, the worker will receive a severance check of $50 and will be asked to leave. If the cost of effort for Rosie can be represented by function $C(e) = (e/1{,}000)^2$, where effort, e, is measured in the number of rivets installed, will Rosie work or shirk?

Answer

If Rosie shirks, her expected payoff is

$$E\pi(\text{shirk}) = (0.7)(1{,}000) + (0.3)(50) = 715$$

where 0.7 and 0.3 is the probability of not being and of being caught.

If Rosie works, her payoff is

$$\pi(\text{work}) = 1{,}000 - (20)^2 = 600$$

where $20^2 = \left(\frac{20{,}000}{1{,}000}\right)^2$ is the cost of effort of installing 20,000 rivets. Because $E\pi(\text{shirk}) > \pi(\text{work})$, Rosie would shirk.

A Revenue-Sharing Plan

Having learned the strengths and weaknesses of motivating workers through a combination of an efficiency wage and randomly monitoring their activities, our entrepreneur decides to examine a different type of plan. She therefore hires another consulting firm, which proposes a revenue-sharing plan.

The idea of a revenue-sharing plan is appealing to our entrepreneur because it would enable her to motivate her workers without paying them excessively high wages and without having a costly staff of managers or inspectors to monitor their activities. With a revenue-sharing plan, there should be no need to maintain an expensive hierarchical organization because the workers should exert the required effort without anyone checking on them. Therefore, on the surface, this plan seems more cost-effective than the plan that combines an efficiency wage and monitoring.

Let us examine a revenue-sharing scheme that has been proposed to our entrepreneur: Each worker will be given a share called s_i of the total revenue collected from sales of the goods produced by the firm. (The subscript i will be used to

---

CONSULTING REPORT   13.3

MOTIVATING WORKERS WITH REVENUE SHARING

The consultants suggest that our entrepreneur can motivate her workers better if she allows them to share in the revenues of her firm. Then the greater the revenues are, the more the workers earn. This arrangement gives the workers an incentive to perform well on the job. They have a personal interest in the success of the firm and should therefore strive to keep production at a high level so that the firm can maintain or increase its revenues.[4] This effort should occur without monitoring by managers or inspectors.

The consultants tell our entrepreneur that by giving her workers a share in the firm's revenues rather than paying them a wage, she will make them feel as if they are "partners" in the firm. She should, of course, keep a larger share for herself because she has to pay for capital goods and other resources needed for production. The sum of the shares of the firm distributed must sum to one, including the share that the entrepreneur gets. ●

---

[4] Some companies have claimed in their advertising that because of employee ownership or because of a profit-sharing plan, they provide better service to customers. For example, a series of television commercials by Avis for its car rental operations made this type of claim.

identify the individual workers so that with n workers in the firm, each will be labeled by some i from 1 to n.) If the firm collects R dollars in revenue from sales, worker 1 will receive $s_1 \cdot (R)$, worker 2 will receive $s_2 \cdot (R)$, and so on. Because our entrepreneur cannot distribute more revenue than the firm collects, it must be that the sum of the s_i for all workers cannot exceed 1 ($\Sigma s_i \leq 1$).

Unfortunately, this revenue-sharing plan will fail. To understand why, let us assume that the plan does work. Each worker actually puts out e^* units of effort, and after receiving their share of the firm's revenue, all workers earn more than their opportunity wage. Let us now assume, however, that one of the workers decides to experiment and provide less than e^* units of effort. Say that he reduces his effort by 1 unit. From our assumption about the cost of effort, we know that this decrease in effort will save the worker ψ dollars. Therefore, reduced effort is beneficial to him in the sense that he does not have to work so hard, but it also has a disadvantage for him. If he reduces his effort, the revenue of the firm will decrease, which means that he will receive less because his earnings are a share of the total revenue. However, this disadvantage is not significant. Every time the firm's revenue decreases by 1 unit, each worker loses only s_i dollars. For instance, if a firm has 100 workers, each with an equal share of the revenue, then a decrease of $1 in the firm's total revenue means a reduction of only $\frac{1}{100}$ of $1 in the earnings of each worker. If the amount of money saved by working less hard is greater than this loss in earnings, each worker will shirk his duties. In other words, shirking is beneficial to the worker because it brings an unshared gain but has only a shared cost.

We can rephrase this analysis in terms of game theory. Consider the game defined by our entrepreneur's revenue-sharing scheme. It is a game in which each player (worker) must decide how hard to work and, given the amount of effort put out by all workers, the firm's revenue is determined. Then the individual payoffs are calculated, given s_i. The logic described previously indicates that an effort level of e^* by all workers does not result in a Nash equilibrium because if everyone else exerts this much effort, an individual worker has an incentive to shirk. Consequently, at the Nash equilibrium for this game, shirking will occur.

The situation may even be worse than this analysis indicates because there may be another equilibrium for this game in which each worker exerts no effort at all. To see why such an equilibrium may exist, say that all workers completely shirk their duties. Given that fact, would anyone have an incentive to deviate and work with positive intensity? Not necessarily, because deviating would increase a worker's expected payoff by only s_i, yet the cost of his effort would increase by ψ, which we will assume is greater than s_i. In other words, this worker would bear the full cost of his effort but receive only a share of the increase in revenue resulting from that effort. Thus, the no-effort strategy array is an equilibrium.

After this analysis, our entrepreneur realizes that the revenue-sharing scheme will not work. It will not solve the moral hazard problem of workers not working.

A Forcing-Contract Plan

forcing contract
An incentive scheme in which a target output is set for the entire group and payments are received by all workers if the group's output exceeds this target.

Our entrepreneur now turns to yet another consulting firm for advice. The consultants propose that she use what they call a forcing contract to deal with the moral hazard problem of workers not working. This idea is based on the work of Bengt Holmstrom.[5]

---

[5] Bengt Holmstrom is an MIT economist whose article, "Moral Hazard in Teams" (*The Bell Journal of Economics* 13 [Autumn 1982]: no. 2, pp. 324–41), created a burst of interest in the type of incentive scheme discussed here.

A forcing contract is basically an incentive scheme in which a target output is set for the entire group, R^*, and payments are received by all workers if the group's output exceeds this target. If it falls short of the target, however, all workers receive either nothing or some very small conciliation price. To understand why a forcing contract will be effective, let us assume that all workers actually do what is expected of them and exert e^* units of effort. If this is the case, we would ask the following question: Will anyone want to deviate by reducing the level of effort he exerts? If we rephrase this question in terms of game theory, we will ask this: Is the choice of e^* a Nash equilibrium for the forcing-contract game? When we analyzed the revenue-sharing plan for motivating workers, we saw that it was in the interest of an individual worker to reduce his level of effort. However, with a forcing contract, the situation is different.

When all workers exert e^* units of effort, the firm produces revenue of exactly R^*. Each worker will therefore earn $w - \psi \cdot (e^*)$, which we will assume is greater than zero. If one worker then decides to reduce her effort from e^* to e' with $e' < e^*$, the total revenue of the firm will fall below R^*, and the workers will be paid nothing. The payoff to the worker who shirks her duties will be $0 - \psi \cdot (e')$, which is clearly worse than her payoff if she exerts e^* units of effort. Therefore, if this scheme is adopted and all workers agree to exert e^* units of effort, no worker will want to deviate. In other words, the choice of e^* is a Nash equilibrium. If the workers expect one another to exert e^* units of effort, they will all perform at the expected level. Note that this is a symmetrical Nash equilibrium because all workers supply the same amount of effort.

CONSULTING REPORT 13.4

MOTIVATING WORKERS WITH A FORCING CONTRACT

The consultants tell our entrepreneur that to motivate her workers to exert the level of effort she desires, she will have to act like a boss and force them to work by punishing them if they fall short of their targeted output. This is what the consultants mean by a forcing contract.

To implement a forcing contract in her firm, the consultants suggest the following scheme to our entrepreneur: Because you can easily monitor the total output of the firm but not the effort of the individual workers, specify a critical amount of revenue for the firm, which we will call R^*. If the revenue of the firm meets or exceeds R^* in the given period, then pay all workers their opportunity wage.[6] However, if the revenue of the firm is less than R^* in the given period, pay the workers nothing. This harsh contract will force the workers to exert the desired level of effort. ●

[6] Actually, we can assume that the workers will be paid a little more to entice them to agree to the scheme.

Criticisms of the Forcing-Contract Plan. While the forcing-contract plan may sound good theoretically, there are several problems with it. One problem is the harshness of the plan. All workers lose their wages for a given period if just one worker shirks his or her duties during that period. Another problem is that such harshness may lead to no effort rather than the desired level of effort. While it is true that exerting the desired level of effort and producing the specified amount of revenue constitute a Nash equilibrium for the forcing-contract game, exerting zero effort and producing nothing also constitute a Nash equilibrium for this game. Obviously, if a worker knows that the other workers will not fulfill the terms of the forcing contract, he will not exert any effort because he will realize that his effort will be wasted. It will not bring him any payoff. Therefore, all workers will understand that they are better off working elsewhere at their opportunity wage.

Still another problem with the forcing-contract plan is that it requires the workers to trust that their employer will be truthful when she reports the firm's revenue to them. If she is not truthful, they will receive no payoff for their work. While the forcing-contract plan may solve the moral hazard problem of workers not working, it creates another moral hazard problem because the employer now has an incentive to lie to the workers about the firm's revenue.

Proponents of the forcing-contract plan have arguments to counter these criticisms. Let us now examine their contentions.

The Forcing-Contract Plan Defended. While the no-work equilibrium for the forcing-contract game does indeed exist, it is unlikely that we will ever see this equilibrium occur. If workers actually accept such a contract and agree to work under its terms, we must conclude that they intend to exert the necessary effort and that they expect their coworkers to do the same. Otherwise, they would be better off obtaining a job elsewhere at their opportunity wage and not wasting their time pretending that they will work hard. Clearly, anyone who chooses to work under such conditions must intend to meet the terms of the forcing contract even though these terms are harsh. There is probably some self-selection taking place here. It may be that people who are willing to work hard tend to choose jobs at firms with forcing contracts and that people who are not willing to work hard tend to choose jobs at firms that pay the opportunity wage regardless of output.

The moral hazard problem created by the forcing-contract plan is a serious one. Obviously, employers have an incentive to be dishonest when reporting revenue to workers. However, there are risks involved in this strategy of cheating that will limit its use. In the short run, a firm will save money by understating its revenue and therefore not paying its workers the wages they earned. In the long run, the firm runs the risk of losing its workers because they cannot make a living no matter how hard they work. Furthermore, it will be very difficult to hire replacements because the firm will have a reputation for not paying its workers fairly. The firm also runs the risk of incurring legal action. If the workers uncover evidence of the firm's dishonesty, they can bring a lawsuit against it for fraud and breach of contract.

| SOLVED PROBLEM 13.2 | **Question (Application and Extension: Forcing Contracts and Nash Equilibria)** |

Question (Application and Extension: Forcing Contracts and Nash Equilibria)

In the forcing contract described earlier, is the outcome where each worker chooses the effort level e^* the *only* Nash equilibrium?

Answer

No. In fact, there may be many equilibria. Any arrangement of effort levels that determines a revenue of exactly R^* will be an equilibrium as long as no one receives less than zero as a payoff. To understand why this is so, consider an arrangement of effort levels that is very uneven; in this arrangement, some people put in a lot of effort while others shirk. Still, assume that the target R^* is reached exactly. Then any agent has the following alternatives: He or she can increase effort, but this makes no sense because the worker will have to absorb the full cost of each extra unit of effort and will have to share the benefits of the extra revenue among all the members of his or her group. Alternatively, the agent can reduce his or her effort level, which will cause the firm not to meet the target. In that case, if an agent is going to lower his or her effort level, it would be best to lower it to zero, thereby avoiding all the costs of effort. The payoff in this situation would be zero. Thus, even if some people are working harder than others, as long as each person is getting a payoff that is greater than zero, it is best for workers not to deviate. There is also a Nash equilibrium where nobody works (prove this to yourself). Hence, we can have many different Nash equilibria.

See the Resolving the Teaser feature at the end of this section for a description of an experiment on forcing contracts.

A Plan Involving Economic Tournaments

At this point, our entrepreneur has come to several conclusions about how to organize her firm and motivate the workers. She has reached these conclusions as a result of the advice she received from consulting firms and a subsequent analysis of this advice. First, she has decided to organize her firm as a hierarchy with herself at the top. Second, she has decided that she will not be able to motivate her workers effectively with the plan combining the efficiency wage and monitoring or the plan that involves revenue sharing. The forcing-contract plan seems to be the only one that will generate the level of output that she desires. However, she is not comfortable with the harshness of this plan. She therefore hires another consulting firm in an attempt to find a more satisfactory plan. This firm specializes in the use of economic tournaments to motivate workers and thereby solve the moral hazard problem.

To understand how the proposal of the consultants for an economic tournament would work, let us consider a simple example. This example involves a two-worker organization, but the same principles can be applied to a situation with n workers.

economic tournament (rank-order tournament) A system in which workers are compensated not on the basis of their absolute output but rather on the basis of their output relative to the output of others.

CONSULTING REPORT   13.5

MOTIVATING WORKERS WITH ECONOMIC TOURNAMENTS

The consultants begin by explaining the idea behind tournaments. They tell our entrepreneur that an economic tournament, or more specifically a rank-order tournament, is a system in which workers are compensated not on the basis of their absolute output but rather on the basis of their output relative to the output of others.

Sometimes the output of a worker results not just from the amount of effort the worker exerts but also from some random element such as luck. For example, suppose that an entrepreneur wants to increase the sales of her firm and therefore hires a staff of salespeople to call on potential customers and convince them to buy her product. She will not know how much effort each of these salespeople puts into the job. She will only know the amount of sales each of them has made during a given period. In reality, these sales may be influenced by luck or other random elements and may not involve much effort on the part of the salesperson. For instance, a salesperson might spend all his time in a restaurant drinking coffee but by chance might meet a potential customer who orders a huge quantity of his product. Luck may also work in the opposite way. A salesperson might spend a great deal of time trying to obtain a large order from a customer, and just as the customer is ready to sign the contract, he suffers a heart attack. Luck can be good or bad; in either case, luck makes it difficult to judge the effort of the salesperson.

When the output of workers represents a combination of effort and luck, an economic tournament may be a useful way to induce the workers to exert the desired amount of effort. ●

In a two-worker firm, we must define two prizes for an economic tournament: a big prize M and a small prize m. If these are dollar prizes, then $M > m$ would mean that the winner of the big prize receives more dollars than the winner of the small prize. The workers can exert any level of effort they want during the weekly period that each tournament lasts. At the end of the week, they report the output they have produced. The worker with the greater output receives the big prize, and the worker with the smaller output receives the small prize.

What we see in this example of an economic tournament is a two-person game in which the strategy of each player (worker) is her choice of an effort level. Each player's payoff will be a function not only of her choice of an effort level but also of her competitor's choice. The choice of an effort level influences each player's payoff in two ways. First, given the choice of her opponent, her own choice of a higher effort level increases her chance of winning the big prize. Second, because people do not generally like to work too hard, effort is costly. Thus, the higher the effort level a player chooses, the more her effort costs and the smaller the benefits she will receive from that effort (especially if, ultimately, her opponent is just lucky and wins the big prize anyway). By choosing the prizes for an economic tournament appropriately, a firm can set up tournaments such that, at the Nash equilibrium of the game they define, all workers exert the desired amount of effort. See the Experimental Evidence feature at the end of this section for a description of a laboratory experiment on economic tournaments.

SOLVED PROBLEM 13.3

Question (Content Review: Economic Tournaments and Nash Equilibria)

As described previously, consider a two-person tournament in which there are no random elements. What this means is that when a person chooses an effort level, his or her output is known for sure. Demonstrate that there are no pure strategy Nash equilibrium effort levels in such a tournament. (The same result holds for tournaments with more than two people.)

Answer

The answer here is quite straightforward. Note that there can be no equilibrium where each person chooses zero; if that was the case, there would be an incentive for a player to increase his effort level just a tiny bit and win the big prize. If an equilibrium exists, it must involve positive effort levels. Thus, take any pair of positive effort levels (say we have a two-person tournament), and whichever is higher will win. Hence, either there is an incentive for the lower-effort person to raise his effort level above his opponent's, or if the cost of that higher-effort level is too great, the lower-effort person should drop out and choose zero. However, once the person drops out and chooses zero, his higher-effort opponent will lower her effort level to zero plus a tiny bit (say ϵ) and will win with practically no cost. This is not an equilibrium. However, the lower-effort person will now increase his effort to, for example, zero plus 2ϵ and will win for sure. Effort will now escalate, and the agent's effort will cycle and never settle down. Finally, one might think that there would be a pure strategy equilibrium where each person exerts the maximum effort, e^{max}, and each wins with probability $1/2$. This cannot be an equilibrium, however, as long as $1/2(M) < c(e^{max})$ where $c(e^{max})$ is the cost associated with the maximum effort and M is the value of the big prize.

EXPERIMENTAL EVIDENCE

ECONOMIC TOURNAMENTS

Laboratory experiments provide some evidence about how tournaments might work in the real world. For example, let us consider the results of a series of laboratory experiments devised by Bull, Schotter, and Weigelt to test the tournament scheme.[7] A typical experiment in this series was conducted as follows. A group of 24 college undergraduates were recruited as subjects for the study. They were brought to a room, randomly assigned seats and subject numbers, and then given written instructions. They were informed that they would be divided into pairs and that another subject would be randomly assigned as their "pair member," but they would not know the identity of that person. They were also told that the amount of dollars they would earn in the experiment was a function of their own decisions, the decisions of their pair members, and the realizations of a random variable (luck).

As the experiment began, each subject was first asked to pick an integer between 0 and 100 (inclusive) as his or her "decision number" and to enter that number on a worksheet. Corresponding to each decision number was a cost listed in a table in the instructions. In all experiments in the series, these costs took the form e^2/c, $c > 0$, where e represented the decision number and c was a scaling factor that was used to make sure the payoffs were of a reasonable size.

After all the subjects had chosen and recorded their decision numbers, an experiment administrator circulated a box containing bingo balls labeled with the integers from −30 to +30, including 0. These were called "random numbers." Each subject pulled a random number from the box, replaced it, entered it on his or her worksheet, and then added it to the decision number to find his or her "total number" for that round. The subjects recorded their total numbers on slips of paper, which were then collected and recorded by an administrator, who compared the total numbers for each pair of subjects. It was then announced which member of each pair had the highest total number. The pair members

with the highest and lowest total numbers were awarded, respectively, fixed payments M and m ($M > m$). Each subject then calculated his or her payoff for the round by subtracting the cost of the decision number from the fixed payment. Notice that all the parameters of the tournament were common knowledge except the physical identity of each subject's pair member.

The experiment replicated the simple example of an economic tournament in a two-worker organization that we discussed in the previous section of this chapter. The decision number corresponds to the effort of each worker, the random number to luck, the total number to his output, and the decision cost to the cost of his effort.

Given the parameters for the cost of effort and given the size of the prizes chosen by Bull, Schotter, and Weigelt, the Nash equilibrium effort level of the tournaments in most of the experiments was designed to be 37. Figure 13.2 presents a graph of the round-by-round mean or average effort levels chosen by the subjects in the first experiment conducted by Bull, Schotter, and Weigelt.

Notice that as the number of rounds increased, the mean effort levels of the subjects moved almost consistently toward the predicted equilibrium level. In other words, over time, the subjects acted as if they had learned to behave in a manner that was consistent with the predictions of the theory underlying economic tournaments. In another experiment, the parameters of the tournament were altered so that the equilibrium was 74 instead of 37. Figure 13.3 depicts the mean effort levels for this experiment. Even though the equilibrium level has changed, we again see that the mean effort levels move toward the equilibrium level.

These graphs demonstrate that, at least in the laboratory experiments conducted by Bull, Schotter, and Weigelt, subjects, on average, responded to the incentives provided for them in tournaments and acted according to the Nash equilibrium predictions of the theory. Over time, the effort levels they chose converged to the equilibrium level.

---

[7] Clive Bull, Andrew Schotter, and Keith Weigelt, "Tournaments and Piece-Rates: An Experimental Study," *Journal of Political Economy* 95, no. 1 (1987): 1–33.

(Continued)

Figure 13.2

The Mean Effort Levels in an Experiment Involving Economic Tournaments.

In the first of the experiments conducted by Bull, Schotter, and Weigelt, the actual effort levels of the subjects moved toward the predicted equilibrium level of 37 as the number of rounds increased.

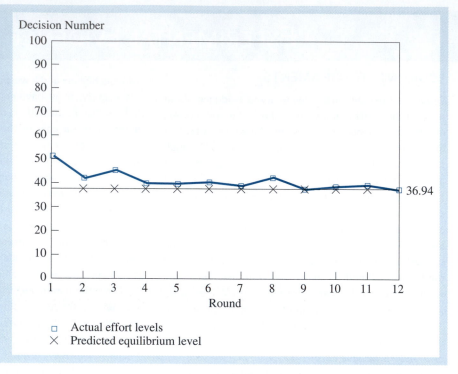

Decision Number

□ Actual effort levels
× Predicted equilibrium level

Figure 13.3

The Mean Effort Levels in an Experiment on Economic Tournaments with a Different Equilibrium Level.

In another of the experiments conducted by Bull, Schotter, and Weigelt, the equilibrium level was changed to 74 but the actual effort levels again moved toward the predicted equilibrium level as the number of rounds increased.

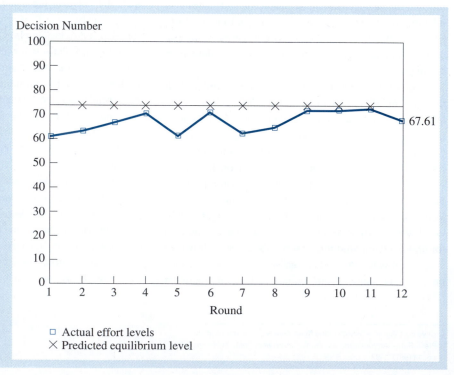

Decision Number

□ Actual effort levels
× Predicted equilibrium level

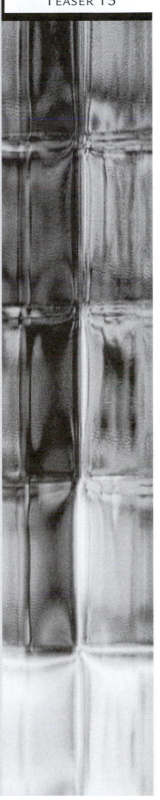

INCENTIVES - Forcing Contracts

The type of contract specified in the Nalbantian-Schotter experiment was a forcing contract.[8] In their experiment, Nalbantian and Schotter looked at exactly the set of incentive programs discussed in this chapter and more—that is, revenue sharing, forcing contracts, profit sharing, and tournaments. What they have found is that, despite the fact that forcing contracts are able to attain an optimal outcome theoretically, they are actually quite poor incentive mechanisms in terms of maintaining high output levels. In fact, they are worse than revenue sharing.

In the Nalbantian-Schotter experiment, 6 subjects chose effort levels—that is, numbers between 1 and 100—for which there was an increasing cost attached (the cost function $c(e) = (e^2/100)$). Each member of the group of six did this simultaneously and in isolation so that no one knew what his or her team members were choosing. Once these numbers were chosen, they were added together, and then a random term was added to the total, with the random number being drawn from the set of integers from −40 to +40 with equal probability. The sum of the effort choices and the random number was called the *group output*. The value of this output was simply the output multiplied by a price of 1.5.

After the value of the output was determined, each subject's payoff was awarded using the payoff formula of the different schemes tested. For example, under revenue sharing, after the team revenue was defined, it was simply divided by 6 and all shared equally. In the forcing-contract experiment, a group target of 675 was defined and the payoff for any subject was the value of the team output divided by 6, if the value of the team's output equaled or exceeded 675. From this payoff, the subject had to subtract the cost of his or her effort. If the team failed to reach the target, then the subjects would be paid zero, and their cost would be subtracted from that payoff. Hence, for example, if everyone put in 75 units of effort and the random term happened to be zero (so the target of 675 is just reached), then each subject would earn $56.25 = 675/6 − (75^2/100)$. However, if one person shirked and put in zero effort while all others put in 75 (and again the random term was zero), then the output of the team would be 375 and its value 562.5. In this case, the target would not be met and all those who put in 75 units of effort would get a payoff of $−56.25 = 0 − 56.25$. The shirker would get zero because he or she exerted no effort and got no payoff. The situation where everyone puts in 75 units of effort is the optimal-effort configuration because it equates the marginal value of output to the marginal cost of effort.

Figures 13.4(a) and 13.4(b) present the mean effort levels of subjects in the experiment over the 25-round horizon of the experiment using the revenue-sharing and forcing-contract schemes. As we can see, as time passes there is little difference between the effort levels of subjects using these two different incentive schemes. Despite the fact that the forcing contract has an equilibrium where each subject should choose 75, effort levels fall toward 20 as time goes on and show no indications of rising above that level.

The reason for this poor performance in the forcing-contract experiments is that forcing contracts, despite their good equilibrium, are risky schemes. If you work hard and exert high levels of effort and either one person in your group shirks or you get a bad random draw (bad luck), the result can be very poor and perhaps even have negative payoffs. In the revenue-sharing experiment, you actually have a dominant strategy

[8] Haig Nalbantian and Andrew Schotter, "Productivity Under Group Incentives: An Experimental Study," *American Economic Review* 87, no. 3 (June 1997): 314–41.

RESOLVING
TEASER 13 *(Contd.)*

to choose—19.1—and no matter what the others do (that is, if they all choose zero), you will always be able to earn approximately 1.17 and more if they decide to exert effort as well. Hence, although forcing contracts promise more, they are risky and wind up offering less. Because neither of these schemes seems to perform well, however, the search is still on for better incentive schemes.

Figure 13.4

(a) Revenue Sharing—Mean Effort Levels. (b) Forcing Contracts—Mean Effort Levels.

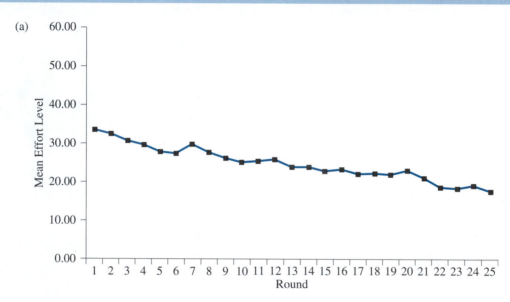

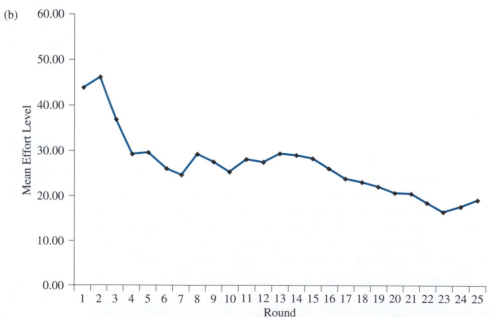

Designing the Optimal Contract—Principal-Agent Problems

All the incentive schemes investigated so far, except for our monitoring scheme, are what we may call group incentive programs in the sense that the rewards to any individual agent depend not only on his or her actions but also on the actions of the other agents in the group or tournament. But in many circumstances you might face in life, you will need to alter the behavior of some person who is acting on your behalf. For example, if you ever renovate a house, you will find that the architect you employ will want to sign a contract in which her compensation is a fixed percentage of the total cost of the project. If the project is $100,000 and she gets a 15% fee, she will earn $15,000. Obviously, such a contract creates the wrong incentives because the architect is given a motive to increase and not decrease the cost of the job. Put differently, she will maximize her payoff by minimizing yours. In contrast, if you ever are unfortunate enough to have to sue someone for damages you have suffered, you will find that personal injury lawyers get 33% of any damages you are paid. While this appears to be as faulty a contract as the architect's, it actually aligns your interests with the lawyer's because it is to the advantage of both for you to collect as much in damages as possible.

The question we deal with in this section is how to write the optimal contract in order to get some other person who is acting on your behalf to maximize your utility. To aid us in this discussion, we will call the person who is acting on behalf of another the agent and the person employing the agent the principal. The principal-agent game is played as follows: First the principal offers the agent a contract, which the agent can either refuse or accept. Obviously, if the contract is rejected, it must be because the agent will be better off rejecting it and accepting another option, which we will call the "outside option." If the agent accepts the contract, however, he will be assumed to behave so as to maximize his own utility and not that of the principal. So the contract offered must be such as to get the agent to behave as the principal wants. As we will see, it will often be the case that no contract will exist that will be the very best for the principal, but we will look for the second-best contract that we can find.

The form of the optimal contract—that is, its terms—are obviously going to be influenced by the amount and type of information available to the principal when it comes time to pay the agent. Two cases are most relevant. In the first case, the principal can observe not only the outcome produced by the agent but also the actions he took in producing that outcome. We assume perfect monitoring of the agent so that his actual effort can be measured on the job. This assumption is obviously most beneficial for the principal and, in general, will allow him to achieve the best outcome, which in this context means getting the greatest utility while paying the agent as little as possible. In the other case, the agent's actions cannot be observed, but what he produces can be. The terms of the contract must then be written conditional only on the output observed because it is impossible to write a contract predicated on actions that cannot be observed. We will deal with these two cases one at a time.

Writing Contracts When Actions Are Observable

Consider a principal who wants to hire a worker to work for her. The agent is currently working and earning $15,000 a year after subtracting the cost (or disutility) of his effort from his wage. Consequently, unless the principal offers at least this amount of money, the agent will not switch jobs. (We will assume that all the

group incentive programs
An incentive scheme in which the rewards to any individual agent depend not only on his or her actions but also on the actions of the other agents in the group or tournament.

agent
The person who is acting on behalf of a principal.
principal
The person employing the agent.

agent and principal care about is money so that the working conditions of both jobs are identical and their utility is linear in dollars. This last assumption, which we have previously called the assumption of risk neutrality, assumes that the marginal utility of dollars is constant always. We will also assume that the disutility of work can be measured in dollars.)

If the agent accepts the job, we will assume that he will either work hard and take action a_H or shirk and take action a_L. The cost of working hard, $C(a_H)$, for the agent is the monetary equivalent of \$5,000, while the cost of shirking, $C(a_L)$, is \$1,000. (Assume that even if he shirks, he must still arrive at work each day and look busy.) If the worker works hard, we will assume there will be a 70% chance the firm will do well and earn \$50,000 and a 30% chance that it will do badly and earn only \$20,000. If the agent shirks, we will assume that there will be only a 50% chance that the \$50,000 will be earned and a 50% chance that \$20,000 will be earned.

The principal wants to maximize profit, which is equal to revenues minus what she has to pay the worker to achieve those revenues. Let $R(a)$ stand for revenues (in this case either \$50,000 or \$20,000) and $w(a)$ the wage paid to the agent. Note that we wrote the wage paid to the agent as a function of the actual action taken by the agent because we have assumed that we can, for the moment at least, monitor the agent's actions. Writing profits as $\pi(a)$, we see that the principal wants to maximize $\pi(a) = R(a) - w(a)$, while the agent prefers to maximize $V(a) = w(a) - C(a)$.

Clearly these interests are not aligned, because the agent would like the big payment and the low level of effort, while the principal would like just the opposite. In this case, however, because actions are observable, it should be clear that the principal is advantaged and can get exactly what she wants at the lowest cost. To see this, consider the following contract.

$$w(a) = \$20,001 \text{ if action } a_H \text{ is taken,}$$
$$w(a) = \$0 \text{ if action } a_L \text{ is taken.}$$

We can see that the principal will maximize her profits while still giving the agent an incentive to join the firm. To demonstrate this, note that if the agent puts forth a high level of effort at the firm, the expected revenues are $E(R) = 0.70 \times \$50,000 + 0.30 \times \$20,000 = \$41,000$, while if shirking occurs so that a_L is taken, $E(R) = 0.5 \times \$50,000 + 0.50 \times \$20,000 = \$35,000$. We know that the agent must expect to earn \$15,000 in order to join the firm and, because it cost \$5,000 to exert the high-effort level, we must pay the agent at least \$20,000 to join and take the high action. Because it costs the agent only \$1,000 to shirk and choose a_L, at least \$16,000 must be paid to get the worker to join the firm and take the low-effort level.

Now compare the principal's profits in each of these situations. If she pays at least \$20,000 (say \$20,001) and hopes for the high-effort level, she will earn \$41,000 − \$20,001 = \$20,999, while if she pays \$16,000 and accepts the low-effort level, she will earn only \$19,000. Clearly, with these numbers she would prefer to have the worker join the firm and work hard. (Note that in some cases it might be preferable to have the worker join the firm and exert a low-effort level, for example, if hard work is so arduous that it costs the workers \$10,000. Explain why.) The contract specified above accomplishes just that. At the stated contract, no agent will join the firm if he intends to shirk. An agent will join the firm and work hard, however, because the payoff for not joining the firm is \$15,000 while the payoff for joining it is \$15,001. (Remember our assumption that the worker only cares about money, so an extra dollar is sufficient to get the worker to make the move.)

This example illustrates a general procedure that we can outline. To derive the optimal contract, first find the smallest amount of money needed to get the agent to choose any particular effort level. In our example, we see that it would take at least $20,000 to get the agent to join the firm and choose a_H and $16,000 to join the firm and choose a_L. Note that we need to induce the agent to actually join the firm, so in addition to simply maximizing her profits the principal must satisfy what is called the participation constraint. The participation constraint ensures, in this case, that the agent is better off joining the firm and taking the prescribed action than not. Further, the agent must be willing to take the prescribed action once he joins, so the contract must offer incentives to do so. This constraint on the contract is called the incentive compatibility constraint.

More formally, to find the minimum amount of money needed to get an agent to join the firm and work at a specified level, say a_H, the principal must solve the following problem:

$$\text{Min } w(a_H)$$

subject to

$$w(a_H) - C(a_H) \geq \$15,000 \qquad \text{Participation Constraint}$$
$$w(a_H) - C(a_H) \geq w(a_L) - C(a_L) \quad \text{Incentive Compatibility Constraint}$$

In this problem, the principal wants to pay as little as possible and still induce the agent to join (the participation constraint), and if the agent joins, the principal wants him to choose the high-effort level (the incentive compatibility constraint).

A similar problem can be solved for the low-effort level, where the principal will see what the minimum is that she must pay a worker to join and choose the low-effort level.

Let $W_{\text{Min}}(a_H)$ and $W_{\text{Min}}(a_L)$ be these minimum wages. After these are defined, we can move to step two of the problem, which is to find the action that maximizes the profits of the principal. In other words, the principal chooses which action she wants the agent to choose by comparing

$$E(\pi(a_H)) = \$41,000 - W_{\text{Min}}(a_H)$$

with

$$E(\pi(a_L)) = \$35,000 - W_{\text{Min}}(a_L)$$

and choosing the maximum. In our example, the maximum occurs when the agent chooses the high-effort level, but this might not always be the case, as we mentioned before.

Writing Contracts When Actions Are Unobservable

The analysis above is less than totally realistic. More precisely, it is often the case that the actions of the agents we hire are not observable. For example, if we hire a salesman who goes on the road to sell our product, once he leaves our office we have little idea of what he is actually doing with his time. While he might say he is devoting great effort to selling our product, he may be playing golf. This realization will force us to write our contracts not in terms of actions, which we cannot observe, but in terms of outcomes. Despite this difference, however, our procedure will be the same. First we will find the minimum amount of money needed to have the agent join the firm and choose any particular action. Then we will compare our profits, decide which action we want him to take, and implement that contract. In the analysis, it is assumed

participation constraint
A constraint in a contract that ensures the agent is better off taking the contract and joining the firm rather than not.

incentive compatibility constraint
A constraint in a contract that ensures the agent will be willing to take the prescribed action once he joins by offering incentives to do so.

that while the firm is risk neutral and able to diversify its risk, the worker is risk averse because all of his income is derived from the job and he cannot easily diversify.

To do this, let w_G be the wage paid if the good outcome occurs ($50,000) and w_B be the wage paid if the bad outcome occurs ($20,000). Then, in order to get the worker to choose the high-effort level, we must find w_G and w_B, which will induce the agent to choose the high-effort level with the minimum amount of compensation. This is equivalent to solving the following problem:

$$\text{Min } 0.7(w_G) + 0.3(w_B)$$

subject to

$$0.7(w_G - \$5,000) + 0.3(w_B - \$5,000) \geq 15,000 \quad \text{Participation Constraint}$$

and

$$0.7(w_G - \$5,000) + 0.3(w_B - \$5,000) \geq 0.5(w_G - \$1,000) + 0.5(w_B - \$1,000)$$
$$\text{Incentive Compatibility Constraint}$$

Note what this problem says. It looks for the minimum payments, w_G and w_B, to make contingent on observing the good and bad outcomes, respectively, which will induce the agent to join the firm rather than choose his alternative employment offering him $15,000. This is the participation constraint. The second constraint gives him an incentive to choose the high-effort action a_H instead of the low-effort action a_L. This is the incentive compatibility constraint.

If we actually solve this problem, we find that $w_B = \$6,000$ and $w_G = \$26,000$. So in order to induce the worker to join the firm, exert a high-effort level, and do so with the minimum amount of compensation, we must pay $26,000 if the good state occurs and $6,000 if the bad state occurs. (Check to see that this solution satisfies the constraints.)

A similar problem can be solved to derive what the contract looks like that gets the worker to join the firm and exert a low level of effort. This can be written as follows:

$$\text{Min } 0.5(w_G) + 0.5(w_B)$$

subject to

$$0.5(w_G - \$1,000) + 0.5(w_B - \$1,000) \geq 15,000 \quad \text{Participation Constraint}$$

and

$$0.5(w_G - \$1,000) + 0.5(w_B - \$1,000) \geq 0.7(w_G - \$5,000) + 0.3(w_B - \$5,000)$$
$$\text{Incentive Compatibility Constraint}$$

The solution to this problem also involves $w_G = \$26,000$ and $w_B = \$6,000$, so that at these sets of wages the agent is just indifferent between joining the firm or not and exerting high- or low-effort levels once he joins the firm. To break this deadlock, we can add a small amount ϵ to w_G and thereby make the agent strictly prefer to choose the high-effort level once employed. This is what we would also prefer to do because the expected profits from having the agent exert a high amount of effort at the minimum cost are $E(\pi_{High\ Effort}) = 0.7(\$50,000 - \$26,000) + 0.3(\$20,000 - \$6,000) = \$21,000$, while the expected profit for the principal if the agent chooses the low-effort level at the minimum cost is $E(\pi_{Low\ Effort}) = 0.5(\$50,000 - \$26,000) + 0.5(\$20,000 - \$6,000) = \$19,000$.

The moral of the principal-agent problem is that you can lead a horse to water but you can't make him drink. In this case, you can induce a worker into your firm but you cannot make him work the way you want him to unless you structure the contract you offer him correctly. Even then, because of the constraints placed upon the work relationship and the limitations on information, you still may not be able to get the worker to perform in the best manner. See the Experimental Evidence feature at the end of this section for an example showing how the incentive problem gets complicated once we introduce more complex preferences for workers.

SOLVED PROBLEM 13.4

Question (Application and Extension: Optimal Contracts)

Tony owns a cafe and needs to hire a new waiter. Paully is considering working for Tony. Currently, Paully is in waste management and can make $20,000 a year without expending any effort. Tony offers to pay Paully a base salary of $16,000 a year plus tips (which are $10 per table served) if Paully serves 1,000 tables over the year. If Paully serves fewer than 1,000 tables, Tony will pay him nothing, but Paully gets to keep his tips. Paully's cost of effort is $c(t) = t^2/200$, where t is the number of tables served. Will Paully accept this contract? Also, prove that, if he does accept it, he will serve exactly 1,000 tables.

Answer

The first thing to do is to figure out what the wage schedule is that Tony is offering. Notice that Paully will get paid $10 per table served no matter how many tables are served plus $16,000 if he serves 1,000 tables. Therefore, the wage schedule is

$$w(t) = 10t, t < 1,000$$
$$w(t) = 10t + 16,000, t \geq 1,000$$

Next, check whether the contract satisfies Paully's participation constraint. Paully will accept the contract and serve 1,000 tables if

$$w(1,000) - c(1,000) \geq \$20,000$$
$$(\$10)(1,000) + \$16,000 - \frac{(1,000)^2}{200} \geq \$20,000$$
$$\$21,000 \geq \$20,000$$

so the contract does satisfy the participation constraint.

What about the incentive compatibility constraint? Paully could choose to serve any amount of tables other than 1,000 if he wanted to. So what we need to show is that

$$w(1,000) - c(1,000) \geq w(t) - c(t)$$

for any other value of t. For values of t less than 1,000, Paully gets only $10 per table. Thus, if he serves 999 tables, he only gets $9,990 less the cost of his effort, which is far less than the $21,000 ($26,000 less the cost of his effort) he gets if he serves 1,000 tables. Therefore, Paully wouldn't want to serve fewer. He also wouldn't want to serve any more than 1,000 tables. To see this, we must know that Paully's marginal cost of effort is $MC(t) = t/100$, whereas his marginal benefit of effort is $10 (as he gets $10 per table served). Setting marginal cost equal to marginal benefit, we see that

$$\frac{t}{100} = 10$$
$$t = 1{,}000$$

Thus, Pauly would not want to serve more than 1,000 tables. Pauly will accept the contract and will become a waiter in Tony's cafe.

EXPERIMENTAL EVIDENCE

SHOULD HOMO ECONOMICUS BE REPLACED BY HOMO RECIPROCANS?

What should be obvious from our discussion so far is that if people are selfish and hate to work, they will need to be motivated and monitored carefully. Also, if they have no moral compunctions about taking a free ride when the opportunity arises, shirking is likely. But if human nature is different—that is, if people feel it is fair to offer a good day's work for a good day's pay or if they are willing to reciprocate with hard work when they are offered a wage that exceeds what the market dictates—then the incentive problems we are discussing in this chapter may not arise. It is exactly this type of reasoning that has motivated Ernst Fehr and his collaborators[9] to rethink the incentive problem and ask how such a problem might be solved if, instead of assuming Homo economicus as our model for human nature, we assume Homo reciprocans. Under this model of human nature, people are willing to reciprocate and to return good acts with good acts and also to punish nasty acts. So if Homo economicus would breach the trust of his employer by taking an above-market wage and shirking on the job, Homo reciprocans would respond to a good wage with high effort levels and would be willing to punish shirking with costly penalties.

To illustrate this point, Fehr and his collaborators have run a set of experiments aimed exclusively at demonstrating how changing our assumptions about human nature may change the type of pay institution we use at the workplace. To explain their experiments,

consider the following laboratory two-stage labor market.

Firms move first in this market and offer a contract to workers. A contract specifies both a wage for work and an effort level. So, for example, a contract would be a pair (w, e'), with w specifying a wage and e' an expected effort level. In the typical experiment performed, there are six firms and eight workers, and the first thing that happens in the experiment is that all six firms offer contracts that are written on the blackboard. Next, a worker is drawn at random, and he or she can choose which contract to take. The worker is anonymous, so if he or she decides to shirk (exert less effort than specified in the contract), his or her identity will not be known to the firm. Hence, if people are selfish and maximizing (that is, Homo economicus is the correct model of human nature), they will accept that contract offering the best wage and will work as little as possible. (There is no punishment possible here for shirking even if a worker puts in the smallest effort possible.) If the firms are rational, however, they will figure this out and will offer the lowest acceptable wage, expecting the lowest possible effort in return. If Homo reciprocans is a better description of what people are really like, then we might expect people to offer more effort in response to a more generous wage offer. More precisely, let $r = [w - c(e)]$ be the surplus or rent that a worker receives when he or she is offered a wage of w and works using the specified effort level, e (given that his or her cost of effort is measured by the function $c(e)$). We will call a contract more generous if it offers a greater surplus.

In addition to this two-stage labor market, Fehr and associates created a three-stage labor market in which the first two stages were identical to the ones we have described above, but a third stage was added in which

[9] Ernst Fehr, Georg Kirchsteiger, and Arno Riedl, "Does Fairness Prevent Market Clearing?: An Experimental Investigation," Quarterly Journal of Economics 108 (May 1993): no. 2, pp. 437–49.

Figure 13.5

Firms' Average Desired Effort in the Two- and Three-Stage Treatment.

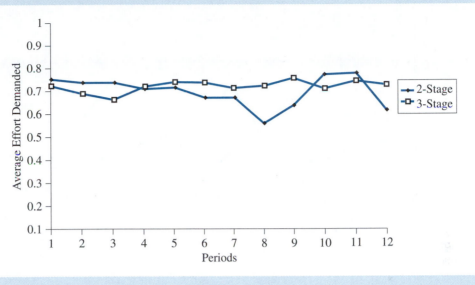

the firm could see if the worker shirked or not and punish him for breach of contract. Here, however, the punishment was costly to the firm and was purely a vindictive act; it did nothing other than exact revenge. Hence, it should never be used by a rational *(Homo economicus)* firm. Knowing this, the worker would not change his or her behavior when the third stage was added and would still shirk just as he or she did in the two-stage experiment. *Homo reciprocans* firms, however, would use the punishment because these firms reward good deeds with good acts and punish bad deeds.

The results of the experiments are summarized by the following figures taken from Fehr and Gachter.[10] In Figure 13.5 we see the average effort desired and specified in the contracts offered by the firms (effort levels could be chosen only in the interval [0.1, 1], with 1 being the highest effort level available). As you can see, they are significantly above the effort level of 0.1 predicted by the theory assuming *Homo economicus* and the parameters used in the experiment.

Figure 13.6 presents the average effort actually provided in the two- and three-stage experiments. Note here that effort levels are again above the level predicted by economic theory based on *Homo economicus*. Note, however, that the three-stage game—the one in which there are punishments available to the firms—elicits a higher effort level from the worker even though any threats of punishments should not be carried out by rational, self-interested firms. Finally, note that in Figure 13.7 we see that the average amount of effort offered by workers is an increasing function of the generosity (or surplus) of the contract offered. Contracts offering more surplus—that is, excess of wage over cost of effort—elicit more effort from workers, which indicates that workers respond to good acts with good deeds themselves.

The point of the experiment is to raise some doubts as to whether economic theory starts out with the correct assumptions about human nature. This is important because there must be a proper match between the institutions we design at the workplace and the types of people who are working there. *Homo reciprocans* may perform poorly in institutions designed for *Homo economicus* and vice versa.

(Continued)

---

[10]   Ernst Fehr and Simon Gachter, "How Effective Are Trust- and Reciprocity-Based Incentives?" in *Economics, Values, and Organizations*, Avner Ben-Ner and Louis Putterman (eds.): Cambridge University Press, 1998.

Figure 13.6

Workers' Average Actual Effort in the Two- and Three-Stage Treatment.

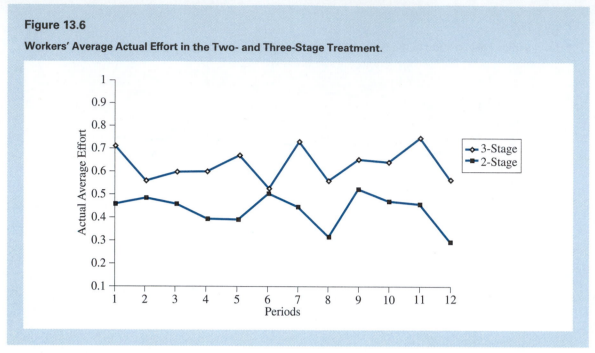

Figure 13.7

Workers' Average Actual Effort Given Firms' Offered Rents.

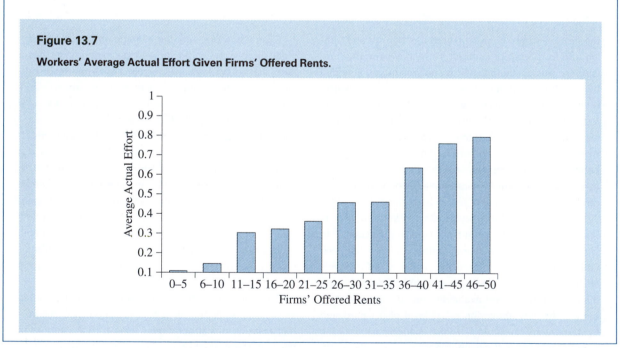

Affirmative Action and Discrimination in the Workplace

In a perfect world, what we have said so far could take us a long way toward solving the work incentive problem. In the real world, however, we face the additional problem that societies have tended to discriminate against certain groups over their history. This discrimination may have the effect of eliminating some groups from the best schools and barring them from other educational and training opportunities to the point that they arrive at the workplace less than equal competitors with groups that have not met such discrimination. One policy that governments have instituted to rectify this situation is an affirmative action program in which groups discriminated against in the past are favored for promotions within the organization. A natural question to ask, therefore, is what the effect of these programs has been, both on the economic opportunities of disadvantaged groups and on the efficient functioning of the organization. We will discuss this below.

uneven tournament
A tournament in which it is more costly for one group of agents to perform the same tasks than for others.

unfair tournament
A tournament in which the rules of the tournament treat people differently, giving an advantage to one identifiable group.

EXPERIMENTAL EVIDENCE

AFFIRMATIVE ACTION AND INCENTIVE

One answer to the question of how effective affirmative action programs are is offered by Schotter and Weigelt[11] in an experiment that phrases the discrimination/affirmative action question as a problem for the theory of tournaments. Think of economic organizations as presenting agents with a set of tournaments in which they compete for prizes, which in this case can be considered promotions. Those who perform best get promoted, while those who do not stay where they are or leave. Such tournaments can be asymmetrical in two ways. They can be uneven tournaments if it is more costly for one group of agents to perform the same tasks than for others. For example, if one group of agents has been discriminated against in the past and deprived of educational or training opportunities that the other has had, then that group can be assumed to find it more arduous—more costly—to perform at the workplace than others who have not been the victims of such discrimination.

A tournament can also be an unfair tournament when the rules treat people differently. Here, possibly because of discrimination, some groups of people have to sufficiently outperform others in order to obtain a promotion. For example, in order for one type of person to be promoted, it might be that his or her output at work not only has to exceed that of competitors' but also must do so by an amount K. An affirmative action program is a program that takes a previously uneven tournament, in which groups of agents with different cost functions are competing for promotions, and turns it into an uneven *and* unfair tournament by giving a preference in

promotion to those groups that have the high cost-of-effort function. Put differently, an affirmative action program skews the promotion rules within an organization toward those groups that have been discriminated against in the past by allowing them to be promoted even if their output falls short of the highest output level by an amount K. By changing the value of K, the affirmative action program can change the degree to which previously disadvantaged groups are favored.

In Schotter and Weigelt,[12] the authors compare the effort choices of agents in uneven tournaments with those in uneven and unfair tournaments (affirmative action tournaments) to see what happens to the promotion rate and output of the laboratory organization. What they find is complex. If the amount of historical discrimination is not great—that is, if the cost asymmetry of the agents is not too large—laboratory affirmative action programs, while increasing the promotion rates of the disadvantaged group, tend to reduce the output of the organization and hence its profitability. However, if the degree of cost asymmetry is great, then instituting an affirmative action program increases not only the promotion rates of disadvantaged workers but organization output and profit as well.

The reason for these results is straightforward. When a group is highly discriminated against, at least in the lab, we find that that group becomes discouraged and "drops out" in the sense that members tend to exert zero effort and do not even try to get a promotion. When an affirmative action program is initiated, these disadvantaged workers start to try again because they see that the playing field is more level. Once they do so, nondisadvantaged workers, in an effort to maintain

---

[11] Andrew Schotter and Keith Weigelt, "Asymmetric Tournaments, Equal Opportunity Laws, and Affirmative Action: Some Experimental Results," *Quarterly Journal of Economics* 107 (May 1992): no. 2, pp. 511–39.

[12] Ibid.

Figure 13.8

Mean Effort Levels Where Disadvantaged Members Dropped Out.

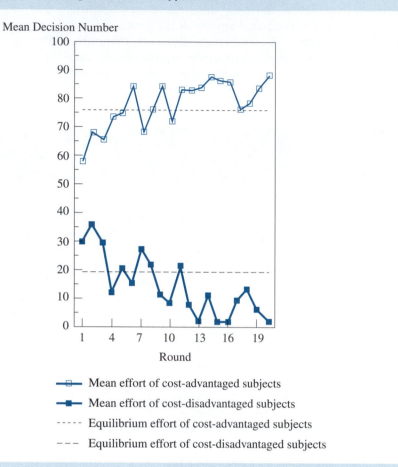

their promotion rate, work hard as well and the output of the organization rises.

To be more precise, consider having a tournament in which one laboratory subject had a cost of effort function of e^2/c while another had the same function but multiplied by a constant, which we will call $\alpha(e^2/c)$. For some groups $\alpha = 2$, while for others $\alpha = 4$. In the case of the second group, setting $\alpha = 4$ turned out to make a significant difference; 8 of 15 such disadvantaged subjects dropped out of the tournament and chose effort levels of virtually zero. Figure 13.8 shows the output levels of these disadvantaged subjects and their advantaged opponents.

Schotter and Weigelt take such a tournament and modify it by instituting a laboratory affirmative action program in which disadvantaged subjects can win the

tournament and hence the big prize (promotion) even if their output is as much as 45 units less than that of their advantaged counterparts.[13] In other words, they set $K = 45$ for disadvantaged subjects. Table 13.1 gives the results of this experiment.

In Table 13.1[14] we can see the impact of the affirmative action program by comparing the results of the $\alpha = 4$ experiment to the experiment where $\alpha = 4$ but where $K = 45$ in an effort to compensate for the severe cost disadvantage. As we see, on average the effort levels of disadvantaged subjects increase from 18.47 to 32.41 because these subjects are now trying harder. In response, advantaged workers also increase their effort

---

[13] Ibid.
[14] Ibid., p. 534.

Table 13.1	Results of the Schotter-Weigelt Affirmative Action Experiment.		
		$(\alpha = 4)$	$(\alpha = 4, K = 45)$
Mean effort levels for rounds 11–20	Cost-advantaged subjects	77.3	85.51
	Cost-disadvantaged subjects	18.47	32.42
Expected probability of winning	Cost-advantaged subjects	0.970	0.797
	Cost-disadvantaged subjects	0.130	0.293
Expected monetary payoff	Cost-advantaged subjects	$1.49	$1.20
	Cost-disadvantaged subjects	$0.92	$0.93

from 77.33 to 85.51. These changes lead to an increase in the probability of promotion for the disadvantaged workers from 0.130 to 0.293, as well as an increase in the output of the organization because of the increased effort levels of both groups of workers.

These results take a step toward disproving a long-held belief among policy makers and economists that there is a sad trade-off between efficiency and equity. In the case of affirmative action, it is assumed that while such programs may increase equity, they *must* do so at the cost of efficiency or loss of output. These experiments demonstrate that this need not be the case. While giving disadvantaged workers hope and leading them to work harder, we can encourage advantaged workers to increase their effort level in an attempt not to be left behind. The result is an increase in the promotion of disadvantaged workers along with an increase in organizational output.

Conclusion

In this chapter, we have touched on one of the central issues of economic theory—the incentive problem. This problem arises when an entrepreneur, like the jam maker in our primitive society, realizes that she must motivate her workers to perform well on the job because it will be too difficult for her to monitor their individual efforts continuously. It is essential that any entrepreneur who is establishing a firm find a satisfactory method of motivating her workers. Otherwise, the firm will not be able to prosper, and it may not even be able to survive. That is the reason we have devoted most of Chapter 13 to a discussion of the issue of motivating workers.

Summary

At the beginning of this chapter, we saw that there are two basic methods of organizing work in business enterprises. All activities can be performed within the firm by employees working under the supervision of a staff of managers, or the necessary goods and services can be obtained from independent contractors outside the business. There is also another alternative: to handle some activities within the firm but use outside sources to complete other activities. We learned that decisions about how to organize work should be made by weighing the costs and benefits of the different methods.

If we assume that people are selfish and that they find work unpleasant, then we can expect that workers will shirk their responsibilities whenever they have an opportunity to do so. Such a temptation is called a moral hazard. This chapter has outlined a number of methods that can be used to solve the moral hazard problem of workers not working. Each of these methods gives workers an incentive not to shirk their duties. One such method—the plan combining the efficiency wage and occasional monitoring—involves both a positive incentive (the attraction of a wage that is above the opportunity wage) and a negative incentive (the fear of being fired if one is caught shirking). The revenue-sharing plan offers the positive incentive of receiving a portion of the firm's revenue so that the more the workers produce, the more they earn. In the forcing-contract plan, the incentive is a negative one—workers receive their opportunity wage only if their output is high enough to meet a predetermined revenue target for the given period.

Economic tournaments can be created in which workers are paid on the basis of their relative output rather than their absolute output. Tournaments are useful when output represents a combination of luck and effort and it is difficult to judge the amount of effort that workers actually exert.

Exercises and Problems

1. Consider a firm that is run in the following manner: Six workers are involved in making the goods the firm sells. Labor is the only input used in the production process, which means that output Y is equal to the sum of the efforts expended by the six workers. Hence, $Y = \Sigma_{i=1}^{6} e_i$, where e_i is the effort of worker i, which is a number between 0 and 100. The output sold commands a price of $P = 1.5$ in a competitive market. All the workers dislike work and have a cost-of-effort function of $C(e_i) = e_i^2/100$. The manager can observe only the total output of the firm. She is not able to monitor the effort levels of the individual workers. Thus, if a worker wants to shirk, he can do so.

   How much should each worker work if the Pareto-optimal level of output is to be achieved?

   (*Hint*: Define the Pareto-optimal level of output as the output that will maximize the social welfare $\pi = P(Y) - \Sigma_{i=1}^{6} C(e_i)$. Note also that the marginal revenue from any worker who expends one more unit of effort is 1.5, while the marginal cost of that effort is $e_i/50$.)

2. Let us assume that the firm described in problem 1 uses a revenue-sharing plan to motivate its workers and divides its total revenue equally among the workers. Hence, for every dollar of revenue generated by the firm, each worker will receive $\frac{1}{6}$ of that dollar. The workers' marginal cost of effort remains at $e_i/50$. (For the sake of simplicity in this problem and subsequent problems, no portion of the firm's revenue is allocated to the owner of the firm.)

   a)   Assume that each worker knows that his effort cannot be monitored, and assume that he chooses his level of effort in isolation without being aware of the choices made by the other workers. What is the Nash equilibrium level of effort of each worker?

   b)   Is the Nash equilibrium level of effort the same as the Pareto-optimal level of effort? If not, why not?

   c)   Is the Nash equilibrium unique? If so, explain why.

3. Let us now say that the firm described in problem 1 uses a forcing-contract plan to motivate its workers. If total output is 450 or more, each worker is paid a wage that is equal to $\frac{1}{6}$ of the total revenue generated by the firm. If total output is less than 450, the workers receive no pay. (If total output is 450, then total revenue is $1.5(450) = 675$.)

   This plan defines a game in which each worker chooses an effort level of e_i (between 0 and 100). If total output (revenue) is greater than or equal to 450 (675), the worker's payoff is $\frac{1}{6}$ of the total revenue. If total output (revenue) is less than 450 (675), the worker's payment is zero.

Prove that the situation in which each worker chooses to expend 75 units of effort is a Nash equilibrium for this game.

(*Hint*: Consider whether any worker has an incentive to choose a different level of effort if everyone else chooses 75 units.)

4. Let us assume that the firm described in problem 1 uses the following plan: If the six workers generate total revenue that is strictly less than $112.50, they receive nothing. If the total revenue is exactly $112.50, each worker receives $18.75 ($\frac{1}{6}$ of the total revenue) minus the cost of his effort. If the total revenue is greater than $112.50, each worker receives $18.75 plus an equal share of the amount of revenue above $112.50. We can depict this plan in the following manner, where R is the total revenue.

$$\text{Payment to worker } i = \begin{array}{ll} 0, & \text{if } R < 112.5 \\ 18.75, & \text{if } R = 11.25 \\ 18.75 + (1/6)(R - 112.5), & \text{if } R > 112.5 \end{array}$$

a) Demonstrate that the situation in which all workers expend 12.5 units of effort is a Nash equilibrium.

b) Prove that no situation in which the total revenue is more than $112.50 can be a Nash equilibrium.

c) Is this plan better than the revenue-sharing plan in Problem 2?

5. Now consider a slightly different version of the plan that we saw in problem 4. Again, R is the total revenue.

$$\text{Payment to worker } i = \begin{array}{ll} 0, & \text{if } R < 112.5 \\ 18.75, & \text{if } 112.5 \leq R < 675 \\ 18.75 + (1/6)(R - 112.5), & \text{if } R \geq 675 \end{array}$$

Under this plan, the workers are paid nothing if the total revenue is below $112.50, are paid $18.75 if the total revenue is between $112.50 and $675, and are paid $18.75 plus an equal share of all revenue in excess of $675 if the total revenue is more than $675. Note that there are two revenue targets in this plan. The lower target is $112.50, which if surpassed allows the workers to be paid $18.75. The higher target is $675, which if surpassed gives the workers an additional revenue-sharing component by allowing them to divide all gains above the higher target.

a) Prove that the situation in which all workers exert 75 units of effort is a Nash equilibrium.

b) Why do you think that this plan is capable of raising the effort level from 12.5 units to 75 units, while the plan described in problem 4 could not do so?

6. Consider a worker whose utility is equal to the amount of dollars she has ($U = \$$) and who can earn $100 a day as a bank teller. However, she takes a job as a worker in a firm that produces shirts. She and her coworkers are monitored at random by their employer to see if they are exerting a target level of effort of $e^* = 15$ units. Assume that the probability of any worker being monitored is p. Also assume that e^* is the same level of effort the worker would have to exert as a bank teller. If she is monitored and her employer finds that she is exerting at least 15 units of effort, she is paid $\bar{w} > \$100$. If she is caught putting in less than 15 units of effort, she is fired on the spot but given severance pay of $w < \bar{w}$. Say that she suffers a disutility of effort of $2, in monetary terms, for

every unit of effort she exerts, so that the dollar cost of exerting the target level of effort of e^* is $-2e^*$. (If she chooses to exert a lower level of effort than e^*, we can assume that she will not exert any effort at all because she loses her job if she is caught working at any level below e^*, no matter what that level is. Of course, she has no incentive to exert more than e^* units of effort.)

a)   Say that her employer gives her a wage of $140 a day if she exerts the required 15 units of effort or gives her severance pay of $60 if she is caught working at a lower level of effort and fired. Will this worker put in the required amount of effort or will she shirk?

b)   Will this worker prefer a job at the shirt factory or at the bank?

7. Wayne Corp. needs to hire a salesperson to sell a new product it has developed. If the salesperson works hard, there is a 90% chance that he will sell $100,000 worth of product and only a 10% chance that he will sell only $50,000 worth of product. If he shirks, there is only a 20% chance that he will make sales of $100,000 and an 80% chance that he will make sales of $50,000.

a)   Assume that any salesperson can easily find a job that pays $20,000 and that requires no effort. Bob, who is a salesperson, is considering working for Wayne Corp. Bob's utility is of the form $U(w, e) = w - e$, where w is the wage paid to Bob and e is the cost of effort in terms of dollars. A high level of effort for Bob is equivalent to a cost of $10,000, while shirking is equivalent to $0. If Bob's actions are completely observable by Wayne Corp., what is the optimal contract they should offer him? Assume contracts can be offered only in whole dollar amounts.

b)   Now assume that Bob cannot be observed by Wayne Corp. What now is the optimal contract they should offer him?

c)   Now assume that Bob's disutility from working hard is $20,000. What is Wayne Corp.'s optimal contract now?

d)   If Bob's disutility of high effort remains at $10,000 but his outside option increases to $30,000, what now would be the optimal contract for Wayne Corp. to offer?

8. Smith & Co., a well-known producer of hand tools, wishes to hire a researcher to speed the development of the next generation of left-handed screwdrivers. If the researcher works hard, there is an 80% chance that she will make the crucial breakthrough and allow her firm to earn $50,000 in revenues and only a 20% chance that she'll make no breakthrough and earn the firm no additional revenue. If the researcher shirks her duties, there is only a 30% chance that she'll be able to make the breakthrough.

a)   If researchers can earn $20,000 in other jobs, what contract should Smith & Co. offer to a researcher? Assume that the hard effort by a researcher is equivalent to a cost of $10,000 and shirking is equivalent to a cost of $0. Also assume that Smith & Co. cannot observe the effort level of the researcher and that there is no cost of effort in the other jobs.

b)   If researchers can earn $45,000 in other jobs, what is the optimal contract that Smith & Co. should offer?

c)   What is the maximum amount that researchers can earn in outside jobs such that Smith & Co. would still find it profitable to hire a researcher?

Markets and Market Structures

In most textbooks, the study of markets is the be all and end all of economics. The study of the consumer and the firm is just looked upon as one of the ingredients needed to study the supply and demand side of markets, the only institution in need of study. While this book takes a slightly broader view of institutions, the study of markets is still central to what we do.

We start our analysis of markets in Chapter 14 by making an artificial assumption that perfectly competitive market institutions are already in place so we can study how firms behave in this very important institutional setting. Here, we will investigate how firms in perfectly competitive markets make their price and quantity decisions and how the market price and quantity are determined in the short run. We will also examine the welfare properties of perfectly competitive markets in the long run in Chapter 15, and we will find that these markets benefit society by maximizing the sum of consumer surplus and producer surplus. Finally, in Chapter 16 we study other various types of market institutions that could be used to allocate goods, namely auctions.

What is left out of this picture is how this institution emerged. In other words, when the world was created, such markets did not exist. Rather, they emerged as time went on and our primitive economy grew. So in Chapters 17 and 20, we investigate how perfectly competitive markets could have evolved from an earlier stage in which all production was concentrated in the hands of one producer—a monopolist. These chapters are like flashbacks in a movie where you are given a glimpse of what is happening in the plot at this moment (perfectly competitive markets) but then are transported back in time to see how we got to where we are today.

As a guide to what we do in this section, as stated above, we start out in Chapter 14 by talking about the properties of perfectly competitive markets. After this, we go back in time to when our entrepreneur in Chapter 8 first discovered the process of production. Because, as you may recall, she was the only person who knew how to produce anything, that entrepreneur was instantly awarded a monopoly in the production of this product—jam. In Chapter 17, we study the theory of monopoly and how monopolists set prices and outputs. We also investigate the welfare deleterious consequences of organizing markets this way. This leads us into Chapter 18, where we study the theory of regulation. The idea here is that if monopoly is welfare decreasing, then there may be a case for government intervention to prevent the welfare losses associated with one-firm markets.

One aspect of monopolies is that they are profitable. Because of this, it is likely that other firms will want to enter such markets and compete. This leads us in Chapter 19 to study the theory of oligopolistic markets with small numbers of firms and in Chapter 20 to study how firms try to prevent other firms from entering their profitable markets. What happens at the end of Chapter 20, however, is that all of the entry-prevention tricks used by firms to limit entry fail and firms start to enter our monopolistic industry. As a result, the number of firms in the industry grows and, in the limit, a perfectly competitive market emerges. It is this market that is assumed to be in place at the beginning of Chapter 14.

In summary, this section studies markets by starting out with the limit case— perfectly competitive markets with an infinite number of firms. It then demonstrates how this market emerged from a process of entry and growth. On the way, we study the theory of monopoly (Chapter 17), monopoly regulation (Chapter 18), oligopoly (Chapter 19), and entry prevention (Chapter 20).

Perfectly Competitive Markets: Short-Run Analysis

EXPERIMENTAL
TEASER 14

MINIMUM WAGES

It is a common argument in public policy debates that minimum wages lower employment. This fact leads opponents to argue against such legislation using the argument that fewer unskilled teenagers will be employed if a minimum wage is instituted. In recent years, using data from New Jersey fast food restaurants, papers by David Card and Alan Krueger have argued that this may not be true.

An experimental paper by Armin Falk, Ernst Fehr, and Christian Zehnder* lends support to the Card-Krueger hypothesis but possibly for different reasons.

So, how can the imposition of a minimum wage increase employment? Why do laboratory firms offer more than the minimum wage once a minimum wage law is instituted?

---

* Armin Falk, Ernst Fehr, and Christian Zehnder, "The Behavioral Effects of Minimum Wages," IZA working paper 1625, June 2005, Zurich.

Perfectly competitive markets are ones with a large number of firms, free entry, a homogeneous product, factor mobility, and perfect information. In addition, each firm has an insubstantial share of the market, and therefore its behavior cannot influence the market price.

In this chapter, we will investigate how firms in perfectly competitive markets make their price and quantity decisions and how the market price and quantity are determined in the short run.

Competitive Markets in the Short Run

We will begin our discussion of such markets by looking at how they operate in the short run in terms of quantity and price.

The Quantity Decision of a Competitive Firm in the Short Run

The major characteristic of perfectly competitive markets is that in these markets, no firm is large enough or can produce enough output to change the price of the good on the market. Put differently, because no firm can influence the market price, they all must take the market price as given and decide how much to produce given that immutable price. Let us now investigate the quantity decision of one of the firms that competes in this industry. Figure 14.1 depicts the firm's average variable, average total, and marginal cost curves as well as a set of possible demand curves that it faces.

Figure 14.1

Cost and Demand for a Competitive Gadget Firm.

In the short run, the optimal quantity equates the marginal cost to the given price, provided that this price exceeds the average variable cost. Thus, at a price of p_1, the firm produces a quantity of q'' but at a price of p_0' the firm produces nothing.

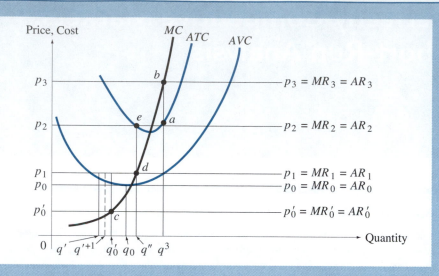

Remember that in the short run a firm has a historically fixed amount of at least one input, which we will call *capital*. In other words, capital represents a fixed cost for the firm that cannot be varied within the time period of our analysis. The number of firms in the industry is also fixed during the time period we are investigating because this period is too short for any new firms to enter. We know that the firm described in Figure 14.1 is functioning in the short run because its average variable cost curve and average total cost curve differ. In the long run, there are only variable costs.

In Figure 14.1, we see a set of straight lines that are virtually horizontal. These are the possible demand curves the firm faces. Each curve represents demand at a different price. At this point in our discussion, we are not interested in how such prices are set by the market; rather, we want to know what quantity the firm will choose to supply, given any one of these prices. Let us say that the prevailing market price is p_1. If this is the case, would q' be the profit-maximizing quantity for the firm to set? The answer is no. To understand why q' is not the profit-maximizing quantity at a price of p_1, let us ask if the firm would benefit from selling one more unit, say unit q'^{+1}. As we can see in Figure 14.1, while the firm receives price p_1 for the additional unit, the marginal cost of producing that unit is equal to only the height of point c. In other words, the marginal revenue from selling unit q'^{+1} is greater than its marginal cost of production. Therefore, unit q'^{+1} should be produced. The same is true for unit q_0 and, in fact, for any other unit at which the price is greater than the marginal cost of production.

However, at a price of p_1, it will not pay to produce as many as q_3 units because unit q_3 has a marginal cost equal to the height of point b in Figure 14.1, but the marginal revenue received for the unit will be only price p_1. Hence, the marginal cost of production for the unit is greater than the marginal revenue that will be obtained from selling it, which means that the unit should not be produced by a profit maximizer. This indicates that the optimal quantity for a competitive firm to sell is the quantity at which the marginal cost of production is equal to the price received for the good because $p =$ marginal revenue.

In the short run, however, this quantity-setting rule must be slightly modified. For example, consider price p_0'. At this low price, our rule indicates that q_0' units is the optimal quantity to sell because it is the quantity at which the marginal cost of producing unit q'_0 equals the price. Note, however, that this price is below the *average variable cost* of production. Hence, if the competitive firm produces the quantity indicated, it will not only have to pay its fixed cost, but it will also incur a loss on each unit because the price it receives from selling q'_0 units will not even cover the average variable cost. Such a firm will be better off not producing any units. If it shuts down, it will still have to pay its fixed cost, but it will avoid losing money on each unit produced. This is true because none of the units produced up to q'_0 yields a price great enough to cover its average variable cost.

Note that the price the firm receives must cover its average *variable* cost but not its average *total* cost in order to make it worthwhile for the firm to produce. To see the truth of this statement, let us look at price p_1 in Figure 14.1, where the demand curve facing the firm is virtually a horizontal line and the optimal quantity to sell is q''. At that quantity, the price received is greater than the average variable cost of production but less than the average total cost of production. If the firm actually produces a quantity of q'' at a price of p_1, it will incur a total loss equal to p_2edp_1. However, in the short run, the firm will continue to produce because if it were to stop doing so, it would still have to pay its fixed cost. (Remember that the fixed cost must be paid whether or not a firm produces.) The fact that price p_1 is greater than the average variable cost of production at a quantity of q'' means that each unit sold more than pays for its average variable cost. The excess of price over average variable cost contributes to the payment of the firm's fixed cost. Thus, despite the loss it incurs, the firm will still produce as long as the price it receives from selling the optimal quantity covers its average variable cost. The excess of price over average variable cost minimizes the loss. These facts yield the following rule for choosing a quantity for the equilibrium of a competitive firm in the short run: The profit-maximizing quantity for a competitive firm to set in the short run is that quantity at which the price received equals the marginal cost of production, provided that this price is greater than the average variable cost of production.

Let us now look at an example of how to apply this rule. We will consider a firm with the following cost structure.

Quantity	Fixed Cost	Marginal Cost	Average Variable Cost
1	$100	$52	$52
2	100	44	48
3	100	37	44.33
4	100	31	41
5	100	26	38
6	100	22	35.33
7	100	19	33
8	100	16	30.875
9	100	15	29.11
10	100	16	27.80
11	100	19	27
12	100	22	26.58
13	100	26	26.53
14	100	31	26.85
15	100	37	27.53
16	100	44	28.56
17	100	52	29.94

Note that this firm has a fixed cost of production of $100. Its marginal and average variable costs are as specified. At what market prices will this firm choose to produce and at what market prices will it choose to shut down? To answer this question, let us say that the market price is $19. The firm will therefore set a quantity of 11 units of output because this is the quantity that equates the price to the marginal cost. However, we see that at a quantity of 11, the price of $19 does not cover the firm's average variable cost, which is $27. Hence, at such a quantity, it will be best for the firm *not to produce* because by producing it will generate a total loss of $188 as follows: quantity · (price − average variable cost) + fixed cost = 11 · ($19 − $27) + 100. The loss on each unit will be $8. If the firm does not produce when the market price is $19, it will lose only its fixed cost of $100. Therefore, at a market price as low as $19, the firm is better off shutting down production.

If we analyze the other amounts in this example, we find that the firm should produce only when the market price is greater than $26.53. Only at prices above that level will the firm be able to cover its average variable cost of production.

MEDIA NOTE

THE INTERNET AND PERFECT MARKETS

Perfectly competitive markets are ones in which many buyers and sellers can meet together with full information about supply and demand, no barriers to entry exist, etc. In such markets, every buyer would be matched with the supplier that could best meet his needs, prices would be at exactly the level that would keep supply and demand in equilibrium, and there would be no "transaction costs," such as time wasted seeking the right product.

Such markets rarely exist in the real world, but in the virtual world of the Internet, there is promise. This is true because the Internet has the ability to bring buyers and sellers together in exactly the circumstances dictated by theory. Buyers and sellers can gather in a virtual place without any information cost and with minimal processing cost. Information and search costs can be minimized as well. Consumers and businesses can take part in competitive auctions on eBay and other venues and buy practically everything and anything they want. In addition, firms and their suppliers can meet in online exchanges, "eHubs," and "business to business" (B2B) markets to auction, negotiate, or compare prices. The better known of these include Ariba, Chemdex, and eSteel.

The Perfect Solution

In an article, Steven Kaplan, of the University of Chicago, and Mohanbir Sawhney, of Northwestern University, identify two main ways in which B2B eHubs can enhance economic efficiency: "aggregation"—bringing together a huge number of buyers and sellers in a relatively costless manner—and "matching"—a dynamic process of matching buyers and sellers.

Drawing on economic theories of efficient auctions, Paul Milgrom, an economist at Stanford University, helped Perfect.com (a Web-based market firm) devise a patented technology, which they hope will become the norm in these markets. It is an automated "request-for-quote" process that allows competition on many factors besides price. The technology aims to allow buyers, in just 30 seconds, to describe what they want in many different respects—such as speed of delivery, supplier's reputation, and warranty period—as well as price. Suppliers will spell out, just as quickly, their capabilities in the same dimensions. The technology will then automatically find the best match of buyer and seller. Milgrom claims that, in more than half of all B2B Internet transactions, this could produce economic gains.

Source: Adapted from "How to Be Perfect: Attempts to create a perfectly efficient market on the Internet sound so ambitious as to be other-worldly. Do they have any chance of success?" as appeared in *The Economist,* February 12, 2000

---

supply function
A function that specifies how much of a good a firm would be willing to sell given any hypothetical market price if all other factors remain constant.

The Supply Function of a Competitive Firm in the Short Run

A supply function specifies how much of a good a firm would be willing to sell given any hypothetical market price if all other factors remained constant. The concept of a supply function for a competitive firm is analogous to the concept of a demand function for a consumer. Instead of describing how much a consumer is willing to buy at each price, it describes how much the firm is willing to supply at each price.

Figure 14.1 provides all the information we need to derive a supply curve for a competitive firm in the short run. To see how this is done, we will apply the optimal quantity rule and see what quantities would be set for any market price offered to the firm. First, let us look at price p_0', for which the optimal quantity to produce is q_0'. However, at a price of p_0' and a quantity of q_0', the marginal revenue received is below the average variable cost of production and the firm would therefore not want to produce any output. This situation is depicted in Figure 14.2, which shows the short-run supply curve for the firm.

Why is the competitive firm in Figure 14.2 unwilling to supply goods to the market in the short run at any price below p_0? As we know from Figure 14.1, p_0 is the price that exactly equals the lowest point on the average variable cost curve, and because the marginal cost equals the average variable cost at this point, it must be that if p_0 is actually the prevailing market price, the firm will be indifferent between not producing at all and producing quantity q_0. Thus, for prices below p_0, the firm will not want to produce because such prices are below its average variable cost. At any price above p_0, we can find the quantity the firm will supply by looking for that quantity at which the marginal cost of production equals the price. However, this equality holds only along the marginal cost curve, so that the supply curve of the firm in the short run must equal the marginal cost curve for all points above the lowest point on the average variable cost curve. The supply curve in Figure 14.2 is nothing more than the marginal cost curve we observed in Figure 14.1 except that it has been drawn to coincide with the vertical axis for all prices below p_0. These facts yield the following rule for the short-run supply curve of a competitive firm: The supply curve of a competitive firm in the short run equals the marginal cost curve of the firm above the lowest point on the average variable cost curve.

The Market Supply Curve

We have just derived the supply curve for a firm in a competitive industry, but if we want to determine how the market price is set, we must also derive the **market supply function or aggregate supply function**. This function tells us how

market supply function (aggregate supply function)
A function that tells us how much of a product all of the firms in an industry will supply at any given market price.

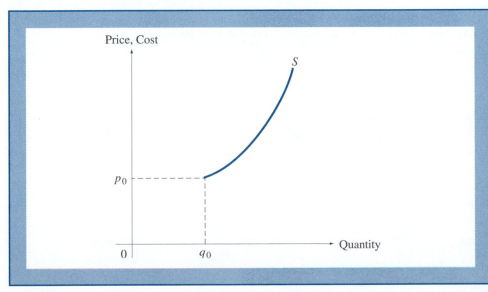

Figure 14.2

A Short-Run Supply Curve for a Competitive Firm.

At prices below p_0, the firm produces nothing because these prices are less than the average variable cost. At prices above p_0, the supply curve is identical to the marginal cost curve.

much of a product all of the firms in an industry will supply at any given market price. Fortunately, deriving the market supply function is a simple matter if we assume that the act of producing by one firm in a competitive industry does not affect the cost of production of any other firm and we also assume that all firms in the industry are so small that they control an insignificant portion of the market. Using such assumptions, we can derive the market supply curve for a firm by horizontally adding the supply curves of all of the firms in the industry, just as we derived the market demand curve in Chapter 4 by horizontally adding the demand curves of all consumers of a good.

Figure 14.3 shows the derivation of the market supply curve for the gadget industry, which is now a competitive industry. In this diagram, we see the individual supply curves of three firms in the industry. For the sake of simplicity, we will say that these are the only firms in the gadget industry despite the fact that such an assumption violates one of the fundamental characteristics of a competitive market—that it consists of a large number of firms. Note that the supply curves for the three firms have different shapes, indicating that not all firms in the industry are identical. The market supply curve tells us how much of the good *all firms in the industry* will supply at each hypothetical market price that may prevail.

To construct a market supply curve for the gadget industry, let us initially assume that p_1 is the prevailing market price. At this price, we see that the only firm willing to produce is firm 1, which produces q_1^1. (The superscript indicates the firm, and the subscript indicates the quantity. For example, q_2^3 means that firm 3 produces a quantity of q_2.) If the price is p_1, the entire industry produces only q_1^1. For all prices below p_2, firm 1 is the only firm willing to produce, so the market supply curve is the same as the supply curve of firm 1 alone. Above price p_2 but below price p_3, both firms 1 and 2 are willing to produce. For example, at a price of p_2', we see that firm 1 is willing to produce $q_{2'}^1$ and firm 2 is willing to produce $q_2^{2'}$. However, firm 3 is not willing to produce at such a low price, so the aggregate amount supplied at p_2' is $q_{2'}^1 + q_2^{2'}$. This amount appears as point A on the market supply curve in Figure 14.3. Above price p_3, we find that firm 3 will enter the

Figure 14.3

Deriving a Market Supply Curve for a Competitive Gadget Industry.

The market supply curve is the horizontal sum of the marginal cost curves of all of the firms in the industry.

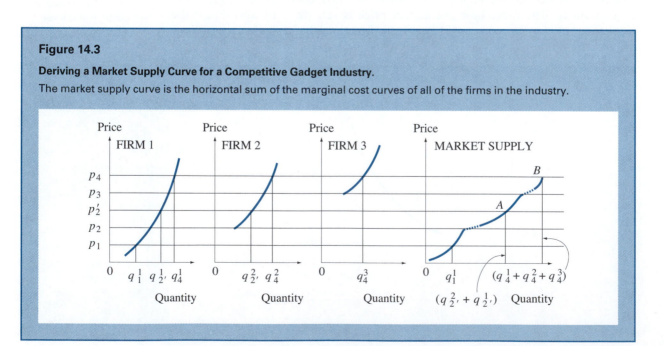

market. Hence, at price p_4, firm 1 will supply q_4^1, firm 2 will supply q_4^2, and firm 3 will supply q_4^3. The aggregate amount supplied will be $q_4^1 + q_4^2 + q_4^3$, which appears as point B on the market supply curve in Figure 14.3.

Note that because the market supply curve is merely the sum of the marginal cost curves of all of the firms in the industry, it represents the aggregate short-run marginal cost of supplying each unit to the market. For example, point B on the market supply curve in Figure 14.3 indicates the cost of the variable inputs that must be bought in order to supply the $(q_4^1 + q_4^2 + q_4^3)$th unit to the market.

Price Determination and the Definition of a Short-Run Equilibrium in a Competitive Market

Up to this point, our analysis has been hypothetical. We have asked questions of the following type: *If* the market price of the good is p, then how much will the industry supply? *If* the market price is p', then how much will the industry supply? Now we want to know what the market price will actually be. To determine this, let us juxtapose the two curves that we see in Figure 14.4: the market supply curve of a competitive industry in the short run and the market demand curve for the good produced. Remember that the market demand curve is derived by horizontally adding the individual demand curves for all of the consumers in the market, and these individual demand curves are the result of the utility-maximizing behavior of the consumers.

We will use Figure 14.4 to derive the **short-run equilibrium** for a perfectly competitive market—the price-quantity combination that will prevail in a perfectly competitive market in the short run. A price-quantity combination constitutes a short-run equilibrium for a competitive market if it is such that (1) no individual firm wishes to change the amount of the good it is supplying to the market; (2) no individual consumer wishes to change the amount of the good he or she is demanding; and (3) the aggregate supply in the market equals the aggregate demand for the good. What we mean in this definition is that a price and its associated quantity (the aggregate amount supplied by all firms and demanded by all consumers) are in equilibrium if there is no tendency or force in the market acting to

short-run equilibrium
The price-quantity combination that will prevail in a perfectly competitive market in the short run.

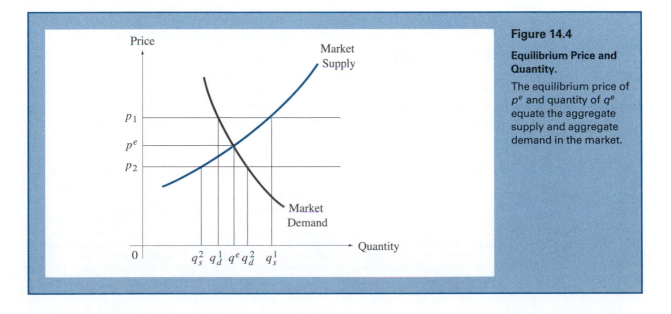

Figure 14.4

Equilibrium Price and Quantity.

The equilibrium price of p^e and quantity of q^e equate the aggregate supply and aggregate demand in the market.

change them. The forces that can change the quantity are profit maximization by the firms and utility maximization by the consumers. If at the existing price all firms are maximizing their profit by choosing the quantity they want to supply to the market and all consumers are maximizing their utility by choosing the quantity they want to demand, then as long as nothing changes, there will be no force acting in the market to alter the aggregate supply and demand.

To ensure that there is no force acting to change the price, we must be certain that the aggregate supply in the market equals the aggregate demand. To understand why this equality of supply and demand is necessary, let us say that in Figure 14.4 the market price is p_1. At this price, firms are willing to supply q_s^1, but consumers demand only q_d^1. Hence, at a price of p_1, all agents are satisfied with their decisions, but supply and demand do not match because $q_s^1 > q_d^1$. There is an excess supply. If the firms actually produce the amount they are willing to supply, it cannot be sold at such a high price, and we would expect the firms to offer the good to consumers at a lower price rather than adding the excess supply to inventory. Therefore, the excess supply will lead to price cutting and will be a force acting to change the price.

At a price of p_2, just the opposite situation will occur. Because $q_s^2 < q_d^2$, there will be excess demand, which will create pressure for prices to rise. The consumers who are not able to obtain the good will offer a higher price for it. Thus, only at p^e is there no incentive for consumers to change their demand and for firms to change their supply, and there is no force acting to change the price because the aggregate supply equals the aggregate demand.[1]

In Figure 14.5, we see the gadget industry, a competitive industry, in a short-run equilibrium.

Note that the equilibrium price in the industry, p^e, appears at the far right in Figure 14.5, where the market supply and market demand curves intersect. The aggregate quantity bought and sold in the market is seen as quantity q^e in that diagram. At price p^e, firm 1 tries to maximize its profit by selling q_e^1 units, firm 2 tries to do so by selling q_e^2 units, and firm 3 tries to do so by selling q_e^3 units. Two of the three firms succeed in earning a profit at this market-clearing price. In fact, firms 1 and 2 earn an extra-normal profit equal to π^1 and π^2, respectively. Firm 3, on the other hand, earns no profit at the short-run equilibrium.

Policy Analysis in the Short Run: Comparative Static Analysis

comparative static analysis
An analysis in which the economist examines the equilibrium of the market before and after a policy change to see the effect of the change on the market price and quantity.

The simple supply and demand diagram presented in Figure 14.5 can be used quite effectively for policy analysis. The way in which economists perform policy analyses is through a method called comparative static analysis. Basically, a comparative static analysis is an analysis in which the economist examines the

---

[1] We can think of this competitive equilibrium as a game played by the firms that supply the good, the consumers who demand the good, and a market auctioneer. The strategy set of the firms consists of all the positive quantities of the good that they can produce; the strategy set of the consumers consists of all the positive quantities of the good that they can demand; and the strategy set of the auctioneer consists of all the positive prices that can be announced to the market. The payoff to the firms is their profit, and the payoff to the consumers is their utility. The payoff to the auctioneer is equal to −1 times the quantity of excess demand or excess supply in the market. When supply equals demand, the auctioneer's payoff is maximized because it is zero. From this description, we can see that a Nash equilibrium for this game consists of a price for the auctioneer at which supply equals demand and at which all consumers maximize their utility and all firms maximize their profit. This is exactly how we defined a competitive equilibrium above.

Figure 14.5

The Short-Run Equilibrium for a Competitive Industry.

The short-run equilibrium for a competitive industry is consistent with positive profits.

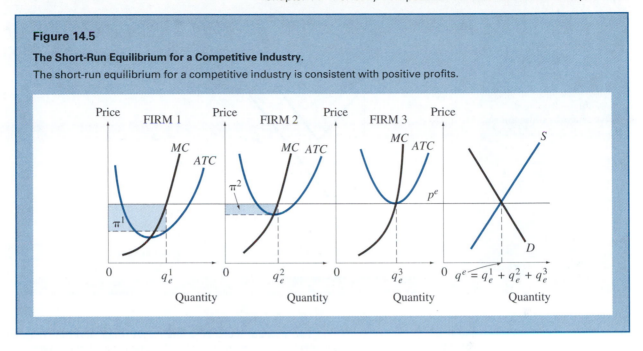

equilibrium of the market before and after a policy change to see the effect of the change on the market price and quantity. In other words, the economist *compares* two *static* equilibria. What is *not* done in a comparative static analysis is to examine the path that the market will follow in moving from one of these equilibria to the other. That would be a dynamic analysis.

To understand how an economist might go about making a comparative static analysis of a policy change, let us consider the following examples.

dynamic analysis
An analysis in which the economist examines the path that the market will follow in moving from one equilibrium to another.

Example 14.1

THE MARKET FOR ILLEGAL DRUGS

The market for illegal drugs is not unlike the market for any good. There exists a commodity, such as cocaine or heroin, that is desired by one group of economic agents, whom we will call the "users," and another group of economic agents, whom we will call the "dealers," is willing to supply the commodity. Obviously, this market is different from most other markets in the sense that it involves the purchase, sale, and use of an illegal substance, which means that anyone who is caught performing such activities will be prosecuted. Still, the fact that the good is illegal does not prevent the market from operating. It simply imposes an additional cost on both the dealers and the users. For example, the dealer's cost of selling cocaine is not only the price paid to buy it from a wholesaler but also the possible cost of being caught and put in jail. The greater the likelihood that these events will occur is, the higher the cost of doing business for the drug dealer. The user faces a similar situation. Thus, for both the dealer and the user, the cost of obtaining an illegal drug is not only the actual cost of buying the drug but also the possible cost of apprehension and punishment.

Because government actions affect the likelihood that any drug dealer or user will be caught, these actions also affect the cost of buying and selling drugs and thereby affect the market price and the quantity bought and sold. To understand the consequences of government actions affecting the market for illegal drugs, let us consider Figure 14.6.

In Figure 14.6, we see the market for illegal drugs portrayed by the familiar supply and demand curves. The market supply curve represents the profit-maximizing decisions of the drug dealers about the quantity of illegal drugs they will provide at each price offered in the market. The market demand curve represents the utility-maximizing decisions of the drug users and illustrates the quantity they will purchase at various prices, assuming that their incomes and the prices of the other goods they purchase remain constant. In Figure 14.6, we

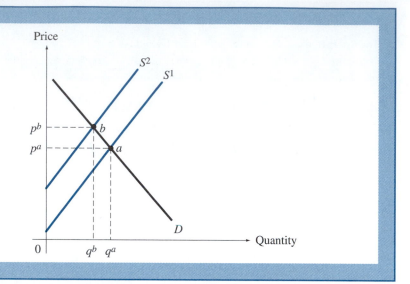

Figure 14.6

The Market for Illegal Drugs.

An increase in the probability that a drug dealer will be caught shifts the supply curve to the left, from S^1 to S^2, raises the equilibrium price from p^a to p^b, and lowers the equilibrium quantity from q^a to q^b.

find that initially, when we take into account the cost of the illegal drugs and the cost of doing business, the market is in equilibrium at a price of p^a and a quantity sold of q^a units.

Now let us say that the government decides to launch a "war on illegal drugs." If the government therefore expands the size of its drug enforcement agency, the probability of drug dealers' being caught and prosecuted will increase. How will this policy change by the government affect the market price of illegal drugs and the quantity sold? To answer this question, we must first investigate how the supply and demand curves for illegal drugs will move as we change the parameters of the market. If we look again at Figure 14.6, we find that the supply curve will *shift* to the right or the left as the cost of doing business decreases or increases. By a shift, we mean a complete displacement of the curve to the right or the left so that at any given price, the quantity sold will now change. For example, if the government hires more drug enforcement agents, the cost of doing business for the drug dealers will increase because the likelihood of apprehension and punishment will increase. The increase in the cost of doing business can be expected to shift the supply curve to the left from S^1 to S^2 because a smaller quantity will be sold at any previous price. What effect does expanded drug enforcement have on demand? When the supply curve shifts to the left, we find that there is no shift in the demand curve because the attitude of the users toward buying drugs does not change. As a result, the market price of illegal drugs will increase to p^b and the quantity sold will decrease to q^b.

From a policy point of view, we can say that an increase in the number of drug enforcement agents will be successful in decreasing drug sales. When we *compare* the old equilibrium at point *a* to the new one at point *b*, we see a fall in the use of illegal drugs in society. Thus, by performing a comparative static analysis, we have been able to evaluate the effectiveness of a policy change that is intended to curb drug sales. What we do not know is whether the policy change is beneficial to society on the whole because that will depend on whether the advantages society reaps from less use of illegal drugs are greater than the cost of the additional drug enforcement agents.

There is another policy question related to the foregoing analysis. Who should the drug enforcement agency spend its time apprehending and prosecuting—the dealer in illegal drugs or the user? As we will see, the answer to this question depends on whether the dealer or the user is more likely to be deterred by the prospect of being punished for a drug-related crime. To examine the issue further, let us consider Figure 14.7.

In Figure 14.7, we see a set of four supply and demand curves for the illegal drug market. If we start our analysis with demand curve D^1 and supply curve S^1, we find that this market reaches an initial equilibrium at point *a*. However, as we know from our previous analysis, when the government increases its drug enforcement effort and aims it strictly at the dealers, the supply curve will shift to the left, as we see in the shift from S^1 to S^2. This shift takes place because the dealers now have a higher cost of doing business. If the expanded drug enforcement is aimed at users only, the shift will occur in the demand curve rather than the

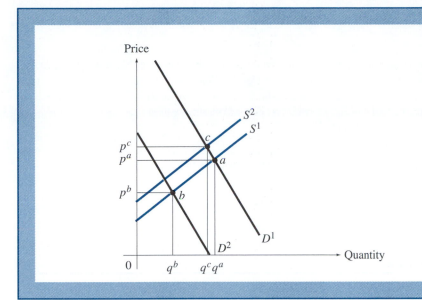

Figure 14.7

The Decision About Whom to Prosecute.

A policy of prosecuting illegal drug dealers shifts the supply curve from S^1 to S^2 and the equilibrium from point a to point c. A policy of prosecuting illegal drug users shifts the demand curve from D^1 to D^2 and the equilibrium from point a to point b.

supply curve. Further, if we assume that the greater prospect of punishment actually decreases the desire of users to continue taking drugs, the demand curve will shift down and to the left as is shown by the shift from D^1 to D^2 in Figure 14.7.

Now let us assume that the selling of illegal drugs is carried out by organized crime groups. We might expect that these groups will be able to absorb the increased cost of doing business. For example, they probably have lawyers on retainer who can handle the greater number of drug prosecutions. Under these circumstances, the expanded enforcement effort against drug dealers should cause a relatively small shift in the supply curve. However, the emphasis on punishing drug dealers rather than drug users will move the market equilibrium from point a to point c, where the price of illegal drugs will rise from p^a to p^c and the quantity sold will fall.

As we saw previously, an emphasis on punishing the users of illegal drugs will lead to a big shift in the demand curve from D^1 to D^2, but the supply curve will remain at S^1. As a result, the market equilibrium will move from point a to point b, where the price of illegal drugs will actually *fall*, but the quantity sold will undergo a substantial decrease from q^a to q^b. Obviously, a policy of prosecuting the users of illegal drugs will be much more successful in curbing drug consumption in society than a policy of prosecuting the dealers.

MEDIA NOTE

CRIME PREVENTION

What's the best way to cut down on prostitution? One solution is to arrest the prostitutes, but another is to embarrass the johns by posting their pictures in newspapers. Which do you think is more effective? Economic theory might suggest that the latter is more effective because prostitutes are in business and one of the costs of doing this business is occasionally spending the night in jail. But prostitutes are also backed by their pimps, so once in jail they are bailed out and back on the streets in a matter of hours. As a result, if police step up their

enforcement of prostitution laws, it is unlikely to shift the supply curve of prostitute services very far. Just the opposite can be expected to happen if the policy is aimed at those who frequent prostitutes. These are men of varied economic and social backgrounds, but one thing they have in common is that they do not want it known that they solicit for prostitutes. Hence, if the cost of visiting a prostitute increases because of potential embarrassment, we can expect that the demand curve for such services will shift to the left, causing the amount of prostitution to fall (as well as its price).

MEDIA NOTE *(Contd.)*

This is the solution the Chicago Police Department has chosen. It started putting photographs, names, and partial addresses of arrested johns on its Web site and keeps them there for 30 days. Dave Bayless, a police department spokesman, said, "If we can do anything to get a john to think twice about coming into Chicago communities to solicit a prostitute, we think we're addressing the problem."

In total, about 16,000 women and girls are involved in prostitution in the Chicago area, which led to 3,204 arrests with 950 customers on solicitation charges.

Several cities, including Durham, North Carolina; Akron, Ohio; and Denver, Colorado, post names and photographs of people who are arrested in or convicted of prostitution-related crimes on police Web sites or local television.

Source: Adapted from "Chicago Police Put Arrest Photos of Prostitution Suspects Online," as appeared in the *New York Times,* June 23, 2005

Example 14.2

THE INCIDENCE OF A TAX

As we just observed, government can affect the workings of a market by the way in which it enforces laws. Another, and perhaps more common, way in which government can affect the workings of a market is through its ability to impose a tax. For example, let us say that the government imposes a tax on the producers of a certain type of good. Will the consumers end up paying this tax through higher prices, or will the producers simply absorb it? This question involves the issue of tax incidence—the ultimate distribution of the burden of a tax. As we will see, the answer to the question depends on the elasticity of demand for the product being taxed. In general, the *more* elastic the demand, the *less* the incidence of the tax will fall on the consumers. Let us consider Figure 14.8, which illustrates the relationship between tax incidence and elasticity of demand.

In Figure 14.8(a), we see a market in which the elasticity of demand is zero. This probably means that consumers treat the good as an absolute necessity and there is no substitute for the good. Superimposed on the demand curve in Figure 14.8(a) are two supply curves, S^1 and S^2. Let us start our analysis at the intersection of S^1 and D, where we see point a. This point constitutes a market equilibrium in which the price is p^a and the quantity sold is q^a. Now let us say that the government imposes a tax on the producers that amounts to α on each unit of the good. As a result, the supply curve of the producers will shift up and to the left by the amount of α. The new supply curve will be S^2, which is parallel to S^1 but above it by the amount of α.

Note that the tax shifts the supply curve in a *parallel* manner because the height of the old supply curve S^1 above any quantity indicates the minimum amount of money it will take for the producers to be willing to supply a unit of the good. When the government imposes the per-unit tax of α, the producers will demand α more for each unit before they will agree to supply any given unit.

Look again at Figure 14.8(a). When the tax is instituted, we see a new equilibrium established at point b, where the price is $p^a + \alpha$ but the quantity sold is still q^a. Clearly, the imposition of the tax has led to a new equilibrium price that is equal to the old price plus the full amount of the tax. The consumers pay the entire tax, but they continue to buy the old quantity. They have no alternative. Because the elasticity of demand for the good is zero, the consumers cannot substitute another good for this one when the tax is imposed. The producers are therefore able to shift the entire amount of the tax to the consumers.

Figure 14.8(b) presents the opposite situation. Here, demand for the good is infinitely elastic, perhaps because a perfect substitute exists. If the price of the substitute is p^a, then any increase in the price of the original good will cause its demand to fall to zero. The imposition of a tax on the product will again cause the supply curve to shift from S^1 to S^2. However, in this case, the tax will not lead to an increase in the market price of the good. Instead, the market price will remain unchanged, but the quantity sold will decrease. The producers will absorb the entire tax, and the consumers will not pay any of it. However, the producers will no longer want to supply the old quantity, so the amount sold will fall.

tax incidence
The ultimate distribution of the burden of a tax.

Figure 14.8

The Incidence of a Tax and the Elasticity of Demand.

(a) When demand is perfectly inelastic, the incidence of a tax of α per unit falls entirely on the consumer.
(b) When demand is perfectly elastic, the incidence of the tax falls entirely on the producer. (c) When elasticity is intermediate between 0 and $-\infty$, the incidence of the tax falls partly on the consumer and partly on the producer.

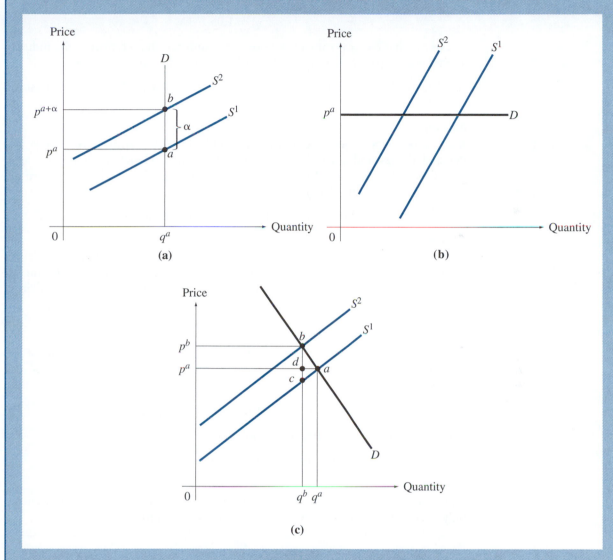

(a)

(b)

(c)

In Figure 14.8(c), we see a situation in which the demand curve has an intermediate elasticity, between 0 and $-\infty$. If we start our analysis at point a, we find that before imposition of the tax, the equilibrium price is p^a and the equilibrium quantity is q^a. When the tax is imposed, the supply curve shifts up from S^1 to S^2, and the equilibrium moves from point a to point b. The new price is p^b, and the new quantity is q^b. Note that the new price is higher than the old price by the amount db, but the tax is equal to the amount $cb > db$. In this case, part of the tax (db) is being paid by the consumers and part (cd) is being paid by the producers.

SOLVED PROBLEM 14.1

Question (Content Review: Tax Incidence)

Assume that an industry exists where the market demand curve is

$$q_d = 100 - 0.5p$$

and the market supply curve is

$$q_s = 1.0p$$

Let us say that the government imposes a per-unit tax on each firm in the industry so that it must pay the government $2.00 for each unit sold.

  a) What is the equilibrium price and quantity in the market before the imposition of the tax?

Answer

Before the imposition of the tax, we simply need to equate the supply and demand curves and solve for the equilibrium price. Hence, $q_d = 100 - 0.5p = q_s = 1.0p$ or $100 - 0.5p = 1.0p \Rightarrow 100 = 1.5p \Rightarrow p = 66.67$. Plugging 66.67 into the demand curve, we find that $q_d = 66.67$.

  b) What is the equilibrium price and quantity after the imposition of the tax?

Answer

After the imposition of the tax, the supply curve shifts up so that in order to induce the same amount of supply, each firm will have to receive a $2.00 higher price to compensate for its increased costs. Hence, the supply curve can be written as

$$q_s = p - 2$$

Given the demand curve $q_d = 100 - 0.5p$, which does not shift as a result of the imposition of the tax, we can equate supply and demand and solve for the new equilibrium:

$$p - 2 = 100 - 0.5p \Rightarrow 102/1.5 = p \Rightarrow 68$$

The new quantity is $q_d = 100 - 0.5(68) = 66$.

  c) How much of the $2.00 tax is shifted to consumers?

Answer

Note that even though the tax imposed was $2.00, the equilibrium price went up only $1.33. Hence, only $1.33 of the $2.00 tax is shifted to the consumer.

Example 14.3

THE MINIMUM WAGE AND MARKETS WITH PRICE FLOORS

The imposition of a maximum or minimum price in a market is another common form of policy intervention by government. If the equilibrium price that the market would naturally set differs from the artificially established maximum or minimum, then this policy of imposing a price ceiling or a price floor interferes with the natural equilibrating forces of the market. Two well-known examples of such intervention are rent control and the minimum wage. In a real estate market where there is rent control, the maximum rent a landlord can charge is set by the government. If the market equilibrium is above that maximum, landlords are prevented from obtaining the full market rent for their property. In labor markets where there is a minimum wage, employers must pay wages to their workers that do not fall below the government-imposed minimum. Thus, the workers are protected from the forces of supply and demand whenever the equilibrium wage is lower than the government-imposed minimum.

To gain a better understanding of how a price floor affects the workings of a market, let us take a closer look at the minimum wage. We will begin by considering the labor market depicted in Figure 14.9.

In the market that appears in Figure 14.9, labor is a key input for the production process of the firms involved. The lower the wage is, the more labor these firms will demand. As a result, the demand curve for labor slopes down and to the right. The supply curve for labor was derived in Chapter 4 and is the outcome of the utility-maximizing decisions that the workers made in dividing their time between leisure and work. The equilibrium for the labor market depicted in Figure 14.9 occurs at point a, where the wage is w^a and the quantity of labor employed is q^a. Let us assume that this wage is extremely low, perhaps because the market consists of unskilled workers with limited education, such as teenage workers. Let us say that the equilibrium wage of w^a is so low that public pressure mounts to force employers to increase this wage. Eventually, the public pressure results in the passage of a **minimum wage law** that prescribes a floor below which wages cannot fall. Such a minimum wage is depicted in Figure 14.9 as a horizontal line at wage rate w^{min}.

Once the minimum wage is imposed, two changes occur immediately in this labor market. First, the wage paid to workers rises from w^a to w^{min}. Then, the number of workers employed falls from q^a to q^{min}. Thus, at the minimum wage rate of w^{min}, there is an excess supply of workers. More people want to work at that wage rate than firms are willing to hire. Further, fewer workers are employed than would be employed if the market were allowed to determine the equilibrium wage. However, those workers who are employed earn more money.

Critics of the minimum wage argue that it is partially responsible for the high incidence of crime among teenagers because it prevents $q^a - q^{min}$ teenagers from obtaining jobs. These critics assert that the minimum wage has placed such teenagers on the streets without anything to do, and this idleness leads to crime. As the old saying indicates, "The devil makes work for idle hands." These critics advocate letting the wage fall to its natural market level of w^a even though that level is low because such a wage will allow more people, especially teenagers, to find jobs, and once employed, they will be less likely to commit crimes. This analysis sounds plausible, but it is incomplete. As we know from our discussion of crime in Chapter 4, criminals can be viewed as rational, utility-optimizing agents who consider their options between honest and dishonest work and decide on how much time to devote to each. At the low market wage of w^a, crime looks relatively attractive. Honest work does not seem very worthwhile. Now let us assume that the government devises a policy to decrease crime among teenagers by increasing their employment opportunities. Instead of imposing a minimum wage or allowing the wage to fall to its natural market level, the government offers to subsidize any firm that hires teenagers. Figure 14.10 describes this situation.

In Figure 14.10, we see our original supply and demand curves S^1 and D^1. As before, the resulting market wage is w^a and the resulting quantity of labor employed is q^a. However, at a wage of w^a, there may be a substantial amount of crime in society because honest work may

minimum wage law
A law that prescribes a floor below which wages cannot fall.

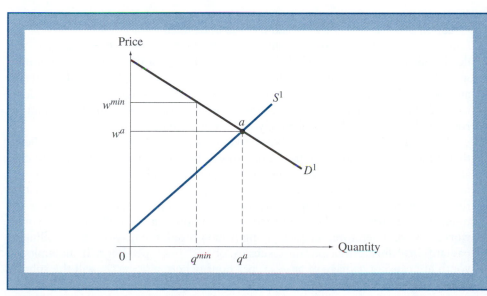

Figure 14.9

The Labor Market and the Minimum Wage.

The establishment of a minimum wage of w^{min} raises the equilibrium wage paid to employed workers from w^a to w^{min} and lowers the number of employed workers from q^a to q^{min}.

Figure 14.10

Government-Subsidized Wages.

A government subsidy of the wages of teenage workers shifts the demand curve for labor from D^1 to D^2, raises the equilibrium wage from w^a to w^b, and raises the number of workers employed from q^a to q^b.

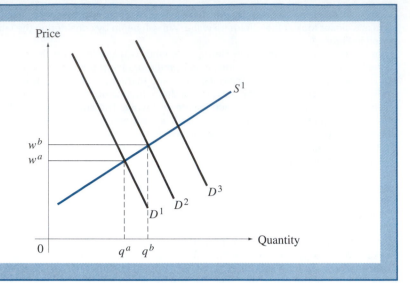

not appear attractive. If the government decides to subsidize wages, that subsidy will shift the demand curve for labor out and to the right, say to D^2. At a demand of D^2, we see a new equilibrium wage of w^b and a quantity of labor employed of q^b, which means that a larger number of people have opted for honest work. A higher subsidy will shift the demand for labor to the right again to D^3 and lead to even more workers' being hired. As an increasing number of workers find jobs, there will be fewer and fewer people who are idle and therefore prone to commit crimes.

From the example that we just analyzed, it appears that instead of eliminating the minimum wage to reduce crime, the government should do the opposite—subsidize the market-determined wage. The problem with this policy is that the subsidy cannot rise indefinitely. There must be a point at which the subsidy is too high. This point is reached when the marginal benefit of an additional dollar spent on subsidizing the market wage creates a reduction in the costs of crime just equal to that dollar. The optimal subsidy will, of course, vary from society to society, and we cannot say that it is represented by demand curve D^2 or D^3. However, the optimal subsidy is likely to be positive and lead to a wage above w^a.

SOLVED PROBLEM 14.2

Question (Application and Extension: Wage Subsidies)

One of the arguments for abolishing the minimum wage is the idea that "the devil makes work for idle hands," meaning that if an artificially high minimum wage leads to a reduction in youth employment, those unemployed will engage in antisocial behavior and, hence, will diminish the quality of life for all of us. However, if that is the argument against the minimum wage, there might be another route to dealing with the problem of youth employment.

Figure 14.11 represents the labor market in Keystone City. The mayor believes that if more people can get jobs, vandalism will be greatly reduced in the city. She also thinks that the market-clearing wage for young people is too low—so low that many might be discouraged from seeking employment. Rather than eliminating the minimum wage and letting the wage fall to its competitive level, the mayor announces that firms will be subsidized by an amount $w^{min} - w^a$ for each young worker hired. Therefore, for each young person hired, the mayor stands willing to pay any firm hiring that person a subsidy of $w^{min} - w^a$ per hour. If unemployed youth are causing damage of $w^v - w^a$ per hour, where $w^v > w^{min}$, will the subsidy actually save the city money?

Figure 14.11

Subsidizing Youth Employment.

A subsidy leads to higher wages and more young employees.

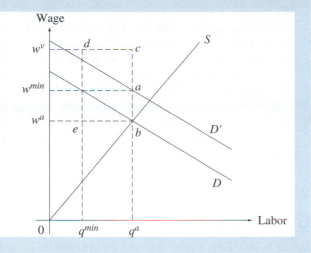

Answer

Consider Figure 14.11. The subsidy may be beneficial. It will save the city money if the amount spent on the subsidy is less than the amount of damage caused by unemployed workers; thus, if $(w^{min} - w^a)q^a < (w^a - w^a)(q^a - q^{min})$, the plan is beneficial. We can see this situation graphically in Figure 14.11.

Therefore, if the area $w^{min} abw^a$ is greater than $dcbe$, the wage subsidy would cost more than the damage; if the opposite were true, the subsidy would benefit society.

MINIMUM WAGES

RESOLVING
TEASER 14

In the Falk et al. experiment, the researchers set up markets where the labor supply curve should be perfectly elastic at a wage of zero. In other words, workers, because they can earn nothing if they do not accept a job, should be willing to accept any wage. In the experiment, there are three workers per firm, which means that each firm should hire three workers. However, workers may reject low wages for reasons of fairness, etc. If firms know this, they can expect that the reservation wages of workers will be upward sloping and not flat. So firms face an upward-sloping supply curve of labor due to the fact that the workers' notion of fairness lead them to reject low wages, and different workers have different reservation wages—some may reject very low offers but accept higher ones, while others may reject even high offers. However, when firms face an upward-sloping labor supply schedule, increases in the minimum wage may not reduce but instead even increase employment.

To see why, assume that there is a fair amount of heterogeneity in the reservation wages of workers and that the marginal revenue received by the firm in hiring its third worker is 260. In such a case, it may be profit maximizing to hire fewer than three workers. For example, if reservation wages of the three matched workers are (0, 10, and 100), hiring three instead of two workers (and paying them all the same wage, that is, the reservation wage of the last person hired) produces marginal costs of $3 \times 100 - 2 \times 10 = 280$, which exceeds the marginal revenue of the third worker, which is only 260. (Remember, we must pay all workers the same wage; so when we hire the third at a wage of 100, we must raise the wages of the other two workers to 100 as well.)

(Continued)

It is therefore optimal for the firm to hire two instead of three workers in this case. The introduction of a minimum wage of 40 reduces the marginal cost of labor from 280 to 220 (because if the firm hired two workers only, it would cost 2×40 and not 2×10), which is less than the marginal revenue of the third worker. Thus, hiring all three workers is profitable in the presence of the minimum wage.

In the Falk et al. experiment, the researchers find that, probably because of fairness motives, firms do in fact face an upward-sloping reservation wage or supply schedule and, as a result, they do find that imposing a minimum wage of 40 in their experiment does in fact lead to more employment.

Conclusion

While most of the welfare properties of perfectly competitive markets involve markets in long-run equilibrium, as Keynes has said, "In the long run we are all dead." We live our lives in a sequence of short runs and hence we need to know how the world functions there. This is what we did in this chapter, but in the next we turn our attention to long-run equilibria and the welfare properties of markets in that hypothetical world.

Summary

This chapter took a look at the theory of competitive markets in the short run. We studied the short-run supply decisions of firms and characterized the conditions needed for a short-run competitive equilibrium. The short-run analysis of markets differs from that of markets in the long run in the sense that, in the short run, the firms are stuck with some factors of production that are fixed in size. This constraint leads to some conclusions that do not hold in the long run. For example, while in the long run all extra-normal profits for firms are competed away by market entry, this is not true in the short run. In addition, policy recommendations made in the short run may differ substantially from those made in the long run. In this chapter, we took a look at a variety of such policy issues, including minimum age policy, policies concerning illegal drugs, and tax incidence.

Exercises and Problems

1. Consider a firm with the following cost structure:

Quantity	Fixed Cost	Total Variable Cost	Marginal Cost	Average Variable Cost
1	2	10		
2	2	18		
3	2	24		
4	2	31		
5	2	40		
6	2	54		

a) In the above table, fill out the Marginal Cost and Average Variable Cost columns.

    b)   If market price is set at \$6.00, how many units would the firm produce? Calculate its profit.

    c)   If market price is set at \$9.00, how many units would the firm produce? Calculate its profit.

2. Consider a firm with a total cost curve of $TC = 1{,}000 + q^3/3 - 2q^2 + 6q$ and the associated marginal cost curve of $MC = q^2 - 4q + 6$.

    a)   What is the lowest price at which this firm will want to supply a positive amount to the market in the short run?

    b)   At the "lowest price," how much will be supplied?

    c)   How much will be supplied in the short run if the price is \$10?

3. Suppose there are 3 identical firms with $TC = 100 + 2q^3 - 4q^2 + 50q$ (where $MC = 6q^2 - 8q + 50$ and $AVC = 2q^2 - 4q + 50$).

    a)   Draw the short-run supply function of each firm.

    b)   Draw the short-run market supply function.

4. Suppose there are 2 firms in the industry. Firm 1 produces with the total cost function $TC_1 = 100 + 2q^3 - 4q^2 + 50q$ (where $MC = 6q^2 - 8q + 50$ and $AVC = 2q^2 - 4q + 50$). Firm 2 produces with the total cost function $TC_2 = 100 + 2q^3 - 8q^2 + 20q$ (where $MC = 6q^2 - 16q + 20$ and $AVC = 2q^2 - 8q + 20$).

    a)   Draw the short-run supply function of each firm.

    b)   Draw the short-run market supply function.

5. Assume that the market demand curve is $q_D = 100 - 0.5p$ and the market supply curve is $q_S = 1.0p$.

    a)   Find the equilibrium price and quantity.

    b)   Suppose the government imposes on each firm a \$1.00 tax on each unit sold. How much of the \$1.00 tax is shifted to the customer?

    c)   Find the tax revenue of the government.

In Chapter 14, we studied how perfectly competitive markets function in the short run. However, much of the argument for laissez-faire economics relies on long-run arguments, so it is that analysis that we now turn our attention to. In the process of defining a long-run equilibrium, we will also examine its welfare properties. As we will see, these markets benefit society by maximizing the sum of consumer surplus and producer surplus.

The Long-Run Equilibrium for Identical Firms

While firms in perfectly competitive markets may earn extra-normal profits in the short run, such profits will not characterize the long-run equilibrium in these markets. In most cases, if the firms in an industry are making extra-normal profits, other firms will become aware of the situation and will want to enter the industry. Hence, the short-run equilibrium we examined previously will not continue indefinitely. For an industry equilibrium to endure, there must be no incentive either for the firms currently in the industry to change their capacity or for other firms to enter the industry. These considerations lead us to the following definition of a

long-run equilibrium
The price-quantity combination that will prevail in a perfectly competitive market in the long run.

long-run equilibrium for a perfectly competitive market—the price-quantity combination that will prevail in a perfectly competitive market in the long run: A price-quantity combination constitutes a long-run equilibrium for a competitive market if it is such that (1) no individual firm wishes to change the amount of the good it is supplying to the market, (2) no individual consumer wishes to change the amount of the good he or she is demanding, (3) no existing firm in the market has any incentive to change the amount of any of the inputs it is using or to exit from the market, (4) no firm outside the market has any incentive to enter it, and (5) the aggregate supply in the market equals the aggregate demand for the good.

This definition takes the definition of a short-run equilibrium in a perfectly competitive market and broadens it to include the concepts of entry, exit, and capital expansion. It is no longer sufficient that no firm wants to change its supply and no consumer wishes to change his or her demand; it is now also necessary that there be no incentive for a firm to enter or exit the market or expand its use of capital.

To see how firms in competitive markets adjust to the long-run equilibrium, let us look at Figure 15.1(a), which depicts the long-run cost situation of such a firm.

In Figure 15.1(a), we see the long-run average and marginal cost curves for a competitive firm along with a series of short-run curves. Each short-run average and marginal cost function is associated with a different amount of capital that the firm might have available. Capital will be the fixed factor in our analysis. For example, the average cost curve labeled K^1 indicates the short-run average cost function for this firm if K^1 is the amount of its capital. Similarly, there are three other short-run average cost curves, each of which is predicated on a different level of

Figure 15.1

The Adjustment to a Long-Run Equilibrium.

Positive profits attract the entry of additional firms and shift the supply curve to the right (Figure 15.1[b]) until each firm has a capacity of K^* and the market supply curve is S^*. In a long-run equilibrium, each firm produces q^* units and earns zero profits because the price of p^* equals the long-run marginal cost.

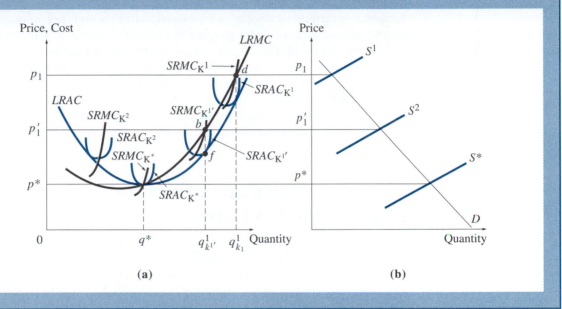

(a)   (b)

capital (K^*, $K^{1'}$, and K^2). Note that when K^* is the amount of capital available and q^* is produced, this is the lowest average cost possible for the firm.

For the moment, assume that all firms in the industry have exactly the same cost structure as this firm. Figure 15.1(b) depicts various market supply and demand conditions. Let us start our analysis when the applicable supply and demand curves are S^1 and D, which determine a market price of p_1. At this price, the firm will decide that in the long run it wants to sell that quantity at which the price equals the *long-run* marginal cost of production. (We are assuming that the firm has enough time to adjust all factors of production to meet any level of demand.) It is the long-run marginal cost that is relevant here. At a price of p_1, the firm produces a quantity of $q_{k_1}^1$, and it will install a capacity of K^1 because that amount of capital will allow it to produce $q_{k_1}^1$ at the lowest possible average cost.

As we see, given the price of p_1, this firm will make extra-normal profits. If the firm is earning extra-normal profits, other firms will decide to enter the industry. This entry can be depicted by a shift of the supply curve from S_1 to S_2. Given the demand curve, the expansion of supply will cause the market price to fall from p_1 to p_1'. If our firm is able to adjust its capital when the price decreases to p_1', it will lower the amount of capital it uses from K^1 to $K^{1'}$ and produce a quantity of $q_{k_1'}^1$. However, after these changes, the firm will still be earning extra-normal profits, so the industry will continue to attract new entrants. The entry of additional firms will shift the market supply curve further to the right, thus depressing the market price even more.

When will this process end? As long as firms in the industry earn extra-normal profits, other firms will be attracted and will decide to enter the industry. There is only one price at which the firms in the industry will not earn extra-normal profits, and that price is p^*. Therefore, entry will continue until the market price is driven down to p^* (until the supply curve has shifted to S^*). At that point, each firm will use K^* amount of capital and produce q^* units, and the market price of p^* will be equal to the firm's marginal cost. The market price of p^* will also be equal to the lowest point of the long-run average cost curve.

The situation that we just described meets all the criteria that we specified for a long-run equilibrium in a competitive industry. At price p^*, no firm will have any incentive to change its output or its capital, no firm will want to exit the industry because it is earning an amount at least equal to its opportunity cost outside the industry, and no firm will want to enter the industry because it will not be able to make extra-normal profits. Hence, we can say that this situation represents a long-run equilibrium. We can characterize this equilibrium as follows: At a long-run equilibrium, all firms in a competitive market are using the amount of capital that allows them to produce at the point of the minimum average cost on their long-run average cost curve, entry into and exit from the market have ceased, the market supply equals the market demand, and the market price equals the marginal cost.

The Long-Run Equilibrium for Heterogeneous Firms

The analysis that we just completed assumes that all firms in a competitive market are identical and have identical long-run average cost curves. In the real world, this is not the case. One factor that can cause a difference in long-run costs is location. Some firms are located in areas where it is less costly for them to produce. For example, in the mining industry, some firms own land with mineral deposits that are close to the surface and therefore easy to work. These firms are likely to be low-cost producers. Other mining companies have mineral deposits that are buried deep in the ground and are difficult to extract. Not surprisingly, such firms are usually high-cost producers. Even if an industry like this is competitive, we would not expect to see the market price driven down to the bottom of each firm's average cost curve. Figure 15.2 illustrates this point.

In Figure 15.2(a), we find a long-run market price of p^* and a firm with what appears to be two long-run average cost curves. The lower curve, $LRAC$, is the long-run average cost curve of the firm exclusive of what we will soon call economic rent. This curve includes all the costs that the firm incurs when it produces its output. Therefore, at the long-run market price of p^*, the firm seems to be earning extra-normal profits that are equal to p^*abc. If these are really extra-normal profits, how can there be a long-run equilibrium in the industry? Why do we not see other firms entering the industry?

The extra-normal profits of the firm depicted in Figure 15.2 occur simply because this firm has land in an unusually good location (like the mining company with land containing an easily accessible mineral deposit), and no other firm entering the industry will be able to replicate this characteristic. Any new entrant will have a higher average cost curve like $LRAC'$ and can earn only normal profits, which means that there is no positive incentive to enter the industry. The difference between the two average cost curves, $LRAC$ and $LRAC'$, is therefore attributable to the fact that the firm we are looking at is in a favored position relative to all other firms that might enter the industry. It has an asset, a well-located piece of land, that no other firm can replicate. The location of its land, then, is the factor that is bringing this firm a return that others cannot obtain. The return from such a special factor is called economic rent. But if this factor is special, the firm should

economic rent
The return to a factor of production over and above what is needed to secure the services of that factor.

Figure 15.2

Rent and Long-Run Competitive Equilibria.

A long-run equilibrium equates the price to the firm's rent-inclusive long-run average cost curve *LRAC′*, which includes the opportunity cost of the firm's location.

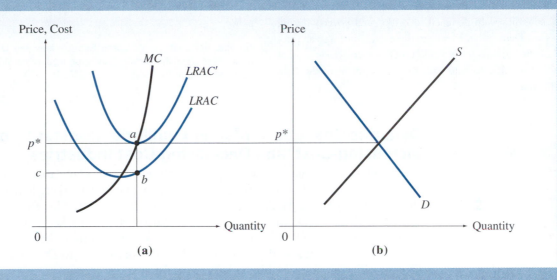

(a)   **(b)**

be able to sell it, because, presumably, there is a market for a factor that brings extra-normal profits to its owner. In some sense, then, there is an opportunity cost to holding this special factor. When this opportunity cost is added to the other costs of production, the relevant rent-inclusive average cost curve for the firm will shift up from *LRAC* to *LRAC′*. In such a situation, the firm will no longer be earning extra-normal profits above its rent-inclusive average cost curve, and so the situation depicted in Figure 15.2(a) is a long-run equilibrium after all.

rent-inclusive average cost
The average cost of the firm when economic rent is included as a cost.

MEDIA NOTE

SUBSIDIES

In 2002, the $118 billion, six-year farm bill signed by President George W. Bush caused a debate among economists. But whether you believe that the government needs to protect the farmers or less government intervention is your motto, you agree that the bill offered will cause a lot of problems.

The bill's purpose was to ensure farmers a designated price on 15 crops by insuring any price fall with federal subsidies. The new bill also raised the number of protected crops and their subsidies.

However, this policy hits the farmers when they are in their most vulnerable state, when harvest is poor. When quantities are low, prices go up, which means less subsidies because these are price-based. Farmers who are in a drought region

with little produce to sell will suffer, while those in the more rich areas will enjoy the rise in prices. In the long run, when the weather is normal, such subsidy structures encourage wasteful production, make the land fragile due to cultivation, and keep crops' prices low at the expense of poor areas.

Another concern is the focus of farmers on subsidized crops exclusively. Subsidies in effect create gluts of specific crops. Some economists suggest that by spending half of the current bill on inventory management rather than subsidies, the government can avoid gluts. Another suggestion is to make the subsidies contingent with idle land. While this means that the government pays the farmer not to farm, this expense is balanced by the savings taxpayers will get by avoiding gluts.

MEDIA NOTE *(Contd.)*

Another problem for economists who want to leave the farmers to the market forces is the fact that most farmers nowadays are wealthier than most taxpayers who pay for the subsidies. Also, subsidies were designed to battle rural poverty during the Great Depression. However, these days, only a small fraction of the rural sector is made up of farmers, meaning that subsidies do little to help with the development of the U.S. rural region.

Even President Bush's own economists suggested shelving the subsidies. However, their suggestions were ignored by the Congress, whose farm-state members control the farm policy.

Source: Adapted from "Some Economists Say U.S. Farm Policy Has Got It All Wrong," as appeared in the *Wall Street Journal,* August 19, 2002

Dynamic Changes in Market Equilibria: Constant-Cost, Increasing-Cost, and Decreasing-Cost Industries

In an industry with an upward-sloping supply curve, we know that in the short run, when demand for the product increases so that the market demand curve shifts to the right, the equilibrium price will increase as well. This fact is demonstrated in Figure 15.3, where we see the initial short-run market supply and demand curves S^1 and D^1, which intersect at point *a*. The equilibrium price-quantity combination at point *a* is p^a and q^a. If the demand curve shifts to D^2, the new equilibrium will be at point *b* with a price of p^b and a quantity of q^b.

As we can see from Figure 15.3, price unambiguously increases when demand increases (shifts to the right) in the short run. The short-run supply curve is upward sloping. In the long run, this need not be the case. The long-run supply curve may be upward sloping, downward sloping, or constant (flat) in response to a shift in demand.

Figure 15.3

The Short-Run Response to a Change in Demand.

When the demand curve shifts from D^1 to D^2, the short-run response is an increase in the price from p^a to p^b and an increase in the quantity from q^a to q^b.

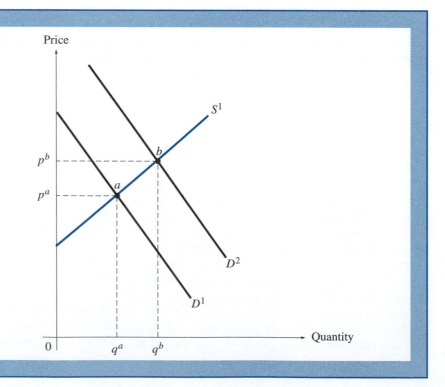

Constant-Cost Industries

To understand how the long-run supply curve of an industry can be flat and not upward sloping, let us consider Figure 15.4.

In the left panel of Figure 15.4(a), we see the market supply and demand curves S^1 and D^1 for an industry intersecting at point a and resulting in an equilibrium price of p^a. In the right panel of this diagram, we see the long-run and short-run average and marginal cost curves for a representative firm in the industry. To make matters simple, let us assume that the cost curves for all firms in the industry are identical to these cost curves. Note that because the price p^a equals the minimum point on each firm's long-run (and short-run) average cost curve, price p^a constitutes a *long-run equilibrium price* for this market.

Now, we will let demand for this product shift to the right from D^1 to D^2. In the short run, this increase in demand will cause the price of the good to increase from p^a to p^b. It will also cause each firm in the industry to make extra-normal profits equal to the area $\eta\lambda\sigma\delta$ in the right panel of Figure 15.4(a). Seeing these profits, other firms will enter this industry, which will cause the supply curve to shift to the right. As the supply curve shifts to the right, the price of the good will fall from its newly established level of p^b. The question is this: How far will the price fall?

The answer to this question depends on what happens to the cost of the inputs to production for the firms in the industry as new firms enter. In part (a) of Figure 15.4, it is assumed that as new firms enter, the cost functions of all firms in the industry will stay the same. This will be true if inputs are in abundant supply and if the industry we are looking at consumes only a small share of the inputs in the market. In this case, the expanded size of the industry will hardly be noticed, and input prices and costs will remain unchanged. As we see in Figure 15.4(a), when costs do not change as new firms enter an industry, the short-run market supply curve will shift to S^2, where the price of p^a is reestablished at point a. Entry into the industry will stop at this point. Note that the resulting *long-run supply curve* (the dark line in Figure 15.4[a]) is flat despite the fact that each short-run supply curve is upward sloping. Industries such as this, in which the long-run supply curve is flat, are called **constant-cost industries**.

Increasing-Cost and Decreasing-Cost Industries: Pecuniary Externalities

Underlying our discussion of constant-cost industries is the assumption that the entry of additional firms into an industry has no effect on the cost curve of the existing firms. This is not necessarily the case. For example, let us say that an industry makes its product from a metal that is mined by digging shafts. When demand for the metal is small, the mining process is quite cheap because the metal can be extracted from deposits that are fairly close to the surface and therefore do not require deep shafts. However, when demand grows, deeper and deeper shafts must be dug, which causes the price to increase. When this occurs, we say that the entry of one firm causes a **pecuniary externality** on the market because the action of one agent (the entrant) has increased the price of a good to other agents (the firms already in the market).

Pecuniary externalities will have a dramatic effect on the shape of the long-run cost curve of an industry. In fact, the long-run cost curve will be upward sloping, and we therefore call industries of this type **increasing-cost industries**. Such a situation is depicted in Figure 15.4(b). In the left panel of this diagram, we again see short-run supply and demand curves S^1 and D^1 and an initial equilibrium at

constant-cost industries
Industries in which the long-run supply curve is flat.

pecuniary externality
Pecuniary externalities exist when the action of one agent increases the price of a good to other agents.

increasing-cost industries
Industries with a long-run cost curve that is upward sloping.

Figure 15.4

Constant-Cost, Increasing-Cost, and Decreasing-Cost Industries.

(a) With constant costs, the long-run response to an increase in demand re-establishes the original price of p^a.
(b) With increasing costs, the long-run response results in a higher price. (c) With decreasing costs, the long-run response results in a lower price.

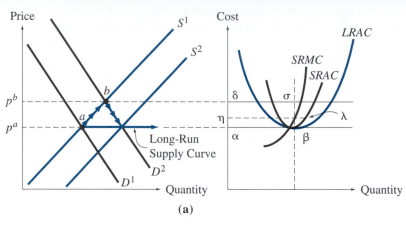

(a)

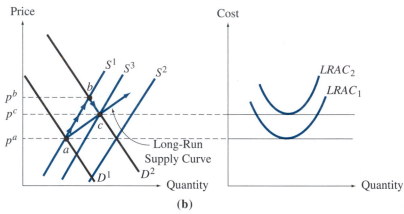

(b)

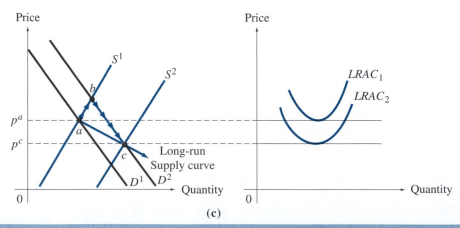

(c)

point *a*, where the price is p^a. When demand shifts from D^1 to D^2, the price rises to p^b and all firms in the industry earn extra-normal profits. These profits attract other firms to the industry, and as entry occurs, the cost of the inputs to production increases because of the pecuniary externalities. The higher cost of the inputs causes the long-run average cost curves of all the firms to shift up from $LRAC_1$ to $LRAC_2$. The short-run supply curve shifts to the right but not all the way to S^2. It stops at S^3, where a new long-run equilibrium price of p^c is established. In response to the shift in demand from D^1 to D^2, the industry equilibrium now moves from point *a* to point *c* along the upward-sloping long-run supply curve.

Figure 15.4(c) depicts a **decreasing-cost industry** in which the long-run cost curve is downward sloping. In this case, the entry of new firms makes the cost of inputs cheaper, and hence the long-run average cost curves of all firms in the industry shift down. This type of situation may occur when the presence of new firms in an industry gives the existing firms stronger bargaining power against suppliers. It may also be that the greater number of firms in the industry allows the suppliers of inputs to benefit from increasing returns to scale in their technology, which decreases their costs and therefore the price they charge for the inputs.

decreasing-cost industries
Industries with a long-run cost curve that is downward sloping.

Why Are Long-Run Competitive Equilibria So Good?

In order to answer the question that is asked in the heading of this section, let us investigate the welfare characteristics of perfectly competitive markets and compare the welfare levels of these markets with the welfare levels of the monopolistic and oligopolistic markets that we studied previously. We know that when markets are organized as monopolies, prices are set above marginal cost. As a result, society experiences a deadweight loss because the amount of goods produced is smaller than the amount that would be beneficial for society if we measure welfare by our usual standard—the sum of consumer surplus and producer surplus. We found that oligopolies provided better welfare performance than monopolies because as more and more firms enter a market, the price in that market is driven down toward the marginal cost. In perfectly competitive industries, we see a market structure that is optimal in terms of welfare and that produces goods in the most efficient manner. In short, the results of perfectly competitive markets serve as a benchmark that economists can use to measure the performance of other market structures. Perfectly competitive markets constitute an ideal for which economists aim.

Let us now consider the following welfare propositions for perfectly competitive markets. These propositions will help us to understand why long-run competitive equilibria are so good.

Welfare Proposition 1: Consumer and Producer Surplus Are Maximized

The first welfare proposition that we will examine is as follows: At the long-run equilibrium of a perfectly competitive industry, the sum of consumer surplus and producer surplus is maximized. This proposition tells us that perfectly competitive markets will set a price and quantity at which there will be no deadweight loss for society. To check the accuracy of this proposition, let us look at Figure 15.5.

In Figure 15.5, we again see simple market supply and demand curves. We know that the equilibrium price-quantity combination for the industry will occur

Figure 15.5

A Competitive Equilibrium Maximizes Consumer and Producer Surpluses.

Triangle *A* is the consumer surplus, and triangle *B* is the producer surplus. In this competitive industry, the sum of the consumer and producer surpluses is maximized because the equilibrium price of p^* occurs at the intersection of the demand and supply curves. Therefore, the price is equal to the marginal cost.

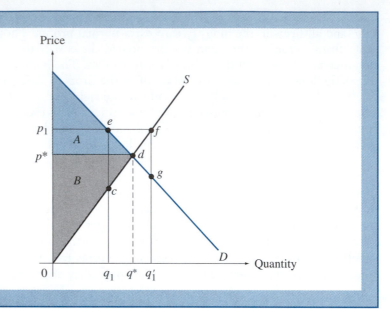

at the point where the demand and supply curves intersect because any excess demand or supply will be eliminated by the overbidding of consumers or the underbidding of suppliers. However, in a competitive industry, the supply curve is simply the sum of the marginal cost curves of all the firms in the industry. The supply curve represents a schedule of prices for providing this good to society. The demand curve, as we know, is equivalent to society's maximum-willingness-to-pay schedule.

At the equilibrium price of p^*, we see two triangles labeled A and B. Triangle A is the consumer surplus in the market because it represents the amount by which society's willingness to pay exceeds the price that buyers have paid for the good. Triangle B is the producer surplus because it represents the amount by which the price received by sellers for q^* units of the good exceeds the marginal cost of producing these units. Note that the sum of these surpluses can only be maximized at price p^*. For example, consider price p_1. At this price, consumers will demand q_1 units of the good even though q_1' will be supplied at that price. At price p_1, society will suffer a deadweight loss equal to the area edc in Figure 15.5. This is the amount by which the surpluses will fall if the price is set at p_1. The optimal quantity to be sold in this market is q^* because it is only at p^* where price equals marginal cost. We would not want to produce a quantity like q_1' because at that quantity, the marginal cost of production (as seen by the height of the supply curve at point f) is greater than the amount that society is willing to pay for the unit (as seen by the height of the demand curve at point g).

SOLVED PROBLEM 15.1

Question (Application and Extension: Long-Run Equilibria)

Central City currently has no restrictions on the number of taxi cabs that can operate in the city. Each cab has an average cost for rides of $AC = \frac{100}{q} + 0.01q$ and a marginal cost of $MC = 0.02q$, where q is the number of rides per day. Because anyone can become a cab driver, there is a 5% probability that a cab will have an accident each time it gives a ride. Each time a cab has an accident, the rider will incur $200 in medical costs due to injuries sustained in the accident.

a) If the demand for taxi rides per day in Central City is $D(p) = 10,000 - 100p$, what is the equilibrium number of cab rides and the number of cabs that will operate in Central City? What is the expected consumer surplus?

Answer

Because there are no barriers to entry for cab drivers, they will enter the market until price is driven to the lowest point possible at which profits are zero and the number of cabs fulfills the demand for rides at that price. Competition drives price down to the minimum point on the average cost curve. This can be found by setting $AC = MC$:

$$\frac{100}{q} + 0.01q = 0.02q$$
$$q = 100$$

Plugging this value back into the average cost curve, we find that the equilibrium price must be

$$p = \frac{100}{100} + 0.01(100) = \$2$$

At this price, the total demand for cab rides each day will be

$$D(2) = 10,000 - 100(2) = 9,800$$

Therefore, the equilibrium number of cabs will be 9,800/100 = 98.

Expected consumer surplus is

$$\frac{1}{2}(9,800)(100 - 2) - (0.05)(9,800)(200) = \$382,200$$

where the first term is the consumer surplus on the 9,800 rides and the second term is the expected accident cost.

b) Now assume that Central City decides to regulate its cabs by issuing licenses. The city will issue only 49 licenses and will require each license holder to take a safety class, which will reduce the probability of an accident to 1%. Price will be regulated to equal average cost. What will the equilibrium price and quantity of cab rides per driver be now? Will society be better or worse off with licensing?

Answer

With 49 cabs, demand will be equal to $49q$, so one equation is

$$49q = 10,000 - 100p$$

Price will be regulated to equal average cost, making profits zero, so

$$p = \frac{100}{q} + 0.01q$$

We now have two equations with two unknowns. Solving these two equations simultaneously, we get $q = 100 + 70\sqrt{2} \approx 199$ and $p = 100/199 + 0.01(199) = \$2.49$. Expected consumer surplus is then

$$\frac{1}{2}(49)(199)(100 - 2.49) - 0.01(49)(199)(200) = \$455,910$$

So cab riders are better off with the licensing plan, even though there are fewer cabs and they are more expensive.

SOLVED PROBLEM 15.2

Question (Content Review: Loss in Consumer Surplus)

Recall Solved Problem 14.1 in the previous chapter. In that problem, we had a demand curve of

$$q_d = 100 - 0.5p$$

and a market supply curve of

$$q_s = 1.0p$$

The government imposed a tax of $2, which raised the equilibrium price in the market from $66.67 to $68 and lowered the quantity bought from 66.67 to 66. What is the loss in consumer welfare as a result of this tax imposition?

Answer

Let us draw a diagram to help us. In Figure 15.6, we see that the demand curve is such that the quantity demanded is zero when the price reaches $200. Hence, the consumer surplus before the imposition of the tax is equal to the area of the triangle *abc*, which is area $abc = \frac{1}{2}(66.67)(133.33) = \$4,444.56$. The consumer surplus existing after the imposition of the tax is the area $dec = \frac{1}{2}(66)(132) = \$4,356$; hence, loss $= 4,444.56 - 4,356 = 88.56$.

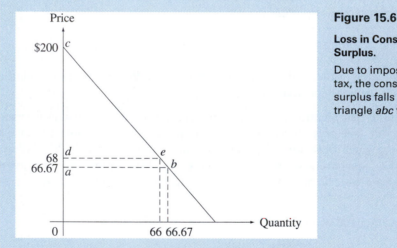

Price

$200 *c*

68 *d* ---- *e*
66.67 *a* ---- *b*

0   66 66.67   Quantity

Figure 15.6

Loss in Consumer Surplus.

Due to imposition of tax, the consumer surplus falls from triangle *abc* to *dec*.

Welfare Proposition 2: Price Is Set at Marginal Cost

The next welfare proposition that we will examine is as follows: At the long-run equilibrium of a perfectly competitive industry, price is set so that it is equal to marginal cost. To confirm the accuracy of this proposition, we can again turn to Figure 15.5. As before, we know that the equilibrium price will be found at the intersection of the supply and demand curves. Therefore, because the supply curve of a competitive industry simply represents the marginal cost curve of the industry, a price that is set at the intersection of the supply and demand curves must be equal to the marginal cost.

Welfare Proposition 3: Goods Are Produced at the Lowest Possible Cost and in the Most Efficient Manner

The final welfare proposition that we will consider is as follows: At the long-run equilibrium of a competitive industry, goods are produced at the lowest possible average cost and in the most efficient manner. Let us look at Figure 15.7(a), which shows the long-run equilibrium for a representative firm in a competitive industry.

At the equilibrium, the firm depicted in Figure 15.7(a) will produce q^* units using a plant that has a capacity of K^*. However, K^* is the capacity level that minimizes the average cost of production, and we know that the process of entry will drive the price down to the point where this capacity is the one that will be chosen by all firms. Competition ensures that the goods sold to consumers will be produced at the lowest possible cost.

Competition also leads to the efficient organization of production. A competitive industry allocates the output to be produced in any given period among firms in an optimal manner. For example, let us say that we are economic planners who must assign to each firm in an industry an amount of output to produce during a certain period, given that the price for this output will be set by the market. In other words, we cannot set a price for the good; but given the market price and a quantity to be produced, we must assign output quotas to the firms and demand that they produce these quantities. Say that we want to maximize the difference

Figure 15.7

A Competitive Equilibrium Results in Efficient Production.

(a) At its long-run equilibrium, this representative firm in a competitive industry will produce q^* units of output at a capacity level of K^*, which minimizes the average cost of production. (b) In a competitive industry, the market allocates production efficiently. Each firm chooses the optimal quantity of q^* to produce by equating its marginal cost to the market price of p^*.

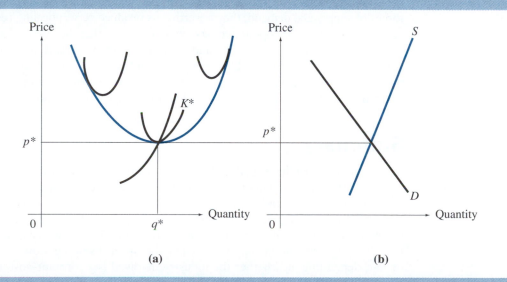

between the revenues of the industry and the costs of production. In short, we want to maximize the following function:

$$\text{Max } \pi = pQ - C_1(q_1) - C_2(q_2) - C_3(q_3) - \ldots - C_n(q_n)$$

In this function, Q equals the sum of the outputs of all the firms. Because we (the planners) are told what p and Q must be, the way we maximize the function is to minimize the cost of producing Q units. Minimizing this cost requires that we distribute output to each firm in such a way that the marginal cost of production is equal in all firms. We now have the rule for optimal allocation of outputs within a competitive industry. To prove that such an allocation is optimal, let us say that we distribute outputs in a different manner, and as a result, the marginal cost of producing the last unit in firm i is different from the marginal cost of producing the last unit in firm j. If the marginal cost is greater in firm i than in firm j, then it pays for us to take a unit of production away from firm i and give it to firm j, which can produce that unit more cheaply. Hence, as economic planners, we would allocate outputs so as to equalize the marginal cost of production among the firms in the industry.

The market does exactly the same thing that we did as economic planners. When the market price of a good is p^*, each firm in the competitive industry finds its optimal quantity to produce by equating its marginal cost to the market price. This optimal quantity occurs at the intersection of the market demand and supply curves, as shown in Figure 15.7(b). Because each firm will equate its marginal cost to the same market price, the marginal cost of production will be equal for all firms in the industry. The market therefore solves the problem of allocating production within an industry in precisely the same efficient manner as a group of economic planners.

Conclusion

The economy we have been examining is well on its way to becoming an advanced economy; like many advanced economies, it is organized around competitive markets. Although these markets are anonymous and work through the impersonal forces of supply and demand, they nevertheless produce very appealing results. They yield outcomes that are optimal for society in the sense that they maximize consumer surplus and producer surplus. In addition, competitive markets provide goods to consumers at the lowest possible average cost and are therefore efficient. Because of this efficiency, competitive markets serve as benchmarks that we can use to judge the performance of other market forms, such as monopoly and oligopoly.

Summary

In this chapter, we have analyzed how firms functioning within the institutional structure of perfectly competitive markets set their prices and quantities. To do so, we investigated the supply function for competitive firms and the nature of short-run and long-run equilibria in competitive markets. We found that while the short-run market supply curve for a perfectly competitive industry is upward sloping, the long-run market supply curve may be upward sloping, downward sloping, or flat, depending on whether the industry involved is a constant-cost, increasing-cost, or decreasing-cost industry. This distinction depends on whether there were pecuniary externalities in the industry or not.

We also discussed how comparative static analysis can be used to examine the effects of policy changes on competitive markets. We applied this analytical method to several examples. At the end of the chapter, we looked at a set of propositions indicating the welfare properties of perfectly competitive markets. We saw that such markets maximize the sum of consumer surplus and producer surplus, set prices that are equal to marginal cost, and produce at the lowest possible average cost.

APPENDIX A

TWO WELFARE PROPOSITIONS

Proposition 1: Price is set at marginal cost by firms in a perfectly competitive industry.

Proof: Because the industry is perfectly competitive, all firms are price takers. Further, in the long run, all inputs are variable.

Each firm chooses output level y to maximize profits.

Formally, each firm solves

$$\text{Max}_{y}\ \Pi = py - c(y)$$

The first-order condition is then $p = c'(y)$; each firm independently sets a quantity at which its marginal cost equals the market price p. However, because all firms are equating their marginal cost to a common price, we know that $MC_i = MC_j = p$ for all firms i and j in the market.

Proposition 2: In a competitive market, goods are produced at the lowest possible cost and in the most efficient manner.

Proof: Assume that society has n firms. The social objective is

$$\text{Max}_{\{q_1,\ldots,q_n\}}\ \Pi = p \sum_{i=1}^{n} q_i - \sum_{i=1}^{n} c_i(q_i)$$

The first-order conditions for society's problem are

$$p = c_i'(q_i) \text{ for } i = 1,\ldots,n$$
$$\text{or, price} = MC \text{ for all firms}$$

This is the same as the competitive outcome. Hence, the market outcome meets the social objectives and is efficient.

To show the lowest-cost part of the proposition, we proceed as follows: The average cost of production for firm i is

$$AC_i = \frac{1}{q_i} c_i(q_i)$$

The first-order conditions for minimizing average cost are

$$-\frac{1}{q_i^2} c_i(q_i) + \frac{1}{q_i} c_i'(q_i) = 0$$
$$\Rightarrow c_i'(q_i) = \frac{1}{q_i} c_i(q_i)$$
$$\Rightarrow MC_i = AC_i \text{ for } i = 1,\ldots,n$$

But the price $= MC$ for a competitive industry, so the price charged for the good is the lowest cost (the minimum point on the average cost curve).

Exercises and Problems

1. Poland wants to privatize its farming industry and will therefore allow 10,000 farms to produce wheat under competitive circumstances. Assume that entry into the wheat-growing segment of the industry will be easy. Also assume that each wheat farm will have a total cost function of the following type: $TC = q^2/2 - 4q + 200$, where q is the farm's output. Associated with this total cost function are an average cost function of $AC = q/2 - 4 + 200/q$ and a marginal cost function of $MC = q - 4$. At present, the government planners are setting a price of $P = 20$ per bushel for wheat.

   a) At the *long-run* perfectly competitive equilibrium for the wheat-growing segment of the farming industry, will the price be lower or higher than the present administered price?

   b) How much wheat will each farm produce?

   c) If each wheat farm had ten acres before privatization and produced a yield of four bushels per acre, should the size of these farms be increased or decreased after the market becomes competitive? In other words, will it be cheaper to grow wheat on larger or smaller farms when the market is competitive?

2. Assume that the taxi industry in the town of New City is perfectly competitive. Also assume that the constant marginal cost of a taxi ride is $5 per trip and that each taxi is capable of making 20 trips a day. We will let the demand function for taxi rides each day be $D(p) = 1,100 - 20p$.

   a) What is the perfectly competitive price of a taxi ride?

   b) How many rides will the citizens of New City take every day?

   c) How many taxis will operate in New City?

   Assume that every taxi that operates in New City has a special license. Therefore, the number of such licenses is the same as the number of taxis that you calculated in part c of this problem. Further assume that the demand for taxi rides has increased and is now $D(p) = 1,200 - 20p$. The cost of operating a taxi is still $5 per ride, and the number of taxis has not changed.

   d) Calculate the price that will equate demand with supply.

   e) Calculate the profit that each taxi will earn on a ride.

   f) Calculate the daily profit of each taxi. (*Hint:* Continue to assume that each taxi can give only 20 rides a day.)

3. A competitive market has an unlimited number of potential suppliers producing the same output, and each supplier has a long-run average cost function of $AC = q^2 - 4q + 6$ and a long-run marginal cost function of $MC = 3q^2 - 8q + 6$.

   a) Find the equilibrium quantity q produced by each firm in the long run.

   b) Find the long-run equilibrium price.

4. Suppose that there is an economy with two firms whose products are completely independent. By "independent," we mean that when one firm changes its price, the other firm's demand is totally unaffected. The only possibilities for employment in this economy are a career running firm 1 or firm 2 or a career as an economics professor who earns $20,000 a year. There are no barriers to entry in these careers, and anyone currently employed in one occupation can change to another without cost.

The only input that either firm needs to make its product is seaweed, which costs $2 a pound. Each firm requires 1 pound of seaweed to produce 1 unit of its product. The cost of the input (seaweed) does not include the cost of an entrepreneur's time. There are no costs involved in being an economics professor. The demand for the product of firm 1 is $P_1 = 2,002 - 4Q_1$, and the demand for the product of firm 2 is $P_2 = 4,004 - 5Q_2$.

a)   If anyone can become an economics professor, what will the long-run equilibrium prices be for firms 1 and 2?

b)   Is the price of each firm's product forced down to the level of the marginal cost of the seaweed?

5. Assume that a certain small town contains a large number of widget-producing firms. All the firms buy oil from the same refinery. Firm 1 is situated very close to the refinery, and the other firms are located 50 miles away. Firm 1 pays $18 per barrel for the oil, while the other firms pay $18 per barrel plus a transportation charge of $0.05 a mile, or a total of $20.50 per barrel.

To produce four widgets, a firm needs $\frac{1}{10}$ barrel of oil, $\frac{1}{2}$ hour of labor, and the use of one machine. The cost of labor is $10 per hour, and the necessary machine can be rented for $5 per hour. No firm has the capacity to produce more than 100 units of widgets.

a)   Derive the supply curve for firm 1. Derive the supply curve for all the other firms.

b)   What is the equilibrium price?

c)   Does any firm earn economic rent (that is, extra economic profit) in the industry?

d)   Does firm 1 affect the price of widgets in the industry? If not, why not?

e)   Suppose that there is no capacity limit. What will the equilibrium price be?

f)   Will firm 1 affect the price when there is unlimited capacity?

6. Consider a competitive industry in which each firm has a demand function of $Q_D = 1,400 - 4P$ and a supply function of $Q_s = 200 + 2P$.

a)   Graph the demand and supply functions.

b)   What is the equilibrium price, that is, the price set by the market?

c)   What is the sum of the producer and consumer surpluses at the equilibrium price?

d)   Say a government bureaucrat sets the price at $300. What is the sum of the producer and consumer surpluses at that price? What about at a price of $100?

7. Assume that a very large number of firms in an industry all have access to the same production technology. The total cost function associated with this technology is $TC(Q) = 40Q - 24Q^2 + 4Q^3$. If the demand function for the industry's product is $Q = 19 - P$, how many firms will produce positive amounts of output at a competitive (that is, zero profit) equilibrium?

MARKET INSTITUTIONS

Many markets in the world are organized markets whose rules are designed by people. For example, the New York Stock Exchange is a market that functions using a given set of rules that are very different from those used by NASDAQ. Dutch flower markets are organized in yet a different manner, using what is called a Dutch Auction, while the commodity exchanges in New York sell their goods in even different ways. When we talk about markets, then, it seems as if we should include in our discussion an analysis of the rules these markets use to sell goods because it may be that different sets of rules—market institutions—yield different results.

The most famous market institution used by experimental economists (which mimics the rules on the New York Stock Exchange) is the double oral auction. In this market institution, both buyers and sellers are symmetric in that they are able to yell out bids and "asks" any time they want in order to buy the goods available. When they see a bid or ask they like, they can accept that as a contract for them. (You may have seen this on the floor of the stock exchange.)

This set of rules can be used to allocate goods among a small number of buyers and sellers when information among them is very limited. As such, it can be used in markets that look very different from competitive markets, where all information is supposed to be perfect and there are a large number of firms. What has been shown is that even with small numbers of buyers and sellers and even with limited information, the outcomes of these markets look very much like the outcomes that would result if these markets satisfied all of the properties of perfectly competitive markets. This fact has been demonstrated again and again, starting with the seminal work on these institutions by Vernon Smith and Charles Plott.

What do you think would happen in these markets if, instead of the buyers and sellers having equal opportunities to yell out bids and asks, only one side of the market could be active while people on the other side would have to sit passively and just wait until they saw a bid or ask they wanted to accept? In other words, what would happen if the sellers could yell out asks while the buyers could yell out only acceptances when they saw an ask they liked (or vice versa)? Would prices and amounts sold be different? If the market converged to the competitive equilibrium, would it converge differently than it did using the double oral auction? We will answer these questions later.

REVENUE EQUIVALENCE

EXPERIMENTAL TEASER 16

Consider four types of auctions that we will examine later in this chapter.

First-Price Sealed Bid Auction (FPA)—In this auction, one good is auctioned off to a set of buyers. Each buyer writes his or her bid on a piece of paper and seals it in an envelope. All the envelopes are then collected and opened, and the highest bidder wins the good and pays the price he or she bid.

Second-Price Sealed Bid Auction—In this auction, one good is auctioned off to a set of buyers. Each buyer writes his or her bid on a piece of paper and seals it in an envelope. All the envelopes are then collected and opened, and the highest bidder wins the good but pays the price of the second-highest bidder.

English or Ascending Auction—In this auction, the price of the good is raised mechanically so that, say, every 10 seconds it goes up a fixed amount. All bidders raise their hands at the beginning and as the price rises above what they are willing to pay, they lower their hands. The last buyer to have his hand raised wins at the price that caused the second-to-last bidder to drop out.

The Dutch or Descending Auction—In this auction, the price of the good is initially set at a very high level and lowered mechanically so that. say, every 10 seconds it goes down a fixed amount. All bidders keep their hands lowered at the beginning of the auction, and the first person to raise his hand wins the good at the price at which he raised his hand.

Which type of auction do you think raises the most revenue for the sellers? Which type of auction do you think is supposed to raise the most revenue? Would you be surprised to find out that, in theory, they all should raise the same amount of revenue? A paper by James Cox, Bruce Robertson, and Vernon Smith suggests that this theoretical result may not hold empirically.*

---

* See James Cox, Bruce Robertson, and Vernon Smith, "Theory and Behavior of Single Object Auctions" in Vernon Smith, ed., *Research in Experimental Economics*, Greenwich, CT: JAI Press, 1982, 2, pp. 1–43.

In all of our analysis so far, we have assumed that the market reaches an equilibrium at the intersection of its demand and supply curves. But how is this equilibrium actually reached? We know that in the real world, markets are organized according to specific sets of rules. For example, on the New York Stock Exchange, buyers and sellers must follow a specific set of rules defining when they can make a bid and exactly what type of bid is acceptable. In other words, our analysis up to this point has been institution-free. We have not mentioned what set of rules is used in the illegal drug market, the labor market, or any other market we have discussed. All that we have stated is that given the derived supply and demand curves, the market will converge toward an equilibrium. This raises some fundamental questions about market institutions and market equilibria: Are the rules that we use to organize a market—to make it an institution—at all important to the eventual convergence of the market price toward its natural equilibrium? Do any rules work in a market? Theoretically, we would expect that the rules used in a market would affect the way the market functions quite dramatically, but this conjecture must be tested.

Actually, this conjecture has been the focus of experimental economists for a number of years. Starting with the work of Vernon Smith and Charles Plott, economists have conducted literally thousands of experiments trying to find a set of market rules that will almost guarantee the convergence of the market price toward its equilibrium. In this chapter, we will look at how such experiments are conducted and review the results of several of them. We will investigate common auction institutions used both in the real world and in the lab and investigate their efficiency properties. Our investigation of these experiments should lead to a greater understanding of the significance of market rules or institutions to the functioning of markets and their equilibrating nature.

MEDIA NOTE

INTERNET AUCTIONS

Economists have long been interested in the "auction theory." Numerous papers have been written on the theory of auctions and bidding; however, lack of data prevented testing of these theories. All this has changed with the emergence of the Internet and auction Web sites, especially eBay. Through eBay, economists now have vast amounts of data on millions of transactions, bidding strategies, and behavior that they did not have before. One piece of information that exists on eBay that rarely exists in other markets is a system where the reputation of sellers can be evaluated by those who have dealt with them in the past. This data provides a kind of naturally occurring experiment, and the question is, What can economists learn from these real-life economic laboratories?

Professor Luis Cabral from the New York University business school found significant importance of the sellers' reputations, especially for the prices they can charge. While this is trivial for any eBay user, this is not obvious to an economist because the ranking system on eBay is anonymous. Moreover, when looking into sellers who have received their first piece of negative feedback, Cabral found that these sellers went into a downward spiral of fewer sales and declining reputation.

Another surprising finding for economists was the strength of brand names in the Internet age. Economists view the Internet as the place where complete information does hold. Customers can check various prices charged and the reliability of various sites at virtually no cost. Despite this, Professor Judith Chevalier from the University of Chicago business school found that Amazon.com can charge higher prices than Barnes & Nobles on the same items. In a different feedback study, Chevalier found that negative feedbacks have a higher impact than positive ones. She explains this discrepancy by the different attitude buyers have to the feedback. Positive feedbacks are viewed with skepticism because these can be posted by the author, while negative feedbacks are viewed as more objective and thus more relevant to the quality of the book.

Some questions regarding the online auction remain unsolved. One such question is about the practice of "sniping," that is, waiting until the last minute of the auction and then making an offer that other bidders can't outdo in time. This practice is very eBay-specific because the auctions on eBay have a time limit. Professor David Reiley for the University of Arizona found that in auctions where there are many different bidders, especially when standard electronic gear is auctioned, snipers do not do better than other bidders either by their success rate or the prices they pay. However, in auctions that are specialized and have few bidders, sniping is a profitable strategy as long as not all the bidders are engaged in sniping.

Source: Adapted from "E-Commerce Sites Make Great Laboratory for Today's Economists," as appeared in the *Wall Street Journal,* October 11, 2004

The Double Oral Auction and One-Sided Oral Auction Market Institutions

double oral auction
A double oral auction is an auction in which both buyers and sellers can make bids or asks as the auction progresses. Contracts per goods are consumated when an agent on either side accepts an outstanding bid or ask.

Let us consider a market institution called the double oral auction. The buyers and sellers of a good sit in a room, and the sellers offer each unit of the good to the buyers in sequence, one unit at a time. The buyers and sellers shout bids and asking prices until a unit is sold. For example, a buyer may shout that he is willing to pay $200 for a unit, and the seller may shout that she wants $350 for the unit. Clearly, in this case, because the asking price of $350 is greater than the bid of $200, neither the buyer nor the seller will enter into a transaction. However, because all bids and asking prices are written on a blackboard at the front of the room for everyone to see, any bid made after this point will have to be higher than

$200 and any asking price announced will have to be lower than $350. The auction process for a unit continues until either the seller is willing to accept a buyer's bid or a buyer is willing to accept the seller's asking price. At that point, the two parties will make a contract for the unit, which removes it from the market. The auction process will then start for another unit and continue until either all units are sold or the market day ends. Now we can see why this type of market institution is called the double oral auction. It allows both buyers and sellers to make verbal offers at any time while the units are up for sale. In other words, it treats both sides of the market symmetrically.

Would the results from the double oral auction type of market be different if the rules were changed? For example, suppose that only the buyers could make offers during the auction and the sellers were not allowed to make counteroffers. They could merely agree to an existing bid by shouting their acceptance of the latest one offered. Or suppose that only the sellers were allowed to make offers and the buyers could accept or reject these offers but could not make counteroffers. We will call such market institutions **one-sided oral auctions**. Look at the resolution of Experimental Teaser 15 to find out the answer.

one-sided oral auctions Market institutions in which buyers can accept or reject offers from sellers but cannot make counteroffers.

RESOLVING
TEASER 15

MARKET INSTITUTIONS

Vernon Smith, Charles Plott, and their collaborators have performed experiments aimed at answering just the type of questions that we have raised here.[1] Each of these economic experiments involves replication of a real-world market institution within a laboratory setting by giving recruited volunteers monetary incentives to act like real buyers or sellers in a market. If there is a need to compare two or three different market institutions, this can be done quite easily by conducting several different experiments, each replicating the specific institution in question. For example, let us consider the following two experiments. In each of these experiments, the organizers use a group of 10 volunteers who are paid for their participation. The organizers re-create a market in the laboratory by assigning half the subjects the role of buyers and the other half the role of sellers. The subjects who are to act as buyers are told that they will receive a certain number of dollars for each unit they purchase. In fact, they are given a schedule indicating the redemption value of each unit purchased. To illustrate, let us say that the organizers of the experiment tell buyer 1 that his schedule of redemption values will be as described in Figure 16.1.

In Figure 16.1, we see that if this laboratory buyer successfully purchases 1 unit, he will be paid $10 by the organizers of the experiment. For the second unit he purchases, he will be paid $8; for the third unit, he will be paid $6; and so on. Hence, if this buyer purchases 3 units, he will receive $24 from the organizers of the experiment. Figure 16.1 also shows that unless the buyer purchases the first unit at a price that is less than $10, he will lose money. Similarly, he must purchase the second unit at a price that is less than $8 in order to avoid a loss. Therefore, the payoff to any buyer for a unit will be the difference between the value defined by his redemption schedule and

(Continued)

1 The content of much of this section and Figures 16.1–16.6 are based on material that appears in several articles written by Vernon Smith, including "The Effect of Market Organization on Competitive Equilibrium," *Quarterly Journal of Economics* 78 (May 1964): 181–201; "Experimental Auction Markets and the Walrasian Hypothesis," *Journal of Political Economy* 73 (August 1965): 387–93; and "Bidding and Auctioning Institutions," in *Bidding and Auctioning for Procurement and Allocation,* ed. Y. Amihud (New York: New York University Press, 1976).

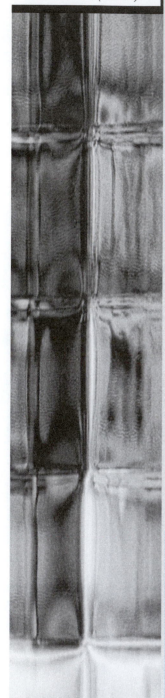

Redemption Value

Figure 16.1

A Redemption Value Schedule for Laboratory Purchases.

The graph depicts the amount of money the laboratory buyer will be paid for each successive unit of the good he purchases.

the price at which he purchases the unit. For example, if this buyer purchases 2 units in a given round of the experiment and pays $5 for the first unit and $4 for the second unit, his payoff will be $9, which is calculated as follows: payoff = ($10 − $5) + ($8 − $4) = $9. In short, the payoff to a buyer is the consumer surplus on the units he purchases.

For a laboratory seller, the situation is similar. The organizers of the experiment tell the subjects who are assigned the role of sellers that any unit they sell during the experiment must be bought from their experiment administrator first. Each of the sellers is given a schedule defining the costs of the units to be sold. A representative cost schedule for a laboratory seller appears in Figure 16.2.

In Figure 16.2, we find that the first unit sold will cost this laboratory seller $3, the second unit will cost her $5, and so on. Hence, if she sells the first unit at a price that is below $3 and the second unit at a price that is below $5, she will lose money. A seller's payoff in any round of the experiment is the difference between the price she receives for the units sold and her cost for obtaining those units. For example, if she sells 2 units in a given round of the experiment and receives $11 for the first unit and

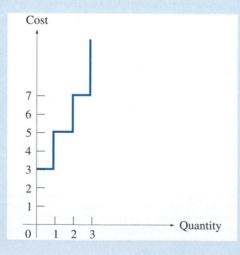

Cost

Figure 16.2

A Cost Schedule for Laboratory Sales.

The graph depicts the amount of money the laboratory seller must pay for each successive unit of the good she sells.

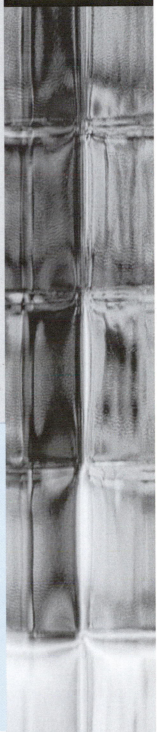

$8 for the second unit, her payoff will be $11, which is calculated as follows: payoff = ($11 − $3) + ($8 − $5) = $11. The payoff to the seller is analogous to the producer surplus on the units sold.

If we want to generate a market demand curve for such an experiment, all we need to do is horizontally add the individual demand curves for the buyers in the simulated market. Figure 16.3 presents a market demand curve that was derived in this manner.

In Figure 16.3, we see a set of diagrams representing the individual redemption value schedules of three laboratory buyers. We can think of these redemption value curves as *induced demand curves* because the organizers of the experiment induce demand for a good by giving each buyer a schedule of redemption values. The diagram on the far right in Figure 16.3 is the market demand curve. It tells us how much of the laboratory good will be demanded at each possible price. For example, if the price is $5, subject 1 will want to purchase up to 3 units, subject 2 will want to purchase up to 2 units, and subject 3 will want to purchase up to 6 units. Hence, at a price of $5, the aggregate demand for the good will be 11 units. This quantity appears at point *A* on the market demand curve. The other points on this curve are generated in a similar manner.

A market supply curve is analogous to a market demand curve and tells us how many units of a good the sellers will want to supply at any given price. It is generated similar to the market demand curve, as we see in Figure 16.4.

In Figure 16.4, we find a set of diagrams representing the individual cost schedules of three laboratory sellers. We can think of these cost curves as *induced supply curves*. The diagram on the far right is the market supply curve. It tells us how much of the laboratory good will be supplied at each possible price. For example, if the price is $7, subject 4 will want to supply up to 3 units, subject 5 will want to supply up to 4 units, and subject 6 will want to supply up to 6 units. Hence, at a price of $7, the aggregate supply will be 13 units of the good. This quantity appears at point *B* on the market supply curve. The other points on this curve are generated in a similar manner.

Figure 16.3

A Market Demand Curve Derived in a Laboratory Experiment.

The market demand curve is the horizontal sum of the individual redemption value schedules assigned to the buyers in the experiment.

(Continued)

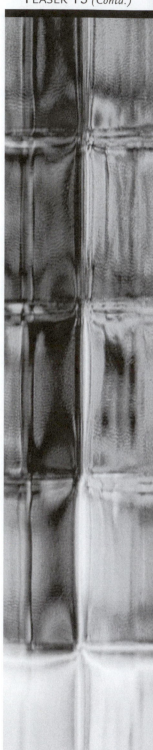

Figure 16.4

A Market Supply Curve Derived in a Laboratory Experiment.

The market supply curve is the horizontal sum of the individual redemption cost schedules assigned to the sellers in the experiment.

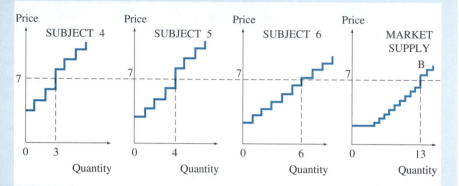

The experiment is conducted in the following way. At a given time, the market opens and the subjects are free to make bids and announce asking prices as described previously. Because the subjects are playing for real money, the ones who are acting as buyers have a strong incentive to purchase goods for as low a price as possible. (Remember that the payoff to the buyers is the difference between the redemption value of each unit they purchase and the price they pay for the unit.) Similarly, the subjects who are acting as sellers have a strong incentive to sell for a price that is as high as possible. The market stays open for five minutes during each round of the experiment. In this period, the buyers and sellers complete their transactions. At the end of the period, the experiment administrator makes the payoffs to the subjects. Then a new round starts, and this round is identical to the previous round in every detail. The subjects are not allowed to carry over goods or cash from one trading period to the next. At the end of the final round, each subject's payoff for the entire experiment amounts to the sum of his or her payoffs for the individual rounds.

For purposes of discussion, let us say that we perform three experiments according to the procedures described in this section. One experiment uses the double oral auction, and two experiments use the one-sided oral auction. In the latter case, one of the experiments has the buyers as the active parties and the other experiment has the sellers as the active parties. In all experiments, we keep the induced supply and demand curves of the subjects constant so that the only difference among the three experiments is the set of rules—the market institution—used. This procedure allows us to isolate (or control for) the effect of the market institution.

There are two ways to evaluate the outcome of such market experiments. One way is to ask which type of market institution would be best for the buyers or the sellers. The other way is to ask which type of market institution is most efficient, that is, which type maximizes the sum of consumer surplus and producer surplus. Clearly, the most efficient market institution is the one that is capable of generating a price for its good at the intersection of the supply and demand curves. In our study of monopoly in Chapter 17, we will see that this is true because only at the price it mentions is the sum of consumer surplus and producer surplus maximized. Note that Figure 16.5 contains laboratory-induced

Figure 16.5

The Market Supply and Demand Curves in the Smith Experiments.

The price-quantity combination that maximizes the sum of consumer surplus and producer surplus appears at the intersection of the market supply and demand curves. This combination consists of a price of $2.10 and a quantity of either 7 or 8 units.

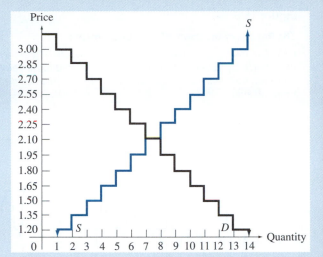

supply and demand curves that are juxtaposed on one graph and intersect at a price of $2.10, where between 7 and 8 units will be sold. Hence, a price of $2.10 and a quantity of 7 or 8 units constitutes the welfare-maximizing price-quantity combination.

The Results of the Experiments

The actual experiments run by Smith involved 14 buyers and 14 sellers, each of whom was given induced supply and demand curves. These individual supply and demand curves were used to generate the market supply and demand curves depicted in Figure 16.5.

As we already know, the price-quantity combination in Figure 16.5 that maximizes the sum of consumer surplus and producer surplus is $2.10 and 7 or 8 units. There is an indeterminacy about the optimal number of units to sell because the cost of the last unit to the seller is equal to the value of that unit to the buyer. Hence, if the eighth unit is sold, it will not generate surplus for anyone.

Figure 16.6 presents the results of the Smith experiments involving three types of market institutions. We see the results of a one-sided oral auction with the sellers active in (a), the results of a one-sided oral auction with the buyers active in (b), and the results of a double oral auction with both buyers and sellers active in (c).

Let us designate the three types of market institutions in the Smith experiments as follows: E_s for the one-sided oral auction in which only the sellers are active, that is, only the sellers can make offers; E_b for the one-sided oral auction in which only the buyers are active; and E_{sb} for the double oral auction in which both buyers and sellers are active. The diagrams in Figure 16.6 show the transactions that were completed in the experiments and the resulting prices, period by period and price by price. For example, in trading period 1 of market institution E_s (Figure 16.6[a]), we see that the first transaction actually completed took place at a price of $1.50, the second transaction took place at a price of $1.65, and so on. By the end of the first trading period, the optimal quantity of 7 units was sold, but the prices charged were consistently below the optimal price of $2.10. Note that when the market institution was E_s (Figure 16.6[a]),

(Continued)

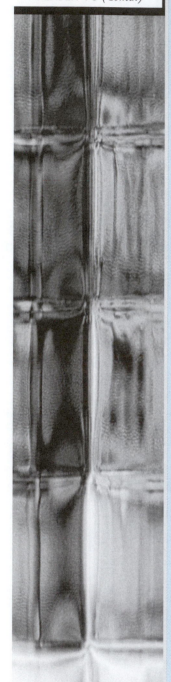

Figure 16.6

The Results of the Smith Market Experiments.

(a) When only sellers made offers, prices tended to be below the optimal level.
(b) When only buyers made offers, prices tended to be above the optimal level.
(c) When both sellers and buyers made offers, prices tended to be closer to the optimal level.

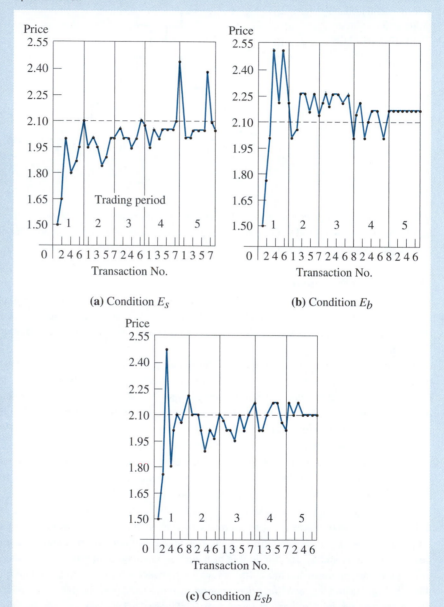

(a) Condition E_s

(b) Condition E_b

(c) Condition E_{sb}

only two transactions completed in any of the trading periods had prices above $2.10. The prices charged tended to be below this level.

For market institution E_b (Figure 16.6[b]), just the opposite is true. Here the buyers were active, but only 8 of the 37 prices charged were below the optimal price of $2.10.

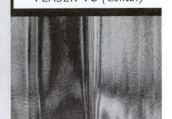

For market institution E_{sb} (Figure 16.6[c]), the result is somewhere in the middle of the results for E_s and E_b, but there is a much stronger tendency for the price to be at the optimal level of $2.10. For example, in Figure 16.6(c), we see that of the 37 prices charged during the five trading periods, 12 were exactly at the optimal level of $2.10, 7 were above that level, and 18 were below that level.

In summary, the Smith experiments demonstrated that the double oral auction (E_{sb}) is an efficient market institution for selling goods. These experiments also demonstrated that the exact set of rules used in each market institution affects the results achieved.

Question (Application and Extension: Auctions and Competitive Markets)

GetItHere.com is a flea market on the Internet. Sellers submit the prices at which they are willing to sell their objects, and buyers submit the prices they are willing to pay. The manager of the Web site matches buyers with sellers to close all transactions. Suppose there are six buyers and six sellers in the market for ceramic elephants. The following table contains the prices they submit.

SOLVED
PROBLEM
16.1

Buyer	Buyer Price	Seller	Seller Price
1	$90	1	$ 20
2	$80	2	$ 40
3	$70	3	$ 50
4	$60	4	$ 70
5	$50	5	$ 90
6	$40	6	$100

a) If the manager of the Web site allows this market to clear as if it were a perfectly competitive market, what will the equilibrium price, quantity, and total surplus be?

Answer

Consider Figure 16.7. As we can see, three ceramic elephants would be sold at a price of p, where $70 \geq p > 60$. The table tells us that buyer 1 buys from seller 1, buyer 2 buys from seller 2, and buyer 3 buys from seller 3. It also tells us that a

Figure 16.7

Matching Buyers and Sellers.

Maximizing the quantity sold does not maximize consumer plus producer surplus.

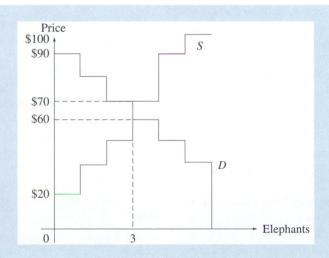

fourth unit will not be sold because buyer 4 is willing to pay only $60 for it but seller 4 wants $70. The exchange of these 3 units gives a surplus of

$$($90 - $20) + ($80 - $40) + ($70 - $50) = $130$$

b) Suppose that the manager adopts a policy in which he will pair buyers and sellers in such a way that the highest possible number of ceramic elephants will be sold. To do this, he pairs buyer 1 with seller 5, buyer 2 with seller 4, buyer 3 with seller 3, buyer 4 with seller 2, and buyer 5 with seller 1. Will society be better off with this scheme than it would be with the perfectly competitive market scheme?

Answer

Society is not better off with this scheme. Even though more elephants are exchanged, the total surplus is less:

$$($90 - $90) + ($80 - $70) + ($70 - $50) + ($60 - $40) + ($50 - $20) = $80$$

MEDIA NOTE

ALLOCATION OF RESOURCES

Using the price system can many times lead to efficiencies not available if other, seemingly more equitable institutions are used. Take the case of the La Guardia airport, which is one of the most crowded in the country. Anyone using the airport knows that you have to sit on the runway for long periods of time before you are allowed to take off. What is the best way to allocate takeoff slots (that is, the right to take off at a specific time) when you have some very large and some very small planes vying for slots?

The Federal Aviation Administration (FAA) authorized the use of a lottery for operating slots that gave preference to nine small airlines that serve small communities. Is this efficient? Obviously not. Slots at crowded airports are a valuable economic resource, much like scarce seats on an oversold flight. To demonstrate that markets might be better, consider how airlines used to allocate oversold seats. Carriers once handled oversold flights on a first-come, first-served basis. If 120 passengers presented tickets for a flight with 100 seats, only the first 100 got to go. For passengers coming from connecting flights, this was like a lottery. If your connecting flight was late, you got bumped. This solution never considered that individuals have different needs. People with urgent schedules were often forced to wait, while those less pressed made their flights.

In 1979, the Civil Aeronautics Board called for carriers to offer cash payments, free tickets, or other rewards to induce volunteers to relinquish their seats on oversold flights. Passengers could decide for themselves how important it was to avoid waiting. Those with pressing business simply wouldn't volunteer. The board's proposal was adopted and soon became widely recognized as both fairer and more efficient than the earlier system.

Parallel issues arise with overcrowded airports. Just as a plane can accommodate only so many takeoffs and landings, so every time a 19-seat Beechcraft 1900 uses La Guardia, the FAA must deny permission to some larger plane—say, a Boeing 757 with several hundred passengers. Today, even among carriers currently authorized to use La Guardia, delays and flight cancellations are legion. More important, a host of carriers would like to provide large-aircraft service to La Guardia but are not authorized to use the airport at all. That means some travelers have to use less convenient airports, just as someone has to wait when flights are oversold. In both cases we have a strong interest in minimizing total inconvenience.

Scarce operating slots at La Guardia can be allocated in essentially the same way the FAA solved the overbooking problem for passengers. Rather than give slots away by lottery, the FAA could sell them to the highest-bidding airlines. If the market value of a slot were, say, $5,000, carriers would have to charge travelers on a 20-passenger flight $250 more for a one-way ticket, while those on a 200-passenger flight would have to pay only $25 extra. Passengers on small flights would thus have a strong incentive to divert to less-crowded times or airports.

Source: Adapted from "Scarce Slots? Hold an Auction," as appeared in the *New York Times,* December 13, 2000

Other Auction Institutions

Simply because the double oral auction appears to yield competitive results in an efficient manner does not mean that it can be used everywhere. In fact, it is used relatively infrequently compared with other auction institutions. For example, in most art auctions and country auctions, we see what is called an English auction, in which the auctioneer starts the bidding at a certain level and people raise their hands to announce new bids. When the cry "Going, going, gone" is heard, the auction is over and the last person to bid wins the good. In Holland, where flowers are sold at auction, a Dutch auction has been followed for many years. Here, rather than have the price increase as time moves on, the auctioneer sets the price arbitrarily high—so high that it exceeds all reasonable bids. It is then systematically reduced, dropping at a constant rate of $k per ten seconds. In this auction, no one speaks at all. The first person to raise his or her hand and accept the good freezes the clock at the current price and wins the good.

In government purchasing, bids to supply military hardware or desks for the Agriculture Department are often written on pieces of paper, sealed in an envelope, and opened on a preannounced day. Such sealed-bid auctions are quite common and can take two different forms. In the first, called a first-price sealed-bid auction, everyone submits a sealed bid. When the bids are opened, the winner is the highest bidder and pays a price equal to his or her bid. In the second-price sealed-bid auction, sealed bids are submitted and the winner again is the bidder with the highest price, but the winner pays not his or her bid but rather the bid submitted by the second-highest bidder.

Many other auction institutions exist, such as "bidding by candle," where anyone can announce a price for the good and the auction stays open until a candle burning at the front of the room goes out. At that moment, the last announced bid wins.[2]

Which auction is used will depend on a number of factors, including the ease with which the buyers can be brought together in one place to bid. One question that arises is whether the auction institution really matters or whether the results would be the same regardless of which rule was used. The answer is that the rule matters but not under all circumstances.

Before we investigate these results in a more systematic manner, let us first classify two types of auctions according to a classification that will prove useful for our results later. Auctions can be private value auctions or common value auctions. A private value auction is typically an auction like a country furniture auction, in which each person has a particular and different value for the good being auctioned. For example, say a blue couch and a yellow couch are both being auctioned at a country fair. People with blue living room walls may care more for the blue couch and be willing to pay more for it than the yellow couch, while people with yellow walls will have opposite tastes. The yellow couch may be Art Deco and the blue may be Victorian, so people with houses decorated in these styles may also have different values for these couches. The point about private value auctions, however, is that each person has his or her own private value for the good, these values differ across people, and they are known only to the individuals themselves.

English auction
An auction, of the type used in common country auctions, in which the auctioneer starts the bidding at a certain level and people raise that bid until no one wishes to increase their bid any further. The last person to bid wins the good at a price equal to that bid.

Dutch auction
An auction in which the auctioneer sets the price arbitrarily high and then systematically reduces it until one bidder stops the falling price and buys the good.

sealed-bid auction
A sealed bid auction is an auction in which bidders enter their bids privately and the winner is that bidder whose bid is highest.

first-price sealed-bid auction
An auction in which bidders submit sealed bids, and the winner is the highest bidder, who pays a price equal to his or her bid.

second-price sealed-bid auction
An auction in which everyone submits a sealed bid and the winner is the highest bidder, but the winner pays a price equal to the second-highest bidder's price.

private value auctions
An auction in which each person has a particular and possibly different value for the good being auctioned.

---

[2] See Ralph Cassady, *Auctions and Auctioneering* (Berkeley: University of California Press, 1967).

common value auction
An auction in which one objectively true value for a good exists, but information about that value is distributed across the population.

In a **common value auction**, one objectively true value for a good exists, but information about that value is distributed across the population. A typical example is an auction of the rights to explore and exploit oil deposits in a newly found oil field. Here, different companies have performed tests on the oil tract and have a sounding indicating the amount of oil present. Because each company has performed this test in a different area under different circumstances, their information is different and so are their estimates of how much the tract is worth. Despite these different estimates, however, there is only one objectively true amount of oil present, and we can assume that no matter who wins the bidding, the value of winning is the same to all bidders. To analyze our different auction rules, we will treat these two types of auctions separately.

MEDIA NOTE

BIDDING CARTEL

Auctions and markets work well when people compete but when they collude, the outcomes can be devastating. Take the recent bid-rigging case in Japan.

Prosecutors suspected the Yokogawa Bridge Corp. and Ishikawajima-Harima Heavy Industries Co. of **bid-rigging** practices related to bridge-construction projects. The companies were charged with violating the Antimonopoly Law, constituting the largest such complaint since a bid-rigging case involving water-meter contracts with the Tokyo metropolitan government in July 2003.

The heads of eight construction companies—Yokogawa Bridge, JFE Engineering Inc., Kawada Industries Inc., Ishikawajima-Harima Heavy Industries, Miyaji Iron Works Co., TTK Corp., Takadakiko Co., and Kurimoto Ltd.—were accused of coordinating for 47 companies in the industry talks

that had been ongoing for at least 40 years. More precisely, the 47 companies had held general meetings in late March each year to elect the organizing company for the next fiscal year. The companies agreed to entrust the organizer to allocate construction projects among member companies, the sources said.

To facilitate their practices, they wrote a manual saying that bridge-construction contracts should be allocated on the basis of the "give-and-take spirit" and documents containing telephone networks for senior officials at the 47 firms. In the manual, the 47 firms said the coordination is intended to "prevent a fall in contract prices."

These practices have serious consequences. The market for steel bridges is estimated at about 350 billion yen a year.

Source: Adapted from "Prosecutors Raid Firms over Rigging Bids on Bridge Works," as appeared on the Japan Economic Newswire, May 23, 2005

bid rigging
Collusion among firms bidding in an auction.

Private Value Auctions

A private value auction can be thought of as a game played as follows. Each player draws a private value from a random distribution of private values indicating what the good being sold is worth to him or her. This private value is known only to the buyer drawing it, yet all bidders know the distribution. To simplify our analysis, we will assume a uniform distribution of values defined over the interval [0, 100]. Uniform distributions are such that all values in this interval are equally likely to be drawn. For instance, a bidder is as likely to draw the value 0 as 33 or 66 or 100.

Given any particular auction rule being used, once all bidders draw their values, they must define a strategy for themselves. A strategy in an auction is a rule indicating at what point the bidder will stop bidding, given his or her private value. It is therefore a function of the private values. For example, a strategy in the Dutch auction would be a rule indicating when to stop the clock and accept a price if no one has yet done so. A strategy for the English auction would be a rule that indicated when to stop bidding and start sitting silently and watching the others compete. A strategy for a sealed-bid auction indicates what bid to write down and seal in the bid envelope given any random cost. Finally, the auction ends when the rules indicate a winner has been found, and payoffs are determined at that point. The payoff to losing an auction will be assumed to be zero, while the payoff to winning will be the difference between the bidder's randomly determined private value and the price he or she had to pay for the good in the auction.

For private value auctions, if you were the auctioneer, which auction form would you prefer? To help answer this question, consider the following two theorems.

> **Theorem 16.1: The outcomes of the English and second-price sealed-bid auctions are identical, as are the prices and allocations determined.**

Proof: The proof is simple. Note that in a second-price sealed-bid auction, it is a dominant strategy to bid truthfully and write your private value on the piece of paper. Recall that your bid determines only whether you win the auction or not; it does not affect the price you pay if you win. That is determined by the second-highest bidder. Therefore, bidding below your value only lowers the probability that you will win without changing the price you pay if you do. Clearly that cannot be optimal. Likewise, raising your bid above your private value increases your probability of winning only when there is a bidder above your true private value; otherwise it has no effect. However, if you win in these circumstances, you will wind up paying more for the good than you value it, and that cannot be optimal either. Therefore, bidding your true value is optimal in a second-price sealed-bid auction.

Likewise, a dominant strategy for bidding in an English auction is to continue bidding until the price in the auction rises to your private value. Obviously you should not stop at a price below your value if others are continuing because that could cause you to lose a good that you value at more than its final selling price. Likewise, bidding beyond your value is silly because, again, you might win a good whose price exceeds your value. Hence, it is a dominant strategy to bid as long as the price is less than or equal to your value.

Given that all bidders in the second-price sealed-bid auction and the English auction will bid their value as a dominant strategy, we see that prices will rise in each case to equal the value of the second-highest bidder because in the sealed-bid second-price auction, the highest value will win at a price equal to that of the second-highest value, while in the English auction the buyer with the second-highest value will not stop bidding until his or her value is reached, at which point the auction will stop and the highest-value bidder will win. This determines a corollary.

> **Corollary: In the English and second-price sealed-bid auctions, the good will be allocated to the highest-value bidder at a price equal to the value of the second-highest bidder.**

> **Theorem 16.2: The outcomes of the Dutch and first-price sealed-bid auctions are identical, as are the prices and allocations determined.**

Proof: Our strategy here will be identical to that in Theorem 16.1. We will first prove that in both auctions, bidders will use identical strategies. Knowing this, it will be obvious that the results of the auctions will be identical.

Before we begin, note that the first-price sealed-bid and Dutch auctions are strategically identical because in the first-price sealed-bid auction, the bidder has no additional information about the other bidders before she is expected to bid. All she knows is her private value and the distribution from which other private values are drawn. The same is true in the Dutch auction. Here, the bidder has drawn a private value, and before the clock is stopped no one has gained any information about the other bidders. Hence, bidders are in a strategically identical situation at the time they are asked to bid and should employ identical strategies.

To understand what this strategy looks like, let us concentrate on the first-price sealed-bid auction and assume that there are n bidders at the auction and that bidder 1 draws value v_1, bidder 2 draws v_2, and so on. Now arrange these values from the highest to the lowest and call V_n the highest of these values no matter which bidder drew it. Call V_{n-1} the second highest and so forth, so V_1 will be the lowest of the n values drawn and $V_n > V_{n-1} > \ldots > V_1$. These values, arranged this way, are the **order statistics** of the sample of n values drawn.

To derive the optimal bid given a value drawn in the first-price sealed-bid auction, note that no bidder will ever bid above her value because if she won, she would do so at the price she bid. Therefore, bidding above her value does nothing but subject her to the possibility of a loss. So if she is going to bid, the question is how much below her value she should bid. Further, note that in equilibrium, the highest-value bidder must win the auction because if her bid strategy ever entails her losing to the second- or third-highest value bidder, she can always increase her payoff by bidding slightly above their value, but below hers, and win the good. So for strategic purposes, once she gets a private value, she might as well assume that she has the highest value or the highest-order statistic.

Knowing that and knowing that no bidder will ever bid above his or her value, you know that you can win if you bid above the value of the second-highest bidder. In fact, your optimal bid will be exactly the expected value of the second-highest bidder, assuming you are the highest, because if you bid below that value, the second-highest value bidder could always increase his bid above your value but below his value and steal the good from you while making a profit for himself. The only problem is that, assuming that you have drawn the highest value, you do not know what the value of the second-highest bidder is.

To figure this out, assume that all values are drawn from a uniform distribution over the interval [0, 100]. If there are six bidders in the auction, we can assume that, on average, the values drawn for the order statistic $V_n, \ldots, V_1$ should be equally spaced on the interval. What this means is that, if we were to draw a million samples of six values from a uniform distribution over [0, 100], the average value of the highest draw in these samples should be $(\frac{6}{7})100 = 85.71$, the second highest should be 71.42, the third 57.14, and so on, and the lowest on average should be 14.28. This is illustrated in Figure 16.8.

What this figure shows are the expected values of the six order statistics for draws of samples of size six from the interval [0, 100]. As you see, on average they are equally spread out along the interval. So if we had three bidders, we would expect to see these expected values at the 25, 50, and 75 values. In general, the expected value of the highest of n order statistics from the interval $[0, I]$ is $[n/(n + 1)]I$, while the second highest is $[(n - 1)/(n + 1)]I$, and so on.

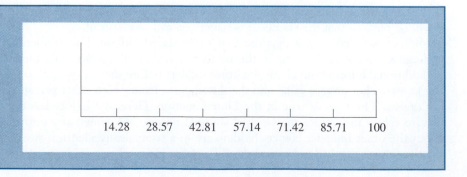

Figure 16.8

Expected Value of Order Statistics.

On average, in a sample of 6 drawn from a uniform distribution, the highest value should be 85.71, the second highest 71.42, the third highest 57.14, and so forth.

order statistics

The Rth order statistic of a sample is the Rth smallest value of the sample.

To complete our derivation of the optimal strategy, let us assume that you draw a value v in the auction. You can derive your optimal bid by assuming that you have the highest bid among the n people in the auction. If this is the case, then there remain $n - 1$ people who have values lower than yours. The highest among them is, on average, $[(n - 1)/n]v$, and that should be your bid. Because the Dutch auction is equivalent strategically, this should be your bid in that auction as well.

To summarize our results so far, we have derived the fact that the bidding strategies and hence the outcomes of second-price sealed-bid and English auctions are identical, as are the bidding strategies and outcomes of the first-price sealed-bid and Dutch auctions. In fact, the expected revenue from the second-price sealed-bid auction and the English auction is equal on average to the expected value of the second-highest-order statistic in the auction. In addition, we have derived the equilibrium bid strategy for the Dutch and first-price sealed-bid auctions and have seen that, in these auctions, bidders should bid $[(n - 1)/n]v$ where v is the value drawn and n is the number of bidders in the auction. The next result ties together these disparate results and says that no matter which auction you use, the revenue generated by the auction is, on average, the same.

> **Theorem 16.3: Revenue Equivalence Theorem** If (1) all bidders are identical and draw their values independently from identical intervals; (2) bidders care only about their monetary rewards and have utility functions that are linear in income; and (3) the payoff of the auction is a function only of the bids made, then the expected revenue generated by the first-price sealed-bid auction, the second-price sealed-bid auction, the Dutch auction, and the English auction is identical and equal to the expected value of the second-highest-order statistic.

This theorem basically says that under the assumptions stated, the actual auction form used has no influence at all on the revenues generated by the auction. This is true because we already know that the second-price sealed-bid and English auctions yield a price equal to the second-highest-order statistic of the distribution. In addition, we know that in the first-price sealed-bid auction and the Dutch auction, bidders will bid $(n - 1)/n$ of their value so that the winning bid will be $(n - 1)/n$ times the highest-order statistic in any auction of this type. It can be proven that, on average, the expected value of the winning bids in the first-price sealed-bid and Dutch auctions equals the expected value of the second-order statistic for the auction and, hence, they are equal. So despite their different appearance, all the auction institutions mentioned so far are equivalent with respect to their revenue-generating abilities.

This does not mean that this result is true for any set of circumstances. For example, if buyers are not identical but draw their values from different intervals, the results mentioned above break down and there are advantages to employing different auction rules.

RESOLVING
TEASER 16

REVENUE EQUIVALENCE

James Cox, Bruce Roberson, and Vernon Smith experimentally demonstrated results in line with the prediction of the theory that English and second-price sealed-bid auctions produced similar revenues. However, first-price sealed-bid auctions provided higher revenue than Dutch auctions. One explanation for this difference might be that the bidders enjoy waiting in the Dutch auction. As they waited longer, the bids became lower, and hence the revenue of the seller was decreased. Can you think of other explanations?

Common Value Auctions and the Winner's Curse

Say that the government is auctioning off a franchise to sell hot dogs at the professional baseball stadium in your town or city. Each firm interested in doing business makes an estimate of its costs and the expected attendance and hot dog consumption of the fans. Each firm then figures out a bid. The government, using a first-price rule, chooses a firm to which it will sell the franchise. A few months later, you are informed that you have won the competition; you will be the sole provider of hot dogs at the ball park. Is this good news or bad news? You might think at first that it is good news because you have won a franchise that you wanted. On the other hand, if you won, it must be true that every other firm bid less than you, so maybe they knew something you didn't or you miscalculated in your bidding. Putting it differently, isn't the fact that you won evidence that you paid too much?

winner's curse
An outcome of a common value auction in which the winning bidder bids more than the true expected value of the good he or she wins.

Such a phenomenon has come to be called the winner's curse, which basically says that the winner of such a good at a common value auction is actually the loser because the winner probably bid too much for the good.

The winner's curse was first pointed out in oil tract bidding in the 1960s, where it was discovered that the winning bidders tended to overestimate the value of oil in the tracts they won by a substantial margin.[3]

A common way to illustrate the point is to show a group of people a jar filled with pennies and have them bid for them. The highest bidder wins the jar and gets to keep the pennies inside after paying his or her bid. In this little experiment, winning bidders tend to overpay substantially for the jar because, after they win, they realize that they must have had an exaggerated estimate of the amount of money in the jar. (You can try this out on friends when you are short on cash because it is almost a guaranteed money producer.)

The question then arises of how to bid in common value auctions so as to avoid the winner's curse. To answer, let us pause and consider why people are subject to the winner's curse in the first place. Say that you make an estimate of how much oil is in the ground on a specific oil tract. Because the winning bidder is likely to be that bidder who has the highest estimate of the value of the oil in the ground, his or her estimate is a biased estimate of the true value of the oil. Hence, making a bid close to that estimate is likely to yield a loss to the winning bidder—he loses if he wins.

The key to solving the puzzle involves the use of order statistics again. Let us say you knew for sure that all the estimates gotten by your opponents in the bidding competition were drawn from a uniform distribution that started at zero and had a mean centered on the true value of the oil tract. No estimate below zero will ever be received by any firm. What you do not know, however, is the largest estimate any buyer might receive. This piece of information will be crucial to you because if you knew the upper limit of the uniform distribution and knew that the true value of the good was equal to the mean of this distribution, you could easily get an unbiased estimate of the true value of the good by estimating what the mean of the uniform distribution of estimates was. But estimating the mean of a uniform distribution is simply finding its midpoint. So, if you knew that the upper limit was 500, you would know that the mean value of the estimates was 250 and, by assumption, that this was the actual value of the tract.

---

[3] See E. Capen, R. Clapp, and W. Campbell, "Competitive Bidding in High Risk Situations," *Journal of Petroleum Technology* 23, no. 6 (June 1971): 641–53.

What you must do to bid in a sophisticated manner is try to use your estimate of the value of the tract to estimate the upper limit of the distribution and then use that estimate of the upper limit to estimate the mean of the distribution. That estimated mean will be your bid, and it will also be the equilibrium bid of bidders in the auction because bidding above that value subjects you to a loss, and bidding below it leaves open the possibility of someone else outbidding you and making a profit.

Say you receive an estimate. If you are worried about avoiding the winner's curse, you should first assume that you have the highest estimate of all the bidders. If there are six bidders, we know from our discussion that the average value of the highest-order statistic among six bidders is six-sevenths of the upper limit of the distribution. For instance, as we demonstrated previously, if the random variable was defined over the interval [0, 100], the expected value for the highest-order statistic in a sample of six is $(\frac{6}{7})100 = 85.71$.

Using this fact in our current example, say that there are six bidders in the oil auction and that you receive an estimate of 500. Then, if that is the highest estimate of the six bidders, we know that the upper limit of the distribution, I, can be estimated as $(\frac{6}{7})I = 500$.

Solving for I, we find that $I = 583.33$. However, because our best estimate of the mean of the distribution, and therefore the true value of the oil, is the midpoint of the interval [0, 583.33], that midpoint equals $(0 + 583.33)/2 = 291.67$; this value of 291.67 should be our bid.

To summarize the procedure, draw an estimate of the value of the good (oil). Assume that this estimate is the highest estimate drawn by any bidder in the auction. This is essential because, in equilibrium at least, the winner will be the bidder with the highest estimate. Now use this estimate to estimate the upper limit of the probability distribution, and once that is found take the midpoint of the interval as your estimate of the common value of the good. Bid that value. Note that as the number of bidders in the auction increases, the highest estimate will converge to the true upper limit and the bids will converge to the true value of the good.

Conclusion

This chapter closes our discussion of perfectly competitive markets and market designs whose aim is to replicate perfectly competitive market outcomes. We study these markets because many real world markets share their features, but also because they set a welfare benchmark upon which we can compare the performance of other market organizations. In the chapters that follow we move on to study markets with fewer numbers of firms, ranging from one (in the case of monopoly), two (in the case of duopoly), and many (in the case of oligopoly). Our focus of attention in these chapters will be on the economic welfare of society when markets are organized in a manner that is less than perfectly competitive, and we will investigate whether intervention in these markets can be socially beneficial.

Summary

In our discussion of perfectly competitive markets, we never specified the rules of trade. In other words, we relied upon the forces of supply and demand to get price and quantity to their short- or long-run equilibrium levels but did not discuss "rules of the market game." In this chapter, we took a look at some very specific ways to organize markets. We saw that some very different-looking auction mechanisms can be expected to generate the same level of revenues for the auctioneer and found that certain market rules, those of the "Double Auction," are reliable in generating efficient competitive outcomes. The problem of market design, however, is a fascinating one and one that has attracted a great deal of attention from economists.

Exercises and Problems

1. Jane, an antiques collector, often participates in sealed-bid auctions through the mail. In her most recent auction catalog, she has seen a set of china that she would dearly love to own. Jane personally values the set at $2,000. She believes that there are four other collectors who will also bid on the set. She does not know at exactly how much each of the other collectors values the set, but she believes that all of the other collectors have drawn their values from a uniform distribution on the interval [$1,000, $3,000].

   a) If the auction house employs a first-price sealed-bid auction, what should Jane bid?

   b) If the auction house employs a second-price sealed-bid auction, what should Jane bid? If she wins, how much should she expect to pay? What is the probability that she will win?

   c) Show that the revenue that the auction house expects to raise is identical, given that the auction house does not know the values of any of the collectors, that it believes that all collectors are drawing their value from a uniform distribution on the interval [$1,000, $3,000], and that five people actually do participate in the auction.

   d) Suppose instead that the auction house employs a third-price sealed-bid auction. This auction is similar to the second-price auction in that the highest bidder wins the auction, but in the third-price sealed-bid auction, the winner pays only the bid of the third-highest bidder. How much should Jane bid in this case? What amount of revenue should the auction house expect to raise in this auction? Is this amount different from that in part c, and if so, why?

2. Elizabeth owns a plot of land out in the country. Recently, four owners of neighboring plots have discovered gold on their lands and have begun mining operations. Elizabeth believes that there probably is gold on her land as well, but she has no desire to mine the land herself, nor does she have any idea just how much gold there is on her land. She has therefore decided to auction off her land to the highest bidder.

   a) Assume that each neighbor desires to bid on Elizabeth's land. Also assume that each neighbor believes that the estimates of the value of the land by all the other neighbors are distributed uniformly on the interval beginning at 0 with a mean centered on the true value of the land. If neighbor A estimates the value of the land to be $200, what amount should he bid in order to try to avoid the winner's curse—that is, winning the land at a price exceeding its true value?

   b) If the true value of the land were actually $150, how high would the auction winner's estimate have to be to subject him to the winner's curse even if he had bid optimally?

   c) Assume Elizabeth has a friend who is an eminent geologist and whose opinion is always believed to be true. She asks her friend to give her an estimate on the value of her land. The geologist reports back to Elizabeth and tells her that the land does indeed have gold on it and that it is worth $100 at a minimum and very likely more. Should Elizabeth make this information known to her neighbors before they submit their bids? Explain. (*Hint*: The formula to determine the upper limit of a uniform distribution, I, given one believes that he has the highest estimate, E, is $E = U + [n/(n + 1)](I - U)$, where n is the number of bidders and U is the lower limit of the distribution.)

17

The Age of Entrepreneurship: Monopoly

EXPERIMENTAL TEASER 17

MONOPOLY AND INSTITUTIONS

This chapter discusses the theory of monopoly. We will define *monopoly* as a situation in which there is one seller selling a homogeneous good to several or many buyers. As we will see, when such a situation occurs, the market will not function efficiently and there will be a loss of consumer surplus as the monopolist attempts to restrict quantity and raise the price of the good.

However, there are many ways that we can organize a monopolistic market. For instance, the usual monopolistic market is one in which the monopolist states or posts a price for its good and any buyer in the market wishing to buy at that price does so. Such a market, known as the *posted offer market*, gives the monopolist a great deal of market power because he or she is able to make a take-it-or-leave-it offer to buyers. But monopolistic markets need not be organized this way. In fact, if we could find another way to organize a monopolistic market that would lead to better results in terms of prices and efficiencies, then it might make good public policy not to regulate price but to legislate the type of market institution required for monopoly.

Vernon Smith* investigated the impact of market organization on the performance of monopolies and discovered that the degree of monopoly power varies greatly with the way a monopolistic market is organized. In fact, the usual posted offer market is generally agreed to be the most favorable to the sellers. Hence, there is room for improvement. Can you think of other ways to organize a one-seller market that will be either better or worse than the take-it-or-leave-it posted price institution?

---

* Vernon Smith, "An Empirical Study of Decentralized Institutions of Monopoly Restraint," in *Essays in Contemporary Fields of Economics in Honor of E. T. Weiler,* eds. J. Quirk and G. Horwich (West Lafayette, IN: Purdue University Press, 1981), pp. 83–106.

Let us return to the situation described in Chapter 8 where our budding entrepreneur, the jam maker, has established a firm to produce and sell her product marks. This is a time before the existence of competitive markets, when the age of entrepreneurship is dawning. Other potential entrepreneurs will soon follow her example by developing their own products and starting their own firms. Meanwhile, no one else has yet discovered how to produce jam, so our potential jam maker will initially have no competition. She will be the sole producer in the market, which means that she will have a monopoly.

In previous chapters, we saw how this entrepreneur learned about the technology and costs of production and the various methods of organizing work and motivating workers. We also saw how she learned about game theory. All this knowledge will help her to produce in a manner that is technologically feasible, efficient, and cost-effective and to behave strategically in the market. However, before she begins the operations of her firm, she must also know the answers to the following questions: What is the *optimal* (profit-maximizing) amount of output to produce? What is the profit-maximizing price to charge? Will my firm be able to earn extra-normal profits (profits in excess of the opportunity cost of my time) because it is a monopoly?

In this chapter, we will investigate how decisions are made about what quantities to produce and what prices to charge for products. We will also examine the effect of monopoly on the welfare of people in our primitive society.

Costs, Demand, and Profits

From our previous analysis of production in the long run, we know that our entrepreneur can determine the least-cost way to produce any amount of output given the technology to be used. The result of this type of analysis is summarized by the cost function for her firm. Let us assume that the average and marginal cost functions associated with the jam-making operation have the shapes shown in Figure 17.1.

In this figure, we see the familiar U-shaped average and marginal cost functions. As our entrepreneur looks at these curves, she realizes that she needs only one more piece of information to be able to answer the three questions posed at the beginning of this chapter. She must know how much people are willing to pay for any quantity of jam. Obviously, the more people are willing to pay for any given quantity (if everything else remains constant), the more profitable jam making will be and the greater the likelihood that our entrepreneur will be able to earn extra-normal profits. From our discussion in Chapter 4, we know that a market demand function presents exactly this type of information. A market demand function tells us what quantity of a good will be purchased at any given price or, conversely, what price the market is willing to pay for any given quantity of the

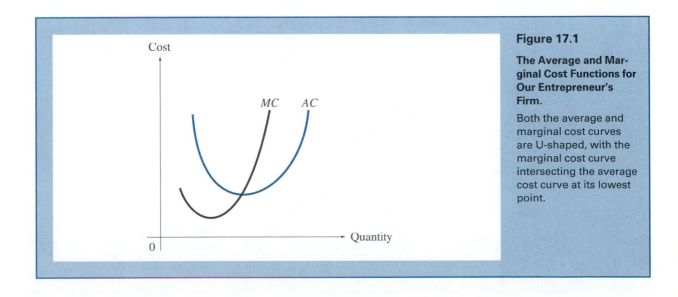

Figure 17.1

The Average and Marginal Cost Functions for Our Entrepreneur's Firm.

Both the average and marginal cost curves are U-shaped, with the marginal cost curve intersecting the average cost curve at its lowest point.

good. For the sake of simplicity, let us say our entrepreneur finds that the market demand for jam is linear, as depicted in Figure 17.2.

This information about demand and cost is all that is needed to allow our entrepreneur to determine what price to set for her product and what quantity to produce.

Pricing and Quantity Decisions

With the help of the demand and cost curves, we can deduce the optimal price for our entrepreneur to charge and the optimal quantity for her to produce. By *optimal*, we mean the price and quantity that will maximize her firm's profits. However, before we proceed any further with our discussion of how to determine optimal prices and quantities, let us consider the topic of arbitrage pricing.

Arbitrage and Pricing

Assume that our entrepreneur makes only one type of jam and that all potential consumers live close to one another so that reselling the jam is a costless process. This means that if a person buys some jam and then decides to resell it to someone else, such a resale can be accomplished without incurring any cost. These assumptions give us the following arbitrage pricing result for a firm that has a monopoly: In a market where it is costless for an agent to resell units of a good purchased previously and where all agents can be contacted cheaply, the good must be sold at the same price to all agents.

More formally, let us define arbitrage as a process of buying a commodity and reselling it at a favorable price. Opportunities for arbitrage exist whenever different agents face different prices for the same good and the cost of contacting an agent and reselling the good to him is less than the difference in prices. This result indicates that if opportunities for arbitrage exist, then the process of arbitrage will continue until all agents face the same price—until these arbitrage opportunities are eliminated. Therefore, arbitrage pricing—pricing that is consistent with the fact that agents *will* engage in arbitrage *if* opportunities exist—entails a uniform price for all agents.

arbitrage
A process of buying a commodity and reselling it at a favorable price.

arbitrage pricing
arbitrage pricing is the price of a good or asset that results after the process of arbitrage has occurred if arbitrage opportunities existed.

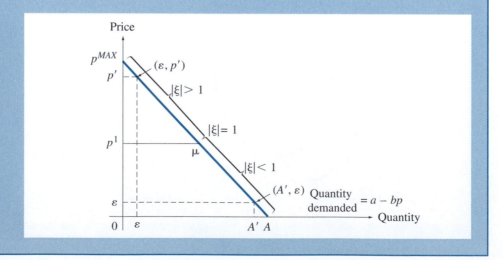

Figure 17.2

Linear Market Demand Function.

Market demand is a linear function $q = A - bp$ of price p.

We can use the following example to illustrate the result of arbitrage pricing. Let us say that a good is sold by our monopolist at different prices to two different people. One person (call him an arbitrageur) buys the good for $3, while the other person (call her the consumer) buys the good for $7. If it is costless to resell goods, we would expect the arbitrageur to contact the consumer and tell her not to buy from the monopolist but rather to buy from him at a lower price—say $5. In such a case, the consumer would benefit because she would be able to buy the good for $5 rather than the $7 the monopolist was asking for it. The arbitrageur would benefit because he would buy the good for $3 and sell it for $5, thereby earning a profit of $2 from the transaction.

While such opportunities for arbitrage exist, we cannot have an equilibrium price in the market because the process of arbitrage will change the prices that are being charged for the good. For example, consider the case that we have been discussing. When the monopolist hears that arbitrage is occurring, she will contact the consumer and offer to sell her the good at a reduced price—say $4.50. The consumer will then cancel the deal with the arbitrageur in order to make the more advantageous deal with the monopolist. Hearing this, the arbitrageur will lower his price, and the process will continue until only one price exists in the market and there are no more opportunities for arbitrage. Note that in this case the result rests on the fact that reselling is costless. If reselling were prohibitively expensive (for example, if jam had to be eaten within five minutes of purchase or else it spoiled), then the argument made here would not be correct and many prices might exist simultaneously in the market. We will turn our attention to this possibility later in the chapter when we discuss price discrimination. For now, however, let us concentrate on the situation where our entrepreneur sets one price for her product and all consumers must pay this price.

Pricing and Elasticity

The relationship between pricing decisions and the elasticity of demand should be obvious. Let us define the revenue from the sale of jam as revenue = (price)(quantity), or $R = pq$. Let us define the profits from the sale of jam as revenue minus costs, or $\pi = R - C$. We know from Chapter 9 that costs are always an increasing function of the quantity produced.

Now let us say that our entrepreneur is pricing her product (choosing a price) on the inelastic portion of the demand curve in Figure 17.2 (at a point below and to the right of point μ).[1] Because demand is inelastic here, we know from Chapter 4 that if she contemplates a 1% increase in price, such an increase will lead to less than a 1% decrease in the quantity demanded. Because revenue equals the price multiplied by the quantity sold ($R = pq$), we see that such an increase in price must increase the revenue at our entrepreneur's jam-producing firm. The 1% increase in price will more than compensate the firm for its small decrease in sales. (Imagine if the elasticity of demand were zero. Then a price increase would cause no decrease in demand.) If our entrepreneur decreases the quantity produced in addition to raising the price, the firm's cost of production will fall and its profit will increase. Because the same argument can be made for any point on the inelastic

---

[1] We know that a point like μ where elasticity equals 1 must exist on a linear demand curve because at point p^{MAX} the elasticity approaches infinity, while at point A it approaches zero. Because the elasticity continuously decreases along the demand curve between these points, there must be a point that separates the elastic portion ($\xi > 1$) from the inelastic portion ($\xi < 1$). This point is μ ($\xi = 1$).

portion of the demand curve, we can now state the following elasticity rule for monopoly pricing.

> **Pricing Rule 1: The Elasticity Rule for Monopoly Pricing.** Never price a commodity on the inelastic portion of the demand curve.

<table>
<tr><td></td></tr>
</table>

SOLVED PROBLEM 17.1

Question (Content Review: Pricing and Elasticity)

Consider a firm facing the following demand schedule:

Quantity	Price
1	15
2	14
3	13
4	12
5	11
6	10
7	9
8	8
9	7
10	6
11	5
12	4

Use the elasticity formula to determine whether the firm would be maximizing its profits by setting a price equal to 5. Also find that point on the demand curve where the elasticity is unitary.

Answer

The firm would not be maximizing its profits if it set a price of 5. At that price, the elasticity is $|\varepsilon| = \left|\frac{\Delta q/q}{\Delta p/p}\right| = \left|\frac{1/11}{1/5}\right| = \frac{5}{11} < 1$. Hence, if the firm were to set a price of 5, it would be pricing on the inelastic portion of the demand curve and, therefore, would not be maximizing its profits.

Demand has unitary elasticity at the point where $p = q = 8$. We can see this using the elasticity formula because $|\varepsilon| = \left|\frac{\Delta q/q}{\Delta p/p}\right| = \frac{1/8}{1/8} = 1$.

Marginal Revenue

While we do not know how our entrepreneur will actually price her product, we do know that she will be forced by the arbitrage pricing result to sell to everyone at the same price. In addition, from the elasticity rule, we know that she will never set a price below p^1 (the price associated with point μ on the demand curve in Figure 17.2). To understand how to determine the optimal quantity to produce and the optimal price to set for jam, let us consider Figure 17.3.

In this figure, we see the downward-sloping, straight-line demand curve for jam along with an associated curve depicting marginal revenue. Marginal revenue is the increase in the total revenue of a firm generated by the sale of an additional unit of output after taking into account whatever adjustment the firm must make in the price of all *previously* sold units as a result of its efforts to sell more of the good.

Using the no-arbitrage result, we know that our entrepreneur will have to sell the jam she produces to all consumers at the same price. The demand curve tells

marginal revenue
The increase in the total revenue of a firm generated by the sale of an additional unit of output.

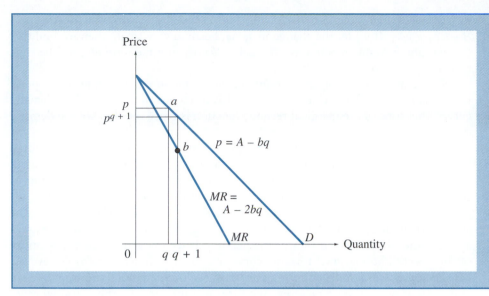

Figure 17.3

Marginal Revenue and Demand.

The marginal revenue curve is steeper than the demand curve. With a straight-line demand curve, the slope of the marginal revenue curve is twice the slope of the demand curve.

her how many units of jam she will be able to sell at each given price. Let us express the demand function as $q = f(p)$, which simply means that the quantity sold is a function of the price charged. Related to this demand function is what we will call the inverse demand function, $p = h(q)$, which indicates the price that would result if any given quantity were placed on the market. Note that in the inverse demand function, price is a function of quantity, while in the regular demand function, quantity is a function of price.

inverse demand function
The function that indicates the price that would result if any given quantity were placed on the market.

Let us assume that our entrepreneur is currently selling q units of jam and wants to sell an additional unit so that the total sold will be $q + 1$. In order to sell this additional unit (the $q + 1$st unit), she will have to set its price below the price for all q units sold previously. It will have to sell at p^{q+1} instead of p. However, because all units of a good must sell at the same price, she will also have to lower the price of the previously sold q units. Hence, her marginal (or additional) revenue from selling the $q + 1$st unit is $MR = p^{q+1} - [(pq) - p^{q+1}q]$. What this expression tells us is that when the $q + 1$st unit is sold at a price of p^{q+1}, the revenue from the sale of that unit increases the total revenue by p^{q+1}. That is the first term in the marginal revenue expression.

Because of the arbitrage result, the price of the q units sold previously must now be decreased in order to maintain uniform pricing for all units of the good. Therefore, if the firm previously sold q units at a price of p, it will now adjust the price of those units to p^{q+1}, which is lower than p. The second term in the marginal revenue expression therefore represents the loss in revenue associated with selling an additional unit.

To understand marginal revenue more thoroughly, look again at Figure 17.3. Note that the marginal revenue curve falls below the downward-sloping, straight-line demand curve. In fact, the slope of the marginal revenue curve is exactly twice as steep as the slope of the demand curve. To prove this, let us consider the straight-line inverse demand curve $p = A - bq$. At quantity q, the revenue is $R = pq = (A - bq)q = (Aq - bq^2)$. Let us now increase the amount of output provided from q to $q + \Delta q$. At this quantity, the price is $p' = A - b(q + \Delta q)$ and the revenue is $R' = (A - b(q + \Delta q))(q + \Delta q)$. Hence, the change in revenue when moving from q to $q + \Delta q$ is $\Delta R = R' - R = [A - b(q + \Delta q)](q + \Delta q) - (Aq - bq^2)$, which can be expressed as $\Delta R = \Delta q(A - 2bq - b\Delta q)$. To calculate the slope of this marginal revenue function, we divide both sides by Δq to obtain $\Delta R/\Delta q = A - 2bq - b\Delta q$. If we let the change in q, Δq, become very small, then we find that the marginal revenue function is $MR = A - 2bq$ because the term $b\Delta q$ will become zero as Δq goes to zero.

Note that the slope of the marginal revenue function is $2b$, while the slope of the demand curve from which it is derived is b. Hence, for straight-line demand curves, the slope of the marginal revenue function is twice the slope of the demand curve.

Look at the quantity-price pair (p, q) in Figure 17.3, which is represented by point a on the demand curve. At that point, the demand curve tells our entrepreneur what price she will have to offer the market if she wants to sell q units of the good. Because she must sell all units at the same price, the demand curve indicates the per-unit revenue generated by the sale of q units of jam. This is the average revenue associated with q units. Thus, the demand curve shows the average revenue of the firm. It tells us the per-unit price needed to sell any quantity of the good. The marginal revenue curve tells us how much the firm's revenue will increase when our entrepreneur sells an incremental (additional) unit. We see that while the average revenue for $q + 1$ units is p^{q+1}, the marginal revenue from the sale of the $q + 1$st unit is $p^{q+1} - (pq - p^{q+1}q)$, or somewhat less than p^{q+1}.

Point b in Figure 17.3 represents the marginal revenue from selling the $q + 1$st unit, which is less than the average revenue of p^{q+1}. More precisely, if we let revenue be $R = pq$ and our entrepreneur decides to increase the amount she sells to $q + \Delta q$, then the firm's marginal revenue can be expressed as $MR = (\Delta p/\Delta q)(q) + p$. Note that a change in quantity in this expression (actually an infinitely small change in quantity) has two effects. First, it lowers the price of the q units that were previously sold ($\Delta p/\Delta q$ tells us how much this price will decrease). Second, it results in a selling price of p for the additional units. (When changes in quantity are infinitely small, the price of each additional unit sold will be very close to the original price.)

Because the demand curve is downward sloping, we know that $\Delta p/\Delta q$ is negative (increasing the quantity sold decreases the price), so the marginal revenue condition can be expressed as $MR = p - |\Delta p/\Delta q|(q)$, where the straight lines around $\Delta p/\Delta q$ represent absolute values. If we were now to multiply the right side of this expression by p/p (which would leave it intact), we would find that $MR = p[1 - |(\Delta p/\Delta q)(q/p)|]$. Note that $(\Delta p/\Delta q)(q/p)$ is nothing more than 1/elasticity of demand $= 1/\xi$. Hence, marginal revenue takes the form $MR = p(1 - 1/|\xi|)$.

As the elasticity of demand for a product becomes greater, the divergence of price from marginal revenue becomes smaller. When the elasticity of demand is infinite, price equals marginal revenue.

SOLVED PROBLEM 17.2

Question (Content Review: Pricing and Elasticity)

Bob's Computer Mania has franchises in several cities across the United States. The New York City store is currently selling its Q3000 model for $1,000. Each store in the other cities sells the Q3000 at a different price. Table 17.1(a) shows the different prices at which each store sells and how many units were purchased.

The New York City store is considering raising its prices. If we assume that consumers are the same in each city, will it be profitable for the store to increase its price?

Table 17.1

(a) Demand for Q3000 Computers.

Price	Quantity Sold
$ 950	225
$ 975	210
$1,000	200
$1,050	190
$1,100	175

(b) Revenues

Price	Quantity Sold	Revenue
$ 950	225	$213,750
$ 975	210	$204,750
$1,000	200	$200,000
$1,050	195	$204,750
$1,100	175	$192,500

Answer

The answer is no. In fact, the New York City store may be better off by lowering its price. As shown in Table 17.1(b), we can see this if we compute the revenues from the data given in Table 17.1(a).

When it is charging $1,000 per unit, the New York City store is on a very elastic part of its demand curve and could increase its revenues by decreasing its price.

Optimal Price and Quantity Results

Let us return to the operations of our entrepreneur's jam-making firm. We are now ready to derive the optimal price for the firm to charge and the optimal quantity for it to produce. As we noted previously, determining the optimal price and the optimal quantity will require balancing the costs and benefits involved in selling particular quantities. Before we delve into the details of this process, let us examine the concepts that underlie the optimal quantity and optimal price rules. We will do this by analyzing profitability on a unit-by-unit basis.

The Profit-Maximizing Quantity

If our entrepreneur already has the necessary capital to produce goods, under what circumstances will she want to sell her first unit of output? Clearly, she will do so only if the amount of dollars she can collect from selling that first unit is greater than the costs involved in producing it. We know from the demand curve that when the first unit is sold, it will generate a certain amount of revenue, the marginal revenue associated with the first unit. Because the necessary capital is already available and is a fixed cost, the marginal cost associated with this first unit is simply the cost of hiring labor. If the marginal revenue is greater than the marginal cost, our entrepreneur will produce and sell the first unit. The same is true for the second unit, the third unit, and subsequent units. In fact, our entrepreneur will continue to produce and sell units as long as the marginal revenue received from sales is greater than the marginal cost of producing those units.

This analysis yields the following quantity-setting rule for firms that have a monopoly in their markets: When the demand curve is downward sloping, a monopolist will produce units of a good until the point where the marginal revenue of the last unit sold is equal to its marginal cost. Figure 17.4 will help us to understand this rule.

In Figure 17.4, we see the marginal revenue and demand curves superimposed on the marginal cost curve of the firm. Note that the marginal revenue received from selling the q^* unit is exactly equal to the marginal cost of producing that unit. For quantities less than q^*, the marginal revenue received from selling these units is greater than the marginal cost of production. The firm will therefore increase its profit by producing these units. For quantities greater than q^*, we see just the opposite situation. In this case, the additional revenue received from selling each unit is less than the additional cost of producing the unit. In other words, the marginal revenue is less than the marginal cost. Hence, these units are not profitable and should not be produced.

The Profit-Maximizing Price

Now that we know the quantity that should be produced (q^* units), what price should be charged? This amount is easily determined because we know from the definition of the demand curve that q^* units can be sold in the market at a maximum price of p^* per unit. (Look at the height of the demand curve above the quantity q^*.) Hence, if q^* is the optimal quantity, then all of these units should be sold at a price of p^*. Any lower price would clearly be suboptimal because our entrepreneur would miss the opportunity to obtain the maximum amount of profit for the quantity she wishes to sell. On the other hand, a higher price is not feasible because the optimal quantity defined by the demand curve (q^* units) cannot be sold at a price above p^*. These considerations yield the following optimal pricing rule for a monopolist.

> **Pricing Rule 2: _The Profit-Maximizing Determination of Price._** The optimal price for a monopolist is the price that is on the demand curve at the optimal quantity point.

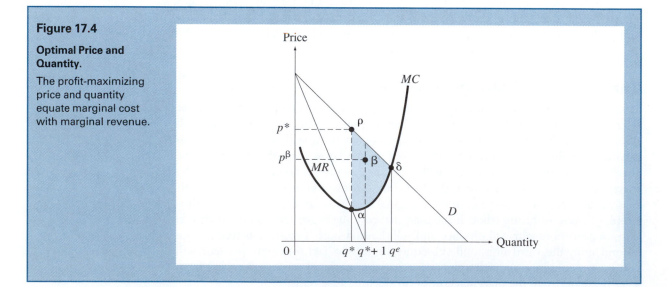

Figure 17.4

Optimal Price and Quantity.

The profit-maximizing price and quantity equate marginal cost with marginal revenue.

This rule tells us that a profit-maximizing monopolist sets a price for her product that is above the marginal cost of producing a unit of the product. How far above the marginal cost should the price be? The answer to this question is determined by how elastic demand is at the optimal quantity point. More precisely, remember that $MR = p(1 - 1/|\xi|)$. Hence, $p = MR(1 - 1/|\xi|)$. However, because at the optimal quantity point $MR = MC$ (where MC stands for marginal cost), we see that $p = MC/(1 - 1/|\xi|)$. The price charged by a profit-maximizing monopolist will therefore be inversely related to the elasticity of demand she faces: The more inelastic the demand is, the greater the price will be above the marginal cost of producing the q^* unit.

SOLVED PROBLEM 17.3

Question (Content Review: The Profit-Maximizing Quantity)
Consider a monopolist facing a demand curve of $p = 100 - 4q$. Suppose that it has a constant marginal cost of 4. What quantity will maximize the firm's profits?

Answer
We know from our discussion of the relationship of marginal revenue and demand that if we have a linear demand curve, then the associated marginal revenue curve has a slope that is twice as steep. Hence, the marginal revenue curve associated with this demand curve is $MR = 100 - 8q$.

The firm will maximize its profits when it sets marginal revenue equal to marginal cost, so it must solve for q in $100 - 8q = 4 \Rightarrow 8q = 96 \Rightarrow q = 12$.

Therefore, $q = 12$ is the profit-maximizing output.

The Socially Optimal Price

We now know that in an effort to maximize her profits, our entrepreneur will set a price of p^* and plan to produce a quantity of q^*. This combination of price and quantity will result in the best outcome for her firm. But is it the best outcome for society? Would society as a whole, including our entrepreneur, be better off with some other outcome? The answer to this question is yes. To understand why, let us again consider Figure 17.4, which depicts the optimal price-quantity outcome determined by our entrepreneur.

We know that our entrepreneur will not want to produce any more than a quantity of q^* if she has to sell all units at one price because the marginal revenue from selling one additional unit is less than the marginal cost of production. However, the market demand curve can be interpreted as specifying the maximum amount of money that society is willing to spend for each unit offered for sale. Consider what would happen if our entrepreneur thought of offering the $q^* + 1$st unit. If we look at the height of the demand curve above the $q^* + 1$st unit, we see that it measures the maximum willingness of society to pay for that unit. The height of the marginal cost curve at $q^* + 1$ measures the marginal cost of producing that unit. If our entrepreneur were to offer the $q^* + 1$st unit, society would place a value on the unit that is higher than its cost of production.

If society could find some way to pay our entrepreneur more than the marginal cost of producing the $q^* + 1$st unit (but less than the price indicated by the demand curve)—say a price measured by the height of the line $(q^* + 1)\beta$—both society and our entrepreneur would benefit. Hence, it would be possible to make everyone in society (including our entrepreneur) better off by producing the $q^* + 1$st unit. The fact that our entrepreneur does not produce this unit must mean that her monopolistic behavior prevents society from reaching its maximum potential welfare. If we consider all the units between q^* and q^e, we see that society's maximum willingness to pay is greater than the marginal cost of producing these units. Thus, society loses when our entrepreneur does not produce these units.

The shaded region $\alpha\delta\rho$ in Figure 17.4 is an approximate measure of what is called the **deadweight loss** to society from the monopolistic behavior of our entrepreneur. It represents a dollar measure of the loss that society suffers when units of a good that would benefit it are not produced because of the profit-maximizing motives of the entrepreneur involved. In short, from society's point of view, the monopolist's price is too high and her quantity is too low.

What price is the socially optimal price? To answer this question, we must first define what *socially optimal* means. Consider Figure 17.5, which presents a demand curve and a marginal cost curve for a monopolist.

With the combination of price p and quantity q in Figure 17.5, we see that the good is sold until the point at which the marginal cost of production equals the maximum willingness to pay for that quantity or until the marginal cost curve intersects the demand curve. At that price-quantity combination, consumers buy q units and pay p per unit. In other words, they pay pq to our entrepreneur for the total quantity.

Consider the triangular area (pbd) under the demand curve and above the line pb in Figure 17.5. This area is analogous to the consumer surplus that we encountered in Chapter 4 when we discussed individual demand. However, now it represents a societal surplus that results when people consume q units at price p. In short, it represents the dollar amount of the difference between what people are willing to pay for q units and what they were asked to pay for those units, namely pq. To understand this difference, consider the first unit sold. It was sold at a price of p, but the maximum price that society was willing to pay for this unit was τ. Hence, $\tau - p$ represents the amount by which consumers benefited because they were able to purchase the first unit, which they valued at τ, for a price of only p. We can use the same logic to analyze the gains on all units up to q; and by adding these gains, we obtain the triangle pbd. We call the amount represented by this triangle the **societal consumer surplus**, or simply the **consumer surplus**.

The area below the line pb and above the marginal cost curve (above that portion of the marginal cost curve bounded by efb) represents another type of

deadweight loss
The dollar measure of the loss that society suffers when units of a good whose marginal social benefits exceed the marginal social cost of providing them are not produced because of the profit-maximizing motives of the firm involved.

societal consumer surplus
The difference between what the consumers would have been willing to pay for a good and the amount the good is actually being sold for.

Figure 17.5

The Socially Optimal Price.

The price-quantity combination that maximizes the sum of consumer surplus and producer surplus equates marginal cost with price (willingness to pay).

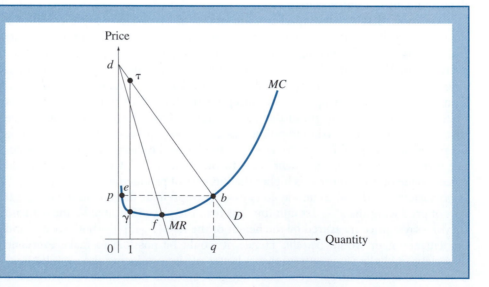

surplus—the producer surplus. It is the amount by which the total revenue received by a firm for units of its product exceeds the total marginal cost of producing those units. For example, consider the first unit produced. The marginal cost of producing that unit is Υ, yet our entrepreneur will receive a price of p for it. Clearly, $p - \Upsilon$ represents the gain to her from the sale of the first unit at price p. By using similar logic for all units up to q, we can define the area below the line pb and above the marginal cost curve as the producer surplus.

A socially optimal price-quantity combination is one that maximizes the sum of the producer surplus and the consumer surplus. For now, let us assume that our entrepreneur must charge a single price to all consumers. In this case, the only single price that can be optimal is the one at which the demand curve intersects the marginal cost curve. This intersection occurs at price p in Figure 17.5. Thus, we can define a socially optimal single price as a price that equals the marginal cost of producing the quantity demanded by the market at that price. These considerations yield our third pricing rule.

producer surplus
The difference between what a producer receives for the goods it produces and the cost of producing them.

socially optimal price-quantity combination
The combination of price and quantity that maximizes the sum of the producer surplus and the consumer surplus.

socially optimal single price
The price that equals the marginal cost of producing the quantity demanded by the market at that price.

SOLVED PROBLEM 17.4

Question (Content Review: The Socially Optimal Single Price)
Assume that you have a market where the demand for the product is linear and equal to $p = 100 - 4p$. Also assume that all firms produce the good using a constant marginal cost function where $MC = 4$, no matter how many units are produced.

a)   What price will maximize the sum of producer and consumer surplus in this market?

Answer
The socially optimal price is where the marginal cost curve intersects the demand curve, or $100 - 4q = 4$. Solving for q, we find that $4q = 96$ and $q = 24$. With this quantity, the associated price is 4 (that is, price is set equal to marginal cost).

b)   What price will be set in the market if a monopolist sets the price to maximize its profits?

Answer
If the market were organized as a monopoly, the monopolist would equate marginal cost to marginal revenue, which is $MR = 100 - 8q$. Thus, a monopolist would solve for q in $100 - 8q = 4 \Rightarrow q = 12$. The associated price is $p = 100 - 4(12) = 52$, which is quite a difference.

c)   What is the loss in consumer surplus resulting from the monopoly?

Answer
To solve for the loss in consumer surplus, let us look at Figure 17.6.

In this figure, we see the demand curve and two associated prices and quantities. At the socially optimal price and quantity, we see that the consumer surplus described is the area of triangle abc. However, this triangle has a base of 24 and a height of $\$100 - \$4 = \$96$, so the area of the triangle (the consumer surplus) is $area = \frac{1}{2}(\$96)(24) = \$1,152$. The consumer surplus existing after the monopoly price is the area of triangle dec. This triangle has a base of 12 and a height of $\$100 - \$52 = \$48$. So its area is $area = \frac{1}{2}(12)(\$48) = \$288$, and the loss of consumer surplus is the difference in these two areas, or $\$1,152 - \$288 = \$864$.

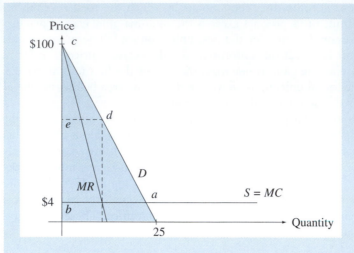

Figure 17.6

Demand and Associated Marginal Revenue.

The optimal quantity is where the demand curve cuts the *MC* curve.

Pricing Rule 3: The Socially Optimal Single Price. If a monopolist must charge one price to all consumers, then the price that maximizes the sum of the consumer surplus and the producer surplus must be the price at which the demand curve intersects the marginal cost curve.

It is clear that our entrepreneur's effort to maximize her own profit does not produce the result that is best for society. The reason is simple. Her objective is not to maximize the benefit to society but rather to make as much money for herself as possible. She does this by selling that quantity at which her *private* marginal cost equals her *private* marginal revenue. If she wanted to maximize the benefit to society, she would choose the quantity at which her private marginal cost of producing equals society's marginal benefit from having one more unit produced. This quantity would occur at the point where the demand curve intersects the marginal cost curve because the demand curve indicates the marginal benefit to society of each additional unit (society's maximum willingness to pay for each unit).

We can now see the disadvantages of monopoly to society. Monopoly results in prices that are too high and quantities that are too low from society's point of view.

MEDIA NOTE

MONOPOLIES

Telecom laws in the United States are mirrors of the times in which they were set. Since 1934, there has been only one major overhaul in telecom legislation. The Telecommunications Act of 1996 required local-phone monopolies to open their systems to rivals in order to gain permission to offer long-distance services. The act also allowed for cable vs. phone competition, a competition we see today where cable companies are offering phone services to their subscribers.

During these years of competition, technologies have evolved and changed the way people communicate with each other. More cell phones are used today than regular land lines at home; broadband Internet access enables long-distance calls at virtually no cost; and phone companies plan to offer video on phone lines. These changes have led the phone companies to call for a change in the regulation because they feel they are at a competitive disadvantage due to the open network requirement.

The change sought is to reverse the separation between regular phone services and other services that the 1996 act designed. Also, the new regulation will have to take into consideration all the new technologies that have come into being and reinterpret the telecom market. This will put the phone companies at the same level as the cable and other communication companies, something that the cable firms aren't really happy with.

Source: Adapted from "Phone Companies Push Telecom Overhaul; Industry Wants Revamp of 1996 Act to Level Playing Field, but Cable Firms Are Cautious," as appeared in the *Wall Street Journal,* January 18, 2005

Question (Application and Extension: The Socially Optimal Price and Quantity)

On Groundhog Island, there is only one source of clean water. The well is owned by Mr. Robinson, who bottles the water for the consumption of the island's occupants. The average and marginal cost of bottling a 5-gallon jug of water is $10. (Average and marginal cost can be the same when there is no fixed cost.) The demand for bottled water on Groundhog Island is $q = 100 - \frac{1}{2}p$, where q is the number of jugs and p is the price for a jug of water.

   a)   Calculate the socially optimal price and quantity of water.

Answer

To calculate the socially optimal price and quantity for water, we must find the point at which the demand function equals the marginal cost. Inverting the demand curve and setting it equal to the $10 marginal cost, we get

$$200 - 2q = 10$$
$$q = 95$$

   Substituting back into the demand curve, we see that $p = 10$. Thus, the socially optimal price is $10. There is no producer surplus here; the marginal cost curve is flat and the price is set at marginal cost, so the only surplus in this economy goes to the consumers. At a price of $200, consumers demand exactly 0 jugs of water. Thus, consumer surplus is $\frac{1}{2}(190)(95) = 9,025$.

   b)   What would the price and quantity be if Mr. Robinson were a monopolist and acted accordingly?

Answer

If Mr. Robinson acted like a monopolist, he would price his water differently. The monopolist equates marginal revenue to marginal cost. Because the demand curve is linear, we know that the marginal revenue curve has a slope that is twice as steep, so that

$$MR = 200 - 4q$$

Setting this equal to marginal cost, we see that

$$200 - 4q = 10$$
$$q = 47.5$$
$$p = 105$$

Therefore, a monopolist would sell only 47.5 jugs of water and would charge $105 per jug. At this price and quantity, producer surplus grows to $(95)(47.5) = 4,512.5$, while consumer surplus falls to $\frac{1}{2}(95)(47.5) = 2,256.25$, with overall surplus dropping to 6,768.75.

SOLVED PROBLEM 17.5

Pricing and Profits

We now have all the information we need to determine whether our entrepreneur's jam-making operation will be profitable. We know that she will produce q^* units of jam and charge p^* for each unit. At this quantity and price, can she cover her costs? Will she make a profit? Will her monopoly position in the jam market bring extra-normal profits? We have already defined profit as the difference between revenue and costs. Alternatively, we can say that our entrepreneur will make a positive profit if the price she receives from selling a certain number of units exceeds the average cost of producing those units. If the average cost includes all of the fixed costs of production and our entrepreneur's opportunity cost, then she will earn an extra-normal profit on each unit she sells. The total amount of the extra-normal profit will be equal to the quantity sold times the excess of price over average cost.

$$\text{Extra} - \text{normal profit} = (\text{price} - \text{average cost})(\text{quantity})$$

To see whether our entrepreneur will earn an extra-normal profit from her jam-making operation, we will use information about price and quantity from Figure 17.5 and add information about her average cost function. Then we can determine whether the profit-maximizing price exceeds or falls short of the average cost of production. Figure 17.7 depicts the profitability of jam production.

In Figure 17.7, we see our entrepreneur's demand and marginal cost curves along with the result of her profit-maximizing strategy of selling q^* units at price p^*. This strategy produces total revenue from sales of p^*q^*, which is represented by the rectangle p^*gq^*0. Her average cost for producing q^* units is measured by the height of the line p^*d above the quantity q^*. Note that the average cost of producing q^* units is greater than their price, which means that there is a loss on each unit. The total cost of producing q^* units is q^*e. This amount is represented by the rectangle edq^*0. The total loss incurred is represented by the rectangle $edgp^*$.

Obviously, our entrepreneur's first plan for producing and selling jam is a failure. At her profit-maximizing price, she is not able to cover her fixed production costs and the opportunity cost of her time.

See the Resolving Experimental Teaser 17 feature at the end of this section for a study that discusses how the degree of monopoly power varies with the way a monopolistic market is organized.

MEDIA NOTE

PRICE DISCRIMINATION

The best example for third-degree price discrimination can be found in the prescription drugs market. For example, an arthritis medicine costs $108 when sold to humans, while dog owners can buy the same drug for $38. Another example is that an AIDS drug costs $18 in the United States, while costumers in Uganda pay $9. (Meanwhile, the generic version is sold for $1.50 in Brazil).

This pricing structure is due partly to the cost structure of the drug companies and partly to the bargaining power of the customers. Although research for a new drug can cost millions of dollars, the marginal cost of producing one more pill is very small. While the temptation to cut prices to the cost exists, cutting prices across the board will lead the pharmaceutical companies to lose money in the long run on the development of new drugs. Here is where differential pricing comes into play.

One reason for the fact that prices in the United States are higher than those in Europe is the structure of the health care systems. While in European countries there is one governmental health care provider that bargains over prices and is thus able to reduce them, in the United States the health

care system is fragmented across various agencies. This lowers the customers' bargaining power.

The other reason for the high prices is the sheer size of the American market. Imagine that there are only two countries—the United States and Uganda—both in need of an AIDS medicine, which is sold at $18 in the United States and $9 in Uganda. Now let us assume that politicians have forced the drug companies to charge only one price. What price will the drug company choose? More likely the price will be closer to $18 than $9. The reason is that the market in the United States is much larger, and reducing the price to $9 in the United States will cause a higher loss of revenues than increasing the price to $18 in Uganda.

This example can work in the other direction as well. Take the same example as before, but instead of an AIDS drug, the drug will be an antimalarial medicine. In this case, if there will be only one price, the price will likely be closer to $9 because the market in Uganda is much larger for this type of drug than the U.S. market.

In essence, when companies engage in third-degree price discrimination, the customers paying the higher price are sure that if the practice is abolished and the companies are forced to charge one price, that price will be the lower one. That is not necessarily true.

Source: Adapted from "Examining Differences in Drug Prices," as appeared in the *New York Times*, September 21, 2000

Two-Part Tariffs and Nonuniform Pricing

Clearly, our entrepreneur needs a new business plan for her jam-making operation. She therefore decides to obtain advice from a consulting firm.

To understand the logic behind the two-part tariff system that the consultants are proposing, consider Figure 17.8.

two-part tariff

A two-part tariff is a price discrimination technique in which the price of a product or service is composed of two parts—a lump-sum fee as well as a per-unit charge.

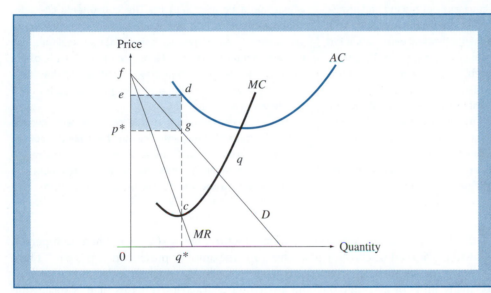

Figure 17.7

The Profitability of Production.

If the price that equates marginal cost and marginal revenue is below the average cost, the entrepreneur cannot operate profitably while charging a single price to all consumers.

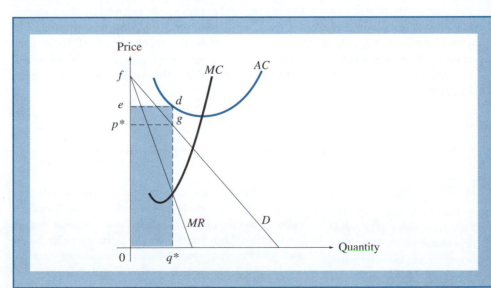

Figure 17.8

Two-Part Tariffs.

The producer charges each consumer, in addition to the per-unit price, a fixed fee equal to her share of the consumer surplus.

The diagram in Figure 17.8 is almost identical to the one in Figure 17.7. We see the uniform price strategy of the monopolist at (p^*, q^*). The loss incurred by this strategy is represented by the rectangle $edgp^*$. Note, however, that at the price of p^*, there is a consumer surplus (CS) as represented by the triangle fgp^*. Because only one price is charged, the people who actually buy the good pay less for it than they are willing to pay. The consumer surplus is a dollar measure of the benefit these people receive from consuming the good at price p^*. Our monopolist would like to capture this surplus for herself. One way to do so is to charge each of these people an equal share of the consumer surplus as a fee in addition to the per-unit price they must pay.

CONSULTING REPORT   17.1

USING TWO-PART TARIFFS TO INCREASE PROFITABILITY

After the consultants study the issues of pricing and profitability at our entrepreneur's firm, they tell her that there is *no single price* that she can charge that will earn a profit for the firm. She needs a different pricing structure. They suggest a two-part tariff instead of the uniform pricing structure that she had previously planned to use.

The consultants explain that the two-part tariff system is simple. Rather than charging just a price of p^* for each unit, she will charge a fixed fee and a per-unit price. All consumers must pay the fixed fee before they are allowed to buy any units of the good. So for each jar of jam they want to buy, they will pay a per-unit price of p', which might be less than p^*. The consultants cite telephone companies that provide local service as an example of firms with monopoly power that successfully use the two-part tariff system. (Note that in most areas of the United States today, people pay a fixed fee for their telephone service each month and then pay a price for each call they make.)

The consultants state that this two-part tariff system should be better for our entrepreneur because the combination of a fixed fee and a per-unit price will allow her to capture more revenue. With the additional revenue, she should be able to cover her costs and earn a profit. ●

If N people consume jam at price p^*, let the fee $= (CS/N)$. Then each person will pay a total of $CS/N + p^*q$, where q is the amount purchased at price p^*. Thus, consumers will be charged the fixed fee of CS/N, which is independent of how many units of jam they buy and a per-unit charge of p^*. If this plan is successful, our entrepreneur will capture the entire surplus previously enjoyed by the consumers plus revenue of p^*q^* for all units sold. Her total revenue will therefore be given by the area fgq^*0, and her total cost will be the rectangle edg^*0. If the total revenue is greater than the total cost, the two-part tariff system should allow our entrepreneur to earn an extra-normal profit. We will assume that this is what happens.

MEDIA NOTE

PRICE DISCRIMINATION I

Most consumers applauded the arrival of Priceline.com. The idea of setting your own price for a good seems to be a gold mine for consumers. Ironically, Priceline.com works in a way that has many of the features of a very clever price discrimination device. Let's look at how it works.

With Priceline you name your price. That sounds great since it seems to put the buyer in the driver's seat. Actually, it might do just the opposite since it allows the seller to price discriminate. When you name your price, the seller has already told Priceline what minimum price he is willing to accept but you do not know that price. Hence, different buyers will state different prices and will buy at different prices as well. But this is merely a clever way to perform what we have called third-degree price discrimination.

As you recall, for this to work, there are two requirements. One is a way to smoke out the different amounts different people are willing to pay. The second is to make arbitrage difficult. This is just what Priceline offers sellers. Airlines are a good example. As you know when you fly it is not unlikely that the person sitting next to you paid a different fare. The

airlines have historically done this separating customers into different groups (based on their elasticity of demand) and selling to each group at a different price. Priceline accomplishes the same thing much more simply. It finds out how much each customer is willing to pay by simply asking them. And you thought you were clever in using them.

Source: Adapted from "The Economics of Priceline," as appeared on Slate.com, May 19, 2000

Criticisms of the Two-Part Tariff System

While the two-part tariff system sounds good, there are some problems with it. For example, it will discourage sales to certain types of people. Every society contains many different types of people. However, for the sake of simplicity, let us assume that there are only two types in our primitive society, Geoffreys and Elizabeths, and that they differ in their level of income and their taste for jam. If they are asked to pay the same fee and the same per-unit price, some of these people will decide not to consume any jam at all because they cannot afford the high cost or because their liking for jam is not strong enough to induce them to buy if the cost is high. Under these circumstances, institution of a two-part tariff may actually cause revenue to fall. Let us now consider Figure 17.9, which illustrates such a situation.

In Figure 17.9, we see a demand curve for the Elizabeths and a demand curve for the Geoffreys. The demand curve for the Elizabeths is to the right of the one for the Geoffreys, and we will interpret this arrangement to mean that the Elizabeths are willing to pay more for any quantity of jam than the Geoffreys are. In the uniform pricing plan devised by our entrepreneur, each person will be able to buy the good for a price of p^*. At that price, the Geoffreys will consume q_1 units and will obtain the consumer surplus represented by area A. The Elizabeths will

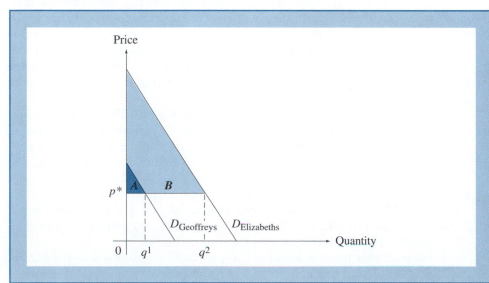

Figure 17.9

Consumer Resistance to the Two-Part Tariff.

The Elizabeths are willing to pay the fixed fee, but the Geoffreys are not.

consume q_2 units and will obtain the consumer surplus represented by areas A and B. The two-part tariff plan proposed by the consultants will be beneficial to the Geoffreys and the Elizabeths only if the fee they pay, CS/N, is less than the consumer surplus they enjoy by buying the good at price p^*. In other words, the Geoffreys will be better off consuming the good under the two-part tariff plan only if $CS/N < A$, whereas the Elizabeths will be better off only if $CS/N < A + B$. However, if the fee is set at CS/N, it will be too high to allow the Geoffreys to benefit from consuming the good. They will all forgo consumption rather than buy the good on these terms. The reason is simple. Say there are $N/2$ Elizabeths and $N/2$ Geoffreys. At price p^*, each Geoffrey enjoys a consumer surplus equal to area A, while each Elizabeth enjoys a consumer surplus equal to areas $A + B$. The total consumer surplus is therefore $CS = (N/2)A + (N/2)(A + B)$. Because the fee is set at CS/N, each person will pay the following:

$$\text{Fee} = \frac{CS}{N} = \frac{\left[\dfrac{N}{2}(A) + \dfrac{N}{2}(A + B)\right]}{N} = A + \left(\frac{N}{2N}\right)B = A + \frac{B}{2}$$

Note that the fee charged will then be greater than the consumer surplus of A enjoyed by the Geoffreys under the uniform pricing plan. Obviously, if our entrepreneur uses the two-part tariff plan, no Geoffrey will choose to consume jam. They will be better off not buying it. The situation with the Elizabeths is different. They can benefit from the two-part tariff plan because the fee is less than their consumer surplus of $A + B$. However, it is unlikely that our entrepreneur can make money with this plan, because all the Geoffreys, who are one half of the population, will refuse to buy her goods.

One possible remedy to this problem is to charge different fees to different types of people. Why not charge the Elizabeths the higher fee and the Geoffreys a lower fee? For example, charge each Geoffrey a fee of A and each Elizabeth a fee of $A + B$. If our entrepreneur keeps the per-unit price at p^*, she should be able to capture the entire consumer surplus and still retain the Geoffreys as consumers of jam (or at least have them in a state of indifference between buying and not buying, in which case we can assume that they will buy).

But why stop there in making the two-part tariff system flexible? We know that at p^*, the monopoly price, there are people ready to pay more than the marginal cost for additional units of the good. Why not decrease the price below p^*, attract new consumers, and then increase the fee to capture the new consumer surplus generated by the lower price? In fact, it may even be possible for our entrepreneur to charge the socially optimal price of p if she charges a large enough fee so that she can make a profit. To see how this pricing arrangement might be possible, let us consider Figure 17.10.

In Figure 17.10, we see the same situation as in Figure 17.7, except for the introduction of the lower per-unit price. At this price of p, there are losses equal to the areas $E + C$. If the fee is set so as to capture all the consumer surplus under the demand curve, then our entrepreneur will receive an amount of dollars equal to the area acp. If this area is greater than the loss incurred by selling q units at a price of p (areas $E + C$), then it will be possible for our entrepreneur to provide the socially optimal level of output and the socially optimal price and still make a profit. In fact, although society benefits from this arrangement, our entrepreneur benefits even more because she obtains the entire consumer surplus.

There is another problem with the two-part tariff system. Assume that our entrepreneur uses a plan that consists of a per-unit price of p and fees of A for the Geoffreys and $A + B$ for the Elizabeths. The Geoffreys consume q' units, and the

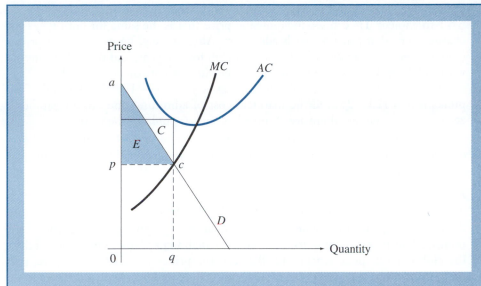

Figure 17.10

Two-Part Tariffs at the Socially Optimal Price.

A two-part tariff enables the monopolist to earn positive profits under marginal-cost pricing.

Elizabeths consume q'' units, with $q'' > q'$. Therefore, the cost of each unit of jam to the Geoffreys is $(A + pq')\, q'$, while the cost to the Elizabeths is $(A + B + pq'')q''$. It is very unlikely that the costs for each group will be equal under this plan. Assume that the cost per unit is less for the Geoffreys than for the Elizabeths. If this is the case and if it is costless for the Geoffreys to contact the Elizabeths and resell units that they buy, the Geoffreys will say to the Elizabeths, "Don't buy any jam from our entrepreneur. We will give you a better deal. Because the cost to us is less than it is to you, we will buy all the jam you want and then resell it to you at a lower price than she will charge you."

Note that as the quantity bought by a Geoffrey becomes large, the cost to him approaches p per unit because the fee, which is fixed, is now spread over many more units. Under such conditions, the two-part tariff system will fail. Our entrepreneur will not be able to keep the two groups separate and maintain different price structures for them. Therefore, the revenue received from the sale of each unit will approach a uniform price of p. This is an example of the arbitrage pricing result that we discussed earlier.

In regard to arbitrage pricing, it is now clear that the situation at the jam-making firm is very different from the situation of local telephone companies, which the consultants cited as successful users of the two-part tariff system. Although some classes of consumers may receive lower rates for telephone service, there is little chance that such consumers can benefit by reselling the services to other consumers who pay higher rates. Obviously, most people want their own telephones so that they can make and receive calls in their home. It is not practical for them to visit someone else's home every time they must make a call. Therefore, arbitrage pricing does not undermine the two-part tariff system at local telephone companies.

Question (Application and Extension: Two-Part Tariffs)

John is thinking of opening a dance club in a small college town. There are two types of students in the town—the punks and the preppies—and each type has different demand curves for attending his club. He is not allowed to price

SOLVED PROBLEM 17.6

discriminate, so he can't charge the preppies differently than the punks. Thus, he has two choices. He can set an admission price that is the same for both types and charge them that price for each admission. Alternatively, he can create a private club, charge each person a fee to join the club for the year, and then allow anyone with a club card in free. (You can go into the club only if you are a member.)

Assume that the demand of the preppies is $q = 120 - 10p$, the demand of the punks is $q = 120 - 2p$, and the marginal cost of admitting one more customer is zero. Also assume that there are 20 preppies and 20 punks in the town.

a)   What is the profit-maximizing price and quantity for John if he simply charges one price for each admission? How many preppies will be in the club and how many punks?

Answer

To find the profit-maximizing price for John, we first need to construct his total demand curve, which is the demand he faces after aggregating all the preppies and punks. Note that according to the preppie demand curve, there is no demand for the club once its price reaches 12. Between the prices 12 and 60, therefore, only the punks will go. For prices below 12, both will go and we simply need to add the two demands to get the total demand curve for all prices between 0 and 12. Hence, the demand curve can be written as

$$Q = 20(120 - 2p) \text{ if } 12 \leq p \leq 60, \text{ and}$$
$$Q = 20(120 - 2p) + 20(120 - 10p) \text{ if } 0 \leq p \leq 12.$$

To find the profit-maximizing price, note that if we set a price in the interval between 12 and 60, then the demand would be $p = \frac{2400}{40} - \frac{Q}{40} = 60 - \frac{Q}{40}$, and the associated marginal revenue curve would be $MR = 60 - \frac{Q}{20}$ because marginal revenue falls at twice the rate of the demand curve for a linear demand curve. Hence, the optimal price would be 30 because that would equate the marginal revenue to the marginal cost, which we have assumed is zero. At $p = 30$, only the punks would come to the club. They would each come 60 times but because there are 20 of them, there would be 1,200 trips to the club, which at \$30 each would yield a profit of \$36,000 (cost is zero). If a price below 12 were set, then the demand curve faced would be $Q = 20(120 - 2p) + 20(120 - 10p) = 2,400 - 200p + 2,400 - 40p = 4,800 - 240p$. By inverting this function, we see that $240p = 4,800 - Q \Rightarrow p = \frac{4800}{240} - \frac{Q}{240} = 20 - \frac{Q}{240}$. The associated marginal revenue curve is $MR = 20 - \frac{Q}{120}$. Setting this equal to 0 implies $Q = 2,400$ and $p = 10$. (Remember $p = 20 - \frac{Q}{240}$, which at $Q = 2,400 \Rightarrow p = 10$.) This, however, yields a profit of only \$24,000 = \$10 \cdot 2,400. So $p = 30$ is the best price. At that price, only the punks go to the club and each punk would make 60 trips.

b)   Say that John wants to set up a club and charge a yearly fee. After the fee, he will admit each person for free. If he sets a fee of \$600 per year, how many preppies will join? How many punks will join? How much money will he collect? Will he be better off?

Answer

If admissions were free but each person had to pay \$600 for a club membership, then any preppies or punks would join only if the value of the consumer surplus received by being able to be admitted to the club at a zero price were greater than the club membership fee.

To make this comparison, let's draw the demand curves for the preppies and the punks. In Figure 17.11(a) we see the demand curve for the preppies. Note that at a zero price, each preppie would go to the club 120 times, while if the price

Figure 17.11

Demand of Preppies and Punks.

The areas of these triangles represent maximum willingness to pay to join the club.

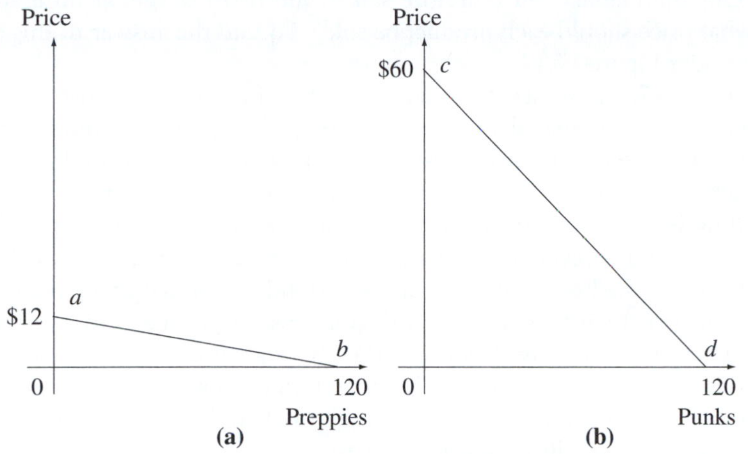

(a)   (b)

were above 12, no preppies would go. The consumer surplus that any preppy would get from going to the club 120 times at $p = 0$ is, therefore, the area of the triangle $0ab = \frac{1}{2}(12)(120) = 720$. In other words, the most a preppy would pay to join the club and be allowed to go there for free would be $720, which is greater than the $600 being charged. Hence, preppies would join and make 120 trips. The punks, as shown in Figure 17.11(b), would perform a similar calculation, and we would find that their consumer surplus would be the area of triangle $0cd = \frac{1}{2}(120)(60) = 3,600$. Thus, the punks would eagerly join because they value their 120 visits per year at $3,600 and are being asked to pay only $600 to join. The total revenue of the club owner is $24,000 = 20 \cdot \$600 + 20 \cdot \$600$.

Obviously, this pricing scheme is not beneficial for the club because, using one price, it earned $36,000.

Price Discrimination

We now know that the two-part tariff system will fail in our entrepreneur's jam-making firm because of arbitrage pricing and the fact that consumers cannot be prevented from reselling the goods to one another. Is there some way to overcome these problems? What if consumers have different tastes in jam? For example, suppose that the Geoffreys take the existing jam and add apples to it while the Elizabeths add raspberries to it. Also suppose that the Geoffreys hate the Elizabeth-style jam, and the Elizabeths hate the Geoffrey-style jam. In such a situation, our monopolist can *separate* the two groups of consumers into different markets and thereby prevent the arbitrage that made it impossible for her to earn a profit with the two-part tariff system.

Let us say that instead of producing one type of jam that contains an equal amount of both fruits, our monopolist decides to create two products—apple jam and raspberry jam. She will make the two types of jam from an identical blend of fruits, but at the end of the production process, she will costlessly add a little more of one fruit or the other to produce the different flavors. Our monopolist will sell the apple jam to the Geoffreys and the raspberry jam to the Elizabeths. Because the two products are distinct and each is tailored to the tastes of a particular group, no Elizabeth or Geoffrey will be able to resell jam to someone in the other group. Our monopolist can therefore sell to the two markets at different prices. But at what price should each product be sold? To find the answer to this question, let us consider Figure 17.12.

In Figure 17.12, we see the demand curves for the two types of jam. The apple jam is the one created to suit the tastes of the Geoffreys, and the raspberry jam is the one created to suit the tastes of the Elizabeths. Associated with each demand curve is another curve that indicates the marginal revenue to be derived from selling various amounts of jam in each market. Figure 17.12 also includes the firm's total marginal revenue curve and its marginal cost curve. The total marginal revenue curve is the horizontal sum of the two individual marginal revenue curves. The marginal cost curve depicts the marginal cost of producing one more unit of jam *no matter where it is eventually sold*. (We have assumed that adding apples and raspberries is a cost-free process.) The first question that must now be considered is how much jam to produce and sell in each market. The answer to this question is summarized by the following pricing rule.

> **Pricing Rule 4: Price Discrimination in Segmented Markets**. A good should be produced until the point at which the marginal revenue received from selling it in any market is equal to the marginal cost of producing it. At the profit-maximizing quantity, the marginal revenue from selling the last unit in one market should be equal to the marginal revenue from selling the last unit in the other market (and equal to the common marginal cost).

To understand this rule, let us look at an example. We will assume that our entrepreneur sells jam in each market in such a way that the marginal revenue she receives from selling the last unit of apple jam to the Geoffreys is greater than the marginal revenue she receives from selling the last unit of raspberry jam to the Elizabeths. We will also assume that the marginal revenue obtained from selling the last unit of apple jam to the Geoffreys is $5, but the marginal revenue obtained from selling the last unit of raspberry jam to the Elizabeths is only $2. Then if our entrepreneur transfers one unit of sales from the raspberry jam market to the apple jam market, she will have a net gain of $3. She will lose $2 by reducing her sales in the raspberry jam market but will gain $5 by increasing her sales in the apple jam market. Whatever the marginal cost of producing that unit, she is better off selling it in the apple jam market rather than in the raspberry jam market.

In Figure 17.12, we see the optimal quantity to produce depicted by q^o and defined by point o, where the marginal cost curve intersects the total marginal revenue curve. This intersection determines the marginal cost associated with the optimal quantity of each good. Therefore, to find the optimal quantity to sell in each market, our entrepreneur simply looks for the quantity that equates the marginal revenue for the good to its associated marginal cost. In the apple jam market, which consists of the Geoffreys, we see that q^g units will be sold; and in the raspberry jam market, which consists of the Elizabeths, we see that q^e units will be sold. To find the optimal price in each market, our entrepreneur simply sets the price at the height of the demand curve above the desired quantity. In the apple jam (Geoffrey) market, the price will be set at p^g, and in the raspberry jam (Elizabeth) market, the price will be set at p^e. Algebraically, the pricing rule is as follows:

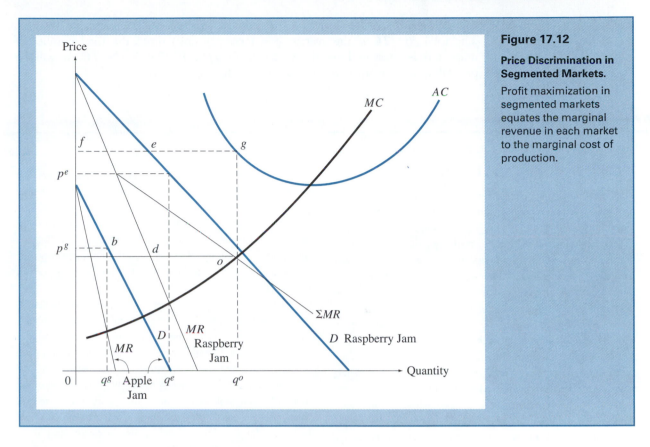

Figure 17.12

Price Discrimination in Segmented Markets.

Profit maximization in segmented markets equates the marginal revenue in each market to the marginal cost of production.

$MR^e = MR^g = MC^t$, where MR^e and MR^g are the marginal revenues in the raspberry jam (Elizabeth) market and in the apple jam (Geoffrey) market, respectively, and MC^t is the marginal cost in the total market (producing $q^e + q^g$). However, from the definition of marginal revenue, we know that $MR^e = p^e(1 - 1/|\xi^e|)$, and $MR^g = p^g(1 - 1/|\xi^g|)$. Hence, $p^e = MR^e(1 - 1/|\xi^e|)$ and $p^g = MR^g(1 - 1/|\xi^g|)$.

Note that the more inelastic the demand for a product in any market is (that is, the smaller ξ is), the higher the price will be in that market. We will refer to the practice of charging different prices to different consumers as **price discrimination**. Hence, a price-discriminating monopolist sets prices that vary inversely with the absolute value of the elasticity of demand. This pricing rule applies whether the entrepreneur is selling different goods in different markets, as in the case of our jam maker, or the same good in different markets. Of course, we know from our study of arbitrage pricing that price discrimination in the latter situation depends on the nonexistence of arbitrage opportunities. Otherwise, by buying in the low-price market and selling in the high-price market, arbitrageurs would force the monopolist to set a uniform price. Therefore, when we refer to price discrimination, we will be assuming **segmented markets**—markets whose physical separation or other characteristics make arbitrage impossible.

Will our entrepreneur's latest pricing strategy, which is based on price discrimination, make it profitable for her to produce jam? Let us look again at Figure 17.12 and find the answer by comparing the total revenue generated by this price-discrimination plan with the total cost of producing q^o units. As we see from the diagram, the total revenue generated from the apple jam (Geoffrey) market is $R^g = p^g \cdot q^g$ and is depicted by the rectangle $0q^g bq^g 0$. The total revenue generated by the raspberry

price discrimination
The practice of charging different prices to different consumers.

segmented markets
Markets whose physical separation or other characteristics make arbitrage impossible.

jam (Elizabeth) market is $R^e = p^e \cdot q^e$ and is depicted by the rectangle $0q^e d^e f 0$. The total cost TC is the average cost (cost per unit) times the total number of units and is measured by the rectangle $0q^o g f 0$. If $R^e + R^g \geq TC$, it will be profitable for our entrepreneur to carry on her operations.

MEDIA NOTE

PRICE DISCRIMINATION II

The new electronic age has brought with it many benefits, but there are also some downsides. One is the practice of "dynamic pricing." While in the good old days, firms practiced price discrimination as best they could by judging the types of customer they were dealing with, the new electronic age has made the practice much more sophisticated. For example, it has recently come to light that Amazon.com has been charging different customers different prices (for movies, not books). Customers accused the online retailer of tailoring its prices to the consumers' characteristics.

As described by Paul Krugman, dynamic pricing is a practice used by electronic Web sites to price discriminate. When you log on, the computer checks out your "electronic fingerprint" to look at your previous purchases, where you live, etc., and sizes you up as to whether you are likely to balk at a high price. If you look like a person with low demand elasticity, you get charged a high price.

The need for price discrimination comes from the fact that books must be sold at a price well above the actual cost of producing one more copy—their marginal cost—because if

they did not, the publisher could not cover its fixed costs. But when the price is set high, the publisher loses many potential customers.

In the old days, publishers used to deal with this in a number of ways. One was to issue a hard copy of the book first at a high price and soak up all the sales to those impatient people who could not wait until the eventual lower-priced paperback was issued.

E-commerce, however, offers new price discrimination techniques. Using a person's electronic fingerprint, a Web site can make a guess as to whether the person will be repelled by a high price or not. Using that information, it can tailor a price to each person separately. Krugman argues that this may be good for everyone. Publishers would be willing to publish more titles, and book buyers who would otherwise have delayed their purchases until the thing came out in paperback would be spared the wait. He also says it may be fair because those who pay more actually subsidize those less fortunate ones who want to read the book but can only afford a lower price.

Source: Adapted from "What Price Fairness?" as appeared in the *New York Times,* October 4, 2000

SOLVED PROBLEM 17.7

Question (Application and Extension: Price Discrimination)

Sal sells T-shirts for the Rolling Stones concert. He sells them at a retirement community and a high school. The people in the retirement community really love the Rolling Stones and have a lower price sensitivity than do the teenagers, who have more substitutes and less money. Assume that the marginal cost of producing each T-shirt is $2.00 and that Sal sells the shirts for $6.00 at the retirement home and $3.33 at the high school. At these prices, is Sal maximizing his profits if the elasticity of demand of the senior citizens is -1.5 and the elasticity of demand of the teenagers is -2.5?

Answer

Yes. To maximize profits, Sal must equate the marginal revenue in each market to the common marginal cost. Given a demand curve, the marginal revenue associated with it at any point is $MR = p[1 - (1/|\xi|)]$, where ξ is the elasticity of demand. Let p_r and p_{hs} be the prices charged in the retirement and high school markets, respectively; let MR_r and MR_{hs} be the associated marginal revenues; and let ξ_r and ξ_{hs} be the elasticities of demand in each market. Then in order for Sal to be profit maximizing, he must set prices such that $MR_r = p_r[1 - (1/|\xi_r|)] = MR_{bs} = p_{bs}[1 - (1/|\xi_{bs}|)] = MC = 2$. Using the values assumed in the problem, we see that $MR_{bs} = 6[1 - (1/|1.5|)] = MR_r = 3.33[1 - (1/|2.5|)] = 2 = MC$, which satisfies our maximizing condition.

Question (Application and Extension: Segmented Markets)

SOLVED
PROBLEM
17.8

The Apex Corporation, a monopolist in the waterproof paint market, sells its water-resistant paint to two distinct types of customers for two distinct purposes. One type of customer buys the paint for painting kitchens and bathrooms. The other type of customer builds model ships and uses Apex's paint to paint the hulls of the ships. To Apex, the paint is the same product regardless of the market to which Apex sells it, and the marginal cost of its production is $5 per gallon. Apex is able to successfully segment its markets.

The demand for paint for kitchens and bathrooms is

$$D_K = 5,000 - 500p_K$$

where D_K is the demand for paint for kitchens and bathrooms in gallons and p_K is the price. The demand for paint for model ships is

$$D_S = 95 - p_S$$

where D_S is the demand for paint for model ships in gallons and p_S is the price.

If Apex is selling paint to the kitchen and bathroom market at a price of $6 per gallon and at a price of $60 per gallon to the model ship builders, is it maximizing its profits?

Answer

The answer is no; Apex is not maximizing its profits. To maximize profits, Apex must choose quantities to supply each market that equate the marginal revenues it receives in each market to the common marginal cost. To find the marginal revenue, we must invert each demand curve, so

$$p_K = 10 - \frac{q_K}{500}$$
$$p_S = 95 - q_S$$

Now using the rule to find marginal revenue when we have linear demand curves, double the slope and keep the intercept the same:

$$MR_K = 10 - \frac{q_K}{250}$$
$$MR_S = 95 - 2q_S$$

Next, set these marginal revenues equal to marginal cost and solve for quantities in each market:

$$5 = 10 - \frac{q_K}{250}$$
$$q_K = 1,250$$
$$5 = 95 - 2q_S$$
$$q_S = 45$$

Plugging these quantities back into their respective demand curves, we get the profit-maximizing prices Apex should charge in each market:

$$p_K = 10 - \frac{1,250}{500} = \$7.50$$
$$p_S = 95 - 45 = \$50$$

Thus, Apex should sell its paint to the kitchen and bathroom painters at a price of $7.50 per gallon and at a price of $50 per gallon to the model ship builders.

Conclusion

Even though it is a monopoly, the first entrepreneurial venture in our primitive society has had difficulty earning a profit. The problem stems from the firm's high average costs. We investigated several different pricing strategies to see if any of them could overcome this problem. We were looking for a pricing strategy that would provide enough revenue to cover the firm's cost of production and the opportunity cost of the entrepreneur's time and also allow the firm to make a profit.

We found that uniform pricing failed to generate positive profits, but a two-part tariff plan seemed promising. However, the arbitrage pricing result caused the firm to lose money with the two-part tariff system. Only after our entrepreneur changed her product line in order to create segmented markets for the goods and then instituted a price-discrimination plan was the firm able to earn a profit.

In the next chapter, we will turn our attention to another type of monopoly: a natural monopoly. We will investigate the economic effects of such a monopoly and the attempts of society to regulate this form of monopoly.

Summary

This chapter has examined the pricing and quantity-setting policies of a monopolist. We saw that in a nonsegmented market, the arbitrage pricing result forces the monopolist to charge a uniform price for all goods sold. When a monopolist must sell at a uniform price, two pricing rules describe how such a price will be determined: the elasticity rule and the profit-maximizing rule.

We also discussed why the profit-maximizing prices set by a monopolist would not be optimal from a societal point of view. We saw that such prices lead to a decrease in the amount of consumer surplus and producer surplus generated when prices are set at marginal cost. In fact, monopoly produces a deadweight loss, a loss in consumer surplus not captured by the monopolist. From society's perspective, monopolistic behavior results in prices that are too high and quantities that are too low.

RESOLVING
TEASER 17

MONOPOLY AND INSTITUTIONS

Vernon Smith investigates the various ways we can organize monopolistic markets. In his experiment, he recruits 6 subjects and designates 1 subject to be a seller and the 5 other subjects to be buyers, each having a demand for 2 units of the good. Each buyer is given a resale value for the goods: If he or she purchases a good during the market operation, the experimenter stands willing to pay an amount of money to redeem that good. For example, assume that you are buyer 2 in the market and have a

(Continued)

demand for 2 units. You might be told that if you buy 2 units, you will be paid a redemption price of $150 for the first unit you buy and $60 for the second unit. Hence, if you buy the first unit at a price of $50 and the second at a price of $40, your final payoff from the market will be $\pi_{buyer} = (150 - 50) + (60 - 40) = 120$, which represents the amount of consumer surplus you have received from your two purchases. (Remember that consumer surplus is the difference between what you are willing to pay for a good and what the market requires that you pay.) The monopolist, on the other hand, is given a marginal cost schedule (there is no fixed cost) indicating the cost of producing each additional unit. If the monopolist sells, for example, 5 units of the good each at the posted price of $50, and the marginal cost of each of the units is $10 for the first, $15 for the second, $20 for the third, $25 for the fourth, and $30 for the fifth, then his or her profits from the market will be the sum of the differences between the price he or she receives for each unit of the good sold and its marginal cost of production; that is, $\pi_{monopolist} = (50 - 10) + (50 - 15) + (50 - 20) + (50 - 25) + (50 - 30) = 150$.

In the Smith experiment, buyers and sellers are given the marginal cost functions and resale values shown in Table 17.2.

These costs and resale values generate the supply and demand diagrams on the left-hand side of Figures 17.13(a) and 17.13(b).

Note that in the diagram we have located both the monopoly price and the quantity defined by the intersection of the marginal cost and marginal revenue curves and the competitive price and quantity defined by the intersection of supply and demand. Given this market setting, Smith allows trade using a number of different trading institutions. In one called the double oral auction, instead of the monopolist simply posting a price and presenting the buyers with a take-it-or-leave-it ultimatum, the goods are auctioned one at a time. As each good is brought up, both buyers and the seller yell out bids and asks. More precisely, any buyer can yell out how much he is willing to pay for the good, and the monopolist can yell out how much he is willing to accept. When a buyer or the monopolist likes the price he sees, he simply yells out that he will consummate a deal at that price; that good is then taken off the market, and a contract is formed. The next good is then brought up for sale.

While Smith goes on to test a variety of other institutions—including what he calls the "posted-bid market," an "offer auction," and so on—for our purposes here we will

Table 17.2   Marginal Cost and Demands.

Quantity	Seller Marginal Cost	Resale Value	Buyer No.
0	0		
1	60	150	2
2	60	140	3
3	60	130	4
4	60	120	5
5	65	110	6
6	70	100	6
7	75	90	5
8	80	80	4
9	85	70	3
10	90	60	2

(Continued)

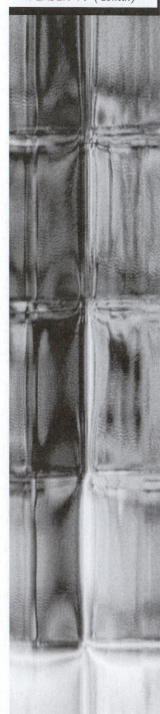

Figure 17.13

Two Monopoly Sessions: A Comparison of Double Auction and Posted Offer Outcomes.

Source: Constructed with data from Smith 1981a.

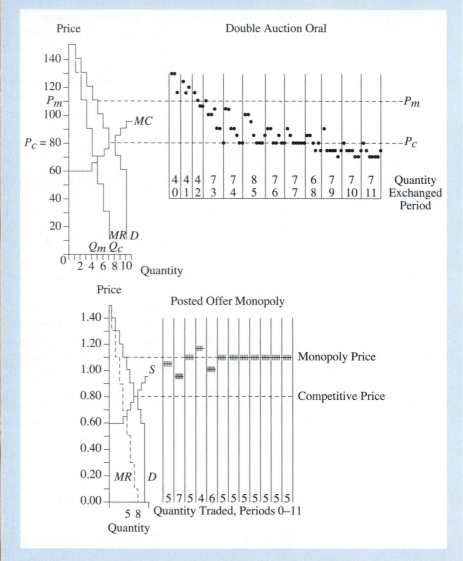

stop and compare these two institutions alone, that is, only the double oral and posted offer auctions.

Probably the best way to make this comparison is to present the sequence of prices formed in both of these markets. For example, in Figure 17.13(a), we present the actual sequence of contracts formed for the goods in the 11 market periods over which the double oral auction experiment was run.[2] A market period is a totally new replication

(Continued)

---

[2] Smith ran other experiments with this institution, all of which had the same general conclusions.

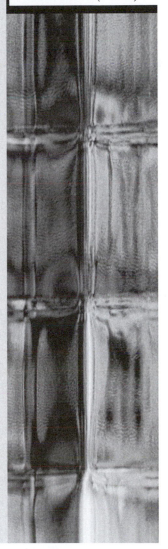

RESOLVING
TEASER 17 *(Contd.)*

of the market starting fresh each period. So as one moves to the right, one sees 11 repeated trials of the same experiment with the same subjects, each having the same valuations and costs. Each market period lasts about five minutes, and trading resumes in the next period with fresh (but identical) supply and demand curves. No unsold goods can be carried over from one period to the next, so goods that are unsold go out of existence at the end of the market period.

As we can see, while prices start above the monopoly level in period zero (which was a practice round where no payoffs were paid), they continually fall as the market progresses to the point where, in period 11, all of the contracts made are at or below the competitive level. In short, despite their monopoly, subjects in these experiments using the double oral auction market institution were not very successful in exploiting their market power.

This result is in contrast, however, to the results of Smith's monopoly experiments using the posted offer institution. In these experiments, using the same supply and demand conditions, prices converged nicely to the monopoly price and stayed there after period five. These results are presented in Figure 17.13(b).

These results are rather startling. They seem to indicate that just having a monopoly is not a sufficient condition for prices to reach monopoly levels and to show how important the institution used to run the monopolist market is. The reason is simple. In the double oral auction, buyers have some strategic weapons. As the monopolist states her price, the buyers can simply not reply and let the clock for the market period keep ticking. After a while of facing nonresponses, a monopolist might get nervous and decide to lower her price, fearing that the buyers simply will not buy at the monopoly price. If the buyers understand that their nonresponse can lead the monopolist to lower her price, that is exactly the course they will follow. If the monopolist does not lower her price, then near the end of the period the buyers can always buy the good—by waiting they incur very little cost. In the posted offer institution, however, no such strategy is available. The seller simply states the price and buyers cannot get her to lower it during a market period. All they can do is refuse to buy and hope she will lower it in future periods—but this strategy is costly.

These results leave open the possibility that we can regulate monopolists by forcing them to use particular types of market institutions, as opposed to allowing them to use the posted offer institution (which is almost universal) and then regulating the price they can charge.

APPENDIX A

THE MONOPOLY PROBLEM

The only constraint a monopolist faces on pricing behavior is the demand function. Let $D(p)$ be the demand function (demand as a function of price) and let $p(y)$ be the inverse demand function, specifying price as a function of demand. The monopolist's profit function can then be written as

$$\Pi = p(y)y - c(y)$$

Then the monopolist's problem is

$$\underset{y}{\text{Max}} \ \ p(y)y - c(y)$$

The first-order condition equates marginal revenue and marginal cost:

$$p(y) + y\frac{dp(y)}{dy} - \frac{dc(y)}{dy} = 0$$

or

$$p(y) + p'(y) \cdot y - c'(y) = 0$$

Because the first two terms in the above expression are simply the marginal revenue of the monopolist while the third is the monopolist's marginal cost, this first-order condition is equivalent to

$$MR = p(y) + p'(y)y = c'(y) = MC$$

This can be rewritten as follows:

$$p(y)\left[1 + \frac{dp}{dy} \bigg/ \frac{p}{y}\right] = c'(y)$$

$$\Rightarrow p(y)\left(1 + \frac{1}{\epsilon(y)}\right) = c'(y)$$

$$\Rightarrow MC = p(y)\left(1 + \frac{1}{\epsilon(y)}\right)$$

Here, $\epsilon(y)$ is the elasticity of demand facing the monopolist, which is a measure of the proportional change in demand as price changes. Further,

$$\epsilon(y) = \frac{dy}{dp} \bigg/ \frac{y}{p} < 0$$

because demand is downward sloping and $dy/dp < 0$.

We therefore write the price-marginal cost relationship as

$$MR = MC = p(y)\left(1 - \frac{1}{|\epsilon(y)|}\right)$$

Consider the special case of linear inverse demand and linear costs:

$$p(y) = \alpha - \beta y$$
$$c(y) = cy$$

Note that this is the same as having linear demand and costs because the corresponding demand curve is

$$y = -\frac{1}{\beta}p + \frac{\alpha}{\beta}$$

Then the problem is

$$\underset{y}{\text{Max}}\ y(\alpha - \beta y) - cy$$

and the first-order conditions are

$$\alpha - 2\beta y - c = 0$$

or

$$MC = c = \alpha - 2\beta y$$

Therefore,

$$y^* = \frac{\alpha - c}{2\beta}$$

and

$$p^* = \frac{\alpha + c}{2}$$

PRICE DISCRIMINATION

Price discrimination arises when a monopolist is able to charge different prices to different groups of buyers.

Consider the situation when the monopolist sells goods in two markets, labeled 1 and 2, with respective demand curves $p_1(y_1)$ and $p_2(y_2)$. Suppose costs are linear as before, and the marginal cost of producing an extra unit of output is c; further, it costs the same to produce a unit of the good whether the good is sold in market 1 or in market 2.

The monopolist's problem is

$$\underset{\{y1, y2\}}{\text{Max}} \quad y_1 p_1(y_1) + y_2 p_2(y_2) - cy_1 - cy_2$$

The first-order conditions are

$$p_1(y_1) + y_1 p'_1(y_1) = c$$
$$p_2(y_2) + y_2 p'_2(y_2) = c$$

Note that the revenues earned from each of the markets are

$$R_1 = y_1 p_1(y_1) \quad \text{and} \quad R_2 = y_2 p_2(y_2)$$

and the marginal revenues are

$$MR_1 = p_1(y_1) + y_1 p'_1(y_1)$$
$$MR_2 = p_2(y_2) + y_2 p'_2(y_2)$$

Thus, the optimizing conditions for the firm require that the two marginal revenues be set equal to the marginal cost:

$$MR_1 = MR_2 = MC$$

Let ϵ_1 and ϵ_2 represent the price elasticities of demand in markets 1 and 2. Then we can rewrite the first-order conditions (as in Appendix A) as

$$p_1(y_1)\left[1 - \frac{1}{|\epsilon|}\right] = c$$
$$p_2(y_2)\left[1 - \frac{1}{|\epsilon|}\right] = c$$

Hence, $p_1(y_1) > p_2(y_2)$ if and only if $|\epsilon_1| < |\epsilon_2|$, or the market with more elastic (more price-sensitive) demand gets charged the lower price.

Exercises and Problems

1. Assume that a monopolist can produce each unit of his product at constant average and marginal costs of $10. His firm faces a market demand curve of $Q = 100P$.

a) What price and quantity should the firm choose in order to maximize its profit? What is the maximum profit the firm can earn?

b) How much will the firm produce under perfect competition (where price is equal to marginal cost)?

2. Suppose that a monopolist faces a demand curve of $P = 100P - 2Q$. Her firm has costs of $C(Q) = 5Q^2$.

a) What is the revenue function for this monopolist?

b) What is the marginal revenue function?

c) What is the marginal cost function?

d) If the marginal revenue function is $MR(Q) = 100 - 4Q$ and the marginal cost function is $MC(Q) = 10Q$, what is the profit-maximizing output for this monopolist?

e) What is the maximum profit this firm can make?

f) If this monopolist has to pay a permission fee of $150 to the state government in order to start the business, will her optimal level of output change? If not, why not?

3. Suppose you are in charge of a toll bridge that is essentially cost-free. The demand for bridge crossings, Q, is given by $P = 12 - 2Q$.

a) Draw the demand curve for bridge crossings.

b) What is the socially optimal price for crossing the bridge? How many people will cross the bridge at that price?

c) If you were a monopolist, what price would you charge?

d) What is the elasticity of demand at the monopoly price?

4. Say that a monopolist faces a market demand curve of $Q = 50 - P$.

a) If the monopolist can produce each unit of his product at constant average and marginal costs of $10, how much will the firm produce to maximize its profit? What price will it charge? What is the monopolist's profit at this price and this quantity?

b) Suppose the firm has a total cost function of $TC = (Q^2/2) - 10Q + 200$. The corresponding marginal cost function is $MC = Q - 10$. (The marginal cost function can be found by differentiating the total cost function.) If the monopolist is facing the same market demand as before, what is his profit-maximizing level of output and price? How much profit will the firm earn?

c) Now suppose the firm has another total cost function, which is $TC = (Q^3/3) - 11Q^2 + 150Q + 200$. The associated marginal cost function is $MC = Q^2 + 22Q + 150$. If the firm faces the same demand as before, how much will it produce and what price will it charge? What will its profit be? Will it continue to operate at that level of profit? Explain why or why not.

5. Consider an island served by one ferry company. There are two types of people who visit the island, day trippers who come in the morning to enjoy the island's beaches on a Saturday or Sunday (or sometimes a weekday) and permanent summer residents who work in the city during the week but come to the island on Friday night to spend the weekend and then leave on Monday to return to work. The ferry has the following rate schedule: $6.50 for a same-day round trip and $5 for a one-way trip. There are no round-trip savings for people who do not travel both ways on the same day.

a)   Given the description of the two groups who visit the island, do you think that price discrimination could work here?

b)   Is the rate schedule of the ferry company an effective price-discrimination device? Why or why not?

c)   If so, what will be the round-trip cost for the permanent summer residents? What will be the round-trip cost for the day trippers?

6. Suppose a mail-order business has a monopoly on video games in the towns of Alexandria and Babylon. These two towns are quite a distance away from each other. The demand for video games in Alexandria is $Q_A = 55 - P_A$, and the demand for video games in Babylon is $Q_B = 70 - 2P_B$. This monopolist can produce video games at the constant marginal (and average) cost of $5 per unit.

a)   If the firm can ensure that video games sold in Alexandria are not resold in Babylon and vice versa, how many video games will it sell in these two cities? At what prices will the firm sell the games? What will its total profit be? (Assume that the firm can produce video games in fractional quantities.)

b)   Now suppose that it costs $5 to mail a video game from Alexandria to Babylon and vice versa. How will the monopolist's behavior change? In particular, how much total profit will she make in this new situation?

c)   How would the answer to part B of this problem change if the mailing cost between the two towns was *zero*?

7. Mr. Drip has $150 pocket money a year, which he spends on items such as cigarettes, candy bars, and coffee. Drip has been in the habit of drinking 2 cups of coffee a day on most business days, or 500 cups a year, at the Downtown Koffee Klub, where the price of coffee is $0.10 a cup.

a)   Draw a diagram with indifference curves to show Drip's equilibrium position.

b)   The Koffee Klub now offers Drip a membership that will entitle him to drink as many cups as he wishes without charge; however, he will have to pay membership dues of $75 a year. Should Drip join the club? How many cups will he drink each year if he joins the club? If you have concluded that Drip will not join the club, how low would the annual membership dues have to be to induce him to become a member?

c)   The Koffee Klub is considering the adoption of an associate membership plan in which coffee will sell for $0.05 a cup. Using your indifference curve diagram, show how much Drip would be willing to pay for such a membership. (*Hint:* Assume that there are no benefits from membership other than coffee. Use your indifference curves throughout.)

8. The Polaroid company sells both cameras and film. It must decide how to price each product. One group of managers suggests that the company should charge a high price for its cameras and a very low price for its film (so that the film is almost a giveaway). Another group of managers takes the opposite position. They say that the company should set a high price for the film and a very low price for the cameras (so that the cameras are practically a giveaway). Assume that Figure 17.14 depicts the demand for Polaroid film by any consumer, that the cost of producing the film is v, and that the cost of producing the cameras is zero. Also assume that the consumer represented in Figure 17.14 does *not* own a camera and that the price of the film is set at p_1.

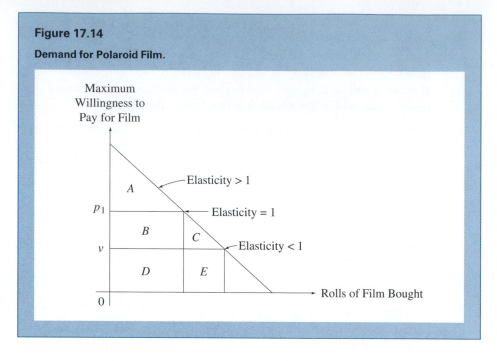

Figure 17.14

Demand for Polaroid Film.

a) How much profit will Polaroid make from sales of the film? Indicate your answer by using the appropriate capital letter or combination of capital letters from Figure 17.14 (such as D or $C + E$) to describe the relevant area in the diagram.

b) If the price of film is p_1, what area in Figure 17.14 represents the maximum that the consumer would be willing to pay for the camera? Explain your answer.

c) Taking into consideration your answers to parts A and B of this problem and assuming that no consumer yet owns a camera, what price for both film *and* a camera would maximize Polaroid's profit?

d) Now assume that *all* consumers own cameras and that Polaroid wants to maximize the revenue (not profit) it receives from film sales. What price would maximize the revenue?

9. Assume that a firm needs 1 unit of capital and $\frac{1}{2}$ unit of labor to produce each unit of output that it sells. Also assume that the price of capital is $6 per unit and the price of labor is $4 per unit. Further assume that the firm faces the marginal revenue, total revenue, and demand functions from the chart on page 413.

a) What are the total cost, average cost, and marginal cost functions for this firm?

b) What quantity would be produced and sold by a monopolist if he wanted to maximize his profit? What would the price be?

c) What quantity would be produced and sold by a perfectly competitive industry if each firm had the production function stated previously? What would the price be?

10. A monopolist sells a good to three consumers who have the following demand curves: $Q_1 = 120 - 5P$, $Q_2 = 50 - 10P$, and $Q_3 - 150 - 5P$. She produces the

good with a technology that has the following cost structure: $C = 8 + 4Q^2$ and $MC = 8Q$.

a) Derive the aggregate demand curve facing the monopolist.

b) If this monopolist must charge the same price to each consumer, what is the profit-maximizing price?

c) Will this monopolist make a profit at the profit-maximizing price you found in part B?

d) Suppose this monopolist requires that each consumer who wants to buy her product pay a fee in order to join a club and then pay the monopoly price for the good.

Q	Marginal Revenue	Total Revenue	Price
1	18	18	18
2	17	35	17.5
3	16	51	17
4	15	66	16.5
5	14	80	16
6	13	93	15.5
7	12	105	15
8	11	116	14.5
9	10	126	14
10	9	135	13.5
11	8	143	13
12	7	150	12.5
13	6	156	12
14	5	161	11.5
15	4	165	11
16	3	168	10.5
17	2	170	10
18	1	171	9.5
19	0	170	9
20	−1	168	8.5
21	−2		8

Is there any positive membership fee she can charge so that all three of her existing consumers will *stay* in the club? Of course, consumers have the option of not joining the club if they decide not to purchase her product. (*Hint:* Think about the absolute maximum a consumer would be willing to pay for this product.)

e) What is the socially optimal price?

f) Suppose that the monopolist still requires that consumers who want to buy her product pay a fee to join the club in addition to paying for the good. However, she is now charging the socially optimal price. Is there any positive membership fee the monopolist can charge so that all three of her existing consumers will stay in the club?

g) Compare the profit the monopolist would earn by charging a membership fee and the monopoly price and by charging a membership fee and the socially optimal price.

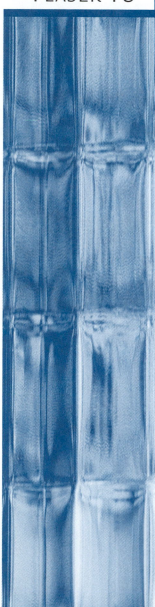

NATURAL MONOPOLY

If you have ever seen old western films, you know it was common for the bad guy (dressed in black) to say to the good guy (dressed in white), "This town is not big enough for both of us." While in westerns this typically meant that the bad guy was likely to kill the good guy if he did not leave, in economics it is more likely to mean that the market cannot support two enterprises profitably so one will have to leave. (There are not often good and bad guys in markets, although some may think they are all good while others may think that they are all bad.) However, if a market has room for only one firm, then it is unlikely that that market will be competitively organized. In fact, by definition, it would have to be a monopoly.

There are many reasons monopolies arise, and if they arise because the cost structure in the industry can support only one firm due to the existence of economies of scale (decreasing average costs) in production, they are called natural monopolies.

So it would appear from what we have just said that a logical scenario for a market whose cost structure exhibits decreasing average costs is for monopoly to arise. This is a testable hypothesis, however, and actually was tested by Charles Plott, Alexander Borges Sugiyama, and Gilad Elbaz.*

While we will discuss the results of their experiment later, after we learn more about natural monopolies, consider the setup of their experiment. Say you have a set of 7 firms who can enter one of two markets. In market A, if they were to enter, they would almost always earn a safe profit of 300. If they decided to enter market B, how much they earn would depend on whether another firm (or firms) entered as well and what price and quantity they offered to the market. However, if one firm entered and offered to satisfy all buyers who wanted to buy a good, given the cost structure, that firm could set a price that was so low that no other firm could make a profit by entering and setting a lower price. After the other firms were scared out of the market, the remaining firm could act like a monopolist and set a high price. This is the sense in which there is no room for more than one firm in the market.

Now think of what could happen in this situation. One outcome is for one firm to enter market B, all the other firms to enter market A, and the firm in Market B to have an implicit (or explicit) threat to undersell any firm that would enter. If the other firms believe this, they will stay out and this firm will set a monopoly price. So under this scenario (the "natural monopoly scenario"), market B would be organized as a monopoly with all the bad welfare characteristics that that implies.

(Continued)

---

* "Economies of Scale, Natural Monopoly, and Imperfect Competition in an Experimental Market," *Southern Economic Journal,* vol. 61, October 1994, pp. 261–87.

EXPERIMENTAL
TEASER 18 *(Contd.)*

Another possible outcome is again for one firm to enter market B but for the firms in market A to implicitly say, "We are watching you. If you set a price too high, we will enter your market and steal your customers." Here, the price in market B will actually be driven down to the average cost of production and profits driven down to zero under the threat of potential entry by firms in market A. This is what has been called the "contestable market scenario." Which outcome do you think is more likely? Stay tuned.

In many societies, public utilities like electricity, gas, water, and telephone service are government-regulated monopolies. In this chapter, we will ask a very fundamental question about such monopolies: Why did they ever develop in the first place? Or, to put it another way, why were competitive markets not used to provide such goods and services (as long-distance telephone service was supplied in the United States until its deregulation)? To answer this question, we will investigate the technological reasons societies prefer that certain goods and services be supplied to consumers through the structure of government-regulated monopolies rather than the structure of competitive markets.

Because regulation of prices is an essential feature of society's control over such monopolies, we will also study a number of different regulatory methods in this chapter. These methods include a rate-of-return regulation, average-cost pricing, and price-cap regulation. As we will see, none of these regulatory methods proves to be ideal.

The Costs of Market Entry

Consider a new entrepreneur in our primitive society who is thinking of building a water treatment and supply plant for the community. This venture will involve purifying the water from an existing source and providing it to consumers at a price they are willing to pay. Pure water will produce a great advance in public health and should therefore be welcomed by the community. Our entrepreneur believes that he can make a good profit if he is the sole supplier of water—in other words, if he has a monopoly in this market. However, if he has to share the market with another firm, he does not think he can make a return that will reward him sufficiently for all his effort and for the resources that he will have to invest. He quickly realizes that if other entrepreneurs attempt to follow his example and enter the water supply market, he must try to keep them out.

When he gives more thought to the problem of competition, he concludes that the technology he will use to purify water and deliver it to consumers is the key to successfully preventing other firms from entering the market. This conclusion makes him stop and contemplate what his costs are likely to be. It appears that the business of purifying and transporting water will be rather capital-intensive; that is, it will involve substantial capital expenditures for the treatment plant itself and for equipment such as pipes, filters, and storage tanks. These are all fixed costs. The variable costs are quite small in comparison because just a few employees can easily monitor a well-designed water treatment plant. Therefore, it is very likely that the firm's costs will be composed mostly of fixed costs and that these costs will be heavy. Because the average fixed cost of each unit of output decreases as the total quantity of output increases (as we discussed in Chapter 9), the more the firm can produce, the more it can spread its heavy fixed costs. Thus, if the firm

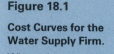

Figure 18.1

Cost Curves for the Water Supply Firm.

Where the average total costs are falling (rising)— that is, for the output levels below (above) 120,000 gallons—the marginal cost is below (above) the average total cost.

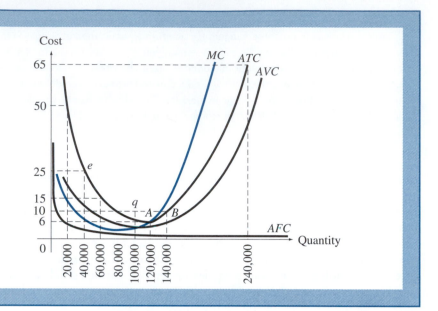

can prevent others from entering its market, its average total costs will decline over a large amount of output. Figure 18.1 depicts this type of cost function.

In Figure 18.1, we see a set of short-run marginal, average fixed, average variable, and average total cost curves for the water supply firm that our entrepreneur wants to establish. Note that because of the heavy fixed costs, the average total costs fall as the output levels become higher and the fixed costs therefore have less influence. Average total costs increase only after point A is reached. By then, the fixed costs are so thoroughly spread over the previous units of output that the variable costs start to dominate. Because these costs increase rapidly as more and more units of variable input are added, they eventually pull up the average total costs. Note also that because the average total costs decrease over such a large range of output, the marginal costs must be below the average costs along this same range. (We know that when average costs are falling, marginal costs must be below them.) Figure 18.1 shows the behavior of the marginal costs.

Natural Monopoly

At first, our entrepreneur thinks that he will be able to prevent other firms from entering the market if he can purify water and deliver it to consumers more cheaply than the other firms can. He makes this idea more precise by defining what is called a **subadditive cost function**. To understand such a function, we will assume that our entrepreneur produces a given level of output, such as q. We will also assume that $C(q)$ is the least-cost way to produce an output of q using the technology available and that q' and q'' are two other levels of output that are smaller than q but are such that $q' + q'' = q$. This leads us to the following definition: A cost function is subadditive if $C(q) < C(q') + C(q'')$ for all levels q, q', and q'', such that $q = q' + q''$.

This cost function indicates that it is cheaper for our entrepreneur to produce q units of water than it is to have those units produced by two smaller firms with output of q' and q'', respectively. (The same situation holds if we consider more than just two other potential suppliers.) Based on the subadditive cost function,

subadditive cost function
A cost function that indicates that the cost of producing x units of output, $C(x)$, is less than the cost of producing A units and B units separately where $A + B = x$, that is, $C(x) \leq C(A) + C(B)$.

our entrepreneur believes that he will be able to repel any potential competitors from entering the market. He also believes that his monopoly will benefit society. He sees it as a natural monopoly—a monopoly that develops because the cheapest way to produce any given level of output in this market is to have one firm do it. Furthermore, he argues that consumers will like having their water supplied by a monopoly because they will pay a lower price than they would in a competitive market. We will soon see that this claim is not totally correct.

natural monopoly
A monopoly that develops because the cheapest way to produce any given level of output in a market is to have one firm do it.

Question (Content Review: Subadditive Cost Function)

Assume that a multinational corporation has two plants in two different countries. The plants are identical, as are the wages paid and the cost of all inputs. In fact, the cost of production is summarized by the following cost function:

$$c(q) = 3q^{1/2}$$

Assume that the manager of the firm is thinking of two plans. Plan 1 calls for the firm to produce 100 units of output in plant 1 and 900 units of output in plant 2, while the other plan calls for plant 1 to produce all 1,000 units. Which plan is cheaper?

Answer

This cost function is subadditive. Hence, it will be best to produce all 1,000 units in plant 1. To see this, note that

$$c(900) + c(100) = 3\sqrt{900} + 3\sqrt{100} = 90 + 30 = 120$$

while

$$c(1,000) = 3\sqrt{1,000} = 3(31.62) = 94.86$$

SOLVED PROBLEM 18.1

Let us now look more closely at the conditions that are necessary for natural monopolies. Specifically, we want to know what types of cost functions lead to such monopolies. A sufficient condition for a natural monopoly is to have an average total cost curve that is falling. This condition can be seen in Figure 18.1 for quantities below 120,000. For example, if average total costs are always falling, then consider output q, which consists of 100,000 gallons of water. We see that it costs our monopolist $6 a gallon, or a total of $600,000, to produce these 100,000 gallons. Now let us say that we want to explore the possibility of using two smaller firms to produce these 100,000 gallons of water. One firm will produce 60,000 gallons, and the other firm will produce 40,000 gallons. We see that the average cost of producing 40,000 gallons (point e in Figure 18.1) is $25 a gallon, while the average cost of producing 60,000 gallons is $15 a gallon. Therefore, the total cost of having the two smaller firms produce the 100,000 gallons is $(40,000 \cdot 25) + (60,000 \cdot 15)$, which totals $1.9 million, or more than three times as much as it would cost to have our monopolist produce that amount of water. With falling average costs, the monopolist is able to produce in the least-cost way at all output levels.

However, average costs need not fall everywhere in order to have the conditions for a natural monopoly. *It is a sufficient condition, but not a necessary one, for average costs to decrease at all levels of output.* Figure 18.1 illustrates the accuracy of this statement. Look at point B, and note that average costs have not fallen for all output levels up to that point, which we will say represents 140,000 gallons. After point A, average costs rise. Yet if the demand for water is no greater than B, the firm supplying this water will be a natural monopoly.

The reason the firm will be a natural monopoly is simple. Let us assume that instead of having a single firm produce the 140,000 gallons, two smaller firms are used. One firm produces 120,000 gallons, while the other firm produces the remaining 20,000 gallons. The total cost of having a single firm (a monopoly) produce the 140,000 gallons is $1.4 million: $C(140,000) = 140,000 \times 1,400,000$. The total cost of having two firms produce the 140,000 gallons is $1.72 million: $C(120,000) + C(20,000) = (120,000 \cdot 6) = 1,720,000$. The fact that average costs do not decrease for all levels of output up to 140,000 gallons at our entrepreneur's firm does not mean that the firm cannot produce the 140,000 gallons more cheaply than several smaller firms and therefore still be a natural monopoly. We can do a similar analysis for any number of firms with different combinations of output that add up to 140,000 gallons, and we will come to the same conclusion.

Clearly, however, a firm that has a technology that produces the cost function shown in Figure 18.1 is not a natural monopoly at *every* level of output. For example, consider the output of 240,000 gallons. If this amount is produced by one firm, it will cost $15.6 million: $C(240,000) = 240,000 \cdot \$65 = \$15,600,000$. However, the same output can be produced more cheaply by two smaller firms, each of which supplies 120,000 gallons. In this case, the 240,000 gallons will cost $1.44 million: $C(120,000) + C(120,000) = (120,000 \cdot 6) + (120,000 \cdot 6) = 1,440,000$. Hence, there is a level of output beyond which a firm with the cost function depicted in Figure 18.1 is no longer a natural monopoly.

SOLVED PROBLEM 18.2

Question (Content Review: Monopoly, Costs, and Profit)

The Pinewood Lumber Company has a cost function $c(q) = 25 \ln q$, where q is the quantity of two-by-fours produced, and $\ln q$ is its natural logarithm. This means that Pinewood has a marginal cost function of $MC(q) = 25/q$. The demand for two-by-fours is $D(p) = 20 - 2p$. If Pinewood sets its price and quantity by equating marginal revenue and marginal cost, could it make a profit?

Answer

Pinewood's marginal revenue is found by inverting the demand curve and doubling the slope because it faces a linear demand curve. Marginal revenue is $MR(q) = 10 - q$. Setting marginal revenue equal to marginal cost and solving for the quantity of two-by-fours, we get

$$10 - q = \frac{25}{q}$$
$$q = 5$$

Substituting back into the demand curve, we find the price, $p = \$7.50$.

The average cost for producing these 5 two-by-fours is

$$AC(q) = \frac{c(q)}{q} = \frac{25 \ln q}{q} = \frac{25 \ln 5}{5} = \$8.05$$

Thus, Pinewood cannot make money here because the price it sets is below its average cost of production due to decreasing marginal costs.

Sustainable Monopoly

Our entrepreneur is under the impression that his water supply firm will be protected from market entry by rival firms because it is a natural monopoly. As we will now see, this idea is erroneous. Consider point *B* in Figure 18.2.

Figure 18.2 depicts the same average total cost curve as Figure 18.1, except that an aggregate demand curve for purified water has now been superimposed over the cost curve. If the demand for water is 140,000 gallons, $10 a gallon is the lowest price that will allow our monopolist to cover his cost of production. As we see in the diagram, the demand curve for purified water intersects the average total cost curve at *B*. We also see that for output at levels lower than *B*, any producer is a natural monopolist. Does it then follow that another firm can enter the water supply market, take customers away from our existing monopolist, and make a profit if that firm discovers how to purify water using the same technology as our existing monopolist? The answer is yes. To understand why, let us consider a firm that enters the water supply market and produces 120,000 gallons at an average cost of only $6 a gallon. Such an entrant can therefore set a price between $6 and $10 (the existing monopolist's lowest price), sell 120,000 gallons of water, and make a profit. This firm will be successful because it need not supply the entire market when it enters but rather can provide only 120,000 gallons and enjoy the low costs associated with producing that quantity. Such a strategy for market entry will drive our existing monopolist out of business. Hence, just having a natural monopoly does not guarantee that a firm will be able to prevent competitors from entering its market.

A natural monopoly that can erect barriers that keep others out of its market is called a **sustainable monopoly**. We can define such a monopoly more precisely

sustainable monopoly
A natural monopoly that can erect barriers that keep others out of its market.

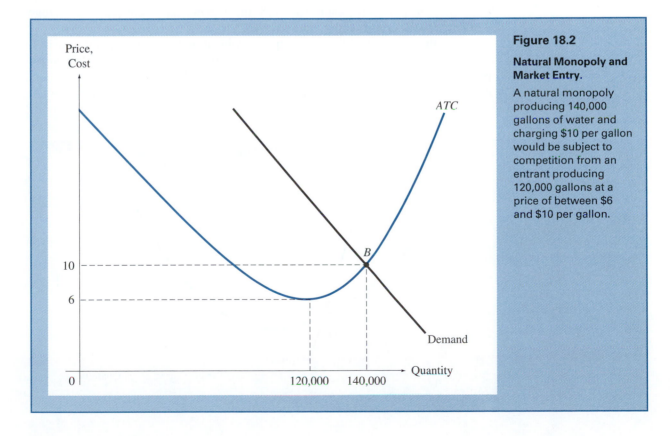

Figure 18.2

Natural Monopoly and Market Entry.

A natural monopoly producing 140,000 gallons of water and charging $10 per gallon would be subject to competition from an entrant producing 120,000 gallons at a price of between $6 and $10 per gallon.

as follows: A natural monopoly that has a cost function of $C(q)$ and faces a demand function of $D(p)$ is sustainable if there is a price of p and an output of q such that (1) $q = D(p)$, (2) $p \cdot q = C(q)$, and $p' \cdot q' \leq C(q')$ for all $p' < p$ and all $q' \leq D(p')$. What this definition tells us is that a natural monopoly is sustainable if at any price the firm satisfies all the demand in the market (condition 1); covers its cost (condition 2); and sets a price of p such that any competing firm that tries to enter the market by selling a smaller quantity at a lower price will incur a loss (condition 3).

From this definition, it follows that a natural monopoly is sustainable if, for an output of q, average costs are declining at every level up to that quantity. To understand this idea, let us consider the demand and cost situation depicted in Figure 18.3.

In this figure, we see that the demand curve intersects the average cost curve at point A. Because average cost is declining up to that point, the firm has a sustainable natural monopoly for that quantity. For example, let us say that the firm sets a price of p^a and sells a units as demanded at that price. Now let us assume that another firm wants to enter the market and sell some quantity that is less than a. To avoid losing money, the entrant must set its price above p^a. For example, say that it chooses a price of p^c and hopes to sell c units. However, because this price of p^c is higher than the price of p^a that the existing monopolist charges, consumers will not buy from the entrant. Therefore, the only way the entrant can take customers away from the existing monopolist is by setting a price below p^a. If the entrant does so and wants to increase the quantity it will sell from a units to b units, its price will have to be below its average cost, which means that it will lose money. On the other hand, a price and quantity below a will not cover the cost of production, as we can see at point d. Therefore, an output of a is sustainable for the monopolist, as is any quantity at which the demand curve intersects the average cost curve to the left of point C in Figure 18.3.

Note that a sustainable price-output combination must be a point at which the demand curve intersects the average cost curve. In other words, if our entrepreneur wants his natural monopoly to be sustainable, he must set a price and quantity at which demand equals average cost. At such a price and quantity,

Figure 18.3

A Sustainable Monopoly.

Point A is a sustainable monopoly price-output combination because a potential entrant would either set a higher price and fail to take away customers or set a price lower than its average cost and lose money.

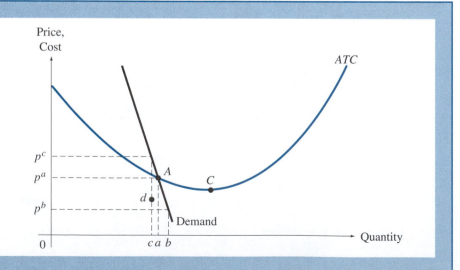

however, our entrepreneur will just cover his average cost. There will be no extra-normal profits. Will he actually want to supply water at such a low profit level? The answer is yes because the cost curve of the firm includes his opportunity cost. His time is treated as one of the inputs into the production process, which means that he is being compensated for it. Hence, while he would like to earn extra-normal profits, he is willing to supply water at the sustainable price and quantity.

The Inertia Shopping Rule

After considering the conditions under which a natural monopoly must operate, our entrepreneur decides to establish his water supply firm. Figure 18.4 depicts the costs and demand that he expects to face when the firm begins its activities.

Our entrepreneur believes that the firm's natural monopoly is sustainable. As Figure 18.4 illustrates, given the situation the firm faces, its profit-maximizing price is p^m and its profit-maximizing quantity is q^m. As we know from our study of monopoly in Chapter 17, q^m is that quantity at which the marginal revenue from production equals the marginal cost. The price is set above the marginal cost, depending on the elasticity of the demand curve. Remember that $p = MC/(1 - 1/|\xi|)$. According to the business plan devised by our entrepreneur, he should make extra-normal profits equal to the area $p^m dcf$ in Figure 18.4. However, these extra-normal profits may attract other firms to the water supply market. Our entrepreneur is prepared for such an event. If a competitor should try to enter this market, he will immediately lower his price to p^s, which is the sustainable price for the market. (Price p^s is identical to price p^a in Figure 18.3.) Our entrepreneur assumes that customers suffer from inertia and will therefore not shift their

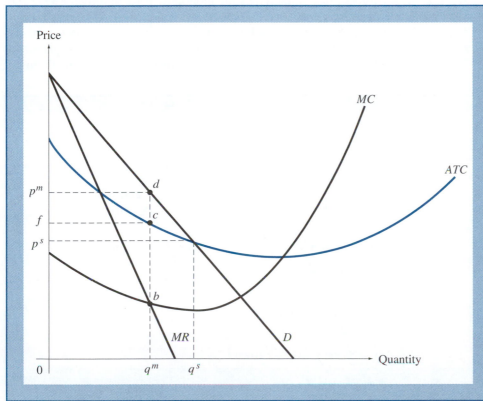

Figure 18.4

Monopoly Price and Quantity.

The monopoly price-quantity combination determined by equating marginal revenue and marginal cost is p^m and q^m, and p^s and q^s are the sustainable price-quantity combination determined by equating price and average cost.

demand to the entrant immediately even though that firm's price is lower. As a result, he should have enough time to decrease his price and prevent the entrant from taking away any of his customers.

Figure 18.5 presents our entrepreneur's strategic analysis of the situation he thinks his firm will face in trying to prevent a competitor from entering the water supply market. He sees this situation as a *game* in which he and the potential entrant are the players. The first move in the game occurs when he sets a price, which we will assume is either the monopoly price of p^m or the sustainable price of p^s.

In making his strategic analysis of the game, our entrepreneur assumes that customers will behave according to the **inertia shopping rule** when they decide from which firm to buy. This rule is as follows: Buy from the firm that charges the lowest price, but if you are already buying from a firm and another firm enters the market and offers you a lower price, give your current firm a chance to meet the entrant's price before shifting your business.

The second move in the game belongs to the potential entrant. Seeing the price that our entrepreneur's firm (the incumbent firm) has set and knowing that consumers will probably act in accordance with the inertia shopping rule, the potential entrant then decides whether to enter the market or stay out. If this firm decides to enter, it must charge the sustainable price. If the existing price in the market is the monopoly price, the incumbent firm will have time to decide whether to lower its price. If entry occurs when the existing price is the sustainable price, then both firms will split the market at that price.

To see the payoffs from the game, look at the terminal nodes of the game tree in Figure 18.5. The first amount under each node represents the payoff to the incumbent firm, and the second amount represents the payoff to the potential entrant. If the incumbent firm initially sets the monopoly price and then lowers it to the sustainable price after entry occurs, the entrant will gain no customers (assuming that the inertia shopping rule holds true). However, because the entrant incurred fixed costs of $100,000 in order to establish a water treatment plant, this firm's payoff will be −100,000. In other words, the firm loses the $100,000 that it

inertia shopping rule
The rule that states that buyers will buy from the firm that charges the lowest price but that if they are already buying from a firm and another firm enters the market and offers a lower price, they give their current firm a chance to meet the entrant's price before shifting their business.

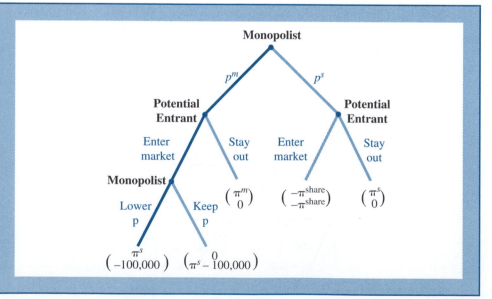

Figure 18.5

The Entry-Prevention Game of a Sustainable Monopoly.

The incumbent moves by choosing either the monopoly price of p^m or the sustainable price of p^s. The potential entrant moves by choosing either to enter the market or to stay out.

invested in the plant. Of course, we are assuming that there is no market in which the firm can sell its water treatment equipment and recover some of the money it invested. In the case of a primitive society, this assumption is almost certainly correct. Costs of fixed factors, such as equipment, that are not recoverable because the items have no resale value or alternative use are called sunk costs. (In this analysis of the strategic situation our entrepreneur faces, we have assumed that customers will behave according to the inertia shopping rule and that the costs of a failed attempt at market entry will all be sunk costs. Later we will investigate this same situation with a different set of assumptions and see how the results change.)

sunk costs
Costs of factors that are not recoverable because the items have no resale value or alternative use.

Look again at the game tree in Figure 18.5. The darkened path at the left depicts the following three moves in the game: the incumbent firm initially sets the monopoly price, entry occurs, and the incumbent firm then lowers its price to the sustainable level. As a result of these moves, the incumbent firm will earn the sustainable-price payoff of π^s. The entrant is driven from the market. As we saw previously, this firm will have a payoff of $-100,000$ because the failure of its attempt at market entry brings about the loss of its investment.

If the incumbent firm maintains its monopoly price after the other firm enters the market and offers the sustainable price, then the incumbent firm will lose the market to the entrant. In this situation, the entrant will earn the sustainable-price payoff minus the cost of entry, or $\pi^s - 100,000$. Note that the payoff to the incumbent firm when it loses the market is zero rather than $-100,000$ because we are assuming that the incumbent firm paid for its capital in the past. If the incumbent firm initially sets the monopoly price and no entry occurs, the payoffs will be monopoly profits of π^m for the incumbent firm and zero for the potential entrant.

Now look at the right side of the game tree in Figure 18.5. If the incumbent firm initially sets the sustainable price and entry occurs, then both the entrant and the incumbent firm will have to share the market at the sustainable price. Thus, each of them will receive $-\pi^{share}$ as a payoff. If the incumbent firm initially sets the sustainable price and no entry occurs, the payoffs will be sustainable profits of π^s for the incumbent firm and zero for the potential entrant.

In the situation described by this game, we can conclude that there is only one subgame perfect equilibrium. This equilibrium occurs when the incumbent firm sets the monopoly price and the other firm decides not to enter the market. We can easily verify that this is the only subgame perfect equilibrium by using backward induction. For example, let us say that the incumbent firm sets the sustainable price (that is, moves to the right on its first move). We can see that the best response the potential entrant can make to this move is not to enter the market because entering yields a payoff of $-\pi^{share}$ while not entering yields a payoff of zero. The value to the incumbent firm of choosing the sustainable price is therefore π^s. If the incumbent firm chooses the monopoly price of p^m, the other firm must decide whether to enter the market. If this firm does not enter, it receives a payoff of zero. If it does enter, the next move belongs to the incumbent firm, which now controls the outcome of the game. Because of the inertia shopping rule, the incumbent firm has some time to decide whether to lower its price to p^s. We can assume that the incumbent firm will make this change because by selecting the sustainable price, it will earn a payoff of π^s, but maintaining the monopoly price yields it a zero profit.

It should be clear to any firm contemplating entry that if it enters the market after the incumbent firm sets the monopoly price, this firm will subsequently lower its price, force the entrant out of the market, and cause the entrant to lose its investment. Hence, a monopoly price will deter the entry of any potential competitor. Because no entry will occur when the price is either p^s or p^m, the incumbent firm will set the monopoly price.

Question (Application and Extension: The Entry Game)
Consider the game tree shown in Figure 18.6, which depicts a situation of potential entry by a firm and an incumbent.

Figure 18.6

The Entry Game I.

The game without the inertia shopping rule.

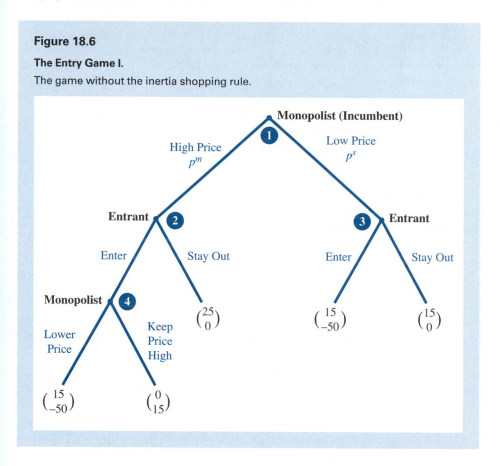

In this game, the incumbent monopolist firm moves first and sets either a low price, p^s, or a high price, p^m. Seeing this price, the entrant decides whether to enter or not; if it does enter, it does so at the low price. If entry occurs, the monopolist can adjust its price to match that of the entrant. The inertia shopping rule says that if the monopolist does meet the price of the entrant, it will retain all of its customers. The numbers at the end of the game tree depict the payoffs.

a) Solve this game by backward induction.

Answer
Looking for a subgame perfect equilibrium, we start at the back of the tree and work toward the front. Note that if the game ever reached node 4 (that is, if the monopolist set a high price and the entrant entered), the monopolist, whose turn it is to move there, would lower its price. The monopolist would lower its price because keeping its price high would mean it would lose the market; on the other

hand, lowering it would mean that, given the inertia shopping rule, it would retain the entire market at a lower price. Moving up to node 2 and knowing what the monopolist would do at node 4, we see that the entrant at node 2 would stay out; this is true because 0 is greater than −50, which is what it would get if it had to pay a fixed cost to enter (just to have the monopolist lower its price and keep the entire market). Thus, the monopolist then knows that if it sets a high price, the entrant would not enter and the monopolist would get a payoff of 25 from setting such a price. Setting a low price will get it only 15 because the entrant will not enter there either.

b) At the equilibrium of the game, does the entrant enter?

Answer

As seen previously, the entrant does not enter when the inertia shopping rule is in place.

c) Now assume that the inertia shopping rule does *not* exist so that if the entrant enters at a low price and the monopolist matches that low price after entry, the entrant and previous monopolist share the market. Solve this new game and determine whether in this game there is an equilibrium where the entrant enters.

Answer

If the inertia shopping rule is not in place, then we will assume that whenever the entrant and monopolist set the same price, they share the market. This yields the game tree shown in Figure 18.7.

Figure 18.7

The Entry Game II.
The Entry Game I without the inertia shopping rule.

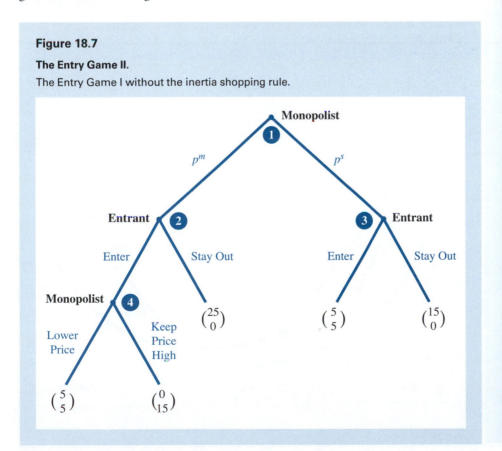

Using backward induction again on the tree, we can see that there are two equilibria. In one, the monopolist sets a high price, the entrant enters, the monopolist lowers its price, and they share the market. In the other, the monopolist sets a low price, the entrant enters, and they share the market.

The Need for Regulation

Monopoly and the Deadweight Loss

Armed with the preceding analysis, our entrepreneur makes two important decisions. He decides to establish his water supply firm, and he decides to charge the monopoly price. As time passes, he finds that things have worked out exactly as he planned. No other firms have entered the water supply industry, and as a result, his firm has been able to earn large monopoly profits. Society is not very happy about this situation. Consumers complain about the high price of water even though they realize they are better off because of the pure water that the firm is providing to them. They agree that our entrepreneur should be rewarded for his ingenuity and effort, but they believe that the present economic arrangement is not satisfactory, and they sense that there may be a better way to handle pricing and profits in the water supply industry. Figure 18.8 explains their concerns.

In Figure 18.8, we see the demand, marginal revenue, average cost, and marginal cost curves of a natural monopoly—the water supply industry. The monopolistic quantity is q^m, and the monopolistic price is p^m. This price-quantity

Figure 18.8

The Social Waste of Monopoly.

The monopoly price-quantity combination is p^m and q^m. The socially optimal price-quantity combination is p^{mc} and q^o. Hence, society would be willing to pay more for additional units than the cost of producing those units.

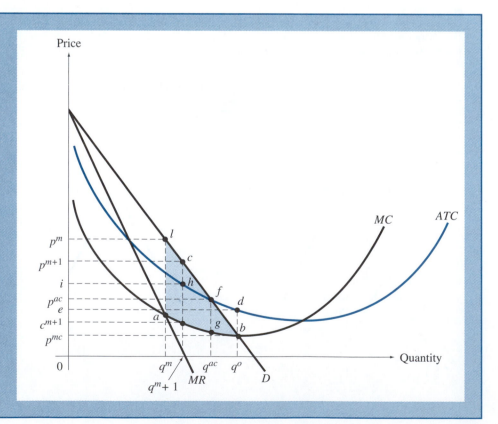

combination is not optimal from society's point of view. Consider what happens if the firm sells one more unit than the monopolistic quantity—the $q^m + 1$st unit. For this unit, society is willing to pay $p^m + 1$, but the marginal cost of producing that unit is only $c^m + 1$. Although society is willing to pay more for the $q^m + 1$st unit than its production cost, the unit is not being sold. This fact means that there are people in society who want more pure water and are willing to pay our entrepreneur at least his production cost but are not able to obtain the water. The reason for this difference between what society wants and what is produced is simply that our entrepreneur's objective is not to maximize society's welfare but rather to maximize his own profits, which leads him to restrict output to q^m.

The total loss to society from having a monopoly set the current price and quantity in the water supply industry is represented by the blue-shaded area *lba* in Figure 18.8. This amount is the deadweight loss associated with monopoly. Only at a quantity of q^o and a price of $p^{mc} = MC$ will the welfare of the consumers be maximized. This welfare-maximization requires **marginal-cost pricing**.

marginal-cost pricing
To set a price that is equal to the marginal cost.

Average-Cost Pricing

After this analysis becomes known, there is a public outcry and a consumer movement emerges. People see no reason that a monopolist should make huge profits and yet not provide pure water to all the consumers who want it. Soon, people ask the government to intervene in the water supply industry. Government officials realize that this is a hot political issue, and because there are many consumers but only one monopolist, they quickly agree to form a regulatory agency to set the price of water and ensure that there is an ample supply of pure water for everyone who wants it.

The regulatory commission calls our entrepreneur to a hearing and demands that he charge the welfare-optimal price of p^{mc} (the marginal-cost price) and sell a quantity of q^o (see Figure 18.8). Our entrepreneur tells the members of the commission that their demands are not feasible—that if he implements these demands, he will lose money and have to go out of business. As a result, society will lose its source of pure water.

The reason that marginal-cost pricing will cause losses is that the average cost falls over the entire range of outputs we are looking at (between 0 and q^o), and we know that the marginal cost will always be below the average cost. (Remember that when the average cost falls, the marginal cost is below the average cost.) If the price of water is set at p^{mc}, this price will be less than the average cost by the distance *bd* in Figure 18.8. The total losses that will occur are represented by the rectangle $p^{mc}edb$. Our entrepreneur then explains that if the commissioners want him to break even, they either have to allow him to set his price above the marginal cost or, if they insist that he use the welfare-optimal price, they must pay him a subsidy to cover his losses so that he can stay in business. He suggests that they finance the subsidy by placing a tax on some other goods. Because the commissioners do not have the authority to tax other goods, they realize that they must consider the situation further before making a decision. They recess the hearing with our entrepreneur and then meet privately to discuss the problem.

average-cost pricing
To set a price that is equal to the average cost.

second-best result
A market outcome that is optimal given existing constraints in the market but worse than the outcome that would result if those constraints were removed.

The commissioners conclude that the most feasible solution is to use **average-cost pricing**—to set a price that is equal to the average cost. They will therefore direct our entrepreneur to set a price of p^{ac} and sell a quantity of q^{ac}. This plan will not produce the welfare-optimal result for society, but it will achieve the **second-best result**. When it is not possible to obtain the most desirable economic outcome in a situation—marginal-cost pricing in this case—society has to compromise and accept the next most desirable outcome.

Our entrepreneur does not like the plan devised by the regulatory commission and therefore decides to hire a consulting firm to advise him and to represent him at the appeals hearing. This firm comes up with a rather clever response that argues against the need for any regulation in the water supply market.[1]

SOLVED PROBLEM 18.4

Question (Application and Extension: Pricing with Decreasing Cost)

Consider a benevolent monopolist that has a cost function of the following type:

$$C = 10,000 + 2q$$

In this cost function, we see that the fixed cost of production is 10,000, while the variable (or marginal cost) is 2. Assume that the firm faces a market demand curve of the following type:

$$p = 10,002 - 4q$$

Because the monopolist is benevolent, it tries to set the socially optimal price.

a) If it does so, could it make a profit?

Answer

No. The socially optimal price is where price equals marginal cost. Here, marginal cost is 2. So let us find that quantity the monopolist will sell if it sets price equal to marginal cost. We do this by setting $p = 2$ in the demand function and solving:

$$2 = 10,002 - 4q \rightarrow q = 2,500$$

At the socially optimal price, the firm will sell 2,500 units of the good. Its cost of producing that quantity is $C(2,500) = 10,000 + 2(2,500) = 15,000$. Its revenue is $R = p \cdot q = 2 \cdot 2,500 = 5,000$. Hence, because its revenues are less than its costs, it will lose money by trying to be benevolent.

b) What is the lowest price it could charge and still cover its costs?

Answer

In order for the firm not to incur a loss, it must set price and quantity such that its revenue equals its costs, or $pq = c(q)$. In terms of the demand and cost functions listed above, this means that the following condition must be satisfied:

$$(10,002 - 4q)q = 10,000 + 2q$$

It is only for quantities of q that satisfy this equation that the firm will exactly cover its costs. Rewrite this equation as follows:

$$10,002q - 4q^2 - 10,000 - 2q = 0 \Rightarrow 4q^2 - 10,000q + 10,000 = 0$$

---

[1]   The work upon which this section is based appears in a number of articles and books. The two that were relied on most heavily here are William Baumol, John Panzar, and Robert Willig, *Contestable Markets and Industry Structure* (New York: Harcourt Brace Jovanovich, Inc., 1982) and William Baumol, Elizabeth Bailey, and Robert Willig, "Weak Invisible Hand Theorems on the Sustainability of Prices in a Multiproduct Monopoly," *American Economic Review* 67 (June 1977): 350–65.

Using the quadratic formula to solve, we find that

$$q = 1,250 + 200\sqrt{39} \text{ and } q = 1,250 - 200\sqrt{39}$$

or

$$q = 2,499 \text{ and } q = 1$$

Because we are looking for that solution where the price is lowest, we need only to substitute 2,499 into the demand function to see that $p = 10,002 - 4q = 10,002 - 4(2,499) = 10,002 - 9,996$ so that $p = 6$. Hence, the lowest price the monopolist could charge and still break even is 6 with an associated quantity of 2,499. Note how close this solution is to the optimal one. The monopolist basically sells the same quantity but merely must raise its price from 2 to 6 to cover costs.

Ask yourself the following questions: What feature of this problem makes these solutions so close? Is this always the case?

CONSULTING REPORT   18.1

USING THE CONCEPT OF A CONTESTABLE MARKET TO ARGUE AGAINST REGULATION

The consultants assert that there is no need for regulation at all in the water supply market because the threat of entry by other firms will be enough to discipline the behavior of the incumbent firm (our entrepreneur) and bring about a socially desirable price and level of service (the second-best welfare-optimal price and quantity). The consultants argue that other firms will closely monitor this market, looking for an opportunity to enter it. Knowing that such monitoring is taking place, the incumbent firm will set a price that is equal to its average cost because any price above that level will attract entry. In short, the threat of entry is all that is needed to drive the price down to the level of the average cost.

The consultants state that the water supply market is a *contestable market* and that no firm can dominate it for long with a monopoly price. ●

Our entrepreneur is surprised by the consulting firm's analysis of the strategic situation in the water supply market. This analysis is based on a different set of assumptions than the ones he used when he previously made his own analysis (see Figure 18.5 and the surrounding discussion). Remember that his analysis was based on the following two assumptions: that consumers will behave according to the inertia shopping rule and that the costs of a failed attempt at market entry will all become sunk costs for the firm involved. These assumptions led our entrepreneur to conclude that he would be able to set the monopoly price and maintain it because the threat of entry by other firms is not a credible one.

The inertia shopping rule indicates that the incumbent firm can quickly force an entrant out of the market by simply lowering its price. Sunk costs mean that the price of a failed attempt at market entry is high—a total loss of the amount invested. If these assumptions are true, they represent a powerful deterrent to market entry by competitors and therefore protect the ability of the incumbent firm to charge a monopoly price.

The Theory of Contestable Markets

The consultants tell our entrepreneur that his assumptions are not realistic. They explain that, in their opinion, the theory of contestable markets provides a more accurate description of the nature of the water supply market. According to this theory, customers have no loyalty to any sellers and especially not to monopolists who charge high prices. As soon as a new firm enters a market and charges a lower price, the customers will flock to that firm. The theory of contestable markets also assumes that once a monopolist sets his price, it becomes costly for him to change it quickly. For example, he will have to inform all of his customers of the price change. Thus, it is difficult for a monopolist to force a competitor out of the market soon after entry by quickly lowering his price.

Another key assumption of the theory of contestable markets is that the costs incurred in a failed attempt at market entry will not become sunk costs because the capital equipment that was acquired can easily and without cost be taken elsewhere and used. If this is the case, then a potential entrant monitoring a market and seeing that the monopolist who controls the market has set a price above the sustainable or average-cost price of p^{ac} will quickly be able to move the necessary capital into the market, start operations, and take away the monopolist's customers by charging a lower price. If the monopolist eventually responds by decreasing his price below the entrant's price and he therefore regains his customers, the entrant can easily exit the industry and deploy her capital elsewhere because there are no sunk costs. The consultants call this process hit-and-run entry, and they say that it will prevent the monopolist from charging a high price. A market that competitors can easily enter and leave is known as a contestable market. The consultants claim that the water supply market is such a market. This type of market is characterized by a lack of customer loyalty so that low price becomes the determining factor for buying decisions, and it is characterized by a lack of any harsh penalties for leaving the market so that fear of losing one's capital investment does not serve as a barrier to market entry.

The consultants say that in a game defined by the contestable market assumptions, the only equilibrium is one in which the monopolist sets a price of p^{ac} (the average-cost price) and no one enters the market. Because the possibility of successful entry by other firms exists if the monopolist charges a higher price, society can obtain its desired second-best welfare-optimal result without having to impose any regulation. Figure 18.9 depicts the contestable market entry game, which illustrates the analysis that the consultants have made of the water supply market.

In this figure, we see that the incumbent firm (the monopolist) has the first move. For the sake of simplicity, let us assume that this firm can set either the monopoly price of p^m or the average-cost price of p^{ac}. (Obviously, there are other

hit-and-run entry
When a potential entrant monitoring a market sees an opportunity to enter a market and does so but then exits when the incumbent firm responds.

contestable market
A market that competitors can easily enter and leave because there are no sunk costs.

contestable market entry game
A game defined by the contestable market assumptions.

Figure 18.9

The Contestable Market Entry Game.

The monopolist moves by choosing either the monopoly price of p^m or the average cost price of p^{ac}. The potential entrant moves by choosing either to enter the market or to stay out.

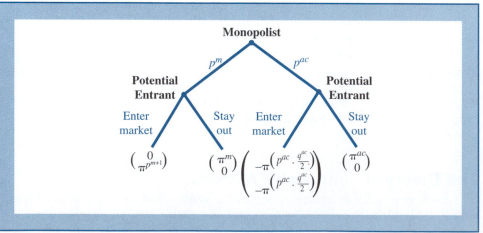

possible prices, but by restricting our discussion to just two prices, we can simplify the situation without changing its ultimate outcome.) After seeing the price set by the incumbent firm, its potential competitor must decide whether or not to enter the market. If the incumbent firm sets the monopoly price and entry occurs, the entrant can set a price just below the monopoly price, take all the customers away from the incumbent firm, and make huge profits. For example, if we use data from Figure 18.8, we see that if the incumbent firm sets a price of p^m, the entrant can choose a price of p^{m+1}, sell a quantity of q^{m+1}, and make profits of π^{pm+1} equal to the rectangle p^{m+1} *chi*. The incumbent firm's profits will be zero. Of course, the incumbent firm will eventually respond to the entry of a competitor, but that response will not eliminate the short-term profit of the competitor. If the competitor does not enter the market, it will have a payoff of zero. Clearly then, setting the monopoly price will attract the entry of a competitor and cause the incumbent firm to lose its customers and earn no profit at all. In fact, according to this logic, the incumbent firm will continue to earn no profit as long as it uses any price above the average-cost price of p^{ac}.

If the incumbent firm sets the average-cost price of p^{ac} and entry occurs, we will assume that both firms will share the market and both will lose money. Because of decreasing average costs, if each firm sells only a quantity of $q^{ac}/2$ at a price of p^{ac}, the average cost of production for each must be above p^{ac}. If we call the total profit $-\pi^{[pac\cdot(qac/2)]}$, then the profit of each firm that shares the market is $-\pi^{[pac\cdot(qac/2)]}$. If the incumbent firm sets a price of p^{ac} and no entry occurs, the incumbent firm will earn its normal profit, which we will denote as π^{ac}.

From this description of the contestable market entry game, we see that if the incumbent firm sets the monopoly price, it can expect that a competitor will enter its market and that it will earn no profit, while if it sets the average-cost price of p^{ac}, it can expect that no competitor will enter its market and that it will earn normal profits. Hence, the subgame perfect Nash equilibrium for the contestable market entry game is the situation in which the incumbent firm, because it fears the entry of a competitor, sets the average-cost price, while the potential entrant, seeing that the average-cost price is being used, decides that no opportunity exists and does not enter.

Note that it is the *threat* of entry by a competitor that makes our entrepreneur set the second-best welfare-optimal price. There is no need for entry actually to occur. Similarly, the optimal result is accomplished without the intervention of a regulator. It is almost as if an invisible hand—in this case, the invisible hand of potential competition—sets the price optimally.

Criticisms of the Theory of Contestable Markets. While the theory of contestable markets sounds convincing, there are some problems with it.[2] One fundamental problem is that the results of this theory are very sensitive to the accuracy of the assumptions that underlie it. A perfectly contestable market is one in which competitors can enter and leave easily and in which no harsh economic penalty exists for leaving because there are no sunk costs. The incumbent firm (the monopolist) cannot react quickly to the entry of a competitor, and the competitor can therefore engage in a hit-and-run strategy by monitoring the incumbent's price, entering the market if the price is above the average cost, making huge short-term profits, and

---

[2] The arguments in this section are based on Marius Schwartz and Robert Reynolds, "Contestable Markets: An Uprising in the Theory of Industry Structure: Comment," *American Economic Review* 73 (June 1983): 488–90.

then exiting if the incumbent firm lowers its price. The competitor makes its decision about market entry on the basis of the *before-entry* price and does not fear a price war after entry because it knows that the incumbent firm cannot adjust its price quickly enough. Thus, there is at least a short-term opportunity for large profits.

However, if any one of the underlying assumptions of the theory of contestable markets proves to be inaccurate, then the entire structure of the theory falls apart. For example, if the incumbent firm can react quickly to entry by changing its price, the potential competitor should not base its decision about market entry on the currently existing price but rather on its perception of what the incumbent firm's price will be *after* entry. Such a perception may prevent entry and may allow the incumbent firm to keep its price above the average cost. Further, say that the incumbent firm and its competitor can exist costlessly, but the competitor cannot enter quickly when it sees an excessively high price. It must wait to plan and execute its entry strategy. Then the incumbent firm can set a high monopoly price and enjoy monopoly profits while its potential competitor prepares to enter, and just as entry occurs, the incumbent firm can leave the market. In this case, because of the lag in entry, the price will remain above the average cost both before and after entry. Obviously, one assumption of the theory of contestable markets—that competitors can enter quickly—is not valid in this particular situation and the theory therefore does not work here.

See the Experimental Evidence feature at the end of this section for an application of contestability theory to the airline industry plus a laboratory experiment on the same theory.

RESOLVING
TEASER 18

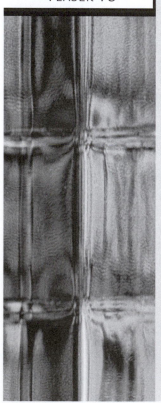

CONTESTABLE MARKETS

As you recall, in the Plott et al. experiment, firms could enter one of two markets, A or B. In market A, they were fairly sure to make a safe outcome, while in market B firms faced a cost structure that had decreasing average costs throughout the entire range of demand. The research question was, What outcome would occur? Would one and only one firm enter market B and set itself up as a natural monopoly? Would one and only one firm enter market B and set a price equal to average cost as contestable market theory says it should? Would several firms enter market B and collude, setting a high price, or would several firms enter and compete by setting a low price?

The data indicates that while no one theory properly explains all the data correctly, the contestable market theory does the best job. For example, the contestable market theory makes predictions about what the price will be in market B, how many firms will enter, and what quantity will be sold. Looking at these variables one by one, we see a fairly close fit between the theory and the data. For example, in 53 of the 57 periods in which the market was run, no more than one firm had positive sales in market B. In 41 of these periods, prices were within 10 experimental dollars of the predicted price of 325. In contrast, the natural monopoly theory failed to predict prices. In no period was the price within 10 experimental dollars of the natural monopoly price of 684. Also, the contestable market theory says that the quantity sold should be at the quantity where the price defined by the demand curve equals the average cost of production (31 units in this experiment). As it turned out, the quantity sold was within 3 units of the predicted quantity in 49 of 57 periods. It was never that close to the natural monopoly quantity of 17. When comparisons are made between the contestable market theory and other explanations, it is similarly superior. In short, this experiment offers support for the contestable market theory.

Rate-of-Return and Price-Cap Regulation

Rate-of-Return Regulation

While average-cost pricing sounds simple, it requires that the regulatory commission have all the relevant information about the producer's costs. Because this information may be difficult to obtain, the commission suggests the use of **rate-of-return regulation**, which is not only very simple to administer but also requires less information than the regulatory schemes discussed previously (marginal-cost pricing and average-cost pricing). The idea behind rate-of-return regulation is as follows: When people invest their money in an enterprise, they expect to receive a rate of return that is at least as good as the rate of return they could have earned by investing their money elsewhere, perhaps in a savings account at a bank. If they do not obtain such a rate of return, they will probably conclude that the investment was not a wise one and should be ended. Therefore, a regulatory commission must allow any firm under its jurisdiction to earn a rate of return for the firm's investors that is sufficient to warrant their keeping their capital investment in the firm. However, to prevent large monopoly profits, the firm will not be allowed to earn more than some *fair* rate of return. Hence, if profits are large enough to create an *excessive* rate of return for investors, the firm will be directed to reduce the price of its regulated product.

> **rate-of-return regulation**
> Regulation in which a regulatory commission must allow any firm under its jurisdiction to earn a rate of return for the firm's investors that is sufficient to warrant their keeping their capital investment in the firm.

Let us assume that when our entrepreneur organizes his water supply firm, he obtains some of the necessary capital from a group of investors. If we let K stand for the amount of capital contributed by our entrepreneur and his investors, then after the firm has paid its variable costs, it must earn enough money to pay its investors rK, where r is the rate of return allowed by the regulators. In choosing this rate, the regulators wanted to make sure that it would be sufficiently large to satisfy the investors. Note that K, the amount of capital in the firm, is something *observable*, so a regulatory commission should find it relatively easy to *measure* that amount. If we assume that the inputs for the production of purified water are capital and labor and if we let w_1 be the wage rate for labor, L, let Q be the output of the firm, and let p be the price of pure water, then rate-of-return regulation tells us that $pQ - w_1L \leq rK$. This means that after the firm subtracts its labor costs from its revenues, the amount that is left must not be greater than is necessary to pay a rate of return on capital of r. To help it decide on the merits of rate-of-return regulation, the commission hires its own consulting firm.[3]

To understand the reasoning of the consultants, say that our entrepreneur's water supply firm is allowed to earn $(100 \times r)\%$ on its capital. Say that the firm decides to produce $\overline{Q}$ units of purified water at a price of $\overline{p}$ per unit. Hence, the firm's revenue will be $\overline{p}\,\overline{Q}$. If the firm is efficient, it will produce this output with a certain combination of capital and labor that we will denote by (K^*, L^*). Assume, however, that if the firm uses this combination of inputs, it will make a rate of return greater than r on its capital. What this means is that $\overline{p}\,\overline{Q} - w_1L^* - rK^* > 0$, or $\overline{p}\,\overline{Q} - w_1L^* > rK^*$. If the firm is forced to earn a lower return and if we assume that $\overline{p}$ and $\overline{Q}$ are fixed, the only way to satisfy this regulatory constraint is to change the input mix.

---

[3] H. Averch and L. L. Johnson, "Behavior of the Firm Under Regulatory Constraint," *American Economic Review* (December 1962): 1,053–69.

CONSULTING REPORT 18.2

EVALUATING THE EFFECTIVENESS OF RATE-OF-RETURN REGULATION

The consultants are not favorably disposed toward rate-of-return regulation. They tell the members of the regulatory commission that this type of regulation will not cure the problem of excessive cost that average-cost pricing creates, and it will lead to inefficient production. They explain their response as follows. In choosing among the different combinations of labor and capital that can be used to produce any given quantity, a regulated firm will tend to select an inefficient mix of inputs that gives it a desired rate of return rather than the mix of inputs that represents the most efficient method of production. Rate-of-return regulation encourages a firm to use more capital than is necessary or efficient to produce its product. ●

rate base
The amount of capital of a firm upon which its rate of return is calculated.

There are two ways that the firm can alter its combination of inputs. One way is to use more labor and less capital. Let us call such a bundle (K', L'). The other way is to use more capital and less labor. We will call such a bundle (K'', L''). Now assume that at both (K', L') and (K'', L''), the firm exactly satisfies the regulatory constraint. This means that both $\bar{p}\bar{Q} - w_1 L' = rK'$ and $\bar{p}\bar{Q} - w_1 L'' = rK''$ are true. However, because (K'', L'') is the bundle using more capital, the firm will keep rK'' as its return and pay only $w_1 L$ to its workers. If the firm uses (K', L'), it will keep only rK' as its return and will pay much more to its workers. From this example, we see that rate-of-return regulation forces a firm to produce outputs in an inefficient manner. The firm has an incentive to satisfy the regulatory constraint by using more capital than it actually needs because capital is the rate base on which its return is calculated. Rate-of-return regulation biases the use of inputs toward the one on which the rate of return is calculated.

Figure 18.10 illustrates the point that we have just been discussing. In this we see an isoquant of the firm depicting all the combinations of inputs that exactly produce output $\bar{Q}$.

The straight line RR' represents the rate-of-return constraint in the sense that along all points on RR', we have $\bar{p}\bar{Q} - w_1 L - rK = 0$. Points above the constraint, like B, imply a lower rate of return than r. (With p and Q fixed at $\bar{p}$ and $\bar{Q}$, any increase in the use of labor and capital to produce $\bar{Q}$ will imply lower profits.) The opposite is true for points below line RR'. Points above the line more than satisfy the constraint, but we can presume that a profit-maximizing regulated firm will not choose them because the firm is allowed a return of r and will presumably try to obtain at least that return for its investors. Points below the line imply a rate of return greater than r, which is not allowed by the regulatory commission.

Note that point A is the cost-minimizing input combination (K^*, L^*) for producing $\bar{Q}$. However, this input combination cannot be chosen as a way to produce $\bar{Q}$ because it will create too high a rate of return for the firm. If the firm wants to satisfy the regulatory constraint in a manner that produces the best return for its investors, it will choose point C, where the input combination is (K'', L''). This input combination is on isocost line $C^2 C^2$. Note that the optimal input combination for output Q (point A) is on isocost line $C^1 C^1$. (Point D, which contains the combination $[K', L']$, will also satisfy the regulatory constraint but will yield less return for the firm because it pays so much money to labor and involves so little capital; that is, it provides such a small rate base.) While an unregulated firm will choose the cost-minimizing input combination at point A, a regulated firm will select the capital-maximizing input combination at point C to obtain the allowable

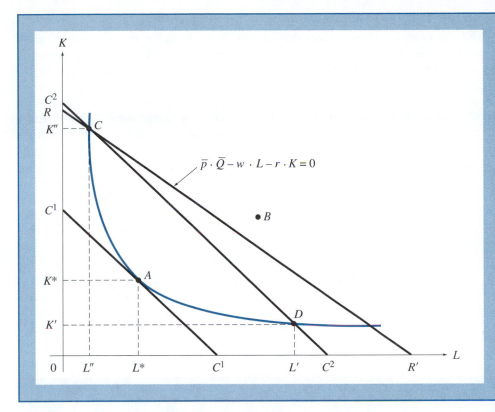

Figure 18.10

The Averch-Johnson Analysis.

Rate-of-return regulation forces the firm to choose a point on or above line RR'. The input combination that maximizes profits subject to the rate-of-return constraint is point C, at which the firm is producing in a more capital-intensive manner than is optimal for that output (point A).

rate of return. Hence, regulation forces a firm to produce outputs in an inefficient manner.

This weakness of the rate-of-return method prompts the members of the regulatory commission to look for another way of solving the regulatory problem. They now turn their attention to schemes that will give a regulated firm an incentive to hold down its costs. One member of the commission suggests price-cap regulation.

CONSULTING REPORT   18.3

USING PRICE-CAP REGULATION AS AN INCENTIVE FOR EFFICIENCY

The consultants are favorably impressed with price-cap regulation because it gives firms an incentive to improve the efficiency of their operations, and more efficient operations can lead to lower prices for consumers and higher profits for producers. The consultants explain that the idea behind price-cap regulation is simple. As firms continually produce the same product or service, they should become better and better at it. Over time, if a firm wants to minimize its costs, it can learn to do so and produce more efficiently. Price-cap regulation tries to give regulated firms an incentive to do just that by allowing them to keep at least a portion of the cost savings they create.

The consultants then explain to the members of the regulatory commission how the price-cap method works.

Suppose you find that the productivity of the water supply firm increases by 3% each year so that the cost of purified water drops by that amount. To implement the price-cap method, you announce that you will adjust the price of purified water to consumers each year by the difference between the rate of increase in the cost of the inputs and 3% (the expected yearly increase in the productivity of the water supply firm). If the input costs increase at a faster rate than 3%, the price of water will rise, while if the input costs increase at a slower rate than 3%, the price of water will fall. Therefore, if the water supply firm can increase its productivity at a rate that is greater than 3%, it can keep the additional cost savings for itself. ●

Price-Cap Regulation

All the methods of regulation that we have studied so far create a *moral hazard* with respect to cost containment because they provide an incentive to maximize costs. The greater a firm's costs are, the greater the price it can charge or the greater the rate of return it can receive. For example, under average-cost pricing, the amount a firm is permitted to charge for a product is based on the average cost of producing that product. A higher cost leads to a higher price. Why should a firm regulated in this manner care about holding down its costs when it knows it can always pass on cost increases to the consumer by raising its price? Similarly, rate-of-return regulation provides an incentive to use excessive amounts of capital in order to increase the firm's rate base. The regulatory commission recognizes that this is a significant problem and therefore decides to have its consulting firm study the idea of price-cap regulation—a method of regulation that is designed to encourage efficient production by allowing firms to share in any cost savings they achieve in producing their product.[4]

A monopolist faced with price-cap regulation will quickly realize that the more he can decrease his operating costs, the more he will benefit because all cost savings beyond the "cap" belong to his firm. This type of regulation creates a real incentive for the monopolist to reduce his costs. Of course, the public also benefits because of lower prices or at least smaller increases than would occur with another regulatory method.

price-cap regulation
A method of regulation that is designed to encourage efficient production by allowing firms to share in any cost savings they achieve in producing their product.

EXPERIMENTAL EVIDENCE

DOES CONTESTABILITY WORK?

Though one can argue that contestability seems to be a good model of how the world works, it would be nice to have an empirical basis upon which to make a judgment. One way to accomplish this is to look at the real world and try to find situations where the assumptions upon which the theory is based are satisfied and then try to determine if the theory's predictions are supported in practice. Another approach would be to run a laboratory experiment where the environment can be controlled and behavior can be tested in that controlled setting. Let us talk about both.

Remember that there are two major assumptions that need to be satisfied if a market is to be contestable. One is what we can call the *sticky price assumption*, or an assumption that specifies that when an incumbent firm sets a price, its potential competitors can enter the market and underprice it without that firm being able to change its price in the short run. The other assumption is a *no sunk cost* assumption.

A real-world industry that satisfies these assumptions is the airline industry. Before the 1970s, the airline industry was fairly heavily regulated. Rates were controlled and service was dictated for many localities, which were not especially profitable. However, during the Carter administration, the industry was deregulated and competition was allowed to rule. One reason such a move was considered possible is that the airline industry looks somewhat contestable. For example, say that you are a firm that has 20 planes and you are serving only the New York–California route, but you notice that there is little competition in the New York–Florida corridor where prices are high. In order to enter the new route, you need only to arrange for airport landing rights at Florida—a relatively minor cost—and take one of your planes from your California route and move it to the Florida route. In other words, because your planes on the New York–California route have the option of a low-cost Florida business, they are not sunk costs. In fact, there are few sunk costs in this case. Thus, if the incumbent firms on

---

[4] The idea of price-cap regulation was first developed by Peter Linhart, a mathematician, and Roy Radner, an economist, at the Bell Telephone Laboratories in Murray Hill, New Jersey.

that route eventually lower their prices after you enter and force you out, you can always take your planes and go elsewhere. Because of the lack of sunk costs, the Florida route is subject to "hit-and-run" entry, which is the basis of the theory of contestability. (Although airlines can change their rates quickly in response to entry, there is typically a lag that is long enough to allow an entrant to attempt to become entrenched.)

The history of airline deregulation is difficult to evaluate and is filled with price wars and erratic movements. One thing that is clear, however, is that the competition created by deregulation, given the relative ease with which airlines can switch routes if profits seem available elsewhere, has lowered considerably the cost of travel to the consumer.

Another approach to testing the theory of contestability is to run an experiment where the assumptions upon which the theory is based can be controlled in the laboratory to see if the predictions of the theory are supported. Though many such experiments have been conducted, one summarized by Glenn Harrison[5] captures the two features of the theory that characterize it—no sunk costs and sticky prices. (The actual experiment performed was conducted by Harrison and McKee.[6])

The Harrison-McKee experiment took place in the following manner. Two or three subjects were designated as firms. The firms were presented with three schedules indicating their marginal costs and the marginal and average revenue derived from the demand curve in the market. These are presented in Table 18.1.

Given these marginal cost and marginal revenue schedules, each laboratory firm had to choose a price and quantity to offer to the market. Once these prices and quantities were offered, the buyers in the market, who were represented by computer programs in the experiment instead of live subjects, were chosen randomly and were able to buy all they wanted in the market; they first purchased from the lowest-price firm and then worked their way up to higher- and higher-price firms if their demands were not satisfied. High-price firms were shopped at last and faced the possibility of never being able to serve the market if all demand was previously satisfied by lower-price firms. After the computerized shopping occurred, the profits of each firm were derived and the next market period began. In the next period, however, the firm that had sold the largest quantity the period before was designated as the incumbent and had

Table 18.1   Marginal Revenue and Costs.

Unit	Average Revenue	Marginal Revenue	Marginal Cost
1	$6.23	$5.98	$4.98
2	5.98	5.48	4.73
3	5.73	4.98	4.48
4	5.48	4.48	4.23
5	5.23	3.98	3.98
6	4.98	3.48	3.73
7	4.73	2.98	3.48
8	4.48	2.48	3.23
9	4.23	1.98	2.98
10	3.98	1.48	2.73
11	3.73	0.98	∞

to publicly list a price for that period before the other firms had to list theirs. In other words, after the incumbent listed its price, that price could not be changed and the other "entrant firms" could choose their prices, given the knowledge of the incumbent's price. By this device, Harrison and McKee emulated the sticky price assumption we have listed before. (Note, of course, that there are no sunk costs in the experiment.)

Before we proceed, it is important to note that this market institution is an example of the posted offer institution common among many retail stores in the United States. In such an institution, firms post prices, and consumers search among them and shop from the lowest-price firm. In this experiment, the buyers were computers and had perfect information about prices, so they didn't really need to search but simply went to the lowest-price firm to satisfy their demands. As we have seen in the Smith monopoly experiments, such an institution is favorable to the monopolist; thus, if we get more competitive results in this experiment, they should be a result of the contestability features built into the experiment by Harrison and McKee.

To measure the performance of these experimental markets, Harrison and McKee devised the following monopoly performance index:

$$M = \frac{p - p_c}{p_m - p_c} 100$$

where p is the actual profit made by the firms in one or more periods, and p_c denotes the trading profits that

(Continued)

[5] Glenn Harrison, "Experimental Evaluation of the Contestable Market Hypothesis," in *Public Regulation*, ed. E. Bailey (Cambridge MA: MIT Press, 1986).

[6] Glenn Harrison and Michael McKee, "Monopoly Behavior, Decentralized Regulation, and Contestable Markets," *The Rand Journal of Economics* 16 (1985): 51–68.

would be made if the market were at the competitive equilibrium, which, as we will see, is defined by price being equal to marginal cost. (This is also the price at the intersection of the market supply and demand curves.) The theoretical monopoly profit defined by equating the marginal cost and marginal revenue in the market is p_m. Clearly, if the market converges to the competitive equilibrium, then $M = 0$ because the numerator in M will be zero. If the market reaches the monopoly solution, then $M = 100$ because the numerator and denominator in M will be equal. Looking at Table 18.1 on marginal costs and revenues, we can see that the monopoly price in the market is $5.23 and the monopoly quantity is 5. (The competitive price is $2.61 and the competitive quantity is 10, but this is not easily determined from the table.)

If contestability is functioning in this market, we should see the monopoly index, M, converging toward zero over time as incumbent firms learn that setting a price above the competitive price will attract entry and yield lower profits. Figure 18.11 demonstrates exactly that as it presents the average monopoly index, M, pooled over all experiments run with the contestable market conditions.

As we can see, after only two periods the monopoly index is practically zero and stays there for the remainder of the experiment. In other experiments run by Harrison and McKee elsewhere, when the contestability feature is removed—that is, where there is no incumbent and no sticky prices—M is considerably higher,

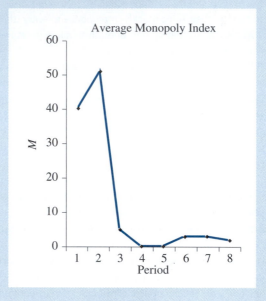

Figure 18.11

The Harrison-McKee Experiment.
The market performs better as subjects learn.

showing how sensitive the results of the experiment are to deviations from the assumptions of the theory.

In short, Harrison and McKee give stunning evidence that the contestability theory may be predictive in the real world if we can ever find circumstances that match those outlined in the theory.

Other Regulatory Issues

Regulating Multiproduct Monopolies

When a monopolist faces a technology with decreasing average costs, we know from a previous discussion in this chapter that the problem of natural monopoly is bound to arise and that it will be necessary for the firm to use some form of pricing other than marginal-cost pricing. For example, the firm may have to set a price that is equal to the average cost of the product even though such a price will cause a deadweight loss in welfare. If a monopolist produces several different types of goods under conditions of decreasing average costs, the problem becomes even more complex. We will now turn our attention to this problem.

Let us say that our primitive society must deal with the issue of regulating a multiproduct monopolist. This firm produces two types of goods, which we will call good 1 and good 2. How can the regulatory commission determine the second-best welfare-optimal price for each of these products? The regulatory

---

[7] The Ramsey pricing rule is named for Frank Ramsey, the famous British mathematician who devised it.

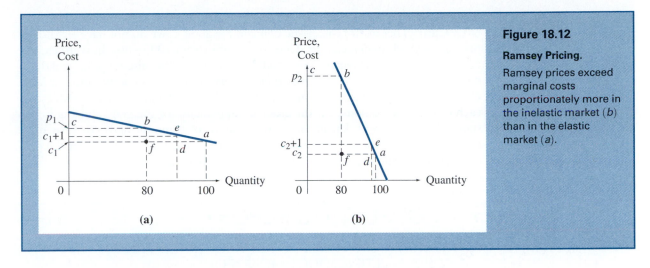

Figure 18.12

Ramsey Pricing.

Ramsey prices exceed marginal costs proportionately more in the inelastic market (*b*) than in the elastic market (*a*).

commission seeks advice from its consulting firm about the situation. The consultants suggest the use of a pricing formula called the **Ramsey pricing rule**.[7] The formula makes it possible to set prices that will cover the common fixed cost of the producer but also minimize the loss of consumer surplus.

Let us now take a closer look at the Ramsey pricing rule so that we can better understand the pricing policy that the consultants are suggesting to the members of the regulatory commission.

Ramsey pricing rule
The pricing formula that makes it possible to set prices that will cover the common fixed cost of the producer but also minimize the loss of consumer surplus.

The Ramsey Pricing Rule

The Ramsey pricing rule can be stated as follows: The prices of a regulated multiproduct monopolist should be set so as to curtail the production of all outputs in the same proportion from the hypothetical levels they would have reached if the prices had been set at the marginal cost of the products.[8] To see what this means, let us say that, at the regulated prices, p_1 and p_2, the demands for good 1 and good 2 are $D^1(p_1)$ and $D_2(p_2)$. Further assume that the demands for these goods if the prices were set at marginal costs c_1 and c_2 would be $D_1(c_1)$ and $D_2(c_2)$. Then the Ramsey pricing rule dictates $D_1(p_1)/D_1(c_1) = D_2(p_2)/D_2(c_2)$.

This rule shows that the less elastic the demand for a good is, the more its price will diverge from (rise above) its marginal cost. For example, consider Figure 18.12, which depicts the demand curves for goods 1 and 2. Note that the demand for good 1 is rather elastic, while the demand for good 2 is rather inelastic.

As we raise the price of each good above its marginal cost, a surplus develops. This surplus can be used to cover the firm's common fixed cost. The Ramsey pricing rule indicates that we should continue raising prices proportionately until enough surplus exists to cover the common fixed cost completely. Assume that if prices are set at the marginal cost, the demand for both good 1 and good 2 will be 100. Further assume that if we raise the prices so that there is a 20% decrease in the quantity sold of each good (that is, we raise the prices of the two goods above their marginal costs to p^1 and p^2), the sum of the surpluses generated (*cbfc*$_1$ for

[7] The Ramsey pricing rule is named for Frank Ramsey, the famous British mathematician who devised it.

[8] For an elaboration of this rule, see William W. Sharkey, *The Theory of Natural Monopoly* (Cambridge, England: Cambridge University Press, 1982).

good 1 and $cbfc_2$ for good 2) will be just enough to cover the common fixed cost of c_0. Clearly, because of the elastic demand for good 1, we do not have to raise its price very much to decrease its demand by 20% (from 100 to 80). In contrast, because of the inelastic demand for good 2, we will have to raise its price greatly to decrease its demand by 20%. From these observations, we can derive another form of the Ramsey pricing rule: $(p_1 - c_1)/p_1 = -k/\xi_1$ and $(p_2 - c_2)/p_2 = -k/\xi_2$. In each of these expressions, ξ is the elasticity of demand for the good and k is a constant whose value will depend on c_0, the amount of common fixed cost that must be covered. As we can see, the greater the elasticity of demand, the smaller the percentage by which the price of a good will diverge from its marginal cost.

CONSULTING REPORT 18.4

USING THE RAMSEY PRICING RULE TO SET REGULATED PRICES FOR A MULTIPRODUCT MONOPOLY

The consultants explain the derivation of the Ramsey pricing rule by referring to the monopolist who produces two types of goods, which we have called good 1 and good 2. We will assume that the cost of producing q_1 units of good 1 and q_2 units of good 2 is $C(q_1 + q_2) = c_0 + c_1 q_1 + c_2 q_2$. The consultants point out that in this cost function, there is a common fixed cost, c_0, which must be paid no matter which good is produced. The marginal cost of producing good 1 is c_1, and the marginal cost of producing good 2 is c_2. We will assume that the demand for good 1 and the demand for good 2 are independent of each other so that $q_1 = D(p_1)$ and $q_2 = D(p_2)$. With these demand functions, it is almost as if the monopolist sells each of his goods to a separate group of consumers so that the price charged to group 1 (for good 1) has no effect on the demand for good

2 and the price charged to group 2 (for good 2) has no effect on the demand for good 1.

The consultants remind the members of the regulatory commission that the welfare-maximizing solution to their problem is to have the monopolist price each good at its marginal cost so that $p_1 = c_1$ and $p_2 = c_2$. However, this is not a feasible solution because such prices will not cover the common fixed cost of c_0 and the monopolist will therefore lose money. Clearly, the prices to be used must diverge from the marginal cost of the goods. The consultants emphasize that the prices set for a multiproduct monopolist should diverge from marginal cost in an optimal way that minimizes the loss of surplus to society. The Ramsey pricing rule accomplishes this objective. ●

To see why the Ramsey pricing rule works, consider Figure 18.12 again. In order to minimize the welfare loss from having the prices of goods 1 and 2 diverge from their marginal costs, we will want to continue raising their prices until the resulting welfare loss is equal for each group of consumers and the common cost is covered. In this example, we are measuring welfare as the sum of the consumer surpluses of the two groups (the marginal cost is constant here, so there is no producer surplus when the price charged is the marginal cost). Thus, it should be clear that if the marginal welfare loss from a price increase is different for each of the two groups (let us say greater for group 1 than for group 2), then it is worthwhile to alter these price changes and have a smaller price increase for the group that is hurt relatively more.

To see how this situation leads to the Ramsey pricing rule, assume that we are considering an increase of one unit above marginal cost in the prices of goods 1 and 2. As a result, in Figure 18.12(a), the price for group 1 will rise from c_1 to $c_1 + 1$. Similarly, in Figure 18.12(b), the price for group 2 will rise from c_2 to $c_2 + 1$. Note that the price increase for group 1 causes a loss of welfare, or consumer surplus, equal to the area ead in (a), which is much greater than the loss of welfare that occurs when group 2 receives the same price increase (as shown in area ead of [b]).

Such price increases are sufficient to cover the common fixed cost of the firm, but clearly, they are not optimal. By lowering the price to group 1 and raising the price to group 2, we can decrease the loss in welfare that results and still obtain the same surplus to cover the common fixed cost. Price must rise more in an inelastic market than in an elastic one. This logic yields the Ramsey pricing rule.

SOLVED
PROBLEM
18.5

Question (Content Review: Ramsey Pricing)

All-Sport is the sole producer of replica baseball and football jerseys. The production of baseball jerseys has a cost function of $c(q_B) = 1,000 + 75q_B$, where q_B is the number of baseball jerseys produced. The production of football jerseys has a cost function of $c(q_F) = 2,000 + 50q_F$, where q_F is the quantity of football jerseys. The demand for baseball jerseys is $D_B(p) = 5,000 - 2p$, and the demand for football jerseys is $D_F(p) = 4,000 - p$. The government has decided that the sports fan is an important part of the economy and should not be overcharged by a monopolist. It decides that it will employ Ramsey pricing to regulate All-Sport's production of jerseys. What two equations must the regulator solve to determine at what price and quantity All-Sport should sell under Ramsey pricing?

Answer

The first equation is the zero-profit equation. For All-Sport, this would be

$$\left(2,500 - \frac{q_B}{2}\right)q_B + (4,000 - q_F)q_F - (1,000 + 75q_B) - (2,000 + 50q_F) = 0$$

The second equation is the Ramsey pricing equation:

$$\frac{D_B(p_B)}{D_B(MC)} = \frac{D_F(p_F)}{D_F(MC)}$$

To translate this in terms of quantities, first recognize that $D_B(p_B) = q_B$ and $D_F(p_F) = q_F$. Looking at the cost functions, we see that each additional baseball jersey costs $75, so the marginal cost of baseball jerseys is $75. Likewise, the marginal cost of football jerseys is $50. Plugging these two marginal costs into the respective demand curves, we get

$$D_B(MC) = 5,000 - 2(75) = 4,850$$
$$D_F(MC) = 4,000 - 50 = 3,950$$

Thus, the Ramsey pricing formula is

$$\frac{q_B}{4,850} = \frac{q_F}{3,950}$$

Solving both of these equations simultaneously for q_B and q_F and plugging these values back into their respective demand curves will give the Ramsey prices for each market.

Conclusion

One type of institution that we see in many societies is the government-regulated natural monopoly. This type of institution is often used to supply public utilities such as electricity, gas, water, and telephone service to consumers. The society that we are studying in this book was forced to deal with the issue of regulating a natural monopoly because of the technological realities of that monopoly. In the next chapter, we will investigate what happens in a world where the technological conditions for natural monopoly do not exist. As we will see, in such situations, the case for government regulation is diminished but does not totally disappear.

Summary

In this chapter, we examined several techniques that societies use to regulate monopolistic firms. Although monopolies can be created in a number of different ways, we concentrated on those that develop when there is a technology that leads to a natural and sustainable monopoly. We saw that monopoly pricing produces results that are not socially optimal; that is, monopolies do not set the best (the welfare-optimal) prices, which are equal to the marginal cost of the products. Monopoly pricing therefore creates a deadweight loss for society. We investigated a number of schemes that are used in an effort to eliminate part of this deadweight loss by inducing monopolists to charge the second-best welfare-optimal price.

We analyzed the theory of contestable markets, which says that no regulation is needed because the fear of potential competition will keep the behavior of monopolists under control. We also examined three methods of regulating prices: rate-of-return regulation, price-cap regulation, and Ramsey pricing. We saw how rate-of-return regulation attempts to achieve both a socially desirable price for consumers and a fair return on capital for investors. However, this method of price regulation tends to encourage excessive use of capital and discourage efficient production. Price-cap regulation is designed to overcome these problems. It offers monopolists an incentive for efficiency by allowing them to share any cost savings with consumers. The Ramsey pricing rule is intended to set prices that will be sufficient to cover the common fixed cost of a multiproduct monopolist but will also minimize the welfare loss of consumers.

APPENDIX A

THE ALLOCATION OF COMMON COSTS: CROSS-SUBSIDIZATION

The path of regulation of natural monopolies is strewn with many economic and political dangers. For example, the regulatory commission in our primitive society is becoming very aware that there are identifiable groups of people in this society who have different ideas about which rate structure is optimal for purified water. The commission must meet with representatives of these groups to hear their grievances, and it must hold public hearings to solicit a wide range of opinions whenever it is time to re-evaluate the rate structure.

The Problem of Allocating Common Costs Among Customers

Although everyone in our primitive society pays the same rate for water, the cost of serving customers varies a great deal. This situation has led to the biggest problem that the regulatory commission now faces—the problem of the fairness of a uniform rate. Some customers who are less costly to service feel that, because everyone is charged the same price for water, they are being treated unfairly. For example, if the water supply firm has to pump water through its pipes to people living 100 miles from its plant, then these people are more costly to service than people who live 50 miles from the plant. Clearly, there is a cost connected with building and maintaining each mile of the firm's pipeline. The people who live closer to the plant see no reason why they should have to subsidize the customers who live farther away by paying the same price for water. In other words, the costs of delivering water to customers from the plant are shared, or **common costs**, and are currently allocated equally among the customers regardless of where they are located along the pipeline. The issue that the regulatory commission must now deal with is whether there is a more fair way to divide these costs. This is the same type of problem that the commission faced when it used the Ramsey pricing rule in regulating the prices of a multiproduct monopoly so that no one group of consumers would suffer too great a loss of welfare by paying an excessive share of the firm's common fixed cost.

common costs
Costs that are shared among customers.

To make the issue of fairness in setting water rates even more compelling, assume that the people who live at the end of the water supply pipeline are the wealthiest people in society. Let us also assume that all groups agree that they will pay their fair share of the expense of building and maintaining the pipeline, but they differ as to what *fair share* means in this context.

Determining a Fair Price

At first, the regulatory commission considers a *fair price* to be one that provides water to customers at a lower cost than they can provide it to themselves. For example, the members of the commission reason that if the people living 50 miles from the plant were not customers of the water supply firm, they would have to set up their own plant to purify the water and their own pipeline to deliver the water to their homes. This might be very costly. If it will cost them more to provide themselves with water than they are paying the water supply firm, then they should not complain about the fairness of the firm's price. Basically, this type of fairness test is called a stand-alone test. It asks consumers not to think about the price being charged to others, but rather to compare the price they are paying for the service with the price they would have to pay if they provided it for themselves. If consumers are currently paying less for water than it would cost them to obtain it for themselves, they cannot claim that they are subsidizing others. In fact, the existence of other consumers is what makes it possible for the water supply firm to offer such low rates.

Now assume that a representative of the community located 50 miles from the water treatment plant reacts to the stand-alone test as follows: We know that we *alone* cannot provide water more cheaply for ourselves than we can obtain it from the water supply firm. However, if we form a water-producing coalition or cooperative with other communities, we can provide ourselves with water more cheaply. For example, if we get together with the communities located 35 and 45 miles from the existing plant, we can build our own small plant and distribution system and, by splitting the necessary costs, we can actually pay less than we are currently paying.

In a sense, this group of communities is subsidizing the high-cost areas because it can do better by operating its own water supply system. The group therefore demands that a **generalized stand-alone test** be used and that a rate structure be developed that satisfies the test. This type of rate structure must be such that no individual community or group of communities can do better for itself than to obtain its water at the rates offered by the water supply firm.

generalized stand-alone test
The test that asks a group or individual community of similar consumers to compare the price they are paying for the service with the price they would have to pay if they provided it for themselves.

We can explain this rate structure more formally as follows.[9] Assume that there is a town that has a pure water well at its center. Two communities (communities 1 and 2) are located to the east of this well, and two communities (communities 3 and 4) are located to the west of the well. The annual cost of maintaining the well and the above-ground storage tank used to hold water after it is pumped from the well is $100. The water supply system also includes an eastern pipeline that is used to serve communities 1 and 2 and a western pipeline that is used to serve communities 3 and 4. Each of these pipelines has a yearly maintenance cost of $100. Further, there is a $100 cost attributable to each community for distribution of the water. The total yearly cost of operating this public utility is therefore $700 ($100 for the well and the storage tank, $200 for the two pipelines, and $400 for the four distribution systems). Let r_1, r_2, r_3, and r_4 be the revenues collected from each of the four communities. If the regulated utility is to break even, then it must be that $r_1 + r_2 + r_3 + r_4 = 700$.

To find a set of prices for these communities that will satisfy the generalized stand-alone test, we must search for prices that are such that once they are set (and the revenues r_1, r_2, r_3, and r_4 are determined), no individual community or group of communities can do better for itself than simply buying water at the prices offered by the regulated utility. More precisely, we are looking for prices that will determine the revenues to be collected from the communities in such a way that the following set of inequalities will be satisfied. (Remember that revenues earned by the regulated utility are costs to the communities in which it operates.)

$$r_i \leq 300, \quad i = 1, 2, 3, 4$$
$$r_1 + r_2 \leq 400$$
$$r_3 + r_4 \leq 400$$
$$r_1 + r_3 \leq 500$$
$$r_2 + r_4 \leq 500$$
$$r_i + r_j + r_k \leq 600$$
$$r_1 + r_2 + r_3 + r_4 = 700$$

These inequalities have a simple explanation. Any single community can supply itself with water each year by paying $100 for maintenance of the well and the storage tank, $100 for maintenance of the pipeline, and $100 for distribution expenses. Therefore, the total cost to any individual community for supplying itself with water is $300. The first inequality tells us that the prices charged (which determine the revenues to be collected by the utility) must not total more than $300 for any individual community. If the total is greater than $300, the community will simply set up its own water supply system and obtain the water it needs at a lower cost. In terms of the concept of the core discussed in Chapter 21, any individual community can block prices that will cost it more than $300. Similarly, any two communities on the same side of the well, communities 1 and 2 or communities 3 and 4, can band together to supply themselves with water each year by paying $100 to maintain the well and the storage tank, $100 to maintain the pipeline, and $200 for the expenses connected with the two distribution systems. The total cost to any such group of two adjacent communities is $400, so the revenues that the utility collects from them must be less than $400. Otherwise, such a group will block the prices that generate these revenues and will provide water for itself.

---

[9] The material presented here is based on Gerald Faulhaber, "Cross Subsidization: Pricing in Public Enterprise," *American Economic Review* 65 (December 1975): 966–77.

It is more expensive to supply communities on opposite sides of the well because two pipelines must be built and maintained—an eastern pipeline and a western pipeline. In fact, we see from the inequalities that it will cost $500 for a coalition consisting of two such communities and $600 for a coalition consisting of three such communities. If prices can be found that produce revenues satisfying these inequalities, then no community or group of communities can object. The prices will be "fair" in the sense that they will be *subsidy-free*. In fact, many such prices exist. For example, say that the regulated utility charges individual communities $175. Clearly, at this price, each community will do better obtaining its water from the regulated utility than it can do by itself because the cost of providing its own water is $300. Similarly, if the utility charges any group of two adjacent (or nonadjacent) communities $350 rather than the $400 (or $500) that it will cost such a group to operate its own water supply system, then the group is better off buying its water from the utility. The same is true for any group of three communities if the utility charges $525 and the group will have to pay $600 to provide its own water. No individual community or group of communities can block this symmetric price schedule. Other nonsymmetric price structures also exist.

One question that arises is whether there are subsidy-free prices in all such pricing situations. The answer to this question is no. However, it still makes sense to put pricing structures to a generalized stand-alone test and see if subsidy-free prices exist. If these prices are available, then they should be considered. If they do not exist, then it is at least clear that some subsidies will be necessary.

The preceding analysis bears some similarity to our analysis of exchange in Chapter 21, which uses the concept of the core of an economy. In that situation, we looked for an allocation that was such that no individual or group of individuals could form a coalition and block the proposed allocation. Obviously, our current analysis involves a similar issue, but instead of allocations, we are dealing with prices and with shares of common costs.

APPENDIX B

FRANCHISE MONOPOLY

Consider the problem of setting up a telephone system in a community that has never had one before. If the community simply allows different telephone companies to sell their services and the companies cannot agree to share a common wiring system, then each company will wire the houses of its customers separately. As a result, the various telephone companies will have incompatible systems; unless people obtain their service from the same company, they will not be able to talk with each other by telephone. The only other alternative will be for people to subscribe to all companies and have many telephones in their homes, which will be wasteful and costly. Obviously, this is not a practical arrangement. The government therefore decides that it will grant a license, or **franchise**, to one company to set up a monopoly that will provide telephone service to the community.

franchise
The license a government grants to a company that allows it to set up a monopoly.

Using a Demsetz Auction to Overcome the Problem of Franchise Monopoly

The decision to grant a franchise for telephone service raises another problem. By giving just one company the right to provide telephone service to the community, the government is creating a monopoly, and we know that monopolies tend to set high prices and restrict output, which leads to a deadweight loss for society.[10] One possible solution is for the government to announce publicly that it will create a monopoly involving telephone service and that this monopoly will be awarded in the following way: On a given date, there will be an auction at which people will be able to bid for the right to operate the telephone monopoly for a certain number of years, which we will call T. The amount of the winning bid will be paid to the government. After T years, the government will again seek competitive bids for the telephone franchise. This type of auction is called a **Demsetz auction**.[11] Figure 18.13 illustrates how a Demsetz auction works.

Demsetz auction
An auction in which the right to be the exclusive franchisee of a good or service is auctioned by the government.

In Figure 18.13, we see the typical situation of a monopolist facing a linear demand curve and a U-shaped marginal cost curve. As we know, the monopolist will sell the quantity at which the marginal cost equals the marginal revenue (point a) and will price the product on the demand curve at that point. The welfare loss to society from this solution is the triangular region *dea*, which represents the deadweight loss from the monopoly. Note, however, that at the monopoly price the firm's profit is equal to the area $p^m dfc$. Let us call this amount π^m. If the right to be a monopolist is auctioned off, then any potential monopolist should be willing to bid up to the amount π^m for that right. The reason is simple. Once the potential monopolist obtains the franchise, he will be able to earn π^m. If he wins the auction with a bid that is less than this amount, say b^*, then he will be earning extra-normal profits equal to $\pi^* - b^*$. In fact, the only Nash equilibrium bid in the auction will be equal to π^m. To see why this is true, let us assume that a bidder actually wins the auction with a bid that is lower than π^m, say b^*. Then if there are n bidders, there will be $n - 1$ losers and one winner, which means that one of the losers will have an incentive to bid $b^* + \varepsilon, b^* < b^* + \varepsilon < \pi^m$, where ε is some small positive number. If this bid wins, then again there will be $n - 1$ losers and one winner, and a loser will have an incentive to bid above $b^* + \varepsilon$. We can assume that this process will continue until all participants in the auction bid π^m. At that point, the situation is in equilibrium. (Let us say that if all participants in the auction bid the same amount, a random device is used to choose the winner.)

The equilibrium for the auction occurs at a bid of π^m because no bidder will want to bid more than that even though a higher bid would surely win the auction; however, such a bid would cost more than the monopoly is worth. Similarly, no bidder will want to bid less than π^m. At a bid of π^m, each bidder can expect to win with a probability of $1/n$ and can expect to earn $(1/n)(\pi^m)$. A lower bid will surely lose and produce earnings of zero (which is what we assume losing is worth).

We can therefore expect that a franchise auction will raise π^m in revenue for the government. This money can be used to compensate the consumers who suffer from the deadweight loss because of the pricing practices of the monopolist. If the area $p^m dfc = \pi^m$ in Figure 18.13 is larger than the area representing the deadweight loss, *dea*, then the amount of revenue raised by the auction can compensate society for the fact that this industry is being run by a monopolist.

Criticisms of the Demsetz Auction

Like all the other schemes for overcoming the effects of monopoly that we have investigated, the Demsetz auction presents some problems. One problem is that all

---

[10] The material discussed here is based on Harold Demsetz, "Why Regulate Utilities," *Journal of Law and Economics* 11 (April 1968): 55–65.

[11] The Demsetz auction is named for the economist who devised it, Harold Demsetz of the University of California at Los Angeles.

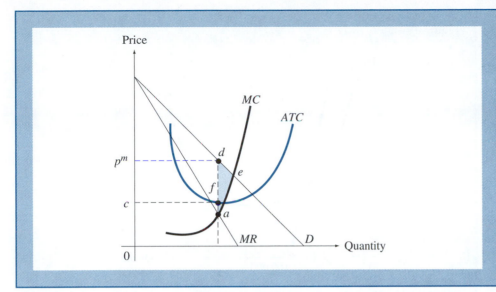

Figure 18.13

A Demsetz Auction.

A potential monopolist would be willing to bid up to the amount represented by the area $p^m dfc = \pi^m$, the monopoly profit, for the right to be a monopolist.

bidders may not be in an equal position after several years when the second auction is held. Before the first auction, all bidders may be in an identical position. However, by the time the second auction is held, a monopolist has been in control of the industry for T years, and it is very likely that this incumbent monopolist will be in a better position than the other bidders to win the auction on advantageous terms. Therefore, in the future, we can expect the auction to raise less and less money.

The second problem with the Demsetz auction is very fundamental. After the auction is over, society will have to live with all the disadvantages of having a monopolist in charge of an industry. In fact, it will have to face a monopolist who is protected by government sanction.

Exercises and Problems

1. A firm that makes widgets must build a plant that will cost $10,000. The plant will be able to produce up to 10,000 units, at which point its capacity will be reached and a new plant will be needed. The total cost function for each plant (including the fixed cost of building the plant) is $C(q) = \$10,000 - q^{1/2}/100$.

   a) Determine the cost function for this firm.

   b) Is this cost function subadditive over the range of outputs from 1 unit to 10,000 units? Is it subadditive for all levels of output?

2. Consider the information about demand and cost that appears in Figure 18.14.

   a) If a firm faces the demand and cost situation depicted in Figure 18.14, will it be a sustainable monopoly at the price and quantity combination of $p = 10$ and $q = 100,000$?

   b) Will the firm be a sustainable monopoly at the combination of $p = 14$ and $q = 90,000$? What about the combination of $p = 11$ and $q = 90,000$?

   c) If the firm tries to produce 95,000 units and charge a price of $12 a unit, could a potential entrant take away any of its market?

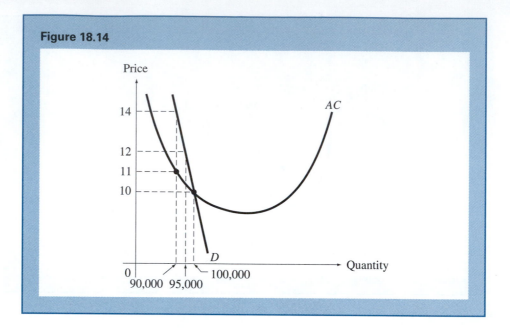

Figure 18.14

d) Describe a strategy that would allow a potential entrant to take away this firm's market (that is, describe a price and quantity choice for the potential entrant).

3. Consider Figure 18.15, which depicts the demand and cost situation of a monopolist. Is the monopoly price sustainable in this situation?

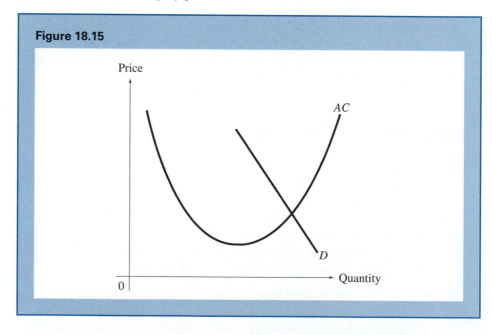

Figure 18.15

4. Can one potential entrant police the behavior of many monopolists? Consider a case in which there are two monopolists in different industries. Figure 18.16 depicts the demand and cost situations faced by these monopolists.

   As we can see, each monopolist is capable of setting a monopoly price and earning extra-normal profits. The potential entrant is capable of entering either

Figure 18.16

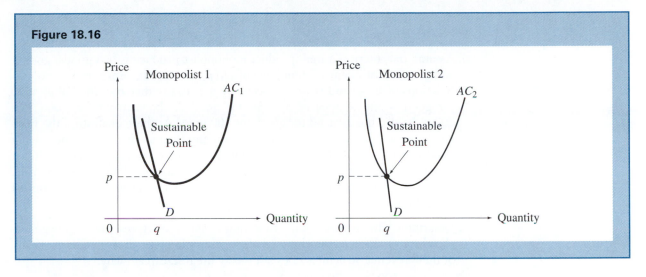

industry and can use the same technology as the existing firm in the industry. Let us assume that the potential entrant has perfectly mobile capital and that there are no sunk costs involved in leaving either industry. By perfectly mobile capital, we mean that the potential entrant can move his capital from one industry to the next without any cost. Let us assume that he has only enough capital to enter one industry at a time, so he will have to choose which industry, if any, he wants to enter now.

Consider the following game played by the potential entrant and the two monopolists. In the first move, each monopolist sets a price for her product. Next, the potential entrant looks at these prices and decides whether either industry offers him an opportunity to make a profit. If there is no opportunity for profit, he will stay out of both industries. If both industries offer an opportunity for profit, he will decide which one will provide the bigger profit and enter that industry. When entry occurs, the incumbent monopolist will not be able to respond quickly. Hence, the entrant will be able to take away the entire market and make a profit, at least temporarily.

The game described here is one in which the prices that the two monopolists set for their goods determine not only the profits they will make from selling their goods but also the likelihood that the potential entrant will come into their markets. Despite the fact that the potential entrant can come into just one market at a time, an observer of this game claims that its only equilibrium is one in which both monopolists set their prices at the sustainable (average-cost) level. The observer concludes that one potential entrant can police the behavior of two monopolists under contestable-market assumptions. Prove that this conclusion is true.

5. Say that a monopolist has a cost function of the following type: $C(q) = bq$, which indicates that there are no fixed costs and that the marginal costs are constant. A regulatory agency claims that setting the price of this firm's product so that it is equal to the average cost will provide the "best" outcome for society.

   a)   Demonstrate that the claim of the regulatory agency is correct given the firm's cost function.

   b)   Is it true that average-cost pricing produces an optimal result for all cost functions?

c) What is special about this particular cost function that makes the agency's claim true?

6. Assume that there is a multiproduct monopolist producing two goods, good 1 and good 2, with demand functions of $D_1(p)$ and $D_2(p)$, respectively, and cost functions of $C_1(q)$ and $C_2(q)$, respectively. Let us say that at a price of $p_1^* = 20$ for good 1 and a price of $p_2^* = 30$ for good 2, the demand for good 1 is 200 units and the demand for good 2 is 300 units. At these quantities, the marginal cost of producing good 1 is $15 a unit and the marginal cost of producing good 2 is $20 a unit. The firm has a common fixed cost of $4,000, which must be met in order for the firm to stay in business. Using the Ramsey pricing rule, demonstrate that this price structure produces the second-best welfare-optimal result for society.

7. Determine whether each of the following revenue structures satisfies the generalized stand-alone test in the case of the example given in Appendix A. If any of these revenue structures does not satisfy the test, explain why.

a) $r_1 = 300$, $r_2 = 200$, $r_3 = 100$, $r_4 = 100$
b) $r_1 = 100$, $r_2 = 300$, $r_3 = 200$, $r_4 = 100$
c) $r_1 = 200$, $r_2 = 300$, $r_3 = 200$, $r_4 = 0$
d) $r_1 = 250$, $r_2 = 100$, $r_3 = 250$, $r_4 = 100$

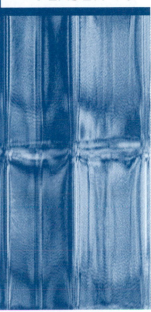

OLIGOPOLY

Consider an experimental market with only two firms of the type investigated by Steffen Huck, Wieland Mueller, and Hans-Theo Normann.[*] Let us say that these firms produce an identical good and do so by producing a quantity of the good and putting it on the market. After both firms produce their quantity, the price is determined by the market demand function and each firm then can calculate its profits by multiplying the market price by its output and subtracting its cost of production.

Think of this market being played as follows. In one version, firm 1 produces its output first and announces it, and then firm 2, knowing the announcement of firm 1, produces its output. In the second version, both firms, without knowing the choice of the other, produces an output.

The question for you to think about is under which set of rules, the sequential or the simultaneous choice rules, is total welfare highest where welfare is defined as the sum of consumer plus producer welfare? Under which set of rules are firms less likely to collude? Say the experiment is repeated for many periods. In one treatment, each firm receives a randomly chosen opponent while in the other its opponent stays fixed. Under which treatment would you think collusion among the firms would be least likely?

---

[*] Steffen Huck, Wieland Mueller, and Hans-Theo Normann, "Stackelberg Beats Cournot: On Collusion and Efficiency in Experimental Markets," *Economic Journal* 111 (474), 2001, 749–65.

IMITATION IN OLIGOPOLISTIC MARKETS

While the theory of oligopoly we learn in this chapter will be an equilibrium theory—that is, we will study the Nash equilibrium of the game defined by the market—economic agents like firms or people don't start out acting as if they were in equilibrium. Rather, through repetition and experience they learn about the situation they are in and their behavior converges to or approaches that defined by the theory.

One way to learn is to imitate others. But whom should you imitate? In an interesting paper by Theo Offerman, Jan Potters, and Joep Sonnemans,[*] the researchers indicate that, depending on whom firms imitate, the market converges to a different outcome. (By *imitating*, we mean copying that firm's output level.) For example, firms might

(Continued)

---

[*] Theo Offerman, Jan Potters, and Joep Sonnemans, "Imitation and Belief Learning in an Oligopoly Experiment," *Review of Economic Studies,* 2002, vol. 69., pp. 973–97.

EXPERIMENTAL
TEASER 20 *(Contd.)*

imitate the firm that received the highest profit last period, or they could imitate the firm whose output would be best for all of them if they all adhered to it. In theory, one of these imitation rules will lead to a competitive outcome where profits are zero, while the other will lead to a collusive outcome. Which imitation rule leads where, and do you think we would observe these outcomes in a laboratory experiment?

The economy that we are studying in this book is still extremely primitive. At the present time, we are studying productive enterprises, all of which are monopolies. This economy is certainly far from the type of highly competitive free enterprise system that we are familiar with in the United States and that we studied previously in Chapters 14 and 15. So the question is how competitive markets emerge from either monopolistic markets or markets with small numbers of firms. To find the origins of competitive markets, we will have to investigate other industries in which the technology is such that several firms, if not many firms, can survive simultaneously at the equilibrium.

In this chapter, we will see a new industry that is not a sustainable or natural monopoly developed in our primitive society. This industry produces a recently discovered product called a gadget. The first entrepreneur in the industry quickly realizes that once she establishes her firm and begins to sell her product, other firms will attempt to imitate the product and enter the industry. Unless she can prevent the entry of such potential competitors, the industry will rapidly undergo a transformation from a monopoly to a *duopoly* and then to an *oligopoly*. As we investigate the events that occur in this industry, we will examine the theory of duopoly and oligopoly—the theory of markets with two or a few competing firms. This theory will be of major importance in Chapter 20 when we see our gadget maker plan a strategy to keep potential entrants out of her market.

Production in a Nonnatural Monopoly Situation

Let us assume that an agent in our primitive society comes upon a technology to make a product that we will call a gadget. This technology is such that the marginal cost of producing gadgets rises as more are produced and rises at an increasing rate. Figure 19.1 shows such a marginal cost curve along with the assumed average cost curve for the firm producing the gadgets.

Remember that we usually depict marginal cost curves as being U-shaped, like the average cost curve shown in Figure 19.1. We could easily have done so again, but, for the sake of simplicity, we will assume that in this case the marginal cost is always increasing. There is no contradiction between a U-shaped average cost curve and a constantly rising marginal cost curve because the firm presumably has fixed costs that make the average cost of production high at low levels of output. As these average fixed costs fall with the increase in output, so does the average cost until the rising marginal cost of production pulls the average cost up again.

We will assume that the inverse demand for gadgets is a simple linear function $p = A - bq$, where p is the market price of the good, A is a constant, b is the slope of the inverse demand function, and q is the total output placed on the market.

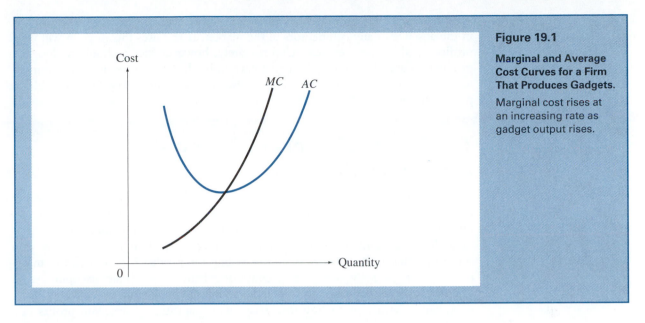

Figure 19.1

Marginal and Average Cost Curves for a Firm That Produces Gadgets.

Marginal cost rises at an increasing rate as gadget output rises.

This function tells us the maximum price attainable for any given quantity sold and is therefore called the *inverse demand function*.

Our gadget maker sees immediately that if she can keep competitors out of her market, she will be able to make a substantial profit for herself. Figure 19.2 demonstrates this fact by showing her demand function superimposed on her cost function.

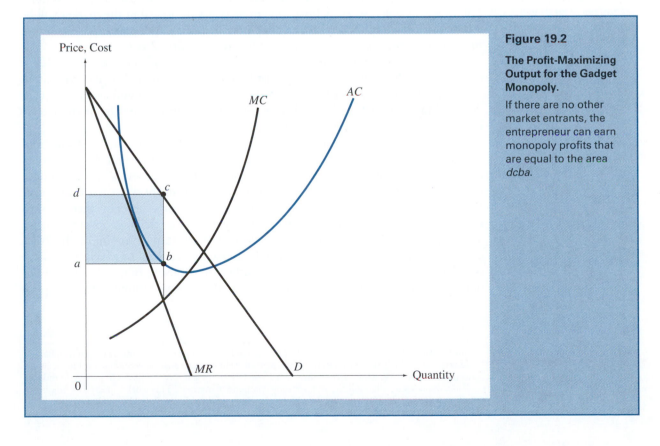

Figure 19.2

The Profit-Maximizing Output for the Gadget Monopoly.

If there are no other market entrants, the entrepreneur can earn monopoly profits that are equal to the area *dcba*.

Figure 19.2 also indicates the monopoly price that the gadget maker can set in the absence of any competitors in the market. If she uses this price, it will yield profits equal to the area *dcba*. Unfortunately, however, her technology does not give her a natural monopoly. She will have to battle to keep competitors from entering her market because, presumably, two or even more firms will be able to profitably coexist in this market.

The Cournot Theory of Duopoly and Oligopoly

As our gadget maker starts to plan a strategy for keeping other firms out of her market, she realizes that in order to know how to prevent entry, she needs an understanding of what the industry might be like with competition present. For example, what kind of market equilibrium might she face if the industry is a duopoly—that is, if there are two firms selling the product? To obtain this information, our gadget maker hires a consulting firm, which bases its opinions on Cournot's theory (or model) of duopoly, a famous theory that was devised in the nineteenth century to analyze the behavior of quantities, prices, and profits in a two-firm market.[1]

duopoly
An industry in which there are two firms selling a product.

The consultants issue a report that summarizes the essential features of the Cournot model. (Although this model is for a duopoly, it can be, and often is, extended to an oligopoly—a market that is dominated by a few sellers of a product.)

Cournot model
A model in which firm 1 and firm 2 choose a quantity simultaneously, and after both firms have chosen their outputs, the price of the good on the market and the profits of both firms are determined.

To understand the Cournot model better, let us assume that there are two firms in the gadgets market and that these firms face a linear inverse demand function of $p = A - b(q_1 + q_2)$. Clearly, the price that will prevail in the market will be a function of the outputs of *both* duopolists, q_1 and q_2. We can express the cost function for firm 1 as $C(q_1)$ and the cost function for firm 2 as $C(q_2)$.

oligopoly
A market that is dominated by a few sellers of a product.

Note that while the demand function and the price depend on the output levels of both duopolists, each duopolist's cost function is determined by its own output level. We will assume that both cost functions have marginal and average costs as depicted in Figure 19.1. Marginal costs rise as output grows and rise at an increasing rate, while average costs are U-shaped.

Given a two-firm industry with the linear demand function and cost functions shown in Figure 19.1, we want to use the Cournot model to find the answers to the following questions: What will be the *equilibrium* output levels of the two duopolists? What price will prevail in the market? What profit will each firm make? By *equilibrium*, we mean a pair of output levels, one for each firm, that are such that after they are chosen, neither firm has any incentive to change its output level. This type of equilibrium is called a Cournot equilibrium. It is simply the Nash equilibrium that we defined in Chapter 11 applied to a model in which duopolistic or oligopolistic firms compete with each other by choosing output levels. To understand how a Cournot equilibrium is reached, we must examine the concept of reaction functions.

Cournot equilibrium
The Nash equilibrium applied to a model in which duopolistic or oligopolistic firms compete with one another by choosing output levels, that is, the Nash equilibrium of a Cournot oligopoly model.

---

[1] Antoine Augustin Cournot (1801–1877) was a French mathematician, economist, and philosopher. He was one of the first scholars to use mathematical techniques to analyze economic problems. In his most noted work, which was published in 1838, Cournot examined problems of pricing in monopolistic, duopolistic, oligopolistic, and perfectly competitive markets. This work appeared in English as *Researches into the Mathematical Principles of the Theory of Wealth*, translated by Nathaniel Bacon (New York: Macmillan, 1897).

Reaction Functions

In every market, there is a strategic interaction among firms. Each firm in the market will respond to the actions of the other firms in some manner. These responses are summarized by what are called reaction functions or best-response functions. The reaction function specifies a firm's optimal choice for some variable such as output, given the choices of its competitors.

Using the Cournot model, let us assume that both firms in a duopolistic market want to make as much profit as they possibly can. However, each firm has a problem because its profit depends on the output level its competitor chooses as well as the output level it chooses, and it does not know what the choice of its competitor will be when it makes its own choice. We can summarize this situation by saying that both duopolists (firms 1 and 2) want to maximize their profits, as indicated by the following profit functions: $\pi_1[A - b(q_1 + q_2)] \cdot q_1 - C(q_1)$ and $\pi_2[A - b(q_2 + q_2)] \cdot q_2 - C(q_2)$.

reaction functions (best-response functions)
A function that specifies a firm's optimal choice for some variable such as output, given the choices of its competitors.

CONSULTING REPORT   19.1

USING THE COURNOT MODEL TO DETERMINE AN EQUILIBRIUM FOR A DUOPOLISTIC MARKET

The consultants explain that the Cournot model is based on two key concepts about the firms in a duopolistic market: that each will behave in a profit-maximizing manner and that each will assume that the other firm will keep its output constant at the existing level when it changes its own output. We can think of the Cournot model as one in which firms alternate making decisions about the quantity they wish to produce. First, one firm chooses what it considers to be a profit-maximizing level of output. Then, given that firm's choice of a quantity and assuming it will not change, the other firm sets its own profit-maximizing quantity.

This process of adjustment continues through several stages of action and reaction until the two firms reach an equilibrium and have no further incentive to change their outputs. During the entire process of adjustment, each firm believes that the other firm's current level of output is fixed and uses this assumption in selecting its own level of output.

In the Cournot model, the quantity, price, and profits produced at the equilibrium for a duopolistic market will be between those that occur in a monopolistic market and those that occur in a perfectly competitive market. ●

Note that the price that either duopolist faces, $[A - b(q_1 + q_2)]$, and the profit it will earn depend on the output of both duopolists. Note also that each profit function is composed of two parts. The first part is the revenue component of profit, which is represented by the price of the good, $[A - b(q_1 + q_2)]$, times the output of the firm, q_1 or q_2. The second part of the profit function is simply the duopolist's cost, $C(q_1)$ or $C(q_2)$.

Let us now say that firm 2 decides to produce $\bar{q}_2$ units of output. Under the Cournot model, firm 1 assumes that no matter what output choice it makes, firm 2 will not change its own output choice in response. Economists today call this assumption the Cournot conjecture. More generally, we will let the conjectural variation denote the change that a firm expects in its competitor's choice of an output level in response to a change the firm made in its own output level. Using this definition, we can say that the conjectural variation in the Cournot model is zero. (Later we will consider oligopoly models with nonzero conjectural variations.)

Given firm 2's decision, firm 1's profit is now solely determined by its own output choice, which means that we can express its profit function as $\pi_1 = [A - b(q_1 + \bar{q}_2)] \cdot q_1 - C(q_1)$. In a sense, firm 1 is now a monopolist because, with

Cournot conjecture
In a Cournot duopoly, the Cournot conjecture is an assumption that no matter what change in output a firm makes, the other firm will not change its own output choice in response.

conjectural variation
The change that a firm expects in its competitor's choice of an output level in response to a change the firm makes in its own output level.

firm 2's output fixed at $\bar{q}_2$, the price of the good is only a function of the output choice of firm 1. Given firm 2's decision, firm 1 should now choose an output level that equates its marginal revenue to its marginal cost. To see how the optimal output for firm 1 is derived, consider Figure 19.3.

Figure 19.3 shows the demand function and the associated marginal revenue function facing firm 1 at different levels of output set by firm 2. To understand how these functions are determined, consider what happens when firm 2 chooses an output of $\bar{q}_2$. If the inverse demand curve for the product is $p = A - b(q_1 + q_2)$, then with an output of $\bar{q}_2$ for firm 2, the inverse demand curve facing firm 1 will be $p = (A - b\bar{q}_2) - bq_1$. In other words, if firm 2's output is fixed at $\bar{q}_2$ and firm 1 sets an output of zero, then the price will be $A - b\bar{q}_2$. The output of firm 2 reduces the price from A, which is what it would be if *both* firms set a zero output. As firm 1 raises its output, the price will fall even further and the slope of the demand curve will be $-b$.

In Figure 19.3, the demand curve labeled D_1 is the one that will result when firm 2 sets its output at $\bar{q}_2$. If firm 2 chooses a higher level of output, say q_2', then the demand curve for firm 1 will shift toward the origin, as shown by D_2. The reason for this shift is that the price that will result now if firm 1 sets an output of zero is $A - bq_2'$, which is less than $A - b\bar{q}_2$, because $q_2' > \bar{q}_2$. Note, however, that the slope of the demand curve remains the same. If firm 2 chooses a level of output that is lower than $\bar{q}_2$, say q_2^*, then the demand curve for firm 1 will be further from the origin, as depicted by D_3. In this case, if firm 1 sets an output of zero, the market price will be $A - bq_2^*$, which is greater than $A - b\bar{q}_2$, because $q_2^* < \bar{q}_2$.

In Figure 19.3, we also see the marginal cost curve for firm 1. Depending on the output level chosen by firm 2, we can now define the output level that represents the best response—the profit-maximizing choice—for firm 1. Finding the best response is a simple matter. First we locate the demand curve for firm 1 that is associated with the quantity chosen by firm 2, and then we find the output level at which firm 1's marginal revenue equals its marginal cost. For example, say that $\bar{q}_2$ is the quantity set by firm 2. We therefore look at the demand curve labeled D_1 and the marginal revenue curve labeled MR_1 in Figure 19.3 and see that q_1^1 is the optimal level of output for firm 1. It is firm 1's best response because it is the output level that maximizes the firm's profit. Similarly, if firm 2 sets a quantity of q_2',

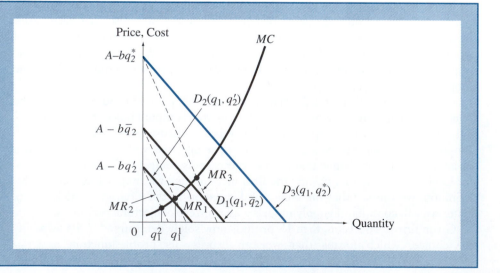

Figure 19.3

The Optimal Output for a Gadget Duopolist.

Given firm 2's production of $\bar{q}_2$, firm 1 maximizes its profit by choosing output level q_1^1, which equates its marginal cost to its marginal revenue given that $\bar{q}_2$ units are already in the market.

the relevant demand and marginal revenue curves for firm 1 are D_1 and MR_1, and its best response is to choose an output level of q_1^2. In this way, we can define a best response for firm 1 to every hypothetical output level of firm 2. The reaction function for firm 1 is formally presented in Figure 19.4.

Note that in Figure 19.4 the output level of firm 1 is inversely related to the output level of firm 2. The more firm 2 produces, the less firm 1 will produce. It is important to realize that each point on this reaction function represents the *optimal (profit-maximizing) choice or best response* of firm 1 to a possible output level of firm 2.

A similar analysis can be made for firm 2 in order to derive its reaction function and find its best response to each level of output that firm 1 might choose. Such a curve appears in Figure 19.5.

In Figure 19.5, we again see that the optimal or profit-maximizing output level for one duopolist (firm 2) is a decreasing function of the output level chosen by the other duopolist (firm 1), given the Cournot conjecture. For convenience, we can express these reaction functions for the duopolists in the gadgets market as $q_1 = f_1(q_2)$ and $q_2 = f_2(q_1)$.

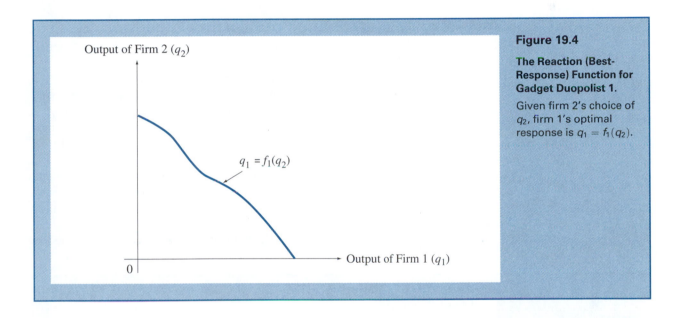

Figure 19.4

The Reaction (Best-Response) Function for Gadget Duopolist 1.

Given firm 2's choice of q_2, firm 1's optimal response is $q_1 = f_1(q_2)$.

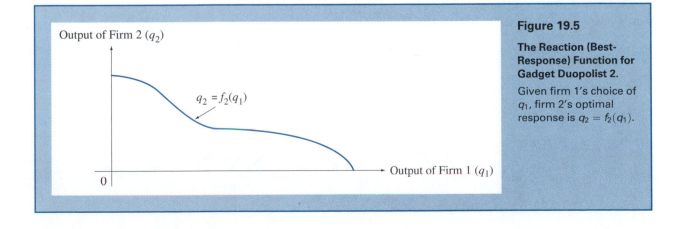

Figure 19.5

The Reaction (Best-Response) Function for Gadget Duopolist 2.

Given firm 1's choice of q_1, firm 2's optimal response is $q_2 = f_2(q_1)$.

SOLVED
PROBLEM
19.1

Question (Application and Extension: The Best Responses)

Assume that there are two firms, each producing with a constant marginal cost function of $MC = 2$. Assume that the demand function for the product is defined as follows: $p = 100 - 0.5(q_1 + q_2)$. If firm 2 sets a quantity of $q_2 = 100$, what is the best response quantity for firm 1?

Answer

If firm 2 sets a quantity of $q_2 = 100$, then the residual demand curve facing firm 1 is $p = 100 - 0.5(q_1 + 100) = 100 - 0.5q_1 - 50 = 50 - 0.5q_1$. If the marginal cost of production is constant at 2, then the firm should set a quantity at which the marginal revenue associated with the residual demand curve is equal to the constant marginal cost. We know that the marginal revenue curve associated with this demand curve has the form $MR = 50 - q_1$ because it has a slope with twice the steepness of the demand curve. Setting $MR = MC$ means setting $50 - q_1 = 2$. Solving, we see that $q_1 = 48$, and this is the best response.

An Alternative Derivation of Reaction Functions

There is an alternative, and perhaps simpler, way to derive the reaction function for a firm. Consider Figure 19.6.

In Figure 19.6, each point, like point x, represents output levels for firm 1 and firm 2. For example, at point x, firm 1 produces q_1' and firm 2 produces q_2'. At point q_1^m, the output of firm 1 is q_1^m, and the output of firm 2 is zero. In other words, q_1^m is firm 1's monopoly output. This output combination of $(q_1^m, 0)$, in which firm 1 produces its monopoly output and firm 2 produces zero output, yields profits for firm 1 that are greater than the profits it can earn with any other output combination.

Now look at the output combination at point a of Figure 19.6. At that point, firm 1 continues to produce its monopoly output of q_1^m, but now firm 2 produces a positive output. Clearly, firm 1 will receive lower profits at point a than it will at point q_1^m because the positive output of firm 2 decreases the price that firm 1 can obtain for its output. Let us now locate the **isoprofit curves** in this space—the sets

Isoprofit curves
The set of outputs for all firms in a market that yield a given firm the same profit level.

Figure 19.6

Reaction Function.

For each level of q_2, firm 1's reaction function gives the level of q_1 that places firm 1 on the lowest attainable isoprofit curve (that is, the level of q_1 determined by the tangency of the isoprofit curve and a horizontal line). Given $q_2 = q_2'$, firm 1 chooses $q_1 = q_1'$; given $q_2 = \bar{q}_2$, firm 1 chooses $q_1 = \bar{q}_1$.

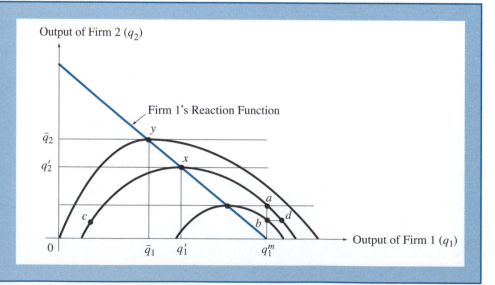

of points that yield the same profits to firm 1. We will start by looking for those output combinations that yield the same profits as point a. Let us examine point b, where again firm 1 produces the monopoly output of q_1^m, but now firm 2 is producing less than it did at point a. Clearly, the reduction in firm 2's output raises firm 1's profits above what they were at point a. To bring the profits of firm 1 back to what they were at point a, we have two options. We can move to either point c or point d. At point c, firm 1 has lower output than it did at point b, which raises the price of gadgets but lowers the firm's profits because it is now selling a smaller quantity of the product. At point d, firm 1 has higher output than it did at point b, which allows it to sell a greater quantity, but the additional output lowers the price and also increases the firm's costs. The net result is that points c, a, and d all have the same profit levels. In general, the isoprofit curves for firm 1 have the shape shown in Figure 19.6. The curves closer to the horizontal axis (and closer to the monopoly output level) contain higher levels of profit.

To derive the reaction functions for firms 1 and 2, let us look first at firm 1. For any given output level chosen by firm 2, the reaction function should tell us the profit-maximizing output level for firm 1. Say that firm 2 sets an output level of q_2'. Given this choice by firm 2, firm 1 will want to choose the output level that places it on the lowest possible isoprofit curve because profits increase as firm 1 moves toward the horizontal axis. This output level will be characterized by the tangency of the isoprofit curve and the line drawn parallel to the horizontal axis at the height of q_2'. Such a tangency occurs at point x in Figure 19.6, where the output level is q_1'. When firm 2 chooses a higher level of output, such as $\bar{q}_2$, tangency occurs at point y and the optimal level of output for firm 1 falls to $\bar{q}_1$. By successively choosing different levels of output for firm 2 and finding the tangency points for firm 1, we can trace firm 1's reaction function. A similar analysis can produce firm 2's reaction function.

Deriving a Cournot Equilibrium

To find the Cournot equilibrium for this duopolistic market, we can simply take the two reaction functions for firms 1 and 2, place them on the same diagram, and see where they intersect. The point of intersection represents the equilibrium, as shown in Figure 19.7.

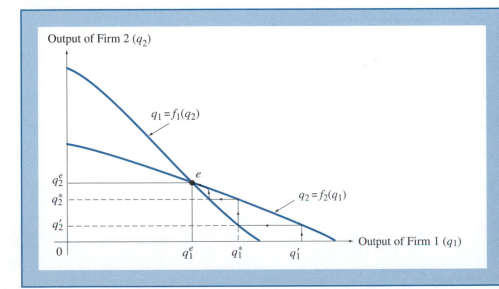

Figure 19.7

The Reaction Function Equilibrium (Nash Equilibrium) for the Gadget Duopoly.

The intersection of the two firms' reaction functions at (q_1^e, q_2^e) is the point at which each firm is responding optimally to the other's choice.

Note that the two reaction functions intersect at point e in Figure 19.7. At this point, firm 1 is producing an output of q_1^e and firm 2 is producing an output of q_2^e. If firm 1 produces q_1^e, then the best response for firm 2 is to produce q_2^e. Similarly, if firm 2 produces q_2^e, then the best response for firm 1 is to produce q_1^e. In short, q_1^e and q_2^e are the best responses of the two firms to each other. If both firms choose these output levels, neither firm will have an incentive to change its choice. Put differently, if these output levels are set, they will remain unchanged—the market will be in equilibrium.

Stable and Unstable Cournot Duopolies

At this point in our analysis, the following question arises. According to the Cournot theory of duopoly, the gadgets market will be in equilibrium *if* firms 1 and 2 choose output levels q_1^e and q_2^e, but what guarantee do we have that the two firms will actually choose these output levels? There are two responses to this question. The first response is that the Cournot theory does not claim that the duopolists will choose these output levels. All it says is that *if* they do choose these output levels, the market will be in equilibrium. The second response goes further and says that we can actually expect that the output levels in the market will eventually reach q_1^e and q_2^e.

Let us examine the reasoning behind the second response. Say that we are not at the equilibrium in Figure 19.7. Also say that firm 1 chooses an output level that is higher than its equilibrium output level of q_1^e, such as q_1'. From firm 2's reaction function, we see that it will then choose an output level of q_2', which is lower than its equilibrium output level of q_2^e. However, when firm 2 chooses q_2', firm 1's reaction function indicates that it will decrease its output from q_1' to q_1^*. With the output of firm 1 at q_1^*, the reaction function of firm 2 shows that it will now increase its output from q_2' to q_2^*, and so on. This process is *convergent*. If allowed to continue, it will lead the firms to converge on q_1^e and q_2^e, which are the equilibrium output levels for the market.

Does convergence on the equilibrium depend on how we draw the reaction functions? The answer to this question is yes. In Figure 19.7, the reaction functions are drawn in such a way that the one for firm 2 is flatter than the one for firm 1. If the opposite is true, then we will have the situation depicted in Figure 19.8.

Figure 19.8

An Unstable Cournot Equilibrium.

The reaction function of the firm whose output is measured on the vertical axis is steeper than the reaction function of the firm whose output is measured on the horizontal axis. In this case, the reactions of the two firms to a disequilibrium situation will take them further and further away from the equilibrium point.

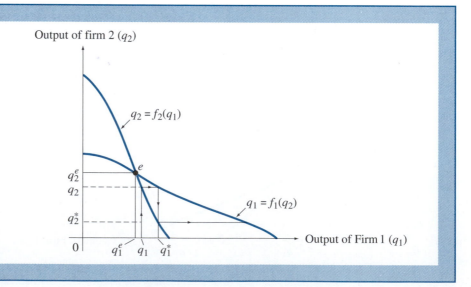

If the reaction functions are shaped as shown in Figure 19.8, it will be difficult for the market to converge to the equilibrium. In this case, it is still true that if the market ever reaches the equilibrium, it will remain there, but we cannot rely on the process of convergence to bring about the equilibrium.

To illustrate this point, let us say that the two firms are not at the equilibrium in Figure 19.8. We will assume that firm 1 chooses an output that is higher than its equilibrium output of q_1^e, such as q_1'. From firm 2's reaction function, we can see that it will then choose q_2', which is lower than its equilibrium output of q_2^e. When firm 2 chooses q_2', firm 1's reaction function shows that it will increase its output from q_1' to q_1^*, moving it further away from the equilibrium. With the output of firm 1 now at q_1^*, the reaction function of firm 2 indicates that it will decrease its output from q_2' to q_2^*, moving it further away from the equilibrium as well, and so on. This process is *divergent*. At each stage, it moves the two firms further away from the equilibrium.

SOLVED PROBLEM 19.2

Question (Application and Extension: Nash Equilibrium Quantities)

Assume that you have two firms competing in a market and that these firms have the following reaction functions:

$$q_1 = 50 - \frac{1}{2}q_2$$
$$q_2 = 50 - \frac{1}{2}q_1$$

a) For what quantity produced by firm 2 would firm 1 prefer to shut down and produce nothing?

Answer

Obviously, if firm 2 set a quantity of 100, then $q_1 = 50 - \frac{1}{2}(100) = 0$ and firm 1 would shut down.

b) What quantity would firm 1 produce if firm 2 never existed?

Answer

If firm 2 never existed, then $q_2 = 0$ and the best output for q_1 would be 50.

c) Verify that $q_1 = 33.3$ and $q_2 = 33.3$ is a Nash equilibrium.

Answer

We can verify that 33.3 for each firm is a Nash equilibrium by seeing if those quantities constitute a best response for each firm. Plugging 33.3 into each reaction function, we see that $33.33 = 50 - \frac{1}{2}(33.33)$; thus, if firm 1 is choosing 33.33, firm 2 will also want to choose 33.33, and vice versa. That is the definition of an equilibrium.

Using Game Theory to Reinterpret the Cournot Equilibrium

Our previous analysis of the Cournot equilibrium can be restated in terms of game theory. We can think of the strategic interaction between firms in a duopolistic market as a game, which we might call the **simultaneous-move quantity-setting duopoly game**. In this game, there are two players, firms 1 and 2, and each player has a strategy set from which it can choose a feasible strategy whenever

simultaneous-move quantity-setting duopoly game
The strategic interaction between firms in a duopolistic market as a game where each firm chooses its quantity simultaneously.

it must make a move. These strategy sets are equivalent to all the positive output levels in the Cournot model. However, to simplify the game, it might make sense to restrict the strategy sets to those output levels between 0 and A/b. Because A/b drives the price of the good to zero, we can presume that rational firms will never choose output levels above A/b. The payoff functions for this game are presented in two equations that we used previously: $\pi_1 = [A - b(q_1 + q_2)] \cdot q_1 - C(q_1)$ for firm 1 and $\pi_2 = [A - b(q_1 + q_2)] \cdot q_2 - C(q_2)$ for firm 2. These are the components of the game's normal form.

The game is played as follows: First, both firms choose their output levels simultaneously, with neither firm knowing what level the other firm has chosen. Once these quantities are placed on the market, the demand curve tells the players what the price will be, and each firm calculates its payoffs (profits) accordingly. The equilibrium defined by the Cournot model is nothing more than the Nash equilibrium in this simultaneous-move quantity-setting duopoly game.

SOLVED PROBLEM 19.3

Question (Application and Extension: Best-Response Functions and Nash Equilibria)

Bob and Art live next door to each other and share a driveway between their houses. Both men are botanists and love flowers. Each has decided to plant pansies on his side of the driveway. On one Saturday morning, each announces to the other that he is going to his own favorite gardening shop to purchase pansies. Because each man will plant the flowers so close to each other, both will get enjoyment from his own and his neighbor's pansies.

Art's preferences for how many pansies to purchase depend on how many Bob has bought and can be described by the best-response function

$$A = 20 - \frac{1}{2}B$$

where B is the number of pansies bought by Bob. Bob's preferences can be described by his best-response function

$$B = 24 - \frac{1}{4}A$$

where A is the number of pansies Art buys.

a) If Bob finds out that Art is going to buy 12 pansies, how many should he buy?

Answer

If Art buys 12 pansies, Bob's best response is

$$B = 24 - \frac{1}{4}(12) = 21$$

Thus, Bob should buy 21 pansies.

b) What is the equilibrium amount of pansies the men should buy if neither knows how many the other is going to purchase?

Answer

The equilibrium is found by solving the two best-response functions simultaneously—that is, solving the following two equations:

$$A = 20 - \frac{1}{2}B$$

$$B = 24 - \frac{1}{4}A$$

for A and B.

This can easily be done by substituting Bob's function into Art's function and solving

$$A = 20 - \frac{1}{2}\left(24 - \frac{1}{4}A\right)$$

$$= 8 + \frac{1}{8}A$$

$$\frac{7}{8}A = 8$$

$$A = \frac{64}{7}$$

and substituting back into Bob's best-response function

$$B = 24 - \frac{1}{4}\left(\frac{64}{7}\right)$$

$$= \frac{152}{7}$$

Thus, assuming that pansies (like all other goods) are perfectly divisible, in equilibrium Art buys $\frac{64}{7}$ pansies and Bob buys $\frac{152}{7}$. Because Art's best response is to buy $\frac{64}{7}$ pansies if Bob is going to buy $\frac{152}{7}$ pansies and Bob's best response is to buy $\frac{152}{7}$ pansies if Art is going to buy $\frac{64}{7}$, each pansy decision is a best response to the other. This is the definition of an equilibrium.

Criticisms of the Cournot Theory: The Stackelberg Duopoly Model

An Asymmetric Model

Our gadget maker thinks that she now understands the Cournot theory and its game theory interpretation quite well. However, she questions the relevance of the Cournot theory to her situation because she is worried about preventing potential competitors from entering the market in which she is already entrenched. As a result of this entrenchment, she believes that any entrant will view her as a kind of leader and will view himself, a relative upstart, as a follower. In other words, she feels that the Cournot theory treats firms or players symmetrically, but, in reality, the situation she faces is *asymmetric*, with her firm established as the leader and any firm that enters the market now taking the role of a follower. (Imagine a new firm starting to manufacture automobiles in the United States and having to compete with General Motors and Ford. Clearly, a theory that treats all firms in this type of market symmetrically would be unrealistic.) To obtain information about how an asymmetric market functions, our gadget maker turns to another consulting firm, one that bases its opinions on the work of Heinrich von Stackelberg, another economist who studied the problem of

Stackelberg model
A model in which one firm, firm 1, chooses its quantity first, and then the other firm, *knowing what firm 1 has done*, makes its choice. After both firms have sequentially chosen their outputs, the price of the good on the market and the profits of both firms are determined.

duopoly and developed a well-known duopoly model.[2] The new consulting firm issues the following report in which it describes the main features of the Stackelberg model.

Let us now take a closer look at the Stackelberg model by applying it to the gadgets market. We will assume the same demand, cost, and profit functions as we did with the Cournot model. We will say that demand is linear, that marginal costs are strictly increasing, and that profits are represented by the following two equations: $\pi_1 = [A - b(q_1 + q_2)] \cdot q_1 - C(q_1)$ for firm 1 and $\pi_2 = [A - b(q_1 + q_2)] \cdot q_2 - C(q_2)$ for firm 2. We will also assume that each firm has a Cournot reaction function defining its best response to any given output level chosen by its competitor. We will denote these reaction functions as $q_1 = f_1(q_2)$ for firm 1 and $q_2 = f_2(q_1)$ for firm 2.

CONSULTING REPORT 19.2

USING THE STACKELBERG MODEL TO DETERMINE AN EQUILIBRIUM FOR A DUOPOLISTIC MARKET

The consultants explain that the Stackelberg duopoly model is an extension of the Cournot model but allows for asymmetric behavior by the two firms in a duopolistic market. The Stackelberg model assumes that one firm will play an aggressive role in the market (be the leader) and the other firm will play a passive role (be the follower). The leader will choose its level of output first. It will set a profit-maximizing quantity, taking into consideration the quantity it expects the follower to set in reaction to its own choice. The leader assumes that the follower will also want to maximize its profits but that it will accept the leader's output choice as a given. This assumption permits the leader to predict the follower's output choice and take that choice into account when it makes its own output choice. ●

Stackelberg leader
The firm to move first in the Stackelberg model.
Stackelberg follower
The firm to move second in the Stackelberg model.

To make our example asymmetric, assume that firm 1 chooses its quantity first. Then, firm 2, *knowing what firm 1 has done*, makes its choice. After both firms have sequentially chosen their outputs, the price of the good on the market and the profits of both firms are determined. Because firm 1 moves first, it is the Stackelberg leader and can commit itself to a fixed output. Firm 2, the Stackelberg follower, then takes firm 1's output as a given and chooses a best response. In such a model, there is an advantage to moving first, as depicted by Figure 19.9.

In Figure 19.9, we see the reaction function of firm 2, the Stackelberg follower in this market. Firm 1, the Stackelberg leader, knows that for any output level it might set, firm 2 will set the output level that represents its best response to firm 1's choice. Therefore, firm 1 can predict firm 2's choice of an output level from its reaction function. If firm 1 is rational, it will choose the output level that maximizes its profits *after taking into consideration firm 2's best response to that output level*.

The Stackelberg Equilibrium

To understand what output level would be consistent with a Stackelberg equilibrium, let us look at Figure 19.9 again. Note that the isoprofit curves of firm 1 are

---

[2] Heinrich von Stackelberg was a German economist who examined market organization and the strategic interaction of firms. He proposed the leader-follower concept for duopolistic markets in *Marktform und Gleichgewicht* (Vienna: Julius Springer, 1934). This work appeared in English as *The Theory of the Market Economy*, translated by A. T. Peacock (New York: Oxford University Press, 1952).

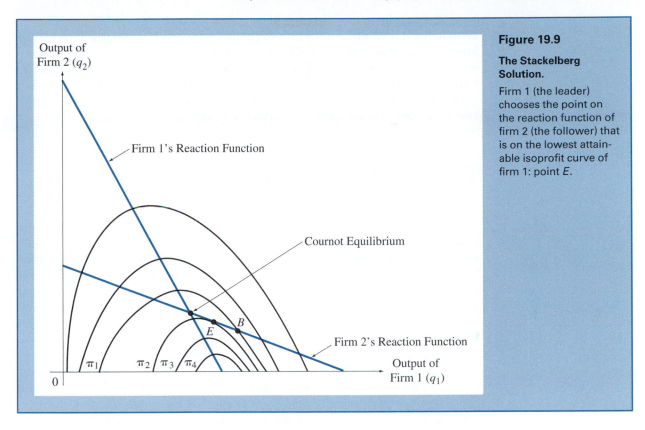

Figure 19.9

The Stackelberg Solution.

Firm 1 (the leader) chooses the point on the reaction function of firm 2 (the follower) that is on the lowest attainable isoprofit curve of firm 1: point E.

superimposed on firm 2's reaction function. The task for firm 1 is to choose the output level that will place it on the lowest possible isoprofit curve consistent with firm 2's choice of an optimal (profit-maximizing) quantity. In short, by moving first, firm 1 can actually choose at which point on firm 2's reaction function it wants the market to be—the point where its own profits will be greatest. In Figure 19.9, this profit maximization occurs at point E, where firm 1's isoprofit curve is tangent to firm 2's reaction function. Such a point represents a **Stackelberg equilibrium**.

To demonstrate that point E in Figure 19.9 must be a Stackelberg equilibrium, consider any other point such as B. Note that point B is on isoprofit curve π_1, which involves lower profits than isoprofit curve π_2, the one where point E is located. No output combination on isoprofit curves like π_3 and π_4 can be the equilibrium because it is not on firm 2's reaction function and therefore does not fit our assumption that firm 2 will act in a rational manner.

Algebraically, we can describe the Stackelberg model as follows: Let $q_2 = f_2(q_1)$ be firm 2's reaction function and let $\pi_1 = [A - b(q_1 + q_2)] \cdot q_1 - C(q_1)$ be firm 1's profit function. However, because firm 1 knows that firm 2 will respond to its output choice by choosing a best response, we can replace q_2 in firm 1's profit function with $f_2(q_1)$. Firm 1's profit function now reads $\pi_1 = [A - b(q_1 + f_2(q_1))] \cdot q_1 - C(q_1)$. Firm 1's problem is simply to maximize this profit function by choosing q_1, knowing that firm 2 will respond optimally to its choice.

As we see in Figure 19.9, at the Stackelberg equilibrium, firm 1 chooses a higher level of output than it previously did at the Cournot equilibrium and receives greater profits. This is the essence of the **first-mover advantage** that the leader has in the Stackelberg model.

Stackelberg equilibrium
The equilibrium prices and quantities of a Stackelberg game.

first-mover advantage
The advantage the leader (first mover) has in the Stackelberg model, which allows him to produce a higher level of output than he previously did in the Cournot equilibrium, thus receiving greater profits.

sequential-move quantity-setting duopoly game
A duopoly game in which firms alternate in setting quantities.

The Stackelberg model matches our gadget maker's view of her market as an asymmetric one in which her firm will be the leader and an entrant will be the follower. Remember that we characterized the Cournot model as a simultaneous-move quantity-setting duopoly game. Similarly, we can think of the Stackelberg model as a sequential-move quantity-setting duopoly game that results in a greater payoff for the leader and a smaller payoff for the follower than they would receive at the Cournot equilibrium of the same market.

The Welfare Properties of Duopolistic Markets

As our primitive society begins to develop markets where two or a few firms compete, a question naturally arises about the welfare aspects of the Cournot equilibrium: Do such markets produce a better welfare outcome than monopolistic markets? The answer to this question is as follows: The Cournot equilibrium outputs for firms in duopolistic markets yield better welfare results than those that occur in markets characterized by monopoly (when welfare is measured in terms of consumer surplus plus producer surplus), but the welfare results in such markets are not optimal. They are in between the welfare levels produced in perfectly competitive markets and those that occur in monopolistic markets. To prove this statement, let us again turn our attention to the gadgets market—a duopolistic market. As we did previously, we will assume that the inverse demand for gadgets is linear and is represented by $p = A - b(q_1 + q_2)$. For the sake of simplicity, we will also assume that the marginal cost of production is zero. (The results that we derive would not be different if we were to assume that the marginal cost is U-shaped or strictly rising, as in Figure 19.1.) Because each firm has zero marginal cost, it will set its marginal revenue equal to zero when the other firm chooses a level of output. Reformulating the problem with the assumption of zero marginal cost, we can express the profit function for the duopolists as follows: $\pi_1 = [A - b(q_1 + q_2)] \cdot q_1$ for firm 1 and $\pi_2 = [A - b(q_1 + q_2)] \cdot q_2$ for firm 2. Note that when the marginal cost is zero, maximizing profits is the same as maximizing revenue.

We can derive the reaction functions for the two firms from these profit functions by equating the marginal revenue for each firm to zero after the other firm has set its level of output. Using partial derivatives, we find that the marginal revenue is $MR_1 = A - 2bq_1 - bq_2$ for firm 1 and $MR_2 = A - 2bq_2 - bq_1$ for firm 2. Solving for q_1 and q_2 will give us the reaction functions of the two firms. These reaction functions will specify the profit-maximizing output that each firm should set for any given output of the other firm. We can express the reaction functions as follows: $q_1 = (A - bq_2)/2b$ for firm 1 and $q_2 = (A - bq_1)/2b$ for firm 2.

If a monopolist with the same cost structure were to provide all the gadgets for this market, then she would have to determine how much of output q to produce so as to maximize her profits. This problem can be stated as Max $\pi = (A - bq)q$. Note that because there is only one producer, the total output (q) for the market is the same as the sum of the firms' output ($q = q_1 + q_2$). To maximize this function, we take the derivative and make it equal to zero. We then find that the optimal monopoly output is $q = A/2b$.

Figure 19.10 represents the monopolistic market by our familiar inverse demand and marginal revenue curves. However, note that in this example, the marginal cost curve is flat and moves along the horizontal axis.

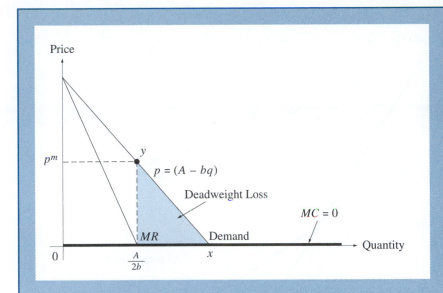

Figure 19.10

The Monopoly Solution with Zero Marginal Costs.

The monopolist will choose output $A/2b$, at which the marginal revenue equals the marginal cost of zero. At the welfare-optimal output level, x, the price equals zero. The deadweight loss is area $(A/2b)xy$ under the demand curve and between the monopoly and welfare-optimal output levels.

In Figure 19.10, we see the market or aggregate demand for the product along with the marginal cost curve of the monopolist (which is the same as the marginal cost curve of each duopolist). We also see that the monopolist will choose an output of $A/2b$ and a price of p^m. This monopoly price-quantity combination will create a deadweight loss of consumer surplus equal to the area in the triangle $(A/2b)xy$. The welfare-optimal price will be zero, and the welfare-optimal quantity will be x units. Note that with an inverse demand curve of $p = A - bq$, a zero price results when $A = bq$ so that $q = A/b$, which is the output at point x. In other words, because the marginal cost is zero, any consumer willing to pay more than a price of zero should be allowed to buy gadgets, which means that the optimal price must be zero. The monopoly and welfare-optimal price-quantity combinations therefore represent the two extremes between which prices and quantities can fall. Let us now demonstrate that in a duopolistic market, the price and the quantity will be between these two extremes. Consider Figure 19.11.

In Figure 19.11, we see our familiar reaction functions, this time for firms that have a zero marginal cost. Note that the horizontal axis represents the output of firm 1, while the vertical axis represents the output of firm 2. From the re-action functions of these two firms, which we previously saw in equation form as $q_1 = (A - bq_2)/2b$ and $q_2 = (A - bq_1)/2b$, we find that when firm 2 produces a zero output, firm 1's best response is to set the monopoly output because, in effect, firm 1 is a monopolist. The monopoly output for firm 1 occurs at point $A/2b$ along the horizontal axis. If firm 1 produces a zero output, firm 2's best response is to choose the monopoly output at point $A/2b$ along the vertical axis. Similarly, if either firm were ever to choose the welfare-optimal output of A/b, the other firm's best response would be to set an output of zero. For example, suppose that firm 1 is at point A/b on the horizontal axis. At this point the price would be zero, so firm 2's best response is to produce zero (see point x in Figure 19.10).

Now consider the line drawn between the two monopoly outputs in Figure 19.11 (the line between points $A/2b$ and $A/2b$). Any output combination along this line is such that the *total* output on the market will be the monopoly

Figure 19.11

The Equilibrium Price and Quantity Compared.

The Cournot equilibrium, with a total quantity of $2A/3b$, is on an iso-output line strictly between the monopoly line (a total quantity of $A/2b$) and the welfare-optimal line (a total quantity of A/b).

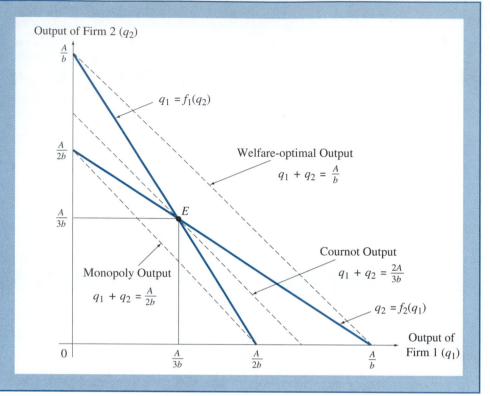

Output of Firm 2 (q_2)

$q_1 = f_1(q_2)$

Welfare-optimal Output

$q_1 + q_2 = \dfrac{A}{b}$

Cournot Output

$q_1 + q_2 = \dfrac{2A}{3b}$

$q_2 = f_2(q_1)$

Monopoly Output

$q_1 + q_2 = \dfrac{A}{2b}$

Output of Firm 1 (q_1)

iso-output line
The set of output combinations for two duopolistic firms that has the property of the sum of the outputs being constant.

output. The points along this line differ only according to the amount that each firm individually supplies to the market. A line of this type is called an iso-output line. Because the market price depends on the *sum* of the outputs produced, the price at any point on the iso-output line will be the same. For example, the price at any point on the line between the monopoly outputs $A/2b$ will be the monopoly price. Similarly, consider the line between the welfare-optimal outputs A/b. At any point along this iso-output line, the *total* output is equal to the welfare-optimal quantity and the price is equal to the welfare-optimal price. The only thing that differs at any point on the line is the portion of the welfare-optimal quantity that each firm supplies.

SOLVED PROBLEM 19.4

Question (Application and Extension: The Equilibrium Price and Quantity Under Duopoly)

a) The town of Deadeye has only one chicken farmer to supply eggs. Assume that the marginal cost of egg production is zero and that in Deadeye the inverse demand for eggs (measured in cents) is $p = 100 - 2q$. At what price and quantity will the chicken farmer sell eggs?

Answer
The chicken farmer will set the quantity that equates marginal revenue to marginal cost. Because demand is linear, marginal revenue will be $MR(q) = 100 - 4q$. Thus, to find the optimal quantity

$$100 - 4q = 0$$
$$q = 25$$

Putting the quantity back into the demand curve, we find that the price of eggs is

$$100 - 2(25) = 50¢$$

b) Now assume that a second chicken farmer who also has zero marginal cost moves to Deadeye. Taking demand into consideration, this means that chicken farmer 1 has a reaction function of

$$q_1 = 25 - \frac{1}{2}q_2$$

where q_1 and q_2 are the quantities of eggs supplied by chicken farmers 1 and 2, respectively. Chicken farmer 2, likewise, has a reaction function of

$$q_2 = 25 - \frac{1}{2}q_1$$

What will the quantities supplied and price for eggs be now?

Answer

To find the quantities, simultaneously solve the two reaction functions.

$$q_1 = 25 - \frac{1}{2}\left(25 - \frac{1}{2}q_1\right)$$
$$0.75q_1 = 12.5$$
$$q_1 = 16\frac{2}{3}$$

Substituting back into farmer 2's reaction function, we find that q_2 is also equal to $16\frac{2}{3}$. This is a result of the fact that the two chicken farmers are symmetric; they face identical demands and marginal costs. Whenever this occurs, both firms in the Cournot duopoly game will produce identical amounts.

The price of eggs, then, is

$$p = 100 - 2\left(16\frac{2}{3} + 16\frac{2}{3}\right) = 33\frac{1}{3}¢$$

Notice that the price has gone down and the total quantity supplied of eggs has gone up as compared to the case when there was only one chicken farmer. In the case when there was only one chicken farmer, consumer surplus was $6.25. When the second chicken farmer entered the market, consumer surplus increased to $11.11. This shows that increased competition lowers the price for the consumer.

Finally, note that point E in Figure 19.11, the Cournot equilibrium quantity $(2A/3b)$, is on an iso-output line strictly between the monopoly line and the welfare-optimal line.[3] Because price decreases as quantity produced increases, it must be true that at the Cournot equilibrium, the price and the quantity are between the monopoly and welfare-optimal levels. This proves our premise that in a duopolistic

---

[3] Note that the Cournot output $(2/3)(A/b)$ can be written as $[n/(n+1)] \cdot A/b$, where n is the number of firms in the market. As n becomes larger and moves toward infinity, $[n/(n+1)] \cdot A/b$ approaches A/b, the competitive result. We will derive this result more formally in Chapter 20.

market, the outcome for society (as measured by the consumer surplus plus the producer surplus) will be between the monopoly outcome and the welfare-optimal outcome. Note that this result will occur for any technologies that produce reaction functions with the same general shape as the ones in Figure 19.11, not just for technologies with zero marginal costs.

RESOLVING
TEASER 19

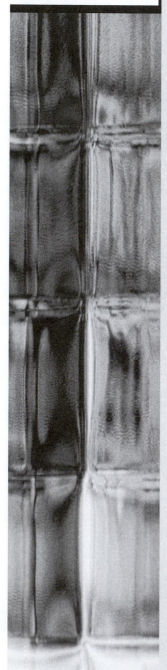

OLIGOPOLY

The Huck, Mueller, and Normann experiment sets up a very clean test of the performance properties of the Cournot and Stackelberg models. They perform an experiment with a classic 2 × 2 design, changing both the rules of the market and the matching technology of subjects. What this means is that they ran four experiments. In one, the Cournot simultaneous rules were used and subjects were matched in fixed pairs for ten rounds. In another experiment, the Cournot rules were used again with another set of subjects, but here, after each of the ten periods, subjects' partners were randomly rematched. Obviously these treatments differ in the facility they provide for subjects to collude because it is easier to collude with the same partner in a repeated game context because knowing you have the same partner lets you punish him for transgressions and also allows you to coordinate on a collusive strategy. Another two experiments were done using Stackelberg rules with fixed and random matching.

The results of the Huck et al. experiments are clear. With respect to Cournot markets, they find that little or no collusion existed with random matching and quantities chosen that are consistent with the predictions of the Cournot theory. In contrast, when the matching is fixed, collusive results are obtained.

In Stackelberg markets, they find that output increases when compared with the Cournot results. In addition, Stackelberg markets create higher consumer surpluses and higher welfare levels regardless of whether subjects are randomly matched or not. Under random matching, Stackelberg markets yield outputs that are higher than the theoretical prediction, and under fixed pairings, there is less collusion in Stackelberg markets.

To summarize these results, consider the following two tables that provide the theoretical predictions for subject firms in these markets along with the realized outcomes.

Table 19.1	Theoretical Predictions for the Huck, Mueller, and Normann Experiment.		
Variable	**Cournot**	**Stackelberg**	**Collusion**
Individual Quantity	$q = 8$	$q_{leader} = 12$ $q_{follower} = 6$	$q = 6$
Total Quantity	$Q = 16$	$Q = 18$	$Q = 12$
Profits	$\Pi = 64$	$\Pi_{leader} = 72$ $\Pi_{follower} = 36$	$\Pi = 72$
Consumer Surplus	128	162	72
Welfare	256	270	216

(Continued)

Table 19.2   Realized Outcomes in the Huck, Mueller, and Normann Experiment.

Variable	Stackelberg Random	Stackelberg Fixed	Cournot Random	Cournot Fixed
Individual Quantity	Lead = 10.19 Foll = 8.32	Lead = 9.13 Foll = 7.92	8.07	7.64
Total Quantity	$Q = 18.51$ Std dev = 2.86	$Q = 17.05$ Std dev = 3.67	$Q = 16.14$ Std dev = 3.12	$Q = 15.27$ Std dev = 4.08
Total Profits	$\Pi = 93.48$ Std dev = 45.59	$\Pi = 105.01$ Std dev = 45.99	$\Pi = 116.60$ Std dev = 36.02	$\Pi = 116.73$ Std dev = 42.87
Consumer Surplus	175.37 Std dev = 56.70	152.14 Std dev = 66.12	135.38 Std dev = 55.04	124.91 Std dev = 68.74
Welfare	269.85 Std dev = 13.51	257.16 Std dev = 23.96	251.98 Std dev = 24.28	241.64 Std dev = 31.39

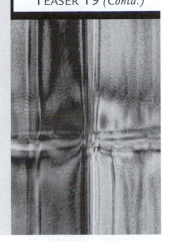

Question (Application and Extension: Monopoly, Duopoly, and Consumer Surplus)

SOLVED
PROBLEM
19.5

Consider a market with a demand curve for a product produced by two firms, firms 1 and 2. The demand for the products can be summarized by the following demand function:

$$p = 50 - \frac{1}{2}(q_1 + q_2)$$

There is zero marginal cost.

Given this demand function, the reaction function for each firm is $q_1 = 50 - \frac{1}{2}q_2$ and $q_2 = 50 - \frac{1}{2}q_1$. As discussed in Solved Problem 19.2 earlier in the chapter, the Nash equilibrium for this market is one where each firm sets a quantity of 33.3. The monopoly solution is one where the total quantity on the market is 50. What is the improvement in consumer surplus by having the market organized as a duopoly?

Answer

Let us answer this question with a diagram (see Figure 19.12). In this diagram, we have the market demand curve

Figure 19.12

Welfare Comparisons of Monopoly and Duopoly.

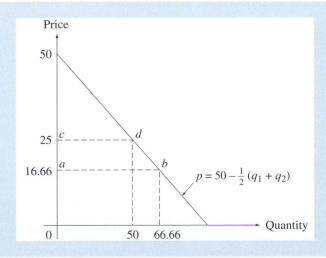

$$p = 50 - \frac{1}{2}(q_1 + q_2)$$

and we have the two quantities of 66.66 and 50. As we see, if the price for the good in the market is 50 or more, the quantity demanded is zero. No one is willing to pay more than 50 for the good. Using the demand curve, we see that if both firms produce 33.33, the total quantity is 66.66 and the market price is $p = 50 - \frac{1}{2}(66.66) = 16.66$. At the monopoly quantity, the market price is $p = 50 - \frac{1}{2}(50) = 25$. Now in the diagram we see that the consumer surplus is represented by the triangle above the line ab for the duopoly situation (that is, the line representing a quantity of 66.66 and a price of 16.66) and the triangle above the line cd in the monopoly situation (that is, the line representing a price of 25 and a quantity of 50). The areas of these triangles are as follows:

$$CS_{monopoly} = \frac{1}{2}(50 - 25)(50) = 625$$

$$CS_{duopoly} = \frac{1}{2}(50 - 16.66)(66.66) = 1,111.22$$

Criticisms of the Cournot Theory: The Bertrand Duopoly Model

One feature of the Cournot model that often strikes people as odd is the fact that it assumes that firms compete in a market by choosing the quantities of a good they will produce. Our usual perception is that firms compete through the prices they charge for their goods. For example, when we look at the advertisements in a newspaper, we see automobile dealers, consumer electronics stores, supermarkets, and many other types of firms competing on the basis of price. Clearly, the view that firms compete through the prices they choose is at variance with the assumption of the Cournot model that they compete through the quantities they decide to produce. Our gadget maker is one of the people who questions the validity of the Cournot model for just this reason. She therefore asks for advice about the nature of a duopolistic market from still another consulting firm. This firm bases its opinions on the work of Joseph Bertrand, who had the same reservations about the Cournot model and, as a result, developed a different kind of duopoly model.[4] In their report, the consultants summarize the basic features of the Bertrand model.

Bertrand model
A model of oligopolistic competition where firms compete by setting prices.

Let us use a simple example to look at the Bertrand model more closely. Say that two firms, i and j, sell an identical product. According to the Bertrand model, these firms can think of themselves as facing a demand function with the following characteristics: If one firm charges a price that is above the price set by its competitor, the demand for its product will be zero. If it charges a price below the price set by its competitor, it will capture all the demand in the market. (In the Bertrand model, it is assumed that all firms have enough production capacity to supply the

---

[4] Joseph Bertrand was a nineteenth-century French mathematician and economist. His critique of the Cournot model and presentation of an alternative model appears in "Theorie Mathematique de la Richesse Sociale," *Journal des Savants* (September 1883): 499–508.

entire market. Later, we will see what happens when this assumption is violated.) If both firms set the same price for the product, they will split the demand in the market. This type of demand function can be depicted in algebraic terms as follows:

$$D_i(p_i, p_j) = \begin{cases} D(p_i) & \text{if } p_i < p_j \\ (1/2)[D(p_i)] & \text{if } p_i = p_j \\ 0 & \text{if } p_i > p_j \end{cases}$$

CONSULTING REPORT   19.3

USING THE BERTRAND MODEL TO DETERMINE AN EQUILIBRIUM FOR A DUOPOLISTIC MARKET

The consultants tell our gadget maker that the Bertrand model is based on a number of assumptions. The most important of these assumptions is that if two firms are selling an identical product, consumers will buy from the firm that charges the lower price. Therefore, in the Bertrand model, firms set prices and allow the market to determine the quantities. Of course, this is the opposite of what happens in the Cournot model.

According to the Bertrand model, each firm in a duopolistic market sets a profit-maximizing price in the belief that the price chosen by its rival will not change. This belief encourages the two firms to engage in a process of competi-tive price-setting until the market arrives at an equilibrium. Thinking that the price set by its rival is fixed, first one firm and then the other firm changes its price in order to take customers and profits away from its rival. Eventually, the two firms reach an equilibrium at which neither has an incentive to change its price any further. This equilibrium occurs when the price of the product falls to its marginal cost.

In the Bertrand model, a duopolistic market produces the same equilibrium as a perfectly competitive market in terms of price, quantity, and profits. The two firms share the market and earn zero profits. ●

The first line of this demand function tells us that if firm i sets a lower price than firm j, all consumers will buy from firm i at price P_i, and firm i will be able to sell as much as the market wants at that price, $D(P_i)$. The second line of the demand function tells us that if firms i and j set the same price, they will split the market demand between them at that price. Finally, the third line of the demand function tells us that if firm i sets a higher price than firm j, it will sell nothing. If we assume that each firm can produce the product at a constant marginal cost of c, then the payoff to each firm will be $\pi_i = p_i[D_i(p_i, p_j)] - c[D_i(p_i, p_j)]$.

The Bertrand Equilibrium

If we think of our example of the Bertrand model in terms of a game, the players are firms i and j, their strategy sets are all the pairs of positive prices they can charge, and their payoffs are the ones just described. We can characterize this game as a simultaneous-move price-setting duopoly game. In the first move of the Bertrand game, each firm sets a price. Seeing these prices, the consumers then decide which firm to buy from. They do so according to the demand function specified previously. The payoffs from the game are determined by the pricing decisions of the two firms and the buying decisions of the consumers. An equilibrium for this game is a pair of prices that, once they are set, are such that neither firm has any incentive to change its price given the price of its opponent. Just as the Cournot equilibrium is a Nash equilibrium for the quantity-setting game, the Bertrand equilibrium is a Nash equilibrium for the price-setting game.

Bertrand equilibrium
An equilibrium to an oligopoly game played by firms' setting prices (Bertrand competition) such that competition forces the price down to the marginal price.

Even though the Cournot and Bertrand equilibria are applications of the same equilibrium concept, they lead to very different outcomes. The Cournot equilibrium produces a price and a quantity that are intermediate between the monopoly and welfare-optimal levels, but the Bertrand equilibrium results in the welfare-optimal price and quantity. We can express the latter outcome as the Bertrand proposition: At the equilibrium of the simultaneous-move price-setting duopoly game, the price of the product is driven down to its marginal cost and the quantity sold in the market is the welfare-optimal quantity.

Proving the Bertrand Proposition

We can prove the Bertrand proposition without too much difficulty. As we do so, note that our proof illustrates the central idea of price competition in a free-market economy.

Let us say that, contrary to the Bertrand proposition, the equilibrium price is not the same as the marginal cost of the product for either firm. Indeed, we will assume that $p_i > p_j > c$, so that the price set by firm i is greater than the price set by firm j. In this case, firm i will sell no goods and receive no profit (assuming that the firm produces only after it knows its demand), but firm j will earn a positive profit because its price is above c. Clearly, firm i's best response to this situation is to set a price for its product that is just below the price of firm j. To be more specific, let us say that firm i will set a price of $p_i = p_j = \epsilon > c$, where ϵ is some arbitrarily small decrease in firm j's price, because, by slightly underpricing its competitor, firm i can capture the entire market and make a positive profit (because $p_i - \epsilon > c$). Firm j will then respond in a similar way by setting a still lower price, such as $p_j = p_i - \epsilon - \epsilon$, and thereby recapture the market from firm i. Hence, a pair of unequal prices above the marginal cost of the product cannot be a Bertrand equilibrium. The two firms involved will simply continue to make competitive price reductions until the price reaches the marginal cost.

Can a pair of equal prices above the marginal cost of the product be a Bertrand equilibrium? The answer to this question is no. At $p_i = p_j > c$, both firms will share the market. However, such an arrangement is not stable because if either firm merely reduces its price by ϵ, it will capture the entire market. An infinitesimal reduction in price can produce much higher profits. Hence, there is again an incentive for both firms to decrease their prices until they reach the marginal cost of the product.

Because we cannot have a Bertrand equilibrium if the two firms set different or equal prices that are above marginal cost, the only other arrangements left are for one firm to set a price at marginal cost while the other firm sets a price above it, or for both firms to set their prices at marginal cost. To prove that the former arrangement is impossible, let us assume that $p_i > p_j = c$. In this case, firm j will earn no profit because it is setting a price exactly at marginal cost and firm i will also earn no profit because it will have no customers. However, because $p_i > p_j$, firm j will have an incentive to raise its price (but still keep it below p_i). By using this strategy, firm j will be able to capture the entire market at a price above marginal cost, which will yield positive profits. Therefore, the only way that the market can arrive at a Bertrand equilibrium is for both firms to set a price that is equal to the marginal cost of the product. At this outcome, the two firms will not earn positive profits but will be indifferent between staying in the market and exiting the market because normal or zero economic profits include an amount necessary to keep entrepreneurs in the market. If either firm increases its price above marginal cost (the equilibrium level), it will lose all sales to its competitor. If either firm decreases its price below marginal cost, it will incur losses.

By simply changing the basis of competition from quantity to price, the Bertrand model produces a dramatically different outcome for duopolistic markets than the Cournot model. At the Bertrand equilibrium, the prices in such markets are driven down to marginal cost, a level far below what we observed at the Cournot equilibrium.

Question (Content Review: Bertrand and Cournot Equilibria)

Consider two oligopolists producing an identical product with identical cost functions $C = q^2$ (that is, $MC = 2q$) who face a demand curve $p = 1 - (q_1 + q_2)$.

SOLVED PROBLEM 19.6

a) What is the Cournot equilibrium in this market?

Answer

Denote firm 1's output by q_1 and firm 2's output by q_2. Firm 1's total revenue function is $R = p \cdot q_1 = [1 - (q_1 + q_2)]q_1 = q_1 - q_1^2 - q_2 q_1$. The associated marginal revenue curve is given by $MR_1 = 1 - q_2 - 2q_1$. Equating firm 1's marginal cost to its marginal revenue, we get its reaction function:

$$2q_1 = 1 - q_2 - 2q_1$$

That is,

$$q_1 = \frac{1 - q_2}{4}$$

Because firm 2 is identical to firm 1 in all respects, we can immediately deduce that firm 2's reaction function is

$$q_2 = \frac{1 - q_1}{4}$$

Substituting firm 1's reaction function into firm 2's, we see that

$$4q_2 = 1 - q_1 = 1 - \frac{1 - q_2}{4} = \frac{3 + q_2}{4}$$

That is,

$$16q_2 = 3 + q_2 \rightarrow 15q_2 = 3$$

Therefore, $q_1 = q_2 = \frac{1}{5}, p = \frac{3}{5}$.

b) If firm 1 can choose its output first, what will the outcome be?

Answer

If firm 1 produces first, it will take firm 2's reaction to its own output into account. Therefore, we can rewrite the demand curve faced by firm 1 as

$$p = 1 - q_1 - q_2 = 1 - q_1 - \frac{1 - q_1}{4} = \frac{3}{4} - \frac{3q_1}{4}$$

Firm 1's marginal revenue function is

$$MR_1 = \frac{3}{4} - \frac{3q_1}{2}$$

Equating marginal cost to marginal revenue, we get

$$2q_1 = \frac{3}{4} - \frac{3q_1}{2} \rightarrow q_1 = \frac{3}{14}, q_2 = \frac{11}{56}, p = \frac{33}{56}$$

c) Suppose the two firms choose *price* instead of *quantity*. What will the market outcome be?

Answer

No matter what price one firm sets, the other firm can always do better by setting a slightly lower price and capturing the whole market. Therefore, the only possible equilibrium occurs when both firms set a price equal to marginal cost. Because the two firms produce an identical product, consumers have no reason to discriminate between the two firms, so the two firms will split the market. Thus, the demand curve can be rewritten as $p = 1 - 2q$, where q is the amount produced by each firm. Then setting price equal to marginal cost, we get $q = \frac{1}{4}$ and $p = \frac{1}{2}$.

Collusive Duopoly

There is something that does not sound right about the results of the Bertrand model. With only two firms in a market, it is hard to believe that the price will be driven down to a level that will maximize the welfare of consumers but minimize the profits of the firms. The Cournot model seems more intuitively correct because it tells us that as more firms enter a market, the price will *gradually* drop from the monopoly level to the welfare-maximizing level. In the Bertrand model, the addition of just one firm brings about a dramatic change in price level.

One simple reason we find it difficult to believe that price will decrease to marginal cost in a duopolistic market is that we expect the two firms involved to get together and work out a more favorable pricing arrangement between themselves. In other words, we expect the two firms to collude on price. In such a collusive duopoly, both firms agree to set the same price at some level above marginal cost and to split the market and its profits. The problem with arrangements of this type is that each firm has a great incentive to cheat and sell to some customers at a price below the agreed price of p. Hence, collusive arrangements are usually not stable. At some point, most firms involved in such arrangements will cheat; and once cheating starts, it usually continues until the price is driven down to marginal cost.

To understand this situation more clearly, let us consider the following simple matrix game between two Bertrand duopolists who have agreed to collude at a price above marginal cost. Once the agreement is in effect, each firm is tempted to cheat by offering secret deals to some customers at slightly lower prices in order to obtain their business.

The game matrix in Table 19.3 illustrates the situation that our colluding duopolists face. Each of them has two possible strategies: cheat or honor the agreement. If both firms honor the agreement, each will receive a payoff of $1 million. However, if one firm honors the agreement and the other firm cheats, the cheater

collusive duopoly
A duopoly in which the two firms collude on a price to set.

Table 19.3	Matrix of the Payoffs from a Game Involving a Collusive Pricing Arrangement.				
		FIRM 2			
		Honor Agreement		**Cheat**	
Firm 1	**Honor Agreement**	$1,000,000	$1,000,000	$200,000	$1,200,000
	Cheat	$1,200,000	$ 200,000	$500,000	$ 500,000

will do relatively better. That firm will receive $1.2 million, but the firm that honors the agreement will receive only $200,000. Mutual cheating will yield a payoff of $500,000 for each firm.

Note that this game is nothing more than another example of the prisoner's dilemma game described in Chapter 11. Each firm has a dominant strategy, which is to cheat; consequently, cheating by both firms forms the only equilibrium for the game. However, as in all prisoner's dilemma games, the equilibrium is worse for both firms than is honoring the collusive agreement. The lesson that this game teaches us is that collusive agreements are inherently unstable and very vulnerable to cheating by all parties involved. In recent years, the failure of the OPEC cartel to control oil prices effectively because of disagreements among its members has provided an example of the instability of cartels. Widespread cheating on production quotas is just one of the many problems that OPEC has faced in trying to enforce its price-fixing rules. These problems are merely a reflection of the basic weakness of collusive arrangements as illustrated by the simple matrix game in Table 19.3.

SOLVED PROBLEM 19.7

Question (Application and Extension: Collusive Duopoly)

The city of San Dimas offers franchises for street taco stands for bid. The demand for tacos in San Dimas is $q = 2,000 - 200p$, and the marginal cost of a taco is $1 (there are no fixed costs). The bids, which must be submitted in a sealed envelope, must state the price at which bidders intend to sell the tacos. Whoever submits the lowest price will win the franchises. There are only two prospective bidders, Bill and Tina. They both know each other very well and decide to meet and discuss how they should bid before their weekly round of golf at the local country club. They agree to enter the same bid so that they can each get half the stands and maximize their profits.

If Bill and Tina do collude, what price would both announce? Is the arrangement stable? If not, what is the equilibrium price each will bid?

Answer

If Bill and Tina do collude, they would each bid the monopoly price. The inverse demand curve is $p = 10 - q/200$, which means that the marginal revenue curve is $MR = 10 - q/100$. Setting marginal revenue equal to marginal cost, we see that

$$10 - \frac{q}{100} = 1$$
$$q = 900$$

Plugging this quantity back into the demand curve, we see that the monopoly price is $5.50. This is what Bill and Tina would both bid if they colluded, and both would earn the following profit:

$$\pi = \frac{1}{2}[(5.50)(900) - (1)(900)] = \$2,025$$

Collusion here is not stable, though, because there is no way to enforce it. Imagine that Bill goes through with the plan but Tina bids $5.49 instead. Then Tina will win all of the franchises and will get the following profit:

$$\pi = (5.49)(902) - (1)(902) = \$4,049.98$$

Therefore, each would have incentive to cheat on the deal. The only equilibrium is for them to bid $1, their marginal cost. At any higher bid there would be incentive for the other bidder to undercut. This situation is nothing more than the Bertrand oligopoly game.

Making Cartels Stable: The Kinked Demand Curve Conjecture

From our discussion in the previous section, it would appear that all cartels are doomed to failure because they are inherently unstable. However, that instability is predicated on certain assumptions; if these assumptions are relaxed, it may turn out that collusive arrangements are more viable than we thought. For example, our analysis of the prisoner's dilemma game at the end of the previous section presents a collusive arrangement as a game that is to be played once and only once between the two firms involved. However, in the real world, we know that firms that enter into a collusive arrangement meet each other regularly in the marketplace and interact repeatedly. It is natural to expect that this repeated interaction will facilitate collusion because it permits firms to *punish* a cheater by lowering their prices once they become aware of the cheater's defection from the collusive agreement. Consequently, if we treat a collusive arrangement as a repeated game and not a one-time game as we did previously, then we may find that such an arrangement can have a more stable outcome. (The appendix to this chapter presents a model of repeated interaction between Cournot-like firms and demonstrates that if a market has an infinite life, collusion is an equilibrium outcome. This discussion has been relegated to the appendix because it is more technical in nature than the rest of our analysis and is probably best suited to those students who have a taste for mathematics.)

Even without ascribing infinite life to markets, we can envision the emergence of stable collusive agreements if we relax the definition of what constitutes an equilibrium for these markets. The Cournot and Bertrand models define an equilibrium as a situation in which no firm or player has any incentive to change its behavior (either the quantity it is producing or the price it is charging), given the actions of its opponents and *given the assumption that its opponents will not respond to any action that it takes*. We earlier called this assumption the Cournot conjecture. Actually, it might make more sense for a firm to expect its opponents to react when it changes its strategy; such reactions, if taken into account before the players make their moves, might change the outcome of the game and make collusion more likely. This line of reasoning allows us to see how a stable collusive arrangement might emerge even if a game is not repeated an infinite number of times. For example, let us make the logical assumption that in a Bertrand game, any action by one firm to raise the prevailing price in the market will not be matched by its competitors, but any action by one firm to lower the prevailing price will be matched. Hence, a firm that raises its price will find that its demand will drop to zero. Because the firm's competitors will not match the price increase, they will be able to take away its market share. On the other hand, a firm that lowers its price will experience an increase in demand but will see its profits fall because its competitors will match the price reduction, pushing profits further from their joint maximum.

To make our example more precise, let us say that at present both firms in our duopolistic industry are charging a price of p, which is between the marginal cost and the monopoly price, $c < p < p^m$. At a price of p for the product, the demand facing firm i can be expressed as follows:

$$D(p_i) = \begin{cases} 0 & \text{if } p_i > p \\ \dfrac{D(p)}{2} & \text{if } p_i = p \\ \dfrac{D(p_i)}{2} & \text{if } p_i < p \end{cases}$$

Clearly, with this demand function, neither firm will want to raise or lower its price. According to our conjecture about behavior in a Bertrand game, any attempt by one firm to change the prevailing market price will be of no advantage to that firm. In fact, the firm will be worse off. If the firm raises its price, its competitor will not match the increase and it will lose all its sales. If the firm lowers its price, say from p to $p' < p$, then its competitor will react by matching the reduction. As a result, firm i's demand will rise from $D_i(p, p)/2$ to $D_i(p', p')/2$, but because p is already below the monopoly price of p^m, a further reduction will only serve to decrease the profits of both duopolists. Profits will fall because the increased demand will lead the two firms to expand production to units whose marginal cost is even further above marginal revenue. Therefore, neither firm will choose to make such a price reduction. The assumption that firms will match a reduction but not an increase in the prevailing price is called the kinked demand curve conjecture and is responsible for the stability of duopolistic and oligopolistic markets.

The kinked demand curve conjecture establishes any price between c and p^m as an equilibrium price as long as all firms choose it. This will be true even if the game is played only once as long as the firms behave according to the kinked demand curve conjecture. In short, the Cournot and Bertrand models exclude the possibility of a stable collusive arrangement because they use a conjectural assumption about the behavior of competing firms that is too restrictive.

kinked demand curve conjecture
The assumption that firms will match a reduction but not an increase in the prevailing price that is responsible for the stability of duopolistic and oligopolistic markets.

RESOLVING
TEASER 20

IMITATION IN OLIGOPOLISTIC MARKETS

In the Offerman, Potters, and Sonnemans paper, the researchers attempt to investigate whether different imitation and learning rules lead oligopolistic markets to converge to different outcomes. The starting point for their experiments is the idea that firms may attempt to learn in different ways in markets. In each period, they may imitate the firm that did the best last period in the market. If they do this, however, it can be shown that such an imitation rule, if followed by all firms, will lead to the completive equilibrium outcome where all firms earn zero profits. Hence, this is self-destructive. Knowing this, firms may decide to act more cooperatively and imitate the firm that last period took an action that, if followed by all firms, would have been best for the entire industry (the exemplary firm). Such a rule would lead to the collusive outcome. Finally, firms may simply form beliefs about what the other firms are likely to do this period based on what they did last period, using a Cournot assumption that no firm will change their output, and simply best respond to last period's market output. This rule will lead to the Nash-Cournot equilibrium.

To sort this all out, Offerman et al. run a set of three firm markets where, in each of three treatments, firms receive different feedback. In Treatment Q, subjects receive feedback information on total quantity, price, own revenue, and own cost and profit. In treatment Q_q, firms receive additional information on the outputs produced by the other firms last period. Finally, in Treatment $Q_{q\Pi}$, firms also receive yet more information about the

(Continued)

profits of the other firms. Obviously, these three treatments are run in an effort to focus the subject's attention on different things and hence lead them, via imitation, to different outcomes.

If the theory works, we would expect that with the first treatment, we would observe the Cournot-Nash outcome because firms have no information to imitate other firms. In the third treatment, we would expect the competitive outcome because here firms can see the most profitable firm last period and imitate them, while in the second treatment firms should be led, via imitation, to the collusive outcome.

A rough summary of the Offerman et al. results offers substantial support for the theory. Table 19.4 presents the mean quantities, prices, and profits across the three treatments.

As we see in Table 19.4, when information is available that, if followed, would lead to the competitive outcome, Treatment $Q_{q\Pi}$, we see that outputs are higher and prices and profits are lower. But when information is available about the exemplary firm, Treatment Q_q, profits tend to be the highest, as suggested by the theory, because this condition is most conducive to collusion. Treatment Q, the Cournot-Nash treatment, falls between these two extremes, as it should.

A note of caution is needed here because the results summarized above are crude, qualitative results and the authors of this paper make many, many qualifications. Still, the general punch line is characterized properly.

Table 19.4	Results of the Offerman, Potters, and Sonnemans Experiment.		
Treatment	**Quantity**	**Price**	**Profits**
Q	77.84 (std dev 16.19)	18.59 (std dev 1.76)	731.43 (std dev 109.09)
Q_q	74.63 (std dev 17.27)	19.17 (std dev 2.05)	748.73 (std dev 116.47)
$Q_{q\pi}$	82.43 (std dev 20.06)	17.90 (std dev 2.72)	667.08 (std dev 147.12)

The Edgeworth Model

To find a more profitable equilibrium for a duopolistic industry than the welfare-optimal prices and quantities in the Bertrand model, we have had to resort to the kinked demand curve conjecture or to the idea of markets with infinite horizons. Our gadget maker is not satisfied with this analysis or with our previous analysis of duopolistic markets, especially because the results differ so dramatically depending on whether we use a price version or a quantity version of the duopoly model. Our gadget maker therefore decides to obtain the views of one more consulting firm. This firm bases its opinions on the work of Francis Ysidro Edgeworth, whose name will reappear in our study of exchange in Chapter 21.

The logic behind the Edgeworth model is simple. Let us say that both firms in the gadgets industry do indeed charge the marginal cost price, and together, they have enough capacity to satisfy demand so that all consumers who want gadgets can obtain them. As a result, neither firm makes a profit. But what will happen if one firm, say firm 1, raises its price above marginal cost? Obviously, all consumers will attempt to buy their gadgets from firm 2. However, because firm 2 is capacity-constrained, it will not be able to serve everyone, so there will be some unsatisfied customers willing to pay more than marginal cost to buy gadgets. Firm 1 can now offer gadgets to these customers at a price above marginal cost and thereby make a profit. The marginal cost solution is not an equilibrium in this situation. The exact nature of the solution will depend on how we define the rationing rule that tells us who will obtain gadgets from firm 2 when it keeps its price at marginal cost after firm 1 has deviated from this price.

Although a full description of the pricing process in the Edgeworth model is beyond our needs here, the following example will provide an intuitive understanding of this process. Assume that both firms in the gadgets industry have enough capacity individually to satisfy demand for the monopoly quantity of q^m but not enough capacity to satisfy demand for the welfare-optimal quantity of q^c when the price is equal to the marginal cost. Further, assume that prices are set such that $p^m > p^1 > p^2 > p^c$, so that firm 1's price is above firm 2's price. In this case, all consumers will want to buy from firm 2. If firm 2 can satisfy the entire market at a price of p^2, then firm 1 will have no customers. As a result, firm 1 will surely lower its price from p^1 to $p^2 - \epsilon$ and attract all the demand. This price reduction by firm 1 will cause prices to fall until both firms are charging the marginal cost price. However, we already know that a situation in which both firms charge the marginal cost price is not an equilibrium in the Edgeworth model. Hence, one firm will raise its price and the process of changing the price to maximize profits will start all over again. If, however, at the original price configuration, firm 2 cannot satisfy the entire demand, then firm 1 will receive some customers. There will then be an incentive for firm 2 to raise its price to $p^1 - \epsilon$ because, by doing so, it will increase its profits even though the higher price will drive some customers away. (We know that this is true because as the firm raises its price, p^2 comes closer to the monopoly price and the firm's profits increase.) The price configuration in the gadgets industry will now be firm 1 charging p^1 and firm 2 charging $p^1 - \epsilon$. Again, there is no equilibrium. After the two firms establish this pair of prices, firm 1 will want to lower its price to $p^1 - \epsilon - \epsilon$ because this small price reduction will bring a large increase in demand. As the low-cost firm in the market, firm 1 will now be able to capture sales from firm 2.

CONSULTING REPORT   19.4

USING THE EDGEWORTH MODEL TO DESCRIBE PRICE BEHAVIOR IN A DUOPOLISTIC MARKET

The consultants tell our gadget maker that the Edgeworth model presents both good and bad news about price behavior in a duopolistic market. The good news is that this model offers a solution to the problem of price competition in which prices do not fall to marginal cost. The bad news is that this model does not have an equilibrium of the type we expect to see. In other words, a game defined by the Edgeworth model will not have a pair of prices that constitute an equilibrium. The consultants explain that this lack of an equilibrium occurs because underlying the Edgeworth model is the assumption that the two firms in a duopolistic market are capacity-constrained, which means that neither firm has enough capacity to produce the quantity that would be demanded at the marginal cost price of c. This rather realistic assumption is all that is needed to establish a situation in which the prices set by the two firms do not inevitably fall to marginal cost and remain there.

Instead, the Edgeworth model describes a market in which prices move in cycles. As each firm attempts to maximize its profits, prices rise and then fall, but they never settle permanently at one level. If prices reach marginal cost, they always move back to a higher level. ●

Prices will continue to fall until marginal cost is reached, and then they will rise again when one firm decides to increase its price. Thus, in the Edgeworth model, capacity constraints cause prices to cycle endlessly and never settle at any particular level. An industry will go through periods when prices fall ("price wars") and periods when prices rise.

Conclusion

Our primitive society will soon make the transition to markets that are composed of many competing firms. However, at the moment, its markets are still dominated by a few large firms. We would expect such firms, knowing that more competition is on the way, to try to develop strategies to keep other firms from entering their markets. Naturally, incumbent firms fear that the entry of new firms will lead to lower prices and lower profits. In the next chapter, we will see how the battle is waged between the new firms that want to enter an established market and the incumbent firms that are attempting to prevent such entry. We will also see what happens when the number of firms in a market goes to infinity. This next chapter, then, will lay the groundwork for our study of perfectly competitive markets, or markets inhabited by a great many small firms.

Summary

In this chapter, we saw how competition for profits affects quantity and price in duopolistic and oligopolistic markets. We studied various well-known models for such markets: the Cournot quantity-setting model, the Stackelberg leader-follower model, the Bertrand price-setting model, and the Edgeworth model. To describe the equilibria or lack of equilibria envisioned by these models, we have defined the concept of a reaction or best-response function. We observed that each model makes a very different prediction about how prices and quantities will behave. We also analyzed the welfare properties of duopolistic and oligopolistic markets and found that they varied according to the model used to describe the market.

We investigated collusive arrangements (cartels) in which firms agree to set certain prices or quantities in order to ensure profitability for each participant. Although such arrangements are normally considered unstable, we saw that it was possible to envision stable collusive arrangements by using the kinked demand curve conjecture or the idea of markets with infinite horizons.

APPENDIX A

NASH EQUILIBRIUM IN DUOPOLY

In markets with few firms, each firm must take into account not only the parameters it faces—that is, the market demand and its costs—but also the anticipated actions of its competitors. When the anticipated actions of each firm are realized in the market, an equilibrium is established. To see this, assume the market consists of two firms that produce the same (homogenous) product—the two firms, labeled 1 and 2, produce quantities q_1 and q_2, respectively. Hence, the aggregate quantity on the market is $Q = q_1 + q_2$. Let

$$P(Q) = a - Q \quad \text{for } Q < a$$
$$= 0 \quad \text{for } Q \geq a$$

be the inverse demand function, which just indicates the market-clearing price when quantity Q is on the market.

Suppose the total cost to firm i of producing the quantity q_i is $C_i(q_i) = c_i q_i$, $i = 1, 2$; that is, firm 1's marginal cost is c_1 and firm 2's marginal cost is c_2. The payoff is the same as profits, and

$$\pi_i(q_i, q_j) = q_i[P(q_i + q_j) - c_i] = q_i[a - (q_i + q_j) - c_i]$$

1. Best-Response Functions

The best-response functions describe the profit-maximizing output of firm i, given any output by firm j. Hence, the best-response function for firm 1 is obtained by maximizing the profit function for firm 1 given that firm 2 is known to produce the (arbitrary) amount q_2; q_1^{BR} solves

$$\text{Max}_{\{0 \leq q_1 < \infty\}} \ \pi_1(q_1, q_2) \Rightarrow \text{Max}_{\{0 \leq q_1 < \infty\}} \ q_1[a - (q_1 + q_2) - c_1]$$

The first-order condition can be written as

$$q_1^{BR} = R_1(q_2) = \frac{1}{2}(a - q_2 - c_1)$$

Similarly, the best response q_2^{BR} for firm 2 is obtained as the solution to

$$\text{Max}_{\{0 \leq q_2 < \infty\}} \ \pi_2(q_1, q_2) \Rightarrow \text{Max}_{\{0 \leq q_2 < \infty\}} \ q_2[a - (q_1 + q_2) - c_2]$$

and the first-order conditions yield

$$q_2^{BR} = R_2(q_1) = \frac{1}{2}(a - q_1 - c_2)$$

$R_1(q_2)$ and $R_2(q_1)$ are the best-response functions. See Figure 19.7 in the text.

2. The Cournot Model

In the Cournot model, both firms make their production decisions simultaneously, and then the total quantity is brought to the market. Each firm chooses its output q_i from a set of nonnegative real numbers $(0, \infty)$; that is, $0 \leq q_i < \infty$.

The quantity pair (q_1^*, q_2^*) is a Nash equilibrium if,

(i) for firm 1, q_1^* solves

$$\text{Max}_{\{0 \leq q_1 < \infty\}} \ \pi_1(q_1, q_2^*)$$

or

$$\text{Max}_{\{0 \leq q_1 < \infty\}} \ q_1[a - (q_1 + q_2^*) - c_1]$$

(ii) for firm 2, q_2^* solves

$$\text{Max}_{\{0 \leq q_2 < \infty\}} \ \pi_1(q_1^*, q_2)$$

or

$$\text{Max}_{\{0 \leq q_2 < \infty\}} \ q_2[a - (q_1^* + q_2) - c_2]$$

In other words, if both firms anticipate (q_1^*, q_2^*) in the market, then their best response to that anticipation is in fact to choose (q_1^*, q_2^*).

The first-order conditions yield the best response of firm 1 to firm 2's equilibrium output q_j^*, $j = 2, 1$. These best responses can be written as

$$q_1^* = \frac{1}{2}(a - q_2^* - c_1)$$
$$q_2^* = \frac{1}{2}(a - q_1^* - c_2)$$

The intersection of the reaction curves (derived in the previous sections) is the Nash equilibrium of the Cournot game (see Figure 19.7 in the text); clearly, at (q_1^*, q_2^*), the best reactions of the two firms match one another. To calculate the Nash equilibrium, we simply solve the pair of simultaneous equations for q_1^* and q_2^*. This procedure yields

$$q_1^* = \frac{1}{3}(a + c_2 - 2c_1)$$
$$q_2^* = \frac{1}{3}(a + c_1 - 2c_2)$$

Consider the symmetric case, when $c_1 = c_2 = c$. Then

$$q_1^* = q_2^* = \frac{1}{3}(a - c)$$
$$Q^* = q_1^* + q_2^* = \frac{2}{3}(a - c)$$
$$P(Q) = a - Q = \frac{1}{3}(a + 2c)$$

It is important to note that the total production under the Nash outcome is higher than that in the collusive outcome. In this case, the joint profits are maximized:

$$\text{Max}_{\{0 \le (q_1, q_2) < \infty\}} \ q_1[a - (q_1 + q_2^*) - c_1] + q_2[a - (q_1^* + q_2) - c_2]$$
$$\text{Max}_{\{0 \le (q_1, q_2) < \infty\}} \ (q_1 + q_2)a - (q_1 + q_2)^2 - (q_1 + q_2)c, \quad \text{assuming } c_1 = c_2 = c$$

The first-order conditions yield $Q = q_1 + q_2 = (\frac{1}{2})(a - c)$, which is lower than the output $(\frac{2}{3})(a - c)$ of the Cournot equilibrium and $P(Q) = (\frac{1}{2})(a + c)$, which is higher than the price $(\frac{1}{3})(a + 2c)$ associated with the Cournot equilibrium.

3. The Stackelberg Model

In the Stackelberg model, one of the firms (called the dominant firm) moves first and chooses output, and then the other firm makes its output decision; that is, (i) firm 1 chooses $q_1 \ge 0$, and then (ii) firm 2 observes q_1 and chooses $q_2 \ge 0$. Assume that all costs, demands, and profits are identical to those in the Cournot case.

To compute the subgame perfect equilibrium of this game, we proceed backward. Given that firm 1 has produced quantity q_1, firm 2's decision problem is to

$$\text{Max}_{\{q_2 > 0\}} \ q_2[a - (q_1 + q_2) - c_2]$$

which yields a reaction function

$$R_2(q_1) = \frac{1}{2}(a - q_1 - c_2)$$

as before.

Firm 1 should anticipate that its quantity choice of q_1 will be met by the reaction $R_2(q_1)$. This implies that firm 1's problem is

$$\text{Max}_{\{q_1 > 0\}}\ \pi_1[q_1, R_2(q_1)]$$

or

$$\text{Max}_{\{q_1 > 0\}}\ q_1[a - (q_1 + R_2(q_1)) - c_1)]$$

Substitution for $R_2(q_1)$ yields

$$\text{Max}_{\{q_1 > 0\}}\ q_1 \left(\frac{a - q_1 + c_2 - 2c_1}{2} \right)$$

which yields

$$q_1^* = \frac{1}{2}(a + c_2 - 2c_1)$$

$$q_2^* = R_2(q_1^*) = \frac{1}{4}(a - 3c_2 + 2c_1)$$

In the symmetric case, where all costs are identical, $q_1^* = \frac{1}{2}(a - c)$ and $q_2^* = \frac{1}{4}(a - c)$.

Graphically, what this means is that firm 1 chooses its output such that firm 2's reaction curve $R_2(q_1)$ is tangent to firm 1's isoprofit curve. See Figure 19.9 in the text.

APPENDIX B

IMPLICIT COLLUSION AND REPEATED GAMES

Most duopolistic situations are repeated over and over again and involve the same two firms. We cannot properly analyze these situations by using the Bertrand model (or even the Cournot model) because such models assume that duopoly games will be played only once and therefore provide a static view of these games. However, as we learned in this chapter, if duopolistic games are repeated, there may be more of a chance to establish stable collusive arrangements because there will be a greater opportunity to punish firms that cheat. Hence, the proper game to analyze is the supergame (see the appendix of Chapter 11), which we will define here as the one-time Bertrand game played repeatedly for an infinite number of periods. If the Bertrand game is played in this manner, then a strategy will involve a rule dictating behavior at each point in time, possibly as a function of what has happened in all periods in the past history of the game.

A Strategy for Achieving a Collusive Equilibrium in the Bertrand Supergame

To prove that implicit collusion that is self-enforcing can occur in a market, let us consider the following strategy. We will assume that both firms in the gadgets industry use this strategy.

1. Choose the monopoly price of *pm* in period 0.

2. Continue to choose the monopoly price of *pm* in period *t* as long as one's opponent has chosen *pm* or a higher price in every period from period 0 to period *t* − 1.

3. If one's opponent has deviated and chosen a price of $p < pm$ in period $t - 1$, then choose the marginal cost price of $p = c$ in period t and every period thereafter.

Our gadget maker claims that if both firms in the industry follow such a strategy and if the discount factor used by both firms is sufficiently large, then this strategy will provide an infinite stream of choices, in which each firm will select the monopoly price of p^m in each period. Neither firm has any incentive to cheat and choose a lower price. Perfect collusion at the monopoly price is a Nash equilibrium for the Bertrand supergame.

Proving the Collusive Equilibrium

Our proof of this proposition follows along the same lines as the proof given in Chapter 11 for the existence of a supergame equilibrium in a repeated prisoner's dilemma game. We will assume, as the one-time Bertrand model has us do, that when both firms set the monopoly price, they will share the market and receive the profit denoted by $\pi^m/2$. At this outcome, the price is p^m and each firm produces $D(p^m, p^m)/2$. Clearly, because p^m is greater than the marginal cost of the production of c, both firms will make a positive profit. Now, let us call π^c the profit that is earned when both firms set a price equal to marginal cost, and let us call $\pi^i(p^m - \epsilon, p^m)$ the profit to firm i when it chooses a price of $p^m - \epsilon < p^m$ and firm j chooses a price of p^m. Obviously, the profit to firm i in the latter case is larger than either $\pi^m/2$ or π^c because $\pi^i(p^m - \epsilon, p^m)$ represents a situation where firm i is serving the entire market at a price only slightly below the monopoly price, which must be better than serving only half the market at p^m.

Let us say that our gadget maker's proposed strategy is used by both firms. As a result, they will receive the payoff of $\pi^m/2$ in each period. The present value of receiving this payoff forever is $(\pi^m/2)(1 - \delta)$, where δ is the discount factor used for both firms. If perfect collusion at the monopoly price is to be an equilibrium for the game, it must be that neither firm has an incentive to deviate. We can demonstrate that this is so for the following reasons. Let us say that firm 1 contemplates cheating in period t by choosing a lower price than p^m. (We will assume that neither firm will want to cheat by choosing a higher price because such a deviation can never be beneficial. The other firm will not respond to a price increase, and the deviating firm will therefore lose all its sales.) The deviating firm's strategy can be summarized in the following way: "I will choose p^m for all periods until period t. In period t, I will deviate and choose $p^m - \epsilon < p^m$. From that point on, I know that my opponent will try to punish me forever by choosing $p = c$. My best response to such punishment is to choose $p = c$ also, which is what I will do starting in period $t + 1$."

Such a deviation strategy will yield firm 1 a payoff stream of $\pi^m/2$, $\pi^m/2, \ldots \pi^m/2, \pi_t^1(p^m - \epsilon, p^m), \pi^c, \ldots$ to the original strategy, then firm 1 will receive a payoff of $\pi^m/2$ for all periods until period t. In period t, when firm 1 cheats by lowering its price to $p^m - \epsilon$, it will receive a one-period cheater's payoff of $\pi^1(p^m - \epsilon, p^m)$. From then on, both firms will choose a price that is equal to marginal cost and receive a payoff of π^c. Is such a deviation profitable for firm 1, given that firm 2 will not change its planned strategy? Put differently, is the one-period cheater's payoff sufficiently enticing to make firm 1 want to risk eternal marginal cost pricing?

To identify the conditions under which no deviation is profitable, we will let P_1 be the payoff to firm 1 in the supergame. If firm 1 deviates and firm 2 adheres to its strategy, then firm 1's supergame payoff when discounted to the beginning of time is as follows:

$$P_1 = \sum_{\rho=0}^{t-1} \frac{\delta \rho \pi^m}{2} + \delta^t \pi_t^1(p^m - \epsilon, p^m) + \sum_{\rho=t+1}^{\infty} \delta^\rho \pi^c$$

The payoff for adhering to the proposed strategy is $P_1 = \sum_{\rho=0}^{\infty} \delta^\rho \pi^m / 2$. Note that until period t, the two strategies yield the same payoff because they both dictate the same actions. In period p, however, the actions differ and so do the payoffs. The question then is whether a planned deviation in period t would be profitable when contemplated in period 0. Such a deviation is profitable under the following conditions:

$$\delta^t \pi_t^1(p^m - \epsilon, p^m) + \sum_{\rho=t+1}^{\infty} \delta^\rho \pi^c \geq \sum_{\rho=t}^{\infty} \frac{\delta^\rho \pi^m}{2}$$

Hence, it is profitable to deviate if the payoff stream from deviating in period p (the terms on the left side of the inequality) is greater than the payoff from not deviating (the term on the right side of the inequality). This inequality can be rewritten in the following manner:

$$\frac{\delta^t(\pi^m/2)}{(1-\delta)} \leq \delta^t \pi_t^1(p^m - \epsilon, p^m) + \frac{\delta^{t+1}\pi^c}{(1-\delta)}$$

After algebraic manipulation, we find that a deviation is profitable only under the following circumstance:

$$\delta < \frac{\pi_t^1(p^m - \epsilon, p^m) - \pi^m/2}{\pi_t^1(p^m - \epsilon, p^m) - \pi^c}$$

If this duopolistic situation is repeated over an infinite horizon and if the discount factors of the firms are large enough, then it will be possible to support an infinite history of monopoly prices, with no firm having any incentive to deviate. Infinite horizons plus high discount factors equal collusive behavior.

Exercises and Problems

1. Consider a duopolistic market with a demand function of $p = 10 - 2(q_A + q_B)$. Firm A has a cost function of $C_A = 4 - q_A + q_A^2$, while firm B has a cost function of $C_B = 5 - q_B + q_B^2$. Assume that these firms can choose only their output levels and that their choices are constrained in the following way: Firm A can produce either $q_A = 0.92$ or 0.94, while firm B can produce either $q_B = 0.41$ or 0.74.

   a) Assuming that payoffs are identical to profits, supply the information that is missing from the matrix given below. In this matrix, Π_A and Π_B are the payoffs to firms A and B, respectively.

		q_B	
		0.41	0.74
q_A	0.92	(Π_A, Π_B)	(.,.)
	0.94	(.,.)	(.,.)

b)   Say that firms A and B are players in a game where they can choose only the output levels specified previously. Does the choice of 0.94 by firm A and the choice of 0.74 by firm B constitute a Nash equilibrium for the game?

2. Assume that two firms, A and B, compete with each other in the same market. They produce a commodity that has the following demand: $p = 1 - q_A - q_B$. Each firm must decide what fraction of the market to supply by choosing an output level between 0 and 1. There are no fixed costs of production, and the marginal costs are zero. The profit of firm A is $\pi_A(1 - q_A - q_B)q_A$, and the profit of firm B is $\pi_A(1 - q_A - q_B)q_B$.

a)   If firm B sets output levels of $q_B = \frac{1}{4}, \frac{1}{2}, \frac{3}{4}$, and 1, what is the demand function facing firm A in each case?

b)   What is firm A's marginal revenue function for each output level of q_B chosen by firm B? (*Note:* The slope of the marginal revenue curve for a firm facing a linear, downward-sloping demand curve is twice the slope of the demand curve.)

c)   Using the Cournot conjecture, assume that after firm B sets its output levels, firm A will consider these output levels to be fixed. What is the best response of firm A to firm B's choice of the output levels of $q_B = \frac{1}{4}, \frac{1}{2}, \frac{3}{4}$, and 1 in each case? (*Hint:* Remember that firm A will set $MR = MC = 0$ for each level of output chosen by firm B.)

d)   What will the Cournot-Nash equilibrium be in this example? What will the corresponding equilibrium price be?

e)   On a graph, plot the market demand curve, the equilibrium output for the industry, and the consumer surplus generated at this equilibrium. Also, calculate the deadweight loss.

3. Consider two firms, A and B, that produce a commodity with the same demand and cost structure as in problem 2. However, assume that instead of choosing a quantity like Cournot duopolists, the firms choose a price like Bertrand duopolists. The game they play is as follows. If firm A's price is lower than firm B's price, firm A obtains all the customers in the market who are willing to pay its price (or more). Firm A will therefore sell $q_A = 1 - p_A$ units, and firm B will sell zero units. Firm A's profit will be $\pi_A = (1 - p_A)p_A$, while firm B's profit will be zero. The opposite happens if firm B sets a lower price than firm A. If the two firms set the same price, $p_A = p_B$, they will split the market demand equally and will receive profits of $\Pi_A = \left(\frac{1}{2}\right)(1 - p_A)p_A = \pi_B = \left(\frac{1}{2}\right)(1 - p_B)p_B$.

a)   If firm A sets a price of $\frac{1}{3}$ and so does firm B, what profit will each firm make?

b)   What output will each firm sell when they both set a price of $\frac{1}{3}$?

c)   Is this pair of prices an equilibrium?

d)   What is the only pair of prices that constitutes an equilibrium for this game?

e)   Is this equilibrium the one that maximizes the sum of consumer welfare and producer welfare?

4. Consider a duopolistic market with two firms, A and B, facing a demand curve of $p = 1 - q_A - q_B$. Assume that initially each firm has access to the same technology with constant returns to scale and that the cost of production is $C_A = q_A/2$ for firm A and $C_B = q_B/2$ for firm B. Also assume that the two firms can only set output levels that are between 0 and $\frac{1}{3}$.

a) What is the profit function for each firm?

b) Assume that you are told that the reaction functions are $q_A = \frac{1}{4} - q_B/2$ for firm A and $q_B = \frac{1}{4} - q_A/2$ for firm B. Graph these reaction functions in a box like the one shown below.

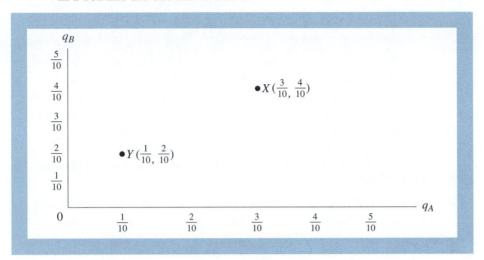

c) What is the Nash equilibrium for this game?

d) Assume that the initial output levels of the two firms are given by points X and Y in the box illustrated here. Show the process of change in the output levels of the two firms and the point at which their output levels converge.

e) On the basis of the two paths, one leading from point X and the other leading from point Y, do you think that the Nash equilibrium of this game is stable?

5. Assume that two firms, A and B, have the same demand function as in problem 4, but their cost functions are $C_A = \left(\frac{1}{2}\right)q_A - \left(\frac{3}{4}\right)q_A^2$ for firm A and $C_B = \left(\frac{1}{2}\right)q_B - \left(\frac{3}{4}\right)q_B^2$ for firm B.

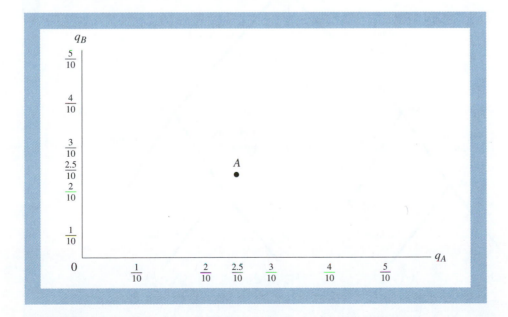

a)   The reaction functions of the two firms are as follows:

$$q_A = \begin{cases} (1/2), & \text{if } 0 < q_B < (1/4) \\ 1 - 2q_B, & \text{if } (1/4) \le q_B \le (1/2) \end{cases}$$

$$q_B = \begin{cases} (1/2), & \text{if } 0 \le q_A \le (1/4) \\ 1 - 2q_A, & \text{if } (1/4) \le q_A \le (1/2) \end{cases}$$

Graph these reaction functions in a box like the one given below. Assume that the output of each firm is restricted to levels between 0 and $\frac{1}{2}$.

b)   What are the Nash equilibria for this game? How many are there? (*Hint:* Find the point where the reaction functions of the two firms intersect.)

c)   Assume that $(\frac{1}{3}, \frac{1}{3})$ is a Nash equilibrium. If we start at point $A = (\frac{1}{4}, \frac{1}{4})$, do the output levels of the duopolists converge at the equilibrium point $(\frac{1}{3}, \frac{1}{3})$? What might we conclude about the stability of the equilibrium point $(\frac{1}{3}, \frac{1}{3})$?

6. Consider an industry that consists of two firms: the Nice firm and the Nasty firm. The demand in this industry is $p = 1 - q_{Nice} - q_{Nasty}$, and the two firms have cost functions of $C_{Nice} = (\frac{1}{2})q_{Nice}$ and $C_{Nasty} = (\frac{1}{2})q_{Nasty}$. Assume that there is a Nash equilibrium of $(\frac{1}{6}, \frac{1}{6})$ in the industry. Then the Nasty firm announces that unless the Nice firm produces no more goods and leaves the market (thus allowing Nasty to be a monopolist and produce an output of $\frac{1}{4}$), it will "flood the market" by producing an output of 1 and will therefore drive the price to zero. The game tree in Figure 19.13 depicts this situation. In the first stage of the game, Nasty announces its intention to produce either 1 or $\frac{1}{6}$. In the second stage, Nice decides whether to leave the market or not after hearing Nasty's announcement. In the third stage, Nasty chooses its output after observing Nice's decision. Note that Nasty's announcement at

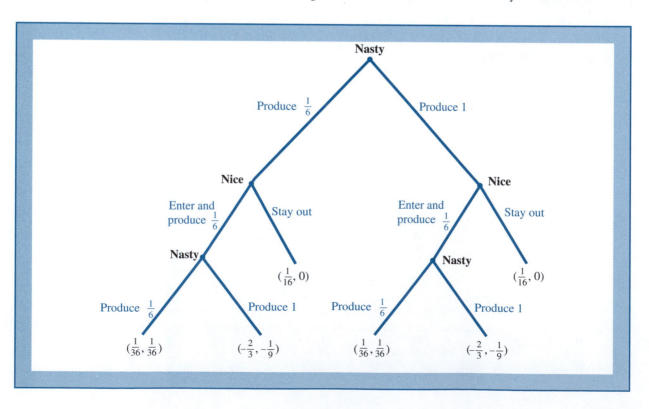

the first stage of the game is nonbinding because Nasty does not have to carry out its threat.

    a)   Is the threat of the Nasty firm to produce an output of 1 and flood the market credible? If not, why not? (*Hint:* Start at the end of the game tree, and work backward to find the subgame perfect equilibrium.)

    b)   Does Nasty's ability to announce an intended strategy increase its equilibrium payoff compared to the Cournot-Nash equilibrium payoff?

    c)   Now assume that the game is played by allowing Nasty to choose an output level first and then having Nice choose a response. In other words, Nasty is a Stackelberg leader. Find the Stackelberg equilibrium. Does it pay for Nasty to be a Stackelberg leader? (*Hint:* The best response of Nice is $\frac{1}{4} - \left(\frac{1}{2}\right)q_{Nasty}$.)

7. Assume that there are two firms in a market, firms 1 and 2. The total demand for the identical product they make is $p = 200 - 2(q_1 + q_2)$, where q_1 is the output of firm 1 and q_2 is the output of firm 2. The production costs of firms 1 and 2 are $C_1 = q_1^2$ and $C_2 = q_2^2$, respectively.

    a)   Assume that firm 2 decides to produce either 20, 40, 60, or 100 units of output. Show the demand curve and the marginal revenue curve facing firm 1 in each of these situations, assuming that the output levels will remain unchanged once they are chosen.

    b)   Define the output that represents the best (the profit-maximizing) response of firm 1 to each of the output levels chosen by firm 2. (*Hint:* Given the output of firm 2, define the demand and marginal revenue functions. Then set the marginal revenue so that it is equal to the marginal cost, where the marginal cost of the two firms is $MC_1 = 2q_1$ and $MC_2 = 2q_2$.)

8. Consider a monopolist facing a demand curve of $p = 1 - q_M$, where q_M is the monopolist's output. The firm has no marginal cost, but it must bear a fixed cost of $\frac{1}{4}$ in order to produce. Thus, its cost function is $C(q_M) = \frac{1}{4}$.

    a)   Determine the monopolist's profit-maximizing output.

    b)   Suppose that another firm is thinking about entering the market. It also has a zero marginal cost, but its fixed cost is $\frac{1}{10}$. If the second firm does decide to enter the market, what will the Nash equilibrium profits of the two firms be after entry occurs?

    c)   Suppose that the monopolist commits itself to a monopoly output (the output it was producing before there was any threat of competition), and it will produce this output no matter what the entrant does. Can the entrant make a positive profit by choosing the *best response* to the monopoly output?

    d)   What is the smallest output that the monopolist can choose that will prevent entry by the rival firm? In other words, what is the smallest output that will deny the rival firm a positive profit if it does enter the market and the monopolist actually produces its chosen output?

9. Consider the following matrix, which shows the payoffs for a game between two firms in a duopolistic industry.

		Firm II	
		Low Price	High Price
Firm I	**Low Price**	0, 0	20, −8
	High Price	−8, 20	5, 5

a) What is the only Nash equilibrium in pure strategies for this game?

b) Are there dominant strategies for each firm?

c) Now suppose that the cost structure in the industry has changed so that the new payoffs for the game are as shown below. Is the Nash equilibrium determined in part A of this problem still an equilibrium?

		Firm II	
		Low Price	High Price
Firm I	**Low Price**	0, 0	0, −10
	High Price	−10, 0	5, 5

d) Are there now any other equilibria?

e) If there are now several equilibria for the game, which one do you think is likely to be chosen? Why?

Market Entry and the Emergence of Perfect Competition

ENTRY PREVENTION

While misery may love company, monopolists do not. By definition they like to be alone in markets. Hence, we might expect that when a monopoly exists, it will do its best to keep other firms—potential entrants—out. One way to do this, as we will see when we study the Dixit model in this chapter, is to invest in production capacity.

For example, let us say that there is an industry with one incumbent firm—the monopolist—and another firm whose objective is to enter. Say that the "entry game" is played as follows. In order for any firm to produce, it must build a plant that costs $F. First, in stage 1, the incumbent monopolist moves and decides how much of $F it wants to invest by choosing a fraction, a, $0 \leq a \leq 1$, of $F to commit to. In stage 2, the entrant can see the investment or lack of investment made by the incumbent. Then both firms have to decide whether to be in or out of the market. Being in means spending the entire $F on capacity. Being out for the incumbent monopolist means deciding not to produce and losing the a $F invested so far.

This game has the following two subgames defined by whether the incumbent invested or not. Note that if nobody enters, both firms earn zero. If one firm enters and one does not, the entrant gets the whole market (1) and the other firm gets nothing (0). If both firms enter, they both pay $F but compete profits away, so each loses $F ($-F).

INCUMBENT MONOPOLIST DOES NOT BUY CAPACITY

		Entrant	
		Out	In
Incumbent	Out	0, 0	0, 1
	In	1, 0	$-F, -F$

INCUMBENT MONOPOLIST DOES BUY CAPACITY

		Entrant	
		Out	In
Incumbent	Out	$-aF, 0$	$-aF, 1$
	In	1, 0	$-F, -F$

An experiment by Brandts, Cabrales, and Charness* tried to test the idea of whether a pre-committed investment can deter entry. They ran an experiment in which subjects

(Continued)

---

* Jordi Brandts, Antonio Cabrales, and Gary Charness, "Entry Deterrence and Forward Induction: An Experiment," mimeo, August 2004.

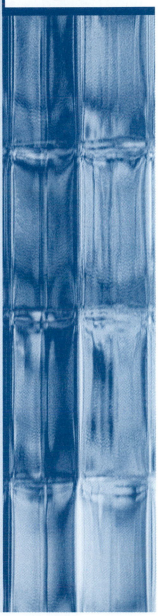

EXPERIMENTAL
TEASER 21 *(Contd.)*

played a game identical to the one described above. Do you think that an incumbent can deter entry by building capacity in this game? Use the notion of forward induction and the two payoff matrices above to help you answer this question.

Just as countries battle for territory, firms battle to defend or capture market share. The struggle to defeat business rivals is sometimes waged so aggressively that it brings to mind the old saying "all is fair in love and war." In this chapter, we will discuss the tactics that firms use to keep potential competitors from entering their markets and taking away their customers.

We will begin by examining an early model of entry prevention, and we will find that this model is flawed because it does not take into account the concept of subgame perfection, which we studied in Chapter 11. After discussing the weaknesses of this early model, we will investigate a later model that was created to strengthen the theoretical foundation for the idea of entry prevention. At the end of the chapter, we will ask what happens when an entry-prevention strategy fails and many competing firms successfully enter a market. As we will see, this event changes the nature of the market. From an oligopoly in which competition is limited to a few large firms, it becomes a perfectly competitive market in which price and quantity are set by an infinite number of small firms.

The Appendix to this chapter contains some advanced material on entry prevention in situations where there is uncertainty because of incomplete information. This material is recommended only for students who have a good understanding of the mathematical techniques of economic analysis and are very comfortable with the concepts of game theory presented in Chapter 11.

The Need for Entry-Prevention Strategies

Consider a monopolist such as the gadget maker we encountered in Chapter 19. She controls the market for her product and has no competition. As we know from the theory of monopoly, she is in a very advantageous position and will want to maintain that position. However, other firms will almost certainly be attracted to the monopolist's market because of the extra-normal profits she is earning. These firms will devise strategies for entering her market and capturing her customers and profits.

The monopolist must be prepared to defend her market. She must develop a strategy that will allow her to prevent the entry of potential rivals. The successful entry of a few competing firms will transform the market from a monopoly to an oligopoly and thereby decrease her profits. If additional firms enter the market, it may eventually become a perfectly competitive market, in which case the profits of the former monopolist will diminish even further.

Limit Pricing in the Bain, Modigliani, Sylos-Labini Model

A monopolist such as our gadget maker must ask herself the following question: Is there a way that I can behave in terms of setting a level of output to produce or a price to charge that will deter potential competitors from entering my market? Let us assume that our gadget maker hires a consulting firm to help her find an answer to this question. The consultants base their opinions on the early work of the economists Joe Bain, Franco Modigliani, and Paolo Sylos-Labini.[1] In their report, the consultants outline a model that uses a pricing strategy to make it unprofitable for any potential competitor to enter a market. We will call this model the Bain, Modigliani, Sylos-Labini model.

Let us look more closely at the Bain, Modigliani, Sylos-Labini model and see how our gadget maker might use limit pricing to maintain her monopoly. We will assume the following conditions for this example.[2]

1. There are two periods: the pre-entry period ($t = 0$) and the entry period ($t = 1$). During period 1, the potential entrant can decide to enter the market or stay out. If entry does not appear to be profitable, the potential entrant will stay out.

2. There is a single established firm, the *incumbent*, which we will designate as firm i, and a potential entrant, which we will designate as firm e.

3. Consumers are not loyal. They do not care from which firm they purchase the product, and there is no cost to switching firms.

4. Demand does not change over time.

5. In period 0, the incumbent firm commits to an output level x_1, which it will maintain in all future periods.

6. The potential entrant believes that if it enters the market, the incumbent firm will continue to produce at its pre-entry level of output regardless of any actions the entrant takes and regardless of the prevailing market price.

Of these assumptions, the first four are rather innocuous, but the fifth and sixth are not. Assumption 5 tells us that in period 0, the incumbent firm will *commit* itself to an output that it will not change in period 1 *no matter what the potential entrant decides to do*. Assumption 6 tells us that the potential entrant believes that this commitment will be kept if it enters the market. We will see later that, because of the idea of a subgame perfect equilibrium, it may not be rational for the incumbent firm to adhere to the commitment it made in period 0 if entry actually occurs in period 1.

Blockading Market Entry

Let us now consider Figure 20.1, which shows the demand for gadgets and the costs of the incumbent firm (our monopolist) in period 0, the pre-entry period.

Specifically, Figure 20.1 depicts the demand curve of the incumbent firm and its marginal and average cost curves. Note that this is the demand curve of a monopolist. It portrays the demand that will exist if the potential entrant stays out of

Bain, Modigliani, Sylos-Labini model
A model where an incumbent firm uses a pricing strategy to make it unprofitable for any potential competitor to enter a market.

---

[1] Joe S. Bain, who was a professor of economics at the University of California at Berkeley, did pioneering work on the subject of oligopolistic industries and the barriers to entry they raise. Franco Modigliani, an Italian-born U.S. economist who spent much of his teaching career at the Massachusetts Institute of Technology, has made many significant contributions to economics, especially to the theory of consumption, financial theory, and monetary theory. He was awarded the Nobel Prize in economics in 1985. Paolo Sylos-Labini is an Italian economist who investigated various aspects of oligopoly including oligopoly and technical progress. He is probably best known in the United States for his work on the forces of economic growth.

[2] The assumptions used here follow the presentation given in the survey article "Mobility Barriers and the Value of Incumbency" by Richard J. Gilbert, which appeared in *Handbook of Industrial Organization*, edited by R. Schmalensee and R. D. Willig (New York: Elsevier/North-Holland, 1989).

CONSULTING REPORT 20.1

USING THE LIMIT-PRICING STRATEGY OF THE BAIN, MODIGLIANI, SYLOS-LABINI MODEL TO DETER MARKET ENTRY

The consultants explain that the concept behind the Bain, Modigliani, Sylos-Labini model is quite simple. The established firms in an oligopolistic market can deter entry by setting their output at such a level that the remaining demand in the market is too low for a potential entrant to earn a profit at any price it can charge. This strategy, which is known as limit pricing, may make it necessary for the established firms in the market to raise their output above the profit-maximizing level in order to prevent entry. However, even with the resulting decrease in profitability, the established firms will still be able to earn extra-normal profits. ●

limit pricing
A strategy in which the established firms in an oligopolistic market can deter entry by setting their output at such a level that the remaining demand in the market is too low for a potential entrant to earn a profit at any price it can charge.

residual demand curve
The demand curve that describes the demand remaining for the potential entrant after the incumbent firm has set its output level.

the market. For the sake of simplicity, we have used a linear demand curve, which means that we can express the demand as $p = A - b(q_i + q_e)$, where q_e is the output of the potential entrant and q_i is the output of the incumbent firm. This function equals $p = A - bq_i$ when q_e is assumed to be 0. We know that a monopolist will normally want to set the profit-maximizing quantity of q^m and its associated price of p^m. Our gadget maker does just that in period 0. She ignores the possibility of entry and chooses the monopoly quantity-price combination of (q^m, p^m). Figure 20.2 depicts the situation a potential entrant will therefore face in the gadgets market.

As we know from our discussion of duopoly in Chapter 19, when one firm sets a positive output level in a two-firm market with a linear demand curve, this choice shifts the demand curve facing the other firm toward the origin while keeping the slope of the curve unchanged. In Figure 20.2, we see that the potential entrant faces a new demand curve *after* the incumbent firm has set its output of q^m. We will call this demand curve, which can be expressed as $p = (A - bq^m) - bq_e$, the residual demand curve because it describes the demand remaining for the potential entrant after the incumbent firm has set its output level. Note, however, that we are assuming that the potential entrant faces the same cost functions as the

---

Figure 20.1

Limit Pricing in the Bain, Modigliani, Sylos-Labini Model.

As a monopolist, the incumbent firm faces a demand curve of $p = A - bq_i$ and chooses the monopoly quantity of q^m and the monopoly price of p^m.

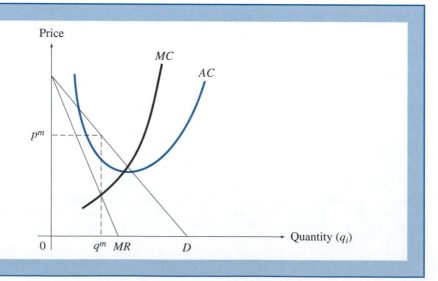

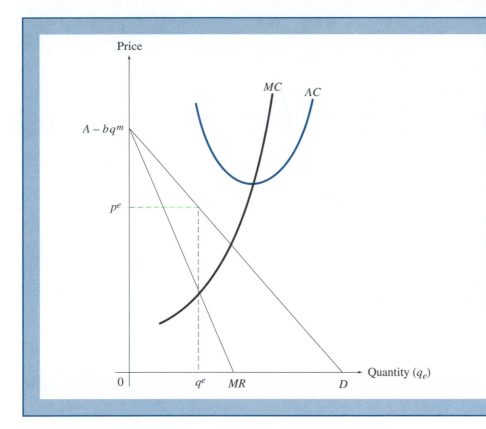

Figure 20.2

The Residual Demand for the Potential Entrant: A Case of Blockaded Entry.

Once the incumbent firm has set its output level at q^m, the potential entrant faces a residual demand curve of $p = (A - bq^m) - bq_e$. In this case, because the average cost curve is above the demand curve for all output levels, profitable entry is impossible.

incumbent firm because they both use the same technology. As we can see from Figure 20.2, the demand and cost functions have been drawn in such a way that when the incumbent firm sets its monopoly quantity of q^m, the demand curve facing the potential entrant shifts down so far that it is always below the average cost curve of that firm. Thus, no matter what quantity the potential entrant sets, it can never charge a price that will allow it to earn enough money to cover its average cost of production.

In such a case, the potential entrant will stay out of the market. Bain calls this outcome a blockaded entry because the incumbent firm is able to deter entry by simply pursuing a policy that is best for itself as a monopolist. Note, however, that this conclusion is reached only if we accept assumptions 5 and 6 of the Bain, Modigliani, Sylos-Labini model. If the potential entrant assumes that the incumbent firm will not change its output from the monopoly quantity of q^m, then it will stay out of the market. A different belief on the part of the potential entrant might lead to a different conclusion.

blockaded entry
When the incumbent firm is able to deter entry by simply pursuing a policy that is best for itself as a monopolist.

Impeding Market Entry

The example that we just investigated is rather extreme because it assumes that a monopolist can prevent entry by simply setting the monopoly output. However, in some cases, this is not possible, and the monopolist must choose a less advantageous level of output in order to deter entry. Bain calls the outcome of such situations an impeded entry.

To understand the use of the limit-pricing strategy to impede entry, let us consider Figure 20.3, which depicts the demand and costs of another hypothetical

impeded entry
A situation where the monopolist must choose a less advantageous level of output in order to deter entry.

Figure 20.3

Another Hypothetical Monopoly.

The incumbent firm sets an output level of $q^{m'}$ and a price of $p^{m'}$.

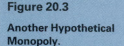

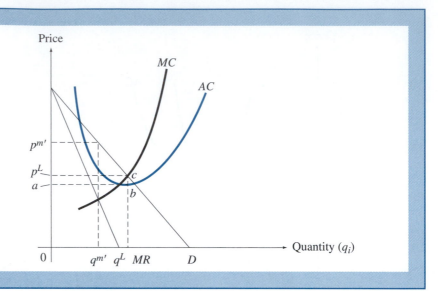

Figure 20.3

Another Hypothetical Monopoly.

The incumbent firm sets an output level of $q^{m'}$ and a price of $p^{m'}$.

monopolist. This firm faces the same demand curve that we saw in Figure 20.1 but has a different average cost curve.

In Figure 20.3, we observe that our new monopolist has set a monopoly output of $q^{m'}$ and a monopoly price of $p^{m'}$. This quantity-price combination will yield a demand curve for the potential entrant as depicted in Figure 20.4.

Figure 20.4, which is analogous to Figure 20.2, shows the residual demand curve for the potential entrant when the incumbent firm sets its monopoly output of $q^{m'}$. Note that the potential entrant can now enter the market and make a profit if the incumbent firm does not change its output in response. For example, if the entrant sets a quantity of $q^{e'}$ and a corresponding price of $p^{e'}$, then it will make a profit of $\pi^{e'}$, which is equal to the area $p^{e'}cba$ in Figure 20.4. In this case, the incumbent firm cannot blockade entry by setting its monopoly output. However, it can impede entry by raising the level of its output. Let us look again at Figure 20.3 and consider Figure 20.5, which presents the residual demand function for our potential entrant based on a higher output level, q^L, set by the incumbent firm, and an associated price of p^L.

In Figure 20.3, we see that at an output level of q^L and a price of p^L, the incumbent monopolist earns extra-normal profits equal to the area p_Lcba. However, the residual demand curve in Figure 20.5 shows that the remaining demand in the market is now so low that there is no price that the potential entrant can set that will yield a profit, assuming that the incumbent firm will keep its output level fixed at q^L. If we look again at Figure 20.5, we find that when the incumbent firm sets a quantity of q^L, the profit-maximizing response by the potential entrant is to choose a quantity of q^e, but this quantity will make the potential entrant indifferent between entering the market and staying out. At a quantity of q^e and a price of p^e, the potential entrant can just cover its average cost. Thus, the incumbent monopolist is able to impede entry by setting a quantity of q^L, which we will call the limit quantity, and an associated price of p^L, which we will call the limit price.

Note that it is possible to use higher output levels than q^L to deter entry; q^L is the lowest one that will serve the purpose. Hence p^L, the limit price, is the highest price consistent with entry deterrence, while q^L is the lowest output level consistent with entry deterrence.

limit quantity
The quantity an incumbent monopolist sets that enables it to impede entry into the market.

limit price
The price an incumbent monopolist sets that enables it to impede entry into the market.

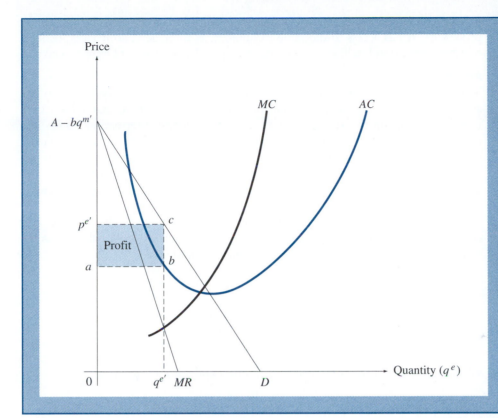

Figure 20.4

The Residual Demand for the Potential Entrant: A Case of Impeded Entry.

In this case, profitable entry is possible as long as the incumbent firm continues to produce the monopoly quantity of q^m. If the potential entrant sets a quantity of $q^{e'}$ and a price of $p^{e'}$, it will earn profits that are equal to the area $p^{e'}cba$.

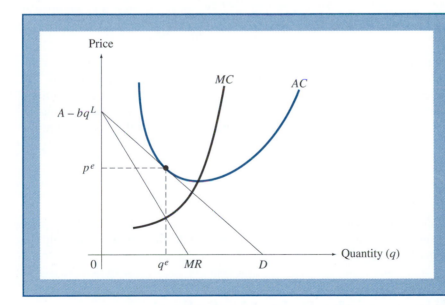

Figure 20.5

The Residual Demand for the Potential Entrant: A Case of Impeded Entry.

Instead of setting the monopoly quantity of q^m and the monopoly price of p^m, the incumbent firm sets the limit quantity of q^L and the limit price of p^L. This lowers the residual demand curve so that it is tangent to the potential entrant's average cost curve, making profitable entry impossible.

Question (Content Review: Impeding Entry)

Intelligent Computing produces processors for personal computers. It has an average cost function $AC = q + 10{,}000/q$ and a marginal cost function $MC = 2q$. It faces demand $q = 540 - p$ for its processors and is currently the sole supplier.

SOLVED PROBLEM 20.1

A potential competitor, Orange Computers, is considering entering the market for processors. It has access to the same technology as Intelligent, so it faces identical cost functions. Can Intelligent sustain its monopoly by blockading Orange's entry?

Answer

The key to solving this problem is to find the highest quantity at which the average cost curve intersects the demand curve and to compare that value to the minimum point on the average cost curve. If the highest intersection occurs at a quantity less than the quantity at the minimum point of the average cost curve, then the monopoly is sustainable if the monopolist sets its price equal to the average cost at that point of intersection. If the highest intersection occurs at a quantity higher than the quantity at the minimum point of the average cost curve, then the monopoly is not sustainable.

We know that the marginal cost curve always intersects the average cost curve at its minimum point, so equating the two and solving for q will give us the quantity at the minimum point of the average cost curve:

$$q + \frac{10{,}000}{q} = 2q$$
$$q^2 = 10{,}000$$
$$q = 100$$

Next we need to determine where the average cost and demand curves intersect. Again, set the two equal to each other and solve for q:

$$q + \frac{10{,}000}{q} = 540 - q$$
$$2q^2 - 540q + 10{,}000 = 0$$
$$2(q - 250)(q - 20) = 0$$
$$q = 20 \text{ or } 250$$

Thus, the quantities at which the average cost and demand curves intersect are 20 and 250. We are interested in the highest quantity of intersection, which is 250. The highest intersection is at a greater quantity than the quantity at the minimum point of the average cost curve; thus, the monopoly will not be sustainable. Intelligent might try to blockade entry by setting its price at the point where the average cost curve intersects the demand curve:

$$p = 250 + \frac{10{,}000}{250}$$
$$= 290$$

Orange Computers could enter the market and sell, say, 100 processors at a price of $280 and make a profit of $8,000. Intelligent would then be left with only the residual market.

Criticisms of the Bain, Modigliani, Sylos-Labini Model: Subgame Perfection

There are some problems with the Bain, Modigliani, Sylos-Labini model and its limit-pricing strategy for entry prevention. For example, if we analyze this model in terms of game theory, we will find that it fails because the equilibrium it defines is not what we called a subgame perfect equilibrium in Chapter 11.

Using Game Theory to Analyze the Bain, Modigliani, Sylos-Labini Model

To understand why the Bain, Modigliani, Sylos-Labini model cannot produce a subgame perfect equilibrium, let us consider Figure 20.6.

In Figure 20.6, we see an extensive-form game that describes the entry-prevention situation in the gadgets market. Because the complete game tree would be extremely complicated, Figure 20.6 portrays only one path through the game tree. Of course, in theory, there should be branches emanating from all the choices available to the incumbent firm at the first move of the game. At this first move, the incumbent firm must select a quantity to produce from the set of all possible output levels, ranging from a low of $\underline{q}$ to a high of $\bar{q}$. This choice is made in period 0, the pre-entry period and, according to assumption 5 of the Bain, Modigliani, Sylos-Labini model, should be adhered to in both periods of the game.

The second move of the game involves the potential entrant and takes place in period 1, the entry period. Having observed the output level chosen by the incumbent firm, the potential entrant must decide whether to enter the market or stay out. If the potential entrant chooses to stay out, the incumbent firm will continue to earn the profits associated with the quantity set in period 0. If the potential entrant chooses to enter the market, there is a third move in the game. The incumbent firm must decide whether it actually wants to continue to adhere to the quantity it set in period 0. According to the Bain, Modigliani, Sylos-Labini model, the incumbent firm has made a commitment to keep its output at this level. However, it may not be in the best interest of the incumbent firm to do so *if* entry occurs. In other words, the incumbent firm makes an implicit threat in period 0 but may not want to carry out the threat in period 1. We can state this threat as follows: I will

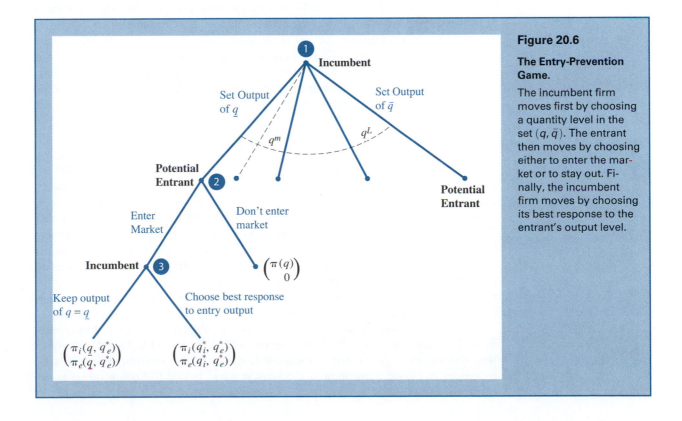

Figure 20.6

The Entry-Prevention Game.

The incumbent firm moves first by choosing a quantity level in the set $(\underline{q}, \bar{q})$. The entrant then moves by choosing either to enter the market or to stay out. Finally, the incumbent firm moves by choosing its best response to the entrant's output level.

set a limit quantity of q_L in period 0, and *I will continue to produce that amount in period 1 even if you enter the market.*

To define payoffs for this game, we will assume that if entry occurs and the gadgets market is thereby transformed from a monopoly to a duopoly, the entrant will choose the output level that corresponds to the Cournot equilibrium output level for a duopoly game. To be more specific, the entrant will not choose the quantity that is a best response to the output set by the monopolist in period 0, but rather it will choose the equilibrium output level for the duopoly game that will be defined between the incumbent firm and the entrant. We will restrict the choice of the incumbent firm at this point to either maintaining the quantity it set in period 0 or selecting a best response (a Cournot equilibrium response) to the output level set by the entrant. The final payoff to the incumbent firm is the sum of its profits in both periods 0 and 1, while the payoff to the entrant is just its profit in period 1. If the entrant enters and chooses the Cournot quantity, the monopolist prefers to choose Cournot too rather than the limit quantity q^L.

The Lack of a Subgame Perfect Equilibrium

As we can see from the game tree in Figure 20.6, the only subgame perfect equilibrium is one in which the incumbent firm sets the monopoly output in period 0, entry occurs, and the incumbent firm then changes its output in period 1 to the Cournot equilibrium output. To reach this conclusion, we need only use the backward induction technique for analyzing extensive-form games. For any output chosen by the incumbent firm in period 0, we can look at the subgame defined by the entrant's move. For example, let us look at the subgame defined by the node labeled 2 in Figure 20.6. At this move, the incumbent firm has a very low level of output that it set in period 0. If the potential entrant decides to enter the market and does so at a level equal to the Cournot equilibrium output, then the incumbent firm must choose between two alternatives. It can either continue to adhere to the output level selected in period 0, as assumption 5 in the Bain, Modigliani, Sylos-Labini model says it will, or it can abandon this output level and choose the output level that is best, *given that entry has occurred.* By the definition of the Cournot equilibrium, we know that once entry takes place, the incumbent firm should set the quantity that represents its best response to the equilibrium choice of the entrant. Therefore, if the incumbent firm is rational, it will abandon the output level it chose in period 0 and behave like a duopolist in period 1.

Knowing this, the potential entrant will decide to enter the market because if it does so, its payoff will be the Cournot equilibrium profits of $\pi(q_i^*, q_e^*)$, while if it stays out of the market, it will receive a zero payoff. Note that in this backward induction analysis, the potential entrant's decision about entering the market or staying out is unaffected by the price the incumbent firm established in period 0. The potential entrant's decision is based only on what it expects the incumbent firm to do if it enters the market, not on what the incumbent firm has done in the past. Knowing that the potential entrant will make its decision in this way, the incumbent firm will be best off setting the monopoly price in period 0 because the price chosen in that period will have no effect on the decision of the potential entrant. Hence, the incumbent firm might as well maximize its profits in period 0.

This outcome is very different from the one predicted by the Bain, Modigliani, Sylos-Labini model. Basically, it demonstrates that the model is flawed because its limit-pricing strategy involves a noncredible threat by the incumbent firm to keep its output in period 1 constant at the level it set in period 0. Such a threat is not credible because when the two players reach the subgame in which the potential entrant is to move, the potential entrant will ignore the threat, knowing that a rational incumbent will not carry it out if entry occurs. Hence, the outcome predicted by the Bain, Modigliani, Sylos-Labini model, in which the incumbent firm prevents entry by setting a limit price, does not constitute a subgame perfect equilibrium for the game described by this model.

Question (Application and Extension: Impeding Market Entry)

SOLVED PROBLEM 20.2

Mrs. Donut is currently the only donut shop in the town of Colfax. Freddie's Fried Dough is considering opening a franchise there to compete with Mrs. Donut. Both would face the same cost functions to operate in Colfax. It will take Freddie's some time to move in and to set up its store, so Mrs. Donut will have time to set a quantity to maximize its profits, either by blockading Freddie's entry or by optimally responding to an inevitable entry.

To simplify this game, assume that this is a two-period game. In the first period, Mrs. Donut can choose one of three possible quantities of donuts to produce: high, medium, or low. In the second period, Freddie's decides whether or not to enter. If Freddie's does enter, then the two firms must play the "entry game," where they simultaneously choose the quantities they will supply—again, high, medium, or low. If Freddie's does not enter, Mrs. Donut will simply decide on its own volume, just as in the first period. The game tree depicted in Figure 20.7 represents this problem.

Figure 20.7

The Donut Game.

Backward induction leads to high output in period 1, entry, and both firms' choosing M in the last stage.

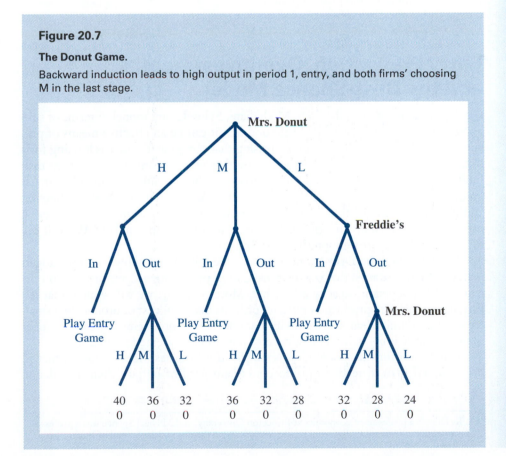

The game that is played if Freddie's decides to enter is as follows:

			Freddie's	
		H	M	L
Mrs. Donut	H	10, 10	8, 12	6, 14
	M	12, 8	10, 10	9, 9
	L	14, 6	9, 9	6, 6

THE ENTRY GAME

In addition to these payoffs, Mrs. Donut will receive in period 1 an additional 20 if it chooses high, an additional 16 if it chooses medium, and an additional 12 if it chooses low. Will Freddie's enter or stay out?

Answer

It should be clear that Freddie's will enter because it will get a positive payoff no matter what the outcome, as opposed to a zero payoff if it stays out. Using backward induction to solve the game, we must first solve the period 2 matrix game. (M, M) turns out to be the Nash equilibrium of the game. This gives both firms a payoff of 10 for period 2, no matter what Mrs. Donut does in the first period. Moving back to the first period, it should be clear that Mrs. Donut will choose to produce the high quantity because this quantity will give it an additional 20 in profit. Therefore, the subgame perfect equilibrium is for Mrs. Donut to produce the high quantity in period 1, for Freddie's to enter, and for both to produce the medium quantity in period 2.

Entry Prevention, Overinvestment, and the Dixit-Spence Model

Clearly, an evaluation of the Bain, Modigliani, Sylos-Labini model in terms of subgame perfection diminishes the likelihood that it can be an effective means of preventing entry. As a result, it is not surprising that our gadget maker is looking for a different method of entry prevention—one that uses a more subtle strategy than limit pricing. She therefore seeks advice from another consulting firm. This firm is guided by the more recent work of economists A. K. Dixit and Michael Spence, and it suggests a model that is based on a strategy of overinvestment in production capacity by the incumbent firm in order to make entry unprofitable.[3] We will call this model of entry prevention the Dixit-Spence model.

Dixit-Spence model
A model of entry prevention where the strategy of the incumbent monopolist is to overinvest in production capacity in order to make entry unprofitable.

To understand the Dixit-Spence model more fully, let us apply it to the gadgets market. We will assume that the marginal cost of producing gadgets depends on the amount of production capacity a firm has. More precisely, we will assume that if a firm has an installed production capacity of K, its marginal cost of producing a smaller number of units than K is υ, and its marginal cost of producing a greater number of units than K is $\upsilon + s$. This marginal cost function is presented in Figure 20.8.

The reason for this assumption is simple. If a firm has excess capacity, that is, more capital than it needs to produce a certain level of output, then in order to

---

[3] A. K. Dixit is a professor of economics at Princeton University, and Michael Spence was a professor of economics at Harvard College and subsequently became the dean of the School of Business at Stanford University.

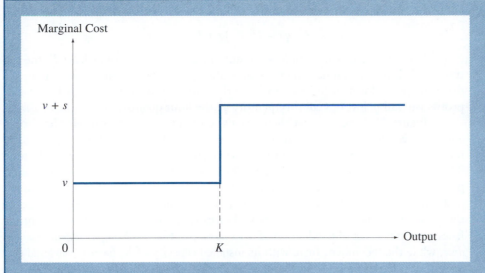

Figure 20.8

The Marginal Cost Function for a Capacity-Constrained Firm.

At output levels that are lower than the firm's installed capacity of K, the marginal cost is merely the variable marginal cost of v. At higher output levels, the marginal cost also includes the cost of additional capacity, s.

produce one more unit of output, the firm will need to buy more variable inputs such as labor. We will let v be the cost of the inputs needed to produce one more unit of output, and we will assume that this level is constant no matter how much output is produced. When a firm has excess capacity, its marginal cost of producing one unit is v. However, when there is no excess capacity, the firm must buy not only more variable inputs but also more capacity in order to produce one more unit of output. We will assume that the cost of the capacity needed to produce one more unit is s and that this cost is independent of the amount produced. Hence, when a firm must produce beyond its capacity, its marginal cost must be $v + s$.

overinvestment strategy
An entry-prevention strategy for an incumbent firm in which the incumbent monopolist overinvests in production capacity to make a credible threat to increase its output beyond the limit quantity (and thereby sell the goods at a price below the limit price) if any competitor enters the market.

CONSULTING REPORT   20.2

USING THE OVERINVESTMENT STRATEGY OF THE DIXIT-SPENCE MODEL TO DETER MARKET ENTRY

The consultants tell our gadget maker that any effective strategy for entry prevention must be consistent with sub-game perfection. The overinvestment strategy of the Dixit-Spence model meets this criterion. An incumbent firm that overinvests in production capacity can make a credible threat to increase its output beyond the limit quantity and sell the goods at an associated price beyond the limit price if any competitor enters the market. With the excess production capacity created by overinvestment, the incumbent firm is in a position to carry out such a threat and make entry unprofitable for a potential competitor. ●

Figure 20.8 illustrates the marginal cost function facing a firm that has an installed production capacity of K. In other words, the firm is capacity-constrained beyond the level of K.

In addition to these assumptions, both firms are assumed to have a fixed cost F, making the cost function of the incumbent

$$C_i(q, K) = vq + F, \text{ if } --q \leq K$$
$$vq + s(q - K), \text{ if } --q > K$$

while the cost function for the entrant is

$$C_e(q) = (v+s)q + F.$$

Note that with fixed cost F, unless the entrant earns a profit of at least F, the entrant will drop out. Hence, there is an output level for the incumbent that will drive the price down sufficiently to force the entrant out of the market because its profits will fall below F. Call this quantity q^L the limit quantity.

In Figure 20.8, we see that the marginal cost is v up to the capacity level of K and then rises to $v+s$ beyond the capacity level of K. Why should this type of technological assumption allow a firm to prevent entry more easily in a credible way? The reason is that there is an important difference between an incumbent firm and a potential entrant because the incumbent firm, having produced the product in the past, *already has installed capacity*, but the potential entrant, having never produced the product before, does not possess such a capacity. Hence, the potential entrant faces a marginal cost of production of $v+s$ *no matter how much output it decides to produce*, while the incumbent firm, with its installed capacity of K, faces a marginal cost of v for all output up to K and a marginal cost of $v+s$ for all output above K. To see why this difference in production capacity and marginal cost is the key to entry prevention in the Dixit-Spence model, let us consider Figure 20.9.

Figure 20.9 shows a single reaction function for a potential entrant, which is marked R_e, and a series of reaction functions for the incumbent firm, each of which is indexed to a different level of installed capacity. The potential entrant's reaction function is easily explained. It is the reaction function that we would expect to see for a firm faced with a marginal cost of $v+s$. Because the potential entrant has only one marginal cost, it also has only one reaction function. Note, however, that this reaction function has a jump in it at quantity q^L because, if the

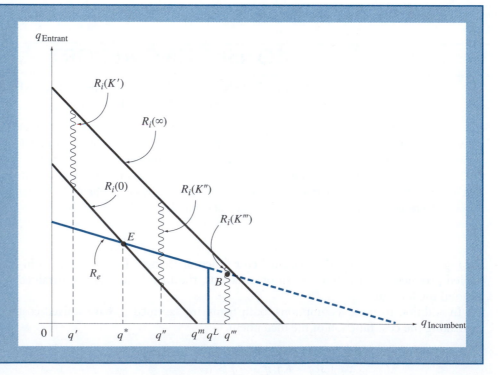

Figure 20.9

Reaction Functions in the Dixit-Spence Model.

The potential entrant has reaction function R_e. The incumbent firm chooses R_i from a series of reaction functions by setting a capacity level. The incumbent firm can credibly deter entry by choosing a reaction function such that its optimal response to entry is to produce at an output level higher than the limit quantity of q^L.

incumbent sets an output equal to q^L (or more), the entrant will not enter because it will be unable to cover its fixed costs. The incumbent firm can choose among different levels of installed capacity and therefore can actually decide on which reaction function it wants to be.

To understand these reaction functions, note that the lower the marginal cost faced by a duopolist is, the higher its output will be, given any level of output produced by its rival. We know that this is true because when one firm has chosen its output, the other firm will equate the marginal revenue associated with its residual demand curve to its marginal cost of production. The lower the marginal cost is, the higher the level of output at which this will occur. Hence, firms with lower marginal cost curves will have reaction functions that are shifted out, and that implies a higher level of output for any given level of output set by the rival firm. In this model, there are only two marginal costs: υ if the firm produces below its installed capacity and $\upsilon + s$ if the firm produces above its installed capacity.

In Figure 20.9, we see two reaction functions for the incumbent firm. One of these reaction functions, $R_i(0)$, is predicated on the assumption that the incumbent firm has *no* installed capacity and faces a marginal cost of $\upsilon + s$ for every unit produced starting with the first unit. The other reaction function, $R_i(\infty)$, is predicated on the assumption that the incumbent firm has an infinite amount of installed capacity, or at least a capacity so large that it will never be fully used in the normal course of interaction in the gadgets market. The marginal cost associated with this reaction function is only υ for all units of output. Hence, this reaction function shifts to the right. Connecting the two reaction functions are a series of squiggly lines that represent the fact that the incumbent changes from one reaction function, $R_i(\infty)$, to the other, $R_i(0)$, when its output exceeds its installed capacity.

For example, let us say that the incumbent firm has an installed capacity of K', so it can produce $q' = K'$ units without having to add any more capacity. Its marginal cost is therefore υ for all quantities up to q' and $\upsilon + s$ for all quantities above that level. If we look again at Figure 20.9, we find that $R_i(\infty)$ is the relevant function for all output up to q' and $R_i(0)$ is the relevant reaction function for all output above q'. In Figure 20.9, we see that an increase in output above q' is portrayed by the first squiggly line marked $R_i(K')$ because at $K' = q'$ the reaction function jumps from $R_i(\infty)$ to $R_i(0)$. Similarly, if capacity is higher at $K'' = q''$, then the relevant reaction function is $R_i(\infty)$ for quantities up to q'' and $R_i(0)$ for quantities above q''. Other reaction functions can be defined for different levels of installed capacity.

To analyze the strategic situation faced by the incumbent firm and the potential entrant in this example, let us think in terms of a game that is taking place in three stages or periods. In period 0, the incumbent firm decides what production capacity to build. In period 1, the potential entrant sees the result of the incumbent firm's decision and decides whether to enter the market or stay out. In period 2, the output is set. Of course, if no entry occurs in period 1, only the incumbent firm will choose a quantity in period 2. If entry does take place in period 1, then the incumbent firm and the potential entrant will each select a quantity in period 2. According to Dixit and Spence, the decision that the potential entrant makes to enter the market or stay out depends on the amount of production capacity built by the incumbent firm in period 0. This capacity must be large enough that the threat of the incumbent firm to produce an entry-preventing level of output in period 2 is credible.

To see exactly how the Dixit-Spence model works, let us say that the incumbent firm has no capacity at all. Hence, the relevant reaction functions in Figure 20.9 will be $R_i(0)$ for the incumbent firm and R_e for the potential entrant. If entry occurs, these reaction functions will define point E as the equilibrium for the duopoly game that develops *after* entry. As we saw previously, the problem with the Bain, Modigliani, Sylos-Labini model is that it assumes that the incumbent firm will choose q^L, the limit quantity, before entry and continue to choose it after entry. However, if the incumbent firm has no installed capacity and entry occurs, we can see that the incumbent firm will change its output from q^L to q^*. Consequently, the threat to continue to adhere to the limit quantity of q^L is not credible. Now let us say that the incumbent firm builds a capacity of K'''. In this case, its reaction function will be $R_i(\infty)$ up to $K''' = q'''$, and then it will drop along the squiggly line marked $R_i(K''')$. Notice that when the installed capacity is at this level, the reaction functions of the potential entrant and the incumbent firm cross at point B, where the incumbent firm produces output that is greater than the limit quantity of q^L. Now, because of the excess capacity installed by the incumbent firm, the potential entrant knows that the equilibrium of the duopoly game defined *after entry* will involve such a high level of output for the incumbent firm that entry will not be profitable. The potential entrant realizes that it will be better off staying out of the market. Thus, entry is prevented.

Note that because entry does not occur at the equilibrium for this game, the incumbent firm will set the monopoly output of q^m in period 2 and therefore will have unused capacity. The overinvestment strategy of the Dixit-Spence model requires the incumbent firm to build excess capacity in period 0 so that it can *commit* itself to producing an output larger than the limit quantity in period 2 if entry occurs. The existence of this excess capacity makes the incumbent firm's threat credible. However, a disadvantage of overinvestment is that the incumbent firm builds capacity it never uses. Hence, this strategy is somewhat wasteful of resources.

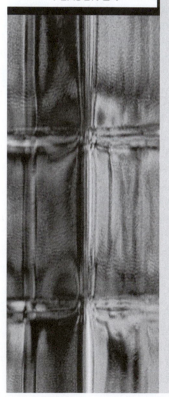

RESOLVING
TEASER 21

ENTRY PREVENTION

Now that we know something about entry prevention, let us turn once again to the Brandts, Cabrales, and Charness experiment. Remember that in this experiment the incumbent goes first and commits to a certain capacity in stage 1 of the experiment. In stage 2, both firms decide whether to go in or stay out. The payoffs are presented in the two matrices below.

		Incumbent Monopolist Does Not Buy Capacity	
			Entrant
		Out	In
Incumbent	Out	0,0	0,1
	In	1,0	$-F, -F$

		Incumbent Monopolist Does Buy Capacity	
			Entrant
		Out	In
Incumbent	Out	$-aF, 0$	$-aF, 1$
	In	1,0	$-F, -F$

Note that the strategy of the incumbent to buy capacity and then not enter the market (stay out) is dominated by the strategy of not buying capacity and staying out because, for that strategy, he or she can guarantee him- or herself 0, while building capacity and then staying out would get him or her $-aF$. Consequently, when the

(Continued)

entrant sees that the incumbent has built capacity, he should infer that the incumbent intends to stay in the market and, hence, he should stay out. This is what theory predicts and why, in this experiment, committing to capacity on the part of the incumbent is an entry-prevention strategy.

The results of the Brandts et al. experiment are consistent with the theory. Overall, the incumbent becomes the monopolist in these experiments 69% of the time as opposed to the entrant, who becomes the monopolist only 8% of the time. When the incumbent buys capacity, it leads to his being the monopolist 88% of the time, while for the entrant it is only 2% of the time. Even without pre-commitment to capacity, the incumbent became the monopolist 56% of the time as opposed to 12% for the entrant. Capacity is installed 42% of the time.

These results tend to support the idea that investment can be a device to help an incumbent firm prevent entry.

Question (Application and Extension: Incumbent Firm Capacity and Market Entry)

SOLVED
PROBLEM
20.3

Assume that McGwire's hot dog stand is the only stand selling hot dogs to fans going to Wrigley Field in Chicago. It has a grill that can serve 50 hot dogs an hour at a marginal cost of 0. After 50 hot dogs, however, it has to install a larger capacity, and its cost increases to $50q$, where q is the number of hot dogs served ($q > 50$). A potential competitor, Sosa's Hot Dogs, Inc., is thinking of entering. Because it has no installed capacity like McGwire's, its cost is $50q$ for all $q \geq 0$. The demand for hot dogs is

$$p = 100 - (q_E + q_S)$$

where q_E and q_S are the quantities sold by McGwire's and Sosa's, respectively. Knowing that Sosa's wants to enter the market, what capacity will McGwire's set? Will Sosa's enter?

Answer

Let's look at Sosa's first. It faces a demand function $p = 100 - (q_E + q_S)$ and has a cost of $50q_S$. Hence, Sosa's revenue can be written as $R = pq = [100 - (q_E + q_S)]q_S = 100q_S - q_E q_S - q_S^2$. The marginal revenue associated with this revenue function is $MR_S = 100 - q_E - 2q_S$. To find Sosa's reaction function, we know that for any output set by McGwire's, Sosa's will equate its marginal revenue (derived from its residual demand curve) to its marginal cost, which is 50. This yields

$$100 - q_E - 2q_S = 50$$

or

$$2q_S = 50 - q_E \Rightarrow q_S = \frac{50 - q_E}{2}$$

Note, however, that if McGwire's sells 50 or more hot dogs, Sosa's will not want to go into the market. McGwire's can keep Sosa's out by committing to a capacity of 50 (which it already has) and selling that amount. However, because this is exactly the amount it would want to sell if it were a monopolist (check this out for yourself), it would gladly sell 50. Hence, Sosa's will not enter.

Perfect Competition as the Limit of Successful Entry—When Entry Prevention Fails

Let us assume that our gadget maker is unsuccessful in defending her monopoly against competition; she is not able to prevent entry. We will further assume that after the entry of the first few competing firms, many other firms decide to enter the gadget industry in search of extra-normal profits. What effects will this unrestricted entry have on the price of gadgets and on the quantity of gadgets produced? We will now investigate this question.

The Effects of Successful Entry on Price and Output

Let us say that the inverse demand curve for gadgets is $p = p(Q)$, where Q is the total output of the industry and is made up of the output produced by firms $i-1, 2, \ldots, n$. The output of firm 1 is q_1, the output of firm 2 is q_2, and so on. There are n firms. When the industry was a monopoly, its elasticity of demand was the same as the elasticity of demand of the only existing firm and its prevailing price was the price set by that firm. We will let $\xi(Q)$ be the elasticity of demand for the industry when it was organized as a monopoly, and, as we know from our previous discussion of monopoly in Chapter 17, $p^m = MR/(1 - 1/|\xi(Q)|)$ will be the monopoly price for the industry, where MR is the marginal revenue received from the Qth unit sold. As we will now see, the situation changes when there are n firms in the industry.

Consider the marginal revenue for any one firm, given the output set by the other firms:

$$MR_i = p(Q) + \left(\frac{\Delta p}{\Delta Q} \right) q_i \qquad \text{(1)}$$

Note that when a number of firms are producing a product, the marginal revenue received by any single firm from selling one more unit of the product is less than it would be if the firm were a monopolist because the impact of its change in quantity is smaller when the other firms are already selling a large quantity. To see this effect more clearly, multiply the second term in the equation for the marginal revenue (1) by $p(Q) \cdot Q/[p(Q) \cdot Q]$. The result, which is shown in the following equation, is innocuous because $p(Q) \cdot Q/[p(Q) \cdot Q] - 1$.

$$MR_i = p(Q) \left[1 + \left(\frac{\Delta p}{\Delta Q} \right) \cdot \left(\frac{Q}{p(Q)} \right) \cdot \left(\frac{q_i}{Q} \right) \right] \qquad \text{(2)}$$

If we now let $q_i/Q = s_i$ be the share of the total output sold by firm i and $\xi(Q)$ be the elasticity of demand for the industry, we find the following:

$$MR_i = p(Q) \left[1 - \frac{s_i}{|\xi(Q)|} \right] = p(Q) \left[1 - \frac{1}{\frac{(|\xi(Q)|)}{s_i}} \right] \qquad \text{(3)}$$

A profit-maximizing oligopolist, after observing the output set by its competitors, will choose a quantity such that its marginal revenue equals its marginal cost, which we can express as follows:

$$MR_i = p(Q) \left[1 - \frac{1}{\frac{(|\xi(Q)|)}{s_i}} \right] = MC_i \qquad \text{(4)}$$

or

$$p(Q) = \frac{MC_i}{\left[1 - \frac{1}{\underset{s_i}{(|\xi(Q)|)}} \right]}$$

Note that these equations tell us how far the firm will set its price above its marginal cost as its share of the market varies. For example, when the firm is a monopolist, its share of the market will be 1, and we see the typical monopoly pricing solution: $p = MC_i/(1 - 1/|\xi(Q)|)$. However, as the number of firms grows, s_i will go to 0 and, as we can see from the equation labeled (4), price will move toward marginal cost. Note also that as an increasing number of firms enter the market, the demand curve facing any given firm must become more and more elastic. We can see this effect by interpreting $|\xi(Q)|/s_i$ as the elasticity of demand facing the ith firm and observing that as s_i goes to zero, the elasticity goes to infinity.

The Characteristics of Perfectly Competitive Markets

The fact that price will converge on marginal cost as the number of firms in the industry grows is significant because we know that setting a price equal to marginal cost maximizes the sum of the consumer surplus and the producer surplus in the industry. Hence, something good happens when many competing firms enter an industry, and this is what we will now investigate.

Let us assume that the gadget industry has already grown to the point where it contains a large number of firms. By "large," we mean a number so big that the demand curve facing any given firm is infinitely elastic or flat. (The s_i of each firm is close to zero.) As a result, each firm has such a small share of the market that its behavior cannot influence the price. As we saw earlier, such a firm is called a *price taker* because the market determines a price for it and the only decision it makes is how much to produce given the price set by the market. An industry composed of price-taking firms constitutes a **perfectly competitive market**. This type of market has the following characteristics:

1. There are many firms, each of which has an insubstantial share of the market.

2. There is free entry into the market. No barriers exist to prevent entry.

3. There is a homogeneous product. All firms in the industry produce exactly the same product.

4. There is perfect factor mobility. The factors of production (that is, capital and labor) are free to move between this industry and one or more other industries.

5. There is perfect information in the sense that all participants in the market are fully informed about its price and about its profit opportunities.

Because price is beyond the control of any firm in a perfectly competitive market, the only decision that a firm must make is how much output to produce *given* the market price. But if all firms are price takers, how is the market price determined? In the next chapter, we will see how the prevailing market price determines the quantity supplied and how that quantity, given the demand for the good, determines the new market price. We will first investigate the quantity-setting decision of each firm and then proceed to demonstrate how all these decisions together, along with the current state of demand, determine the market price.

perfectly competitive market
A market in which there are many firms, each of which has an insubstantial share of the market; there is free entry into the market and no barriers exist to prevent entry; there is a homogeneous product and all firms in the industry produce exactly the same product; there is perfect factor mobility and the factors of production (that is, capital and labor) are free to move between industries; and there is perfect information in the sense that all participants in the market are fully informed about its price and about its profit opportunities.

Conclusion

Our monopolist has failed to prevent competing firms from entering her industry. Despite her attempts to use the limit-pricing strategy and the overinvestment strategy to keep competitors out of the industry, a large number of firms have gained entry and driven her extra-normal profits down to zero. The process of entry has changed the gadgets market from a monopoly to a duopoly to an oligopoly and finally to a perfectly competitive market. In the next chapter, we will investigate the nature of perfectly competitive markets and discover how they set price and quantity.

Summary

In this chapter, we examined two entry-prevention models. The Bain, Modigliani, Sylos-Labini model involves a limit-pricing strategy in which the incumbent firm threatens to increase its output to a level that will depress the price of the good to the point that a potential entrant will not be able to make a profit if it enters the market. We found that this model is unsatisfactory because it does not result in a subgame perfect equilibrium. The threat of the incumbent firm is not credible. The Dixit-Spence model is more satisfactory. It uses an overinvestment strategy in which the incumbent firm builds excess capacity so that its threat to make entry unprofitable by greatly increasing its output is credible. Finally, in the last section of the chapter, we discussed what happens to an industry when there is unlimited entry. We found that in such a case, the equilibrium market structure consists of an infinitely large number of small firms. This type of market—a perfectly competitive market—will produce prices that are equal to marginal cost. Other important characteristics of such a market are free entry, homogeneous product, perfect factor mobility, and perfect information.

APPENDIX

Incomplete Information and Entry Prevention

One of the troubling aspects of the entry-prevention[4] strategies discussed in this chapter is that they assume that all firms in a market are completely informed about one another and have identical cost structures. This means that every firm has full knowledge of the cost and profit functions of the other firms in its market. Such assumptions are often unrealistic. Most firms do not know what type of technology a potential entrant will have if it enters the market or what its cost and profit functions will be. Having studied game theory in Chapter 11, we understand that a firm attempting to prevent entry may be in a situation that is more like a game of incomplete information than like the games of complete information we observed in this chapter. It is possible, however, that lack of complete information is not a disadvantage. Instead, incomplete information might allow an incumbent monopolist to prevent entry. To see how such a situation

---

[4] For more information about the topic discussed in this appendix, see Reinhard Selten, "The Chain-Store Paradox," *Theory and Decision*, vol. 9 (Norwell, Massachusetts: Kluwer Academic, 1978), pp. 127–59, and Paul Milgrom and John Roberts, "Predation, Reputation, and Entry Deterrence," *Journal of Economic Theory* 27 (1982): 280–312.

might occur, let us examine a simple model of entry prevention where there is incomplete information. This model was first presented by the economists Paul Milgrom and John Roberts, and we will therefore refer to it as the Milgrom-Roberts model.[5]

Using the Milgrom-Roberts Model: A Game of Incomplete Information

Let us say that there are two technologies that the incumbent can use to produce gadgets. One technology has a low constant marginal cost of $0.50, while the other technology has a high constant marginal cost of $2. The potential entrant also has two possible technologies with different marginal costs. These costs are $1.50 and $2. There is a probability of p that the potential entrant will have the high marginal cost and a probability of $1 - p$ that it will have the low marginal cost, while there is a probability of q that the incumbent will have the high marginal cost and a probability of $1 - q$ that it will have the low marginal cost.

The entry-prevention game begins in period 0 when nature determines what technology the incumbent and the potential entrant will use. Therefore, in period 0, each firm learns what its marginal cost will be, but it does not know the other firm's marginal cost. In period 1, the incumbent selects a quantity of x_i to produce and earns the expected profit from this choice without any interference from the potential entrant. During period 2, the potential entrant observes the output choice of the incumbent and decides whether to enter the market or stay out. If the potential entrant does decide to enter the market in period 2, it incurs an entry cost of K and learns what the marginal cost of the incumbent is. Similarly, the incumbent learns what the marginal cost of the entrant is. Both firms then play a Cournot quantity-setting game in period 2.

If entry occurs, the payoff that the incumbent receives from this game is the sum of its profits in periods 1 and 2, while the payoff to the entrant is its profit in period 2. If no entry occurs, the incumbent continues to enjoy the monopoly profit in period 2.

The strategies for the two players in this game are simple. The incumbent's strategy consists of a rule that specifies what quantity it should set depending on whether it is a low-cost or high-cost producer. The potential entrant's strategy consists of a rule that indicates whether to enter the market given its cost function *and* the quantity chosen by the incumbent. For the sake of simplicity, let us say that entry occurs and the following payoffs are defined for the entrant at the Cournot equilibrium of the post-entry duopoly game that takes place in period 2.

$$\pi_e^c(c_i^{low}, c_e^{low}) - 7 = -0.75$$
$$\pi_e^c(c_i^{low}, c_e^{high}) - 7 = -2.31$$
$$\pi_e^c(c_i^{high}, c_e^{low}) - 7 = 2.00$$
$$\pi_e^c(c_i^{high}, c_e^{high}) - 7 = 0.11$$

(5)

In these payoffs, the 7 represents the fixed cost that the potential entrant must bear in order to enter the industry. Let us also assume that the incumbent's reward for deterring entry in period 2 is the difference between the monopoly

---

[5] Paul Milgrom and John Roberts are both professors at Stanford University and experts in the field of game theory.

profit earned if there is no entry and the Cournot equilibrium profit earned if entry occurs. We will let R denote this reward, which is as follows:

$$R(c_i^{low}, c_e^{low}) = 10.31$$
$$R(c_i^{low}, c_e^{high}) = 9.12$$
$$R(c_i^{high}, c_e^{low}) = 9.75 \tag{6}$$
$$R(c_i^{high}, c_e^{high}) = 8.89$$

Remember that each of these numbers represents the difference between the monopoly profit that any high-cost or low-cost incumbent will receive if there is no entry in period 2 of the game and the Cournot equilibrium profit it will receive if there is entry by either a high-cost or a low-cost entrant.

The monopoly output for the incumbent when it has a low cost is 4.75, which yields a profit of \$22.56; whereas the monopoly output for the incumbent when it has a high cost is 4, which yields a profit of \$16.

Note that if the incumbent has a low cost, then no potential entrant, whether it is a high-cost or low-cost producer, will want to enter the market because it will not be able to make a profit at the Cournot equilibrium of the post-entry duopoly game. The main reason for this lack of profitability is the fixed entry cost of 7. Hence, there is an incentive for a low-cost incumbent to try to signal this information to the potential entrant by setting an output in period 1 that indicates what its cost structure is. The problem in such a situation is that a high-cost incumbent might attempt to mislead a potential entrant by imitating the signal of a low-cost incumbent in order to deter entry.

In an entry-prevention game of incomplete information, the equilibrium must be defined as a pair of strategies, one for the incumbent and one for the potential entrant, that are such that, given the strategy of the other firm, neither the incumbent nor the potential entrant will want to deviate. The strategy for the incumbent is a rule stating its output in period 1 as a function of its costs. The strategy for the potential entrant is a rule indicating whether to enter the market or stay out, given its costs and the quantity set by the incumbent.

There are two types of equilibria that exist in this example—a *pooling equilibrium* and a *separating equilibrium*, which we will discuss in turn.

A Pooling Equilibrium

In a pooling equilibrium, both the high-cost and low-cost incumbent set the same output level in period 1. Hence, when the potential entrant observes this output level, it does not learn what type of cost structure the incumbent has. In other words, the incumbent's signal in period 1 offers no information to the potential entrant. The best that the potential entrant can do in such a case is to assume that the incumbent has a low cost with a probability of q and a high cost with a probability of $1 - q$. (These are the original or *prior probability* beliefs of the potential entrant.) The expected profits if entry occurs are as follows, with $c_i = c_i^{low}$ and $\bar{c}_i = c_i^{high}$.

$$\text{Expected profits from entry} = q\pi_e^c(\bar{c}_i, c_e) + (1 - q)\pi_e^c(c_i, c_e) - K \tag{7}$$

What this equation tells us is that if the potential entrant decides to enter the market, there is a probability of q that the incumbent will have a high cost. In this case, the equilibrium payoff to the entrant in the post-entry duopoly game will be $\pi_e^c(\bar{c}_i, c_e)$. On the other hand, there is a probability of $1 - q$ that the incumbent will have a low cost, in which case the equilibrium payoff to the entrant will be $\pi_e^c(c_i, c_e)$. K represents the fixed cost of entry, which is 7 in our example.

Obviously, the potential entrant will want to enter the market if it can expect positive profits after entry. Given the numbers in our example, positive profits for an entrant will depend on q, the prior probability that the incumbent has a high cost. When $0.273 < q < 0.954$, then profits, as specified in the equation labeled (3), will be positive for only a low-cost entrant. Hence, in this case, entry will occur with a probability $1 - p$. When $q < 0.273$, profits will not be positive for either a high-cost entrant or a low-cost entrant, so entry will not occur. However, when $q > 0.954$, just the opposite is true. Because there is such a strong probability that the incumbent has a high cost, both a high-cost entrant and a low-cost entrant can expect to earn positive profits and will therefore want to enter the market.

To be more precise about this equilibrium, let us assume that the strategy of the incumbent, whether it has a high cost or a low cost, is to choose an output of 4.75 in period 1. This is the monopoly output for a low-cost firm. The strategy of the potential entrant is to enter the market no matter what output is set in period 1 if it is a low-cost firm but to enter only when an output other than 4.75 is set in period 1 if it is a high-cost firm. Hence, by setting an output of 4.75 in period 1, the incumbent will definitely keep a high-cost firm from entering the market, but by setting an output other than 4.75, the incumbent will induce entry by both high-cost and low-cost firms.

Let us now show that this strategy forms an equilibrium—that neither the incumbent nor the potential entrant will want to deviate from its announced strategy no matter whether it has a high cost or a low cost. We will consider the incumbent first. A low-cost incumbent will not want to increase its output in period 1 because the higher output will lower its profits in period 1 and induce entry in period 2. Similarly, a decrease in output will also lower the profits of the incumbent in period 1 and induce entry. For a high-cost incumbent, an increase in output will result in even lower profits because the additional quantity will move its output in period 1 even further away from its monopoly level and induce entry in period 2. A decrease in output can increase the profits of a high-cost incumbent in period 1, especially if it brings the output down to the monopoly level. However, this decrease in output is certain to induce entry, which will lead to a profit in period 2 that is sufficiently small to create a net loss for the firm. (Check for yourself that the profit received in period 2 when entry is certain is less than the profit received in period 2 when the probability of entry is $1 - p$ if the pooling equilibrium is adhered to.)

We already know that when the pooling equilibrium exists, only a potential entrant with a low cost will want to enter the market, which is exactly what the strategies of the two players call for. Hence, the two strategies specified here do constitute a pooling equilibrium for the entry-prevention game of incomplete information.

A Separating Equilibrium

The **separating equilibrium** for this game involves the following strategies for the two players: If the incumbent has a low cost, it sets an output of 7.2 in period 1. (Note that this output is way above the monopoly output of 4.75 for a low-cost incumbent.) A high-cost incumbent sets its monopoly output of 4.0 in period 1. After seeing the output set by the incumbent in period 1, the potential entrant will decide to enter the market in period 2 only if this output is less than 7.2. Otherwise, the potential entrant will stay out of the market.

Notice that the strategy of the incumbent is to set a different output level in period 1 depending on whether it has a high cost or a low cost. The strategy of the potential entrant is to enter the market only if the output set by the incumbent

separating equilibrium
An equilibrium to a game of incomplete information where players of different types take different actions so that others are able to learn their type from the action they take. This is the opposite of a pooling equilibrium, where different types play identically and hence no information can be inferred from their actions.

signals that it has a high cost. We can easily show that these two strategies form an equilibrium. Let us take the incumbent first. If it is a high-cost firm, it will not want to deviate from the stated strategy. Setting an output level of 4.0 in period 1 allows it to obtain monopoly profits in that period before entry can occur and share the market at the Cournot equilibrium after entry takes place in period 2. In order to deter entry in period 2, a high-cost incumbent must set a huge output of 7.2 in period 1 and earn rather small profits in that period. The profits the incumbent will earn in period 2 as a result of deterring entry will not compensate it for the reduced profits in period 1. Hence, a high-cost incumbent will not choose an output of 7.2 in period 1.

A low-cost incumbent can benefit from not setting such a large output as 7.2 in period 1, but if it sets a smaller output (like 4.75), it will surely induce entry in period 2. Entry will so reduce a low-cost incumbent's profits in period 2 that it is not worthwhile for this type of incumbent to set a smaller output than 7.2. Hence, neither a high-cost incumbent nor a low-cost incumbent will want to deviate from the specified strategy.

What about the potential entrant? It is obvious that whether the potential entrant has a high cost or a low cost, it will not want to deviate because, in a separating equilibrium, it will learn what the cost structure of the incumbent is. Knowing that it is profitable to enter only when the incumbent has a high cost, both types of potential entrant will do so at this equilibrium and, hence, neither has an incentive to deviate.

Exercises and Problems

1. Let us assume that there is an industry with an incumbent monopolist and a potential entrant. The demand in this industry is $P = 20 - b(q_i + q^e)$, where q_i is the output of the incumbent monopolist, q^e is the output of the entrant, and b is a constant equal to $\frac{1}{2}$. Let us also assume that the constant average cost is $10 a unit for the entrant and zero for the incumbent monopolist.

   a) What is the residual demand curve for the entrant?

   b) Will the incumbent monopolist be able to blockade entry by setting its monopoly price? (*Hint:* Solve for the monopoly price and the monopoly quantity. Then insert that quantity into the residual demand curve and compare the residual demand curve to the average cost function.)

   c) Is the monopoly price equal to the limit price for this monopolist?

2. Consider an incumbent monopolist that has branches in 20 cities. In each city, there is a potential entrant that is trying to decide whether to enter the market and compete with the incumbent monopolist. Each of these firms will make its decision in sequence; that is, the potential entrant in market 1 will decide first, the potential entrant in market 2 will decide next, and so on. Hence, the potential entrant in market t will see the entire history of entry in the previous $t - 1$ periods before it has to make its decision. If a firm decides to enter, then the incumbent monopolist will have to decide whether to fight entry in that market or accept entry and collude with the entrant. The payoffs from these decisions appear in the following game matrix and are the same for each of the 20 markets in which the monopolist does business.

		Potential Entrant	
		Enter	Stay Out
Incumbent	Collude	50, 40	100, 0
Monopolist	Fight	0, −10	100, 0

Note that the first number in each cell of the matrix is the payoff to the incumbent monopolist, and the second number is the payoff to the potential entrant. If the potential entrant stays out of the market, its payoff is 0 and the payoff to the incumbent monopolist is 100. If entry occurs and the incumbent monopolist colludes, it receives a payoff of 50 and the entrant receives a payoff of 40. If entry occurs and the incumbent monopolist decides to fight it, the payoffs are 0 to the incumbent monopolist and −10 to the entrant.

a) Assume that the first move in the game is the decision of the potential entrant to enter the market or stay out and the next move is the decision of the incumbent monopolist to fight or collude if entry occurs. Draw the extensive form of this game.

b) What is the only subgame perfect equilibrium in this game?

c) Assume that this game is played for 20 periods, one period for each potential entrant. What is the only subgame perfect equilibrium in the 20-round game? The total payoff to the incumbent monopolist is the sum of its payoffs from the 20 markets in which it operates, but each entrant receives a payoff from just its own market. (*Hint:* Use backward induction to analyze the game. Start with period 20 and decide what will happen in that round, then do the same for period 19, and so on until you reach period 1.)

3. Say that an incumbent monopolist faces a demand function of $D(p) = 9 - p$, has a constant marginal cost of \$1, and pays a fixed cost of \$2.25. A potential entrant exists with exactly the same technology.[6]

a) If the incumbent monopolist ignores the possibility of entry, it will set a quantity of 4 and a price of \$5 and will earn profits of \$13.75. Verify these figures before proceeding.

b) If the incumbent monopolist produces a quantity of 4 and does not vary that output after entry occurs, what will the residual demand curve of the entrant be?

c) Given this residual demand curve and the assumption that the incumbent monopolist will not respond to the output of the entrant, what output will the entrant set?

d) Under these assumptions, will the incumbent monopolist be better off setting a higher output than the monopoly output and hence a lower price?

e) If we allow the incumbent monopolist to respond to the quantity set by the entrant, what will the Cournot equilibrium of the post-entry duopoly game be?

4. Let us assume that a firm is contemplating entry into the widgets industry, which has an incumbent monopolist. The potential entrant has two choices. It can stay out and put its capital into another industry where it will earn a profit

---

[6] This problem is taken from David Kreps, *A Course in Microeconomic Theory* (Princeton, NJ: Princeton University Press, 1990).

of $45,000 a week, or it can enter the widgets industry and play the game indicated by the following matrix. The first number in each cell of the matrix is the profit that the entrant will earn each week.

There are two equilibria for this game. In the first equilibrium, the incumbent monopolist threatens to set a low price if entry occurs, and hence the best the potential entrant can do is to set a high price and earn a profit of $20,000 a week. If this is the case, the potential entrant will be better off staying out of the widgets industry because it can obtain a profit of $45,000 a week in another industry. In the second equilibrium, the incumbent monopolist sets a high price when entry occurs, allowing the entrant to set a low price and earn a profit of $80,000 a week.

		Incumbent Monopolist	
		High Price	Low Price
Entrant	High Price	−1,000, −1,000	20,000, 80,000
	Low Price	80,000, 20,000	10,000, 10,000

Obviously, this profit would make entry worthwhile for the potential entrant. Both of the equilibria are subgame perfect, yet the one in which the potential entrant rejects the option to earn $45,000 a week in another industry and enters the widgets industry is more appealing. Explain why in such a situation we might expect the potential entrant to decide to enter the widgets industry and the incumbent monopolist to choose a high price when entry occurs. (*Hint:* Because the entrant rejects an opportunity to earn a profit of $45,000 a week in another industry, it must anticipate a favorable outcome for itself in the post-entry duopoly game. Think about what that outcome might be!)

5. Consider the following matrix of the payoffs for a price-setting game between two firms in a duopolistic market.

		Firm II	
		Low Price	High Price
Firm I	Low Price	0, 0	4, 1
	High Price	1, 4	0, 0

a) What are the equilibria for this game?

b) Suppose that we change the rules of the game so that before the game begins, firm I can destroy some of its production capacity. The following matrix shows the new payoffs for the game.

		Firm II	
		Low Price	High Price
Firm I	Low Price	−2, 0	−2, 1
	High Price	−1, 4	−2, 0

Note that firm I's destruction of capacity diminishes its payoff by 2 everywhere in the game matrix. Let us assume that the option to destroy capacity is part of the two-stage game outlined below.

	FIRM I						
	Destroy Capacity				**Don't Destroy Capacity**		
	Firm II				Firm II		
		Low Price	High Price			Low Price	High Price
Firm I Low Price		$-2, 0$	$2, 1$	Firm I Low Price		$0, 0$	$4, 1$
High Price		$-1, 4$	$-2, 0$	High Price		$1, 4$	$0, 0$

It has been argued that the only satisfactory equilibrium for this two-stage game is the "don't destroy" (4, 1) outcome. Explain why this is the only satisfactory equilibrium.

6. Let us say that there is an industry where firm I, the incumbent monopolist, has a constant marginal cost of $6 a unit and a current profit-maximizing price of $8 a unit. Firm II, a potential entrant, has a constant marginal cost of $7 a unit. The president of the incumbent firm tells the president of the potential entrant, "If you come into our market, we will lower our price to $4 a unit and drive you out." Both firms have equal assets.

   a) Is firm I's threat credible? Explain why or why not.

   b) If firm II drives firm I out of the market and becomes a monopolist, will the market price increase or decrease?

7. Suppose that an industry consists of two firms with identical cost functions. They produce identical products and face a joint demand curve of $D = D(q_1, q_2)$, where q_1 is the output of firm 1 and q_2 is the output of firm 2. If firm 1 announces its intended output first and commits itself to producing that output, will its profits be at least as high as the profits of firm 2?

8. Suppose that an incumbent monopolist has to decide its actions over two periods. In period 1, it must commit itself to a technology that will limit its output choices in period 2. It can select technology A, which will force it to choose an output of $\bar{q}$ in period 2, or it can select technology B, which will allow a number of possible output choices. In period 2, the potential entrant, knowing which technology was chosen by the incumbent monopolist, must decide whether to enter the market or stay out. The potential entrant is aware that the selection of technology A will require the incumbent monopolist to produce $\bar{q}$ in period 2, but the selection of technology B will give the incumbent monopolist a number of output choices and therefore cause the two firms to play a Cournot quantity-setting game. The following diagram illustrates the complete game involving both technologies. Note that the Cournot game is part of this larger game.

   At the subgame perfect equilibrium for this game, what technology will the incumbent monopolist choose? Will the potential entrant want to enter the market or stay out?

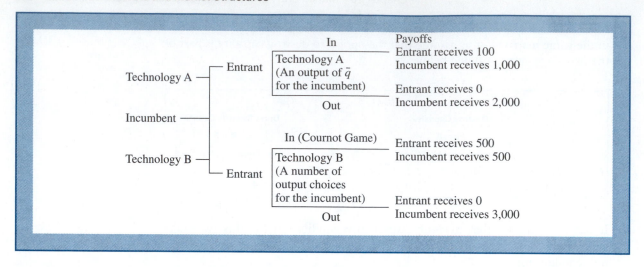

9. Suppose that there is an industry with n identical firms, each of which has a market share of $1/n$. Each firm also has a constant marginal cost of production of $10 a unit, and the elasticity of demand in the industry is constant (for all output levels) at 2. What will the Cournot equilibrium price be when n is equal to 1, 2, 100, or 1,000?

Welfare, Exchange, and General Equilibrium

At the close of Chapter 15, we saw that competitive markets, if left alone, in the long run can determine results that are optimal in the sense of maximizing the sum of consumer plus producer surplus. But if you noticed, that analysis was done for the production and distribution of only one good in isolation. In that sense, the analysis was a partial equilibrium analysis. But economies consist of many markets whose demands are interrelated. The question then arises as to whether we can generalize the beneficial results of competition to economies consisting of many markets simultaneously. This is called general equilibrium analysis, and this is what we will discuss in Chapter 22.

Before we do that, however, we will discuss a special general equilibrium problem called the problem of exchange in Chapter 21. In an exchange problem we have an economy in which nothing is produced but goods costlessly fall down from the heavens and land on people's property. You may keep what lands on your property, but you may want to exchange some of what you have received with others who have received other goods you may desire. The questions here are how the goods that are dropped are reallocated by the process of free and perfect competition, whether the results of this reallocation are optimal and, if so, in what sense they are optimal. After this discussion, we will proceed to Chapter 22, where we introduce production into our economy and again ask the same welfare questions.

The questions asked in these two chapters are fundamental to the question of whether governments should intervene in economies because, if the process of competition determines outcomes that are generally deemed as acceptable, then the case can be made that no intervention is needed. As you will see in this section and in Section 7, the case against intervention is one that must be carefully constructed.

CHAPTER 21
The Problem of Exchange

CHAPTER 22
General Equilibrium and the Origins of the Free-Market and Interventionist Ideologies

The Problem of Exchange

In Chapter 4, we assumed the existence of perfectly competitive markets even though we had no idea how such markets developed in our primitive society. We made this assumption because we were interested in analyzing how consumers with the preferences described in Chapter 2 would behave if they were placed in large impersonal markets—markets where prices are set anonymously and trading does not involve personal interaction. In this chapter, we will turn our attention to the process by which competitive markets emerged.

We know that competitive markets did not always exist. They emerged at some point in history to solve an economic problem that society faced. To help us understand how and why competitive markets were created, we will investigate a primitive, two-person economy inhabited by the types of people discussed in Chapter 2. We will begin our study of this two-person economy by examining the process of barter exchange. Our analysis will involve the use of a construct called the *Edgeworth box*, which will allow us to define a set of *efficient trades*. Using a concept known as the *core*, we will also be able to define a set of *equilibrium trades*.

As the chapter progresses, our simple two-person economy will grow in size. Each of our two agents will multiply proportionately into many agents of the same type. Competitive markets will emerge at the limit of this process when the size of the economy approaches infinity. At this point, we will formally define the idea of a *competitive equilibrium*.

Harvesting and Gathering: The Need for Trade

Consider a primitive, two-person economy where every day people spend the morning harvesting and gathering fruit that grows on the trees and bushes around them. Individual property rights exist and are respected by both agents. Neither of them steals the fruit harvested by the other. Transfers of fruit between our agents are made only through trades voluntarily entered into by both parties.

Let us begin our analysis by looking more closely at the agents who constitute our two-person economy—Geoffrey and Elizabeth. They harvest two types of fruit: apples and raspberries. Because apples grow on tall trees but raspberries grow on bushes close to the ground, Geoffrey, the taller of the two, usually picks more apples and fewer raspberries than Elizabeth. For the sake of simplicity, let us assume that Geoffrey picks 8 pounds of apples and 2 pounds of raspberries every day, while Elizabeth picks 2 pounds of apples and 6 pounds of raspberries every day. Therefore, because all the harvesting is done in the morning, by the end of each morning, this economy consists of 10 pounds of apples and 8 pounds of raspberries. Geoffrey and Elizabeth have two options in disposing of these goods. Either they can consume exactly what they pick, or they can change the mix of fruit they have by trading with each other. Which option will they choose?

Constructing the Edgeworth Box and Finding Feasible Trades

Let us say that our agents have the type of preferences we assumed in Chapter 2. They are selfish and nonsatiated, so we must presume that they will want to trade with each other *if, and only if*, they think that they will benefit from trading. Figure 21.1 demonstrates possible outcomes of the trading process for Geoffrey and Elizabeth.

Figure 21.1 presents a diagram known to economists as the **Edgeworth box**.[1] This graphical device permits us to analyze the process of trade between two parties. We can use the Edgeworth box to answer the following question: What outcomes will result from a voluntary trading process that involves two agents and two goods in an economy? This box will also allow us to define an equilibrium for the trading process.

In Figure 21.1, the two parties to the trading process are Geoffrey and Elizabeth. The two goods involved are the apples and raspberries that Geoffrey and Elizabeth pick each day. The height of the Edgeworth box shown in Figure 21.1 represents the quantity of apples in the economy, while the width represents the quantity of raspberries. When we look at the box from point *A* toward point *B*, we see that there are 10 pounds of apples in the economy; and when we look at the box from point *A* toward point *D*, we see that there are 8 pounds of raspberries. Hence, the size of the Edgeworth box represents the *total* amount of the designated goods available for consumption in the economy.

Each point in the Edgeworth box represents a possible **allocation** of the two goods involved—a specification of the quantity of each good to be consumed by each of the two agents. For example, in Figure 21.1, point *A* is the origin or zero point for Geoffrey's consumption. At this point, he is consuming neither apples nor raspberries. Looking at the box from Geoffrey's perspective (from point *A*), we see that as we move from point *A* to point *B*, his allocation of apples grows larger, while as we move from point *A* to point *D*, his allocation of raspberries grows larger. At point *e*, Geoffrey's allocation consists of 3 pounds of apples and 3 pounds of raspberries. Point *C* is the point of origin or zero point for Elizabeth's consumption. If we look at the box from Elizabeth's perspective (from point *C*), we find that movement in the direction of point *B* increases her allocation of raspberries and that movement in the direction of point *D* increases her allocation of apples. For Elizabeth, point *e* represents an allocation of 7 pounds of apples and 5 pounds of raspberries.

Notice that the total amount allocated at point *e* is 10 pounds of apples and 8 pounds of raspberries (3 pounds of apples and 3 pounds of raspberries to Geoffrey and 7 pounds of apples and 5 pounds of raspberries to Elizabeth). This total is exactly the amount of fruit that Geoffrey and Elizabeth harvested in the morning. Point *e* is therefore a **feasible allocation** for our two agents because it does not

Edgeworth box
A graphical device that permits us to analyze the process of trade between two parties.

allocation
A specification of the quantity of each good to be consumed by each agent in the economy.

feasible allocation
An allocation that does not allocate more than the total amount of goods available in the economy.

---

[1] The Edgeworth box was invented by Francis Ysidro Edgeworth (1845–1926), who was a professor of political economy at Oxford University from 1891 to 1922. Edgeworth also devised two other analytical tools that are widely used by economists—indifference curves and the contract curve.

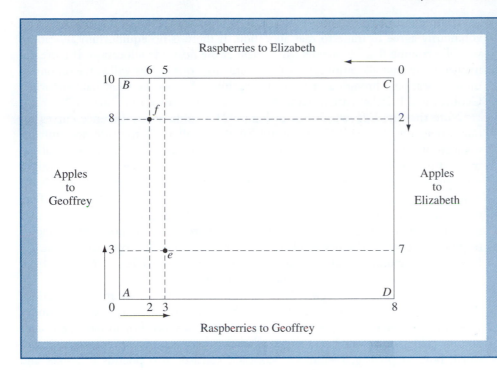

Figure 21.1

The Edgeworth Box: The Benefits of Trade.

Each point in the box represents a different way of allocating the two goods in the economy to the two agents. Quantities of apples are measured on the vertical axis and quantities of raspberries on the horizontal axis. Geoffrey's consumption levels are measured from point A and Elizabeth's from point C.

exceed the goods available in the economy. There are enough resources to give each of our agents precisely the amounts called for at point e.

Now look at point f in Figure 21.1, which shows another feasible allocation. This point represents the allocation of apples and raspberries that exists just after the daily harvest is completed and before any trade has taken place. At point f, Geoffrey and Elizabeth have the amounts they picked (8 pounds of apples and 2 pounds of raspberries for Geoffrey and 2 pounds of apples and 6 pounds of raspberries for Elizabeth). This type of feasible allocation is called a **no-trade allocation**—an allocation in which the two agents consume exactly the quantities of the two goods that they initially possessed. Also notice the allocations at points A and C of Figure 21.1. At point A, all goods are allocated to Elizabeth, and at point C, all goods are allocated to Geoffrey. These are also feasible allocations.

Any point in the Edgeworth box defines a feasible allocation of goods for the economy. Hence, all points in the box represent possible outcomes of the trading process.

no-trade allocation
A feasible allocation in which agents consume exactly the quantities of the goods that they initially possessed.

Finding Equilibrium Trades

In order to analyze the possible outcomes of the trading process that the Edgeworth box describes, we must ask the following question: Is there an outcome that is more beneficial to the parties involved than keeping the goods they initially possess (the no-trade allocation)? In the case of Geoffrey and Elizabeth, we want to know whether there exists a point in the Edgeworth box—a feasible allocation—that our agents both agree is better for them than point f, their no-trade allocation. If there is such an allocation that also has the property that, once the parties reach this point, they have no further incentive to continue trading, then it is called an **equilibrium allocation**.

equilibrium allocation
An allocation that has the property that, once the parties reach this point, they have no further incentive to continue trading.

If there is an equilibrium allocation, we will presume that our agents will both voluntarily agree to trade to that allocation. If there is no equilibrium allocation, we will presume that our agents will remain at the no-trade allocation. If there are many equilibrium allocations, we will presume that our agents will agree on one of these allocations through a process of bargaining. Let us see what happens when Geoffrey and Elizabeth are faced with the allocations shown in Figure 21.2.

Note that the Edgeworth box in Figure 21.2 contains indifference curves for our two agents. To see if Geoffrey and Elizabeth will agree to trade, we must investigate whether there is an allocation that will increase their utility levels above those at the no-trade allocation. In Figure 21.2, the indifference curves for both of our agents go through point f—the no-trade allocation. Note that Geoffrey's indifference curve is bowed in toward the origin at point A, and Elizabeth's indifference curve is bowed in toward the origin at point C. Indifference curves farther away from the point of origin for Geoffrey's indifference curve (point A) and closer to point C represent higher levels of utility for him. Just the opposite is true for Elizabeth. Her utility level increases as we move closer to point A and away from the point of origin for her indifference curve (point C).

By simply looking at Figure 21.2, we can see that there are many allocations that will allow both Geoffrey and Elizabeth to increase their utility levels above those they can achieve at point f—the no-trade allocation. For instance, consider point g. This point must be a feasible allocation because it is a point in the Edgeworth box. At point g, Geoffrey's allocation consists of 6 pounds of apples and 4 pounds of raspberries, and Elizabeth's allocation consists of 4 pounds of apples and 4 pounds of raspberries. Notice that at point g, Geoffrey is on indifference curve I_{2g} instead of indifference curve I_{1g}, which goes through the point of the no-trade allocation. Because I_{2g} is farther from Geoffrey's point of origin than I_{1g}, it is clear that he will prefer to trade to point g rather than remain at point f—the no-trade allocation. Similarly, Elizabeth will prefer to trade to point g rather than remain at point f

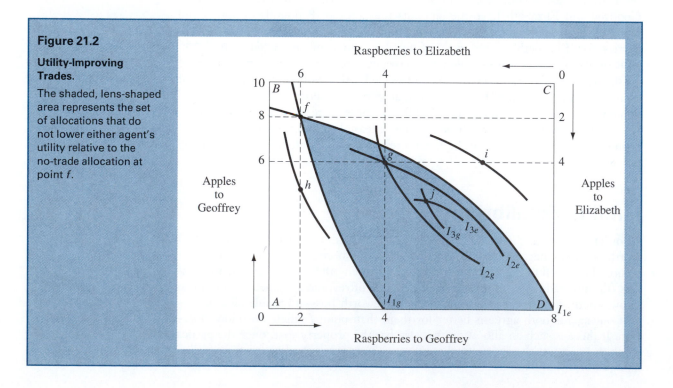

Figure 21.2

Utility-Improving Trades.

The shaded, lens-shaped area represents the set of allocations that do not lower either agent's utility relative to the no-trade allocation at point f.

because she is on indifference curve I_{2e} at point g instead of on indifference curve I_{1e} where point f is located.

Blocking Trades

Let us consider Figure 21.2 again. The allocation at point g is not the only allocation that will make both Geoffrey and Elizabeth better off than they were at the no-trade allocation. In fact, any allocation in the shaded, lens-shaped area of Figure 21.2 is an allocation that both Geoffrey and Elizabeth prefer to their no-trade allocations. But what about allocations outside this area? For instance, what about an allocation like the one at point h? Does that allocation make *both* agents better off? Clearly not, because although Elizabeth is on a higher indifference curve at point h, Geoffrey is on a lower indifference curve than he was at point f. Of course, we are assuming that our agents trade by mutual agreement, so we must presume that Geoffrey will block, or prevent, any trade below indifference curve I_{1g}. A trade of this type is not an individually rational trade for Geoffrey. Making such a trade would lower his utility level because he could guarantee himself a position on I_{1g} by not trading at all. Similarly, an allocation such as the one at point i would benefit Geoffrey but not Elizabeth and would therefore be blocked by her. All trades below indifference curve I_{1e} are not individually rational for Elizabeth. Hence, if a trade is going to occur, it must benefit both of our agents, which means that it will have to take place at an allocation inside the shaded, lens-shaped area of Figure 21.2.

An Efficient, or Pareto-Optimal, Allocation

As we have seen, the trades that take place inside the shaded, lens-shaped area of Figure 21.2 are those that are individually rational for *both* agents. But where in this area will the final trade occur? To help us narrow down the set of possibilities, we need an additional assumption about allocations. This assumption is that the final allocation agreed to must be efficient, or what economists call Pareto optimal.[2] By *efficient* or *Pareto optimal*, we mean that there must not be another feasible allocation that could make both agents better off—or one agent equally well off and the other better off—than the proposed allocation. A more formal definition of this type of allocation follows: A feasible allocation is efficient, or Pareto optimal, if there does not exist another feasible allocation that makes at least one party (or perhaps both parties) to the trade better off (on a higher utility level) and makes neither party worse off. An efficient trade is one leading to an efficient allocation.

Let us look at Figure 21.2 to find an example of an efficient allocation. Although the allocation at point g makes both Geoffrey and Elizabeth better off than they were at the no-trade allocation, it is not an efficient allocation because there is another allocation at point j that places both agents on even higher indifference curves (I_{3g} and I_{3e}). It is clear where efficient allocations can and cannot exist in the Edgeworth box. Whenever we see an allocation for which the agents' indifference curves define a lens-shaped area such as the one at point g, there will exist other allocations that make both agents better off. Hence, only allocations that eliminate such lens-shaped areas can be efficient allocations.

block
To prevent a trade from occurring by forming a coalition and offering each person in the coalition more than they receive from the current proposed trade.

individually rational trade
A trade that offers a trader a higher level of utility than he or she could receive by not trading.

Pareto-optimal (efficient) allocation
An allocation of goods across people such that there are no other feasible allocation that could make all agents better off—or all agents equally well off and at least one strictly better off—than the proposed allocation.

---

[2]   Pareto-optimal allocations are an outgrowth of the work of the Italian economist Vilfredo Pareto (1848–1923). Pareto held the Chair in Economics in the Faculty of Law at the University of Lausanne in Switzerland from 1892 to 1907. He was originally trained as an engineer and made many contributions to the application of mathematics and statistics to economics.

SOLVED PROBLEM 21.1

Question (Content Review: Efficient [Pareto-Optimal] Allocation)

A vegetarian and a carnivore eat at Morton's Steak House. The vegetarian eats no meat, and the carnivore refuses to allow anything green to enter his mouth (he does not even eat potatoes). Morton's Steak House serves only steak dinners, and each dinner comes with a potato, a salad, and broccoli. They both order steak dinners.

a) After their meal is served, does the food on their plates constitute a Pareto-optimal allocation?

Answer

The food on their plates is certainly not a Pareto-optimal allocation. The vegetarian would like the carnivore's potato, broccoli, and salad, while the carnivore wants the vegetarian's steak and would gladly trade for it. Hence, because both could be made better off by a trade, the existing allocation cannot be optimal.

b) What is the Pareto-optimal allocation?

Answer

The only Pareto-optimal allocation is one in which the vegetarian has all of the potatoes, salad, and broccoli, while the carnivore has all of the steak.

SOLVED PROBLEM 21.2

Question (Content Review: Efficient [Pareto-Optimal] Allocation)

Alberto and Raphael are on a desert island. While Alberto merely owns a small vegetable patch that provides him with subsistence, Raphael owns everything else on the island and is extremely well off. Is this allocation Pareto optimal?

Answer

Yes. A Pareto-optimal allocation is one in which no person can be made better off by reallocating resources without someone being made worse off. Here, when we take anything from Raphael and give it to Alberto, we make Alberto better off, but we also make Raphael worse off. Hence, the original allocation must have been Pareto optimal.

The Marginal Conditions for Efficient Trades. In order for an allocation to exist for which no lens-shaped area can be defined, the indifference curves of the agents at the point of that allocation must be tangent to each other. To help understand why efficient trades require indifference curves that are tangent, remember that the slope of an agent's indifference curve at any point measures the marginal rate of substitution for that agent of goods 1 and 2. When the indifference curves for two agents are tangent, these marginal rates of substitution are equal for both agents.

Now suppose that the marginal rates of substitution for two agents are not equal. Then the existing allocation cannot be efficient because we will be able to find another allocation that makes both agents better off or one agent better off and the other no worse off. To demonstrate the validity of this claim, let us look at the allocation at point g in Figure 21.2. At that point, we see that Geoffrey's marginal rate of substitution of apples (good 2) for raspberries (good 1) is greater than Elizabeth's rate. (Compare the slopes of their indifference curves at point *g*.) For purposes of illustration, let us say that the following inequality holds.

$$MRS_{\text{Geoffrey}} = \frac{4}{1} > \frac{3}{1} = MRS_{\text{Elizabeth}}$$

What this inequality means is that at point *g*, Geoffrey is willing to give up 4 pounds of apples in order to obtain 1 pound of raspberries, while Elizabeth is willing to give up 1 pound of raspberries in order to obtain 3 pounds of apples. If Geoffrey gives up 4 pounds of apples and receives 1 pound of raspberries in exchange, he will be at exactly the same level of utility after this trade as he was before it. If he receives 1 pound of raspberries and has to give up only $3\frac{1}{2}$ pounds of apples in exchange, he will be better off than he was before the trade. Similarly, if Elizabeth receives $3\frac{1}{2}$ pounds of apples in exchange for 1 pound of raspberries, she will be better off than she was before the trade.

Given the preceding facts, let us say that at point *g* Geoffrey proposes a trade in which he will give Elizabeth $3\frac{1}{2}$ pounds of apples in exchange for 1 pound of raspberries. If Elizabeth agrees, both of them will be better off after the trade than they were before it. Geoffrey will give up only $3\frac{1}{2}$ pounds of apples in order to obtain 1 additional pound of raspberries. (Remember that he was willing to give up 4 pounds of apples.) Elizabeth will receive $3\frac{1}{2}$ pounds of apples in exchange for 1 pound of raspberries. (She was willing to accept only 3 pounds of apples and would have remained on her original indifference curve.) Hence, because the indifference curves of these two agents are not tangent at point *g* (and, as a result, their marginal rates of substitution are not equal), there must be another trade that will produce an allocation that makes both agents better off than they are at point *g*. The allocation at point *g* cannot be an efficient, or Pareto-optimal, allocation. To further explain the nature of an efficient allocation, let us consider Figure 21.3.

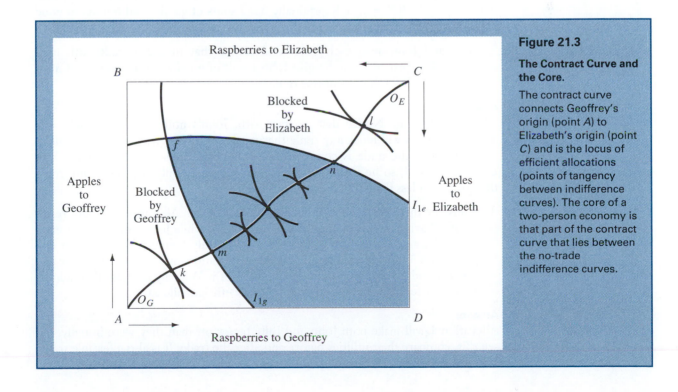

Figure 21.3

The Contract Curve and the Core.

The contract curve connects Geoffrey's origin (point *A*) to Elizabeth's origin (point *C*) and is the locus of efficient allocations (points of tangency between indifference curves). The core of a two-person economy is that part of the contract curve that lies between the no-trade indifference curves.

In Figure 21.3, we see our original Edgeworth box with the no-trade allocation at point f. We also see a curve that starts at point A (the origin of Geoffrey's indifference curve) and ends at point C (the origin of Elizabeth's indifference curve). This new curve, which extends from A to C, is called the contract curve. It is characterized by the fact that along this curve, the indifference curves are tangent. Therefore, all trades along the contract curve are efficient trades.

contract curve

A curve in the Edgeworth box that traces out all the efficient trades.

The Relationship between Efficient Trades, the Contract Curve, and the Core.

The following statement sums up the results of our study of efficient trades until now: In our two-agent economy, which is defined by the no-trade allocation at point f and the tastes of the agents as described by their indifference curves, the set of trades defined by the contract curve leads to the set of efficient allocations for our agents.

Although the contract curve defines the set of efficient trades, it does not define the set of *equilibrium* trades. There are certain trades on the contract curve that would not be acceptable to *both* Geoffrey and Elizabeth. For example, we know that Geoffrey would not agree to any trade like the one at point k in Figure 21.3, which is on the contract curve but places him at a lower level of utility than he can achieve with the no-trade allocation at point f. He would block such a trade because it is not individually rational. For the same reason, Elizabeth would not accept a trade like the one at point l on the contract curve.

SOLVED PROBLEM 21.3	**Question (Application and Extension: Efficient Trades)**

There are two goods in the economy—x and y. Billy has a utility function $U^B = x^2 y$. His marginal utility for good x is $MU_x^B = 2xy$, while his marginal utility for good y is $MU_y^B = x^2$. John also has utility over the two goods, $U^J = xy$, with $MU_x^J = y$ and $MU_y^J = x$. Billy originally has 2 units of good x and 6 units of good y. John originally has 5 units of good x and 1 unit of good y.

a) Billy and John meet each other and realize that they can trade with each other. Billy proposes that he give John 1 unit of good y in exchange for 3 units of good x. Will John accept this trade?

Answer

The answer is no. Notice that to start with, John's utility is $U^J = (5)(1) = 5$. Therefore, John will block any trade that results in his receiving less than 5 units of utility after the trade is complete. The proposed trade will leave John with $U^J = (2)(2) = 4$, so he will block the trade. Likewise, Billy will block any trade that gives him less than $U^B = (2)^2(6) = 24$.

b) Consider three other allocations for Billy and John. Allocation 1 would result in Billy having 3 units of good x and 5 of good y, while John would have 4 units of good x and 2 of good y. Allocation 2 gives Billy 6 units of x and 3 of y and gives John 3 units of each good. The final allocation gives Billy 4 units of x and 2.8 of y and gives John 3 units of x and 4.2 of y. Will any of these final allocations be a feasible, individually rational, and efficient allocation?

Answer

Allocation 1 will make both John and Billy better off than they were initially. To see this, compare their utilities before and after the trade. It is also a feasible trade. Initially there are 7 units of good x and 7 units of good y between the two individuals. After the trade, the final allocations also add up to 7 units of each good. However, the final allocation is not efficient because it does not equate John's and Billy's marginal rates of substitution (MRS). Billy's MRS is

$$MRS^B = \frac{MU_x^B}{MU_y^B} = \frac{2x_B y_B}{x_B^2} = \frac{2y_B}{x_B} = \frac{10}{3},$$

while John's MRS is

$$MRS^J = \frac{MU_x^J}{MU_y^J} = \frac{y_J}{x_J} = \frac{2}{4}$$

Allocation 2 also makes both better off and does equate the marginal rates of substitution:

$$MRS^B = \frac{2y_B}{x_B} = \frac{6}{6} = 1$$

$$MRS^J = \frac{y_J}{x_J} = \frac{3}{3} = 1$$

But it is not a feasible allocation. It has a total of 9 units of good x and only 6 of good y.

The final allocation, Allocation 3, is efficient.

$$MRS^B = \frac{2y_B}{x_B} = \frac{5.6}{4} = 1.4$$

$$MRS^J = \frac{y_J}{x_J} = \frac{4.2}{3} = 1.4$$

Both are made better off by the trade; the total sum of each good in the final allocation is equal to the sum of each good in the initial allocation, and therefore it is feasible.

In order to find the set of trades that represents both efficient allocations and equilibrium allocations, we must look at the portion of the contract curve that lies between the no-trade curves I_{1g} and I_{1e}. This portion of the contract curve contains the set of equilibrium trades because it represents a set of allocations that are individually rational (produce a higher level of utility than the no-trade allocation) and that cannot be blocked by any single agent or group of agents. (Of course, our two-person economy does not have groups of agents. There can only be one group of two agents.)

Economists call the set of equilibrium trades or allocations that we have just described the **core** of the economy. A more formal definition of this term is as follows: The core of an economy is that set of efficient (Pareto-optimal) allocations that cannot be improved upon by any agent acting alone (in an individually rational manner) or by any group of agents acting together. In terms of the Edgeworth box, the core is the portion of the contract curve that lies between the no-trade indifference curves.

Look at Figure 21.3 again. Notice that the set of equilibrium allocations in our two-person economy is very large. In fact, because of our assumption of divisibility, there are an infinite number of allocations that are equilibrium allocations. Further notice that the allocation at point m in the core leaves Geoffrey with the same level of utility that he had before the trading process started, while Elizabeth is doing

core
The set of efficient (Pareto-optimal) allocations that cannot be improved upon by any agent acting alone (in an individually rational manner) or by any group of agents acting together.

much better. In fact, at point *m*, Elizabeth has captured all the gains from trade. There does not exist another equilibrium trade that Geoffrey would not block and that could make Elizabeth any better off. Similarly, point *n* represents an allocation at which Geoffrey captures all the gains from trade. Hence, as we move from point *m* in the core along the contract curve to point *n*, we see that Geoffrey's utility is constantly increasing while Elizabeth's is constantly decreasing.

The actual point on the contract curve at which our agents finally agree to trade will depend on how well they bargain. If Elizabeth is a strong bargainer, then she will attempt to force a trade as close to point *m* as possible. Likewise, if Geoffrey is a strong bargainer, he will attempt to force a trade as close to point *n* as possible. Thus, while the identification of equilibrium allocations on the contract curve narrows down the trading possibilities, it still leaves the outcome of the trading process a little indeterminate.

SOLVED PROBLEM 21.4

Question (Application and Extensions: The Core of a Two-Person Economy)

Assume that Eddie and Jim are the only people in an economy that has just two goods—peaches and plums. Let us say that before trade is allowed in the economy, Eddie has 3 peaches and 6 plums and Jim has 6 peaches and 3 plums. However, let us also assume that for both of them, peaches and plums are perfect substitutes; that is, the marginal rate of substitution is 1 between peaches and plums for both Eddie and Jim.

a) Draw an Edgeworth box depicting this economy, which includes Eddie's and Jim's indifference curves.

Answer

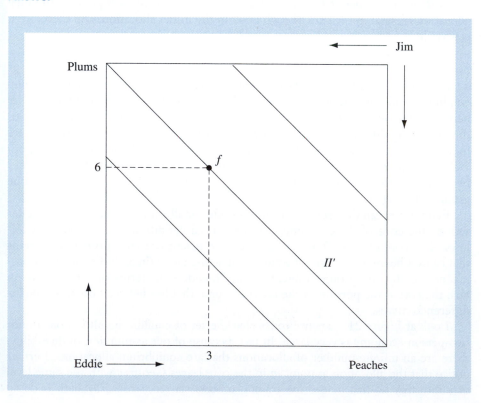

b) What is the core of this economy?

Answer

The Edgeworth box in this example is somewhat special. As you can see, Eddie's and Jim's indifference curves are simple, straight lines that overlap. Through the initial endowment point f, you can see that Eddie's and Jim's indifference curves are right on top of each other. Call the common indifference curve II'; then any point below II' will be blocked by Eddie, and any point above II' will be blocked by Jim. Also, because both Eddie and Jim are indifferent along the line II', they won't block any such point. Hence, the core is the line II', and any point on the line is in the core.

One of the reasons we cannot narrow down the range of possible equilibrium trades any further is that we are dealing with a two-person economy. Trading outcomes in such a small economy depend on the personalities involved. For example, if Elizabeth is strong-minded and knows how to bluff effectively and Geoffrey is meek and mild-mannered, we can expect Elizabeth to dominate Geoffrey and obtain more favorable trades. Hence, one logical question to ask is whether the set of equilibrium trades will decrease when we increase the number of people in our economy. For example, in a larger economy, if Elizabeth were to drive too hard a bargain with Geoffrey and force him to point m, his no-trade indifference curve, he might refuse to trade with her and instead make a trade with someone else who will allow him to achieve at least some gains from the trade. Hence, the addition of other agents can be expected to decrease the bargaining power of any single agent and eliminate extreme core allocations such as points m and n.

Another way to address the issue of how the trading process might change in a larger economy is to ask the following question: What happens to the size of the core as we increase the number of agents in the economy? As we will see, there is a dramatic change in the size of the core when the economy grows. As we increase the size of the economy by adding more and more agents of each type (that is, many duplicates of Geoffrey and Elizabeth), the core will "shrink" until, ultimately, when we have an infinite number of duplicates of Geoffrey and Elizabeth, there will be only one allocation in the core that remains an equilibrium allocation. Note, however, that we will increase the size of the economy in one specific way by assuming that there are many identical copies of the two traders with whom we started—Geoffrey and Elizabeth. Clearly, this is not the only way to envision an economy growing. However, it does successfully present the idea that as the number of people in an economy increases, there is a greater amount of competition, which can be expected to narrow down the possible outcomes from the trading process. Let us now look at the changes that occur in the core and the trading process when an economy grows in size.

A Growing Population and the Core

In order to study the types of social and economic institutions that develop as economies grow, we will have to introduce a larger number of agents into our model economy. Many institutions, such as the competitive markets we will see emerging in this section, would not arise without the existence of large numbers of people. Let us assume that our economy grows through a process of **replication**, by which we mean that the duplicates of Geoffrey and Elizabeth will develop simultaneously so that at first we will have an economy with two Geoffreys and two

replication
The process of increasing the size of an economy proportionately.

Elizabeths, then four Geoffreys and four Elizabeths, then eight of each type, and so on. As this process occurs, we will look at the set of core allocations and see what happens.

An Economy with Four Agents

When we add just one more agent of each type to our economy, we will immediately see the set of core allocations shrinking because the allocations at points m and n, in which agents of one type capture all the gains from trade, are eliminated. In other words, when the economy has two Geoffreys and two Elizabeths, there will no longer exist any core or equilibrium allocations in which all the advantages of a trade will go to the agents of one type. The equilibrium of the trading process will now guarantee that traders of all types benefit in the sense of achieving final utility levels strictly greater than the ones they could obtain if they remained at their no-trade allocations.[3]

We will use Figure 21.4 to examine how trading relationships change when the economy grows and the size of the core shrinks. However, for the moment, let us imagine that in our expanded four-person economy, it is still possible for the agents of one type to receive no benefits from trade. Look at Figure 21.4, which contains the Edgeworth box for the two-person economy that we studied previously, but assume that there are now four agents in the diagram.

Let us say that the two Elizabeths propose a trade at point m to the two Geoffreys. Remember that in our two-person economy, the allocation at this point was an equilibrium allocation—it was in the core of the economy. Because there are two agents of each type in the four-person economy, the supply of available goods has doubled. There are now 20 pounds of apples and 16 pounds of raspberries to be traded each day. Therefore, the allocation at point m will be as shown below. (For convenience, we will designate the first Geoffrey as Geoffrey 1 and the second Geoffrey as Geoffrey 2. Similarly, we will designate the first Elizabeth as Elizabeth 1 and the second Elizabeth as Elizabeth 2.)

Geoffrey 1 receives 3 pounds of apples and 3 pounds of raspberries.

Geoffrey 2 receives 3 pounds of apples and 3 pounds of raspberries.

Elizabeth 1 receives 7 pounds of apples and 5 pounds of raspberries.

Elizabeth 2 receives 7 pounds of apples and 5 pounds of raspberries.

As we can see, Geoffrey 1 and Geoffrey 2 have not achieved any gains from the trade at this allocation because they have merely moved along their no-trade indifference curve from point f to point m. Hence, we might expect that they would be eager to explore the possibilities of bettering their situation. One way to do this is to see if they can play one of the Elizabeths off against the other by negotiating a special deal with her. This special deal would have to make each Geoffrey and the Elizabeth at least as well off as they were at the no-trade allocation. Otherwise, they would have no incentive to agree to the deal. Such a special deal can indeed be found, so it is worthwhile for a coalition of the two Geoffreys and one Elizabeth to block the trade at point m.

---

[3] Note that when we have more than two people in our model economy, there is an increase in the number and size of the possible coalitions. For example, while we can still form our original two-person groups, coalitions of three and even four members are now possible. However, our original definition of the core still applies to this more general case.

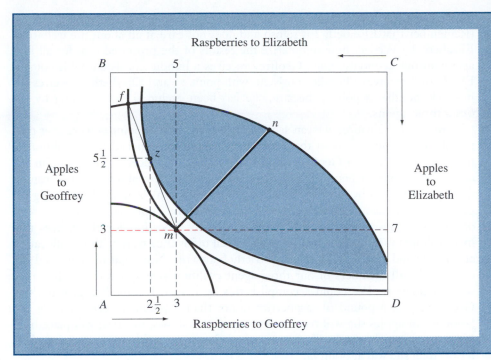

Figure 21.4

The Core of a Four-Person Economy.

The core is the set of efficient (Pareto-optimal) allocations that cannot be blocked. Adding agents shrinks the core. Point m belongs to the core of a two-person economy but not to the core of a four-person economy.

Let us see how this group might negotiate a better deal for themselves. Suppose that the two Geoffreys say to Elizabeth 2: "Look, form a coalition with us. We will give you the same allocation that you would receive from a trade at point m. You will end up with 7 pounds of apples and 5 pounds of raspberries. We will do this by giving you 5 pounds of the apples we picked, which you can add to the 2 pounds you picked. We will divide the 5 pounds of apples that we are giving you so that each of us has to contribute only $2\frac{1}{2}$ pounds. In return, you will give us 1 pound of raspberries, which we will divide evenly between us. As a result of this trade, we will all be better off than we were before." The allocation produced by such a trade among the three members of the coalition is as follows.

Elizabeth 2 receives 7 pounds of apples and 5 pounds of raspberries.

Geoffrey 1 receives $5\frac{1}{2}$ pounds of apples and $2\frac{1}{2}$ pounds of raspberries.

Geoffrey 2 receives $5\frac{1}{2}$ pounds of apples and $2\frac{1}{2}$ pounds of raspberries.

Notice that this trade is feasible for the three agents in the coalition because it does not allocate to them more apples or raspberries than they pick each morning. The proposed allocation contains exactly the amounts harvested by the two Geoffreys and the one Elizabeth—18 pounds of apples and 10 pounds of raspberries.

Figure 21.4 indicates the effects of the proposed trade on the three agents in the coalition. Each Geoffrey moves from his no-trade allocation to point z. He does this by giving up $2\frac{1}{2}$ pounds of apples in exchange for the $\frac{1}{2}$ pound of raspberries that he receives from Elizabeth 2. Because point z is on a higher indifference curve than point m, each Geoffrey is better off at this allocation. However, Elizabeth 2 is still at point m. She remains there because she gives up 1 pound of raspberries in exchange for 5 pounds of apples. Hence, she is just as well off after the trade as she was before it, and she might as well go along with the trade. (Remember that Elizabeth 2 is selfish and does not care at all about the welfare of Elizabeth 1.) We can now summarize the results of the proposed deal for all four agents in our economy. Each Geoffrey receives a bundle consistent with point z, Elizabeth 2 receives a bundle consistent with point m, and Elizabeth 1 receives the no-trade bundle at point f because she has been excluded from trading by the other three agents.

From our evaluation, we can see that if an allocation at point m were ever proposed to the four agents in this economy, it would be blocked by a coalition of three agents—the two Geoffreys and one Elizabeth. Hence, m cannot be in the core of the economy because the core is that set of efficient allocations that cannot be improved upon by any individual or group (coalition) of individuals acting together. In our example, however, we see that m can be improved upon by a group of agents because they can find another feasible allocation for themselves that makes all members of the group at least as well off as they were with the allocation at point m and makes some of them strictly better off. Note that if we wanted, we could make all members of our three-agent coalition strictly better off than they were at point m. We could accomplish this by having Elizabeth 2 give the two Geoffreys $\frac{7}{8}$ of a pound of raspberries rather than 1 pound in exchange for the 5 pounds of apples she will receive. As Figure 21.5 shows, this deal will place both Geoffreys at point w and will place Elizabeth 2 at point y, where she is strictly better off than she was at point m.

As we have seen, by simply adding one more agent of each type, we have begun to shrink the set of allocations in the core of the economy. Why does this happen? If we look again at Figure 21.4, we see that the final allocation selected by our three-agent coalition places Elizabeth 2 at point m but places each Geoffrey at point z. Point z is on a straight line between points f and m. In fact, it is halfway between these two points because the two Geoffreys are dividing

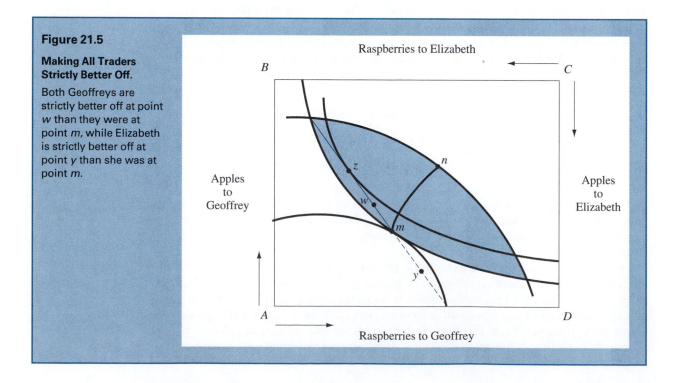

Figure 21.5

Making All Traders Strictly Better Off.

Both Geoffreys are strictly better off at point w than they were at point m, while Elizabeth is strictly better off at point y than she was at point m.

equally the amounts they give to and receive from Elizabeth 2. Note that the slope of that line describes the deal offered to Elizabeth 2, which involves 5 pounds of apples for 1 pound of raspberries. This deal places Elizabeth 2 back at point m. However, because we have assumed that our agents have convex preferences and hence indifference curves that are bowed into their origins, it must be that point z (which is halfway between points f and m, two equally good bundles) provides our agents with more utility than either point f or point m. This is one of the many advantages of having assumed that the preferences of our agents are convex.

An Economy with Many Agents

As we increase the number of Geoffreys and Elizabeths proportionately, we can demonstrate that other points besides m in the original core of our model economy are eliminated. In fact, as stated previously, we will see that when the number of Geoffreys and Elizabeths in the economy approaches infinity, only one type of allocation remains in the core. All other points will be eliminated along the way. We will call these remaining allocations the *competitive equilibrium allocations* because they will represent exactly the same allocation that would result if perfectly competitive markets existed for the allocation of goods 1 and 2 and a set of *competitive prices* had been defined, which facilitated the allocation. We will shortly discuss what we mean by a competitive equilibrium allocation and a set of competitive prices. First, however, let us demonstrate that as an economy grows larger, the set of core allocations shrinks down to only one point. Consider Figure 21.6.

In Figure 21.6, we see the Edgeworth box again with the no-trade allocation depicted by point f. We also see two other allocations on the contract curve, one depicted by point q and the other depicted by point e. Note that at point e, not only are the indifference curves tangent to each other, but the line fe from the no-trade allocation to point e is also tangent to the indifference curves. This is not true,

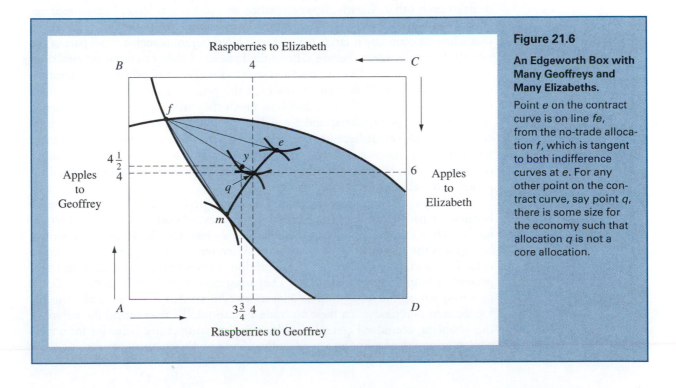

Figure 21.6

An Edgeworth Box with Many Geoffreys and Many Elizabeths.

Point e on the contract curve is on line fe, from the no-trade allocation f, which is tangent to both indifference curves at e. For any other point on the contract curve, say point q, there is some size for the economy such that allocation q is not a core allocation.

however, of point q where, while the indifference curves are certainly tangent (q is on the contract curve), the line fq is not tangent to the indifference curves. (Note that in Figure 21.4, the line fm is *not* tangent to the indifference curves at point m.)

We will now examine the idea that as our model economy approaches an infinite size, the only core allocations that will remain will be the allocations at points like e where the price line is tangent to both indifference curves, which will represent what we are calling the *competitive equilibrium allocations*. Consider the allocation at point q in Figure 21.6. Appendix A of this chapter shows that through a process of coalition formation identical to the one described previously, for any allocation not on a line from the no-trade allocation that is tangent to the indifference curves, there will exist a size for the economy at which such an allocation is not in the core. Hence, we can always choose a size for the economy (a certain number of Geoffreys and Elizabeths) for which a point such as q is no longer a core allocation.

Now look at the allocation at point e of Figure 21.6. Note that all the allocations on the line between points f and e make the Geoffreys worse off than they are at point e. This means that even if we were to play the same game we played before in our four-person economy by finding larger and larger coalitions and then trying to block a trade at point e, we would not be able to do so because we could never find an allocation on line fe that would make our agents as well off as they are at point e. (Line fe is where all such blocking allocations would lie as they did on the line fm in our four-person economy.) We can conclude that the allocation at point e is the only allocation that cannot be blocked by the process described previously and is the only allocation that remains as our model economy approaches an infinite size.

Competitive Behavior. What special significance does the allocation at point e of Figure 21.6 have? Notice that throughout our analysis, the agents achieved their allocations through a bargaining process in which they met face to face and offered deals to each other. Clearly, however, when an economy is large, face-to-face negotiations would be very costly and time consuming. Let us suppose, therefore, that when an economy is large, because each single agent is such a small part of the overall economy, agents behave differently. Instead of trying to organize coalitions and block allocations, they sit home and wait to see the set of prices (trading ratios) that exist for goods. When they know what the prices are, they decide how much of each good they will demand and how much they will supply. We will refer to such agents as price takers, and we will refer to such price-taking behavior as competitive behavior because it is the type of behavior envisioned by economists for agents who function in large markets where it is reasonable to assume that no one agent can have any appreciable influence on the prices that are determined for goods or the allocations that are chosen.

It is ironic that such mechanical and nonstrategic behavior is called *competitive* because we usually think of competition as a process of deal making or deal blocking, which is exactly opposite to the behavior we just described. Still, competitive behavior is the term that we will use here. When our agents engage in competitive behavior, then, given their no-trade allocation, each set of prices they might face presents a simple problem for them. They must choose the bundle of goods that is best for them in the set of feasible allocations (the set that is economically feasible for them to purchase given their no-trade allocation). To understand the nature of this problem, consider Figure 21.7, which depicts competitive behavior for a two-person economy consisting of one Geoffrey and one Elizabeth.

competitive behavior
Price-taking behavior.

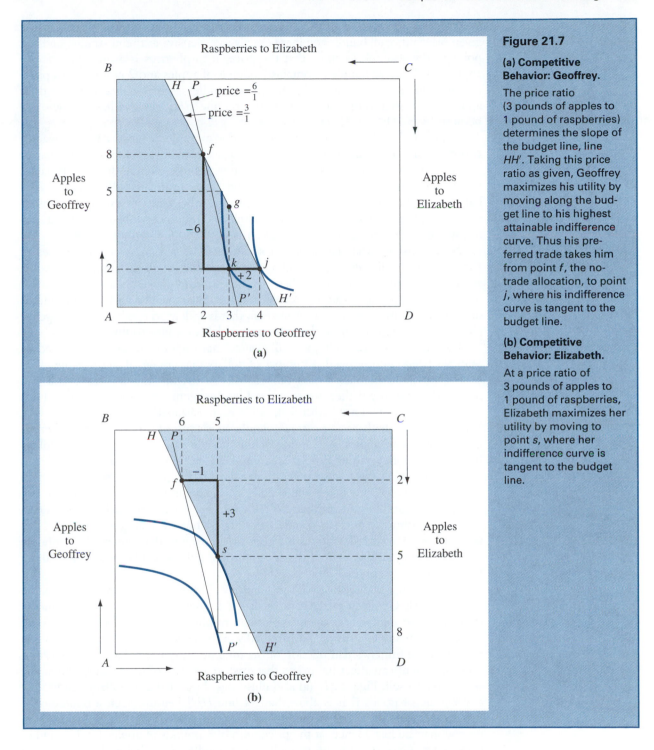

Figure 21.7

(a) Competitive Behavior: Geoffrey.

The price ratio (3 pounds of apples to 1 pound of raspberries) determines the slope of the budget line, line *HH'*. Taking this price ratio as given, Geoffrey maximizes his utility by moving along the budget line to his highest attainable indifference curve. Thus his preferred trade takes him from point *f*, the no-trade allocation, to point *j*, where his indifference curve is tangent to the budget line.

(b) Competitive Behavior: Elizabeth.

At a price ratio of 3 pounds of apples to 1 pound of raspberries, Elizabeth maximizes her utility by moving to point *s*, where her indifference curve is tangent to the budget line.

Let us say that at a given time, the prices of apples and raspberries are in the ratio of 3:1. This means that any Geoffrey or Elizabeth must give up 3 pounds of apples to purchase 1 pound of raspberries. Thus, raspberries are three times as expensive as apples. At those prices, each Geoffrey faces a budget line depicted by the straight line *HH'* in Figure 21.7(a). This line has the property that, at the given price ratio, all bundles on it are exactly as expensive as the no-trade bundle at point *f*. For example, assume that the price of raspberries is 3 and the price of apples is 1. Because bundle *f* contains 8 pounds of apples and 2 pounds of raspberries, its value is $14 = 8(1) + 2(3)$. Note that bundle *g*, which contains 5 pounds of apples and 3 pounds of raspberries, is also on line *HH'* and also has a value of 14 because $14 = 5(1) + 3(3)$.

Barter trading is an inefficient process. For example, let us say that instead of two types of goods, our economy has three types: apples, raspberries, and bananas. If a particular Geoffrey picks only apples and wants to exchange them for bananas, he will have to take his apples to market and locate someone willing to exchange bananas for apples. Whenever he finds someone who wants to exchange raspberries for apples, he cannot make a trade. Exchange requires two parties who are interested in obtaining each other's goods, or a **double coincidence of wants**.

double coincidence of wants

The requirement of trade where two parties must be interested in obtaining each other's goods.

Now consider what happens if a society uses a certain good, like pieces of paper or metal called *dollars*, as legal tender acceptable for all exchange. Then when someone who picks apples wants bananas, he can simply take dollars to the market to obtain the bananas because he knows that the dollars will be an acceptable means of purchasing any type of good. A medium that is widely acceptable in exchange for all goods and services and for the settlement of debts is called **money**.

money

A medium that is widely acceptable in exchange for all goods and services and for the settlement of debts.

For the sake of simplicity, we will assume that each of the agents in our economy has been endowed with a number of dollars that are equal to the value of his or her no-trade bundle. These dollars will be useful only for trade and will not yield any utility if they are consumed by the agents in some other way. Each Geoffrey will be endowed with $14, while each Elizabeth will be endowed with $20. (Each Elizabeth has a no-trade bundle consisting of 6 pounds of raspberries and 2 pounds of apples. The value of this bundle is $20 = 6(3) + 2(1)$.) Dollars function as money in our simple economy because they are a commodity that is readily acceptable for trade among all agents. At this point, we will not go into such questions as who issues these dollars, who guarantees that people are not given more than the value of their no-trade bundle, and so on. Such questions certainly lie within the purview of microeconomics, but we will ignore them at this point in order to avoid a digression. Let us simply say that our model economy now has money in the form of dollars, and these dollars will be used as a medium of exchange in the trading process.

The fact that budget line *HH'* in Figure 21.7(a) is a *straight* line illustrates the fact that each Geoffrey can always exchange 3 pounds of apples for 1 pound of raspberries no matter how many apples and raspberries he has. In short, because there are so many Geoffreys and Elizabeths in the economy and because each one has only an infinitely small fraction of the total quantity of apples and raspberries, no single agent can affect the prices that exist, regardless of the amounts he or she would like to sell. Figure 21.7(a) also illustrates the fact that Geoffrey cannot buy any bundle of goods that is above budget line *HH'* because such a bundle costs more than $14, the value of his no-trade bundle, and therefore requires more money than he has. Hence, at the price ratio of 3 pounds of apples for 1 pound of raspberries, Geoffrey can afford to buy any bundle on or below line *HH'*—any bundle in the shaded area of Figure 21.7(a).

Given the indifference curve for Geoffrey, we know from the assumptions discussed in Chapter 2 that he will choose the point on budget line *HH'* at which his indifference curve is tangent to that line—the point at which his marginal rate of substitution is equal to the price ratio. This point is depicted as point *j* in Figure 21.7(a). As we can see, the bundle at point *j* consists of 2 pounds of apples and 4 pounds of raspberries. Because Geoffrey's no-trade bundle contains 8 pounds of apples and 2 pounds of raspberries, the fact that at the stated prices he wants a bundle consisting of 2 pounds of apples and 4 pounds of raspberries means that he is willing to give up 6 pounds of apples if the market provides him with 2 more pounds of raspberries. Put differently, at the price ratio of 3 pounds of apples for 1 pound of raspberries, Geoffrey is willing to supply 6 pounds of apples and, in exchange, he demands 2 pounds of raspberries. Note that his supply is depicted as −6, while his demand is depicted as +2. Therefore, he is a *net demander* of raspberries and a *net supplier* of apples. Let us record this data in row 1 of Table 21.1.

Now let us look at each Elizabeth. At the price ratio of 3 pounds of apples for 1 pound of raspberries, each Elizabeth has a no-trade bundle worth $20. She can consume any bundle in the shaded area to the right of budget line *HH′* in Figure 21.7(b). From this figure, we see that she chooses her bundle by picking one at a point where her indifference curve is tangent to budget line *HH′*—a point where her marginal rate of substitution is equal to the ratio of the prices. This bundle occurs at point *s*. It consists of 5 pounds of raspberries and 5 pounds of apples. However, because she started at her no-trade bundle of 6 pounds of raspberries and 2 pounds of apples, her selection of a bundle at point *s* means that she is willing at those prices to supply 1 pound of raspberries and, in return, she demands 3 pounds of apples. Her supply is, therefore, −1 pound of raspberries, and her demand is +3 pounds of apples. At the price ratio of 3:1, Elizabeth is a *net supplier* of raspberries and a *net demander* of apples. This fact is depicted in row 1 of Table 21.1.

A Competitive Equilibrium. At the existing prices for apples and raspberries, Elizabeth and Geoffrey cannot completely satisfy their demands or dispose of their supplies. Geoffrey is demanding 2 pounds of raspberries, but Elizabeth is willing to supply only 1 pound. On the other hand, Geoffrey is willing to supply 6 pounds of apples, but Elizabeth is demanding only 3 pounds. Hence, we see that there is an excess demand for raspberries amounting to 1 pound and an excess supply of apples amounting to 3 pounds. Such trades cannot be consummated because they are not consistent. They are not *equilibrium* trades.

What are equilibrium trades? At the current prices, both Geoffrey and Elizabeth are choosing the bundles of apples and raspberries that make them most happy. The problem is that their choices create an imbalance between supply and demand. Geoffrey is demanding more raspberries than Elizabeth is willing to supply, and he is supplying more apples than she is demanding. To achieve an equilibrium, we

Table 21.1	Net Supplies and Demands.						
	GEOFFREY			**ELIZABETH**			
Price Ratio	**Demand**	**Supply**	**Demand**	**Supply**	**Excess Demand**	**Excess Supply**
3 lbs. of apples for 1 lb. of raspberries	2 lbs. of raspberries	6 lbs. of apples	3 lbs. of apples	1 lb. of raspberries	1 lb. of raspberries	3 lbs. of apples
6 lbs. of apples for 1 lb. of raspberries	1 lb. of raspberries	6 lbs. of apples	6 lbs. of apples	1 lb. of raspberries	0 for any good	0 for any good

competitive equilibrium
A price vector stating one price for each good in the economy along with an associated vector of supplies and demands for each good at which no agent has any desire to change their supplies or demands and at which supply and demand are consistent (equal for each good) and hence trades can be carried out in a coordinated way.

competitive prices
Prices that equate the supply and demand for each good.
competitive equilibrium allocation
The allocation of goods determined by a competitive equilibrium.

must find a price ratio at which our agents have no desire to change their selections, but at which supply and demand are consistent and hence trades can be carried out in a coordinated way. In short, we are seeking a competitive equilibrium.

For our simple exchange economy, we can define a competitive equilibrium as a set of prices (one price for each good) at which the agents can choose the bundles that maximize their utility (can behave as price takers). These prices will be such that no agent will have any desire to change his or her chosen bundle and the supply of each good will equal the demand for the good so that trades can be carried out consistently.

Note that this definition implies that our agents and the market have certain characteristics. First, it implies a particular type of behavior on the part of our agents, which we have called *competitive behavior* or *price-taking behavior*. In a market with an infinite number of agents, the trading process is simplified. Each agent spends his or her time calculating his or her supply and demand at the announced prices. The bargaining and coalition formation that we saw previously are now gone. Next, our definition implies that at the equilibrium, there is no incentive for any agent to change his or her supply or demand, which means that his or her behavior will repeat itself forever as long as the economy does not undergo changes or shocks. Moreover, all trades desired can actually be carried out because there is no excess supply or demand. Finally, our definition of a competitive equilibrium implies that the prices charged for goods are competitive prices because they are the prices that equate the supply and demand for each good. The allocation of goods determined by a competitive equilibrium is called a competitive equilibrium allocation.

To determine where the competitive equilibrium is for our model economy, let us see what happens when we raise the price of raspberries and lower the price of apples. Assume that our agents must now give up 6 pounds of apples to obtain 1 pound of raspberries. If we look at Figure 21.7(a), we observe that at the new prices depicted by budget line PP', Geoffrey chooses to consume the bundle containing 2 pounds of apples and 3 pounds of raspberries, which is located at point k. This is his best bundle in the new economically feasible set defined by budget line PP'. In other words, Geoffrey chooses to supply 6 pounds of apples and, in return, he demands 1 pound of raspberries. According to Figure 21.7(b), Elizabeth now decides to consume the bundle containing 8 pounds of apples and 5 pounds of raspberries, which is her best bundle in the new economically feasible set defined by budget line PP'. Hence, at these prices, she is willing to supply 1 pound of raspberries and demands 6 pounds of apples in exchange. This information about the new supply and demand appears on the second line of Table 21.1. Note that at the revised prices, the amount of apples supplied by Geoffrey is exactly equal to the amount demanded by Elizabeth, while the amount of raspberries supplied by Elizabeth is exactly equal to the amount demanded by Geoffrey. Hence, these prices are competitive prices and the economy is in balance.

To see how a competitive equilibrium looks in terms of the Edgeworth box, consider Figure 21.8.

In Figure 21.8, we see our familiar Edgeworth box with the initial no-trade allocation at point f. We also see price line GG' going through point f as well as the contract curve. Finally, we see an allocation at point e, which is on the contract curve and also has the property that the indifference curves of both agents are tangent to price line GG' at this point. GG' has a slope of -6 and, hence, represents the competitive price ratio. At these prices, we see that Geoffrey moves from point f to point e by giving up 6 pounds of apples and receiving 1 pound of

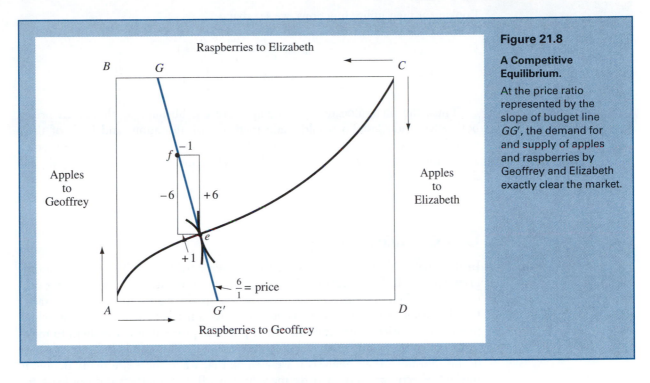

Figure 21.8

A Competitive Equilibrium.

At the price ratio represented by the slope of budget line *GG'*, the demand for and supply of apples and raspberries by Geoffrey and Elizabeth exactly clear the market.

raspberries in return, while Elizabeth moves from point *f* to point *e* by doing just the opposite—giving up 1 pound of raspberries in order to receive 6 pounds of apples in exchange. At point *e*, Geoffrey and Elizabeth have no desire to change their supply and demand and, because supply and demand are equal, the allocation at point *e* represents a competitive equilibrium allocation.

SOLVED
PROBLEM
21.5

Question (Application and Extension: A Competitive Equilibrium)

Consider a two-person economy with two people, Elvis and Costello. There are two goods in the economy—*x* and *y*. Elvis has a utility function $U^E = x^2 y$. His marginal utility for good *x* is $MU_x^E = 2xy$, while his marginal utility for good *y* is $MU_y^E = x^2$. Costello also has utility over the two goods, $U_{\mathcal{J}} = xy$, with $MU_x^C = y$ and $MU_y^C = x$. When the economy starts, Elvis has 7 units of *x* and 2 units of *y*, while Costello has 2 units of *x* and 4 units of *y*. Competitive markets are opened, and Elvis and Costello trade at the market prices of $p_x = 1$ and $p_y = 1$. After their trade, Elvis has 6 units of *x* and 3 units of *y*, while Costello has 3 units of *x* and 3 units of *y*. Do the final prices and allocation constitute a competitive equilibrium?

Answer

Yes. To constitute a competitive equilibrium, we must satisfy certain conditions. First, both Elvis and Costello must be maximizing their utility at the market prices, given their incomes. In this case, at the market prices, Elvis's initial income is $7(p_x) + 2(p_y) = 7(1) + 2(1) = 9$, while Costello's initial income is $2(p_x) + 4(p_y) = 2(1) + 4(1) = 6$. After they make their final purchases, Elvis has spent $6(1) + 3(1) = 9$, and Costello has spent $3(1) + 3(1) = 6$. Hence, both Elvis and Costello could afford the bundles they bought. Now we must verify that they are maximizing their utilities; this would occur if their marginal rates of substitution between goods *x* and *y* equaled the ratio of the prices (which in this case is 1).

Looking at their utility functions, we see that

$$MRS^{Elvis} = \frac{2y_E}{x_E} = \frac{6}{6} = 1$$

$$MRS^{Costello} = \frac{y_C}{x_C} = \frac{3}{3} = 1$$

Thus, the final allocation is a competitive equilibrium. At the stated prices, both Elvis and Costello would trade to this final allocation, and both of them would be maximizing their utility in doing so. Also, because both of them could afford this final allocation, it is feasible. Finally, note that the excess supply and demand for x and y are zero.

Conclusion

In the final analysis, we have come to a rather startling result. As our economy grew larger, all the allocations in the core were eliminated by the blocking process until only one allocation was left—the competitive allocation. This is exactly the allocation that should be reached if we have a market for each good in which people act as price takers and offer their goods at prices that allow them to maximize their utility and balance supply and demand. This result indicates that we do no injustice to our analysis if we assume that when there are many people in our model economy, competitive markets exist. If such markets did not exist and people made their trades by bargaining (a very costly and time-consuming process when an economy involves so many people), we would reach the same competitive allocation anyway. Hence, from now on, we will assume that we have an economy with a large number of agents and, consequently, that markets for goods exist. What type of markets these are, however, will change as we proceed.

Summary

In this chapter, we have investigated the process of exchange. We started out by considering a world with two agents who have different utility functions and different initial endowments of two goods (raspberries and apples). We then asked the following questions: Do mutually beneficial trades between these two agents exist? If so, what do such trades look like? These questions led us to define the concept of an efficient, or Pareto-optimal, trade. Using the geometrical construct of an Edgeworth box, we established the fact that the set of efficient trades occurs along the contract curve inside the Edgeworth box. This curve is the locus of allocations that are efficient. We presented an algebraic condition characterizing efficient trades.

After examining the nature of efficient trades, we then turned our attention to defining the set of equilibrium trades. To do this, we introduced the idea of the core of an economy. This core was defined as a set of efficient allocations that cannot be improved upon by a trader acting in an individually rational way or by a group of traders acting together to further their own interests.

In the remainder of the chapter, we investigated the relationship between the core of an economy and the idea of a competitive equilibrium. We found that as the economy grew larger through a process of replication (a proportionate increase in the number of agents of each type), the set of allocations in the core shrank. As the number of agents in the economy approached infinity, the core was reduced to a single competitive equilibrium allocation. In this way, we observed that competitive markets emerge from a process of bargaining as the number of agents in the economy becomes larger.

THE SHRINKING OF THE CORE

In this appendix, we will take a closer look at why the core shrinks as the size of an economy increases. We will use an example drawn from Figure 21.6.

Let us demonstrate that an allocation such as the one at point q in Figure 21.6 cannot be a core allocation if the size of the economy is allowed to grow large enough. At point q, each Geoffrey is receiving 4 pounds of apples and 4 pounds of raspberries, while each Elizabeth is receiving 6 pounds of apples and 4 pounds of raspberries. Hence, the Geoffreys are better off than they were at point m in Figure 21.4, but the Elizabeths are worse off. While this allocation (as well as the one at point m) was stable when we had only one Geoffrey and one Elizabeth, it is not stable when the size of the economy increases. For example, assume that the economy has grown to contain eight Geoffreys and eight Elizabeths. What we want to show is that even with just eight Geoffreys and eight Elizabeths, it is possible to form a coalition of Geoffreys and Elizabeths that will do better for themselves than they are currently doing at point q. Such a coalition would block a trade at point q and eliminate that allocation from the core.

Suppose that eight Geoffreys and seven Elizabeths form a coalition at the urging of the Geoffreys, who propose the following deal to the Elizabeths: "Your no-trade allocation is 2 pounds of apples and 6 pounds of raspberries. We will improve this allocation by giving each of you 4 pounds of apples if each of you gives us 2 pounds of raspberries." As a result of this deal, each Elizabeth will end up at point q. She will have 6 pounds of apples and 4 pounds of raspberries, which is exactly the allocation provided at point q. Hence, the special deal proposed by the eight Geoffreys yields the seven Elizabeths the same level of utility they would achieve from a simple trade at point q.

For the Geoffreys, the effects of the special deal are quite different. This deal places them on a higher level of utility than they would obtain at point q. Collectively, the eight Geoffreys will receive 14 more pounds of raspberries (2 pounds from each of the seven Elizabeths) in return for giving up 28 pounds of apples (4 pounds to each of the seven Elizabeths). Therefore, because of the deal, each Geoffrey will end up with an allocation consisting of $4\frac{1}{2}$ pounds of apples (the 8 pounds he picked less $3\frac{1}{2}$ pounds to the Elizabeths) and $3\frac{3}{4}$ pounds of raspberries (the 2 pounds he picked plus $1\frac{3}{4}$ pounds from the Elizabeths). This allocation moves the Geoffreys to point y.

Let us summarize the outcome of the special deal negotiated by the coalition of eight Geoffreys and seven Elizabeths. Each Geoffrey will be at point y in Figure 21.6, and each Elizabeth will be at point q. Again, as in Figure 21.4, all eight Geoffreys are strictly better off at point y than they were at point q, while all seven Elizabeths are just as well off. It would be in the interests of this coalition to block a trade at point q because no member is worse off at y than at q, y is feasible for all members, and some members (the Geoffreys) are strictly better off at y than at q. Note that again we were able to improve the satisfaction of the Geoffreys because we could find an allocation on the line between the no-trade allocation at point f and, in this case, point q, which makes each of these agents better off. Whether we can find a point such as y depends on whether we can locate a large enough coalition whose composition makes it possible to achieve a higher level of utility for at least some of the members. Of course, the greater the size of an economy, the easier it is for large coalitions to form.

APPENDIX B

PARETO OPTIMA AND THE CONTRACT CURVE

A Pareto optimum is an allocation of commodities such that no one individual can be made better off without making another worse off. In formal terms, this requires that if we fix the utility level of $n-1$ people in an n-person society, the allocation for which we are searching must maximize the utility level of the remaining person. We compute the Pareto-optimal allocations in an Edgeworth box by finding that feasible allocation that maximizes the utility of any one agent while keeping the utility level of the other constant at a fixed predetermined level. The contract curve is then simply the collection of all points that are Pareto optima.

Formally, we have two agents labeled A and B with utility functions $u^A(x_1^A, x_2^A)$ and $u^B(x_1^B, x_2^B)$ defined over their consumption of the two goods labeled 1 and 2, the total amounts of which are w_1 and w_2.

The problem is

$$\text{Max}_{\{x_1^A, x_2^A\}} u_A(x_1^A, x_2^A)$$
$$\text{s.t. } u_B(x_1^B, x_2^B) = \bar{u}$$
$$\text{and } x_1^A + x_1^B = w_1$$
$$\text{and } x_2^A + x_2^B = w_2$$

The Lagrangian of this problem is

$$L(x_1^A, x_2^A x_1^B, x_2^B) = u_A(x_1^A, x_2^A) + \lambda(\bar{u} - u_B(x_1^B, x_2^B)) + \mu_1(w_1 - x_1^A - x_1^B)$$
$$+ \mu_2(w_2 - x_2^A - x_2^B)$$

Maximizing the Lagrangian with respect to x_1^A, x_2^A, x_1^B, and x_2^B, we have the following first-order conditions:

$$\frac{\partial u_A}{\partial x_1^A} = \mu_1 \qquad \frac{\partial u_A}{\partial x_2^A} = \mu_2$$

$$-\lambda \frac{\partial u_B}{\partial x_1^B} = \mu_1 \qquad -\lambda \frac{\partial u_B}{\partial x_2^B} = \mu_2$$

Combining the two sets of results, we have

$$\frac{\partial u_A}{\partial x_1^A} \bigg/ \frac{\partial u_A}{\partial x_2^A} = \frac{\mu_1}{\mu_2} = \frac{\partial u_B}{\partial x_1^B} \bigg/ \frac{\partial u_B}{\partial x_2^B}$$

that is,

$$MRS_A = MRS_B$$

Further, we can simplify the above expression by substituting in for $x_1^B = w_1 - x_1^A$ and $x_2^B = w_2 - x_2^A$. This yields an expression $x_1^A = f(x_2^A)$, where $f(.)$ is some function. This is the equation of the contract curve.

As an example, consider the following problem with multiplicative utilities:

$$u_A(x_1^A, x_2^A) = x_1^A x_2^A$$
$$u_B(x_1^B, x_2^B) = x_1^B x_2^B$$

The Lagrangian of this problem is

$$L(x_1^A, x_2^A, x_1^B, x_2^B) = x_1^A x_2^A + \lambda(\bar{u} - x_1^B x_2^B) + \mu_1(w_1 - x_1^A - x_1^B)$$
$$+ \mu_2(w_2 - x_2^A - x_2^B)$$

The first-order conditions are

$$x_2^A = \mu_1 \qquad x_1^A = \mu_2$$
$$-\lambda x_2^B = \mu_1 \qquad -\lambda x_1^B = \mu_2$$

so that we have

$$\frac{x_1^A}{x_2^A} = \frac{x_1^B}{x_2^B}$$

which is the equality condition for the marginal rates of substitution. Eliminating x_1^B and x_2^B, we get

$$x_2^A = \frac{w_2}{w_1} x_1^A$$

which is the equation of the contract curve.

APPENDIX C

COMPETITIVE EQUILIBRIUM AND PARETO OPTIMALITY

In an exchange economy, prices perform the task of allocation. Consider, as in the previous appendix, two agents labeled A and B with utility functions $u^A(x_1^A, x_2^A)$ and $u^B(x_1^B, x_2^B)$ defined over their consumptions of the two goods labeled 1 and 2, the total amounts of which are w_1 and w_2.

Let (w_1^A, w_2^A) and (w_1^B, w_2^B) be the original endowments of the two agents. Let p_1 and p_2 be the prices of the two goods.

In a competitive equilibrium, the following must be true:

1. Agent A maximizes her utility subject to her budget constraint.

$$\text{Max}_{\{x_1^A, x_2^A\}} u_A(x_1^A, x_2^A)$$
$$\text{s.t. } p_1 x_1^A + p_2 x_2^A = p_1 w_1^A + p_2 w_2^A$$

2. Agent B maximizes his utility subject to his budget constraint.

$$\text{Max}_{\{x_1^B, x_2^B\}} u_B(x_1^B, x_2^B)$$
$$\text{s.t. } p_1 x_1^B + p_2 x_2^B = p_1 w_1^B + p_2 w_2^B$$

3. Total allocation equals total endowment.

$$x_1^A + x_1^B = w_1^A + w_1^B$$
$$x_2^A + x_2^B = w_2^A + w_2^B$$

Define the Lagrangians:

$$L_1(x_1^A, x_2^A) = u_A(x_1^A, x_2^A) + \lambda_1(p_1 w_1^A + p_2 w_2^A - p_1 x_1^A - p_2 x_2^A)$$
$$L_2(x_1^B, x_2^B) = u_B(x_1^B, x_2^B) + \lambda_2(p_1 w_1^B + p_2 w_2^B - p_1 x_1^B - p_2 x_2^B)$$

Then (1) is equivalent to

$$\text{Max}_{\{x_1^A, x_2^A\}} L_1(x_1^A, x_2^A)$$

whose first-order conditions are

$$\frac{\partial u_A}{\partial x_1^A} = \lambda_1 p_1 \qquad \frac{\partial u_A}{\partial x_2^A} = \lambda_1 p_2$$

And (2) is equivalent to

$$\text{Max}_{\{x_1^B, x_2^B\}} L_2(x_1^B, x_2^B)$$

whose first-order conditions are

$$\frac{\partial u_B}{\partial x_1^B} = \lambda_1 p_1 \qquad \frac{\partial u_B}{\partial x_2^B} = \lambda_1 p_2$$

Eliminating λ_1 and λ_2 from the two sets of first-order conditions, we get

$$MRS_A = \frac{p_1}{p_2} = MRS_B$$

Hence, in competitive equilibrium (as in Pareto optima), the marginal rates of substitution are equalized. As a result, all competitive equilibria are Pareto optimal.

Exercises and Problems

1. Consider an economy of 10 individuals who are located in a straight line. Each person has one neighbor to the right and one neighbor to the left (except for the two people at the ends of the line). There are two goods in this economy: apples and oranges. Each person has the following preference between apples and oranges: If the neighbor on the left eats an apple, the person will lose one unit of utility, while if the neighbor on the right eats an orange, the person will gain one

.	.	.	.	.	.	.	.	.	.
1	2	3	4	5	6	7	8	9	10

unit of utility. Any other possibility (either an apple on the right or an orange on the left) yields zero utility. People do not care what they themselves consume, only what their neighbors consume. Let us depict the economy as follows.
Assume that five people in this economy are endowed with one orange each and the other five are endowed with one apple each.

a)   What is the Pareto-optimal distribution of apples and oranges; that is, how should we place the five holders of apples and the five holders of oranges?

b)   Is it true that the holder of an orange must be placed in slot 10 in any Pareto-optimal arrangement? Explain.

c)   Which arrangement maximizes the sum of the utility of all the people? Does this arrangement have to be the Pareto-optimal arrangement? What is the sum of the utility in such an arrangement?

d)   Which arrangement minimizes the sum of the utility? What is the sum of the utility in such an arrangement?

2. Assume that because of a world food crisis, it becomes necessary to ration food. Further assume that there are n kinds of food and m types of people. (Each type of person has a different utility function, but all people of each type are identical.) Two rationing schemes are offered.

i.   Take stock of n foods and divide that stock equally among all the people. Do not allow anyone to trade in food after the distribution in order to prevent people from ending up with a poor diet.

ii.   Count the number of units of each kind of food. Issue a different type of ration ticket for each kind of food and as many ration tickets of each type as there are units of that kind of food. Then give each consumer the same bundle of ration tickets. When a consumer wants to purchase one unit of food of a specific kind, have him or her present the appropriate type of ration ticket for that kind of food to the government store. Allow trading in ration tickets.

a)   Will scheme i determine Pareto-optimal allocations? Why or why not?

b)   Show that for any individual, scheme ii is at least as good as scheme i.

3. Assume that we have an exchange economy consisting of two traders, 1 and 2, and two goods, X and Y. Suppose that trader 1's utility function is $U^1 = 3Y_1$ and trader 2's utility function is $U^2 = 5X_2$. Assume that the initial allocation of goods X and Y to traders 1 and 2 is $X_1 = \frac{1}{2}$, $Y_1 = \frac{1}{2}$, and $X_2 = \frac{1}{2}$, $Y_2 = \frac{1}{2}$.

a)   Draw the indifference curves for traders 1 and 2 in an Edgeworth box.

b)   Is the initial allocation Pareto optimal? Explain why or why not.

c)   Identify any Pareto-optimal allocation or allocations. In other words, draw the contract curve.

d)   Finally, suppose that traders 1 and 2 can trade with each other, given their initial allocations. Assuming that they are utility maximizers and price takers, what allocation would be a competitive equilibrium? At what rate would they exchange good X for good Y at the equilibrium?

4. Consider an economy with two people who have right-angle indifference curves of the type shown in Figure 21.9. Explain why the contract curve in Figure 21.9 is "thick"; that is, explain why the contract curve is a thick shaded area rather than a thin line.

5. Say that we have a society with n androgynous people, that is, people who can instantly change their sex from male to female and back again. Any two people can marry and create 1 unit of utility, which they share. (Assume that utility is transferable, and any utility gained when people marry can be split just as dollars can be divided. Also assume that money is equivalent to utility for these people.) Hence, the value of a coalition of two people is 1. The value

Figure 21.9

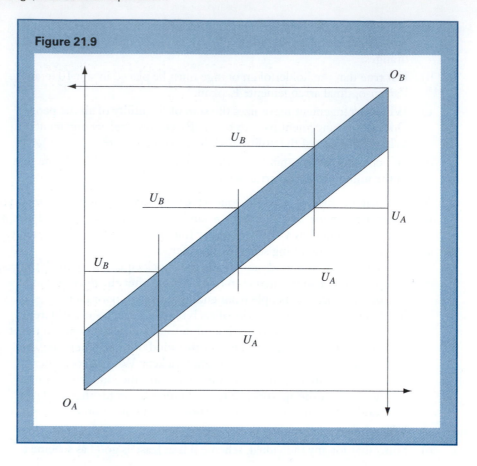

of not marrying (being single) is zero. Because polygamy is outlawed, a coalition formed by three people creates only 1 unit of utility. Therefore, when a coalition involves an odd number of people, they will be better off if they break up into pairs and marry each other, leaving the odd man (or woman) out. Show that when the number of people in this society is odd, the core of the marriage game is empty, but when the number of people is even, the core is not empty. Explain your answer. (*Hint*: Think of what would happen if there were an odd number of people and everyone was married except one person, who would receive a zero-utility payoff from being single.)

6. Arnold and Brigitte are marooned on a deserted island. For sustenance, Arnold has exactly 1 unit of Xylose and Brigitte has exactly one unit of Yam. Their preferences between these two items are represented by the following two equations:

$$U^A = X_A^{1/3} \cdot Y_A^{2/3}$$
$$U^B = X_B^{1/2} \cdot Y_B^{1/2}$$

In these equations, X_A and Y_A are the consumption of Xylose and Yam by Arnold. Similarly, X_B and Y_B are the consumption of Xylose and Yam by Brigitte. Given these utility functions, the marginal utilities of Xylose and Yam are as follows:

$$MU_X^A = \left(\frac{1}{3}\right)X_A^{-2/3} \cdot Y_A^{2/3}, \ MU_Y^A = \left(\frac{2}{3}\right)X_A^{1/3} \cdot Y_A^{-1/3}$$
$$MU_X^B = \left(\frac{1}{2}\right)X_B^{-1/2} \cdot Y_B^{1/2}, \ MU_Y^B = \left(\frac{1}{2}\right)X_B^{1/2} \cdot Y_B^{-1/2}$$

a) Is the following allocation Pareto optimal? Explain why or why not. (*Hint*: Use the conditions on the marginal rates of substitution.)

$$X_A = \frac{1}{2}, Y_A = \frac{2}{3}, \ \text{and} \ X_B = \frac{1}{2}, Y_B = \frac{1}{3}$$

b) If Arnold and Brigitte were to trade between themselves, would they be able to attain this allocation as a competitive equilibrium? What would be the equilibrium price ratio of Xylose to Yam? Would Arnold and Brigitte

Price	Demand	Demand	Demand	Demand	Excess Demand	Excess Demand
(p_x/p_y)	for X_1	for Y_1	for X_2	for Y_2	for X	for Y
1. 3						
2. $\frac{3}{2}$						
3. 1						
4. $\frac{2}{3}$						
5. $\frac{1}{3}$						

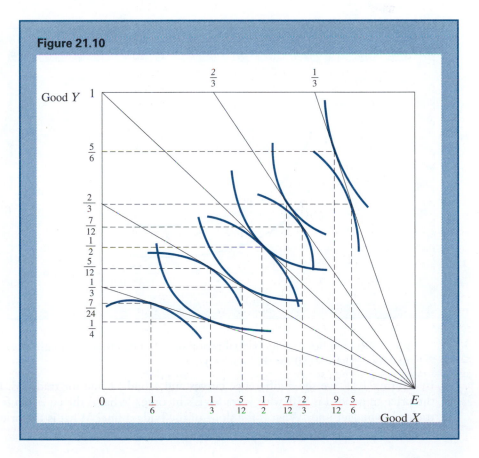

Figure 21.10

be able to afford this allocation at the equilibrium prices, given their endowments? If not, what kind of income transfer would be necessary?

7. Consider the Edgeworth box shown in Figure 21.10. Point E in Figure 21.10 represents the initial endowments of goods X and Y for consumers 1 and 2. The total amount of each good available is 1 unit. Given the family of indifference curves for consumers 1 and 2, complete the following table.

8. Say that Marty the monopolist has one orange that he purchased for $0.30. Both Geoffrey and Elizabeth want that orange. Geoffrey is willing to pay up to $0.60 for it, while Elizabeth is willing to pay up to $0.50 for it. If the orange is sold to Geoffrey for $0.35, the payoffs are as follows: Marty would earn $0.05 because the orange cost him $0.30 and he sold it for $0.35 (Marty's payoff = price − cost). Geoffrey would earn $0.25 because he valued the orange at $0.60 and paid $0.35 for it (Geoffrey's and Elizabeth's payoff = value − cost). Elizabeth would earn nothing because she did not purchase the orange and therefore did not receive or pay anything.

   a)   What coalition would block this arrangement?

   b)   If the orange is sold to Geoffrey for $0.31, is the outcome in the core of the market game? What if the orange is sold for any price p such that $0.30 \leq p \leq 0.50$?

   c)   Which coalition could block the following outcome: Elizabeth purchases the orange for $0.49 and Geoffrey gets nothing?

   d)   Can there *ever* be a core allocation in which Elizabeth purchases the or-

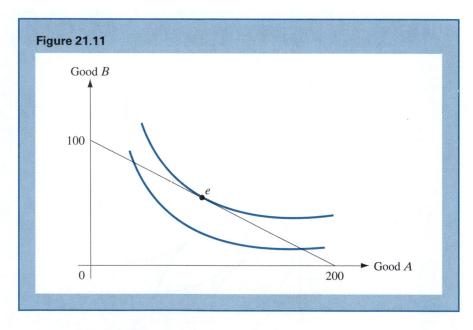

Figure 21.11

ange? (Remember that individual rationality dictates that Elizabeth *never* pay more than $0.50 for the orange.)

9. In Figure 21.11, we see indifference curves and a budget line for trader E. If the price of good A is $50, what is trader E's income? What is the equation for trader E's budget line? What is the slope of the budget line? What is the price

General Equilibrium and the Origins of the Free-Market and Interventionist Ideologies

The development of competitive markets in a society leads to friction among the members of that society. Some people, whom we will call free-market advocates or laissez-faire advocates, feel strongly that the government should not interfere with the functioning of perfectly competitive markets. These free-market advocates argue that such markets are efficient and will supply goods to consumers at the lowest possible average cost if left alone (see Chapter 15). Other people, whom we will call interventionists, feel that there is a flaw in this argument. They claim that in many situations free markets do not really exist, or if they do exist, they fail to work as well as expected. Further, these people claim that even when free markets operate efficiently, they may not produce outcomes that are *equitable* or *fair*. Some members of society may do very badly at the equilibrium of a perfectly competitive market. The interventionists feel that the government has a responsibility to correct the inequities and failures of perfectly competitive markets and that, therefore, some types of government intervention in an economy are desirable.

The interventionists also claim that the case for nonintervention has not been proved. Although they admit that in certain instances, a particular competitive market may have undesirable welfare characteristics, they feel that these are *isolated* cases. They argue that an economy consists of many interconnected markets and that it has not been demonstrated that a perfectly competitive economy *as a whole* has the same beneficial welfare properties as a single market within that economy.

In the remaining chapters of this book, we will be concerned with the ideological debate between free-market advocates and interventionists. We will look closely at the basic arguments of the two economic adversaries in this chapter.

The Free-Market Argument

The free-market argument starts with the assumption that at one point in time, there is an existing economy with a given stock of capital and labor and large numbers of people who function as both producers and consumers. All the consumers have convex indifference curves, which indicate a decreasing marginal rate of substitution between goods. All the producers have convex isoquants, which indicate a decreasing marginal rate of technical substitution between inputs. To simplify our discussion, we will further assume that there are only two people in the economy, person 1 and person 2, and that the economy produces only two goods, good 1 and good 2. These assumptions are merely a convenience and will not restrict our analysis in any way.

The problems that the economy must solve are (1) how to allocate the existing stock of capital and labor efficiently between the production of good 1 and

free-market advocates (laissez-faire advocates)
People who feel strongly that the government should not interfere with the functioning of perfectly competitive markets.
interventionists
People who feel that there is a flaw in the idea that markets are efficient.

Pareto-efficient allocation
An allocation of inputs (capital and labor) where it is not possible to reallocate these inputs and produce more of at least one good in the economy without decreasing the amount of some other good that is produced.

the production of good 2, which will determine how much of each good is produced, and (2) how to distribute these goods efficiently among the population once they are produced. When we refer to efficiency here, we mean Pareto efficiency. An allocation of inputs (capital and labor) is a **Pareto-efficient allocation** if it is not possible to reallocate these inputs and produce more of at least one good in the economy without decreasing the amount of some other good that is produced. Similarly, a distribution of goods is Pareto efficient if it is not possible to redistribute these goods and make at least one person in the economy better off in terms of utility without making someone else worse off.

The free-market argument rests on three beliefs:

1. Perfect competition will allocate inputs to the production of goods in an efficient manner.

2. Once goods are produced, they will be distributed in an efficient manner by the forces of supply and demand in competitive markets.

3. The final mix of goods produced will be determined by the distribution of income generated by the competitive market process; whatever the final mix of goods turns out to be, these goods will be distributed among the population in an efficient manner.

Let us now review the various stages in the free-market argument one by one. We will begin by describing the conditions that must be satisfied to ensure the efficient distribution of goods once they have been produced. We will then discuss the conditions that must be satisfied to ensure the efficient allocation of inputs to production. Finally, we will prove that a set of perfectly competitive markets will exactly satisfy such conditions. This result is the basis of the argument of free-market advocates that government interference with the competitive process may reduce the efficiency of that process.

MEDIA NOTE

GOVERNMENT INTERVENTION: PATERNALISM

When should governments intervene in our lives? One view is that there is a certain type of paternalism that might benefit us if government can determine incentives for us that lead us to do things that are good for us but that we would not do otherwise. One case in point may be cigarette taxation. Other than the need for revenue, one argument against taxing cigarettes is that if a person has a preference to smoke, that is his or her business and he or she should be left alone to weigh the benefits and costs of doing so. In addition, a tax on cigarettes is considered to put a higher burden on the lower and middle classes than other taxes (e.g., property taxes) because people in those classes spend a higher portion of their income on cigarettes.

Further, allowing people to smoke may not inflict a cost on the rest of us because if they do choose to smoke, then they will probably die prior to running up hefty Medicare bills that healthy people who live long lives would incur.

Recent economic research finds the analysis above to be wrong. Jonathan Gruber and Sendhil Mullainathan from MIT found in their research that after taxes increased, many smokers quit or cut down on their smoking and were pleased about it. Also, poorer people were more likely to quit smoking than rich people, making the tax less regressive than suggested above. Later research showed that when the price of cigarettes increases by 10%, it is followed by a 5% drop in smoking. This makes the cigarette tax the only tax that can increase revenues while cutting costs—a case for governmental paternalism.

Source: Adapted from "How a Tax on Cigarettes Can Help the Taxed," as appeared in the *New York Times,* April 14, 2002

Efficiency in Consumption

In Chapter 21, we examined the conditions that must be satisfied for a distribution of goods to be efficient. We saw how two people, Geoffrey and Elizabeth, spent their mornings picking apples and raspberries and their afternoons exchanging bundles of fruit. We found that the efficient distribution of this fruit fell along the contract curve of the appropriately defined Edgeworth box. Remember that the contract curve was the locus of points along which the marginal rates of substitution for the two types of fruit were equal in the minds of Geoffrey and Elizabeth. Thus, at each point on the contract curve, the indifference curves of Geoffrey and Elizabeth were tangent. (You may want to review the material relating to the Edgeworth box in Chapter 21.)

In the economy that we are discussing here, goods 1 and 2 are produced rather than merely picked. We will assume that the total output of this economy is 18 units of good 1 and 20 units of good 2. (We will see shortly why these particular amounts of the two goods have been produced.) Our task now is to allocate these goods efficiently between persons 1 and 2. To do so, we will use the Edgeworth box shown in Figure 22.1.

Each point in the Edgeworth box in Figure 22.1 represents an allocation of goods 1 and 2 between persons 1 and 2. For example, in the allocation at point *a*, person 1 has 6 units of good 1 and 12 units of good 2 and person 2 has 12 units of good 1 and 8 units of good 2. As we know, the efficient set of allocations is located along the contract curve. At each point on this curve, the marginal rates of substitution of persons 1 and 2 are equal. These allocations are Pareto efficient; that is, once we choose an allocation on the contract curve, there is no other allocation in the Edgeworth box that can make both persons better off. In other words, once we move away from any allocation on the contract curve, either one person will be better off and one worse off or both will be worse off. For example, as we move

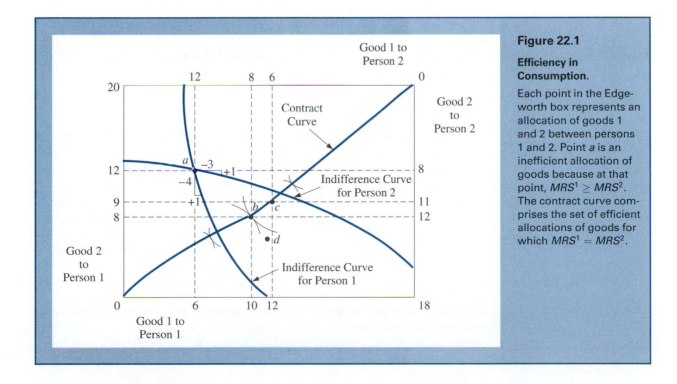

Figure 22.1

Efficiency in Consumption.

Each point in the Edgeworth box represents an allocation of goods 1 and 2 between persons 1 and 2. Point *a* is an inefficient allocation of goods because at that point, $MRS^1 \geq MRS^2$. The contract curve comprises the set of efficient allocations of goods for which $MRS^1 = MRS^2$.

along the contract curve from the allocation at point b to the allocation at point c, person 1 is better off but person 2 is worse off. Similarly, as we move along the contract curve from the allocation at point b to the allocation at point d, persons 1 and 2 are both worse off.

Because all Pareto-efficient allocations fall along the contract curve, we can now state the condition for efficiency in consumption: A given set of goods in an economy should be allocated across a set of consumers until the marginal rate of substitution for each pair of goods is equal for each consumer. We can also express this condition as $MRS^1_{2 \text{ for } 1} = MRS^2_{2 \text{ for } 1} = \cdots = MRS^i_{2 \text{ for } 1}$, where $MRS^i_{2 \text{ for } 1}$ is the marginal rate of substitution of good 2 for good 1 for consumer i in the economy.

> **condition for efficiency in consumption**
> The condition that a given set of goods in an economy should be allocated across a set of consumers until the marginal rate of substitution for each pair of goods is equal for each consumer.

Why the Condition for Efficiency in Consumption Must Be Satisfied. To understand why the condition for efficiency in consumption must be satisfied, let us say that we are considering an allocation that does not meet this condition. Such an allocation cannot be Pareto efficient because we will be able to find another allocation that will make both persons better off. For example, let us look at the allocation at point a in Figure 22.1. By comparing the slopes of the indifference curves at this point, we can see that the marginal rate of substitution of good 2 for good 1 for person 1 is greater than that for person 2: $MRS = \frac{4}{1} > \frac{1}{3} = MRS^2$. This means that person 1 is willing to give up 4 units of good 2 in order to obtain 1 unit of good 1, whereas person 2 is willing to give up 3 units of good 1 in order to obtain 1 unit of good 2. If person 1 does give up 4 units of good 2 in exchange for 1 unit of good 1, he will stay at exactly the same level of utility. If he obtains 1 unit of good 1 and has to give up only 1 unit of good 2 for it, he will increase his utility. Similarly, if person 2 receives 1 unit of good 2 in exchange for 1 unit of good 1, she will be better off.

Because the indifference curves of persons 1 and 2 are not tangent at point a (and hence the marginal rates of substitution are not equal), there must be another allocation that makes both of these people better off than they are at point a. Therefore, the allocation at point a cannot be efficient. The same logic applies to any two people in the economy and any two goods, so we can easily generalize this rule to many people.

Efficiency in Production

We are also interested in knowing what conditions are necessary for the efficient allocation of inputs to production. As we will now see, these conditions are analogous to the conditions for the efficient allocation of goods to consumers after the goods are produced. Let us consider the Edgeworth box shown in Figure 22.2.

The inputs to production, which we will call labor (L) and capital (K), appear along the horizontal and vertical axes of Figure 22.2. The size of the Edgeworth box is determined historically; that is, the box depicts an economy at a certain point in time when the labor force and the capital stock are of a certain size as a result of past events. The size of the labor force is determined by previous birth and death rates in the population, and the size of the capital stock is determined by previous amounts of investment and depreciation. In any case, we must consider the existing labor force and capital stock as fixed elements that will not be affected by anything we do in our analysis.

Our task is to allocate these inputs to the production of goods 1 and 2 in a Pareto-efficient manner. Remember that an allocation of inputs is Pareto efficient

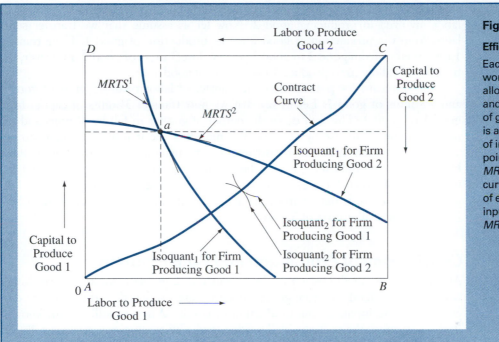

Figure 22.2

Efficiency in Production.
Each point in the Edgeworth box represents an allocation of inputs L and K to the production of goods 1 and 2. Point a is an inefficient allocation of inputs because at that point, $MRTS^1_{K \text{ for } L} > MRTS^2_{K \text{ for } L}$. The contract curve comprises the set of efficient allocations of inputs for which $MRTS^1_{K \text{ for } L} = MRTS^2_{K \text{ for } L}$.

if there is no other allocation that will allow the economy to produce more of one good without producing less of another good.

At point A in Figure 22.2, we see that the economy has allocated all its inputs to the production of good 2. At point C, we find just the opposite situation—the economy has allocated all its inputs to the production of good 1. The points that appear inside the Edgeworth box indicate allocations of inputs to the production of both goods. Note that the isoquants inside the box are analogous to the indifference curves in Figure 22.1. The slopes of these isoquants at any point represent the marginal rate of technical substitution of input K for input L.

Where in the Edgeworth box in Figure 22.2 does the efficient allocation of inputs to production occur? The answer to this question is obvious if we again make an analogy with the condition for efficiency in consumption. The efficient allocation of input occurs along the contract curve of the Edgeworth box. Hence, the **condition for efficiency in production** is as follows: A given set of inputs available in an economy should be allocated across a set of producers until the marginal rate of technical substitution for each pair of inputs is equal for each producer. We can also express this condition as $MRTS^1_{K \text{ for } L} = MRTS^2_{K \text{ for } L} = \cdots = MRTS^i_{K \text{ for } L}$, where $MRTS^i_{K \text{ for } L}$ is the marginal rate of technical substitution of capital for labor for producers in the economy.

condition for efficiency in production
The condition that a given set of inputs available in an economy should be allocated across a set of producers until the marginal rate of technical substitution for each pair of inputs is equal for each producer.

Why the Condition for Efficiency in Production Must Be Satisfied. Let us now examine the reason this condition is necessary for efficiency in production. We will say that we are at point a in Figure 22.2, an allocation of inputs that is not on the contract curve and therefore does not satisfy the condition for efficiency in production. Keeping in mind that the marginal rate of technical substitution is simply the ratio of the marginal product of labor to the marginal product of capital, we will assume that at point a, $MP^1_L/MP^1_K = \frac{5}{1} > \frac{3}{1} = MP^2_L/MP^2_K$. This means that

at point *a*, the labor involved in producing good 1 is more productive than the labor involved in producing good 2. Now let us assume that we transfer some labor from the production of good 2 to the production of good 1. If we transfer 1 unit of labor from good 2 to good 1, we will lose 3 units of good 2. However, the transfer will allow us to produce 5 more units of good 1.

Our scorecard for point *a* after the transfer of labor reads +5 units of good 1 and −3 units of good 2. Let us say that we now transfer $3\frac{1}{2}$ units of capital from good 1 to good 2. This will cause the output of good 1 to fall by $3\frac{1}{2}$ units and the output of good 2 to rise by $3\frac{1}{2}$ units (assuming that the marginal products do not change very much after the redistributions are made). The net result of these transfers of labor and capital is that the output of good 1 increases by $1\frac{1}{2}$ units and the output of good 2 increases by $\frac{1}{2}$ unit. Because the output of both goods is greater after a redistribution from the allocation at point *a*, that point cannot be a Pareto-efficient allocation of inputs.

Consistency of Production and Consumption

At this stage in our discussion of the free-market argument, we know two things: (1) how to efficiently allocate goods once they are produced, and (2) how to efficiently allocate inputs to the production of goods. What we still do not know is how many goods the economy will produce and why competitive markets will allocate inputs to production and distribute finished goods in the most efficient manner. Let us now pursue the answers to these questions.

We will start by looking again at Figure 22.2, where we will move from point *A* to point *C* on the contract curve. At point *A*, the economy is producing only good 2. At point *C*, it is producing only good 1. Thus, as we move from *A* to *C*, the amount of good 1 available increases and the amount of good 2 decreases. This trade-off is illustrated by the production possibilities frontier of the economy, which we see in Figure 22.3. Note that good 2 appears on the vertical axis in this figure, and good 1 appears on the horizontal axis. A production possibilities frontier shows the maximum amounts of goods that an economy can produce if it allocates its inputs efficiently—that is, if it allocates its inputs so that all points on the frontier satisfy our condition for efficiency in production.

production possibilities frontier

A curve that shows the maximum amounts of goods that an economy can produce if it allocates its inputs efficiently—that is, if it allocates its inputs so that all points on the frontier satisfy our condition for efficiency in production.

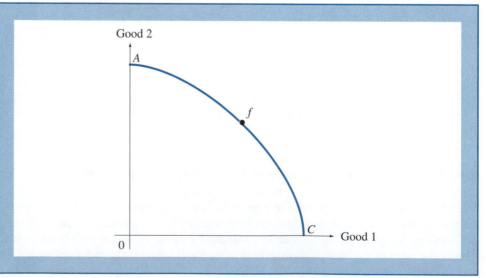

Figure 22.3

The Production Possibilities Frontier.

The production possibilities frontier comprises the set of efficient allocations of inputs between goods 1 and 2.

The slope of the production possibilities frontier in Figure 22.3 indicates how many units of good 2 the economy would have to sacrifice (by transferring inputs from the production of good 2 to the production of good 1) in order to obtain 1 more unit of good 1. This trade-off is called the marginal rate of transformation (MRT) of good 2 into good 1. From a societal point of view, the MRT is equal to the ratio of the marginal costs of goods 1 and 2 because the cost to society of producing 1 more unit of good 1 is the amount of good 2 that must be sacrificed to produce that unit. Hence, $M_{2 \text{ for } 1} = MC^1 / MC^2$.

Now let us say that the economy has produced the product mix represented by point f in Figure 22.3. This bundle of goods defines the Edgeworth box depicted in Figure 22.4.

The contract curve shows all the efficient allocations of goods that total the bundle located at point f of Figure 22.4. The optimal way to distribute this bundle is to find the point on the contract curve at which the marginal rate of substitution of good 1 for good 2 equals the marginal rate of transformation of the two goods. This occurs at point g because the slopes of the two indifference curves at point g are the same as the slope of the production possibilities frontier at point f. Thus, we can now state the condition for consistency of production and consumption as follows: For any mix of outputs produced, the marginal rate of transformation of those goods in production (as defined by the slope of the production possibilities frontier) must equal the marginal rates of substitution for all consumers using those goods. We can also express this condition as $MRS^1_{2 \text{ for } 1} = MRS^2_{2 \text{ for } 1} = \cdots = MRS^i_{2 \text{ for } 1} = MRT_{2 \text{ for } 1}$, where $MRS^i_{2 \text{ for } 1}$ is the marginal rate of substitution of good 2 for good 1 for consumer i and $MRT_{2 \text{ for } 1}$ is the marginal rate of transformation of good 2 into good 1.

Why the Condition for Consistency of Production and Consumption Must Be Satisfied. The reason this condition must be satisfied is easy to understand. For the sake of discussion, let us say that there is a situation in which the condition is not satisfied. The marginal rate of transformation (which is equal to the ratio of the marginal costs of goods 1 and 2) is much less than the common marginal rate of substitution so that $MRT_{2 \text{ for } 1} = MC^1 / MC^2 = \frac{2}{1} < MRS_{2 \text{ for } 1} = \frac{9}{1}$.

marginal rate of transformation (MRT) The slope of the production possibilities frontier that indicates how many units of good 2 the economy would have to sacrifice (by transferring inputs from the production of good 2 to the production of good 1) in order to obtain 1 more unit of good 1.

condition for consistency of production and consumption The condition that for any mix of outputs produced, the marginal rate of transformation of those goods in production (as defined by the slope of the production possibilities frontier) must equal the marginal rates of substitution for all consumers using those goods.

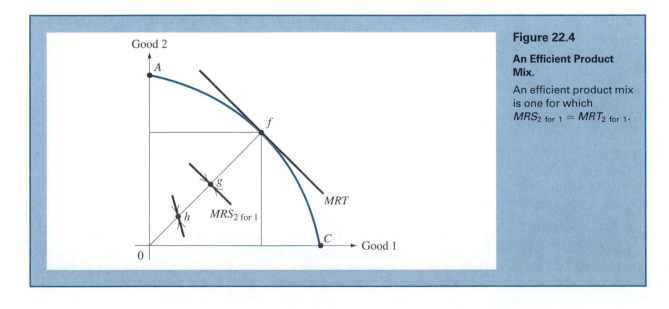

Figure 22.4

An Efficient Product Mix.

An efficient product mix is one for which $MRS_{2 \text{ for } 1} = MRT_{2 \text{ for } 1}$.

This situation can be represented by point h in Figure 22.4. What we will find is that the product mix allocation pair represented by points f and h cannot be Pareto optimal because there is another product mix allocation pair that will make all consumers and producers better off. To prove the validity of this claim, let us start at points f and h and make a change in the product mix. We produce 2 fewer units of good 2 and 1 more unit of good 1, which is what the marginal rate of transformation at point f dictates. At point h, the marginal rate of substitution tells us that consumers are willing to give up 9 units of good 2 to obtain 1 more unit of good 1. Hence, by changing the product mix, we can make both producers and consumers better off. Because the producers are willing to increase the production of good 1 by 1 unit if they can decrease the production of good 2 by 2 units and the consumers are willing to give up 9 units of good 2 in order to receive 1 more unit of good 1, there is plenty of room for a mutually beneficial reallocation between producers and consumers. Only when $MRT = MRS$ is such a reallocation not possible.

MEDIA NOTE

GOVERNMENT INTERVENTION

A form of government intervention that is less visible than others is subsidies. Here, certain industries are given tax breaks, export credits, loan guarantees, etc. Inevitably, such subsidies cause distortions and misallocations of resources. A good example is the aerospace industries of Canada and Brazil and the airline firms of Bombardier and Embraer, who make regional jets. Both firms, both profitable and competently run, still receive and lobby for subsidies.

But there are economic costs for such subsidies. As we know, economic activities should be increased up to the point where the marginal benefit from increased activity equals their marginal cost. If governments subsidize industries, they disguise the true marginal costs involved in production and hence can lead to increases in the size of these industries beyond what is economically efficient. Hence, with subsidies, the industries have a tendency to grow to a size that is greater than they should under normal economic calculations. In addition, taxpayer money is being poured into ventures that are inherently risky, and when things turn bad, the situation can get ugly politically.

Source: Adapted from "Keep Subsidies Out of Aircraft Competition," as appeared in the *Financial Post,* June 28, 2004

SOLVED PROBLEM 22.1

Question (Content Review: Pareto Optimality)

Robinson Crusoe has invented a machine that can make two mangoes out of one coconut. Conversely, the machine can make one coconut out of two mangoes. Crusoe's utility function over mangoes and coconuts is given by $U(c, m) = cm$. Note that for his utility function, the marginal utilities are $U_m = c$ and $U_c = m$ for mangoes and coconuts, respectively.

a) Suppose Crusoe has four mangoes and four coconuts. Is that a Pareto-optimal allocation?

Answer

Because the machine can make two mangoes out of one coconut and vice versa, the marginal rate of transformation of mangoes for coconuts is $MRT_{m \text{ for } c} = 2$. For Crusoe's utility function, the marginal utilities are $U_m = c$, $U_c = m$, and $MRS_{m \text{ for } c} = U_c/U_m = m/c = 1$ for $c = m = 4$. Therefore, $MRT_{m \text{ for } c} \neq MRS_{m \text{ for } c}$, and the allocation is not Pareto optimal.

b) If four mangoes and four coconuts is not a Pareto-optimal allocation, what would Crusoe have to do with his current holdings of mangoes and coconuts to get a Pareto-optimal allocation?

Answer

For a Pareto-optimal allocation, we must have $MRT_{m \text{ for } c} = MRS_{m \text{ for } c} = 2$. Let u be the number of coconuts used to make mangoes. Then $4 - u$ is the number that is left to consume directly. Using his machine, Crusoe can make mangoes and coconuts and can have combinations of them (m, c) that satisfy $m = 4 + 2u$ and $c = 4 - u$, where u is the number of coconuts Crusoe uses as inputs in his machine; that is, for every coconut he gives up, he gets two mangoes. For $MRS_{m \text{ for } c} = 2$, we must have $(4 + 2u)/(4 - u) = 2$. Solving for u, we find $u = 1$. Thus, Crusoe can achieve a Pareto-optimal allocation by using his machine to produce two mangoes with one coconut. He will be left with six mangoes and three coconuts, in which case

$$MRS_{m \text{ for } c} = m/c = 2 = MRT_{m \text{ for } c}$$

Perfectly Competitive Markets Satisfy the Conditions for Pareto Efficiency

The next stage in the free-market argument is one of the crowning achievements of economic science. It is the demonstration that perfectly competitive markets will satisfy all three of the conditions for Pareto efficiency. Let us examine this part of the free-market argument step by step.

Satisfying the Condition for Efficiency in Consumption. As we saw in Chapter 14, all consumers in perfectly competitive markets are able to buy goods at common and identical prices. For example, if oranges sell for $1 a pound and apples sell for $3 a pound, all consumers can buy as many oranges and apples as they like at these prices. We also know from Chapter 4 that given a budget constraint and a set of fixed, perfectly competitive prices, people will maximize their utility. That is, they will buy goods up to the point at which their marginal rate of substitution equals the ratio of the prices of the goods. Hence, if there are n people in society, each will purchase oranges and apples in such a way that $MRS_{oranges \text{ for } apples} = p_{apples}/p_{oranges}$. If every person does this, then the following condition will be satisfied: $MRS^1_{oranges \text{ for } apples} = MRS^2_{oranges \text{ for } apples} = MRS^3_{oranges \text{ for } apples} = \cdots = MRS^i_{oranges \text{ for } apples} = P_{apples}/P_{oranges}$, where $MRS^i_{oranges \text{ for } apples}$ is the marginal rate of substitution of oranges for apples of person i. In other words, if every person in society is equating his or her private marginal rate of substitution to the same fixed and common price ratio, then all marginal rates of substitution will be equal, which is what is required by our condition for efficiency in consumption.

Satisfying the Condition for Efficiency in Production. A similar argument proves that perfectly competitive markets will satisfy the condition for efficiency in production. In this case, we will rely on the fact that the markets for factors of production—capital and labor—are also perfectly competitive. The prices of capital and labor will therefore be equal for all firms wishing to produce. We know from our discussion of the theory of the firm in Chapter 9 that a firm wanting to maximize its profits will hire inputs up to the point at which the marginal rate of technical substitution equals the ratio of the factor prices. If all firms behave this way, then we can express the resulting equality as follows: $MRTS^1_{capital\ for\ labor} = MRTS^2_{capital\ for\ labor} = MRTS^3_{capital\ for\ labor} = \cdots = MRTS^i_{capital\ for\ labor} = w_{labor}/w_{capital}$, where $MRTS^i_{capital\ for\ labor}$ is the marginal rate of technical substitution of capital for labor of firm i and $w_{labor}/w_{capital}$ is the ratio of the prices of labor and capital. Because all firms are equating their marginal rates of technical substitution to the same price ratio, these rates are equal, as is required by our condition for efficiency in production.

Satisfying the Condition for Consistency of Production and Consumption.

Our final condition for efficiency requires that the marginal rates of substitution in consumption be equal to the marginal rate of transformation in production. We know from Chapter 6 that at the long-run equilibrium of a perfectly competitive market, the prices of all goods will be driven down to their marginal cost by the process of market entry. Hence, at the equilibrium, $p_{apples}/p_{oranges} = MC_{apples}/MC_{oranges}$. Because all consumers are equating their marginal rates of substitution to the price ratio, when the price ratio equals the ratio of marginal costs, the consumers are also equating their marginal rates of substitution to the ratio of marginal costs, which is in turn equal to the marginal rate of transformation. Thus, $MRS = MRT$, which satisfies our final condition for efficiency.

SOLVED PROBLEM 22.2

Question (Application and Extension: Pareto Optimality)

Ally and Ling have access to a machine that can convert 1 apple to 1 banana and vice versa. Ally has a utility function over apples and bananas given by $U^A(a, b) = a^{1/3}b^{2/3}$, and Ling has the utility function $U^A(a, b) = a^{2/3}b^{1/3}$. The associated marginal rates of substitution of b for a for Ally and Ling are $MRS^{Ally}_{b\ for\ a} = U^A_a/U^A_b = b/2a$ and $MRS^{Ling}_{b\ for\ a} = U^L_a/U^L_b = 2b/a$, respectively.

Which of the following allocations is Pareto optimal?

a) Ally: (2 apples, 4 bananas), Ling: (3 apples, 3 bananas)

Answer

Note that for Pareto optimality, we must have $MRS^A_{b\ for\ a} = MRS^L_{b\ for\ a} = MRT_{b\ for\ a}$. Because a machine can convert 1 apple into only 1 banana, $MRT_{b\ for\ a} = 1$. $MRS^A_{b\ for\ a} = U^A_a/U^A_b = b/2a$, and $MRS^L_{b\ for\ a} = U^L_a/U^L_b = 2b/a$.
$MRS^A_{b\ for\ a} = 1 \neq 2 = MRS^L_{b\ for\ a}$. This is not a Pareto-optimal allocation.

b) Ally: (2 apples, 2 bananas), Ling: (4 apples, 1 banana)

Answer

$MRS^A_{b\ for\ a} = \frac{1}{2} = MRS^L_{b\ for\ a} \neq 1 = MRT_{b\ for\ a}$. This is not a Pareto-optimal allocation.

c) Ally: (2 apples, 4 bananas), Ling: (4 apples, 2 bananas)

Answer

$MRS^A_{b\ for\ a} = MRS^L_{b\ for\ a} = MRT_{b\ for\ a} = 1$. This is a Pareto-optimal allocation.

Question (Application and Extension: Pareto Optimality)

Karen and Julie have preferences over apricots and books given by the following utility functions: $U^K(a, b) = a^{1/3}b^{2/3}$, $U^J(a, b) = a^{2/3}b^{1/3}$. The marginal rates of substitution of books for apricots for Karen and Julie is $MRS^K_{b \text{ for } a} = U^K_a/U^K_b = b/2a$ and $MRS^J_{b \text{ for } a} = U^J_a/U^J_b = 2b/a$. Karen has neither books nor apricots, but Julie has 10 of each.

a) Is this allocation Pareto optimal?

Answer

The allocation is Pareto optimal. The only way that Karen can be better off is for Julie to be worse off because for Karen to be better off, Julie must give her some of her apricots and books.

b) Suppose you wanted to divide the allocation of apricots and books more evenly between Karen and Julie. For instance, say you would like Karen to have 4 of Julie's apricots. How many books should Julie give Karen for the final allocation to be Pareto optimal?

Answer

Again, for Pareto optimality we must have $MRS^K_{b \text{ for } a} = MRS^J_{b \text{ for } a}$, where $MRS^K_{b \text{ for } a} = U^K_a/U^K_b = b/2a$, and $MRS^J_{b \text{ for } a} = U^J_a/U^J_b = 2b/a$. Let a and b be Karen's allocations of apricots and books. Because Karen must have 4 apricots, $a = 4$. Then Julie's allocation of apricots and books must be 6 and $(10 - b)$. To ensure Pareto optimality, we must have $MRS^K_{b \text{ for } a} = MRS^J_{b \text{ for } a}$, which means that we must have $b/(2a) = 2(10 - b)/(10 - a)$, with $a = 4$. Solving for b, we get $b = 80/11$. Therefore, Karen would have 4 apricots and 80/11 books, and Julie would have 6 apricots and 30/11 books in a Pareto-optimal allocation.

SOLVED PROBLEM 22.3

The Two Fundamental Theorems of Welfare Economics

The free-market argument culminates in two theorems that summarize it and provide its ideological punch. The first fundamental theorem of welfare economics tells us that every competitive equilibrium is a Pareto-optimal equilibrium for the economy. When an economy reaches a competitive allocation, the supply of each good on the market equals its demand. Further, the price of each good is such that no consumer wishes to change his or her demand for that good and no firm wishes to change its production of that good. Thus, the first fundamental theorem of welfare economics indicates that when a competitive equilibrium exists, the allocations of inputs and outputs in the economy define a Pareto-optimal outcome.

The second fundamental theorem of welfare economics tells us that every Pareto-optimal allocation for an economy can be achieved as a competitive equilibrium for an appropriately defined distribution of income. Therefore, the second theorem is, in a sense, the converse of the first. It begins with the assumption that we have somehow determined that a particular Pareto-optimal outcome is desirable for an economy. (How this outcome is selected need not concern us here.) The second theorem of welfare economics indicates that we can achieve a Pareto-optimal allocation by redistributing income and then allowing the perfectly competitive economy to work uninterrupted. In other words, for any Pareto-optimal allocation of goods, there is a distribution of income that will allow the economy to achieve that allocation of goods as a competitive equilibrium.

first fundamental theorem of welfare economics
Indicates that when a competitive equilibrium exists, the allocations of inputs and outputs in the economy define a Pareto-optimal outcome.

second fundamental theorem of welfare economics
Tells us that every Pareto-optimal allocation for an economy can be achieved as a competitive equilibrium for an appropriately defined distribution of income.

These two theorems seem to nail shut the coffin on the interventionist argument. If one believes in the concept of Pareto optimality (which is a very weak optimality concept), then one is forced to agree that government intervention is senseless because any Pareto-optimal state can be achieved as an equilibrium of a perfectly competitive economy. One must be willing to redistribute income, but there is no need to intervene in the price system.

Consumer and Producer Surplus at a Pareto-Optimal Equilibrium

At a competitive equilibrium, consumers are equating their marginal rates of substitution to the ratio of all the prices they face. Firms are also equating their marginal costs to these prices, and supply is equal to demand. This means that in each market in the economy, the price of a good will be equal to its marginal cost and consumers will purchase the good at that price. These conditions guarantee that the sum of the consumer surplus and the producer surplus in each market will be maximized. Because such competitive equilibria are Pareto optimal, we see that a Pareto-optimal allocation is one in which the sum of the consumer surplus and the producer surplus is maximized.

The Interventionist Argument

The interventionist argument centers on equity considerations and the belief that free-market advocates give too much weight to Pareto optimality as the criterion for judging the outcomes of an economy.

To understand the interventionist argument better, let us consider Figure 22.5.

In Figure 22.5(a), we see a production possibilities frontier. From our condition for the consistency of production and consumption, we know that for every bundle of goods indicated by a point on the production possibilities frontier, there is a point in the associated Edgeworth box at which the marginal rates of substitution equal the slope of the production possibilities frontier. This point defines the Pareto-optimal allocation of that bundle of goods. Assuming that such a point always exists,[1] it represents the allocation that will be determined by a perfectly competitive economy. For example, say that product mix a on the production possibilities frontier in Figure 22.5(a) is chosen by society. The Pareto-optimal allocation of this bundle is indicated by point A. If a society chooses a different product mix, say the one depicted at point b, then a different allocation, point B, will result.

Figure 22.5(b) shows all the possible utility levels associated with the Pareto-optimal allocation for each product mix point on the production possibilities frontier in Figure 22.5(a). This set of utility levels is called the **utility possibilities frontier** of the economy. Note that for some points on the production possibilities frontier, the associated utility levels are high for one consumer but low for the other. At allocation A, for example, consumer 2 has a utility level of 20, whereas consumer 1 has a utility level of only 2. At other production points, both consumers do quite well.

The point that is eventually reached on the production possibilities frontier depends on how well endowed with labor and wealth consumers are when they start the process. These endowments vary from consumer to consumer. Some consumers

utility possibilities frontier
All the possible utility levels associated with the Pareto-optimal allocation for each product mix point on the production possibilities frontier.

---

[1] Proof of this assertion is beyond the scope of this book.

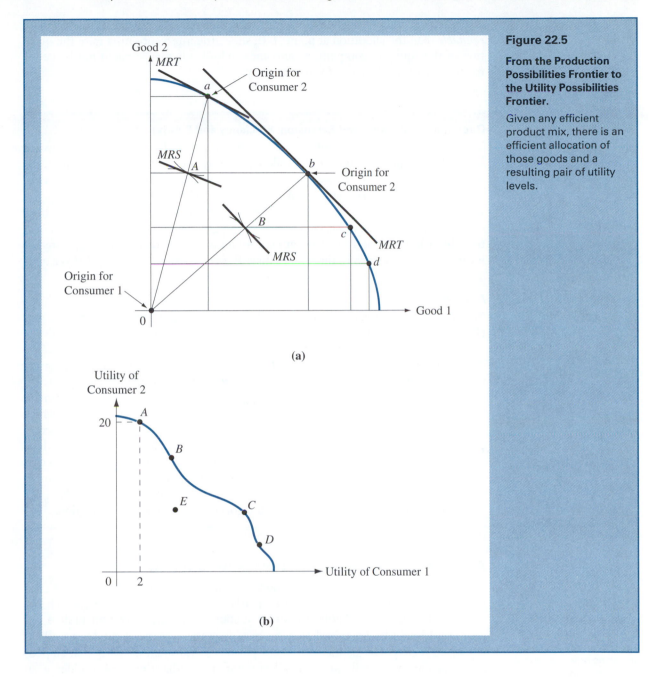

Figure 22.5

From the Production Possibilities Frontier to the Utility Possibilities Frontier.

Given any efficient product mix, there is an efficient allocation of those goods and a resulting pair of utility levels.

start out with more wealth than others. Similarly, some start out with a larger endowment of labor; that is, they are more productive than others and hence have more "effective" labor units to sell. These consumers will receive more income and so will be able to purchase more goods and services at the equilibrium of the economy than consumers who are less amply endowed. The consumers with the larger endowments will do quite well for themselves, while the others will do rather poorly.

The interventionists do not believe that a person's inherited wealth or endowment of labor should determine how well he or she lives. In fact, they suggest that it might be better for the government to intervene in the economy portrayed in Figure 22.5(b) and determine a point such as E. Although the allocation at point E

is not on the utility possibilities frontier and hence is not efficient, it is far more *equitable* than the allocation at point A. In short, the interventionists raise the question of the equity of competitive outcomes and ask whether it might not be better to sacrifice some efficiency for more equity.

<table>
<tr><td>

SOLVED PROBLEM 22.4

</td><td>

Question (Application and Extension: Efficiency and Equity)

There are 100 pounds of coffee and 100 gallons of milk to be divided between Ian and Jim. Ian and Jim have the following utility functions over coffee and milk: $U^I(c, m) = c^{1/5}m^{4/5}$, $U^J(c, m) = c^{4/5}m^{1/5}$. The marginal rates of substitution for Ian and Jim are, respectively, $MRS^I_{c \text{ for } m} = U^I_m/U^I_c = 4c/m$ and $MRS^J_{c \text{ for } m} = U^J_m/U^J_c = (100 - c)/4(100 - m)$. Say that the government intervenes in this little economy, and because of fairness concerns, the government says that in any allocation, both Jim and Ian must have at least 40 units of each commodity. Can any allocation both be Pareto optimal and satisfy the government regulation? If yes, give an example of one.

Answer

No. To see this, consider an allocation where Ian gets (c, m) and, therefore, Jim gets $(100 - c, 100 - m)$, where c and m represent units of coffee and milk, respectively. The marginal rates of substitution for Ian and Jim are $MRS^I_{c \text{ for } m} = U^I_m/U^I_c = 4c/m$ and $MRS^J_{c \text{ for } m} = U^J_m/U^J_c = (100 - c)/4(100 - m)$. To satisfy the government regulation, we must have $40 \leq c \leq 60$, $40 \leq m \leq 60$. To satisfy Pareto optimality, it must be that $MRS^I_{c \text{ for } m} = MRS^J_{c \text{ for } m}$. But because of the government regulation, the smallest that $U^J_m/U^J_c = (100 - c)/4(100 - m)$ can be is $\frac{1}{6}$, which occurs when Jim gets $c = 60$ and $m = 40$, while the largest it can be is $\frac{3}{8}$, which occurs when $c = 40$ and $m = 60$. Likewise, for Ian the smallest $4c/m$ can be is $\frac{8}{3}$, which occurs when Ian gets $c = 40$ and $m = 60$, while the largest it can be is 6, which occurs when $c = 60$ and $m = 40$. Thus, for any allocation that satisfies the government regulation, we have $(100 - c)/4(100 - m) < 4c/m$, and $MRS^I_{c \text{ for } m} \neq MRS^J_{c \text{ for } m}$. No Pareto-optimal allocation exists once the government imposes its regulation.

</td></tr>
</table>

A Basis for Intervention: Rawlsian Justice

According to the philosopher John Rawls, equality of income should have a higher moral standing than it is given by free-market advocates.[2] In his view, which has come to be known as **Rawls' maximin justice** or simply **Rawlsian justice**, an economy should be organized so as to maximize the welfare of the least well-off person in society. His justification for this idea is as follows: Let us say that all people in society are initially under a veil of ignorance in that they have no idea what their productive capabilities are. They are therefore unable to predict what their incomes are likely to be in a free market. If they are asked to choose a scheme for distributing income, they will probably choose one that ensures that the people who turn out to be very productive transfer some of their income to those who turn out to be less productive. Rawls claims that people would willingly agree to a scheme that maximizes the income of the least well-off person in society because they can imagine themselves as being that person.

Rawls' maximin justice *or* Rawlsian justice
The idea that an economy should be organized so as to maximize the welfare of the least well-off person in society.

---

[2] John Rawls is a moral philosopher at Harvard University. His ideas about what constitutes a just society are presented in *A Theory of Justice* (Cambridge, MA: Harvard University Press, 1971).

The Rawlsian position holds that inequality may sometimes be tolerated, but only when it serves to increase the welfare of the least well-off person in society. For example, if lower taxes for wealthy people will make them work harder and invest more money so that ultimately they create more jobs for poor people, then such an inequality is justified in Rawlsian terms. However, any other type of inequality—one that does not contribute to an increase in the welfare of the least well-off person—is not justified. In essence, then, Rawls supports the following interventionist view: Points that are not on the utility possibilities frontier and therefore represent inefficient allocations may be desirable from a moral perspective if they are more equitable than points representing efficient allocations.

A Free-Market Rebuttal to Rawls: Nozick's Process Justice

The free-market argument also has its philosophical foundations. One of the leading free-market philosophers is Robert Nozick, who offers the following rebuttal to Rawls.[3]

Nozick claims that we should judge the performance of perfectly competitive economies and other types of economies not on the basis of the outcomes they determine, but rather on the basis of the *process* by which those outcomes are determined. For instance, let us say that the outcome of an economy—a certain distribution of income or a certain allocation of goods—is determined by a noncoercive process; that is, people are not forced to make any trades or to offer their labor for sale against their will. Nozick would argue that any outcomes from such an economy are justified because they are achieved by the voluntary agreement of all the parties involved in the process. Hence, Nozick's theory is sometimes referred to as process justice.

Nozick uses the following example to illustrate his ideas: Suppose that three people survive a shipwreck and are marooned on a desert island. One of these people is an avid boxing fan, and the other two are famous heavyweight boxers—Muhammad Ali and Joe Frazier.[4] Each has only $100, which he managed to salvage from the ship before it went down. When the boxing fan realizes that his companions on the desert island are Ali and Frazier, he immediately offers them the following proposition. "If you fight each other, I will pay the winner $90." If the two boxers agree to fight and Ali wins, the distribution of income on the island will leave Ali with $190, Frazier with $100, and the boxing fan with $10. If Frazier wins, the distribution of income will leave Ali with $100, Frazier with $190, and the boxing fan again with $10. An interventionist looking at this distribution of income would probably say that it is unfair because it is so unequal. Nozick, however, would argue that this distribution of income is fair because it was arrived at through a noncoercive process. Further, we must assume that viewing the fight brought an increase in utility to the person with the lowest income—the boxing fan—because he was the one who voluntarily proposed the deal that led to the inequality. Any market outcome is justifiable under this theory as long as the process that leads to the outcome is voluntarily agreed to by all the parties who are involved.

process justice
The idea that performances of perfectly competitive economies and other types of economies should be judged not on the basis of the outcomes they determine, but rather on the basis of the process by which those outcomes are determined.

---

[3] Like Rawls, Robert Nozick is a philosopher at Harvard University. The approach to economic justice discussed here was originally presented in Nozick's book *Anarchy, State, and Utopia* (New York: Basic Books, 1974).

[4] This example was devised in the early 1970s and therefore includes boxers who were prominent at the time. A fight between these two boxers would have been considered a major sporting event and would have commanded high ticket prices.

The Weakness of Nozick's Argument. Although Nozick's argument is persuasive, it does present some difficulties. For one thing, many people would question the idea that a competitive process can be considered fair when the starting point for the competition is not fair. Some individuals inherit large amounts of money that they can invest to produce income. Other individuals come from families that are sufficiently well-off to provide them with the type of education that is needed to enter high-income occupations. These lucky people clearly have a significant advantage in the competition for income. Thus, even though the poor people in an economy may not be coerced, they still may be unable to compete fairly. In short, Nozick's argument does not deal successfully with the problem that people start the competitive process in unequal positions.

The free marketeers enter the argument at this point. They say that this criticism of Nozick's views does nothing to diminish the strength of the free-market argument. The second fundamental theorem of welfare economics states that if an outcome of a competitive process is not desirable for any reason, then the way to rectify the situation is to change the income distribution that prevails when the process starts but not to intervene in the process itself. Hence, some free-market advocates will tolerate a redistribution of income before the competitive process starts *but not after the process has begun*.

Equitable Income Distribution: Varian's Envy-Free Justice

A free marketeer would not like the path that this chapter has taken because it has put so much emphasis on income redistribution. True libertarian free marketeers will not tolerate any redistribution. They feel that people with high incomes work hard for their money and therefore have the right to leave it to their heirs or do anything else they wish with it. To switch the debate to grounds that are less controversial, the free marketeers might want to exploit the idea of fairness developed by the economist Hal Varian.[5]

Varian's idea of fairness has to do with the notion of envy and is therefore known as envy-free justice. To understand this idea, let us say that we have a two-person economy with two goods. We can depict this economy with an Edgeworth box. As we know, any point in the Edgeworth box represents an allocation of goods between the two people. If person 1 prefers person 2's bundle of goods to his own bundle, we can say that person 1 *envies* person 2. An envy-free allocation is one in which no one envies the bundle of anyone else. Do such allocations really exist? Varian explains that it is possible to prove the existence of at least one envy-free allocation in the following manner. Let us assume that both people in our economy begin with equal shares of all the goods available for allocation. If they have different tastes and are allowed to trade in the market at fixed competitive prices, both will choose bundles that maximize their utility, given the income generated by their initial endowments and given the prevailing prices in the economy. Thus, after exchange takes place, each person will have a different bundle of goods. Because both started out with equal incomes, any bundle available to person 1 was available to person 2. The fact that person 1 chose a different bundle than person 2 means that he prefers his bundle to the one chosen by person 2. Hence,

envy-free allocation
An allocation in which no one envies the bundle of anyone else.

---

[5] Hal R. Varian is the Dean of the School of Information Management and Systems at the University of California, Berkeley, a professor in the Haas School of Business, and a noted author of economics textbooks. The views discussed here originally appeared in Varian's article "Equity, Envy, and Efficiency," *Journal of Economic Theory* 9 (1974): 1–23.

he cannot envy person 2. Similarly, person 2 cannot envy person 1. The allocation resulting from trade is therefore envy free, and we have proved that such an allocation can exist. Further, our establishment of the fact that an envy-free allocation of goods can exist suggests that we might also be able to justify inequalities in the distribution of income on envy-free grounds.

The Weakness of Varian's Argument. There are two main problems with Varian's argument. First, the fact that an allocation of goods is envy free does not mean that it is appealing on other grounds. For example, one person may be extremely happy with his allocated bundle, whereas another person may be miserable. The happy person will certainly not envy his miserable neighbor. However, it is possible that the miserable neighbor is also not envious. She may find that the happy neighbor's bundle includes goods that she hates. Hence, an allocation can be envy free even though one person is happy with his bundle and the other person is miserable with hers. In short, the fact that an allocation is envy free tells us nothing about the distribution of utility.

The second problem with an envy-free allocation is that it may not be Pareto optimal. There may be another allocation that would make everyone better off than the current envy-free one. Furthermore, not all Pareto-optimal allocations are envy free.

SOLVED PROBLEM 22.5

Question (Content Review: Envy-Free Allocation)

Mr. Friday and Mr. Gannon are police detectives. Each man originally has an allocation of 5 pounds of coffee and 6 dozen donuts. Mr. Gannon has a utility function $U_G(c, d) = cd$, and Mr. Friday has a utility function $U_F(c, d) = c + 3d$, where c is pounds of coffee and d is dozens of donuts.

Friday offers to trade 1 pound of coffee to Gannon for $\frac{1}{2}$ dozen donuts. Will Gannon accept the trade? Will the final allocation be envy free?

Answer

Gannon's original utility is

$$U_G(5, 6) = (5)(6) = 30$$

If he accepts Friday's offer, his utility will be

$$U_G\left(6, 5\frac{1}{2}\right) = (6)\left(5\frac{1}{2}\right) = 33$$

so Gannon will accept the trade.

The allocation after the trade is then 6 pounds of coffee and $5\frac{1}{2}$ dozen donuts for Gannon and 4 pounds of coffee and $6\frac{1}{2}$ dozen donuts for Friday. If Gannon had Friday's allocation, he would have the following utility:

$$U_G\left(4, 6\frac{1}{2}\right) = (4)\left(6\frac{1}{2}\right) = 26$$

Because this is less than the 33 of his final allocation, Gannon will not envy Friday.

Friday's utility from the final allocation is

$$U_F\left(4, 6\frac{1}{2}\right) = 4 + 3\left(6\frac{1}{2}\right) = 23\frac{1}{2}$$

If he had Gannon's allocation, his utility would be

$$U_F\left(6, 5\frac{1}{2}\right) = 6 + 3\left(5\frac{1}{2}\right) = 22\frac{1}{2}$$

Thus, he doesn't envy Gannon. The final allocation is envy free.

Institutional Failure: Another Interventionist Argument

Every time our model society has come upon a problem, it has created an institution to deal with that problem. When people needed an efficient means of exchanging goods, competitive markets arose. When people were troubled by the uncertainty in their lives, insurance and risk-sharing mechanisms developed. When monopolists threatened to reduce economic welfare, regulatory agencies were established. In short, our agents have proven quite resourceful in creating economic institutions to cope with the vagaries of modern economic life.

We have seen that society is best off in terms of welfare when the institution created to deal with a problem is a competitive market because competitive markets are characterized by good welfare performance. As a result, free marketeers concluded that when society faces a problem that can be solved by the creation of a competitive market, it should allow such a market to function without any external intervention. However, not all economic problems can be solved by the creation of competitive markets. In some circumstances, the prerequisites for the creation of such markets do not exist. In most of the remaining chapters of this book, we will investigate the circumstances under which we can expect that competitive markets will not be established in the first place or will fail to function properly if they are established. These circumstances include markets with asymmetric information, public goods, externalities, moral hazard, and incomplete information. Hence, these chapters present counterarguments to the free-market ideology that are based on *efficiency* rather than *equity*.

When markets fail, other institutions are usually created to fill the gap. For example, health insurance may at times be unavailable because of the peculiarities involved in selling insurance. When this occurs, groups of people may enter into risk-sharing agreements or even insure themselves to obtain coverage. When such nonmarket institutions are created and function in an efficient manner, efficiency can be restored. However, there is no guarantee that the institutions created to fill the void left by market failure will function properly. In this case, there is a general institutional failure, and intervention may be necessary to remedy the situation.

EXPERIMENTAL EVIDENCE

GOVERNMENT INTERVENTIONS AND THE AFFIRMATIVE ACTION DEBATE

One of the most controversial issues facing our economy and society in recent years is affirmative action. The debate centers on a conflict about equity, with the rights of the majority depicted as compromised by programs designed to increase the welfare of underprivileged minorities. Implicit in this discussion is the assumption that all affirmative action programs increase costs and reduce productivity. This result, it is claimed, is demonstrated trivially by economic analysis because any interference in the competitive process that prevents the most capable from being chosen must be wasteful and costly.

Andrew Schotter and Allan Corns challenge this claim by demonstrating that auctions in which high-cost minority firms are given preferential treatment in the award of contracts (by allowing them to win even if they are not the lowest bidders but are within, say, 5% or 10% of the lowest bid) can simultaneously enhance equity and decrease the cost of government procurement.[6] The experiments show that the imposition of an appropriate price-preference rule can lead both to an increase in equity and to cost effectiveness if the degree of price preference is chosen correctly.

Experimental Design

The experiment performed was a straightforward price-preference auction. Student volunteers were told to come to a classroom that was reserved for the experiment. Upon arrival, six students were randomly selected for each experimental session, and each subject was randomly assigned to be either a type *A* or a type *B* bidder. You can think of the experiment as a market where firms are competing for government contracts by submitting sealed bids. The cost to any firm of completing the contract is random. However, type *B* bidders were *low-cost* bidders, which meant that, although their costs were random, they were drawn from a somewhat lower interval of potential costs than were type *A* bidders. More specifically, type *B* bidders drew their costs in any round of the experiment from the set of integers ranging in value from 100 to 200, each with an equally likely probability. Type *A* subjects, or *high-cost* bidders, drew their costs from the interval 110 to 220. There were four type *B* bidders and two type *A* bidders.

In the beginning of each round of the experiment (there were 20 rounds in all), an experimental administrator walked around the room with two bags of chips marked *A* and *B*. Each bag contained a number of chips representing the distributions for the cost ranges of the two types of distributions. An *A* subject was given the *A* bag, at which point he or she pulled out a chip containing a number; each chip had a different cost number on it. This number was to be the cost for the subject in that round. Subjects made money when they "won" the contract, and their payoff was the difference between their winning bid and their randomly drawn cost.

After a cost was drawn, each subject recorded that cost on his or her worksheet and then took out one of the 20 bid slips and wrote the bid on that slip. These bids were collected by the experimental administrator; depending on the rules of the auction run, a winner was determined. The experimental administrator then wrote on the blackboard the number of the subject who had won, the price at which he or she won, and whether that subject was an *A* or *B* type. (Actually, subjects numbered 1 or 2 were *A* types, while those numbered 3, 4, 5, or 6 were *B* types.) Subjects then recorded their payoffs, and the next round would start in an identical manner. In each experiment, there were 20 rounds and the final payoff to subjects was the sum of their payoffs over the entire 20-round history of the experiment. Subjects were paid at the end of the experiment and were dismissed.

Four different experiments that differed only in their rules were run. In other words, in all experiments the number of *A* and *B* types, the cost distributions, and so on remained the same. The preference rules used were a 0%, 5%, 10%, and 15% preference for type *A*. For any *x*% preference rule greater than 0%, after the bids were submitted, the bids of the *B* types were increased by *x*% before any comparison of bids was made. The lowest post-preference bid was then awarded the contract at the price of the submitted bid, and the experiment proceeded to the next round.

Auction Performance: Does Price Preference Decrease Cost and Increase Equity?

It was found that the adoption of an appropriate price-preference rule can not only decrease the cost of government purchasing but can also raise the probability that a high-cost firm will win an auction. In short, if an appropriate price-preference rule is chosen, one can increase both cost effectiveness and equity. The descriptive results of the experiment are shown in Table 22.1, which is used here to discuss both the equity and the procurement-cost outcomes of the experiment.

Table 22.1 lists the number of winners of each type in the four auctions run (Winners), the number of type *A* winners who won because of the preference rule (Wins by Preference), the average cost drawn by winning subjects in each (Avg. Cost Winners), the average bid entered by these winners (Avg. Bid Winners), as well as the average profit realized by these winning bidders

(Continued)

---

[6] Andrew Schotter and Allan Corns challenge this claim in their paper, "Can Affirmative Action Be Cost Effective? An Experimental Examination of Price-Preference Auctions," *American Economic Review* (March 1999).

Table 22.1   Descriptive Results of Price-Preference Auctions

Auction Type	0%	5%	10%	15%
WINNERS				
A-types	12	22	28	43
B-types	87	78	52	57
WINS BY PREFERENCE	—	10	19	23
AVG. COST WINNERS				
A-types	117.17	120.68	127.64	123.74
B-types	113.82	111.44	112.62	112.77
AVG. BID WINNERS				
A-types	124.42	126.95	137.14	131.56
B-types	120.80	117.13	117.92	119.02
HIGHEST COST WINNER	A's—125	A's—151	A's—160	A's—148
	B's—151	B's—155	B's—144	B's—146
AVG. PROFIT PER UNIT				
A-types	7.25	6.27	6.50	5.47
B-types	6.99	5.69	5.31	5.68
AVERAGE PRICE	121.24	119.29	122.78	124.41

(Avg. Profit per Unit). The table also lists the average price paid by the auctioneer to purchase goods in each auction (Average Price).

Equity

In terms of equity, it is shown that as the price preference given to high-cost firms increases, the fraction of contracts awarded to them increases from 12% in the 0% or no-price-preference auction to 43% in the 15% preference auction. More importantly, however, it appears that as the price preference is increased, it becomes responsible for more and more of these wins as it turns what would have been losing high-cost bidders under lower-preference regimes into winners. For example, while 10 out of 22, or 45.4%, of the type A winners in the 5% experiment won because of the price preference, 63.6% of the wins for type A subjects in the 10% experiment were the result of the preference rule. This percentage falls from 63.6% to 53.4% in the 15% case, probably the result of random selection of high-cost draws for the B group in the 15% experiment where (at least in one experiment) the random cost draws for the low-cost B types were particularly high. Hence, there is little doubt that, at least in the laboratory setting, price preference increases the probability that high-cost (minority) firms win contracts.

Procurement Cost Comparisons

Table 22.1 also shows that the average price paid per auction in the four experiments was 121.24, 119.29,

122.78, and 124.41 for the 0%, 5%, 10%, and 15% preference auctions, respectively. Looking simply at the average price paid per auction, the 5% price-preference rule seems to be the best, followed by the 0% auction and then the 10% and 15% auctions.

Why Price Preferences Lower Costs: Why Affirmative Action Can Be Cost-Reducing to Taxpayers

The reason price-preference rules can lower the cost of government purchasing is straightforward. Price preferences, while often considered anticompetitive, actually increase competition among the firms, strengthening those firms the government wants to spur to compete more effectively against the low-cost firms. To see why, consider an auction with two high-cost firms and four low-cost firms. Low-cost firms draw their costs from a uniform distribution ranging from 100 to 200; high-cost firms draw their costs from a uniform distribution ranging from 110 to 220. Note the asymmetry in the situation. When there is no price preference, high-cost firms face one other high-cost firm and the severe competition of four low-cost firms, while each low-cost firm faces three other low-cost firms and the ineffective competition of two high-cost firms. In other words, low-cost firms face less effective competition than high-cost firms. When price preferences are instituted, high-cost firms become more like low-cost firms, and as a result of this increase in "effective" competition, the low-cost firms' bids become more aggressive. While, by analogy, high-cost firms now face less competition and hence bid less aggressively, if the preference is chosen correctly, the reduction in bids by low-cost firms (the firms that are more likely to win) more than compensates for the increased bids of high-cost firms, which are less likely to win.

Conclusion

Asymmetric information, public goods, externalities, moral hazard, and incomplete information are problems our developing society will be dealing with in the chapters that follow. These problems furnish the ideological ammunition for the political battles that will divide a heretofore tranquil population. When markets or other institutions fail, debates arise about what should be done to fix or replace them. The central question in these debates is this: Can individuals who are maximizing their utility solve these problems by themselves or do they need outside (governmental) help? The interventionists will argue that government intervention is necessary, whereas the free marketeers will insist that society should either do nothing or do the minimum possible so that the markets can work. In the next chapter, we will look at problems of adverse selection and moral hazard, using a number of different examples to see how the debate between free-market advocates and interventionists plays itself out.

Summary

In this chapter, we discussed how perfectly competitive economies determine Pareto-optimal outcomes, and we examined the conditions that must be met to obtain such outcomes.

The first and second fundamental theorems of welfare economics establish that every competitive equilibrium is a Pareto-optimal equilibrium and that every Pareto-optimal equilibrium can be achieved as a competitive equilibrium as long as income is distributed appropriately. However, even though free markets are efficient, efficiency is not the only criterion that one might apply in evaluating markets. The idea of equity, which is most often raised by philosophers, is also important. We discussed several different concepts of economic justice: Rawlsian justice, Nozick's process justice, and Varian's envy-free justice.

The last section of the chapter mentioned a number of circumstances under which we might expect that perfectly competitive markets will not be established or will fail. These circumstances include the existence of asymmetric information, public goods, externalities, and incomplete information. Asymmetric and incomplete information are likely to lead to problems of moral hazard and adverse selection, both of which kill the Pareto optimality that makes perfectly competitive markets so desirable.

Exercises and Problems

1. Let us say that there is a two-firm economy in which firm 1 produces good X_1 using capital K_1 and labor L_1 and firm 2 produces good X_2 using capital K_2 and labor L_2. The marginal products of capital and labor in the production of good X_1 are $MP_K^1 = (\sqrt{K_1}\sqrt{L_1})/2K_1$ and $MP_L^1 = (\sqrt{K_1}\sqrt{L_1})/2L_1$. For good X_2, the marginal products are $MP_K^2 = (\sqrt{K_2}\sqrt{L_2})/2L_2$ and $MP_L^2 = (\sqrt{K_2}\sqrt{L_2})/2L_2$.

a) If the economy has 100 units of capital and 100 units of labor, is $K_1 = 50$, $L_1 = 50$, $K_2 = 50$, and $L_2 = 50$ an efficient allocation?

b) Demonstrate that $K_1 = 64$, $L = 36$, $K_2 = 36$, and $L_2 = 64$ is not an efficient allocation.

2. Consider an economy with only two firms. Firm 1 produces good 1 using capital K_1 and labor L_1 with the production function $Q_1 = \min(K_1/6, L_1/2)$. Firm 2 produces good 2 using capital K_2 and labor L_2 and the production function $Q_2 = \min(K_2/4, L_2/2)$. Assume that the economy has 800 units of capital and 600 units of labor.

a) Is an allocation of inputs in which firm 1 receives all the labor and firm 2 receives all the capital efficient? Why or why not?

b) Is the allocation in which firm 1 receives all the labor and all the capital efficient?

c) What if firm 2 receives all of both inputs?

d) Is the allocation $K_1 = 650$, $L_1 = 200$, $K_2 = 150$, and $L_2 = 200$ efficient?

3. Let us say that in a two-firm economy, firm 1 has a constant marginal cost $MC_1 = 2$ for producing good 1 and firm 2 has a constant marginal cost of $MC_2 = 3$ for producing good 2. All 100 people in this economy have a utility function of $U = X_1 X_2$, where X_1 is the quantity of good 1 consumed and X_2 is the quantity of good 2 consumed. The marginal utility of good 1 in this utility function is $MU_{x2}, = X_2$, and the marginal utility of good 2 is $MU_{x2}, = X_1$. Assume that the economy produces 3,000 units of good 1 and 2,000 units of good 2.

a) Would it be consistent with a competitive equilibrium for each person to consume 30 units of X_1 and 20 units of X_2?

b) Would it be consistent with a competitive equilibrium for half the population to consume 10 units of X_2 and 15 units of X_1 and half to consume 30 units of X_2 and 45 units of X_1? Explain your answer.

c) If the prices of goods 1 and 2 are $P_1 = 2$ *and* $P_2 = 3$, respectively, what income is needed by each person to achieve the competitive equilibrium allocation in part b of this problem?

d) If each person had the utility function $U = 4X_1 + 2X_2$, would it ever be efficient for society to produce good 2? Explain your answer.

4. Consider the social utility functions in Figure 22.6. These functions assign a "societal utility" to every set of individual utilities.

a) Suppose that a utility possibilities curve is added to Figure 22.6. What type of utility possibilities curve (concave, convex, or linear) would be most likely to give all utility in society to one person at a welfare optimum?

b) In part iii of Figure 22.6, moving from point b to point a places society on a higher level of utility. Explain why.

5. Let us say that in a two-person society, person 1 has a utility function of $U = 4X_1 = 2X_2$ and person 2 has a utility function of $U = X_1 \cdot X_2$. There are two goods, X_1 and X_2. The marginal cost of producing good X_1 is 4, and the marginal cost of producing good X_2 is 2. In a perfectly competitive economy, the relative price of goods 1 and 2 is 4 to 2.

a) An egalitarian free-market politician suggests that prices be set by the market but income be distributed equally. If each person receives an income of $100, what would the distribution of goods be at the competitive equilibrium?

Figure 22.6

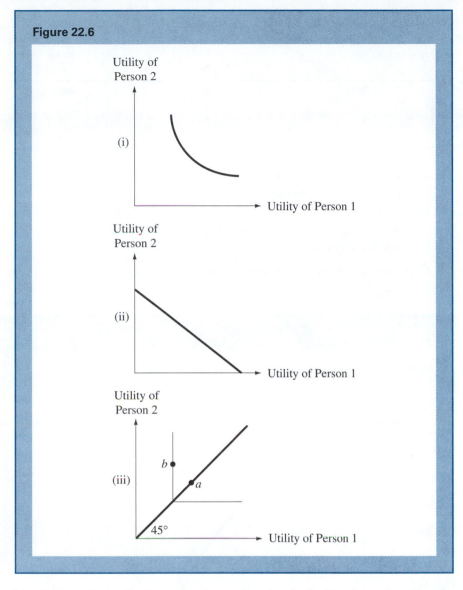

b) A libertarian politician wants the *market* to set both the prices of goods and the incomes of people. If person 1 consumes 50 units of good X_1 and 25 units of good X_2 and person 2 consumes 25 units of good X_1 and 50 units of good X_2 at the libertarian outcome, how much income will each have?

c) Why are the competitive prices in parts a and b of this problem independent of the distribution of income?

6. Consider the following four distributions of income in a four-person society. Which distribution of income would a believer in Rawlsian justice consider the best distribution? Explain your answer.

Person	DISTRIBUTION			
	1	2	3	4
1	200	600	900	1,000,000
2	200	800	400	1,000,000
3	200	100	201	201
4	200	400	300	201

7. Assume that Bob has a utility function of $U = 8X_1 + 1X_2 - 3X_3$ and Joan has a utility function of $U = -2X_1 + 7X_2 + 5X_3$. Consider the following allocation:

Good	Bob	Joan
X_1	4	1
X_2	2	3
X_3	1	4

a) Is this allocation envy free?

b) Is this allocation Pareto optimal?

c) Find a Pareto-optimal allocation, and determine whether it is envy free.

d) Do you think that the allocation in part c of this problem is desirable? Why or why not?

8. Consider the utility possibilities function for a two-person society given in Figure 22.7.

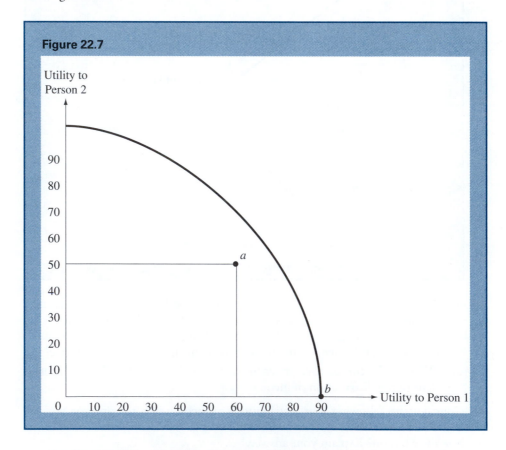

Figure 22.7

a) At point b, how much utility does each person receive?

b) At point a, how much utility does each person receive?

c) Which point, a or b, is Pareto optimal?

d) Which point, a or b, do you think would be better for the society in which you live? Explain.

9. Assume that a firm produces a good at a constant marginal cost of \$4 and that it must pay a \$1 tax for each unit it produces. The price of the good to the consumer is \$4.50. Does such a situation satisfy the conditions for Pareto optimality? If not, which condition or conditions are violated?

10. Suppose that the production possibilities frontier for cheeseburgers (C) and milkshakes (M) is given by $C + 2M = 600$.

   a) Graph this function.

   b) Assuming that people prefer to eat two cheeseburgers with every milkshake, how much of each product will be produced? Indicate this point on your graph.

   c) Assuming that this fast-food economy is operating efficiently, what price ratio (P_C/P_M) will prevail?

Breakdowns and Market Failure

While competition is likely to lead to socially beneficial results, there are a number of situations in which it can be expected to fail. These breakdowns of the market process are investigated in this section.

Markets can fail for many reasons. In Chapter 23, we investigate how the competitive process fails when it is faced with information that is not perfectly distributed. You may have noticed that in all that we have said until Chapter 23, it was assumed that agents were perfectly informed about all the key variables of the economy. Even in our chapter on uncertainty, our economic agents at least knew the probability distribution governing the states of the world, and such information was symmetrically available to everyone. Here, we look at what are called the problems of moral hazard and adverse selection, which occur when some agents have more or better information than others, and will demonstrate that such informational asymmetries can create problems for the proper functioning of markets. We repeat this analysis in Chapters 24 and 25, where we investigate the problems of externalities and public goods, respectively. Along the way, we stay informed about what types of remedies would restore the efficiency properties of markets and ask whether these can be achieved without intervention by the state.

Moral Hazard and Adverse Selection: Informational Market Failures

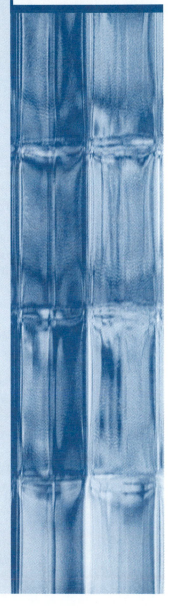

ADVERSE SELECTION

Ever open your mail and find that a credit card company is offering you a new credit card at a "special" introductory offer? These offers are sent to you from banks and other issuers of credit cards to try to get you to use their cards. If you were to send a random sample of people different offers in the mail, with some better than others, and you knew who were the better customers in terms of who was more likely not to default on the loans you are giving them, do you think that those who responded and wanted the card would be better or worse risks than those who did not respond? Further, if you offered some potential customers better terms than others, do you think that those who accepted the worse terms would be better or worse risks?

If the credit risk of customers is a function of the terms you offer them, then, as we will see in this chapter, you have a problem of adverse selection. This is a problem faced by insurance companies and credit card companies all the time and occurs when you cannot observe the characteristics of the people with whom you are dealing.

For example, while credit card companies might make a lot of money if they offered high interest rates to customers, if the only ones that accepted such poor terms were the bad default risks, then the companies may actually do worse than they would if they offered better terms.

To investigate this problem, Lawrence Ausubel* performed a field experiment in which he got the credit records of many hundreds of thousands of customers and, in conjunction with a set of credit card issuers, sent credit card offers with different sets of terms (introductory interest rates, length of the introductory offer, and ultimate interest rates after the introductory period expired). Because he knew how good the credit ratings were for each person solicited, he could look at who responded to the solicitations and see if there was adverse selection in the credit card market; that is, he could see if people who accepted the offer were worse risks than those who did not respond and if there was a relationship between the terms they were offered and the credit ratings of those who accepted.

This experiment is different from the types of laboratory experiments we have discussed so far in that this experiment was done with real customers in real markets. As such, it is very appealing and offers an insight into how real people would make decisions in real markets as opposed to the laboratory settings discussed so far.

What do you think Ausubel found?

---

* Lawrence Ausubel, "Adverse Selection in the Credit Card Market," Mimeo, June 1999, University of Maryland.

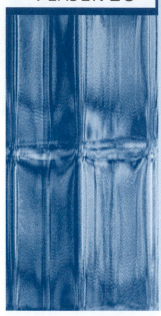

MORAL HAZARD

Say that your car breaks down and you need to get it fixed. The problem can be either minor or major. If you own a car, then you must be aware of the reputation of car mechanics—it is not very good. The problem you have is that car mechanics come in many flavors. They can be honest or dishonest and competent or incompetent. In fact, they can be combinations of those, so you may bring your car to an honest and incompetent car dealer and be told the car has a major problem or you can bring your car to a dishonest but competent mechanic and be told the same thing. In fact, no matter what is wrong with your car, given the types of mechanics, you can be told either that it has a minor or a major problem. Knowing this, dishonest firms have an incentive to lie. To combat against such lies, consumers search for second and sometimes third opinions. The policy question is, given that a certain fraction of firms are honest, dishonest, competent, and incompetent (and all combinations thereof), can market forces be relied upon to police these markets or are government interventions, like price controls and licensing, necessary? Andrew Schotter and Carolyn Pitchik[*] have studied this question both theoretically and experimentally and have come to mixed conclusions. See their analysis later in this chapter.

---

[*] Carolyn Pitchik and Andrew Schotter, "Norms and Competition in Markets with Asymmetric Information: An Experimental Study of the Development of Industry Ethics," *Metroeconomica*, vol. 2, 1994.

As we discussed at the end of Chapter 22, if all of the prerequisites for perfect competition are not satisfied, the economic outcomes of markets may be less desirable than the first and second fundamental theorems of welfare economics predict. The theory of perfect competition assumes that economic agents have complete and perfect information about all of the variables that affect their well-being. In this chapter, we will examine the effects of deviating from the informational assumptions that form the basis of free-market ideology. More precisely, we will explore the problems of moral hazard and adverse selection that arise when the agents in an economy have incomplete information available to them or when there is an asymmetric distribution of information.

This chapter uses examples from the insurance, car repair, and restaurant industries to illustrate the problems of moral hazard and adverse selection. We will see that when informational scarcities exist, competitive markets may either fail to develop or, if they do develop, may not yield the expected types of Pareto-optimal results. While these failures might seem to justify intervention by the government, we will find that there are free-market solutions requiring no intervention. We will examine some of these solutions.

Moral Hazard in the Insurance Industry

When insurance companies were first established, they encountered a number of unexpected difficulties. The companies noticed that after they insured an individual against a simple risk, that individual changed his or her behavior in a way that made the insured loss more likely to occur. In other words, once people purchased insurance, they became more careless in their behavior because they knew that if they incurred a loss, the insurance company would reimburse them for that loss. This change in behavior resulted in more claims and more payouts for the insurance company and made it less profitable to issue insurance. As we might expect, the insurance companies sought ways to discourage careless behavior. They developed *co-insurance* or *deductibles* on the policies they wrote. Let us see how such arrangements work.

Market Failure Due to Moral Hazard

Remember that the inhabitants of our primitive society originally earned their living by picking fruit. To reach the fruit growing in the upper branches of trees, they had to use ladders. Sometimes these ladders tipped over, and as a result, people were injured. Now let us assume that there are two types of ladders available in this society. Each person can choose either the *safe ladder* or the *risky ladder*. The safe ladder costs $6, and there is a 10% chance of an accident occurring with this ladder. The risky ladder costs only $4, but users have a 40% chance of an accident. We will say that an accident is equivalent to a loss in income of $8. For example, the income of a person earning $20 will decrease to $12 if an accident occurs. (We assume that this monetary loss expresses the total disutility of the event for the person and that he is not any worse off due to injury.) Finally, we will say that each person has the same *Von Neumann-Morgenstern cardinal utility function*, which assigns utility numbers to dollars as shown in Table 23.1.

Before a person purchases insurance in this society, he must decide which ladder to buy. Clearly, he will choose the ladder that will maximize his expected utility. For example, the expected utility of choosing the risky ladder is $(0.40)u(\$20 - \$8 - \$4) + (0.60)u(\$20 - \$4) = 8.10$, whereas the expected utility of choosing the safe ladder is $(0.10)u(\$20 - \$8 - \$6) + (0.90)u(\$20 - \$6) = 8.60$. Hence, if there were no insurance, the person would choose the safe ladder, and the probability of his having an accident would be 10%.

An insurance company will view the prospect of insuring such a person as a gamble that offers a 10% chance that it will have to pay out $8 against a 90% chance that it will not have to pay out anything ($0). If the insurance company is risk neutral, it would be willing to sell insurance for any price above $0.80 because $0.80 is the expected loss from the gamble it faces $(\$0.80 = 0.10 \cdot \$8 + 0.90 \cdot \$0)$. However, a risk-averse person, by definition, would be willing to pay more than $0.80 for such insurance. To be more precise, the person who owns a safe ladder faces a gamble in which there is a 90% chance that he will receive a utility of 9 $[u(\$14)]$ and a 10% chance that he will receive a utility of 5 $[u(\$6)]$. This gamble yields an expected utility of 8.60. Note, however, that according to the cardinal

Table 23.1	The Von Neumann-Morgenstern Cardinal Utility Function.
	Utility (Dollars)
	$u(\$0) = 0.00$
	$u(\$6) = 5.00$
	$u(\$8) = 6.00$
	$u(\$10) = 6.50$
	$u(\$11) = 7.50$
	$u(\$12) = 8.10$
	$u(\$13) = 8.60$
	$u(\$14) = 9.00$
	$u(\$15) = 9.25$
	$u(\$16) = 9.50$

utility function, receiving \$13 for sure yields a utility of 8.60. Hence, paying a premium of \$3 for insurance and a price of \$4 for the risky ladder is just as good as not buying insurance and risking an accident with the safe ladder because the person is guaranteed an income of \$13.

If the insurance could be bought for a price between \$0.80 and \$3, then anyone would be willing to buy it. Similarly, any insurance company would be willing to sell it. However, if the insurance company agrees to pay the *full* \$8 cost of any accident that occurs, then everyone will buy the risky ladder because after paying π for insurance, their expected utility from the risky ladder is $u(\$20 - \$4 - \pi) = u(\$16 - \pi)$, whereas their expected utility from the safe ladder is $u(\$20 - \$6 - \pi) = u(\$14 - \pi)$. Obviously, in this situation, being risky is better than being safe. As a result, once insurance is available, people will shift from the safe ladder to the risky ladder.

Thus, the existence of insurance changes the behavior of the people who are insured. This situation is an example of moral hazard. When people alter their behavior after purchasing insurance, they cause a change in the gamble faced by the insurance company. Now that everyone uses the risky ladder, the insurance company faces a 40% chance that it will pay out \$8 and a 60% chance that it will not pay out anything. Because the company is risk neutral, it will insure such a risk if the agents involved are willing to pay a premium equal to the expected value of the loss, which is \$3.20. But people are not willing to pay more than \$3 for insurance. Hence, this market will *fail* because of a moral hazard problem.

Market Solutions to the Moral Hazard Problem: Co-Insurance and Deductibles

For the first time, our model society has encountered market failure. The reason for this market failure is incomplete information. The insurance companies do not have the information that would make it possible for them to monitor the actions of their policyholders after they issue the policies. How can the insurance companies remedy this situation? For instance, does the failure of the market to provide incentives for people to behave in a safe manner mean that the government must enter the market? Advocates of the free-market approach say that no intervention is warranted. They claim that insurance companies can solve the problem themselves by including a deductible in their policies so that any policyholder who has an accident must pay a portion of the loss that arises from the accident.

co-insurance (deductible)
The amount any agent will have to pay in the event that the situation being covered by the insurance company occurs.

In essence, the insurance company is saying to the policyholder, "We will insure you for a premium of \$1, just as we promised; and we will not check on the type of ladder you are using. However, if an accident occurs, instead of paying you \$8, we will pay you only k dollars, where $k < \$8$. You will be responsible for the remaining loss." Given the existence of this co-insurance or deductible provision of $8 - k$, each person must decide whether it is worthwhile for him or her to purchase insurance and, if so, whether to buy the safe ladder or the risky ladder. The decision about the ladder involves an evaluation of whether the expected utility of the safe ladder with deductible insurance is greater than the expected utility of the risky ladder with deductible insurance. For example, let us say that \$20 is the income of any person if no accident occurs, \$6 is the cost of the safe ladder, \$4 is the cost of the risky ladder, $\$(8 - k)$ is the amount paid by the insured after the deductible is paid, and \$1 is the cost of insurance. We can therefore express the utility for each type of ladder in the following way: Expected *utility*$_{SL}$ = $(0.10)u[\$20 - \$6 - \$(8 - k) - \$1] + (0.90)u(\$20 - \$6 - \$1)$. Expected *utility*$_{RL}$ = $(0.40)u[\$20 - \$4 - \$1 - \$(8 - k)] + (0.60)u(\$20 - \$4 - \$1)$, where SL is the safe ladder with deductible insurance and *RL* is the risky ladder with deductible insurance.

If we let the deductible equal $5, we see that the expected utility for the safe ladder with deductible insurance is 8.34 [(0.10)u($8) + (0.90)$u$($13)] and the expected utility for the risky ladder with deductible insurance is 8.15 [(0.40)u($10) + (0.60)$u$($15)]. Clearly, after the introduction of the deductible, policyholders must bear some of the risk of suffering a loss if an accident occurs and therefore have an incentive to act cautiously. As a result, they will want to buy the safe ladder, which provides a better chance of avoiding an accident. The insurance companies will again want to sell insurance because we know that they are willing to do so at a premium of $1 *if* people behave in a safe manner.

In this situation, market failure due to moral hazard was solved *without* the intervention of any outside authority. As we will see later, this may not always be the case.

MEDIA NOTE

ADVERSE SELECTION AND MORAL HAZARD

Banks are sometimes viewed as an unnecessary evil. They are big institutions whose sole purpose is to charge fees to their small consumers. But banks do serve a purpose because they furnish a solution to the adverse selection and moral hazard problems in the loans market.

The adverse selection problem arises from the fact that the more eager borrowers are, as indicated by the higher interest rate they are willing to pay, the higher the risk they pose to the lenders. The second problem, the moral hazard problem, is the inability of the lenders to process the vast information needed to monitor the borrowers.

The incentives to solve adverse selection and moral hazard problems in the free market—for example, the bonds market—are small. Consider a lender that has managed to solve the problems above at some cost and decided that a specific borrower is a good risk for him to take. The result is that the lender will buy that specific borrower's bonds. The upshot of such a buy is that other lenders will see that the bonds of the borrower are bought, realize that the problems of adverse

selection and moral hazard are solved, and buy the bonds as well. In effect, the other lenders take a free ride on the appraisal and monitoring efforts of the first lender. But if lenders can take free rides on the monitoring of others, then there is no incentive for them to monitor; thus, the free-riding problem causes market failure.

Here is where the banks come to the rescue. Banks have specialized in dealing with adverse selection and moral hazard. They have developed tools in order to recognize the risks each borrower presents and, if the borrower is already a customer, they have full information about her. This helps curb the adverse selection problem. The easy access to information also enables the bank to monitor the borrower very effectively. Indeed, by tracking the uses of the money borrowed and deposited in the bank, the bank has full disclosure on the borrower's activities. So because of the special role that banks play and the information they are able to acquire cheaply, they help solve what would otherwise be a very complicated problem.

Source: Adapted from "The Trouble with Banks," as appeared in *The Economist,* May 1, 2003

Question (Application and Extension: Insurance and Deductibles)

The Federal Insurance Company offers an auto insurance policy that costs $1,000 minus a $200 deductible for full coverage for an accident. The Union Insurance Company offers a policy that costs $900 minus a $600 deductible for full coverage. Drivers in this society are either safe or reckless. If a driver is safe, he has a 5% chance of having an accident that will total his car. If a driver is reckless, he has a 50% chance of having an accident that will total his car. Mr. Landis owns a car worth $20,000 and has a utility function $U(x) = x$, where x is his wealth.

SOLVED PROBLEM 23.1

If Mr. Landis is a safe driver, will he buy insurance? If so, from which company will he buy? What about if he is a reckless driver? If he could choose to be safe or reckless, what would he do?

Answer

If Mr. Landis is a safe driver, his expected utility without insurance is

$$EU(\text{No Insurance}) = (0.05)(0) + (0.95)(20{,}000) = 19{,}000$$

If he buys from Federal,

$$EU(\text{Federal}) = (0.05)(20{,}000 - 1{,}000 - 200) + (0.95)(20{,}000 - 1{,}000) = 18{,}990$$

and if he buys from Union,

$$EU(\text{Union}) = (0.05)(20{,}000 - 900 - 600) + (0.95)(20{,}000 - 900) = 19{,}070$$

Thus, Mr. Landis will buy insurance from Union if he is a safe driver.

If Mr. Landis is a reckless driver, his expected utility without insurance is

$$EU(\text{No Insurance}) = (0.05)(0) + (0.50)(20{,}000) = 10{,}000$$

If he buys from Federal,

$$EU(\text{Federal}) = (0.50)(20{,}000 - 1{,}000 - 200) + (0.50)(20{,}000 - 1{,}000) = 18{,}900$$

and if he buys from Union,

$$EU(\text{Union}) = (0.50)(20{,}000 - 900 - 600) + (0.50)(20{,}000 - 900) = 18{,}800$$

So if Mr. Landis is reckless, he will buy insurance from Federal.

If Mr. Landis could decide to be reckless or safe, he would choose to be safe and buy from Union as that would give him the highest expected utility.

---

adverse selection
Adverse selection occurs in situations where one economic agent (say an insurance company) cannot observe the characteristics of another (potential clients) and offers a contract that is accepted by a set of people in the population that has less than average desirability (bad risks).

Adverse Selection

We have just observed how the inability of one party in a trade (the seller) to monitor the behavior of the other party (the buyer) because of a lack of information can lead to the problem of moral hazard and ultimately to market failure. Similarly, the inability of the party on one side of a trade to recognize certain characteristics of the party on the other side of the trade because of a lack of information can also lead to a problem that may cause market failure—the problem of adverse selection.

MEDIA NOTE

ADVERSE SELECTION

Adverse selection is not merely a textbook abstraction. It affects life on a daily basis. Consider the case of the mortgage lender American Business Financial Services company (ABFS) and the problems it faced because of adverse selection.

In this case, the City of Philadelphia tried to lure firms into the city by offering them lucrative tax breaks in hopes that they would locate in the Center City area and provide jobs. At first, the city was proud of its decision, but ultimately the ABFS story only illustrated the adverse selection problem.

The problem was that by offering subsidies and tax breaks, the city attracted those firms that were most in need of help rather than the more healthy firms that could have survived with less help. In other words, the selection of firms that initially bit at the bait being dangled by the city was worse than the average firm that could have been attracted by the policy. These firms were also the least likely to grow in the future but the most likely to need a short subsidy fix.

In order to finance its move, ABFS engaged in a number of suspect practices that eventually led to its being investigated by the city. In the end, the city attracted exactly those types of firms that it would least like to do business with.

It's not just a Philadelphia problem. The point is that governments frequently mess up when they try to boost economic growth by targeting particular companies or industries for favored treatment. They fail because they start out with the deck stacked against them, thanks to the principle of adverse selection.

Source: Adapted from "A Tale of Woe, but Not Surprise," as appeared in *The Philadelphia Inquirer,* April 6, 2005

Market Failure Due to Adverse Selection in the Insurance Industry

The insurance industry is an obvious example of a market in which the problem of adverse selection can arise. Given limited information about the characteristics of potential buyers, an insurance company may be unable to distinguish between good risks and bad risks. If the company issues too many policies to bad risks, it will have to pay an inordinate number of claims. In other words, if the company selects its risks from the population in an adverse way, it will probably suffer severe losses and may even fail.

To gain a better understanding of the problem of adverse selection, let us return to the story of how the insurance industry developed in our model society. We will now assume that all the inhabitants of this society bought ladders before anyone applied for insurance. Some people bought safe ladders, and others bought risky ladders. Let us say that a fraction (λ) of the population bought the safe ladders and the rest ($1 - \lambda$) bought the risky ladders. It is impossible to tell by looking at the ladders which ones are safe and which ones are risky. We will classify the people in this society into two groups, *safe* and *risky*, based on the type of ladder each person owns. Note that the situation here differs from the situation in the previous section, where people chose to behave in either a safe or a risky manner.

What we now want to know is how the insurance industry in this society will deal with the different and unknown levels of risk in the population. Can it distinguish between the safe and risky groups and price its products appropriately for the two groups? If not, can the industry operate successfully?

Question (Application and Extension: Insurance and Moral Hazard)

Tanya has a car that will be stolen with probability 0.1 if an antitheft device is not used and 0.05 if the device is used. The value of the car is $10,000, and the cost of the antitheft device is $10. Suppose that Tanya can only insure the car for its full value, and the insurance company cannot tell if she has bought the antitheft device. In addition to the value of her car, Tanya has $1,000 in her bank account. Let her Von Neumann-Morgenstern utility function over total wealth be $U(w) = \sqrt{w}$.

SOLVED PROBLEM 23.2

a) If Tanya is not using the antitheft device, what premium will the insurance company charge her?

Answer

If she does not use the antitheft device, the probability of theft is 0.1. Then the risk-neutral insurance company will charge a premium equal to the expected loss due to theft. Thus, the premium will be $10,000(0.1) = $1,000.

b) Will Tanya purchase the theft insurance for her car, given the premium calculated in part a?

Answer

No, Tanya will not purchase theft insurance for her car. Given full coverage by an insurance company, it is never in Tanya's interest to purchase the antitheft device because, either way, she retains the full value of the car. (Assume that there is no inconvenience to her if her car is stolen. She only cares about money.) Therefore, the insurance company will always assume that Tanya is not using the antitheft device and will charge her a premium of $1,000. If Tanya purchases the insurance policy, her expected utility is 100 because, whether her car is stolen or not, her wealth will be $10,000 (*car*) + $1,000 (*bank account*) − $1,000 (*insurance premium*) = $10,000, and $\sqrt{10,000} = 100$. But if Tanya does not purchase insurance and uses the antitheft device, her expected utility will be $0.95(10,990)^{1/2} + 0.05(990)^{1/2} = 101.16$. In case the car is not stolen, her wealth will be $10,990 = $10,000 (*car*) + $1,000 (*bank account*) − $10 (antitheft device). If the car is stolen, her wealth will be $990 = $1,000 (*bank account*) − $10 (antitheft device). Therefore, Tanya has a higher expected utility if she does not purchase the insurance policy but purchases the antitheft device instead.

c) If Tanya can convince the insurance company that she will purchase the antitheft device and she buys the insurance policy, what will be her expected utility?

Answer

If Tanya purchases the antitheft device, the expected payment for the insurance company is $10,000(0.05) = $500. If she convinces the insurance company that she will purchase the device, Tanya's premium will be $500. Therefore, her expected utility will be $(10,490)^{1/2} = 102.42$.

Question (Application and Extension: Insurance and Moral Hazard, Continued)
Let Tanya of Solved Problem 23.2 have access to an insurance policy with a 10% deductible.

a) If she purchases the deductible insurance and uses the antitheft device (and the insurance company knows it), what will be her insurance premium?

Answer

The premium will equal the expected payments by the insurance company. If the car is stolen, the insurance company will pay $9,000. Then the premium will be $9,000(0.05) = $450.

b) If Tanya purchases the 10% deductible insurance for the premium computed in part a, will she also buy the antitheft device?

Answer

If Tanya purchases the antitheft device, her expected utility will be $0.95(11,000 - 450 - 10)^{1/2} + 0.05(10,000 - 450 - 10)^{1/2} = 102.41$. If she does not buy the antitheft device, her expected utility will be $0.9(11,000 - 450)^{1/2} + 0.1(10,000 - 450)^{1/2} = 102.21$. Therefore, Tanya will buy the antitheft device if she purchases the deductible policy.

c) Will Tanya purchase the 10% deductible insurance?

Answer

If Tanya purchases the deductible policy as well as the antitheft device, her expected utility will be 102.41. If she does not purchase any insurance policy and uses the antitheft device, her expected utility will be 101.16 (from Solved Problem 23.2). If she purchases neither the insurance nor the antitheft device, her expected utility will be $0.9(11,000)^{1/2} + 0.1(1,000)^{1/2} = 97.56$. Therefore, Tanya will choose the action that gives her the highest expected utility, which is to purchase the deductible policy and to buy the antitheft device.

Determining the Minimum Acceptable Price for the Insurance Companies.

In this case, the insurance companies do not know which people fall into the risky group and which fall into the safe group, that is, which ones have a 40% chance of an accident and which ones have a 10% chance of an accident. This lack of information forces the insurance companies to sell insurance on the assumption that they will face the *average* number of accidents for the population. When an individual wants to purchase insurance, the companies will assume that he or she is the *average* person. Therefore, they will calculate the probability of an accident (P) for that individual as $\lambda(0.10) + (1 - \lambda)(0.40)$. Note that when $\lambda = 1$ (everyone belongs to the safe group), $P = 0.10$, but when $\lambda = 0$ (everyone belongs to the risky group), $P = 0.40$. Risk-neutral insurance companies will then face a gamble for each person in which they will have to pay $8 with a probability of P and nothing ($0) with a probability of $(1 - P)$. The expected monetary loss of such a gamble is $[\lambda(0.10) + (1 - \lambda)0.40]($8) + \{1 - [(\lambda(0.10) + (1 - \lambda)0.40)]\}(0) = $3.20 - 2.40λ.

When $\lambda = 1$, everyone owns a safe ladder. Then, as before, the insurance companies are willing to sell insurance to any applicant for $0.80. When $\lambda = 0$, everyone owns a risky ladder, and the minimum price acceptable to a risk-neutral insurance company is $3.20.

Determining the Maximum Acceptable Prices for Safe and Risky Customers.

Now let us look at the situation from the point of view of the potential buyers of insurance. Assuming that everyone has an income of $20, we can see that safe people (the ones who own the safe ladders) face a gamble in which there is a 10% chance of losing $8 and thereby having a final income of $6 (after we deduct the $6 cost of the ladder) and a 90% chance of losing nothing and having a final income of $14 (again, after we deduct the $6 cost of the ladder). If we use the cardinal utility function in Table 23.1, we find that this gamble has an expected utility of $(0.10)u($6) + (0.90)u($14) = (0.10)(5) + (0.90)(9) = 8.60$. This utility of 8.60 is the equivalent of having $13 for sure, as shown in Table 23.1. Therefore, we know that safe people would be willing to pay up to $1 for insurance. (Remember that after buying the safe ladder, these people have a 90% chance of earning an income of $14.)

Risky people (the ones who own the risky ladders) face a gamble in which there is a 40% chance of having a loss of $8 and a final income of $8 (after we deduct the $4 cost of the ladder) and a 60% chance of having no loss and a final income of $16 (again, after we deduct the $4 cost of the ladder). Their expected utility is therefore $(0.40)u(\$8) + (0.60)u(\$16) = (0.40)(6) + (0.60)(9.5) = 8.10$. This utility of 8.10 is equivalent to having $12 for sure, as shown in Table 23.1. Hence, we can see that risky people would be willing to pay up to $4 for insurance. It is not surprising that risky people are willing to spend more to obtain insurance protection. Because of their 40% chance of having an accident, insurance is certainly worth more to them.

Why Does the Market Fail? If the fraction of safe people in the population is $\frac{1}{4}$, then we can see that the average probability of an accident in the population is $P = (0.25)(0.10) + (0.75)(0.40) = 0.325$ and the price that a risk-neutral insurance company would charge is $2.60 $[(0.325)(\$8) + (0.675)(\$0) = \$2.60]$. This price will produce a long-run competitive equilibrium for the insurance industry because it is the price at which profits are driven down to zero. (The expected loss of $(0.325)(\$8) + (0.675)(\$0)$ equals the price of $2.60.)

There is a problem with this equilibrium price of $2.60. It exceeds the price of $1 that safe people are willing to pay for insurance and falls below the price of $4 that risky people are willing to pay: maximum price for insurance (safe people) $<$ $2.60 $<$ maximum price for insurance (risky people) because $1 < \$2.60 < \$4$. If insurance companies cannot distinguish between the safe people and the risky people in a population because of a lack of information, they must charge everyone the same average premium. As a result, the safe people will not buy insurance, and the insurance industry will be selling only to risky people. However, because there is a 40% chance that risky people will have an accident and each accident costs the insurer $8, the companies can expect to pay $3.20 $[(0.4)(\$8) + (0.6)(\$0)]$ to these people. Yet the companies are collecting a premium of only $2.60. Under these circumstances, the insurance companies will either suffer losses and go bankrupt or increase their price sufficiently so that they can afford the high level of claims that occurs when only risky people buy insurance.

Clearly, the problem that we just examined is a problem of adverse selection. There is not enough information in the market. One side in insurance transactions (the seller) does not have adequate information about the characteristics of the other side (the buyer) to price its policies appropriately. The insurance companies therefore end up selling only to risky people, and the safe people must do without insurance. Obviously, this market is not yielding Pareto-optimal results. There are safe people who are willing to pay for insurance and insurance companies that are willing to sell to these people at low premiums. However, the insurance companies cannot write such policies because the risky people ruin the market. This situation exists because the companies cannot identify good and bad insurance risks; and as a result, they must charge all customers a uniform rate that reflects the *average* cost of insuring any individual in the population. This average cost is too high to attract good risks but too low to fully cover the losses produced by the bad risks who do buy insurance. Thus, the market fails.

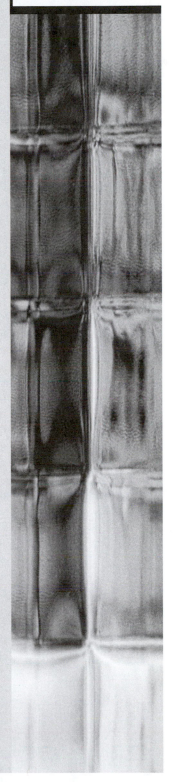

ADVERSE SELECTION

In the Ausubel experiment, three sets of mailings were done offering different terms to different sets of customers. We will examine only Experiment 1. In that experiment, 600,000 customer names were randomly assigned to six equal markets, and different credit card offers were made to each group. The offers varied by their introductory interest rates and the duration of the introductory offer. All solicitations were for gold cards (although if a customer responded and was not qualified for a gold card, he was offered something less) and, for the entire post-introductory period, offered an interest rate of 16%.

The Ausubel data set had information on the characteristics of the customers, including their incomes and a full analysis of their credit ratings so the researchers knew the types of people they were dealing with.

The results of Experiment 1 are presented in Table 23.2 (Table 4A of Ausubel). A set of statistical tests run on these means (and the associated standard deviations) indicate that there are significant differences in a number of the treatments as the terms of the credit card contracts change, indicating evidence of adverse selection. For example, comparing the results of treatments A and D, the average income of customers was $43,019 in market treatment A, whereas it was only $39,702 in market treatment D. Gold cards were awarded to 84.0% of customers in market treatment A but to only 76.7% of customers in market treatment D. An average credit limit of $6,446 was assigned to customers in market treatment A, while an average of only $5,827 was assigned in market treatment D. While average revolving balances were essentially the same ($5,290 vs. $5,152), customers in market treatment A had $19,209 in average revolving limits, while customers in market treatment D had only $16,422. Customers in market treatment A were utilizing 32.2% of their credit limits, while those in market treatment D were utilizing 35.1% of their credit limits. All of these results are significant, meeting at least the 5% level of significance.

The adverse selection seen above was entirely observable to a credit card issuer at the time that the customers responded to the solicitation and therefore could have been avoided. But there may still be adverse selection across credit card offers even if companies hold the characteristics of people constant and vary the contracts offered them. In other words, even after controlling for the deterioration in observable characteristics yielded by an inferior offer, does the inferior offer still yield a customer pool that is more likely to default?

Ausubel's analysis provides strong evidence of adverse selection on hidden information. For example, even after controlling for all information known to the card issuer at the time that the account is opened, respondents to a solicitation with an introductory interest rate that is 1% higher have a delinquency probability that is 1.2 percentage points higher, while respondents to a solicitation with an introductory offer that lasts 3 months longer have a delinquency probability that is 1.7 percentage points lower. In addition, even after controlling for all information known to the card issuer at the time that the account is opened, respondents to a solicitation with an introductory interest rate that is 1% higher have a bankruptcy probability that is 0.4 percentage points higher, while respondents to a solicitation with an introductory offer that lasts 3 months longer have a bankruptcy probability that is 0.8 percentage points lower.

It clearly appears that the poorer credit card terms draw out a worse set of borrowers and that this adverse selection cannot be seen in the observable characteristics of the borrowers that the banks could observe before making the loan.

Table 23.2   Market Experiment 1 (Respondent Characteristics)

Treatment	Resp Rate Income	Income	Gold Credit	Limit	Rev. Balance	Rev. Limit	Util Rate	Debt Burden
A. Intro rate 4.9%—6mo	0.01073	43019.20	0.8397	6446	5240.32	19209.26	0.32172	0.13371
B. Intro rate 5.9%—6mo	0.00903	41896.14	0.80177	6206.90	4923.39	18987.80	0.31520	0.13470
C. Intro rate 6.9%—6mo	0.00687	41232.76	0.00058	5972.54	4806.17	16677.68	0.33707	0.13058
D. Intro rate 7.9%—6mo	0.00645	39702.43	0.76744	5827.24	5152.29	16421.54	0.35056	0.14278
E. Intro rate 6.9%—9mo	0.00992	41782.08	0.81149	6278.99	5247.73	18161.04	0.33360	0.14185
F. Intro rate 7.9%—12mo	0.00944	42122.87	0.82309	6295.60	5768.35	18039.49	0.35175	0.14874

Market Solutions to the Adverse Selection Problem: Market Signaling

When the insurance market in our model society failed because of moral hazard, the insurance companies instituted a deductible provision in their policies that helped them solve the problem by forcing customers to share in the risk against which they were being insured. As we will see in this section, the market also provides a solution to the adverse selection problem—market signaling, which indicates the hidden characteristics of a class of agents in the market. However, we will find that this solution is not totally satisfactory.

The problem of adverse selection has made it impossible for safe people to obtain insurance at a price they consider acceptable. Because the insurance industry could not successfully identify these people as good risks, it was forced to charge them the average loss rate of $2.60 rather than the rate of $0.80 that is appropriate for good risks. This situation raises the following question: Is there a way that the good risks in the population can signal the insurance industry that they own safe ladders so that they can buy insurance at a lower cost? Remember that there is only a 10% chance that safe people will have an accident, which is why the expected cost of insuring them is only $0.80; but there is a 40% chance that risky people will have an accident, which is why the expected cost of insuring them is at the high level of $3.20.

To illustrate how the people who own the safe ladder might successfully signal this information, let us say that the insurance industry sets up a school that will provide instruction in the safe operation of ladders. We will assume that, as a public service, the insurance industry pays the tuition of anyone who wants to attend the school. Thus, the only cost of attending the school is the opportunity cost that people must bear because the time spent at the school could be used to earn a living. Let us also assume that the market options of safe people are worse than the market options of risky people; and, consequently, safe people have lower opportunity costs.

Both safe and risky people must decide whether to attend the school. Will such attendance serve as a signal that a particular person is safe or risky? Obviously, if only safe people go to the school, then school attendance will function as a reliable signal that the insurance companies can use to set their rates. However, if both safe and risky people enroll in the school, then school attendance will serve no signaling purpose at all. Whether a safe or risky person attends the school will depend on the cost of doing so and the insurance premium savings that will result if signaling is successful.

Another way to envision this situation is as a game between the safe and risky people in which their strategies are to attend the school or not and their payoffs are the prices they are charged for insurance after they and all others have made their schooling choice. If there is a Nash equilibrium for this signaling game in which only safe (or only risky) people go to the school, then it is a **separating equilibrium** and insurance companies will be able to set their prices by observing whether a person has attended the school or not. Given the costs and benefits of attending the school, if both risky and safe people do so, then a **pooling equilibrium** exists and school attendance is no longer an informative signal.

The Conditions for a Separating Equilibrium in a Signaling Game.

Our analysis of signaling in the insurance market leads to the following proposition: If the opportunity cost of attending school for risky people is greater than $2.40 and the opportunity cost of attending school for safe people is less than $0.20, then a separating equilibrium exists in which only safe people will go to the school and only risky people will not.

To prove this proposition, let us say that the opportunity cost of attending the school is $2.80 for risky people and $0.15 for safe people. We will also say that at these opportunity costs, all safe people go to school and all risky people do not, which means that the insurance companies can use schooling as a signal. If the insurance industry is competitive, the presence of this signal will force it to charge each safe person a price of $0.80 for insurance and each risky person a price of $3.20. Hence, our proposition claims that in such a situation, given the opportunity costs of attending the school and the insurance prices faced by each group, if all safe people go to school and all risky ones do not, no safe or risky person will want to change his or her schooling decision. To see that this is true, let us look first at the safe people. By attending school, they pay an opportunity cost of $0.15 and a price of $0.80 for insurance. Thus, they pay a total of $0.95. If they drop out of the school, the insurance companies will assume that they are not safe and charge them a price of $3.20. Hence, they are better off staying in the school because they can buy insurance more cheaply that way. Even after we add the opportunity cost of attending the school to the price charged by the insurance companies, the final cost of insurance for these people ($0.95) is less than the maximum of $1 they are willing to pay for insurance. As a result, they will want to attend the school. (We can now see why $0.20 is the cutoff point for the opportunity cost of attending the school for safe people. An opportunity cost of $0.20 plus an insurance price of $0.80 equals $1, the maximum that safe people are willing to pay for insurance.)

Risky people pay a price of $3.20 for insurance but have no opportunity cost because they do not attend the school. If they were to change their decision about school, they would have an opportunity cost of $2.80. The insurance industry would then classify them as safe people and charge them a price of $0.80 for insurance. However, this change would actually raise the final cost of insurance for risky people. They would have to pay a total of $3.60 ($2.80 + $0.80) instead of the $3.20 they are currently paying with no school attendance. Hence, given opportunity costs of less than $0.20 for safe people and more than $2.40 for risky people, a separating equilibrium exists for the signaling game in the insurance market.

Is There a Pooling Equilibrium?

Under these conditions, there is no pooling equilibrium for the signaling game. At the pooling equilibrium, risky people would have to pay $2.60 for insurance and $2.80 to attend the school. However, if they do not attend school, they are identified as risky people and have a total cost of only $3.20 for insurance. Hence, risky people would never participate in a pooling equilibrium in which everyone attends the school. What about a pooling equilibrium in which no one attends the school? This type of pooling equilibrium for the signaling game in the insurance market will also not exist, but for a slightly different reason.

---

separating equilibrium
An equilibrium where different types play differently so their types can be inferred by their actions.

pooling equilibrium
An equilibrium to a game of incomplete information where players of different types take identical actions so that others are not able to learn their types from observing the actions they take.

Let us say that no one attends the school, and both safe people and risky people pay $2.60 for insurance. (Note that the price of insurance is the same if everyone attends the school or no one attends the school. In either case, schooling or the lack of schooling does not send an informative signal about any individual to the market.) Now let us say that the insurance companies will interpret a decision to attend the school as proof that the individual who is doing so is a safe person. In such a situation, a safe person will want to go to the school because, as we saw previously, that person will pay the low premium rate of $0.80 and have a total cost of insurance of only $0.95, which is clearly better than the $2.60 currently being paid. Hence, if no one goes to the school, safe people will want to deviate and do so.

Does Market Signaling Produce Pareto-Optimal Results? Note that in the situation we just examined, the existence of a potential signal that one group can buy insurance at a lower cost than the other group allows the existing market failure to be eliminated. Note also that the safe people are the main beneficiaries of this signaling because they are now able to purchase insurance, whereas previously they were not. The risky people are worse off. Before the creation of the school, they paid $2.60 for insurance, but now they are paying $3.20 at the separating equilibrium. Hence, the institution of market signaling does not produce Pareto-optimal results. Signaling is not a Pareto-improving institution. Some people are helped, but others are hurt. Furthermore, there is no guarantee that such a separating equilibrium will even exist. In our simple setting, the existence of a separating equilibrium requires that the opportunity costs of safe and risky people be sufficiently different, and this may not always be the case. Hence, while market signaling may provide a solution to the adverse selection problem, it is no panacea.

SOLVED PROBLEM 23.4

Question (Application and Extension: Self-Selections)

Miller's, a producer of fur coats, wishes to hire a salesperson. Fur coats are sold for $1,000 each. A good salesperson can sell 50 coats a month, and a bad salesperson can sell only 10. Salespeople at Miller's earn a base salary of $1,000 each month plus a commission per coat sold. If we assume that good salespeople can earn $5,000 a month at another job and bad salespeople can earn $2,000 a month at another job, in what range must the commission percentage fall if Miller's wishes to hire only good salespeople and if it can't tell good salespeople from bad during the initial interview?

Answer

Let c be the commission percentage. Good salespeople will work for Miller's only if

$$\$5,000 \le \$1,000 + (50)(1,000)c$$
$$c \ge \frac{4,000}{50,000} = 8\%$$

Bad salespeople will not want to work for Miller's if

$$\$2,000 \ge \$1,000 + (10)(1,000)c$$
$$c \le \frac{1,000}{10,000} = 10\%$$

So if Miller's wishes to hire only good salespeople, it must offer a commission on sales between 8% and 10%.

Adverse Selection in Employment: The Institution of Tipping

Employers face a problem that is similar to one that insurance companies face. While insurance companies must be able to distinguish between good and bad risks, employers must be able to distinguish between good and bad workers. If employers can identify good (high productivity) workers, they can offer higher wages to such workers than they offer to bad (low productivity) workers. It might even be possible for employers to hire only good workers. However, if employers cannot distinguish between good and bad workers, then they must offer all workers a wage that reflects the *average* productivity of all workers in the population. Such a wage may be too low to attract good workers. If this happens, the labor market will fail. Although there are employers who are willing to pay high wages to good workers, such employers cannot identify the good workers and therefore end up hiring only bad workers who will accept a low wage.

Based on our previous discussion of signaling in the insurance industry, it might seem logical to consider signaling as a market solution for the problem of adverse selection in employment. For example, if we develop a signaling model to deal with this problem, we would probably expect good workers to attend some type of post-secondary school (perhaps a college or a vocational school) in order to obtain a credential that sets them apart from the bad workers. If the cost of education is lower for good workers, we might expect to find a separating equilibrium for this model, just as we did for the signaling model we constructed for the insurance industry. However, societies are very resourceful, and they often find several different institutional solutions for a particular problem they face. To illustrate how an adverse selection problem in employment may be solved by the creation of a non-signaling institution, let us examine the employment situation in the restaurant industry.

Adverse Selection in the Restaurant Industry. Let us assume that there is a restaurant in our society that serves only one type of meal—a fried chicken dinner. The restaurant needs ten waiters and therefore places an advertisement in the help wanted section of a local newspaper. When applicants arrive at the restaurant, the owner is unable to identify whether they are good waiters or bad waiters. In this case, good waiters can serve ten meals a night, while bad waiters are capable of serving only five meals a night. The restaurant is very popular and normally serves 100 meals a night. If the owner hires ten good waiters, they should have no trouble handling the typical nightly workload.

We will also assume that good waiters are not only capable of serving ten meals a night but are also more able people all around and hence have better outside opportunities for employment than bad waiters. We will call the outside opportunity wage of the good waiters w_g and the outside opportunity wage of the bad waiters w_b. Finally, let us assume that the owner of the restaurant cannot afford to hire bad waiters because a reputation for bad service will ruin her business.

Question (Application and Extension: Lemons)

SOLVED PROBLEM 23.5

Izzy's Auto Sales deals in used cars. Used cars are either of good or bad quality. Izzy values good cars at $5,000 and bad ones at $1,000. Consumers value good-quality cars at $8,000 and bad-quality ones at $1,500. Consumers cannot determine the quality of a car until they buy it, but they do know that 50% of available used cars are good quality and 50% are bad quality. Izzy is aware of the quality of his cars, but he will not reveal this information. How much would a risk-neutral consumer be willing to pay for a car on Izzy's lot? At this price, would Izzy be willing to sell both types of cars? What if the population of cars were split—60% good and 40% bad?

Answer

A consumer's expected value for a car is

$$(0.50)(8,000) + (0.50)(1,500) = \$4,750$$

Because this is the maximum the consumer would be willing to pay for a car if he or she doesn't know its quality, Izzy will put only bad-quality cars on his lot. The good-quality cars are worth more to him than consumers are willing to pay.

If the population of good and bad cars were 60% and 40%, respectively, rather than 50% and 50%, consumers would be willing to pay

$$(0.60)(8,000) + (0.40)(1,500) = \$5,400$$

In this case, Izzy would put both types of car on the lot.

Tipping and Self-Selection: Will Tipping Allow a Restaurant to Separate the Good Waiters from the Bad Waiters?

There are two employment policies that a restaurant can use. It can pay each waiter a salary (S) and allow no tipping, or it can pay each waiter a smaller salary (S_L) and allow tipping. When tipping occurs, we will assume that it is equal to 15% of the price of each meal, which we will say is P. The final nightly income for a waiter when there is no tipping is S whether the waiter is good or bad. When there is tipping, the final nightly income is $S_L + (10 \cdot P \cdot 0.15)$ for good waiters and $S_L + (5 \cdot P \cdot 0.15)$ for bad waiters. (Note that good waiters do not receive better tips from their customers; they simply serve more meals.) Can tipping enable the restaurant to attract only good waiters by discouraging the bad ones from applying for a job? Will tipping allow the restaurant to maximize its profits?

We will assume that the outside opportunity wage of good waiters is greater than the outside opportunity wage of bad waiters: $w_b < w_g$. Hence, if a restaurant does not allow tipping and sets salary S below w_b, it will attract no waiters at all. If it sets salary S between w_b and w_g, then it will attract only bad waiters, while if it sets salary S equal to or greater than w_g, it will attract both good and bad waiters. However, for the restaurant, a salary of w_b is better than any salary between w_b and w_g. All salaries in that range will attract only bad waiters (and hence will allow the restaurant to serve only 50 meals a night), but a salary of w_b will at least minimize the costs of the restaurant.

If the restaurant wants to attract good waiters, then its best policy would be to set a salary of w_g because that is the lowest salary at which it can obtain such waiters. Note, however, that by setting a salary of w_g, the restaurant will attract *both* good and bad waiters. If we assume that the population contains an equal number of good and bad waiters, we would expect the applicants to reflect this distribution. The restaurant will then hire five good waiters and five bad waiters and be able to serve 75 meals each night (ten meals each by the five good waiters and five meals each by the five bad waiters). The profits from setting a salary of w_b are $\pi_{wb} = P \cdot 50 - 10w_b$, and the profits from setting a salary of w_g are $\pi_{wb} = P \cdot 75 - 10w_g$.

Although good waiters serve more customers, it is costly for the restaurant to have to pay the same high wage to all waiters, both the good ones and the bad ones. It is profitable to set the high wage only if $\pi_{wg} = P \cdot 75 - 10w_g > \pi_{wb} =$

$P \cdot 50 - 10w_b$ or only if $w_g - w_b \leq P(75 - 50)/10 = 2.5P$. Thus, if there is no tipping, the best policy for the restaurant is to set a high salary of w_g only if the difference between the outside opportunity wages of the waiters is less than 2.5 times the price of a meal.

Under what conditions will a worker want to be a waiter at the restaurant rather than taking an outside employment opportunity? Clearly, with no tipping, good waiters will offer their services to the restaurant only if $S \geq w_g$, and bad waiters will do the same only if $S \geq w_b$. When tipping is permitted, good waiters will agree to work at the restaurant only if $S_L + (10 \cdot P \cdot 0.15) \geq w_g$, while bad waiters will agree to work at the restaurant only if $S_L + (5 \cdot P \cdot 0.15) \geq w_b$. Hence, when the restaurant allows tipping, it can set the base salary of its waiters low enough so that only the good waiters will find it advantageous to work there. The bad waiters will decide to take their best outside employment opportunities. As we can now see, tipping is a mechanism that makes it possible for the restaurant to separate the good waiters from the bad waiters.

To see how this policy might work, let us assume that $w_g = \$4$, $w_b = \$3$, $S_L = \$1$, and $P = \$2$. Seeing this base salary and knowing their abilities as waiters, applicants will decide to take a job at the restaurant or work elsewhere. A good waiter will earn $S_L + [(10)(\$2)(0.15)] = 1 + \$3 = \$4$, while a bad waiter will earn $S_L + [(5)(\$2)(0.15)] = \$2.50$. Given these parameters, the good waiters will be indifferent between working at the restaurant and working elsewhere because they earn \$4 in each case. The bad waiters will strictly prefer to work elsewhere. Hence, if the restaurant allows tipping, it will attract only good waiters.

The restaurant will institute a tipping policy if the profits from such a policy are greater than the profits from just paying a salary to the waiters. We know that when the restaurant pays only a salary, it will set that salary at w_g and therefore will attract both good and bad waiters. Its profits will be $\pi(salary) = [(75)(\$2) - 10w_g] = [(75)(\$2) - (10)(\$4)] = \$110$. With a policy of tipping, however, its profits will be $\pi(tipping) = [(100)(\$2) - 10S_L] = [(100)(\$2) - 10] = \$190$.

Given the parameters of this simple example, it is clear that if the restaurant institutes a policy of tipping, it will solve its adverse selection problem and simultaneously maximize its profits. Note that the restaurant industry and other industries created the institution of tipping to solve a recurrent adverse selection problem in employment. While signaling could have been used to solve this problem, tipping illustrates an important point. Societies develop a variety of different institutions to help them solve the same types of problems. Finally, we should note that tipping is a *nonmarket solution* to the problem of adverse selection in employment. Tipping changes the institution by which people are paid, but it does not create a new market to rectify the inefficient outcome from adverse selection in employment.

Moral Hazard and Adverse Selection: Expert Opinion in the Car Repair Business

Although automobiles provide a very useful means of transportation, they sometimes present maintenance problems for their owners. To help the owners deal with these problems, certain individuals have established themselves as car repair experts. If a car breaks down, the owner takes it to one of these experts for a diagnosis of the problem and an estimate of the cost of the repairs that the expert says are necessary. If the owner agrees, the expert then makes the repairs. This process would be quite simple if all experts were competent in diagnosing the problems and offered honest opinions. However, if we are realistic, we must assume that this is not the case. Let us say that one-half of the car repair experts are competent, by which we mean that they always make a correct diagnosis, and the other half of the car repair experts are incompetent, by which we mean that they sometimes make mistakes. (We will assume that they are incorrect 20% of the time.)

When a car breaks down, most owners must rely on the judgment of an expert about what repairs are necessary because they have no knowledge of the inner workings of their vehicles. This ignorance on the part of the car owners provides an incentive for the experts to lie. Economists analyze this type of situation by saying that there is **asymmetric information** in the market. The experts understand the problems, but the car owners do not. In other words, the buyers and sellers in this market have different amounts of information.

Let us say that problems with cars fall into two categories: major problems and minor problems. A major problem costs a great deal of money to repair, and a minor problem costs very little. Because of the asymmetric information in this market, the expert may be tempted to tell an owner whose car has a minor problem that it is a major problem, charge a large amount for the repair, and then simply fix the minor problem. If the car runs properly after the repair, the owner will be satisfied and will never know about the misrepresentation. Hence, asymmetric information causes *moral hazard* for car repair experts. They are tempted to lie to their customers in order to earn more money than is justified by the amount of repair work actually needed.

Owners of cars are aware that moral hazard exists in the car repair market. They also know that some experts are honest but incompetent. As a result, car owners often seek opinions from several experts and decide what repairs to make only after they consider all the opinions they have collected. Obviously, this search for information can be costly. For example, it costs the owners something if they have to take time off from work whenever they must take their cars to an expert. Hence, car owners will continue to seek information until the marginal cost of obtaining one more opinion equals the expected marginal benefit from the information contained in that opinion. The marginal benefit arises from the added probability that the car owners will make the correct decision about what repairs are needed.

Determining the Equilibrium of the Car Repair Market

At this point, it is logical to ask what the equilibrium honesty level of firms will be in the car repair market. Will the dishonest experts eliminate the honest ones because their lies make it impossible for the honest experts to earn profits, or will there be a mixture of honest and dishonest experts at the equilibrium of the market? The adverse selection problem raised here is similar to the adverse selection problem involving good and bad waiters. We want to know whether honest and dishonest experts can coexist in the car repair market, just as we wanted to know whether good and bad waiters can coexist in the restaurant industry.

In order to find the equilibrium of the car repair market, it is helpful to think of this market as a game between the experts and the car owners. In such a game, the experts must choose an honesty level h, where $0 \leq h \leq 1$ determines the degree to which they will be honest (the fraction of time they will report honestly to the car owners). The car owners must choose a strategy for obtaining information and reaching a decision about what repairs to make. The payoffs to the experts will depend on how many cars they fix and how many owners they can deceive, while the payoffs to the owners will depend on how honestly and competently their car repairs are made. An equilibrium for this market (or game) will be an honesty level for competent and incompetent experts and a strategy of

asymmetric information
When the buyers and sellers in a market have different amounts of information.

information search and decision making for car owners such that the following conditions are present:

1. Given the honesty level of incompetent experts and the strategy of information search and decision making of the car owners, no competent expert will wish to change his or her honesty level.

2. Given the honesty level of competent experts and the strategy of information search and decision making of the car owners, no incompetent expert will wish to change his or her honesty level.

3. Given the honesty levels of competent and incompetent experts, no car owner will wish to change his or her strategy of information search and decision making.

A substantial amount of analysis is needed to determine the equilibrium of the car repair market under the conditions just described. However, we can summarize certain obvious points in two propositions.

No All-Competent and All-Honest Equilibrium Exists. This proposition states that the car repair market can never have an equilibrium in which all experts are both competent and honest. It is quite simple to prove this proposition. Let us say that all car repair experts are expected to be competent and honest. In such a situation, there would be no incentive for car owners to search for opinions because they would expect to receive the same diagnosis from all the experts. Hence, car owners would seek just one opinion and believe that opinion. However, if this is the procedure the owners use, we can expect that some experts will lie because they know that their opinions will never be checked. Thus, an equilibrium in which car repair experts are all competent and honest can never exist.

An All-Dishonest Equilibrium Exists. This proposition states that the car repair market can always have an equilibrium in which all experts are dishonest. It is also quite easy to prove this proposition. If all experts are dishonest, they will always tell owners that their cars have a major problem. Faced with this fact, the owners will not want to obtain other opinions because they know that all opinions will be dishonest. The owners will therefore have car repairs made on the basis of their own analysis of what is wrong. Clearly, because the owners are not experts, they will make a lot of bad decisions.

Is This a Case for Government Intervention?

Faced with such a bleak outlook in regard to honesty and competence, government leaders might decide that a market like the car repair market requires government intervention. They know that such a recommendation will stir an ideological debate, but they are prepared to argue that the consumer must be protected. However, before taking any action, the government leaders seek advice from a consulting firm. This firm bases its opinions on the experimental work of Carolyn Pitchik and Andrew Schotter.[1]

---

[1] Carolyn Pitchik is an economist at the University of Toronto. The work summarized here was done jointly by Pitchik and Andrew Schotter and appears in Carolyn Pitchik and Andrew Schotter, "Norms and Competition in Markets with Asymmetric Information: An Experimental Study of the Development of Industry Ethics," *Metroeconomica*, vol. 2, 1994.

CONSULTING REPORT   23.1

DETERMINING WHETHER GOVERNMENT INTERVENTION CAN INCREASE LEVELS OF COMPETENCE AND HONESTY

The consultants explain that *licensing* and *price controls* are two common forms of government intervention in markets where there are problems of incompetence and/or dishonesty. A licensing law requires that people who practice certain professions such as medicine and dentistry and certain trades such as auto mechanics and plumbing must obtain a license before they can offer their services to the public. Typically, an applicant for a license must successfully complete a specified educational program or training program and must achieve a passing grade on a licensing examination. The primary purpose of licensing laws is to ensure an adequate level of competence in the market.

Price control laws limit the prices that can be charged for specified types of goods and services. These laws are intended to combat dishonesty by making it less profitable for firms to lie.

The experimental work of Pitchik and Schotter indicates that licensing can have significant beneficial effects on a market by increasing the levels of competence and honesty. Pitchik and Schotter concluded that licensing is a more effective form of government intervention than price controls. ●

RESOLVING
TEASER 23

MORAL HAZARD AND THE PITCHIK-SCHOTTER EXPERIMENTS

Pitchik and Schotter conducted a set of experiments to see if two types of government intervention—licensing and price controls—can increase the levels of competence and honesty in a market. They recruited college undergraduates as subjects for the experiments. They brought these subjects into a laboratory where they had them play a game very similar to the game involving the car repair market that we discussed in this chapter. Each subject was assigned one of the following three roles: a competent car repair expert, an incompetent car repair expert, and the owner of a malfunctioning car who is seeking opinions about what repairs the car needs. The experts earned money by giving opinions (which, of course, were fictitious), and the car owners earned money by deciding what repairs to make. The better the decisions of the car owners, the more money they earned. The results of these experiments are summarized in the sections that follow.

The Effects of Licensing

The goal of a licensing policy in the car repair market is to decrease the fraction of incompetent experts (firms) and to increase the level of honesty. Pitchik and Schotter performed two experiments to test the effects of a licensing policy. They established a market of six firms in each of these experiments. The market in experiment 1 consisted of three competent firms and three incompetent firms, while the market in experiment 2 was made up of four competent firms and two incompetent firms. Because the market in the second experiment had a higher proportion of competent firms, Pitchik and Schotter reasoned that comparing the results of the two markets would be equivalent to comparing the effects of a licensing policy that reduces the number of incompetent firms in the market.

Table 23.3 shows that the licensing policy has an unambiguously beneficial effect. The mean honesty levels of both the competent and incompetent firms rise when the proportion of competent firms in the market increases from one-half to two-thirds. For the competent firms, the mean honesty level rises from 71% in experiment 1 to 77% in

(Continued)

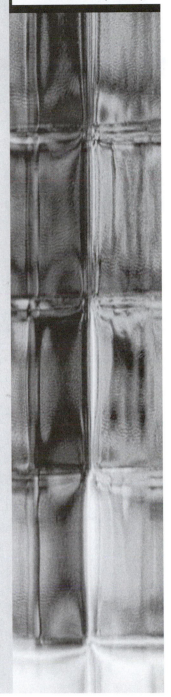

experiment 2. For the incompetent firms, the level rises from 71% in experiment 1 to 79% in experiment 2.[2] Consequently, Pitchik and Schotter concluded that, in their experiments, licensing had a significant beneficial effect on the honesty of firms.

The Effects of Price Controls

The next phase of the Pitchik-Schotter experiments was to study the effects of price controls on the honesty levels of markets. Pitchik and Schotter again used two experimental markets. However, in this case, one market had a significantly higher price for the most costly type of repair than the other market. The experimenters reasoned that by comparing the results obtained from these two markets, they would be able to assess the impact of government efforts to use price controls as a means of increasing the level of honesty.

The two simulated markets involved in this part of the study were identical except for the fact that the most costly type of repair had a higher price in experiment 2 than in experiment 3. Hence, the market in experiment 3 functioned like a market in which the price of a major repair had been administratively reduced. The results that emerged from these experiments were paradoxical, as Table 23.4 shows.

In Table 23.4, we see that the reduction in the price of the major repair that occurs in experiment 3 has an unambiguously detrimental effect on the levels of honesty in

Table 23.3	The Effects of Licensing: A Comparison of the Results of Experiments 1 and 2 Conducted by Pitchik and Schotter.		
	Experiment 1	**Experiment 2**	**Difference**
Mean Honesty of Competent Firms	0.71	0.77	0.06
Variance	0.05	0.04	
Number of Observations	20	30	
Mean Honesty of Incompetent Firms	0.71	0.79	0.08
Variance	0.02	0.02	
Number of Observations	40	30	

Table 23.4	The Effects of Price Controls: A Comparison of the Results of Experiments 2 and 3 Conducted by Pitchik and Schotter.		
	Experiment 2	**Experiment 3**	**Difference**
Mean Honesty of Competent Firms	0.77	0.68	0.09
Variance	0.04	0.05	
Number of Observations	30	30	
Mean Honesty of Incompetent Firms	0.79	0.69	0.10
Variance	0.02	0.02	
Number of Observations	30	30	

(Continued)

---

[2] These differences were found to be statistically significant at the 6% level for competent firms and the 4% level for incompetent firms using a Wilcoxon-Mann-Whitney one-tailed test. Such a statistical test investigates whether we can accept the hypothesis that the samples of honesty levels that we observed in these two experiments came from populations with the same mean or average honesty. Saying that they are significantly different means that we can reject the hypothesis that experiments 1 and 2 had mean honesty levels that were the same.

RESOLVING
TEASER 23 *(Contd.)*

the market. The mean honesty levels of both the competent and incompetent firms fall. For the competent firms, the mean honesty level decreases from 77% in experiment 2 to 68% in experiment 3. For the incompetent firms, the level decreases from 79% in experiment 2 to 69% in experiment 3.[3]

These results are paradoxical because we usually expect that a reduction in price will have beneficial effects for consumers. However, this perception does not take into account the secondary aspects of the situation. For example, a fall in the price of a major repair implies that there is also a decrease in the cost of mistakenly having a major repair done when a minor repair would have been sufficient. Hence, the fall in the price of a major repair makes consumers less cautious about agreeing to such a repair. They are less likely to carry out a thorough search for information (seek many opinions from different experts) in order to avoid a mistake, and they are more likely to make a quick decision. Under these circumstances, it is reasonable to expect that some firms will take advantage of the letdown in consumer vigilance and will lower their level of honesty.

Table 23.5 indicates the average number of information searches by the car owners in these experiments and the average number of opinions they obtained from experts before they were willing to agree to a major repair.

Table 23.5 shows that the car owners tended to make fewer searches for information in experiment 3 than in experiment 2. The mean number of information searches decreased from 2.11 to 1.96.[4] In addition, the car owners tended to agree more easily to a major repair in experiment 3. The mean number of expert opinions that they used before deciding to make a major repair decreased from 2.03 to 1.66.[5]

What conclusion can we draw from the paradoxical results of these experiments? It may be that price controls are a "two-edged sword" in terms of consumer welfare. Lower prices increase welfare by allowing consumers to purchase more goods for a given amount of money, but higher prices may cause consumers to be more diligent in seeking information about possible purchases and more careful in the decisions they make about their purchases. Apparently, the secondary effects of lower prices were dominant in experiment 3.

Table 23.5	The Information Search and Decision-Making Behavior of Consumers: A Comparison of Experiments 2 and 3 Conducted by Pitchik and Schotter.		
	Experiment 2	**Experiment 3**	**Difference**
Mean Number of Information Searches per Consumer	2.11	1.96	0.15
Variance	0.41	0.34	
Mean Number of Expert Opinions Needed to Decide on a Major Repair	2.03	1.66	0.37
Variance	0.57	0.45	

(Continued)

---

[3] These differences were statistically significant at the 10% level for competent firms and at the 3% level for incompetent firms.

[4] While this decrease was small in absolute terms, it was statistically significant at the 16% level, using a Wilcoxon-Mann-Whitney one-tailed test.

[5] This difference was significant at the 8% level, using the Wilcoxon-Mann-Whitney test.

Based on these experiments, Pitchik and Schotter advocate the use of licensing as a means of increasing competence and honesty in markets, such as the car repair market, where one side (the buyers) must depend on the technical knowledge of the other side (the sellers).

A Free-Market Rebuttal to the Pitchik-Schotter Recommendation

The Pitchik-Schotter recommendation is more interventionist than many free-market advocates would want. They would argue that there is no need for government intervention because free-market forces can be relied on to rectify the problems of incompetence and dishonesty. Theoretically, it may be impossible to have total honesty and competence at the market equilibrium, but it is possible to have high levels of honesty. Advocates of the free-market solution point out that even in the Pitchik-Schotter experiments, honesty levels averaged more than 70% before intervention. Such levels might not be so bad as to require intervention.

Free-market advocates would also suggest that we use signaling to solve problems of adverse selection. For example, firms might try to signal their competence and honesty by offering guarantees on their work and by building a reputation for good work and fair dealing in the community. Finally, in a field like car repair, firms providing only diagnostic services might develop. These firms would not do any repair work and therefore would have no incentive to recommend unnecessary repairs to car owners. Such an arrangement would remove the moral hazard problem that currently exists in the car repair field. With a variety of market safeguards available, free-market advocates feel that licensing and other types of government intervention are not needed to ensure competence and honesty in markets.

Conclusion

In this chapter, the idea that perfectly competitive markets are such an adaptable institution that they can handle all economic problems has suddenly come into doubt. This doubt will grow in succeeding chapters. While a lack of information caused market failure here and led to a conflict between supporters of interventionist solutions and supporters of free-market solutions, we will see similar dilemmas develop when we examine problems such as externalities and public goods in coming chapters.

Summary

This chapter has presented an analysis of what happens in an economy when a perfectly competitive market cannot be relied on to yield Pareto-optimal results. We saw how such a market failure can arise because of incomplete information and asymmetric distribution of information and how informational deficiencies lead to problems of moral hazard and adverse selection. We investigated several market solutions to these problems: signaling, self-selection, and reputation building. We found that such solutions are created within a market by its participants. For example, the practice of tipping in the restaurant industry is a market-generated solution to an adverse selection problem in the employment of waiters.

We also examined licensing and price controls, two forms of government intervention that are sometimes used to deal with the moral hazard problem that arises in markets like the car repair market where consumers with little or no technical knowledge must face experts. Finally, we reviewed a set of experiments that were conducted to test the effectiveness of licensing and price controls. The results of these experiments indicated that licensing has beneficial effects on a market but that price controls may produce secondary effects that cause a decrease in honesty levels rather than the intended increase.

Exercises and Problems

1. Consider a town that has equal numbers of two types of residents. The type 1 residents are careful people who conduct their daily affairs with reasonable caution. In contrast, the type 2 residents are careless people who often behave like "absent-minded professors." All the residents own identical houses that are currently worth $200,000, and all of them have a utility function of the following type: $u(\$0) = 0$, $u(\$50,000) = 4.5$, $u(\$75,000) = 6.5$, $u(\$100,000) = 10$, and $u(\$200,000) = 15$.

   All houses face the risk of fire. If a fire occurs, the resulting damage will be classified as either a total loss (worth $0) or a partial loss (worth $100,000). A type 1 (careful) resident has a 40% probability of no fire, a 40% probability of a fire that results in a total loss, and a 20% probability of a fire that results in a partial loss. A type 2 (careless) resident faces a 60% probability of total loss, a 30% probability of a partial loss, and a 10% probability of no loss.

   a) If *all* residents want to buy insurance, at what price would the insurance company be willing to sell it to them? (At what price would the premium equal the expected loss?) We will call this price the fair premium.

   b) Will both types of residents buy insurance at the fair premium that you calculated in part a? If not, determine which residents will purchase insurance, and calculate the resulting expected loss for the insurance company.

2. Suppose that a person wants to buy a used car. She knows that half of the available used cars are good cars and the other half are "lemons." She is willing to pay $10,000 for a good car and $2,000 for a lemon. Finally, assume that the seller values the car at $1,000 if it is a lemon and $6,000 if it is not a lemon.

   a) Assume that this buyer cannot distinguish the good cars from the bad cars. How much would she be willing to pay for any car?

   b) What types of cars will be offered for sale in the market at the price calculated in part a?

   c) Based on your answer in part b, calculate the ultimate equilibrium price of a car in this used-car market.

3. John M. Bezzle wants to start a business, and he therefore asks investors for money. When he receives the money, he can either use it in the business or embezzle it (use it for his own purposes). The business may succeed, with probability 2/3, or it may fail, with probability 1/3. If it fails, the investors receive a payoff of -100, no matter whether funds were embezzled or not. (We can express this payoff as -100.) A success will yield $500 if Bezzle is honest and $+\$100$ if he is dishonest. Assume that Bezzle will earn $100 more if he embezzles than if he is honest no matter what the outcome is.

a) Is there a moral hazard problem for the investors? If so, explain what it is.

b) Suppose that the investors specify the following terms in their contract with Bezzle: "We will pay you $20 if the outcome is a payoff of $+500$ or -100, but we will sue you for $10,000 if the outcome is a payoff of $+100$." Will this contract cause Bezzle to be honest? Why does the contract pay more for an outcome of -100 than an outcome of $+100$?

4. Assume that used-car dealers index the quality of the cars they sell by a parameter θ. This parameter is uniformly (equally) distributed in the interval $(b, 3b)$ for some number $b > 0$ so that the best car has an index that is three times the index of the worst car. The dealers know the quality of the cars they sell. If a dealer sells a car of quality θ at price P, the dealer's profit is $P - \theta$. Dealers will sell a car only if they are assured of making a positive profit.

If a buyer purchases a car of quality θ at price P, the buyer will make a profit of $k\theta - P$, where k is a constant no less than 1 and represents the fact that the buyer values quality more than the dealer does. Buyers cannot observe quality directly, but they infer the quality of a car from its price. Buyers will purchase a car only if they can expect a nonnegative profit. Because there are many buyers and few dealers in the market, any gains from trade are taken entirely by the dealers.

a) If P is the equilibrium price, what is the range of quality of the cars that will be traded in the market?

b) Determine the equilibrium price in terms of k and b.

c) Determine the equilibrium price and the fraction of cars that will be brought to the market when i) $k = 1.2$, ii) $k = 1$, and iii) $k = 1.5$.

d) Is the equilibrium ever the best, or is it always the second best? Explain carefully.

e) When $k = 3$, what is the equilibrium price and what fraction of cars will be traded in the market? *Note:* When a variable is uniformly distributed over an interval $[x, y]$, the mean value taken by that variable is $X = (x + y)/2$.

5. It has been observed that investment bankers in New York who ride bicycles for recreation or exercise face a greater risk of having their bikes stolen than professional bicycle messengers. Specifically, there is an 80% chance that a banker will lose a $1,000 bicycle during a given year but only a 20% chance that a messenger will lose a bicycle. An equal number of bankers and messengers own bicycles in New York.

a) If an insurance company cannot distinguish a banker from a messenger, it *must* therefore charge the same premium to everyone. What will the actuarially fair insurance premium be?

b) Let us say that bankers and messengers both have the logarithmic utility functions $u(C) = log\ C$ (they are risk averse), and they both earn $10,000 a year. Will the bankers and messengers purchase bicycle insurance at the fair premium? Explain.

c) Given the answer to part b, does the insurance company make any profits or incur any losses? (Remember that the insurance company exactly breaks even with a fair insurance policy.) If the insurance company does not break even, what should the premium be for a fair policy? Would the new premium cause the bankers and messengers to change their decisions about purchasing insurance?

   d) Suppose that the insurance company charges different premiums for bankers and messengers. Would the answers to parts a and b change?

6. The Happies, a family of four, bought a 100-year-old house that needs major renovations. They hired an architect who agreed to do the job for a fee that is equal to 10% of the total cost of the renovations.

   a) Does this contract create a moral hazard on the part of the architect? If so, explain what the moral hazard is.

   b) If you answered yes to part a, devise a contract that could avoid such a moral hazard.

7. Assume that there are two types of radios on the market: good radios and bad radios. Of the firms that manufacture radios, 50% produce good radios and 50% produce bad radios. A good radio does not break for five years, while a bad radio has a 50% chance of breaking when it is first used. If the bad radio does not break immediately, it works for five years, just like the good radio. A good radio is worth $100 to consumers, and a bad radio is worth nothing.

   a) What is the maximum price any consumer would be willing to pay for a radio if both types of firms produce radios?

   b) If it costs $55 to manufacture each radio, will any firms want to produce radios?

   c) If it costs $50 to manufacture each radio, which firms will want to produce radios?

   d) Suppose that it costs $50 to manufacture each radio and $20 to repair a broken radio. Also suppose that the firms that produce good radios give a warranty in which they promise to repair any radio that breaks within five years of purchase. If the price of radios were to rise above $50, which type of firm would issue a warranty? If the price rose to $60, which type of firm would offer a warranty? Can warranties signal quality? What is the equilibrium price for radios in the market?

8. Ed Bull works in a china shop and can choose to be either careful or careless (act like "a bull in a china shop"). If he is careful, there is a 50% chance that he will break some china. If he is careless, the chance of his breaking some china rises to 75%. If Ed breaks china, he will be fired and have no wealth; but if he avoids breaking any china, he will keep his job and have wealth of W. Ed dislikes being careful and values being careless by E, a lump sum of utility that is added to his utility of wealth function. He has a strictly concave utility of wealth function. Now let us assume that an insurance company decides to sell unemployment insurance to Ed. If he is fired, this insurance will restore his wealth to W.

   a) Suppose that the insurance company can observe Ed's actions. Thus, if any china is broken, the company will know whether Ed was careful or careless. Assume that π is the cost of each unit of insurance (that is, it costs π to insure one unit of wealth W). If $u(W/2) > u(W/4) + E$, show that an insurance contract that sets $\pi = \frac{1}{4}$ when Ed is careful and $\pi = \frac{3}{4}$ when Ed is careless will lead him to be careful and buy full insurance coverage (that is, buy W units of insurance for πW).

   b) Now, suppose that the insurance company cannot observe Ed's actions. As a result, if any china is broken, the company will not know whether Ed's carelessness caused the accident. Determine the optimal insurance contract in this situation.

Externalities: The Free Market–Interventionist Battle Continues

EXPERIMENTAL TEASER 24

GOVERNMENT INTERVENTION

Consider the following three methods of dealing with pollution. In method 1, we tax polluters for each unit of pollution they create. In the second, the government sets a standard or a limit to the amount of production allowed and presumably sets it optimally. Finally, in the third method the government runs a market for pollution permits where if a firm wants to produce, and therefore pollute the air, it has to buy a permit for each unit of pollution dumped. Which method do you think was the most successful when these three methods were compared in an experiment run by Charles Plott?*

---

* Charles Plott, "Externalities and Corrective Policies in Experimental Markets," *Economic Journal* 93 (1983): 106–27.

EXPERIMENTAL TEASER 25

THE COASE THEOREM

Say that I take an action, produce a product, and as a result of my production you are damaged; that is, I pollute your air. As we will see in this chapter, such a situation is called an externality. The question is how society can attain the optimal level of economic activity under these circumstances. One solution, the interventionist solution, is to have the government control the production of the polluter in some way—taxes, quotas, etc. Another way is to leave the parties alone and let them bargain. Presumably, if the damage created by the pollution were greater than the profits earned by production, the damaged party would be able to pay the polluter to stop producing or cut down on the amount. This would restore optimality without government intervention. This assertion is the logic behind the famous Coase theorem named for Ronald Coase, an economist at the University of Chicago.

Does this work? If left alone, will people solve their own externality problems? Consider the following experiment run by Elizabeth Hoffman and Matthew Spitzer ("The Coase Theorem: Some Experimental Tests," *Journal of Law and Economics 25* [1982]: 93–98.)

The experimenters brought pairs of subjects into a room, one pair at a time. One of the subjects in the pair was designated the controller by the flip of a coin. The subjects were then given a payoff schedule like that shown in Table 24.1. The controller was told that she had two options. She could pick a row unilaterally, in which case

(Continued)

EXPERIMENTAL TEASER 25 *(Contd.)*

Table 24.1   Payoff Schedule for the Hoffman-Spitzer Experiment.

Row Number	Controller	Noncontroller
1	$ 0.00	$12.00
2	$ 4.00	$10.00
3	$ 6.00	$ 6.00
4	$ 8.00	$ 4.00
5	$ 9.00	$ 2.00
6	$10.00	$ 1.00
7	$11.00	$ 0.00

she and her partner would receive the payoffs indicated. Alternatively, she and her partner could jointly select a row and then bargain as to how they would split the total payoff indicated in that row. Note that because the controller can affect the payoff received by her partner, her position is equivalent to that of an agent causing an externality.

Suppose that the controller unilaterally chooses row 7. In this case, she receives $11 and her partner receives nothing. The total payoff to the pair is $11. This choice is consistent with the competitive market outcome in a market with an externality.

Now let us assume that the controller selects row 2, which gives the pair a total payoff of $14. Because this is the highest possible total payoff, row 2 is the Pareto-optimal choice and the choice predicted by the Coase theorem. That is, from our discussion of the Coasian solution, we would expect the controller's partner to offer her sufficient compensation out of his payoff so that she will want to choose row 2. When this experiment was done, what do you think happened? Did the controller bargain and reach an efficient outcome with her pair member? Because the controller could guarantee herself $11 by unilaterally determining the outcome, do you think that any controllers ever agreed to an outcome where they received less than $11? Would concerns about fairness intervene here and cause a more even split of the $14?

Economic development brings great increases in the standard of living of all the inhabitants of our no-longer-primitive society. Unfortunately, it also brings a major problem—pollution. As our model society becomes more productive, its factories begin to pollute the air and water. At first, the pollution is tolerable and no one pays any attention to it. But after a number of years, it begins to have adverse effects on people's health and lifestyles. On bad days, pollutants in the air cause some people to have difficulty breathing and make almost everyone's eyes itch and burn. "No swimming" signs have been posted along the river because the water is so badly polluted. As a result of these events, some members of our model society have begun demanding that government leaders do something about the pollution problem. Others argue against government intervention, claiming that the economy can solve the pollution problem by itself if given the chance to do so. Thus, free-market advocates and interventionists are resuming the ideological battle that racked our model society in Chapter 22.

In this chapter, we will investigate the economic causes of such problems as pollution and the challenges they present to a free-market economy. We will then examine some solutions, both interventionist and noninterventionist, and evaluate the effectiveness of these solutions.

The Externality Problem Described

To understand the economic causes of social problems like pollution, we will make use of the society envisioned by Edward Dolan in his book *TANSTAAFL: Economic Strategy for the Environmental Crisis*.[1] This society produces only two products: clean water and paper. As Figure 24.1 shows, this society is situated on the banks of a river, with the paper mill upstream from the water treatment plant. Below the water treatment plant is the city, where all the people live.

This society has a problem because the paper mill dumps its wastes into the river, and such wastes make it more expensive for the water treatment plant to produce clean water for the inhabitants of the city. In other words, the paper mill imposes a cost on the water treatment plant. Because this cost has no direct effect on the paper mill, it is *external* to the paper mill. In general, we will use the term externality to describe any cost or benefit generated by one agent in its production or consumption activities but affecting another agent in the economy. The paper mill does not take the external cost created by its wastes into account when making its production decisions. As we will see shortly, this myopia causes the market to fail to determine an efficient outcome for society.

To make the situation more concrete, let us say that the paper mill is producing 10 tons of paper. Its marginal cost (the cost of the capital and labor required to produce an additional pound of paper) is \$0.005 per pound. Note that this is the

externality
Any cost or benefit generated by one agent in its production or consumption activities but affecting another agent in the economy.

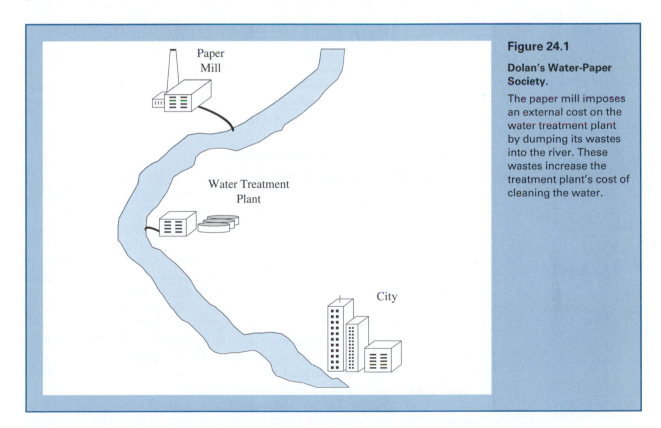

Figure 24.1

Dolan's Water-Paper Society.

The paper mill imposes an external cost on the water treatment plant by dumping its wastes into the river. These wastes increase the treatment plant's cost of cleaning the water.

---

[1] Edward Dolan, *TANSTAAFL: Economic Strategy for the Environmental Crisis* (New York: Holt, Rinehart & Winston, 1969), pp. 24–27. *TANSTAAFL* stands for "There ain't no such thing as a free lunch."

private marginal cost
Cost, excluding
externalities.

mill's private marginal cost. It does not include the external cost that the wastes from the mill impose on the water treatment plant. Assuming that paper production is a competitive industry, we know that the price of paper will be forced down to its marginal cost, so paper will sell for $0.005 per pound in this economy.

Now, let us say that the water treatment plant's marginal cost is $0.50 per 1,000 gallons when the paper mill is idle and therefore generating no waste. (This is the cost of the capital and labor needed to treat the unpolluted river water to make it suitable for drinking.) However, when the paper mill is operating, the water treatment plant has an additional cost of $0.05 per 1,000 gallons for each ton of paper produced. Because the paper mill is currently producing 10 tons of paper, the cost of treating the river water has increased by $0.50 per 1,000 gallons— 10 tons · $0.05 per ton = $0.50. Adding this marginal externality cost of $0.50 per 1,000 gallons to the water treatment plant's marginal cost for capital and labor inputs of $0.50 per 1,000 gallons raises its total marginal cost to $1 per 1,000 gallons. Assuming that water treatment is a competitive industry, the price of water will be $1 per 1,000 gallons, or $0.001 per gallon. At this price, let us assume that 1 million gallons are demanded, so society spends $1,000 on water.

The Effects of an Externality on Output

Given the externality created by the paper mill's wastes, can we expect our model society to produce Pareto-optimal amounts of clean water and paper? (Recall from Chapters 21 and 22 that a Pareto-optimal outcome requires that there be no other amounts of clean water and paper that, if produced, would make someone in society better off without making anyone worse off.) Intuitively, we might expect the answer to be no. The paper mill is imposing an additional cost on the water treatment plant, but there is no mechanism to make the mill accountable for this cost, so it seems unlikely that the outcome for society will be Pareto optimal. Indeed, it is not. To understand why this is so, we must analyze the problem.

Another Look at the Conditions for a Pareto-Optimal Outcome

In Chapter 22, we saw that there are three conditions that must be met by a perfectly competitive economy for the outcome it determines to be Pareto optimal. In our water-paper economy, the first condition is that the marginal rate of substitution of paper for water must be the same for each individual in the society. That is, $MRS^1_{w \text{ for } p} = MRS^2_{w \text{ for } p} = \cdots = MRS^i_{w \text{ for } p}$, where $MRS^i_{w \text{ for } p}$ is the marginal rate of substitution for person i. For each person, the marginal rate of substitution is equal to the ratio of the marginal utility of paper to the marginal utility of water, which is in turn equal to the ratio of the price of paper to the price of water. That is, $MRS_{w \text{ for } p} = MU_p/MU_w = P_p/P_w$. In our model society, the price of paper is $0.005 per pound and the price of water is $0.001 per gallon, so $P_p/P_w = \$0.005/\$0.001 = \frac{5}{1}$. If we assume that each consumer is maximizing his or her utility, then all consumers will set their marginal rates of substitution so that they are equal to the same price ratio, $\frac{5}{1}$. Thus, our first condition is met.

The second condition has to do with production inputs. It requires that the marginal rate of technical substitution of the paper mill be equal to that of the water treatment plant. We need not concern ourselves with this condition at the present time.

It is in fulfilling the third condition that our model society runs into trouble. This final condition states that the marginal rate of substitution of water for paper must equal the marginal rate of transformation of water for paper. That is,

$MRS_{w \text{ for } p} = MRT_{w \text{ for } p}$. The marginal rate of transformation is supposed to be equal to the ratio of the marginal cost of producing paper to the marginal cost of producing clean water. That is, $MRT_{w \text{ for } p} = MC_p/MC_w$. From our earlier discussion, we know that the marginal cost of producing paper is \$0.005 per pound and that the marginal cost of producing clean water is \$0.001 per gallon. The ratio of these costs is $\$0.005/\$0.001 = \frac{5}{1}$. Thus, at first glance, it would appear that $MRS = MRT = \frac{5}{1}$ and so our third condition is met. In reality, however, it is not met.

A marginal rate of transformation of $\frac{5}{1}$ implies that we must give up 5 gallons of water in order to obtain 1 more pound of paper. Unfortunately, this is not actually the case. To see why, let us take \$1 away from the production of clean water. *When the mill is producing 10 tons of paper*, the marginal cost of water production is \$0.001 per gallon. The water treatment plant will therefore be producing 1,000 fewer gallons of water, or 999,000 gallons instead of 1 million gallons. Our model society will then be spending only \$999 on water purchases.

Now let us give the \$1 to the paper mill. Because its marginal cost is \$0.005 per pound of paper, this change allows the mill to produce 200 more pounds of paper. Note that it still looks like our marginal rate of transformation is $\frac{5}{1}$ because we appear to have given up 1,000 gallons of water in order to obtain 200 pounds of paper. But the story is not over yet.

When the paper mill produces the extra 200 pounds of paper, it will be producing 10.1 tons of paper instead of 10 tons. Recall that for each ton of paper it produces, the mill imposes a cost of \$0.05 per 1,000 gallons on the water treatment plant. The mill's additional output of 0.1 tons will therefore increase the marginal cost of the water treatment plant by another \$0.005 per 1,000 gallons. The marginal cost, and hence the price, of water will be \$1.005 per 1,000 gallons, not \$1. Thus, with the \$999 that society has available to spend on water, it can purchase only about 994,000 gallons rather than 999,000 gallons.

Because society must actually give up almost 6,000 gallons of water, not 1,000, to obtain 200 more pounds of paper, the true marginal rate of transformation of paper for water is $\frac{6,000}{200} = \frac{30}{1}$ rather than $\frac{1,000}{200} = \frac{5}{1}$. We might call the ratio of $\frac{30}{1}$ the social marginal rate of transformation because it takes into account the full marginal cost of producing 1 more pound of paper—the mill's input costs plus the cost it imposes on the water treatment plant.

Once we have determined the true marginal rate of transformation of paper for water *for society*, we can see that the third condition for a Pareto-optimal outcome is not met. Rather than being equal, $MRS_{w \text{ for } p} = \frac{5}{1}$ is much less than $MRT_{w \text{ for } p} = \frac{30}{1}$. In other words, because of the external cost imposed by the paper mill on the water treatment plant, individuals in society are purchasing units of paper with a marginal utility of \$0.05 but a *social marginal cost* of \$0.30. In short, the competitive market is determining the wrong set of prices. The price of paper is too low; it does not reflect the true social marginal cost of paper production.

An Externality Causes Market Failure

We can now answer our original question about whether our water-paper economy will produce Pareto-optimal amounts of clean water and paper. Obviously, the answer is no. At production levels of 10 tons of paper and 1 million gallons of water, this society's competitive market has failed. It is producing too much paper and not enough water. To prove to ourselves that the amounts of clean water and paper are not Pareto optimal, all we need to do is find new amounts of water and paper that will make at least one party better off without making any party worse off.

Let us assume that we reduce the production of paper by 200 pounds. Because the price of paper is \$0.005 per pound, this is equivalent to asking the paper mill to sacrifice $0.005 per pound · 200 pounds = $1 in revenues. Note, however, that the reduction of paper production by 200 pounds will lower the cost of producing water by $0.005 per 1,000 gallons. This means that the cost of producing clean water will fall from $1 per 1,000 gallons to $0.995. Hence, it will cost only $995 instead of $1,000 to produce 1 million gallons of water—a savings of $5 for the water treatment plant.

In other words, asking the paper mill to cut its production by 200 pounds will decrease the mill's revenues by $1, but it will lower the costs of the water treatment plant by $5. Clearly, then, the cost savings of the water treatment plant will be enough to allow it to produce more water *and* compensate the paper mill for its lost revenues. For instance, if the water treatment plant spends $3.50 of the $5 to produce more clean water, it can still give the paper mill $1.50, which will more than cover the mill's $1 loss in revenues. Thus, it appears that both parties will be better off. The problem is that the impersonal forces of the competitive market will fail to reach this solution.

The realization that externalities can cause the competitive market to determine the wrong set of prices and, hence, cause the market to fail to determine a Pareto-optimal outcome is a matter of grave concern to interventionists and free-market advocates alike. As is usually the case, the agents in our model society call on an economic consulting firm to help them think through the problem.

CONSULTING REPORT   24.1

HOW CAN THE MARKET FAILURE CAUSED BY AN EXTERNALITY BE RECTIFIED?

Following a thorough search of the economic literature, the consultants suggest that the agents in our model society consider three interventionist solutions to the externality problem. The first is the use of Pigouvian taxes, the second is the use of standards and charges, and the third is the creation of marketable pollution permits. Further, they suggest that the agents take a look at the experiments performed by Charles Plott in evaluating these three forms of intervention.

The consultants do not go so far as to say that intervention is inevitable, however. They suggest that our agents also consider the Coase theorem and the experimental evidence provided by Elizabeth Hoffman and Matthew Spitzer. •

SOLVED PROBLEM 24.1

Question (Application and Extension: Negative Externalities)

Two firms are located next to each other. They both manufacture steel. The cost function of firm 1 is given by $c(Q_1) = (1 + Q_2)Q_1^2$, where Q_1 is the output of firm 1 and Q_2 is the output of firm 2. Similarly, the cost function of firm 2 is given by $c(Q_2) = (1 + Q_1)Q_2^2$. The associated marginal cost curves are $MC_1 = 2(1 + Q_2)Q_1$ and $MC_2 = 2(1 + Q_1)Q_2$, respectively. Note that in these cost functions, the output of each firm affects the costs of the other (perhaps through pollution) and makes it more expensive for the other firm to operate. The firms are able to sell steel at the market price of 12 per unit of steel.

a) What level of output will each firm choose to produce?

Answer

Under perfect competition (the case here), the firm will choose the output level for which marginal cost will equal the price. Note that $MC_1 = 2(1 + Q_2)Q_1$ and $MC_2 = 2(1 + Q_1)Q_2$. Then in equilibrium, $12 = 2(1 + Q_2)Q_1 = 2(1 + Q_1)Q_2$. Solving for Q_1 and Q_2, we get $Q_1 = Q_2 = 2$.

b) Calculate the profit that each firm gets at the competitive equilibrium and when each firm chooses an output of 1.9. Is the competitive equilibrium level Pareto optimal?

Answer

The profit of each firm when $Q_1 = Q_2 = 2$ is $12(2) - (1 + 2)4 = 12$. Suppose $Q_1 = Q_2 = 1.9$. Then the profit of each firm is $12(1.9) - (1 + 1.9)1.9^2 = 12.33$. Thus, $Q_1 = Q_2 = 2$ is not Pareto optimal.

Question (Application and Extension: Positive Externalities)

Two firms are engaged in the production of cellular telephones. The cost functions are given by $c(Q_1) = (10 - Q_2)Q_1^2$ and $c(Q_2) = (10 - Q_1)Q_2^2$, where Q_1 and Q_2 are the outputs of firm 1 and firm 2, respectively. Note that $MC_1 = 2(10 - Q_2)Q_1$ and $MC_2 = 2(10 - Q_1)Q_2$. Also note that the more one firm produces, the lower the marginal cost of production to the other firm. There are positive externalities in the technology, which might be the result of the fact that each firm can watch the other and learn from what it is doing. The market price of cellular telephones is 18. The current technology does not allow either of the firms to manufacture at an output level greater than 5.

a) What are the output levels and profits of each firm?

Answer

Note that $MC_1 = 2(10 - Q_2)Q_1$ and $MC_2 = 2(10 - Q_1)Q_2$. Setting the marginal cost to price, we have $18 = 2(10 - Q_2)Q_1 = 2(10 - Q_1)Q_2$. Solving for Q_1 and Q_2, we get $Q_1 = Q_2 = 1$. The profit of each firm is then $1(18) - 9(1) = 9$.

b) Are the output levels Pareto optimal? (*Hint*: Check the profits of each firm if each produces an output of 1.1.)

Answer

$Q_1 = Q_2 = 1$ is not Pareto optimal. Let the output levels be $Q_1 = Q_2 = 1.1$. Then the profit of each firm is $(1.1)18 - (8.9)(1.1)^2 = 9.03$, which is higher than the profit for $Q_1 = Q_2 = 1$.

SOLVED PROBLEM 24.2

Interventionist Solutions to the Externality Problem

Pigouvian Taxes

The economist A. C. Pigou argued that when an externality exists, the government should tax the party causing the externality by an amount equal to the externality.[2] To understand how such Pigouvian taxes would work, let us look again at the paper mill in our water-paper society.

Pigouvian taxes
Government taxes that tax the party causing an externality by an amount equal to the externality.

---

[2] Arthur Cecil Pigou (1877–1959) was an English economist who held the chair of political economy at Cambridge University from 1908 to 1944. He did extensive work in the area of welfare economics. He provided the basis for the theory of externalities by making a distinction between private and social costs and proposing taxes and subsidies to remedy situations where such costs differ.

Figure 24.2 shows the demand curve for paper faced by the paper mill as well as two marginal cost curves. The lower marginal cost curve, *MC*, is the mill's private marginal cost curve. It reflects all input costs for producing paper. This marginal cost curve intersects the demand curve at point *A*, which means that the mill will produce 10 tons of paper. This is the level of production that will result with a competitive market.

Recall, however, that each time the mill produces one more ton of paper, the costs of the water treatment plant increase by $0.05 per 1,000 gallons. In a competitive market, this additional cost is external to the paper mill, so the mill does not take it into account in deciding how much paper to produce. Society, however, must take this cost into account. The higher marginal cost curve, *MC'*, in Figure 24.2 is the social marginal cost curve. It represents the marginal costs faced by society for paper production. It reflects the private input costs of the paper mill *plus* the external costs that the mill imposes on the water treatment plant.

We can now see that the competitive solution at point *A* of Figure 24.2 is not optimal for society. The social marginal cost of producing the tenth ton (the distance *BC*) is greater than the social marginal benefit to consumers of receiving that ton (the distance *BA*). Clearly, production at point *D* would be socially optimal, but the competitive market will not achieve this solution on its own.

According to Pigou, the solution to the problem is to tax the paper mill by an amount equal to the marginal externality, or the difference between the private marginal costs of the mill and the social marginal costs for paper production (the distance *EF*). This tax will force the paper mill to *internalize* the externality and take it into account when deciding how much paper to produce. As a result, the mill will reduce paper production to the socially optimal level represented by point *D* of Figure 24.2.

Figure 24.2

Pigouvian Taxes.

The imposition of a tax equal to the marginal externality (distance *EF*) equates the private marginal cost *MC* faced by the paper mill with the social marginal cost *MC'* and thereby induces the mill to produce at the optimal level for society (point *D*).

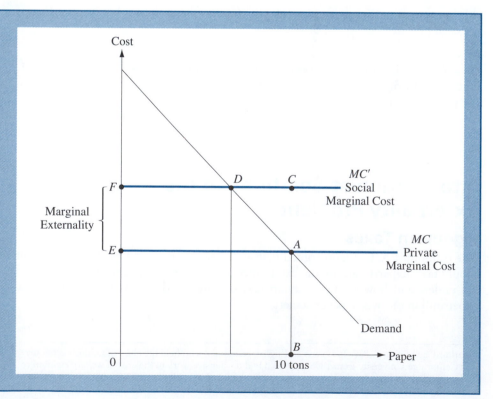

The Weakness of the Pigouvian Tax Solution. Although the Pigouvian tax solution to the externality problem may seem ideal in theory, there is a major practical problem in administering it. If the government is to set the externality tax at its optimal level, it must know the exact amount of the externality. This information is very difficult for the government to obtain. In fact, the party affected by the externality may not even know exactly how much it is being damaged. And, even if it does know, it might not report the amount to the government accurately. The affected party has a great incentive to exaggerate the amount of damage it experiences with a view toward reducing this damage as much as possible. Thus, unless the government can obtain accurate information about the amount of an externality, the Pigouvian tax solution is unlikely to be effective.

Standards and Charges

Another way the government can intervene in a market with an externality in order to reduce the effects of the externality is through a system of standards and charges. The government first determines a standard—the amount of damage caused by the externality that it considers acceptable. It then levies charges on the agents causing the externality in order to force them to reduce the externality to the acceptable level.

Note that the system of standards and charges is not equivalent to the Pigouvian tax solution. If the government knows the extent of the damage caused by the externality, it can set the Pigouvian tax at a rate that will ensure that the agents causing the externality will reduce their production and, hence, reduce the cost of the externality to the optimal level. With standards and charges, the government sets a charge that it hopes will cause these agents to reduce the externality to the predetermined level.

standards and charges
A system for a government to intervene in a market with externalities in order to reduce its effects by levying charges on the agents causing the externality in order to force them to reduce the externality to the acceptable level.

Implementing Standards and Charges for a Single Firm. To see how a system of standards and charges would affect a single firm, let us say that the government of our water-paper society decides that the paper mill is dumping too much waste into the river. The government conducts a study to determine how much waste is tolerable. It then levies an environmental charge (a type of tax) on each gallon of waste the paper mill dumps into the river in the hope that this charge will cause the mill to reduce its waste to the desired level.

Figure 24.3 shows how the environmental charge will affect the paper mill. This figure depicts the demand curve for paper that the mill faces as well as two marginal cost curves. The lower marginal cost curve, MC, represents the mill's private marginal cost before the government imposes the environmental charge. As long as the mill is on curve MC, it will set its output at point A, where its marginal cost equals the market price. At this point, the mill's output is q_0.

When the government imposes the environmental charge on the paper mill, the mill's marginal cost function increases by an amount equal to the charge. Its marginal cost curve therefore shifts upward to MC'. On curve MC', the mill's marginal cost equals the market price at point B and the mill reduces its output to q_e. Ideally, at this lower output, the mill will have decreased the amount of waste it dumps into the river to the standard established by the government—the level the government feels is tolerable.

Implementing Standards and Charges for Two or More Firms. Suppose there are several agents that are creating an externality. How should the government apply the system of standards and charges to reduce the effects of the

Figure 24.3

The Effect of an Environmental Charge on a Single Firm.

The imposition of an environmental charge equal to the distance between the marginal cost curves MC and MC' induces the firm to cut back its output from q_0 to q_e.

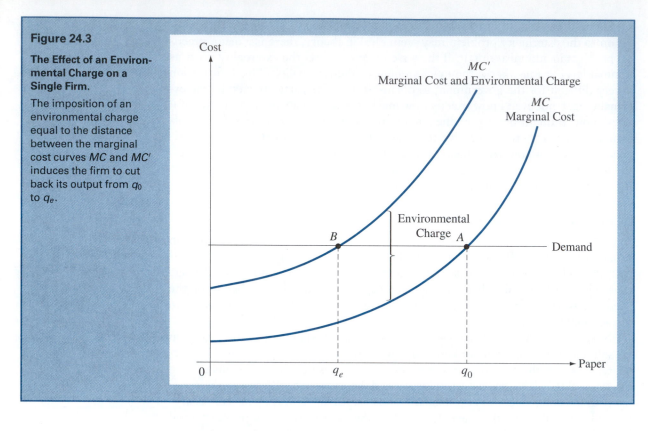

externality in this case? To answer such a question, let us begin by assuming that there are two paper mills in our water-paper society. Each day, mill A is dumping 70 gallons of waste into the river and mill B is dumping 30 gallons of waste. The government decides that this pollution should be cut in half. What should it do? An obvious possibility is to require across-the-board cuts of 50% in the waste that the two mills dump. Although this would reduce pollution by the desired amount and would be simple to administer, it is not the least-cost way to achieve the desired reduction and, hence, is not the most efficient solution.

The reason across-the-board cuts are not efficient is that different firms have different abilities to reduce pollution. For instance, let us say that firm A has a new plant that includes a modern pollution abatement system, whereas firm B has an old plant with an obsolete pollution abatement system. Firm A's marginal cost of abatement function will be lower than firm B's, so firm A will be able to reduce pollution more efficiently than firm B.

Now, let us assume that the government does mandate across-the-board pollution cuts of 50%. It requires firm A to reduce its pollution by 35 gallons and firm B to reduce its pollution by 15 gallons. At these levels, let us say that firm A can decrease its pollution by one more gallon at a cost of $5 and firm B can do the same at a cost of $8. Thus, if the government requires firm A to reduce its pollution by 36 gallons instead of 35 gallons, the cost to society will be $5. If, at the same time, the government allows firm B to dump an additional gallon of waste—that is, it allows firm B to reduce its pollution by 14 gallons instead of 15 gallons—society will save $8. At these new levels, the same total reduction in pollution is achieved, but society realizes a net savings of $3. Obviously, then, the across-the-board cut is not the least-cost way to achieve the desired reduction in pollution.

The efficient way to achieve any given set of pollution standards is to have the firms with a lower cost of abatement reduce their emission of pollutants by more than the firms with a higher cost of abatement. This is exactly what an environmental charge per unit of pollution accomplishes.

Figure 24.4 illustrates the effects of an environmental charge on our two paper mills. In that figure, the horizontal axis measures the amount of abatement; larger quantities of abatement mean fewer emissions and less pollution. The figure depicts the marginal cost of abatement curves for firms A and B, both of which slope upward. Note that at each level of abatement, firm A has a lower marginal cost than firm B. The environmental charge is represented by a horizontal line because it is constant at all levels of abatement. Once this charge is set, each firm will reduce its emission of pollutants to the point where its marginal cost of abatement equals the environmental charge. Because firm A has a lower cost of abatement function, it will choose a level of abatement (a_{high}) that is much higher than the level of abatement chosen by firm B (a_{low}). Note, however, that at the equilibrium, the marginal costs of abatement for firms A and B are equal.

In summary, government intervention through a system of standards and charges works as follows when there are a number of firms polluting the environment. The government sets a standard—an acceptable level of pollution. That is, it determines just how much pollution it feels is tolerable. The government then levies an environmental charge per unit of pollution. In response, the polluting firms reduce their emission of pollutants to the point that their marginal cost of abatement equals the charge (and the marginal cost of abatement of the other firms). Then, if the government has selected an appropriate charge, the total pollution emitted by all the polluting firms will be at the desired level.

The Weakness of the Standards and Charges Solution. The standards and charges solution is even more difficult to administer than the Pigouvian tax

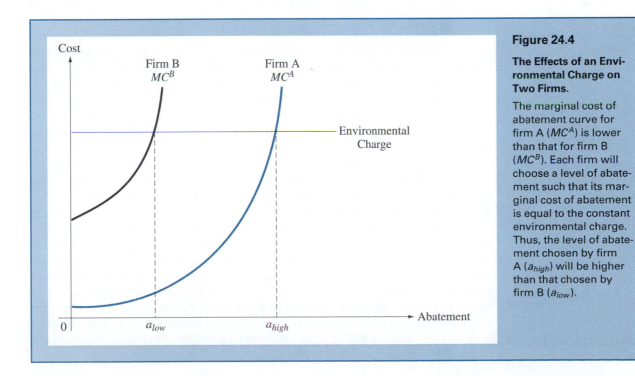

Figure 24.4

The Effects of an Environmental Charge on Two Firms.

The marginal cost of abatement curve for firm A (MC^A) is lower than that for firm B (MC^B). Each firm will choose a level of abatement such that its marginal cost of abatement is equal to the constant environmental charge. Thus, the level of abatement chosen by firm A (a_{high}) will be higher than that chosen by firm B (a_{low}).

solution. Again, the government must somehow determine the exact amount of damage caused by the externality. Otherwise, it will not be able to set a standard. As we have seen, obtaining this information can be very difficult. Then the government must decide on the environmental charge to be levied. To set the optimal charge, the government would have to know the cost functions of all the agents causing the externality, which it obviously cannot know. Thus, when the government determines the charge, it actually has little idea of how much the agents will reduce production and, hence, reduce the damage caused by the externality. All the government can do is levy a charge and wait to see its effects.

If the charge is set at too high a level, the agents will decrease their output too much and reduce the damage caused by the externality more than is required. Similarly, if the charge is too low, the damage caused by the externality will still be excessive. True, the government can "fine-tune" the charge by raising and lowering it until the optimal effects are achieved, but all these changes are likely to be confusing.

Marketable Pollution Permits

marketable pollution permits
A method of government intervention to prevent externalities whereby a government-issued permit allows a firm to pollute the environment by a specified amount.

The final method of government intervention to correct the effects of the externality caused by pollution that we will discuss is the creation of marketable pollution permits. Each permit allows a firm to pollute the environment by a specified amount. Thus, if a polluting firm wants to produce one unit of a product, it must buy not only the labor and capital it needs to produce that unit but also a permit that will allow it to pollute the environment. Clearly, a firm with a high marginal cost of abatement would be willing to pay a substantial amount to buy such a permit because it would otherwise have to spend a substantial amount to clean up its own pollution. Conversely, a firm with a low marginal cost of abatement would be willing to pay less for the permit because it can always clean up its own wastes at a lower cost.

To establish the pollution permit market, the government first determines the amount of pollution it considers tolerable, just as it does in setting pollution standards. It then offers for sale the number of permits that will result in this amount of pollution. One major advantage of this method of intervention should already be obvious. Because firms can pollute only if they have a permit and because the government decides how many permits it will make available, the government knows exactly how much pollution there will be after the permits are sold.

To see how a market in pollution permits would work, let us consider an industry in which there are two polluting firms, firm A and firm B. These firms have the marginal pollution abatement cost functions shown in Figure 24.5. The government determines that pollution should be limited to 2 units and decides to sell permits allowing only this much pollution. Each firm has a clear choice. It can either buy the permits and continue to pollute as it produces or pay the cost of cleaning up its own pollution. If firm A does not buy the permits, it will have to pay $4 to clean up the first unit of its pollution and $6 to clean up the second unit, a total of $10 in pollution abatement costs. This amount is indicated by area A on the left side of Figure 24.5. Firm B, on the other hand, has a higher marginal cost of abatement function. It will therefore have to pay a total of $14 to clean up its own pollution—$6 for the first unit and $8 for the second unit. This amount is indicated by area B on the right side of Figure 24.5.

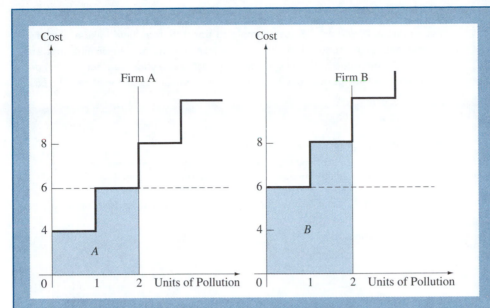

Figure 24.5

A Market for Pollution Permits.

The cost to clean up 2 units of pollution is $10 for firm A and $14 for firm B. In a market for permits giving the right to emit 2 units of pollution, firm A would bid up to $10 and firm B would bid up to $14.

RESOLVING
TEASER 24

AN EVALUATION OF THE EXTERNALITY PROBLEM AND THE INTERVENTIONIST SOLUTIONS—THE PLOTT EXPERIMENTS

We have now seen that economic theory predicts that a competitive market will fail to arrive at a Pareto-optimal outcome in the presence of an externality. We have also examined, on a theoretical basis, three interventionist solutions to the externality problem—Pigouvian taxes, standards and charges, and marketable pollution permits. At this point, it seems reasonable to wonder just how well the theories we have studied approximate reality. For a sense of this, let us take a look at a series of experiments conducted by Charles Plott.[3]

Plott's Basic Laboratory Model

Plott set up his experiments by creating a laboratory model of a market with an externality. (Except for the inclusion of the externality, the procedures he used were identical to those used by Vernon Smith in the experiment discussed in Chapter 16.) In Plott's experimental market, the subjects buy and sell units of a fictitious good using the double oral auction mechanism. Each buyer is paid a redemption value for every unit he or she purchases according to a predetermined redemption schedule, and each seller must pay a premium for each unit he or she sells according to a predetermined cost schedule. (These procedures and the auction mechanism are discussed in more detail in Chapter 16. You may want to review this material.) To introduce the externality into the market, Plott stipulated that each transaction completed would impose an additional cost on all subsequent transactions. This cost increases with the number of units sold.[4]

(Continued)

---

[3] Charles Plott, professor of economics at the California Institute of Technology, is one of the foremost pioneers in the field of experimental economics. The experiments discussed here are reported in Charles Plott, "Externalities and Corrective Policies in Experimental Markets," *Economic Journal* 93 (1983): 106–27.

[4] Plott's experimental market might be thought of as a model of the market for crack cocaine. In that market, people buy the good and then commit crimes to obtain money to pay for their next purchase. Thus, the more people who buy the good, the more crime there is in society.

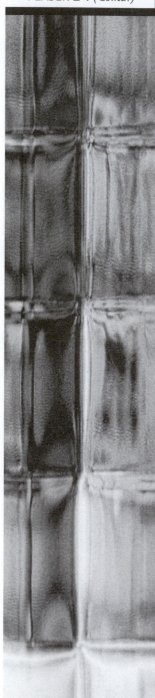

RESOLVING
TEASER 24 *(Contd.)*

For example, if we think of each completed transaction as being like a unit of a good that has been produced, then in this market the more transactions that are completed, the more costly it will be to complete each succeeding transaction. This behavior is depicted in Figure 24.6, where the social marginal cost curve shows the cost

Figure 24.6

Plott's Laboratory Model of a Market with an Externality.

Economic theory predicts that the market, if left alone, will ignore the externality and will reach its equilibrium at point *B*, where the private marginal cost curve *MC* and the demand curve intersect. Point *A*, where the social marginal cost curve *MC'* and the demand curve intersect, is the optimal solution for society.

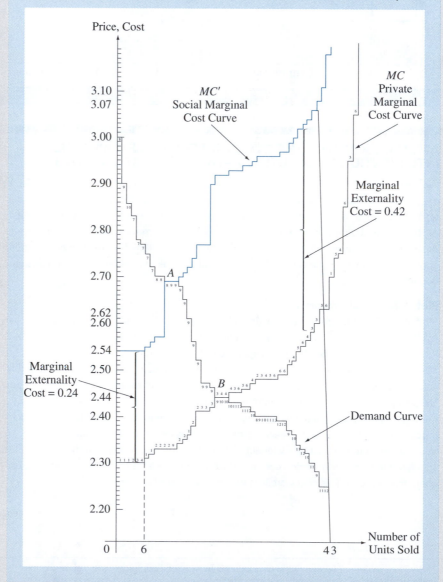

(Continued)

situation for an individual. Note that after 6 transactions are completed, the difference between the private and social marginal costs is $0.24; while after 43 transactions are completed, the difference between the private and social marginal costs has grown to $0.42. Hence, not only is there an externality, but its magnitude increases as more transactions are completed.

Plott's experimental market is illustrated in Figure 24.6. The redemption and cost schedules Plott used result in the demand curve and the private marginal cost curve *MC* (also the supply curve for this market). The curve *MC'* is the social marginal cost curve, which takes into account the externality. It reflects the private marginal cost of each unit of the fictitious good plus the marginal damage done to society with each trade.

Will the Competitive Market Really Fail?

As we know from our discussion in the section titled "The Effects of an Externality on Output," the Pareto-optimal level of production of the fictitious good for society occurs where the social marginal cost curve *MC'* intersects the demand curve. This point is labeled *A* in Figure 24.6. It indicates an expected output of 13 units and an expected equilibrium price of $2.69. However, economic theory tells us that the market will ignore the externality if left to its own devices. Therefore, the market will reach equilibrium at its competitive outcome. This occurs at point *B*, where the private marginal cost curve *MC* intersects the demand curve. At point *B*, the expected output is 24 units and the expected equilibrium price is $2.44.

In his first experiment, Plott investigated whether the predictions of economic theory were accurate. Would the participants in this experimental market ignore the fact that their actions carry with them an externality that hurts all the agents in the market, including themselves, as the theory predicts? Or would they modify their behavior to take the externality into account?

Plott ran this experiment twice, with two different groups of subjects. The session with each group consisted of five market periods. The results are shown in Figure 24.7. Each graph summarizes the market activity that took place during the five periods of each session. At the top of the graph, we see the mean price determined in each period and the number of units of the good that were sold. During both sessions, the volume sold tended to move toward the competitive output level of 24 units and the price tended to move toward the competitive equilibrium price of $2.44. Based on these results, Plott was able to conclude that the predictions of economic theory were accurate. The market failed. The subjects ignored the externality, and the market came to equilibrium at the competitive level of output rather than at the Pareto-optimal level for society.

Evaluating the Interventionist Solutions

Having established that his experimental market would fail in the absence of a mechanism requiring the subjects to take the externality into account, Plott then ran additional experiments to evaluate the efficacy of three interventions—Pigouvian taxes, permits, and standards.

For his experiment to evaluate Pigouvian taxes, Plott increased the cost schedule by a tax equal to the amount of the marginal externality generated by each trade. This internalized the externality by shifting the private marginal cost curve *MC* in Figure 24.6 upward so that it was congruent with the social marginal cost curve *MC'*. Under these conditions, we would expect the market to reach equilibrium at point *A*, the Pareto-optimal level of output for society.

(Continued)

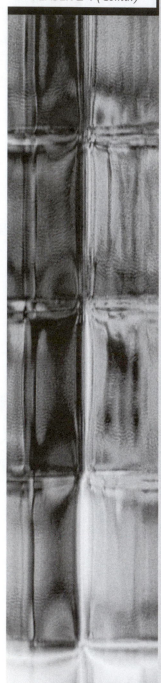

RESOLVING
TEASER 24 *(Contd.)*

Figure 24.7

The Results of Plott's Experiment to Investigate the Behavior of a Market with an Externality.

As economic theory predicts, the prices in the experimental market moved toward the competitive equilibrium price of $2.44 and the quantities sold moved toward the competitive equilibrium volume of 24 units rather than toward the optimal price and volume for society of $2.69 and 13 units.

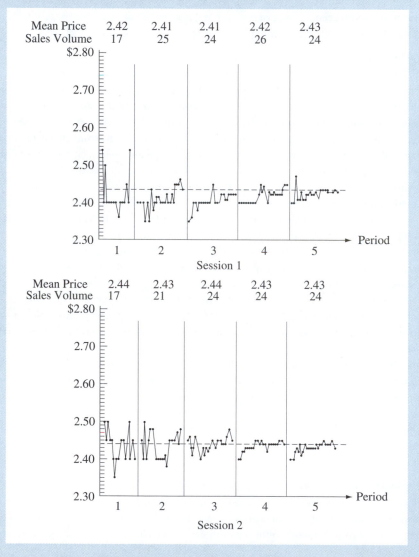

In the experiment to evaluate permits, Plott created a secondary market for permits alongside the primary market for the fictitious good. In order to purchase a unit of the good in the primary market, a buyer first had to purchase a permit in the secondary market. The expected equilibrium price for permits was $0.36, and the expected equilibrium sales volume was 13. At the equilibrium of the primary market, which is shown

(Continued)

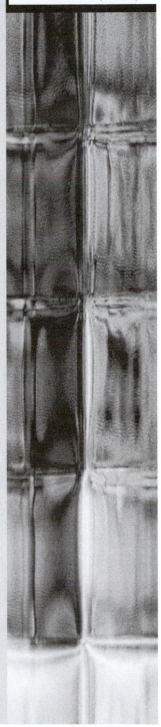

by point *A* in Figure 24.6, the expected price of each unit of the good was $2.69 and the expected sales volume was 13 units. The price of $2.69 is equal to the marginal cost of $2.33 for producing the 13th unit of the good plus the $0.36 cost of the permit.

To evaluate the standards solution, Plott limited the volume of trade on the primary market to the Pareto-optimal level of 13 units. Because of this limitation, he could anticipate that the equilibrium price would be set at $2.69 and that all units would be sold.

The results of these experiments are shown in Figures 24.8, 24.9, and 24.10.[5] The Pigouvian tax intervention (Figure 24.8) and the permit intervention (Figure 24.9) were both effective in pushing the volume down to the Pareto-optimal level of 13 units and the price up to the optimal equilibrium price of $2.69. In addition, in the permit experiment, the prices paid for permits converged on the equilibrium level of $0.36. (Hence, the equilibrium price of $2.69 for the product was equal to the marginal cost of producing the 13th unit, $2.33, plus the cost of the permit, $0.36.) The permit intervention was more efficient than the Pigouvian tax intervention in terms of the fraction of consumer surplus plus producer surplus captured by the subjects.

The least effective intervention was the standards and charges intervention (Figure 24.10). Because the number of units of the good that could be sold was limited to 13, the buyers and sellers in this experiment rushed to conclude their transactions early in each period, before the limit was reached. This rush led to prices that were not at the equilibrium level. Note that the mean prices arrived at in this experiment are comparable to those for the experiment in which there was no intervention.

Figure 24.8

The Results of Plott's Experiments to Evaluate the Interventionist Solutions to an Externality: The Pigouvian Tax.

The Pigouvian tax intervention pushed prices and quantities toward the optimal levels for society of $2.69 and 13 units.

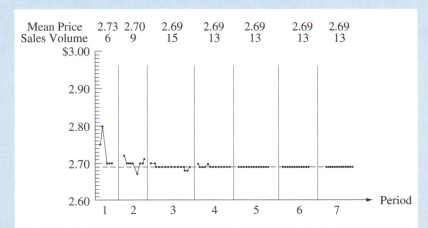

| Mean Price | 2.73 | 2.70 | 2.69 | 2.69 | 2.69 | 2.69 | 2.69 |
| Sales Volume | 6 | 9 | 15 | 13 | 13 | 13 | 13 |

(Continued)

---

[5] Due to space limitations, not all of the diagrams included by Plott in his paper appear in Figures 24.8, 24.9, and 24.10. However, the outcomes depicted in those that are shown are representative of Plott's results.

Figure 24.9

The Results of Plott's Experiments to Evaluate the Interventionist Solutions to an Externality: Permits.

Like the Pigouvian tax intervention, the permit intervention succeeded in pushing prices and quantities toward the optimal levels for society. However, the permit intervention was more efficient in terms of the amount of consumer and producer surplus captured.

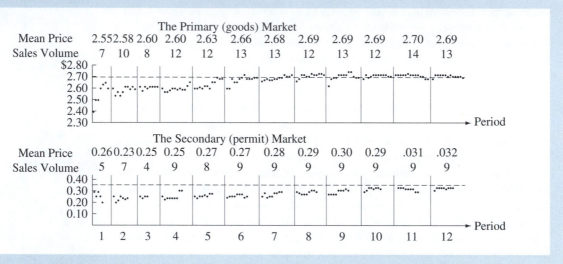

Figure 24.10

The Results of Plott's Experiments to Evaluate the Interventionist Solutions to an Externality: Standards.

The standards and charges intervention was the least effective of the three forms of intervention tested by Plott. It led to prices that were not at the optimal level for society.

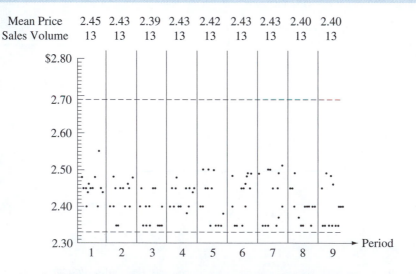

The best solution for society is the one that will reduce total pollution to 2 units for the least amount of money. If society requires firm B to clean up its own pollution, the total cost to society will be $14. Clearly, then, society is better off if it requires firm A to clean up its own pollution, which will cost only $10, and allows firm B to continue to pollute. Indeed, this is exactly the result that a competitive market in pollution permits will achieve, as we will now see.

Let us say that the government holds an auction to sell the two pollution permits, and both firms A and B participate in this auction. Bids are to be offered in increments of $0.10. The bidding will continue until neither firm bids any higher, at which point the permits will be awarded to the firm that has made the highest bid. Firm A will keep bidding until it has bid a total of $10. It will stop bidding at that point because the next bid would be greater than $10, which is what it would cost firm A to clean up its own pollution. Firm B, on the other hand, has a total pollution abatement cost of $14, so it would be willing to bid up to $14 to buy the two permits. However, firm B will not have to bid that high. Because firm A will drop out of the bidding at $10, firm B can win the two permits for a total cost of $10 or slightly more than $10. Thus, the market in pollution permits achieves society's aim of reducing pollution by 2 units for the least amount of money. Firm B is allowed to pollute because it bought the permits; and firm A, the least-cost abater, must cut its level of pollution.

Although the use of marketable pollution permits must be considered a government intervention, it is a rather minor one. Essentially, it simply creates a new market—a market for pollution permits—where one did not previously exist.

A Noninterventionist Solution to the Externality Problem: The Coasian Solution

Given our discussion thus far, it might appear that only through some sort of government intervention can our model society solve its externality problem. Naturally enough, the interventionists in our model society readily accept this idea. But the free-market advocates say, "Not so fast." Referring to Consulting Report 24.2, they point out that Ronald Coase (an economist whose work we have already discussed several times) has developed a strong argument against the need for the interventionist solutions to the externality problem.

Coase argues that when an externality exists, the agents involved will be able to correct the effects of the externality by private agreement if they can costlessly negotiate among themselves.[6] The reason is simple. If the market has not determined a Pareto-optimal outcome, then, by definition, another outcome must exist that will make at least one of the parties (and perhaps all of them) better off without making any party worse off. Hence, if the agents simply talk with each other, they should be able to agree on a mutually beneficial way to split the gains that could be achieved by altering the market outcome to its Pareto-optimal level.

For example, in "The Effects of an Externality on Output," we saw that our water-paper society would be better off if the paper mill were to reduce its output by 200 pounds. As we calculated, this reduction would cost the paper mill $1 in revenue, but it would save the water treatment plant $5 in costs. Clearly, both parties would be better off if they negotiated a deal in which the water treatment plant pays the mill to reduce its paper production. Because the paper mill stands to lose only $1 in revenue, any payment greater than $1 would make it better off. Furthermore, because the water treatment plant stands to save $5 if the mill makes the reduction, it should be willing to pay up to that amount to have the mill do so. Any

---

[6] Coase's views on the externality problem are presented in his seminal article "The Problem of Social Cost," *Journal of Law and Economics* (1960): 1–44.

payment from the water treatment plant to the paper mill that is greater than $1 but less than $5 will make both parties better off. Then, after the 200-pound reduction is negotiated, the two parties will want to see if a further reduction would be mutually beneficial. If so, they will continue their bargaining. According to Coase, the two parties will eventually arrive at a mutually beneficial solution that will also be Pareto optimal for society.

However, what happens if the paper mill owns property rights allowing it to use the river for dumping wastes? Won't it simply ignore the offer made by the water treatment plant? Not at all, Coase would contend. As long as the mill is sufficiently compensated for reducing its output, doing so will make it better off even if it owns property rights that allow it to pollute the river. What if the situation is reversed and the water treatment plant owns the rights to use the river for whatever purposes it wants? Won't it simply forbid the mill to dump its wastes? Again, Coase would say no. In this case, the mill would be willing to pay the water treatment plant to allow it to dump its wastes as long as the mill's marginal revenues are greater than the marginal costs these wastes impose on the water treatment plant. Hence, no matter who owns the property rights to use the river, we will always arrive at a Pareto-optimal solution *if the parties can costlessly negotiate*. (Of course, we would expect the agent owning the property rights to be able to negotiate the better deal, but that is a distribution issue, not an efficiency issue.)

Coase theorem

In markets with externalities, if property rights are assigned unambiguously and if the parties involved can negotiate costlessly, then the Coase theorem suggests that the parties will arrive at a Pareto-optimal outcome regardless of which one owns the property rights.

Coase's views can be summarized in what has come to be known as the **Coase theorem**: *In markets with externalities, if property rights are assigned unambiguously and if the parties involved can negotiate costlessly, then the parties will arrive at a Pareto-optimal outcome regardless of which one owns the property rights.*

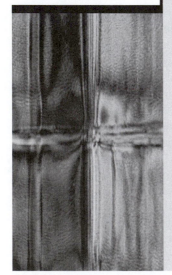

RESOLVING
TEASER 25

EXTERNALITIES—THE HOFFMAN-SPITZER EXPERIMENT

Basically, the Coasian solution to the externality problem rests on the idea that rational individuals in a situation where an externality exists will find a way to rectify the damage done by the externality if they are allowed to negotiate among themselves.[7]

The results of the Hoffman-Spitzer experiment show overwhelming support for the viability of the Coasian solution. Indeed, Hoffman and Spitzer found that only 1 of the 24 pairs of subjects who participated in this type of experiment failed to choose the Pareto-optimal outcome.

One aspect of the results was surprising, however. As we saw in Chapter 2, two fundamental assumptions of the free-market argument are that people are selfish and that they behave rationally when making economic decisions. Thus, we would expect that the controller would never agree to a split of the $14 that would give her less than the $11 she would receive by unilaterally choosing row 7. This did not turn out to be the case. Of the 24 subjects acting as controllers in this experiment, all but 7 agreed to an even split of the $14 between themselves and their partners so that each received $7. This finding would seem to challenge the assumptions of selfishness and rationality.

---

[7] Actually, Hoffman and Spitzer performed a number of different experiments to investigate the Coase theorem. Information about these experiments can be found in Elizabeth Hoffman and Matthew Spitzer, "The Coase Theorem: Some Experimental Tests," *Journal of Law and Economics* 25 (1982): 93–98.

Conclusion

Our hypothetical society has once again struggled with a challenge to the free-market ideology of laissez-faire as it debated the proper response to the market failure caused by the externality problem. As is usually the case, the debate pitted interventionists, who feel government action is necessary to rectify the problem, against free-market advocates, who feel the problem can be rectified by market or quasi-market means. In the next chapter, this society will face an even more difficult challenge to the ideology of laissez-faire—the problem of public goods. The debate will again reflect the familiar party lines of the interventionists and the free-market advocates. This time, however, there will be no Coase theorem to remedy the problem, so some sort of intervention will seem inevitable.

Summary

In this chapter, we have investigated externalities and how they can cause free markets to fail in determining optimal outcomes for society. The interventionists in our model society argued that government action was necessary and debated the most efficient way to intervene. The possibilities considered were Pigouvian taxes, standards and charges, and marketable permits. Based on the evidence of the Plott experiments, marketable permits appear to produce the best results. The free-market advocates in our model society relied on the famous Coase theorem to argue that government intervention was not necessary. Their position was that the market can rectify the problems caused by externalities if agents are free to negotiate costlessly. An experiment by Hoffman and Spitzer seems to support this view.

APPENDIX

EXCESS PRODUCTION UNDER EXTERNALITIES

In the presence of negative external effects, a firm would produce more than the socially optimal output level if (as is usually the case) it does not take the external effect into account. One way to rectify this antisocial behavior is to tax the firm on its output or require it to "buy" the right to produce the external effect.

To illustrate these ideas, consider two firms labeled 1 and 2 that produce goods 1 and 2, respectively. For simplicity, assume that the firms act as perfect competitors in their respective product markets; thus, firm 1 faces price p_1 for its output x_1 and firm 2 faces price p_2 for its output x_2.

Let $c_1(x_1)$ and $c_2(x_2)$ be the cost functions of the two firms. Further, let $e(x_1)$ be the external cost imposed on firm 2 by the production of x_1 by firm 1.

Then their profit functions are

$$\pi_1 = p_1 x_1 - c_1(x_1)$$
$$\pi_2 = p_2 x_2 - c_2(x_2) - e(x_1)$$

The first-order (profit-maximizing) conditions are

$$p_1 = c_1'(x_1^*)$$
$$p_2 = c_2'(x_2^*)$$

That is, the firms set price = marginal cost, but firm 1 ignores the cost that it imposes on firm 2.

The socially optimal solution is obtained by maximizing total profits jointly; that is,

$$\max{}_{\{x_1, x_2\}} W = [p_1 x_1 - c_1(x_1)) + (p_2 x_2 - c_2(x_2) - e(x_1)]$$

The first-order conditions of this problem yield

$$p_1 = c_1'(x_1^S) + e'(x_1^S)$$
$$p_2 = c_2'(x_2^S)$$

Comparing the market solution and the social welfare solution, we see that firm 2 produces the socially optimal level of output $x_2^* = x_2^s$ but firm 1 produces too much: $x_1^* > x_1^s$. To see this more clearly in an example, assume that the cost functions are simple quadratic functions.

$$c_1(x_1) = \frac{1}{2} c_1 x_1^2$$

$$c_2(x_2) = \frac{1}{2} c_2 x_2^2$$

$$e(x_1) = \frac{1}{2} e x_1^2$$

Then, $p_1 = c_1 x_1^* \Rightarrow x_1^* = p_1/c_1$, while $p_1 = c_1 x_1^s + e x_1^s = (c_1 + e) x_1^s \Rightarrow x_1^s = p_1/(c_1 + e)$. Hence,

$$x_1^* = \frac{c_1 + e}{c_1} x_1^S > x_1^S$$

In order to force firm 1 to produce the socially optimal output, we can levy a tax on its output. Let the tax be $t(x_1)$. Then, with the tax, firm 1 will maximize:

$$\pi_1 = p_1 x_1 - \frac{1}{2} c_1 x_1^2 - t(x_1)$$
$$p_1 = c_1 x_1^* + t'(x_1^*)$$

If a tax rate $t'(x_1) = e x_1$ is imposed, then in equilibrium,

$$p_1 = c_1 x_1^* + e x_1^*$$
$$\Rightarrow x_1^* = x_1^S$$

Hence, the total tax on firm 1 should be $\frac{1}{2} e x_1^2$, so in equilibrium, firm 1 pays $\frac{1}{2} e(x_1^*)^2$. In equilibrium, firm 2 incurs a cost of $\frac{1}{2} e(x_1^*)^2$ from the externality, so if the tax amount is transferred to firm 2, the externality is fully internalized. Such a tax is called a Pigouvian tax.

Markets for Externalities

As noted in the text, in practice such taxes are difficult to apply because they require the government or the regulatory body to know the exact cost function for the external cost. If the government knew the exact cost functions, it could simply calculate the equilibrium amounts and instruct the firms to produce accordingly.

A more practical alternative is to introduce a market for the externality. Let us say that firm 1 must "buy" the right from firm 2 to produce amount x_1 at price q—that is, firm 1 pays amount $q x_1$ to firm 2 to produce its output.

The profit functions in this case are

$$\pi_1 = \max{}_{\{x_1\}} p_1 x_1 - c_1(x_1) - q x_1$$
$$\pi_2 = \max{}_{\{x_2\}} p_2 x_2 - c_2(x_2) - e(x_1) + q x_1$$

where

$$c_1(x_1) = \frac{1}{2}c_1x_1^2$$

$$c_2(x_2) = \frac{1}{2}c_2x_2^2$$

$$e(x_1) = \frac{1}{2}ex_1^2$$

Hence, firm 1 chooses output x_1, taking into account the cost qx_1 that it incurs by paying for the right to produce the externality, while firm 2 chooses output x_2 and the output x_1 it is willing to accept at price q. Finally, q is determined by market equilibrium.

The first-order conditions are

$$p_1 - q = c_1x_1^* \quad \text{for firm 1}$$
$$p_2 = c_2x_2^* \quad \text{and}$$
$$q = ex_1^* \quad \text{for firm2}$$

In equilibrium,

$$\frac{p_1 - q}{c_1} = \frac{q}{e}$$

$$q = \frac{p_1e}{c_1 + e}$$

The outputs of the firms are

$$x_1^* = \frac{p_1}{c_1 + e}$$

$$x_2^* = \frac{p_2}{c_2}$$

which are the socially optimal quantities. Firm 1 pays the amount

$$qx_1^* = \frac{p_1^2e}{(c_1 + e)^2}$$

Exercises and Problems

1. Let us say that there is a class in which a weekly exam is given. The class has one genius, who always scores 100%, and 19 "regular" students, who always score 85%. The teacher grades the exam on a curve by taking the difference between the highest score and 100 and adding the result to each student's score. For example, if the highest score is 78, each student will have 22 points added to his or her score. The parents of these students pay them $1 for each point scored on the exam.

   a) Does the genius impose externalities on the rest of the class? If so, what is the value of the marginal externality for each exam?

   b) What is the Pareto-optimal configuration of grades?

   c) If the highest scoring student on each exam could be taxed for each point he or she scores above the second-highest scoring student, what marginal tax would result in the Pareto-optimal distribution of grades?

   d) If the 19 "regular" students were to bribe the genius to start scoring 85 instead of 100, what is the maximum amount of money they could offer?

2. A soot-spewing factory that produces steel windows is next to a laundry. We will assume that the factory faces a prevailing market price of $P = \$40$. Its cost function is $C = X^2$, where X is window output, so the factory's marginal cost is $MC = 2X$. The laundry produces clean wash, which it hangs out to dry. The soot from the window factory smudges the wash, so the laundry has to clean it again. This increases the laundry's costs. In fact, the cost function of the laundry is $C = Y^2 + 0.05X$, where Y is pounds of laundry washed. The demand curve faced by the laundry is perfectly horizontal at a price of $10 per pound.

   a)   What outputs X and Y would maximize the sum of the profits of these two firms?

   b)   Will those outputs be set by a competitive market?

   c)   What per-unit tax would we need to set on window production to obtain the outputs found in part a of this problem?

3. Suppose that the speed limit on a four-lane highway is 60 miles per hour. An accident has occurred in the southbound lanes, and people in the northbound lanes tend to slow down and look at it. This reduces the speed in the northbound lanes from 60 to 40 miles per hour. All the people in the northbound lanes are on their way to work and are driving 40 miles. If they agree not to slow down, they can get to work in 40 minutes. However, if they slow down, the trip will take 60 minutes. The people in the northbound lanes all obtain private satisfaction from slowing down and looking at the accident.

   a)   Will an informal agreement not to slow down be stable?

   b)   What is the externality in this situation?

4. Assume that a society has three firms, A, B, and C, situated in a row. The society faces the following problem. Every unit of output that firm A produces creates a benefit for firm B of $7 and a cost to firm C of $3. The marginal cost of production for firm A is $MC = 4q^a$, where q^a is firm A's output. The market price for the output of firm A is $16. (Assume that this is the marginal benefit to society of consuming each unit.)

   a)   What total amount of output will firm A produce in a competitive market?

   b)   What output is the optimal output for society?

   c)   Suppose that firms A and B merge and then set the output that is best for them. What would that output be? Would it be the socially optimal output?

5. Let's say that there are three firms in a community that pollute the environment. The government has decided that 21 units of pollution must be abated and that each firm must cut pollution by 7 units. The marginal cost of pollution abatement is $MC^A = \frac{1}{3}q$ for firm A, $MC^B = \frac{1}{2}q$ for firm B, and $MC^C = \frac{1}{4}q$ for firm C, where q is the quantity of abatement. The government wants the total amount of pollution to be reduced by 21 units and demands that each firm reduce its pollution by 7 units.

   a)   Is this solution efficient? Explain why or why not.

   b)   If the solution is not efficient, how much pollution should each firm reduce at the efficient outcome?

   c)   If each firm must abate 7 units of pollution, what is the maximum firm A would be willing to pay firm C to cut 2 additional units of pollution so that firm A could cut its pollution by only 5 units?

Input Markets and the Origins of Class Struggle

When Karl Marx said, "Workers of the world unite; you have nothing to lose but your chains," he created a powerful slogan that became a rallying cry for workers around the world for more than 100 years. Economists now know that a more accurate, though much less effective, version of Marx's message would be, "Workers of the world unite so that you can raise your wage above your marginal revenue product." In this section, we will learn why such a reinterpretation of Marx's message is appropriate.

The society that we have been studying in this book has thus far been a classless one. Everyone has had an equal chance of being either a worker or a capitalist. But we know that this is not a true picture of what happens in the world. In most Western societies where capitalism prevails, some people have only their own labor services to sell to the market, whereas other people also have capital goods and perhaps land. With property distributed unequally, we would expect to find an unequal distribution of income among the population, and we do.

In this section, we will investigate how the returns to the owners of each factor of production—labor, capital, and land—are determined in markets that are organized competitively and in those that are not. When we examine noncompetitive markets, we will investigate the theory of alternating offer sequential bargaining and will look at some experimental results pertaining to this theory.

We will also examine the origins of class conflict in our model society. We will see that this conflict develops as the owners of the various factors of production compete with each other to gain a larger share of the economic pie. Naturally, each group devises arguments to justify the claim that it deserves greater economic rewards.

Public Goods, the Consequences of Strategic Voting Behavior, and the Role of Government

PUBLIC GOODS

Let's say that your college wants to build a swimming pool and asks all current students to contribute. Once the pool is built, no one can be excluded from it whether they contributed or not. Say that you like to swim and will use the pool if it is built. The college asks you to voluntarily write out a check and send it to the college and says the college will build the size of pool it can afford given the contributions. Say there are 10,000 students in your college and the suggested contribution is $100, although you are free to give as much or as little as you'd like. If all people gave $100, that would make a $1,000,000 swimming pool. Say finally that contributions are anonymous, so no one will ever know if you contributed or not.

Under these circumstances, would you contribute to the pool? If you think of this situation as a game, how much money do you think would be given at the (symmetric) equilibrium of the game?

This situation is characteristic of what economists call a public goods situation. Public goods are goods that, once constructed, are available to everyone, regardless of their contribution. (We will give a more complete definition later.) The game theoretical prediction is that people will "free ride" on the contributions of others, hoping that all other people give the prescribed $100 so they can enjoy a swimming pool worth $999,900 without contributing anything—have their cake and eat it too.

Public goods games have been the focus of a huge amount of attention by experimental economists for a long time. Later in this chapter, I will summarize some early experiments aimed at figuring out whether people take free rides.

PUBLIC GOODS WITH PUNISHMENT

In the teaser above, notice that no one can be punished for not contributing to the public good. But what do you think would happen if people could see who did not contribute and punish them at a cost to themselves? Because many people have a strong aversion to being a "sucker" in social dilemma situations, those who cooperate and contribute may be willing to punish free riders, even if this is costly for them and even if they cannot expect future benefits from their punishment activities. The main purpose of an experiment by Ernst Fehr and Simon Gachter* was to show experimentally that

(Continued)

---

* Ernst Fehr and Simon Gachter, "Cooperation and Punishment in Public Goods Experiments," *American Economic Review*, vol. 90, no. 4, September 2000, pp. 980–94.

EXPERIMENTAL
TEASER 27 *(Contd.)*

there is indeed a widespread willingness to punish the free riders. Their results indicate that this holds true even if punishment is costly and does not provide any material benefits for the punisher. In addition, they provide evidence that free riders are punished more heavily the more they deviate from the cooperation levels of the cooperators. Potential free riders, therefore, can avoid or at least reduce punishment by increasing their cooperation levels. This, in turn, suggests that in the presence of punishment opportunities, there will be less free riding. Let's see what happens.

In this chapter, we will see our model society face another and far more difficult challenge to free markets. In previous chapters, when free markets were challenged by problems such as incomplete or asymmetric information or externalities, agents in our model society sought and usually found ways to remedy the problems so that the free markets could remain virtually intact. It will now be much harder to find such solutions because the challenge to free markets comes from the properties of the goods being allocated. The agents in our model society must find a way to allocate *public goods*—goods that are in some sense shared among all the members of society—without requiring intervention by the government. This task will be extremely difficult for our agents, and much of our discussion in this chapter will center on how society can optimally coordinate the sharing of the costs of public goods.

To understand the problems that public goods present, we will ask several questions in this chapter: What is the optimal amount of a public good to produce, and what conditions must be satisfied at such an optimum? After this optimum is known, how can an economy achieve it? Will free markets be able to achieve this optimum, or must the government help the economy to coordinate its activities? Not surprisingly, these questions will spark an ideological battle in our model society that is similar to the battle that was fought over the externality problem (see Chapter 24). We would expect such a battle to occur because economic questions are often closely linked to questions of ideology.

This chapter is not concerned only with the problems that public goods pose for free markets and the solutions to those problems. In later sections of the chapter, we will consider the role that government plays in other areas of social discourse where it is assumed that society cannot rely strictly on market institutions to solve its problems. Instead, government takes the role of problem solver. It acts as an institutional architect that designs various types of institutions for society to use. We will discuss the problems that government faces when it attempts to play such a role.

private goods
Goods that have the properties of excludability and rival consumption.

excludability
When consumption of a good is restricted to certain people, such as people who are willing to pay for the good.

rival consumption
When consumption of a good by one person decreases the quantity of the good available for consumption by others and therefore deprives someone else of the good.

Public Goods and the Free-Rider Problem Defined

All the goods we have discussed so far are considered private goods because they have the properties of *excludability* and *rival consumption*. By excludability, we mean that consumption of a good is restricted to certain people, such as people who are willing to pay for the good. By rival consumption, we mean that consumption of a good by one person decreases the quantity of the good available for consumption by others and therefore deprives someone else of the good. An apple is an example of a private good. Only an individual who is willing to pay the price set by the seller can obtain it, and once the buyer consumes that apple, it is no longer available for consumption by anyone else.

As we would expect, public goods are just the opposite of private goods; that is, they have the properties of nonexcludability and nonrival consumption. If one person consumes such a good, others cannot be excluded from consuming it; and consumption of such a good by one person does not diminish the amount available for consumption by anyone else. An example of a public good is a national defense system. Once the system is operating, no member of society can be excluded from the protection that it provides. Furthermore, the extent to which it protects one person does not diminish the extent to which it protects all the other people in society.

Some goods are not purely public or private. Instead, they are "mixed" goods; that is, they have properties of both public and private goods. For example, there are goods that are excludable but nonrival in consumption. Cable television service falls into this category. It is available only to people who pay for it, but its use by one subscriber does not diminish either the quantity or the quality of the service received by any other subscribers. There are also goods that are nonexcludable but rival in consumption. For instance, no one can be excluded from a public park, but if too many people use the park, it becomes less enjoyable for everyone. We will not be concerned with mixed goods in this chapter.

The Free-Rider Problem

One problem raised by public goods is that the individual members of a society have no incentive to contribute their fair share of the costs of producing these goods because they know that they cannot be excluded from using the goods once they are produced. In fact, each member of society has an incentive to take a "free ride" by not contributing to the costs of public goods. This situation is known as the free-rider problem.

For example, once a society decides that it needs a national defense system, its government must determine how much money to spend on the system. Should the government establish a huge military complex or a small one? To answer this question correctly, the government needs complete and accurate information about the costs of national defense and the maximum willingness of *each* member of society to pay these costs. How can the government obtain this information? One way would be to simply ask all the members of society to write on a piece of paper how much they would be willing to spend for each level of military protection. A government official or some sort of public goods coordinator would collect these pieces of paper and use them to choose the level of national defense that is optimal (in a sense to be defined later).

Now, suppose that you know that all the other people in society are reporting their true maximum willingness to pay. You also know that there are so many people in society that your response, no matter what it is, will not affect the level of national defense chosen in any meaningful way. Under these circumstances, you will have a great incentive *not* to report truthfully. In fact, your rational response would be to write on the piece of paper that you are not willing to pay anything for national defense. Note, however, that if all the people in society followed the same logic, which they would if they were rational agents, then no one would offer to pay for the national defense system; as a result, society would have no military force to protect it.

public goods
Goods that have the properties of nonexcludability and nonrival consumption.

free-rider problem
When members of a society have incentives to take advantage of a public good by not contributing to paying its costs.

MEDIA NOTE

POSITIVE EXTERNALITIES

To Catch a Thief [Op-Ed]

The LoJack security system has been introduced in many states with great consequences for crime prevention.

Sold for $695, the LoJack is a radio transmitter that is hidden on a vehicle and then activated if the car is stolen. The transmitter then silently summons the police—and it is ruining the economics of auto theft. A car containing a LoJack system is not marked, so no potential thieves know if a car they are looking at is a LoJack car. This fact has big consequences for the car theft industry because car theft, it turns out, is a volume business. As a result, if even a small percentage of vehicles have LoJack, the professional thief will eventually steal a car with one and get caught.

The thief's challenge is that it's impossible to determine which vehicle has a LoJack (there's no decal). So stealing any car becomes significantly more risky, and one academic study found that the introduction of LoJack in Boston reduced car theft there by 50 percent.

Two Yale professors, Barry Nalebuff and Ian Ayres, note that this means that the LoJack benefits everyone, not only those who install the system. Professor Ayres and another scholar, Steven Levitt, found that every $1 invested in LoJack saves other car owners $10.

Professors Nalebuff and Ayres note that other antitheft devices—such as the Club, a pole-like device that locks the steering wheel—help protect a car, but only at the expense of the next vehicle.

"The Club doesn't reduce crime," Mr. Nalebuff says. "It just shifts it to the next person."

The problem with this line of thinking, however, is that if the LoJack system is undetectable, then there is little incentive to buy one yourself. You might as well free ride on the purchases of others and let them spend the $695. In other words, the benefit from crime prevention is a public good, and we know that people free ride in such circumstances.

In their clever book *Why Not?*, the two professors propose measures to shift people away from devices like the Club and toward LoJack. For example, they urge regulators to require insurers to give discounts to LoJack users. Massachusetts does that, so LoJack use is high in Massachusetts and car theft is now low.

Another solution is clever pricing or tax breaks for those who install a silent system. For example, suppose we apply the LoJack model to home burglary alarms. Conventional home alarms are accompanied by warning signs and don't reduce crime but simply shift the risk to the next house. What if we encouraged hidden silent alarms to change the economics of burglary?

Source: New York Times, June 28, 2005

SOLVED PROBLEM 25.1	**Question (Application and Extension: Public Goods and Externalities)**

Question (Application and Extension: Public Goods and Externalities)

Ten years ago, most commercial software applications were copy protected, which made them rather difficult to copy. Nowadays, software packages are hardly ever copy protected; that is, you can very easily copy software applications that others paid for and use them at home for free. On the other hand, most software manufacturers offer generous "upgrade policies," whereby legal owners of software can get more recent versions of that software at a special discount, and "support services," whereby legal owners get technical assistance from the manufacturer's technical experts. These facilities are, of course, not available to users of illegal copies of software. Explain this business practice in terms of public goods and externalities.

Answer

The problem with computer software is that it is exclusive but not excludable. In other words, if one person is using one copy of a software application, no one else can use the same copy, but one can always make a new copy and use it. Thus, it is very difficult to prevent free riding in the use of software because one can use software without paying for it. The upgrade policies and support services have to be viewed as additional enticements in this context. Although one's use and enjoyment of the software is presumably not contingent upon paying for it, these extra benefits are available only to the legitimate owners. Note that of the two additional benefits, an upgrade policy is not a great inducement to pay for one's software. When one can get the software for free, offers of discounts mean very little. The other policy of offering assistance only to bona fide users, however, can be critical in encouraging people to pay for their software.

The Pareto-Optimal Conditions for an Economy with Public Goods

In Chapter 22, we studied the conditions that must be met to ensure a Pareto-optimal allocation of private goods. We found that in an economy with only private goods, a Pareto optimum is reached when (1) the marginal rates of substitution between any two goods are equal for all agents in the economy; (2) the marginal rates of technical substitution for any two inputs are equal for all firms in the economy; and (3) the marginal rates of substitution equal the marginal rates of transformation for any two goods. In an economy that has public goods as well as private goods, these conditions will have to be modified, mostly because once a public good is produced, *all* people in the economy consume the same quantity of that good.

For example, let us consider a simple economy with one public good, one private good, and two consumers. Consumer 1 has an income of B_1, and consumer 2 has an income of B_2. We will assume that the private good is produced by a large number of competitive firms at a constant marginal cost of $5 per unit. The public good is provided by a firm that produces it on demand for the government at a constant marginal cost of $13 per unit. The utility functions of the consumers, which depend on the amounts of the private good and the public good they use, are $U_1[x_1(private), \bar{x}(public)]$(public)] for consumer 1 and $U_2[x_2(private), \bar{x}(public)]$ for consumer 2. Note that the amounts of the private good used by consumers 1 and 2 (x_1 and x_2, respectively) can differ (as indicated by the subscripts), but the amounts of the public good used by both ($\bar{x}$) must be the same.

With this information, we can derive the demand curves of our consumers for both the private good and the public good by the process of utility maximization (as discussed in Chapter 4). These demand curves are shown in Figure 25.1.

Figure 25.1(a) shows the demand curves of consumers 1 and 2 for the private good along with the marginal cost of providing the good. Note that every point on these demand curves indicates the maximum willingness of the consumer to pay for each unit purchased. We know that in a perfectly competitive economy, the price of the private good will be driven down to $5, so $5 is the price that both of our consumers will face. As we will soon see, at the Pareto-optimal arrangement, the prices charged to our consumers for the public good will be different.

Figure 25.1(b) shows the demand curves of consumers 1 and 2 for the public good, given that the price of the private good is $5. Curve D_1, for example, indicates the amounts of the public good that consumer 1 will demand at various prices if he has to pay $5 for the private good. Put differently, curves D_1 and D_2 show the maximum willingness of our consumers to pay for various quantities of the public good, given their budget constraints and the fact that they have to pay $5 for each unit of the private good they buy.

What amounts of the public and private goods are optimal for our model society to provide? We can easily find the answer to this question by looking at Figure 25.1(a). From this diagram, it is clear that our agents should purchase the private good until that point at which their marginal benefit from consuming one more

Figure 25.1

The Pareto-Optimal Conditions for a Public Goods Economy.

(a) The marginal benefit received by each person from consumption of the private good equals the marginal cost of providing the private good. (b) The *sum* of the marginal benefits received by all people from consumption of the public good equals the marginal cost of providing the public good.

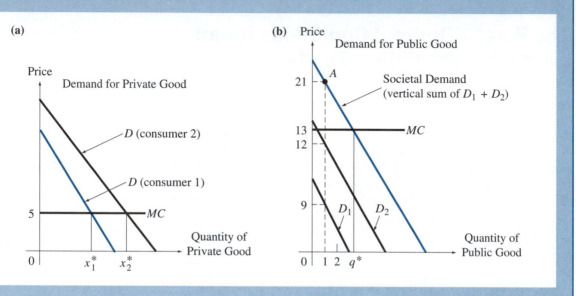

unit (as indicated by their demand curves) equals the marginal cost of providing the good. Hence, consumer 1 will use x_1^* and consumer 2 will use x_2^*. But what quantity of the public good should be provided? As a general rule, society should provide the public good until that point at which the marginal benefit to society of having one more unit produced equals the marginal cost of the good. However, each time society provides one unit of a public good, that unit is consumed by our two agents simultaneously because neither can be excluded from consuming it. Hence, while each unit of the public good costs \$13, the marginal benefit it provides to society is the *sum* of the marginal benefits received by our two agents. We can see this by looking at Figure 25.1(b). It shows the demand curves of consumers 1 and 2 for the public good along with the societal demand curve, which is obtained by vertically adding the individual demands at each quantity. For example, if one unit is provided, consumer 1 would be willing to pay \$9 for it, whereas consumer 2 would be willing to pay \$12. Thus, the societal benefit from having one unit of the public good provided is \$9 + \$12 = \$21, as we see at point A on the societal demand curve. From Figure 25.1(b), it is clear that at q^* units, the societal marginal cost of providing the q^*th unit of the public good equals the societal marginal benefit. Hence, q^* is the optimal quantity of the public good to produce.

We can now state the Pareto-optimal conditions for an economy with public goods:

1. Private goods should be allocated until that point at which the marginal rate of substitution between any two goods equals their price ratio.

2. Because we want efficient production, the marginal rates of technical substitution of the inputs to production of all goods must be equal.

3. Wherever public goods exist, the *sum* of the marginal rates of substitution (for all people in society) of private for public goods must equal the marginal rate of transformation between these goods.

Question (Application and Extension: Pareto-Optimal Conditions for an Economy with Public Goods)

SOLVED PROBLEM 25.2

A summer community with three people has to decide on the size of swimming pool it wants to build for its citizens. The marginal cost of increasing the pool size by 1 square foot is $3.50. The consultant they hired has decided that a 400-square-foot pool is the right size. The three people have marginal rates of substitution between pool size and other income of 2, $\frac{1}{2}$, and 1, respectively.

a) Is the 400-square-foot pool the optimal size?

Answer

Yes. The condition for an optimally sized public good is met because the sum of the marginal rates of substitution equals the marginal cost of the public good.

b) Assume now that the people have utility functions defined over the public good, *PU*, and a private good (income), *PR*, as follows:

$$\text{Person 1}: U_1 = PR^{1/2}PU^{1/2}$$
$$\text{Person 2}: U_2 = PR^{1/3}PU^{2/3}$$
$$\text{Person 3}: U_1 = PR^{1/5}PU^{4/5}$$

Assume that after their contributions to the public good, person 1 has $200 left to spend on private goods, person 2 has $400 left, and person 3 has $500 left. Is a 400-square-foot pool optimal for these people?

Answer

These people have Cobb-Douglas utility functions. As we have derived before, with these utility functions the marginal rates of substitution (between private and public goods) are as follows:

$$MRS_{person\ 1} = \frac{PU}{PR}$$
$$MRS_{person\ 2} = \frac{1}{2}\frac{PU}{PR}$$
$$MRS_{person\ 3} = \frac{1}{4}\frac{PU}{PR}$$

where *PU* and *PR* are the amounts of public and private goods each of these people have. Plugging these amounts into their marginal rates of substitution, we find that

$$MRS_{person\ 1} = \frac{PU}{PR} = \frac{400}{200}$$
$$MRS_{person\ 2} = \frac{1}{2}\frac{PU}{PR} = \frac{400}{800}$$
$$MRS_{person\ 3} = \frac{1}{4}\frac{PU}{PR} = \frac{400}{2,000}$$

Note, then, that the sum of these marginal rates of substitution is $2 + \frac{1}{2} + \frac{1}{5} \neq 3\frac{1}{2}$, which is the marginal cost of building the public good. Hence, the optimal conditions are not satisfied here.

The Lindahl Solution to the Public Goods Problem

Can the Pareto-optimal conditions for an economy with public goods be met by a competitive, free-market system? In other words, if we leave our agents alone to pursue their self-interest in an economy with public goods, will they determine allocations of public and private goods that satisfy Pareto-optimal conditions? To investigate this question, let us look at the work of Erik Lindahl.[1]

Let us assume that the members of a society always tell the truth about their preferences when they are asked. (We will return to this assumption later, but for now let us simply accept it.) We can then envision the economy of this society working as follows: There is no intervention in any private goods market because competitive forces should be sufficient to drive the price down to the marginal cost. For each public good, a government agent announces individual shares of the good's cost for the people in the economy. These cost shares represent the fraction of the cost of the public good that each person will have to pay if the good is provided. Hence, the people in this economy will face prices for all goods just as they would in a purely private goods economy. The only difference is that some of these prices—the cost shares of the public goods—will be announced by the government. Given these prices, people will maximize their utility and state their demand for the private and public goods. An equilibrium will be reached when the prices for private goods and the cost shares for public goods are such that no one wishes to change his or her demand for the private and public goods, the supply of private goods equals the demand, and everyone demands the same amount of each public good.

Note that at the equilibrium cost shares for a public good, everyone demands the same amount of the good because public goods are nonexcludable. Thus, once a quantity is supplied, everyone will consume the same amount of the good. At the private goods equilibrium, each person faces the same price but consumes a different quantity. This is just the opposite of the situation that exists at the public goods equilibrium, where each person faces a different price but consumes the same quantity. Hence, we must find cost shares that make all people want to consume the same quantity. Otherwise, someone will wish to change his or her demand.

Although Lindahl's scheme is not a totally free-market scheme, it involves the government simply as a *coordinator* for the public goods markets. It is therefore not as much a market intervention as it is a market aid. Lindahl's scheme is illustrated in Figure 25.2.

In looking at Figure 25.2, we will assume that there are just two goods in the economy, one public and one private, and only two people, person 1 and person 2. Part (a) of the figure shows the amount of the private good consumed by person 1 or person 2 along the vertical axis and the amount of the public good consumed along the horizontal axis. The preferences of the person are represented by the indifference curves. The budget and prices faced by the person are indicated by the slope and placement of the budget line.

To make matters simple, let us assume that the price of the private good is equal to 1. In this way, changes in the slope of the budget line will reflect changes in the person's cost share for the public good. When the cost share of the public

---

[1] Erik Lindahl was a noted Swedish economist who did extensive work in the area of public goods. He developed an approach to the provision and financing of public goods that is known as the Lindahl solution or the voluntary exchange model. This approach is noncoercive; it involves a unanimous voluntary agreement by the members of society. The Lindahl solution builds on ideas originally advanced by Knut Wicksell, another famous Swedish economist.

Figure 25.2

The Lindahl Solution.

At the Lindahl equilibrium, point D, both agents demand the level of the public good provided (g^* units), given their assigned cost shares ($\bar{h}$ for person 1 and $1 - \bar{h}$ for person 2).

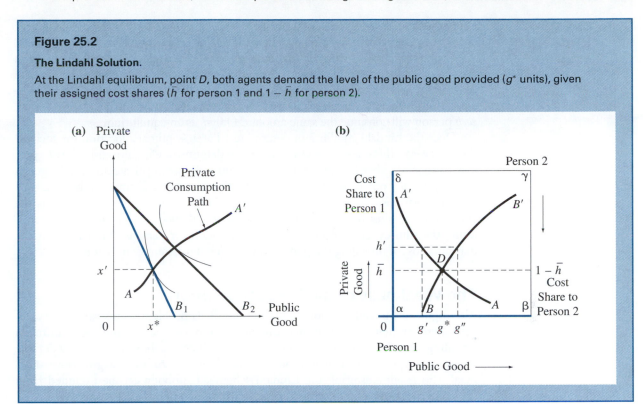

good is relatively high, we will be on budget line B_1 and the person will consume a bundle containing x^* units of the public good and x' units of the private good. When this person's cost share decreases, the budget line will rotate outward and he or she will consume more of the public good (assuming that the public good is a normal good).

In part (b) of Figure 25.2, the origin for person 1 is at point α and the origin for person 2 is at point γ. The horizontal axis shows the amount of the public good provided, reading from left to right. Hence, at α no public good is provided, while at β a large amount is provided. The vertical axis shows the cost share of each person. The cost share of person 1 is h and the cost share of person 2 is $1 - h$. (Note that $h + (1 - h) = 1$.) In moving up the vertical axis from point α to point δ, person 1's cost share, h, increases, while person 2's cost share, $1 - h$, decreases. Line AA' is the demand curve of person 1 for the public good, and line BB' is the demand curve of person 2 for the public good. Note that line AA' is simply the private price consumption path derived in Figure 25.2(a). At point δ, person 1 faces a cost share that is equal to 1. Hence, she must bear the entire cost burden but demands none of the public good, as the graph has been drawn. Note that because she demands none of the public good, she will spend all her income, B_1, on the private good.

Any point in part (b) of Figure 25.2 determines an allocation in our mixed economy consisting of both private and public goods. At point D, for example, g^* units of the public good are provided. Person 1's cost share is $\bar{h}$, whereas person 2's cost share is $1 - \bar{h}$. If the price (marginal cost) of the public good is \$1, person 1 will spend $\pi_1 = (\bar{h} g^*)(\$1)$ on the public good and the remainder of her budget, $B_1 - \pi_1$, on the private good. Similarly, person 2 will spend $\pi_2 = (1 - \bar{h})g^*(\$1)$ on the public good and $B_2 - \pi_2$ on the private good. Point D is not just any point, however. It indicates what we will call the **Lindahl equilibrium** for the economy. To see why it is an equilibrium, let us say that we raise the cost share of person 1 from $\bar{h}$ to h' and,

Lindahl equilibrium
A competitive equilibrium for a market with both private and public goods.

hence, lower the cost share of person 2 from $1 - \bar{b}$ to $1 - b'$. Because the cost share of person 1 has increased, her demand for the public good falls from g^* to g'. The opposite is true for person 2. Because of his decreased cost share, his demand for the public good increases from g^* to g''. However, at b' we see that the demand of person 1 and the demand of person 2 for the public good are unequal. Such a situation cannot be an equilibrium because, whatever level of public good is provided, *each* person will consume the same amount. Only $\bar{b}$ is an equilibrium.

Does the Lindahl equilibrium determine a Pareto-optimal allocation for society? The answer to this question is yes, and we can demonstrate it quite easily.[2] At $\bar{b}$, person 1 is equating her marginal rate of substitution between private and public goods to her price for public good $\bar{b}$. At the same time, person 2 is equating his marginal rate of substitution to $1 - \bar{b}$. Hence, $MRS_1 + MRS_2 = \bar{b} + 1 - \bar{b} = 1$, which is the condition that must be satisfied for a Pareto-optimal allocation. That is, at the optimum, the sum of the marginal rates of substitution for persons 1 and 2 equals the marginal cost of providing the public good, which, by assumption, is equal to 1.

The Weakness of the Lindahl Solution

Although the Lindahl solution to the public goods problem seems satisfactory, let us remember that it is predicated on the assumption that people are truthful in revealing their preferences for public goods. There is, however, a considerable incentive for people in such an economy not to tell the truth to the government official who is administering the Lindahl scheme. If nobody can be excluded from the enjoyment of a public good once it is produced, then the less a person contributes to the cost of the good, the more he or she will have to spend on private goods. In the extreme, when people falsely claim no demand and therefore contribute nothing to the cost of the public good, they are able to retain their entire budget for the purchase of private goods. This strategy is called *taking a free ride* because the people who do not contribute are being carried along without cost by the other members of society who do contribute. Obviously, if everyone takes a free ride, society will not be able to provide any public goods.

The Lindahl scheme can be treated as a game of strategy. This normal-form game involves the two-person economy with two goods, one private and one public, which we have been using in our discussion of the Lindahl solution to the public goods problem. At the beginning of the game, the government administrator asks each person to indicate his or her demand curve for the public good, assuming

---

[2] The proof that a Lindahl equilibrium is Pareto optimal is easily demonstrated using a little calculus. Let the utility function of person 1 be represented by $U_1 = U_1(B_1 - bg, g)$. In this utility function, we see that person 1 obtains utility from the public good consumed, g, and that all money not spent on the public good, $B_1 - bg$, is spent on the private good, which also yields utility. (b is the cost share for the public good that person 1 must bear.) Having substituted the budget constraint for this utility function, person 1 will maximize the following to achieve her optimal utility given $b : MaxU_1 (B_1 - bg, g)$. The first-order condition is $\partial U_1/\partial g = \partial U_1/\partial g + (\partial U_1/\partial x)(dx/dg) = \partial U_1/\partial g + \partial U_1/\partial x(-b) = 0$, where x is the amount of the private good consumed by person 1. This can be rewritten as $\partial U_1/\partial g = (\partial U_1/\partial x)b$ or $(\partial U_1/(\partial g)/(\partial U_1/\partial x) = b$. Note that $(\partial U_1/\partial g)/(\partial U_1/\partial x)$ is the marginal rate of substitution between public and private goods for person 1. Person 2 goes through the same maximization process: $MaxU_2[B_2 - (1 - b)g, g]$. The first-order condition here is $\partial U_2/\partial g = \partial U_2/ g + (\partial U_2/\partial y)(dy/dg) = \partial U_2/\partial g + (\partial U_2/\partial x)(1 - b) = 0$, where y is the amount of the private good consumed by person 2. This can be rewritten as $\delta U_1/\delta g = (\delta U_1/\delta x)(1 - b)$ or $(\partial U_2/\partial g)/(\partial U_2/\partial y) = (1 - b)$. Because from person 1's maximization, $b = (\partial U_1/\partial g)/(\partial U_1/\partial x)$, and from person 2's maximization, $(\partial U_2/\partial g)/(\partial U_2/\partial y)$, we see that at the Lindahl cost share b, $(\partial U_1/\partial g)/(\partial U_1/\partial x) = 1 - (\partial U_2/\partial g)/(\partial U_2/\partial y)$ or $(\partial U_1/\partial g)/(\partial U_1/\partial x) + (\partial U_2/\partial g)/(\partial U_2/\partial y) = 1$. Hence, as the Pareto-optimal condition dictates, at the Lindahl equilibrium, the sum of the marginal rates of substitution between private and public goods equals the marginal cost of providing these goods.

that the price for the private good will remain fixed (perhaps because this good is produced at a constant marginal cost). After collecting information about demand for the public good, the government administrator searches for a set of cost shares that will result in a Lindahl equilibrium. The administrator then assigns the cost shares to the members of society.

In this game, the strategy of each player is embodied in the demand function that he or she submits to the government administrator. The payoff to each player depends on the demand functions submitted by *all* the players.

At this point in our discussion, two questions arise about the Lindahl game: At the Nash equilibrium for the game, do people submit their true demand functions, or do they lie? If they lie, does the resulting equilibrium determine a Pareto optimum, or does the utility of the people in the economy decrease because they lie? The answers to these two questions are quite simply that truth-telling is not a Nash equilibrium strategy for the Lindahl game and that less than the Pareto-optimal amount of the public good will be provided if the Lindahl scheme is implemented. To see why this is so, let us consider Figure 25.3.

In Figure 25.3, we see the demand curves for persons 1 and 2 that were previously shown in Figure 25.2(b). We also see a set of indifference curves for person 1. Each indifference curve depicts the combinations of amount and cost share of the public good that will make person 1 indifferent. For example, at point a on indifference curve I_2, society produces g_a units of the public good and asks person 1 to contribute h_a. If we move from point a to point b, we see that person 1 receives more of the public good, which is beneficial, but has to pay more for it, which is unfavorable. On balance, therefore, person 1 is indifferent between points a and b. The lower indifference curves are better for person 1 than the higher ones. To see this, compare points b and c.

Point c in Figure 25.3 corresponds to the same amount of the public good as point b, but point c is on a lower indifference curve than point b. Thus, the cost share that person 1 must pay in order to receive the same amount of the public good is lower: h_c rather than h_b. We can therefore conclude that point c is better for person 1 than point b. Indeed, all the points on indifference curve I_1 are better than all the points on indifference curve I_2.

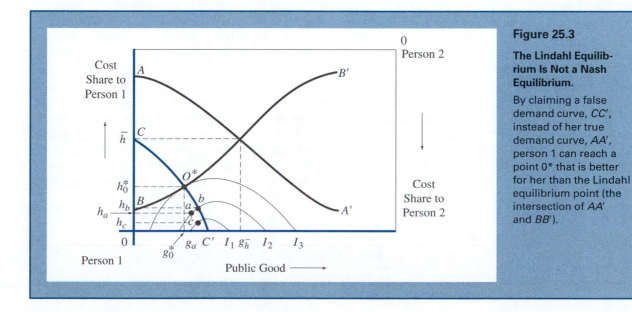

Figure 25.3

The Lindahl Equilibrium Is Not a Nash Equilibrium.

By claiming a false demand curve, *CC'*, instead of her true demand curve, *AA'*, person 1 can reach a point 0* that is better for her than the Lindahl equilibrium point (the intersection of *AA'* and *BB'*).

Let us say that person 1 assumes that person 2 will submit his truthful demand curve BB' to the government administrator. Person 1 can then act like a Stackelberg oligopolist and choose the combination of amount and cost share of the public good along demand curve BB' that will make her most happy. Put differently, person 1 will want to choose the point on demand curve BB' that places her on the *lowest* indifference curve. Such a point is point 0^*. If person 1 then submits a false demand curve, say CC', to the government administrator, the Lindahl equilibrium will be at point 0^*. At this point, person 1's cost share will be h_{0^*}, and g_{0^*} units of the public good will be produced. However, at the Pareto-optimal Lindahl equilibrium, which results when everyone in society tells the truth, person 1's cost share will be $\bar{h}$, and $g_{\bar{h}}$ units of the public good will be produced. Clearly, then, the Lindahl equilibrium is not a Nash equilibrium.

If everyone else tells the truth in the Lindahl game, then person 1 has an incentive to lie. Hence, the outcome of the Lindahl scheme is likely to be suboptimal for society. The free-rider problem causes this scheme to fail.

Theoretical Solutions to the Free-Rider Problem

The research of Mark Isaac, Kevin McCabe, and Charles Plott seems to indicate that free riding is a real problem that society must address in order to achieve an optimal sharing of the costs of public goods. We therefore need a scheme for allocating the costs of public goods that can replace the Lindahl solution. This scheme must be one that will give people an incentive to reveal the truth about their public goods preferences to the government. To find such a scheme, we will now take a look at the work of Theodore Groves and John Ledyard as well as that of Nicholas Tideman, Gordon Tullock, and Vernon Smith.

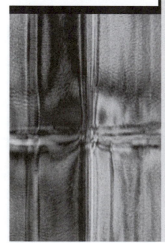

RESOLVING
TEASER 26

To what extent is free riding really a problem? To find the answer to this question, let us quickly survey some of the early experimental evidence that has been accumulated about the propensity of people (or at least laboratory subjects) to free ride.

Early in the modern debate about free riding, Leif Johansen stated, "I do not know of many historical results or other empirical evidence which show convincingly that the problem of correct revelation of preferences has any practical significance."[3] This view was supported by an early experiment conducted by Peter Bohm.[4] In Bohm's study, adults were asked to come for an interview for which they would be given a fee. During the interview, they were asked how much of the fee they would be willing to pay to watch a film featuring two popular comedians. They were told that they would be shown the film only if the sum of the contributions made by all the people interviewed was greater than the cost of showing the film. However, if the film was shown, all the subjects could view it. Clearly, the showing of the film was a public good because it had the properties of nonexcludability and nonrival consumption. Nobody

(Continued)

---

[3] This statement appears in Leif Johansen, "The Theory of Public Goods: Misplaced Emphasis?" *Journal of Public Economics* 7, no. 1 (February 1977): 147–52.

[4] Peter Bohm, "Estimating Demand for Public Goods: An Experiment," *European Economic Review* 3 (1982): 111–30.

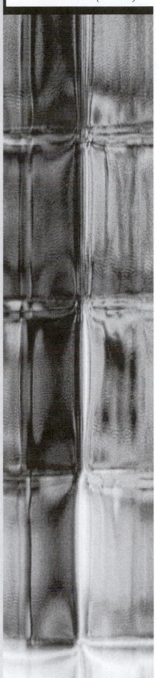

could be excluded from viewing the film, and one person's enjoyment of the film would not diminish anyone else's enjoyment of the film.

Five different rules were used to determine how much the subjects would be charged. For example, under one rule, the subjects were charged whatever amount they offered; under another rule, they were charged a percentage of that amount; and under still another rule, they were charged nothing at all. Clearly, these different rules lead to different incentives to tell the truth. (Consider how you would respond to a rule that requires you to pay the full amount you offer versus a rule that allows you to pay nothing.) Bohm found that the subjects tended to offer equal contributions no matter which rule was used. He took this as evidence of the subjects' propensity to tell the truth and not take advantage of the opportunities to free ride. Thus, Bohm's experiment can be viewed as supporting the idea that free riding is not a relevant problem. Other experiments by Friedrich Schneider and Werner Pommerehne and by Gerald Marwell and Ruth Ames reached similar conclusions.[5]

Most of these studies had two weaknesses. First, they measured the willingness of subjects to pay for a public good instead of controlling this willingness to pay in the laboratory. Second, they were performed only once. Hence, the subjects did not have the opportunity to learn that dishonesty might be the most profitable policy.

Isaac, McCabe, and Plott performed a series of experiments that remedied the weaknesses of the earlier studies.[6] In this study, the subjects were given demand and payoff schedules for a public good. Each of the subjects was then asked to indicate what contribution he or she wanted to make to the cost of the public good. The subjects wrote the amounts of their contributions on pieces of paper; and the experiment administrator collected these pieces of paper, totaled the contributions, and calculated how many units of the public good could be produced. The quantity to be produced was determined by equating the marginal aggregate contributions of the subjects to the assumed marginal cost of $1.30 per unit.

The net payoff to the subjects was the difference between the value of the units produced and the amount they contributed to the cost of the good. For example, let us say that the subjects were told that they would be paid $3 if one unit of the good was produced, another $2 if two units were produced, another $1 if three units were produced, and nothing more for any additional units produced. If two units were produced and a subject contributed $1 per unit, her net payoff would be the sum of the values of the first two units ($3 + $2 = $5) minus her contribution ($1 + $1 = $2), *or* $5 − $2 = $3.

This experiment was repeated ten times. The researchers found that the contributions were significantly higher the first time the experiment was run than they were in later stages. In fact, as the number of stages increased, the amount that the subjects were willing to contribute came closer and closer to zero, the pure free-ride point. However, it never reached that point. The researchers interpreted these results as indicating that repetition and learning tended to increase free riding. Because repetition and learning are features of the public goods situation in the real world, we might view the results of this study as evidence that the free-riding problem is a matter of legitimate concern.

[5] F. Schneider and W. Pommerehne, "Free Riding and Collective Action: An Experiment in Public Microeconomics," *Quarterly Journal of Economics* 116 (1981): 689–704. G. Marwell and R. Ames, "Economists Free Ride, Does Anyone Else? Experiments on the Provision of Public Goods," *Journal of Public Economics* 15 (1981): 295–310.

[6] Mark Isaac, Kevin McCabe, and Charles Plott, "Public Goods Provision in an Experimental Environment," *Journal of Public Economics* 26 (1985): 51–74.

The Demand-Revealing Mechanism

demand-revealing mechanism
A mechanism that creates the incentive for people to reveal their public goods preferences in a truthful manner.

A demand-revealing mechanism creates the incentive for people to reveal their public goods preferences in a truthful manner. Let us see how such a mechanism works.

Assume that there are four houses on a dark street and that the people who own these houses decide that they want streetlights. The president of the street association proposes three lighting plans, all of which cost the same amount of money. Plan A calls for one very bright streetlight, plan B calls for two somewhat less bright streetlights, and plan C calls for three streetlights that are considerably less bright. It is agreed that the four members of the association should indicate their preferences by stating how much they would be willing to pay to implement each plan. The true willingness of the association members to pay for the three plans is summarized in Table 25.1.

This table tells us, for instance, that member 3 most prefers having two streetlights and would therefore be willing to contribute up to $80 for plan B, but he would be willing to contribute only $20 for plan A (he thinks one streetlight will do little good even if it is very bright) and would be willing to contribute only $25 for plan C (he fears that the extra streetlight will prevent him from sleeping).

The problem now is to devise a scheme that will force the members of the street association to report their preferences truthfully so that the president can choose the optimal plan. Using our free-market utilitarian assumption from Chapter 2, we will consider the "optimal" plan to be the one that maximizes the difference between the total amount the members are willing to pay for a plan and its cost. Because we are assuming that the costs of the three plans are the same, the optimal plan is simply the one that maximizes the members' willingness to pay. Hence, the optimal plan is plan B, for which the total willingness to pay is $220, as opposed to $150 for plan A and $205 for plan C.

Schemes of this type were first investigated by William Vickrey, Theodore Groves, Edward Clarke, Nicholas Tideman, and Gordon Tullock. We will use Tideman and Tullock's demand-revealing scheme as an example here. Let us see how it works. First, each member of the street association writes on a piece of paper the maximum amount of money he or she would be willing to pay to implement each of the three plans for installing streetlights. The president of the street association accepts this information as true and then chooses the plan for which the total reported willingness to pay is the highest. Next, the president must specify how much each member will have to pay. To do this, she identifies the plan that will be chosen when any member's report is included in her calculations and the plan that would be chosen if that member's report were not included. If the same plan would be chosen in both cases, then the member is charged nothing. If

Member	A	B	C	Tax
Table 25.1	**A Demand-Revealing Mechanism Based on a True Willingness to Pay for Streetlights.**			
		PLAN		
1	$60	$50	$40	0
2	30	70	50	5
3	20	80	25	40
4	40	20	90	0
Total willingness to pay	**150**	**220**	**205**	

the report changes the association's choice, then the member is charged the difference between the total willingness to pay for the plan chosen without his or her report and the total willingness to pay for the plan chosen when his or her report is included.

For instance, if all members of the street association report truthfully as shown in Table 25.1, the costs will be nothing for member 1, $5 for member 2, $40 for member 3, and nothing for member 4. These costs are determined as follows: The president chooses plan B because the total reported willingness to pay for plan B is the highest. If we eliminate member 1's report, then the total willingness to pay for plan A is $90, that for plan B is $170, and that for plan C is $165. Again, plan B is chosen, so the same plan is adopted with or without member 1's report. Hence, member 1's cost is zero. Now, let us look at member 2. When her report is included, the association's choice is plan B. However, when her report is eliminated, the association's choice is plan C, for which the total willingness to pay is then $155 as opposed to $150 for plan B and $120 for plan A. Because member 2's report changes the choice from plan C to plan B, she is charged the difference between the total willingness to pay of $155 for plan C and the total willingness to pay of $150 for plan B without her. Similar calculations are made for members 3 and 4.

Why does such a scheme work? Why are the selfish, utility-maximizing members of the street association forced by this scheme to tell the truth? To understand why this type of scheme is effective, let us look at the calculations for member 3. He likes plan B the most, then plan C, and then plan A.

Let us say that the three other members submit reports such that the president of the association would choose plan B without member 3's report. In this case, it would clearly be best for member 3 to submit a truthful report. If he does, plan B (his first choice) will be selected and he will not have to pay a share of its costs. If he were to lie and say he would be willing to pay more for plan A or plan C, he would then run the risk of changing the association's choice from plan B to something else and having to pay part of the cost.

Now let us say that the other three members of the association send reports such that plan C would be chosen without member 3's report. Then if member 3 submits a report that keeps the choice at plan C, he will not be charged and his net benefit will be $25 ($25 minus a cost of zero). If plan C is the association's choice, then member 3's cost will be independent of his report, no matter what it says. Assume that he is thinking of submitting a report that changes the choice from plan C to plan B. If he does so, his cost will be either more than $55 or less than $55. If it is more than $55, then he would be better off to tell the truth and let plan C remain the choice because his payoff from changing the choice from plan C to plan B will be less than $25, the payoff he receives when plan C is selected and he is not charged. Similarly, if member 3's cost is less than $55, he is better off reporting his true preferences because plan B will then be chosen and his cost will be less than $55, which means that his payoff will be more than $25. This line of reasoning indicates that when such a demand-revealing mechanism is used, honesty becomes the best policy among a set of rational economic agents.

Question (Content Review: Demand Revelation)

Consider the preferences of four people—persons 1, 2, 3, and 4—in the following society. In this society, they must choose between three public goods projects—projects A, B, and C.

SOLVED PROBLEM 25.3

		Project		
		A	B	C
Person	1	60	30	80
	2	70	100	30
	3	80	50	70
	4	50	40	50
Total		**260**	**220**	**230**

a) Calculate the Clarke-Groves-Tullock taxes for each person.

Answer

To calculate the Clarke-Groves-Tullock taxes, let us proceed in steps.

First, assuming that the numbers in the table are the truthful numbers, we see that project A would be chosen because it has the largest collective willingness to pay. Now let us calculate the taxes of each person. We do this by eliminating each player separately, seeing if each elimination changes the social choice, and then taxing the person the amount of money needed to restore the public choice to its former alternative. If person 1 were eliminated, we see that the public alternative would remain at project A because in the society without him, project A would have a total of $200, project B a total of $190, and project C a total of $150. Hence, the addition of person 1 to society would have no effect on the public choice, and his tax is zero. Proceeding in a similar manner for the other three people, we find that if person 2 were eliminated, the public choice would change from project A to project C. In that case, project A would have a total of $190, project B a total of $120, and project C a total of $200. To restore project A to the social choice, we would need to add $10 to choice A. Hence $10 is the tax for person 2. The taxes of person 3 and person 4 would be zero as well because eliminating either of them would not alter the social choice.

b) Say that person 1 lied about his true preference and stated that project C was worth 100 to him and not 80. Would this lie change his payoff? Would it change the payoff of anyone else? If so, decide whose payoff would change and by how much.

Answer

If person 1 lied and reported 100, his tax would not change, but the tax on person 2 would increase from $10 to $30. Run through the calculations listed above and verify this fact.

The Weakness of the Demand-Revealing Mechanism. While seemingly satisfactory, the demand-revealing mechanism, like many of the schemes presented before in this book, is not devoid of problems. There is nothing in the demand-revealing mechanism that guarantees that the sum of the subsidies paid and the costs imposed by the scheme will add up to zero. Hence, the government may run a huge surplus in administering the mechanism. This surplus cannot be divided among the citizens because that would ruin the incentive properties of the scheme. Thus, it will have to be destroyed (perhaps dumped in the ocean), and that will conflict with Pareto optimality.

The Auction Election Mechanism

Vernon Smith has pioneered experimental studies in a variety of fields. In Chapter 16, we surveyed his work in the design of market institutions. We will now examine a scheme that Smith has developed for forcing people to reveal their true preferences for public goods. He calls this scheme the auction election mechanism. In this scheme, a group of N people must decide how much of a public good is to be produced. The value of X units of the public good to person i is given by $V_i(X)$ with $V_i(0) = 0$, meaning that the value of not producing any amount of the public good is equal to zero. The scheme works as follows:

1. Each person submits a two-element bid (b_i, X_i), in which b_i is the amount of money person i is willing to pay for the public good and X_i is the amount of the public good he or she would like produced. If the good is produced, then person i's cost share will be $(q - B_i)X$, where $B_i = \Sigma_{j \neq i} b_j$ and $X = \Sigma X_k/N$. In other words, people submit bids, and *if* any quantity of the public good is produced, then each person pays the difference between the cost of the good, q, and the sum of the bids made by all other people, B_i, times the average quantity of the public good demanded by all N people, X.

2. Each person has an unqualified right to reject or agree to his or her cost share $(q - B_i)X$.

3. If *all* the people agree to their cost shares and the quantity X, then X units of the public good are produced and person i pays $(q - B_i)X$. If no agreement is reached, no amount of the public good is produced and the payoff to each person is $V_i(0)$.

Note that this scheme is like the demand-revealing mechanism in that the cost share of an individual depends not on his or her bid but on the bids of all the other people in society. It is different from the demand-revealing mechanism in that it requires unanimity in order for society to reach a decision. In addition, the subsidies or costs implied by the equilibrium of this scheme are not necessarily those of the demand-revealing mechanism. However, the Lindahl equilibrium is an equilibrium in both the demand-revealing scheme and this one.

Smith ran a set of experiments to find out whether the auction election mechanism would successfully determine the optimal amount of a public good to produce.[7] In these experiments, three public goods projects were under consideration. One of the projects was the "best" in the sense that the sum of money people were willing to pay for it was greater than the sum they were willing to pay for any other project. In each experiment, the three projects were considered by a group of six subjects, who participated in the auction election scheme for up to ten rounds.

Table 25.2 shows the valuation placed on each project by each subject. For example, we see that subject 1 is willing to pay up to $60 for project 2. (Of course, he would like to pay less for it, but $60 is his maximum willingness to pay.) On the other hand, subject 1 would have to be paid $20 in compensation if project 3 were built. (The valuation of −$20 implies that subject 1 would be damaged by the construction of that project.)

According to the subject valuations in Smith's experiments, project 2 is clearly the best project for society. What we would now like to know is whether the mechanism used in these experiments induced people to reveal the truth about their preferences. Although telling the truth is not a dominant strategy in the auction election mechanism, truth-telling does constitute a Nash equilibrium strategy. However, many other Nash equilibria exist here as well. Let us consider Figure 25.4, which presents the results of Smith's experiments.

In Figure 25.4, we see the round-by-round bids of each subject in each experiment along with the sum of the bids of the groups. Only the bids on project 2 are shown because that is the project with which we are primarily concerned. Looking

---

[7] Vernon Smith, "The Principle of Unanimity and Voluntary Consent in Social Choice," *Journal of Political Economy* (December 1977).

Table 25.2	Subject Valuations of Three Public Goods Projects in Smith's Experiments.						
	SUBJECT						
Project	**1**	**2**	**3**	**4**	**5**	**6**	**Total**
1	$ 5	−$ 30	−$ 30	$ 25	$ 25	$ 0	−$ 5
2	60	5	5	−10	−10	55	105
3	−20	45	45	0	0	−25	45

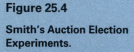

Figure 25.4

Smith's Auction Election Experiments.

The auction election experiments usually result in the rational group choice, but they do not always induce truth-telling.

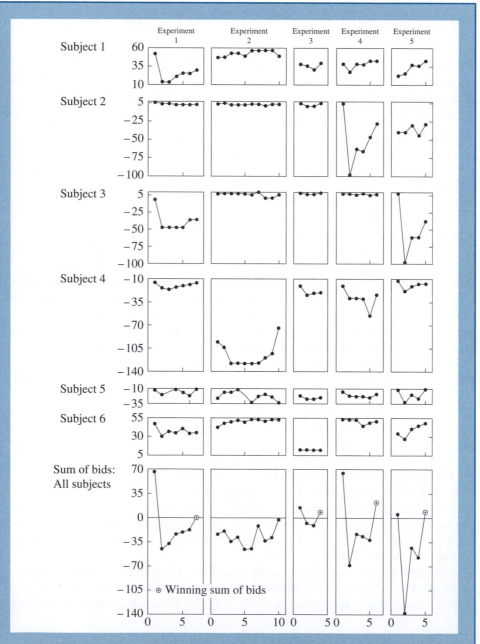

at the bottom set of graphs, we find that the groups usually came to a unanimous decision, as indicated by the circle in the graphs for four of the five experiments. Hence, the auction election mechanism does quite well in facilitating a rational choice by a group. In terms of individual behavior, the subjects often told the truth, but truth-telling does not appear to have been the general rule. Thus, the auction election mechanism is satisfactory at the group level, but it does less well at the level of the individual.

After all our discussions of theories and experiments, the free-rider issue seems as murky as it was in the beginning. Although free riding is apparently a problem that must be dealt with in allocating the costs of public goods, the mechanism that should be used for this purpose is still an open question.

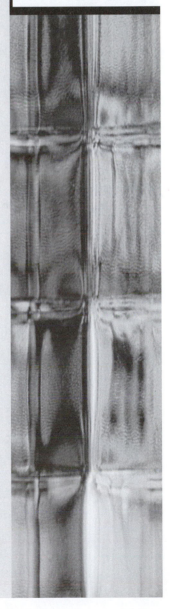

RESOLVING
TEASER 27

The Fehr-Gachter experiment consists of a public good experiment with four treatment conditions. There is a "stranger" treatment with *and* without punishment opportunities and a "partner" treatment with *and* without punishment opportunities. In the partner treatment, the same group of $n = 4$ subjects plays a finitely repeated public goods game for ten periods; that is, the group composition does not change across periods. Ten groups of size $n = 4$ participated in the partner treatment. In contrast, in the stranger treatment the total number of participants in an experimental session, $N = 24$, is randomly partitioned into smaller groups of size $n = 4$ in each of the ten periods. Thus, the group composition in the stranger treatment is randomly changed from period to period. The treatment without punishment opportunities serves as a control for the treatment with punishment opportunities. In a given session of the stranger treatment, the *same N* subjects play ten periods in the punishment and ten periods in the no-punishment condition. Similarly, in a session of the partner treatment, all groups of size *n* play the punishment and the no-punishment condition. Each group of subjects played the game for ten periods with (or without) punishment and then, for the last ten periods, they switched to the other condition.

The actual game played in the experiment is as follows. In each period, each of the *n* subjects in a group receives an endowment of *y* tokens. A subject can either keep these tokens for him- or herself or invest g_i tokens ($0 \leq g_i \leq y$) into a project. The decisions about g_i are made simultaneously. The monetary payoff for each subject *i* in the group is given by $\Pi_i = y - g_i + a(\sum_{j=1}^{n} g_j)$ where $0 < a < 1 < na$. In all treatment conditions, the endowment is given by $y = 20$, groups are of size $n = 4$, the marginal payoff of the public good is fixed at $a = 0.4$, and the number of participants in a session is $N = 24$.

What this payoff function says is that a payoff for a subject is equal to the amount of money the subject starts out with, $y = 20$, minus what he or she contributes, g_i, plus $a = 0.4$ times the total amount contributed by all the other subjects. This is a standard game used in public goods experiments called the "voluntary contribution game." Given these parameters, contributing zero is a dominant-strategy Nash equilibrium

The major difference between the no-punishment and the punishment conditions is the addition of a second decision stage after the simultaneous contribution decision in each period. At the second stage, subjects are given the opportunity to simultaneously punish each other after they are informed about the individual contributions of the other group members.

Group member *j* can punish group member *i* by assigning so-called punishment points p_{ji} to *i*. For each punishment point assigned to *i*, the first-stage payoff of *i*, Π_i, is reduced by 10%. However, the first-stage payoff of subject *i* can never be reduced

(Continued)

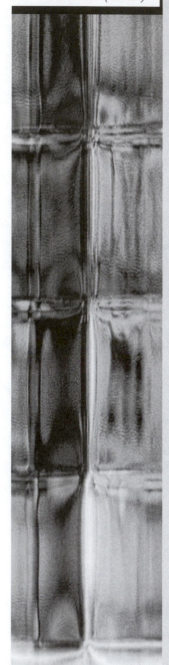

RESOLVING
TEASER 27 *(Contd.)*

below zero. The total payoff from the punishment condition is the sum of the period-payoffs, which include how much subjects earn in the stage one game, how much they are punished, and how much they punish others. (For more details, see Ernst Fehr and Simon Gachter, "Cooperation and Punishment in Public Goods Experiments," *American Economic Review,* vol. 90, no. 4, September 2000, pp. 980–94.)

The basic results of the experiment can be seen in their Figures 1A and 1B and Figures 3A and 3B.

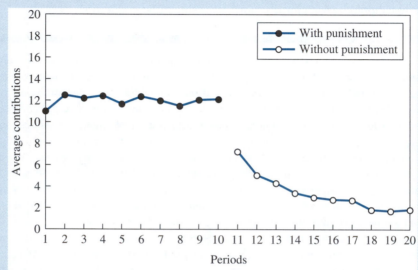

Figure 1A. Average Contributions over Time in the Stranger-Treatment (Sessions 1 and 2)

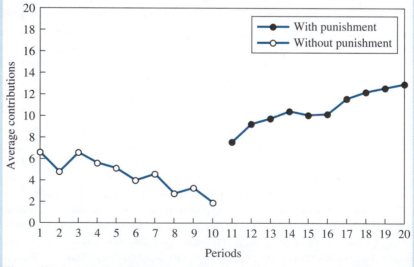

Figure 1B. Average Contributions over Time in the Stranger-Treatment (Session 3)

(Continued)

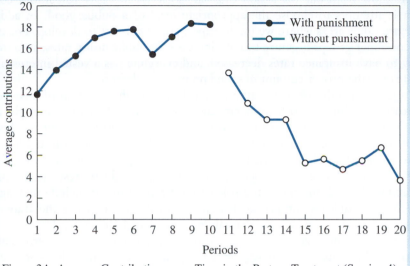

Figure 3A. Average Contributions over Time in the Partner-Treatment (Session 4)

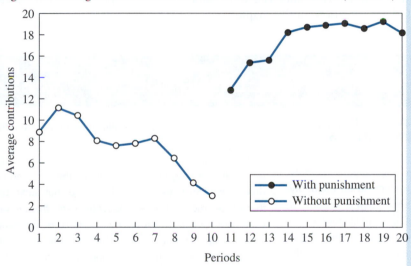

Figure 3B. Average Contributions over Time in the Partner-Treatment (Session 5)

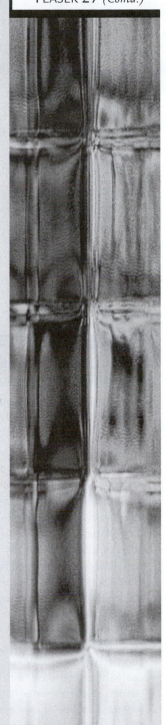

These figures tell a very dramatic story. The ability to punish free riders, in both the stranger and partner treatments, significantly increases the contributions that people make to the public good. In the partner treatment, the level of contributions tended toward the full 20 units, which is the efficient amount, while in the stranger treatment it seemed to tend toward about 12. Without punishment, there is a clear tendency to converge toward zero, the dominant-strategy equilibrium.

The Role of Government

As we know from our discussion thus far, society can easily run into a conflict when it attempts to choose the appropriate level of a public good. In addition, there are other areas where we might expect social conflict to develop. For example, consumer groups organize to fight increases in public utility rates, auto owners lobby to have insurance rates decreased, and everyone has a vested interest in the debate over the proper amount to spend on national defense.

In the remainder of this chapter, we will discuss the function of government in creating institutions to help its citizens solve such conflicts. Some might argue that the role of government in this capacity should be kept to a minimum because people have the ability to settle their conflicts by themselves without the intervention of government. Indeed, the Coase theorem (Chapter 24) implied that if there were no transaction costs in society, most conflicts could be resolved by private bargaining. In such instances, the role of government might include making sure that the prerequisites for private bargaining exist and reducing the transaction costs that might impede the bargaining process. Ultimately, however, such bargaining becomes a zero-sum game. At that point, some type of government mediation might be necessary to aggregate the preferences of individuals and reach a socially desirable outcome. We will examine some mechanisms for mediation in the following sections of the chapter.

EXPERIMENTAL EVIDENCE

WHY PEOPLE CONTRIBUTE TOO MUCH TO PUBLIC GOODS: WARM GLOW VS. COLD PRICKLE

Think for a moment about an oligopoly or duopoly problem and a public goods problem. In an oligopoly problem, firms have to decide how much of a good to produce and place on the market. In a public good situation, people have to decide how much of their private funds they will contribute to the construction of the public good instead of use for their own private consumption. Both decisions involve externalities, as described in Chapter 24. In the oligopoly situation, each time you produce more output and place it on the market, you decrease the price for all firms and hence lower their profits. Producing generates a *negative* externality. In the public good case, however, contributing to the public good generates a positive externality. If you contribute, everyone else gets more of the public good. In both situations, there exists a Nash equilibrium outcome to the public goods or oligopoly game in which the Nash equilibrium is not efficient. In the oligopoly game, the Cournot-Nash equilibrium involves more production than should be produced in order to maximize the joint profits of the firms in the market, while in the public

goods situation, the Nash equilibrium involves too little public good contribution.

In laboratory experiments, there is a curious set of facts. While in oligopoly experiments, the Nash equilibrium prediction does well in the sense that subjects in these experiments choose production levels that are basically consistent with the theory, in public goods experiments, people contribute more than is predicted. In other words, while people have the opportunity to free ride in public goods games, they rarely take advantage of the opportunity to the full extent possible. In laboratory experiments, for example, subjects tend to start out contributing about 50% of their income to public good construction and then, as they gain experience, lower these contributions to about 25% toward the end of the experiment. Because in these experiments they have a dominant strategy of contributing zero, such overcontribution is striking.

This tendency to overcontribute is evident in data on charitable giving. Obviously, giving to charities is a public goods game. If others give, you will receive the benefits even if you do not give. If, for example, cancer is cured or the homeless housed, you benefit even if

(Continued)

you do not contribute. Yet data indicate that people give way beyond the selfish free-ride level. For example, James Andreoni[8] summarizes some statistics indicating that 85% of households contribute to charities, with 50% of all tax returns taking charitable deductions. These gifts are large, as well, with charitable contributions equaling about 2% of the gross national product. No such altruistic results are found either in oligopoly experiments or in the world of oligopolistic competition where, even in the absence of antitrust enforcement, cartels seem to find it hard to collude in a stable manner (witness OPEC, for example). What explains this seeming paradox between the willingness of people to free ride in oligopoly games and their reluctance to do so completely in public goods games?

According to Andreoni, the paradox can be explained by realizing that in the way public goods games are explained to subjects in the lab (and in the real world of charitable giving), contributing to the public good generates a positive externality—that is, it benefits others—while in oligopoly games producing one more unit generates a negative externality. Hence, in public goods games, contributing is the nice thing to do and should provide a "warm glow" of altruism for anyone who attempts it; in the oligopoly game, on the other hand, producing (because it generates a negative externality) produces a "cold prickle," and there is little incentive to do so because it will not make you feel good about yourself if you do.

To test this hypothesis, Andreoni performed a very simple public goods experiment. In this experiment, which is the standard type of public goods experiment performed in the profession, subjects are recruited and given an initial endowment of 60 tokens or experimental dollars. They are told that they will be randomly placed in groups of five, and they will then have to decide how much of their 60 tokens they will want to allocate to the public good and how much they will want to keep for themselves. Keeping a token will earn them 1 cent after the experiments are over, while for every token allocated to the public good, all subjects will earn $\frac{1}{2}$ cent. So, for example, if you allocate a token toward the public good and no one else does, then you receive $\frac{1}{2}$ cent; keeping it for your private consumption, on the other hand, would have yielded 1 cent. In other words, it never pays to contribute. However, for every token someone else contributes, you receive $\frac{1}{2}$ cent whether you contributed or not. Thus, if the other 4 subjects in

your group all contribute a token, your payoff will increase by 2 cents ($\frac{1}{2} \times 4$).

In such a situation, it should be clear that the Pareto-optimal level of contributions is for all people to contribute all of their 60 tokens to the public good. Each person's payoff will then be $150 = (\frac{1}{2} \times 300)$. If they all keep their tokens, they all earn only 60. However, if all others contribute 60 and you keep your tokens for yourself, then you will earn even more ($180 = 60 + [\frac{1}{2} \times 240]$). In fact, it is a dominant strategy for you to keep all of your tokens, so the Nash equilibrium here is for no one to contribute.

The innovation of Andreoni is in the way he presents this experiment to the subjects. What he does is to take two different groups of subjects and give them different instructions describing the game. In one he describes the game in such a way that contributing is seen as a nice thing to do; that is, he states that you are given 60 tokens that you can keep (that is, be selfish) or contribute to the public good. In the other set of instructions, subjects are told that all of their 60 tokens are initially contributed to the public good so that their only decision is how greedy to be in taking these tokens away from the group. In this set of instructions, allocating tokens to yourself is a nasty thing. In other words, Andreoni frames the allocation decision two ways. In the positive frame, he tries to generate a "warm glow" from giving, while in the negative frame, he accentuates the "cold prickle" of being selfish. The two key paragraphs in the instructions are as follows (italics added for explanation):

Positive Frame:

Every token you invest in the Individual Exchange (*i.e., keeping your tokens for yourself*) will yield you a return of one. The other members of your groups are not affected by your investment in the Individual Exchange.... Your return from the Group Exchange (*contributing to the public good*) will depend on the total number of tokens that you and the other four members of your group invest in the Group Exchange. The more the group invests in the Group Exchange, the greater the return to each member of the group.

Negative Frame:

Every token you invest in the Individual Exchange (*i.e., keeping your tokens for yourself*) will yield you a return of one. However, each token you invest in the individual exchange will reduce the earnings of the other players by one half of one cent each.... Every token you invest

---

8 "Private Giving to Public Goods: Proceedings from the 1987 Annual Conference of the National Tax Association Tax Institute of America," 1988, pp. 69–74.

in the Group Exchange yields a return of $\frac{1}{2}$ cent for you. The other members of your group are not affected by your investment in the Group Exchange.

Obviously, these two framings change the way the problem is perceived. The results are summarized in Figure 25.5(a) and Figure 25.5(b).

Figure 25.5

(a) Average Percentage of Endowment Contributed to Public Good Due to the Negative Frame Contributions.
(b) Percentage Free Riding: The Positive Frame Has Fewer People Free Riding.

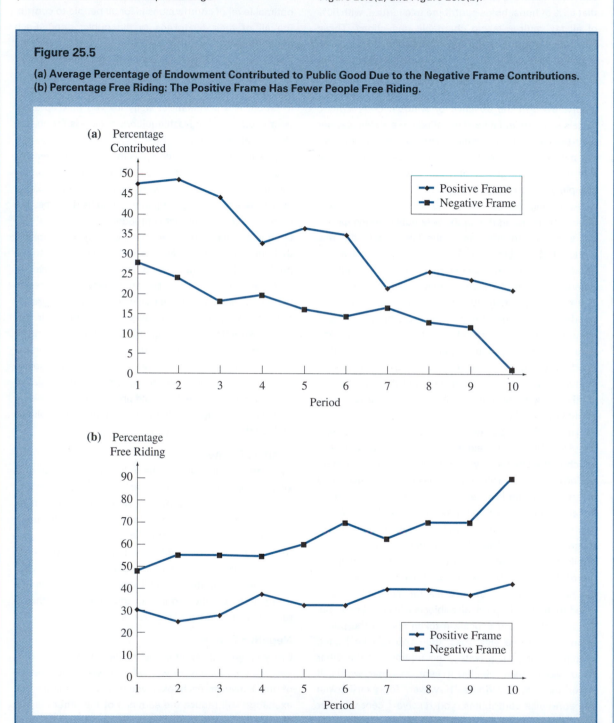

(Continued)

In Figure 25.5(a), we see the average percentage of the 60-token endowment contributed to the public good over the ten rounds of the experiment. (The subjects played the game ten times each with a randomly chosen group of five subjects so that no one knew the others with whom they were grouped and no reputations could be established among the subjects.)

As we can see, the results are striking. Using the positive frame, we get the typical public goods results. Subjects start off by contributing about 47.5% of their endowment to the public good, but as time goes on, this amount diminishes—but not all the way to zero. In round ten, subjects are still contributing 20.9%. For the negative frame, the results are quite different. Subjects start by contributing only 27.8% and, on average, this rate fell to only 1% by the end. If we look at the percentage of subjects taking a free ride over time —that is, contributing 0% of their endowment—we see in Figure 25.5(b) that in the positive frame, 30% of the subjects start out by taking a free ride, and this percentage increases to 42.5% in round ten. In the negative frame experiment, on the other hand, 47.5% of the subjects start out by taking a free ride, and that percentage increases to 90% by round ten—quite a dramatic difference!

In summation, this experiment is one of a number indicating that the way a situation is presented to people or the way in which people interpret such situations for themselves may dramatically affect the way they behave. Framing a public good problem positively seems to call forth the best in people, while framing it negatively seems to bring out their worst.

The Problem of Preference Aggregation: Arrow's Impossibility Theorem

Ideally, when it is necessary or desirable for the government to aggregate the preferences of individuals to make some decision that will affect the welfare of everyone in society, the mechanism the government uses will result in rational social choices that accurately reflect the true preferences of the individuals in society. By *rational*, we mean that the choices the government makes should obey the same axioms of rationality that we imposed on individual preferences in Chapter 2. In other words, these choices should be complete and transitive. However, as we will soon see, it is very difficult for the government to make such choices.

The Voting Paradox

One might think that if all the individuals in society have complete and transitive preferences, then it must follow that social preferences based on these individual preferences will also be complete and transitive. Unfortunately, this is not at all true. For example, say that society uses a majority voting rule to choose between pairs of alternatives; that is, whenever one of two alternatives must be chosen, the alternative that receives more than 50% of the votes is selected. The voting paradox tells us that this majority voting rule will not necessarily lead to transitive social preferences even when each individual's preferences are transitive. To understand the voting paradox, let us consider the preference matrix given in Table 25.3.

The society that we are dealing with in Table 25.3 consists of three people who face three alternatives, which, for the sake of simplicity, we will call alternative

Table 25.3	A Preference Matrix for a Three-Person Society.		
	PERSON		
Rank of Preference	**1**	**2**	**3**
First	x	z	y
Second	y	x	z
Third	z	y	x

x, alternative *y*, and alternative *z*. These alternatives might be three different levels of spending on national defense, three different school-tax rates, or three different schedules of operating hours for the public library. Person 1 prefers *x* to *y* to *z*, person 2 prefers *z* to *x* to *y*, and person 3 prefers *y* to *z* to *x*. We will assume that each person's preferences are transitive (and complete). As a result, each person has a unique best alternative. Let us see whether the use of the majority voting rule when individual preferences are transitive (and complete) will lead to a set of social preferences that are also transitive.

For the moment, we will assume that *people vote honestly and do not try to disguise their true preferences*. (We will return to this assumption later.) If our three-person society is asked to choose between *x* and *y*, then *x* will be chosen because two people (persons 1 and 2) prefer *x* to *y*. If *y* and *z* are now ranked, majority voting will lead to the choice of *y* because two people (persons 1 and 3) prefer *y* to *z*. So far, society has indicated that *x* is preferred to *y* (*xSy*) and *y* is preferred to *z* (*ySz*). For social preferences to be transitive, we should find that *x* is preferred to *z* (*xSz*), but such is not the case. When *x* and *z* are put up for a majority vote, we find that *z* is chosen because two people (persons 2 and 3) prefer *z* to *x*. The resulting social preferences are *xSy* and *ySz* but also *zSx*. This result is not transitive. Hence, what we have here is an example of the voting paradox.

The voting paradox was first discovered in 1785 by the Marquis de Condorcet, a French philosopher.[9] Its implications have been generalized by Kenneth Arrow, the noted U.S. economist.[10] As we have seen, the voting paradox holds that even if all the people in a society have transitive preferences, the preferences of society taken as a whole need not be transitive. This creates a big problem for society. Even though government should merely reflect the preferences of the individuals under its jurisdiction, it may not be able to make its choices in a transitive manner. To break the cycling of social preferences that results, society might have to rely on some external authority, and that is exactly what we have been trying to avoid.

Although the voting paradox seems to have disturbing implications about the ability of government to aggregate individual preferences, perhaps the picture is not so bleak. We have looked at only one voting institution—the majority voting rule. Maybe another voting rule would not be subject to the same intransitivity and hence would allow government to function as we would like. Unfortunately, this hope is in vain. As we will see shortly, no voting institution exists that is not subject to the voting paradox.

Conditions for an Ideal Voting Mechanism

In our search for voting mechanisms that will lead to transitive social outcomes, we do not want to obtain transitive social preferences at any cost. For example, let us look at a mechanism in which one person is chosen at random from the population and his or her preferences are considered to represent the preferences of everyone in society. This mechanism leads to transitive social preferences because each person's preferences are assumed to be transitive in the first place. In a sense,

---

[9] See Marquis de Condorcet, *Essai sur l'Application de l'Analyse aux Probabilities des Decisions Rendue à la Pluralite des Voix* (Paris: 1785). A reprint of this work is available (New York: Chelsea Publishing Company, 1973).

[10] See Kenneth Arrow, *Social Choice and Individual Values* (New York: Wiley, 1951). Arrow is a Nobel Prize–winning economist who has taught at Harvard and Stanford. He has made significant contributions to general equilibrium theory, the theory of decision making under conditions of uncertainty, and growth theory.

the social preferences determined by this mechanism are based strictly on individual preferences because everyone has an equal chance of being chosen. However, this mechanism violates our democratic ideals. Social choices are supposed to represent the preferences of all individuals. They should not be based on the preferences of a dictator, even if that dictator is randomly chosen.

The mechanism we want to find should not only yield transitive social preferences, but it should also satisfy the following conditions.

Condition 1: Group Rationality. The social preferences generated by any voting procedure should define a complete and transitive ordering of the set of alternatives. In other words, when a voting rule is used to aggregate individual preferences, the resulting social preferences should look like they came from a rational individual; that is, they should be complete and transitive.

Condition 2: Unrestricted Domain. Every ordering of individual preferences that is complete and transitive should be allowed. This condition means that society should not rule out certain types of preferences. All preferences should be allowed as inputs into the aggregation process as long as they are rational, that is, transitive and complete.

Condition 3: Pareto Optimality. If there is an alternative, x, that all people prefer to another alternative, y, x should be preferred to y in the social ranking as well.

Condition 4: Independence. The social ranking of two alternatives, x and y, should depend only on the preferences of individuals between these two alternatives. That is, the social ranking of x and y should be independent of the rankings individuals give to some other alternative, say z. For example, say that society has a set of alternatives, A, to choose among and there are two preference profiles, R and R'; that is, there are two possible groups of individual rankings indicating the preferences of people over set A. Assume that these profiles each rank x and y identically but differ over the other alternatives. Then any voting mechanism that ranks x as being socially preferred to y under profile R should also rank x as being socially preferred to y under profile R'.

Condition 5: Nondictatorship. No individual in society should be so powerful that the voting mechanism reflects only his or her preferences over every set of alternatives put up for a vote.

Voting Mechanisms and the Ideal Conditions

We could examine a number of different types of voting mechanisms to see whether they meet all the conditions that we just specified for an ideal voting mechanism, but according to Kenneth Arrow, we would be wasting our time if we did so. Arrow's impossibility theorem tells us that there is no voting mechanism that determines transitive social preferences and also satisfies the five conditions for an ideal voting mechanism.

We can look at this theorem in many ways. One way is to view it as an indication that if we want a voting mechanism that satisfies conditions 1, 2, 3, and 4, then we must be ready to accept a dictatorial voting mechanism and thereby violate condition 5. In a sense, this solution tells us that our desire for transitive social preferences can be attained only if we are willing to abandon our desire for democracy.

Arrow's impossibility theorem
A theorem that demonstrates that there is no voting mechanism that determines transitive social preferences and also satisfies the five conditions for a desirable voting mechanism.

Viewed in such a manner, Arrow's impossibility theorem is quite pessimistic and disturbing.

Another way of looking at Arrow's impossibility theorem is more hopeful. Remember that condition 2 requires that there should be no limitations on the types of preferences people can have. This condition is clearly desirable from a philosophical point of view. No outside authority should have the right to rule that anyone's preferences are not permissible. However, from a practical point of view, we know that certain types of preferences are often just not accepted in real societies. In such cases, there might be hope that we can find a voting mechanism that satisfies all of our conditions except, of course, condition 2.

Economists have investigated the types of restrictions on preferences that would allow the simple majority voting rule to yield transitive social preferences. For example, let us say that the issue under consideration is one-dimensional; that is, the alternatives differ in only one characteristic. Such an issue might be how much money to spend on the local public school system, where all the alternatives can be described by dollar amounts arrayed along a continuum, starting at $0 and extending to some upper bound $B. If each person prefers to spend a particular amount of money and has less and less preference for the alternative amounts as they get further and further away from that amount, then we can say that each person has a **single-peaked preference**. Figure 25.6 illustrates such preferences for a four-person society that is debating the school spending issue.

The continuum of alternatives, which ranges from $0 to $B, is shown on the horizontal axis of Figure 25.6. The utility that each person derives from each alternative is measured by the vertical axis. Note that each person has an inverted V-shaped function. This means that the alternative corresponding to the top of the V is the preferred alternative and that all other alternatives are preferred less and less the further they diverge from the preferred alternative.

Clearly, these are very specific types of preferences; and they do not satisfy condition 2, which says that there should be no restriction on preferences. However, if the society we are discussing does in fact have these types of preferences, then all the other conditions for an ideal voting mechanism *can* be satisfied by use of the simple majority voting rule.

single-peaked preferences
In voting for one-dimensional issues—that is, issues like how much money to spend on military expenditures, how high a tax should be set, etc.—preferences are single peaked if a person has a uniquely best alternative he or she prefers and his or her preferences decline as the distance between this best alternative and the alternative under consideration increases.

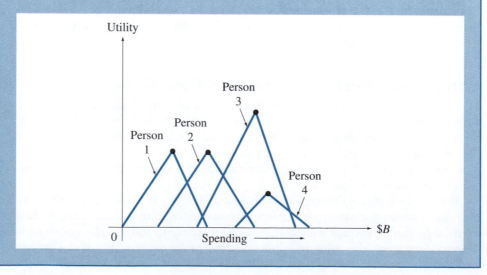

Figure 25.6

Single-Peaked Preferences.

For each person, alternatives become steadily worse as they get further and further away, in either direction, from the preferred alternative.

The Problem of Vote Manipulation

We are searching for a voting mechanism that will result in a socially desirable outcome—an outcome that accurately reflects the preferences of the individuals in society. Unfortunately, our search is further complicated by the fact that voting outcomes can be manipulated in various ways by single individuals who are in positions of power.

Agenda Manipulation

If an individual can control the order in which pairs of alternatives are voted on, then that individual can affect the outcome of the vote. This process is called agenda manipulation. For instance, a leader of a legislative body or a chairperson of a committee can skew the outcome of a vote to his or her desired choice by simply altering the agenda that is presented to the people who will vote.[11]

To see how agenda manipulation works, let us consider Table 25.4. We will assume that the matrix shown in this table represents the preferences of a three-person committee.

We will also assume that person 2 in Table 25.4 is chairing the committee and that alternative solutions for an issue are voted on in pairs using the majority voting rule. The chairperson has control of the agenda, so she decides the order in which the pairs of alternatives are voted on. If the chairperson selects an agenda in which the committee votes first on x versus y and then votes on the winner of that contest versus z, the alternative chosen will be z. By majority vote, x will defeat y, but z will defeat x. Now let us say that the chairperson sets an agenda in which the committee votes first on z versus x and then votes on the winner of that contest versus y. With this agenda, the committee will choose y. If the chairperson selects an agenda consisting first of z versus y and then of the winner of that contest versus x, the committee's choice will be x. Thus, it is clear that any outcome is possible in this example depending on what agenda the chairperson selects. Because person 2 is chairing the committee in this example and her first preference is alternative z, she will obviously set an agenda consisting first of x versus y and then of the winner of that contest versus z. As a result, the committee will choose her first preference of alternative z.

agenda manipulation
The process by which an individual who controls the agenda for a committee or voting body manipulates the order in which pairs of alternatives are voted on in an effort to influence the outcome.

The Levine-Plott Experiment on Agenda Manipulation. The problem of agenda manipulation has disturbing implications for the democratic process. To see whether a clever chairperson can actually manipulate the outcome of a vote as we have indicated, let us look at an experiment conducted by Mike Levine and Charles Plott.[12] Its purpose was to investigate whether the results of a vote taken by a flying club on the composition of its fleet were manipulated by a clever choice of agenda.

The flying club had to decide how many and what types of planes to buy. The types of planes under consideration were the Bonanza E (which we will denote by E), the Bonanza F (F), the Cessna (C), and the Bonanza A (A). Mike Levine, a member of the club, wanted the outcome to be EEEFFCC. That is, he

---

[11] The discussion in this section relies on the work of Peter Ordeshook as presented in his book *Game Theory and Political Theory* (Cambridge, England: Cambridge University Press, 1986).

[12] Mike Levine and Charles Plott, "Agenda Influence and Its Implications," *Virginia Law Review* 63 (May 1977): 561–604.

Table 25.4	A Preference Matrix for a Three-Person Committee.		
		PERSON	
Rank of Preference	**1**	**2**	**3**
First	x	z	y
Second	y	x	z
Third	z	y	x

wanted a seven-plane fleet consisting of three Bonanza E's, two Bonanza F's, and two Cessnas. Levine and Plott attempted to achieve this outcome by manipulating the club's agenda as shown in Figure 25.7.

What was the content of the flying club's agenda? First, the club had to decide whether there should be six or seven planes in its total fleet. After making this decision, the club had to decide if there should be a secondary fleet containing planes other than E's and F's. The next decision was whether the secondary fleet should consist of one or two planes. Finally, the club had to decide whether C's or A's should make up the secondary fleet.

When the club voted, Levine achieved exactly the outcome he desired. We might be tempted to view this result as proof of the proposition that outcomes can be manipulated by manipulating the agenda. However, such a conclusion is not warranted because the voting process did not take place within a controlled experiment. Hence, the outcome could have been a coincidence and could have had nothing to do with agenda manipulation.

To investigate the matter further, Levine and Plott circulated a questionnaire to the members of the flying club after the decisions had been made so that they

Figure 25.7

The Agenda for the Levine-Plott Agenda Manipulation Experiment.

The club voted sequentially on the agenda items, starting with the decision about whether there should be six or seven planes in the fleet.

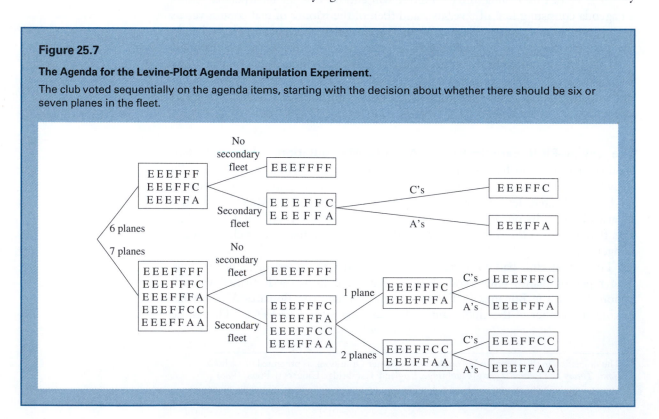

could identify the preferences of the club members. Then Levine and Plott ran an experiment in which they induced these preferences in the subjects (who were college students) by offering them differing monetary rewards depending on the outcome attained in the voting process. The results of this experiment confirmed Levine's supposition that the outcome of the actual club vote was no accident. The result Levine wanted was obtained through his manipulation of the club's agenda. Thus, it is clear that the intransitivities of the majority voting rule can be used by a devious legislative leader or committee chairperson to skew voting outcomes toward the result that he or she wants. The moral of this story is to beware of the agenda. The person who controls the agenda may be able to control the outcome of the voting process.

Strategic Voting

Thus far in our discussion of voting mechanisms, we have assumed that the votes of individuals will truthfully reflect their preferences for the alternatives in question. However, we know that this need not be the case. If a voter thinks that her first choice has no chance of being selected, she may decide to vote for her second choice or even her third choice to prevent an alternative she considers disastrous from being chosen. This process is called strategic voting.

To understand how strategic voting works, let us look once again at the preference matrix for the three-person committee shown in Table 25.4. We will again assume that person 2 is chairing the committee. As chairperson, she has selected the agenda x versus y, winner versus z, because it will result in the selection of z, her first preference, *if all the members of the committee vote according to their true preferences*. Note, however that z is person 1's third preference. If he can assume that the other two members of the committee will vote truthfully, then he can prevent z from being selected by lying on the first vote and voting for y, his second preference, rather than for x, his first preference.

We can see person 1's strategy more clearly by looking at the decision tree in Figure 25.8. When x and y are voted on first, person 1 has the choice of voting truthfully for x or lying and voting for y. If he votes truthfully, alternative x will win the first round of voting. Then, in the second round of voting when the choice is between x and z, alternative z will win no matter how person 1 votes. However, if person 1 lies during the first round of voting and votes for y, then y will win the second round of voting between y and z. Thus, by lying, person 1 can ensure that y, his second choice, is selected over z, his third choice. Clearly, honesty is not the best policy here.

If we think of this situation as a game, another way to analyze the result is to say that the strategy of telling the truth is not a Nash equilibrium strategy. We know that this is true because we have demonstrated that if person 1 is aware of the agenda and expects all the members of the committee to honestly vote their preferences, he would have an incentive to lie and not vote truthfully.

Perhaps vote manipulation through strategic voting is possible only with the majority voting rule. Let us look at another voting rule to see if strategic voting can also occur with that rule. To investigate the question, we will consider Table 25.5, which shows a preference matrix for a five-person committee that is facing five issues.[13]

strategic voting
Voting in a manner that does not reflect one's true preferences in an effort to affect the outcome of a vote.

---

[13] This example is presented in more detail in Peter Ordeshook, *Game Theory and Political Theory* (Cambridge, England: Cambridge University Press, 1986).

Figure 25.8

A Decision Tree for a Player Who Engages in Strategic Voting.

By lying in the first round of voting, person 1 can ensure that y, his second choice, is selected over z, his third choice, in the second round of voting.

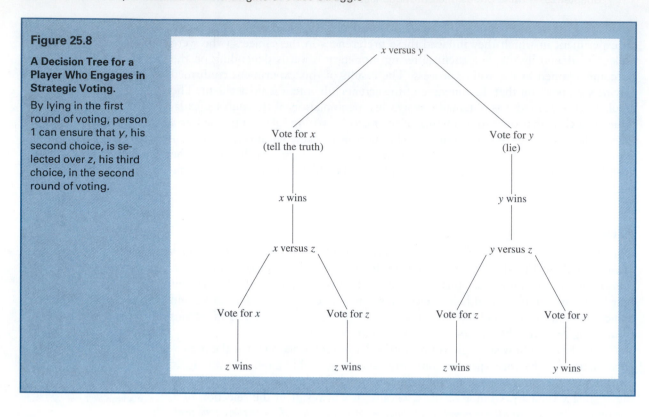

Table 25.5	A Preference Matrix for a Five-Person Committee.				
			PERSON		
Rank of Preference	**1**	**2**	**3**	**4**	**5**
First	x	y	y	c	x
Second	c	c	c	d	y
Third	d	e	x	x	e
Fourth	y	d	e	e	d
Fifth	e	x	d	y	c

Borda count method
A voting method used to choose between k alternatives where the voters allocate k votes to their first alternative, $k-1$ votes to their second, $k-2$ votes to their third, etc. The alternative receiving the largest total number of votes is the one chosen by the voting body.

Instead of using the majority voting rule, the committee uses the Borda count method. In this voting method, each person ranks the five alternatives and gives his or her first choice five votes; the second choice, four votes; the third choice, three votes; the fourth choice, two votes; and the fifth choice, one vote. The alternative receiving the largest total number of votes is the one chosen by the committee.

With the Borda count method, if all five people on the committee vote truthfully, then alternative c will win. It will receive 18 votes, whereas alternative x will receive 17 votes, alternative y will also receive 17 votes, alternative d will receive 12 votes, and alternative e will receive 11 votes.

The question now is whether or not telling the truth is a Nash equilibrium strategy for the Borda count method. To demonstrate that it is not, let us say that person 1 does not vote according to his truthful preferences of $xPcPdPyPe$. Instead, he lies and votes as though his preferences were $xPePdPcPy$. This time, alternative x will receive 17 votes, as before, but alternative c will get only 16 votes. In other words, by altering his vote, person 1 was able to switch the committee's choice from c to x, which he preferred. Clearly, the Borda count method can be manipulated.

Let us cut short our search for a voting mechanism that cannot be manipulated by stating the Gibbard-Satterthwaite theorem: When a single outcome is to be chosen from more than two alternatives, the only voting rule that cannot be manipulated is a dictatorial one. Basically, this theorem tells us that our search for a voting mechanism that cannot be manipulated will be fruitless because none exists.

> **Gibbard-Satterthwaite theorem**
> When a single outcome is to be chosen from more than two alternatives, the only voting rule that cannot be manipulated is a dictatorial one.

Question (Application and Extension: Voting)

As we know, people are liable to vote strategically when they go to the polling booth. In other words, they are likely to vote for a candidate that they do not like simply to block the election of another they dislike more. Consider the following voting scheme called "The Dictator for a Day Scheme." Everyone states which candidate they like the most. They write that candidate's name on a piece of paper and put it into a hat. One slip is drawn randomly from the hat, and that person is elected.

a) Will this scheme get everyone to tell the truth?

Answer

Yes, everyone will tell the truth. There are only two possible outcomes: either a person's piece of paper is drawn, or it is not drawn. If it is not drawn, it does not matter what that person wrote on the paper. If it is drawn, then it is in that person's best interest to have told the truth. Thus, telling the truth is a dominant strategy.

b) Is the outcome Pareto optimal?

Answer

By definition the outcome is Pareto optimal because if everyone tells the truth, the outcome will have to be at least one person's best option. Therefore, because changing the outcome will hurt this person, no Pareto superior move exists.

c) Will the outcome always be "desirable" in the sense that it represents the preferences of the community?

Answer

The outcome may be pretty undesirable. Consider a community with all Republicans, except for one lonely Democrat. When the community has to elect a candidate, the Democrat writes his candidate on the piece of paper, and it is chosen. Even though the Democrat is elected, virtually no one wants him in office.

SOLVED PROBLEM 25.4

The Government as Institutional Architect

The Gibbard-Satterthwaite theorem creates a problem for the government in its role as the architect of the institutions that society uses to allocate goods, choose political leaders, and make other social choices. It implies that any mechanism society uses to make such choices can be manipulated and may therefore result in undesirable outcomes. This problem can be resolved if we forget about nonmanipulable mechanisms and look instead for mechanisms with Nash equilibria that determine satisfactory outcomes. What we mean here is illustrated in Figure 25.9.

Figure 25.9

The Design of Institutions.
Because the government does not have full knowledge of the environment, it cannot construct the performance correspondence indicating which outcomes are desirable for that environment. Instead, the government attempts to specify a voting mechanism such that the citizens will choose the same outcomes that the government would if it had full knowledge of the environment.

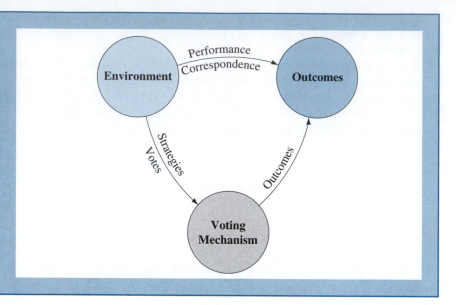

performance correspondence
A relationship between the environment and the set of desired outcomes that tells us which outcomes will satisfy our performance criteria.

The upper left corner of the triangle in Figure 25.9 is identified as the environment. By *environment*, we mean a complete description of the economy or voting body that we are concerned with, including the preferences of each member. Clearly, no government has all the information necessary to describe the environment because it cannot look into the minds of all its citizens and examine their utility functions. However, for the moment, let us assume that we possess all this information. We should therefore be able to choose the exact outcomes we want, and no ambiguity should result as long as we agree on the types of outcomes we want for society. For example, if we insist on efficiency or Pareto optimality, then for any given set of alternatives, we should be able to choose an efficient set of outcomes. We call this relationship between the environment and the set of desired outcomes the performance correspondence and depict it as an arrow going from the environment to the set of outcomes, as shown in Figure 25.9. For any environment, the performance correspondence tells us which outcomes will satisfy our performance criteria.

Because a government does not have all the information needed to construct a performance correspondence, it must take an indirect route and specify a voting institution for the people in society to use. We can then look for a Nash equilibrium set of votes to be chosen by the people in society. The equilibrium set of votes is shown along the arrow on the left side of the triangle in Figure 25.9. Once the people in society cast these votes, the voting institution chosen by the government transforms them into outcomes, which are shown along the arrow on the right side of the triangle.

The question for the government as a designer of institutions is whether it can choose a voting institution for any given environment such that the outcomes achieved at the Nash equilibrium of the institution are the same as the outcomes determined by the performance correspondence. Note that this does not imply that people will tell the truth at the equilibrium. All that is required is that the same outcomes are achieved as would result if full information were available.

A discussion of exactly how such institutions are designed is beyond the scope of this book. Let us simply say that great progress has been made toward constructing a theory that delimits the circumstances under which such mechanisms will exist and outlines what they should look like. Our discussion of the demand-revealing mechanism earlier in this chapter is a good example. The field of institutional economics should offer much excitement in the future.

SOLVED
PROBLEM
25.5

Question (Application and Extension: Public Goods)

a) Suppose a city is trying to decide whether it should build a public library or a public hospital. There is only enough money to build one. If the city asks its citizens to vote on the two projects and says the project receiving more votes is to be chosen, will the scheme induce the citizens to reveal their preferences truthfully? Will the scheme be Pareto optimal? Assume that if there is a tie, one project will be chosen by tossing a coin.

Answer

This scheme will induce the citizens to reveal their preferences truthfully. If a person favors the library but votes for the hospital, this will only increase the chance of the hospital being selected. Therefore, one does not have the incentive to lie about one's preferences. The scheme is also Pareto optimal. If, for example, the library is chosen, it means that a certain number of people (in fact, a majority) chose the library over the hospital. Building the hospital would make these people worse off.

b) Now suppose there are three projects instead of two—a public library, a public gymnasium, and a public hospital. Will the scheme in the previous question succeed in inducing truthful revelation? Again, in case of a tie, a project will be chosen at random with equal probability (that is, $\frac{1}{3}$). To make things simple, you can assume that there are only three citizens—A, B, and C.

Answer

When there are three projects, there is a possibility of deception by the citizens. Suppose A has voted for the library and B has voted for the hospital. Now suppose C prefers the gymnasium over the library and the library over the hospital. If C votes for the gymnasium, there is an even chance ($\frac{1}{3}$) that it will be selected. If C votes for either the library or the hospital, that project will be chosen for certain. Therefore, unless C likes a $\frac{1}{3}$ chance of the gymnasium, the library, or the hospital more than having the library for sure, he has an incentive to lie.

c) Finally, suppose that the city asks its citizens to rank the projects. A first position gives a project 3 points, a second position gives it 2 points, and a third position gives it 1 point. Then all of the points given to the projects are added up, and the project with the highest number of points is chosen. Will this scheme induce a truthful revelation of preferences? Assume again that there are only three citizens—A, B, and C.

Answer

Consider the following situation:

	Library	Gymnasium	Hospital
A	2	1	3
B	2	1	3
C	2	3	1
Total	**6**	**5**	**7**

The previous table shows the true preference rankings of all three individuals. If all three reveal their preferences truthfully, the hospital will be chosen by the city. But note that C prefers the hospital the least and his first preference, the gymnasium, is not chosen. So, if C lies about his preferences and puts the library as his first choice (which is actually his second choice), the library will tie with the hospital. Thus C's second choice now has an even ($\frac{1}{2}$) chance of being chosen, even if his real first choice, the gymnasium, has no chance of being chosen. By a simple manipulation, C has now made the best of a bad situation. This scheme may not result in truthful revelation of preferences, as this particular example shows.

Rent Seeking—The Economics of Interest Groups

rent-seeking behavior
The behavior of interest groups in their attempt to extract rents from the government or other authorities.

Our discussion thus far has treated individuals as if they act in isolation. Each person considered his or her preferences and the voting rule being used and then cast his or her vote alone. But the real world is actually more complex than this. People with common interests often join together to coax, bribe, or threaten their legislators to vote on their behalf. Such lobbying groups may spend considerable amounts of money on their activities. But exactly what are these groups trying to achieve? Why is it so important to them that legislators vote the way they desire? The theory of rent-seeking behavior tries to explain why and how interest groups act as they do. Let us now turn our attention to this theory and the problem underlying it.

For the purposes of our discussion, we will assume that the government has created a regulated monopoly in which the right to produce a good and sell it to the community is bestowed costlessly on a firm. Once this firm starts operations, it is able to maximize its profits subject to some form of regulation or oversight.

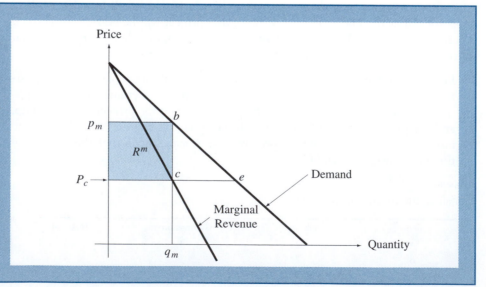

Figure 25.10

Rent-Seeking Behavior.

A firm would be willing to pay an amount equal to the potential monopoly profit, $R^m = area\ p_m bcp_c$, for a government franchise permitting it to operate as a monopolist.

However, for the moment, we will assume that this regulation or oversight is ineffective, as Figure 25.10 indicates.

In Figure 25.10, we see that the monopolist faces a downward-sloping demand curve and a constant fixed marginal cost of production of c. The monopolist maximizes its profits by setting a price of p_m and selling a quantity of q_m. The firm will earn profits of R^m equal to the area $p_m b c p_c$ in Figure 25.10. These profits can be considered economic rent accruing to a monopoly because they exceed the amount the firm needs to produce its product. The opportunity to obtain economic rent is precisely the reason that the monopolist sought the franchise from the government. Therefore, it is no surprise that the monopolist spends money to have lobbyists try to influence legislators to vote against bills that would deregulate the industry or lead to a decrease in the economic rent the monopolist receives. In fact, it is worth R_m to the monopolist to preserve the status quo, and presumably this is the amount the firm is willing to spend on lobbying.

Competitive Rent Seeking

Now let us say that the monopoly franchise has not yet been awarded by the government and that two firms are vying for it. The franchise is worth R^m to each firm, so we might expect each firm to send a lobbyist to the capitol to capture the available rents. We can define a two-firm lobbying game as follows: At the first stage, each firm commits an amount of resources to lobbying. We will let R_1 be the amount committed by firm 1 and R_2 be the amount committed by firm 2. Each lobbyist is equally effective, so the probability of winning the franchise is $p_1 = R_1/(R_1 + R_2)$ for firm 1 and $p_2 = R_2/(R_1 + R_2)$ for firm 2. The expected profits from lobbying are as follows:

$$\pi_1 = [R_1/(R_1 + R_2)]R^m - R_1 \text{ for firm 1}$$
$$\pi_2 = [R_2/(R_1 + R_2)]R^m - R_2 \text{ for firm 2}$$

(25.1)

Assuming that there is an upper limit on the amount that can be spent on lobbying, $\bar{R} > R^m$, we now have a well-defined game in which the strategy sets for the firms are the amounts that they will spend on lobbying and their payoffs are defined by the payoff functions π_1 and π_2.

The equilibrium for this game depends on the assumptions we make about what happens to the resources spent by the losing lobbyist. If those resources are returned, the payoff functions will be $\pi_1 = [R_1/(R_1 + R_2)]R^m$ for firm 1 and $\pi = [R_2/(R_1 + R_2)]R^m$ for firm 2. In this case, each firm will spend an amount equal to the full rent generated by the monopoly franchise. To see why, consider how the lobbying game operates. Each firm can offer a bribe to the government bureaucrat who is in charge of awarding the franchise. At any time, either firm can raise its bribe. At the end of the process, the bureaucrat will take one bribe (presumably the bigger bribe). Clearly, in this bribery game, the only equilibrium is one in which each firm offers a bribe equal to the full amount of the economic rent, R^m, and each has a 50% chance of obtaining the franchise. The reason this is an equilibrium is that there is no cost to the bidding because any rejected bribe remains with the firm that offered it.

Now let us assume that money spent on unsuccessful lobbying is lost forever. In this case, the payoff functions are the ones specified in the equations labeled 25.1; and we can easily determine that the equilibrium amount of money for each firm to spend is $R^m/4$, at which point each firm again has a 50% chance of winning. Hence, in this case, the entire rent would not be dissipated. In fact, together the firms would spend only half the amount of the potential rent on lobbying.[14]

The important point about rent seeking is that it increases the cost to society of monopolies established by the government. In our analysis in Chapter 17, we considered the social cost of monopoly to be the deadweight loss created when monopolies exist. In Figure 25.10, such a deadweight loss is represented by the triangular area bec. Rent seeking implies that the loss is much greater because it includes not only area bec but also all the money wasted on lobbying. In our first model, where the unsuccessful firm regains its lobbying costs, the amount of money spent is $R^m = p_m bcp_c$. The cost of monopoly here is thus the entire area $p_m bcp_c$. In our second model, where the unsuccessful firm loses its lobbying costs, the total loss is the deadweight loss plus half of the area R^m. In either case, rent seeking is a wasteful activity that is often spurred by governmental creation of monopolies.

Conclusion

In this chapter, the ideological battle between interventionists and free-market advocates that began in Chapter 14 has resumed over the issue of public goods and the free-rider problem. Because of this issue, the battle has taken its most serious turn against the free-market ideology. When faced with the free-rider problem, the agents in our model society seem unable to solve the problem without at least some government assistance—government coordination or a demand-revealing mechanism. This issue, among others, raises the question of what the optimal role of government should be in a freely competitive, democratic society. We turned our attention to this question in the last part of the chapter, where we investigated the role of government.

We saw that government can be conceived of as a mediator of the interests of different groups in society. Here, its job is to structure debate and aggregate preferences. Further, in its search for institutions through which the different groups in society can resolve their disputes, government is an institutional architect. The institutions it designs are different from any of the institutions we encountered previously in this book because those institutions were not created by design but rather arose unplanned from the utility-maximizing behavior of individuals. The result is an economy with two types of institutions, planned and unplanned, that interact with each other.

---

[14] To derive the equilibrium in this game, we use the following procedure. We know that at the equilibrium, one firm's marginal benefit from increasing its allocation of resources by one unit must equal the marginal cost of doing so given the amount of resources being spent by the other firm. Because both firms are identical, we will search for symmetric equilibria only. To find the marginal benefits and costs of resource spending, we take the derivative of the π_1 function with respect to R_1 and the derivative of the π_2 function with respect to R_2 in equation 25.1 as follows:

$$\frac{\delta \pi_1}{\delta R_1} = \left[\frac{R_2}{(R_1 + R_2)^2}\right] R^m - 1 = 0$$

$$\frac{\delta \pi_2}{\delta R_2} = \left[\frac{R_1}{(R_1 + R_2)^2}\right] R^m - 1 = 0$$

Looking at the first equation, we see that $R^m R_2 = (R_1 + R_2)^2$ or $R_2 = (R_1 + R_2)^2 / R^m$. However, at a symmetric equilibrium, we know that $R_1 = R_2$, so $R_2 = (2R_2)^2 / R^m$ or $(R^m)^{1/2} = (2R_2 / R_2^{1/2})$. Squaring both sides, we find $R^m / 4 = R_2$. By symmetry, we also know that $R_1 = R^m / 4$.

Summary

In this chapter, our model society faced another market failure—an inability to allocate public goods efficiently. This failure arose because public goods have special characteristics. They are nonexcludable and nonrival in consumption. We found that it was necessary for policy planners to develop demand-revealing schemes to help them allocate public goods in efficient ways. The reason these mechanisms were required is that people, if left to their devices, have an incentive to free ride when asked to pay for public goods. We reviewed the literature about the free-rider problem to try to discover whether it is a real problem or whether it is merely theoretical. We found that the results of certain experiments seem to indicate that free riding really exists. We also investigated a number of experimental studies that evaluated the effectiveness of various schemes to solve the free-rider problem.

In later sections of the chapter, we looked at some processes by which individual preferences are aggregated to make social choices. Our discussion was motivated by the famous voting paradox of Condorcet. This discussion used the Arrow impossibility theorem to demonstrate that vote manipulation is not an exotic event but rather a real danger to be avoided. We explored the conditions under which the problems raised by the voting paradox would not hold. Finally, we looked at the problem of competitive rent-seeking behavior. We found that lobbyists waste resources in their efforts to influence the processes of government.

Exercises and Problems

1. Let us say that each person in a society values the construction of a public swimming pool at $100. (The $100 represents each person's true maximum willingness to pay.) There are 20 people in this society, and the pool costs $1,600. The government suggests the following scheme to finance the pool: Each person will send a check to the government, and if more than $1,600 is collected, the government will have the pool built. (To make things simple, we will assume that any excess money the government receives is burned.) If the pool is not built, all the money will be returned to the members of society who contributed it.

    a) Suppose that no one sends any money. Is that situation an equilibrium?

    b) Suppose that the 20 members of society send $80 each. Is that situation an equilibrium?

    c) Suppose that 16 members of society send $100 each and 4 members send nothing. Is that situation an equilibrium? Explain.

2. Consider a three-person society in which the demand functions of persons 1, 2, and 3 for a public good are $P^1 = 100 - 3q$, $P^2 = 200 - 4q$, and $P^3 = 400 - 10q$, respectively. These functions show the maximum amount of money each person would willingly pay for each unit of the public good, q.

    a) Plot the three demand functions.

    b) If the marginal cost of providing the public good is $20, what is the optimal quantity of the public good for society to produce?

3. The citizens of Xanadu have to choose among three projects: a bridge, a school, and a hospital. There is enough money to build only *one* of these projects. The members of the Citizens Council are well versed in political theory and

are aware that there is no method of choosing the project to be built that will satisfy the entire population. Consequently, they have designed the following ingenious scheme: Each citizen is asked to write on a piece of paper the project he or she likes *most*. All the pieces of paper are put in a hat, and a member of the council pulls one out. The project written on that piece of paper is the one that is built.

a) Prove that if the citizens of Xanadu are selfish and are rational utility maximizers, each of them will indeed write down the project he or she likes the most; that is, none of the citizens will lie.

b) Prove that the choice determined by this scheme is a Pareto-optimal choice.

c) Does the outcome of this scheme lead you to think that Pareto optimality alone is a sufficient criterion for making social choices? Can it facilitate the "tyranny of the minority"?

4. In real life, people do not always take a free ride when they are able to. Social norms and pressures often prevent it. Let us assume that a society consists of only two people, persons A and B. (You should be able to generalize this problem to any number of people.) Each person can either contribute to a public good or free ride each year of his adult life (which we will assume to be 50 years). In a given year, if one person contributes and the other does not, then the person who contributes receives a payoff of 5 and the person who free rides receives a payoff of 15. If both contribute, then both receive a payoff of 12. If both free ride, the public good is not provided and both receive a payoff of zero. This information is summarized in the following game matrix:

		Person A	
		Contribute	Free Ride
Person B	Contribute	12, 12	5, 15
	Free Ride	15, 5	0, 0

We will call the game described by this matrix the "stage game" because it is played every year. In other words, every year represents a stage in a continuing game that should last throughout the 50-year adult lives of the two players: persons A and B. Thus, the extensive form of the game is derived by repeating the stage game 50 times. We will assume that A and B do not discount their future payoffs; that is, each person's payoff over the entire 50 years is simply the sum of his yearly payoffs. We will also assume that each can find out about the other's actions only in the following year. Now suppose A and B are using the following strategies:

Strategy 1: Each player contributes in the first year and continues to contribute every year until year 48 as long as the other player has contributed in the previous year. In year 49, A contributes and B free rides. In year 50, A free rides and B contributes.

Strategy 2: If A free rides in any year before year 50, then B free rides from the next year until year 50. If B free rides in any year before year 49, then A free rides from the next year until year 50.

a) Does the stage game have Nash equilibria? If so, what are they? Are the Nash equilibria Pareto optimal?

b) Show that the pair of strategies for the extensive-form game constitutes a subgame perfect equilibrium. What will be the equilibrium outcome?

5. Assume that luck and $10,000 are needed to create a technological break-through in the production of ink. Inky Products, Inc., has achieved such a breakthrough. Acting as a monopolist, the firm can earn $5,000 a year from this innovation. However, if other firms copy the ink, all profits will be eliminated within a year. Any other firm will be able to copy the ink by simply buying a bottle and analyzing it, which can be done at a negligible cost.

   a)   What is the public good in this example?

   b)   Would any firm want to invest $10,000 for the research necessary to create the technological breakthrough that leads to the initial production of the ink?

   c)   Using this example, explain why patents exist in the world.

6. Determine whether each of the following items is a public good. For any item that is not, give the property of a public good that it lacks.

   a)   Television shows broadcast over the airwaves

   b)   Cable television shows

   c)   Community swimming pools with entry restricted to community residents

   d)   Computer software

   e)   Economics textbooks

7. Dewey, Cheatum, and Howe is a law firm organized as a partnership. Profits are divided equally among the partners no matter what the productivity of each partner is.

   a)   Does a public good exist in this law firm?

   b)   Assume that instead of having a partnership, the three lawyers simply share the rent on the office they occupy and conduct separate private practices. Will they work harder or less hard under this arrangement? Explain your answer with reference to public goods and their properties.

8. Consider the following situation described by A. K. Sen in *Collective Choice and Social Welfare*:

   Let the social choice be between three alternatives involving Mr. A reading a copy of *Lady Chatterley's Lover*, Mr. B reading it, or no one reading it. We name these alternatives a, b, and c, respectively. Mr. A, the prude, prefers most that no one read it, next that he reads it, and last that "impressionable" Mr. B be exposed to it; that is, he prefers c to a, and a to b. Mr. B, the lascivious, prefers that either of them should read it rather than neither, but further prefers that Mr. A should read it rather than he himself, for he wants A to be exposed to Lawrence's prose. Hence he prefers a to b, and b to c.

   How should society rank these alternatives so that the ranking is consistent with Pareto optimality?

Input Markets and the Origins of Class Conflict

Why It Is Important to Determine the Return on Each Factor of Production

The fall of communism in Eastern Europe has been interpreted as proof of the proposition that free-market economies work better than centrally planned economies. Rather than making us complacent, however, the failure of communism should cause us to investigate free-market economies more closely. The fact that these economies are more efficient than centrally planned economies does not mean that free markets are optimal in every respect. It also does not mean that workers, capitalists, and landowners are always happy with the economic rewards they receive for their services.

For the model economy that we are examining in this book, the division of society into workers, capitalists, and landowners creates potential sources of conflict. Society will have to find ways to prevent or handle such conflict. The issue that underlies the conflict is obviously whether the returns on labor, capital, and land are fair and reasonable. We will investigate how these returns are determined in both competitive and noncompetitive markets according to economic theory. Only then can we evaluate whether the returns are fair and reasonable.

The Return on Labor

In a perfectly competitive economy, the prices of all goods, be they inputs or outputs, are determined by the forces of supply and demand in the markets for those goods. To study these markets, we must first identify the economic agents who demand the goods involved and those who supply the goods. In the labor market, individual firms demand the services of labor and individual workers supply those services. Let us now look at demand and supply function in the labor market.

The Demand for Labor Services by Individual Firms

The demand for labor by a firm is motivated strictly by its desire to maximize its profits. Firms hire labor because they need it to produce output and thereby have a product to sell in the market. Consequently, we call the demand for labor a **derived demand** of a firm—it is derived from the process of profit maximization.

To understand the demand for labor more thoroughly, let us consider a firm that has already hired a certain amount of capital (K) and is contemplating an increase in its use of labor. The more labor the firm uses, the more output it can produce. The benefit to the firm of one more unit of labor is the marginal increase in its output. Figure 26.1(a) presents the short-run production function for the

derived demand
Demand for labor that is derived from the process of profit maximization.

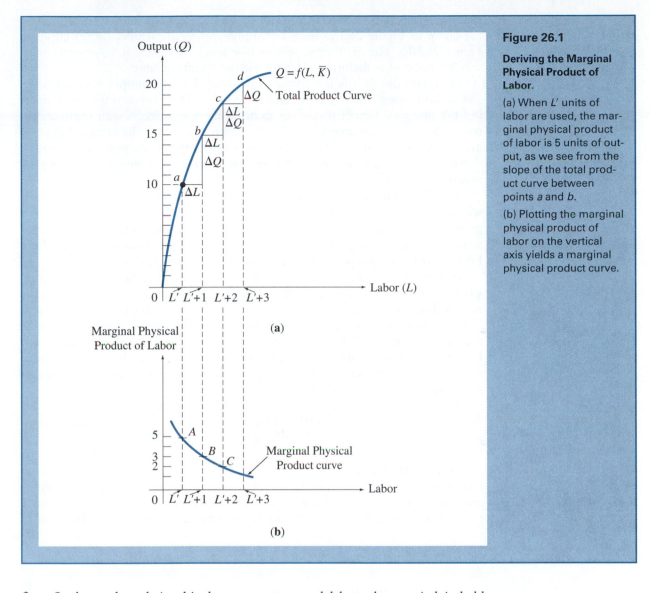

Figure 26.1

Deriving the Marginal Physical Product of Labor.

(a) When L' units of labor are used, the marginal physical product of labor is 5 units of output, as we see from the slope of the total product curve between points a and b.

(b) Plotting the marginal physical product of labor on the vertical axis yields a marginal physical product curve.

firm. It shows the relationship between output and labor when capital is held constant.

We want to see how the output increases as the firm progressively adds more and more labor. At point a in Figure 26.1(a), we find that the firm is using L' units of labor and producing 10 units of output. If the firm could add an infinitesimal amount of labor at point a, we could record the resulting output and define the marginal product of labor exactly at that point. Because it is not possible to divide labor in this way, let us say that the firm decides to use an additional unit of labor, which increases the total number of workers from L' to $L' + 1$. As we can see in Figure 26.1(a), this incremental increase of 1 unit of labor results in a 5-unit increase in output. Letting $\Delta Q / \Delta L$ approximate the marginal physical product of labor at point a, we find that $\Delta Q / \Delta L = \frac{5}{1}$ or 5. This marginal physical product is recorded in Figure 26.1(b) as point A.

A move from point b to point c in Figure 26.1(a) increases labor by another unit, $\Delta L = 1$. However, because there are diminishing returns for each factor, the resulting increase in output is only 3 units, so $\Delta Q / \Delta L = 3$ at point b. This marginal

**marginal physical
product (MPP) curve**
The curve that tells us
how much extra output,
in physical units, will be
produced as the firm adds
more and more units of
labor.

**marginal revenue
product (MRP)**
The firm's marginal physical product the new work-
ers will produce times the
marginal revenue *(MR)* the
additional units of output
will earn.

**optimal quantity of labor
rule**
The rule that indicates that
a profit-maximizing firm
will hire labor up to the
point at which the marginal
revenue product it receives
from the last unit of labor
hired equals the marginal
cost of labor (the wage
the firm must pay to the
last worker hired).

physical product is shown as point *B* in Figure 26.1(b). Further moves along the curve in Figure 26.1(a) trace a marginal physical product (MPP) curve in Figure 26.1(b). The MPP curve tells us how much extra output, in physical units, will be produced as the firm adds more and more units of labor.

However, the firm is not trying to produce the most output it can. Rather, like all businesses, it wants to maximize its profits. The firm does this by compar-ing the marginal benefit it receives from hiring new workers with the marginal cost of hiring these workers. The firm's marginal benefit is the marginal physical product the new workers will produce times the marginal revenue (*MR*) the addi-tional units of output will earn. We will call the resulting amount the marginal revenue product (MRP) of labor. Therefore, $MRP = (MR)(MPP)$.

When an industry is perfectly competitive, we know that all the firms in it will be price takers and will face a perfectly horizontal demand curve for their product. Consequently, the marginal revenue they receive from sales will be con-stant and equal to the price (*P*) of the good. The marginal revenue product for a firm in a perfectly competitive industry will therefore be $MRP = (P)(MPP)$.

If an industry is noncompetitive, let us say monopolistic, the situation is some-what different. Hypothetically, when a monopolist sells an extra unit of output, the marginal revenue it receives for that unit is less than the price previously charged. Not only must the monopolist reduce the price of the extra unit so that it can be sold, but the monopolist must also reduce the price on all goods sold previously. Hence, for a monopolist, $MRP = (MR)(MPP)$. Figure 26.2 shows the marginal revenue product curves for a firm in a perfectly competitive industry and for that same firm if it were a monopolist.

Note that because the marginal physical product curves in Figure 26.2 are downward sloping, the marginal revenue product curves are also downward slop-ing. The curve for the monopolist falls faster because its marginal revenue is always less than the price.

When a firm decides to hire additional labor, it determines how much to hire by using the optimal quantity of labor rule. This rule indicates that a profit-maximizing firm will hire labor up to the point at which the marginal revenue product it receives from the last unit of labor hired equals the marginal cost of

Figure 26.2

The Marginal Revenue Product Curve.

The marginal revenue product of a monopolist falls faster than that of a perfectly competitive firm because the monop-olist's marginal revenue is always less than the price.

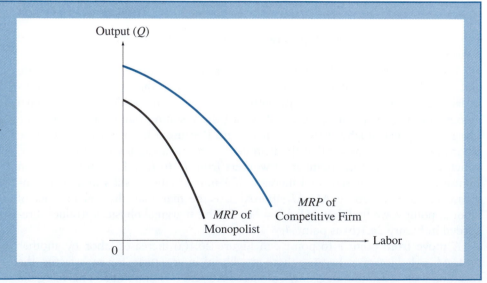

labor (the wage the firm must pay to the last worker hired). To understand the optimal quantity of labor rule, let us consider Figure 26.2. This figure shows the marginal revenue product curves for a firm in a perfectly competitive industry and for a firm that is a monopolist, and it shows the marginal cost curve (supply curve) of labor for a perfectly competitive labor market, that is, a market where there is perfect information about wages and perfect mobility of workers.

Note that the marginal cost curve of labor in Figure 26.3 is horizontal, which means that it is perfectly elastic. This perfect elasticity reflects the fact that a firm hiring workers in a perfectly competitive labor market pays a wage that is constant and fixed by the market. In Figure 26.3, we also see that the marginal revenue product equals the marginal cost of labor at point *a* for the competitive firm and at point *b* for the monopolist. We would expect the monopolist to hire less labor than the competitive firm because we know that monopolists restrict output.

We can now determine the demand curve for labor at a single firm. It is simply the firm's marginal revenue product curve. As we can see in Figure 26.4, this demand curve gives the amount of labor that the firm will hire at any wage. For instance, at a wage of w_a, the firm will hire L_a units of labor. Similarly, it will hire L_b units of labor at a wage of w_b and L_c units of labor at a wage of w_c.

Question (Content Review: The Marginal Product of Labor)

Suppose a firm's production technology is given by the Cobb-Douglas function $Q = L^{1/2}$. The marginal product of labor is $MP = \frac{1}{2}L^{-1/2}$. Suppose the wage rate is \$5. We will talk later about how the wage is determined, but for now assume it is \$5. If the output price is 1, what are the competitive levels of output and input?

Answer

Equating the marginal product to the real wage, we get $\frac{1}{2}L^{-1/2} = 5$; that is, $L^{1/2} = \frac{1}{10}$. Therefore, $L = \frac{1}{100}$ and $Q = \frac{1}{10}$.

SOLVED PROBLEM 26.1

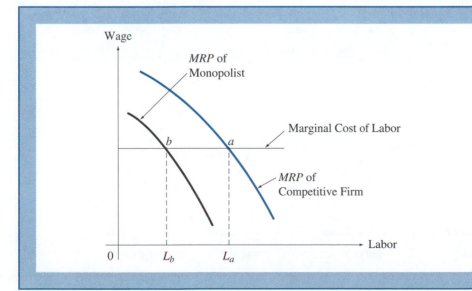

Figure 26.3

A Firm's Decision about Hiring Labor.

A profit-maximizing firm will hire units of labor up to the point at which the marginal revenue product curve intersects the marginal cost of labor curve.

Figure 26.4

The Demand for Labor.

A firm's demand curve for labor shows the amount of labor the firm will hire at various wage rates.

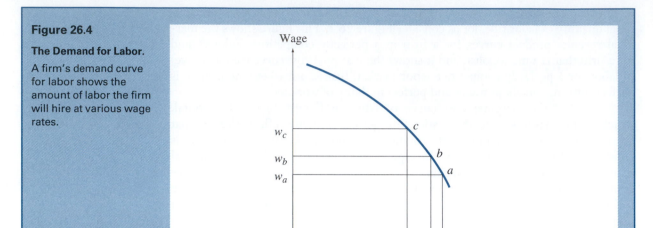

The Market Demand for Labor

The demand for labor in a market is simply the horizontal sum of the demands for labor of all the individual firms in that market. For example, Figure 26.5 depicts three firms, each with a different demand curve for labor. Perhaps these demand curves vary because the firms are using different technologies to produce. The market demand curve appears in the panel at the far right.

Figure 26.5 shows that at a wage of w_a, firm 1 demands 10 units of labor, firm 2 demands 20 units, and firm 3 demands 15 units. Consequently, the total market demand for labor at w_a is 45 units. At a wage of w_b, the demand for labor is 8 units

Figure 26.5

Deriving the Market Demand for Labor.

The market demand for labor is the horizontal sum of the individual labor demand (marginal revenue product) curves of all the firms in the market.

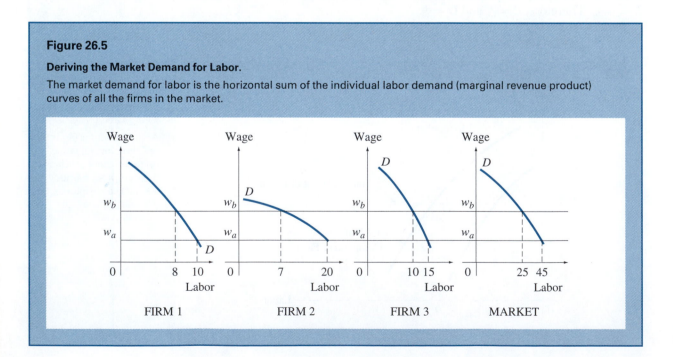

for firm 1, 7 units for firm 2, and 10 units for firm 3. Thus, as the wage rate rises from w_a to w_b, the total market demand for labor falls from 45 units to 25 units.

The Supply of Labor and the Behavior of Individual Workers

Labor is supplied to the market by individual workers who look at the wage rate and decide how they will divide their time between work and leisure. They decide how much labor they are willing to supply and how much leisure they want for themselves. At every wage rate, then, the workers maximize their utility and offer an amount of labor to the market. In Chapter 4, we analyzed how workers make the decision about allocating their time between work and leisure. You may want to review this analysis. Now let us consider Figure 26.6, which illustrates how individual workers will behave in response to different wage rates.

In Figure 26.6, we see the labor supply curve for an individual worker. This curve shows the amount of labor the worker is willing to offer to the market at various wage rates. Note that as the wage rate increases, the worker will choose to devote more hours to labor.

The Market Supply Curve for Labor

The market supply curve for labor is simply the horizontal sum of the individual supply curves of all workers in the market. Thus, it is derived by the same process that is used to derive the market demand curve. This process is illustrated in Figure 26.7.

In Figure 26.7 we see a labor market with three workers, each facing a set of three different wage rates, which were determined by the market. At a wage rate of w_e, worker 1 is willing to supply 4 hours of labor, worker 2 is willing to supply 6 hours of labor, and worker 3 is willing to supply 8 hours of labor. Thus, the total market supply of labor at that wage rate is 18 hours. When the wage rate rises to w_f and then to w_b, the workers offer increasing amounts of labor to the market, as shown by the market supply curve at the far right in Figure 26.7. The kinks in the curve may result from the horizontal aggregation or generally from different reservation wages at which workers participate in the labor market.

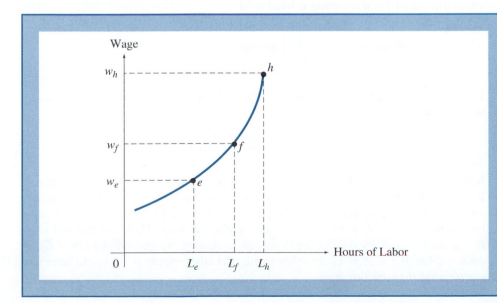

Figure 26.6

The Labor Supply Curve for an Individual Worker.

Plotting the number of hours of labor supplied on the horizontal axis and the wage rate on the vertical axis yields the labor supply curve for an individual worker.

Figure 26.7

Deriving the Market Supply Curve for Labor.

The market supply curve for labor is the horizontal sum of the individual labor supply curves of all the workers in the market.

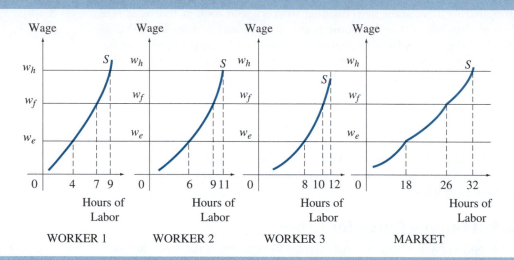

| WORKER 1 | WORKER 2 | WORKER 3 | MARKET |

SOLVED PROBLEM 26.2

Question (Application and Extension: Labor Supply)

Suppose a consumer's preferences over consumption and leisure are given by $U = C^{1/2}Z^{1/2}$, where C is the level of consumption and Z is the level of leisure. The marginal utilities are $MU_C = \frac{1}{2}C^{-1/2}Z^{1/2}$ and $MU_Z = \frac{1}{2}C^{1/2}Z^{-1/2}$. Assuming that the consumer has only 24 hours to divide between leisure and labor, what will the labor supply be when the price of consumption is $1 and the wage rate is $5? On a piece of paper, graph the labor supply curve as a function of the wage rate when the price of consumption is fixed at $1.

Answer

The budget constraint faced by the consumer is

$$C = 5(24 - Z)$$

Equating the marginal rate of substitution of leisure for consumption to the real wage, we get

$$5 = \frac{\frac{1}{2}C^{1/2}Z^{-1/2}}{\frac{1}{2}C^{-1/2}Z^{1/2}} = \frac{C}{Z}; \text{ that is, } C = 5Z$$

Substituting the second equation into the first, we get $5Z = 120 - 5Z$; that is, $Z = 12$. Therefore, the supply of labor is 12 hours. To graph the labor supply curve, we have to assume that the wage rate is w instead of $5. Then the budget constraint becomes $C = w(24 - Z)$. The equality between MRS and the real wage rate gives $C = wZ$. By combining these two equations, we get $wZ = w(24 - Z)$, or $2wZ = 24w$; that is, $Z = 12$. In other words, the labor supply is always 12 hours, *no matter what the wage rate is.*

The Equilibrium Market Wage

Up to now, we have seen how individual firms and individual workers decide on the quantity of labor they wish to demand and supply, but we have not yet learned how the equilibrium market wage is set. In a market with many firms and many workers, we can determine the equilibrium wage by simply juxtaposing the market supply and demand curves for labor as is done in Figure 26.8.

The equilibrium wage rate of w_e for the labor market occurs at point E in Figure 26.8, where the supply of labor equals the demand. If we assume that all labor is of the same quality, then w_e is the wage rate that workers will receive in this industry.

Setting the Stage for Class Conflict

When the market determines the wage rate of w_e, each firm in the industry will hire labor up to the point at which the total wage it pays is equal to its marginal revenue product. This equality is shown in Figure 26.9.

Note that the payment to labor in Figure 26.9 is represented by the rectangular area $0w_eeL_e$. The firm's revenues, however, are equal to the area $0HeL_e$. For each unit of labor the firm hires up to q_e, its revenues increase by the amount represented by the height of the marginal revenue product curve, yet the amount the firm has to pay each worker is only w_e. In other words, the owners of the firm are making a surplus of w_eHe above what they are paying the workers.

Once the workers become aware of the surplus, they might want to claim a portion of it for themselves. The owners of the firm would then argue that they need the surplus to pay for the other factors of production. For instance, say that the owners of the firm must obtain machines for the workers to use in producing output. Obviously, the owners of the machines want to be paid for supplying these capital goods. Similarly, the owners of the land on which the firm's factory building is located want to be paid rent. Thus, before we can arbitrate the claims of the workers for a larger share of the firm's output, we must understand how the returns on capital and land are determined in a competitive market.

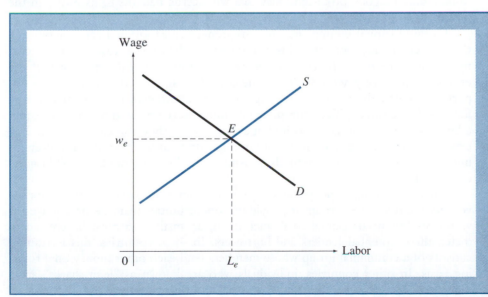

Figure 26.8

Determining the Equilibrium Market Wage.

The equilibrium market wage is the wage at which the market demand for labor equals the market supply of labor.

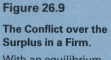

Figure 26.9

The Conflict over the Surplus in a Firm.

With an equilibrium wage rate of w_e, the worker receives a payment equal to the area $w_e e L_e 0$, whereas the firm receives a surplus equal to the area $H e w_e$.

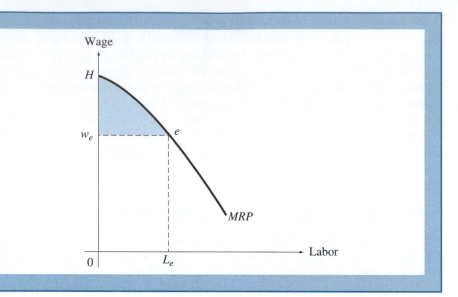

The Return on Capital

We know that there are three inputs to production: capital, labor, and land. Two of these inputs—labor and land—occur naturally, but capital is a human artifact. It consists of goods made by human beings for use in producing outputs that are ultimately intended for consumers. This distinction between natural and manufactured inputs is actually an oversimplification because it is such a common practice in modern economies to enhance the productivity of labor and land by using a variety of methods and devices developed by human beings. For example, workers add to the effectiveness of their natural capacity for labor through education and on-the-job training; that is, they add to their human capital. Similarly, the yield from land is increased by the application of fertilizers and the installation of irrigation systems. However, for our purposes in this discussion, we will consider capital to be a durable good produced today that will accrue benefits to its owner in the future.

human capital
Skills of labor.

To build capital equipment, an entrepreneur must either borrow money in the financial markets or invest his or her own funds. In each case, there is a cost to the entrepreneur. The cost of borrowing the money is the interest that the entrepreneur must pay on the loan. The cost of using one's own money is its opportunity cost—the potential earnings from an alternative investment that one forgoes. For example, if an entrepreneur's funds were not used to start and equip a business, they could be deposited in a bank where they will earn interest. The expected return on capital must therefore be sufficient to entice an entrepreneur into borrowing the necessary funds or using his or her own funds to build capital equipment.

When one group of people in society has money from savings available for investment and another group of people has opportunities to make productive investments but needs capital to finance them, an institution must be created to match these potential lenders and borrowers. In some countries, this institution consists of a communal group whose members lend each other money on a rotating basis. In other countries, individuals who are known as "loan sharks" arise. They lend money at very high interest rates and sometimes use physical force to collect if borrowers fall behind in their payments. In still other countries, organized financial markets develop where loans can be acquired and where money is lent to aspiring (and perhaps risky) firms through venture capitalists.

In this section, we will see how competitive financial markets determine the market rate of interest in an economy. We will use the market rate of interest as a measure of the amount that must be paid to the owners of financial capital to persuade them to lend it to others to invest in production. Once this payment for capital is determined, we will consider it along with the payments that must be made for the other factors of production—labor and land—in order to complete our analysis of whether labor is being paid its equitable share of the commonly created output.

Thus, we are faced with the following question: How is the market rate of interest determined? We will answer this question by investigating the forces that underlie the supply and demand curves for loanable funds in the financial markets.

The Supply of Loanable Funds

On one side of the financial markets are the suppliers of funds. They are mostly individual consumers who make the decision to save a portion of their income today and deposit it in a bank or other savings institution where it will grow by earning interest until they withdraw the accumulated funds at some time in the future. Obviously, these people will save money only if the amount of interest their money can earn is sufficient to make them want to sacrifice some of their present consumption for a future gain. Given this situation, what does the supply curve of loanable funds look like and how is it determined? The answer to this question requires nothing more than a typical exercise in utility maximization analysis. Let us use Figure 26.10 for this purpose.

In Figure 26.10, we see a standard indifference curve diagram with a budget constraint for an individual consumer. The horizontal axis shows consumption today, and the vertical axis shows consumption tomorrow. The budget line *AB* tells us that this person has a wealth of $10,000 a year. She can choose to consume her entire

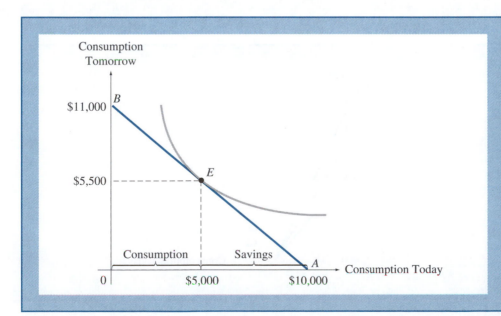

Figure 26.10

The Decision to Save.

The consumer allocates her income between current consumption and saving such that the budget line, whose slope represents the rate of interest, is tangent to an indifference curve reflecting her preferences between consumption today and consumption tomorrow.

wealth today, consume nothing today and all her wealth tomorrow, or divide her wealth between consumption today and consumption tomorrow. If she consumes all her wealth today and saves nothing, she will be at point A in Figure 26.10. At point B, the opposite is true. She saves her entire wealth today and postpones consumption until tomorrow.

Note, however, that if our consumer is willing to wait until tomorrow, she will then be able to consume more than she can today. In fact, by waiting, she can increase the amount she has available for consumption to $11,000. The reason for this increase in her financial resources is that there is a market for loanable funds in which people who have savings can lend money and receive interest on it. In this case, the interest rate is 10%, so every dollar not spent in consumption today will yield $1.10 tomorrow. The slope of the budget line indicates the rate of interest obtainable in the market.

The decision of the consumer about saving will depend on whether she prefers consumption today or consumption tomorrow. These preferences are represented by the indifference curve in Figure 26.10. As we can see, the consumer reaches an equilibrium at point E, where the marginal rate of substitution between consumption today and consumption tomorrow equals the rate of interest. At point E, the rate at which the consumer is willing to postpone consumption today for consumption tomorrow is exactly equal to the rate at which the market is willing to pay her to do so. At this point, she saves $5,000 and consumes $5,000 today. She lends the $5,000 she saves, and because of the interest paid on the loan, she has $5,500 to consume tomorrow. As the interest rate changes, the consumer will be induced to save more or less. Let us now consider Figure 26.11, which shows how the supply curve for loanable funds for our consumer is derived.

In Figure 26.11, we see the interest rate rise from 10% to 15% and then to 20%. As a result, the consumer increases the amount she saves, moving from point E to point F and eventually to point G. Let us now turn our attention to Figure 26.12, which depicts the supply curve for loanable funds for our consumer.

Figure 26.12 shows the rate of interest on the vertical axis and the amount of loanable funds supplied on the horizontal axis. Note that the supply curve for the loanable funds provided by our consumer is upward sloping. As the interest rate

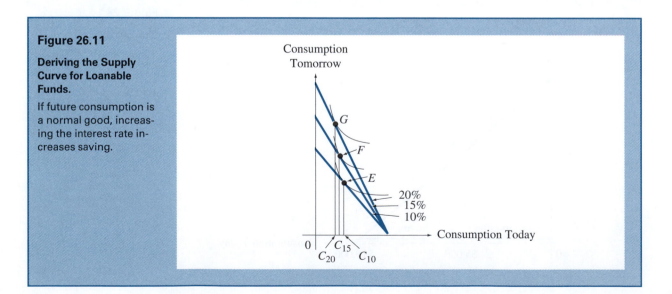

Figure 26.11

Deriving the Supply Curve for Loanable Funds.

If future consumption is a normal good, increasing the interest rate increases saving.

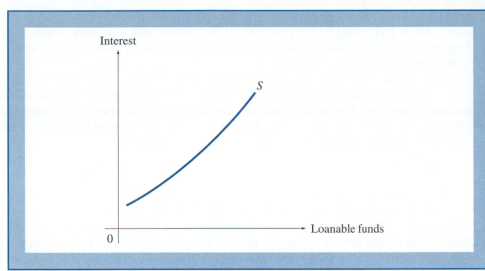

Figure 26.12

The Supply of Loanable Funds.

Plotting the quantity saved on the horizontal axis and the interest rate on the vertical axis yields the supply curve for loanable funds.

rises, the amount she is willing to lend increases. The market supply curve for loanable funds is simply the sum of the individual supply curves for all the people who have savings available for investment, just as the market supply curve for labor is the sum of the individual labor supply curves for all the workers in the market.

The Demand for Loanable Funds

On the other side of the financial markets are the demanders of loanable funds. These people are producers or potential producers who need the funds to purchase capital goods. In other words, these people have opportunities for productive investments. Thus, if they borrow money today and use it in their businesses, the returns should be great enough to repay the loans with interest in the future. To determine how much money to invest in a project and therefore how much to seek in the market for loanable funds, producers must weigh the rate of return they expect to earn on their investments against the cost of borrowing—the interest rate they must pay to obtain the funds.

Calculating the Rate of Return on an Investment. Let us assume that a firm has an opportunity to invest in a capital goods project that will cost $100 today and return $105 in one year. If we let C be the cost today, R_1 be the return in a year, and π be the rate of return on the investment, then

$$C(1 + \pi) = R_1 \text{ or } \pi = R_1/C - 1$$

We are saying that π is the one-period rate of return on an investment of C today that will yield R_1 in a year. In other words, if C is allowed to grow at π percent for one year, it will reach R_1. In our example, $\$100(1.05) = \$105$, so π is 5%. Dividing both sides by $(1 + \pi)$ produces the following:

$$C = R_1/(1 + \pi)$$

If the investment will yield nothing one year from now but R_2 two years from now, the income stream will be $R_1 = 0$ and $R_2 = \$105$. To find the rate of return on the investment, we must solve for the π that equates $C(1 + \pi)^2$ to R_2 because if C dollars are invested at a rate of return of π percent, they will yield $C(1 + \pi)$ after one year, and that $C(1 + \pi)$, if invested at the end of the first year, will yield $C(1 + \pi)^2 = C(1 + \pi)(1 + \pi)$ at the end of the second year. In other words, the rate of return is the rate that equates the discounted value of the income stream generated by the investment to its cost.

Now let us assume that the investment project will yield income in each year of a multiyear period. The firm involved borrows C dollars today to build the project and receives the following income stream: R_1 at the end of year 1, R_2 at the end of year 2, R_3 at the end of year 3, and so on up to year n. To calculate the rate of return on such an investment, we must solve for the π such that

$$O = -C + R_1/(1 + \pi) + R_2/(1 + \pi)^2 + R_3/(1 + \pi)^3 + \cdots + R_n/(1 + \pi)^n$$

A producer will undertake an investment in a capital goods project only if the expected rate of return on the investment is greater than the market rate of interest of r. Obviously, when borrowed funds are used for an investment, the producer will lose money if the rate of return on the investment is less than the rate paid to the lender. When internal funds are available, the producer will also not want to make the investment unless its rate of return is greater than the market rate of interest because there is an opportunity cost to using internal funds. For example, if a firm has $10,000 to invest, it always has the option of depositing the money in a bank and earning interest at the market rate of r, that is, that rate of return determined by the forces of supply and demand in the loadable funds market.

Determining the Demand for Loanable Funds. Once we know how to calculate the rate of return on an investment, we can calculate the demand for loanable funds in a single firm and in the market. Then we can use the market supply and demand curves for loanable funds to determine the market rate of interest and the return on capital. Let us now consider Figure 26.13, which shows the demand of one firm for loanable funds.

In Figure 26.13, we see the market rate of interest on the vertical axis and various amounts of loanable funds on the horizontal axis. The demand for loanable funds describes the relationship between the two. Let us assume that the firm

Figure 26.13

The Demand for Loanable Funds by a Firm.

At each interest rate, the firm will demand a quantity of loanable funds sufficient to finance all those investment projects with rates of return greater than the interest rate.

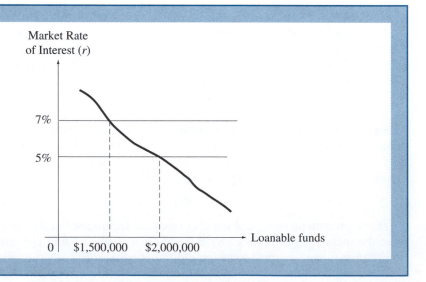

represented in this diagram has a set of investment projects that it can rank by their rates of return. Some projects will yield high rates of return; others will yield low rates. To simplify our analysis, we will assume that the set of projects is infinite and includes every imaginable rate of return. We will also assume that the firm will undertake all projects with rates of return higher than the market rate of interest. For example, as Figure 26.13 shows, if $r = 5\%$, the firm's demand for loanable funds will be $2 million. In other words, the firm has projects totaling $2 million that will yield a return on investment that is greater than 5%. However, at $r = 7\%$, projects totaling only $1.5 million will be profitable investments for the firm. Clearly, the demand curve for loanable funds is downward sloping. Thus, the lower the market rate of interest is, the greater the demand for loanable funds.

The market demand curve for loanable funds is the sum of the demand curves of the individual firms, just as the market supply curve for loanable funds is the sum of the individual supply curves. Figure 26.14 depicts the demand for loanable funds in the market.

Determining the Market Rate of Interest and the Return on Capital

The equilibrium of the market for loanable funds occurs at the intersection of the market supply and demand curves. This point gives us the market rate of interest and the amount of funds that will be invested at that rate, as we see in Figure 26.15, where the market rate of interest is r^* and the amount of funds invested at that rate is K^*. The market rate of interest, in turn, determines the return on capital. At the equilibrium of the market for loanable funds, the marginal rate of return, which is the rate of return on the last profitable project undertaken by society, is just equal to the market rate of interest.

Figure 26.14

The Market Demand Curve for Loanable Funds.

The market demand curve for loanable funds is the horizontal sum of the demand curves for loanable funds of all the individual firms in the market.

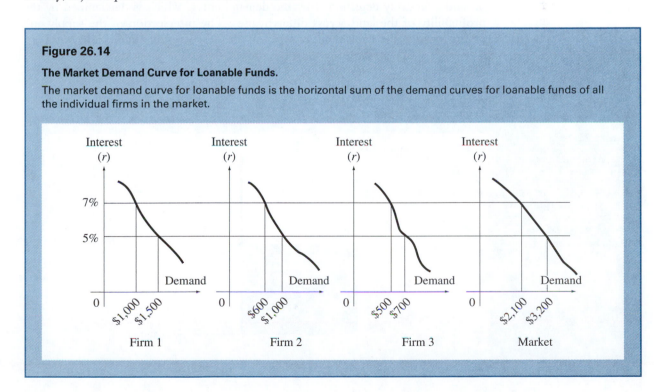

Figure 26.15

The Market for Loanable Funds.

The equilibrium interest rate is determined at the intersection of the market supply curve section for loanable funds and the market demand curve for loanable funds.

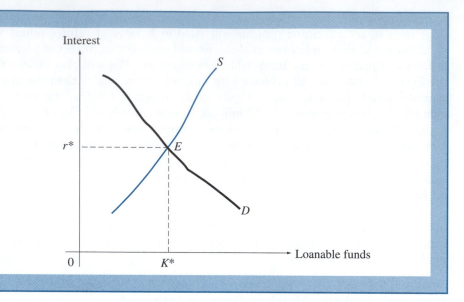

The Return on Land

While the return on labor is in the form of wages and the return on capital is in the form of interest, the return on land is in the form of rent. According to its formal definition, rent is the return on a factor above the amount necessary to entice that factor into the production process.

Figure 26.16 shows that the supply of land is perfectly inelastic, which means that the same amount of land, L_e, is available at any price. Consequently, the price of land is entirely determined by the demand curve, which is determined by the profitability of the land across different uses. The intersection of the supply and demand curves occurs at point e in Figure 26.16, where the equilibrium rent is r_e. At this price of r_e, the return on land is the rectangle $0r_eeL_e$, all of which is rent.

rent
The return on a factor above the amount necessary to entice that factor into the production process.

Figure 26.16

The Market Determination of Rent.

The equilibrium rent on land, r_e, is determined at the intersection of the vertical supply curve for land and the downward-sloping demand curve for land.

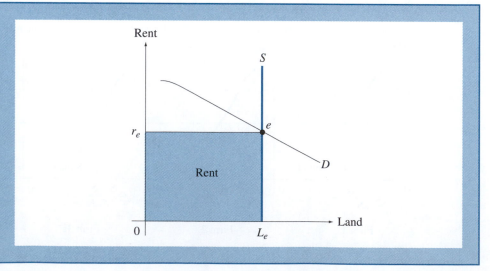

Resolving the Claims of Different Factors of Production: The Product Exhaustion Theorem

Free-market economies determine the returns on the factors of production according to what is called the marginal productivity theory. Each factor is paid its marginal revenue product, which means that each factor is paid its marginal contribution to the total output of society. Thus, labor is paid the marginal revenue product of the last worker hired and capital is paid the rate of return earned on the last unit of capital used. The return on land is determined strictly by demand. This distribution of income is often referred to as the functional distribution of income.

If we are to have a theory of income distribution, we want that theory to explain exactly what portion of the value of the goods produced by society each factor of production will receive. We also want that theory to impute the value of the goods produced fully so that nothing is left over. In other words, we want the payments to the factors of production to fully account for the value of the goods produced, or "exhaust" the value. At first glance, the marginal productivity theory does not seem to meet these criteria. When each factor of production is paid its marginal revenue product, it is not clear that the sum of the payments made will equal the total value of the output produced by society. If the two sums are not equal, then the claims on the total goods produced may exceed the total amount of money available, in which case the claims will be inconsistent. Conversely, the claims may fall short of the total of society's output, in which case there will be an amount remaining after each factor has been paid its marginal revenue product. In either of these cases, it would not be possible to use the marginal productivity theory to justify the distribution of income to the factors of production. We would have to use another rationale to resolve the disputes that would result.

marginal productivity theory
The theory that states how free-market economies determine the returns on the factors of production, whereby each factor is paid its marginal revenue product.

functional distribution of income
The distribution of income across the factors of production: land, labor, and capital.

Product Exhaustion

In a world of perfectly competitive markets, the marginal productivity theory does not run into the difficulties that we just examined. If each factor is paid its marginal revenue product, the total value of society's output will be distributed to the factors of production. This idea is expressed in the product exhaustion theorem, which can be stated as follows: When all the factors of production are paid the value of what they produce, then at the long-run equilibrium of a perfectly competitive economy, the sum of their shares of the value of the socially produced pie must equal 1.

To understand the product exhaustion theorem, we will let $x_1^*, x_2^*, x_3^*, x_4^*, \ldots, x_n^*$ be the vector of inputs chosen by a firm at the long-run competitive equilibrium of a market, where x_1^* is the amount of factor 1 used at the equilibrium, x_1^* the amount of factor 2, and so on. We will let $w_1, w_2, w_3, w_4, \ldots, w_n$ be the prices of these inputs, p be the price of the good produced, and y^* be the quantity produced. We know that all the factors will be paid their marginal revenue product, so we want the following to be true:

product exhaustion theorem
When all the factors of production are paid the value of what they produce, then at the long-run equilibrium of a perfectly competitive economy, the sum of their shares of the value of the socially produced pie must equal 1.

$$py^* = w_1 x_1^* + w_2 x_2^* + w_3 x_3^* + w_4 x_4^* + \cdots + w_n x_n^*$$

This relationship implies

$$p = \frac{(w_1 x_1^* + w_2 x_2^* + w_3 x_3^* + w_4 x_4^* + \cdots + w_n x_n^*)}{y^*}$$

However, this situation merely tells us that the product exhaustion theorem will hold when the factors are paid their marginal revenue product and *the price of the good is set so that it is equal to the long-run average cost.* At the long-run equilibrium of a competitive market, this is exactly what happens. Thus, we can say that in such circumstances, the product exhaustion theorem will prove to be true.

SOLVED PROBLEM 26.3	**Question (Content Review: Hiring Factor Inputs)** Consider a firm that has a production function $Q = KL$, where Q is output, K is capital, and L is labor. For this production function, the marginal product of capital is $MP_k = L$, while the marginal product of labor is $MP_L = K$. The firm sells a product whose price p is \$1. The wage is \$5, while the cost of capital is \$10. If the firm pays all workers the value of their marginal product, $VMP_K = p(MP_K)$, $VMP_L = p(MP_L)$, how much labor will it hire, how much capital will it use, and will it make or lose money? **Answer** It will hire workers up to the point where the value of the marginal product of labor and of capital equal their respective prices. Because the wage rate is constant at \$5 and the cost of capital constant at \$10, the firm will set $MP_k = (\$1)L = \$10$, $MP_L = (\$1)K = \$5$ and hence will use 5 units of capital and 10 units of labor. Its output will be $Q = 5 \times 10 = 50$ and its revenue \$50. Its cost of production is $\$100 = \$5 \times 10 + \$10 \times 5$. Thus, the firm will lose money because this technology has increasing returns to scale. Each unit of input is more productive than the last. Thus, when, for instance, you attempt to pay each worker the value of the marginal product of the last worker employed, you are paying them all the value produced by the most productive worker; hence, you are overimputing value to this factor.

Determining the Return on Labor in Markets that Are Less than Perfectly Competitive

In our analysis so far in this chapter, we have concentrated on how the returns to the factors of production are determined when all markets are perfectly competitive. If the factors of production are purchased and sold under conditions of perfect competition, no agent in the economy is large enough or powerful enough to affect the wages, interest, or rents the factors receive. Everyone is a price taker. In the real world, however, not all markets are perfectly competitive. Workers form unions so that they can present a collective front to employers when they bargain over wages and benefits. Their aim is to try to capture more than their marginal revenue product. On the other side, employers are sometimes in a position to dominate the bargaining process. For example, a big employer in a small town has powerful bargaining strength because it can threaten to close down its factory, which would be devastating to the workers and to the town as well.

In this section, we will see how two powerful entities, such as a monopolist and a monopsonist, might bargain with one another. As we know, a monopolist is the sole seller of a good or service. A labor union with a closed shop arrangement might be considered a monopolist. Being the sole supplier of labor, it is the only entity with which an employer can bargain in order to hire workers. Conversely, a monopsonist is the sole buyer of a good or service. The single employer in an old-style factory town might be considered a monopsonist. At the least, it would have extraordinary bargaining power over labor.

Monopsony

We are already familiar with the characteristics of a monopoly—a market with a single seller. Let us now investigate how a **monopsony**—a market with a single buyer—functions. There are various forms of monopsony. For instance, the Department of Defense is presumably the only domestic purchaser of tanks in the United States. However, our discussion in this section will focus on monopsonistic input markets. The classic example of such a market, as we noted previously, is the once common "company town," a local labor market dominated by a single employer.

A firm that must compete with many other employers to hire workers faces a horizontal, or perfectly elastic, labor supply curve. Offering even slightly less than the equilibrium wage will cause the firm to lose its entire workforce to its rivals. But a firm that is the "only game in town" has leeway in setting wage levels. Lowering its wage will cause only a fraction of its workers to leave the firm; raising its wage will cause a finite increase in its supply of labor. In other words, a monopsonist faces an upward-sloping labor supply curve.

Of course, given the nature of monopsony, the labor supply curve of a monopsonistic firm is simply the market labor supply curve, which we already know is upward sloping. Actually, all the characteristics that we ascribe to monopsonists in this discussion will be analogous to the characteristics of monopolists. Remember that the demand curve of a firm in a competitive market is horizontal, but a monopolistic firm faces a downward-sloping demand curve, and the slope of this curve depends on the elasticity of demand.

What is the optimal wage policy for a monopsonistic firm? To answer this question precisely, we must first make the following assumptions: that the monopsonistic firm takes the labor supply function as given and that it cannot practice **wage discrimination**. By not practicing wage discrimination, we mean that the firm must pay the same wage rate on all units of labor it employs. Each employee earns the same regardless of their individual productivity or personal value for leisure.

Let us assume that labor is the only variable input of the monopsonistic firm, and let us define its **marginal expenditure (ME)** on labor as the change in its total wage bill that results from its hiring of one additional unit of labor. For a firm in a competitive labor market, the marginal expenditure on labor is simply the existing wage rate. But if a monopsonistic firm wishes to attract more workers, it must offer a higher wage because it faces an upward-sloping labor supply curve. Moreover, this higher wage must be paid to all existing employees as well as to the new employees because wage discrimination is excluded. The marginal expenditure on labor curve of the monopsonist must therefore lie *above* the upward-sloping labor supply curve, as shown in Figure 26.17.

The monopsonist's **total expenditure (TE)** on labor is simply the total wage it pays: $TE = wL$, where L is the supply of labor available at a wage rate of w. Suppose that the monopsonist now wishes to attract a labor force of $L + \Delta L$ by offering a wage of $w + \Delta w$. Then the marginal expenditure on labor is $ME = (\Delta w/\Delta L)L + w$, where $\Delta w/\Delta L > 0$ because the labor supply curve is upward sloping. (For infinitely small changes in L, the wage paid new workers will be sufficiently close to w.)

Now we can derive the optimal wage policy for a monopsonist. A profit-maximizing monopsonist will hire additional workers up to the point at which its marginal expenditure on labor is equal to labor's marginal revenue product (*MRP*). Remember that the marginal revenue product of labor is equal to marginal revenue

monopsony
A market with a single buyer.

wage discrimination
When a firm does not pay the same wage rate on all units of labor it employs.

marginal expenditure (ME)
The change in a firm's total wage bill that results from its hiring of one additional unit of labor.

total expenditure (TE)
The total wage a monopsonist pays for labor.

Figure 26.17

A Monopsonistic Labor Market.

A single firm buys labor services in a monopsonistic market. While the wage level in a competitive market would be w_c and the employment level would be L_c, the monopsonist chooses a wage level of w_M and an employment level of L_M.

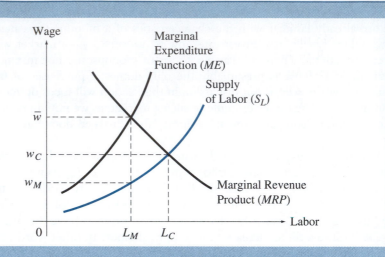

times the marginal physical product of labor. Also remember that diminishing returns to labor ensure that the marginal revenue product of labor declines as the quantity produced increases; that is, the *MRP* curve is downward sloping. The relevant curves are presented in Figure 26.17.

The curve labeled *ME* in Figure 26.17 is the marginal expenditure on labor curve, the curve label S_L is the labor supply curve, and the curve labeled *MRP* is labor's marginal revenue product curve.[1] In the monopsonistic labor market, the equilibrium occurs at the intersection of the *MRP* and *ME* curves because the single employer equates the marginal revenue product of labor to its marginal expenditure on labor by using L_M units of labor. However, the monopsonist does not offer a wage of $\bar{w}$. Instead, it offers only a wage of w_M because the S_L curve indicates that L_M units of labor will be supplied at a wage of w_M.

If we substitute the preceding expression for the marginal expenditure on labor, we see that wage w, which maximizes the profits of the monopsonist, satisfies the following condition:

$$MRP = w + \left[\left(\frac{\Delta w}{\Delta L} \right) \left(\frac{L}{w} \right) \right] w$$

Note that the positive and finite quantity $(\Delta L / \Delta w)(w/L)$ is the elasticity of the labor supply with respect to the wage. Let us denote this elasticity by ζ. We can then rewrite the preceding condition as follows:

$$MRP = w(1 + 1/\zeta)$$

Rearranging this equation gives an interesting result:

$$(MRP - w)/w = 1/\zeta$$

The right side of the equation is zero when ζ is infinite—that is, when the labor supply curve is horizontal—which means that the labor market is competitive.

---

[1] Note that if the labor market were perfectly competitive, then its equilibrium would occur at the intersection of the *MRP* and *SL* curves (because the firms in the market would take the wage rate as given). This situation implies a competitive wage of w_C and an employment level of L_C.

Hence, we can say that a profit-maximizing monopsonist will always pay labor *less* than its marginal revenue product; and the less elastic the labor supply is, the greater the gap between the wage rate paid by the monopsonist and labor's marginal revenue product will be. For this reason, the term monopsonistic exploitation is sometimes used to refer to any situation in which a factor of production is paid less than the value of its marginal revenue product.

Bilateral Monopoly

Let us now combine the features of monopoly and monopsony into a single model by considering a market with only one seller and one buyer. This type of market is called a bilateral monopoly. Although we could cite various examples of bilateral monopoly, we will limit our discussion here to bilateral monopoly in the context of input markets.

Let us assume that all the workers in a small town organize into a single union so that they can bargain collectively with the town's sole employer over wage and employment levels. Obviously, the union, as the only seller of labor, is a monopolist; the firm, as the only buyer of labor, is a monopsonist. The equilibrium wage in such a model is indeterminate unless we make some assumptions that we have not yet made in our discussion of input markets.

For the firm, the effects of bilateral monopoly are identical to those of monopsony. The firm has an upward-sloping marginal expenditure on labor curve and wishes to employ the quantity of labor, say L_F, at which its marginal expenditure on labor equals the marginal revenue product of labor. Under bilateral monopoly, however, the position of labor changes because labor is no longer a price taker. Therefore, the firm cannot be sure, as it was under monopsony, of attracting L_F units of labor by offering the minimum wage that makes it worthwhile for the union to supply that number of units. As a monopolistic supplier, the union is seeking to solve its own analogous optimization problem: choosing the combination of wage and employment levels that is best for labor, subject to the constraint that it be minimally acceptable to the employer. Thus, each party is attempting to set the price by treating the *other* party as a price taker.

Remember that a competitive firm's supply curve for the good it produces is its marginal cost curve because such a firm will want to supply that quantity at which the price it receives is equal to the marginal cost it incurs. Similarly, workers in a competitive labor market will supply that quantity of labor at which their wage rate equals their marginal opportunity cost in terms of forgone leisure. We did not refer to supply curves in our study of monopoly because the existence of a supply function implies that the supplier treats price as a given. If, however, we assume that the buyer in a market regards the supplier (perhaps mistakenly) as a price taker, then we can think of the supplier's marginal cost curve as the "supply curve" that the buyer believes he is facing. Similarly, in a competitive labor market, the employer's labor demand curve is its marginal revenue product of labor curve because the firm will demand that quantity of labor at which the wage rate it pays equals the marginal revenue product of labor. When there is a single employer in a market, no true labor demand curve exists. If labor regards the employer as a price taker, however, then that firm's marginal revenue product of labor curve will be considered by the union as the labor "demand curve."

Therefore, a labor market characterized by bilateral monopoly is similar to a simple monopsony in that the employer faces an upward-sloping marginal expenditure on labor curve that lies above labor's marginal cost curve (the labor "supply curve"). Because labor is a monopolistic supplier, however, there is no true supply

monopsonistic exploitation
Any situation in which a factor of production is paid less than the value of its marginal revenue product.

bilateral monopoly
A market with only one seller and one buyer.

curve. As a monopolist, the union seeks to supply that quantity of labor, say L_U units, at which its marginal revenue equals its marginal (opportunity) cost. The union's marginal revenue, MR_U, is the same as labor's marginal revenue MR_L and is derived in the same way as any monopolist's marginal revenue: $MR_U = w(1 - 1/|\xi|)$, where $\xi < 0$ is the elasticity of demand for labor with respect to the wage rate w. Hence, labor's marginal revenue curve lies below the downward-sloping marginal revenue product of labor curve (the labor "demand curve").

Figure 26.18 combines all four curves: labor's supply (marginal cost) curve (S_L), the firm's marginal expenditure on labor curve (ME), the marginal revenue product of labor curve (MRP), and the marginal revenue to labor curve (MR_L). In a perfectly competitive labor market, the S_L curve is the labor supply curve, while the MRP curve is the labor demand curve. Hence, the competitive equilibrium occurs at a wage of w_C and an employment level of L_C. In a monopsonistic labor market, the firm will choose an employment level of L_F, which is at the intersection of the ME and MRP curves, and it will pay a wage of w_F, which appears on the S_L (labor supply) curve, because w_F is the lowest wage that makes it worthwhile for the union to supply L_F units of labor.

If many competitive firms confront a single union, labor will set an employment level of L_U, which occurs at the intersection of the S_L and MR_L curves, and it will receive a wage of w_U, which appears on the MRP (labor demand) curve, because w_U is the highest wage that makes it worthwhile for firms to hire L_U units of labor. However, when there is a bilateral monopoly, the outcome is indeterminate. There are no true demand or supply curves because neither side is a price taker. Consequently, neither side can necessarily achieve its optimal quantity of labor by offering the other side a minimally acceptable wage level. All we can say is that it seems reasonable that the negotiated wage will lie between w_F and w_U, that the

Figure 26.18

A Bilateral Monopoly.

Bargaining between a single seller of labor services, a union, and a single buyer leads to an indeterminate wage level, which will lie between w_F and w_U, and an indeterminate employment level, which will lie between L_F and L_U.

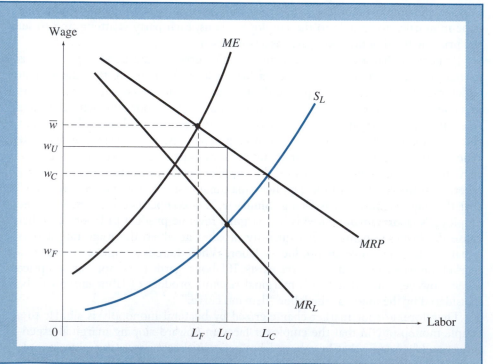

employment level will lie between L_F and L_U, and that the actual outcome will depend on the intangible "bargaining power" of the two parties. Note that if we had drawn the curves differently, we could have had $L_U < L_F$. Also, note that if the wage is set above w_C, then the quantity of labor employed will be constrained by the demand curve, while if the wage is set below w_C, the quantity of labor employed will be constrained by the supply curve.

The Alternating Offer Sequential Bargaining Institution

As we learned from our discussion of bilateral monopoly, that model leaves the final wage and employment levels indeterminate. The wage level will lie between w_F and w_U, and the employment level will lie between L_F and L_U. The exact amounts depend on the bargaining skills of the employer and the union. However, we may be able to anticipate the final wage and employment levels if we know what institution will be used to conduct the bargaining. Different bargaining institutions lead to different outcomes. Therefore, we must choose one bargaining institution to study so that we can gain an understanding of its properties.

The institution that we will investigate is called the **alternating offer sequential bargaining institution**. It has a structure that reflects real-world bargaining to some extent but is also quite stylized. We will be looking for the Nash equilibrium solution to the game defined by this institution.

To describe this institution, let us assume that time is divided into discrete periods in which agreements can be reached. Let us also assume that the parties involved are bargaining over a pie whose value will decrease over time if no agreement is reached. This pie could be the profits of a firm, which will decrease as time passes without an agreement because the firm will lose market share to other firms. Let us say that in the first period, the amount to be divided between the two parties involved—the firm and the union—is $5 million. If no agreement is reached in period 1, the pie shrinks to $2.5 million in period 2. In period 3, if the bargaining proceeds that far, the pie will shrink to $1.25 million. If no deal is reached by the end of period 3, the pie shrinks to zero (the firm closes) and no payments are made. These shrinkages are very dramatic, but they are effective in illustrating the point.

The bargaining game works as follows. In period 1, player A (the representative of the employer) will make an offer to player B (the representative of the union). Player A requests a certain amount of the pie for himself, say α, which leaves $5 million − α for player B. Player B can then either accept or reject the offer. If she accepts it, the game is over and the payoffs are $\pi_A = \alpha$ for player A and $\pi_B = \$5$ million − α for player B. If the offer is rejected, then in period 2 the pie shrinks to $2.5 million and player B makes an offer to player A. Let us say that player B requests an amount β of the pie for the union. This amount leaves $2.5 million − β for player A. Player A then decides whether to accept or reject the offer. If the offer is accepted, the payoffs are $\pi_A = \$2.5$ million − β for player A and $\pi_B = \beta$ for player B. If the offer is rejected, the game moves to period 3, where the pie falls to $1.25 million and player A makes an offer. If this offer is rejected, each player receives a payoff of zero and the game ends. Figure 26.19 presents a game tree that describes the game defined by the alternating offer sequential bargaining institution.

In Figure 26.19, we see the extensive form of the bargaining game that we have just analyzed. The game starts in period 1. Player A moves first and can choose any value of α as an offer as long as $\alpha \leq \$5$ million. The next player to move is player B, who accepts or rejects the offer. An acceptance ends the game.

alternating offer sequential bargaining institution
A structured method of bargaining where each bargainer takes turns making offers. If an offer is accepted, the bargaining stops. If the offer is not accepted, the bargaining proceeds to the next round but, due to the delay, the value of what is being bargained over, "the pie," shrinks.

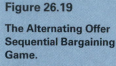

Figure 26.19

The Alternating Offer Sequential Bargaining Game.

In each period, one player proposes a division of the economic pie and the other player either accepts or rejects that division. If the second player rejects the offer, she proposes a division of a smaller pie in the next period.

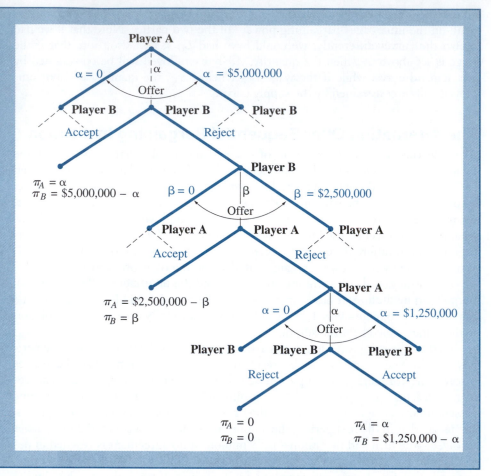

A rejection leads to period 2, in which player B makes an offer. The same process occurs in each period. If no agreement is reached by the time period 3 ends, the payoff to both players is zero.

The equilibrium strategies for this game are given by the **alternating offer sequential bargaining equilibrium theorem**. This theorem is as follows: When the total number of periods in the alternating offer sequential bargaining game is finite, there is a unique subgame perfect equilibrium in which the first offer made is accepted. The equilibrium offer is equal to the sum of the decrements in the pie when the first player makes his offer.

According to this theorem, the subgame perfect equilibrium for the game described in Figure 26.19 occurs in period 1 when the offer made by player A is accepted. The following analysis indicates how the offer is derived: Player A initiates the bargaining in periods 1 and 3, and player B initiates the bargaining in period 2. The size of the economic pie is $5 million in period 1 but drops to $2.5 million in period 2. The decrement from period 1 to period 2 is therefore $2.5 million. When player A again makes an offer in period 3, the pie has shrunk to $1.25 million. The decrement from period 2 to period 3 is therefore $1.25 million. If player A's offer in period 3 is not accepted, the pie will then shrink to zero. Because the theorem tells us that the equilibrium offer is equal to the sum of the decrements in the pie when the first player makes his offer, we know that the subgame perfect equilibrium is reached when player A offers to take $3.75 million

alternating offer sequential bargaining equilibrium theorem

When the total number of periods in the alternating offer sequential bargaining game is finite, there is a unique subgame perfect equilibrium in which the first offer made is accepted. The equilibrium offer is equal to the sum of the decrements in the pie when the first player makes his offer.

($2.5 million + $1.25 million) in period 1 and player B accepts this offer. The payoffs are $3.75 million to player A and $1.25 million to player B.

Backward induction is used to achieve this result, as is true for any subgame perfect equilibrium in a game with perfect information. To understand the reasoning involved, let us go to the last period of the game, period 3, in which player A makes an offer. At this stage, player A knows that player B will end up with a payoff of zero if she rejects his offer. Consequently, player A need offer player B only an infinitely small amount ϵ to obtain her acceptance because $\epsilon > 0$ is better than nothing. Offering zero to player B will actually make her indifferent between accepting and rejecting, so for convenience let us assume that an offer of zero will be accepted. Player A will therefore receive the entire pie of $1.25 million in period 3.

Now let us move back to period 2, in which player B makes an offer. Player B knows that if the game proceeds to period 3, player A can obtain the entire pie of $1.25 million. Consequently, any offer to him of $1.25 million or more should lead to an acceptance. Because the pie is $2.5 million in period 2, player B will offer $1.25 million to player A. When we move back one more stage, which brings us to period 1, we see that player A knows that if the game proceeds to period 2, player B will demand $1.25 million. Thus, player A can expect that any offer to player B in period 1 that gives her at least $1.25 million will be accepted. Player A will therefore offer player B $1.25 million and demand $3.75 million for himself. Note that $3.75 million = ($5 million − $2.5 million) + ($1.25 million − $0), so as the theorem predicts, player A demands the sum of the decrements in the pie.

Question (Content Review: Bargaining)

Suppose the management and the labor union of a firm are bargaining over the share of the firm's product that will go to the two respective parties. The company charter specifies that management and labor must reach an agreement in three rounds of negotiation; otherwise, the dispute will be referred to the court—a long and costly process that both parties would prefer to avoid if possible. The negotiations occur in the following pattern: In the first round, the management proposes. If the labor union refuses the management's proposal, it has to make a counterproposal in the second round. If management refuses labor's proposal, it has to make yet another proposal in the third and final round. If the labor union refuses management's proposal, the case is then referred to the court. Suppose the value of the firm's product is 1 in the first round; that is, we are really interested in the *fraction* of the firm's product that goes to each party rather than its absolute magnitude. We also suppose that both parties discount future earnings by 10%; that is, the firm's product is worth 0.9 in the second period and 0.81 in the third. If an agreement is not reached in the third period, we assume that the value of the firm's product becomes zero. Describe the outcome of the negotiation; that is, at what stage will the negotiation be concluded and with what shares accruing to the two parties?

What will the outcome be if the labor union makes the first proposal?

[*Hint:* Think of the *subgame perfect* equilibrium; that is, think of what happens in the third and last round and then work your way backward to the beginning round.]

Answer

Consider what will happen if the union rejects management's offer in the third round: both parties will end up with zero. Therefore, the union will accept any positive share, however small, offered by management. We will make things simpler by assuming that, in fact, an offer of zero will be accepted by the union

SOLVED PROBLEM 26.4

(because it is indifferent between accepting or rejecting it, in which case it will also end up with zero). Thus, if the negotiation continues on to the third round, management will end up with 0.81 ($= 0.9^2 \times 1$). Then in the second round, the union will offer a share of 0.81 to management (and 0.09 for itself), because management is indifferent between accepting it or rejecting it, in which case it ends up with 0.81 anyway. Then in the first round, the management will offer the union a share of 0.09 ($= 0.9 - 0.81$), because the union is indifferent between accepting it or rejecting it, in which case it ends up with 0.09 anyway. Therefore, the management will propose a share of 0.91 for itself and 0.09 for the union in the first round, and it will be accepted.

Using exactly the same argument as above, if the union makes the first proposal, it will propose a share of 0.91 for itself and 0.09 for management in the first round, and it will be accepted.

An Evaluation of the Alternating Offer Sequential Bargaining Institution: The Neelin, Sonnenschein, Spiegel Experiment

In our analysis of the alternating offer sequential bargaining game, we found that backward induction is the reasoning process used by the players to arrive at the equilibrium offer and acceptance of that offer. When real people are involved in such a situation, will they reason in this way? Much experimental evidence suggests that they will not. We will now review one experiment that illustrates this point. The experiment was conducted by Janet Neelin, Hugo Sonnenschein, and Matthew Spiegel, who paired 80 junior and senior economics students at Princeton University and had the pairs play an alternating offer sequential bargaining game.[2]

After participating in four practice games, the subjects played a series of games for money. The games consisted of two, three, and five periods; during these periods, the economic pie shrank just as we saw in the example that we studied. Table 26.1 describes the design of the games played by the subjects in the experiment.

For each of these games, the subgame perfect Nash equilibrium is a first offer of $3.75 by one player in each pair of subjects and the acceptance of that offer by the other player. Consequently, the subjects were presented with games having identical equilibrium values but different lengths. Because of this structure, the experiment was able to test the length of game over which the subjects could successfully reason by backward induction.

The results of the experiment provided only limited support for bargaining theory. In the two-period game, only 15 of the 40 subjects who moved first made the equilibrium offer of $3.75. However, 33 of the 40 offered amounts ranging from $3.50 to $3.75, so we cannot totally reject bargaining theory on the basis of these results. In the three-period and five-period games, the theory did much worse. In the three-period game, most of the first-period offers were for $2.50, which represents an equal split of the pie. In the five-period game, the first-period offers clustered around $3.25, which is between the equal-split value of $2.50 and the equilibrium value of $3.75.

One interpretation of these results is that the subjects were able to perform backward induction when the horizon of a game was only two periods, but when

---

[2] Janet Neelin, Hugo Sonnenschein, and Matthew Spiegel, "A Further Test of Noncooperative Bargaining Theory: Comment," *American Economic Review* 78, no. 4 (September 1998): 824–36.

Table 26.1	The Design of the Games Played in the Neelin, Sonnenschein, Spiegel Experiment to Evaluate Bargaining Theory.		
	AMOUNT TO BE DIVIDED IN EACH PERIOD		
Period Number	**Two-Period Game**	**Three-Period Game**	**Five-Period Game**
1	$5.00	$5.00	$5.00
2	1.25	2.50	1.70
3		1.25	0.58
4			0.20
5			0.07

the horizon was longer, their minds played a trick that interfered with the backward induction process. The trick was to treat longer games as if they had a horizon of two periods and solve them that way. For example, if the subjects viewed the three-period game as if it were a two-period game, the pie would shrink from $5.00 to $2.50. The equilibrium first-period offer would then be $2.50, which is exactly the offer that the subjects tended to make. Similarly, when the five-period game is viewed as a two-period game, the pie shrinks from $5.00 to $1.70. In this case, the equilibrium first-period offer would be $3.30, which is not significantly different from the $3.25 offer that was the modal choice of the subjects.

In short, the experiment seems to indicate that people are capable of performing backward induction when the horizon of the game is brief, such as two periods. However, people are unable to do so consistently when the horizon is longer. In fact, they seem to transform longer games into two-period games and solve them accordingly. This clearly violates some of the assumptions behind bargaining theory.

Conclusion

In this chapter, we asked a very fundamental question about the way in which the output of society is distributed: Are the factors of production paid their equitable shares of the output of society, or should labor receive more and capital and land receive less? The answer offered was that if the factors of production are paid their marginal revenue products, then the shares they receive can be justified. This happens in competitive markets. In cases of monopsony/monopoly, however, one party can get a larger share. The members of society who believe that this argument makes logical and ethical sense tend to support the resulting distribution of income. However, there are those in society who reject the argument.

Once the subject of equitable distribution of income is put up for debate, a need arises for a mediator who will lead all sides to a compromise. As we saw in Chapter 25, the government often takes on this role. As mediator, it aggregates the preferences of the citizens so that society can make choices about the returns to labor, capital, and land.

Summary

One of our concerns in this chapter was to derive the equilibrium shares of the three factors of production—labor, capital, and land—in the output of society. To do this, we relied on the theory of marginal productivity, which predicts that in perfectly competitive economies, each factor will be paid its marginal revenue product. We also made use of the product exhaustion theorem, which indicates that the total value of what is produced will be paid out exactly and that each factor will be paid its marginal contribution.

However, we noted that many input markets are not perfectly competitive, and we therefore investigated how imperfectly competitive input markets function. We studied the theories of monopsony and bilateral monopoly, and we found that when monopsonistic employers and monopolistic unions bargain over wages, the outcome is indeterminate. To see if we could eliminate this indeterminacy, we examined the alternating offer sequential bargaining institution, which gives precise and determinate predictions. However, a look at some of the experimental evidence relating to bargaining theory raised doubts about its validity under certain conditions.

Exercises and Problems

1. A competitive firm has the production function $Q = 20L - \frac{1}{4}L^2$, where Q is the number of units of output produced and L is the number of units of labor (the only input) used. This production function implies the marginal product of labor function $MP_L = 20 - \frac{1}{2}L$. The output price is $2, the wage rate is $1, and the firm faces a fixed cost of $100.

   a) What is the profit-maximizing quantity of labor demanded by the firm?

   b) What is the firm's profit in the short run?

   c) If, in the long run, the output price changes so that profits are zero, what is the quantity of labor demanded in the long run?

2. A competitive firm has the production function $Q = L^\alpha K^\beta$, where Q is the number of units of output produced, L is the number of units of labor used, and K is the number of units of capital used. This production function implies the marginal product of labor function $MP_L = \alpha L^{\alpha-1} K^\beta$ and the marginal product of capital function $MP_K = \beta L^\alpha K^{\beta-1}$. The output price p, the wage rate w, and the cost of capital r are given. Assume that $\alpha > 0$, $\beta > 0$, and $0 < (\alpha + \beta) < 1$. Remember that a profit-maximizing firm will equate the marginal rate of technical substitution of labor for capital (the ratio of the marginal products of capital and labor) to the ratio of the prices of capital and labor. Similarly, the firm will equate the marginal revenue product of each factor to its cost.

   a) What is the firm's profit-maximizing quantity of labor if the quantity of capital is fixed at K?

   b) What is the firm's profit-maximizing level of capital if both capital and labor are variable? (*Hint:* Use the profit-maximizing capital-labor ratio K/L to substitute for the level of labor.)

3. Consider a competitive firm with the total product schedule given in Table 26.2.

Table 26.2	Total Product Schedule.	
Units of Labor Used		**Units of Output Produced**
1		3
2		5
3		6
4		6.5
5		6.75
6		6.75

a) If the output price is $12 and the wage rate is $3, how many units of labor will the firm use in order to maximize profits?

b) If you know that the output price is $11 and that the firm maximizes profits by using 2 units of labor, what can you say about the wage rate?

c) If you know that the wage rate is $15 and that the firm maximizes profits by using 4 units of labor, what can you say about the output price?

4. Consider a monopoly with the total product and inverse demand schedules given in Table 26.3.

Table 26.3	Total Product and Inverse Demand Schedules.	
Units of Labor Used	**Units of Output Produced**	**Price**
1	4	$10.00
2	7	8.00
3	9	8.00
4	10	6.50
5	10	6.50

a) If the wage rate is $16, what is the profit-maximizing quantity of labor?

b) If you know that the profit-maximizing quantity of labor is 2 units, what can you say about the wage rate?

5. Consider a firm that sells its output in a competitive product market, is a monopsonist in the labor market, and faces the labor supply and total product schedules given in Table 26.4.

Table 26.4	Labor Supply and Total Product Schedules.	
Price	**Units of Labor Used**	**Units of Output Produced**
$4.00	1	4
5.00	2	7
6.00	3	9
7.00	4	10
8.00	5	10.5
9.00	6	10.5

a) If the output price is $7, what wage rate maximizes the firm's profits?

b) If you know that the firm maximizes profits with a wage rate of $5, what can you say about the output price?

6. Consider a firm that is a monopolist in its product market and a monopsonist in the labor market. It faces the labor supply, total product, and inverse demand schedules given in Table 26.5. What wage rate maximizes the firm's profits?

Table 26.5	Labor Supply, Total Product, and Inverse Demand Schedules.		
Wage Rate	**Units of Labor Used**	**Units of Output Produced**	**Price**
$2.00	1	3	$13.00
$3.00	2	5	12.00
$4.00	3	6	11.00
$5.00	4	6.5	10.00

7. Each day an individual must decide how to allocate his 24 hours between labor and leisure. He can choose to supply L hours of labor in order to earn money to buy consumption goods C. The remaining hours, Z, constitute his leisure time. Hence $0 \leq L \leq 24$ and $Z = 24 - L$. The individual takes as given the wage rate w (dollars an hour) and the price of consumption goods, which we will assume is equal to 1. He spends his entire income on consumption goods, so that $C = wL$. He chooses L so as to maximize the value of his utility function $u(C, Z)$, where $u(C, Z) = C^{1/3} \, Z^{2/3}$. This utility function implies a marginal utility of consumption function $MU_C = \frac{1}{3}(C^{-(2/3)}Z^{2/3}) = \frac{1}{3}(Z/C)^{2/3}$ and a marginal utility of leisure function $MU_z = \frac{1}{3}(C^{1/3}Z^{-(1/3)}) = \frac{1}{3}(Z/C)^{-(1/3)}$. Remember that in order to maximize his utility, an individual who consumes two goods will equate his marginal rate of substitution (the ratio of his marginal utility from each of the two goods) to the ratio of their prices. Note that the wage rate can be interpreted as the price of leisure. Derive the labor supply function (L as a function of w). Show that the individual has a vertical labor supply curve and provides 8 hours of labor a day regardless of the wage rate.

8. Suppose that in problem 7 the utility function is $u(C, Z) = 2C + 60Z - Z^2$. This utility function implies a marginal utility of consumption function $MU_c = 2$ and a marginal utility of leisure function $MU_z = 60 - 2Z$. Assuming that w is between \$6 and \$30, derive the labor supply function and show that the labor supply curve is upward sloping.

9. Suppose that in problem 7 the utility function is $u(C, Z) = 1{,}000C + 10{,}000Z - C^2$. This utility function implies a marginal utility of consumption function $MU_c = 1{,}000 - 2C$ and a marginal utility of leisure function $MU_z = 10{,}000$.

   a) Derive the labor supply function.

   b) Show that the individual supplies no labor if the wage rate is \$10, 12.5 hours of labor if the wage rate is \$20, and fewer than 12.5 hours of labor if the wage rate is above \$20.

   c) How can such a "backward-bending" labor supply curve be explained in terms of income and substitution effects?

Answers to Selected Exercises and Problems

Chapter 3

1 (a) Because John must consume gin and vermouth in a certain combination, they are perfectly complementary goods. Therefore, the indifference curves are L-shaped, as shown in Figure 1.

Figure 1

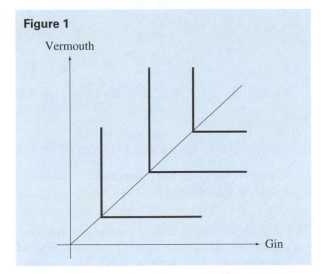

Vermouth

Gin

(b) Steve's indifference curve appears in Figure 2.

Figure 2

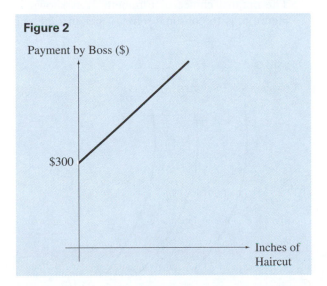

Payment by Boss ($)

$300

Inches of Haircut

(c) From Figure 2, we can see that the indifference curve coincides with the vertical axis until we reach $300, and then the indifference curve is a straight line with slope 8. Therefore, the marginal rate of substitution is equal to infinity between $0 and $300 and is equal to 8 beyond $300.

(d) Because Ann likes both beer and pretzels but becomes sick after she drinks 12 beers, the indifference curve must slope upward beyond 12 beers. In other words, Ann must consume *more* pretzels for each additional beer she drinks after the first 12 beers. Thus, Figure 3 shows that *every* indifference curve is upward sloping after 12 beers.

Figure 3

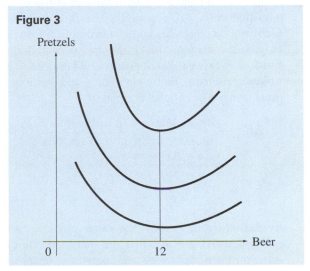

Pretzels

0   12   Beer

3 (a) When the utility function is of the form $U = ra$, the expression for the indifference curve at the level of 2,500 "utils" is $ra = 2,500$. In other words, the area of the rectangle formed by the coordinates of any point on the indifference curve is equal to 2,500, as shown in Figure 4. A curve that has this property is called a *rectangular hyperbola*. It is bowed toward the origin with the two ends getting closer and closer to the respective axes but never actually touching them.[1]

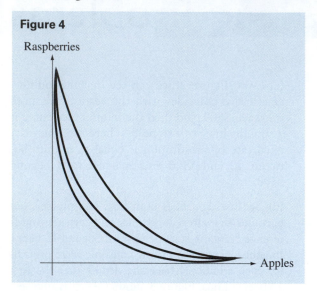

Figure 4

Raspberries

Apples

(b) The marginal utility of consuming an apple is $MU_A = r$, and the marginal utility of consuming a raspberry is $MU_R = a$. To see this, suppose Geoffrey increases his apple consumption from a to $a + \Delta a$, keeping his raspberry consumption fixed at r, where Δa is positive. Therefore, his utility rises from ra to $r(a + \Delta a)$, and his marginal utility from apples is equal to

$$MU_A = \frac{\text{Increase in utility}}{\text{Increase in apple consumption}}$$
$$= \frac{r(a + \Delta a) - ra}{(a + \Delta a) - a}$$
$$= \frac{r\Delta a}{\Delta a} = r$$

By reasoning in exactly the same way, we can prove that $MU_R = a$. Then the marginal rate of substitution of apples for raspberries is equal to $MRS_{RA} = MU_A/MU_R = r/a$. Using this formula, we find that the marginal rate of substitution is equal to 1 when 50 apples and 50 raspberries are consumed and is equal to 2 when 50 apples and 100 raspberries are consumed.

(c) We know that Geoffrey's marginal rate of substitution of apples for raspberries must equal the price ratio at his optimum, provided that the

[1] In mathematical terminology, the two ends are asymptotic to the axes.

optimal bundle represents an interior solution. Together with the budget constraint, this implies that at the optimum, we must have

$$\frac{r}{a} = 1 \qquad \text{(3.1)}$$
$$r + a = 100 \qquad \text{(3.2)}$$

By substituting (3.1) in (3.2), we obtain $a = r = 50$. Because this represents a feasible bundle, the optimum is an interior solution; that is, the marginal rate of substitution equals the price ratio.

(d) If the price ratio of apples to raspberries is ¾, the optimal conditions are

$$\frac{r}{a} = \frac{3}{4} \qquad \text{(3.3)}$$
$$4r + 3a = 100 \qquad \text{(3.4)}$$

By substituting (3.3) in (3.4), we obtain the following:

$$4r + 4r = 100 \Rightarrow r = 12.50$$
$$3a + 3a = 100 \Rightarrow a = 16.67$$

Therefore, Geoffrey will consume 12.5 raspberries and 16.67 apples at the optimum.

4 (a) In Figures 5, 6, and 7, the vertical axis measures "consumption tomorrow" and the horizontal axis measures "consumption today." The optimal choice of Elizabeth 1, as shown in Figure 5, is to consume all her income and save nothing. The optimal choice of Elizabeth 2, as shown in Figure 6, is to consume some of her income and

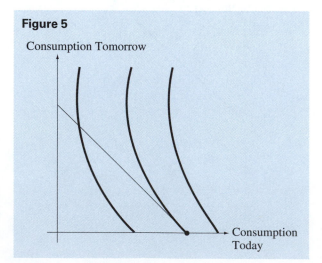

Figure 5

Consumption Tomorrow

Consumption Today

Figure 6

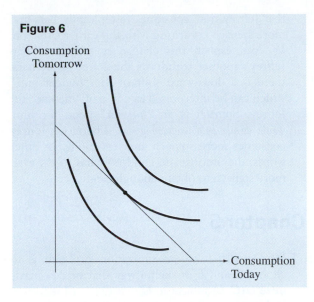

Consumption
Tomorrow

Consumption
Today

Figure 7

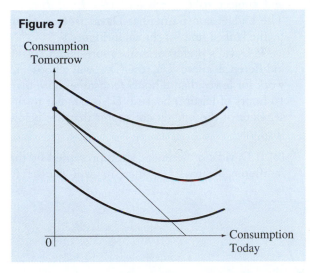

Consumption
Tomorrow

Consumption
Today

save the rest. The optimal choice of Elizabeth 3, as shown in Figure 7, is to save all her income and consume nothing.

The peculiarity of Figures 5 and 7 lies in the fact that the consumer's indifference curves may touch one of the axes. This means that *the consumer's utility from zero consumption or zero savings is not zero.* In technical terms, the consumer is said to have *separable preferences,* so that her marginal utility from one good is independent of her consumption of the other good.

In Figure 5, the consumer's indifference curves touch the horizontal axis. Given a particular budget line, the highest indifference curve reached by the consumer actually meets the budget line *on* the

horizontal axis. As we can see from this figure, the indifference curve is not tangent to the budget line at the optimum; that is, the marginal rate of substitution is not equal to the price ratio.

Similarly, in Figure 7, given a certain budget line, the highest indifference curve meets this line on the vertical axis because all the indifference curves touch the vertical axis.

The indifference curves in Figure 6 are "normal"; that is, they do not intersect either of the axes. In other words, the consumer's preferences are "nonseparable." Consequently, the optimum bundle contains a positive amount of each commodity.

(b) The slope of the budget line (i.e., the price ratio of consumption today to consumption tomorrow) is equal to $1 + r$, where r is the interest rate. This is because \$1 saved today will be worth $\$(1 + r)$ tomorrow. Therefore, \$1 in consumption today can be transferred to $\$(1 + r)$ worth of consumption tomorrow through saving.

Chapter 4

2 (a) Suppose that Elizabeth's monetary income is M. Then, according to her simple rule of thumb, her demand for good x is $M/2p_x$, and her demand for good y is $M/2p_y$, where p_x and p_y are the prices of x and y, respectively. Because her utility function is of the form $U = xy$, her marginal utility of x is equal to y, and her marginal utility of y is equal to x.

Therefore, her marginal rate of substitution of y for x is given by $MRS_{yx} = y/x$. We know that a condition for utility maximization is that the marginal rate of substitution be equal to the price ratio. To verify that this condition exists, we must substitute the demand functions in the expression for the marginal rate of substitution:

$$MRS_{yx} = \frac{y}{x}\left(\frac{M}{2p_y}\right) \div \left(\frac{M}{2p_x}\right) = \frac{M2p_x}{M2p_y} = \frac{p_x}{p_y}$$

This proves that Elizabeth's simple rule of thumb is indeed utility maximizing.

(b) When Elizabeth's income is \$1,000, she spends exactly \$500 on good x. Therefore, her demand for x is given by $500/p_x$.

5 (a) Jeffrey likes candy and hates spinach, which means that he derives positive marginal utility from candy and *negative* marginal utility from spinach. In other words, spinach is a "bad." However, because consumer preferences are represented by ordinal utility rather than cardinal utility, it is not enough to say that Jeffrey obtains negative utility from the consumption of spinach. Therefore, Jeffrey's indifference curves between candy and spinach must be positively sloped, as shown in Figure 8. Why? The slope of each indifference curve at any point can be interpreted as the extra amount of candy we would have to give Jeffrey to keep him on the same indifference curve if he has to consume 1 more ounce of spinach. Note that we cannot call this quantity the "marginal rate of substitution" because Jeffrey is not substituting candy for spinach! Because Jeffrey receives 2 "free" candy bars and then 1 candy bar for every extra ounce of spinach he eats, his spinach-candy consumption must lie on a positively sloped straight line with a vertical intercept of 2 and a slope of $\frac{1}{2}$. We may interpret this line as his "budget constraint." From Figure 8, we can also see that the indifference curves must have increasing slopes because Jeffrey's optimal choice consists of positive amounts of both goods. (Verify this.)

(b) If Jeffrey's mother does not give him 2 "free" candy bars, his consumption forms an upward-sloping straight line that passes through the origin and has a slope of $\frac{1}{2}$. We can see from Figure 8

that Jeffrey now consumes fewer candy bars and more spinach compared with the earlier situation. We can explain this change as follows: When Jeffrey's mother withdraws the 2 free candy bars, there is a downward shift of the "budget line," which can be interpreted as a loss of "income" for Jeffrey. Spinach is an "inferior" good for him, while candy is a normal good. Therefore, Jeffrey consumes more spinach and less candy. In other words, the unfortunate child now has to eat even more spinach to obtain enough candy.

Chapter 5

1 (a) David's utility maximization problem is to choose C and L in such a way that he can maximize $U(C, L)$ subject to $C \le w (24 - L)$ if $L \ge 16$ and subject to $C \ge w8 + w'(16 - L)$ if $L < 16$. The budget constraint that David faces is given by the kinked line *bcd* shown in Figure 9.

If David's preferences are represented by the indifference curve U^1, then he will choose to work for fewer than 8 hours (consume more than 16 hours of leisure) because U^1 is tangent to the segment of the budget constraint that lies below the kink.

(b) If David's preferences are represented by the indifference curve U^2, then he will choose to

Figure 8

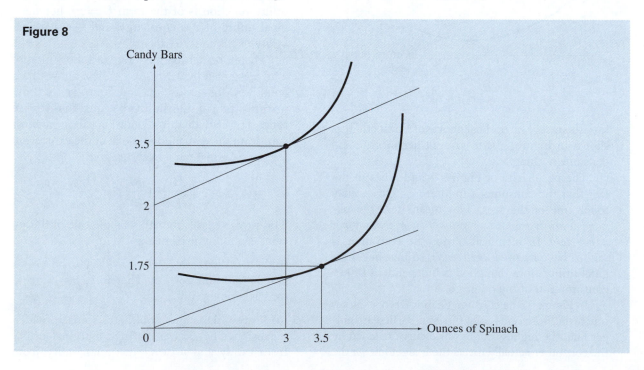

Figure 9

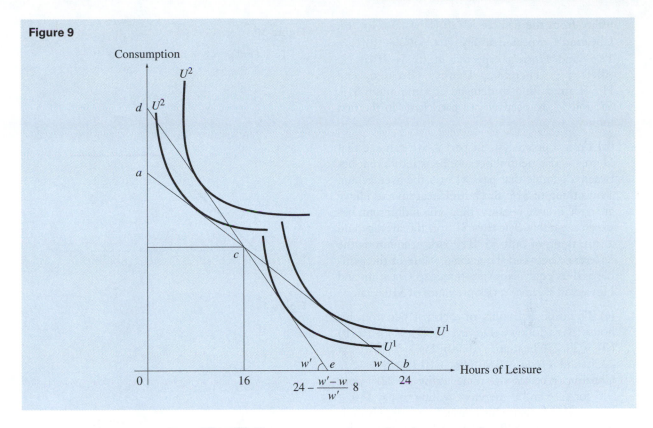

Consumption

work for more than 8 hours (consume fewer than 16 hours of leisure) because U^2 is tangent to the segment of the budget constraint that lies above the kink.

Chapter 6

3 (a) An honest person receives a guaranteed income of $10,000, and a criminal faces a gamble with an expected return of $(0.25)(\$13,000) + (0.75)(\$1,000) = \$4,000$. Therefore, a person who commits a crime must be risk preferring. He prefers a gamble that pays only $4,000 on the average over a sure thing of $10,000. A criminal's utility function must be convex; that is, it must be increasing at an increasing rate.

(b) We cannot say, unambiguously, whether an honest person is risk averse, risk neutral, or risk preferring. All we can say with certitude is that *if an honest person is risk preferring, he must be less risk preferring than a criminal*. In other words, his utility function is less sharply convex than a criminal's.

(c) Because criminals are risk preferring, they will certainly not accept an insurance scheme. In fact,

they will have to be *paid* to accept such a scheme. What we are really saying is that they will have to be paid to make them keep to the straight and narrow!

4 In the simple experiment, choice A has an expected return of -510, while choice B has an expected return of -500. Note that when people choose B over A, we do not learn anything about their attitudes toward risk. All we know is that such people are rational in the sense that they choose the lottery with the higher expected payoff (or lower loss). In the second experiment, choices A and D together have an expected return of $(0.75)(240 - 1,000) + (0.25)(240 - 0) = -510$. Choices B and C have an expected return of $(0.75)(0 - 750) + (0.25)(1,000 - 750) = -500$. If a majority of the people choose A and D over B and C, their choices are a violation of rationality.

Chapter 7

1 (a) The amount that each lawyer demands at a minimum is equal to the sum that gives the same (expected) utility as the gamble. Dewey's expected utility from the gamble is $(30)(\frac{1}{2}) + (0)(\frac{1}{2}) = 15$, Cheatum's expected utility is $(25)(\frac{1}{2}) + (0)(\frac{1}{2}) = 12.5$, and Howe's expected utility is $(14)(\frac{1}{2}) + (0)(\frac{1}{2}) = 7$. Therefore, Dewey, Cheatum, and Howe are willing to demand at a minimum \$15, \$5, and \$5, respectively, to participate in the first lottery.

(b) From our analysis in part a, we can see that Dewey is risk neutral because he is indifferent between a gamble that pays \$15 on the average and a sure thing of \$15. But both Cheatum and Howe are risk averse because they are indifferent between a gamble that pays \$15 on the average and a sure thing of only \$5. The risk premium is the difference between the average value of the gamble and its equivalent sure thing, so Cheatum and Howe will sacrifice a risk premium of \$10 each.

(c) The expected utility of each partner from his house is as follows: Dewey, $(0.90)(30) + (0.10)(0) = 27$; Cheatum, $(0.90)(25) + (0.10)(0) = 22.5$; and Howe, $(0.90)(14) + (0.10)(0) = 12.6$. Cheatum receives the same utility of 22.5 from \$15 for sure and is therefore willing to pay $\$30 - \$15 = \$15$ to insure his house. Similarly, Howe is willing to pay $\$30 - \$10 = \$20$ to insure his house. Finally, because Dewey is risk neutral, as noted in part b, he is indifferent between this gamble (of not insuring) and a sure thing of \$27. Therefore, he is willing to pay $\$30 - \$27 = \$3$ to insure his house.

Chapter 8

3 The total product curve for fasteners is shown in Figure 10, and the associated average and marginal product curves for fasteners appear in Figure 11.

(a) The total product curve is a 45-degree straight line until the point where $Z_1 = 10$. It becomes a horizontal straight line thereafter.

(b) The average product curve is constant at 1 until $Z_1 = 10$ and becomes a rectangular hyperbola thereafter. The marginal product curve is constant at 1 until $Z_1 = 10$ and is equal to zero thereafter.

5 (a) The marginal product of labor of good X is $MP_L^X = L_X^{-1/2}/2$, and the marginal product of labor of good Y is $MP_L^Y = L_Y^{-1/2}/2$. Therefore, you will maximize your profits at the point

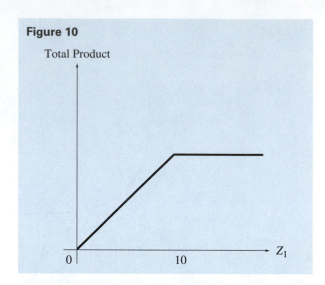

Figure 10

Total Product

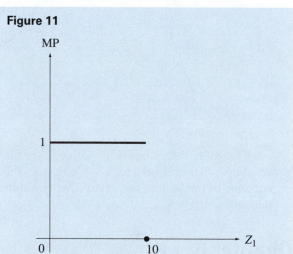

Figure 11

MP

where the value of the marginal product of each good is equal, that is, where $P_X MP_L^X = P_Y MP_L^Y$. Otherwise, you will always have an incentive to use more labor in producing the good that has a higher value of marginal product so that you can increase your profits. The above profit-maximizing condition implies

$$10\left(\frac{L_X^{-1/2}}{2}\right) = 5\left(\frac{L_Y^{-1/2}}{2}\right) \Rightarrow 2L_X^{-1/2}$$
$$= L_Y^{-1/2} \Rightarrow 2L_Y^{1/2}$$
$$= L_X^{1/2} \Rightarrow 4L_Y = L_X$$

But then, you must also have $L_X + L_Y = 100$.

Combining this condition with the previous condition results in $L_X = 80$ and $L_Y = 20$. Therefore, $X = 80^{1/2} = 8.94$ and $Y = 20^{1/2} = 4.47$.

(b) Now you must produce goods X and Y so as to maximize your profits and *then* use your profits to buy a consumption bundle that will maximize your utility. We know from part a that you must produce 8.94 units of good X and 4.47 units of good Y to maximize your profits, which will be $(10)(8.94) + (5)(4.47) = 111.80$. Then your problem is to choose quantities of goods X and Y to consume that will maximize your utility so that $U = 10L^{1/2}{}_X L^{1/2}{}_Y$ subject to the budget constraint of $10X + 5Y = 111.80$. Now, the marginal utility of good X is $MU_X = 5^{-1/2}{}_X Y^{1/2}$, and the marginal utility of good Y is $MU_Y = 5X^{1/2}Y^{-1/2}$. Therefore, the expression for the marginal rate of substitution of good Y for good X is

$$MRS_{XY} = \frac{MU_X}{MU_Y} = \frac{5X^{-1/2}Y^{1/2}}{5X^{1/2}Y^{-1/2}} = \frac{Y}{X}$$

The utility maximization condition is $MRS_{YX} = P_X/P_Y$, or

$$\frac{Y}{X} = \frac{10}{5} \Rightarrow Y = 2X$$

By substituting in the budget constraint, you obtain $(111)(80) = 10X + 5Y = 10 + (5)(2X) = 20X$, or $X = 5.59$ and $Y = 11.18$. So, you must be a net supplier of good X and a net demander of good Y in order to maximize your utility. Because good X costs twice as much per unit as good Y, you must devote more of your efforts to producing good X to maximize your profits, but you must consume more of good Y to maximize your utility.

The curve ab in Figure 12 is the production possibilities frontier, and U is the indifference curve. The isorevenue curve is presented by the straight line cd with slope = price ratio $P_X/P_Y = 2$. You must choose the point on the production possibilities frontier that lies on the highest isorevenue line. This is point g, which is tangent to cd. Therefore, cd also represents the budget line. The utility-maximizing bundle lies on the highest indifference curve, at the point of tangency e between U and the budget line cd. The excess demand for good Y is equal to ef, and the excess supply of good X is equal to fg.

8 (a) The output per worker at a given level of the firm's output is represented by the slope of the straight line connecting the origin to the

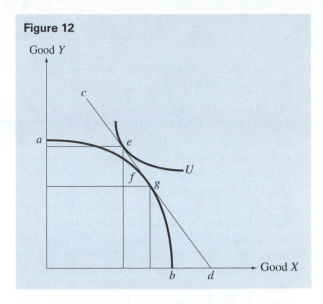

Figure 12

corresponding point on the production function. The highest level of output per worker is achieved at the point where the line connecting the production function and the origin is *tangent* to the production function itself, as shown in Figure 13.

(b) We can also see from Figure 13 that the firm's total output is at its maximum when 100 workers are employed. Hiring more workers at that point only reduces output. For example, the 101st worker the firm employs reduces its output by 62 units. If we take the price of output to be $1 per unit of the good produced (assuming that everything else is measured in terms of that good), the firm's loss in revenue is $62. Therefore, the firm would be willing to pay the 101st worker $62 to leave the job.

Chapter 9

1 (a) When $X = Y = 9$, $MRTS_{YX} = MP_X/MP_Y = (Q/2X)/(Q/2Y) = Y/X = 1$ and the input price ratio is $P_X/P_Y = 8/16 = \frac{1}{2}$. Therefore, the input combination of 9 units of X and 9 units of Y is not cost minimizing.

(b) The input price ratio must be 1 for the input combination of 9 units of X and 9 units of Y to be efficient.

(c) When $P_X/P_Y = \frac{1}{2}$, the cost-minimizing conditions are

$$Y/X = 1/2 \tag{9.1}$$
$$10X^{1/2}Y^{1/2} = 400 \tag{9.2}$$

By substituting (9.1) in (9.2), we find that $X = 56.56$ and $Y = 28.28$.

3 (a) We assume that the "production" of lawn-mowing services exhibits constant returns to scale and fixed proportions. The small lawn mower produces 1 unit of output in 1 hour using $\frac{1}{3}$ of a gallon of gasoline; the large lawn mower produces 3 units of output in 1 hour using 1 gallon of gasoline. Therefore, the small lawn mower produces 1 unit by combining labor hours, gasoline, and lawn mower hours in the ratio of 1:1/3:1. Similarly, the large lawn mower produces 3 units by combining labor hours, gasoline, and lawn mower hours in the ratio of 1:1:1. This analysis confirms that the production functions are of the following form:

$$y = \min\{z_1, 3z_2, z_3\}$$
$$y = 3 \cdot \min\{z_1, z_2, z_4\}$$

In these expressions, z_1 is hours of labor, z_2 is gallons of gasoline, and z_3 and z_4 are the number of hours the small and large lawn mowers are used.

(b) The minimum cost of producing 1 unit of output with the small lawn mower is as follows:

$$\$w_1 + \$w_2/3 + \$w_3$$

This minimum cost is achieved when the three inputs are used in the exact proportion prescribed. Therefore, the total cost function for the small lawn mower is

$$C_s(y) = (w_1 + w_2/3 + w_3)y$$

Similarly, the total cost function for the large lawn mower is

$$C_L(y) = (w_1/3 + w_2/3 + w_4/3)y$$

Remember that a total cost function is defined in terms of the minimum cost of producing a given level of output.

(c) The small lawn mower will be cheaper than the large one if $C_s(y) < C_L(y)$, which means that

$$(w_1 + w_2/3 + w_3)y < (w_1/3 + w_2/3 + w_4/3y)$$
$$\Rightarrow w_1 + w_2/3 + w_3 < (w_1/3 + w_2/3 + w_4/3)$$
$$\Rightarrow 2w_1/3 + w_3 < w_4/3$$
$$\Rightarrow 2w_1 < w_4 - 3w_3$$

Figure 13

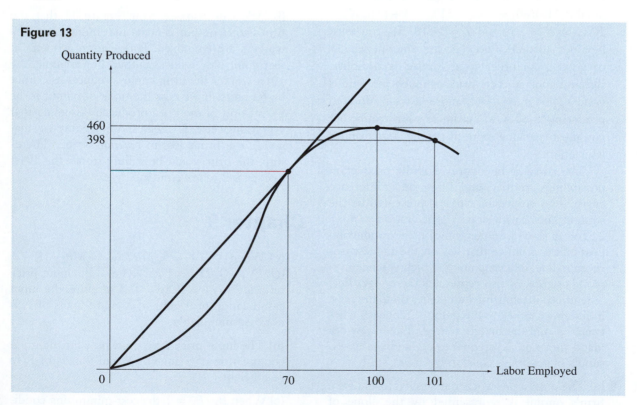

This result is *independent* of the price of gasoline because the cost of gasoline per unit of output is the same for both mowers.

(d) If the college student charges $\$p$ for mowing 10,000 square feet of lawn, her net profit for every hour of work will be as follows if she uses the small lawn mower:

$$p - w_1 - w_2/3 - w_3$$

If she uses the large lawn mower, her net profit will be

$$p - w_1/3 - w_2/3 - w_4/3$$

The college student will set up her own lawn-mowing business only if her profits exceed w_1, her opportunity cost, which is the amount that she can earn by working in the family business. To put it another way, $w_1 \leq p - w_1 - w_2/3 - w_3$, or $w_1 \leq p - w_1/3 - w_2/3 - w_4/3$; that is, $w_1 \leq \max\{p - w_1 - w_2/3 - w_3, \ p - w_1/3 - w_2/3 - w_4/3\}$.

Now, the first inequality implies that $p \geq 2w_1 + w_2/3 + w_3$, and the second inequality implies that $p > \frac{4}{3}w_1 + \frac{w_2}{3} + \frac{w_4}{3}$. Therefore, the two together imply that $p > \max\{2w_1 + w_2/3 + w_3, \ \frac{4}{3}w_1 + \frac{w_2}{3} + \frac{w_4}{3}\}$.

Chapter 10

1 (a) Assuming that the speed of each truck is s miles per hour, it takes $1/s$ hour to move 1 mile. So the labor cost per mile is $\$\%\frac{w}{s}$ and the fuel cost per mile is $\$p(A + Bs)$. With an unlimited number of trucks available, the firm's output is unlimited and its total variable cost function is of the form

$$\left[\frac{w}{s} + p(A + Bs)\right]m$$

The m in this expression is the number of miles moved.

(b) If there is only one truck and it can be driven for a maximum of 10 hours per day at s miles per hour, then the firm's total variable cost is

$$\min\left\{\left[\frac{w}{s} + p(A + Bs)\right]m, \ \left[\frac{w}{s} + p(A + Bs)\right]10s\right\}$$

Chapter 11

2 (a) The game tree for the extensive form of the game is shown in Figure 14.

Figure 14

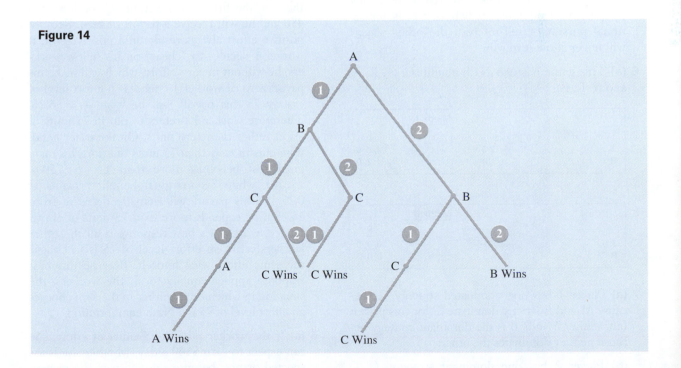

(b) As usual, we must use backward induction to find the subgame perfect equilibria of the game. Because C moves after A and B and everyone has to pick up one or two stones, the game will either end before C can play or he will be faced with one or two stones remaining. If C has the chance to move, he will take the remaining stone or stones. If A takes one stone, B cannot win under any circumstances, whether she takes one or two stones. In either case, C will simply pick up whatever is left after B's move. On the other hand, if A takes two stones, B can assure herself a victory by picking up the two remaining stones. Thus, there are three subgame perfect equilibria in this game.

i. A takes one stone, B takes one stone, and C takes the remaining two stones and wins the game.

ii. A takes one stone, B takes two stones, and C takes the remaining stone and wins the game.

iii. A takes two stones, and B takes the remaining two stones and wins the game.

(c) The only situation in which A can win is when A, B, and C each take one stone, and A therefore has a second move in which he takes the last stone. But C will never take only one stone when there are two left and thus deprive himself of a win. Because equilibrium behavior calls for rational pursuit of self-interest, the other players will never allow A to win.

6 (a) This game has two Nash equilibria: (1, R, A) and (r, L, B).

	Matrix A	
	L	R
l	6, 3, 2	4, 8, 6
R	2, 3, 9	4, 2, 0

	Matrix B	
	L	R
l	8, 1, 1	0, 0, 5
R	9, 4, 9	0, 0, 0

7 (a) Player 1 has one dominated strategy, T, because M and B strictly dominate T for this player, but neither M nor B is the dominant strategy because neither dominates the other.

(b) Player 2 has one dominant strategy, C. C strictly dominates both L and R for this player.

(c) The Nash equilibrium of this game arrived at by the successive elimination of eliminated strategies is (M, C). For player 2, C dominates both L and R. Therefore, rationality dictates that player 2 never play either of the dominated strategies. Similarly, we cannot expect player 1 to play T under any circumstances.

Chapter 13

1 The Pareto-optimal level of output is achieved when one worker's payoff cannot be increased without decreasing some other worker's payoff. This level can be found by maximizing the sum of the payoffs to the six workers. The sum of the payoffs is equal to $PY - \sum_{i=1}^{6} C(e_i)$. The payoffs to the workers must come from the firm's revenue. Thus, the maximum occurs when marginal revenue is equal to marginal cost; that is, $1.5 = e_i/50$. Solving for e_i, we find that $e_i = 75$. This is the Pareto-optimal level of effort. The corresponding output level is 450.

3 To verify that the choice of an effort level of 75 by all the workers is a Nash equilibrium, suppose that everyone except worker 1 makes this choice. Then if worker 1 selects a lower level of effort than 75, the firm's total output will be less than 450 and he will receive a payoff of zero. Because positive effort always results in a positive cost, if worker 1 decides to "cheat" on his fellow workers, he will put in zero effort, which will make his payoff zero. If worker 1 chooses an effort level of exactly 75, his payoff will be $\frac{675}{6} - \frac{75^2}{100} = 56.25$. Therefore worker 1 prefers to put in 75 units of effort rather than zero units. On the other hand, if he puts in *more* than 75 units of effort, his marginal cost becomes more than 1.5 ($= e_i/50 = 75/50$), while his marginal benefit remains at 0.25. So his payoff will actually decrease from 56.25 if he expends more than 75 units of effort. Hence, worker 1's best response if all the other workers select an effort level of 75 is to choose the same effort level himself. Because this best response applies equally to all the workers, the situation in which each worker in the firm chooses an effort level of 75 is a Nash equilibrium.

6 (a) If the worker puts in 15 units of effort, she can expect to earn $140 a day, whether she is inspected or not, because she will pass the inspection anyway. If she is not inspected, her employer will simply assume that she put in the required amount of effort and will pay her \$140. Therefore, if this worker expends 15 units of effort, her expected net payoff is \$110 (\$140 − \$2 × 15). On the other hand, if she shirks, her expected net payoff is $p0 + (1 − p)(140 − 0) = 140(1 − p)$. Therefore, she will not shirk if and only if

$$60p + 140(1 − p) \leq 110 \Rightarrow p \geq 30/80 = 0.38$$

In other words, she will put in the required amount of effort if the probability of inspection is greater than 0.21.

(b) If the probability of inspection is greater than 0.21, the worker will want to exert 15 units of effort at the shirt factory, which will give her \$110. She will prefer to work at the shirt factory because the bank will pay her only \$70. If, however, the probability of inspection is less than 0.21, she will shirk at the shirt factory and will obtain a payoff that is even greater than \$110. Therefore, she will not work at the bank under any circumstance.

Chapter 14

2 (a) In the short run, the firm will keep operating if the price (average revenue) is greater than or equal to the average variable cost. The average variable cost is given by

$$AVC = \frac{TC − 1,000}{q} = \frac{q^3/3 − 2q^2 + 6q}{q}$$
$$= q^2/3 − 2q + 6.$$

On the other hand, price is equal to marginal cost at the short-run equilibrium. The minimum price at which the firm will supply a positive amount is given by the point at which average variable cost is at its minimum, i.e., marginal cost is equal to average variable cost:

$$q^2 − 4q + 6 = q^2/3 − 2q + 6$$
$$\Rightarrow 2q^2/3 − 2q = 0$$
$$\Rightarrow q(q − 3) = 0$$
$$\Rightarrow q = 0, \text{ or } q = 3.$$

AVC is equal to 6 when $q = 0$ and equal to 3 when $q = 3$. Therefore, average variable cost is minimized at $q = 3$. The price corresponding to $q = 3$ is 3, since price is equal to the average variable cost. Therefore, the minimum price at which the firm supplies a positive amount is 3, and the amount supplied is 3 units.

(b) At the short-run equilibrium, price is equal to marginal cost, i.e., the supply schedule is given by the marginal cost curve. Therefore, the output supplied when the price is 3 is given by

$$q^2 − 4q + 6 = 3$$
$$\Rightarrow q^2 − 4q + 3 = 0$$
$$\Rightarrow q = 3.$$

(c) When the price is 10, the supply is approximately equal to 4.83 units.

Chapter 15

1 (a) and **(b)** At the short-run equilibrium, the price is equal to the marginal cost, whereas at the long-run equilibrium, the price is equal to the average cost *and* the marginal cost; that is, production is at the point of minimum average cost. When we set the average cost so that it is equal to the marginal cost, we obtain

$$q/2 − 4 + 200/q = q − 4$$
$$\Rightarrow q/2 − 200/q = 0$$
$$\Rightarrow q^2 − 400 = 0$$
$$\Rightarrow q = 20$$

Therefore, the long-run equilibrium output will be 20 bushels of wheat per farm. The long-run equilibrium price will be equal to the average cost and the marginal cost: $P = q − 4 = 20 − 4 = 16$. This price is lower than the present administered price of $P = 20$.

(c) Because each farm will produce 20 bushels of wheat at the long-run equilibrium and it takes 1 acre to produce 4 bushels, the optimum size for a wheat farm after the industry becomes competitive will be only 5 acres, compared to 10 acres before privatization.

2 (a) At the perfectly competitive equilibrium, price is equal to marginal cost. Therefore, the competitive price of a taxi ride is \$5.

(b) Substituting the price in the demand function, we find that the equilibrium number of taxi rides every day is equal to $1,100 − 20 × 5 = 1,000$.

(c) Given that each taxi is capable of making 20 trips a day, the number of taxis needed in New City is $1,000 ÷ 20 = 50$.

(d) The number of taxi licenses in New City is 50, the same as the number of taxis we calculated in part c, which means that the "supply" of taxi rides every day is 1,000. Equating demand to supply, we find that $1,200 - 20p = 1,000$, or $p = 10$. Thus, each taxi ride costs $10 in New City.

(e) Given that the cost of each taxi ride is $5 and the fare is $10, the profit each taxi earns on a ride is $5.

(f) Because each taxi can make 20 trips a day, its daily profit is $100.

4 (a) We know that at the long-run equilibrium, a competitive firm's *economic* profit is driven down to zero. But in this case, the definition of economic profit must include an entrepreneur's opportunity cost of not being an economics professor, which is $20,000. Therefore, the long-run profit of each firm will be driven down to $20,000.

We can express the two firms' total cost functions as $C_2 = 2Q_1$ and $C_2 = 2Q_2$. When we set the profit so that it is equal to $20,000 for firm 1, we find that

$$20,000 = P_1Q_1 - 2Q_1$$
$$= 2,002Q_1 - 4Q_1^2 - 2Q_1$$
$$= 2,000Q_1 - 4Q_1^2$$

Solving for p_1, we find p_1 equal to either 42.83 or 1,961.63, but at price 42.83 firm 1 produces $Q_1 = 489.8$ at a lower average cost. Solving for firm 2 in a similar manner, we find that firm 2 will produce $Q_1 = 795.4$ at a price of 27.

(b) No. See the answer to part a.

Chapter 17

4 (a) The inverse demand curve is $P = 50 - Q$, and the marginal revenue is $MR = 50 - 2Q$. Equating marginal revenue to marginal cost gives us $50 - 2Q = 10$. Solving this equation for Q, we find that the monopolist's output is $Q = 20$ and its price is $P = 50 - 20 = 30$. The monopolist's profit at that quantity and price is $30 \times 20 - 10 \times 20 = 400$.

(b) In this case, the monopolist's profit-maximizing condition is $50 - 2Q = Q - 10$. Hence, the output level is $Q = 20$ and the price charged is $p = 30$. The monopolist's profit at that quantity is $30 \times 20 - (\frac{1}{2})(20) + (10)(20) - 200 = 400$.

(c) Now the monopolist's profit-maximizing condition is $50 - 2Q = Q^2 - 22Q + 150$; that is, $Q^2 - 20Q + 100 = 0$. This is a simple quadratic equation. Solving it for Q, we find that $Q = 10$ and $p = 40$. The monopolist's profit is $40 \times 10 - 10^3/3 + 11 \times 10^2 - 150 \times 10 - 200 = -533.33$. But if the monopolist shuts down its operation— that is, produces $Q = 0$—it will still incur a fixed cost of 200, which means that it will have a loss of 200. Therefore, the firm will prefer to close its production activities.

5 (b) All the day trippers can avail themselves of the round-trip fare because they return to the city on the same day. The commuters, on the other hand, cannot take advantage of the round-trip fare because they stay on the island for more than a day. The only way a summer resident can take advantage of the round-trip fare is by buying a round-trip ticket from the day tripper. But assuming that one person can buy only one ticket, a day tripper will not be able to sell his *own* ticket. If he did, he would have to pay a regular fare for his trip back to the mainland. Therefore, the fare system is effective as a price-discrimination device.

(c) The round-trip cost of the ferry service for a summer resident is $10, and the round-trip cost for a day tripper is $6.50.

10 (a) The aggregate demand curve is given by

$$P = \begin{cases} 30 - Q/5 & Q \le 30 \\ 27 - Q/10 & 30 < Q \le 220 \\ 16 - Q/20 & 220 < Q \le 320 \end{cases}$$

(b) The aggregate demand curve in this problem is kinked, so we must determine first the marginal revenue function for each of the three sections.

$$MR = \begin{cases} 30 - 2Q/5 & Q \le 30 \\ 27 - Q/5 & 30 < Q \le 220 \\ 16 - Q/10 & 220 < Q \le 320 \end{cases}$$

Setting each of these marginal revenues equal to marginal cost, $8Q$, and solving for Q, we get $Q = 3.57$, 3.29, and 1.98, respectively. Note, though, that the last two quantities do not fall in the proper ranges for those marginal revenue equations to be true. Therefore, the only quantity consistent with optimization is $Q = 3.57$. Thus, $P = 29.28$.

(c) The monopolist's profit level is $(29.28)(3.57) - 8 - (4)(3.57)^2 = \$45.57$.

(d) Because only consumer 3 is willing to purchase the good at the monopoly price, there is no positive fee that the monopolist can charge to induce all three consumers to participate in the market.

(e) The socially optimal (that is, the perfectly competitive) price is equal to the marginal cost. Thus, equating the demand curve to the marginal cost curve, we get $30 - Q/5 = 8q$, (that is, $Q = 3.65$ and $P = 29.27$). Note that the monopolistic and the competitive prices are *approximately* equal (these are approximate results) because the aggregate demand curve is very steep—so much so that the marginal revenue curve is virtually indistinguishable from the demand curve. That is why equating the price or marginal revenue to the marginal cost gives rise to (more or less) the same price.

(f) Again, only consumer 3 will want to participate in the club, so there is no positive membership fee that would entice all three consumers to participate.

(g) Because only consumer 3 is a willing participant in both scenarios, it should be clear that the monopolist will be better off by charging the competitive price along with the fee. By charging this price, the monopolist earns $(3.65)(29.27) - 8 - (4)(3.65)^2 = 45.55$ plus a fee equaling 3's entire consumer surplus of $(\frac{1}{2})(3.65)(0.73) = 1.33$ for a total of 46.88. If she were to charge the monopoly price, she would earn 45.57 as above, plus a fee of $(\frac{1}{2})(3.57)(0.72) = 1.28$ for a total of 46.85. Again, there isn't a lot of difference due to the closeness of the two sets of prices and quantities.

Chapter 18

2 The following answers are based on the information that appears in Figure 15.

(a) At $p = 10$ and $q = 100,000$, the firm is making zero profits. If another firm entered the market and tried to sell any amount below 100,000 units at a price below $10 per unit, it would incur a loss. Therefore, this firm is a sustainable monopoly.

(b) Because the point $p = 14$, $q = 90,000$ is above the average cost curve, the firm would make a positive profit at this point; therefore, the firm's monopoly is not sustainable at this combination. Although the point $p = 11$, $q = 90,000$ is on the

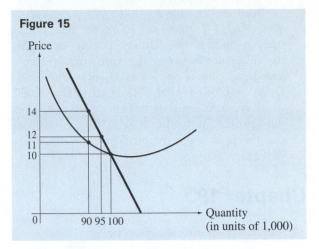

Figure 15

average cost curve, it is not on the *demand* curve (the market is willing to pay up to $14 for 90,000 units). Therefore, the firm's monopoly is not sustainable at this combination either.

(c) If the firm produces 95,000 units and charges $12 per unit, its monopoly is again not sustainable because the firm is earning a positive profit. For example, another firm could enter the market and produce 94,000 units at a price of $11.50 per unit and still make a positive profit.

(d) A potential entrant could take the entire market away from an incumbent that is producing 95,000 units and charging a price of $12 a day unit by choosing any price between $10 and $12 a unit and the quantity on the demand curve associated with the chosen price (say, $p = 11$, $q = 97,000$).

5 (a) The price that represents the "best" outcome for society is usually defined as the price that is equal to the marginal cost. In this case, the claim of the regulatory agency that average-cost pricing is best is correct because the firm's cost function indicates that its average and marginal costs are the same. Both are equal to b.

(b) It is not true that average-cost pricing produces an optimal result for all cost functions. In fact, most cost functions have different average and marginal costs. The only kind of cost function that has the same average and marginal costs is of the form $C(q) = bq$, where b is a constant.

(c) The cost function given in this problem represents the sole exception to a general rule, as noted in the answer to part b. It is a cost function that has identical average and marginal costs.

Because we have $D_1(P_1^*)/D_1(mc_1) = 200/400 = D_2(P_2^*)/D_2(mc_2) = 300/600$, this pricing scheme satisfies the Ramsey pricing rule. Also, the difference between the firm's total revenue and total cost is $(p_1^* - mc_1)D_1(p_1^*) + (p_2^* - mc_2)D_2(p_2^*) = (20 - 15)200 + (30 - 20)300 = 4,000$, which is exactly equal to the firm's fixed cost. Thus, the firm does not suffer a loss. We can conclude that this pricing scheme produces the second-best welfare-optimal result.

Chapter 19

1 (a) Firm A's profits are given by

$$\Pi_A (q_A, q_B) = Pq_A - C_A$$
$$= (10 - 2q_A - 2q_B)q_A - 4 + q_A - q_A^2$$
$$= 11q_A - 3q_A^2 - 2q_Aq_B - 4$$

Similarly, Firm B's profits are given by

$$\Pi_B (q_A, q_B) = Pq_B - C_B$$
$$= (10 - 2q_B - 2q_A)q_B - 5 + q_B - q_B^2$$
$$= 11q_B - 3q_B^2 - 2q_Bq_A - 5$$

Therefore, we can complete the payoff matrix as follows:

		q_A	
		0.41	0.74
q_B	0.92	2.82, −1.74	2.21, 0.135
	0.94	2.98, −1.76	2.29, 0.106

(b) From the payoff matrix in part *a*, we can see that the output combination of $q_A = 0.94$ and $q_B = 0.74$ is a Nash equilibrium. The best that firm A can do when firm B produces 0.74 units is to produce 0.94 units, and the best that firm B can do when firm A produces 0.94 units is to produce 0.74 units. In other words, $q_A = 0.94$ is a best response to $q_B = 0.74$, and $q_B = 0.74$ is a best response to $q_A = 0.94$.

6 (a) To find the subgame perfect equilibrium for the game between the Nice firm and the Nasty firm, we must look at the bottom node of the game tree. Clearly, if Nice remains in the market and produces $\frac{1}{6}$, Nasty would prefer to produce $\frac{1}{6}$ rather than 1. Given this situation, Nice would rather stay and receive a payoff of $\frac{1}{36}$ than leave the market and receive a payoff of zero. Because Nasty's announcement in the first period is nonbinding, Nice will stay regardless of Nasty's declaration. Thus, there are two subgame perfect

equilibria: (i) Nasty announces its intention to produce 1, Nice stays and produces $\frac{1}{6}$, and then Nasty produces $\frac{1}{6}$, or (ii) Nasty announces its intention to produce $\frac{1}{6}$, Nice stays and produces $\frac{1}{6}$, and then Nasty produces $\frac{1}{6}$. Note that although both of these subgame perfect equilibria have the same *outcome*, the *strategies* are different. We can therefore conclude that Nasty's threat to produce 1 is not credible.

(b) As we saw in part a, Nasty's ability to announce an intended strategy does not lead to an outcome that differs from the Cournot equilibrium.

(c) Nasty's profit function can be written as $(1 - q_{Nice} - q_{Nasty})q_{Nasty} - (\frac{1}{2})q_{Nasty}$. By equating Nice's marginal revenue to its marginal cost, we find that its reaction function is $q_{Nice} = \frac{1}{4} - (\frac{1}{2})q_{Nasty}$. When Nasty is a Stackelberg leader, it takes into account Nice's reaction to its own output when it chooses its profit-maximizing output. Substituting this in Nasty's demand curve, we get $P = 1 - q_{Nice} - q_{Nasty} = 1 - \frac{1}{4} + (\frac{1}{2})q_{Nasty} - q_{Nasty} = \frac{3}{4} - (\frac{1}{2})q_{Nasty}$. Therefore, Nasty's marginal revenue is $\frac{3}{4} - q_{Nasty}$. By equating it to Nasty's marginal cost, we obtain $\frac{1}{2} = \frac{3}{4} - (\frac{1}{2})q_{Nasty}$; that is, $q_{Nasty} = \frac{1}{4}$. Nice's output is $q_{Nice} = \frac{1}{4} - (\frac{1}{2})(\frac{1}{4}) = \frac{1}{8}$. In this case, Nasty does gain from being the Stackelberg leader because the outcome is better from its point of view than the Cournot-Nash equilibrium of $(\frac{1}{6}, \frac{1}{6})$.

7 (a) For a given level of output q_2 by firm 2, the demand curve faced by firm 1 is $p = (200 - 2q_2) - 2q_1$. Therefore, the demand curve faced by firm 1 for the various levels of output by firm 2 is indicated by

$$p = \begin{cases} 160 - 2q_1, \text{when } q_2 = 20 \\ 120 - 2q_1, \text{when } q_2 = 40 \\ 80 - 2q_1, \text{when } q_2 = 60 \\ -2q_1, \text{when } q_2 = 100 \end{cases}$$

and the associated, marginal revenue curves are:

$$MR = \begin{cases} 160 - 4q_1, \text{when } q_2 = 20 \\ 120 - 4q_1, \text{when } q_2 = 40 \\ 80 - 4q_1, \text{when } q_2 = 60 \\ -4q_1, \text{when } q_2 = 100 \end{cases}$$

(b) For a given level of q_2, the demand curve faced by firm 1 can be written as $p = (200 - 2q_2) - 2q_1$. Therefore, its marginal revenue curve is indicated by $MR_1 = (200 - 2q_2) - 4q_1$. Its marginal cost is expressed by $MC_1 = 2q_1$. When we equate firm 1's marginal revenue to its marginal cost, we obtain $200 - 2q_1 - 4q_1 = 2q_1$; that is, $q_1 = 100/3 - q_2/3$. This last equation is the general formula for firm 1's reaction function. Thus, the best response of firm 1 to the various levels of output produced by firm 2 is as follows:

$$q_1 = \begin{cases} 80/3, \text{ when } q_2 = 20 \\ 20, \text{ when } q_2 = 40 \\ 40/3, \text{ when } q_2 = 60 \\ 0, \text{ when } q_2 = 100 \end{cases}$$

Chapter 20

2 (a) The extensive form of the game is shown in Figure 16.

(b) If the potential entrant stays out of the market, it receives a payoff of zero and the incumbent monopolist receives a payoff of 100. If the potential entrant does enter the market, the incumbent's best response is to collude, in which case it receives a payoff of 50 and the entrant receives a payoff of 40. Therefore, in the subgame perfect equilibrium of the game, the potential entrant will enter the market and the incumbent will collude.

(c) Suppose that we designate the incumbent as player 0 and the potential entrants as players 1–20. To find the subgame perfect equilibrium for the 20-period game, we must use the usual backward-induction technique. If player 20 chooses to enter

in period 20, player 0's best response is to choose to collude. Long-run considerations do not matter because the game ends after period 20 anyway. Furthermore, player 20's choices are not influenced by what the players in earlier periods did. Even if player 19 chose to enter in period 19 and player 0 chose to fight in response, player 20 would not be deterred. Therefore, it is best for player 20 to choose to enter. Now consider player 19's situation in period 19. Her decision neither influences nor is influenced by the outcome in period 20. (She also does not care about player 20's payoff!) So player 19, like player 20, finds it in her best interest to choose to enter. Continuing in this way, we can conclude that players 1–20 will each choose to enter and player 0 will choose to collude in response to each of them. Thus, players 1–20 will each receive a payoff of 40 and player 0 will receive a payoff of 1,000.

4 Consider the sequence of moves in this game: In the first stage, the potential entrant decides whether or not to enter the market, and the incumbent monopolist observes its actions. In the second stage, if the potential entrant does enter the market, the two firms set their prices without seeing each other's moves. In such a situation, because the potential entrant moves first, it can actually signal its intention in the second stage by its actions in the first stage. Clearly, if the firm decides to enter, it does so with the intention of earning more than $45,000, which means that it intends to set a low price. Hence, the monopolist takes the potential entrant's act of entry as a signal of its willingness to set a low price. The best response of the monopolist is to set a high price. Anticipating such a reaction by the monopolist, the potential entrant will indeed decide to enter. This is a way of rationalizing the second subgame perfect equilibrium.

8 If we look at the last stage of the game, we find that whether the incumbent chooses technology A or technology B, the potential entrant will always prefer to enter rather than stay out. In each case, the potential entrant receives a payoff of zero if it stays out but a positive payoff if it enters. So the outcome is (1,000, 100) if the incumbent chooses technology A and (500, 500) if the incumbent chooses technology B. (The first number in parentheses is the incumbent's payoff, and the second number is the potential entrant's payoff.) Therefore, the incumbent will choose technology A, and the only subgame perfect outcome will be

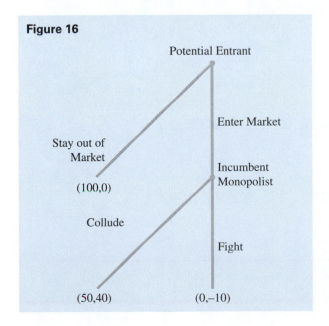

Figure 16

Potential Entrant

Stay out of Market

Enter Market

(100,0)

Incumbent Monopolist

Collude

Fight

(50,40) (0,–10)

(1,000, 100), in which the potential entrant does enter the market.

Chapter 21

3 (a) The first thing to note about the utility functions of the traders is that they depend on one good only. For example, U^1 does not depend on good X and U^2 does not depend on good Y. This situation implies that the indifference curves of trader 1 are horizontal straight lines, with utility increasing in the upward direction like DD', FF', and GG' in the picture below, and the indifference curves of trader 2 are vertical straight lines, with utility increasing in the leftward direction like CC', BB', and AA'. Figure 17 shows such indifference curves.

(b) We cannot apply the criterion of equal marginal rates of substitution to verify the Pareto optimality of an allocation here. The MRS_{YX} of trader 1 is zero, and the MRS_{YX} of trader 2 is infinity everywhere. In fact, because trader 1 cares only about the amount of good Y and trader 2 cares only about the amount of good X, any transfer of good Y to trader 1 by trader 2 in exchange for good X will make both traders better off.

Therefore, it is easy to see that the initial allocation $(\frac{1}{2}, \frac{1}{2})$ to each trader cannot be Pareto optimal.

(c) Using the argument advanced in part b, we can see that the only possible Pareto-optimal allocation occurs at point E in the northwest corner of the Edgeworth box, where trader 1 consumes 1 unit of good Y and no units of good X and trader 2 consumes 1 unit of good X and no units of good Y.

(d) E is the only competitive equilibrium, and the associated price ratio is given by the slope of the straight line EI (the budget line), which is 1. To see this, consider the utility-maximization problems of the two traders. Given a set of prices (p_X, p_Y), trader 1 will choose bundle $[0, (p_X + p_Y)/2p_Y]$ and trader 2 will choose bundle $[(p_X + p_Y)/2p_X, 0]$. (Verify these choices by drawing a diagram.) Such choices indicate that trader 1 will spend all his monetary income on good Y and trader 2 will spend all her monetary income on good X. Because the income of trader 1 is $\frac{P_x + P_y}{2}$ and because he spends all of that income on good Y, he can buy $\left(\frac{p_X + p_Y}{2}\right)\left(\frac{1}{p_y}\right)$ units of Y. Because he is the only person purchasing Y, he gets the total endowment of 1 unit, or $\left(\frac{p_X + p_Y}{2}\right)\left(\frac{1}{p_y}\right) = 1 \Rightarrow p_X = p_Y$.

Figure 17

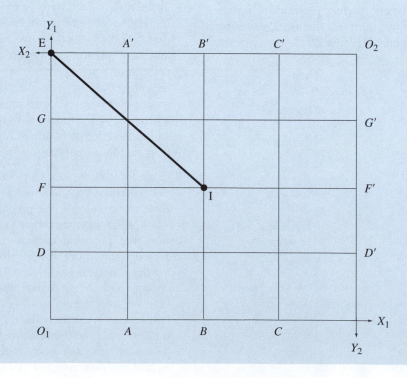

7 (a) The completed table is as follows:

Price (p_1/p_2)	Demand for X_1	Demand for Y_1	Demand for X_2	Demand for Y_2	Excess Demand for X	Excess Demand for Y
3	13/18	5/6	2/9	1/3	−1/12	1/6
3/2	5/9	2/3	7/18	5/12	−1/12	1/12
1	1/2	1/2	1/2	1/2	0	0
2/3	5/12	7/18	5/8	7/12	1/2	−1/4
1/3	3/8	5/24	7/8	17/24	1/6	−1/24

10 Trader S is willing to exchange 1 pound of steak for 3 pounds of hamburger. However, at the current market prices, he can obtain only 2 pounds of hamburger for every pound of steak that he gives up. In other words, his marginal rate of substitution of hamburger for steak is 3, but the price ratio is only 2. Therefore, he should increase his steak consumption and decrease his hamburger consumption. To obtain 1 more pound of steak, he need give up only 2 pounds of hamburger at the current prices, but he would have to give up 3 pounds of hamburger to stay on the same indifference curve. Because he is giving up less, he moves to a higher indifference curve, as shown in Figure 18.

Chapter 22

1 (a) In the case of goods X_1 and X_2, the marginal rates of technical substitution of capital for labor are as follows:

$$MRTS_{KL}^1 = \frac{MP_L^1}{MP_K^1} = \frac{\sqrt{K_1L_1}/2L_1}{\sqrt{K_1L_1}/2K_1} = \frac{K_1}{L_1}$$
$$MRTS_{KL}^2 = \frac{MP_L^2}{MP_K^2} = \frac{\sqrt{K_2L_2}/2L_2}{\sqrt{K_2L_2}/2K_2} = \frac{K_2}{L_2}$$

Therefore, the allocation $K_1 = 50$, $L_1 = 50$, and $K_2 = 50$, $L_2 = 50$ is efficient because

$$MRTS_{KL}^1 = 1 = MRTS_{KL}^2$$

(b) The allocation $K_1 = 64$, $L_1 = 36$ and $K_2 = 36$, $L_2 = 64$ is not efficient because

$$MRTS_{KL}^1 = \frac{16}{9} \neq MRTS_{KL}^2 = \frac{9}{16}$$

3 (a) Profit maximization by the two firms in the economy requires that $MC_1 = P_1$, $MC_2 = P_2$; that is, $P_1 = 2$, $P_2 = 3$. Utility maximization by the consumers requires that

$$MRS_{21} = \frac{MU_1}{MU_2} = \frac{P_1}{P_2} \Rightarrow \frac{X_2}{X_1} = \frac{2}{3}$$

Therefore, consumption of 30 units of good X_1 and 20 units of good X_2 by everyone in the economy is consistent with a competitive equilibrium.

(b) Although each person's marginal rate of substitution is equal to $\frac{2}{3}$, consumption of 10 units of good X_2 and 15 units of good X_1 by half the population and consumption of 30 units of good X_2 and 45 units of good X_1 by half the population may still not be consistent with a competitive equilibrium. Because everyone has the same utility function, people will demand precisely the same amount *if they also have the same income*. Thus, the second example is possible only if the two halves of the population have different incomes.

(c) Given the prices $P_1 = 2$ and $P_2 = 3$, everyone consuming 15 units of good 1 and 10 units of good 2 will need an income of $(2)(15) + (3)(10) = 60$. Everyone consuming 45 units of

Figure 18

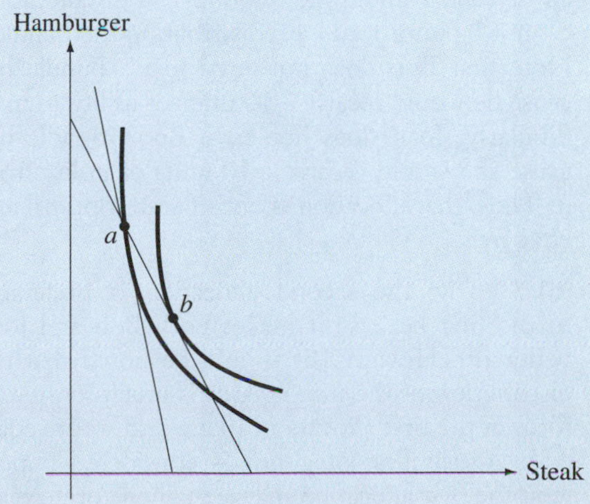

good 1 and 30 units of good 2 will need an income of $(2)(45) + (3)(30) = 180$.

(d) If each person has the utility function $U = 4X_1 + 2X_2$, the marginal rate of substitution is constant at 2. However, because the profit-maximizing price ratio is $\frac{2}{3}$, consumers will spend all their income on good 1 and nothing on good 2 (see Exercise 3 in Chapter 2 for more details). Therefore, good 2 should not be produced.

7 (a) For an allocation to be envy free, Bob must not prefer Joan's bundle and Joan must not prefer Bob's bundle. Bob receives 31 units of utility from his own bundle and -1 unit from Joan's bundle. Joan receives 39 units of utility from her own bundle and 11 units from Bob's bundle. Because neither party prefers the other's bundle, the allocation is envy free.

(b) For an allocation to be Pareto optimal, there cannot be another allocation with the same total amount of the three goods that makes at least one party better off without making the other worse off. The allocation that appears in this problem is not Pareto optimal because there is another allocation that gives Bob a bundle of (5, 0, 0) and Joan a bundle of (0, 5, 5) and therefore makes *both* Bob and Joan better off. With this allocation, Bob receives 40 units of utility and Joan receives 60 units of utility.

(c) The allocation of (5, 0, 0) to Bob and (0, 5, 5) to Joan is Pareto optimal. It is easy to understand why. Because Bob receives the most utility from good 1, he should have all of it; and because he receives negative utility from good 3, he should have none of it. For similar reasons, Joan should have all of good 2 and none of good 1. This allocation cannot be improved by redistributing the bundles. Note that Bob does not envy Joan's bundle because he would receive -10 units of utility from it. Similarly, Joan does not envy Bob's bundle because she would receive -10 units of utility from it. Thus, this allocation is both Pareto optimal and envy free.

(d) Clearly, the second allocation is preferable to the first because it makes both Bob and Joan better off. However, it should be noted that the distribution of the three goods is much more uniform in the first allocation. In a world where equitable distribution of goods is considered important, the first allocation may actually be preferred.

Chapter 23

1 (a) To compute the fair premium, the insurance company assumes that there are equal numbers of careless and careful people in the town. Thus, the insurance company has a $0.50\ [(0.5)(0.4) + (0.5)(0.6)]$ chance of paying \$200,000 for a total loss, a $0.25\ [(0.5)(0.2) + (0.5)(0.3)]$ chance of paying \$100,000 for a partial loss, and a $0.25\ [(0.5)(0.4) + (0.5)(0.1)]$ chance of not paying anything. The fair premium, π, is determined as follows: $\pi = (0.5)(200,000) + (0.25)(100,000) = 125,000$.

(b) A careful person's expected utility from this insurance is $U(200,000 - 125,000) = U(75,000) = 6.5$, while his expected utility from no insurance is $0.4U(200,000) + 0.2U(100,000) + 0.4U(0) = 8$. A careless person also has an expected utility of 6.5 from insurance, but his expected utility from no insurance is only $0.1U(200,000) + 0.3U(100,000) + 0.6U(0) = 4.5$. Clearly, a careful person is better off not buying insurance, but a careless person is better off buying insurance.

4 (a) The range of quality of the cars that will be traded in the market is $[b, P]$ if $b \leq P \leq 3b$, $[b, 3b]$ if $P > 3b$. No cars are brought to the market if $P < b$.

(b) The expected profit of the buyers is $[k(P + b)/2] - P$ if $P \leq 3b$. At the equilibrium, their expected profit is zero. Therefore, $[k(P + b)/2] - P = 0$; that is $P = kb/(2 - k)$. However, this is for $b \leq P \leq 3b$ or $1 \leq k \leq \frac{3}{2}$. If $k > \frac{3}{2}$, all cars are brought to the market, so the expected profit to the buyers is $2kb - P$ and the equilibrium price is $P = 2kb$. If $k < 1$, no cars are brought to the market, but we will ignore this situation.

(c) The equilibrium price and the fraction of cars that will be brought to the market in each case are as follows:

i. When $k = 1.2$, $P = 1.5b$ and the fraction of cars $= 0.2/2 = 0.25$.

ii. When $k = 1.0$, $P = b$ and the fraction of cars $= 0$.

iii. When $k = 1.5$, $P = 3b$ and the fraction of cars $= 1$.

(d) At the first-best equilibrium, there is no asymmetry of information—that is, the buyers and sellers have exactly the same information. In such a case, the equilibrium price will be exactly equal to the quality: $P = \theta$. From part c, we know that when $k = 1.0$ (the buyers' value quality exactly the same as the sellers'), $P = b$. Thus, only the very worst cars would be put on the market. However, because we are dealing with a continuous distribution of quantities, the probability of any car being of quality b is zero, so no cars will sell. Any greater value of k will result in a positive number of cars being put on the market, but there will be uncertainty about their quality for the buyer, so any equilibrium solution will be second best.

(e) When $k = 3$, all cars are on the market, so the expected value to the seller is $2b$ and the expected value to the buyer is $(3)(2b) = 6b$. The equilibrium is therefore $P = 6b$, and all cars are brought to the market.

6 (a) A moral hazard arises in this situation because the higher the cost incurred is, the higher the architect's fee. The architect therefore has no incentive to keep the cost down. In fact, he has an incentive to raise the cost of the renovation work.

(b) The general principle that underlies the successful solution of any moral hazard problem is to make the concerned party's payoff contingent on avoiding the action that creates the moral hazard. For example, if the architect is paid a *fixed* sum that must cover both the cost of the renovation work and his fee, it is in his interest to keep the cost down because he has to bear the cost in this case.

Chapter 24

1 (a) The genius imposes a *negative* externality on the rest of the class. If she always scores 100% on exams, all the other students will have a zero added to their grades; and of course, the fewer points they earn, the less money they will receive from their parents. For each point the genius scores above 85, the "regular" students lose a point and hence receive a dollar less from their parents. Thus, a dollar is the value of the marginal externality for each exam.

(b) The only Pareto-optimal distribution of grades is the one in which *everybody*, including the genius, receives the same points. As long as the scores are unequal, it is possible to raise the grades of everyone, except the highest scorer, without hurting that student. Also, the teacher's method of grading on a curve makes everyone's score exactly 100 if everyone receives the same number of points. Clearly, it is not possible to receive anything more than that.

(c) The highest-scoring student could be taxed at the marginal rate of a dollar for each point she earns above the next highest-scoring student in the class. Then the amount collected from this tax could be divided equally among all the students in the class to make their grades equal and thereby achieve a Pareto-optimal distribution of grades.

(d) If the genius is bribed to score only 85 points, each "regular" student receives 100 points. The genius also receives 100 points, but she would have earned this number of points anyway. Because each "regular" student earns an additional 15 points ($15) if the genius scores 85 points, the class is willing to pay her a bribe of $285 [($15) (19)] to stop her from scoring 100!

2 (a) If the two firms were run by the same management (that is, if they were part of a multiplant monopoly), their total profit would be $\Pi = 40X + 10Y - X^2 - Y^2 - 0.05X$. Equating the marginal revenues of each good to its marginal cost, we find that $40 = 2X + 0.05 \Rightarrow X = 19.75$ and $10 = 2Y \Rightarrow Y = 5$.

(b) In a competitive market, the window factory would not take its externality on the laundry into account. It would simply equate its own marginal cost to its own revenue, which yields $2X = 40$, or $X = 20$. Then the laundry's total cost function would become $Y^2 + 1$. The laundry's profit-maximizing output is given by $2Y = 10$, or $Y = 5$. Thus, in a competitive market, the laundry would produce at the same level, but the window factory would produce more than it does as a monopoly.

(c) If the window factory were taxed at the rate of $0.05 per unit of X, its private cost would be identical to the social cost. Such a tax would make the outcome the same as it was in part a.

4 (a) In a competitive market, firm A will equate its marginal cost to its marginal revenue, $16 = 4q_A$, or $q_A = 4$.

(b) To find the optimal output for society, we must equate the social marginal benefit of q_A to its social marginal cost, which is $16 + 7 = 4_{q_A} + 3$, or $q_A = 5$.

(c) If firms A and B merge and then choose the best amount of q_A for the combined operation, their output would be $16 + 7 = 4_{q_A}$, or $q_A = 5.75$. This amount is higher than the socially optimal output of 5.

Chapter 25

1 (a) If 19 of the 20 members of our hypothetical society do not send any money, then the 20th person's best response is not to send any money either. Even if this person sends some money, it will be returned because there will not be enough money to build the pool. If we apply this reasoning to all the members of society, it becomes clear that no one sending money is a Nash equilibrium.

(b) If 19 members of society send $80 each, the 20th person's best response is to send $80 as well. If she sends more than $80, the excess will be burned. If she sends less, the pool will not be built, and having the pool built is worth $100 to her. Therefore, everyone's contributing $80 is a Nash equilibrium.

(c) If 15 members of society have contributed a total of $1,500 toward the $1,600 cost of building the pool, the 20th person's best response is to send $100. Sending less will not get the pool built, and sending more does not make sense. Similarly, if the other members of society have contributed $1,600, then the 20th person's best response is to send no money because the pool will be built anyway and the government will burn any excess money it receives for the pool. Therefore, 16 people's contributing $100 each and 4 contributing zero is a Nash equilibrium.

3 (a) If each citizen of Xanadu is rational, he or she wants the government to build the project that he or she likes the most. However, if one is not honest when she writes her preferred project on the piece of paper the government collects for the drawing and her piece of paper is selected from the hat, then her first choice will certainly not be built. Of course, if someone else's piece of paper is selected, her favorite project may or may not be chosen. Therefore, it is always best for a citizen to indicate his or her true first choice, no matter what other people do. Obviously, the

more people who vote for a particular project, the more likely it is that the project will be selected. It is in the interest of each citizen to be honest about his or her preference because, by doing so, he or she increases the likelihood that this project will be built.

(b) The method that Xanadu uses for selection of a project is Pareto optimal. Regardless of which project is chosen, no choice of another project can make any citizen better off without making some other citizen worse off. For example, if one or more citizens vote for the bridge and a piece of paper indicating that the bridge should be built is drawn from the hat, then a change from this choice to the choice of the hospital will increase the utility of anyone who voted for the hospital but will decrease the utility of anyone who voted for the bridge.

(c) The scheme used in Xanadu illustrates that even the most *arbitrary* method of making a choice can be Pareto optimal. In fact, far from being the tyranny of the majority, Pareto optimality is sometimes the tyranny of the minority. Under a scheme such as the one used in Xanadu, each citizen has the potential power to determine the choice for society, which is why a solution that favors one or a few people but puts everyone else at a disadvantage can still be Pareto optimal. On the other hand, changing from the minority choice to the majority choice is not enough to guarantee Pareto optimality.

4 (a) The Nash equilibria are (Contribute, Free-Ride) and (Free-Ride, Contribute). Neither is Pareto optimal because (Contribute, Contribute) is the pair of actions that maximizes the total payoffs.

(b) To show that a pair of strategies is subgame perfect, we must check for deviations at every stage of the game, starting with the last stage. In the 50th year, neither person A nor person B has an incentive to deviate because (Free-Ride, Contribute) is a Nash equilibrium. Similarly, nobody has an incentive to deviate in the 49th year because (Contribute, Free-Ride) is also a Nash equilibrium. Therefore, if both players conform to their strategies for all 50 years of the game, each receives a payoff of

$$\underbrace{12 + 12 + \ldots + 12}_{48} + 15 + 5 = 596$$

If a player deviates in any period before the 48th year, say in period t, he or she receives

$$\underbrace{12 + 12 + \ldots + 12}_{t-1} + \underbrace{15}_{t} + \underbrace{5 + 5 \ldots + 5}_{50-1} =$$

$$12(t-1) + 15 + 5\,(50 - t) = 7t + 253$$

When we compare the two payoffs, it is clear that no one will deviate from the prescribed pair of strategies at any stage. Thus, these strategies constitute a subgame perfect equilibrium.

Chapter 26

3 (a) The total product schedule used in this problem is as follows.

The wage-to-price ratio is $3 : 12 = 0.25$. The marginal productivity is 0.25 at 5 units of labor. Thus, the number of units of labor that the firm will use to maximize profits is 5.

(b) At 2 units of labor, the marginal productivity is 2 and so is the real wage. Therefore, the wage rate is $(2)(11) = 22$, or \$22.

(c) At 4 units of labor, the marginal product is 0.5. Because the wage rate is \$15, the output price is $15/0.5 = 30$, or \$30.

7 When we equate the individual's marginal rate of substitution to the price ratio, we find that

$$w = \frac{MU_z}{MU_c} = \frac{(\tfrac{2}{3})(Z/C)^{-1/3}}{(\tfrac{1}{3})(Z/C)^{2/3}} = 2(C/Z), \text{ or}$$

$$Z = 2C/w$$

Units of Labor Used	Units of Output Produced
1	3
2	5
3	6
4	6.5
5	6.75
6	6.75

The budget constraint is $C = wL = w(24 - Z)$. Substituting in the previous equation, we obtain

$$Z = \frac{2C}{w} = \frac{2w(24 - Z)}{w} = 48 - 2Z$$

Therefore, $Z = 16$, $L = 8$.

8 The optimality condition is as follows:

$$w = \frac{MU_z}{MU_c} = \frac{60 - 2Z}{2} = 30 - Z, \text{or } Z = 30 - w$$

Therefore, the labor supply function is given by $L = 24 - Z = w - 6$.

As long as the wage rate w is more than \$6, the labor supply is positive and upward sloping. However, because the labor supply cannot be more than 24 hours, w cannot be more than \$30. Thus, w must be between \$6 and \$30.

Glossary

Additive utility function A utility function that has the property that the marginal utility of one extra unit of any good consumed is independent of the amount of other goods consumed.

Additivity assumption The assumption on consumption sets that states that it is possible to add consumption bundles.

Additivity assumption The assumption that states that if we can produce an output of x using one combination of inputs (capital and labor) and another level of output of y using another combination of these inputs, then we can feasibly produce the output $x + y$.

Adverse selection Adverse selection occurs in situations where one economic agent (say an insurance company) can not observe the characteristics of another (potential clients) and offers a contract that is accepted by a set of people in the population that has less than average desirability (bad risks).

Agenda manipulation The process by which an individual who controls the agenda for a committee or voting body manipulates the order in which pairs of alternatives are voted on in an effort to influence the outcome.

Agent The person who is acting on behalf of a principal.

Allocation A specification of the quantity of each good to be consumed by each agent in the economy.

Alternating offer sequential bargaining equilibrium theorem When the total number of periods in the alternating offer sequential bargaining game is finite, there is a unique subgame perfect equilibrium in which the first offer made is accepted. The equilibrium offer is equal to the sum of the decrements in the pie when the first player makes his offer.

Alternating offer sequential bargaining institution A structured method of bargaining where each bargainer takes turns making offers. If an offer is accepted, the bargaining stops. If the offer is not accepted, the bargaining proceeds to the next round but, due to the delay, the value of what is being bargained over, "the pie," shrinks.

Approximate measure of consumer surplus A measure of consumer surplus determined by the area under the uncompensated demand curve.

Arbitrage A process of buying a commodity and reselling it at a favorable price.

Arbitrage pricing The price of a good or asset that results after the process of arbitrage has occurred if arbitrage opportunities existed.

Arrow's impossibility theorem A theorem that demonstrates that there is no voting mechanism that determines transitive social preferences and also satisfies the five conditions for a desirable voting mechanism.

Asymmetric information When the buyers and sellers in a market have different amounts of information.

Average-cost pricing To set a price that is equal to the average cost.

Backward induction The process of solving a game by going to its end and working backward.

Bain, Modigliani, Sylos-Labini model A model where an incumbent firm uses a pricing strategy to make it unprofitable for any potential competitor to enter a market.

Bayes-Nash equilibrium An equilibrium defined for a game of incomplete information that takes into account the fact that a player may be facing opponents of different, random types.

Bellman's principle of optimality The idea that, in a dynamic economic problem, at any point in time the decision maker can choose an optimal action by comparing the value of stopping versus continuing in an optimal fashion.

Bertrand equilibrium An equilibrium to an oligopoly game played by firms setting prices (Bertrand competition) such that competition forces the price down to the marginal price.

Bertrand model A model of oligopolistic competition where firms compete by setting prices.

Bid rigging Collusion among firms bidding in an auction.

Bilateral monopoly A market with only one seller and one buyer.

Block To prevent a trade from occurring by forming a coalition and offering each person in the coalition more than they receive from the current proposed trade.

Blockaded entry When the incumbent firm is able to deter entry by simply pursuing a policy that is best for itself as a monopolist.

Borda count method A voting method used to choose between k alternatives where the voters allocate k votes to their first alternative, $k - 1$ votes to their second, $k - 2$ votes to their third, etc. The alternative receiving the largest total number of votes is the one chosen by the voting body.

Cardinal utility Utility is said to be measurable in the cardinal sense if not only the utility numbers assigned to bundles but also their differences are meaningful.

Coase theorem In markets with externalities, if property rights are assigned unambiguously and if the parties involved can negotiate costlessly, then the Coase theorem suggests that the parties will arrive at a Pareto-optimal outcome regardless of which one owns the property rights.

Cobb-Douglas production function A production function of the form (with two inputs, capital and labor) $y = K x_{capital}^{\alpha} x_{labor}^{\beta}$.

Co-insurance (deductible) The amount any agent will have to pay in the event that the situation being covered by the insurance company occurs.

Collusive duopoly A duopoly in which the two firms collude on a price to set.

Common costs Costs that are shared among customers.

Common value auction An auction in which one objectively true value for a good exists, but information about that value is distributed across the population.

Comparative static analysis An analysis in which the economist examines the equilibrium of the market before and after a policy change to see the effect of the change on the market price and quantity.

Compensated demand function A hypothetical demand curve in which the consumer's income is adjusted as the price changes so that the consumer's utility remains at the same level.

Competitive behavior Price-taking behavior.

Competitive equilibrium A price vector stating one price for each good in the economy along with an associated vector of supplies and demands for each good at which no agent has any desire to change their supplies or demands and at which supply and demand are consistent (equal for each good) and hence trades can be carried out in a coordinated way.

Competitive equilibrium allocation The allocation of goods determined by a competitive equilibrium.

Competitive prices Prices that equate the supply and demand for each good.

Complete binary ordering An assumption on consumer preferences that implies that if any two bundles in the consumption possibility set (hence the term binary) are chosen, say bundles a and b, then our agents will be able to rank them—tell whether they prefer a to b or b to a or whether they consider a to be exactly as good as b.

Condition for consistency of production and consumption The condition that for any mix of outputs produced, the marginal rate of transformation of those goods in production (as defined by the slope of the production possibilities frontier) must equal the marginal rates of substitution for all consumers using those goods.

Condition for efficiency in consumption The condition that a given set of goods in an economy should be allocated across a set of consumers until the marginal rate of substitution for each pair of goods is equal for each consumer.

Condition for efficiency in production The condition that a given set of inputs available in an economy should be allocated across a set of producers until the marginal rate of technical substitution for each pair of inputs is equal for each producer.

Conjectural variation The change that a firm expects in its competitor's choice of an output level in response to a change the firm makes in its own output level.

Constant returns to scale A feature of a technology that is such that when all inputs are increased by a fixed multiple λ, output increases by the same multiple; that is, if all inputs are doubled, then so is the resulting output.

Constant-cost industries Industries in which the long-run supply curve is flat.

Consumer surplus The net gain that a consumer achieves from purchasing a good at a certain price per unit.

Consumption possibility set The set of bundles feasible for the agents to consume in a society.

Contestable market A market that competitors can easily enter and leave because there are no sunk costs.

Contestable market entry game A game defined by the contestable market assumptions.

Continuity The assumption on utility functions that states that if two bundles are close to each other in the feasible set, then they will be assigned utility numbers that are close to each other as well.

Continuous probability distribution A probability distribution with an infinite number of events.

Contract curve A curve in the Edgeworth box that traces out all the efficient trades.

Convexity The property of consumption sets that implies that it is possible to combine two bundles to produce a third by consuming fractions of them.

Convexity assumption The assumption that states that if there is a production activity y that produces a certain amount of output z using capital and labor in particular amounts and another activity w that produces the same quantity using different amounts of these inputs, then we can always produce at least z by mixing these activities and using y a fraction of the time and w a fraction of the time.

Convexity of preferences A psychological assumption about preferences that states that if a consumer is indifferent between a goods bundle x and a goods bundle y, then he would prefer (or be indifferent to) a weighted combination of these bundles to either of the original bundles x or y.

Coordination game A game in which the players have a common interest in reaching an equilibrium yet, if there are multiple equilibria, their preferences may differ as to which is the best. At the equilibrium of a coordination game, no player wishes any other player to change their actions.

Core The set of efficient (Pareto-optimal) allocations that cannot be improved upon by any agent acting alone (in an individually rational manner) or by any group of agents acting together.

Cost function The function that demonstrates the relationship between cost and quantity that will tell how much it will cost to produce each quantity of a product.

Cournot conjecture In a Cournot duopoly, the Cournot conjecture is an assumption that no matter what change in output a firm makes, the other firm will not change its own output choice in response.

Cournot equilibrium The Nash equilibrium applied to a model in which duopolistic or oligopolistic firms compete with one another by choosing output levels, that is, the Nash equilibrium of a Cournot oligopoly model.

Cournot model A model in which firm 1 and firm 2 choose a quantity simultaneously, and after both firms have chosen their outputs, the price of the good on the market and the profits of both firms are determined.

Credible threats Threats that, if the game ever progresses to the point where the threat is supposed to be carried out, will, in fact, be acted on.

Deadweight loss The dollar measure of the loss that society suffers when units of a good whose marginal social benefits exceed the marginal social cost of providing them are not produced because of the profit-maximizing motives of the firm involved.

Decreasing returns to factor The decrease in the rate that output grows when we increase the usage of one factor but hold the usage of all others constant.

Decreasing returns to scale A feature of a technology that is such that when all inputs are increased by a fixed multiple λ, output increases by less than that multiple; that is, if all inputs are doubled, then the resulting output increases but by less than a factor of two.

Decreasing-cost industries Industries with a long-run cost curve that is downward sloping.

Demand curve A curve that represents graphically the relationship between the quantity of a good demanded by a consumer and the price of that good as the price varies.

Demand-revealing mechanism A mechanism that creates the incentive for people to reveal their public goods preferences in a truthful manner.

Demsetz auction An auction in which the right to be the exclusive franchisee of a good or service is auctioned by the government.

Derived demand Demand for labor that is derived from the process of profit maximization.

Diminishing marginal rates of substitution The property of indifference curves stemming from their convexity that implies that if we move along the indifference curve, hence keeping the consumer at the same utility level, the marginal rate of substitution decreases.

Discount factor Measures how much a player values future payoffs relative to current payoffs.

Discrete probability distribution A probability distribution with a finite number of events.

Divisibility assumption The assumption that states that if an input combination y is a feasible input combination, then so is λy where $0 \le \lambda \le 1$. In other words, if it is feasible to produce a product using 4 units of labor and 8 units of capital, then it is feasible to produce using a constant fraction of those inputs, for example, 2 units of labor and 4 units of capital, if $\lambda = 1/2$.

Divisibility assumption The assumption on consumption sets that states that goods are infinitely divisible.

Dixit-Spence model A model of entry prevention where the strategy of the incumbent monopolist is to overinvest in production capacity in order to make entry unprofitable.

Dominant strategy A strategy that is best for a player no matter what the opposing players do. A dominant strategy dominates all other strategies.

Dominant strategy A strategy that is best for a player no matter what the opposing players do. A dominant strategy dominates all other strategies.

Dominant-strategy equilibrium The equilibrium in a game in which all players use their dominant strategies.

Dominate Strategy A dominates strategy B if it gives a higher payoff than B no matter what the opposing players do.

Dominated strategy A strategy that is dominated by another strategy.

Double coincidence of wants The requirement of trade where two parties must be interested in obtaining each other's goods.

Double oral auction An auction in which both buyers and sellers can make bids or asks as the auction progresses. Contracts per goods are consumated when an agent on either side accepts an outstanding bid or ask.

Duopoly An industry in which there are two firms selling a product.

Dutch auction An auction in which the auctioneer sets the price arbitrarily high and then systematically reduces it until one bidder stops the falling price and buys the good.

Dynamic analysis An analysis in which the economist examines the path that the market will follow in moving from one equilibrium to another.

Economic institutions Conventions developed by a society to help it resolve recurrent economic problems; sets of rules created to govern economic behavior.

Economic models Abstract representations of reality that economists use to study the economic and social phenomena in which they are interested.

Economic rent The return to a factor of production over and above what is needed to secure the services of that factor.

Economic tournament (rank-order tournament) A system in which workers are compensated not on the basis of their absolute output but rather on the basis of their output relative to the output of others.

Economically feasible consumption set The reduced set of consumption bundles economically feasible to consume; that is, each bundle satisfies the budget constraint.

Edgeworth box A graphical device that permits us to analyze the process of trade between two parties.

Efficiency wage Wages paid by a firm to its workers that are above the market-clearing level in order to increase their productivity or efficiency.

Elastic demand A characteristic of demand for a good where, at a given price, a 1% change in the price of a good leads to a more than 1% change in the quantity demanded of that good.

Elasticity of demand Measures the percentage change in the demand for a good that results from a given percentage change in its price.

Elasticity of substitution A measure of how easy it is to substitute one input for another in producing a given level of output.

English auction An auction, of the type used in common country auctions, in which the auctioneer starts the bidding at a certain level and people raise that bid until no one wishes to increase their bid any further. The last person to bid wins the good at a price equal to that bid.

Envy-free allocation An allocation in which no one envies the bundle of anyone else.

Equilibrium A state in which no player will wish to change his or her behavior given the behavior of the other players.

Equilibrium allocation An allocation that has the property that, once the parties reach this point, they have no further incentive to continue trading.

Exact measure of consumer surplus A measure of consumer surplus determined by the area under the compensated demand curve.

Excludability When consumption of a good is restricted to certain people, such as people who are willing to pay for the good.

Expected monetary value The expected monetary return of a lottery, gamble, or investment, determined by taking a weighted average of the monetary prizes offered using the associated probabilities as weights.

Expected utility The expected utility of a lottery, gamble, or investment, determined by taking a weighted average of the utility of the monetary prizes offered using the associated probabilities as weights.

Expected utility hypothesis The hypothesis that states that when people are faced with risk, they assess the possible payoffs in terms of utility and then choose the gamble that yields the payoff with the highest expected utility.

Expenditure function The function that identifies the minimum amount of income that we must give a consumer in order to allow him to achieve a predetermined level of utility at given prices.

Extensive form A description of a game of strategy that provides a detailed description of the rules of the game.

Externality Any cost or benefit generated by one agent in its production or consumption activities but affecting another agent in the economy.

Extra-normal profit Any return above the normal profit to an entrepreneur.

Feasible allocation An allocation that does not allocate more than the total amount of goods available in the economy.

Finite horizon game A repeated game with a finite number of repetitions.

Firm A business entity that hires labor and capital to produce a product.

First fundamental theorem of welfare economics Indicates that when a competitive equilibrium exists, the allocations of inputs and outputs in the economy define a Pareto-optimal outcome.

First-mover advantage The advantage the leader (first mover) has in the Stackelberg model, which allows him to produce a higher level of output than it previously did in the Cournot equilibrium, thus receiving greater profits.

First-price sealed-bid auction An auction in which bidders submit sealed bids, and the winner is the highest bidder, who pays a price equal to his or her bid.

Fixed costs The costs of the fixed factors of production; the costs that do not change with the level of output.

Fixed factor of production A factor of production whose level cannot be adjusted in the time period under investigation.

Forcing contract An incentive scheme in which a target output is set for the entire group and payments are received by all workers if the group's output exceeds this target.

Franchise The license a government grants to a company that allows it to set up a monopoly.

Free disposability assumption The assumption that states that if we can produce a certain output with a given combination of inputs, then with those inputs we can always produce strictly less.

Free-market advocates (laissez-faire advocates) People who feel strongly that the government should not interfere with the functioning of perfectly competitive markets.

Free ride The process of enjoying the benefits of a public good without contributing to its construction.

Free-rider problem When members of a society have incentives to take advantage of a public good by not contributing to paying its costs.

Functional distribution of income The distribution of income across the factors of production: land, labor, and capital.

Game of imperfect information A game in which, when a player reaches a decision point, she does not know all the choices of the other players who preceded her.

Game of perfect information A game in which, when any player makes a move, he knows all the prior choices made by all the other players.

Game of strategy A multiperson decision problem in which an abstract set of rules constrains the behavior of players and defines outcomes on the basis of the actions taken by the players.

Game theory The study of games of strategy and the strategic interactions that such games reveal.

Game tree A visual depiction of an extensive form game that presents the rules and payoff contingencies of the game.

General inputs A capital good that has many uses.

Generalized stand-alone test The test that asks a group or individual community of similar consumers to compare the price they are paying for the service with the price they would have to pay if they provided it for themselves.

Gibbard-Satterthwaite theorem When a single outcome is to be chosen from more than two alternatives, the only voting rule that cannot be manipulated is a dictatorial one.

Giffen good A good whose demand curve is upward sloping.

Group incentive programs An incentive scheme in which the rewards to any individual agent depend not only on his or her actions but also on the actions of the other agents in the group or tournament.

Hit-and-run entry When a potential entrant monitoring a market sees an opportunity to enter a market and does so but then exits when the incumbent firm responds.

Homogeneous production function A particular type of production function that has the property that whenever we multiply its inputs by a factor λ, we simply obtain the same output we started with multiplied by λ^K where K is the degree of homogeneity.

Homothetic preferences Preferences for which the resulting indifference curves have the property that, along any ray from the origin, the marginal rate of substitution between two goods remains constant. This implies that consumers will increase the purchases of goods proportionately as their incomes increase and prices stay constant.

Homothetic production function A production function that has the property that whenever we multiply inputs by a factor λ, the marginal rate of technical substitution remains the same between all inputs.

Human capital Skills of labor.

Hyperbolic preferences A particular way to discount future payoffs that leads to time-inconsistent behavior.

Immediate run A period of time so short that producers are unable to vary any of their inputs to meet changes in demand or other changes.

Immediate run A period of time so short that producers are unable to vary any of their inputs to meet changes in demand or other changes.

Impeded entry A situation where the monopolist must choose a less advantageous level of output in order to deter entry.

Impersonal markets Markets in which the identity of the traders and their size in the market do not affect the price at which they trade.

Incentive compatibility constraint A constraint in a contract that ensures the agent will be willing to take the prescribed action once he joins by offering incentives to do so.

Income effect The impact of an income-induced change in demand caused by a change in price.

Income elasticity of demand The percentage change in the demand for a good that results from a 1% change in the agent's income.

Income expansion path The path connecting optimal consumption bundles that shows how a consumer changes his quantity demanded of specified goods as his income changes and prices remain constant.

Incomplete information A situation in which producers and consumers are not fully informed about the characteristics of all goods consumed and produced in the economy and that can cause uncertainty and market failure.

Increasing returns to scale A feature of a technology that is such that when all inputs are increased by a fixed multiple λ, output increases by more than that multiple; that is, if all inputs are doubled, then the resulting output increases by more than a factor of two.

Increasing-cost industries Industries with a long-run cost curve that is upward sloping.

Indifference curve A curve or locus of bundles in the consumption set for a consumer among which the consumer is indifferent.

Indifference map A set of indifference curves for a consumer.

Individually rational trade A trade that offers a trader a higher level of utility than he or she could receive by not trading.

Inelastic demand A characteristic of demand for a good where, at a given price, a 1% change in the price leads to a less than 1% change in the quantity demanded.

Inertia shopping rule The rule that states that buyers will buy from the firm that charges the lowest price but that if they are already buying from a firm and another firm enters the market and offers a lower price, they give their current firm a chance to meet the entrant's price before shifting their business.

Inferior good A good for which demand decreases as the income of the consumer increases and the relative prices remain constant.

Infinite horizon game A game repeated over an infinite horizon.

Information sets The sets that indicate what a player knows when it is her turn to make a move in a game tree.

Interventionists People who feel that there is a flaw in the idea that markets are efficient.

Inverse demand function The function that indicates the price that would result if any given quantity were placed on the market.

Isocost curves Curves in which all combinations of inputs on the curve are equally expensive. If input prices are fixed, such a curve is a straight line.

Iso-output line The set of output combinations for two duopolistic firms that has the property of the sum of the outputs being constant.

Isoprofit curves The set of outputs for all firms in a market that yield a given firm the same profit level.

Isoquant The set of bundles that most efficiently produce the same output given a production function.

Kinked demand curve conjecture The assumption that firms will match a reduction but not an increase in the prevailing price that is responsible for the stability of duopolistic and oligopolistic markets.

Leontief production function A production function in which inputs (capital and labor) must be used in a certain fixed proportion to produce output.

Limit price The price an incumbent monopolist sets that enables it to impede entry into the market.

Limit pricing A strategy in which the established firms in an oligopolistic market can deter entry by setting their output at such a level that the remaining demand in the market is too low for a potential entrant to earn a profit at any price it can charge.

Limit quantity The quantity an incumbent monopolist sets that enables it to impede entry into the market.

Lindahl equilibrium A competitive equilibrium for a market with both private and public goods.

Long run The period of time long enough to vary all factors of production.

Long-run average cost function A function describing the average cost of producing units of output when no factor of production is fixed so that each can vary accordingly.

Long-run equilibrium The price-quantity combination that will prevail in a perfectly competitive market in the long run.

Long-run marginal cost function A function describing the marginal cost of producing units of output when no factor of production is fixed so that each can vary accordingly.

Long-run production function The production function that allows the producer to vary the levels of all inputs in an effort to produce a given quantity.

Long-run total cost function A function describing the total cost of producing units of output when no factor of production is fixed so that each can vary accordingly.

Marginal expenditure (*ME*) The change in a firm's total wage bill that results from its hiring of one additional unit of labor.

Marginal physical product (*MPP*) curve The curve that tells us how much extra output, in physical units, will be produced as the firm adds more and more units of labor.

Marginal product curve The graph of the marginal product of a factor of production.

Marginal product of capital The amount by which output would increase if we added one more unit of capital to production, holding all other inputs fixed.

Marginal productivity theory The theory that states how free-market economies determine the returns on the factors of production, whereby each factor is paid its marginal revenue product.

Marginal rate of substitution The ratio at which a consumer, at a particular point on the indifference map, would be willing to exchange one good for another; the rate of exchange that would just maintain the consumer's original utility.

Marginal rate of technical substitution The rate at which one input can be substituted for another while keeping the output produced constant.

Marginal rate of transformation (MRT) The slope of the production possibilities frontier that indicates how many units of good 2 the economy would have to sacrifice (by transferring inputs from the production of good 2 to the production of good 1) in order to obtain 1 more unit of good 1.

Marginal revenue The increase in the total revenue of a firm generated by the sale of an additional unit of output.

Marginal revenue product (MRP) The firm's marginal physical product the new workers will produce times the marginal revenue (MR) the additional units of output will earn.

Marginal-cost pricing To set a price that is equal to the marginal cost.

Market A place where agents can go and exchange one good for another at a fixed price.

Market demand curve The aggregate of individual demand curves.

Market supply function (aggregate supply function) A function that tells us how much of a product all of the firms in an industry will supply at any given market price.

Marketable pollution permits A method of government intervention to prevent externalities whereby a government-issued permit allows a firm to pollute the environment by a specified amount.

Mean-preserving spread proposition The proposition that states that if a risk-averse agent is faced with two gambles, both of which have the same expected monetary return but different variances, the agent will always choose the gamble whose variance is smaller.

Minimum wage law A law that prescribes a floor below which wages cannot fall.

Mixed strategies Strategies that define probability mixtures over all or some of the pure strategies in the game.

Mixed strategy equilibrium An equilibrium where players use mixed strategies.

Money A medium that is widely acceptable in exchange for all goods and services and for the settlement of debts.

Monopsonistic exploitation Any situation in which a factor of production is paid less than the value of its marginal revenue product.

Monopsony A market with a single buyer.

Moral hazard Occurs whenever there are incentives for economic agents who cannot be monitored to behave in a manner contrary to what is expected of them.

Multiplicative utility function A utility function in which utility is a function of the products of the various units of goods consumed. In such utility functions, the marginal utility of

consumption for any good depends on the amount of other goods consumed.

Nash equilibrium A set of strategies, one for each player, in which no player wishes to change his behavior (strategy choice) given the behavior (strategy choice) of his opponents.

Natural monopoly A situation that occurs in industries where the cheapest way to obtain a given quantity of output is to have only one firm produce it.

No free lunch assumption The assumption that you cannot get any output from a production process without inputs.

Noncooperative games Games in which there is no possibility of communication or binding commitments.

Noncredible threat A threat in a strategic game that is not believable or would not be carried out if called upon.

Nonreversibility assumption The assumption that states that you cannot run a production process in reverse.

Nonsatiation A psychological assumption about consumer preferences that states that more of anything is always better.

Normal form game A representation of a game of strategy defined by the number of players in the game, the set of strategies each player has, and the payoffs to each player contingent on one strategy choice for each player. This game is often presented as a matrix game when the players have a small and finite number of strategies.

Normal good A good whose demand curve is downward sloping.

Normal profit A return that is just sufficient to recover an entrepreneur's opportunity cost.

Normative (welfare) economics The type of economics that deals with prescriptive rather than descriptive statements.

No-trade allocation A feasible allocation in which agents consume exactly the quantities of the goods that they initially possessed.

Oligopoly A market that is dominated by a few sellers of a product.

One-sided oral auctions Market institutions in which buyers can accept or reject offers from sellers but cannot make counteroffers.

Opportunity cost The cost of engaging in any activity or the opportunity forgone by choosing that particular activity.

Opportunity wage The wage an agent could earn at the next best work opportunity.

Optimal combination of inputs The mixture of inputs that zproduces a particular level of output at the lowest cost.

Optimal consumption bundle The bundle the consumer chooses in order to maximize his utility within the economically feasible set; the bundle that is best according to his or her preferences.

Optimal quantity of labor rule The rule that indicates that a profit-maximizing firm will hire labor up to the point at which the marginal revenue product it receives from the last unit of labor hired equals the marginal cost of labor (the wage the firm must pay to the last worker hired).

Optimal reservation wage The wage set by a worker searching for a job such that if that wage or more is offered, it will be accepted, and the worker will stop searching.

Order statistics The Rth order statistic of a sample is the Rth smallest value of the sample.

Ordinal utility Utility is measurable in the ordinal sense if the utility numbers we assign to objects have no meaning other than to represent the ranking of these goods in terms of a person's preferences.

Output expansion path The curve containing the tangency points between the isocost curves and the isoquants, presenting the set of input combinations that produces any given output level at the least cost.

Overinvestment strategy An entry-prevention strategy for an incumbent firm in which the incumbent monopolist overinvests in production capacity to make a credible threat to increase its output beyond the limit quantity (and thereby sell the goods at a price below the limit price) if any competitor enters the market.

Paradox of crime prevention Illustrates the fact that policies aimed at reducing crime may actually increase it if crime is an inferior enough good and the income effect of the crime prevention policies is big enough.

Pareto-efficient allocation An allocation of inputs (capital and labor) where it is not possible to reallocate these inputs and produce more of at least one good in the economy without decreasing the amount of some other good that is produced.

Pareto-optimal (efficient) allocation An allocation of goods across people such that there are no other feasible allocations that could make all agents better off—or all agents equally well off and at least one strictly better off—than the proposed allocation.

Participation constraint A constraint in a contract that ensures the agent is better off taking the contract and joining the firm rather than not.

Pecuniary externality Pecuniary externalities exist when the action of one agent increases the price of a good to other agents.

Perfect complements Two goods are perfect complements if they must be consumed in a fixed ratio in order to produce utility. In a two-good world, perfect complements have right angle indifference curves.

Perfect substitutes Two goods are perfect substitutes if the marginal rate of substitution between them is constant along an indifference curve. In a two-good world, the indifferent curve is a straight line.

Perfectly competitive market A market in which there are many firms, each of which has an insubstantial share of the market; there is free entry into the market and no barriers exist to prevent entry; there is a homogeneous product and all firms in the industry produce exactly the same product; there is perfect factor mobility and the factors of production (that is, capital and labor) are free to move between industries; and there is perfect information in the sense that all participants in the market are fully informed about its price and about its profit opportunities.

Perfectly elastic demand curve A demand curve that is horizontal and in which a zero quantity will be sold at any price above a given price p while, at price p, any quantity can be sold.

Perfectly inelastic demand curve A demand curve that is perfectly vertical, representing zero quantity response to a price change.

Performance correspondence A relationship between the environment and the set of desired outcomes that tells us which outcomes will satisfy our performance criteria.

Pigouvian taxes Government taxes that tax the party causing an externality by an amount equal to the externality.

Pooling equilibrium An equilibrium to a game of incomplete information where players of different types take identical actions so that others are not able to learn their types from observing the actions they take.

Positive economics The type of economics that deals with descriptive rather than prescriptive statements.

Price discrimination The practice of charging different prices to different consumers.

Price-cap regulation A method of regulation that is designed to encourage efficient production by allowing firms to share in any cost savings they achieve in producing their product.

Price-compensating variation in income A measure of how much income must be given to a consumer after a price change to leave him or her at the same level of utility he or she had attained before the price change occurred.

Price-consumption path The curve representing how consumption will vary when one price changes but all other prices and the consumer's income remain constant.

Principal The person employing the agent.

Prisoner's dilemma game A 2×2 matrix game in which each player has a dominant strategy determining an equilibrium that is Pareto dominated.

Private goods Goods that have the properties of excludability and rival consumption.

Private marginal cost Cost, excluding externalities.

Private value auctions An auction in which each person has a particular and possibly different value for the good being auctioned.

Probability distribution The distribution that tells us the likelihood that a given random variable will take on any given value.

Process justice The idea that performances of perfectly competitive economies and other types of economies should be judged not on the basis of the outcomes they determine, but rather on the basis of the process by which those outcomes are determined.

Producer surplus The difference between what a producer receives for the goods it produces and the cost of producing them.

Product exhaustion theorem When all the factors of production are paid the value of what they produce, then at the long-run equilibrium of a perfectly competitive economy, the sum of their shares of the value of the socially produced pie must equal 1.

Production function A function that describes the maximum amount of output a producer can produce given a certain level of inputs.

Production possibilities frontier A curve that shows the maximum amounts of goods that an economy can produce if it allocates its inputs efficiently—that is, if it allocates its inputs so that all points on the frontier satisfy our condition for efficiency in production.

Public goods Goods that have the properties of nonexcludability and nonrival consumption.

Pure strategy A complete plan of action for the player that tells us what choice he should make at any node of the game tree or in any situation that might arise during the play of the game.

Quantity demanded The quantity of a good that people seek to purchase at a given price.

Ramsey pricing rule The pricing formula that makes it possible to set prices that will cover the common fixed cost of the producer but also minimize the loss of consumer surplus.

Rate base The amount of capital of a firm upon which its rate of return is calculated.

Rate-of-return regulation Regulation in which a regulatory commission must allow any firm under its jurisdiction to earn a rate of return for the firm's investors that is sufficient to warrant their keeping their capital investment in the firm.

Rationality The assumption that economic agents know what they like and behave accordingly, that is, that an agent's preferences exhibit completeness, reflexivity, and transitivity.

Rawls' maximin justice or **Rawlsian justice** The idea that an economy should be organized so as to maximize the welfare of the least well-off person in society.

Reaction functions (best-response functions) A function that specifies a firm's optimal choice for some variable such as output, given the choices of its competitors.

Refinement concept A refinement concept places a set of extra constraints on a Nash equilibrium in order to select among multiple equilibria if they exist or to simply make the equilibrium more plausible.

Reflexivity An assumption on consumer preferences that states that any bundle is at least as good as itself.

Relative prices The ratio that tells how much a consumer in a market would have to forgo of one good in order to receive units of another good.

Rent The return on a factor above the amount necessary to entice that factor into the production process.

Rent-inclusive average cost The average cost of the firm when economic rent is included as a cost.

Rent-seeking behavior The behavior of interest groups in their attempt to extract rents from the government or other authorities.

Repeated game A game in which a fixed set of players repeatedly play the same game against each other.

Replication The process of increasing the size of an economy proportionately.

Residual demand curve The demand curve that describes the demand remaining for the potential entrant after the incumbent firm has set its output level.

Returns to scale Measures the ratio between the resulting change in the output level and the proportionate change in the levels of *all* the inputs.

Risk averse A characteristic of an agent who has a concave utility function (diminishing marginal utility). A risk-averse agent will reject a "fair gamble" (a gamble that asks a decision maker to put up an amount equal to the gamble's expected monetary return in order to play).

Risk neutral A characteristic of an agent who has a linear utility function, which implies that he will choose between gambles strictly on the basis of their expected monetary value. A risk-neutral agent will be indifferent to a "fair gamble" (a gamble that asks a decision maker to put up an amount equal to the gamble's expected monetary return in order to play).

Risk pooling (self-insurance) A method of avoiding risk whereby groups come together to form a pool so as to share a risk if anyone in the group experiences a negative event.

Risk preferrers A characteristic of an agent who has a convex utility function (increasing marginal utility). A risk-preferring agent will pay a premium to accept a "fair gamble" (a gamble that asks a decision maker to put up an amount equal to the gamble's expected monetary return in order to play).

Rival consumption When consumption of a good by one person decreases the quantity of the good available for consumption by others and therefore deprives someone else of the good.

Sealed-bid auction An auction in which bidders enter their bids privately and the winner is that bidder whose bid is highest.

Second fundamental theorem of welfare economics Tells us that every Pareto-optimal allocation for an economy can be achieved as a competitive equilibrium for an appropriately defined distribution of income.

Second-best result A market outcome that is optimal given existing constraints in the market but worse than the outcome that would result if those constraints were removed.

Second-price sealed-bid auction An auction in which everyone submits a sealed bid and the winner is the highest bidder, but the winner pays a price equal to the second-highest bidder's price.

Segmented markets Markets whose physical separation or other characteristics make arbitrage impossible.

Selfishness A psychological assumption about agents that states that they are interested only in their own utility or satisfaction and make their choices with just that in mind.

Separating equilibrium An equilibrium to a game of incomplete information where players of different types take different actions so that others are able to learn their type from the action they take. This is the opposite of a pooling equilibrium, where different types play identically and hence no information can be inferred from their actions.

Separating equilibrium An equilibrium where different types play differently so their types can be inferred by their actions.

Sequential-move quantity-setting duopoly game A duopoly game in which firms alternate in setting quantities.

Short run The time period during which at least one factor of production is fixed.

Short-run average fixed cost function The function that gives the average fixed cost associated with any level of output. Because the fixed costs of production do not change in the short run, the function is given by the total fixed cost divided by the number of units.

Short-run average variable cost function A function describing the average cost of producing units of output counting only the cost of those factors of production that can vary in the short run.

Short-run equilibrium The price-quantity combination that will prevail in a perfectly competitive market in the short run.

Short-run expansion path A curve that depicts the locus of labor-capital combinations that would be used to produce varying amounts of output in the short run when one factor is held constant.

Short-run marginal cost function A function that indicates the incremental cost of producing the $q + 1$st unit of output given that we have already produced q units.

Short-run production function The production function that allows the producer to vary the levels of some but not all inputs in an effort to produce a given quantity.

Short-run total cost function A function that describes the *total* cost of producing any given level of output with a given fixed amount of capital.

Simultaneous-move quantity-setting duopoly game The strategic interaction between firms in a duopolistic market as a game where each firm chooses its quantity simultaneously.

Single-peaked preferences In voting for one-dimensional issues—that is, issues like how much money to spend on military expenditures, how high a tax should be set, etc.—preferences are single peaked if a person has a uniquely best alternative he or she prefers and his or her preferences decline as the distance between this best alternative and the alternative under consideration increases.

Slutsky equation An equation that decomposes a change in demand as a result of a price change in one good, holding all other prices and incomes constant, into income and substitution effects.

Socially optimal price-quantity combination The combination of price and quantity that maximizes the sum of the producer surplus and the consumer surplus.

Socially optimal single price The price that equals the marginal cost of producing the quantity demanded by the market at that price.

Societal consumer surplus The difference between what the consumers would have been willing to pay for a good and the amount the good is actually being sold for.

Specific inputs A capital good that has only one specific use.

Stackelberg equilibrium The equilibrium prices and quantities of a Stackelberg game.

Stackelberg follower The firm to move second in the Stackelberg model.

Stackelberg leader The firm to move first in the Stackelberg model.

Stackelberg model A model in which one firm, firm 1, chooses its quantity first, and then the other firm, *knowing what firm 1 has done*, makes its choice. After both firms have sequentially chosen their outputs, the price of the good on the market and the profits of both firms are determined.

Standards and charges A system for a government to intervene in a market with externalities in order to reduce its effects by levying charges on the agents causing the externality in order to force them to reduce the externality to the acceptable level.

Strategic voting Voting in a manner that does not reflect one's true preferences in an effort to affect the outcome of a vote.

Strong Axiom of Revealed Preference (SARP) The axiom that states that if bundle x is revealed to be preferred to bundle y (either directly or indirectly) and bundle y is different from x, then bundle y cannot be directly or indirectly revealed to be preferred to x.

Subadditive cost function A cost function that indicates that the cost of producing x units of output, $C(x)$, is less than the cost of producing A units and B units separately where $A + B = x$, that is, $C(x) \leq C(A) + C(B)$.

Subgame The remaining portion of the game tree at a given node of the larger game.

Subgame perfect equilibrium A set of strategies, which constitute a Nash equilibrium, where the actions prescribed by these strategies for the players once they reach any subgame constitute a Nash equilibrium for that subgame.

Substitution effect The change in demand that results from an attempt to substitute a good whose price has decreased for another good whose price has remained constant after having nullified the implicit income effect.

Sunk costs Costs of factors that are not recoverable because the items have no resale value or alternative use.

Superior good A good for which demand increases as the income of the consumer increases and the relative prices remain constant.

Supply function A function that specifies how much of a good a firm would be willing to sell given any hypothetical market price if all other factors remain constant.

Sustainable monopoly A natural monopoly that can erect barriers that keep others out of its market.

Tax incidence The ultimate distribution of the burden of a tax.

Technology The set of technological constraints on production defining how one can combine or convert inputs into outputs.

The reflection effect The prediction that changing the sign on a set of choices will result in people's changing their preferences, even if the final outcomes and the probabilities attached to them are the same.

Time inconsistency A decision maker exhibits time inconsistency if, when faced with identical intertemporal choices that are simply separated by time (i.e., $10 today versus $25 in three weeks or $10 in one year versus $25 in one year and three weeks), the choices made differ.

Total expenditure (TE) The total wage a monopsonist pays for labor.

Total product curve The total product curve represents the amount of output that results as we add more and more units of a variable factor to the production of a good, holding one input constant—for example, how much output we get at different levels of labor inputs holding capital fixed at a given level.

Transitivity An assumption on consumer preferences, and the property of preference relationships that states that if agents think that bundle a is at least as good as bundle b and that bundle b is at least as good as bundle c, then they also think that bundle a is at least as good as bundle c.

Trigger strategy (grim strategy) A type of strategy in an infinite horizon repeated game where one deviation triggers an infinite punishment.

Two-part tariff A two-part tariff is a price discrimination technique in which the price of a product or service is composed of two parts—a lump-sum fee as well as a per-unit charge.

Ultimatum game A two-person game in which player 1 divides an amount of money, c, between himself and his opponent and the opponent either accepts or rejects the proposal.

Uncompensated demand function A demand function that represents the relationship between the price of a good and the quantity demanded, which includes both the substitution and income effects of price changes.

Uneven tournament A tournament in which it is more costly for one group of agents to perform the same tasks than for others.

Unfair tournament A tournament in which the rules of the tournament treat people differently, giving an advantage to one identifiable group.

Unitary elastic demand A characteristic of demand for a good where, at a given price, a 1% change in the price leads to exactly a 1% change in the quantity demanded.

Utility function A representation of an agent's preferences that tells the agent how good a bundle is by assigning it a (possibly ordinal) utility number.

Utility possibilities frontier All the possible utility levels associated with the Pareto-optimal allocation for each product mix point on the production possibilities frontier.

Variable costs The costs of the variable factors of production; the costs that change with the level of output.

Variable factor of production A factor of production whose level can be adjusted.

Variance A measure that tries to capture the variability of a random variable by looking at the expected squared deviation of the random variable from its mean.

Wage discrimination When a firm does not pay the same wage rate on all units of labor it employs.

Weak Axiom of Revealed Preferences (WARP) The axiom that states that if bundle x is ever directly revealed to be preferred to bundle y when the two bundles are not identical, then y can never be directly revealed to be preferred to x.

Winner's curse An outcome of a common value auction in which the winning bidder bids more than the true expected value of the good he or she wins.

Zero-sum game A game in which the gain of one player equals the loss of the other player.

Index

Note: Locators in italics indicate figures or tables.